ISLAM

ISLAM

Past, Present and Future

Hans Küng

Translated by
John Bowden

O N E W O R L D
O X F O R D

A Oneworld Book

First published by Oneworld Publications 2007
Translated by John Bowden from the German
Der Islam: Geschichte, Gegenwart, Zukunft
published 2004 by Piper Verlag, Munich
Reprinted by Oneworld Publications 2008
First published in paperback 2009

A CIP record for this title is available
from the British Library

ISBN 978-1-85168-612-4

Typeset by Jayvee, Trivandrum, India
Printed and bound by the Maple-Vail Book
Manufacturing Group, Braintree, MA, USA

Oneworld Publications
185 Banbury Road
Oxford OX2 7AR
England
www.oneworld-publications.com

To my Muslim friends all over the world

THE RELIGIOUS SITUATION OF OUR TIME

Islam

No peace among the nations
without peace among the religions.
No peace among the religions
without dialogue between the religions.
No dialogue between the religions
without investigation of the foundations of the religions.

CONTENTS

C. HISTORY

D. CHALLENGES OF THE PRESENT

The Aim of this Book

The controversy over the Danish publication of cartoons of Muhammad in 2006 and its effects worldwide have made this book about Islam even more topical. A relaxed, objective and understanding approach is possible, not through polarization and the emotional advocacy of extreme positions, but through a balanced discussion of the deeper causes of tensions and constructive proposals for solving the complex and far-reaching problems.

Against the clash of civilizations

'No world peace without religious peace' is a conclusion I drew as early as 1982 in a series of dialogue lectures on Christianity and Islam at the University of Tübingen. Like its predecessors on *Judaism* (1991, ET 1992) and *Christianity* (1994, ET 1995), this book also begins with the programme I have formulated for the global change of consciousness which is vital for our survival:

No peace among the nations
without peace among the religions.
No peace among the religions
without dialogue between the religions.
No dialogue between the religions
without investigation of the foundations of the religions.

In 1993, the US political theorist Samuel Huntington sketched out a counter-programme—at first cautiously, in the form of a question, but later as a new paradigm of foreign politics: 'A Clash of Civilizations'. Is a battle between civilizations the unavoidable world scenario? Huntington, a Pentagon advisor, who was not much concerned with the internal dynamics and diversities of individual cultures and evidently knew little about complex historical interconnections, fluid transitions, mutual enrichment and peaceful co-existence, forecast that the clash between 'the West' and 'Islam' would be particularly dangerous. In this way he provided ideological support, after the end of the Cold War, for the replacement of the hostile image of Communism with the hostile image of Islam, largely to justify a high level of American rearmament and, whether deliberately or not, to create a favourable atmosphere for further wars.

In 1992, a year before Huntington's article was published—immediately after the ignominious end to the first Iraq War (under the first President Bush) and a decade before the second—a small group of American 'neo-conservative' thinkers and politicians had begun to prepare ideologically for a possible preventive war over oil reserves, American hegemony and Israeli security. After the election of President George W. Bush (in 1999) the war was planned in detail and the unprecedented massacre of 11 September 2001 was exploited as a justification for launching an attack against Afghanistan and threatening one on Iraq (which had not been involved in the 11 September attacks). After vainly attempting to gain the support of the Security Council and following an Orwellian campaign of lies about the reasons for a war and its aims, on 18 March 2003 the Bush administration (inexplicably supported by the British prime minister Tony Blair), in the face of international law and world public opinions launched a war against Iraq with massive military force and soon afterwards, apparently, won it.

However, instead of terror being defeated, in Afghanistan, the Middle East and all over the world, it was helped to spread even wider: to Bali, Casablanca, Riyadh and Istanbul. And in Madrid, on 11 March 2004, came the first massacre on European soil. This attack led to the Spanish government, which had been involved in the Iraq war, being voted out of office in the parliamentary elections two days later. Even for European countries not involved in the war it marked a dramatic heightening of an already tense world situation. These wars against two Islamic countries, together with the double standards practised by the West for decades over Israel's contemptuous policy of occupation, which scorns all UN resolutions, have inflamed the whole Islamic world to unspeakable anger and bitterness and hardened its attitudes. The clash of civilizations seems to have become a self-fulfilling prophecy.

We are unquestionably in a difficult but key phase in reshaping international relations between the West and Islam and between the three Abrahamic religions: Judaism, Christianity and Islam. The options have become clear: rivalry amongst the religions, a clash of civilizations, war between nations or a dialogue of civilizations and peace between the religions as a harbinger of peace among nations. Faced with a deadly threat to all humankind, shouldn't we demolish the walls of prejudice stone by stone and build bridges of dialogue, including bridges to Islam, rather than erect new barriers of hatred, vengeance and hostility? I am pleading neither for opposition to be swept under the carpet nor for a syncretistic mixing of religions. I am pleading for an honest approach and an attempt at understanding, based on mutual self-awareness, on objectivity and fairness, and on the knowledge of what separates and what unites.

Is such an effort naïve, as pessimists and cynics in politics, business, science and journalism think? On the contrary, it is the only realistic alternative, if we are not to give up hope for a better world order altogether. I am convinced that the USA, too, will soon find a way out of its war hysteria as it did out of the McCarthy hysteria in the 1950s and rediscover itself and its great democratic tradition. After the manifest failure of the unilateral world-power strategy, the aggressive war policy in Afghanistan and Iraq, the one-sided involvement in Palestine and the worldwide loss of moral credibility, intercultural and inter-religious dialogue has become even more urgent. A battle against a network of religiously misguided men of violence is unavoidable: however, this will not be, as the Bush administration presumably envisages, a war fought on land, sea and in the air, but one fought by the use of police, secret service, diplomatic and financial operations appropriate to the situation. At the same time there must be support above all for political and social reforms in Islamic countries, in order to remove the breeding-grounds of the terrorists among the frustrated and impoverished members of their populations. Only if it proves possible to isolate the violent extremists and strengthen the moderate Muslims; only if it proves possible to build bridges of trust and to stabilize relations between the Western and the Islamic world; only if it proves possible for Israelis, Arabs and 'Westerners', Jews, Christians and Muslims, no longer to treat one another as opponents but as partners, can the apparently insuperable political, economic, social and cultural problems of the present be overcome and a contribution made to a more peaceful world order.

That is why many people today argue that there should be no relapse into the political and military confrontation, aggression and revenge once practised by the Western nations, but happily superseded after the Second World War. Rather, there is a need for a resolute realization of the new 'postmodern' paradigm of political, economic and cultural understanding, co-operation and integration laid down in the UN Charter and at its most advanced in the framework of the European Union. In the long run, peace and freedom can be built up only on the basis of constitutional states, tolerance, human rights and ethical standards. Together with competent political scientists and ethicists, in 2003 I referred to the specifically political problems in a book on 'Peace Politics. Ethical Foundations for International Relations'.[1]

Civilizations or cultures as such cannot be invited to dialogue, since they are not self-contained entities; rather, the invitation must be to individuals, and specific groups, from diverse cultural frameworks; above all to the politically, economically and culturally responsible élites. In respect of Islam, both Christians and non-Christians should ask: why do 1.2 billion people confess to this religion—and the number is increasing—in the middle regions of the Earth, from the Atlantic coast of Africa to the islands of Indonesia, from the steppes of Central Asia to Mozambique? Why is Islam the largest of the world religions after Christianity, and occasionally hopes that one day it may overtake it? Why, in the conviction of its adherents, is it not only the newest and best religion but also the oldest and most universal? Why has it, more than any other religion, been able to bring together people as different as nomadic Berbers, Middle-Eastern Arabs, West and East Africans, Turks, Bosnians, Albanians, Persians, Pakistanis, Indians, Chinese and Malays—in fact people in almost every country in the world—despite their cultural differences? Where does the power and fascination of Islam really lie? What are its sources, its values, its symbols? What are its message, its essence, its constituent elements? What shapes Muslim life, Islamic politics, culture and art? What are its weaknesses and failings? What self-critical questions do Muslims need to ask themselves?

Making people capable of dialogue

Of course in view of the wealth of publications about Islam, one might ask why yet another big book on the subject is needed. If one has worked intensively on Islamic literature, the question becomes even more pressing. What is the real interest, the distinctive profile, indeed the sense of such an undertaking? There are plenty of cultural histories of Islam and religious and political histories in many languages. However, I am not writing this book as a cultural historian or a historian of religion, or a historian of politics or law. I am writing it in order to help people to engage in dialogue in this decisive transitional phase towards a new relationship between the civilizations, religions and nations, so that whether they are Christian, Muslim or secular; politicians, business leaders or culture-makers; teachers, clergy or students, they may be able to assess the world situation better and react to it better. This cannot be done without an understanding of the world religions. I shall work the history of culture and religion, politics and law into a highly complex description, but at the same time I shall keep this programme, with which I have been concerned for decades, transparent. That is the contribution that I, as a theologian and philosopher engaged in religious dialogue, hope to make with this book.

I hope to offer a fair account of Islam in history and the present. The fourteen centuries of Islam are truly no simpler to present than were the thirty centuries of Judaism and the twenty centuries of Christianity in my earlier books. Like them, this book is not a neutral, scholarly, scientific description of the history of Islam, nor simply a systematic theological description of its teaching; rather, in a chronological, objectively argued presentation, it sets out to be a synthesis of both its historical and systematic dimensions. I also want to relate a great history, which is tremendously dramatic and varied. But I shall keep interrupting the narrative to ask critical questions about the result of the changes that Islam has undergone in different paradigms. There will be 'questions' and 'questions for discussion', which arise particularly when a tradition has become fossilized and almost incapable of communication. This book, like its two predecessors, has been conceived in interdisciplinary terms: it dovetails the isolated disciplines and attempts to provide a multidimensional view of Islam.

I have been aware of the risks of such an undertaking on every page. I have had carefully to walk a precarious tight rope: to find the balance between a deep understanding, which cannot, however, be misused to justify the *status quo*, and, in places, open criticism of Islam, though this must not lead to self-righteousness. This book, written by a non-Muslim, is the expression of a hope that Islam will not grow weaker or even disappear, but will undergo an inner renewal. Without any sense of superiority (of a Christian or secular kind), and in awareness of the dialectic of the Enlightenment, it will argue for a renewed Islam.

In the face of the 'info-smog'—it is said that the mass of data in the world is growing by thirty per cent annually—this book offers not only purely factual knowledge but also orientation: it presents Islam, albeit in a differentiated way, as a whole, not schematically. I have been able to venture on this extremely different undertaking only because, using paradigm analysis, I have at my disposal a theoretical approach and conceptual apparatus which, after earlier reflections in *Does God Exist? The Problem of God in the Modern World* (1978), I have developed and reflected on methodologically in my two books *Theology for the Third Millennium* (1987) and *Global Responsibility* (1991). Paradigm analysis proved itself in the 1990s in the historical assessments of Judaism and Christianity and means that I can conveniently dispense with giving a detailed reconstruction of the fourteen hundred-year-old history of Islam in its various periods and territories with all its different tendencies and central personalities; instead, I shall refer at every point to the classic historical works and specialist literature, a literature which has become impossible even for Islamic specialists to survey. Thinking in paradigms means understanding the dominant structures of history together with the figures that shape them. It means analysing the various overall constellations of Islam, how they come into being, mature and often become fossilized and describing how paradigms which have ossified into tradition live on in the present. Finally it means demonstrating the rise of new paradigms and thus possibly new perspectives for the future.

Among Muslims, even more than among Jews and Christians, the view is widespread that their religion has always remained the same, that it has undergone no great revolutions but developed continuously. I shall demonstrate that this impression is false. However, I am not primarily interested in the past but in the present: in how Islam has become what it is today—with a view to what it could be. The specific characteristic of this kind of history-writing is not pure chronology but the dovetailing of times and problems. That raises a challenge on two fronts: for Muslim readers, how can a Christian theologian venture to involve himself so much in 'internal' Muslim discussions and concerns? And for Christian readers: how can a Christian theologian venture to go so far to meet Muslims on many questions? I have never engaged in an inter-religious dialogue which has ruled out the contentious questions: I have tried to avoid the 'inter-religious cosiness' about which church people sometimes complain, though these people have at best a superficial knowledge of other religions. But at the same time I have always opposed the artificial confrontations engaged in by dogmatic theologians on both sides, who do not investigate beyond their own dogmas and claim true belief in God for themselves alone.

I hope that this necessarily broad approach will provide answers to questions of every kind and stimulate Muslims and Christians (and Jews) to understand one another. Of course, I have had to leave out numerous interesting details, attractive anecdotes and even important aspects in order to achieve the necessary sharpness of vision in an ever-changing historical perspective. I have had to put the main centres of Islam, the Arab world, Turkey and Iran, at the centre and deal with the special developments in India, sub-Saharan Africa and South-East Asia only on the periphery. Above all I had to keep in view the development of national and political Islam and could take account of popular Islam only in the background and below the surface. My concern was not to lose myself in a mass of detail but to work out the conditions and causes of each of the great Islamic overall constellations or paradigms, the pressures on them and their constants and variables, against the background of a brief sketch of their historical development. I have done this within the paradigms of the original Islamic community (P I), Arab empire (P II), Islam as a world religion (P III, the classic paradigm), the Ulama and Sufis (P IV) and finally Islamic modernization (P V), in order to be able to survey and understand all the features of the contemporary paradigm (P VI). Since earlier paradigms do not completely disappear with the arrival of a new one, overlaps are not only unavoidable but also illuminating.

A long intellectual journey

Many studies and experiences stand behind my present reflections on Islam, going back to my first visit to an Islamic country in North Africa as a young doctoral student in 1955: this was the time of my first major attempt at an ecumenical dialogue about the central question in dispute between Rome and the Reformation, namely my dissertation on Karl Barth's doctrine of justification (1957): the whole issue is described in the first volume of my memoirs, *My Struggle for Freedom* (ET 2003). I learned much about method for later inter-religious dialogue from this book. The major dialogue lectures on Islam that I gave in the University of Tübingen in 1982 with my colleague Professor Josef van Ess, a specialist on Islam (see *Christianity and the World Religions*, 1986/7), were also fundamental to my scholarly work on Islam. I was able to deepen and expand the insights gained then, above all through countless studies, trips and colloquia, and through travelling for the seven-part television series *Spurensuche*, made in the 1990s by Sudwest Rundfunk (Germany) and DRS (Switzerland). The seventh film in this series is devoted to the various paradigms of Islam. It is available on video, CD-ROM and DVD; English readers will find an English version of the text in the companion volume *Tracing the Way* (2002).

To my great delight, this third volume of my trilogy completes the project 'The Religious Situation of our Time', which concentrates on the three religions of Near Eastern origin—Judaism, Christianity and Islam. The framework was provided by the project 'No world peace without religious peace', sponsored (1989–1997) by the Bosch Jubilee Foundation and the Daimler Benz Fund. I have now fulfilled my promise: to analyse the spiritual forces of the millennia-old history of these three religions which are still effective in the present, i.e. to give a systematic historical diagnosis and from it to offer perspectives on the different options for the future and with them practical and ecumenical approaches towards a resolution of problems. In this third volume, particularly in the systematic chapters, through a trilateral method I have dovetailed description and criticism of Islam with self-criticism of Christianity (and Judaism), so as not only to make dialogue with others possible, but also to hold my trilogy together.

The best theoretical and practical fruit of the research project 'No world peace without religious peace' was *Global Responsibility*, written in 1990 in connection with the epoch-making changes in Europe. This led to further publications: *A Global Ethic for Global Politics and Economics* (1997), *Wissenschaft und Weltethos* (Science and the Global Ethic, 1998) and *Friedenspolitik. Ethische Grundlagen internationaler Beziehungen* (Peace Policy. The Ethical

Foundations of International Relations, 2003), and also in 1995 to the creation of the Global Ethic Foundation (www.welthethos.org), made possible by a generous donation from Count and Countess von der Groeben. Despite comparatively limited personal and financial means, the Foundation has been able to develop an amazing range of activities in areas ranging from schools to international bodies such as the United Nations Organization.

A planned second volume about the present and future of Christianity has proved superfluous. I have presented so many analyses of the present and visions for the future in all my writings on the reform of the church, such as *Reforming the Church Today. Keeping Hope Alive* (1990), that I can spare myself from describing at length in a new volume things that are well known (and unfortunately for the most part unrealized). I have written individual articles on the situation in Africa and Latin America. My *Short History of the Catholic Church* (2002) has opened the eyes of many people to the tremendous number of problems which have accumulated in the 'Roman Catholic' Church and to the structural crisis in which it now finds itself. More recent developments, which are described with historical objectivity in that short history, are expanded and illustrated in *My Struggle for Freedom* (ET 2003), which I mentioned earlier. Now that this volume on Islam has been published, if I am granted enough strength and time, I shall set to work on giving an account of the second half of my life, in which I was exposed to powerful storms, but came through them to reach new shores and wide open spaces.

There is an extended word of thanks to all who have helped me at the end of this volume.

Hans Küng
Tübingen, 2007

A. ORIGIN

The religions of Chinese origin—Confucianism and Daoism—still appear to most Europeans to be remote, alien, 'Far Eastern', but in no way threatening. The religions of Indian origin—Hinduism and Buddhism—seem to many people closer, less alien, sometimes even sympathetic and, because they are usually peaceful and without long frontiers over which there is conflict with 'Christian' countries, are not seen as a threat, despite violent Hindu fundamentalism in India, which has increased since the end of the twentieth century.

The religions of Near Eastern origin—Judaism, Christianity and Islam—are closely related, and in comparison with the two other religious systems, very similar in many respects. However, between no other religions has there been, and is there, so much quarrelling and dispute as between these three monotheistic prophetic religions, which seem to show special aggressiveness and think in terms of friend and foe. I showed that in the case of Judaism and above all of Christianity in the first two volumes of this trilogy 'The Religious Situation of our Time'.[1] How do things stand with Islam?

A I

A Controversial Religion

Islam, which has frontiers with Christianity extending over many thousands of miles, is increasingly felt to be an explicit threat by many people in the West. In 1993, the American political theorist Samuel Huntington, whom I mentioned in my introduction, stated bluntly: 'The frontiers of Islam are bloody.'[2] Aren't the frontiers of Christianity equally so? Thus a notion of Islam as opponent, as enemy, has been produced: very useful for those ideologists (in America and elsewhere) who urgently need an enemy for their imperialistic military policy and hegemonial ambitions: the hostile image of Islam.

1. The hostile image of Islam

Although the fundamental phenomenon has probably existed since the beginnings of human thought, the terms 'hostile image' or 'hostile stereotype' are modern; they emerged when the East-West conflict was losing its tension and became popular in the Second Gulf War. Since the crime against humanity committed on 11 September 2001 by blinkered fanatics, there has been a danger that world politics will be utterly determined by the hostile image of Islam, matched all too easily on the Muslim side by a hostile image of the West.

The usefulness of a hostile image

'The hostile image represents a more or less structured totality of perceptions, notions and feelings which, unified under the aspect of hostility, are foisted on to a person, a group of people or peoples and states.'[3] The hostile image, which always contrasts with the image of a friend (usually one's own group), comprises not only notions and judgements, as is suggested by the English term 'concept of the enemy', but also perceptions, feelings and prejudices—which is why the visual media are particularly important.

A hostile image—in the West formerly Communism, today Islam—has many uses. It has a variety of individual psychological and political-social functions, as can be seen in the 'war against terrorism' governed by the US striving for hegemony and given highly effective support by the media:

– The hostile image provides an excuse: 'we' (Americans, Europeans, our European and Israeli friends) are not to blame; no, it is all the fault of the enemy, Islam! Our repressed feelings of guilt and inferiority, our aggressions and frustrations, can safely be diverted and projected on to it. Hostile images make it easy to think in terms of scapegoats.

– The hostile image stabilizes: 'we in the West' may disagree over many things, but we are allies against the enemy, against the 'evil empire' or the 'axis of evil'! A common enemy reinforces togetherness, NATO, transatlantic friendship. It allows us to stand united, to demonize critics and to exclude deviants. Hostile images encourage thinking in terms of blocks.

– The hostile image polarizes: by a reduction of the possibilities to either-or ('He who is not for us is against us') people can be grouped and exploited for the political and military conflict as friend and foe, nations which are 'for war' and those which are against it. We might not know what values we favour, but we do know what we are against. The fronts are clear: everyone knows where they and the other party stand. Hostile images force everything into a Manichaean friend-foe scheme.

– The hostile image activates: precise information and orientation are unnecessary: intelligence may be exaggerated, falsified, manipulated or, if need be, invented. We may, indeed we must, defend ourselves against the 'others', foreigners, enemies, from without and within. Not only mistrust but also hostility and if need be even force are appropriate against both things and persons: physical, psychological, political, indeed military force. In soldiers, hostile images overcome inhibitions about killing even better than drugs. Hostile images provide motivation for war, cold or hot.

One consolation remains. Hostile images are not eternal ideas, unchangeable necessities. Not only can they be transferred, for example from 'the Russians' to 'the Arabs'; they can be corrected, if enemies become friends (for example France and Germany), or they can lose their object (for example Communism). They can also be overcome, by concentration on great common tasks (for example the nuclear threat or the ecological crisis) and lead to a worldwide community of destiny and responsibility which includes Islam.

Intolerance, militancy, backwardness?

'Peace among the religions as a harbinger of peace among the nations? Peace among the religions even in Jerusalem, the city of three religions? That's an illusion!' This comment was made to me years ago by a television journalist and 'Middle East expert' who was popular at the time.[4] When I asked him what his alternative was, he tersely replied, 'War!' As if five Israeli–Arab wars had not been enough: there was no other solution to Israeli–Arab antagonism. Unfortunately, this man is representative of many journalists and authors in Europe and especially North America who, because of their latently aggressive disposition, communicate current events to an unsuspecting mass public in such words and images as can even create an understanding of the aggressive policies of Ariel Sharon and his ilk. These populist representatives of the media share responsibility for the continuing existence of hostile images. If, for some pious Christians, for a long time Judaism and then Communism were public enemy number 1, for many of them today this place is occupied by Islam. There are people who cannot live without a hostile image. 'Islam wants to rule the world! An anti-Christian, intolerant and aggressive superstition is already spanning half the globe.' That is what we hear from certain Christian fundamentalist quarters.

Such opposition to Islam in principle is not only to be found in right-wing radical groups with a Christian and Jewish stamp. It has infiltrated the industrial nations widely. When the Western media portray Muslims, they love to portray them as fanatical bearded lawyers, extremist violent terrorists, super-rich oil sheikhs and veiled women. No wonder that for many in the West the image of Islam has become darker. Islam seems to be marked by:

- Internal intolerance: as a totalitarian religion which produces passion, irrationality, fanaticism and hysteria, likes to suppress Christian minorities and even engages in bloody persecutions of dissidents like the Baha'is and the Ahmadis.
- Militancy towards the outside world: as a violent religion which wages 'holy wars', is intent on conquering the world and against which we have to be on our guard.
- Backwardness: as a rigid religion that stubbornly clings to the Middle Ages and has reductive, indeed archaic features: it is uncivilized, scorns women and refuses to engage in dialogue.

Some of this criticism needs to be investigated: the extreme expressions of a militant Islam, from Khomeini to bin Laden, have done great damage to the image of Islam in the West. Nevertheless, those generalized, aggressively polemical and cynically disparaging verdicts urgently need to be differentiated and clarified, since they can have devastating effects both on personal dealings and in the wider sphere of politics. Those who have such a stereotyped hostile image of Islam in their heads perceive reality in a selective way, where everything that deviates from this picture is excluded or reinterpreted. For example, some Christians fail to note that the same activities ('mission', financial support, the construction of places of worship on alien territory and aggressive self-assertion) are 'good' when they benefit their group and 'bad' when carried on by 'the others'.

But quite apart from double standards of evaluation, such an image corresponds little with the reality of Islam. The hostile image provokes even more hostile reactions, and in so doing proves to be a self-fulfilling prophecy. It sharpens conflicts, encourages escalation, makes a realistically differentiated estimate of others difficult and understanding apparently impossible, and thus prepares the ground for military conflicts such as those in Afghanistan and Iraq. But can one enter into a serious dialogue with Muslims at all?

Is dialogue impossible?

'Which Muslims do you want to engage in dialogue with?,' a television journalist once asked me in an ironic and superior way. He is highly respected, but his view of the world is formed by experiences of wars and antagonism between religions and cultures; moreover his picture of Islam has been vigorously criticized by Islamic specialists.[5] 'I engage in dialogue with Muslims to whom often you have no access at all,' I replied, as I remembered the many friendly, lively and eager faces of Islamic scholars, professors, intellectuals and students in Islamabad, Lahore and Karachi; Jerusalem, Cairo, Riyadh and Teheran; Algiers, Fez, Lagos and Dar-es-Salaam, not to mention conversations with extremely knowledgeable Muslims in German-speaking countries, in France, Britain and America. I am not prepared to reduce the difference between 'the West' and 'the Islamic world' to an 'essential' dualism between rationality and faith, science and piety, superiority and inferiority, indeed between peacemaking and a readiness for violence.

As if there were only religious fundamentalists, demagogues in power and fanaticized masses in the 'Arab East'. As if one did not have to distinguish, even among fundamentalists, between those who violently wage a 'holy war' (*jihad*) and those who are concerned to establish their identity in a peaceful, religious and cultural identity. As if the violent rebelliousness of popular Muslim groups were grounded utterly in the essence of Islam—and not least also in the political, social and economic abuses and frustrations caused by dictatorships and the corruption of ruling élites who are often wooed by the West. As if today it were not important to develop efficient political, cultural and religious programmes as alternatives to militant fundamentalism: a democratization and modernization and secularization which nevertheless takes seriously the constructive side of religion in society, the opposite of religionless secularism. From a global perspective, European secularism in its forms which exclude religion represents a special way which, particularly in America, is time and again opposed by religious practice (reactionary but also innovative).

On the basis of my own experiences, although every day I too am confronted with negative reports from the Islamic sphere, I must nevertheless firmly object to the '*simplificateurs terribles*' who give tendentious reports of Islam, are silent about many positive aspects, reinforce anti-Islamic prejudices and elevate all controversies between Muslims, Jews and Christians into an eternal 'Abrahamic fight of destiny'. In this way, they foment even more the vague anxieties about an 'empire of evil', an 'axis of evil', and an Islamic global conspiracy, so as to exploit them in a political and military, economic and commercial way. If this is really the case, as is constantly insinuated, directly or indirectly, by certain neo-conservative ideologists, politicians and journalists, then a historic confrontation between the West and Islam, indeed the 'Third World War' so desired in America by the 'neo-cons' of the Israel lobby (supported by Christian fundamentalist 'theo-cons'), could hardly be avoided, and efforts should be made to form an 'alliance of true humanity'. We can only guess at precisely what that means, set against the background of present-day migration driven by work and poverty, in the rich industrial countries. But what sounds so modern is basically a lapse into the Middle Ages. The state of knowledge about Islam among some of our contemporaries is, as it were, at a medieval level. A brief look at history demonstrates what this means: what do Christians know and what did they know then about Islam?

Eastern knowledge, Western ignorance

Early Greek Christian authors, especially those in Muslim territories, show themselves to be relatively well informed about Islamic doctrines and the Prophet Muhammad, but amazingly, in the Latin West, with the exception of Andalusia, no substantive discussion with Islam took place until the twelfth century.

What did people know in the Islamic East? There, the Nestorian, Syrian and Coptic Christians felt Arab rule to be no more oppressive than the Byzantine rule which had preceded it. The first Christian history of the world, written in Arabic by Agapius (Arabic *Mahbub ibn Qustantin*), bishop of Hierapolis (*Manbij*) in Syria in the tenth century, shows that in the Islamic world Christians too could have some knowledge about the life and teaching of the Prophet Muhammad.

Agapius gives a very objective account of the origins of Islam and the Prophet Muhammad.[6] To explain to his fellow-Christians why such large and important Christian territories could be conquered by the Muslims, the bishop refers to a (legendary?) document of the Byzantine emperor Heraklios (610–42), a contemporary of the Prophet, in which, referring to the biblical promise for Ishmael, son of Abraham, the ancestor of the Arabs, the emperor instructed his governors in Egypt, Syria and Armenia to stop resisting the Arabs. Towards the end of the 'Abbasid caliphate, the Jacobite bishop Gregorios Abu'l Faraj (Barhebraeus, 1226–86) took a relatively positive attitude to Islam, offering a very balanced judgement on the prophetic claim of Muhammad.

The supreme head (Catholicos) of the Nestorian church, Mar Timotheos (780–823), even had the honour of spending two days in a learned dialogue on theological differences with the caliph al-Mahdi (775–85).[7] A purely fictitious but very influential dialogue came from a pupil of the pupil of Yuhanna ibn Sarjun, known as John of Damascus, who died around 750. He was the son of a senior Arab Christian finance official of the Byzantine (Melkite) rite who collaborated with caliph Mu'awiyyah. The young John was a private secretary in the financial administration (then Arabized). When caliph 'Umar II prohibited Jews and Christians from holding high offices of state, John became a monk in the famous monastery of St Sabas in Jerusalem. The *Disputatio Christiani et Saraceni*[8] does not come from him, but the section on Islam in his dogmatic *magnum opus Source of Knowledge* does. In this, he gives a brief history of some hundred heresies, largely taken from another work; however, the concluding section on Islam (number 100), the newest heresy, evidently comes from his own hand.[9] The self-confident and often ironic remarks about Islam are full of misunderstandings and the Christian answers lack any self-critical reflection. The section ends with a silly passage about a surah said to be about a female camel. However, because John of Damascus is regarded as the most important systematic theologian of the Orthodox Church, and the last church father, his view of Islam came to be disseminated widely: Islam was not an independent religion, Muhammad was not a genuine prophet, and his revelation was a product of the imagination.[10]

A series of verdicts (Muhammad was a cheat, an epileptic, the Antichrist and a servant of Satan) and legends were disseminated across the Greek world. It was said, for example, that a Christian monk whom Muhammad later had murdered taught him the Qur'an; that he regarded a dove which had eaten grains from his ear as the Holy Spirit and revealer and that his tomb in Mecca had been seen suspended in the air by magnetic forces.

What was the state of knowledge in Western Europe? Here, more than four hundred years after the appearance of Muhammad, people still had no authentic knowledge about Islam: this was the 'age of ignorance'![11] Only when the last important abbot of Cluny, Peter the Venerable, who was convinced that Islam could be conquered only with the power of the word, visited Spain in 1142 following the problematical consequences of the First Crusade, did more precise studies of the sources of Islam begin. The first (Latin) translation of the Qur'an was made by an Englishman, Robert of Ketton, in 1143. Although it was published along with polemical and apologetic writings by Peter against Islam, it is rightly praised as a landmark in Islamic studies which ended the age of ignorance: 'For the first time the West had an instrument for the serious study of Islam.'[12] It was used by the eirenic Renaissance cardinal Nicolas of Cusa, the Spanish Grand Inquisitor Juan de Torquemada, and the Reformer Martin Luther.

Paradoxically the crusades, despite hostility and war, led to a more precise knowledge of Islam and its Prophet. Emperor Frederick II, who was born in Palermo and grew up among Christians and Muslims, had close contacts with oriental Arab culture in Sicily and Southern Italy. The journey by Francis of Assisi to Sultan al-Malik al-Kamil during the siege of Damietta (near the mouth of the Nile) in the middle of the crusade is wrapped in riddles. Francis travelled in 1219, apparently with no knowledge of Islam and no protection, at the risk of martyrdom: 'On reaching Damietta, Francis attempted to dissuade the crusaders from fighting and refused to take part in the attack. But the crusade ignored him; it was the Sultan who was to listen to him! It thus seems fully proven that Francis' action is the exact opposite of any crusade mysticism.'[13]

William of Tyre (1130–86) and William of Tripolis (1220–73) wrote very fairly about Islam. Sultan Saladin of Egypt (1137–93) was also respected in Europe and was widely regarded as the model of a chivalrous man. There was great admiration of the superiority of Arab culture, philosophy, science, medicine and the economic and military power of Islam, but not of Islam as a religion.

Thomas Aquinas was not really a pioneer of dialogue with Muslims in the High Middle Ages. He knew Islam only from the works of the great Muslim philosophers, and thought that he could defend Christian dogmas against Islam philosophically, at a purely rational level,[14] without being interested in the Qur'an or conversing with Muslims (see C IV, 6). The real pioneers were two of his contemporaries, who knew Arabic well: the English Franciscan Roger Bacon (1220–92), a man of encyclopaedic learning, influenced greatly by Avicenna, who worked energetically for a knowledge of Arabic sciences, and the Catalan nobleman Ramon Llull (Raimundus Lullus, 1232–1316), who devoted his life to the conversion of the Muslims, made three journeys to North Africa and engaged in unpolemical, almost Socratic, dialogues with the Muslims, based less on church documents than on rational grounds.[15]

Twice deported, on his third journey he was stoned so badly that he died on the way home.

A devaluation and rejection of everything Arab, including the Arabic language, began as early as the Renaissance, despite the establishment of chairs for Arabic, numerous translations from Arabic and the efforts of such significant scholars and statesmen as Juan de Segovia, Nicolas of Cusa and the later Pope (Pius II) Enea Silvio Piccolomini, who between 1450 and 1460, in what R.W. Southern has called a 'moment of vision',[16] grappled with the problem of Islam in a new, more peaceful, perspective.

From polemical caricature to balanced reassessment

Around a century later, in 1530, the year of the Lutheran Augsburg Confession, because of the steadily increasing threat to Christianity from the Turks (in 1529 they were at the gates of Vienna, in 1541 they captured Budapest), Pope Clement VII (Medici) had the Arabic text of the Qur'an burnt immediately after publication. It had been published in Venice, at that time called 'the Turkish whore' because it had long collaborated in the Eastern Mediterranean with the Ottoman empire. This first printed edition of the Qur'an may have been intended for export to Islamic countries, none of which then knew the art of printing. Be this as it may, in Rome as in Basle (where it was printed), people feared an intensification of an anti-trinitarian tendency (which appealed to the Bible).

Luther had spoken out for the translation and publication of the Qur'an, but only so that everyone could see what—to use his own words—an accursed, shameful, desperate book it is, full of lies, fables and every kind of abomination. There are said to be Lutheran theologians who even today read the Qur'an in this spirit. Because of the acute military threat and his apocalyptic anxiety, Luther demonized the Muslims, the Turkish rulers, as servants of the devil and claimed that in these end times Muhammad was a pseudo-prophet driven by lust and that Islam was a power opposed to Christ.[17]

Before the pioneering work on religious history *Pansebeia* (1650), written by the Scotsman Alexander Ross,[18] people in the West had a completely distorted picture of Islam, as is abundantly demonstrated by Norman Daniel's study *Islam and the West: The Making of an Image* (1960).[19] Such a religion could only be heresy and a deliberate falsification of the truth, a mixture of violence and sensuousness. Muhammad was a cheat, possessed by the devil, even the Antichrist. It was then easy to contrast this caricature of Islam with an ideal image of Christianity as a religion of truth, peace, love and continence. To immunize their own adherents against rival systems of faith, people defamed the rivals.

Another pioneering book was *De Religione Mohammedica* (1705) by the Utrecht Orientalist Adrian Reland.[20] This was, after the *Pansebeia*, the first approximately objective account of Islam and the Prophet and corrected some of the erroneous insights then current in all apologetic; it was promptly put on the Roman Index of Prohibited Books. But it was confirmed by the English translation of the Qur'an by George Sale and his famous *Preliminary Discourse* (1734),[21] commissioned by the Society for the Promotion of Christian Knowledge but committed to the Enlightenment and a reasonable and tolerant religion.

Enlightenment through literature

For after the Thirty Years War the Enlightenment honoured the notion of tolerance, as demonstrated in Germany in exemplary fashion by Gotthold Ephraim Lessing's play *Nathan the Wise* (1779),[22] with its famous parable of the three rings, that is, the three religions of which no one could tell for certain which was authentic. 225 years later it is still highly topical. In 1984, I gave a series of dialogue lectures at the University of Tübingen, with the literary critic Walter Jens, on eight writers of world literature. On 19 November I spoke about *Nathan*, this 'dramatic conversation between the three world religions of Semitic origin and prophetic character, presented in vivid figures full of spirit and understanding'. Lessing gives us an enlightened Jew (after his early play *The Jews* [1749] the first noble Jew in a German play), a likewise enlightened Muslim (the important sultan Saladin) and an immature but ultimately enlightened Christian (a young crusader, a counterpart to the authoritarian patriarch). Who could have guessed what grim topicality this play would continue to have, with its 'inspiring vision of peace between the religions as a harbinger for peace among human beings generally'?[23]

Between 11 September 2001 and the end of 2003 *Nathan* was staged twenty-four times in German theatres (and once in New York). Karl-Josef Kuschel has made a brilliant analysis of the play, which demonstrates convincingly 'why *Nathan* still has no peer': 'Only Lessing's *Nathan* has a "trialogical" structure: only in this play do all three traditions and cultures express their potential for conflict and reconciliation. We have no other great reference text in German literature about the relationship between Jews, Christians and Muslims. And now for the first time since the crusades there is again this conflict between the Jewish, Christian and Muslim world, focused on Palestine.'[24]

Kuschel rightly criticizes the way in which some contemporary directors focus their productions on the problem of the Germans and the Jews and neglect the Muslims. For through the three Muslims who are portrayed positively on the stage, Lessing makes a 'calculated or strategic re-evaluation of those who are despised' in the intercultural or inter-religious discussion, which is the 'opposite of naive idealization'.[25]

Besides Lessing, hardly anyone else in Europe contributed so much to the re-evaluation of Islam as did Johann Wolfgang von Goethe in his 'Western–Eastern Divan' (1819),[26] a collection (Persian *diwan*) of poems which came into being as the result of an encounter with the poetry of the fourteenth-century Persian poet Hafiz. With its 'Western–Eastern', the collection expresses the encounter of two poets, literatures and cultures—with the experience of love in *Suleiman* at the centre and coming to a climax with the religious problems in the last book. Following Goethe, the orientalist and poet Friedrich Rückert used his unusual talent for language and form to imitate the Qur'an.

In England, rather later, Thomas Carlyle,[27] a translator of Goethe, with his striking lecture 'The Hero as Prophet' (1840) developed a psychological portrait which depicted Muhammad as an honest prophet—in complete contrast to the utterly unhistorical tragedy *Mahomet*, first performed in Lille 1741, in which Voltaire expressed his contempt for the Prophet, and showed him as an unscrupulous figure in search of power. From one of the most notable champions of tolerance that is to be regretted.

Oriental studies and orientalism

The nineteenth century—the century of history-writing and European colonial expansion—finally led to a tremendous surge in oriental studies and thus in historical criticism of Islam. paving the way for a less polemical assessment of Islam on the part of Christian theology and the church. In five respects, decisive progress became evident in the nineteenth and twentieth centuries:[28]

- the historical–critical evaluation of the Prophet Muhammad by scholars such as Gustav Weil, Aloys Sprenger, William Muir, Reginald Bosworth Smith, Leone Caetani, Tor Andrae, Régis Blachère, Maxime Rodinson and W. Montgomery Watt;
- Theodor Nöldeke's history of the Qur'an, which remains fundamental today, and the historical-critical editions of the Qur'an and adequate modern translations associated with the names of Gustav Flügel, Richard Bell, Rudi Paret and Adel T. Khoury;
- a comprehensive investigation of Islamic culture from worship and mysticism through law and morality to literature and art, by such significant scholars as Ignaz Goldziher, C. Snouck Hurgronje, Annemarie Schimmel, and above all the great orientalist Louis Massignon, who called on Christians to make a 'spiritual Copernican shift' and argued for

reconciliation between the religion of hope (Judaism), the religion of love (Christianity) and the religion of faith (Islam);

- a historical–critical evaluation of the Qur'anic picture of Jesus—begun by G.F. Gerock 150 years ago and developed by traditio–historical investigations—which, with the comprehensive and more recent studies by Geoffrey Parrinder, Heikki Räisänen, Claus Schedl and Martin Bauschke (and Olaf H. Schumann for the later Arabic Islamic literature) has finally replaced the apologetic missionary approach.
- a multi-volume history of classical Islamic theology by Josef van Ess, made on the basis of a careful study of the sources.

In the nineteenth and twentieth centuries, oriental studies in Europe achieved a tremendous amount, creating the foundations for an understanding of the East in general and Islam in particular; I shall constantly refer to them. However, for a long time orientalists were not aware how much, despite all their efforts to achieve academic objectivity, they were actually in the service of the policy of economic and cultural hegemony practised by the European powers. Since the 1960s, critical reflection on the history and self-understanding of the orientalists (who initially were also admired in the Arab world) has begun in the West; in this connection I must mention Norman Daniel and Jacques Waardenburg.[29]

But above all *Orientalism*[30] by Edward W. Said, a Christian Palestinian of American nationality, professor of English and comparative literature at Columbia University, New York, published in 1978, gave a healthy shock to and laid the basis for a critical discussion of the post-colonial understanding of culture and post-colonial studies. This critic of literature, culture and society, who after 1967 became a champion of the Palestinian cause, certainly went too far when he sought to find in European oriental studies an anti-Arabism comparable to earlier antisemitism and to demonstrate that the 'East' of oriental studies (sensuous, corrupt, vicious, lazy and tyrannical) was a projection of the wishes of a Eurocentric spirit: the East as the central paradigm of the other.[31] Having said this, European oriental studies were indisputably also partly governed by the national and religious interests of the colonial powers: European soldiers, politicians, missionaries and orientalists often worked together, and the overestimation of European civilization went hand in hand with an underestimation of Arab civilization. Thus this was, in many respects, a cultural, 'spiritual' imperialism.[32] After the Second World War and the Holocaust, the Israeli–Arab conflict added another factor: German orientalists, mindful of historic German guilt, for the most part gave unilateral support to the Israelis.[33] Moreover, Said also vehemently objected to the authoritarian leadership style of Yasser Arafat and, with the Jewish conductor Daniel Barenboim, founded the splendid West–Eastern Divan Orchestra, currently celebrating worldwide success as an act of reconciliation between Jews and Arabs.

Edward Said died of leukaemia on 25 September 2003 at the age of sixty-seven. He has been called the 'only Arab thinker of the twentieth century who has notably shaped intellectual discussion in the West'.[34] The last sentences of what was, as far as I am aware, his last article (written after 11 September 2001) seem to me to be his testament: 'The present time is full of tensions, but it is better for us to ask whether communities are powerful or impotent and whether secular policy is based on reason or ignorance, and better to judge according to the universal categories of justice and injustice, than to get lost in violent abstractions which, while they may offer provisional satisfaction, contribute very little to self-knowledge and an objective analysis. The thesis of a "clash of civilizations" is as simplistic a phrase as "the war of the worlds" and it encourages self-righteous arrogance rather than a critical awareness of the perplexing interdependence of present-day societies.'[35]

Leaving aside the fundamentalist Islamic organizations and their spokesmen, the initially very heated discussion of Said's book[36] led to a more objective view and above all to a more critical and differentiated assessment of oriental studies (no Arab form of 'Western studies' has developed). It is no less welcome that the 1990 Gulf War and the journalistic 'panic makers' have contributed to a shift, particularly among German orientalists. Unlike British and French orientalists, they came not from colonial administration but from the scholarly world of linguistics and history and therefore were spared Said's criticism. Respected professionals, who hitherto had contented themselves with being privately horrified at journalistic best-selling authors and had practised their scholarship in ivory towers, now recognized their political responsibilities. They ventured into the public media to correct, with objective information, sweeping and unhistorical caricatures of Islam and the Arabs—which were particularly dangerous at a time of increasing xenophobia.[37]

However, even if as a Christian theologian one resolutely contests the caricature of Islam, this certainly does not mean that one has to cherish an idealized image of it instead.

2. The idealized image of Islam

Indisputably, hundreds of millions of people are fascinated by Islam. Those who, like me, well remember the time of uncritical Roman Catholic apologetic before the Second Vatican Council can imagine why some pious Muslims attempt to depict their own religion in the brightest colours. Quite uncritically, many people describe a 'whole world' of Islam, which hardly differs from the rose-coloured Christian depictions of Christianity.

An invitation to conversion

Thus Muhammad Ahmad Rassoud, a Muslim missionary in Germany, sent me his work 'What is Islam?' with a kind invitation to become a Muslim. He told me that I finally had the opportunity to enter the history of true faith and achieve happiness in this world and the next. In his booklet he sums up 'the essentials' of his religion 'in a brief and clear form': first the 'cornerstones of faith' (in the one God, his angels, his holy books, his messengers and the Last Judgement and predestination) and then the 'five pillars of Islam' (confession of faith, ritual prayer, almsgiving, month of fasting and pilgrimage). The point is made right at the beginning: 'Islam—this Arabic word means "complete submission and surrender" to Allah, the One God. Allah himself in the Qur'an, the holy book of Islam, describes the religion of Muslims with this expression: the word "Muslim"—derived from the same root *slm* as "Islam"—denotes one "who has submitted completely to Allah".'[38]

Here we are presented with an idealized religion. Islam is uncomplicated in life and morality; is reasonable and tolerant, the eternal doctrine of pure monotheism. We are also told this in an official 'Short Islamic Catechism' from Turkey.

> 'The name of our religion is Islam.
> This designation was not devised by human beings,
> but given by God in the Holy Qur'an.
> Therefore Islam is not the religion of just one people, one nation,
> but the religion of all human beings,
> it is the last religion,
> it is the religion of understanding and science,
> it is the religion of morality,
> it is the religion of peace and order,
> to those who believe in it, it is life.
> Islam purged the laws which were already present in the religions, but had been falsified by human hand. It rescued humankind from its spiritual abyss and led it to a moral level that the spirit of human beings could not devise.'[39]

Christians who want to engage in a fruitful dialogue with Muslims will welcome such Islamic confessions, even if they are very well aware that in them Islam is described at the expense of Jews and Christians, who have allegedly 'falsified the laws by human hand'. It is impossible to carry on any inter-religious dialogue, far less write a book on another religion, without empathy, indeed sympathy.

Incorruptible scholarly honesty, which speaks the truth undeterred, and passionate commitment which works untiringly against hatred and misunderstanding and for peace and understanding are not mutually exclusive. And, of course, this should also be shown from the Muslim side.

The fascination of Islam

Jews and Christians can also be fascinated with Islam. A witness who is above suspicion is Ignaz Goldziher, one of the founders of modern Islamic studies. Goldziher, a Jewish scholar of Hungarian descent, lived in Damascus and Cairo in 1873–4. In just a few pages, his diary shows impressively how one becomes a real Middle East expert.[40] The spontaneous friendliness and welcome which anyone can experience even today in Middle Eastern countries quickly made the twenty-three-year-old from a strange country and religion familiar with the 'powerful world religion of Islam'. 'Moreover during these weeks I lived so much in the Mohammedan spirit that ultimately I became inwardly convinced that I myself was a Mohammedan, and shrewdly discovered that this is the only religion which can satisfy philosophical minds even in its official doctrinal form and formulation. My ideal was to raise Judaism to a similar rational level. My experience taught me that Islam is the only religion in which superstition and pagan rudiments are made taboo not by rationalism, but by orthodox doctrine.' He goes on: 'My way of thinking was utterly sympathetic to Islam; my sympathy also pulled me towards it subjectively. I called my monotheism Islam, and I was not lying if I said that I believed in the prophecies of Mohammed. My copy of the Qur'an can attest how I was inwardly drawn to Islam. My teachers earnestly longed for the moment of my open declaration.'[41]

However, Goldziher remained a Jew and became a great scholar in Jewish studies. In this he differed from a philosopher of our day, the Frenchman Roger Garaudy. For a long time Garaudy was a Politburo member of the Communist Party of France before he became a Reform Communist and for a time a Christian. At the end of a long spiritual journey he finally converted to Islam. He then vigorously denounced the self-righteousness and blindness of the Christian West, energetically called for a 'dialogue of civilizations' and, in the face of the wave of Islamic fundamentalism, presented his readers with an idealized Islam which had brought to the dying civilizations the soul of a new common life. The main concern of his book is to emphasize the 'promise of Islam' in a world which is falling apart: 'Islam has not only integrated the oldest and most developed cultures, those of China and India, Persia and Greece, Alexandria and Byzantium, made them fruitful and spread them from the Chinese sea to the Atlantic, from Samarkand to Timbuktu. It has also brought the soul of a new social life to collapsing empires and dying civilizations, restored to people and their societies their specifically human and divine dimensions of transcendence and society and, on the basis of this simple and strong faith, nurtured a new flourishing of the sciences and arts, prophetic wisdom and laws.'[42] Remarks made by Garaudy in the 1990s which were felt to be and in part were antisemitic indicate that such enthusiasm about Islam can also have its dark side.

Is Garaudy a unique case? In Germany, too, the way of a convert is publicly known and vigorously discussed. Murad Wilfried Hofmann aroused attention because he, with a legal and philosophical training, was the German ambassador to Morocco and Algeria. In his account of his conversion he indicates that, for him, classical Sunni Islam (unlike Garaudy, he thinks little of Sufism) embodies an ideal, living, worthwhile religion. Moreover, he regards Islam as the viable alternative for the future. 'As long as the Western world and Communism stood against each other, Islam could be understood as a "third way", as an option between these two worldviews. Today, however, it sees itself as an alternative scheme for dealing with life in a world that again has become dualistic. It is almost self-evident to far-sighted observers that in the twenty-first century Islam will become a dominant religion worldwide. The title of my book indicates why this will be the case, God willing. Islam does not just regard itself as an alternative to post-industrial Western society. It *is* the alternative.'[43]

May we be critical?

Of course I shall be examining this fascination with Islam carefully. Is it really an 'alternative', really the 'promise' that is conjured up? Just as we should not be terrified by a hostile image, so too we should not be blinded by an idealized image. Other converts to Islam also know this: in contrast to modern Western Islamic studies, traditional Islamic scholarship does not regard critical investigation as its task. Its perspective is, above all, the description, explanation and justification of an ideal Islam. So may we seriously criticize Islam from the inside or even from the outside?

Many orthodox Muslims a priori reject any criticism of their religion—just as many narrow-minded Christians or Jews react in an ungracious and emotional way to criticism of theirs. With my books on Judaism and Christianity I experienced how my criticism of the policy of the state of Israel and my criticism of the policies of Pius XII led a knowledgeable Jewish reviewer and a knowledgeable Roman Catholic reviewer to target fragments of the book and punish all the other parts by ignoring them. Conversely, at a very early stage, some Muslim intellectuals have applied the criticism of Western scholarship to their own religion, history and culture, so that today the front line between the critical and the uncritical runs through Islam. Although it is often concealed, this provokes numerous internal conflicts. For in Islam, as in Christianity and Judaism, as well as all the progress isn't there also a great deal of regression? Aren't there also false developments, fossilizations and errors? Just as idealistic and remote depictions of the church are far from the reality of Christianity, is that possibly also the case with similar accounts of Islam? In the long run, all idealizations, mystifications and glorifications are made at the cost of the religion itself. Don't both Christianity and Islam call for truthfulness? Why not then also truthfulness towards oneself?

Neither prohibitions of questions nor lame comparisons

No religious or state authority has the right to hinder the quest for truth by prohibiting questions. Precisely for the sake of the truth of one's own religion, one must be unreservedly truthful, though of course this must be coupled with justice and fairness. Ultimately free discussion cannot be suppressed, even in authoritarian and totalitarian systems: the Pope could not stop the debate about the ordination of women with an 'infallible' statement, and Ayatollah Khomeini could not stop the controversy over Salman Rushdie with a *fatwa*. So it must be permissible to investigate whether and to what extent Islam, perhaps in the form of some of its representatives, encourages intolerance (especially towards religious minorities), inspires militancy (with its universal claims, including plans to conquer the world) and embodies regressiveness (for example in respect of democracy, human rights and the status of women).

I shall also discuss the great historic confrontations between Islam and Christianity: the Arab conquest of originally Christian territories in the Middle East and North Africa and the centuries-long occupation of Spain in the West and the Balkans in the East. And the expansion of Islam in black Africa and South-East Asia and the efforts to produce a single Islamic front against the West cannot be ignored. Likewise, the European counter-offensives against Islam must also be subject to close inspection: not only the crusades and the Spanish *reconquista* but also, and above all, the military, economic, cultural and religious expansion of the West in the time of modern colonialism and imperialism—up to the fatal Iraq war of 2003, the war of the big lies.

I hope to go into all these questions in a spirit of objectivity and fairness. Both adherents of Islam (Muslim scholars) and experts on Islam (Western specialists) should be convinced that they can learn from one another. But should we compare alleged Islamic intolerance with Western 'tolerance' and 'enlightenment' (as often happens from the Christian side, thinkingly or unthinkingly); Islamic militancy with the alleged Western love of peace and democracy; Islamic backwardness with Western 'progress' and 'modernity'; or even Islam as a religion of the law with Christianity as a religion of freedom?

Strong doubts immediately arise over these lame comparisons:

- is a hostile image of Islam being compared with an idealized image of the West?
- isn't there much intolerance, militancy and backwardness in the West, and much tolerance, love of peace and progress in Islam?
- isn't such a friend–foe scheme meant to mock and exclude what is strange to us?
- is a picture of the real Islam really being sought here?

Today, Christianity is quite openly pluralistic and Islam is more pluralistic than it seems. One of the best Christian experts on Islam, Wilfred Cantwell Smith, has constantly emphasized, quite correctly, that Christians must understand Islam as Muslims understand it themselves.[44] However, the question immediately arises: which Muslims? Can we speak of 'Muslims' or 'Islam' just like that?

3. The real image of Islam

There is a middle way between caricaturing Islam and glorifying it. The common failing of these two approaches is that both are attached to a monolithic and unhistorical image of Islam and presuppose that Islam has always been, and is, everywhere the same. However different Wahhabi Saudis, Iranian Shiite mullahs, Egyptian Islamic Brethren, Palestinian Hamas fighters, Pakistani Sufis or American Black Muslims may be, it is thought that there is an eternal unchanging essence of Islam, radically different from everything Western. In the face of such simplification, only a constant, differentiated consideration of two perspectives can help. The image of Islam, like that of Christianity, is governed throughout by a twofold dialectic: that of essence and form and of essence and perversion.

The 'essence' of Islam in changing forms

If some earlier publications on Islam have shown a lack of tension, in forgetfulness of the present, some current publications suffer from short-sightedness in an obsession with the present. Only an up-to-date interpretation, with a historical in-depth dimension, can help in the dialogue between religions and cultures. The concept of Islam is determined by its concrete historical form at any one time, but by way of exaggeration in the opposite direction, one could almost say that Islam has never anywhere been the same. Each age has its own images and realizations of Islam, which have grown out of a particular historical situation, been lived out of and shaped by particular social and regional forces and Muslim communities, and formed both beforehand and afterwards by individual, intellectually stimulating, personalities.

We must recognize that, for all the historical currents and counter-currents, in the various constantly shifting historical images and lived-out realizations of Islam there is an abiding element to which we shall have to devote all our attention: its basic components and basic perspectives stem from an origin that is by no means random but is given with a quite specific historical personality, a holy scripture. This remains an enduring norm. As in the history of Christianity, so too in the history of Islam there is a persisting element, indeed an 'essence', a common substance, or whatever one cares to call it. I am well aware of the misunderstandings bound up with these traditional terms. Therefore, against all rigid 'essentialism', I would immediately add that this abiding essence shows itself only in what is changing: there is an identity, but only in variables; a continuum, but only in the event; a constancy, but only in changing manifestations. In short, the 'essence' of Islam shows itself not in metaphysical immobility and remoteness but only in a constantly changeable historical form of appearance or *Gestalt.* To get a sight of this original, abiding 'essence' of Islam—which is dynamic, not static and rigid—one must note its changing historical manifestation, its *Gestalt.*[45]

Such a historical approach may seem unusual to some Muslims (and also to some Christians), but only if we see the 'essence' of Islam in its changing historical manifestations do we grasp the Islam from which I want to begin in this account: not an idealized Islam in the remote spheres of a philosophical, theological or juristic theory, but real Islam, as it exists in this world and its history. The real essence of real Islam takes place in different historical forms.

That is illuminating: nowhere is there an essence of Islam 'in itself', detached, distilled 'with chemical purity' from the flow of history: essence and form cannot be neatly separated. At the same time, it is important to see essence and form in their different natures. Otherwise how could Islamic 'reformers', who have existed at all times and still exist today, define the abiding in what is taking shape and judge the concrete, historical manifestation? How otherwise could Muslims and non-Muslims have a norm by which to define what is acceptable or reprehensible in a particular historical and empirical form of Islam? The important of this will emerge when we consider the second perspective.

The 'essence' of Islam and its perversion

Not a few Muslims (and Christians) suffer because Islam (like Christianity) can be distorted, falsified and misused both in everyday private life and in the wider world of politics. Like Christianity, Islam often has been and is used by rulers as a political instrument instead of being lived out as faith and ethics. Thus often Islam, like Christianity, has sown hatred and violence and inspired and legitimated oppression and war, instead of disseminating justice and humanity.

Those with a religious orientation should not deny that, as a human phenomenon, religion is ambivalent. In any religion, essence and form, the abiding and the changing, the good and the bad, saving and damning, essence and perversion[46] are interwoven and can never clearly be separated by human beings, who are themselves deeply ambivalent. Religion can be perverted even in its most essential element, the Bible or the Qur'an. Even the best religious idealism and readiness for sacrifice can be abused and be prone to evil. Power-hungry and obtuse representatives of both religions prove that guilt and sin, both personal and 'structural', are possible even in the holiest things. In short, in Islam too, real essence can be perverted. This is not its legitimate but its illegitimate essence, not its authentic but its perverted essence.

The perversion of the essence of every religion is a dark shadow on all historical eras. That is why one can see the history of any religion in a positive or a negative light. If in Islam there is far less public complaint about this, it is because such complaint is far more dangerous than in Christianity: in both religions, over the course of time it is possible to recognize not only a shaping and forcing of history but also a degeneration and capitulation to it. Religion can degenerate into a power apparatus working with very worldly means and a bureaucracy centred on itself and become a superficial traditional religious feeling which is poor in substance. Anyone, historian or war correspondent, who wants to fix on the negative can easily write a 'criminal history' of Islam, of the kind that has been written of Christianity, and completely miss its essentials by focusing on blood and tears, death and acts of vengeance, wrong turns and false developments.

This means that not only historicity in general but all the historical infection of Islam by elements which are contrary to Islam will, even in its earliest history, be lamented by many Muslims (three of the four rightly-guided caliphs were murdered). What some Muslims today are saying in secret, a few are saying publicly. And where an authoritarian political system does not allow people to migrate, they have turned inwards. More recent critical voices, from Salman Rushdie to Taslima Nasrin, may seem one-sided, arrogant, malicious, indeed damnable to many Muslims, but they should be listened to. It would be wrong to counter them only with cowardly apologetic, persecution, even threats of death—instead of with a real apologia, a defence and justification of Muslim faith, which knows how to distinguish between well-founded and unfounded charges and fundamental reforms.

The status quo as a criterion?

I will never simply take the present status quo of Islam as a criterion or justify it (and here I believe that I am in company with many Muslims); after all, many Muslims themselves hope for or urge a renewal of their religion. Rather, writing as, so to speak, their Christian advocate, I will undertake a critical reconnaissance that should be a help towards the renewal of Islam that is constantly necessary. I chose this approach for Judaism and Christianity, without falsely sparing my own religion, and I will attempt it for my account of Islam.

Is this a presumptuous aim? Not at all. What I have said of Christianity applies here: as an ecumenical theologian committed to fairness to all religions and against all the constantly threatening frustration and resignation of reformers of all religions, who sometimes feel that they are dogs baying at the moon or are running up against a brick wall, I would like my analytical approach to contribute towards a diagnosis of the present which, where necessary, attacks abuses, identifies those responsible, increases the pressure for reform and encourages structural changes. No religion—neither Judaism nor Christianity nor Islam (nor the religions of Indian and Chinese origin)—can be satisfied with the status quo in this time of upheaval. Everywhere there are amazingly parallel questions about a future renewal. In the face of antisemitism and increasing Islamophobia, what are called for are not uncritical philosemites or Islamophiles (hardly anyone talks of Christianophiles), but rather authentic, truthful friends of Judaism and Islam.

Like Judaism and Christianity, in this transitional phase of world history Islam is involved in a fundamental conflict of tradition and innovation; how this can finally be resolved in a balanced way is an open question. As with Judaism and Christianity, so with Islam, one asks oneself whether this religion will succeed in preserving its religious 'substance', its 'essence', despite all the differences and conflicts, despite all the different trends and schools and the battles between traditionalists and modernists, and at the same time reshape itself for a new generation. Will the Islamic peoples, who are caught up in a tremendous crisis of existence at the height of modernity as a result of their confrontation with Western imperialism and colonialism and with European science and economics, technology and democracy, succeed in accepting the challenge of a new era and work creatively towards a new postmodern form of Islam? In this globalized world, all the great religions are in transition from the crisis of modernity into a 'postmodernity' of some kind (or under whatever name) and are thus exposed to the same kind of structural problems.

Understanding Islam from the inside

Outsiders can recognize the fruitful development of Islamic studies, which today are being engaged in more and more by Western and Islamic scholars jointly. Along with the political and economic revaluation of the Islamic nations and Islamic immigration into Western Europe and America, this is the premise for the unquestionably epoch-making reorientation of the Roman Catholic Church, documented in the Declaration on the Non-Christian Religions by the Second Vatican Council (1965).[47] After the Council it was also expressed in a variety of meetings between Muslims and Christians, official and unofficial. The World Council of Churches was also concerned with greater openness towards other religions, and in 1979 for the first time published *Guidelines on the Dialogue with People of Living Faiths and Ideologies.*[48]

It is obvious that in Christianity there can be no going back to the old apologetics and polemics, to immunization by defamation. The centuries of isolation and mutual ignorance are in any case impossible for an increasing number of people to take: books, mass media, travel, hundreds of thousands of adherents of another religion in one's own country, have all had their effect. Despite many political acts of violence and wars, contempt for other religions is slowly giving way to understanding, ignorance to information, mission to dialogue. If the West changes its attitude to the Islamic world, that world will sooner or later change its attitude to the West.

Christian theologians will not investigate Islam from a position of self-assurance only from the outside, in detached objectivity. Since they too are involved, they will constantly think of questions for their own religion and formulate them openly. Christians (and often also Muslims themselves) far too often still regard 'Islam' as a rigid entity, as a closed system of religion, rather than as a living religious movement which over the centuries has undergone epoch-making paradigm shifts in a constant process of change. It has developed great internal diversity and shaped a great variety of people with a broad spectrum of attitudes and feelings.

Our concern must be slowly, as best we can, to understand from within why Muslims see God and the world, worship and the service of humanity, politics, law and art with different eyes and experience them with different hearts. First, we should be clear that for the great majority of Muslims, even today, Islam is not simply a part of life, what secularized people are fond of calling the 'religious factor' alongside the 'cultural factors'. For believing Muslims their life and religion, religion and culture, are interwoven in a lively way, as are their religion and politics. Islam seeks an all-embracing view of life, an all-pervasive attitude wand a way of life which determines everything. We shall have to examine how far this can be realized in a new era of world history.

In an age of aroused ecumenical awareness—more than ever after the attacks in New York and Washington on 11 September 2001, in Madrid on 11 March 2004 and in London on 7 July 2005—I want to argue for the overall responsibility of all for all, and especially for government and political responsibility, in view of a world-political situation that has been made worse by a completely perverse policy. Such inter-religious responsibility means that we must all be interested in the well-being of Islam. Respect for Islam, indeed admiration for its fourteen centuries of cultural and spiritual achievement, should be the basis for formulating particular concerns for reform in the light of the nature of Islam—and for inter-religious solidarity with countless Muslim men and women who feel the pressure for reform far more existentially than any Christian theologian.

But—and every author asks this question—where does one begin such an account of Islam? My answer is: where else than at the beginning? But how is the beginning of Islam to be dated? That question isn't easy to answer.

A II

Problems of the Beginning

Who was the first Muslim? The majority of Christians would certainly reply: Muhammad, the Prophet. As a result, there are still many people today who wrongly call this religion 'Mohammedanism' and its adherents 'Mohammedans'—and in so doing greatly offend Muslims. We can read in any elementary introduction to Islam what has already been laid down in the Qur'an: the first Muslim is Adam, the first human being, for he already 'submitted' to the one and only God, as did Noah and Abraham, Moses and all the prophets, indeed finally Jesus. They all, in their own way, already practised 'Islam', 'submission', 'surrender' to the will of the one and only God. Although the developments of this teaching were always adapted to different peoples and times and thus differed in some respects, they were always about the same message: submission to God, surrender to God.

This is precisely what the Prophet Muhammad proclaimed. As the last of the prophets he simply elevated this eternal teaching to its highest, final stage. So Islam is the one, true, perfect, eternal religion of humankind and the religion of the very beginning. It is the teaching of the Qur'an, just as it is the teaching of the Bible, that the first human being believed in the one God. That is the Muslim self-understanding, and the Muslim theology of history. How much of it can be proved historically?

1. Five thousand years of Near Eastern high religions

Before we turn to the personality of the Prophet Muhammad, to be able to see the Prophet's originality we need to picture some defining structures and mark out the framework within which he lived. For this, however, we have to go back a long way. How far? To the beginning of human history? In their early enthusiasm to see a development, ethnologists wanted to go straight back to the very first beginnings of religion. But they have now abandoned the search for a primal religion, whether animistic or monotheistic. Why? Because they simply do not have the necessary sources for a historical explanation of the origin of religion; contemporary nature-peoples have by no means remained pure 'primal peoples', as was once thought. They too have a long, if unwritten, history.[1]

What about the Bible? Christian theologians should openly concede that the Bible contains no historical information about the beginnings of religion. Given their literary genre, stories in the book of Genesis about a paradisal primal state of human beings and their subsequent fall do not set out to be 'remembrances of primal times', historical accounts; they contain a poetic message, in religious garb, about the greatness of the one God and Creator and the fundamental goodness of his creation, and about human freedom, responsibility and guilt. Present-day Christian theology has therefore lost its early interest in a 'primal monotheism': it has no difficulties in accepting an evolution of the world and of human beings from lower organisms, and does not try to make a synthesis between biblical testimony and ethnological evidence. It is enough to know that in the thousands of years of human history no people and no tribe have so far been found that have no characteristics of religion (in the broadest sense of the word, which includes magic).

Arabia on the periphery of the great empires

We are relatively well informed about the earliest high cultures, because they are the first cultures with writing. Although the discussion about where the first human being (*homo sapiens*) appeared, whether in Africa or elsewhere, is still in full swing, the discussion about the first early historical high cultures and high religions which arose around five thousand years ago has long since settled down. The earliest high culture developed long before the Indus culture in the Indus valley, the Shang culture in the valley of the Yellow River and probably before the Egyptian culture in the Nile Delta—in southern Mesopotamia, in the flood plains of the Euphrates and the Tigris; and this culture had offshoots as far as Arabia.

What would Arabia have been without the inventions made in the temple cities of Sumeria: of the wheel, the potter's wheel, the wagon, the oldest system of calculation (used for the temple economy and to establish an order of gods in the cosmic system)? What would Arabia have been without the invention of writing: in Sumer first of all a pictorial script scratched on clay tablets (of a kind invented almost contemporaneously in Egypt), from which cuneiform and finally a syllabic script came into being?[2] Without writing, administrative registers cannot be set up, nor can messages be transmitted over long distances—prerequisites for the organization of large populations and for retaining learning for later generations.

Historical research shows that from the earliest times to the time of Islam a micro-structure and a contrary macrostructure influenced Near Eastern society.

- The fundamental microstructure, which had been shaped by small groups, was held together by kinship and neighbourliness. Families, clans and tribes were responsible for marriages and bringing up children; they settled disputes and formed a common defensive front against the outside world.
- Over above and this, and running contrary to it, was a macrostructure formed on the one hand by religion and on the other by empires which constantly increased in number and replaced one another. This structure was capable of integrating clans, villages and tribes into a single society, leading to great cultural achievements from the invention of writing, through the creation of important works of myth, religion and poetry, to masterpieces of architecture and sculpture.

The gigantic Arabian peninsula, between the Persian Gulf and the Red Sea, lay on the periphery of the first great cultural sphere, which had developed into a great semicircle, the 'Fertile Crescent'.[3] The name of its inhabitants, 'Aribi', appears for the first time in the ninth century BCE, in a cuneiform account of the battle of Qarqar (853 BCE) by the Assyrian king Shalmaneser III; there is some dispute as to precisely what lies behind this name (ethnically or geographically).[4] By the first millennium BCE, Semites from the north had advanced into the south of the peninsula. In the oasis regions of the rainy south-western triangle, well protected by the Arabian Sea and the Red Sea and the great desert within Arabia, they built several city-states with great temples, monuments and irrigation systems. In addition to the northern Semitic civilization of the Fertile Crescent, here was a southern Semitic civilization—an outpost (the 'Phoenicia of the south')—with the longest trade routes in the world at that time. These were the people of Ma'in, Saba', Qataban and Hadramaut, who are usually called Sabaeans, later Himyarites (Homerites), but today also Yemenites. For long centuries this southern Arabia dominated—because of its favourable climate (proximity to the monsoon), its lucrative monopoly in incense, and above all its geographical situation, which in antiquity was outstanding for trade between east (India) and west (Egypt, the Mediterranean countries, Mesopotamia). With good reason, southern Arabia, with its harbours of Aden and Qana', has been called *Arabia felix*.

Northern Arabia was fundamentally different from this rich and 'fortunate Arabia', a producer and importer of luxury goods, but without leaving any great intellectual, artistic or spiritual achievements: it was arid, inhospitable, sandy, stony, rocky and had no lakes and rivers, only wadis. This land required of its plants, animals and human beings, date palms and camels ('the ships of the desert'), the utmost in hardness, endurance and fighting spirit. But it was this particular northern area, with its sandy deserts, steppes and basalt hills, but also its oases, that made it possible for the Bedouins to settle, cultivate the land and trade (and later possibly breed horses, which were important for militarization). This north changed markedly because of the greatly increased caravan trade on the 'incense route', which had to be organized, protected and encouraged. Northern, or to be more precise Western Central, Arabia is the real home of the Arabs; with its rising cities of Mecca, Ta'if, Yathrib (later renamed al-Madinah—Medina, 'the city' of the Prophet—after Muhammad) and Najran it is the birthplace of Islam. The future was to belong to it.

The great Mesopotamian empires (Babylonian, Assyrian, Chaldaean) which replaced the early Sumerian city states perished as early as the seventh century BCE. Their place was taken by the first comprehensive Near Eastern great empire, that of the Persian Achaemenids. This in turn was destroyed in the fourth century BCE by Alexander the Great, who also conquered Egypt and incorporated its independent culture and religion into his Hellenistic empire. It was of decisive long-term significance for Arabia that this first great empire, stretching from west to east, was finally divided again: in the east it became the Persian empire, first that of the Parthians and from the third century CE that of the Sasanians (with its capital Ctesiphon on the Tigris); in the West it became the Roman empire, which since the fourth century CE had been ruled from Byzantium. Arabia, lying so to speak in between, had for a long time been a plaything of the great powers; as well as Persia and Byzantium, Christianized Ethiopia (with its capital Aksum) played a role.

The Arab tribes advanced far from their peninsula, into Syria and as far as the Mediterranean. In the centuries before Islam this did not happen through conquest, but through a slow process of migration and infiltration of Arabic-speaking individuals and tribal groups, some nomadic, some semi-nomadic and some settled. The Arabs were not remote from the great cultures, but on their doorstep.

The opportunity for Arabia to make its mark on world history was still to come—and would be of decisive significance for the spread of Islam—when in the seventh century CE both the Byzantine and the Sasanian empires went into decline. A power vacuum formed, which the expanding Arab forces could fill. This expansion would have been inconceivable had it not been spurred on by a new faith. Yet was this faith really new?

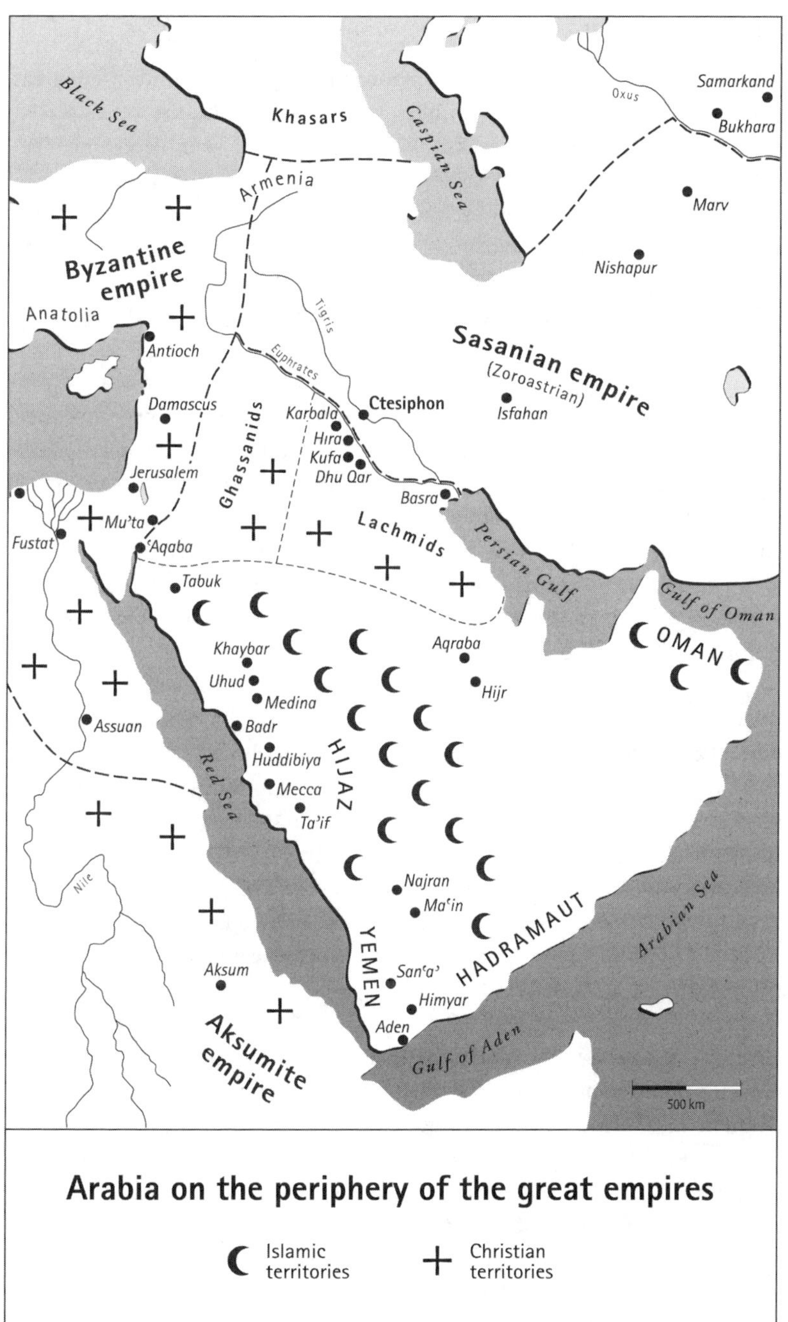

Arabia on the periphery of the great empires

The breakthrough of prophetic monotheism—Israel and Iran

Not only the empires but also the religions in the Near East underwent great upheavals. Often the gods of the families, villages, tribes and cities were replaced by universal gods, the gods of empires, who mostly formed pantheons and hierarchies. From there, as is often asserted, it was only a small step (but even in Israel a long development, for even in Israel polytheism was widespread until the Babylonian exile in the sixth century BCE) to belief in the one God who is the God of the whole universe and the whole of humankind.

Monotheism arose in Israel only on the basis of a whole series of upheavals:[5]

– In the eighth century BCE an initially minority Yahweh-alone movement began the worship of one God (monolatry) but without the denying the existence of other gods outside Israel—hence the sharp polemic of the prophet Hosea against the worship of other gods in Israel and against prostitution in the temple precinct, which was the expression of this alien culture.
– In the seventh century, sole worship of Yahweh became established: in Israel only Yahweh was to be honoured in worship; under King Josiah there was a reform and centralization of the cult on Jerusalem.
– Only in the sixth century did the sole worship of Yahweh (monolatry) develop into a strict belief in one God (monotheism) which denied the existence of all other gods. Thus Second Isaiah (Deutero-Isaiah) proclaims: 'There is no God but me. There is no just and saving God alongside me.'[6] The conquest of Jerusalem by the Babylonians, the destruction of the temple of Solomon and the deportation of the whole upper class to Babylon (587/86 BCE) were interpreted as a punishment for straying into polytheism and the old scriptures were subsequently revised in a strictly monotheistic sense. In the seventh century in the Persian empire, monotheism had likewise become established through the prophetic figure of Zoroaster.

Once Christianity had adopted Jewish monotheism seven centuries later, almost all the peoples around Arabia—the inhabitants of both the Persian Sasanian empire and the Roman Byzantine empire—confessed the one God. And as contacts between the peoples of the Near East deepened, belief in one God, also supported by the Byzantine and the Persian empires, could develop its missionary force. Arab traders and caravans did not have to travel far on any of the great trade routes before encountering monotheistic peoples. As well as the Byzantine imperial church there was the Coptic Church in Egypt, the Jacobite Church in Syria and the Nestorian Church in Iraq.

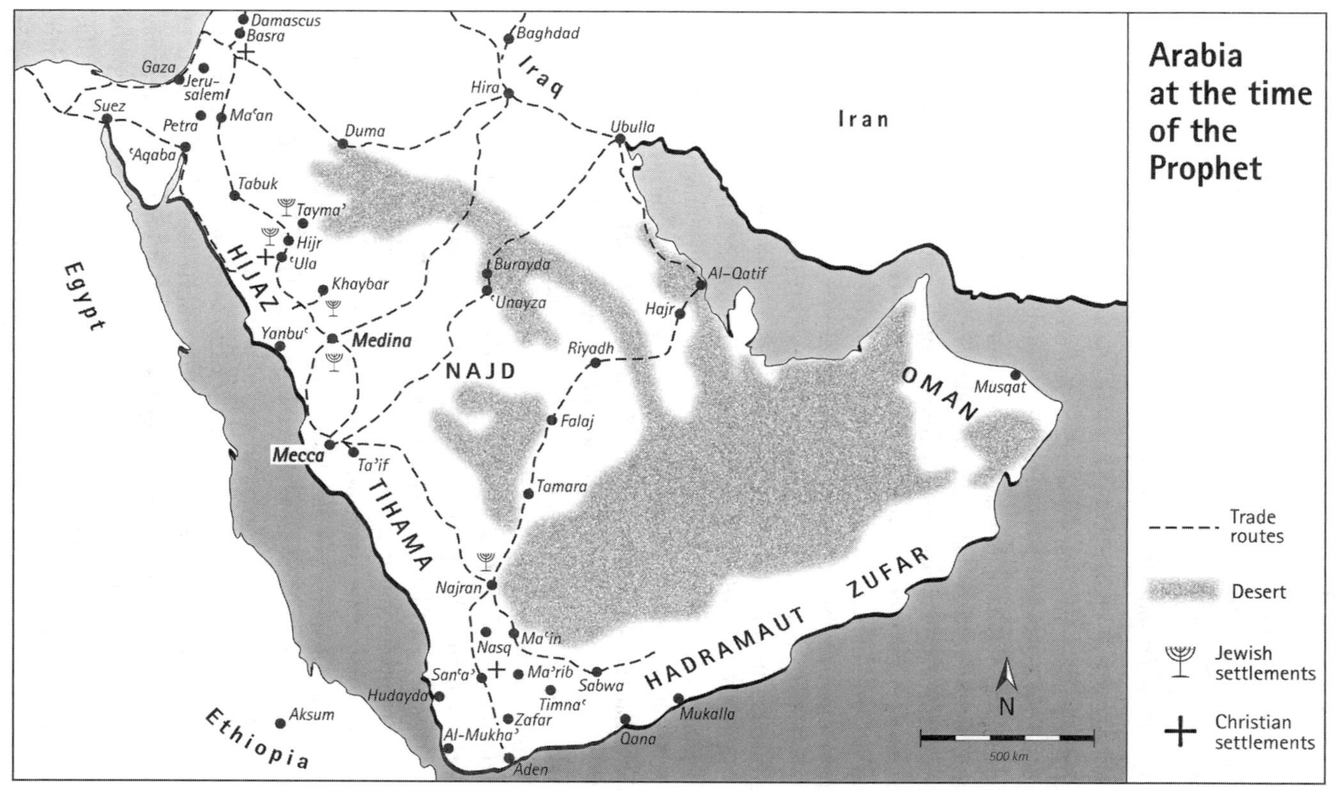
Arabia at the time of the Prophet
Trade routes
Desert
Jewish settlements
Christian settlements
N
500 km
Iran
Iraq
Egypt
Ethiopia
OMAN
ZUFAR
HADRAMAUT
NAJD
TIHAMA
HIJAZ
Damascus
Basra
Baghdad
Hira
Gaza
Jeru-salem
Suez
Petra
Maʿan
ʿAqaba
Duma
Ubulla
Tabuk
Taymaʾ
Hijr
ʿUla
Khaybar
Burayda
ʿUnayza
Al-Qatif
Hajr
Yanbuʿ
Medina
Riyadh
Musqat
Falaj
Mecca
Taʾif
Tamara
Najran
Maʿin
Nasq
Sanʿaʾ
Maʾrib
Sabwa
Hudayda
Timnaʿ
Zafar
Mukalla
Aksum
Al-Mukhaʾ
Qana
Aden

2. Jews, Christians and Jewish Christians in Arabia

In Arabia in 600 CE there were Jews and Christians who believed in one God, but also Arabs who were neither Jews nor Christians. First we shall look at the Jews, then at the Christians in Arabia.

The Jews in the competition over Arabia

Jews had already long been present on the Arabian peninsula before the Christians. They had contacts with the Sabaean kingdom, which is mentioned on several occasions in the Hebrew Bible, in the genealogical lists of the sons of Joktan[7] and Abraham,[8] but especially in connection with the narrative of the visit of the legendary queen of Saba (Sheba in Hebrew) to King Solomon in Jerusalem.[9] The first Jews may have come to southern Arabia as early as the first century BCE, as traders or with the Roman army of occupation in 25.[10] Arabia became even more important for the Jews after the destruction of the Second Temple in 70 CE, their banishment from Jerusalem in 135 CE by the Romans and the rapid expansion of Christianity in the Roman empire. After that, the two great monotheistic religions existed side by side in Arabia, in competition.

In the long centuries of the dominance of south Arabia, Judaism was widely disseminated. There Christianity was associated with Byzantium and Ethiopia, two traditional enemies. However, as early as the fourth century CE Theophilus the Indian (probably an Eritrean, he died in 365), a Byzantine missionary of the Arian confession, allegedly persuaded the Himyarites, who had ruled southern Arabia since the first century BCE, succeeding the Sabaeans, to accept Christianity; he is said to have baptized many people and to have built three churches in Tapharan (*Zafar*?), Aden (*'Adan*) and Hormuz. Yet although Christianity spread widely in the Hadramaut and especially in Najran, which was now Arabized, the position of Judaism remained unshaken.

The competition between Jews and Christians intensified in an ugly way in the first quarter of the sixth century: there was more than one Jewish persecution of Christians in southern Arabia. Clearly, no religion which has come to power is inoculated against the abuse of power. In particular King Yusuf (Dhu Nuwas), who had converted to Judaism, attempted to disseminate Judaism systematically; he persecuted the Christians, provoking a military intervention from Aksum, Christian Ethiopia. Numerous forcible conversions and destructions of churches and villages culminated in the massacre of Christians in Najran, today a city on the frontier between Saudi Arabia and the Yemen.[11] Surah 85.1–9 of the Qur'an is said to refer to this event but the reference is disputed.[12] At any rate this was the turning point: around a thousand years of dominance in southern Arabia was ended when in about 520 an Ethiopian expedition with Byzantine support crossed the strait of Bab al-Mandab, defeated the last Judaizing king of Himyar and for fifty years made southern Arabia an Ethiopian protectorate. Najran became a great Christian centre: a holy city with its holy martyrs Arethas, Elesbaas and Gregentius, and a famous church, an Arabian place of pilgrimage. The Jews had a hard time until the land was finally conquered by the Persians in 575. The Persians then ruled south Arabia for fifty years—until it was conquered by the Arabs. From March 630 to March 631 they received numerous delegations, including 'a delegation of Christians from Najran to God's Messenger, around 60 knights in strength and 14 of the most prominent among them', as Ibn Hisham reports in his biography of the Prophet. What was discussed on this occasion with these Christians, who were manifestly Monophysites, has yet to be discovered, despite intensive research.[13]

However, Judaism had been strongly represented not only in the south, but for a long time also in the north, perhaps since the Babylonian exile and certainly since the first century BCE.[14] Jews lived in several of the fertile palm oases of the Hijaz (Western Arabia) as farmers and craftsmen, apparently not in Mecca but particularly in Yathrib (later Medina). A third of the population of Yathrib is said to have been Jewish: there was even a Jewish clan of goldsmiths and there were armourers and scholars familiar with the Hebrew Bible and the Talmud. The names and works of Jewish poets in Arabia a generation before Muhammad and in his time are preserved in classic Arabic poetry. Arab historians mention that around twenty Jewish tribes lived in the region and there are also reports of Jews in numerous other places in the northern Hijaz. But how were things with the Christians?

Six centuries of Arab Christianity

Ignaz Goldziher, who combined great learning with an insuperable antipathy to Christians, was 'convinced' of 'a lack of any receptivity on the part of the Arab world to the ideas taught in Christianity'. He argued that it was necessary to note 'the superficial way in which Christianity penetrated those few strata of the Arab world into which it found entry, and how completely alien and indifferent the nucleus of the Arab people was towards it, despite the support that this religion found in some parts of Arab territory'.[15]

By contrast, Kenneth Cragg, a leading Christian expert on Islam and the Near East, has demonstrated in a first comprehensive scholarly history of Arab Christians[16] what a role Christianity played in the Near East at a very early stage.[17] Prince Hassan bin Talal of Jordan, the learned spokesman of an Islam ready for dialogue, has confirmed this in a historical investigation.[18] According to Cragg, hardly anything can be inferred from the mention of 'Arabs' in the Pentecost narrative of the Acts of the Apostles;[19] we do not know what Arabs these were, but they were certainly not Arabs from the Arabian peninsula (*jazirat al-'Arab*, 'island of the Arabs'). And the stay in 'Arabia'[20] which Paul says he made does not need to have been a stay on the Arabian peninsula (or in Sinai). In both cases he could be referring to the Syrian desert close to Damascus.

Unquestionably there was considerable Christian influence on pre-Islamic Arabia, above all among the allies of Rome (*confoederati*), not least through Syrian monks, whose monasteries penetrated the desert to a greater extent than did the churches. However, if we are to be able to assess this influence correctly, we must distinguish between three senses of the term 'Arabia':

– In the north-west and north-east of the Arabian peninsula (roughly north of a line between present-day Basra/Kuwait and the Gulf of 'Aqaba), after the annexation of Petra in 106 CE there was the Roman province of Arabia (the Arabic *ar-Rum* could denote the old or new Rome, Byzantium); south of Damascus was the Christian Arab tribe of the Ghassanids (*Banu Ghassan* = 'sons of Ghassan'), who were Monophysites, a buffer state to protect Rome. The Christian Arab princedom of the Lahmids lay on the lower Euphrates (excavations in 1936 in their capital, Hira, revealed two churches decorated with frescoes); this had a Nestorian orientation and was under Persian domination. These Arab princedoms were in constant contact with the centres of Aramaic Christianity: Edessa, Jerusalem, Palmyra and Damascus.

– In the south-west was *Arabia Felix*, which has already been mentioned. It had always been in contact with Monophysite Christian Ethiopia and its capital Aksum, west of the Red Sea. Here, during the fifty-year Ethiopian rule over southern Arabia, Abraha, an Ethiopian upstart, who had killed the Himyarite viceroy of the Negus, had rebelled successfully against Aksum. *De facto* independent, amongst other government measures, he also built a splendid church in San'a'. Indeed, he ventured a military attack on the caravan city of Mecca, in the north, which with its pagan Ka'bah cult was now growing increasingly powerful. However, this was not a success; surah 105 of the Qur'an ('The Elephant') refers to it, and Muslim historians connect the campaign with the year of Muhammad's birth, 570, when Abraha was presumably no longer alive. When southern Arabia then came under Persian rule, the Christian church there became subject to the Nestorian Catholicos in Seleucia-Ctesiphon. But fifty years later (in 634) the last Persian governor went over to Islam, soon to be followed by the whole people.

– Finally there was the east coast of the Arabian Gulf: according to isolated reports, south of the Lahmid territories there was a series of Christian Nestorian dioceses dependent on Hira and Edessa, as far as Bahrain, Qatar and Oman. The Nestorians, who were often engaged in trade, stood out for their intensive missionary activity, which extended as far as Central Asia and China. In this region a prophet Maslama (or Musailima) appeared, who in competition with the Prophet Muhammad proclaimed the one God, 'the Merciful'. From the coast Christianity infiltrated the interior.[21]

We can therefore see that Christian influence was by no means limited to a 'few strata of the Arab world': there were six centuries of Arabic Christianity before the arrival of Islam. According to Cragg, 'a widespread and persisting Christianity did in fact belong in *Jazirat al-'Arab*'. There *was* 'an achievement of Arab and Christian, of this people and that faith'.[22]

Arabic—also a language of Christians

The Arabic language (*al-'arabiyyah*) also attests the presence of Christianity (and Judaism) in Arabia.

– The classical Arabic script developed from the late-Nabataean form of Aramaic. The Aramaic alphabet of the Arab Nabataeans, whose capital was Petra, is the forerunner of Arabic script. The script of Arabic graffiti was predominantly Aramaic or Nabataean.[23] According to the *kitab al-aghani* ('Book of Songs'), two Christians from Hira (Zaid ibn Hammad and his son) were among the very first to invent Arabic script.[24] However, the fact that trilingual Christian inscriptions in Syrian, Greek and Arabic from 512 or 513 CE have been found in Zabad (south-east of Aleppo)—the oldest evidence of Arabic script found so far—is no proof that the script was invented by Christian missionaries.

– What is indisputable is that Christian Arabs played a role in the history of the Arabic language in the sixth century.[25] The earliest texts of a 'classical' Arabic appear in the third century CE and very soon an artistic Arabic poetry developed which is unique in the Semitic sphere. The Arabic language and script were decisively developed further at the court of Hira, an Arab city on the west bank of the southern Euphrates with a bishop's see that is often mentioned, a first great Christian centre even before Najran in southern Arabia. Here, people learned the art of writing long before it was practised generally on the Arabian peninsula. Arabic finally became fundamental to the Arab sense of unity and identity.

On the other hand, it is by no means a slight on the originality of the Qur'an if, for example, one recognizes with the help of A. Jeffrey's *Foreign Vocabulary of the Qur'an*[26] that not only were profane words like *qasr* (from the Latin *castrum*, 'camp', 'castle') borrowed from other languages but also words which became highly relevant for the Qur'an and Muslim use of language, such as *qalam* (from the Greek *kalamos*), which means 'writing instrument', through which God has taught people what they did not know before.[27] The following words come from Semitic Jewish or Christian sources:

sirat—'the right way', 'guidance' (from the Latin *strata*, 'paved street'), which occupies a central place as early as the opening surah of the Qur'an;[28]
surah—'a piece of writing';
rabb—'Lord' (in the Qur'an reserved for God);
'*abd*—'servant' (in the Qur'an reserved for worship);
ar-rahman—'the Merciful' (used twice programmatically in the opening surah, together with the similar sounding *ar-rahim*—the 'One who has mercy', two names for the one God, the all-Merciful).

The Syriac *qeryana* (= 'reading' in the liturgy) demonstrates a connection with the name *al-Qur'an* (through the related verb *qara'a*—'to read aloud'). But even more importantly, the word which the Qur'an knows for the one and only God was manifestly used in Arabia for the supreme God ('high God') well before Muhammad: if it is of purely Arabic origin, *Allah* (Muhammad's father was called *'abd Allah'* = 'servant of Allah') came into being from the combination *al-ilah* (the God). However, according to other authors, it could also have a non-Arabic, Semitic origin (with echoes of the Hebrew *elohim* or the old-Syrian *alaha* = 'the God').[29] Even now Jews, Christians and Muslims know no other Arabic word for God than *Allah*, so *Allah* has to be translated simply as 'God'. Jews, Christians and Muslims worship one and the same God.

No roots in Hellenistic Christianity

'Although Christianity was championed by Byzantium,' says 'Irfan Shahid, 'it remained for the Arabs a Semitic religion, preached to them by Eastern ecclesiastics, whose liturgical language was Semitic, and whose two great centres, Hira and later Najran, were dominated by Syriac culture.'[30] Was Arabia really in process of becoming Christian around 600, as individual Christian historians think?

The old Arab religion was still strong in western Arabia, with Mecca as its cultic centre, which was particularly important for the future. However much Christianity had spread in the north, south and east of Arabia, it must be conceded to Goldziher that neither Orthodox Byzantine, Monophysite nor Nestorian Christianity succeeded in permanently rooting Christian faith in the Arab consciousness. Why not? Monotheism seemed acceptable to many Arabs in the pre-Islamic period, and they were open to prophets and holy writings, but what seemed completely unacceptable was a Hellenistic christology which had deified Jesus, the Messiah/Christ, identified him with God, and proclaimed an incarnate and even crucified 'God'. I shall be investigating this in detail later.

Cragg, too, notes a lack of roots for Christianity in the Arab consciousness and asks: 'Might Arab Christianity, both in the pre- and post-Islamic centuries, have fared more hopefully had the Greek factor in its story been less intellectually fastidious about formulas, more tuned to Arab sympathies and cast of mind?'[31] Cragg is right: 'At stake was the very nature of Christianity as Hebraic in its messianic quality and Greco-Roman in its christological expression. Islam brought an imperious theism, reasserting a Semitic faith that had been not only subtilized but betrayed—as Islam saw it—by Christian theology.'[32]

That still does not focus the problem sharply enough. Cragg has clearly not paid sufficient attention to what could have been the real corrective to this Christianity formed in Greek. This was not only an 'Aramaic-speaking Christianity'—in many respects it was nevertheless a Gentile Christianity which thought in Greek and, having been declared a 'Nestorian' heresy in the fifth century, shifted its focal point east and north, above all to Persia. The corrective could have been provided by the original Jewish Christianity of the first disciples of Jesus, the original Jerusalem community and the communities east of the Jordan: in other words the very first paradigm of Christianity (P I) before the shift to the Greek Hellenistic paradigm that already begins with Paul (P II). I have already referred to the present state of research (which is still by no means complete)[33] and described this in detail in the second volume of this trilogy (on Christianity): lines lead from the very first Jewish Christianity to the seventh century, indeed to Islam.[34]

Traces of Jewish Christianity

In his church history written at the beginning of the fourth century[35] Eusebius reports that after the execution of its head, James, the members of the earliest Jewish–Christian community in Jerusalem left before the outbreak of the Jewish–Roman war in 62 and settled in Pella in Transjordan. Recent investigations[36] have confirmed this information as credible, at least for part of the primitive community.[37]

We can no longer establish how long members of the primitive community remained in Jerusalem or whether they returned there after the war. According to Eusebius' list of bishops, until the ominous year 135 there were no less than fifteen Jewish–Christian 'bishops' in Jerusalem—all circumcised (perhaps this included presbyters and kinsmen of Jesus).[38] Another Jewish revolt then brought the complete destruction of Jerusalem, the expulsion of all Jews, the renaming of the city Aelia Capitolina, and thus also the end of the

Jewish–Christian community of Jerusalem and its dominant position in early Christianity. For the Gentile Christians, its aura had now departed.

Modern church historians do not hesitate to disparage Jewish Christianity as the 'palaeontological period' of church history. Christian dogmatic theologians who note the result of critical exegesis and the history of dogma only so far as they do not disturb their system, constructed as it is on a Hellenistic–Latin basis, usually ignore biblical Jewish Christianity. The further history of Jewish Christianity in the first centuries is among the darkest chapters of church history. There are many reasons for this.[39] 1) European study of the ancient world was initially exclusively orientated on Graeco-Roman antiquity; 2) even the Greek- or Latin-speaking theologians of the first centuries showed little interest in manuscripts in Semitic languages; 3) the Jewish–Christian communities bordering on the Roman empire were a priori suspect of heresy, as they had been in contact with Baptist and Gnostic sects; 4) a large part of the writings was lost, since the moist mud around the Euphrates and Tigris did not preserve the documents of Jewish Christianity as well as the dry sand of the Egyptian desert preserved those of the Coptic Church (at that time in Syria and Palestine people no longer wrote on clay tablets).

Thus, for the Jewish–Christian communities of the Near East, where (to exaggerate somewhat) we have only a few pages of documents covering whole centuries, we are far more dependent on conjectures than for the church of the West, where we often have thousands of pages to assess ten years. And for example, whereas Simon Peter is mentioned by name about 190 times in the New Testament and Saul/Paul about 170, James, the head of the Jewish Christians, is mentioned only eleven times, just three of them in the Acts of the Apostles; this suggests a suppression of Jewish Christianity (and the brothers of Jesus).

However, many specialists are now devoting themselves to the exciting task of discovering traces of Jewish Christianity, with its wide ramifications. It is richly documented in the New Testament writings[40] and can also be traced in the post-New Testament period. There are many pointers to Transjordan. The ongoing existence in the post-New Testament period of Jewish Christians who appealed to Peter or James and who were as yet by no means permeated by Gnosis cannot be denied. This is attested by pieces of tradition which appear incorporated into a Christian romance (attributed to Clement of Rome and therefore called the 'Pseudo-Clementines') about a recognition (the conversion of the Roman Clement, companion of Peter in Palestine and Syria, and the rediscovery of his family, believed to be dead), by the *Kerygmata Petrou* ('Preachings of Peter') and above all by the 'Ascension (*anabathmoi*) of James'.[41]

The background here is made up of Greek-speaking Jewish Christians, probably in Transjordan, in the second half of the second century. They practised baptism in the name of Jesus but at the same time observed the law of Moses (and probably also circumcision). They venerated James as the leader of the Jerusalem community and accused Paul of having hindered the possible conversion of the whole Jewish people to the messiah Jesus by his mission free of the law. Their situation was precarious: their insistence on the observance of the law distinguished this Jewish–Christian community from the new Gentile–Christian community, but belief in Jesus, who was a prophet like Moses and identical with the Messiah whom so many Jews had expected, separated it from the mainstream of Judaism.[42] Furthermore, in Syria there were Jewish–Christian communities faithful to the law who are attested in the *Didaskalia* (Instruction) of the apostles. In the Jordan valley and on the upper reaches of the Euphrates there were the adherents of Elkesai, who represent a sect which was Jewish–Christian and Gnostic–syncretistic at the same time.

Vilification of Jewish Christians

Jewish–Christian customs evidently continued to be widespread for a long time. Even after the shift under Constantine, Christian synods—in Spain the Synod of Elvira (*c.* 305) and in Asia Minor the Synod of Laodicea (between 343 and 381)—opposed them. Around the end of the fourth century the church father Jerome tells of the existence of a small Jewish–Christian community known to him—and evidently not yet separated from the mainstream church: the community of the Nazareans (*Nazareni*) in Beroea (Aleppo, Syria), which recognized Paul as the apostle of the Gentiles but evidently used a Hebrew Gospel of Matthew.[43]

It was the fate of these Jewish–Christian communities that at a very early stage they were ignored, scorned and vilified by Gentile Christians with a classical education. They were attacked first by bishops such as Ignatius of Antioch, who already around 110 had categorically excluded any connection between Christian faith and Jewish practice.[44] In 180–5 they received similar treatment from Irenaeus of Lyons, who also wrote in Greek: he sweepingly called the Jewish Christians 'Ebionites' (this name first appears with him) and explicitly classed them among the 'heretics'.[45]

We know incomparably more about Near Eastern Gentile Christians than we do about this Jewish Christianity. According to the church fathers, sources which need to be read critically, we must differentiate between different groups in different areas and with different names, even if it is difficult to make a historical reconstruction of what is really concealed behind the names.[46] Whereas 'Ebionites' (God's 'poor') was the self-designation of a particular

Jewish–Christian group (there was no 'Ebion'), and 'Cerinthians', 'Symmachians' and 'Elkesaites' point to individual persons (Cerinthus, Symmachus, Elkesai or Elchasai), the Nazoreans (followers of the 'Nazorean' Jesus) go back to the Hebrew–Aramaic designation of Christians by Jews. Isn't it strange that *nasara*, this word of Syrian origin, is also the name of Christians in the Qur'an?

It is important for Christian–Muslim dialogue to note that present-day scholars recognize the continuity of Jewish Christianity with the beginnings of early Christianity more than its heretical distortion. Jewish Christians are regarded as the legitimate heirs of early Christianity, whereas for the most part the New Testament reflects the view of Gentile Christianity as defended by Paul and his followers. The Göttingen exegete Georg Strecker clearly emphasized the current theological significance of Jewish Christianity: 'Though Jewish Christianity may not be identified with a "natural" Ebionite christology (the notion of pre-existence also appears), the return to the historical foundations of Christian faith can help to limit the tendency to docetism or spiritualization in the mainstream church or outside it.'[47] Thus Jewish–Christian theology is a critical corrective to an all too remote christology exposed to the danger of docetism[48] and spiritualization.

For me, the extraordinarily exciting question is whether the Qur'an, which on the whole likewise rejects a docetism in christology, shows Jewish–Christian influences. After the first half of the fifth century, the traces of Jewish Christianity get increasingly lost and syncretistic tendencies become stronger, so the historical question arises: what became of the Jewish–Christian groups? Neither Judaism nor the mainstream church can have absorbed them completely. Perhaps a look at Arabia will help.

Jewish Christianity on the Arabian peninsula?

Finding specific traces of Jewish Christianity among Arabia's major neighbours is important for the question of the possible influence of Jewish Christianity on the Arabian peninsula. Christianity came to Arabia from Syria (as has already been mentioned), Iraq and finally also from Ethiopia:

– In Ethiopia (Arabia's neighbour across the Red Sea, with which there had always been numerous commercial and cultural relations) Christianity was Monophysite: Christians believed only in the one, divine, *physis* or nature in Christ. However, among this Semitic people an earlier Jewish–Christian paradigm seems to have existed beneath the official Monophysite Hellenistic Christianity. I observed this on a visit to Addis Ababa at the feast of the Epiphany: there was veneration of the Mosaic ark of the covenant (*tabot*), a Semitic liturgical language (*ge'ez*), and priests who sang the psalms and danced to the accompaniment of drums and trumpets. Alongside baptism they observe circumcision, and alongside Sunday the Sabbath. They have special regulations about fasting and food: pork is prohibited.[49] It seemed to me that under the precious Hellenistic brocaded garments, embroidered with silver, perhaps there was a simple Jewish-Christian linen cloth.

– In South India there is an ethnically distinct group of around seventy thousand people, the Tekkumbagam Christians or Southists. According to their local tradition seventy-two Christian families were led to Kerala from Syria or Mesopotamia by one Thomas of Cana (Canaan?) in the year 345. These were Jewish Christians who believed in Jesus as the messiah for the Jews, whereas the Christians already living in Kerala were disciples of the apostle Paul.[50] On the other hand, there is a tradition in Eusebius's *Church History*[51] that the apostle Bartholomew (beyond doubt a Jewish Christian) himself proclaimed the Christian message in India and left for the Christians there the Gospel of Matthew in Hebrew (which is now completely lost). This tradition was noted by the Alexandrian philosopher Pantaenus, who went to India as a Christian missionary and successor to the apostle. Therefore some scholars conjecture that there were possibly not only intensive trade relations but also missionary relations between the Christians in southern Arabia and those 'overseas'—in South India.

– Southern Babylonia (Iraq) was the scene of activity of the famous Persian Mani (Greek Manes, Manichaios, 216–276), who in succession to Adam, Seth, Enoch, Noah, Zoroaster, Buddha and above all Christ, understood in Gnostic terms as the final and universal prophet ('seal of the prophets') and the promised paraclete ('comforter'), founded a novel 'Christian' world religion: dualistic and ascetic Manichaeism. In the third and fourth centuries this became a serious rival to Christianity from the Atlantic to China, from the Caucasus to the Indian Ocean. This has long been known to scholars; the new discovery in our day is that, according to the tradition of the Arabic bibliographer Ibn an-Nadim and the Greek Mani Codex[52] recently discovered in Cologne, in his youth Mani belonged to the Jewish-Christian sect of the Arab Elkesai: 'Jewish influences, like legalism and apocalyptic thought, came to him via Jewish Christianity,' remarked the Tübingen Mani specialist Alexander Böhlig at a congress on the Cologne Codex: 'The Baptists, among whom Mani was prominent, were Elkesaites. They saw Elkesai as the founder of their law ... The legalistic character of Judaism is the basis of the legalistic character of Manichaeism.'[53] The Elkesaites are therefore the link between the Palestinian Baptist movement and Jewish Christianity on the one hand and Manichaeism on the other. But there is another much more important trace which takes us further.

If we can trust the research, the Jewish–Christian communities with their theology—despite all the vilification, syncretism and extermination—must have developed an influence which was to be of historic importance in Arabia in particular, through the Prophet Muhammad. Underground links between Jewish Christianity and the message of the Qur'an have long been discussed by Christian scholars.[54] In 1926 the distinguished Protestant exegete from Tübingen, Adolf Schlatter, wrote: 'However, the Jewish church had died out only in Palestine west of the Jordan. In eastern regions Christian communities with Jewish customs continued to exist, in the Decapolis, in Batanaea, among the Nabataeans, on the periphery of the Syrian desert and into Arabia, completely detached from Christianity and without any fellowship with it ... For the Christians the Jew was still an enemy, and the Greek disposition which overlooked the murders by Trajan's and Hadrian's generals as being the well-deserved fate of the malicious and contemptible Jews, also passed over into the church. Its leading men such as Origen and Eusebius, who lived and taught in Caesarea, remained amazingly ignorant about the end of Jerusalem and its church.' However, Schlatter adds: 'None of the leaders of the imperial church suspected that the day would come when this Christianity which they despised would shake the world and destroy a large part of the churches that they had built up; it came at the time when Muhammad took over the possession guarded by the Jewish Christians, their consciousness of God, their eschatology, which preached the day of judgement, their customs and legends, and established a new apostolate as "the one sent by God".'[55]

This thesis of the influence of Jewish Christianity on the Qur'an had already been discussed and reinforced by Adolf von Harnack[56] and later by Hans-Joachim Schoeps.[57] Present-day scholars too have concluded: 'In the course of time the Ebionites together with the Sabaean Baptists seem to have become established in Arabia. This fertilization invites the hypothesis that the Qur'an reflects Ebionite prophetology.'[58] Indeed, Georg Strecker says that it is 'indisputable that Islam was open not only to Jewish and Christian but also to Jewish–Christian influences, even if this is an area of research which so far is largely unexplored'.[59] The original Jewish–Christian paradigm must have been handed on, in whatever form. But is there really a connection with the Qur'an? More than a century lies between the Jewish Christianity of the fourth and fifth centuries and the Qur'an.

When considering possible links between Jewish Christianity and the Qur'an we should probably not think directly of the early Christian Nazoreans. Since Harnack, reference has been made to Jewish Christians of a Gnostic stamp such as the Elkesaites, who according to more recent research must have been identical with the 'Sabians' mentioned in the Qur'an.[60] The existence of

Jewish–Christian writings in Arabic can hardly be disputed any longer. Not only were the Ibadians[61] of Hira and Anbar and some poetic personalities already mentioned by name by Julius Wellhausen,[62] but as the Berlin expert in religious studies, Carsten Colpe, indicates in summary form,[63] sufficient references have been found to liturgical books for an Arabic Christian liturgy to indicate the presence of Christian communities on the Arabian peninsula; evidently there were Arabic translations of the Psalter and the Gospels.

In addition, Colpe made a surprising discovery: the famous Qur'anic designation of the Prophet Muhammad as 'seal of the prophets'[64] already occurs in one of the earliest writings of the earliest Latin church fathers, in Tertullian's *Adversus Judaeos* (before 200)[65]—as a designation of Jesus Christ.[66] Was this title claimed by the Prophet Muhammad in a controversy with Jewish Christians (perhaps in Medina) or Manichaeans?[67] We know from the Qur'an who the previous prophets are: with the exception of Jonah (*Yunus*) they are not Israel's 'minor' prophets (for example, Amos and Hosea) or 'great' writing prophets (such as Isaiah and Jeremiah). Rather, they are biblical figures of whom Muhammad with his interest in religion may possibly have heard on his travels or in other contacts with Christians: Adam (*Adam*) and Noah (*Nuh*), the patriarchs Abraham (*Ibrahim*), Isaac (*Ishaq*) and Jacob (*Ya'qub*), Joseph (*Yusuf*), Moses (*Musa*) and Aaron (*Harun*), Elijah (*Ilyas*) and the kings David (*Dawud*) and Solomon (*Sulayman*), Ezra (*'Uzayr*) and of course Jesus (*'Isa*).

Some other traces can be found. Colpe follows one of them himself, when by means of a text from the Byzantine Sozomen's *Church History* (written between 439 and 450) he describes Jewish Christians who perceived their legitimacy in being descendants of Ishmael and his mother (Hagar), that is, as Ishmaelites or Hagarenes: 'In this way an oriental Jewish–Christian "confession" emerged which is older than Nestorians and Jacobites, and which later continued alongside the latter, predominantly among Arabs. In type they could have been Jews from whom Muhammad received his Jewish traditions—Jews with midrashim but without Talmuds, at the same time Christians who worshipped Jesus and Mary but had no Dyophysite or Monophysite christology. They can have been the vehicles of the biblical and biblical–interpretative traditions of the kind that can be found in the Qur'an.'[68]

The Jewish scholar S. Pines (though criticized by his fellow-Jew S.M. Stern) found a second indicator in an Arabic manuscript of 'Abd al-Jabbar, who worked in Raiy (Iran) between the tenth and eleventh centuries (or of an earlier Muslim scholar), into which a Jewish–Christian text, probably from the fifth/sixth century, had been incorporated. This manuscript contains an early history of the Christian community, laments the split between Judaism and Christianity, criticizes the 'Romanization' of Christianity and claims to be continuing the original uncorrupted tradition of the Jerusalem community as it had been founded by Jesus' first disciples, who believed that he was a man and not a divine being and observed the Mosaic laws.[69] Here is evidence of a Jewish Christianity for the sphere of both Palestine-Syria and Arabia and Babylonia—alive at least until the seventh century.[70]

The fact of Jewish Christianity in Arabia is also recognized by Muslims today. However, Prince Hassan bin Talal, a practising Muslim, educated archaeologist and descendant of an Arab royal house which traces itself back to the Prophet Muhammad, states the challenge which arises for Christianity:

> Such Jewish Christians, possibly of the Ebionite persuasion, still existed in Arabia (as also perhaps in other marginal parts of the Christian world) in the days of the Prophet Muhammad. In Arabic, they were called *Nasara*, which was also the Arabic appellation for Christians in general. From the Qur'an, one learns that the true *Nasara* recognized Jesus as a Messiah (Arabic *masih*), the son of the virgin Mary by the Holy Spirit (a doctrine which the Qur'an fully endorses), and a prophet to Israel, without attributing divinity to his person, as the other *Nasara* did, or conceiving of the One God as a Trinity; also, that the scriptures of these true *Nasara* were a 'gospel' (Arabic *injil*, in the singular). From Muslim tradition one learns that this *injil* of the *Nasara* was not written in Greek, but in *al-'Ibraniyya*: in the Arabic usage of the period, a term denoting Hebrew as well as Aramaic, which were commonly written in the same script. The Qur'an commends the sincerity and modesty of the true *Nasara*, and the affection they demonstrated towards the nascent Muslim community, whose concept of Jesus as a human Christ endowed with the Holy Spirit did not differ much from theirs. Muslim tradition depicts the priests and pious among the *Nasara* as wearing white, apparently as a sign of purity.[71]

We can draw a provisional conclusion:

- There are demonstrable historical references to Christian or Jewish communities or individuals, which are also mentioned quite naturally in the Qur'an. But in terms of source criticism, they do not call in question the originality and authenticity of the revelations of Muhammad.
- It must remain open what historical and genetic affinities the Qur'an displays to any Christian group and with what degree of intensity.
- The analogies between the Qur'anic picture of Jesus and a christology with a Jewish–Christian stamp are perplexing. These parallels are irrefutable and call for more intensive historical and systematic reflection. I shall discuss what all this means, and what inter-religious consequences are to be drawn from it, later in this book (D IV, 2).

However, first we must bring into the foreground a biblical figure of fundamental significance for Jews, Jewish Christians and Gentile Christians, and also for the Prophet Muhammad. To the present day he can unite Jews, Christians and Muslims as the 'father of faith'. His name is Abraham.

3. Abraham—the common ancestor of the 'people of the book'

The fundamental importance of Abraham for the history, piety and theology of Judaism, Christianity and Islam is obvious. It is impressively brought out in the very first book of the Hebrew Bible and in the Gospels, as it is in the Qur'an. According to the texts of the Hebrew Bible, Abram, programmatically renamed 'Abraham', the 'father of many nations' (the later interpretation), is clearly the ancestor of the people of Israel; according to the New Testament, he is also the spiritual ancestor of Christians; and according to the Qur'an he is the physical ancestor especially of the Arabs. But what lies behind this towering biblical and Qur'anic figure? We must first turn to the earlier, biblical evidence.

Who was Abraham?

We have hardly any certain knowledge about his person; a biography is impossible.[72] The patriarchal narratives of Genesis 11–35[73] are our oldest sources and they are not biography or history in our sense. In the case of all the patriarchs, they are a series of short stories, loosely linked together, with doublets and contradictions. More precisely, they are sagas which were handed down orally long before they were fixed in writing.[74] Sagas are not fairy tales:[75] as a rule they have a historical nucleus, for all their brevity, simplification and concentration on a few persons. Abraham, Isaac and Ishmael seem to have been historical figures, not least because of their common West Semitic personal names, even if attempts to date them have so far failed.

The social and cultural conditions that must have prevailed in the Near East in the time between 1900 and 1400 BCE glimmer through the patriarchal stories (their '*Sitz im Leben*'). We are informed to some degree about them by the story of Sinuhe the Egyptian, who lived there among semi-nomads (in the twentieth century BCE); by Egyptian execration texts, which cursed rebellious rulers (in the nineteenth/eighteenth centuries); by the Mesopotamian texts from Mari on the middle Euphrates (eighteenth century) and from Nuzi near Kirkuk (in the fifteenth/fourteenth centuries); and by the letters from the state archive of Pharaohs Amenophis III and Amenophis IV Akhenaten (whose novel belief in one god threw the Egyptian kingdom into a deep crisis), discovered in Amarna on the Middle Nile.[76]

In the case of Abraham, his sons and grandsons, we do not, as is sometimes claimed, have just a private family history extending over three generations. The religious and political implications of these stories, which are hinted at in the Bible and in the Qur'an, are too serious for that; the world–political horizon is also part of the picture. We cannot overlook the fact that in the book of Genesis the story of Abraham is bound up with the prehistory and universal history of humankind, which initially seems to have concluded with the building of the 'tower' of Babel.[77] According to the biblical tradition, which attempts to combine two traditions,[78] Abraham's family migrated from the rich mercantile city of Ur in southern Mesopotamia (whose ziggurat or high temple, dedicated to the moon god Sin, was excavated between 1922 and 1934) and the north Mesopotamian city of Haran on the great bend in the Euphrates, to the land of Canaan, as did so many people from Mesopotamia and the wilderness of Syria and Arabia in the second millennium BCE.[79]

This origin repeatedly took on great symbolic significance in Jewish history with its many changes. From the beginning Abraham was not an indigenous inhabitant but an immigrant: 'a stranger and sojourner'.[80] The only property that he is said to have acquired is a tomb in Hebron;[81] to the present day Jewish, Christian and Muslim pilgrims are shown 'Abraham's tomb' and mark it with religious observances, even in the midst of the Israeli–Palestinian conflict. As a semi-nomad, moving between towns and villages, Abraham certainly had some contact with the indigenous population. But he must have kept some distance from them; his way of life did not allow him, like the other patriarchs, to enter into any marital alliances with indigenous families. Granted, Abraham is described as a 'Hebrew' (*'ibri*[82]). But according to the most recent scholarship that is not simply synonymous with 'Israelite', for the *habiru* or *hapiru* of the Mesopotamian cuneiform texts and the *'prw* of the Egyptian texts, who are probably identical with the 'Hebrews', are less a particular people and more those in a lower social stratum or way of life: often foreigners, vagrants, mercenaries or forced labourers, 'outlaws' who nevertheless could rise to the highest positions.[83]

Abraham, Isaac and Ishmael: biblical perspectives

Something else is of no less importance for the present-day situation of the religions: Abraham's genealogy.[84] Abraham seems to be incorporated into Semitic 'kinships': with Abraham, his son Isaac and his grandson Jacob—possibly brought together in this way only at a later stage—are regarded as the original ancestors of Israel. Today, especially Christian critics of Islam should note that polygamy was taken for granted by the early biblical tribal cultures as well: as is well known, Abraham himself had several concubines.[85]

According to the book of Genesis, by his wife Sarah Abraham fathered Isaac,[86] the father of Esau and Jacob (later called Israel), who was regarded as the father of the twelve tribes. However, first, by his Egyptian concubine, the slave Hagar, Abraham fathered Ishmael,[87] the ancestor of the twelve groups belonging to the Ishmaelite alliance.[88] The Bible does not use the expression 'Arabs', but certainly means the desert dwellers of the north-west Arabian desert (scholars speak of proto-Arabs). Finally, with his second concubine Keturah, Abraham, became the ancestor of sixteen (proto-)Arab nomadic groups.[89] This is significant for present-day questions: Israel originally felt related to the Semitic Arameans of the late second millennium and to the (proto-)Arabs of north-west Arabia in the first half of the first millennium, who were likewise Semitic. The genealogies (the details of which are hardly historical) seek to state at least this: we read in the book of Deuteronomy (26.5) that 'My father was a wandering Aramaean.'

But in the Hebrew Bible isn't Abraham's son Ishmael, son of the wilderness, totally devalued by comparison with Isaac and treated contemptuously in the New Testament, in Paul's letter to the Galatians, with its Sarah–Hagar allegory?[90] That is indisputable, but is only one aspect. The firm biblical preference for Isaac over Ishmael in the Jewish–Christian tradition is a fact, but we should not fail to note that the Hebrew Bible makes not only 'biographically' interesting statements about Ishmael but also theologically relevant ones. Karl-Josef Kuschel is right in his book on Abraham when he works out precisely the positive statements about Ishmael in the interest of an Abrahamic ecumene:[91]

- Ishmael, not Isaac, was the firstborn son of Abraham (at the wish of his wife Sarah). Ishmael—'God (hears)'.[92]
- Even before Isaac, Ishmael receives the sign of God's covenant: circumcision.[93]
- Both Isaac's survival and Ishmael's survival are under God's special protection. Ishmael's rescue from the wilderness, narrated twice, corresponds to the rescue of Isaac from the threat of being sacrificed.[94]
- God's promise of fertility and numerous descendants applies to both Isaac and Ishmael: 'I will so greatly multiply your (Hagar's) descendants that they cannot be counted for multitude.'[95] Like the sons of Jacob, Ishmael's descendants form a group of twelve tribes. God explicitly says to Hagar: 'As for Ishmael, I have heard you; behold, I will bless him and make him fruitful and multiply him exceedingly; he shall be the father of twelve princes, and I will make him a great nation.'[96]
- Not only Isaac but also Ishmael is present at Abraham's burial: even though Hagar and Ishmael have been cast out into the wilderness,[97] surprisingly

> Ishmael reappears at the death of his father Abraham: 'His sons Isaac and Ishmael buried him ...'[98]

What kind of a God is being spoken of in these patriarchal narratives? From the beginning, the God of patriarchal religion was not bound either to heaven or to a sanctuary. He is the one 'God of the father' (the patriarch) to whom he has communicated his revelation: the God of Abraham, the God of Isaac, the God of Jacob, the God of the fathers. After the settlement this God took on elements of the Canaanite God El (under different names, such as 'El Shaddai'), so that the God of Genesis can be described both as the God of the fathers and as El, and at the same time presents himself as a personal and a cosmic God.[99] Thus today there is agreement among biblical critics that, like the lofty ethic of the Bible, its strict monotheism cannot have prevailed as early as the time of the patriarchs; from a historical perspective Abraham was certainly a henotheist who presupposed the existence of several gods but accepted only one God, his God, as the supreme and compelling authority.

What about circumcision?[100] This was not a completely new rite, introduced at that time, but an age-old custom (performed with a stone knife), originally widespread not only among Israel's Semitic neighbours in Canaan and in Egypt, but also in Africa, America and Australia. It was not, however, practised by the Philistines, Babylonians and Assyrians. Circumcision was practised either for hygienic and medical reasons or for social and religious reasons (that is, as a rite of initiation). The Israelites took this rite for granted from the time of the settlement in Canaan; it does not appear at all in the earliest strata of Israelite law and is mentioned only once in the book of Leviticus,[101] without any special emphasis. However, after the downfall of the kingdoms of Israel and Judah and the exile among the Babylonians (who were not circumcised), circumcision, which had previously been taken for granted, became a special religious sign of membership of the Israelite people. Only now did it take on its special significance as an indelible mark of belonging to God and as a sign of the covenant, finally formulated almost as a legal precept in Genesis 17.

If we follow the book of Genesis, what is more important for Abraham is trust in God. Unconditional trusting faith is fundamental. It is said that this faith is 'reckoned to Abraham for righteousness'.[102] Throughout the Hebrew Bible faith (Hebrew *aman*—be firm; causative form *he'emin*—believe, trust) is never understood as acceptance of a truth which has been laid down, as holding the unprovable to be true, but as unshakable trust in a promise which cannot be realized in human terms: as faithfulness, as confidence, as saying 'Amen'. Abraham is the prototype of someone who believes in this sense, a man who, on the basis of this faith, can then withstand the greatest test: the sacrifice of his son Isaac, which is asked of him but in the end is not willed by God.[103]

A first, welcome conclusion is that, with good reason, the three religions which refer to Abraham and in which human beings stand 'before' God, wholly devoting themselves to God and thus believing 'in' God (in contrast to the mystical unity religions of India or the wisdom religions of China), are called religions of faith. Thus Abraham appears as the common ancestor of all three great religions of Semitic origin, which are therefore called the three Abrahamic religions. They can be understood as a great religious river system of Near Eastern origin, essentially different from the river systems of Indian or Far Eastern origin.[104]

Yet we cannot overlook the fact that for all that they have in common, already with Abraham, the one ancestor, a conflict between the three Abrahamic religions is also developing, Why? How is Abraham regarded in Islam?

Dispute over the Abrahamic heritage: Qur'anic perspectives

In the Qur'an Abraham (Ibrahim) is the most frequently mentioned biblical figure after Moses. Around 245 verses in 25 surahs refer to him. There are striking parallels not only to biblical depictions of Abraham but also to rabbinic depictions outside the Bible. Historically, it is important that even before Muhammad's emergence as Prophet there was a monotheistic reform movement among Arabs that appealed to the 'religion of Abraham'. Its adherents were called *hanif*, meaning something like 'God-seeker' or 'devoted to God'. Reports about the *hanif*, which appear at an early stage in Islamic historiography, are also accepted by critical historical research today: 'Here and there in ancient Arabia even before Muhammad there must have been reflective people, prone to brooding, who no longer found any satisfaction in the indigenous religious tradition and took up all the more readily ideas which were currently offered by Christians and Jews—if we may put it this way –, making them their own. It can be indirectly inferred from the language of the Qur'an that in particular they confessed monotheism. Here the term *hanif* has the meaning of something like "Muslim monotheist".'[105]

The patriarch Abraham plays an important role in the Qur'an: one surah even bears his name (surah 14).[106] In the early Meccan surahs Abraham appears above all as a fighter against the idolatry of his father Azar (according to Genesis 11.26, Terah) and of his fellow countrymen and thus for Muhammad proves himself to be the prototype of a speaker of the truth and a great prophet. In the later Medinan surahs Ishmael then appears; he has been mentioned with no close reference to Abraham. The Arabs are his descendants, whereas the Jews stem from Isaac and his son Jacob. Ishmael supports his father Abraham in the effort to build the Ka'bah in Mecca and to make it a place of pure monotheistic worship of God and a pilgrimage centre.[107] This justifies the adoption in Islam of the Ka'bah cult, which is intrinsically pagan.

There is no historical evidence that Abraham, who also according to the Qur'an was active in Palestine and whose tomb is generally thought by Muslims to be in Hebron, travelled so far south. Since the Dutchman Christiaan Snouck Hurgronje, who visited Mecca, explicitly developed the thesis in his 1880 dissertation *Het Mekkaansche Fest* that it was only in Medina that the Prophet Muhammad put forward the view of Abraham as *hanif* and the first Muslim[108] to support his position against critical Jews, the dispute has never ceased.[109] In the meantime, even Western scholars have had to recognize that the association of Abraham with Mecca appears even in the early Meccan surahs,[110] and that the expression 'religion of Abraham' (*millat Ibrahim*) 'does not go back exclusively to the early polemic with Jews (and Christians) in Medina', but arises from a development 'which extends back deep into the Meccan period'.[111] The general position is that Muslims assume as a historical fact that Abraham was in Mecca and according to one verse in the Qur'an[112] built the Ka'bah, the Islamic central sanctuary, with his son Ishmael, or according to another verse[113] merely 'cleansed' it of idolatry. Non-Muslims regard this as a pious legend,[114] though it cannot be proved to be impossible.

The Qur'an, too, calls Abraham the 'friend of God'.[115] However, it is above all important for the Qur'an that Abraham 'was neither a Jew nor a Christian, but was a *hanif*, having surrendered himself unto God: and he was not of those who ascribe divinity to aught beside Him'.[116] It was Abraham who, chosen by God, converted to the one God and opposed all idolatry.[117] In this way he already practised *islam*, unconditional 'submission' to the will of God, especially when he undertook the sacrifice of his own son (Isaac's name is not mentioned at this point,[118] traditional Islamic exegesis thinks here of Ishmael).

The picture of Abraham in the Qur'an, especially from the second Meccan period, can be defined by the following fixed points (I am again following the systematic analysis by Karl-Josef Kuschel):[119]

- Abraham stands for a consistent and unambiguous monotheism which the Prophet himself has rediscovered and revived: the 'religion of Abraham'.
- Abraham is the archetypal figure of rejection of idolatry, who repudiates radically as hostile to God any form of religious veneration or glorification of earthly values or persons (idols).
- Abraham is the model for the deliverance of a monotheistic champion of the faith by God himself and the promise of descendants to him.
- Abraham appears as the intercessor for the righteous, as is shown by the rescue of his brother Lot at the destruction of Sodom.[120]

Thus from the beginning Abraham has been a great prophet of the one God for the Muslims. It is therefore understandable that the claims of Judaism and Christianity to be the only true religion should be undermined by the Qur'an for, according to its understanding, Abraham was neither Jew nor Christian but, after Adam, the exemplary Muslim: 'I shall make thee a leader of men.'[121] Abraham was a believing monotheist, chosen by God, long before the Torah (Arabic *tawrah*) and the Gospel (Arabic *injil*)—the other two books which are holy, but unfortunately have been falsified by Jews and Christians. Islam can thus legitimate itself through Abraham as the oldest and most authentic religion, taught by all the prophets (the same thing was revealed to all of them) and finally proclaimed in a new and definitive way by Muhammad, the confirming 'seal' of the prophets, after the Prophet had received it directly through an angel from the one true God, without the errors and distortions of the Jews and Christians. For the Qur'an, it is clear that Muslims stand closest to Abraham; in the descent from Abraham they are not the only worshippers of God but they are his only true worshippers. They owe much to Abraham: their 'name' (Muslim), their faith, their rites in Mecca, their theocentricity and their universalism.

A second, less welcome conclusion is that, even with apparently so harmless an example as Abraham, it is clear that there are questions between the religions which are extremely difficult, vigorously disputed and also politically explosive; indeed here the very identity of each of the three religions is at stake.

Does that mean that Abraham represents 'a common point of reference' for the three religions only at first glance, while at a second glance 'from the perspective of each religious tradition he is also the embodiment of what distinguishes them from one another and divides them', so that Abraham can hardly be regarded as 'an ideal starting point for present-day dialogue'?[122] If we look more closely, Abraham does not necessarily appear to be an ideal starting point for what today can be called a 'trialogue' (a philological neologism) between Jews, Christians and Muslims. However, he is a real starting point.

What binds Jews, Christians and Muslims together

Looking yet more closely, it emerges that while there is not total accord between the three religions in respect of Abraham, there is not total dissent either, but rather a convergence which makes a dialogue seem meaningful. Might one of the three religions lay exclusive claim to Abraham? Doesn't Abraham 'belong' to all three religions, indeed today couldn't he even be a challenge for them all?

Jews must not overlook the fact that even in the worst times of either medieval or modern anti-Judaism, Christianity could never completely forget that it came from Judaism, which appealed to Abraham, sharing with it at least

Abraham

Ancestor of all three Semitic religions
of Near Eastern origin
Primal representative of monotheism
Archetype of the prophetic religions:
the believer **before** God, friend of God

Physical father of Isaac, whose son Jacob was called Israel. God made an eternal covenant with him. So he is the ancestor of the **Jewish people**.	Spiritual father of all believers, whose promises have been fulfilled in Christ. So he is the ancestor of **Jews and Christians**.	Physical father of Ishmael, with whom he founded the Ka'bah in Mecca as the central sanctuary of the one God. So he is the ancestor of the **Arabs**.
A model of true obedience to the law: the ideal Jew; justified by works, which prove his steadfastness in faith.	A model of unshakeable steadfastness in faith; the one who announces Christ; justified by the faith which precedes works.	A model of unconditional submission (= Islam): the first Muslim; he attains righteousness through faith in God, the service of God and a life pleasing to God.
The sacrifice of Isaac as a prototype for withstanding the most difficult trial of faith.	The sacrifice of Isaac as a prototype for the handing over of God the Son by the Father.	Setting out from Ur as the prototype of the Prophet's migration from Mecca (*hijrah*).
Recipient of the promises of Israel: **people and land**.	Recipient of the promises for all peoples: **Jesus Christ** as the heir of Abraham.	Recipient of the original revelation, which is set down unfalsified only in the **Qur'an**.

the Hebrew Bible, the Psalms and many Hebrew elements of worship (from 'Hosanna' to 'Amen'). The two great Gospels of Luke and Matthew (who himself came from Judaism) explicitly recalled through Jesus' genealogy that Christ Jesus had been a descendant of Abraham.[123] And the God who 'glorified his servant Jesus' was none other than 'the God of Abraham, Isaac and Jacob'.[124] If Christianity after Paul insisted on justification by trusting faith, on the model of Abraham, the father of faith,[125] it did not want to dispense with good works: according to Paul, faith should be active in love.[126] Finally, with the Gospel of John, which calls for an action like that of Abraham,[127] the letter of James in particular emphasizes the necessity of works extraordinarily sharply over against a 'faith' which consists only in inactive confessing.[128]

Conversely, Christians should note that in Judaism, while the rabbis emphasize the significance of Abraham's obedience to the Torah[129] and regard only the children of Isaac as the legitimate children of Abraham, among them there is also the idea that physical descent by no means decides exclusively who are children of Abraham. Members of Gentile peoples can also become children of Abraham as 'proselytes' (literally 'those who come in', converts). Evidently the argument in the Qur'an has touched on a correct point here: before Abraham became the first monotheistic 'missionary', for long years he had been a 'convert' to the true faith. According to the explanations of rabbis, precisely because of his very late circumcision (at the age of ninety-nine!) Abraham had opened up also to non-Jews for all the future the possibility of going over to Judaism, thus becoming the model not only for the Jews but also for Gentiles who go over to Judaism (proselytes), and thus the ancestor of all nations. So, at least to some extent, for Judaism too a spiritual descent from Abraham has been possible for some time. To the present day the convert summoned to read the Torah is addressed as 'X, son of our father Abraham'.[130] Furthermore, according to present-day Jewish theology, Christians who want to remain Christians, together with Muslims, may be regarded as 'children of Abraham'. As the Jerusalem scholar David Flusser remarks: 'In the Jewish religion the existence of Christianity (and Islam) can be understood as a fulfilment of God's promises to Abraham, to make him the father of many peoples.'[131]

Finally, Muslims should not overlook the close relations between Islam and Judaism—despite all the special teachings of the Qur'an. Muslims appeal for their faith to the same Abrahamic origin. Conversely, Israelites felt related to the early Arabs in origin. As we saw, from a historical perspective, from the time of King Solomon at the latest there were numerous demonstrable economic ties between Canaan and Arabia which lasted to the time of the Prophet Muhammad, when numerous Jewish communities lived in Arabia. Moreover, Islamic Qur'an exegesis and historiography, without any inhibitions, supplement the statements of the Qur'an about Abraham in the Hebrew Bible or the Jewish Haggadah, and influence Jewish tradition and interpretations. The Hebrew Bible itself contains a series of allusions to the close relations between Jews and Arabs: numerous Arabic words have found their way into the books of Job and Proverbs and the later Mishnah also contains sections which refer to the conduct of Jews in Arabia. Thus it is not so surprising that all through their history the Jews have felt a certain affinity with Arab culture. The most flourishing centres of medieval Judaism could develop in Muslim countries in particular: under the 'Abbasids in Iraq, under the Moorish rulers in Spain and, after the expulsion from Spain, among the Ottomans in Istanbul and Saloniki.

What unites the religions of the Near Eastern river system beyond all the more or less chance historical relationships? What in principle unites Jews, Christians and Muslims? What can be regarded as the real foundation of an Abrahamic community which is emerging into consciousness and, given the independence of all three religions, has to be realized anew? What unites the three Abrahamic religions now? In inter-religious dialogues with Jews and Muslims one need only sit opposite representatives of the Indian and Chinese river systems to note how much is common to Jews, Christians and Muslims despite all the disputes: a largely similar basic understanding of God, human beings, the world and world history.

A fundamental and at the same time anticipatory conclusion is that Judaism, Christianity and Islam are linked by great common features associated with the name of Abraham: a kind of Abrahamic ecumene rooted in a long history, which hostility and wars could not obliterate. Kurt Rudolph called it 'an inherited history of the utmost extent, which here comes to light in the history of the religion of our cultural circle and which to the present day governs the relationship of the three great religions of the Near East, even if this is often not perceived by believers (whether deliberately or not)'.[132]

One question arises in the face of this Abrahamic 'ecumene' and the similar basic understanding of God and human beings, the world and world history in the three Abrahamic religions. The Christian understands Christianity as the way to eternal salvation but the Muslim also understands Islam, this all-determining way of life, as a way to eternal life, to 'paradise', to eternal salvation. What can a Christian theologian say to this claim? This is a basic question of the first order for a better understanding of Christians and Muslims and accordingly also for Christians and Jews.

Is Islam a way of salvation?

I put this question so bluntly, not least in view of the divided attitude of the World Council of Churches. Neither in its 1979 *Guidelines on Dialogue with People of Living Faiths and Ideologies* nor at its general assemblies has it been able to respond to what today is the extremely urgent question of salvation outside Christianity, so opposed are the standpoints of the member churches, with utter rejection from the Eastern Orthodox and even more some fundamentalist Protestant churches. To put it pointedly, what would 'dialogue' be with those who are going to hell unless they are converted to the Christian faith?

The traditional Catholic position up to the twentieth century—prepared for in the early Christian centuries by Origen, Cyprian and Augustine—is generally known: *extra ecclesiam nulla salus*, no salvation outside the church. *Extra ecclesiam nullus propheta*, no prophet outside the church. The ecumenical council of Florence in 1442 issued an unequivocal definition. 'The Holy Roman Church ... firmly believes, confesses and proclaims that no one outside the Catholic Church, whether pagan or Jew or unbeliever or one separated from the church, will participate in eternal life; rather he will fall into the eternal fire prepared for the devil and all his angels, unless he joins it (the Catholic Church) before his death.'[133] For Catholics, doesn't that settle the claim of Islam? For more than 1200 years it seemed to.

However, in the twentieth century Catholic theology attempted to 'understand anew' that uncompromising '*extra*' dogma, which usually meant reinterpreting it, indeed turning it into its opposite. It was never corrected openly, because it was 'infallible'. Rome had already had to condemn the statement *extra ecclesiam nulla gratia* (outside the church no grace) when faced with the rigorist Jansenists in seventeenth-century France.[134] So if there is grace, charis, charisma outside the church, could it not be that there is also prophecy—according to the New Testament clearly a charisma—outside it?

The traditional Catholic position is now no longer the official Catholic position. In its Constitution on the Church (1964) the Second Vatican Council quite unequivocally declared: 'Those who through no fault of their own, do not know the Gospel of Christ or His church, but who nevertheless seek God with a sincere heart, try in their actions to do His will as they know it through the dictates of their conscience—those too may achieve eternal salvation.'[135]

Explicit mention is made here of those who, by virtue of their origin, have most in common with Jews and Christians through believing in the one God and doing his will, the Muslims: 'But the plan of salvation also includes those who acknowledge the Creator, in the first place among whom are the Muslims: these profess to hold the faith of Abraham, and together with us they adore the one, merciful, God, the merciful, mankind's judge on the last day.'[136]

According to Vatican II Muslims, too, need no longer 'fall into the eternal fire prepared for the devil and his angels'; they can 'attain eternal salvation'. That means that in the Christian view too Islam can be the way to salvation.

This insight must be a good presupposition for now going on, after clarifying the origin and prehistory of Islam, to deal with the question of essence: what is the centre, what is the central message of Islam?

B. CENTRE

By 'centre' I do not mean a 'basic concept' or a 'basic idea' (in Hegel's sense), by comparison with which all other concepts and ideas of the Islamic religion are only historical phenomena and developments. Nor do I mean a 'fundamental principle' from which the whole of Islamic faith could be constructed systematically (as in an orthodox dogmatics). Talk of a 'centre' of Islam is not focused on the theoretical question of a systematic unitary conception. Rather, it is focused on the quite practical question of what is permanently valid and binding in Islam.

For Christians and Jews, but also for Muslims, it is important and legitimate to ask what the difference is between the Islamic religion and other religions and what is its specific characteristic. The specific characteristic of Judaism is Israel as God's people and land.[1] The specific characteristic of Christianity is God's Messiah and Son.[2] But what, in the case of Islam, is:

- the abiding premise (not principle);
- the normative basic idea (not dogma);
- the driving force (not law)?[3]

B I

God's Word has Become a Book

It was always a fundamental Christian misunderstanding of Islam to think that the Prophet occupied the same position in Islam as Jesus Christ in Christianity. This misunderstanding was emphasized by the designation of Islam as 'Mohammedanism' and the Muslims as 'Mohammedans'. Muslims rightly repudiate such designations. In Christianity one can say, with the words of the Prologue of the Gospel of John, 'The Word has been made flesh,'[4] God's Word and Wisdom has 'incarnated' itself in a human being, Jesus of Nazareth. However, in Islam one cannot say this sort of thing about the Prophet Muhammad, and no Muslim has. Here, rather, God's Word has become a book. That, by way of anticipation, gives the basic answer to the question of the centre of Islam: for Muslims the specific character of their religion is that the Qur'an is God's word and book.[5]

1. The Qur'an—the specific feature of Islam

'In the name of God (*bi-smi llah*), the Most Gracious (*ar-rahman*), the Dispenser of Grace (*ar-rahim*). All praise is due to God alone, the Sustainer of all the worlds, the Most Gracious, the Dispenser of Grace, Lord of the Day of Judgement! Thee alone do we worship; and unto Thee alone do we turn for aid. Guide us the straight way—the way of those upon whom Thou hast bestowed Thy blessings, not of those who have been condemned [by Thee], nor of those who go astray.'[6]

So runs the first surah of the Qur'an, 'the opening' (*al-fatihah*), which also regularly introduces Muslim mandatory prayer. Some classical and contemporary Muslim authors see in it the foundation, the sum and the quintessence of the Qur'an: 'It (the opening) contains, in a condensed form, all

The distinctive features of the three monotheistic religions

What they have **in common**:

Belief in the one and only God of Abraham,
the gracious and merciful Creator,
Sustainer and Judge of all human beings.

What **distinguishes** them:

Israel as God's **people** and **land**.	**Jesus Christ** as God's **messiah** and **son**.	The **Qur'an** as God's **word** and **book.**

the fundamental principles laid down in the Qur'an: the principle of God's oneness and uniqueness, of His being the originator and fosterer of the universe, the fount of all life-giving grace; the One to whom man is ultimately responsible, the only power that can really guide and help; the call to righteous action in the life of this world; the principle of life after death and of the organic consequences of man's actions and behaviour; the principle of guidance through God's message-bearers and, flowing from it, the principle of the continuity of all true religions; and, finally the need for voluntary self-surrender to the will of the Supreme Being and, thus, for worshipping him alone.'[7]

But cannot this *fatihah*, the foundation, sum and quintessence of Islam, also be prayed by a Jew or a Christian? I have done so, with conviction, in a Muslim context, and such prayer is reported from trialogue meetings all over the world. But that makes even more pressing the fundamental question: what is it that really distinguishes Islam? What is its particular character, its centre, its 'essence'?

A definition of essence that goes beyond essence

Definitions of Islam by sociologists and political theorists, philologists and historians, are important, but they often show significant limitations of understanding. The British social scientist Ernest Gellner begins his book *Muslim Society* with the words 'Islam is the blueprint of a social order'.[8] The Göttingen political theorist Bassam Tibi, who is of Syrian Muslim origin, writes: 'Islam is not only a political ideology but also and above all a cultural system.'[9] Islam is certainly also all that, but do the majority of Muslims understand Islam primarily in this way?

The Heidelberg Semitic scholar and expert on Islam, Anton Schall, writes: 'I vigorously reject this view, not as a retarding representative of the orchid specialists who are hostile to the social sciences in a way that seems anachronistic' and who therefore reject Bassam Tibi's view, but 'because Gellner and Tibi are mistaken about Muhammad's religious beginnings'.[10]

One may agree with this verdict but then hesitate when one reads Schall's own definition of Islam in his article in the current multi-volume Protestant reference work *Theologische Realenzyklopädie* XVI (1987). His first sentence runs: 'Islam is the religion founded by Muhammad ibn 'Abdallah ibn al-'Abdalmuttalib, whose followers call themselves Muslim or Muslims. Islam is a syncretistic and eclectic collection of several religions from the world of Muhammad. The centre of the religion of Islam is Allah, generally thought to derive from the Arabic *al-Ilah*, the supreme or high God of the city of Mecca before the appearance of Muhammad.'[11]

This description is hardly a good starting point for a sensible conversation with Muslims about their religion. Indeed, for many Muslims these statements might be as blasphemous as the 'Satanic verses' condemned by Ayatollah Khomeini to which the novel by the British Indian writer Salman Rushdie refers.[12] Like the sociologist and the political theorist, this Semitist is wrong about 'Muhammad's religious beginnings'; that helps us to understand rather better why some orientals have something against orientalists.

Christian theologians would begin from too constricted an understanding of Islam if they examined exclusively 'Muhammad's religious beginnings' and in so doing overlooked on the one hand the social and political dimension of Islam and on the other its historical involvement with other religions. That is why I have discussed the 'problems of the beginning' against the widest possible historical and political horizon before venturing on a description of its essence, its 'centre'.

The Qur'an—an Arabic, living, holy book

The Qur'an (*al-Qur'an*) is the centre of Islam. Over fourteen hundred years Islam has time and again fundamentally changed its social order; one political ideology has given way to another and cultural systems have undergone epoch-making paradigm changes. What remained in all the changes of persons, structures, institutions and interpretations? The Qur'an is the origin, source and norm of all that is Islamic, all Islamic faith, action and life. It is given the highest, absolute, authority. Western sociologists, political theorists, philologists and historians must take seriously what the Qur'an means in the lives of believing Muslims.

The foreigner in Fez or Kairouan, in Cairo, Amman, Kabul or Lahore, who hears the prayer-calls and verses from the Qur'an recited from the minarets in the dawn's glow may have no inkling of the fascination the Qur'an can have for Muslims. Even a sober Muslim scholar such as the Arab Toufic Fahd can write what is almost a hymn to the Qur'an: 'It seems to be the last witness to an old Semitic tradition in which the world of images is combined with reality, where the word evokes the magic of the expression and where the physical is transformed by the metaphysical; a discursive thought which is expanded in statements set side by side, often without grammatical supports, without reference to causality, finality, consistency; ideas which repeat themselves, become entangled, permeate one another in a word-whole of the same textual connection; a harmony of a monotonous wealth of sound, wearisome in the long run but often beguiling, soothing, forming itself on the rhythm of breathing and the effect of emptiness and abstraction: that is how the Qur'an appears to the reader who is initiated into the subtleties of the Arabic language and sensitive to the poetic rhythm which the Semitic soul bears through all the incarnations of cultures that it has known now for more than five thousand years.'[13]

For Muslims the Qur'an is not a relic of the past. It is a living, holy book in Arabic. Every word in this description is important.

– It is a *book*. That has the advantage that every believer knows where he is. Here is everything that God has revealed directly. Here one can unequivocally hold on to what God wills. So nothing can be changed here. On the contrary, the Muslim is to stamp everything on his memory as early as possible, as a school child. This book proclaims 'Islam', 'submission to God'; it regulates the life of Muslims and teaches them their obligations.

– It is *one* book. Unlike the Hebrew Bible, the Qur'an is not a collection of very different writings which to the outsider initially seem to have no common denominator. Nor is it like the New Testament, which offers its message in four very different Gospels that contradict one another in many details and are therefore the occasion for some confusion. The Qur'an is a single book, handed down by one and the same prophet within twenty-two years, and therefore is a coherent unity, despite differences in period and style. It was put in order later (by and large according to length) in 114 sections denoted by the Arabic term *surah*, plural *suwar*; these in turn consist of verses, the smallest textual units ('signs': *ayah*, plural *ayat*). There is mention of a book (*kitab*) in the Qur'an itself.

– It is an *Arabic* book. Its 6666 verses form the oldest Arabic prose work: more than anything else it promoted the dissemination of the Arabic language and script; to the present day it has a normative function in syntax and morphology. But the Qur'an is above all the book of revelation given to the Arabs, so that now they too, like Jews and Christians, are possessors of scripture, 'people of the book' (*ahl al-kitab*). They have their own holy book—'the Book' (*al–kitab*), 'the book of God' (*kitab Allah*)—which through the impressive melody and often passionate rhythm of this language can even bewitch and charm even non-Arab Muslims. For them, too, Arabic is the language of worship, and for them, too, Arabic script is to some degree their own. 'In the history of the Arabic language there is no event which has had a more persistent influence on its fate than the rise of Islam.'[14] Apart from Turkish (in which Arabic script was replaced by Latin script in 1928 under Atatürk) and the central and south-east Asian languages (following reforms of scripts since around 1920), Arabic remains the script for Berber, Persian and Kurdish, and also for Indian Urdu and Sindhi; numerous Arabic loan words in all these languages attest to the dominance of Arabic Islamic culture. To the present day Arabic literature is extraordinarily strongly stamped by the Qur'an in its metaphors, quotations, motifs and forms. Even Muslims inclined towards reform think that only those who understand pure Arabic can understand the Qur'an, so every Muslim has to labour to learn Arabic. Be this as it may, through the Qur'an Arabic became the sacred language of the whole Muslim world.

– It is a *living* book. The Qur'an is not a book which sits on the bookshelf like a rarely used household Bible or is mainly read silently. It is a book which is recited aloud in public time and again: *qur'an* comes from the word *qara'a*, 'read aloud, recite', and means 'reading' or 'lecture' in all (fundamentally four) senses of the word: first the act of presenting the revealed text (revelation to Muhammad, then handing down by Muhammad), then the presented text itself, and finally the book of reading and lecture. The Prophet handed down precisely what he heard.

It is a book which, made to resound with the rhyming prose of its surahs and verses, can and should be recited rhythmically.[15] Its words and sentences accompany Muslims from the hour of their birth, when the Qur'anic confession of faith is spoken in their ear, to their last hour, when the words of the Qur'an accompany them into eternity. By hearing, memorizing and reciting, Muslims both confess God's revelation and make it their own. Some Muslims, who began learning as children, know the whole Qur'an by heart; they have the honorary title 'guardian, preserver' (*hafiz*). Famous professional reciters who present the whole text in song are highly regarded as artists. When the Qur'an is presented beautifully with dedication it can fascinate a Muslim, much as the words of a good preacher can fascinate a Christian or the singing of a gifted cantor can a Jew. Anyone who hears the German translation of the famous surah 97 about the sending down of the Qur'an, poetically assimilated to the Arabic text by Friedrich Rückert, can have some inkling of the aesthetic quality of Qur'anic Arabic:

> We sent it down into the night of power,
> Do you know what is the night of power?
> The night of power is
> Better than a thousand months.
> The angels came down in haste and the spirit in it,
> At their Lord's bidding that all might be planned.
> Salvation full is it and peace until the day dawns.[16]

– It is a *holy* book. The Qur'an is not a book like any other, that one can also touch with dirty hands and read in an unclean spirit. Before reading it, one is to cleanse one's hands with water or sand and open one's heart by a humble prayer. It is not a profane book, but sacred through and through and therefore omnipresent: artistically chiselled in stone, embroidered or painted on tiles, its verses adorn Islamic buildings and works of metal and wood, ceramics, miniature paintings and tapestry. Impressively aesthetic, written in different scripts, the copies of the Qur'an tower above all else; they are often housed in precious bindings and usually decorated with coloured patterns. The Muslim house of God, the mosque, has no pictures—the calligraphy of the Qur'an is enough. Muslim worship has neither instruments nor choral singing—the recitation of the Qur'an is music enough. For Muslims the Qur'an is, in Christian terms, word and sacrament in one, a word which can be heard and seen, giving spiritual guidance, warning and admonition and bringing about recollection and discernment—all this in an incomparable way, because it comes directly from God. It is not only 'inspired' by God but 'revealed' by God and therefore directly 'the word of God' (*kalimat Allah*).

How are we to think of a book on earth being God's word? Muslims see few problems here, at any rate far fewer than when Christians claim that a human being is God's word. To accept one or the other is ultimately a matter of faith, but for Muslims, as for Christians, it is a matter not of a blind faith but of an understanding faith.

The Qur'an—God's word

We sometimes read that the Qur'an is the holy scripture of Islam, which contains the revelations of the Prophet Muhammad. That is correct, but is ambiguous for Muslims: does 'revelations of the Prophet Muhammad' mean that the Prophet is the subject and the author of this revelation? As the Qur'an understands it, certainly not! The Prophet is nothing but an object, the one to whom this revelation is addressed, and the subject and author is the one God alone. The revelation indicates how this is to be thought of. At the beginning of the Joseph surah God tells the prophet: 'These are messages of a revelation clear in itself and clearly showing the truth: behold, We have bestowed it from on high as a discourse in the Arabic tongue, so that you might encompass it with your reason. In the measure that We reveal this Qur'an unto thee, We explain it to thee in the best possible way, seeing that ere this thou wert indeed among those who are unaware [of what revelation is].'[17]

It is historically certain that between 610 and 632 Muhammad proclaimed the prophetic message set down in the Qur'an in the Arab trading cities of Mecca and Medina on the incense road. According to his own words—and here an appeal is made to faith—the Qur'an was transmitted to the Prophet Muhammad by the angel Gabriel: 'Gabriel (*Jibril*), verily, by God's leave, has brought down upon thy heart this [divine writ] which confirms the truth of whatever there still remains [of revelation], and is a guidance and glad tiding for the believers.'[18]

According to the current Muslim view, the original book ('the mother of the Book': *umm al-kitab*), which is regarded as the original of all holy scriptures, is not kept on earth but in heaven, as one can read in the Qur'an itself: 'Behold, it is a truly noble discourse, [conveyed unto man] in a well-guarded divine writ which none but the pure [of heart] can touch: a revelation from the Sustainer of all the worlds!'[19] Or at another point: 'Nay, but this [divine writ which they reject] is a discourse sublime, upon an imperishable tablet [inscribed].'[20]

Thus God's word has become book: in the 'night of power' (*laylat al-qadr*)—solemnly commemorated in the fasting month of Ramadan—Muslims celebrate the revelation of the Qur'an, sent down by God to human beings for 'guidance'. Where in Christianity there is the divine Logos who has become human, in Islam there is the word of God which has become book: 'It was the month of Ramadan in which the Qur'an was [first] bestowed from on high as a guidance unto man and a self-evident proof of that guidance, and as the standard by which to discern the true from the false.'[21]

So the Qur'an manifests itself as the constant foundation of Islam that we have been looking for, its normative basic concept, its driving force. As the foundation document of God's final revelation, the Qur'an has deeply stamped all areas of Islam. What the Torah means for Jews and Christ for Christians, the Qur'an means for Muslims: 'the way, the truth and the life'. Indeed for all Muslims the Qur'an is:

- the truth: the original source of the experience of God and piety and the mandatory criterion of right faith;
- the way: the true possibility of coping with the world and the eternally valid standard for correct action (ethic);
- the life: the abiding foundation of Islamic law and the soul of Islamic prayer, already the material for the instruction of Muslim children, the inspiration of Islamic art and the all-permeating spirit of Islamic culture.

The Qur'an is at the same time a religious, ethical and legal-social codex, which however is only the way, the truth and the life to the degree that it is the word of God. That the Qur'an is the word of God has important consequences: it is marked by divine attributes. According to traditional Muslim teaching (and here we are talking about what are virtually Islamic dogmas), the Qur'an is:

- *linguistically perfect*: through the Qur'an, Arabic has attained the status of a divine language which is holy and exalted, without defect and unevennesses, but not without mysteries which interpreters can never decipher completely;
- *unique, inimitable and unsurpassable*: for Muslims the Qur'an is a miracle which transcends human capacities. The Qur'an itself tells us that unbelievers could not produce any similar writing, not even ten surahs, indeed not even one.[22] Therefore the Prophet does not need any miracles to authenticate himself, since the Qur'an itself is one great miracle of authentication;
- *untranslatable*: every young Muslim has to learn the Qur'an by heart in Arabic. But as this is impossible in practice, translations have to be used, which people prefer to call interpretations or paraphrases. In fact, with its rhythm and rhyming words the Qur'an is extraordinarily difficult to translate. Translations by Muslims usually have the Arabic text printed in parallel;[23]
- *infallible and absolutely reliable*: as the revelation was given to the Prophet word for word, it must be free from all errors and also free from all

contradictions: 'Will they not, then, try to understand this Qur'an? Had it issued from any but God, they would surely have found in it many an inner contradiction.'[24]

So, we may ask, is the Qur'an a book 'fallen from heaven', not of this world and therefore not to be subjected to worldly scholarly criteria?

2. The Qur'an—a book fallen from heaven?

In the West, the Qur'an is often spoken of as a book 'fallen from heaven'. In a secularized world, in which at best a meteorite or the debris of a rocket falls from heaven, but not a holy book, that is to dismiss the Qur'an a priori as incredible. But according to the Islamic view, did the Qur'an indeed really fall from heaven as a book? Not at all. Rather, it descended into the Prophet's 'heart',[25] was proclaimed by him and only then written down and collected together. Even orthodox Islamic Qur'anic scholarship has never disguised the fact that the holy book as we have it today was written decades after the death of the Prophet.

There is a process of canonization in all 'books of religion'

All three prophetic religions received their holy books only on the basis of a lengthy process of formation and canonization. Whereas the writings of the Hebrew Bible came into being over a period of perhaps a thousand years and those of the New Testament in less than a hundred years, the Qur'an was formed within twenty-two years. Accordingly, the process of canonization which led up to the precise extent of the holy scripture as it is acknowledged today was shorter:

– In Judaism the 'Torah' (the five books of Moses) came into being at the earliest after the Babylonian exile, possibly only after the end of the fourth century BCE; the 'Prophets' (Nebi'im) only at the end of the third century; and the 'Writings' (Ketubim: Psalms, Job, Song of Songs, etc.) even later. Only in connection with the theocracy paradigm of post-exilic Judaism (Jewish P III) may one speak of a holy book, the Hebrew Bible (the Tanakh, consisting of Torah, Nebi'im and Ketubim) and of a 'religion of the book'.

– In Christianity the first letters of the apostle Paul existed only twenty years after the death of Jesus and all four Gospels by the end of the first century, but about nine-tenths of the final canon was not fixed until the end of the second century. In the case of some secondary writings it was only decided at synods towards the end of the fourth century (Christian P II) that they corresponded to the church's 'guidelines' (Greek *kanon* = 'guideline, measure'), were therefore 'canonical' and so could be read aloud in worship.

– In Islam the process of canonization did not last so long. Here it was not a matter of collecting and recognizing the writings of different ('apostolic') authors but of collecting, ordering and editing different surahs of the one Prophet. In this process of canonization it was not bishops and synods which decided but the caliph (the representative of the Prophet after his death), the scholars and finally the courts.

According to tradition the Qur'anic revelation was initially recorded only on palm leaves, stones, bones and pieces of leather and wood. It is questionable whether the Prophet himself had anything to do with gathering the scattered revelation if (as is assumed by many Muslims) he did not know how to read or write and finally dictated to secretaries. At all events, he did not complete this work and left no official book to posterity.

Many Muslims knew by heart some of the surahs that were regularly recited, and some perhaps the greater part of the future book. Some may have written down whole passages for themselves. But who was to collect all this, write it down, order it and edit it? In the course of time, when the Prophet had died and his companions were growing older and older, this question became urgent. It was decided to collect what had been handed down into a manageable book.

A wearisome process of collecting and editing

First, I shall sketch out briefly the process by which the canonization took place according to the information in Muslim tradition:[26]

– *A provisional edition*: was there already such an edition of the Qur'an under the first caliph, Abu Bakr? Historians doubt whether a collection of surahs was ordered in his brief reign of only two years (632–4) or by the later caliph 'Umar for several reasons, above all because the name of Abu Bakr is missing from another account.[27] However, the possibility cannot be excluded that a former secretary of Muhammad, Zayd ibn Thabit, began his work of writing down and collecting under the second caliph, 'Umar (634–44). 'Umar's daughter Hafsah, a widow of the Prophet, seems to have owned some sheets, perhaps a codex. This codex would have been by no means the only one, since many people knew the Qur'an, different versions of which were already circulating in the different provinces of the new empire that deviated markedly from one another in numerous texts and in the ordering of the surahs. Establishing an order was an urgent matter.

– *The canonical edition*: Caliph 'Uthman's unitary Qur'an. Especially during the Arab campaigns to Armenia and Azerbaijan, disputes had arisen between Muslims from Syria and Muslims from Iraq over the correct reading of the surahs. Beyond any doubt, under the third caliph, 'Uthman (644–56), an authoritative text of the Qur'an was made, a unitary Qur'an that in future was to be the only binding text and thus something like a 'Qur'anic Vulgate' ('in common use'). To the present day, all editions of the Qur'an are essentially copies of 'Uthman's Qur'an. This was made possible through the great literary and editorial achievement of Muhammad's secretary Zayd ibn Thabit in Medina, who with three prominent Meccans brought together the numerous, sometimes very small, fragments and material that had often only been handed down orally. However, in many cases surahs could have been taken over as already separate units. The editors did not take much trouble at some points to avoid unevennesses and breaks, but the way in which they put the elements of the text together was not arbitrary.[28]

'Uthman sent copies of this unitary text from Medina to the most important centres of the empire, Damascus in Syria, Kufa and Basra in Iraq, and probably also Mecca. No resistance worth mentioning was shown to the new canonical text by those who recited the Qur'an there. It was probably generally assumed that this edition contained the essentials of the revelation granted to the Prophet for the Islamic community. However, people did not follow the caliph's instructions to destroy all previous versions of the Qur'an for these were preserved at least in fragments. Subsequently Qur'anic scholars time and again speak of other 'readings' (*qira'at*) and codices (*masahif*). And the classic commentaries—the giant commentary of at-Tabari or the concentrated and therefore popular commentary of al-Baydawi (there are more than eighty Arabic and around seventy Ottoman Turkish commentaries on it)—continually list small variants. In the early tenth century some Muslim scholars even produced a study of these variants, though it showed no important or even fundamental differences. Yet in many respects even 'Uthman's unitary edition was still inadequate. Philologists call it a *scriptio defectiva.*

– *From the defective to the complete edition*: the standard edition of 1923 was made, at the request of the Egyptian King Fu'ad, by scholars of al-Azhar university on the basis of the Iraqi textual tradition. The number and sequence of the surahs had been unambiguously laid down by 'Uthman's edition but the whole text was in a consonantal script (without vowels) and with no diacritical signs, so that numerous words and verses were ambiguous and open to misinterpretation. In many respects this text was more an *aide-memoire* than a clear authoritative document. Moreover, the ways of presenting the text were often very different. So there was an urgent need once again to improve the edition of the Qur'an: this happened in stages by the addition of vowel signs, of signs to distinguish consonants with the same form and signs for erasing (pauses, etc.). All in all there was now no longer a *scriptio defectiva* but a *scriptio plena*, a complete edition, without fault or blemish.

This made the problems of 'Uthman's edition even more evident: manifestly there was no complete uniformity, and manifestly such a uniformity could not be forced on the text. In the important centres of Qur'anic scholarship—Medina and Mecca (for Arabia), Damascus (for Syria), and Basra and Kufa (for Iraq)—the Qur'an was still recited differently in some respects, with textual variants and different modes of presentation, giving different 'readings' (*qira'a*, plural *qira'at*) of the Qur'an. So an attempt was soon made to limit the individual choice of the various 'Qur'an readers' (*qari'*, plural *qurra'*); these reciters were like the old rhapsodists, who delivered the texts of others by heart.

There are seven readings, no more and no less, and seven famous reciters, said Ibn Mujahid from Kufa around 900—for theological reasons (Catholic theologians are reminded of the Council of Trent in the sixteenth century, with its dogma of the seven sacraments, no more and no less). His view gained wide assent: seven readings of the Qur'an were accepted, among which there did not need to be perfect unity. Yet in the course of time for practical reasons a single reading became established, the reading of 'Asim of Kufa (died 744) in the tradition of Haf (died 805). This reading finally formed the basis for the standard edition of the Qur'an published in Egypt in 1923, which today enjoys the utmost respect and is therefore used almost everywhere.

Even the Shiites follow 'Uthman's unitary Qur'an,[29] though they sometimes accuse it of suppressing material about their 'ancestor' 'Ali and the family of the Prophet. However, this is a dogmatic and not a historically qualified charge of falsification, which cannot shake the authority of 'Uthman's version and what is now the standard edition. Of course it is possible that early revelations were forgotten even in Muhammad's lifetime; a hadith concedes that on one occasion the Prophet forgot a particular verse of the Qur'an. However, on the whole Muslims assume that the revelations of the Prophet have been preserved for them complete and unfalsified and this is confirmed by some Western scholars: 'The findings of modern scholarship endorse the view that the text of the Qur'an in its present form is in all essential points the text which Muhammad left to his followers.'[30] We shall go into the most recent form criticism later.

Were the surahs really also put in the right order? What about the chronology of individual surahs, which is after all of decisive importance for understanding them? Isn't there a demonstrable history of this revelation? To a limited degree this is also affirmed by traditional teaching.

Periods of revelation

With the standard edition we now have a perfectly-formed text of the Qur'an: the 114 surahs with vowel signs, diacritical points and information for recitation, sometimes subdivided into sections and quarter-sections. Generally, the surahs are arranged by decreasing length: the longest, surah 2, after the opening surah, has 286 verses, and the shortest, at the end, no more than three. All are given short headings, added later: these are not titles but key words, *aides memoire* in recitation. The heading can either be taken from the name of the chief figure in the surah or simply be a word from it (often from the first verse).

However, more is required than the history of the text and its perfect rendering if the individual surahs are really to be understood. Readers may want to know when and on what occasion the revelation took place and how the occasion sheds light on it. What could give more information about the personality of the Prophet and the development of the message of the Qur'an than a reasonably certain chronology of the Qur'anic texts? Wouldn't this also put particular emphases on the content of the texts and explain some roughnesses and breaks in the given text?

Muslim Qur'an study is well aware of the question of chronology. A chronology already emerges from the information about the places of origin of the surahs, which makes possible a rough division into periods: surahs from Mecca from 610 to 622 (the migration to Medina) and surahs from Medina from 622 to 632 (Muhammad's death). Moreover, the surahs themselves contain references to particular historical events: to the life of Muhammad (above all the experience of his call), to conflicts with opponents and enemies in the city of Mecca, to the fate of the community (above all the migration from Mecca to Medina), and to events during the time in Medina (for example, particular battles or the expulsion of the Jews). In the Qur'an there are further statements that have led Muslim interpreters to investigate the particular occasion of a revelation, so that a whole literature has developed on 'occasions of revelation' (*asbab an-nuzul*). However, this literature sometimes has contradictory and legendary elements and cannot be wholly relied on for historical research. Be this as it may, on the basis of the Egyptian standard edition of 1923 a traditional-chronological listing of many surahs is now possible.

European study of the Qur'an has accepted the results of the Muslims as far as possible, but has gone beyond them. This was made possible by the methods of philological historical criticism developed in Europe above all in connection with the study of the Bible, but which in Islam are largely stuck at their beginnings, despite the efforts of Islamic and Arabic scholars.[31] Could it be possible, one asks, that in the case of the Qur'an too, which was revealed over the course of around twenty years, a development could be established on the basis of inner evidence, content, style and vocabulary (of course in the context of public events)?

A truly pioneering work of 1860 arrived at this conclusion, prepared for by the 'historical–critical introduction' by Gustav Weil:[32] this was the 'History of the Qur'an' by Theodor Nöldeke which I have already mentioned (see A I, 1). It was revised and expanded by Nöldeke's master pupil Friedrich Schwally and others in three volumes (1909, 1919, 1948),[33] and adopted, with few changes, by the leading French Qur'an scholar Régis Blachère.[34] The chronological framework of this work is still the basis for a far-reaching international consensus in historical criticism of the Qur'an.[35] Nöldeke and Schwally do not reject the traditional Muslim division into surahs from Mecca and surahs from Medina but refine and differentiate it on the basis of formal, i.e. linguistic and literary, characteristics of the text of the Qur'an. Three Meccan periods and one Medinan period can be distinguished and with them a slow change in style from emphatically poetic, short, rhythmic verses in Mecca to gradually longer and finally lengthy prose statements in Medina. Without reproducing the tables of surahs and verses that can be found in Nöldeke-Schwally and Blachère,[36] the four periods of revelation according to Nöldeke-Schwally can be described briefly, whilst appreciating that Nöldeke wanted to understand them not as absolute chronology but as 'stages of development'.

The surahs of the *first, early Meccan period* (610–15: a minor emigration of Muslim families to Ethiopia) focus on the conversion of unbelievers to the one true God. The torments of hell for sinners and the paradisal bliss of the pious are vividly depicted. The numerous oaths recall the language of pagan soothsayers or seers. The surahs are brief, and the language of the rhythmic verse is poetic. 'The language is noble, exalted and full of bold images; the rhetorical verve still has a completely poetic colouring.'[37]

In the surahs of the *second, middle Meccan period* (615–20: Muhammad's return from the city of Ta'if) oaths are rarer, verses and surahs increase in length but have no common characteristic: 'We see in them the transition from grandiose enthusiasm to the greater repose of later more prosaic surahs.'[38] There are, above all, illustrations from nature and history (especially the earlier prophets of the Hebrew Bible), which call for trust in God's omnipotence and goodness.

The surahs of the *third, late Meccan period* (620–22: the great emigration to Medina) are longer, seem less inspired and sometimes repetitive: 'The language is drawn-out, flat and prosaic.'[39]

The surahs of the *Medinan period* (622–32: the death of the Prophet) are focused on the consolidation of the community of Muslims and the activity of

Muhammad as its recognized spiritual and secular head. On the one hand these surahs attack the polytheism of the pagans, but on the other they ward off the claims of Jesus and Christians. Stylistically they are not very different from the surahs of the third Meccan period, but they contain numerous laws, ritual precepts and administrative ordinances.[40]

These definitions are approximate. Much Qur'an research is hypothetical and as yet there is no solid verification. However, we exaggerate the illumination brought by textual criticism if we dissolve the surahs accepted without dispute at the time into verses or tiny units which then in turn have to be fitted together according to the (allegedly objective) criteria of the scholar concerned! Nevertheless, important insights into the Qur'an have been achieved in this way. And however many details may be disputed or uncertain, there can be no uncertainty as to what the central message of the Qur'an is, down the centuries and also today. Muslim faith is rooted in it.

The Qur'an as the Islamic constant

The Qur'an is more than a word that has been handed down orally and so can easily be changed. It is the written word set down once and for all, which therefore cannot be changed subsequently: in this, it is like the Bible. Being fixed in writing has ensured the Qur'an an amazing constancy in the changing and varied history of Islam from century to century, from land to land, from generation to generation, from person to person. What has been written remains written.

The Muslim theologian Mahmoud M. Ayoub remarks: 'Although it was shaped by the Muslim community, the Qur'an in fact created that community and remains the foundation-stone of its faith and its morality. Many of its verses were circumstantially determined by the social and religious conditions and questions of the Prophet's society; yet the Qur'an is believed to transcend all considerations of time and space.'[41] In all the different interpretations, commentaries, social orders, ideologies and systems, in all the shaping of Islamic law, the Shariah, the Qur'an remains the common denominator: the 'green thread' which seems to be woven into all Islamic forms, rites and institutions. If we want to know not only what the Islam is that has grown up through history but also what normative Islam is, we cannot avoid going back to the origin, the Qur'an of the seventh century, recognized by all Islamic groups as divine revelation. For Islam and its legislation it approximates to a God-given constitution, a revealed basic law, which cannot be interpreted randomly, despite the breadth of interpretation depending on place, time and person.

The Qur'an has not predetermined the development of Islam, but time and again has inspired it anew. It has permeated the whole of the religious law and shaped jurisprudence and mysticism, art and people's general attitude to life. Commentators have come and gone, but the Qur'an remains: given the many variables in space and time, it is the great constant in Islam. If we want to answer the question raised in the introduction, that is, what the power of Islam is based on, then we will have primarily to point to the Qur'an. It is the main source and criterion of Muslim faith and action. It communicates to Islam ethical obligation, external dynamics and religious depth but also quite specific convictions of faith, and ethical principles which have constantly been maintained: human responsibility before God, social justice and Muslim solidarity.

Thus the Qur'an is the holy book of Islam, understood not as a human word that has been written down, but quite pragmatically as the word of God. The question for Christians, though, is this: can they too acknowledge this book as the word of God?

Is the Qur'an also the word of God for Christians?

For centuries it was forbidden to raise this question at all seriously: Muslims (like Christians in respect of the Bible) were threatened with excommunication and all its consequences if they did. From the first Islamic conquests, the crusades, the capture of Constantinople and the siege of Vienna to the Iranian revolution under Ayatollah Khomeini, this question has deeply divided humanity politically. For just as naturally as Muslims, from West Africa to Central Asia, said yes to the Qur'an as the word of God and orientated their living and dying on it, believing Christians all over the world said no. They were not the only ones: later came the secularist Western scholars of religion, who just as naturally understood the Qur'an not as the word of God but always as the word of Muhammad.

The Canadian scholar Wilfred Cantwell Smith was the first, in 1963, to make a careful analysis of this question, which is still a threatening one.[42] We have to agree with him: remarkably, he says, both answers, given by intelligent, critical and completely honest people, are ultimately based on a dogmatic preconviction, about which no questions are asked. The conflicting views then appear either as unbelief—the Christian 'no' to the question for Muslims– or as superstition, the Muslim 'yes' for Christians.

Is the remark which Smith's American colleague Willard Oxtoby used to make as a warning to students beginning on the study of religions then a true one? 'You get out what you put in.' Will someone who regards the Qur'an as the word of God feel constantly confirmed in reading it—and vice versa?

But I ask myself this: are we stuck with this contradiction, which in the long run can never prove intellectually satisfying? Aren't there more and more Christians, and perhaps Muslims, who have gained improved information about their own position and about the faith of others and therefore ask self-critical questions? I want first and foremost to put a critical question to Christians: as a Christian may one regard the Qur'an at all as the word of God to Muslims?

For too long Christian theology simply dismissed the Qur'an as a 'book of lies' made up of biblical elements. In 1772 Professor David Friedrich Megerlin, the famed author of the 'very first German translation from the Arabic original', presented the Qur'an on the title page as 'The Turkish Bible'; on the opposite page was an etching of 'Mohammed, the False Prophet'.[43] The first person to translate it directly into a European vernacular, the Frenchman André du Ryer (1647), had presented it in a similar way. Happily, the Catholic Tübingen theologian Johann Adam Möhler in 1830 was the first to bring out the independence of the Qur'an as a religious document in an article on Jesus and Muhammad. On the assumption that Muhammad is nothing but a cheat and a false prophet, 'the origin of the Qur'an, in which we often find a quite original piety, a touching devotion and a quite characteristic religious poetry, would be utterly inexplicable. It is impossible for this to be something artificial and forced, which would have to be assumed if we wanted to see Muhammad as a mere cheat ... Many millions of people feed and nurture a laudable religious and moral life from the Qur'an, and I do not believe that they draw from an empty spring.'[44]

Historically the Christian mission to Islam proved completely fruitless, as did (and does) the Muslim mission to Christians. The more Christians and Muslims got to know one another and did not simply attempt to 'convert' one another, the more doubts arose among Christians as to whether their own negative attitude to the Qur'an was correct. The decisive issue for present-day theological problems is not *how* Muhammad received the revelation, but *whether* he received a revelation from God.

May Christians put this sort of question at all? In the light of the Bible mustn't they fundamentally reject it? Aren't there a wealth of negative statements in the New Testament about the error, darkness and guilt of the non-Christian world? These judgements are passed on people who culpably refuse to accept the message of the Bible. However, they are less definitive condemnations than invitations to conversion. And it should not be overlooked that alongside these negative statements there are quite a number of positive statements about the non-Christian world, according to which God originally made himself known to the whole of humankind. Indeed, according to both Old and New Testaments, non-Jews and non-Christians can know the true God: they can recognize what these texts themselves understood as a revelation of God in the creation.

Against this biblical background, can we exclude the possibility that, on the basis of God's revelation in Christ, countless men and women from prehistory to the present have experienced, and still experience, the mystery of God?[45] Can we exclude the possibility that here individuals are also given special knowledge, entrusted with a particular task or given a special charisma? Couldn't this also have been the case with Muhammad, the Prophet from pagan Arabia? '*Extra ecclesiam nulla conceditur gratia*—no grace is granted outside the church': this view has been expressly condemned by the Roman magisterium.[46] If we recognize Muhammad as a post-Christian prophet, to be consistent we must concede the most important concern of Muslims: that Muhammad did not simply make up his message himself, that his message is not simply his word, but God's.

But what is God's word? What is revelation? Has God's revelation really been not only inspired directly word for word by God but dictated by God? This is believed not only by Muslims but also by some Christians—of the Bible. We shall be discussing this point, which has become explosive only in modern times, at length in a later chapter on present-day theological controversies (D IV, 1).

B II

The Central Message

As I explained fully in my book on Judaism,[1] the Jewish confession of faith can be expressed in one sentence: 'Yahweh is the God of Israel and Israel is his people.' So too can the creed of Christianity, as I explained in my book on Christianity:[2] 'Jesus is the Christ (of God).' Yet neither the Jewish nor the Christian confessions of faith have been able to establish themselves in as pointed, exclusive and universal way as that of Islam, although the Islamic confession does not yet appear in the Qur'an in this two-membered form: 'There is no God but God, and Muhammad is his Prophet.' Anyone who confesses this is a Muslim; anyone who does not confess it is not. Every believing Muslim introduces this confession with the words: 'I bear witness that ...'

No God but God and Muhammad his Prophet: this confession of faith (*shahadah*—testimony) is indisputably the central message of Islam, its cornerstone, its first 'pillar'. I shall now investigate the two articles of the confession of faith in more detail: 1) the understanding of God and 2) the understanding of the Prophet.

1. There is no God but God

As I explained in the previous chapter, all three prophetic religions refer to the one God, the Creator of the world and the God of Abraham. However, it is significant that while Judaism takes its name from a people, 'Israel' (or from the tribe of 'Judah'), and Christianity is named after its central figure, 'Christ' (Jesus of Nazareth), Islam—from the Arabic verb *aslama*, 'to submit, hand oneself over, surrender'—by its very name confesses none other than God: 'submission, handing over, surrendering' to God. Belief in the one God (*tawhid*[3]), from the verb 'declare to be one' (*wahhada*) derived from the noun 'one, only'(*wahid*), is the basic dogma of Islam, and is meant quite practically.

The practical theocentricity of Islam

Since Arabic has no capital letters, the word *islam*[4] can mean two things:

- *islam*, with an initial lower-case letter, means the act of submission to God: 'Your God is the One and Only God: hence, surrender yourselves unto Him.'[5]
- *Islam*, written as it were with an initial capital, means the religion of those who confess such submission under God: 'God proffers evidence ... that there is no deity save Him, the Upholder of Equity; there is no deity save Him, the Almighty, the Truly Wise.'[6]

The Qur'an time and again addresses those who believe in God as 'Muslims' (*muslimun*, feminine *muslimat*) and obviously not as 'Mohammedans' (the name of the Prophet is mentioned only four times in the Qur'an).

If the typical symbol for Jews must still be the pious Jew with the Torah scroll and for Christians the eucharist, for Islam it is the shared ritual prayer of Muslims as they prostrate themselves before God with their foreheads touching the ground. This is a tangible expression of the central concern of Islam: not a new social system nor a political ideology, not an anthropology nor even a theology, but rather the quite practical surrender to God which is expressed in prayer, in the attitude of faith and in particular rites and obligations. The 'throne verse' (surah 2. 255) is quite often depicted calligraphically and is a popular pendant for necklaces:[7]

'God, there is no deity save Him,
the ever-Living, the Self-Subsistent Fount of All Being.
Neither slumber overtakes Him, nor sleep.
His is all that is in the heavens and all that is on earth.
Who is there that could intercede with Him,
Unless it be by His leave?
He knows all that lies open before men and all that is hidden from them,
Whereas they cannot attain to aught of His knowledge save that which he wills.
His eternal power overspreads the heavens and the earth,
And their upholding wearies Him not.
And he alone is exalted, tremendous.'

This implies a quite practical theocentricity that has an effect throughout individual and social lives: from education, business, the legal order, science and art to politics and the state. Theocentricity—concentration on God—but does God exist? This is not a question for the average Muslim even today: of course God exists! The existence of God is nowhere proved in the Qur'an—any more than it is in the Hebrew Bible and the New Testament—but is everywhere taken for granted. From the beginning God attests himself through his creation and all the natural phenomena that are 'signs' of his goodness, and above all through his concern for human beings and his saving acts in history. Above all, God attests himself by his revelations to the prophets. Human beings are not to theorize and speculate too much about God: certainly Islam also understands theology as scholarly reflection on God but, by comparison with Christianity, that is very much of secondary significance. Human beings are to honour, worship and obey God; in Islam religious law, which shows people the right way of obeying God in all things, is more important than theology.

Like Judaism and Christianity, Islam is a religion of faith. Human beings are to encounter God neither with detached rational arguments nor in striving for mystical unity, but in trusting faith (*iman*, 'faith', is often used in the Qur'an in the same sense as *islam*).[8] Belief in the one God is therefore:

- the first and foremost obligation of every Muslim: the foundation and meaning of their existence as Muslims;
- the unshakable foundation of the Muslim community and its legal order; the spiritual bond of unity for all Islamic tribes and peoples;
- the sole content of Muslim prayer, addressed to God and no one else;
- the premise of any Muslim theology: God is the only God, both outwardly (in the world) and inwardly (in his being).

I have already named an essential property of God. As we shall see, God has a hundred different names. But it is absolutely fundamental for Islam that God is the One, indeed the Only One.

Monotheism as a core concern and fighting programme

In Judaism, strict monotheism, belief in one God who does not acknowledge the existence of other gods, took centuries to establish. It had first to counter polytheism, belief in and worship of many gods and goddesses, and then henotheism, which presupposes the existence of several gods but accepts only 'one' God as the supreme and binding authority (see A II, 1).

In Christianity, with its Jewish roots, strict monotheism was a given from the start. However, it can hardly be disputed that the increasing Hellenistic equating of the Christ Jesus and the one God of Abraham (I have described at length the paradigm change in christology and the Trinity which is unknown to most Christians and even theologians[9]) made Christian monotheism doubtful, at least for Jews and probably also for Jewish Christians: how can one God in two, even three, 'persons' still be one God?

In Islam, strict monotheism is a core concern and a fighting programme: a single God without peer and or partner! So we read in the Qur'an: 'There has never been any deity side by side with Him: [for, had there been any,] lo! each deity would surely have stood apart [from the others] in whatever it had created, and they would surely have [tried to] overcome one another!'[10] Several gods would compete and dispute over spheres of influence. Here the Prophet's fight is directed first against true polytheism, which was widespread above all among the Arab nomads, who from old accepted a whole series of more or less equal gods (such as forces of nature or tribal rulers). However, increasingly it was also directed against the special form of henotheism which prevailed above all in the neighbourhood of Mecca in which Allah is the supreme God, but there are other divine beings subordinate to him, whether these are intercessors before the highest God, angels, spirits or the 'daughters of God', including one even with the feminine name *Allat*, which corresponds to *Allah*. These evidently played a special role in connection with the pilgrimage centre of Mecca and the Ka'bah.

The first article of the two-membered Islamic confession of faith is directed against subsidiary deities of any kind. Precisely what it says is: 'There is no deity (*ilah*) beside God (*allah*).' *Allah* is a contraction of *al-ilah* (the deity); it is not a proper name like Zeus but an appellative like '*theos, Deus, Dieu*' and therefore is to be translated 'God'. 'Allah' has a plural form (as does '*el*', the Hebrew word for God), but *aliha* is used only for the 'gods' of the pagans and never for the one true God. Unlike the Jews, who only at a late stage began to avoid pronouncing the name Yahweh out of reverence, Muslims do not have the slightest inhibitions about pronouncing the word Allah directly. On the contrary, they cannot use it often enough. To the present day it occurs in names such as 'Abd-allah' ('servant of Allah') or word-combinations such as the *insh'allah* (if God wills) which is constantly used in everyday life. Even those who know no Arabic can feel the powerful sonority of the confession 'No God but God': *la ilaha illa' llah*. These very words can be found in the Qur'an itself;[11] often there are also analogous formulations like 'Your God is one.'[12] The oneness of God is given classic formulation in the short surah 112 entitled *Ikhlas* (Sincerity), which is often quoted by Muslims:

> Say: He is the one God:
> God the Eternal, the Uncaused Cause of All That Exists.
> He begets not, and neither is He begotten;
> and there is nothing that could be compared with Him.

The negative side of this positive confession of faith is the polemical repudiation of *shirk*, the 'association' of any being with God. It later became the general view in Islam that the only sin that excludes a person from the Muslim community is *shirk*, association: the worst form of 'unbelief' (*kufr*). For by claiming that God has an associate (*sharik*), the Muslim becomes an 'associationist' (*mushrik*), a 'polytheist', an unbeliever (*kafir*).

Is that said against the Christians? All the verses in the Qur'an against association are primarily directed against Arab polytheists and henotheists and not against Christians. Yet they were also applied to Christians as early as in the Qur'an. The Umayyad caliph 'Abd al-Malik stamped such words on the first silver and gold coins inscribed in Arabic and used them as an inscription on the Dome of the Rock in Jerusalem (an Islamic response to the Christian Church of the Holy Sepulchre). For isn't the Christ of Hellenistic christology utterly identified with God ('of the same being') and thus 'associated' with him? The Qur'an protests energetically not against Jesus as the Messiah but against his being made equal with God: 'And yet some people assert, "God has taken unto Himself a son!" Limitless is He in His glory! Nay, but His is all that is in the heavens and on earth, all things devoutly obey His will.'[13] Or: 'Indeed, the truth deny they who say, "Behold, God is the Christ, son of Mary"... Indeed, the truth deny they who say, "Behold, God is the third of a trinity"—seeing that there is no deity whatsoever save the one God.'[14] Accordingly, Christians too appear as 'associationists' and we shall have to investigate whether the Qur'an simply misunderstands Christian dogma, as is often claimed by Christians (see D IV, 2).

No wonder that unity (*tawhid*) has become a programmatic word for Islam, although the word does not appear in the Qur'an. Belief in the one and only God forms something like the *articulus stantis vel cadentis Islamismi*: the belief by which Islam stands and falls. There will regularly be Islamic renewal movements which have 'unity' written on their banners. Of course with the unity and oneness of God there are other attributes, above all God's eternity and omnipresence. However, two other characteristics must be more important for Islam, and we shall now look more closely at their significance: God's omnipotence and God's justice.

The creation of the world and human beings

If the media have made one Arabic phrase familiar to non-Arabs and non-Muslims it is the cry '*Allahu akbar!*', often translated 'God is great.' However, as this statement is understood God is not just 'great'. *Allahu akbar!* is an elative and literally means 'God is the greatest'—great everywhere, in all events, absolute. Nothing is like God and nothing can be compared with God.

God's greatness is expressed in his omnipotence, first manifested in his creation. The alleged gods of the pagans could not even create a fly, even if they all collaborated,[15] but Allah, the one God, is the creator of heaven and earth and all that is between them. The whole world is God's work. Like Judaism and Christianity, Islam, for all its belief in spiritual beings, angels and demons, knows of no second creative principle alongside the one good principle, no dualism, and no primal evil alongside the primal good. Rather, the one and only God is the creator of all: 'Say: "God is the Creator of all things"; and He is the One who holds absolute sway over all that exists.'[16]

The Hebrew Bible says of God's act of creation, 'And God said, "Let there be light," and there was light.'[17] Likewise the Qur'an says: 'It is He who grants life and deals death; and when He wills a thing to be, He but says unto it, "Be"—and it is.'[18] However, this very verse, to which there are many parallels, shows that the Qur'an has a different perspective. The Bible is intensely interested in the beginning of the creation; the Qur'an is very much more interested in its progress and continuation, in God's creative power today. God not only created the world but sustains it as long as he wills.

Sometimes Muslims claim that the Qur'an says nothing about the six-day work of the Creator and therefore does not conflict with modern science. But the Qur'an also says: 'It is God who has created the heavens and the earth and all that is between them in six aeons, and is established on the throne of His almightiness (to rule the world).'[19] However, whereas the 'six-day work' in the Bible, related at length and in detail, is programmatically put right at the beginning, in the Qur'an it is mentioned briefly and almost in passing in the middle of other discussions;[20] only at one point is it described at rather more length.[21] The Qur'an says nothing about a seventh day of creation on which God rested, since the Creator knows 'no weariness',[22] but rather, as the Eternal One, is constantly there for the world.

The creation of the first human being from clay or earth is generally reported independently of the six days of creation.[23] The famous beginning of surah 96, regarded as the oldest in the Qur'an, with the title 'The Embryo', shows how strongly the Qur'an is also interested in God's creative power in the creation of human beings in the present: 'Read in the name of thy Sustainer, who has created—created man out of a germ-cell!'[24] God creates every individual and brings about each new stage of development (according to the present state of knowledge in fidelity to nature: sperm, embryo, foetus, bones, flesh).[25] The world and human beings are constantly brought forth from God and sustained anew. In this way God obligates human beings to faith and gratitude and one day will require an account of them. Life is a unique and unrepeatable opportunity that human beings can use or waste. As in the whole of the Near Eastern

Semitic religious river system (and in the Far Eastern Chinese river system)—and in contrast to the religions of Indian origin—there is no notion of a cycle of rebirths on earth.

This also expresses the purpose of the creation of human beings. They are created to be servants of God: 'And I have not created the invisible beings and men to any end other than that they may worship me.'[26] The basic principle of Islamic anthropology is expressed with the service of God, worship: 'Not one of all [the beings] that are in the heavens or on earth appears before the Most Gracious other than as a servant.'[27] In the Qur'an, as in the Bible, the word 'servant' must not be misunderstood. The Arabic '*abd* becomes an extremely positive designation because it is associated with God: *'abd allah*, servant, not of another human being, and therefore unfree, but of God himself and therefore free and set in the creation with dignity. The paradoxical anthropological key statement of the Qur'an is grounded in the fact that as the servant of God, the human being is at the same time God's *khalifah*, his 'successor', 'representative on earth'.[28] But what is the relationship between God and human beings?

God's supremacy—and human responsibility?

Aren't there statements in the Bible, as in the Qur'an, which emphasize God's omnipotence as God's supremacy, to which human beings seem simply to be handed over? Aren't human beings here so totally subordinated to the will of God that they can do nothing more without God's will? Don't human beings seem virtually predestined as those in whose actions God is the real agent? This is how God is presented as the real victor of the battle of Badr against the Meccans in 624: 'And yet it was not you (the Muslims) who slew the enemy, but it was God who slew them; and it was not thou (Muhammad) who cast [terror into them] when thou didst cast it, but it was God who cast it.'[29] Doesn't it seem to follow from such faith in God's supremacy that no misfortune can overcome human beings unless God wills it?[30] In his later years, faced with people complaining about their misfortune, Muhammad required them to say: 'Never can anything befall us save what God has decreed! He is our Lord Supreme; and in God let the believers place their trust!'[31]

So aren't those right who claim that the Qur'an teaches total predestination and that in the Muslim view human beings are in debt to God not only for guidance, grace and help but also when they are led astray and abandoned? Think about this verse of the Quran: 'For, had God so willed, He could surely have made you all one single community; however, He lets go astray him that wills [to go astray] and guides aright him that wills [to be guided].'[32]

We can also read in the Bible that God himself hardened Pharaoh's heart, indeed his people,[33] and created darkness and disaster alongside light and salvation.[34] But anyone who sees only these or similar passages in the Bible or the Qur'an and concludes from them that God is arbitrary fails to recognize the basic message of the Bible and the Qur'an. For part of the fundamental basic message of the Qur'an, too, is that God's omnipotence and the responsibility of the human individual are not contradictory. God's action is not independent of the belief or unbelief, good and evil deeds, of human beings: 'None does He cause to go astray save the iniquitous.'[35] The revelation to the Prophet Muhammad specifically also includes the threat that all human beings must account for themselves at the last judgement and be punished for their evil deeds. I shall be discussing this later.

Initially, it is enough to say that in the Qur'an, as in the Bible, the statements about divine omnipotence and human responsibility are juxtaposed and nowhere balanced. Thus interpreters speak of two complementary truths, both of which should be taken seriously. These truths cannot be rationally reconciled anywhere and would offer to later Muslim theology—as they did to later Christian theology—material for intensive and wearisome arguments and occasions for very different solutions to the problem of God's predestination and human self-determination (see C II, 7). Only if we take into account the statements of the Qur'an not only about the omnipotent Creator and human responsibility but also about the just judge and the final destiny of human beings can we understand the full scope of all this. So we need to consider the Qur'anic protology (the doctrine of the 'first things') and eschatology (the doctrine of the 'last things').

The last judgement and the final destiny of human beings

God is not only the All-mighty but also the All-merciful. In the opening surah, as we saw, God is called 'the most Gracious, the Dispenser of Grace' and most surahs are proclaimed 'In the name of God, the Most Gracious, the Dispenser of Grace'. *Ar-rahman*, 'the one who has mercy' or 'the merciful', became almost a kind of proper name for God, so that there was a danger that naive people could understand *allah* and *ar-rahman* as two different deities.[36] It would also be a misunderstanding of the term 'all-merciful' if we were to take this Qur'anic expression to mean 'having mercy upon all' or even 'the reconciliation of all' (Greek *apokatastasis ton panton*), in other words the salvation of all human beings without exception, which is suggested by Paul.[37]

According to the Qur'an the 'Day of Judgement' (*yaum ad-din*) is the 'Day of Reckoning' (*yaum al-hisab*). On this last day of human history the graves will open and the dead will be raised to life. God, who has created the world and constantly sustains it, is capable of new creation and resurrection. Therefore in the Qur'an protology and eschatology seem to be closely connected. In concrete terms this means that at the end all humankind will be gathered before God. God is nowhere described but appears with his angels to make the great division between the saved and the damned.

As in Jewish apocalyptic and in the apocalypses of the New Testament, this gathering together of all human beings to God, the universal judge and consummator, is depicted in a great picture of judgement. It is introduced by the sound of trumpets and horns and by cosmic catastrophes: seas overflow, mountains crash down, the sun is darkened and clouds fall from heaven.[38] Then the righteous judge appears, who will open for everyone the Book of Life, in which all good and evil deeds are listed. His judgement takes place incorruptibly and precisely: no one will bear another's sins. The possibility that grace can precede judgement is no more indicated in the Qur'an than in the judgement discourses of the Gospels. The good (believers) are welcomed into eternal bliss, into paradise, but the evil (unbelievers) go into eternal damnation, into Hell. Either/or: there is no middle state.[39] The Qur'an describes both paradise and hell in very concrete terms.

A concrete paradise and hell

Whereas later Christian descriptions of eternal bliss made it seem too spiritual and beyond the senses, the descriptions in the Qur'an are highly sensual. There are statements about a blessed vision of God and about forgiveness and peace, but they are very sparse and marginal[40] by comparison with the extraordinarily vivid depictions of a paradise full of earthly bliss. In the 'Garden of Delight' ('Garden of Eden') the just will be granted 'great happiness' under God's good pleasure: a life of completely untroubled sensual joy. They will lie on couches decorated with precious stones, eat delicious food, and drink cups of water and milk which never go stale, with clarified honey and even delicious wine. All this is served by boys who are eternally young. The blessed may even enjoy the company of charming, untouched paradisical virgins ('companions pure, most beautiful of eye').[41]

Are we to understand all these statements (those about the houris have attracted special interest among scholars, both of an earlier period and more recently) symbolically, like the parables of the New Testament, which also mention the end-time feast with new wine,[42] the wedding,[43] the great banquet to which all are invited?[44] Many present-day Islamic warriors for God have undoubtedly taken them literally. The descriptions of paradise in the Qur'an are images of hope, not yet afflicted by paleness of thought, images which express the deepest longings of the human heart and even include intense human relationships. I shall be coming to discussions by theologians about this later (see C II, 7).

No less concrete are the descriptions of hell, which is usually called 'the fire' (*an-nar*), but sometimes also 'Gehenna' (*ghahannam*: a Hebrew or Ethiopian loan word). There is vivid talk of the torment of the damned, with 'hell-fire scorching the skin',[45] for whom a food is prepared 'that chokes';[46] they must eat from the tree (well known in Arabia) whose fruit is 'like molten lead' and will 'boil in the belly'.[47]

The Qur'an clearly talks of eternal damnation but there is no mention of Muhammad's intercession in the judgement for the believers whom he was able to save from the fire of hell (an important theme in the later tradition); intercession cannot help. God distributes salvation and damnation in accordance with people's previous lives. Yet the Qur'an holds firm to a basic conviction and so in the Qur'an the question of the final destiny of the damned is perhaps in the last resort left open: God is incalculable, 'above all schemers';[48] he always reserves the judgement for himself.

In all his revelations God remains the inscrutable one; in all the miracles and parables of his creation he is enigmatic. God remains at a superior distance from the world, though he is by no means rigid and immovable as in some Greek philosophers. He is not Aristotle's 'unmoved mover' but, as in the Bible, a living God with whom a dialogue is possible.

The most beautiful names of God

'God's are the attributes of perfection. Invoke him then by these,' we read in the Qur'an.[49] According to later pious traditions God has a hundred names: ninety-nine are known to human beings but the hundredth has not been disclosed to them. God's being lies beyond human reflection and speculation. Here—and only here—according to Islamic faith lies the great mystery: not in some dogmatic 'mysteries' which are contrary to reason (like oneness and threeness), but in God's transcendence, which is to be respected and not speculated about. It is perfect, as God's superiority to the world is absolute.

Nowhere in the Qur'an are human beings called God's 'image and likeness'[50]as they are in the Bible, and nowhere does a 'covenant' (*mithaq*) between God and human beings appear. Where there is an indication of such an idea, this must be understood as a 'pledge'[51] made by the human being. In the light of the Qur'an one may speak even less of a 'self-communication' or an 'incarnation' of God, but 'only' of his revelation of the 'right way' for human beings. Human beings can, may, should worship God. But in the last resort they can never know how God is in himself. Even if concepts revealed to human beings apply to God, they do not know what, in themselves, these mean when applied to God. Yet they express the fullness of God's properties and are present in the everyday world of Muslims, in the giving of names and in calligraphy.

God is addressed directly with many of these names. The Qur'an—although the discourse of God himself—also contains direct prayers,[52] addresses to God, to the 'Lord' (*rabb*[53]), and more rarely to 'God' (*allahummah*).[54] There is no model prayer in the Qur'an like the 'Our Father' in the New Testament. The name 'Father' for God is strictly avoided, as it could imply sons and daughters. Yet according to the Qur'an God possess attributes such as goodness and mercy, which in the biblical perspective one would call 'fatherly'. Indeed, his mercy (*rahma*) is just as fundamental a property of God as his justice (*'adl*). This God cannot be fitted into the (Lutheran) interpretative framework of 'law' (the God who demands) and 'gospel' (the God who gives). The God of the Qur'an cares for human beings with his mercy, which is mentioned in many hundreds of passages.

All the prayers of the Qur'an are addressed to God, who can and will help. Therefore most of them are intercessions in need, oppression and danger, for forgiveness of sins and preservation from the punishments of hell, but also for good in this world and the world to come: 'O our Sustainer! Grant us good in this world and good in the life to come.'[55] Prayers of praise are rarer and there are hardly any prayers of thanksgiving, though thanksgiving is sometimes included in intercession: 'O my Sustainer! Inspire me so that I may forever be grateful for those blessings of Thine with which thou has graced me and my parents, and that I may do right [in a manner] that will please Thee!'[56] Many prayers are formulated in a particular situation, but they are often so general that they can be prayed by anyone at any time. Countless prayers are put into the mouths of figures from the Hebrew Bible (for example, Adam, Noah, Abraham, Lot, Moses, Solomon, Job) or the New Testament (such as Zechariah, Jesus, the disciples of Jesus), the companions of the Prophet in Mecca and Medina and finally Muhammad himself. Thus, a saying of his has been handed down: 'Say, Lord of all dominion ... Verily, Thou hast the power to will anything.'[57]

The common belief in God in the three Abrahamic religions

Judaism, Christianity and Islam are religions of faith, united by living faith in the one God and his activity in the world. What is the meaning of this 'living faith' that Abraham already showed (see A II, 3)? Is faith a matter of understanding, an act of the will or a movement in the disposition? Certainly, for Jews, Christians and Muslims, faith is not merely a matter of understanding, neither simply holding biblical or Qur'anic texts to be true nor even assenting to more-or-less improbable assertions. That would be utterly to misunderstand faith. On the other hand, for Jews, Christians and Muslims faith is also not just the product of an effort of the will, a blind venture, a leap with no basis, even a

The most beautiful names of God

GOD

The Merciful, the Compassionate.

The King, the Holy One, the Embodiment of Peace.

The Giver of Certainty, Who has everything firm in His hands.

The Powerful, the Proud.

The Creator, the Fashioner (surah 59.22–3).

The Oft-Forgiving (38.66; 39.5; 40.42).

The Compeller (12.39; 13.16; 14.48).

The Generous (3.8; 38.9, 35), the Donor of Livelihood (51.48).

He Who judges justly, Who knows the truth (34.26).

The Equitable, Who bestows generously (2.245).

He Who brings down and exalts (56.3).

He Who gives power, Who humbles (3.26).

The All-Hearing, All-Seeing (17.1; 40.20, 56; 42.11).

The Judge, the Righteous.

The Sensitive, Who has knowledge of all things (6.103; 21.63).

The Patient (3.105), the Majestic (2.255).

He Who is full of forgiveness, Who makes himself known (35.30, 34; 42.11).

The Exalted, the Great.

The Guardian (11.57; 34.21), Who cares for and watches over all things (4.85), Who keeps an account (4.6, 68; 33.39).

The Exalted, the Venerable (55.27, 78)

The Watcher, Who is ready to hear (11.61).

The All-Embracing, the Wise (4.130).

The Loving (11.90; 85.14), Who is worthy of honour (11.73).

The Resurrecter.

The Witness, the Truthful, the Advocate.

The Strong, the Firm.

The All-Embracing Friend, Who is worthy of praise.

He Who makes (creation) at the beginning and repeats (it) (85.13; 10.4, 34; 39.19).

He Who brings human beings to life and makes them die (3.156; 15.23).

The Living, the Existing (3.2).

He Who calls into being, the Highly Praised.
The One, the Impenetrable (112.2).
The Mighty, the Almighty.
He Who sends (things) ahead and puts (them) back.
The First, the Last, the Visible, the Hidden (57.3).
The Protector (13.11).
The Transcendent (13.9).
The Gracious.
He Who shows grace (2.37, 54, 128).
The Avenger (32.22; 43.41; 44.16).
He Who is full of forgiveness (4.43, 99, 149), Who has compassion (2.143; 24.20).
He Who exercises kingly rule (3.26).
He Who is exalted and venerable (55.27, 78).
He Who acts justly, Who gathers together.
He Who is dependent on no one (2.263; 10.68), Who makes rich.
He Who wards (things) off (or grants protection).
He Who brings harm, Who brings what is useful.
The Light that gives right guidance.
The Incomparable Creator (2.117; 6.101).
He Who has existence, Who inherits all (15.23).
He Who shows the right way (or leads on the right way).
He Who is full of patience.

After Abu Hurayra (a companion of the Prophet),
Handed down in the collection of hadith by Tirmidi.[58]

credo quia absurdum: 'I believe precisely because it is absurd' would be a deliberate misunderstanding of faith. Finally, faith is not a subjective movement of the disposition, an act of faith (*fides qua creditur*, 'faith') without any content (*fides quae creditur*, 'belief'). To think that the fact that one believes is more important than what one believes would be an emotional misunderstanding.

For Jews and Christians, as for Muslims, faith is an unconditional entrusting and reliance of the whole person on God and God's word with all the forces of the spirit and disposition here and now. Faith is thus at the same time an act of knowing, willing and feeling: a trust which includes believing something to be true. It is an attitude—simple or very complicated—which is personal, lived out and trusting: a believing attitude to life and way of life by which people live and think, act and suffer.

Neither the Hebrew Bible, the New Testament nor the Qur'an want to 'prove' God, but they constantly and everywhere refer to him. Islam, too, emphatically stresses that belief in God is not irrational, but (to use my own conceptuality) is a highly reasonable trust (not a rational proof). Because the Qur'an, too, is so utterly concerned with human beings and their ways, God is a central concern: the name 'Allah' alone is mentioned more than 2500 times in the Qur'an. So, precisely what are the beliefs that Jews, Christians and Muslims have in common?

– First and fundamental is belief in the one and only God who gives meaning and life to all. For Islam, such belief is a primal truth given with Adam; the unity of the human race and the equality of humankind before God are grounded in the one God. Whatever will have to be said about the Christian doctrine of the Trinity, this too certainly does not want to question belief in the one and only God but to expound it and develop it concretely. Judaism, Christianity and Islam were as much one in their confrontation with old polytheism as they are in the confrontation with modern idols of all kinds which take possession of human beings and threaten to enslave them. Indeed, Judaism and then Christianity cast down the old gods of the pantheon long before Islam.

– Second is belief in the God who acts in history, in a God who is not only the *arche*, the first principle of nature (as in Greek thinking), the primal ground of all, but who, as creator of the world and human beings, is active in history: the one God of Abraham who speaks by the prophets and reveals himself to his people, though time and again his action remains an unfathomable mystery. God transcends history but is also immanent. As the Qur'an so vividly puts it, God is closer to a human being 'than his neck-vein'.[59]

– Third is belief in the one God who, although invisibly embracing and permeating all things, is someone whom they can address in prayer and meditation, praise in joy and thankfulness and complain to in distress and despair. He is a God before whom one can 'fall on one's knees in reverence', 'pray and sacrifice', 'make music and dance', to refer here to a famous saying of the philosopher Martin Heidegger about the future.[60]

– Last is belief in the merciful, gracious God, who accepts human beings. In the Qur'an, as in the Bible, human beings are called 'servants of God': this does not mean slavery under a despot but expresses elementary human creatureliness before the one Lord. The Arabic *ar-rahman* (the 'merciful') is etymologically connected with the Hebrew *rahamim*, which together with *hen* and *hesed* represents the word-field of the New Testament *charis* and our word grace. Some statements in the Bible and the Qur'an can make God appear arbitrary, but the overall testimony of the Bible and the Qur'an is decisively that God is a God of grace and mercy.

Thus Judaism, Christianity and Islam together represent belief in the one God; they all are part of the one great monotheistic world movement. We should not underestimate the political significance of this shared belief in the one God, but be aware of it.

We are now sufficiently prepared to be able to understand better the second part of the Islamic confession of faith: the confession that Muhammad is God's Prophet, the messenger of the one God. Who was this Prophet, and what was the revelation to him?

2. Muhammad is his Prophet

All three Abrahamic religions are prophetic religions, in which prophetic figures who proclaim the word and will of God play a central role. It is striking that:

– For Judaism the 'Torah', the great 'instruction' allegedly written down by Moses himself in five books, is more fundamental than the prophets. Judaism is fundamentally a Torah religion.

– In Christianity, Moses and the prophets of the Hebrew Bible retreat behind the one who, while also called 'prophet',[61] in the New Testament is more than a prophet:[62] Jesus, the 'Christ', the anointed one, the Messiah. From its origin, Christianity is a messianic religion.

– Islam recognizes Moses and Jesus as prophets, but sees even the last of the prophets, Muhammad, the 'seal of the prophets', as no more than a prophet: Islam is and remains a prophetic religion *par excellence*. Despite these different accents it is important not to overlook what the three religions have in common, especially in ethics.

The common basic ethic of the three prophetic religions

As a typically prophetic religion, Islam, like Judaism and Christianity, differs both from the Indian mystic and the Chinese wisdom religions: from Hinduism and Buddhism and from Confucianism and Daoism.[63] In Islam, too, the decisive initiative has been taken by the one God with whom human beings are not one, either by nature or through any kind of effort. In the prophetic religions, human beings stand and act 'before' God, before God's 'face'. They may entrust themselves to God in faith: Islam, too, is a religion of faith.

In order to emphasize this prophetic character of Islam (like that of Judaism and Christianity) even more precisely, we need to recognize that by contrast while in India the basic religious mood is a mysticism of union and in China a harmony of the world, in Islam—to put it metaphorically—human beings and God stand over against one other. Thus Islam, like the two other prophetic religions, is a religion of the confrontation of the holy God and the human beings whom he has created. However, through the one word of God to human beings and through human faith in the one God, it becomes a religion of relationship, of dialogue.

What Islam has in common with Judaism and Christianity can now be defined more precisely. Islam is:

- a religion of revelation, in which God's revelation is given once and for all in the abiding and normative form of a written revelation, the Qur'an;
- a religion which thinks historically, not in mythological cycles of return but with a purposeful view of history which has its beginning in God's creation and is orientated on its end through God's consummation;
- an ethically orientated religion which, like Judaism and Christianity, embraces a basic ethic of elementary humanity grounded in God's word and will.

It is of fundamental importance for the shared life of Muslims, Jews and Christians that for Islam, too, God himself is the advocate of humanity—true humanity. The Qur'an does not contain impersonal laws but God's demands: everything is said 'in the name of the merciful and gracious God'. The imperatives of humanity initially formulated for the people of Israel in the 'Ten Words' (Decalogue) are indispensable for an ethic of humanity. Christianity has taken them over literally (apart from the ritual law of the Sabbath). At the end of the Meccan period the Qur'an, too, presents a summary of the most important ethical obligations, which show many striking parallels to the 'Ten Commandments' of Judaism (again apart from the Sabbath).

Thus—as I said earlier in connection with Judaism and Christianity—we can speak of a common basic ethic of the three prophetic religions which can make a historic contribution to the global ethic which is developing. However, now I shall investigate the specific characteristics of Islam more closely.

A prophetic religion par excellence

Though Judaism and Christianity also were and are prophetic religions, Islam is a prophetic religion in a quite special way, for only in Islam is the Prophet himself part of the confession of faith: 'There is no God but God, and Muhammad is his prophet.' For Muhammad to be the prophet of God means two things:

The common basic ethic

The Jewish–Christian Decalogue (Exodus 20.1–21)	**The Islamic Code of Duties** (Surah 17.22–38)
I am the Lord, your God.	In the name of God, the most Gracious, the Dispenser of Grace.
You shall have no other gods before me.	Do not set up any other deity side by side with God.
You shall not make for yourself an image of God. You shall not misuse the name of the Lord, your God.	For thy Sustainer has ordained that you shall worship none but him.
Remember the sabbath day, to keep it holy.	
Honour your father and mother.	And do good unto [thy] parents. And give his due to the near of kin, as well as to the needy and wayfarer.
You shall not kill.	And do not kill your children for fear of poverty... and do not take any human being's life.
You shall not commit adultery.	And do not commit adultery.
You shall not steal.	And do not touch the substance of an orphan.
You shall not bear false witness against your neighbour.	And be true to every promise.
You shall not covet your neighbour's house.	And give full measure whenever you measure, and weigh with a balance that is true. And never concern thyself with anything of which thou hast no knowledge.
You shall not covet your neighbour's wife, nor his slave, nor his ox, nor his ass, nor anything that is your neighbour's.	And walk not on the earth with haughty self-conceit.

– In the Qur'an Muhammad is presented as prophet in the strict sense: he is not just a *nabi*, not just a usual kind of prophet, but a *rasul*, a messenger of God who—like Moses, David (the Psalms) and Jesus—has brought his people a book.
– At the same time the Qur'an emphasizes that Muhammad is no more than a prophet, no more than a human being. It explicitly states: 'I am but a mortal like you. It has been revealed to me that your God is the One God.'[64]

Some non-Muslims are amazed when, in a mosque, they see two names written equally large on huge tablets or shields: Allah and Muhammad. Doesn't putting them side by side like this endanger the incomparability of God? Hasn't this led to Muhammad sometimes seeming to be divinized, like Christ, in later Muslim piety? According to the Qur'an itself, at any rate, two things need to be borne in mind.

– God and Prophet belong together. The connection we find in the confession of faith is already expressed time and again in the Qur'an: 'Truly spoke God and His Apostle'[65] and therefore: 'We believe in God and in the Apostle, and we pay heed!'[66] Hell is threatened for those who refuse to obey: 'Now as for him who rebels against God and His Apostle—verily, the fire of hell awaits him, therein to abide beyond the count of time.'[67]
– However, the person of the Prophet is completely subordinate to his prophetic office: there is not the slightest indication in the Qur'an that Muhammad might be the object of veneration, even worship. In one of four passages in which the Qur'an mentions the name of Muhammad, there is an explicit stress on his mortality—like that of all previous prophets: 'And Muhammad is only an apostle; all the [other] apostles have passed away before him.'[68]

That means that though Muhammad as the last of the prophets may be the 'seal of the prophets' (*al-khatim al-anbiya'*), who confirms and concludes the missions of earlier prophets, he is nevertheless no more than God's mouthpiece, God's instrument. To further emphasize this, Muhammad is denied all literary knowledge; therefore the Qur'an cannot have been put together from books. When his opponents later compared him tendentiously with Arab poets or storytellers, Muslim scholars vigorously disputed this, emphasizing that Muhammad was an uneducated prophet (*an-nabi al-ummi*) who had no knowledge of poetic art and rhetoric.

For believing Muslims this means that the Qur'an cannot come from the Prophet. It comes from God. The Prophet does not attach the slightest value to intellectual originality but to divine authority. He does not want to be a genius, merely a spokesman. The Qur'an is not an ingenious 'literary' invention of the Prophet but God's gracious revelation. How, we may ask, must we imagine this revelation taking place? What happened at the Prophet's call? How could such a revelation come about?

How the Prophet was called: the messenger of God

What does the Qur'an say about this? It is the most important source for the life of the Prophet, though because of its lack of chronological order and the sparse biographical information it leaves many questions unanswered. What is said in the classical biography (*sirah*) of Muhammad ibn Ishaq (*c.* 704–68), author of the first comprehensive four-volume history of the Islamic world, written around 120 years after Muhammad's death? Parts II and III give a lively and relatively sober account of the life of Muhammad, making use of much old source material. This biography was edited by Ibn Hisham (died 833), tightened up and provided with brief explanations.[69] And what is said in the history of the military campaigns (*kitab al-maghazi*), composed by al-Waqidi (died 822)?[70] Whatever historical disputes there may be, there is a basic framework of the most important dates[71] in the life of the Prophet:[72]

Dates in the life of Muhammad

c. 570	Born in Mecca
c. 595	Marriage with Khadijah
c. 610	First revelation
c. 613	Beginning of public preaching
c. 619	Death of his wife and his uncle Abu Talib
622	Emigration (*hijrah*) to Medina: beginning of the Islamic reckoning of time (on 16 July 622 = Day 1 of Year 1)
September 622	Arrival in Medina
c. February 624	Alteration of the direction of prayer (*qiblah*) from Jerusalem to Mecca (the Ka'bah)
March 624	Victory in the battle of Badr
March 625	Defeat in the battle of Uhud
April 627	Siege of Medina
March 628	Cease-fire of al-Hudaybiyah near Mecca
January 630	Peaceful occupation of Mecca: victory over Ta'if near Hunayn
Oct.–Dec. 630	Military campaign to Tabuk
March 632	Farewell pilgrimage to Mecca
8 June 632	Death in Medina

As in the case of other 'founders of religions', numerous legends cluster around Muhammad's birth and childhood. During her pregnancy his mother is said to have seeing a light going out from her which shone as far as Syria; a Jew proclaimed a star under which Ahmad (= Muhammad) would be born; two men clothed in white cast the child Muhammad on the ground in the desert, took his heart from his body, purified it in the snow from a black lump and replaced it; the Christian monk Bahira in Syria discovered the 'seal of prophecy' between Muhammad's shoulders, and so on.[73]

To non-Muslim readers, some short biographies of the Prophet Muhammad seem to be a very simple success story, but if we read the earliest Muslim traditions and interpret them with the help of historical criticism, it quickly becomes clear that Muhammad, too, experienced a true prophetic destiny—a life with years of struggle and defeats, doubts and depressions—in many respects very similar to the fate of the prophets of Israel.

For decades Muhammad (born around 570) led a completely private life in the trading city of Mecca on the west of the Arabian peninsula (*Hijaz*). He came from the tribe of the Quraysh which had settled here, a tribe less of warriors than of merchants,[74] and the clan of the Hashim,[75] beside which there were more powerful and richer clans. His father, 'Abd Allah, died before his birth, and he was orphaned soon afterwards when his mother Amina died. He was brought up first by his grandfather 'Abd al-Muttalib and then by his uncle Abu Talib, the head of the clan. First he was a shepherd, then became a merchant travelling to Palestine and Syria and finally was head of a business; after five years he also became the husband of a rich widow, Khadijah. Then suddenly, at the age of forty, this businessman claimed that he had had a revelation from God. How is this to be 'explained'?[76]

This revelation did not really take place 'suddenly'. A 'prehistory' has also been handed down to us.

– Before his fortieth birthday Muhammad was accustomed to retreat to a nearby mountain, to a cave or a hill; there, far from the polytheistic bustle of the pilgrim city of Mecca, he devoted himself to meditation and prayer (not an unusual practice at that time).

– In Mecca, and on his travels, Muhammad not only got to know the polytheistic religion of the Arab merchants, pilgrims and poets but also discovered much from, and about, Jews and Christians.

– Muhammad manifestly sympathized with those 'God-seekers' (*hanif*) already known to us and mentioned in the Qur'an. Outside the traditional polytheistic religion, which was so unsatisfactory, they longed for a purer faith, belief in the one God of Abraham.

So God's revelation did not come to Muhammad unprepared. But how does such a revelation take place? The earliest extant report, which goes back to the nephew of Muhammad's favourite wife 'A'ishah, describes a first vision which took place when Muhammad returned to his family after many days and nights of solitude in the wilderness and prayer. It so terrified Muhammad that he sought protection with his wife. This is what the account says:

> At last unexpectedly the Truth came to him and said: O Muhammad, you are the messenger of God.
>
> The messenger of God said: I had been standing, but I sank to my knees; then I crept away and my shoulders trembled; then I entered Khadijah's room and said: Cover me up, cover me up, until the fear has left me. Then he came to me and said: O Muhammad, you are the messenger of God.
>
> He (Muhammad) said: I had thought to cast myself from a ledge of the rock, but while I was contemplating this he appeared to me and said: O Muhammad, I am Gabriel, and you are the messenger of God.
>
> Then he said: Speak. I said: What shall I say? He (Muhammad) said: Then he took me and pressed me vigorously three times until exhaustion overcame me; then he said: Speak in the name of your Lord who has created you. And I spoke.
>
> And I came to Khadijah and said: I am full of anxiety, and I told her my experiences. She said: Rejoice! By God, God will never put you to shame; you do good to your own, you speak the truth; you return what has been entrusted to you; you tolerate toils; you give hospitality to the guest; you help the helpers of the Truth.'[77]

We can no longer know whether this report is accurate. Strikingly, however, in the Qur'an itself, at the beginning of surah 74, there is mention of a veiling or unveiling, so that the biography could be a subsequent exegesis of the Qur'anic passage. The basic substance of the report finds further confirmation in the Qur'an, where two visionary experiences are reported at the beginning of the revelations. In surah 53, 'The Star', the first is described like this:

> This fellow-man of yours (Muhammad) has not gone astray, nor is he deluded, and neither does he speak out of his own desire: that [which he conveys to you] is but a [divine] inspiration with which he is being inspired—something that a very mighty one has imparted to him: [an angel] endowed with surpassing power, who in time manifested himself in his true shape and nature, appearing in the horizon's loftiest part, and then drew near, and came close, until he was but two bow-lengths away, or even nearer. And thus did [God] reveal unto His servant whatever He deemed right to reveal. The [servant's] heart did not give the lie to what he saw: will you, then, contend with him as to what he saw?[78]

Most Muslims now assume that this was a vision of the angel Gabriel—not of God. However, some early Muslim exegetes thought that this was a vision of God himself, as the wording of the text itself indicates (the reference of the pronouns). Another passage of the Qur'an says: 'No human vision can encompass Him, whereas He encompasses all human vision.'[79] According to an old tradition, when asked by a contemporary whether Muhammad really saw God, 'A'ishah, the Prophet's widow, replied, 'My hair stands on end at what you say.'[80] The Qur'an knows three modes of revelation: 'And it is not given to mortal man that God should speak unto him otherwise than

- through sudden inspiration' (*wahy*): without a vision the recipient is often given not a verbal instruction but simply an indication of how to act;
- 'from behind a veil' (*hijab*): again a voice is perceived without a vision;
- 'or by sending an apostle to reveal, by His leave, whatever He wills [to reveal].'[81]

This third mode of revelation is mentioned at another point, where it is said that the angel Gabriel 'has brought down [the Qur'an] upon thy heart'.[82] When the different 'kinds of revelation' were discussed by Muslim scholars in lengthy treatises this came to be regarded as the usual mode of revelation. Muhammad himself was convinced that he could distinguish between a revelation of God and his own thoughts. These revelations must have been visions (in which there was something to be 'seen') only in exceptional cases; rather, they were 'prophetic auditions', 'which Muhammad believed he had received in the wording as revelations and which he felt called to present in the same form to his fellow countrymen and those who shared his faith'.[83] There is still no complete agreement as to which surah was revealed first.[84]

Who was the first, after his wife Khadijah, to encourage Muhammad to take the experience of his personal revelation seriously, because it was like the revelatory experience of Moses? Remarkably it was a Christian, Waraqah, a cousin of Muhammad's wife. Waraqah ibn Nawfal (he has already been mentioned), 'who became a Christian, had read the holy scriptures and had learned from the adherents of the Torah and the Gospel',[85] was probably a Jewish Christian, as he clearly did not read the Bible in Greek but in Aramaic (at that time there was not yet an Arabic translation of the Bible). Waraqah compared Muhammad's experience, not with that of Jesus, but with that of Moses, speaking of a *namus* (for the Greek *nomos* = 'law' of Moses), which was handed on to him.

The battle for justice: the threat to the status quo

The call to be a messenger radically changed Muhammad's life. Dogged by fears and doubts (which touchingly emphasize his humanity), Muhammad at first proclaimed his message only in the circle of his family and friends. It took time for him to become clear about all that his prophetic commission embraced. From then on he constantly received new revelations that he 'presented' or 'recited' to his followers (the verb *qar'a*, from which the noun *qur'an* is derived, is a word which originally was presumably used for the individual revelations which 'came down'). It was three years before he made a public appearance. Only then did he definitively understand himself as 'God's messenger', called on to preach publicly: 'Arise and warn![86] Remind, then, whether this reminding [would seem to] be of use [or not].'[87]

What did the prophet 'warn' of? Fearlessly, Muhammad proclaimed the power and goodness of God to the Meccans and called for gratitude, generosity and social solidarity in face of the coming judgement. By contrast (if we follow Nöldeke, Bell and Watt), the oneness of God does not seem to have stood so much in the foreground (though this assessment is largely dependent on decisions about datings within the Qur'an). The message that the 'messenger of God' presented to the Meccans, 'warning and admonishing', was anything but a comfortable message. On the contrary, at a time of great prosperity, when rich Mecca controlled the caravan trade from the Yemen as far as Gaza and Damascus, Muhammad's proclamation of an alternative manner of life, his preaching of a 'narrow way', was extremely unwelcome. It meant 'the freeing of one's neck, or the feeding, upon a day of hunger, of an orphan near of kin, or of a needy [stranger] lying in the dust—and being, withal, of those who have attained to faith, and who enjoin upon one another patience in adversity, and enjoin upon one another compassion'.[88] The constantly renewed threat of hell is particularly striking: 'Woe unto him who amasses wealth and counts it a safeguard, thinking that his wealth will make him live forever.'[89]

No wonder that Muhammad's message provoked not only curiosity but above all misunderstanding among the Quraysh. It found acceptance only among a very few: members of Muhammad's family and clan and friends (a series of above all younger men, also from influential clans) and some members of the lower class (slaves and aliens). Muhammad accepted them into his community without discrimination. Certainly, none of them were social revolutionaries but they were serious and pious people, discontented with the changing social and moral climate in Mecca (they included Abu Bakr and 'Ali, the later caliph). So the first small community took shape. Its basis was not a particular social status but a common faith, ritual prayer, eschatological piety and an ethic of justice. This too emphasizes the spiritual energy it needed for the Prophet, now as leader of a highly marginalized community, to continue on a way that was questioned from many sides. There were plenty of difficulties, resistance and rejection, which often resulted in inner tribulations and doubt. Why?

Muhammad by no means became the Prophet immediately, as he had hoped; rather, he became a dangerous, and endangered, outsider. His main opponents in Mecca were the great merchants and leading members of the powerful clans, such as the Makhzum and the Umayyah (from which the dynasty of the Umayyads would later emerge), who were affected by his warning. A prophet from the insignificant Hashim clan? Unthinkable! This explains why Muhammad was initially dismissed as a 'seer' (*kahin*), poet (*sa'ir*) or magician (*sahir*)—a man with special capacities transcending the senses, of a kind common in old Arabic religion. A divine commission to a fellow member of the tribe? In Mecca people joked about such bizarre notions as resurrection and last judgement and called for miracles as a proof of his message. The establishment in Mecca felt the message of the new prophet to be a dangerous threat to the *status quo* and thus to its position of economic, social and religious power.

Muhammad's plea for an ethic of justice in the face of the coming judgement, his call to repentance and social solidarity, made with sharp words, threats of punishment and solemn oaths, threatened the selfish and materialistic attitude of the rich merchants and traders.

Nor was this social confrontation all. Social problems were closely bound up with the religious problems. Business life, social structure, religion and moral views formed an entangled system of ideas and attitudes. Muhammad's only reply to the demand for proofs was the message itself, the Qur'an. With its content and the beauty of its language this is a unique miracle, *the* sign of the revelation of God and the credibility of the Prophet.

The battle for the oneness of God: 'Satanic verses'

Very soon there were also clashes in Mecca over the one God and the many deities. It is important to note that Muhammad's own tribe, the Quraysh, supervised (through a variety of offices) the age-old central sanctuary of Mecca, the Ka'bah, which presumably formed the focal point of the settlement and communal life of the various Quraysh clans. The Ka'bah is a rectangular building in the form of a cube measuring ten by twelve metres, housing the famous black stone (which may be basalt or lava or possibly a meteorite), which to the present day is covered with a black carpet. According to the Muslim view, the foundation walls of the Ka'bah were built by Abraham and his son Ishmael (or, according to a later legend, by Adam), and the pilgrimage to this sanctuary was prescribed by Abraham. However, in the time of Muhammad the Ka'bah was still full of images and statues of gods.

The historical reconstructions of the precise nature of the controversies over strict monotheism in Mecca remain very hypothetical. In the view of many scholars, the background to the early Meccan surahs is a notion of God which shows only the beginnings of monotheism but is prepared to tolerate other, subordinate gods. A not insignificant role was played in these controversies by the 'Satanic verses' in the Qur'an (the novelist Salman Rushdie did not invent them in his famous/notorious novel). According to these verses, Muhammad at first tolerated the veneration of the three 'daughters of Allah' (*banat Allah*) in the Ka'bah. In any case, their relations with the 'high God' Allah are more abstract and not of a sexual nature (as in Greek mythology; there are no 'sons of Allah'). Wasn't such a compromise—the one God and subordinate deities—possible with the clan chiefs and merchants of the Quraysh? Initially, they were ready to fall in with it.

But any prophet or messenger of God has notions whispered into his ear by Satan, which must then be corrected by God. We read in the Qur'an: 'Yet whenever We sent forth any apostle or prophet before thee, and he was hoping [that his warnings would be heeded], Satan would cast an aspersion on his innermost aims; but God renders null and void whatever aspersion Satan may cast; and God makes His messages clear in and by themselves—for God is all-knowing, wise.'[90] What are these 'Satanic verses' in the case of Muhammad? They begin in surah 53.19f., the 'Star' (the very one which contains the report of Muhammad's vision at the beginning!): 'Have you, then, ever considered [what you are worshipping in] Al-Lat and Al-'Uzza, as well as [in] Manat, the third and last (of this triad]?'[91]

According to the Annals of at-Tabari (died 923)—based on a report by 'Urwa ibn az-Zubayr to the caliph 'Abd al-Malik (685–705)—and other Muslim commentators, these two verses were followed by two or three others. They are not in the Qur'an but they certainly cannot have been invented: 'They are exalted cranes (*gharaniq*, heron, high-flying bird, angelic being?). For their intercession one may hope.' There is a variant: 'Their intercession is acceptable (to God).'[92] According to the merchants Muhammad recited these fatal verses (in the Ka'bah?) and then even bowed in reverence, readily followed by the merchants.

Some time later (that same evening or after some days?), however, Muhammad recognized the verses as the whisperings of Satan and as a correction received the verses surah 53.21–3: 'Why—for yourselves [you would choose only] male offspring, whereas to Him [you assign] female: that, lo and behold, is an unfair division! These [allegedly divine beings] are nothing but empty names which you have invented—you and your forefathers—[and] for which God has bestowed no warrant from on high.'[93] It has now become quite clear that not only is the intercession of such divine beings denied, but even their existence. Alongside God whom Muhammad worships as Lord (*rabb*), as the creator and redeemer God, sustainer and judge, other, lower gods are inconceivable as intermediaries, only angels as God's servants ('*abd*, plural '*ibad*), his court. Interpreters say that the 'Satanic verses' are 'abrogated', done away with, by those that follow.

At the latest from this moment, Muhammad's fight for the one God thus became a decisive fight against all more lowly deities, who were to intercede before the 'high God' Allah. The 'legends about prophets and punishments' of the middle Meccan surahs are full of polemic against polytheism. The prophetic message is an uncompromising one: 'Say: "O you who deny the truth! I do not worship that which you worship, and neither do you worship that which I worship. And I will not worship that which you have [ever] worshipped, and neither will you [ever] worship that which I worship. Unto you, your moral law, and unto me, mine".'[94] 'Association' becomes the one great sin which is not forgiven: 'Verily, God does not forgive the ascribing of divinity to aught beside Him, although He forgives any lesser sin unto whomever He wills.'[95]

Such an uncompromising stance had its costs. We can understand the opposition of the Quraysh to Muhammad's message.[96] This was not just a matter of belief or unbelief but a 'question of life', a highly political question for the whole tribe, in which the tribal sanctuaries, symbols and traditions, and thus the tribal identity, were at stake. As long as people could remember, Mecca's sanctuary had had a holy, protected time and a holy, protected precinct. Both—in connection with the annual 'pilgrimages' ('time of peace')–were the basis for the great market at which all tribes and clans, whether settled, nomadic or semi-nomadic, could gather together peacefully: for worship and trade, settling disputes and making all kinds of agreements.

And now here was this Qurayshi, questioning the foundation of his own tribe! This was unheard of: for through his demand for 'submission' (*islam*) to Allah alone he

- mocked the venerable cult of the gods of his forefathers;
- rejected the highly respected legends, customs and traditions of the tribe;
- made the whole tribe seem ridiculous to outsiders by his criticism, instead of identifying himself unconditionally with it according to good old custom;
- endangered the unity and cohesion of the clan and the identity of the tribe.

Moreover, each of the three goddesses (*al-Lat*, goddess; *al-'Uzza*, the Strong One and *Manat*, dispenser or goddess of fate) was identified with a famous sanctuary in the neighbourhood of Mecca, on the great trade routes to Medina and Iraq. A denial of the existence of these goddesses would lead not only to a diminution of the cult in the Ka'bah but also to a closing of these sanctuaries (and indeed they were destroyed later, after the victory of the Muslims).

All in all Muhammad's prophetic message was a political factor of the first order: overthrowing gods and violating taboos, reforming society and bringing equality. This was a radical threat to the clan solidarity that had previously been practised, to the authority of the clan heads and to the appeal of the Ka'bah and the other sanctuaries in West Arabia. In short, it was a threat to the economic domination of Mecca and the political dominance of the Quraysh throughout the region.

Muhammad's plea for subordination to the one and only God threatened all the cult and commerce around the Ka'bah, not only the veneration of other gods or goddesses there but also the pilgrimage business and the market—and thus Mecca's financial and economic systems, foreign and trade policy and existing religious, social and political institutions, indeed the venerable tradition, inner unity and external prestige of the tribe itself.

Here an individual with a small group stood up against a whole tribe. How would things end? There were threats and harassment and financial support was refused, but this did not persuade the Prophet to fall into line. The religious, social and political dispute dragged on for years. Finally, however, a decision was needed: either the whole tribe would have to convert to the Prophet and his message—or the Prophet and his followers would have to leave the tribe. A dozen or so years after Muhammad's call there was indeed a decision and a separation.

Emigration: the turn of the ages

Every Arab tribe understands itself to be a community whose solidarity is based on blood; often (as in the case of the Ka'bah) it is a cultic community. The clan is almost a tribe within a tribe. Each clan observes a strict clan solidarity which obligates every member to help against enemies, and which is even stronger than the solidarity with the tribe as a whole. The clan takes blood vengeance on any attack on life or limb—the usual means of law in a nomadic society. As long as Muhammad's uncle, stepfather and head of the Hashim clan, protected him, there was no threat to Muhammad's life. But the situation became increasingly dangerous, so much so that in 615, as leader of his small community, the Prophet recommended that individual members should emigrate to Christian Ethiopia for a time; the emigrants are said to have numbered eighty-nine men and eighteen women, and evidently they received a very friendly welcome from the Negus. However, in Mecca the insults and harassment of the other clans directed against the Hashim clan culminated in a boycott of marriage and trade (616–18). This was an insult but it was dropped, presumably because it was not very effective.

In 619 the controversy reached a critical stage.

First, Muhammad's wife Khadijah died. She had not only brought him wealth and respect but was the first Muslim woman to give him constant and incomparable support in his faith, particularly in the depressing periods when revelations were interrupted.

Soon afterwards Muhammad's uncle Abu Talib died. With him Muhammad lost his most influential protector who, although he himself did not become a

Muslim, resisted all the pressure from the Quraysh to withdraw clan protection from Muhammad.

Another uncle, Abu Lahab, became clan chief; during the boycott he took the side of Muhammad's opponents and married a wife from the hostile Umayyah clan. He yielded to the pressure of leading Qurayshi and finally removed Muhammad's obligatory protection.

The quest of the now 'vagrant' Prophet for a place of refuge outside his tribe in the neighbourhood of Mecca (among nomadic tribes or in the city of Ta'if) proved fruitless; he was mocked and driven away. Someone seeking protection might perhaps have been accepted, but not a 'messenger of God' claiming to be a leader, someone who rejected all their gods. On his return Muhammad, in flight and an outlaw, had difficulty in winning the necessary guarantee of protection from any clan leader at all. He had no political support and won over very few new adherents: the Muslim community numbered probably little more than one hundred members.

A turning point came when, around 620, at the annual pilgrimage and market, a group of six men from Yathrib, about one hundred and eighty miles to the north—possibly at that time it was already called 'the city', 'al-Madinah', Medina by strangers to the place—were persuaded by Muhammad's revelations and became his courageous and steadfast companions. A year later, at the time of the pilgrimage, there was a secret meeting outside Mecca, in 'Aqaba, between twelve delegates from Yathrib/Medina and Muhammad. They came to a provisional agreement. The next year, 622, this agreement was definitively sealed (again in 'Aqaba)—with the oaths of seventy-three new converts that they would practise Islam. Specifically, they vowed that they would believe in the one God, reject theft, calumniation, adultery and infanticide, obey the Prophet and give him a guarantee of protection. Here Muhammad already had a combined religious and political function.

In view of his hopeless situation in Mecca, for Muhammad Yathrib/Medina was a gift from heaven. The Muslims emigrated in small groups, moving away from their own tribe and breaking off natural relations with their own clan—for the sake of their faith. Finally, in complete secrecy, with his companion Abu Bakr (later to become the first caliph) Muhammad himself followed. On 24 September 622 they arrived in Quba', in the southern region of the oasis of Medina. This is called the Hijrah (emigration, not flight) of the Prophet. It was not just a harmless change of place but a critical turning-point. Indeed, it was a dramatic transition to another world: no longer the tribal community but a community of faith; no longer polytheism but Islam. Because the Hijrah marks such a fundamental turning-point not only in the life of the Prophet but in Islam as a whole, the Muslim tradition began a new, Islamic, calculation of the date with this year, Year 1 (16 July 622).

3. The Prophet as leading figure

Yathrib was later called 'Medina', the 'city of the Prophet' (*madinat an-nabi*). It was less a city of trade, pilgrimage and the market than an oasis of date palms and corn: agriculture was successfully practised here above all by the numerous Jews. It was not the city of a single Arab tribe, like Mecca, but the city of several rival tribes and clans (two pagan and three Jewish tribes—the Jewish tribes, too, were Arab). There were disputes lasting decades, anarchic clan fights and blood feuds, especially between the Aws and Khazraj tribes, over the territory which could be utilized for agriculture; these threatened security in the fields and threatened to destroy Medina. But no one was able to settle things.[97]

How the Prophet became the statesman: the founding of a community

Could the Prophet, who had been called to Medina as an arbitrator (*hakam*) and peacemaker by members of two warring tribes (customary among Arabs), bring about a settlement?[98] Muhammad showed political wisdom by making the men of Medina swear an oath in Mecca and concluding an agreement with them there, since in Medina there was neither a common law nor a central government. Soon after his arrival he confirmed this agreement with the inhabitants of the place and fixed it in writing. It has sometimes, exaggeratedly, been called a 'constitution' and the 'community order of Medina'. However, what the historian Ibn Ishaq relates in his biography immediately after the Hijrah is not the original agreement—the three large Jewish tribes no longer appear in it—but a document which was produced very much later and is evidently composite (because of the repetitions in it).

This is one of a kind of treaty quite customary between Arab tribes; it is, as it states: 'a document of Muhammad, the Prophet of God, about relations between the believing Muslims of Quraysh and Yathrib (Medina), those who follow him, who have attached themselves to them and fight together with them.'[99] It is a 'protection and shelter' alliance, about the payment of blood money and ransom, about relations with the Jews, about obligations in negotiations in battle and the prohibition against making a separate peace. But it contains specifically Muslim statements:

- 'They (the Muslims of Quraysh and Medina) are one community (*ummah*) in distinction from other men.'[100] *Ummah* can be rendered community, fellowship or confederation.
- 'The wrath of God on the day of resurrection' is threatened on those who act contrary to the document.[101] (Thus this is an ordinance which is legitimated and sanctioned in political and religious terms at the same time.)

- 'In any question on which you are not agreed, turn to God and Muhammad.'[102] (Muhammad had been called to Medina not only as an arbiter but also as a 'messenger of God'.)

The Prophet succeeded in reconciling the two hostile tribes of Medina and they became his most loyal 'helpers' (*ansar*). At first, they welcomed the 'emigrants' (*muhajirun*, people of the Hijrah) from Mecca. Many of the inhabitants of Medina had already accepted Islam before the arrival of the Prophet and very soon the Muslims were in a majority. For the first time, the tribal groups of Medina, which had been so much at odds with one another, had a common basis of faith. Muhammad now had the unique chance to build up a fully functioning Muslim community: the community or confederation (*ummah*) of Medina as the core of what later became the great Muslim community (likewise *ummah*). Originally Muhammad had, quite naturally, seen his Medinan compatriots and the Arabs generally as his Ummah, but now he had to build up a new political and religious Ummah. 'The religious foundation on which it was based was essential. The Ummah of the Arabs turned into the Ummah of the Muslims.'[103]

The second period of Muhammad's prophetic activity, which was of a very different kind, had now begun. For many interpreters this seems to reveal a completely different Muhammad. The Muhammad who was formerly the preacher of God's goodness, omnipotence and justice in the face of the coming judgement had now turned into the admired and feared politician, a man of war and the senses? But did his personality and principles really change?

We should not overlook either the continuity of a faith so firmly rooted in the omnipotent and merciful God in Muhammad's life or the change in his living conditions and tasks. The former outsider now saw himself suddenly in charge, leader of the community, and the minority which had been hardly tolerated in Mecca now became the controlling majority. Muhammad was not an absolute ruler over the different clans. At first, as clan chief of the emigrants, he remained dependent on the assent of the other clan chiefs; the tribal order was preserved. Yet at the same time he was the unique Prophet who proclaimed God's revelations and therefore could be the supreme arbiter, commissioned by God, in the disputes that continued to break out. The Prophet received more, largely new, revelations relating both to the founding of a righteous society and to the shaping of a worthy form of worship. These became elements of the Qur'an and thus the core of the Islamic religious system that subsequently was to establish itself everywhere.

Muhammad grew into new tasks, and the Prophet became a 'statesman'—here of course he was unlike the prophets of Israel—who proved equal to the high demands of the new confederation. For him, prophetic mission and political capabilities were not mutually exclusive. His political followers were to become Muslim believers. The Prophet saw himself confronted with enormous tasks. The new community or confederation had to be organized:

– domestically, by forging a 'brotherhood' between the 'Hijrah people', the 'emigrants', and those already settled and by assigning new tasks to the 'emigrants', who could not permanently remain dependent on the 'helpers'. Muhammad himself bought a piece of land and built a house which served as a dwelling for him and his family, and became the place of assembly for his followers, the first mosque;

– abroad, by giving the new Islamic community military security. From the beginning there was bitter fighting with the Quraysh and raids were made on the caravans of the Meccans (this became the new task and source of income for the emigrants). Defence of the city against the threatened revenge of the Meccans had to be arranged. And finally, martial enterprises had to be planned and carried out, particularly with the help of the emigrants.

Who were Muhammad's opponents? Even in Medina they took four forms:

- a *polytheistic* opposition made up above all of small clans whose members mocked the Medinans for had subjecting themselves to a foreigner;
- a *Muslim* opposition, directed against the power of Muhammad, which was growing with his successes and his provocative anti-Meccan politics: these hangers-on, followers who were unreliable in crises and sympathized with the Jews, were called 'doubters' and 'hypocrites' (*munafiqun*);
- a *Bedouin* opposition (*a'rab*) around Medina and Mecca, restless and disunited, often involved on both sides and ready to change sides; they were against any religious regulation, for example of prayer and support of the poor; they were unruly and, precisely for that reason, were wooed by the Prophet and used in countless minor military operations;
- a powerful *Jewish* opposition, which I shall consider separately in the next section.

The break with the Jews

The inhabitants of Mecca seemed almost predestined to 'unbelief'; in twelve years the Prophet had achieved nothing. But in Medina his experiences were precisely the opposite. Why? Why was the readiness of Meccans to accept the radical monotheistic faith greater? In the view of most scholars, this is to be explained by the strong influence of a religious group, organized into its own clans but also widespread among the others, which for centuries had already practised strict monotheism and for generations had been settled in Medina: the Jews. Muhammad regarded them, as he did the Christians, as his natural allies, since they possessed a scripture and thus were 'people of the book' (*ahl al-kitab*). Jewish tribes were included in the treaty of Medina as associates.[104]

However, Muhammad experienced fearful disappointment: only exceptionally did Jews convert to Islam. To begin with, he waited. His hopes for support from the adherents of this age-old religion of revelation were nourished by thoughts such as: just as there is only the one God, isn't there fundamentally only the one revelation? Won't the different revelations agree in the course of time? Doesn't his new revelation confirm the Jewish revelation which had preceded it? Why should the Jews reject his revelation? After all, in many respects—such as ritual prayer, eschatological expectation (judgement)—Muhammad's religion strongly resembled Judaism. How often he had appealed to its 'prophets', from Adam to David, from Abraham to Joseph. The Jews need not all become Muslims, but they should accept Muhammad as a true prophet. In that way, he would be an Arab prophet also for the Jews and Christians of Arabia.

As in Mecca, in Medina Muhammad was at first ignored by the Jews and then—behind his back—criticized, attacked and ridiculed. He was said not to be an expert on the Hebrew Bible; he did not know, or only half knew, much of what they, the Jews, knew very precisely from their Holy Scripture. In any case prophecy had been long quenched! After more than a year Muhammad could not deny that the Jews of Medina were rejecting his prophetic claim: for them, he was no prophet. In practical terms, that meant there could be no question of integrating them fully into the new Islamic Ummah.

This brought about a momentous change in the Prophet's basic attitude: his image of the Jews became negative. From his perspective, the fault lay entirely with the Jews since, as Prophet, he was proclaiming none other than the truth of God. The Jews had isolated themselves and were now unreliable allies for the military enterprises of the Muslim community. Disappointment and bitterness probably made the Prophet reflect, at a very early stage, on far-reaching consequences, extending to the expulsion of the Jews, especially as important clan chiefs of his contributed anti-Jewish polemic. The Prophet had originally taken over some religious customs from the Jews (both the ritual times of prayer and the Friday prayer); now he undertook two reorientations that considerably accelerated the process of the formation of Islam as an independent religion alongside Judaism and Christianity:

- Instead of fasting for a day on the Jewish Day of Atonement, the Muslims now observed a mandatory time of fasting lasting a whole Islamic month, in Ramadan.
- Instead of the direction of their prayer (*qiblah*) being towards Jerusalem (as also happened in Eastern Christianity), it now became towards Mecca and the Ka'bah.

However, that does not mean that, theologically, Muhammad completely rejected the Jews. Rather, in the Medinan surahs an independent theology of history develops in which both Judaism and Christianity are assigned a special place.

The Islamic theology of history

Muhammad saw himself as the Arab prophet who, in succession to the prophets of the Old and New Testaments, would lead the Arabs from a time of 'ignorance' (*jahiliyah*) on to the right path. In the now-developed Muslim view, the history of revelation took place in three stages:[105]

– First, Moses brought the Torah, the revelation for Judaism: 'Verily, it is We who bestowed from on high the Torah, wherein there was guidance and light. On its strength did the prophets, who had surrendered themselves unto God, deliver judgement unto those who followed the Jewish faith; and so did the [early] men of God and the rabbis, inasmuch as some of God's writ had been entrusted to their care.'[106]

– Then, Jesus brought the Gospel, the revelation for Christianity: 'And We caused Jesus, the son of Mary, to follow in the footsteps of those [earlier prophets], confirming the truth of whatever there still remained of the Torah; and We vouchsafed to him the Gospel, wherein there was guidance and light, confirming the truth of whatever there still remained of the Torah, and as a guidance and admonition unto the God-conscious. Let, then, the followers of the Gospel judge in accordance with what God has revealed therein.'[107]

– Finally, Muhammad brought the Qur'an, the revelation for Islam: 'And unto Thee [O Prophet] have We vouchsafed this divine writ, setting forth the truth, confirming the truth of whatever there still remains of earlier revelations and determining what is true therein. Judge, then, between the followers of earlier revelation in accordance with what God has bestowed from on high, and do not follow their errant views, forsaking the truth that has come unto thee.'[108]

In the light of the Qur'an, which brings the full, unfalsified truth, the other possessors of scripture—and this cannot be overlooked—are necessarily in a religious twilight. For according to this view, Jews and Christians have falsified scriptures. This is not only asserted in the Qur'an itself but also becomes evident wherever these scriptures do not correspond to the Qur'an. So Jews and Christians are not full believers. However, the Qur'an recognizes different ways to salvation more clearly than Christians normally do: 'Unto every one of you have We appointed a [different] law and way of life.'[109] Indeed, the differences of religion within humankind are expressly grounded in the will of God himself: 'And if God had so willed, He could surely have made you all one single community (*ummah*): but [He willed it otherwise] in order to test you by means of what He has vouchsafed unto you. Vie, then, with one another in doing good works!'[110]

The new Qur'anic theology of history goes one stage further: to the beginning of humankind. According to the Qur'an all three religions are preceded by the 'religion of Ibrahim', the religion of Abraham, whom, as I have remarked, the Qur'an designates *hanif*, one who seeks God and is submissive to God in an exemplary way, as a model of authentic Muslim believing. In this way, the priority of Islam over the two other religions of revelation is claimed in time (and in content). Islam, historically the youngest of the three religions, appears to be both chronologically older and truer in content, in so far as it authentically restores the original religion of humankind.

If, as we saw,[111] during the time in Mecca Muhammad represented Abraham above all as a monotheistic champion of the faith, while his son Ishmael, the ancestor of the Arabs, played no special role, in Medina the roles of both Abraham and Ishmael were decisively strengthened. For we are now told that Abraham and his son Ishmael built the foundations of the Ka'bah together, purified it of idolatry and made it a place of pure monotheistic worship of God, a place of pilgrimage. Abraham and Ishmael stand at the origin of the Muslim pilgrimage to Mecca and are the spiritual leading figures of pilgrimage generally. However, the statements about the Abrahamic origin of Mecca and the Ka'bah cannot be checked and, as we have also seen, led to a historical controversy. This showed that there is no historical evidence for a stay of Abraham (who was buried in Hebron!) in Arabia, but that Abraham is mentioned in the Qur'an even before the time in Medina and the controversy with the Jews.

Whatever may be thought about the historical roots of the Islamic theology of history (which I shall be discussing later), the Bible and the Qur'an agree at least on the basic theological statement that Abraham embodied pure belief in God even before Moses (the 'religion of Abraham'). And if *islam* (with a lower-case *i*) means submission, dedication to God, we can call Abraham a *muslim* (like Noah, and even Adam, before him): a representative of belief in one God long before the Prophet Muhammad and the new religion of 'Islam' (with a capital I). Jews and Christians also appeal to this Abraham who is likewise the model of their faith: they all want to be Abrahamic religions and none should dispute that either of the others is. However, from the beginning the controversies of the new Abrahamic religion with the two others were accompanied by the use of force.

How the Prophet became the general: purges and wars

Even if the aggression of the early Muslims was not directed against the Jews as a people or a 'race' but, for religious and political reasons, 'only' against the three large Jewish tribes (*banu*—sons, tribe) in Medina, today one would probably call it ethnic cleansing. As elsewhere, the Jews were pioneers in agriculture; presumably they all spoke Arabic, had many customs in common with the Muslims and were initially allied with Muhammad. However, after their rejection of his religious claim, they became politically suspect to the Prophet and, in military terms, an unpredictable factor in the fight with the Meccans: they did not want to be members of the Muslim confederation. So in the end Muhammad did not hesitate to get rid of the Jewish tribes one by one; this was all the easier, as they were disunited among themselves. After every victory over the external enemies there was also a battle against the 'enemies' within! In their districts within Medina the Jewish tribal units were attacked, besieged and defeated. There were purges and massacres:

- After their subjection in 624, the Qaynuqa' (most of whom were armourers and goldsmiths) had to give up all their possessions and emigrate.
- In 625 the tribe of Nadir, some of whose palms Muhammad had felled—violating an unwritten law of Arab warfare—had to leave Medina without their possessions.
- In 627 around 600 men from the Jewish tribe of Qurayzah, which had maintained neutrality in a preceding war ('the trench war'), were slaughtered in a single day and their wives and children were distributed among the Muslims. Muhammad, who had a claim to a fifth of the booty, sent some of the wives due him to Najd (in central Arabia) in exchange for horses and weapons.

There is no doubt that the Prophet was directly (or in the third case indirectly) responsible for these actions, as the Muslim sources themselves attest. What was his motivation? Much of Muhammad's crude power politics, like those of the Hebrew Bible, can be explained in terms of the time, which as yet knew no human rights and was accustomed to brutal methods of waging war without mercy. Muhammad nurtured the suspicion that the Jewish tribes were unreliable and, with further military concentration, could stab the 'messenger of God' in the back. But does that justify the massacre of the men and the enslavement of the women and children? In the view of contemporary Muslims, the felling of the palms, which take decades to replace, could not be justified. However, the Prophet—and this makes the unprejudiced observer think—could justify even this by a divine revelation: surah 59.5 reads: 'Whatever [of their] palm trees you may have cut down, [O believers,] or left standing on their roots, was [done] by God's leave.'

The real threat to the security of Medina, though, did not come from the Jews but from Mecca, which had been deliberately provoked. For the whole strategy of the Qurayshi Muhammad in these years was aimed at gaining control over his home city and his home tribe. As the Qur'an itself testifies, this too was not achieved without violence. First of all there were 'raids' (an old Bedouin-Arab custom of plundering attacks as a law of the desert) at the expense of the Quraysh, with Muhammad's assent and co-operation; those who had been forced to emigrate were particularly happy to join in, simply to provide a basis for their economic existence. These raids, undertaken for primarily economic reasons, soon became a war of faith waged at God's command—against the unbelievers of Mecca: 'fighting on the way to God'.

In the Qur'an, which does not set out to be a chronicle of events, at most there are allusions to these military actions, which are assumed to be known about (there is information about the division of plunder of war and the purpose to which the Prophet's share is put). However, these martial actions are not mentioned for human self-glorification; such an anthropocentric view is far removed from the Qur'an. They are for the glory of God. A theocentric perspective prevails, to make it clear that contemporary history is at the same time salvation history, brought about according to God's counsel for human salvation: 'If God succours you, none can ever overcome you, but if He should forsake you, who could succour you thereafter? In God, then, let the believers place their trust!'[112]

With interruptions, the real war with Mecca was to last six years (624–30). Now Muhammad showed himself to be not only an important statesman but also a consummate general:

– In 624 the numerically far inferior Muslims defeated the Meccan relief troops at the watering place of Badr—after a failed attack (before the end of the holy month of Rajab) on a large caravan returning from Syria to Mecca. This was a powerful boost to Muhammad's prestige, because the victory over the strongest tribe of Arabia (praised in the same way as the miracle of the exodus of Israel from Egypt) could be regarded as 'deliverance' (*furqan*) and a sign that Muhammad was indeed the Prophet. The expulsion of the Jewish Qaynuqa' took place soon after this.

– But in 625, in the battle on Mount Uhud north of Medina, the Meccans were victorious, their vengeance for Badr. However, they were unable to shake Muhammad's position in Medina (he was wounded in the battle). Soon after that the Jewish Nadir were driven out.

– In 627 the 'trench war' (when 10,000 Meccans attacked the defensive trenches which had been dug out at Medina) was indecisive, as the Bedouin tribes, skilfully recruited from the Meccan front by Muhammad, left him. This was followed by the extermination of the Jewish tribe of the Qurayzah.

– In 628 (evidently as the result of a dream) Muhammad boldly undertook a pilgrimage to Mecca, with fifteen hundred followers. Stopped at the boundary of the holy precinct in al-Hudaybiyah, with consummate diplomacy he negotiated a ten-year ceasefire and a concession from the Meccans that the Muslims might make a three-day pilgrimage in the following year.

– In 629 (in March) there was a pilgrimage to Mecca, but the attempt to penetrate Byzantine Christian territory failed: there was a defeat at Mu'ta (south-east of the Dead Sea in present-day Jordan).

– In 630, breaking the ceasefire, Muhammad marched on Mecca with a powerful army of 10,000 men: leading Meccans (above all his former chief opponent Abu Sufyan, commander of the caravan which was attacked at Badr and of the Meccan army in the 'trench war') made it possible for Muhammad to enter his ancestral city in triumph without a fight (on 11 January). The images in the Ka'bah were destroyed but there was a very wide amnesty for the Quraysh (there were only isolated executions) and Muhammad took over the administration. Furthermore, together with the Quraysh, Muhammad that same year defeated the army of the city of Ta'if, which was twice as large as his, along with kindred tribes, at Hunayn. From the massive plunder, every man in his army received four camels or their equivalent, but the clan chiefs of Mecca received fifty or a hundred camels depending on their rank. This led to a reconciliation between Muhammad and the Meccans, who now quickly turned to Islam. However, Muhammad returned to Medina with no plunder—and his helpers from there were left empty-handed. Now the Meccans were more important to him.

What could have crowned the amazing career of the Prophet more appropriately than rule over the city of his fathers, over the tribe from which he came? The Quraysh, who had first rejected him, finally accepted him. Muhammad was now not just one of the Arab tribal leaders; he was the sole ruler authorized, by God, against whom no one in southern and central Arabia could bring 20,000 men. The decisive factor was that now the Muslims controlled the most important religious sanctuary of Arabia, the Ka'bah. The consequences were obvious: Islamization of the Ka'bah and the Hajj:

– For the future the cultic centre for Islam no longer lay in distant Jerusalem but in the middle of Arabia, the Ka'bah, to which Jews and Christians soon ceased to have access.

– The pilgrimage to Mecca took on fundamental significance for Islam; the pre-Islamic ceremonial, purged of idolatry, was essentially commandeered for Islam, but the Hajj was now a purely Islamic feast, from which Jews and Christians were excluded.

Muhammad's legacy

After the conquest of Mecca the Prophet Muhammad had barely two years to live. But he was able to use them intensely, at different levels:

– *The unification of the Arabs*: Muhammad did all he could to bring Arabia as far as possible under his control. The tribes defeated at Hunayn—whether nomadic, semi-nomadic or settled—were treated generously. Where the other Bedouin tribes did not take a place in Islamic society, they were subjected to military discipline. The news of Muhammad's message and success had reached as far as Bahrain, Oman and Yemen and tribes which came voluntarily to join him for economic, political or religious reasons. Year 9 of the new reckoning (April 630–April 631) was later called the 'Year of the Delegations (*wufud*)', because so many delegates sought to be accepted into the alliance. While respecting the autonomy of the individual tribes, Muhammad was lord of Arabia and the Muslim community was the greatest power factor in this. In a very short time Arabia had become Muslim: the Bedouin tribes were incorporated and Arabia became the heartland of Islam.

– *The consolidation of Muslim society*: the essential element of this community, the Ummah, was now well developed:

- anyone who wanted to take part in the great pilgrimage (*hajj*) had to confess the one and only God;
- only the one confession of faith (*shahadah*) in the one God and the Prophet Muhammad was tolerated;
- the Prophet strictly required ritual prayer (*salat*) of all Muslims, even the Bedouins, who were opposed to regimentation;
- the alms (*zakat*) due every year were collected by Muhammad's agents (this contributed substantially to the great apostasy movement, the *riddah*, among the Bedouins of Central Arabia after Muhammad's death);
- the month of Ramadan became established as the time of fasting (*siyam*).

These central structural elements of Islam would later be called the 'five pillars'; we shall be looking at them more closely in the next chapter.

– *A declaration of war on Jews and Christians*: Muhammad had been hostile to the Jews ever since the early years in Medina. What about the Christians? Muhammad would have come across Christians, and especially monks (such as the famous monk Bahira), on his business travels to Syria; his first revelation was first confirmed by a Christian (Waraqah)and his followers received a very friendly welcome in Christian Ethiopia. This explains Muhammad's originally friendly attitude to the Christians (who were sparsely represented in western and central Arabia): 'Thou wilt surely find that, of all people, the most hostile to those who believe are the Jews as well as those who are bent on ascribing divinity to aught beside God; and thou wilt surely find, that of all people, they who say, "Behold we are Christians," come closest to feeling affection for those who believe: this is so because there are priests and monks among them, and because these are not given to arrogance.'[113] Muhammad's attitude to Christians presumably deteriorated when he fought for an expansion route to Syria and was defeated by the Byzantines or their Arab allies in 629 at Mu'ta. Moreover, the Qur'an does not show the slightest comprehension of Christian dogma (the Trinity and the divinity of Jesus).

Thus finally there was an explicit declaration of war not only on the Jews but also on the Christians: 'Fight against those who—despite having been vouchsafed revelation—do not believe either in God or the Last Day, and do not consider forbidden that which God and His Apostle have forbidden, and do not follow the religion of truth, till they [agree to] pay the exemption tax with a willing hand, after having been humbled. And the Jews say, "Ezra is God's son," while the Christians say, "The Christ is God's son." Such are the sayings which they utter with their mouths, following in spirit assertions made in earlier times by people who denied the truth. "May God destroy them!" How perverted are their minds! They have taken their rabbis and their monks—as well as the Christ, son of Mary—for their lords beside God, although they had been bidden to worship none but the One God, save whom there is no deity.'[114]

– *The expansion of the Islamic confederation*: Qur'anic exegetes[115] have investigated the text quoted above in many ways (it is said to be a composite text, certain clauses are said to have been inserted later, Ezra is nowhere divinized in Judaism, and so on). However, their conclusions make little difference to the historic significance of these statements: Muslims later obeyed this instruction of the Prophet everywhere on their campaigns of conquest—as early as the military expedition to Tabuk (in 630), where many Christian and Jewish communities became tributary: Christians and Jews were to be fought against until they recognized the political (not the religious!) rule of Islam! So while there were no forcible conversions of those who had been subjected ('There is no compulsion in religion'), all non-Muslims were obliged to pay a poll tax (*jizyah*), an essential source of income for the Muslim rulers. This was first imposed after the conquest of the oasis of Khaybar (sixty miles north of Medina), which belonged to the Jewish Nadir tribe, who had been driven out. The poll tax made a provisional co-existence between Muslims and Jews possible, on the basis that while the Jews continued to be allowed to cultivate the land, as tenants they had to pay tribute to the Muslims (in Khaybar, half the date harvest). In this way the economic and political power of Judaism, which had previously been so significant, was liquidated, and the military, economic and political foundation laid for an Arab–Islamic hegemony.

It is hard to say how many campaigns, major or minor (not mentioned at all in the Qur'an) were waged against Bedouin tribes during the lifetime of

Muhammad: the historian al-Waqidi (died 823) lists seventy-four in his history of the campaigns.[116] Under Muhammad, major military campaigns were carried on in Byzantine frontier territory. The extension of Muslim rule to the region of Syria–Palestine, which though ruled by Byzantium was mostly populated by Arabs, was an attractive prospect. Muhammad himself prepared the operation, in which an irresistible army of three thousand men finally penetrated as far as the Gulf of 'Aqaba.

Among other things, the consequences of this policy, which was domestically monarchical and externally expansive, were:

- Absolutist centralism as the form of rule for the Arab Islamic empire was legitimized by Muhammad's religious and political sole rule.
- While Jews and Christians were tolerated in the Arab-Islamic empire, it was only as 'protected minorities' (*dhimmi*) with markedly reduced rights.

In 632 Muhammad was determined to take part in the pilgrimage from Mecca to Medina. Although he did not know it, this was to be his farewell pilgrimage; on it, once again he took over the direction of the great ceremony. After his return his health deteriorated greatly and he was tormented by headaches and fevers. He became so weak that he handed over leadership of the daily prayers to his loyal companion Abu Bakr. He no longer spent his nights alternating between the rooms of his wives. Tradition has it that he asked permission to remain with his favourite wife 'A'ishah, Abu Bakr's daughter. With his head cradled on her lap, the Prophet died, unexpectedly, aged about sixty, in the tenth year of the Hijrah, on 8 June 632. He did not nominate a successor or representative.

Achievements and virtues of the Prophet

If we look back on the life's work of 'God's messenger', we can understand the judgement of Muslims. Muhammad's achievements were tremendous, indeed epoch-making, and matched by very few others, before or since. This should be recognized, without reservation, even by Christian theology and the Christian churches.

– The Prophet united the Arabia of tribes and clans, which had been rent by constant political disputes and feuds and, because of their different tribal deities, were also split in religious terms. He united it in religion by his message of the oneness of God and politically by his novel form of rule. Islam, which combines religious authority and political power, was the foundation of the unity of Arabia.

– In this way the Prophet brought the Arabs—measured against the this-worldly polytheism of the old Arab tribal religions—to a religious plane comparable to that of the neighbouring great empires. Islam was a monotheistic, ethical high religion.

– Through the Qur'an the Prophet gave countless people in his century and in the centuries that followed infinite inspiration, courage and power to make a new religious beginning: a move towards greater truth and deeper knowledge and a breakthrough towards enlivening and renewing traditional religion. Islam was the great help in life.

So, shouldn't people in seventh-century Arabia have listened to Muhammad's prophetic voice? Shouldn't they have seen the Prophet as the moral example for their behaviour and their way of life? Muhammad was *the* great religious reformer: in him the Islamic tradition sees the embodiment of all the virtues that are important for human beings before God.

Just one significant testimony: in his biography of Muhammad, the Pakistani Muslim Muhammad Ali compiled a whole list of virtues for which Muhammad was exemplary: honesty, simplicity of lifestyle and clothing, love of friends, generosity towards enemies, justice towards everyone, humility, sympathy for the poor and tormented, hospitality, friendliness, strength of faith, readiness to forgive, modesty, adaptability, respect for others and courage. Ali's catalogue ends with a description of the Prophet's steadfastness (and who could deny this?): 'The biographies of the Prophet, whether written by friends or foes, all agree in their admiration for his bold courage and unshakable steadfastness in the face of the most difficult strokes of fate. Despair and despondency were unknown to the Prophet. Shut in as he was on all sides by a gloomy future prospect and by resistance, his belief in the final triumph of the truth was never for a moment shaken. The mightiest storms of distress, deprivation and persecution could not move him an inch from his standpoint. He made the best of all the available God-given means and left the rest to the grace of God. Surprising changes of fortune could never weaken or dampen his courage. Even after the horrific disaster of the battle of Uhud he was ready to pursue the enemy the next day. In a word: even in the most hostile and difficult circumstances his heart was always filled with firm conviction that the truth must triumph in the end.'[117] Really? Was it really so simple, so smooth?

A Christian theologian who shows some understanding for the Prophet's significance, not only for Muslims but for the history of all religions, may ask critical questions about the person and work of Muhammad without offending Muslims. To ask those questions in a spirit of truthfulness is to serve honest understanding between Christians and Muslims. These questions come, not out of a lack of respect for the Prophet and Islam, but out of a concern for their credibility. However rightly Muhammad's virtues may be emphasized, critical questions about his morality cannot simply be suppressed. They relate to the truthfulness of the Prophet, his use of force and his relationship to women.

Immoral? The traditional charges

These charges have long played a role in Christian–Muslim polemic. But does that necessarily mean that they are untrue? I shall look briefly at the traditional charges and attempt to give as balanced an answer as possible.[118]

– *Untruthfulness*? Muhammad undoubtedly had an unerring, unshakable sense of mission that went with his sober disposition, acute understanding and political shrewdness.

Over the centuries Christian criticism (like early Meccan criticism) has charged him with untruthfulness: Muhammad is said to have drawn his wisdom from other, even foreign, informants, Jews and Christians, and simply proclaimed it in Arabic. He is said to have been a deceiver who lied deliberately by proclaiming human ideas as God's revelation.

However, Muhammad was unquestionably convinced that he was not proclaiming his word but the word of God, and that he could distinguish between the two. So it is unjustified to doubt the authenticity of Muhammad's revelatory experiences. Instead we must ask soberly:

- couldn't a well-to-do merchant such as he very easily have led a far more comfortable life he did, first as a solitary 'God-seeker' and then as 'God's messenger'?
- would he have accepted such a life full of sacrifice, and all its dangers, for a false message?
- if we dispute the authenticity of Muhammad's revelation, mustn't we also dispute the authenticity of the revelations of the prophets of Israel, indeed many of the religious claims of Jesus of Nazareth?

The Prophet's subjective honesty may not be doubted. In principle, one can agree or disagree with the content of his revelations but one shouldn't cheapen the disagreement by disparaging Muhammad as a person. Muslims could possibly have countered the moral criticism of Muhammad's truthfulness better had they emphasized more that Muhammad did not travel through the world blind, deaf and mute. As a fundamentally religious man, on his travels and in his personal encounters he spoke not only about merchandise and prices, personal and political conditions, but also about religion. So why dispute that things that he heard and learned elsewhere found their way into his experience of revelation, that on occasions his own reflections preceded it and that only the concluding formulation of the surahs has the authority of the 'word of God'? Didn't the Prophet himself concede that in principle self-deception was possible (as in the case of the Satanic verses) and that in some circumstances corrections and revisions of earlier surahs by later revelations were necessary? This is a central problem which I shall discuss in more detail later. In the case of Muhammad, precisely how are the human word and the word of God related?

– *Violence*? Muhammad combined unusual strength of will with his consciousness of mission and his power to resist his opponents and give positive form to a new community—despite all the enmity. As a leader with extraordinary political and diplomatic gifts, he could win through against enemies outside and within, and also put forward constructive solutions for building up the Islamic Ummah.

Over the centuries Christian critics have raised the charge of violence. It is said that, at least in his second Medinan phase, Muhammad behaved like an unscrupulous power politician: he broke promises solemnly given, acted faithlessly, spoke with a double tongue and was even responsible for political murder, plundering raids, purges of whole tribes and countless wars.

However, it is impossible to reduce Muhammad's life and teaching to a hunger for power or unscrupulous power politics. We do justice to Muhammad only if we see that his own driving force was the proclamation of a religious message, the experience of being grasped and sent. The Prophet was not the messenger of an introverted religious individualism; he did not want to remain a solitary God-seeker like the *hanifa*, solely concerned for the well-being of his soul. Rather, for religious motives, he wanted to shape the life of the individual and community and used all the means of power available at that time to achieve his aim. He was a highly realistic politician who, like any human being, has the right to be measured by the standards of his time and his land, even if today we disapprove of the use of violence as a means to an end, especially when the motives are religious. Muhammad did not want to trust only in the power of faith, like the Christian monks, explicitly praised in the Qur'an, who had withdrawn into the Syrian desert and who through their humble piety had exercised a strong attraction for the Christian nomads in their neighbourhood; nor, in an extremely violent society, did he want to renounce the use of violence. But this is no reason for denying his religious credibility as a 'messenger of God'. Rather, we should consider that:

- Muhammad did not attribute any political and military successes to himself, but always to God; his unshakable faith remained his basic attitude in all his enterprises.
- for him, religion and politics belonged together, though the secular sphere was to be shaped by fundamentally religious intentions.
- the minority status of the 'small flock' was not his ideal but at best the initial stage.
- his Ummah was a power group which had to fight for its position with the same means as the other tribes and groups if it was not to go under.

- at that time plunder was largely tolerated as a means of getting a livelihood; often it was the only way of surviving, especially for the Prophet's companions, who had left all their worldly goods behind in Mecca.
- Muhammad could not have followed a policy which was so successful in the long term without the use of force.
- despite his militant energy and harshness, the Prophet was skilled in negotiation and compromise and was shrewd and tactful (in particular in his personal policies). After his triumphal entry to Mecca the feared head of the new community showed a striking readiness for reconciliation in granting a general amnesty.

Perhaps Muslims would have done better to say more unequivocally that even the Prophet was not a morally perfect man; that possibly he submitted too much to the unwritten laws of old Arab society; that he broke treaties both with the Jews and the Meccans simply out of suspicion; that at least in two cases he failed to observe recognized rules of war (for example attacking at a holy time and felling palms); and that he did not shrink from political murder (of Jews), thus causing widespread fear. Many Muslims have come to recognize that war for the sake of their faith is a pernicious aberration. Even if *jihad* by no means exclusively has the sense of a 'holy war' (this is a Christian invention; the term does not occur in the Qur'an), but initially means 'effort' for God, moral effort towards self-perfection before God, it is worth remembering that in several passages in the Qur'an violent 'effort on the way of God' (*al-jihad fi sabili' llah*) is not only allowed by God but even required. A justification of warlike actions, an Islamic theory of war, can easily be derived from these verses, especially in the fight against Jews and Christians. This is a second problem for later discussion: the problem of religion and power, religion and violence.

– *Licentiousness*? Muhammad, a deeply religious man, was beyond doubt also a very vital, robust man. He was capable of extraordinary physical achievements, first on his travels, then in warlike conflicts. Until his fatal illness he remained fully able-bodied.

However, down the centuries no charge has been repeated as constantly and as penetratingly by Christian critics as that of sexual licentiousness. The arguments were easy to find. In Medina Muhammad initially had four wives—the maximum number which the Qur'an allows a man—and slave girls as concubines.[119] But in the year 626 Muhammad took another wife (who died soon afterwards and therefore is not reckoned in the number), in 627 a fifth and sixth, in 628 a seventh and eighth, and in 629 a ninth—over the years a total of thirteen wives in all, not to mention the many concubinages with slave girls. He had no inhibitions about marrying the wife of his adopted son Zayd ibn Harithah, a freeman, after he had seen her in his house dressed only in an undergarment. This is often trivialized apologetically in Muslim literature. (For example Zaynab is said to have been married to Zayd against her will; Muhammad is said initially to have rejected Zayd's offer and to have married her only when the marriage with Zayd had been broken off. Indeed, it is said that in this way he even raised the lowly status of married women.) The Prophet had a veritable harem, and it is no coincidence that this set a precedent for Islamic potentates.

But all this needs to be assessed fairly. Must we necessarily feel unsympathetic to Muhammad for not adopting asceticism (largely derived from pagan roots), that asceticism which has done so much damage in Christianity (including compulsory celibacy for the leading class)? He rejected the attempts of ʻUthman ibn Mazʻun, who led the small group of Muslim emigrants to Ethiopia, to give Islam more markedly ascetic features (possibly borrowed from Christian monasticism). And during his time in Mecca, where his economic and social superior, Khadijah, had offered him marriage, Muhammad lived a monogamous life.

We should no more castigate Muhammad for having adapted to the polygamous system of the Arab society of the time than we should castigate the patriarchs of Israel, Abraham, Isaac and Jacob, all of whom had several wives. In those societies this was a matter of prestige. It makes little sense to compare those living in polygamy at that time with present-day Christian monogamy (in so far as it is practised). Muhammad entered into some of these marriages for political reasons and into others to protect the women (women whose husbands had fallen in the battles of Badr and Uhud). That Muhammad was susceptible to female charms need not be disputed; he himself spoke of the women and perfumes of Arabia as the earthly gifts he loved most, besides which money and wealth were unimportant. Does that put the truth of his message in doubt? 'The blessing of children' was granted to the Prophet by his many wives only to a limited degree. His only son died in childhood and of his daughters only Fatimah, as the spouse of ʻAli, was to make history: she was his daughter from his first marriage with Khadijah.

Again, it would probably have been better if Muslims had granted Muhammad's human fallibility without much apologetic. This fallibility is even attested in the Qur'an, where God accuses Muhammad of having roughly refused a poor blind man explanations of the faith while seeking to win the favour of the great men of Mecca.[120] Something can be said in defence of the Prophet in the case of the fair Zaynab: the episode is not mentioned at all by Ibn Ishaq and only in passing by Ibn Hisham. However, non-Muslims become suspicious when this marriage is justified by divine revelation, simply so that future believers may follow the Prophet's example and may also marry the wives of adopted sons (though not true daughters-in-law, which is strictly forbidden).[121] 'Then, when Zayd had come to the end of his union with her, We gave her to thee in marriage, so that [in future] no blame should attach to the believers for [marrying] the spouses of their adopted children when the latter have come to the end of their union with them. And [thus] God's will was done.'[122] Here the Prophet had secretly already cherished the wish that Zayd would divorce Zaynab so that he could marry her, but had suppressed this wish out of fear of public reaction, as is said clearly in the preceding verse of the Qur'an: 'Thou didst say unto the one to whom God had shown favour and to whom thou hadst shown favour, "Hold on to thy wife, and remain conscious of God." And [thus] wouldst thou hide within thyself something that God was about to bring to light—for thou didst stand in awe of [what] people [might think], whereas it was God alone of whom thou should have stood in awe.'[123] The view of the pious Hasan al-Basri (died 728) is that this was the worst verse revealed to the Prophet, yet he did not suppress it.[124]

It makes one even more sceptical when, once again, a revelation grants formal permission to the Prophet to marry as many wives as he wants: not only his previous wives, the female cousins who emigrated with him and all the slaves but 'any believing woman who offers herself freely to the Prophet and whom the Prophet might be willing to wed: [this latter being but] a privilege for thee, and not for other believers'.[125] The remark made by Muhammad's favourite wife 'A'ishah in this connection can hardly have been invented: 'God is anxious to do your will.'[126] And it does little to reassure a sceptical non-Muslim when the Prophet's delight in marriage is finally limited by a renewed revelation: 'No [other] women shall henceforth be lawful to thee—nor art thou [allowed] to supplant [any of] them by other wives, even though their beauty should please thee greatly–: [none shall be lawful to thee] beyond those whom thou [already] hast come to possess.'[127] This is the third problem: the relationship between religion, sexuality, man and woman. I shall discuss all three problems later in the context of the three Abrahamic religions.

Like the prophets of Israel

Many religions do not have prophets in the strict sense: the Hindus have their gurus and sadhus, the Chinese their sages, the Buddhists their masters; but none of them have their prophets as do Jews, Christians and indeed Muslims. However, there is no doubt that if one person in the whole history of religion is called simply 'the Prophet', because he claimed this status (but certainly not more), it was Muhammad. Even the orthodox Christian (or Jew) should take note of certain parallels. Like the prophets of Israel, Muhammad:

- did not act on the basis of an office bestowed on him by the community (or its authority) but on the basis of a special personal relationship to God;

- was strong willed and steeped through and through in his divine call, seeing himself totally claimed and exclusively commissioned by it;
- spoke in a religious and social crisis; his passionate piety and revolutionary proclamation stood in opposition to the well-to-do ruling caste and the tradition that it guarded;
- usually calls himself a 'warner' and sought simply to be the spokesman of God and God's word, not of his own;
- indefatigably proclaimed the one God, who tolerates no God alongside himself and who is the gracious creator and merciful judge;
- required unconditional obedience, surrender, 'submission' (*islam*) to this one God: that includes gratitude to God and generosity towards fellow men and women;
- combined his monotheism with a humanism, with belief in the one God and his judgement and the resultant demand for social justice: there are threats against the unrighteous, who will go to hell, and promises to the righteous, who will be gathered to God's paradise.

Anyone who puts the Bible and the Qur'an side by side and reads them will recognize that the three revelatory religions of Semitic origin—Judaism, Christianity and Islam—and especially the Hebrew Bible and the Qur'an all have the same basis. One and the same God speaks clearly in both. 'Thus says the Lord' in the Hebrew Bible corresponds to the 'Say' (*qul*: 332 times) of the Qur'an; the biblical 'Go and proclaim!' corresponds to the Qur'anic 'Arise and warn!' And finally, the millions of Arabic-speaking Christians know no other word for God but Allah!

So isn't it perhaps simply a dogmatic prejudice for Christians to recognize Amos and Hosea, Isaiah and Jeremiah and the extremely violent Elijah as prophets, but not Muhammad?

Is Muhammad also a prophet for Christians?

In our time, there has been much discussion whether individuals make history or vice versa. Today's historiography is more than ever social history, which is not primarily orientated on what Hegel called 'historic' individualities, but on structural conditions and social change. In Muhammad's rapid rise to power the structural conditions—in both foreign and domestic policy—for such an epoch-making change were fulfilled. The problems of sociology, social anthropology and historical geography which are always present in any comprehensive consideration of history must be noted, as I did in my remarks on the problems of the beginning (A II). But particularly in the case of Muhammad it is evident that the description of long-term social forces must not neglect the individuals who act within the framework that they create. In other words, history is always about the dialectic of structures and persons. The 'factual history' of contingent individual events or active persons is by no means just on the surface, but at the centre of the historical processes of 'social history'.

Muhammad is an example of a man who really made history when the time was ripe. In Arnold Toynbee's terminology, a 'challenge' was given; it was matched in the person of Muhammad by the 'response'. What would Arabia have been without Muhammad, a man with a call, charisma, vision and bravura?

For the people of Arabia and finally far beyond, Muhammad was and is *the* religious reformer, *the* Prophet. For those who follow him, Muhammad, who wanted only to be a human being, is more than a prophet in the Jewish or Christian sense: he is a model of that form of life which Islam seeks to be. If according to the Second Vatican Council's Declaration on the Non-Christian Religions (1964) the Roman Catholic Church—here I hope I will be allowed a more than ritual quotation—'also has a high regard for the Muslims', then in my view this same church—and all Christian churches—must also 'have a high regard' for the one whose name perplexingly fails to appear in that declaration, although he and he alone led Muslims to worship the one God, who has now 'spoken to humankind' through him: Muhammad, the Prophet.

Any Jew who disputes that Muhammad has the qualities of a prophet should reflect that in the Hebrew Bible there are already very different prophets, and perhaps they, too, were not all great human examples. Any Christian who disputes that a prophet can come after Christ should reflect that, according to the New Testament, there were also authentic prophets after Christ: men and women who confirmed him and his message, interpreted them and stated them in a new time and situation.[128] Thus in the Pauline communities (as emerges from 1 Corinthians)[129] the 'prophets' occupied second place after the apostles. However, prophecy—a phenomenon above all of Jewish-Christian origin—disappeared soon after the end of the Pauline mission and, with the retreat of Jewish Christianity, disappeared from the profile of most Christian communities; after the Montanist crisis in the second and third centuries (the teaching of Montanus, inspired by earliest Christianity and apocalyptic, claimed to be 'the new prophecy') the prophets and above all prophetesses largely fell into disrepute.

But from the perspective of the New Testament we must not make dogmatic objections to Muhammad's understanding of himself as an authentic prophet *after* Jesus, and claim to be in fundamental accord with him. Details of the relationship between Jesus the Christ and Muhammad the Prophet remain to be clarified. Yet wouldn't this recognition of the title Prophet for Muhammad have major positive consequences for an understanding between Christians and Muslims, and especially for the message that Muhammad proclaimed, which is set down in the Qur'an?

B III

The Central Structural Elements

One of the great strengths of Islam is its clear theoretical and practical structure. Fundamental to that is the simple, easily understandable and unambiguous confession of faith (*shahadah*) in the one God, the omnipotent and all-merciful creator and judge, and in Muhammad his Prophet. This public confession of faith is also one of the five pillars (*arkan*) or essential elements of Islam, which developed very early in the Muslim community on the basis of the Qur'an. However, in the worldview of the Arabs in the seventh century, belief in God also included belief in numerous superhuman spiritual beings:

- in angels (*mala'ika*): God's messengers (especially Gabriel, who brings revelations);[1]
- in the devil or demons (*shayatin*) who lead people astray to evil (especially 'the Evil One': *ash-shaytan* = Satan, also called *iblis* = devil, from the Greek *diabolos*);[2]
- in djinns (*jinn*): those countless localized forces of nature, born of fire, which are intermediate beings between human beings and angels and for which the message of Muhammad is likewise given.[3]

To be a Muslim therefore means above all (as I have shown in detail) to make the confession of faith in God and his messenger and then to fulfil the four main obligations: the obligations of prayer, almsgiving, fasting and the great pilgrimage. These five are the pillars of Islam, on which the house of Islam is built, its central structural elements. I shall now look at them more closely. Islam is meant to embrace the whole of human life and the life of the Muslim is governed, ordered, shaped and marked out from that of non-Muslims by the fundamental obligations.

1. Mandatory prayer

In all three prophetic religions, prayer, both personal and ritual, plays a central role. It is typical of Judaism, Christianity and Islam that in order to find God human beings do not primarily go 'inwards' in meditation as in most religions of Indian origin, but stand 'before God', before God's 'face', and that they speak to God and listen to him. Not the externals but the orientation of the heart are the most important. What are the specific features of Islamic prayer?

Daily ritual prayer—the essential symbol of Islam

Pious Jews entrust themselves to their creator in silence, when they lie down and when they get up. Apart from the Sabbath and the great festivals, for Jews personal prayer or family prayer stand in the foreground. Believing Christians, too, apart from church worship, above all practise personal and family prayer: the 'Our Father' can and should also be prayed in a 'quiet room'—but no regulations are made about it.

However, the Muslim is under an obligation (*fard*) to perform the ritual prayer that is announced publicly every day at particular times. This is the second main duty of Muslims after the confession of faith. At the important hours of the day the call to prayer rings out over Muslim towns and villages, as it has done for centuries. Mandatory prayer takes place five times a day: *salat*—which can be translated 'prayer' and also 'worship'—is beyond doubt the most important religious action in Islam and the specifically Islamic type of prayer. What in Christianity is a binding practice only in monasteries and communities as the 'canonical hours', in Islam affects every belief. However, for the daily mandatory prayers Muslims are not tied to a particular place: the prayers can be offered at home, in the mosque or on the way.

If we follow the Qur'an, mandatory prayer evidently developed only gradually during the life of Muhammad as the basic ritual of the Muslim community.[4] Mandatory prayer is not mentioned in the earliest parts of the Qur'an and occurs first in the middle Meccan surahs. Especially after the battle of Badr, it must have taken on greater significance, and then in the middle of the Medinan period it became a fixed institution and an obligation for all Muslims. According to the Qur'an, Muhammad originally ordained prayer only three times daily, twice during the day and once at night.[5] Later, a third prayer in the middle of the day was introduced; the night vigil was voluntary.[6]

'When, where and how the number of prescribed *salat* increased from the three clearly mentioned in the Qur'an to the five of Islamic law has yet to be satisfactorily explained.'[7] However, the great Muslim law schools agree that there are five mandatory times of *salat*, for which quite precise instructions are given: dawn, midday, afternoon, sunset, evening.

The premise, the 'key', for prayer is purification (*tahur*) from any form of ritual impurity (relieving oneself, sexual intercourse, menstruation or even sleep), which every Muslim performs for himself or herself. This is not primarily a hygienic regulation but a symbolic purification of the person who comes before God. And this is achieved by ritual washing (*wudu*): hands, mouth, nose, face, arms to the elbow, head and feet (where there is no water, sand suffices).[8] It has sometimes been compared with Christian baptism, but wrongly, for neither self-baptism nor repeated baptism is possible in Christianity. Conversely, Islam does not know any divine mediation of grace in the sacrament. Islam has no sacraments. The washing of the body is simply a symbol of the cleansing of the soul from sins: in Islamic understanding every man or woman needs it, but without any special sacrament—whether baptism or confession. Cleansed by washing, the Muslim may come before God without dramatizing the guilt of his sins by an explicit confession of guilt. However, in later tradition this ritual washing turned into a highly complicated system which I shall be discussing later.

Characteristics of Islamic prayer and worship: no priesthood

Any Jew or Christian who is interested in deriving everything in Islam from Judaism or Christianity need only look at Islamic worship: nothing could be more different. Of course, Islam has public prayer, prostrations, forms of address to God, praises, thanksgiving and intercessions, as in the other prophetic religions. However, because of its theocentricity and its largely egalitarian character, Islamic worship displays distinctive characteristics which set it apart from Judaism and especially from Christianity. They are of the utmost importance for the whole of Islamic piety. For example, in Islam there is:

- no priesthood, no priestly ordination and no altar: only someone who leads the worship, the imam, who can be a respected layman;
- no special dress for religious dignitaries and no place in the mosque for a clerical caste but only a platform for the muezzin, who calls the people to prayer; a pulpit and a separate place for the local ruler;
- no distinction between 'celebrant' and 'congregation', the active and passive in worship;
- no solemn music, no singing, no candles, no processions, no sacral drama.

All Muslims are active in this community of prayer in precisely the same way: with their lips and their whole bodies, praying with exactly the same gestures and words. All are included in the closed ranks of the praying community (though women and men are separated): each individual becomes absorbed in the powerful rhythm of this great simple and direct rite of personal and communal worship of God. The following characteristics of everyday prayer are striking:

– Prayer is *disciplined*: not only are ritual washing and dress regulated in detail (for women the whole body except face and hands must be covered and for men at least everything between the navel and the knee), but also the individual parts and movements (each of which has its own designation). The media picture those at prayer in their ordered ranks, first always standing, then bowing with palms on knees, then again upright: seventeen bows in all, then two prostrations in which those who pray touch the ground with their foreheads, knees, both palms and the tips of their fingers.

– Prayer is *concentrated*: it always begins with the declaration of purpose (*niyah*) that this prayer is for God alone, and the words *Allahu akbar*, God is the greatest. Then Muslims pray the opening surah of the Qur'an, including the words 'Thee alone do we worship; and unto thee alone do we turn for aid.'[9] Praise follows, usually with another surah of the Qur'an. An utterly theocentric understanding of prayer is evident, based on God's sovereignty, greatness and unity, undisturbed by any association, deviation or division. Eating, walking or speaking makes the prayer invalid. Only if the prescribed bodily postures are observed precisely is the prayer right (*sahih*); otherwise it is void (*batil*) and therefore has to be repeated.

– Prayer is *universal*: it is performed everywhere in precisely the same way, learned by heart in Arabic—whether or not that is understood (like Latin prayers earlier in the Roman Catholic Church)—and thus binds together Muslims all over the world. Wherever people go, they can feel at home in this prayer. There is a sense of community in the horizontal that is grounded in a consciousness of God in the vertical. The only petition expressed in mandatory prayer is the petition for 'right guidance': 'Guide us the straight way!'[10] This is about the great worldwide 'community' (*ummah*) of Muslims who go the 'right way': 'the way of those upon whom Thou hast bestowed Thy blessings, not of those who have been condemned [by Thee], nor of those who go astray!'[11]

– Prayer is *authentically human*: if performed rightly, it can express the human condition. In the series of humble postures alternating with standing, those who pray express the sense that human beings owe their existence wholly and utterly to God, that in their destiny they are constantly dependent on a higher power but are also responsible to their God. How could Muslims better express their *islam*, their submission, indeed their humility and 'surrender' to God, than with this prayer? Thus mandatory prayer expresses quite tangibly the innermost essence of Islam: submission to the will of God. It can therefore be called the essential symbol of Islam.

The mandatory *salat* for all adult male Muslims includes weekly Friday prayer (at the time of the mandatory midday prayer). It was first introduced by the Prophet who, as imam, usually led prayer, in Medina, neither in imitation of the Jewish Sabbath nor in polemic against it. Friday, the 'day of assembly', was not originally associated with the assembly for worship but with the assembly for the weekly market,[12] the day of the week when it was easiest for the Prophet to gather the people for prayer and instruction (preaching).

That also explains why worship was fixed at noon (the market was finished and those attending it could still get home before dark), why work was to stop only for the time of worship (before and after this mid-day reflection people could get on with their business), and why Friday prayer must take place only in a town, in a single mosque (the great or Friday mosque) and not in the villages (villagers had to come to the towns).[13]

Thus originally Friday was not a Muslim solemn day, even if today in some countries, under Western influence, it has been declared the official rest day, with schools, business and offices closed. But everywhere this Friday worship is a typical characteristic of Islamic life. It is the only Muslim form of worship at which there is preaching: an 'admonitory sermon' and then a 'descriptive sermon' which takes the form of praise; although both are highly ritualized, at any time they can assume explosive political significance: on Fridays, mosques can easily become places of agitation.

Finally, *salat* includes not only the five mandatory daily prayers with the weekly Friday prayer but also prayers which are not mandatory (*fard*) but only customary (*sunnah*) or 'supernumerary' (*nafl*), such as festival prayers, the burial ritual, prayers for rain, prayer at solar and lunar eclipses and prayer on setting out on a journey and returning. There is also prayer (*du'a*= 'call', 'invocation') on every possible occasion on which Muslims turn to God whenever, wherever and however it meets their needs, to worship him, to thank him and above all to ask him for forgiveness of their sins and the fulfilment of their wishes. Prayer is a spontaneous expression of praise, thanksgiving and intercession. Islam has prayer books, but the prayers in them are not mandatory.

Physical manifestations: mosque—muezzin—minaret

Mandatory prayer must be performed as soon as possible after the call to prayer. This can happen anywhere, not just in the mosque. Muslim faith does not need a holy house to express itself. Wherever Muslims prostrate themselves and pray (at home, at work, in school, in the open air), the place becomes a mosque for them: they enter a holy time and a holy place. The Prophet is said to have remarked that the whole world is given to Muslims as a mosque. The place must not be made unclean; bringing along a small carpet can help here. The elementary, natural, character of this ritual prayer undoubtedly contributed to the spread of Islam.

Why then was there need for a mosque, as an Islamic house of God? The English 'mosque', like the German *Moschee*, is a loanword from the French: however, mosque goes back via the Italian *moschea* and the Spanish *mezquita* to the Arabic *masjid*.[14] This word, which occurs almost thirty times in the Medinan surahs of the Qur'an, there means simply 'place of worship' and refers to various sanctuaries. If the word does not come from Aramaic, like the Ethiopian *meshgad* ('church', 'temple'), it can certainly be derived from the Arabic *sajada*, 'prostrate oneself', and therefore means the 'place of casting oneself down', the 'place of worship'.[15] In Mecca, where ritual prayer was evidently not mandatory before the emigration, the Muslims did not even have their own place of worship.

The original model for all mosques is the house that Muhammad had built for himself in Medina: a rectangular courtyard surrounded by clay walls, and in it a hall (later two) with canopies supported by palm branches. After the Prophet's death, in his place of prayer was a sign indicating the orientation of prayer towards Mecca (*mihrab*) and a simple pulpit; attached to the east wall there were huts made of palm branches for the Prophet and his wives.

Here already we can see the multifunctional character of the mosque—very different from a Christian church—that in principle has still been maintained. A mosque, which is primarily a place and not a building, serves at the same time as:

- a place for worship;
- a place for political meetings, negotiations and judgement;
- a place for personal prayer;
- a place for theological instruction and study.

After the Prophet's death, his house became his burial place, the place for bestowing the office of caliph, the seat of government and a meeting place, until these functions were given their own rooms. Soon people were building mosques on the model of Muhammad's mosque in all the towns, great and small. These mosques had both religious and administrative functions; their architecture could differ greatly from region to region. At least the larger ones consisted of a courtyard and one or more covered halls with one side turned towards Mecca. To the present day the furnishings of a mosque include:

- the prayer niche (*mihrab*, possibly taken over from church architecture), which shows the direction (*qiblah*) of Mecca;
- the pulpit (*minbar*), originally probably an elevated seat from which Muhammad gave his speeches and then a place for the leader of Friday worship;
- a stand for the Qur'an, lampstands and lamps, and finally also mats and carpets, since the floor had to be kept cultically clean for prayers (that is why worshippers remove their shoes);
- only calligraphy as decoration (verses of the Qur'an or dedicatory sayings) and non-figurative ornaments;
- in the courtyard or in front of the mosque an ablution fount with a pool or merely taps for ritual washing: mosque and water belong together.

Every mosque has one or more muezzins (*mu'addin*). The muezzin is the one who 'announces' or 'calls', the person who makes the public 'call' (*adhan*) to mandatory prayer. Muhammad is said to have preferred such a caller to instruments such as trumpets, gongs or bells. Presumably at the time of the Prophet, in accordance with old Arab custom, the man who made the call to prayer (women were not admitted to this post) simply went through the streets or called from the flat roof of a house to remind believers of their duty with a brief 'Come to prayer'. Today, there are usually seven short phrases that are announced as loudly and as widely as possible:

'God is the greatest (*Allahu akbar*).
I bear witness that there is no God but God.
I bear witness that Muhammad is God's messenger.
To prayer!
To salvation!
God is the greatest.
There is no God but God.'[16]

Today the announcement is very often made by tapes through loudspeakers and sometimes there is loud competition between several mosques, despite what the Qur'an itself gives as an instruction for prayer: 'By whichever name you invoke Him, His are all the attributes of perfection. And be not too loud in thy prayer nor speak it in too low a voice, but follow a way in-between.'[17]

To begin with, the mosque did not have a tower: only from the time of the Umayyads (usually in formerly Christian territories) did this become an essential element. Minaret comes from the French *minaret*, which in turn comes via the Turkish *minaret(t)* from the Arabic *manara* (lighthouse).[18] This means 'the place where fire (light) is', so a lighthouse like the famous Pharos of Alexandria is the model. The minaret is the tower of the mosque (it can be rectangular, round or polygonal) from which the muezzin calls the time of prayer, from a gallery which is usually richly decorated and is important for the form and proportions of the minaret.[19] Like the church tower, the minaret has less a practical purpose than a symbolic character: it epitomizes the presence of Islam.

2. Almsgiving, fasting, pilgrimage

Prayer, the outflow of the confession of faith, stands at the centre of Muslim practice. But it must not be seen in isolation: that would be prayer with no practical action, and practical action is the aim of Muslim almsgiving. What would be prayer without bodily discipline? That is the aim of fasting in the month of Ramadan. But the climax of every Muslim's life is the great pilgrimage to Mecca—to be made at least once in a lifetime. I shall end this account of the essence of Islam with a brief description of these three further pillars.[20]

Annual almsgiving for the poor

All three prophetic religions aim not only at a new relationship to God but also at a new attitude to fellow human beings: responsibility before God and responsibility for one's fellow men and women belong together. 'Justice' plays as great a role in Islam as in Christianity and there is an awareness in all three religions that here much depends on the voluntary commitment of the individual, on that voluntary benevolence which has long been called 'almsgiving', a word which derives via the church Latin *eleemosyna* from the Greek *eleemosyne* ('compassion'), and means 'giving to the needy'.

However, to a greater degree than Judaism and Christianity, Islam prescribes the giving of alms, in the form of a payment which is laid down by law, as an obligation.[21] In the Qur'an there is as yet no conceptual distinction between voluntary benevolence and mandatory giving: *sadaqah* and *zakat* are often treated as synonyms. But in both concepts we should note a shift of meaning from a voluntary gift to mandatory contribution. *Sadaqah* becomes the word for voluntary giving, and *zakat* (used around thirty times, above all in the Medinan surahs) becomes the classical term for the obligation of all converts to pay a tax for the benefit of the needy.[22] This is how the double verse in the Qur'an has been understood: 'You shall be constant in prayer (*salat*); and you shall spend in charity (*zakat*).'[23]

Amazingly, however, the Qur'an does not contain any concrete regulations as to which possessions are to be taxed and how highly (as it does, say for inheritance and divorce). There is a list of recipients only in one surah:[24] almsgiving is to be above all for the poor and needy; for debtors who have fallen into difficulties which are not of their own making; for slaves who want to ransom themselves; for volunteers to fight for the faith and for travellers without means. So the *zakat* is not just a tax on behalf of the poor; it is intended for society as a whole, and initially it could also be paid cumulatively.

The motivation for such a tax is clear:

- Muslims are to show their gratitude for the good things which the Creator has given them: *zakat* is a visible expression of the earnestness of faith towards God; originally it meant 'cleansing' (from the verb *zakka*, 'to cleanse', 'to purify').[25]
- Through almsgiving Muslims are to express penitence for omissions and pray for divine forgiveness; all Muslims are brothers and sisters.
- Muslims are to further mutual respect and solidarity by their generosity: the Muslim Ummah is a community of solidarity.
- In this way they are to help to reduce the social contrasts by balancing things out between the well-to-do and the needy. If everything in nature is ultimately the property of the Creator, it follows that as God's representatives, human beings have to ensure a better distribution of goods.

It is obvious that the implementation of almsgiving raised some legal and organizational questions. What the Qur'an did not regulate was left for the Sunnah to organize. In working out Islamic law (*shari'ah*) people arrived at some very complicated regulations for individuals (exemptions, different professions and incomes), quite a few of which were subsequently attributed to the Prophet or to Abu Bakr. It was stated that the social tax applied to fruits of the field, vegetables, cattle (around a tenth of their value) and also to precious metals and merchandise (around a fortieth of their value if they were kept in the house for more than a year). In the time of Muhammad, however, the regulations were still so undefined that after his death Bedouin tribes refused to pay anything. They did not see almsgiving as a universal religious obligation of Muslims but as a special element of their agreement with Muhammad, which need not apply after his death. Nevertheless, almsgiving in solidarity became the irrevocable obligation of Muslims, just as the poll tax (mentioned earlier) became an obligation for non-Muslims. This was the original form of Muslim taxation. The coming Islamic state would have a lot to do with both of them.

In addition to mandatory almsgiving another institution came to play an increasingly significant social and political role; it is not one of the five pillars and is voluntary. This was the foundation (*waqf*, plural *awqaf*, 'blockade', that which does not move and thus can be sold, inherited or disposed of), in Islam a permanent, inalienable foundation for the welfare of all. There were already foundations in Egypt, Greece and Rome, and according to Muslim scholars the holy building of the Ka'bah was itself a religious foundation. There is a reference to surah 3.96: 'Behold, the first Temple ever set up for mankind was indeed the one at Bakkah (= Mecca): rich in blessing, and [a source of] guidance unto all the worlds.' In the history of Islam the first mosque in Medina is also the first foundation. As well as religious foundations there are charitable and above all family foundations. They have developed as a religious category since the seventh and eighth centuries on the basis of prophetic tradition (*hadith*).[26]

I shall be go into these special elements of Islamic economic life, *zakat* and *waqf*, later (E IV, 1–2).

The annual period of fasting

All three prophetic religions, and many others, have the practice of fasting, and in Judaism, Christianity and Islam specific times are prescribed for it. According to Jewish law, fasting takes place on the Day of Atonement,[27] and on national days of mourning, but not on the Sabbath or on feast days. The Christian community practised fasting from the beginning, but there was a clear instruction in the Sermon on the Mount that people should 'not observe that you fast, but only your Father, who also sees what is hidden'.[28] Yet at a very early stage the church observed a complete 'public' fast on Good Friday and Holy Saturday: a complete renunciation of food and drink.

Soon fasting was extended to the whole of Holy Week, which became a special time of fasting, and to other festivals, but not as a complete fast. Instead, Christians were to eat no more than one meal a day and to abstain from meat and wine (later also from other foods). However, since the Middle Ages and especially since the Reformation and in modern times, fasting has been increasingly reduced in Christianity. Days of fasting and abstinence have been abolished in the Protestant world, and in the Roman Catholic Church since the Second Vatican Council are prescribed only for Ash Wednesday and Good Friday. The Orthodox churches observe longer and stricter periods of fasting. Most recently, however, the traditional pre-Easter fast (Passiontide) has been promoted again, particularly by evangelical churches in Western consumer society, as a time of voluntary abstinence from consumption.

Islam, too, has voluntary fasts. As in traditional Catholicism, fasting can be a meritorious work or a penance. The Prophet introduced and regulated the obligation of fasting (*siyam*) as a divine commandment for all Muslims in his first year in Mecca.[29] We have already seen that he replaced fasting on the Jewish Day of Atonement (Yom Kippur) by fasting in the month of Ramadan because of his conflict with the Jews. As a result of his victory at Badr on 17 Ramadan of Year 2 after the Hijrah this month had assumed a special solemnity; it is no coincidence that the Qur'an is said to have been sent down in Ramadan.[30]

The motivation for fasting is similar to that in Judaism and Christianity:

- Fasting is an expression of penitence and the eradication of sins.
- Fasting serves towards the mastery of the body and its drives by the spirit.
- Fasting promotes piety and a mutual readiness for forgiveness.

What is special about Muslim fasting? Three characteristics are particularly striking:

– It is not just eating less or giving up certain foods, as in Christianity, but a complete fast, complete abstinence from food and drink and from sexual intercourse.

– It is not just restraint at meal times; rather, restraint is to be practised for the whole day from dawn (the moment when one can distinguish a white thread from a black one) to dusk; it is not even possible to rinse out one's mouth with water or to smoke.

– Fasting is to be practised not just on particular days but for a whole month, the month of Ramadan (between 28 and 30 days). Fasting is made more difficult by the fact that Ramadan, the ninth month of the Islamic lunar calendar, moves through the year and therefore in high summer, when water is necessary for life, refraining from drinking causes considerable difficulties. (The lunar calendar, introduced as the result of a revelation shortly before Muhammad's death,[31] loses eleven days every year because the lunar year is shorter than the solar year, so that Ramadan begins around eleven days earlier every year and the month of fasting can fall in any season.)

The command to fast, for a period that lasts considerably longer in summer than in winter, applies to all adult Muslims, men and those women who are not menstruating. There are concessions over this strict fasting: for the old and sick, for pregnant women and those who are breast-feeding, for travellers and for those involved in hard manual work. However, they are to make up the days of fasting they miss, which cannot always be easy.

Today the beginning of Ramadan, the month of fasting, is indicated according to ancient custom by the observation of the light of the new moon and is announced with pomp in the media. Special Ramadan carpets are laid out in the mosques, and the minarets are also illuminated all night. How is it, then, that for Muslims the time of fasting is not a gloomy time of penitence but rather a time of celebration? This is explained by the two aspects of the month of fasting—its day side and its night side. Fasting (and sexual continence) are practised only during the day; by night people are free. Moreover, according to a revelation the Prophet is said to have abrogated the prohibition against sexual intercourse on the nights of Ramadan.[32] There is eating, lots of feasting, usually more and longer than usual, and sometimes a lavish meal (*fatur*), immediately before which a great deal of shopping is done. The next day one can sleep it off, which makes the daytime fast considerably easier. Fasting and celebrating together helps the community and leads many Muslims who otherwise are not particularly observant to join in.

All in all, Ramadan is more a time of feasting than of repentance, full of countless religious and social activities in mosques and coffee houses. It is a time of fasting and celebrating for the whole Muslim community, a great symbol of the unity of Muslims all over the world and an invitation to non-Muslims to join the Ummah. Like its beginning, the end of Ramadan is established by the sighting of the new moon and the feast of breaking the fast (*'id al-fitr*), one of the two main Islamic festivals.

The great pilgrimage to Mecca

All three prophetic religions and many others also have the practice of pilgrimage. In Judaism, people were to go up to Jerusalem or from Jerusalem to the Temple Mount three times, at the three harvest festivals (the Feast of Unleavened Bread, the Feast of Weeks and the Feast of Tabernacles[33]). However, at an early stage there was a dispute as to whether one had to appear personally and whether one had to fulfil the commandment literally or depending on circumstances. Even after the destruction of the Second Temple Jews made pilgrimages to Jerusalem, though now their joy over Jerusalem was combined with a lament over the destroyed sanctuary and the Herodian western wall, which was all that remained. All through modern times Jews have made pilgrimages to Jerusalem, even more in the age of Zionism, and now after the new foundation of the state of Israel.

In Christianity, too, pilgrimage was customary at an early stage. However, there are no specific instructions about it in the New Testament (there is only a report of Jesus' traditionally Jewish 'pilgrimage' to Jerusalem). A person, not a place, is decisive for Christianity. Yet Christian pilgrimages developed in the early Christian centuries: to the places of martyrdoms or to martyrs' tombs (especially to the tombs of Peter and Paul in Rome), and to the scenes of Jesus' activity in Palestine. The pilgrimage to Compostela, to the tomb of the apostle James, was particularly important in the Middle Ages—it has recently been revived. Very much later, in the Catholic tradition, there were also pilgrimages to particular places where appearances of Mary and other saints were said to have taken place.

From early times there were annual and semi-annual pilgrimages in pre-Islamic Arabia, at the beginning of the spring and the autumn harvest. Mecca was a particularly prominent destination because of the Ka'bah and the other sanctuaries in the vicinity. This old Arabian practice of pilgrimage was continued under a Muslim monotheistic aegis. The various old places and ceremonies were preserved by the Prophet. Cleansed of polytheistic references and re-interpreted, the ceremonies were fused into one group of rituals and made fruitful again for Islam by their association with the history of Abraham and Ishmael (*maqam Ibrahim* = Abraham's footprint by the Ka'bah).[34]

This pilgrimage was of the utmost significance not only for the reconciliation of Muhammad with Mecca but also for the integration of the constantly growing Muslim populations.Their prayer niches (*mihrab*) in the direction (*qiblah*) of Mecca constantly reminded Muslims of their starting-point, their origin, the home of their religion. They needed only to remember or imagine the line as the crow flies extended forwards to know where Muslims 'who are able to undertake it' should travel.[35]

It is understandable that the great pilgrimage (*hajj*) to Mecca became the fifth pillar of Islam. Every adult Muslim is required to undertake this pilgrimage once in his lifetime, though in fact even now only a small number of Muslims can afford it (therefore, as in the case of almsgiving, representation is allowed). Often a family or even a whole village saves so that at least one of them can join in the pilgrimage, to the blessing of all, and later bear the honorific title 'pilgrim' (*hajj*) before his name. Mecca, where formerly Muslims, Jews and Christians lived peacefully together, became the 'mother of the cities' (*umm al-qura*): a 'holy inviolable place' (*harim*) but now for non-Muslims a forbidden city because of its holiness (*al-haram*, 'the sanctuary', has a minimum radius of five kilometres from the Ka'bah in all directions). Medina, too, is an exclusively holy city, but a visit to the tomb of the Prophet is not mandatory for Muslims.

The great pilgrimage of Muslims to Mecca bears little resemblance to a relatively comfortable pilgrimage to Rome or Lourdes, even if some Muslims like to combine a business, study or holiday trip with it. The pilgrimage makes special demands. It is valid only if the pilgrim, of whatever status or class, submits to a ritual that has been very precisely prescribed:

– First of all pilgrims must put themselves in a special state of dedication (*ihram*): with specific ritual actions (the key words are *labbayka allahumma*— 'at your service, O God') put on a white, seamless garment and stop shaving and combing the hair, stop cutting hair and nails, use no perfume, not cover the head, not wear a veil, at most have sandals on their feet, and refrain from sexual intercourse.

– Then a series of sometimes very strenuous and complicated rituals must be performed (usually with the help of a pilgrim guide). These are the rites of the 'little pilgrimage', the 'visit' (*'umrah*) to the Ka'bah in the central mosque of Mecca with a circumambulation of the Ka'bah seven times, which is possible at any time of the year; and the rites of the 'great pilgrimage' (*hajj*), which are possible only on fixed days of the pilgrimage month (*du 'l-hijja*) and are performed at the various holy places round Mecca (Mina, Muzadlifah and 'Arafat).

The most important stations of the great pilgrimage are: the circumambulation of the Ka'bah seven times; the walk, repeated seven times, between the hills of Safa and Marwa; climbing Mount Rahma ('the Mount of Grace') on the plain of 'Arafat; picking up pebbles in Muzdalifah and throwing them at a stone monument; the animal sacrifice in Mina and the sacrificial meal which follows; and finally the repetition of the circumambulation of the Ka'bah .[36] All this is God's command, to be obeyed reverently; like many religious rites it can be understood rationally only to a certain degree.

Some of these Islamic rites, mentioned in the Qur'an and in the Muslim tradition associated with Abraham, Hagar or Ishmael, still clearly show their pre-Islamic origins:

- the throwing of forty-nine pebbles (*jamrat*) in Mina at three stone pillars, which is understood as a symbolic stoning of the devil;
- the kissing, touching or greeting of the black stone in the extreme eastern corner of the Ka'bah (for many centuries now it has been broken and is held together by a stone ring and a silver fastening);
- the sacrifice of sheep, goats or even camels, performed at the same time by all pilgrims; the throats of the animals are cut in the direction of the Ka'bah (by slaughterers or by the pilgrims themselves); today, with more than one million pilgrims, this costs hundreds of thousands of animal lives an hour. Then follows the great sacrificial feast with the distribution and eating of the sacrificial meat, after which the men shave, have their hair cut and put on new clothes. Together with the breaking of the fast, this day of sacrifice (*yawm al-adha*), celebrated all over the Islamic world, is the highest religious festival in Islam.

Islam is the only Abrahamic religion that has preserved blood sacrifices (these are also performed in the fulfilling of vows). However, it is not the externals that are important for Muslims but the religious and spiritual attitude that can be attained with the pilgrimage: complete submission to God and a temporary turning away from the world.

With increasing numbers of participants the organization of the pilgrimage became a growing challenge to the political authorities. Initially the caliph of Damascus was responsible and then the caliph of Baghdad; from the tenth century the Fatimid caliph and the later sultans of Cairo, who were followed finally by the Ottoman sultans and last of all the kings of Saudi Arabia, as guardians of the holy places. It is always the same pilgrimage—though governed by constantly changing political and social circumstances. It goes on year after year, and year after year the giant curtain (*kiswah*) of the Ka'bah is rewoven, while the old is cut into pieces which are sold as souvenirs for the pilgrims.

We have now occupied ourselves sufficiently with the essence and centre of Islam, its central figure and its central structural elements. Before we embark on the tremendous history of fourteen centuries, I would like to pause a moment to sum things up and to ask a few further questions.

A change in the substance of faith

What are the centre and foundation, what is the abiding substance in the Islamic religion or Muslim faith? Whatever historical, political, sociological and anthropological interpretations may rightly or wrongly emphasize, in the light of the basic documents of Islamic faith which have become normative and historically influential, the central content of faith is: 'There is no God but God, and Muhammad is his prophet.' Without this confession there can be no Islamic faith, no Islamic religion.

The whole as it were elliptical testimony of the Qur'an revolves round these two focal points: God and his Prophet. Of course it can be argued that the one God himself forms the centre of the Qur'an, its 'theocentricity'. However, the significant thing about the Qur'an is that this God is never seen alone but always together with the one who is constantly addressed by his revelation. The surahs of the Qur'an do not circle round the 'mysteries of the deity' but round the message which the Prophet has to proclaim to his people.

More precisely, the distinguishing structural elements and abiding guidelines of Islamic faith are:

- belief in the God whom Muslims worship in common with Jews and Christians, who allows no associates;
- belief in the Prophet Muhammad who, as the 'seal of the prophets', confirms the prophets before him;
- belief in the Qur'an proclaimed by the Prophet as the uncorrupted, definitive revelation of God.

The special relationship of Muhammad to his God, resulting in the Qur'an, is the nucleus, starting point and focal point of Islam. Despite the initial refusals of Muhammad's fellow tribesmen and all the developments and entanglements of Islamic history, this would nevertheless remain the basic notion of the Islamic religion that was never given up. For Islam, this constant centre—God and his message in the Qur'an—which is the motive force for everything is the basis of:

- its originality from earliest times;
- the continuity in its long history down the centuries;
- its identity despite all the differences of language, race, cultures and nations.

Anyone who wants to pass a well-founded judgement on the present situation of Islam must know its history, for with the 'essence' and its structure we have as yet by no means grasped living Islam. Just as a static architectural formula cannot show us the imposing building resting on five pillars, a description of its essence cannot show us the concrete religion. Unquestionably, like Judaism and Christianity, Islam is not a static entity. It is a living history, in which 'the essence' of Islam, its 'substance of faith', has repeatedly assumed new and different forms. I shall now turn to this history.

C. HISTORY

In some respects what forms the centre of Islam, its foundation, the abiding substance of its faith, has become clear in a more evident and concentrated way than in the case of Judaism and Christianity: God's word has become a book and the message of this book is that there is no God but God and Muhammad is his Prophet. Islamic faith is imposingly simple and compact; Islamic society is amazingly capable of integration and of offering resistance; and by comparison with Christianity and even more with Judaism the history of the formation of Islamic religion is extraordinarily short and compressed. So, we can ask, doesn't this unique history show incessant expansion until the nineteenth century, a history of victors and victories, a direct development without any deep breaks and contradictions, without a change of paradigms?

C I

The Original Paradigm of the Islamic Community

For a long time Roman Catholicism also paid homage to an organic, idealistic, understanding of history. Although, century by century, new rings kept being added to the trunk of the church tree, there were no breaks or eruptions. Such an understanding of history, which is hardly advocated seriously in Christianity today, comes to grief on historical reality. Doesn't it also come to grief in the case of Islam? Though they are often overlooked, aren't there also epoch-making crises and revolutions in Islam that in the end also explain the stagnation of the Islamic world in the nineteenth and twentieth centuries?

1. Abiding substance of faith—changing paradigms

Though Islam carried on the historic legacy of Judaism and Christianity—belief in the one God—it posed a new challenge with which they had their problems: Muhammad as the definitive Prophet of the one God. However, this centre, this foundation, this substance of faith (in my schematic description indicated in each paradigm by a circle with a line through it) never existed in abstract isolation but has, time and again, been reinterpreted and put into practice to meet the changing demands of the time. Because of that, in this section the systematic–theological and historical–chronological descriptions (without which the former cannot be given a convincing basis) will be combined and regularly interspersed with current reflections, as in my accounts of Judaism and Christianity.

Is there also a paradigm change in Islam?

Islam is no more a monolithic entity than are Judaism and Christianity. Just as a new overall constellation had to come about when the Israelites became a settled people, or when the simple belief of Jewish Christianity in Jesus the Messiah (Christ) was translated into the Hellenistic world of the Roman empire, so too the faith and life of the original Islamic community underwent a great revolution after the peaceful death of the Prophet, when the Islamic movement definitively spread beyond the bounds of Arabia. Again and again, new epoch-making constellations of the time forced the one community of faith to reinterpret and realize one and the same centre of the proclamation of faith and put it into practice.

I follow Thomas S. Kuhn in understanding a paradigm as 'an entire constellation of beliefs, values, techniques, and so on shared by the members of a given community'.[1] I have explained at length in earlier publications[2] that a transfer of the paradigm theory (in the sense of a 'macroparadigm') from the realm of the natural sciences to the sphere of religion and theology is possible, important and urgently necessary, and how far it may be made, and have demonstrated this in my earlier books *Judaism* and *Christianity*. We shall see that the history of Islam is no less dramatic. In it, an initially small community of faith, which then grew extraordinarily quickly in response to renewed great historic challenges, underwent a whole series of fundamental religious changes, indeed in the longer term a revolutionary paradigm change.

My analysis of the more than 3000-year history of Judaism produced the following influential epoch-making constellations (macroparadigms):

- the tribal paradigm before the formation of the state;
- the paradigm of the kingdom: the monarchical period;
- the paradigm of theocracy: post-exilic Judaism;
- the medieval paradigm: the rabbis and the synagogue;
- the modern paradigm: assimilation;
- the developing paradigm of the postmodern period.

Although the history of Christianity is only two-thirds as long, my paradigm analysis, based on the historical evidence, likewise produced six epoch-making constellations:

- the Jewish apocalyptic paradigm of earliest Christianity;
- the ecumenical Hellenistic paradigm of Christian antiquity;
- the medieval Roman Catholic paradigm;
- the Reformation Protestant paradigm;
- the paradigm of modernity orientated on reason and progress;
- the paradigm of a postmodern period which is taking shape.

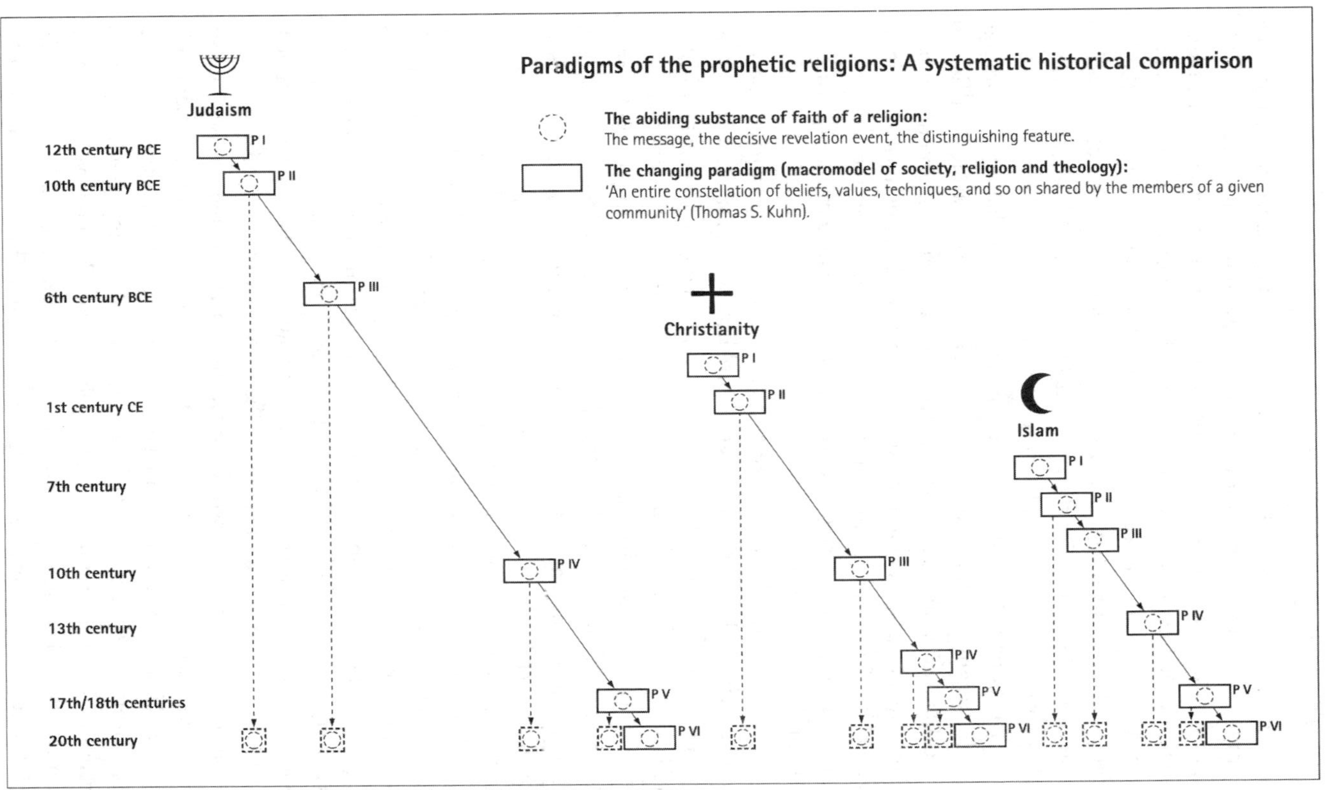
Paradigms of the prophetic religions: A systematic historical comparison
The abiding substance of faith of a religion:
The message, the decisive revelation event, the distinguishing feature.
The changing paradigm (macromodel of society, religion and theology):
'An entire constellation of beliefs, values, techniques, and so on shared by the members of a given community' (Thomas S. Kuhn).
Judaism
Christianity
Islam
P I
P II
P III
P IV
P V
P VI
12th century BCE
10th century BCE
6th century BCE
1st century CE
7th century
10th century
13th century
17th/18th centuries
20th century

New epoch-making constellations

The history of Islam is about a third shorter than that of Christianity, but no less complex. Here too the historical evidence shows similar macroparadigms (or epoch-making overall constellations) to those in Judaism and Christianity. Here too paradigm analysis makes it possible to work out the great historical structures and transformations: by concentrating at the same time on the fundamental constants and the decisive variables. Here too we cannot overlook the historic breaks from which the epoch-making basic models of Islam emerged. They govern the situation of Islam even today.

I shall begin with an analysis of the first overall constellation: the paradigm of the original Islamic community (P I). For Islam, as for Judaism or Christianity, it would have made little sense to construct some models or paradigms in advance. Here too the strictest orientation on empiricism is indispensable. That means that it is important to note the evidence as comprehensively as possible and to utilize for the paradigm analysis what historians have discovered.

In this difficult enterprise (apart from the relevant sections of specialist works on individual periods, aspects or problems which I shall mention where relevant) I shall base myself on the more recent general accounts of the history of Islam.[3] *The Cambridge History of Islam*,[4] a two-volume handbook by internationally known authors, edited by P.M. Holt, Ann K.S. Lambton and Bernard Lewis, is still fundamental. The *Oxford History of Islam*, edited by J.L. Esposito, is more recent and has a more thematic construction.[5] The history of Islam by the French Islamic scholar Claude Cahen, which for its time was innovative in the way in which it also integrated non-political aspects, is still worth reading.[6] The three-volume work *The Venture of Islam* by Marshall G.S. Hodgson of the University of Chicago offers an extensive overall history and takes special account of religious, literary and existential aspects.[7] The composite work by German-language authors edited by Ulrich Haarmann of the University of Freiburg, *Geschichte der arabischer Welt*, covers the political, economic and social history of Arab Islam.[8] For the social history of all Islam I have referred to the great work by Ira M. Lapidus of the University of California, Berkeley, *A History of Islamic Societies*, which, both comprehensively and precisely, investigates especially the institutional systems on the basis of the *Cambridge History*.[9] The compact account by Tilman Nagel of the University of Göttingen, *Geschichte der Islamischen Theologie*,[10] is particularly important. Also indispensable is the monumental multi-volume work by Josef von Ess of the University of Tübingen, *Theologie und Gesellschaft im 2. und 3. Jahrhundert Hidschra* (Theology and Society in the Second and Third Centuries after the

Hijrah),[11] which describes the classical period of Islamic history in six volumes rich in text and analysis. For names, terms, phenomena and events the second edition of the *Encyclopaedia of Islam*,[12] edited by leading orientalists, is an indispensable and inexhaustible source of information. In addition, there are more recent large encyclopedias (see the List of Abbreviations) and shorter reference works (see my note on general accounts of Islam in B I).

2. A religious vision realized

Many prophets had visions—of an event, a person, a development or a new time but few experienced the realization of their vision. Muhammad did. Not only had he to communicate his vision to the people of his time, he was also able to accomplish it. On the basis of the revelations of the Qur'an he called for the establishment of an Islamic community and succeeded in realizing and shaping it. The result was a social transformation of Arab society generally. I shall now investigate more closely what we already know to be the essence and centre of Islam with respect to its realization in its very first era. What did this vision mean for the community and for the individual?

The new Islamic community

There are important differences between Islam and Christianity here:

- The paradigm of earliest Christianity (P I of Christianity)[13] developed only after Jesus' death, whereas the foundations for the paradigm of original Islam (P I of Islam) were laid quite decisively during Muhammad's lifetime.
- In the paradigm of earliest Christianity one could appeal only to the spirit of Jesus Christ, who though dead lived through the power of God, whereas in the paradigm of original Islam the Prophet was still present in person for a whole decade.
- The paradigm of early Christianity was a paradigm dominated by the Christ who had been exalted to God and would soon return (apocalyptic), whereas in its foundational phase the paradigm of original Islam was one of direct 'guidance' by the Prophet Muhammad, who gradually realized his religious vision in person.

However, this utterly earthly leader of the community had very much greater authority than the chief or sheikh (*shaykh*) of a tribe, who held office above all as an arbiter and could act only together with his council. As we saw, the Prophet respected the right of the clans and tribes to their own life and customary law—they were to regulate their own internal affairs. To that degree he was no absolute ruler. However, for questions going beyond the tribe, and in some minor disputes, he was now the supreme authority, who could make final, unassailable judgements. As the one who received, proclaimed and carried out the divine revelation, he spoke in God's name, holding office as a legislator and at the same time as a commander and judge. There was no separation of powers and no place for a purely 'secular' authority alongside the Prophet! Moreover the Prophet had a legitimation that constantly renewed itself through new revelations.

Muhammad left the old Arab family, clan and tribal relationships intact as a basis for the new community. But this blood-relationship was relativized, or better, had another layer put on it, so that it was transformed by a new kind of kinship. The emigration (*hijrah*) from the tribal alliance which ushered in the new time made clear once and for all that another affinity is ultimately more significant than blood kinship: the affinity of faith. We already know very well what constituted this:[14]

- a fellowship of belief in the one God and his Messenger;
- a fellowship of daily ritual prayer;
- a fellowship of concern for the poor and needy;
- a fellowship of discipline through fasting;
- a fellowship of inner purification through pilgrimage to the spiritual centre of Islam.

All these make up the substance of Islam and became the foundation for the Ummah, the new community of Muslims. But this community had to be realized under the conditions of a quite specific historical constellation of seventh-century Arab society[15] which, living on the periphery of the highly civilized world, had little cultural and religious organization. Apart from the areas bordering on the Byzantine or Sasanian Persian empires, it was united neither by religion nor an empire—the two overarching factors which brought order to the society of the time. Therefore pre-Islamic Arab society showed little political and social coherence. It was burdened and endangered by the:

– political splits into rival families, clans and tribes (with confederations, monarchies and kingdoms only in the zones on the periphery of the great empires), which often travelled together with hundreds of tents, operated autonomously and recognized no external authority;

– tensions between these warlike nomads or semi-nomads of the desert, who were mostly shepherds and camel breeders, and those settled at the oases, who worked as farmers, merchants and craftsmen;

– constant weakening and shaking of Bedouin society by persistent hostility, warlike conflicts, plundering campaigns and endless acts of vengeance.

A religion of law?

The new Islamic society had to embrace this splintered, 'fragmented' society of families and clans, towns and Bedouin groups, open its spiritual horizons and integrate it, in terms of religion and culture, through a new brotherliness. The aim was to create a better order and greater harmony within society—on the basis of belief in the one God. The Qur'an is primarily concerned with the relationship of human beings to their Creator and thus with their relationship to their fellow human beings.

Muhammad, who had been brought to Medina as an arbitrator (*hakam*), soon rose, on the basis of his political and military might, to be a legislator. However, he did not exercise his power within the existing legal system but without a system. His authority was not legal; for believers it was religious and for sceptics political. Muhammad changed and expanded the Arab system of arbitration and the old Arab customary law. Yet the Prophet–legislator did not want to provide a comprehensive, complete legal system for regulating the whole of life by means of the Qur'an; he was not concerned with casuistry. The Qur'an is silent on many legal questions, leaving them to Arab customary law. Joseph Schacht, author of the fundamental history of Islamic law, remarks: 'Generally speaking, Muhammad had little reason to change the existing customary law. His aim as a Prophet was not to create a new system of law; it was to teach men how to act, what to do, and what to avoid in order to pass the reckoning on the Day of Judgement and enter Paradise.'[16]

So is Islam a religion of the law? Originally it was not a religion of the law but the religion of an ethic. The Qur'an is concerned with ethical imperatives for human society, not all of which were new. However, on the new basis of faith these norms worked in favour of more justice, fairness, restraint, moderation, mediation, compassion and forgiveness, though this was not transposed into a legal structure of rights and responsibilities. As Schacht remarks: 'Had religious and ethical standards been comprehensively applied to all aspects of human behaviour, and had they been consistently followed in practice, there would have been no room and no need for a legal system in the narrow meaning of the term. This was in fact the original ideal of Muhammad; traces of it, such as the recurrent insistence on the merits of forgiveness, in a very wide meaning of the word, are found in the Koran, and the abandonment of rights is consequently treated in detail in Islamic law. But the Prophet eventually had to resign himself to applying religious and ethical principles to the legal institutions as he found them.'[17]

It is striking that only around six hundred of the 6666 verses of the Qur'an are concerned with legal questions and most of these with religious obligations and practices (such as ritual prayer, fasting and pilgrimage); only around 80 verses contain directly legal material.[18] We could therefore say, apparently paradoxically, that even where the Qur'an has legal material, it uses it in an ethical and not a legal way. Even in family law, which to some extent is discussed comprehensively (but in very different places), the Qur'an is primarily concerned with the questions of the relationship between men and women, and of how children, orphans and relatives, dependents and slaves are to be treated—without addressing the technical legal consequences. The same is true of criminal law and the Qur'anic statements about three particularly problematical areas: violent clashes, business relationships and intoxicating substances. No real detailed legal regulations with punitive sanctions are laid down; rather, moral demands are made and ethical instructions for action are given.

Test cases: blood vengeance, the prohibition of usury, the ban on alcohol

Although they are less fundamental than the 'five pillars' of Islam, quite specific rules of behaviour were visibly to shape the inner life of the Islamic community and bring it under control. They became characteristics which set Muslims apart from 'unbelievers' and gave them a sense of belonging, of being different—and probably better.

– At the time the age-old Arab custom of *blood vengeance*, killing the guilty party as 'retribution' (*qisas*[19]), was not the expression of a primitive blood-lust but an archaic legal means of establishing a minimum bodily security. Individuals were protected by the solidarity of family, clan and tribe. At least after the event, a balance was achieved by the right to equivalent compensation. This was less a matter of justice than of the 'honour' (prestige, reputation) of the tribe or clan, which had to be restored.[20] However, this kind of vengeance could easily lead to a series of reciprocal killings and a limitless blood feud: the object of the blood vengeance need not necessarily be the perpetrator himself but could be some member of his community.

The Qur'an does not do away with blood vengeance, which is also practised by the Jews:[21] 'In just retribution there is life for you.'[22] However, it limits retribution in two ways: only the perpetrator may be killed and only the closest relative of the dead person (blood advocate, *wali ad-dam*) is authorized to exact blood vengeance.[23] Above all, the Qur'an does not allow blood vengeance as the sole legal means where blood has been shed. These are the Qur'anic requirements for the new community:

- the punishment may not be greater than the act to be punished;[24]
- 'forgiveness' should be practised: if possible, money is to be accepted instead of blood (blood money or atoning money: *diyah*).[25]
- if punishment takes place, the dispute is regarded as settled.[26]

– The revelation given to the merchant Muhammad is specially focused on *business morality*. Deadlines for the payment of interest were customary in Mecca at the time of Muhammad and initially the Qur'an sets usury (*riba*[27]) over against almsgiving, without directly prohibiting it: 'Whatever you may give out in usury so that it might increase through [other] people's possessions will bring no increase in the sight of God—whereas all that you give out in charity, seeking God's countenance, [will be blessed by Him;] for it is they [who thus seek His countenance] that shall have their recompense multiplied!'[28] Usury is presumably first forbidden in Medina: 'O you who have attained to faith! Do not gorge yourselves on usury, doubling and redoubling it.'[29]

Thus commercial activity is endorsed in principle but usury is forbidden: 'Those who gorge themselves on usury behave but as he might behave whom Satan has confounded by his touch ... God has made buying and selling lawful and usury unlawful.'[30] This represented a considerable change from the practice, then customary in Mecca, of doubling the sum of money or quantity of goods owed, along with the interest, if it could not be repaid at the due time. We cannot discover whether the arguments with the Jews of Medina had any influence on the prohibition of usury, but the Jews are severely censured because they 'took interest although it had been forbidden to them'.[31] The regulations for business dealings are no less important:

- Contracts entered into before witnesses or in writing are to be observed honestly.[32]
- Weighing and measuring is to be accurate and fair: 'And give full measure whenever you measure, and weigh with a balance that is true.'[33]
- Work is to stop only at the time of the Friday midday prayer.[34]

I shall consider the question of usury and the Islamic economy at length in E IV, 1.

– The Qur'anic *prohibition of wine* was evidently prompted by certain abuses. In the pre-Islamic period wine-drinking was very popular and widespread; wine was made almost everywhere in Arabia.[35] However, the wine was not necessarily wine from grapes (*khamr*), which was an expensive luxury drink imported from Syria and Lebanon. In Yemen people drank honey wine and in Medina (*nabidh*) date wine. There were not only inns selling wine on the margins of the towns but also wine merchants, mainly Jews and Christians, with transportable tent shops and wine in jars and skins, who visited the cities and the Bedouins. Places with women singers and very often games of chance (*maysir*) were not uncommon. Muhammad's companions also held drinking parties.

So, the prohibition against wine does not come from the very first period of Islam but was gradually introduced by the Prophet. In the early days (probably in the Meccan period) wine was called the gift of God.[36] Then a prohibition which was at first conditional was stated: 'In both [intoxicants and games] there is great evil as well as some benefit for man; but the evil which they cause is greater than the benefit which they bring.'[37] A prohibition against attempting 'to pray while you are in a state of drunkenness' follows.[38] Finally, as people did not change their habits, there is a direct prohibition: 'O you who have attained to faith! Intoxicants, and games of chance, and idolatrous practices, and the divining of the future are but a loathsome evil of Satan's doing: shun it, then!'[39]

Thus games of chance (*maysir*[40]), often associated with drinking wine and pre-Islamic practices, were likewise forbidden. We should remember that games of chance very often involved the slaughtering and cutting up of a whole camel (the Bedouins' real wealth) with the drawing of lots deciding who got which part and who had to pay for the camel.

Jews and Christians, who used wine in rituals, were explicitly allowed to consume it. And as the word *khamr* (= grape wine) is used in the Qur'an, while Arabic has around a hundred names for wine, the prohibition against wine was easily evaded. Therefore quite a few Islamic scholars have disputed that the Qur'anic prohibition of wine includes all alcoholic drinks. This is just one indication of how burdensome many Muslims over the centuries have found this particular precept. On the other hand the Islamic food regulations, being relatively few by comparison with the numerous Jewish ones, and which probably mostly had to do with hygiene, caused hardly any difficulties within the Muslim community. The Islamic food laws allowed the enjoyment of 'the good things' that God gives to men and women. Only the flesh of animals which have died, been sacrificed to idols or have not been ritually slaughtered, together with blood and pork, was forbidden food.[41] It is not difficult for Muslims to refrain from pork, since this meat is as repulsive to them as dog meat is to most Europeans. Like the Jews, they regard the pig, wallowing in the mire, as an unclean animal, and therefore pig-keeping is almost unknown in Islamic countries. But in contrast to Judaism, the food laws in Islam are no more complicated than those in Christianity.

The new responsibility of the individual

Through the Qur'an, individual Muslims were directly called on to change their lives. That was new. In Arab tribal society, loyalty was primarily to the wider family and secondarily to the clan. The individual counted for relatively little; in the desert the individual was in any case lost; without the protection of the family or the clan individuals were nothing. Therefore individuals had to do everything they could to preserve group solidarity (*'asabiyah*) towards their family and their clan and devote themselves uncompromisingly to this. Bedouins have no term for individuality or personality. The nearest term, 'face' (*wajh*), applied above all to the head of the clan, the sheikh—not, though, as an individual person but as representative of the clan who, usually having been chosen by the elders of the most respected and richest families, always ruled together with his council. So, at the level of leadership, it was not an individual who ruled (monocracy) but a group of people, exclusively male (collegiality).

The consistent monotheism that Muhammad proclaimed was aimed not only at a new community but also at a new individual responsibility. Muslims were to achieve this in a better way: if there is only one God and this God is the creator, sustainer and judge of human beings, then individuals assume a special dignity; they are no longer playthings in the hands of several rival deities, nor mere objects in an all-determining system of clans and tribes but the creatures of this one God, indeed his 'successors' (representatives),[42] responsible to him.

Direct responsibility before God: original Islam does not know mediators, whether priests or saints; even the Prophet himself is no mediator. The *islam* of men and women, their submission, is to God alone. They bow before the face of God in daily prayer and make the great pilgrimage of their lives for God's sake. Before God they humble themselves in fasting and at God's command they give alms, symbolic of a renunciation of greed and of responsibility for other members of the community. More than any others, these practices make it clear that a person is a Muslim, takes his or her place in the community of faith, and is on the right path.

Thus all individuals stand in a personal relationship to God, who has created them, sustains them and will judge them, indeed who keeps a precise account of their deeds, good and evil. This book will be opened at the Day of Judgement. All individuals are responsible for their salvation. And even the performance of particular rites, including daily prayer, is not sufficient to put one's relationship with God in order. The recognition that human beings are creatures of the one God calls for a reversal of thought and a change of lifestyle: no more conceit and arrogance, no more showing off with possessions and powerful relatives; no more discrimination against the weak; no more embezzling of the property of others and no more lying, deception and unbridled violence, but firm belief in God and obedience to God's will, which leads to true wisdom and the attainment of valuable virtues: 'Whoever is granted wisdom has indeed been granted wealth abundant.'[43]

Arab and Muslim virtues

Thus, against the glorification of clan and tribal group, the martial pride and sometimes also the hedonism of the Bedouin, the Qur'an sets out an ideal of modesty and restraint. This is not a morality of weakness, softness and cowardice; the old Arab virtues are not denied but deepened. In this way there is a far-reaching revaluation of traditional notions of values which seems to be legitimized by God:

- The courage of the seasoned Bedouins in battle and in the defence of their own clans is revived, becoming dedication to the new faith and a readiness for sacrifice for one's faith community.
- Patience in the face of all the adversities of unpredictable desert life is made fruitful again for an unshakable faith in God in the face of all tribulations and temptations.
- The generosity of spontaneous giving is re-orientated and focused on a limited and therefore regular giving to the poor and weak.

The recognition of the nature of human beings as God's creatures also brings forth new, specifically Islamic, virtues:

- If human beings are God's creatures, then humility, not arrogance, must be shown: God does not love those 'who, full of self-conceit, act in a boastful manner'.[44] God 'does not love those who are given to arrogance'.[45]
- If human beings are God's creatures, then their basic attitude must be gratitude: not just calling on God in distress and forgetting him when the danger is past.[46] 'God will requite all who are grateful to him.'[47]
- If God is the creator of all human beings, then graciousness and brotherliness ('brotherliness and sisterliness' would be anachronistic) is to be shown between people: through faith, God has made former enemies friends, indeed brothers.[48] Believers, men and women, are friends with one another,[49] and generosity and friendliness are to prevail.

What about the law of retribution? It is by no means typical of Islam, for the Qur'an also knows of forgiveness. One may recompense evil with evil, but forgiveness is better.[50] God is ready to forgive anyone who is ready to forgive.[51] Muslims are even recommended to recompense evil with good: 'But [since] good and evil cannot be equal, repel thou [evil] with something that is better—and lo! he between whom and thyself was enmity [may then become] as though he had [always] been close [unto thee], a true [friend]! Yet [to achieve] this is not given to any but those who are wont to be patient in adversity; it is not given to any but those endowed with the greatest good fortune!'[52] Will such a new ethic of the individual also have an effect on society?

3. The religious and social transformation

The new vision of the community, like that of the individual, resulted in a transformation of society. The new shared convictions, rites and ethical standards bound together the families, clans and tribes which had previously been segmented and also markedly antagonistic into a new Arab society. The traditional tribal structures were not suppressed but given another layer. Muhammad did not want to abolish the existing social structure; he was no revolutionary. However, he did want to make decisive changes and improvements; he was a radical reformer and renewer. Thus, he sparked off a movement that, in this fundamental phase of Islamic history, did not primarily bring outward expansion and mission but renewal and consolidation within. The economic institutions responsible for the production and distribution of material goods hardly changed in this new society. However, on the basis of changed religious and cultural aims, values, standards and institutions—the family institutions (the wider family, clan, tribe) and the political institutions responsible for the organization of rule, the resolution of conflicts and defence (the founding of a state), were changed. This resulted in the beginning of a new Arab civilization.

The stabilization of marriage and family

On the basis of recent research,[53] one thing becomes clear about marriage and the family in pre-Islamic Arabia: it was hardly a fixed system. In the period immediately before Muhammad the patrilinear system of kinship seems to have predominated but, beyond doubt, there was also the matrilinear system, where only descent from the mother counted. Polyandric marriage was also customary: a woman could have several husbands, with different degrees of permanence and different degrees of responsibility towards any offspring. Temporary marriages (*mut'a*) were also permitted; here the borderline with prostitution was fluid and promiscuity was easily possible.

By contrast, the Qur'an decisively affirms the institutions of marriage and family. The family is particularly emphasized as being among the many good things that God has given human beings: 'And God has given you mates of your own kind and has given you, through your mates, children and children's children.'[54] All in all, the Qur'an brought about considerable stabilization of the family, through the following precepts:

- strict regulations against incest, important not only for the biological legacy but also for the creation of ties of marriage between the different families;

- condemnation of polyandric marriage, because it undermines the stability of the family (the parallel question of marriage to several wives is not put);
- physical paternity must be acknowledged, hence the insertion of periods of waiting, for example, in the case of divorce.

What are the purposes of marriage? First, the procreation of descendants, which, corresponding to a deeply-rooted human tendency, were of vital importance for clans and tribes, at that time more threatened with dying out than with over-population. Having children accords with the will of God, who is himself the real creator of all children.[55]

Second, the fellowship between man and woman, parents and children. The bond between husband and wife is a sign of God in his creation: 'And among His wonders is this: He creates for you mates out of your own kind, so that you might incline towards them, and He engenders love and tenderness between you.'[56]

In view of widespread promiscuity, a third purpose is the satisfaction, institutionalization and regulation of sexual intercourse. The unmarried, whether man or woman, are to 'live in continence'.[57] Sexual intercourse outside marriage is not allowed.[58] However, men are allowed concubines from the ranks of their slave girls as they wish—and also several wives. This brings us to a point that is difficult to explain to non-Muslims.

The affirmation of polygamy is regarded as typically Islamic, though it was widespread in the ancient Near East, as, say, the Hebrew Bible shows (for example, Abraham!). In these warrior societies polygamy probably also had the purpose of providing for the widows of warriors and dealing with the surplus of women brought about by war which was usually high. This is what the Qur'an says about polygamy: 'And if you have reason to fear that you might not act equitably towards orphans, then marry from among [other] women such as are lawful to you—[even] two, three, or four.'[59] However, the husband is to treat all his wives equally and fairly; otherwise he is to marry only one wife: 'But if you have reason to fear that you might not be able to treat them with equal fairness, then [only] one—or [from among] those whom you rightfully possess. This will make it more likely that you will not deviate from the right course.'[60]

As an excuse for polygamy, it has sometimes been asserted that the Qur'an restricted the polygyny previously customary in Arabia. However, first, we know hardly anything about any polygyny in pre-Islamic Arabia (though we do know of polyandry, marriage with several husbands). Secondly, the Qur'anic passage does not impose a limitation. Translated literally, it says: 'Marry what women please you, two, three, and four.'[61] The regulation that a Muslim may have only four legal wives (plus an unlimited number of slave-girls as concubines) would then be a later ruling by Islamic jurists. What, then, is the role of the woman in the Qur'an?

Women—highly valued or discriminated against?

What was new in the Qur'an, and a positive improvement for many women, was that several wives were not to live together (usually with their brothers), with their husbands visiting them for longer or shorter periods. Rather, several wives (some certainly widows, whose husbands had perished in the numerous warlike clashes) were to have their own rooms in a new husband's household ('virilocal polygyny'), in order to find support and protection.[62]

In principle in the Qur'an husband and wife are equal before God, because both have been created by God:[63] 'As for anyone—be it man or woman—who does righteous deeds, and is a believer withal—him shall We most certainly cause to live a good life; and most certainly shall We grant unto such as these their reward in accordance with the best that they ever did.'[64] Nevertheless, there can hardly be any question of equal rights for women and men. The husband's privileges in the wider family dominated by the patriarch and comprising the father, his sons and their family, remain intact. The husband takes the initiative in making and dissolving a marriage and has the say in financial and other matters.

The far superior legal position of the husband should not lead us to overlook the fact that the Qur'an calls for even greater mutual respect and sensitivity. The relative independence of the individual in the family alliance is also important. In particular, rights are secured for women that they did not have in pre-Islamic times:

- The wife can own property in her own name and need not contribute to the support of the family from it.
- The wife has the right to inherit up to a quarter of her husband's property.
- If a rapid or arbitrary divorce threatens, postponement, reconciliation and mediation is required from the families.
- In the case of divorce the wife retains her dowry.

Thus we can understand why many Muslim women concerned for reform today are calling for a return to the Qur'an, for some legal restrictions customary for women do not in fact derive from the Qur'an, but are later juristic rulings by men. For example, there is not a word in the Qur'an about that custom which today Muslims and non-Muslims regard as typically Islamic: the wearing of the veil or headscarf by women. We shall be discussing all the problems posed here for the present day in Part D.

The Islamic constitution—a divine state

Even had Muhammad wanted it, given all the anarchic and separatist tendencies it would have been an illusion to think that the tribal society of Arabia could be replaced by a completely new society. Therefore the Prophet, a great realist, strove not for the replacement but for the federation of the Arab clans and tribes. In the Prophet's lifetime an Islamic constitution developed from this in the form of a confederation the core of which was the community of Medina. Muhammad succeeded in extending this confederation not only to Mecca but also to the whole of western and central Arabia, through the more or less willing association of various Bedouin tribes. Naturally the supreme head of this new constitution was the Prophet himself as 'God's messenger'. Thus in a short time the leader of a persecuted minority had become the organizer of a relatively tightly-ordered community.

This Islamic community did not yet have the legal and administrative features of a modern state. But we are surely right to speak of a state, the 'effective structure of an institutionalized rule extending over a wider area'.[65] This was a fairly closed and sovereign community which was:

- independent of external control and at the same time aimed at the control of neighbouring territories;
- no longer a fragmented society of rival and warring tribes and clans but a relatively united and centralized political structure.[66]

Among the Bedouin tribes, some of which were proud 'noble' warrior tribes, Muhammad's agents, with the introduction of almsgiving (usually paid in camels), marked the beginnings of a political integration. This was later continued by the recruitment of contingents of troops (through agents of the caliph) for the armies of conquest and by their regular payment, along with shares of plunder and land. But whatever worldly motives may also have been at work here, without Islam as an ideological basis this political integration would have been inconceivable. 'Ideologically and organizationally, then, the Islamic state had resources upon which it could draw to override the tribal loyalties that had traditionally been the stumbling block in the path of successful political integration in pre-state Arabia.'[67] Conversely, Islam deeply shaped the state that was coming into being. From the beginning its characteristics were exclusivity, theocracy and militancy:

– *Exclusivity*: on the basis of the treaty of Medina, non-Muslims too were originally members of Muhammad's community, especially the Jews, so strongly represented in Medina. However, after the successive elimination of the Jewish tribes the community became exclusively Muslim. At first, Jews and also Christians were tolerated in Arabia, until they were driven out under the second caliph, 'Umar. He wanted Arabia to be purely Muslim. This is a decisive point for understanding Islam: though initially the intensity of the religious and political following of the Prophet differed considerably—and the Qur'an tells us there were also some 'hypocrites' (unreliable people) as well as the true 'believers'—soon it was no longer disputed that the whole of the religious and political life of the state was subject to laws which did not come from man but from God.

– *Theocracy*: here the difference from Christianity is evident. The Christian community or church was outside the state (whether Jewish or Roman), even in conflict with it, and sometimes persecuted by it (Christian P I). Even in the Byzantine mode of a 'symphony' of throne and altar it remained completely distinct from the state (P II). In the Roman Catholic model, under the influence of Augustine and the popes there was an explicit antagonism between church ('God's state') and state ('the worldly state'). Things were quite different right from the beginning in the Muslim community (Islamic P I). It formed the core around which the Islamic state was built up. Here religious and state institutions were, in principle, identical. The Islamic commonwealth is both a religious community and a political community, a 'divine state', where there is no separation between state and religion. They are fused in an indissoluble unity. This Islamic state is a theocracy, the rule of God, in the full sense of the word. However, we should note that time and again in Christianity, too, there were models of the integration of political and religious community: church state/Vatican state, the Anabaptist kingdom of Münster, Geneva in the time of Calvin, and others.

Given the circumstances, it was not surprising that, in Islam, alms for the poor and needy, initially left to the discretion of the individual and then mandatory in Medina, in fact developed into a kind of state tax, though in view of the tremendous amount of plunder from the conquests and the rich tax income from the subjected peoples which soon flowed in, this eventually represented a somewhat modest sum. As we saw, Muhammad sent agents to the nomadic tribes to raise taxes there; after the Prophet's death some of them attempted to withdraw. Muslim legal scholars worked out the most precise guidelines for this state tax with a religious basis.

– *Militancy*: here a further difference from the Christian community or church is striking. The Christian community is committed, by the message, behaviour and fate of its founder, to non-violence—despite what violent 'Christian' rulers (emperors, kings, bishops and popes) and believers made of the original

Christian ideal once Christianity became a state religion. The Islamic community, in which state and religion coincided from the beginning, is quite different: Muhammad understood it to be a fighting community which was allowed to fight with the sword. Indeed, war as a political means was not only affirmed in principle but, when necessary, waged without any great inhibitions. Thus from its origins Islam has had a militant character, fighting for God—in this respect it is closer to early Judaism and its 'Yahweh wars' than to early Christianity.

However, to counter widespread clichés, at the same time it should be added that alongside readiness for war there is an unmistakable Muslim readiness for peace. Muhammad himself already made peace with the Meccans through the treaty of Hudaybiyah. This illustrates that in Islam military clashes can also be avoided and settled. The peace treaties which the Prophet made with the Christian communities of Najran in the south and Dumat al-Jandal in the north and with the remaining Jews in Medina and Khaybar formed the basis for the behaviour of Muslim conquerors and for a coming Islamic international law. Jews and Christians (and then also the Zoroastrians) were explicitly assured tolerance (not equal rights!) as 'people of the book', who had likewise received a revelation from God. Tolerance (not equal rights!) was explicitly assured, whereas the polytheism against which the Prophet had campaigned was uncompromisingly contested.

Quite apart from any theology, in the face of the quite concrete history of the Prophet and his community a fundamental historical question arises: what is Islamic and what is Arab–Bedouin?

What is Islamic and what is Arab–Bedouin?

In my description of the foundation of the paradigm of the original Islamic community (P I), I hope it became evident that, even in its very first realization, the essence of Islam must not be identified with its historical form. Rather, a distinction must be made between the substance (essence) of Islamic faith and the historical constellation of convictions, values and modes of procedure (the paradigm) current at the time. Some things that flowed into the realization of Islam in this first phase of Islamic history evidently did not follow from its essence of Islam, as laid down in the Qur'anic revelation, but were the consequence of the historical constellation given at the time.

As the Hamburg Islamic expert Albrecht Noth has remarked, from the beginning there was a 'juxtaposition—which could express itself as symbiosis, alternation or even opposition—of new Islamic regulations and older tribal norms of behaviour': the 'tension between Islam and tribalism' is 'an essential, if not *the* essential, characteristic of early Islamic history'.[68]

In other words, the first paradigm of Islam is the result of the radical religious impulses, values and requirements of the Qur'an on the one hand and the circumstances of pre-Islamic Arabic Bedouin tribal culture, which it overlaid and embraced, on the other. Ira M. Lapidus has demonstrated this in investigations which are both compact and highly differentiated. In the creation of a Muslim community in Mecca and Medina we have 'the formation of an overarching religiously defined community as an integrating force in a lineage society'.[69] According to Lapidus, two levels can be distinguished in the complex value system which came into being here: 'In principle the Qur'an introduced a concept of transcendent reality which was opposed to the values of tribal culture'; but 'in practice the family and lineage structures of Arabian peoples became part of Islamic society'.[70]

From this double perspective, even at this initial stage we can hardly avoid questioning the first paradigm of Islam. Those of a traditional frame of mind may not perhaps want to hear them but, in a historical perspective, they must also be pressing for Muslims. Indeed many Muslims raise them—not to write off the past or even a whole paradigm but to gain a new horizon for the future.

Questions: Tensions between Islam and the Bedouins

- What in Islam was introduced by the Qur'an and what was given by the Arab society of the time?
- What in this first concrete historical realization of Islam (P I) is, in principle and essentially, Islamic, and what is, in practice and in fact, Arab–Bedouin?
- May structures, values and norms that manifestly come from Arab tribal culture claim the same validity for all times as the truths and principles which stem directly from the Qur'anic revelation?

At the end of his life the Prophet could look back on a vision that had been fulfilled and on an amazing work. However, the first paradigm of Islam that he himself had grounded so solidly had to stand its first test. This came with his death, in 632.

4. From the Prophet to the Prophet's representative

'The greatest misfortune'? The death of the Prophet? We read this often on Muslim tombstones.[71] The young Islamic community found it difficult to cope with Muhammad's death. However far-sighted the Prophet had been in many respects, he had neglected to arrange his successor in time. Did he think that because of the uniqueness of his call and the direct divine legitimization of his office he would not be able to find a successor? He did not need one for worldly 'interests' such as finances, law and war: surely his closest companions, the 'Prophet's companions' (*ashab*), would be able to cope with these matters? Be this as it may, the Muslim community, which was only ten years old—dating it from the emigration—and organized only in broad outline, needed leadership if it was to survive.

Who is to lead?

Scarcely was Muhammad buried in his house in Medina (in the place where today his tomb is within the 'Mosque of the Prophet') than disputes over his successor began. On the one hand there were the 'helpers' of Medina, who felt disadvantaged by comparison with the Meccans, whom Muhammad had preferred in the distribution of plunder. Should they simply nominate their own leaders for the warlike actions that were envisaged? On the other hand were many Bedouin tribes. They had promised the Prophet personal allegiance but always rejected the efforts of his tribe, the Quraysh, to gain dominance. Should they continue to feel bound to their promise of loyalty after the death of Muhammad? Why constantly pay taxes and permanently perform possibly unpopular religious duties? So an apostasy movement (*riddah*: 'apostasy' from Islam), whether with primarily political or religious motivation, began to gain ground rapidly. A decade after the Hijrah the community, composed of so many elements, threatened to fall apart.

How was this crisis in leadership to be resolved? By a new Prophet? But such a person could not be seen, either in Medina or in Mecca, and was hardly to be expected. According to the Qur'an Muhammad is 'the seal of the prophets', though at first 'seal' was not understood as 'conclusion' but as 'confirmation'.[72] Yet efficient leadership was now desperately needed if the community was to survive.

I intend to trace the history of Islam through the four caliphs of Medina,[73] not because I am overestimating the rulers[74] and neglecting the development of the structures. As I have already emphasized, the concrete history can be comprehensively described only in the dialectic of structures and persons. The 'factual history' of the actions of individuals or contingent individual events does not lie on the surface but is at the centre of the historical processes of social history.[75]

The question of the prophetic succession is also a question of structures and persons. The companions of the Prophet, one might call them the Prophet's apostles, were clearly aware of the danger of a split: after the Prophet's death the Bedouin tribes apostatized, fell away from the faith, and the old murderous tribal realities threatened to break out again, particularly in Medina. If tribes were once again to choose their own leaders, the smaller tribes and those who had emigrated from Medina would suffer. The consequences would be devastating. So there was pressure to find a rapid solution.

The choice of a successor: Abu Bakr, the first caliph

The debate lasted a whole night and it was decided that a 'successor', a 'representative' for Muhammad, a caliph (*khalifah*), must be chosen.[76] The choice fell on a man who was one of the first in Mecca to believe in the Prophet's mission: Abu Bakr.[77] Muhammad's father-in-law (the Prophet married his daughter 'A'ishah), he was originally a Qurayshi and an emigrant. He had been a friend of Muhammad all his life and was one of his closest administrative and military advisers. But probably the decisive factor in choosing him was that the Prophet himself had appointed him leader of the farewell pilgrimage and during his terminal illness leader of the prayers (*imam*).

So Abu Bakr followed Muhammad in leading the community. His election, by a larger group without special authority, was ratified next day by the whole community. In the mosque in Medina Abu Bakr simply declared that he wanted to follow the *sunnah* (custom, example) of the Prophet and as long as he obeyed that, all were to obey him. He had been given the nickname 'the truthful' (*as-siddiq*). By all accounts he was a personally modest, unpretentious man but also capable of energetic action. Now he was concerned not only with the daily ritual prayer and Friday prayer but also and above all with worldly political matters: law, finances and the waging of war. It is important for the whole history of Islam that from the beginning, in the original community and now also among the caliphs, there was no place for a purely worldly authority. The introduction of the caliphate (*khalifah*) meant that

- immediate guidance by the Prophet as the one who received, proclaimed and carried out divine revelations was replaced by guidance from the Prophet's representative (*khalifah*);
- there was no longer a legitimation that renewed itself through new divine revelations. There was only the derived human authority of a non-prophetic leader: no longer a 'spokesman' of God but at best a 'conversation partner' with God;
- the institution of the caliphate took the place of the charismatic leader, office the place of charisma, and tradition the place of prophecy. Charismatic rule was legalized, made traditional and everyday.[78]

The Prophet's representative was not himself a prophet, nor even primarily a religious authority, but a political and legal authority, something like a supreme tribal sheikh who had to lead the whole Muslim community, mediate and make decisions in disputes and assume the supreme leadership. The tasks of the caliph were so new that they had not been laid down. Nor is there anything about them in the Qur'an. The word 'caliph' certainly occurs often in the Qur'an, but at no point does it clearly stand for a possible political and religious successor to the Prophet in leading the community. Surely it isn't surprising that, at a very early stage, there was a dispute among Muslims about the characteristics and competences of the caliph and the way of appointing him?

However, now Muslims became more and more aware of one thing (later, appeals about this were made even to Abu Bakr[79]): though the Prophet was no longer among the living, the Qur'an remained, alive and indestructible, as the eternal word of God. In these new circumstances loyalty to the person of the Prophet was replaced by loyalty to his message (kerygma). Though, in Islam, the religious has a political dimension and the political has religious premises, two aspects of the succession need to be distinguished:

- In the political succession the caliph, as permanent successor to God's messenger, replaced Muhammad the statesman. The caliphate had to become an institution which was primarily political.
- In the religious succession, the Prophet Muhammad was replaced by the Qur'an (only later brought together as a book) and the example of God's messenger, the Sunnah. There was no supreme teaching office. In the long run the Qur'an (part of the essence of Islam) became *the* religious (and indirectly also the political) authority.

The Prophet, who had brought about this fundamental shift by comparison with the pagan prehistory of 'ignorance' (*jahiliyah*), thus remained the spiritual leader, the model for perfect ritual and ethical behaviour. In the political sphere, though, it was the caliphs who, with their conquests and inner disputes (schisms), drew the guidelines for the future: the eschatological ideas and the Bedouin ideal of freedom retreated in favour of a structured government, a 'state'.[80]

Abu Bakr was to be granted a reign of only two years, yet in those years something decisive happened for which the Prophet himself had already prepared: the transition from the desert to the high cultures.

From the desert to the confrontation with the high cultures

If we do not simply take over uncritically the retrospective accounts of later Muslim historians, according to whom Abu Bakr initiated the conquest by sending out four emirs, the question necessarily arises: how could the amazingly successful campaigns of conquest which now followed have come about? How could a people from remote desert cities on the periphery of the high cultures all at once possess giant territories of the two great empires of the time, Byzantium and Persia?

Recent research has shown that developments within domestic policy led to the advances in foreign policy. The tasks of the caliph were primarily domestic policy, and Abu Bakr seems to have tackled them with energy, shrewdness and consistency: the apostasy movement (*riddah*) had to be stopped, the rule of the Islamic community re-established and the true religion of Arabia consolidated everywhere.[81] Evidently the power of the message of the Qur'an was not, in itself, enough to hold together the tribes won over by the Prophet: military force was needed and indeed, in the future, military successes often helped the message to break through.[82]

With a few well-aimed blows Abu Bakr subjected the apostate Bedouin tribes, enforced the payment of alms and established Islam beyond the territories dominated by Muhammad. It would become even clearer in the future that unless the now ruling Muslim élites of Medina and Mecca exercised moderate political control over the Arab tribes, above all the Bedouins, no political integration and no formation of a state would be possible. For these enterprises the caliph depended on the leadership qualities, military knowledge and wide-ranging relationships of the Meccan elite which, a short time previously, had been hostile to the Muslims and especially to the 'helpers' of Medina. However, all now had shared interests in the act of subjection. Thus united, the Muslims defeated a very hostile tribal federation in the battle of al-'Aqraba' (in Central Arabia) in 633.

These victories had consequences. The subject tribes continued to put pressure on the neighbouring tribes and attempted to take advantage of them. The effects could be observed as far as Bahrain and Oman in the east and Yemen and Hadramaut in the south. An increasing number of tribes associated themselves with the powerful Islamic confederation, which now also conquered rival tribal units which had their own 'prophets' (among the four there was even a 'prophetess'), so that very soon all Arabia was Islamicized. The Islamic Ummah finally established itself as the new Arab order of power.

Furthermore, Abu Bakr supported efforts to gain plunder beyond Arabia, in Syria, Iraq and Iran, by raids and surprise attacks. In this way, after the battles within Arabia against the apostasy (the *riddah* wars), the Bedouin powers, which had been thus set free, were diverted outwards and especially northwards. What had begun as 'raids' (*ghazawat*) against original tribes soon became a war against the great power of Byzantium, which of course could not tolerate such attacks and therefore sent an army to southern Palestine. Abu Bakr sent his most competent general, Khalid ibn al-Walid (the 'sword of God'), from

Iraq to Palestine to take supreme command against the Byzantines. For the first time the Arabs were now operating not only as separate bold fighting squads but also as a real army consisting of many small units. Finally—probably to the surprise of both sides—this army defeated the Byzantine troops at the battle of Aghnadayn in 634.

This victory immeasurably increased the enthusiasm for war and the certainty of victory among the Arabs. People were no longer content with individual campaigns for plunder. Now they could set out on the conquest of territories previously controlled by the great powers. Without the two sides really being aware of it, this was to lead to a great confrontation between Islam and Christianity.

5. The original community expands

During the lifetime of the Prophet Muhammad, as we saw, the Qurayshi, who were the leading stratum of Muhammad's ancestral city, were first threatened with force of arms, then won over with shrewd diplomacy, and finally rewarded with the rich plunder of war. However, for the companions of the Prophet in battle, who had already vigorously complained about their small share of the plunder, it was now even more important that after the death of the Prophet the religious message of Islam was not completely sold out to the Qurayshi aristocracy of merchants and warriors. Long before Muhammad, their main interest was the economic and political control of the greater part of Arabia. But after the joint subjugations by the Meccans and Medinans under the leadership of the first caliphs, a renewed emphasis on the religious aspect of Arab politics was particularly urgent. A specifically Islamic policy was called for.

Islamic politics: 'Umar, the second caliph

People learned from the crisis after the death of the Prophet, so before his death (in 634) the first caliph, Abu Bakr, nominated a specific successor. Although a Meccan, unlike the aristocrats of Mecca this successor seemed to guarantee the continuation of the religiously motivated politics of the Prophet. His name was 'Umar ibn al-Khattab.

'Umar was one of the oldest of the Prophet's Meccan companions in battle, who had taken part in the Hijrah. Like Abu Bakr, he had been a father-in-law (through his daughter Hafsah) of Muhammad and his constant adviser. He, too, had supported the election of Abu Bakr and had acted in constant agreement with the first caliph. He now proved to be an excellent leader and organizer and thus in every respect suited for the succession. Popular Western historical accounts liked to suggest that the history of the first caliphs was a history only of intrigues, violent actions and murder. That is not the case. ‘Umar, like Abu Bakr before him, became a successor to the Prophet in a peaceful consensus, and largely fulfilled the expectations pinned on him, in religion, politics and military activities.

The second caliph began by limiting the influence of the powerful Qurayshi politicians:

– In both Medina and Mecca he favoured the most distinguished ‘companions of the Prophet’ (*sahaba*) and the Medinan ‘helpers’ (*ansar*). He gave them posts as governors, military commands and administrative positions, with the highest salaries (the earlier the conversion to Islam, the higher the payment), and allowed them to put to their own use plunder which really belonged to the community. At the same time he attempted, as far as possible, to limit the involvement of the Qurayshi élite in the new campaigns of conquest.

– He called himself not only ‘Successor to the Messenger of God’ (*khalifat rasul Allah*, or *khalifat Allah*: ‘God’s representative’), like Abu Bakr, but also ‘commander of the faithful’ (*amir al-mu’minin*). In this way, he combined the new authority of the supreme head of the Muslim community with the traditional authority of the elected tribal leader.

– Finally, he introduced the specifically Islamic reckoning of time ‘after the Hijrah’. This was constantly to bring to mind the bond between the conquered territories and the original community and to banish the old Qurayshi history into the dark age of idolatry now past. This must have added to the offence taken by the leading Meccans at the political course of the second caliph. They therefore attempted, in their own way, to gain influence in the newly-conquered territories. Indeed, in the long run they could not be avoided, since the conquered territories were enormous.

A shift of political balance from the desert to cultivated areas began to become evident here:

– The political centre of gravity of the original Islamic community was increasingly formed by the desert cities of Mecca and Medina. The political and military ambitions and operations of the generation of the Prophet’s companions were initially still concentrated on the Arabian peninsula. The internal union and renewal of Arab society was at first in the foreground.

– However, the more the Muslims came in contact and confrontation with the cultivated land of the great empires, the more the current leadership of the original community had to concentrate on the newly-conquered provinces: Syria, Iraq and Egypt. Thus external expansion also increasingly governed the development of early Islamic rule.

A question arises that is important for us, to which scholars have given very different answers: what are the reasons for the amazing expansion of the Arabs from the desert into cultivated land?

How was Arab–Islamic expansion possible?

One answer lies with their opponents. Byzantium and Persia, the great powers of the region, had been fatally weakened by a policy of revenge which lasted for decades and were also internally unstable. In 614 the Persians had so thoroughly defeated the Byzantines that they were able to occupy Syria and Egypt and advance to the Mediterranean, the *Mare nostrum* ('our sea') of the Romans (soon after that, the rise of the Frankish empire began to fill the power vacuum in the West). Only fifteen years later the Byzantine emperor Heraklios, using all his forces, won back all the Eastern territories and in 639 the cross was triumphally brought back to Jerusalem. Jerusalem—Christian? Not for long.

The Byzantines had, as it were, celebrated the wrong victory and exhausted their forces on the wrong enemy. It must certainly be a legend that during his lifetime the Prophet Muhammad sent a letter to the Byzantine emperor (and to the Persian great king) inviting them to submit and accept Islam, for in 630 Muhammad would have been glad simply to be able to enter Mecca for the first time. But it is certainly true that now, in the middle of the 630s, a power was developing in the Arabian desert that had been underestimated in the glittering capitals of the Byzantine and Persian empires. After the victory of Aghnadayn, in 634, the new caliph 'Umar was able to exploit the success for the Muslim cause.

Does the weakness of the opponents explain the force of this sudden and powerful military expansion? This thrust must not be confused with the earlier and slow Arab infiltration and migration into the cultivated lands of the north (mentioned in connection with the pre-Islamic period), as is often done in recent Western research. Sceptical scholarship (not always free from anti-religious and anti-Islamic resentment) has attempted to play down the religious factor in the conquests as far as possible and bring together all the possible non-religious factors. In the introduction to his excellent book on the *Early Islamic Conquests*, Fred McGraw Donner of Chicago reports all earlier attempts to explain the conquest and then makes a thorough investigation of the causes of the Arab expansion. His conclusion is that neither hunger, over-population, the drying out of the Arab pastureland (none of which have been verified), the collapse of the luxury trade (which at best would affect only certain circles) nor the efforts of the Bedouins (who notoriously despised agricultural life and farmers) to settle are sufficient explanations of the organized military expansion of the Arabs.

By contrast, there seems good reason to suppose that, behind the expansion, there was a deliberate policy of conquest and settlement on the part of the leading Islamic élites in Medina and Mecca, the 'helpers' and the Quraysh, particularly to keep the Bedouin tribes under control. As many members of the tribe as possible were to be recruited for the army, enticed by every conceivable attraction (such as a regular income, an interesting life or plunder) and be settled in the new garrison cities. In this way, the considerable warlike energy of the Bedouins, who otherwise would have been rivals waging little wars in Arabia, could be exploited for greater political and economic ends.

The organizational concentration and unprecedented penetrative power with which the policy was implemented could not have been achieved without the capacity of the new Islamic state for integration and the spiritual power of the new religion. Fred Donner's conclusion has become established among scholars: 'The Muslims succeeded, then, primarily because they were able to organize an effective conquest movement, and in this context the impact of the new religion of Islam, which provided the ideological underpinnings for this remarkable breakthrough in social organization, can be more fully appreciated. In this sense, the conquests were truly an *Islamic* movement. For it was Islam—the set of religious beliefs preached by Muhammad, with its social and political ramifications—that ultimately sparked the whole integration process and hence was the ultimate cause of the conquests' success.'[83] Thus Western research today can no longer exclude as a possibility what has always been the traditional Islamic view: 'the possibility that the ideological message of Islam itself filled some or all of the ruling élite with the notion that they had an essentially religious duty to extend the political domain of the Islamic state as far as practically possible: that is, the élite may have organized the Islamic conquest movement because they saw it as their divinely ordained mission to do so'. So how was the Arab expansion possible? Even where worldly factors played a role, 'it was Islam that provided the ideological sanction for such a conviction'.[84]

There were three main reasons why the Islamic Arabs were such dangerous opponents to the two great powers of the time:[85]

– *A religious motivation for war.* This was a struggle (*jihad*) for 'God's cause' against the 'unbelievers': a highly meritorious battle for which the Qur'an campaigns (or threatens) intensively. It promises the individual warrior—quite apart from wages and the attraction of plunder—heavenly rewards and, if he dies, immediate entry into paradise.

– *Voluntary associations.* There was no universal conscription. The troops mostly consisted of groups of adult and free Muslims, often ready to die, who had resolved to join the army because of the convincing attractions. The armies were amazingly small (no mass migration of whole tribes, but no wild hordes) but received constant personal support and reinforcement from their tribal homeland.

– *Superior tactics.* Using fast camels and horses (initially few), lusting for battle and tried in warfare, they operated in the same area in several small, autonomous, well-formed units. That explains the unusual mobility, great flexibility and art of rapid improvisation. As a fighting force they were difficult to defeat, and could not be defeated at all by heavy armies of a traditional kind.[86]

The first wave of conquest and the great confrontation with Christianity

Christian Constantinople and Persian Ctesiphon soon felt the Muslim superiority. For an amazing thing had happened: after their first victory over the Byzantines in 634 the Arabs were capable of advancing in three directions at almost the same time. They achieved this without seeming to have anything like a general staff plan or a broad strategic concept with clear war aims and well-thought-out military tactics; certainly there was no central supreme command. Unlike the Prophet, the caliph took no part in waging war. Yet Caliph ʻUmar showed himself to be a great strategist, not least in leaving his capable generals sufficient legal and military scope for their military conquests (*futuh*). It is impossible to ascertain how far the caliph's influence extended, given the highly fragmentary information about both troop movements and the system of reporting between Medina and the 'front'. It is about six hundred miles from Medina to Syria or Iraq, at that time about twenty days' journey.[87] Everything happened on the constant premise of the recognition of the authority of the caliph, the 'commander of the faithful'. He was at the head of the far-reaching system of alliances which some Arab tribes and clans from the marginal zone (as yet not Islamicized) now joined.

The first thrust was against the Christian Byzantine province of Syria. Its capital, Damascus, fell as early as 635, soon followed by Baalbek and other cities, though some strongly fortified cities resisted for longer. The decisive battle was fought as early as 636 at the Yarmuk river, which flows into the Jordan south of Lake Genessaret. On the Muslim side between 20,000 and 40,000 fighters (*muqatila*) are said to have taken part (though numbers from this period must always be treated with caution). Jerusalem was captured in 638 and this city, holy to Jews and Christians, has remained in Muslim hands until our time (interrupted only by the century of the crusades). Called Al-Quds ('the sanctuary'), Jerusalem is also holy to Muslims; after Mecca and Medina it is the third holiest city of Islam, the place of the rock on which Abraham almost sacrificed his son and from which Muhammad is said to have embarked on his ascension. It should not be forgotten that the Muslims allowed the Jews to re-enter the city (they had been prohibited access after the complete destruction of Jerusalem in 135, a ban which the Christian emperors). So it is not surprising that some of the Jews who remained in Palestine felt the Muslim conquest of Palestine to be a liberation. Two years later, the Mediterranean port of Caesarea also fell; it was a centre of Christian education and theology, associated with the school of the first scholarly theologian, the Alexandrian Origen, with the names of the church historians Eusebius and Procopius, and the church teacher Basil the Great. The church library there, regarded as the most comprehensive in antiquity, was destroyed. With the conquest of the west Syrian/north Mesopotamian cities of Harran (associated with the patriarchal narratives of the Bible) and Edessa, the conquest of Syria was complete.

The conquest of the Sasanian empire (first Mesopotamia and then Persia) is regarded as the second thrust, and caused considerably fewer difficulties. The decisive battle between the Arabs (with only 6,000 to 12,000 men) and the Persians took place at al-Qadisiyyah in Iraq, south-west of Hira, at the latest in 636, resulting in the conquest of the Sasanian capital of Ctesiphon. As early as 644, not only Isfahan and other Persian cities but even Azerbaijan had been conquered. The Persian empire was destroyed, though some remote princedoms continued to offer resistance, and the Islamization of the administrative structures took decades.[88] The last important Persian great king, Yazdegerd III, was murdered by his own people as he fled. In passing, it is worth knowing that in the twentieth century the Persian Shah Reza Pahlawi, son of a Cossack commander and instigator of a coup, staged a bombastic festival in Persepolis on the anniversary of the accession of Cyrus the Great to the throne to stabilize his rule. In 1976 he wanted to replace the Islamic calendar ('after the Hijrah') with a new one (2535 'after the accession of Cyrus') to link up with the tradition of the Persian great kings, thus deliberately going back before Islam. Beyond doubt, this hastened his fall three years later at the hands of the Shiite leader Ayatollah Khomeini. As if one could simply turn back more than thirteen hundred years of Islamic rule and the shaping of society!

The conquest of Egypt – the third thrust – took place as early as 641.[89] This happened without the knowledge of the caliph, on the initiative of the Arab general 'Amr ibn al-'As. It was a particularly clear example of the largely autonomous actions of individual bodies of troops and their leaders both in waging war and concluding treaties. As a Byzantine province cut off from Byzantium since the conquest of Syria, Egypt was easy prey for the Arabs, for this granary of Byzantium was hardly urbanized and politically was utterly centralized. For the Arabs it was important not only because of its proximity to Mecca and Medina but also because of its shipyard and its strategic situation for the whole of North Africa. 643 saw the fall of Alexandria, a foundation of

Alexander the Great, cultural capital of the known world and centre of Jewish and Christian Hellenism, where philosophers and theologians such as Philo, Clement and Origen had been active. The Monophysite Copts welcomed its conquest as liberation from the yoke of Byzantine Orthodoxy, just as the Jews welcomed the conquest of Jerusalem.

After the loss of Syria and Egypt, the eastern half of Christian Byzantium was reduced to Anatolia, roughly the area of present-day Turkey. However, Anatolia and the Balkans formed the two most densely populated and richest regions of the empire, so that an attempt would ultimately be made to reconquer the lost provinces. For six centuries these had been under Roman and for three centuries under East Roman–Christian rule. The Arabs aimed at the heart of the Byzantine empire at a very early stage: as early as 660 an Arab fleet appeared before Constantinople but had to depart to settle unfinished business; two further expeditions took place in 672 and 715–18, both equally unsuccessful. Yet the situation had completely changed for Byzantium. The old frontier between the Roman and Persian empires, the Euphrates, had been done away with and there was now a new frontier between Anatolia and Syria, which had formerly belonged to one state. These two boundary changes resulted in a diversion of the flow of trade and considerable shifts in the location of the important economic centres.

All these conquests raised a second fundamental question: how could a desert people, comprising the Prophet's companions from Medina, Meccan merchants and warriors and undisciplined Bedouins, succeed not only in conquering such a giant empire but also in controlling it in the long term? The answer lies in the policy of Caliph 'Umar and the Muslim élite.

Neither assimilation of the Muslims nor conversion of the Christians

The Christian caricature of Islam, still widespread to the present day, includes the idea that Islam spread with nothing but 'fire and sword'. Historically, Arab power certainly spread, with warlike violence, over vast areas that had formerly been Christian (or Zoroastrian). But what about the Islamic religion? Were whole villages, cities, regions and provinces forcibly converted to Islam? Muslim historiography knows nothing of this and would have had no reason to keep quiet about it. Western historical research, too, has understandably not been able to shed any light here either. In reality, everything happened quite differently—at any rate in this first paradigm of Islam. We can start from the fact that the territorial extension of the Islamic state did not mean the spiritual extension of the Islamic religion.

The caliphs were not lawgivers. They had only to ensure the observance of the norms given through the Qur'an and the instructions and modes of behaviour of the Prophet and enforce customary law. But as early as 637 (after Syria had been conquered) Caliph 'Umar had taken counsel with the most important members of the original Medina community and laid down political principles to be followed in the conquered territories:

- the Bedouins were to be prevented from inflicting damage on the settled agricultural society;
- the Arab conquerors were to collaborate with the experienced chiefs, nobility and officials of the conquered lands.
- the Arabian peninsula was to be inhabited exclusively by Muslims. Jews and Christians living here were to leave the country unless they wanted to become Muslims.

We cannot discover precisely how far Caliph 'Umar was personally a great organizer but under his rule the conquered regions were militarily safeguarded, financially and politically stabilized in respect of taxation and had their legislation developed. However, the appointment of the judge, the qadi, and some expansion of the doctrine of responsibilities and the penal law were attributed to 'Umar only after the event, to provide legitimacy. The regulations of the time meant two things for the relationship between Muslims and non-Muslims outside Arabia:

– in the conquered territories the Muslims were not to assimilate to the inhabitants but to co-exist with them as an élite military caste. In 'Umar's view the Arabs were to be a 'nation in arms' and they did indeed exercise a military rule in the conquered territories. 'Umar achieved the consolidation of this rule through the establishment of large military camps (*misr*, plural *amsar*) at important crossroads where the Bedouins were 'settled' (first in tents and then in huts). This happened both through three completely new garrison cities at highly strategic points (Basra on the Persian Gulf, Kufa on the Euphrates and Fustat, the predecessor of present-day Cairo, on the Nile) and through other larger or smaller garrison towns on the periphery of existing towns or in suburbs or in villages.

'Umar thought it of the utmost importance that his Arabs, who were possibly all too impressed by alien cultures, should not be corrupted in their nature and alienated in their faith. The army was to keep to itself in these military camps or the later garrison towns, divide the plunder, gather in the alms and distribute supplies to fighters and administrators in accordance with particular rules. This was done on the Medinan model: those entitled to receive were listed by name in a tribal roll or register (*diwan*) of the army (*diwan* later became the designation for departments and, with additional qualifications, for the supreme organs of administration). In principle, the conquered territories were to be the possession of all Muslims. The conquerors were to share only in the produce of those they had subjected (often as much as half). Here the Islamic faith made an important contribution, by giving the whole system 'divine' legitimacy and thus making the regime of the caliphate also acceptable to foreigners. So, was it in the interest of the conquerors to convert the subjected non-Muslims? Not at all, for:

– Non-Muslims were not to convert to Islam but, in the first instance, to pay taxes (*jizyah*[90]) to the conquerors. Islam was understood primarily as an Arab religion, a religion for Arabs, and so it was to remain. Economic exploitation was another matter: the Muslims had few scruples here, and acted shrewdly. They had learned from the Prophet that they had to negotiate at the right moment. If people were politically submissive to them, they showed an amazing readiness to enter into treaties that often let the inhabitants (who previously had been heavily burdened with taxes by the Byzantines) live better than before. Muslims at the centre of power understood that the new empire could be stabilized economically and financially only if the earlier social and administrative order, including the tax system, remained as far as possible intact and able to function, though now in favour of the new rulers. Depending on the area and the situation, quite different agreements could be made with the subject people; very favourable treaties could be negotiated and the old Byzantine (or Sasanian) élites integrated into the new system. Without these, an ordered administration and regular tax collecting would have been impossible. As long as the governors nominated by the caliphate, key figures who were also leaders in ritual prayer and in war, kept everything under control, along with their administration, all was well.

What about the missionary religious zeal for conversion? The Arabs did not develop such zeal. Nowhere are there reports of the conversion of whole towns, villages or regions, far less of forcible conversions. There are reports that the Arabs, who levied only moderate taxes, were hailed in many places as liberators; by contrast the Orthodox Christians were extraordinarily unpopular among the Monophysite and Nestorian peoples in Egypt, Syria and Mesopotamia.

The Arabs practised segregation everywhere in this first phase of the conquests. Conversions were not wanted; Christian children were not to read the Qur'an. Conversions meant a loss of taxation and led to unnecessary problems of status among the Muslim elite and demands for the same financial privileges. At most the conversion of some Christian Arab Bedouin tribes in the marginal zones was accepted (others remained Christian) or the conversion of important individuals, for example officials, scribes or soldiers in the service of the new power. This rapidly growing number of new Muslims who were not of Arab origin (*mawali*) made an essential contribution to the gradual Islamization of the traditional institutions, though they by no means enjoyed equal rights. Conversely, conversions from Islam to another religion were strictly forbidden, later on pain of death.

In this way the new regime outside Arabia could show great tolerance. 'Unbelievers' in the strict sense, polytheists, had to be converted but those who had scriptures, who already possessed a revelation, did not. The Prophet himself had set the example when he left the cultivation of the soil to the 'people of the book'—who pragmatically included the Zoroastrians in Iran—to make for easier integration. Similarly, the caliphate regime left the non-Muslims in the conquered lands—all Christians, Jews and Zoroastrians—in peace to practise their religion. This even helped the Christian churches—such as the Nestorian Church in Iraq or the Coptic Church in Egypt—to reorganize.

This tolerance was exercised on the basis of a strict subordination:

– Muslims ruled non-Muslims and 'protected' them by granting them local religious and political autonomy. Non-Muslims had the status of 'protected minorities'; they enjoyed internal autonomy and the bodies, lives and possessions of those 'commanded to be protected' (the *dhimmi*) were protected.

– Non-Muslims were, and remained, second-class citizens, usually excluded from the uppermost ranks of government even when they formed the great majority of the population. As farmers, tradesmen and workers they paid taxes (a per capita poll tax, rent for the land and other offerings), whereas the Muslim (as agents, administrators, landlords and soldiers) distributed them. In return the non-Muslims were exempt from military service and from almsgiving (*zakat*).

However, in Egypt, until the thirteenth or fourteenth century, the tax administration was in the hands of Coptic Christian officials, as it was in Syria (where there were also many Jews). These officials also had to suffer the numerous complaints of Muslim subjects about the burden of taxation. All in all, this tolerance with subordination was a compromise between conquerors and conquered, something that always happened in the conquest of settled areas by nomadic peoples. The question was whether the kind of segregation practised by 'Umar could be maintained in the long term. It was not a good sign for the existing regime that the rule of this second caliph, known for his piety, modesty and sense of justice, who still represents the ideal of a Muslim ruler, which had proved so successful, was ended abruptly after only ten years: the 'successor of the messenger of God' and the 'commander of the faithful' was violently killed, it was said, by a slave. 'Umar died in November 644. For Muslims that was a shocking event but it was not to be the only political murder of a caliph.

6. The beginnings of Islamic theology and law

Would the companions of the Prophet and the 'helpers' in Medina be able to continue the Arab policy on a strictly Islamic course? To begin with it looked as if they would, for immediately before his murder 'Umar is said to have made provision for his followers by appointing a six-member advisory college (*shurah*). This included the two main aspirants to the succession: 'Ali ibn Abu Talib, Muhammad's cousin and son-in-law, and 'Uthman ibn 'Affan, likewise a son-in-law of the Prophet, who took part in the emigrations to Ethiopia and then to Medina but was a rich merchant from the powerful Meccan family of the Umayyah, long hostile to the Prophet.

A Meccan, not an Islamic policy: 'Uthman, the third caliph

In 644, 'Uthman ibn 'Affan (caliph from 644 to 656), an ideal candidate for the reconciliation of the two tendencies—the Meccan and the Islamic—within the Muslim community, was chosen as caliph. However, even today he remains a controversial figure. That does not have so much to do with the fact that, for the first time, the great wave of conquests diminished under his rule. Syria, Palestine, Lower Egypt, Iraq and Western Persia already belonged to the Arab empire. After he had conquered the remotest territories of the Persian empire (above all Armenia) and made the first advances in North Africa along the Mediterranean coast beyond Tripolis (which had been conquered under 'Umar in 643), 'Uthman evidently had no further ambitions in foreign policy. He evidently did not want to go down in history like his predecessor, as the great conqueror.

Rather, the third caliph is controversial because he is accused of having abandoned 'Umar's course in domestic policy and, at least in the second part of his twelve years in office, of having given priority to the interests of his family, the Umayyads, and other rich Meccan families. 'Uthman was said to have betrayed the companions of the Prophet and the Medinans and that can hardly be disputed. Depicted in the sources as a pious, gracious and generous ruler, he steered a centralist course. This meant that the members of once-leading clans, above all the Quraysh, rose to become governors, though quite a few of them were to prove to be failures and came to be surrounded with scandal. The incomes from the provinces were redistributed in favour of the great clans which had newly settled there. At the same time the central financial control of the caliphate over income was intensified and accounts were required from the state lands (*sawafi*) which had been conquered.

To excuse 'Uthman, in the long run he could hardly restrict the Quraysh élites to Mecca and exclude them from the positions of power in the provinces, but as the authority of this somewhat inefficient caliph declined, he increasingly went back to the old Arab tribal customs and relied on members of his wider family. Evidently he did not oppose their luxury, hedonism and escapades sufficiently. 'Uthman was not the energetic leader needed at the time. He did not prove to be up to the task of ensuring the just and fair distribution of the enormous plunder of war. He revived the pre-Islamic coalition between Meccan and Arab tribal aristocrats at the expense of the specifically Islamic elements and claimed greater autonomy for the caliphate in financial and social matters without being able to exploit it.

A further element has to be added to the charge of nepotism: the centralization of administration and finances was accompanied by a standardization of the Qur'an, which was unwelcome to some.

From word of mouth to writing: the Qur'an as a book

As I have described (see B I, 2), the Qu'ran was first proclaimed and recited in individual surahs (presumably the individual revelations were already called 'Qur'an'). Only later were the parts gathered together and edited in a book: 'the Qur'an'. Following some preliminary work (probably already under 'Umar) the collecting and editing was done, at the command of Caliph 'Uthman, by an editorial commission, thus publicly bypassing the previously established Qur'an reciters or readers (*qurra'*). What at first sight looks like a purely religious action, aimed at remembering of the exact text and eliminating the differences between the different readings, undoubtedly also had a political significance. For in this way the caliph stripped of power those Qur'an readers, the 'guardians' of the holy book, who were recognized as religious and indirectly also political authorities, because they could recite the Qur'an orally and thus keep it alive.

Why did the Qur'an need to be edited? 'Uthman's critics inevitably understood this work as a further element of a centralizing strategy:

– The state founded by Muhammad was a confederation and, for all its unitary leadership, rested on the division of the tribes. By contrast, the state envisaged by the third caliph, 'Uthman, was to be much more centralized, to enable the caliphate to carry through the necessary economic, social and religious changes.

– The Qur'an was initially recited by many people, and the Prophet had given no instructions for producing a book, though he may have considered this. The book edition of the Qur'an by 'Uthman served to standardize the religion and centralize the political leadership.

However, neither an organization of clerics nor a kind of church came into being and in this first paradigm one can speak of a theology and a legal system only with qualifications.

An Islamic theology?

During the Prophet's lifetime the Qur'an had not existed as a book; there was only, as some modern scholars like to put it, not very piously, 'Qur'anic material', or more accurately, individual 'Qur'anic revelations'. These revelations sometimes contained dialectical arguments, conversations in opposites, for example: 'Say: Who ... They say ... Then say: ...'[91] This style of thinking is not only to be found in the environment of the first Muslim community, in the practice of disputation in ancient rhetoric (and therefore among Christians, Jews and Muslims). It also occurs in the Qur'an itself, so Muslims were quite prepared for disputations and a controversy theology which grew out of them.[92]

However, the leading scholar of classical Islamic theology, Josef van Ess, emphasizes that there was no controversy theology either in the time when the original community was forming or when it was expanding: 'Only from the period of confusion shortly before the fall of the Umayyads do we have clear references to the institution of disputations and the purposeful involvement of people who had been trained in them.'[93] This is also true of the first period of Islam: no 'tradition' can yet be established alongside 'scripture'; beyond the biographical literature (see B II, 2) there was as yet no collection of sayings or episodes involving the Prophet. This so-called hadith literature appears only later.

A comparison with the New Testament might be helpful, since it already contains theology. The 'holy book' of the Christians has a fundamentally different character from the holy book of the Muslims. According to its own self-understanding, the New Testament contains human testimonies to God's word and activity, mediated through Jesus Christ. Being human, these testimonies already contain individual interpretations of one and the same saving event. The three synoptic Gospels (though these were written between four and five decades after Jesus' death) and often the early traditions collected and worked over in them (some of which go back to Jesus) are shaped by particular theological conceptions. This is even more true of the Fourth Gospel, that of John, written more than sixty years after the death of Jesus, which interprets the life, discourses and death of Jesus in a profound yet arbitrary way.[94] The letters of the apostle Paul were written a good two decades after Easter; in them Paul interprets for his Hellenistic recipients the way and work of Jesus in great theological schemes, with all the consequences for communities and individuals. Thus he makes possible the early transition from the Jewish–Christian paradigm (Christian P I) to the Gentile–Christian Hellenistic paradigm (P II).

By contrast, the Qur'an contains no human interpretation of the message communicated by God to the Prophet Muhammad. In the Muslim understanding of faith, the Qur'an is, from beginning to end, a direct message from God, God's word from first to last. However, the great difficulty is that, under 'Uthman, the various Qur'anic revelations were included in the book of the Qur'an solely according to the length of the surahs, without any ordering of their content. Thus from the beginning, Muslims faced the challenging task of showing that the message of the Qur'an is internally coherent and of presenting it to people in an understandable synthesis. What is the Qur'an really about, what is decisive and what is not, and how are apparent contradictions for human reason to be resolved? Or is that perhaps impossible?

One thing is certain: the Qur'an does not concern itself with clever hair-splitting, of the kind that often appears in later theology, but simply with God and human beings, or more precisely, with God the Lord and human responsibility. This is a central question for the everyday life of any Muslim and for high politics: since the Qur'an emphasizes both (as I mentioned in B II,1), what is the relationship between the omnipotence of the Creator and human freedom? Is everything really predestined by God—or is everything a matter of human responsibility? In his history of Islamic theology Tilman Nagel calls this the 'core problem': 'They (the Muslims) struggled over the solution of the core problem which the Qur'an had posed to Muslims—thinking about both causality within the world and thus responsibility for action alongside the omnipotence of the one Creator which realizes itself without interruption.'[95]

The germs of local theologies

There is scarcely any trace of what is traditionally called theology in the first phase of the expansion after the death of the Prophet either. Given the concentration of the whole Arab nation on the conquests, this is not surprising. The foundation of Islamic theology was first laid by the editing of the Qur'an as a book. This provided the basis for an exegesis (*tafsir*) with methods and rules and thus with a thought-out way of dealing with the revelation. Josef van Ess explains that the word *qurra'* was apparently first used not only for those who recited the Qur'an but for all Muslims who had a religious education.[96] Nor is there a general concept of 'religious scholar' ('*alim*, plural '*ulama*', 'the one who has the knowledge). All that we can say is that in this paradigm the later differentiation in religious training gradually took place. There was a distinction between:

- exegetes (*mufassirun*), who would become responsible for the exegesis of the Qur'an;
- jurists (*fuqaha'*), who would become responsible for the application of the legal regulations in the Qur'an (which often conflicted with customary law);
- tradition scholars (*muhaddithun*), who would become responsible for gathering and interpreting the traditions (*sunnah* = 'report, tradition') which were slowly forming alongside the Qur'an.

At this time, however, Sunnah or tradition does not mean the sayings and actions of the Prophet himself which were given for guidance, as it did later; the 'Sunnah of the Prophet' (*sunnat an-nabi*) as a body of specific examples did not exist at all then.[97] Sunnah generally meant local custom: the old custom of a city or region (the *sunnah* of Medina, Kufa, Basra, and so on). But the second caliph, 'Umar, is said to have warned against the uncontrolled growth of oral tradition, of the kind that can be found in the Jewish Mishnah with its many rabbinical opinions. From the perspective of the caliph, this is understandable, if he wanted to maintain the level of interpretation and did not want to be bound by too authoritative a tradition.[98] Presumably the question of whether and how far the ordinance of the first caliphs corresponded to the 'Sunnah of the Prophet' and consequently whether they were or were not binding arose as early as with the succession to 'Umar and the controversies surrounding him.

The parties which were now forming in opposition to the ruling caliph had two possibilities for a theological foundation to their opposition: like the caliphs, they could refer to the Qur'an (a fundamental scripturalism) while rejecting certain accepted local traditions (for example, the punishment of stoning) or they could quote quite specific statements and episodes from the Prophet's life as their authority. However, at a very early stage the question arose whether all these now increasingly widespread traditions about the Prophet were authentic. At that time there was virtually no procedure for deciding (the term hadith, used for the traditions about the Prophet, became customary only in the subsequent paradigm). Nevertheless, critical Western research must not rule out the possibility that authentic hadith were also handed down in this period and passed on to the next generation.

From a present-day perspective, we must avoid one obvious mistake in the quest for the beginnings of Islamic theology: it would be wrong, whether consciously or unconsciously, to take as a model an 'orthodox' theology with a claim to be the sole binding authority. There could not have been such a theology at the time of ʿUthman. Because of the conquests, the original community was largely dispersed over the conquered territories, and by its own will had literally become a diaspora ('dispersion'); from then on its members were active in very different centres. Josef van Ess demonstrated this in detail in his great work on classical Islamic theology using his 'prosopographic method' (presupposing the dialectic of persons and structures). Certainly, no unified theology formed in the controversies over the Prophet's successors at the end of the 'golden age' of Islam. Rather, religious movements formed, containing the nuclei of theologies that, from the perspective of the later Islamic sources, would appear sectarian. However, at the places where they arose, these religious currents and their theologies were mostly seen as 'orthodox'. That means that orthodoxy originally existed locally and was self-sufficient. Given the different centres and groups remote from one another, who could have created a binding consensus? There was no universal Islamic 'magisterium', far less an 'ecumenical council', as among the Christians. But was that necessarily a disadvantage?

We should reflect that as in Christian theology, so too in Islamic theology, the 'history of dogma' has been written by the victors. Is it really true that the losers are always wrong? We can see early Islamic theology for what it really was only if we do not see the whole history of Islamic theology through the spectacles of later orthodoxy. That also applies to the history of Christian theology. Up to the end of this era there is only what one can only call, with van Ess, an 'implicit theology'. But what about Islamic law? That is another question. Hadn't this development already progressed further?

Still no specifically Islamic system of law

Unquestionably, a Sunnah consisting of fundamental decisions of the caliph made on his authority (which was more legal) began to form alongside the Sunnah as local custom (which was more ethical and political). Pre-Islamic customary law, with a style of arbitration that had largely already been followed by the Prophet himself, was further modified and made specific. The caliphs, as political leaders of the Islamic community, held office less and less as arbitrators and more and more as legislators—since administration and legislation largely coincided. Of course, their legislative activity was not focused on the customary law of the Arabs but primarily on the organization of the conquered territories in favour of the Arabs. Individual emphases were introduced into criminal law, for example the flogging of authors of satirical poems directed against other tribes, and stoning for illicit sexual intercourse, penalties which were not prescribed in the Qur'an but possibly introduced under the influence of the Jewish Torah)—an explosive innovation, with fatal consequences down to the present day.

The first caliphs did not appoint distinctive Muslim judges, qadis; 'Umar's alleged instruction for the qadis demonstrably comes from a later century. Nor were the foundations of a specifically Islamic legal system laid, even under the first four caliphs. The leading expert on the development of Islamic law, Joseph Schacht, explains: 'During the greater part of the first [Islamic] century Islamic law, in the technical meaning of the term, did not as yet exist. As had been the case in the time of the Prophet, law as such fell outside the sphere of religion, and as far as there were no religious or moral objections to specific transactions or modes of behaviour the technical aspects of the law were a matter of indifference to the Muslims.'[99]

The Qur'an is hardly more than a preamble, a preface to an Islamic book of law. We may ask how it was possible, at that time, to dispense with specifically Islamic regulations. The simple reason is that, as I have already indicated, the Arabs largely took over the legal and administrative institutions and practices of the conquered territories, both Roman–Byzantine and Sasanian–Persian, whose cultures were highly developed. Just as the Romans had earlier learned from the Greeks, so the militarily superior Arab conquerors learned from the culturally superior Byzantines or Persians whom they conquered—for instance about the taxation system, the treatment of the members of other religions, the establishment of foundations (*waqf*) and much else.

The Muslims took over not only legal institutions and legal practices but also particular juristic terms and maxims, methods of argument and basic ideas. For example, the Roman legal idea of the *opinio prudentium*, expert opinion, became the model for the concept of the 'consensus of the scholars' which was later so important. Therefore there was no need for a distinctive Muslim legal science. New, educated, non-Arab Muslims served as natural mediators in this somewhat unplanned process. To the countries of the Fertile Crescent, along with the Hellenistic education which was widespread everywhere ('rhetoric'), they brought at least a basic legal training which, often at important administrative centres, benefited the new order. Thus both Roman–Byzantine, Talmudic–rabbinic and ultimately also Sasanian–Persian concepts and maxims can be seen in rising Islamic law.[100] But we must return from theology and law to political history.

7. The great crisis in the original community: the split into parties

In Arabic, 'sect' (*firqah*) simply means a closed religious or ideological group but in English 'sect' has negative, heretical connotations. However, it was not a dispute over the 'right faith' that caused the Muslim Ummah to split into two, even three 'parties', but a dispute over the Prophet's legacy as leader, which was to result in a first civil war, disastrous for the whole history of Islam. The fundamental issue was the question of succession to the Prophet: who was his true follower in the office of leader and which group of persons was to be involved?

'Ali, the fourth caliph—disputed

Centralization often destroys the unity it seeks. The centralizing family policy of Caliph 'Uthman caused unrest first among the Qur'an reciters in Kufa and then in Egypt. In 656 the discontented gathered in Medina, with a few hundred protesters from Fustat alone. The conflict heightened: crowds assembled before the caliph's house, loudly accusing him of simony and the embezzlement of state funds. Long negotiations followed but finally the group from Egypt made short shrift of things: they stormed the house and murdered 'Uthman.

One can imagine the new upheaval. For a second time the 'representative of God's messenger' had been murdered; this time not by a frustrated or over-excited slave, as in the case of 'Umar, but by a fellow-believer. That went down in Islamic history as 'the great visitation' (*al-fitnah al-kubrah*) by God on believers. It put the unity of the Muslim community radically in question; indeed, it split it. To the present day the Ummah remains split. How could that come about?

Many were urgently concerned that 'Ali ibn Abu Talib[101] (656–61) should be chosen as 'Uthman's successor. He had not seriously been taken into account in the election of the first and second caliphs because he was too young. In the election of the third caliph he had worked in the electoral body for 'Uthman (but at around forty-five had still been too young by comparison with the almost seventy-year-old 'Uthman).[102] Now, however, a cousin and son-in-law of the Prophet and one of the first to be converted in Mecca, he was elected caliph. This was clearly on the basis, not of a designation or a hereditary claim but of the will of those forces in Medina who wanted to restore the original Muslim élite to power in the face of the Meccan aristocrats (and their Syrian interests) who had become all too powerful. Thus, despite a number of disputes, 'Ali became caliph. He proved to be a very capable, energetic man. He removed—to the great annoyance of the Umayyah family—various unsuitable governors who had been given grace-and-favour appointments by 'Uthman. He also reversed 'Uthman's centralized control of the incomes of the provinces and ensured a more equitable distribution of the income from taxation and the plunder from war.

But 'Ali's election as caliph was marked by a fatal mistake. He had already discredited himself in the eyes of some by having himself elected with the support of

'Uthman's murderers, instead of arresting them and punishing them. For many, the murder cried out for vengeance, for blood vengeance in good Arab style. The prime candidate for blood vengeance was a cousin of 'Uthman, the Umayyad Mu'awiyyah ibn Abu Sufyan, the powerful Muslim governor of Syria, with his headquarters in Damascus. His army had come too late to support 'Uthman, but he avoided paying homage after 'Ali's election and finally made objections to it with the backing of Syria and Egypt. He claimed that the election had been held by a minority, without consulting the provincial nobles (it appears that the members of the Umayyah clan had fled from Medina after 'Uthman's murder) and he demanded that the caliph's murderers be handed over and severely punished.

But how was 'Ali to hand over those who had elected him? He was caught between two stools. He was not isolated and at first must have had the majority of Arabs behind him—not only the tribal warriors who had settled in Kufa (and Egypt) but also the Medinan 'helpers' and their descendants, who saw themselves as having been handed over to Meccan power politics by 'Uthman. As time went on, there was less and less agreement between 'Ali and the companions of the Prophet and their descendants in Medina. Since he found most supporters in Kufa, the garrison town on the Euphrates, 'Ali shifted the residence of the caliph there: contrary to all tradition to a place outside Arabia. This was a momentous decision and a symptom of the far-reaching crisis of the original Islamic community paradigm (P I), which would make a paradigm change unavoidable. We should remember that:

- Mecca remained the religious centre of Islam and the Ka'bah its central sanctuary. But the political centre, the government of the Islamic state, was for the first time (and for ever remained) outside Arabia, which became peripheral to the state.
- For the first time Muslim armies opposed each other in hostility (which would have been unthinkable in the time of the Prophet). A war between believers went against the Qur'an.

The first civil war

'Ali's whole caliphate was dogged by the civil war (*fitnah*[103]—temptation or test) which, as his 'party' (*shi'ah*) later saw it, was one long tragedy. To put things somewhat schematically, it could be said that 'Ali was victorious in the first act of this drama, reached a stalemate in the second and had to accept final defeat in the third.

The *first act* took place in 656: 'Ali, and his political course, was opposed by the Prophet's influential widow 'A'ishah, daughter of Abu Bakr, who lived in Mecca, and by two Meccan aristocrats and important companions of the

Prophet: 'A'ishah's kinsman Talhah and Zubayr, a relation of Muhammad's first wife Khadijah. With armed supporters, they invaded southern Iraq, to stir up the garrison towns of Kufa and Basra against 'Ali. So the caliph had to turn to Iraq instead of to Syria. In the famous 'Battle of the Camel' near Basra he defeated his opponents. Talhah and Zubayr fell; the Prophet's widow (who according to old Arab custom had encouraged her supporters from a camel) was taken prisoner and sent back to Medina. For a long time she remained the last Muslim woman to exert such an influence on public affairs.

The *second act* took place in 657. A much more dangerous opponent, the Umayyad Mu'awiyyah, with his Syrian army, fell upon 'Ali's troops on the upper Euphrates, east of Aleppo at Siffin. Despite weeks of skirmishing and minor battles the clash proved indecisive. Finally arbitration was agreed on, to clarify whether the murder of 'Uthman was justified or not.

The *third act* took place in 659. After long negotiations and vigorous arguments the arbitration (though reports of it are confused) decided for Mu'awiyyah and thus for the election of a new caliph. Some of 'Ali's supporters, especially those old fighters for Islam who had long devoted their lives to the cause and received little thanks for it, felt deeply disillusioned: they thought that 'Ali had handed over Allah's cause to human arbitration and indirectly put his caliphate under human disposition.

In fury, the opponents left the garrison towns of Basr and Kufa. These 'secessionists' or Kharijites (*khawarij*, from *kharaja*—'to go out, leave') gathered by the Nahrawan canal on the Tigris. There the caliph fell on the 'separated ones' and decimated them. Thereafter the Kharijites, originally 'Ali's most loyal followers, became his most bitter enemies, with the result that the caliph had repeatedly to deal with these extremely aggressive 'apostates'. One of their number finally took blood vengeance on the unfortunate fourth caliph: in 661 'Ali was struck down at the door of a mosque in Kufa with a poisoned sword and died a painful death a few days later. This was the third murder of a caliph and again no problems had been solved. Since the middle of the eighth century 'Ali's tomb in Najaf (an-Najaf, a town south of Baghdad and a few miles west of Kufa) has been the crystallization point and central place of pilgrimage for the Shiites, a separate party. Ayatollah Khomeini, who was banished from Iran, taught at its theological high school from 1956 to 1978 and there prepared for the Islamic revolution.[104] Najaf became the centre of Shiite resistance to the American occupation of Iraq between 2003 and 2004.

The split between Sunnis, Kharijites and Shiites

From then until now, Muslims have remained split over 'Ali. He has given his name to an important party that still exists today: 'Ali's party (*shi'at 'Ali*), today called Shiah for short. The 'Shiites' believe that 'Ali was designated 'patron' and supreme head (*imam*) of the Ummah on his return from the farewell pilgrimage, at the pool of Khumm on 16 March 632 (which later became the annual Shiite festival). However, the Sunni interpretation of the same prophetic saying is that Muhammad only wanted to protect 'Ali, who was too strict and therefore unpopular, Much must necessarily remain unexplained here because the sources are obscure.[105]

One thing is certain: Mu'awiyyah, and with him the Umayyads, remained the victor. In 600, after the arbitration, the governor of Syria had homage paid to him as caliph in the holy city of Jerusalem, piously praying on Golgotha, in the Garden of Gethsemane and at the tomb of Mary. After the murder of 'Ali his caliphate was recognized almost everywhere and would become the first of another paradigm of Islam (P II).

What had been, from the beginning, a simmering dispute over the succession to the Prophet, the justification for leadership of the Ummah and the question of legitimizing Islamic rule, now irredeemably broke out. What was to be decisive for the succession in the future: former service of Islam (*sabiqah*) or genealogical proximity to the Prophet (*nasab*) and his family? That was the main question. The unity of the Ummah broke apart over three different theories of the caliphate and concepts of rule.[106] Three parties (plural *firaq*) were in dispute:

- The Sunnis, who to the present day comprise the great majority (around ninety per cent) of the Muslim people. They live by the 'Sunnah', the 'custom', the 'tradition': for them succession to the Prophet should be determined by the Islamic community or its competent representatives. Therefore they recognize all four caliphs of Medina, but only much later called them the 'rightly-guided caliphs'—for the Sunnis the embodiment of ideal rule.
- The Shiites, the minority (today around ten per cent) Muslim population of the world. They live mostly in Iran, Iraq and Lebanon. For them, succession to the Prophet is dependent on divine commission and proclamation by the Prophet Muhammad. Therefore, they acknowledge only 'Ali as the successor chosen by God and allegedly determined by the Prophet and after him those of his descendants who fulfil the preconditions for office, the imams.
- The Kharijites, with a puritanical orientation, who for a long time fought extremely unwelcome battles against the Sunni caliph. Today, having become peaceful, they are widespread among the Berbers, in Zanzibar and above all in Oman. For them a caliph has not just to be a member of the Quraysh (following the Sunnah), nor simply a descendant of Muhammad and 'Ali (following the Shiah); rather, the best Muslim, independent of tribe or family, should be the successor, 'even if he be an Abyssinian slave'.

In view of this split in the great Muslim community that came about so early and has been a burden to the present day, and in view of the later idealization of the 'golden age', which prevents its overcoming, three questions arise.

Questions: The split in Islam

- Three of the four 'rightly-guided' caliphs were murdered. Countless Arab tribal feuds, in which the honour of the tribe and vengeance were put above everything and rivers of blood flowed, took place. Didn't blood vengeance, which derives from a pre-Islamic time and society, prove a penal measure which even at that time provoked rather than hindered serious conflicts? Surely it belongs to Arab Bedouin remnants rather than to the substance of Islam and therefore cannot be a legitimate legal means for a modern legal order?
- The rights and duties of the caliph, the mode of succession and the whole power structure were barely settled by the political end of the first Muslim paradigm. Didn't the Qur'an exclude a split in the community, seeing it at work only among the 'unbelievers', above all among Christians? Wasn't the unity and solidarity of Muhammad's community the original political idea of Islam? So should the dispute over the succession to the Prophet forever split the Ummah, especially as the caliphate no longer exists?
- Should the genealogical-tribal principle (for Sunnis, the caliph, a member of the Quraysh), the genealogical–personal principle (for Shiites, a descendant of 'Ali) and the charismatic principle (for the Kharijites, the most worthy) be played off against each other for ever? Should the split be made eternal in this way?

The memory of the golden age

A new paradigm would emerge from this fundamental crisis but neither the Shiites nor the Kharijites managed to form the dominant structures for the next period and thus determine the essentials of the rising paradigm. They remained important as extremely lively opposition movements within the one Islamic paradigm. For a long time the Shiites lived in close contact with the overwhelming Sunni majority; only very much later did they constitute a community which was separated and closed in on itself. If we leave aside the law of inheritance of the so-called 'Twelver Shia', which differs for ideological reasons (I shall be discussing it later), the positive doctrines of rising Islamic law are represented by both Shiites and Kharijites. In theology, too, there are countless interconnections. These two groups barely differ more from the Sunni majority than they do from each other.

The original Islamic community paradigm remained in the memory of most Muslims as the golden age: a time when the world of Islam was still in order, the community was still one, guided in the spirit of the Qur'an, first by the Prophet and then by the 'rightly-guided' caliphs. But there was a concern to explain the regrettable schism: this was the starting-point for Islamic historiography. The Muslim chroniclers usually reported the controversies and violent acts of this era quite openly and asked how good Muslims could have done better: this was the starting point for Islamic political theory. Despite the negative features, the original community remained a model. Questions arose of religious criteria, of the divine will and human responsibility: this formed the problem for Islamic theology.[107] For the most different traditions, and especially for the Islamic renewal movements, the original community remained the court of appeal.

But the golden age had finally run its course and a paradigm change followed.

C II

The Paradigm of the Arab Empire

Half a century after the Hijrah, who could have imagined that Arabia, the origin and homeland of Islam, would again find itself right on its periphery—that it would again become a hinterland and no longer the scene of political events which affected the future?

- Mecca remained a great place of pilgrimage, but now had become something of a backwater away from the important trade routes.
- Medina was an enclave of pious conservatives who did not want to join in the new development and would have preferred to keep to the original Islamic paradigm (P I).

But in Islam, too, time does not stand still.

1. From Medina to Damascus: the new centre of power

This reminds me, as a Christian, of Jewish Christianity (Christian P I). With the destruction of Jerusalem it had forfeited its centre and had lost itself in the remote Syrian desert, in Mesopotamia and possibly also on the Arabian peninsula, cut off from the revolutionary upheavals brought about by Hellenistic–Byzantine Christianity (Christian P II). Islam now faced no less a revolution: for the conservative pious Muslims in Arabia an unprecedented change in the overall constellation, which they rejected. This change was shaped and accelerated by the encounter with Hellenistic-Byzantine culture, a change from the original Islamic community paradigm (P I) to the paradigm of the Arab empire (P II). As the Montreal Islamic scholar, Donald P. Little, remarks: 'It had become apparent during the reigns of the first caliphs that tribal tradition and the practices of Muhammad in Medina were inadequate resources for administering a vast empire.' What was the practical solution? It consisted in the 'imitation of administrative procedures that had evolved during the centuries of Roman and Byzantine rule there'.[1]

The Umayyads come to power: Mu'awiyyah

A clear indication of this paradigm change was the shift in the political and religious centres of power. This took place formally and lasted almost a century. Not just any city replaced the desert city of Medina (not counting the episode of Kufa when 'Ali resided in Kufa) but an age-old cultural centre at the eastern foot of the Antilebanon, a city which could look back on four millennia of history: Damascus (*Dimashq*).[2]

First mentioned as early as 1470 BCE as a conquest of Pharaoh Thutmosis III, this oasis city, for a short time under the dominion of King David, had been the capital of a great Aramaean empire at the time of King Solomon. It then came under Syrian, Persian, Hellenistic–Seleucid and Arab–Nabataean rule and finally Roman and Byzantine rule. As capital of the Byzantine province of Syria and headquarters of the eastern defence of the empire since the fourth century, Damascus had been a Christian episcopal see, but from 634 it had been in the hands of the Arabs and was the residence of the Muslim governors of Syria.

Damascus became centre of a new Arab dynasty, which was to rule the vast Arab empire for eighty-nine years (661–750) and produce fourteen caliphs. I have already reported the events of the revolution: the governor of Syria, Mu'awiyyah,[3] from the Umayyah clan (*banu umayyah*), had refused to pay homage to the fourth caliph 'Ali, himself claimed the dignity of caliph, fought for it, won, and finally had himself proclaimed caliph. This introduced a paradigm change:

- Instead of the companions of the Prophet and the earlier Muslim élite, the dynasty of the Umayyads was to rule for almost a century. However, they had, opportunistically, confessed Islam only after the conquest of Mecca.
- The interests of the Umayyad caliphs were concentrated on the political leadership and organized administration of the new empire rather than on the religion and theology of Islam.
- Syria replaced Arabia, in religious and political terms, as the dominant power. Here was holy Jerusalem, here the Jewish and Christian prophets had been active, and now here the caliphs had their homes.
- Instead of the desert city of Medina, the Syrian cultural city of Damascus became the political centre of the Islamic Arab empire and the capital of Islam: a victory of the urban state over the Bedouin.

- Instead of the Sasanian traditions with which the Arabs living in Iraq found themselves confronted, the Byzantine traditions, adapted by the Syrian Arabs, became influential across the empire.

Muʿawiyyah was the son of Muhammad's most important Meccan opponent, Abu Sufyan, from the clan of ʿAbd Shams, which was hostile to the Prophet. Probably as a sign of reconciliation, he had been appointed the Prophet's scribe, had then commanded the advance guard of his brother Yahid's army that invaded Syria and, after his brother's early death, had been governor in Syria since 640. As caliph he finally found recognition among the great majority of Muslims, not because he was an Umayyad (and Sufyanid), but because at a difficult time he had proved to be the right man in the right place. As governor of Syria he had long been the most powerful man in the Ummah.

In Syria, Muʿawiyyah had found a relatively well-ordered Byzantine administration which he left intact. He had a strong household and disciplined military forces, formed of tribes settled in different smaller garrison towns. Thus, in just a few years, Muʿawiyyah was able to build up from tribal warriors an army as effective as it was loyal. He also created a war fleet which not only warded off Byzantine attacks but was capable of the conquest of Cyprus (in 672) and Rhodes (in 674) and of a seven-year long sea blockade of Constantinople. However, Muʿawiyyah also seems occasionally to have paid tribute to Constantinople, as he was over-committed elsewhere.

Under his leadership, Arab rule now extended considerably: in North Africa as far as present-day Tunisia, where the new garrison town of Kairouan (*al-Qairawan*) soon became the basis for campaigns of conquest. Eastwards, the frontiers of Islam advanced to the Oxus, and Khorasan, in north-east Iran, became an Umayyad province. Even where there were no great conquests to be made, for example in Anatolia, where the Taurus mountains formed a natural protective wall for Byzantium, Muʿawiyyah ensured, through raids and lesser campaigns, that the troops remained ready for battle.

Hardly any other caliph put into action the Prophet's invitation to *jihad* as energetically and tenaciously as did Muʿawiyyah. He did not understand *jihad* just as moral effort or defensive war, which was intrinsically possible, but as a battle of faith which in Syria was regarded not only as a good work, as it was in the Hijaz, but as the obligation of every Muslim. Questions of war were in the foreground, even in jurisprudence. All the cities on the Mediterranean, such as Ashkelon, Tyre, Beirut, Byblos and Tripolis, were garrison cities and saw themselves as the frontier guard against the superior Byzantine fleet. Worship and asceticism were also connected inwardly with the battle of faith, which, as one hadith has it, is 'the monasticism of Islam'.[4]

A centralist monarchy develops

Mu'awiyyah's power base was and remained the Arab tribes, especially the tribal federation of the Quda'a, led by the warlike tribe of the Kalb. The Kalb had become Christians, but Monophysite because of their independence from Byzantium. Therefore Mu'awiyyah did not hesitate to marry the daughter of the tribal leader, who then bore him his successor, Yazid. At that time there was still a numerically strong Christian population in Syria: only the upper class of the main church (the 'Melkites' or 'Imperials') had moved away to Byzantium. With great skill and shrewd moderation Mu'awiyyah deliberately extended the military and administrative power of the state, not as an absolute ruler but as the 'supreme tribal patriarch' of the Arabs. He cultivated a style of rule characterized by the traditional Arab virtues of negotiation and mediation, generosity and respect for the tribal traditions. He seems to have taken over two tribal institutions directly for his government:

- the council of notables (*shurah*) summoned by the caliph for consultation;
- the delegations (*wufud*) of the tribes, who kept the caliph informed of their concerns.

In this way Mu'awiyyah involved the tribal heads (*ashraf*) in consultation; he had a gift for negotiation which, while respecting the dignity of others, made opposition impossible. His *hilm*, the gentleness, calm, relaxation and self-control with which he disarmed opponents, was famous.

Mu'awiyyah was aware of the dangers of Bedouin tribal particularism and Arab anarchy. Although he respected the tribal structures, he promoted the organization of the empire by adopting Roman and Byzantine patterns of administration and making use of the Byzantine administrative apparatus for the centralization of existing tribal structures. He and his successors 'took over the existing administration and practised the indirect rule of their own tribes'.[5] Thus, even though everything was still within very modest (Syrian!) bounds, the beginnings of the bureaucratization of the Islamic state took place in Damascus, above all to simplify communication with the remote provinces of the empire. This happened through:

- the establishment of a chancery (*diwan al-khatam*) and
- the introduction of a postal service (*barid*).

The establishment of the dynastic principle

In a reign of almost twenty years (661–80) Mu'awiyyah succeeded, by practising 'collegiality', in combining the strong particularist tribal interests with the demands of a state which increasingly had a central government. In Syria he exercised his rule directly but in Iraq he had loyal governors acting largely independently. However, he did not lose control of this region. It had become unruly and difficult; the fanatical Kharijites had strong support in Iraq; they often operated in small terrorist bands of between thirty and a hundred men and waged a holy war against the caliphs, whom they regarded as illegitimate. At the same time the Shiites, who were beginning to form an opposition to be taken seriously, had to be kept in check; I shall discuss this later.

I should point out that many key positions in the developing bureaucracy (which was Syrian and not imperial) were traditionally held by Christians. Some Christians heaped high praise on the caliph's domestic policy, which on the whole was just and peaceful, and made two decades of peaceful development possible for the empire. The Nestorian monk John of Phenek, a contemporary of Muʿawiyyah from north Mesopotamia, attests: 'Righteousness flourished in his time, and great peace prevailed in the regions under his control ... As soon as Muʿawiyyah had come to the throne, there was a peace all over the world unheard of and unseen either by our parents or our grandparents, of an unparalleled kind.'[6]

As is attested for the first time by his predecessor but one, the Umayyad ʿUthman, Muʿawiyyah bore the title not only of 'representative of the Prophet' but also of 'representative of God' (*khalifat Allah*) on earth, thus claiming, as scholars have shown,[7] not only political but also religious authority. At this time the rights and duties, the legitimacy and structure of the rule of the caliphate were far from established. Moreover, Muʿawiyyah was shrewd enough to bring his divine legitimacy and authority into play only rarely. He preferred an efficient policy to sacral theatricality. Granted, his caliphate, too, remained a theocracy, reinforced and applied to the new situation by adopting Byzantine or Persian forms and structures. But this gave it a more secular, 'royal' touch. Later Muslim historians, who in the ʿAbbasid period preferred to present the preceding Umayyads as un-Islamic, therefore describe Muʿawiyyah in purely worldly terms as 'king' (*malik*) and in religious terms as 'caliph'.

The undoubtedly more secular character of Muʿawiyyah's caliphate, and his unusual qualities of leadership, become evident in the rules for his successor. Although the Arabs did not have a monarchical tradition, he succeeded, through 'homage' during his lifetime, in having his well-prepared son Yazid recognized as his successor. Unquestionably it helped that Yazid's mother came from the clan of Kalb, which led the tribal federation. And although his caliphate was by no means regarded by contemporaries as the precedent for an Umayyad succession in office, he laid its foundations. In the next seventy years thirteen Umayyad caliphs succeeded him: sons (in five cases), a cousin or other relatives. The collective rights of the ruling family had precedence over the individual right of a relative. This uncertainty in the succession was time and again to be the occasion for disputes over heredity.[8]

Islamic and Western scholars agree that after the time of Muhammad and the four 'rightly-guided' caliphs (P I) the overall constellation fundamentally changed: 'Mu'awiyyah transformed the caliphate into a monarchical institution of the Persian or Byzantine type, in other words into the kind of institution that the Muslims had been sent out to destroy.'[9] Through Mu'awiyyah's changes to the political structure the foundation for a new paradigm of Islam (P II) had been laid:

- The tribal confederation was replaced by a kingdom in the form of a centralist monarchy.
- The succession to the Prophet was now regulated by the dynastic principle, hitherto unknown in Islam, instead of by acclamation. Succession (with great scope for the choice of person) took place independent of either personal qualities (contrary to the view of the Kharijites) or membership of family or clan (contrary to the view of the Shiites).
- The change to the dynastic principle threw up the question of the legitimacy of such a successor to the Prophet. To many pious people the Umayyads were not legitimate successors but 'usurpers of power'; not caliphs but 'kings'.
- In this new constellation, although the caliph was a 'representative of God', the caliphate took on a more religious than secular character.

Mu'awiyyah, this ruler of extraordinary spiritual superiority, energy and cleverness, united the Arab empire and thus created the presuppositions for the political and military consolidation of the territories conquered two decades before. By combining an Islamic religious ideal and the Umayyad power of government he created the framework for a novel Arab–Muslim society. However, while his long period of rule could conceal the immanent problems of the empire, it could not solve them: the resentment of the Medinans towards the Meccan Umayyah, who had come to power, the manifold tensions between the different tribal groups and the efforts of the Shiites to take over the caliphate were too great. From the beginning Shiite opposition manifested itself, especially in Iraq.

2. The Shiite opposition

No dynastic power and no central authority could persuade the 'party of 'Ali', the Shiites, to believe that the caliphate legitimately belonged to the Umayyads and not to 'Ali (and after his premature death to his firstborn son Hasan).

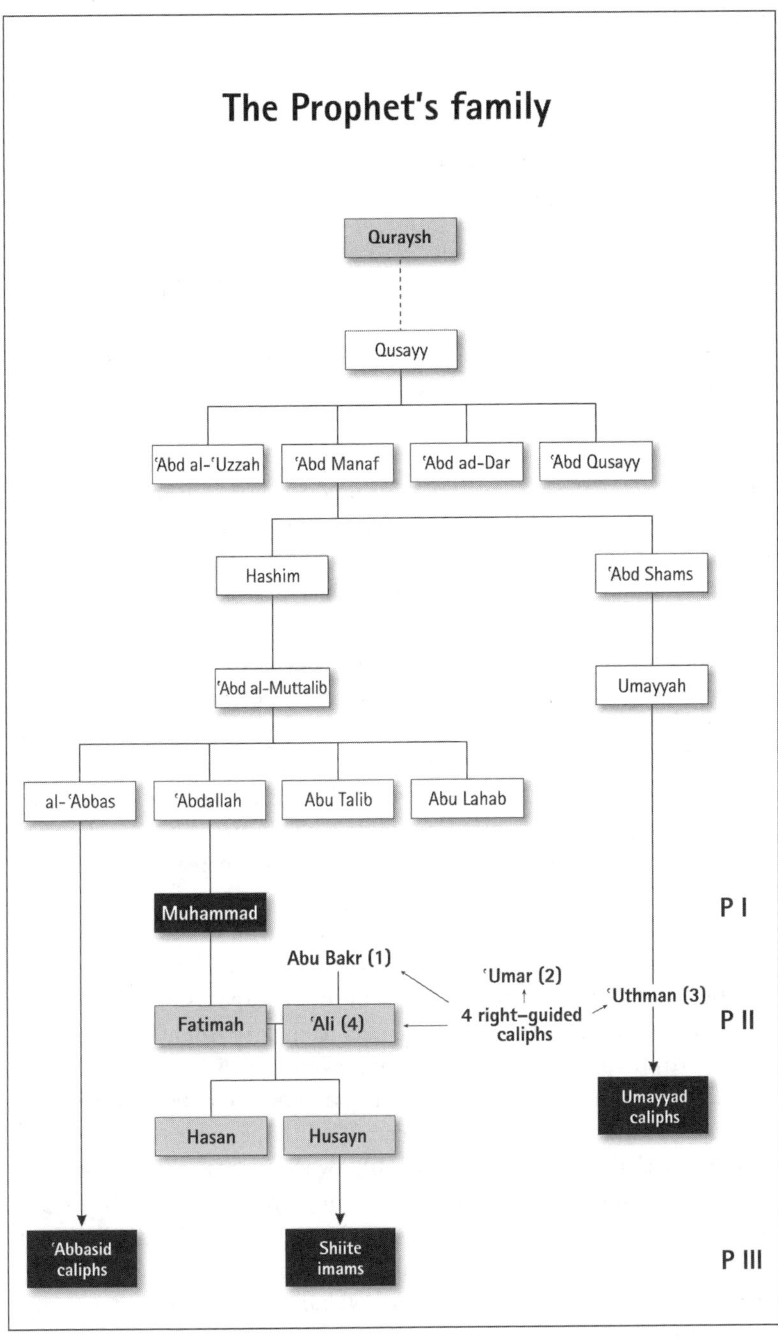
The Prophet's family
Quraysh
Qusayy
'Abd al-'Uzzah
'Abd Manaf
'Abd ad-Dar
'Abd Qusayy
Hashim
'Abd Shams
'Abd al-Muttalib
Umayyah
al-'Abbas
'Abdallah
Abu Talib
Abu Lahab
Muhammad
P I
Abu Bakr (1)
'Umar (2)
'Uthman (3)
Fatimah
'Ali (4)
4 right-guided caliphs
P II
Umayyad caliphs
Hasan
Husayn
'Abbasid caliphs
Shiite imams
P III

However Hasan, grandson of the Prophet and son of 'Ali, refused the caliphate; his place was taken by 'Ali's younger son Husayn. Husayn was tragically killed in the battle for the caliphate. I must briefly tell his story, since even today it is part of the 'past which is omnipresent' for millions of Muslims, especially those of the Shiite tendency.[10] To begin with, we turn to the firstborn.

Husayn—the model for all martyrs

In 661, near the Persian metropolis of Ctesiphon (*al-Mada'in*) on the Tigris, al-Hasan ibn 'Ali[11] clashed with the army of Mu'awiyyah, advancing from Syria. He began negotiations—with the master of negotiations—and conceded little. Why? Sunni historians say it was because he regarded his cause as hopeless. The Shiite version is that out of a love of peace, he did not want to shed more Muslim blood.

Mu'awiyyah, generous and far-sighted, had left the Prophet's nephew large sums of money and the income from the tribute of a district in Persia. This must have made him change his mind, to the dismay of many followers. When Mu'awiyyah entered Kufa, Hasan came to pay homage and, in the mosque, publicly renounced the caliphate. Now around thirty-six years old, he thereupon left Iraq and led a luxurious and sensual life in Medina until his death in 670 (or 678). Because of his countless marriages (there is talk of between sixty and ninety wives and between three and four hundred concubines) and even more numerous descendants, he is called the 'record-holder in divorces' (*al-mitlaq*). However, the Shiite view is that Hasan—destined by his father 'Ali for the succession—never renounced the succession, and indeed was exposed to up to seventy attempted poisonings by Mu'awiyyah. Accordingly, in Shiite texts Hasan's history is accompanied by an increasing number of miracles.

Mu'awiyyah's caliphate began formally with the 'year of the reunion of the Muslim community' in 661, but the Shiite resistance to the Umayyads remained lively. In 671, the governor of Kufa had some of their spokesmen arrested and sent to Damascus, where they were executed. Yet open rebellion broke out only when, shortly before his death in 680, Mu'awiyyah established his son Yazid as successor. As caliph (680–3) Yazid continued the efficient policy of his father.[12] The Shiites of Kufa finally resolved to act. Their hopes were pinned on 'Ali's younger son, al-Husayn ibn 'Ali (626–680),[13] who was by then fifty-four years old. There were already secret contacts with him, so he was invited to Kufa to be proclaimed caliph. Despite all the warnings, Husayn set out. It must have been a very adventurous enterprise, since Husayn travelled from Mecca to Iraq—on the pilgrimage route right across Arabia—with his whole family but with only a few faithful from Mecca.

When they arrived in Iraq, the small group numbering about fifty was stopped, shadowed and finally imprisoned by government troops. The governor of Kufa called on Husayn to pay homage to the caliph, Yazid. He refused and with his small group, reinforced only by a few Kufis, engaged in an armed clash in the plain of Karbala,[14] fifty miles south of Baghdad. It was a catastrophe: Husayn, his oldest son and all the men were slaughtered, wiping out most of the direct male descendants of Muhammad. They were buried in Karbala but their heads, which had been cut off, were taken to Kufa, as were the wives and children they had brought with them. Husayn's head was sent to Damascus, where it was ridiculed by Yazid's followers until it was finally given back to his family. No one knows for certain where it finally lies: in Karbala, where his body is buried, in Damascus, Ashkelon or Cairo, or in some other place. To the present day Husayn's head is venerated in Medina, Najaf and Marv. For 'Ali's party, to confess Husayn is central.

A separate 'confession': the Shiah

Had they not been those of Husayn and his family, these deaths would have caused little stir, but Husayn was the sole surviving son of the sole living daughter of the Prophet. Not only was his death later elaborated as martyrdom, with ever more fanciful features, but his birth and childhood were also exaggerated in legendary fashion. Indeed, for the party of 'Ali, the Shiites, the grandson of the Prophet became the object of a martyr cult unique in Islam, which can compete with the veneration of any martyr in medieval Christianity and even recalls the veneration of the crucified Jesus. Therefore one can meaningfully apply the term 'confession', the term used in Christianity, to them. In Husayn, the believers saw the model of all sufferers: 'the prince of the martyrs' (*sayid ash-shuhada'*) who, like Christ, deliberately went to his death to show people the right way. Verses of the Qur'an therefore came to be interpreted in terms of Husayn and his fate.

By contrast, the Prophet Muhammad, whom the Sunnis also confess, retreated into the background. 'Ali too is venerated by the Shiites. Although, according to Shiite texts, he was a stout, short-sighted 'baldhead', as 'lion' and 'father of the dust' he embodied all youthful virtues: the model of bravery and eloquence. However, the Prophet's grandson Husayn is much closer to Shiite hearts than his father, who was not descended from the Prophet and did not die such a pitiful death. No wonder, then, that Husayn's tomb in Karbala, with its imposing mosque, became the most popular pilgrimage place of the Shiites and the day of Husayn's death, the tenth day of the month of Muharram of the year 61 after the Hijrah (10 October 680 CE), later became the great public annual day of mourning (*'ashurah*). On this day, not only are prayers, hymns and songs offered to 'Husayn, Fatimah's son, the martyr', but there are also passion plays (*ta'ziya*), which are often combined with processions marked by the bloody self-flagellation of those who take part.

Where does the Shiah have its spiritual roots? Earlier Western scholarship thought that the Shiah, which today is widespread above all in Iran and southern Iraq, was the product of an Iranian spirituality, even the revenge of Arian Iranianism on the Arabs and Islam. Today, Ignaz Goldziher's view prevails that the Shiites, who arose in the Arabian milieu of Kufa, are 'as Arabian in their roots as Islam itself.'[15] The Shiah is thus not a movement outside the paradigm of the Arab empire. Rather, as Julius Wellhausen put it in his investigation which opened up scholarly research into the Shiah, it is a 'religious political and opposition party in ancient Islam'[16] which strove with all its might for the caliphate but never seized it. Therefore:

- the split in the Ummah which arose through the fight with 'Ali was deepened; indeed it was perpetuated by the violent death of Fatimah's son Husayn, venerated as a martyr for all time;
- the Shiah was now definitively established as a separate 'confession' in Islam: 'Ali as the true caliph and imam of the Shiah and Husayn as its key witness, proclaimed again and again;
- the dynastic principle was undermined by the Shiite opposition through its direct appeal to the family of the Prophet: instead of the hereditary dynasty of Umayyad caliphs there was the succession of imams (spiritual supreme heads);
- the Shiah can therefore be understood adequately only as an opposition movement within the paradigm of the Arab empire (P II).

With Husayn's death, the Shiite dream of rule over the Ummah seemed over. But the battle went on. For the Shiites held to their conviction: only four people could be regarded as legitimate successors to the Prophet, as 'imams' (the Shiah specialist Heinz Halm speaks of the 'Fourer' Shiah): 'Ali, Hasan, Husayn and a certain Muhammad whom I shall discuss in due course.

The new bearer of the hope of the opposition, the Mahdi; the second civil war

Husayn, the rival, was dead but the opposition of 'Abdallah ibn az-Zubayr, representative of the primacy of Mecca and the Qurayshi aristocracy, was to prove even more dangerous. Having taken his father's side against 'Ali in the 'Battle of the Camel', he was able secretly to assemble an army from holy Mecca, come forward as an anti-caliph and (at least nominally) gain control of a large part of the Islamic world. There followed a second civil war, which was to last twelve years (680–92). Yazid's troops were able to defeat 'Abdallah's followers at Medina, lay siege to Mecca and even set the Ka'bah on fire but that only reinforced the widespread view that the Umayyads were fundamentally godless. The Shiites saw this confirmed in the unexpected death of Yazid (at the end of 683), after which the besieging troops withdrew, and emphasized further by the surprising death of his young son and successor Mu'awiyyah II (in 684). It was only thanks to the subsequent disputes in the house of Umayyah and the tensions between the Yemenite and Qaysitish tribes in Syria that Ibn az-Zubayr was not immediately attacked again and was able to hold power for twelve years.

The Shiites of Kufa, above all the 'repenters' (*tawabun*) who wanted to atone for Husayn's death with the sword and the battle-cry 'vengeance for al-Husayn', likewise turned against the Umayyads. But though some 4000 Shiite Arabs from all over Iraq had spent a day and a night weeping and wailing at Husayn's tomb, their march on Syria once again ended in catastrophe: at the beginning of 685, near Karbala, they were torn to pieces by government troops.

The new spokesman of the 'repenters', al-Mukhtar,[17] a pro-'Ali rebel from Ta'if, who had remained behind in Kufa, met with the same fate two years later when he rebelled against the governor of Kufa. Granted, he was able to bring the citadel under his dictatorial control for a year and, after a counter-revolution, ordered the execution of all those blamed for the Karbala massacre. However, in 687 he was besieged by an army of the governor of Basra. Mukhtar and many Arab tribal warriors fell in the battle; countless non-Arab clients who had converted to Islam (*mawali*), craftsman and tradesmen who had probably supported Mukhtar to improve their legal and financial status, also paid with their blood.

The ideological background to this movement is important. Mukhtar and his followers appealed to someone who was able to help them: Muhammad, the third son of 'Ali, in distant Medina.[18] In him they saw the fourth imam, the only legitimate successor to the Prophet after 'Ali, Hasan and Husayn. Muhammad was not an authentic descendant of the Prophet, as he was born from the marriage of 'Ali with a Hanafite (hence Muhammad ibn al-Hanafiyah), which weakened his authority. He wanted to have nothing to do with the Kufa rebellion and remained in Medina, although a throne had already been prepared for him in Kufa. Nevertheless, Mukhtar unswervingly maintained that, as distinct from the two 'wrongly-guided' caliphs (the Umayyad in Damascus and the anti-caliph Ibn az-Zubayr in Mecca), Muhammad was 'rightly-guided', in Arabic *al-mahdi* (from *hada*, 'to lead or guide').[19] This is the origin of the title Mahdi, which was to prove historically significant.

This had nothing to do with Muhammad ibn al-Hanafiyah, since he explicitly condemned the rebellion in Kufa after its failure; indeed, after the end of the anti-caliphate, in 692 he travelled from Mecca to Damascus, to pay homage to the caliph who had acceded to power there. This man, 'Abd al-Malik, turned out to be another great caliph. In 700 Muhammad died peacefully in Medina but the idea of the Mahdi lived on among the Shiites and underwent a remarkable transformation.

Initially this title had no kind of eschatological meaning but simply designated the legitimate caliph or imam. However, after the death of Muhammad ibn al-Hanafiyah, the Shiites of Kufa (who had been driven underground by the strict regime of the Umayyad governor) became increasingly convinced that the Mahdi proclaimed by Mukhtar was not dead but had been transported from the world. He lived, hidden in a ravine, on Mount Radwah near Medina, well guarded and fed by wild animals. Soon he would soon return, to establish his rule and, with it, true Islam. From the eighth century this idea of the 'transportation', 'absence' and 'return' of the true imam was increasingly developed in the Shiah, but from the beginning it was also alive among the Sunnis.[20] Now, it has an explicitly messianic character: the advent of a worldly ruler who will restore the justice of the early days. Many Muslims still await the return of the Mahdi.

How far Jewish, Christian, Gnostic and Iranian influences were at work in this process can hardly be determined, but—in view of the numerous non-Arab mawali involved—it cannot be ruled out. The one thing that is certain is that the 'Fourer' Shiites finally shrank into small groups, whereas most Shiites turned to other imams:

- The Fiver Shiites or Zaydiyyah split off, with Zayd ibn 'Ali as the fifth imam.
- The Sevener Shiites or Ismailis recognize a seventh imam in the person of Isma'il (died 765), son of Ja'far as-Sadiq; they spread most widely with the Karmates and Fatimids in the tenth and eleventh centuries but were repressed by the Ayyubids and the Seljuks, so that only remnants remained, such as the Druse in the Near East and the Nizaris in India, who recognize the Aga Khan as their supreme head. The present Aga Khan, Karim al-Husayni Shah, has become well known for his charitable activities.[21]
- The Twelver Shiites or Imamis, found mostly in Iran, are by far the largest group: they recognize a series of twelve imams, free from sin and infallible, the twelfth of whom has lived in secret since 873 and will come again as Mahdi at the end of time. Until then, the most senior religious scholars of the Shiite 'clerical' hierarchy represent him: the Ayatollahs (Arabic *mujtahid*), who are authorized to decide in religious or political disputes (by *ijtihad*). They became the normative religious and political power in Persia in the sixteenth century under the Safavids. In the twentieth century, Ayatollah Khomeini, as a key

figure in this Shiite hierarchy, led the revolution against the Westernized Shah of Persia.[22]

Thus the Shiites stepped on to the stage of world politics; they also played a prominent role in Iraq after the 2003 war, where they form more than sixty per cent of the population.

For my analysis of the prevailing paradigm I shall turn again to the dominant convictions, values and patterns of behaviour of the vast majority of Muslims, the Sunnis. After some complications, Sunni Islam and the dynasty of the Umayyads reached its climax under its fifth caliph, who in many respects can be compared with the first.

3. Imperial religious politics under the aegis of Islam

Only around six decades had passed since the Prophet Muhammad had made the great leap from Mecca to Medina but in those few generations how much the world had changed for the Arabs! Vast territories from North Africa to east Persia had fallen under their rule, though as yet their language, administration and culture had not been Arabized. The new generations knew the Prophet Muhammad only by hearsay. Whereas Mu'awiyyah had been the Prophet's scribe (at least for a short time), the fifth caliph of the Umayyad dynasty in Damascus, 'Abd al-Malik, was born in Medina more than ten years after the Prophet's death.

A pious autocrat: 'Abd al-Malik

To put an end to the confusion over the caliphate and the second civil war, the leaders of the Umayyad regime in Damascus had proclaimed a new caliph in Damascus in 684. Marwan was descended from a different Umayyad line; instead of the Sufyanids there were now the Marwanids. When Marwan died the following year, his son 'Abd al-Malik (caliph from 685 to 705)[23] succeeded him without any difficulty. He proved to be such a capable politician, administrator and general that he has been called the second founder of the Umayyad empire.

'Abd al-Malik has often been compared with Mu'awiyyah and these two are by far the most significant caliphs of the Umayyad dynasty. If Mu'awiyyah united the Arab empire after the first civil war, 'Abd al-Malik restored the unity of the empire after the confusions surrounding Yazid's succession to the throne and the second civil war. And if Mu'awiyyah, and his son Yazid, created the foundation of a centralist monarchy through political and military measures, 'Abd al-Malik, together with his son Walid, introduced a significant epoch of reform, the high point of the Umayyad period.

Both caliphs ruled for two decades and were able to get things moving. They did not rule only by consent but often also had issues decided by force of arms, for example the exclusion of the anti-caliphs—'Ali under Mu'awiyyah and Ibn az-Zubayr under 'Abd-al-Malik. Both undertook larger or smaller campaigns against Byzantium in the spirit of *jihad* and to train their own troops and also waged wars on their own territories, Mu'awiyyah in Iraq and 'Abd al-Malik in Syria and Arabia.

However, Mu'awiyyah seems to have been better able than 'Abd al-Malik to cut short violent clashes by negotiations (as he did with 'Ali) or to avoid such clashes altogether (as he did with Hasan). Whereas Mu'awiyyah was charming and attractive and dominated the discussions of his advisory body by his intellectual superiority, 'Abd al-Malik behaved in a lordly and detached way even towards the heads of the tribes, reserving the most important decisions for himself. Unquestionably, under him the caliphate became considerably more autocratic, hierarchical and bureaucratic.

'Abd al-Malik was more religious than Mu'awiyyah, who had confessed Islam only when Muhammad succeeded in capturing Mecca. By contrast, 'Abd al-Malik had spent half his life with his father, in thoroughly Muslim Medina, and had been given a very religious upbringing there. He knew the Qur'an and took great delight in cultivating friendly relations with the pious and with Qur'anic scholars. Moreover, his private life corresponded very closely to Muslim ideals.

That explains why 'Abd al-Malik paid more heed to the religious feelings of his subjects than did his predecessors. He was anxious that his subjects, like him, should really know the Qur'an. He would have liked to transfer the cultic centre of Mecca—for so long in the hands of the anti-caliph—to Syria but he had to drop this plan, and his plan to bring the Prophet's pulpit to Syria, so as to raise the religious status of Damascus. The outrage over that in Medina would have been too great. He had to content himself with encouraging pilgrimages to Jerusalem, which was rather nearer than Mecca and the only city in the world which could compete with it in holiness. The Dome of the Rock, which he had built, and which later became so famous, is both the expression of this high esteem for Jerusalem and a religious and political symbol.

Not only did 'Abd al-Malik have an acute knowledge of human nature; he was also a great power politician, able to rein in the northern tribes and capable of being unscrupulous, indeed cruel, when it came to the caliphate. He did not hesitate personally to murder his cousin when the latter dared to seek to rule. Yet he favoured his kinsmen more than any of his predecessors: the whole wider Umayyad family lived in Damascus. He gave them governors' posts but did not hesitate to keep a strict eye on them and deposed them mercilessly when he thought them inefficient. He was also skilful enough to comfort Khalid, son of the caliph Yazid, who had been excluded from succession to the caliphate, by marrying him to his daughter. He himself married a daughter of Yazid, ʿAtikah, who became his favourite wife.

In domestic politics, ʿAbd al-Malik's most important aim was to restore the unity of the empire and the caliphate. That meant, first, ending the second civil war with the Meccan anti-caliph Ibn az-Zubayr and, second, restoring the authority of the caliphate in refractory Iraq. His highly qualified, and utterly loyal, commander for the two operations was the general and governor al-Hajjaj ibn Yusuf,[24] who later became famous, a man who was fearless and feared, but not cruel. Al-Hajjaj besieged and conquered Mecca in 692 (in the process the already ageing anti-caliph, who had hidden in the Kaʿbah, was killed). Then he proceeded against Iraq: the caliph nominated him governor of Basra in order to gain control of the Iraqi province and its army, which were competing with Syria, and then subdue the Kharijites. This he did. Al-Hajjaj, an outstanding organizer, deservedly became viceroy, with dictatorial authority over all the eastern provinces. From the newly-built garrison city of Wasit, with the support of the Syrian army he now ruled Iraq virtually as a hostile territory. Later, however, he did much to develop the canal system and to encourage agriculture. He also extended his rule further east, as we shall see.

The conquest of North Africa also made progress, since ʿAbd al-Malik's governor succeeded in attracting the Berbers to the Arab side against the Byzantines and in 697 captured Carthage, the capital of the Byzantine province. However, even in the time of ʿAbd al-Malik it was evident that the paradigm change introduced by the caliphate of Muʿawiyyah did not just relate to a change of political structure but had an effect on the social and religious structure of the Ummah.

More than any of his predecessors ʿAbd al-Malik advanced the Arabization of the conquered territories, to make his empire increasingly free from foreign influences and to emphasize his equality with (or even superiority to) the earlier empires. This Arabization had a thoroughly religious dimension: it was aimed, deliberately, at Islamization.[25] The caliph, strongly moulded by the harsh experiences of the second civil war, was aware that peoples in the provinces, so different and remote from one another, had to be made to realize the unity and distinctive character of the Islamic state, which had grown so quickly. That could come about only on the basis of religion. ʿAbd al-Malik acted as ʿUmar, two generations before him, had acted with his new calendar: 'he did it not with manifestos but with symbols'[26] and thus aroused both the political and the military interest of the Arabs. Three of his measures had numerous consequences for people of the time: they related to currency, official language and art.[27]

Introduction of a Muslim currency

The currency reform (presumably in the context of a renewed conflict with Byzantium) was aimed at Arabization and Islamization: the introduction of a distinctive Muslim currency in place of Greek gold and Persian silver. In the Persian sphere of influence, first a marginal legend, *bismi'llah* ('in the name of God'), later expanded with the word *rabbi* ('my Lord'), was added to the traditional Sasanian coins.[28] Likewise, at a very early stage, the cross was obliterated from the Byzantine coins which had initially been taken over.[29] Formerly, the paper money introduced into Byzantium from Egypt—the only place with the relevant specialist workshops—had Christian inscriptions and the cross or a trinitarian formula as watermarks. Now by order of the caliph, the Arabic saying from the Qur'an, 'Say, He alone is God!', was put on them.

Byzantium did not accept this and threatened to stamp insults to the Prophet on the gold coins, all of which came to Arabia from Byzantium. This led 'Abd al-Malik to carry out a plan which Mu'awiyyah seems already to have conceived: he had Arabic gold coins minted in the name of Allah with Qur'anic sayings about the authority of the Prophet (similarly, al-Hajjaj had silver coins minted in Kufa). However, this move did not find immediate approval; the coins had the same weight as the Byzantine gold pieces which had already been discontinued and therefore could not immediately suppress the earlier money. However, eventually the Arab dinar became established as a leading currency in international trade.

There is no doubt that the replacement of the cross or a trinitarian formula with a verse from the Qur'an understood to be anti-Christian had high symbolic value. This is emphasized by the fact that the same thing happened with Egyptian luxury goods (*tiraz*), ceramics and glass weights. 'Abd al-Malik even had milestones and signposts Arabized and Islamized, which makes it more understandable that even in our day, for example in Saudi Arabia, care is taken that street lights or traffic signals do not display the form of the cross.

Arabic becomes the official language

The administrative reform was likewise aimed at Arabization and Islamization. The introduction of Arabic as the official language of the administration in place of Greek and Persian was a highly symbolic change for non-Muslims, who hitherto had despised Arabic as an uncultivated, incomprehensible, unspeakable Bedouin language. Were those with a Greek or Persian education now to deal with the chancelleries only in Arabic? Hitherto, in the official financial world—the main activity of the government—Greek had been used in Damascus and Persian in Kufa. Now the whole system of accounting was changed (somewhat laboriously) by translating the tax register: summaries, copies and reports now appeared in Arabic.

The Greek and Persian government officials, who of course also spoke Arabic, at first remained in office, since one had to be able to understand Greek and Persian to translate into Arabic. Christian officials thus remained influential in the Muslim Arab financial world for a long time (and were often hated as a result). These Greek- and Persian-speaking officials, taken over from the old empire, were gradually replaced by a new generation of Arabic-speaking clients, whom they had trained. This undoubtedly raised the cultural and religious awareness of the Arabs: ultimately the mandatory official language indicated that the true and better Arab religion had prevailed.

The reverse side of this development was that as a result of the growing Greek and Persian influence on it, Arabic itself changed—its vocabulary, certain grammatical rules, syntax and style—away from the Qur'an![30] It is significant that, to his father's great sorrow, Walid, 'Abd al-Malik's son and successor, could not speak the high Arabic of the Qur'an. A problem arose which was to cause great difficulties for Islam (and still does): classical Arabic was now spoken only on solemn occasions; otherwise its use was limited to the realm of literature. The Qur'an had to be proclaimed as a writing of revelation, but because of its antique language it was often understood only vaguely by the people—like Latin in the medieval churches of Italy and Spain. In the courts of the Arab princes, the Arabic heritage was cultivated in Bedouin poetry, in romantic reminiscence of earlier times, but new themes were added: praise of the princes, party struggles, city life and also love poetry.

Art is Islamized

The beginnings of Islamic art could be seen in the previous paradigm (P I); however, we known them only from literature, some inscriptions and coins. In the following paradigm (P II) Umayyad art developed especially in Syria, Palestine, Transjordan and Iraq. Many famous mosques were built, in Damascus, Jerusalem, Medina, Kufa and Wasit, as were numerous palaces and villas and the unique monument of the Dome of the Rock in Jerusalem.[31]

Did Islamic art contribute anything new? That is a much-discussed question. It has sometimes been asserted that Islamic art took over practically all the existing forms and techniques of the artistic traditions of the Near East and the Mediterranean: direct prototypes can be shown for every decorative motif, every unit of planning and every detail of construction. However, this is only one side of the truth. Under Islam, a new ceramic art and a novel ornamental Arabic script came into being which—together with ornamental plaster work—spread across the empire and became the hallmark of Islamic art.

Certain other symbols (Christian and Persian) disappeared and the depiction of human beings and animals was deliberately avoided. So, while individual elements of architecture might have been borrowed, the buildings as a whole were very different from all that had preceded them.

The originality and uniqueness of Islamic art cannot be disputed. As the Harvard art historian Oleg Grabar has convincingly shown, it is based on two parallel and mutually supplementary activities within a single process: on the one hand people adapted the Hellenistic or Iranian traditions which they found, preserving them or rejecting them; on the other they adopted, developed and integrated new forms and techniques inspired by the new social and religious milieu.

> The creation of an Islamic art was not the result of an artistic or aesthetic doctrine, inspired by the new religion or even by social or other consequences of the prophetic message, but consisted in transforming preceding traditions compatible with the as yet barely formulated identity of the Muslim community and at times trying to serve its needs or to proclaim its presence (as in the minaret and tiraz [luxury fabric]).[32]

Just as the tower became a minaret, in Islamic architecture everything took on a new, Islamic, meaning.

What was the aim of the intensive Umayyad building policy?[33] The erection of monumental buildings was quite deliberately a 'Byzantine' demonstration of power against Byzantium. The quasi-imperial character of the caliphate and the sovereignty of the Islamic state were to be demonstrated to Christians and Jews, particularly in Jerusalem. According to the most recent research, it is certain that the Dome of the Rock in Jerusalem (*Qubbat as-sakhra*), though often called the Mosque of 'Umar, was not built by 'Umar (who did not actually capture Jerusalem) but in 692 by 'Abd al- Malik, when the financial situation of the empire had stabilized after the second civil war. The Dome of the Rock was not built as a mosque (in this circular building with a prominent rock in the middle Muslims would not have been able to carry out their usual strict instructions about prayer), but as a great representative building.[34]

Why was it built? To make clear to all the world here, at its holiest place, on the bare rock of Mount Moriah, where according to tradition God demanded the sacrifice of Abraham's son, that Islam likewise is directly connected with the ancestor of Jews and Christians. Indeed Islam has the primacy, because it has renewed the original religion of Abraham, contrary to Jewish and Christian falsifications. With triumphalist and propagandist intent, the Dome of the Rock was therefore provided with an inscription running round it in two bands, on which, as on the coins, the unity and oneness of God is proclaimed—over against the Christian doctrine of God as Trinity. Jesus is mentioned, in good Qur'anic style, not as God's son but as God's servant and Muhammad is praised as the Prophet who—as the notion now is—will intercede for his people on the Last Day.

Greek specialists above all, architects and artists, were taken into service for the mosques, and Greek forms and motifs were borrowed. In Byzantium, people had always been skilled in using decorative splendour as part of mission: this was seen as a way of disseminating Byzantine Christian culture. However, that was a delusion: the opposite happened, and Byzantine art was Islamized. The elements of Byzantine architecture and style, now also used for countless palaces and other buildings, were given a new function and put at the service of the Islamic faith—just as Christians had done previously with Graeco-Roman art and would do later in Spain with Islamic buildings.

Here and there,there were excesses in the direction of religious fanaticism. 'Abd al-Malik prohibited the depiction of crosses throughout the empire and his brother, the governor of Egypt, even had bands of Muslim script attached to Christian churches. And it seems to be more than a rumour that all pigs were slaughtered a year before 'Abd al-Malik's death.

'Abd al-Malik's son, al-Walid (caliph from 750 to 715), now enjoyed the internal peace that his father had brought about by force of arms. Al-Walid is said for the first time to have demonstrated his majesty by pomp. A passionate architect, he did not hesitate to strip the gilding from a Christian church in Baalbek and use it for the al-Aqsa mosque in the temple court in Jerusalem. Not only did he thoroughly rebuild the mosque of Medina but, as his father would have liked to do, he took the church of St John in Damascus away from the Christians in order to enlarge the adjoining main mosque in the Syrian basilica tradition and restore it to splendour. In good Islamic fashion all human figures were omitted from mosaics but the idyllic Byzantine houses and landscapes in the background were soon brought into the foreground—were they images of paradise? Two- or three-dimensional pictorial representations were now taboo, although individual instances had been tolerated in the early period. Pictures of angels, human beings and animals were replaced by floral and geometric forms. Calligraphy began its triumphal progress. In the Umayyad mosque of Damascus we see, for the very first time in an inscription on a building, the classic Islamic confession, but here in three parts: 'Our Lord is God alone, our religion is Islam, and our Prophet Muhammad.'[35]

Everywhere—as also in the new mosques of Medina—what the Byzantines had thought to be an expression of cultural and political superiority became a demonstration of the triumph of Islam over Byzantium. At the same time the mosque became a compact testimony to the unity of political and religious authority in the caliphate. The caliphate gave Islam political splendour and Islam gave the caliphate religious authority. In view of this development it is no surprise that Islamization was extended to the sphere of law.

4. The origin of Islamic law

It has already become clear that neither in the Qur'an nor in the time of the first caliphs (P I) can one speak of a specifically Islamic law in the narrow sense. The paradigm change (P II) had an effect in the sphere of law, as I shall attempt to demonstrate, using the pioneering studies of the history of law by Joseph Schacht,[36] critically supplemented by those of N.J. Coulson.[37] Schacht's position is largely shared by Muslim scholars such as F. Rahman[38] and A.A.A. Fyzee,[39] but criticized severely on some points, for example by M.M. al-Azami.[40]

State judges: the qadis

'Few societies in history can have been subject to such swift changes and have been so ill-equipped to deal with them as were the Muslim Arabs,' remarks the British legal historian Noel Coulson. This is meant as praise: 'That Umayyad legal practice achieved a workable synthesis of the diverse influences at work in the Islamic empire was a real achievement.'[41] The caliphs were very interested in preserving the administrative structures they found in the provinces as far as possible, and had no inhibitions about taking over alien legal concepts and institutions.

In the course of their energetic political leadership and organization of the administration of the new empire the Umayyads could not avoid also developing the legal system. Their vast empire was held together spiritually only by Islam. Under their leadership arose:

- the beginnings of a common Islamic law, the Shariah (*shari'ah*, 'way to the watering hole' or holy law), though this underwent a long development;
- the appointment of state judges (*qudat*, singular *qadi*) and the training of Islamic legal scholars (*fuqaha'*, singular *faqih*), but on a complete private basis;
- the formation of an Islamic jurisprudence (*fiqh*, 'knowledge', jurisprudence) which had not previously existed.

Christians may be surprised that jurisprudence, and not knowledge generally, is honoured with the great word 'knowledge'. However, in P II what would become even clearer in the following paradigms was already becoming evident: law (albeit often practised by theologians) and not theology stands at the centre of Islam. So one can say of later paradigms, but not of the essence of Islam nor even of its early paradigms, that Islam, originally the religion of an ethic, became a religion of the law.

The Umayyads appointed a series of new officials (like the originally Byzantine market inspectors). Typical of the period is the first mention of state judges, the qadis.[42] In the new society they supplemented, or even replaced, the old arbiters (*hukkam*, singular *hakam*[43]) of pre-Islamic Arab society. The great difference from the independent *hakam*, whose office was *ad hoc* and who still existed in the tribes, was that the qadi was a delegate of the governor. This put the qadis in a framework of competences given to them by the caliphs, though with the support of the tribes, so that in fact authentic Arabs were always nominated. The governor had a decisive advantage: he could remove qadis if they did not follow his policy.

The qadis were thus legal officers of the governor; initially they were subordinate and often honorary but towards the end of the Umayyad period they occupied a relatively independent and important position in the government apparatus. Their decisions laid the foundation of what would later be called Islamic law. Their judgements did not have the character of precedents, from which the judgements of later judges had to be derived, as in other legal systems. The practice of justice was still fluid. Iyas ibn Mu'awiyyah (who died in 740 at the age of seventy-six)[44] was typical of these first judges. In forming his decisions, he went neither by the Qur'an nor by a tradition of the Prophet but relied on sound common sense, knowledge of character and his intuition. In contrast to later legal practice, he did not attach much importance to the statements of witnesses (which were often misused) and rejected conclusions by analogy (*qiyas*), which did not allow differences.

However, this led to serious differences in jurisprudence: on the one hand different customary justice was practised in different places and on the other, each judge decided according to his personal view (*ra'y*). There was no superior law and no effort on the part of the central government to unify the law. In the light of circumstances, which grew more and more complicated, the qadis were increasingly forced to specialize and by the last Umayyad decades in practice only specialists were appointed to the office of judge. Where did these specialists come from?

Islamization of the law: pious specialists

By 'pious specialists'[45] we are not to imagine systematic scholarly professionals or even professionals trained by the state. They were more interested in religion than in law, initially more in ritual practices than in legal decisions. They were religiously committed 'lay people', who reflected on questions about the Qur'an and law and discussed them privately in their leisure time, mostly in groups with like-minded friends, and then gave legal information and opinions (*fatwah*, plural *fatawa*), similar to the 'answers' which the Jewish Gaons (heads of schools) had long been accustomed to provide for their fellow believers. It was not a 'faith authority' that was responsible for the interpretation of the Qur'an but the individual, who could develop considerable knowledge. There were many new Muslims among these religious specialists and their groups, but to begin with their access to the office of judge was barred. What determined their real interest?

The interest of the pious legal experts and advisers was not primarily the legal practice of the courts but an Islamic way of life for everyone. They had the impression that the original impulses and elements of Islam were being overlaid by a mass of administrative regulations and foreign legal precepts. The judgements of the qadis were often arbitrary and the government had done little to guarantee the application of the original Islamic criteria; on all sides an Islamic spirit and content was lacking. As religious idealists they investigated soberly and precisely whether, and to what extent, existing customary law corresponded with Qur'anic, or generally Islamic, norms. For them, the basis of all legal findings was not sound common-sense and perspicacity but the Qur'an (and in the course of time also the 'Sunnah of the Prophet'). They wanted to decide from a religious (or more precisely an ethical and ritual) perspective whether and how far particular customs (for example usury, inheritance customs and the sale of slaves) were to be preserved or rejected. To begin with they had little influence on the official pronouncements of the qadis, which followed other categories, since they did not take part in court sessions as advisers. Yet, slowly but surely, they created the foundations the Islamization of existing customary law.

If here too we follow Joseph Schacht, we find that: 'They impregnated the sphere of law with religious and ethical ideas, subjected it to Islamic norms, and incorporated it into the body of duties incumbent on every Muslim. In doing this they achieved on a much wider scale and in a vastly more detailed manner what the Prophet in the Qur'an had tried to do for the early Islamic community of Medina. As a result the popular and administrative practice of the late Umayyad period was transformed into the religious law of Islam. The resulting ideal theory still had to be translated into practice; this task was beyond the power of the pious specialists and had to be left to the interest and zeal of the caliphs, governors, qadis or interested individuals. The circumstances in which the religious law of Islam came into being caused it to develop, not in close connection with the practice, but as the expression of a religious ideal in opposition to it.'[46]

Islamization began quite modestly through legal experts such as Ibrahim an-Nakha'i (who died in 715),[47] the first juristic personality in Kufa with a tangible profile (alongside ash-Sha'bi). Other legal experts in Medina gave legal information to people with qualms of conscience, for example in matters of marriage or divorce, almsgiving or fasting, i.e. more in moral than in really technical legal questions. These religious legal experts, who were highly prized by the people (and often by the rulers) for their pious commitment and their activity as advisers and givers of rulings, often criticized decisions of the government or customs of the people. However, they were not fundamentally opposed to the Umayyad government and state. What was important for the future was that they possessed the trust of the people.

The theoretical foundation of the law

The old so-called old legal schools formed in the last decades of the Umayyad period, when there were more and more legal scholars. They were active in many places: in Iraq, where Kufa was a leading centre, but also in Medina and Mecca and in Syria. These legal schools had no official status, no strict organization, no unified orientation of teaching; they worked on a voluntary, private basis, supported by the veneration and financial resources of the people. Differences between them arose only because of the great regional differences in the cultures of the provinces, not because of particular legal principles or methods. In this earliest stage of Islamic jurisprudence there was 'a considerable body of common doctrine which was subsequently reduced by increasing differentiation between the schools'.[48]

The norms of the Qur'an had never before been taken as seriously. Conclusions in a variety of spheres were formally derived from them, from family and inheritance law to fasting and ritual prayer. Each school represented its own living tradition and established teaching, which was designated as 'Sunnah' or by some such term, but a local consensus (*ijma'*) of scholars could be established, extending far beyond the general basic consensus of Muslims. Whereas the Muslim consensus related only to the essentials of faith and was held generally, the consensus of the scholars, despite local or regional differentiation, was very specific and definite. When it came to determining the content, schools elsewhere that saw some things differently were not excluded, but the consent of all schools was sought. This seemed to guarantee something like infallibility.

However, people were not satisfied with founding Islamic religious law theoretically on the consensus of scholars. It also needed to be safeguarded historically. Since it was a widespread custom in antiquity to put one's own work under the name of a great master (for example in the New Testament the so-called Pastoral Epistles addressed to Timothy and Titus were put in the mouth of Paul), Muslim scholars saw nothing wrong in giving a name to something that was originally anonymous. So the consensus of unnamed legal scholars which existed in the present was increasingly attributed to a famous figure of the past, to emphasize the continuity and authority of the tradition. For example in Kufa, about which we are best informed, the whole doctrine of the school was attributed to Ibrahim an-Nakha'i, mentioned earlier, who in his time, as a man of the centre, had only imparted legal advice. In Medina, people referred to the 'seven jurists' of prehistory, though we know virtually nothing about their teaching. The first jurists about whose teaching we can establish anything authentic come from the last decades of the Umayyad period, that is, the first half of the eighth century, some hundred years after the death of the Prophet.

The scholars went still further. In Kufa, which is a good example, the basis of Islamic law was finally connected with the beginnings of Islam in the city, attributed to a companion of the Prophet, Ibn Mas'ud. The same thing happened in Mecca in connection with Ibn Abbas and in Medina with Caliph 'Umar, both companions of the Prophet. We cannot exclude the possibility that authentic material from the legal practice and oral tradition of the early Islamic period (P I) was preserved, but in the judgement of at least Western historians 'the great mass of the alleged doctrines of the ancients were anachronistic ascriptions'.[49] The last step was then a connection with the Prophet himself. First in distant Iraq and then in Syria (not so much in Medina, the Prophet's home city), the teaching of the jurists and the practice of the local community (which at first existed only as an ideal) were identified with the 'Sunnah of the Prophet'. This 'tradition' was thus understood not primarily theologically and politically but juristically. However, to begin with this happened only generally, with no reference to particular sayings or actions of the Prophet.

This tendency only became established in the next period, so we can now turn again to the political developments, or rather complications, under the Umayyad caliphs.

5. A new community of many peoples

At the climax of Umayyad rule it became clear that the more strongly the empire was Arabized, the more pressing it was to decide what attitude to adopt to the non-Arabs and non-Muslims, above all the Christians. A decision was urgently needed and a turning point for the relationship between Arabs and non-Arabs, Muslims and Christians, may be said to have come about in this paradigm. The policy of segregation pursued by the rightly-guided caliphs (P I) could not be sustained under the conditions of a great empire. The transformation of the patriarchal regime into an imperial government was the basis for this change.

From patriarchal regime to imperial government

Political and religious loyalty to the Islamic regime now replaced loyalty to the person of the caliph. This not only led to an accelerated centralization of the state but also served a 'new ideological policy'.[50] In Mu'awiyyah's time a supreme Arab tribal leader had resided in Damascus, surrounded by other tribal heads. Now an 'emperor' ruled from a richly adorned and well-guarded palace: the 'caliph or representative of God' in the political and religious sense, also called 'God's trustee' (*amin Allah*), 'God's shepherd' (*ra'i Allah*), 'God's authority' (*sultan Allah*) or 'God's lieutenant' (*na'ib Allah*).[51] Sometimes he was even presented as 'pantocrator' (as a parallel but counterpart to the Byzantine depictions of Christ as ruler of all).

The caliph granted festal audiences, crowned and clad in royal garments, surrounded by the most senior court officials, scribes and guards. His daily work consisted of deliberations, receptions and hours of prayer. There was also private entertainment of every kind: hunting, poetry readings, musical performances, wine and dancing girls. People were admitted to the caliph only through a complicated and specific protocol. The great ruler had to be addressed in a subservient tone, and was praised by poets in hymns. The tribal rulers still had important tasks but the imperial government now lay in the hands of professional officials who were responsible to the caliph alone. Their oaths of loyalty to the caliph showed that, in this court, everything depended on obedience and discipline.

In short, the former patriarchal regime (P I) had been transformed into an impartial government (P II). 'Whereas the early Caliphate had been a series of individual reigns deeply dependent upon the personal religious or patriarchal qualities of the Caliphs, the new Caliphate was an institution independent of individual office holders. The Umayyads had managed to turn the Caliphate into a state regime, but at the same time they had kept alive and incorporated into the symbolism of the empire its specifically Islamic heritage.'[52] This now had considerable consequences for the whole of society.

The dividing walls collapse

I cannot report here the dramatic effects of the Arab conquests on agriculture and the regional development of the economy. In Iran the economy boomed while in Mesopotamia, Syria and Egypt it deteriorated and in Iraq the whole structure changed. More important for my paradigm analysis are the general social upheavals that came about under the pressure of wars, migrations and economic changes. Briefly, these were:[53]

– The Arab military élites became a new class and there were enormous class differences between the ordinary members of a tribe and their leaders. The leaders could afford private palaces, estates and an expensive life of luxury, and this aristocracy strengthened its position by suitable marriages.

– The Arab tribal culture that had preceded Islam dissolved. Military and administrative needs (for example, resettlements and new regiments) resulted in new artificial units. The great clans were divided into groups of thousands and smaller ones were put together.

– As a result of immigration the purely Arab garrison and government towns, no longer consisting of tents or huts but of walled houses, lost their specifically Arab character and became ethnically and religiously mixed centres of administration, trade and production. Countless non-Arab officials, craftsmen and soldiers (including whole Iranian regiments) sought lodging and employment in them.

– The Bedouin Arabs and soldiers became an economically differentiated mercantile class of shopkeepers, merchants, craftsmen, workers and farmers. The new religion provided the opportunity for the rise of a new educated class consisting of theologians, teachers and legal scholars, whose functions were further differentiated.

The segregation between conquerors and conquered established by the second rightly-guided caliph ʿUmar collapsed and the assimilation of Arabs and non-Arabs steadily progressed.

Arabs and non-Arabs mix

At the end of the seventh century the greater part of the Arab army had turned to civilian professions; these people no longer wanted to perform military duties or cut themselves off from the rest of the population. For example, in the city of Marv, in 670 about 50,000 families had been settled but by around 730 only 15,000 still did military service. The more people adapted professionally, the greater the social assimilation. Nowhere did this go further than in highly-civilized Persia, where most of the sons of the 'sons of the desert' now spoke Persian, dressed like Persians, joined in celebrating Persian feasts, drank Persian wine and married Persian wives.

Thus a reciprocal interpenetration of the Arab and non-Arab populations could be detected everywhere. The further the conquests extended, the more ethnic groups were incorporated into the Arab empire: no longer just Aramaeans, Iranians and Jews but, albeit in smaller numbers, also Africans, Turks, gipsies and Indians. How was their position in relation to the Arabs to be defined? What legal status were they to be given?

For a long time the system of mawali or clients, associates, affiliates (*mawlah*, plural *mawali*), which came from pre-Islamic times, seemed to provide a model. For example, former slaves had always been accepted by a tribe, not as full members with equal rights but as 'protected' associates. They remained subordinate: they might not marry any members of the tribe and their children continued to have a subordinate status. Converts or new Muslims also assumed this status, which was legally and socially second-class: they were accepted into a client relationship (*wala'*) usually as the clientele of an eminent guardian, whose personal prestige increased with the number of those he was bound to protect.

However, because of increasing conversions, these mawali, from every possible population, whether prisoners of war or indigenous, became ever more numerous. They often converted in large groups, so that the Arab tribes came to consist less and less of tribal members. Many new Muslims brought the knowledge gained in their cultures, a technical knowledge alien to the Arabs, and technical and organizational experience. The Muslim population thus came to have more and more layers and became increasingly diverse. Aristocratic clans accepted better-off mawali (e.g. the Persian cavalry) as associates, whereas more lowly clans had to content themselves with slave workers and weavers.

But we have to ask: why only as associates, second-class people? Where the mawali came to be in the majority they developed a class consciousness and increasingly clearly made known their demands. Could a dual-class society divided in this way still be the brotherly Ummah originally willed by the Prophet and the Qur'an? Isn't a class society among Muslims really un-Islamic? In view of Arabian exclusiveness, what remained of Islamic solidarity? Isn't the Qur'an, revealed to the Arabs in Arabic, explicitly addressed to all human beings?

To put it bluntly, this represented an attack on the Arab hegemony in the name of Islam. In this situation no one was more interested in methodical reflection on their own religion than the dissatisfied mawali, who had lost their bond with their old society and now possessed an identity only through Islam. In the second and third generation some had enough money to sit in the mosque and discuss their theology and legal knowledge. A time bomb was ticking everywhere for domestic policy, and the mawali played no small role in the situation.[54] But before that the military expansion of the Arab empire went even further.

6. A world empire comes into being

'Abd al-Malik is called father of the kings because—as we can see from the genealogy of the Umayyads below—four of his sons succeeded to the caliphate. Only two of the later Umayyad caliphs were not descended directly from him. His oldest son al-Walid (705–15) succeeded him and could use the

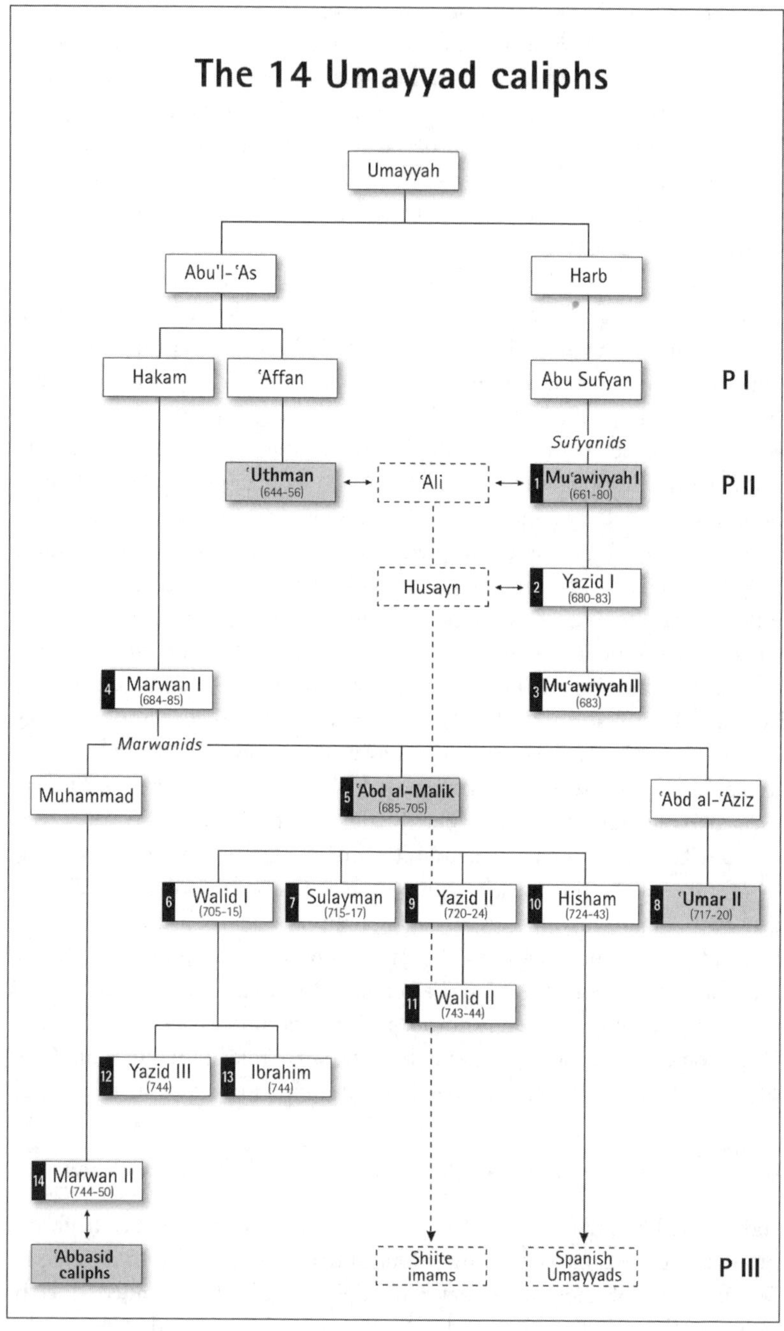
The 14 Umayyad caliphs
Umayyah
Abu'l-'As
Harb
Hakam
'Affan
Abu Sufyan
P I
Sufyanids
'Uthman (644-56)
'Ali
1 Mu'awiyyah I (661-80)
P II
Husayn
2 Yazid I (680-83)
4 Marwan I (684-85)
3 Mu'awiyyah II (683)
Marwanids
Muhammad
5 'Abd al-Malik (685-705)
'Abd al-'Aziz
6 Walid I (705-15)
7 Sulayman (715-17)
9 Yazid II (720-24)
10 Hisham (724-43)
8 'Umar II (717-20)
11 Walid II (743-44)
12 Yazid III (744)
13 Ibrahim (744)
14 Marwan II (744-50)
'Abbasid caliphs
Shiite imams
Spanish Umayyads
P III

consolidation achieved by his father in domestic policy to support powerful external expansion.[55]

Paradigm change in foreign and military policy

During Mu'awiyyah's twenty-year reign (661–80) Arab rule in the east had extended to Khorasan in north-east Iran, to the river Oxus, and in the west as far as present-day Tunisia in North Africa and the Mediterranean islands of Cyprus and Rhodes. However, a seven-year sea blockade of Constantinople came to nothing.

As had happened with the first wave of conquest by the rightly-guided caliphs, for a long time there was nothing more than Arab tribal migrations and the annual deployment of Arab forces from the garrison towns into the neighbouring lands. Now, however, came real wars, motivated by the imperial ambitions of the Umayyads and planned on a world scale. As they were waged further and further from the central Arab areas of settlement, they interested only a part of the population, chiefly those living on the frontiers. In general, resistance to further Arab conquests and the technical expenditure on sieges increased, and plunder and enthusiasm decreased.

A paradigm change, particularly in foreign and military policy, is unmistakable:

- The conquests of the early caliphs (P I) were expansionary wars of the Arab tribes, with enthusiastic tribal warriors and militant leaders around the Arabian peninsula; wages were low but plunder was vast.
- The conquests of the Umayyad caliphs (P II) were strategically-planned imperial wars, aimed at remote goals and carried out with the help of non-Arabian troops and troop leaders (new Muslims or mawali); the wages for these professional soldiers were high, but so was the burden to the taxpayers.

Under Caliph al-Walid the military goals were even more remote than under Mu'awiyyah, the lines of communication and provision were longer and so the tempo of the conquests was slower. Nevertheless, there was again an amazing extension of the Muslim sphere of rule, both eastwards and westwards.

The second wave of conquest: an empire from India to Spain

We shall first look eastwards, where the viceroy al-Hajjaj, fully trusted by al-Walid, determined the strategy of expansion:

– Under Khorasan's governor Qutaybah ibn Muslim, from north-east Persia the Arabs penetrated the lands beyond the Oxus, Central Asian Transoxania

(Turkestan, present-day Uzbekhistan). In 712, they captured Bukhara and Samarkand, but only after long battles. Here, too, the Arabs profited from the weakness of a great power, China, where the Buddhist Tang dynasty was in decline and the Chinese aristocracy could not maintain rule over the more remote parts of Turkestan. This conquest meant the establishment of Islam in central Asia, where it still persists, and the Islamization of the Turkic peoples.

– From southern Persia the Arabs advanced (in the footsteps of Alexander the Great) to Baluchistan, the eastern part of the Iranian highlands, and finally reached the region of the Indus. Al-Hajjaj had paid an unusually large sum of money for his well-equipped troops but allegedly the expedition brought back twice as much. In 712 the Arabs established the emirate of Multan in the Punjab, in present-day Pakistan; for a long time this remained the eastern outpost of Islam. This conquest created the nucleus of Islamic India, from which a great Muslim empire, the Mughal empire, would come into being 700 years later. Since that time Islam (in contrast to Christianity) has had a strong position on the Indian sub-continent.

If we look westwards, to North Africa and then to Europe:

– As early as 697 the Arabs had captured Carthage, the capital of the remote Byzantine province of Africa (now called *Ifriqiya* by the Arabs)—despite the resistance and counter-offensives of the Berbers, only part of whom converted to Islam. Then they moved out from the operational base of Kairouan (= 'camp town'), whose position in central Tunisia protected it against Byzantine attacks by sea, right through the Maghreb to the shores of the Atlantic.

– On the orders of the governor of Ifriqiya, Musa ibn Nusayr, his Berber client Tariq ibn Ziyad crossed the strait and landed in Spain from Berber Africa, near the mountain which since then has been called 'Mountain of Tariq' (*Jabal Tariq*), Gibraltar. On 19 July 711, in a historic battle near Jerez de la Frontera, Tariq and his mostly Berber troops defeated Roderich, the last king of the Christian West Gothic kingdom, at that time riven by internal disputes (in the same year the advances in the east towards central Asia more or less reached their goal). After forced marches, Tariq captured the capital, Toledo. Because of the fall of the king and the capture of the capital, it was easy for Musa, following up with a large Arab army, to bring almost all the Pyrenean peninsula under his power—less by force than by treaty. This meant a far-reaching Islamization of Spain which lasted for more than seven centuries—as long as the Muslims occupied Spain. The '*perdida de España*', the loss of Spain, caused a trauma in the Christian West which still affects it today (for example, in the fear of a 'green flood from Africa to Europe').

What an amazing development! Barely a century after the death of the Prophet, the Arab empire now extended from India to Spain, from the Himalayas in the east to the Pyrenees in the west. In 732 Charles Martel, the founder of the Carolingian dynasty, finally succeeded in stopping the constant Arab advances into France (in the south as far as the Rhône valley and the Garonne, in the north as far as the Loire) in a famous, but badly documented, battle near Tours and Poitiers. Even so, the Islamic conquest—which I have described at length in my book on Christianity[56]—represented a defeat of historic proportions.

The second great confrontation with Christianity

The Arab conquest must not be confused with the total Islamization of the population. There were no mass conversions in the conquered territories: that was not the aim of the Muslims. Large parts of the population remained Christian and many churches continued to be used. A witness to this Christian survival is the most important Byzantine theologian of this period, who was active not in Christian Byzantium but in Muslim Damascus: John of Damascus, a senior official at the Umayyad court who wrote in Greek and who later withdrew into the monastery of Mar Saba near Jerusalem (see A 1, 1).

What about the once-flourishing Christianity of North Africa? With the exception of the Egyptian Coptic Church, after the eighth century it had no chance of survival. The great Latin-speaking churches of Tertullian, Cyprian and Augustine succumbed and the once-important patriarchates of Alexandria, Antioch and Jerusalem sank into insignificance. The areas in which Christianity originated (Palestine, Syria, Egypt) were 'lost' to Christianity. At length, after the conquests the Christianity of North Africa disappeared almost completely. This was a notable development, quite different from that in northern Europe: whereas there the Germanic invaders had adopted the faith of the cultivated Christian residents, in the Near East most of the settled population, with a superior culture, finally accepted the faith of the invaders. Why? I shall consider this later (see C IV, 7, 8).

In the history of the religions did any religion pursue a victorious course as rapid, far-reaching, tenacious and permanent as that of Islam? Scarcely one. So is it any wonder that to the present day Muslim pride is rooted in the experience of the early period that I have just described? Islam is 'a religion of victory'. Is it surprising that the contrast between then and now has been even more painful since nineteenth-century colonization? 'Why have we Muslims in the present remained so culturally and economically backward?'

In his famous 1937 book on *Mohammed and Charlemagne*,[57] the Belgian economic and social historian Henri Pirenne for the first time demonstrated the importance of the Islamic invasion of the Mediterranean world of late antiquity: Islam was so to speak indirectly responsible for the rise of the Frankish kingdom. Undoubtedly there had been a shift in the focal point of Christian history in Europe from the south to the north. This may not have been the case economically, but in political, cultural and religious terms it was. The consequences of the victorious course of Islam (P II) for the formation of the medieval paradigm of Christianity (Christian P III) cannot be overlooked:

- the unity of the Mediterranean world was shattered for ever: to the present day the Mediterranean is no longer a Christian *mare nostrum*;
- the East Roman empire remained permanently weakened even by comparison with the West as a result of the loss of its southern and south-eastern lands;
- the papacy in West Rome was offered the possibility of detaching itself from East Rome and gaining independence from the state. It would develop into one of the main opponents of Islam;
- in the north of Europe the kingdom of the Franks had the historical opportunity to form a new Christian empire.

To put it pointedly, we can say, with Henri Pirenne, that Muhammad made Charlemagne possible. However, this victorious history of early Islam had positive effects not only for Europe but also for Islam itself. The Arab-Islamic empire, which was expanding so powerfully, found itself in an almost life-threatening internal crisis. The time bomb ticking away in domestic politics began to become threatening. There was a first great theological controversy in Islam.

7. A theological controversy with political consequences

The theological dispute had essentially to do with two different cultures that had formed in the course of Umayyad rule:[58]

– On the one hand, there was the court culture of the caliphs and the political élites. In this remote court milieu, people were mainly concerned with architecture, art, philosophy, science, Hellenistic and Persian literature. The Arab aristocracy, whose ideal was the warrior and whose highest values were glory and praise, lived by plunder and state pensions and used possessions and money above all to win themselves praise for their generosity and hospitality;

– On the other hand, there was the urban culture of the new mercantile and educated classes. In this urban milieu, people were more interested in the interpretation of the Qur'an, Islamic law and Arabic literature and mysticism. The

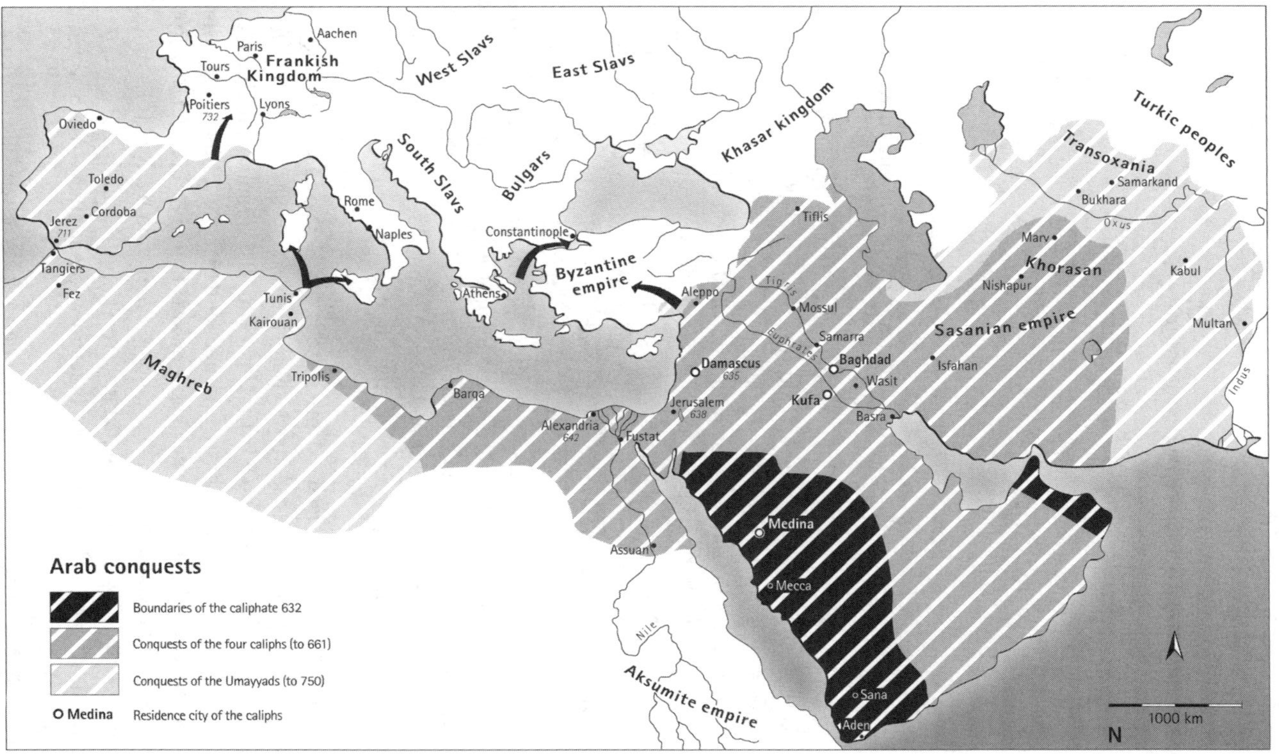
Arab conquests
Boundaries of the caliphate 632
Conquests of the four caliphs (to 661)
Conquests of the Umayyads (to 750)
O Medina Residence city of the caliphs
N
1000 km
Aachen
Paris
Frankish Kingdom
Tours
Poitiers
732
Lyons
Oviedo
Toledo
Cordoba
Jerez
711
Tangiers
Fez
West Slavs
East Slavs
South Slavs
Bulgars
Khasar kingdom
Turkic peoples
Transoxania
Samarkand
Bukhara
Oxus
Rome
Naples
Tunis
Kairouan
Maghreb
Tripolis
Barqa
Constantinople
Athens
Byzantine empire
Aleppo
Tiflis
Tigris
Mossul
Euphrates
Samarra
Damascus
635
Baghdad
Wasit
Kufa
Basra
Jerusalem
638
Alexandria
642
Fustat
Assuan
Nile
Aksumite empire
Medina
Mecca
Sana
Aden
Marv
Khorasan
Nishapur
Sasanian empire
Isfahan
Kabul
Multan
Indus

mawali in particular used their wealth to a remarkable degree to do good works, giving the merchant a central position within the religious intelligentsia and in missions abroad.

Predestination by God—theologically disputed

However, in both milieus people were interested in theology, which now developed slowly in the provinces of the giant empire with their different cultures, though out of very different interests. In dealing with these increasingly far-ranging and complex questions I shall again follow the comprehensive six-volume work by Joseph van Ess and the briefer accounts by W. Montgomery Watt[59] and Tilman Nagel.[60]

In pre-Islamic Arabia, there was a widespread notion that everything was predetermined: by the stars, or by 'fate' (*dahr*). The Qur'an corrected this 'pagan' fatalism in the light of the personal image of God:[61] the personal and living God was now the one who predetermined everything. However, the Qur'an leaves open the question how God's predestination relates to human freedom of decision and responsibility. As I already remarked in connection with the original Islamic community paradigm, the clarification of the relationship between God and human beings, and specifically between divine dispensation and human responsibility, became the core problem of early Islamic theology.

Both divine predestination and human self-determination could be denoted by the word *qadar*, which complicated the problem.[62] Originally, however, *qadar* denoted 'God's cause'; in the Qur'an it denotes the measure of a matter laid down by God[63] and thus God's disposition, providence and predestination: God's determination of destiny. The question now was: wasn't there also a personal responsibility, disposition, human self-determination in the everyday life of the new mercantile and educated classes? Alongside God's *qadar* wasn't there also a human *qadar*? The perspectives 'from above' and 'from below' were different.

'From above': for understandable reasons the Umayyad caliphs and the political élites were interested above all in God's *qadar*. For unlike their four 'rightly-guided' predecessors (P I), the Umayyads (P II) found many difficulties in providing a convincing basis for their authority as caliphs. Following 'Uthman's example, from Mu'awiyyah onwards they did this by designating themselves representatives of God (*khalifat Allah*), who were 'rightly-guided' (*mahdi*). In this way they could signal that everything the caliphs did was rightly guided by divine predetermination, indeed was predestined—in things both good and bad.[64]

Possibly Mu'awiyyah was a predestinarian but the essentially more pious 'Abd al-Malik certainly was: at least for the second half of his reign we may assume that he saw a close connection between the princely grace of God and religious determination. What that means is clarified by a hadith that is said to have circulated under al-Walid I: God would write down only the good deeds of the ruler and not the evil ones. At his accession, Yazid II formally confirmed that a caliph need not give an account of his actions before God, since all that the 'rightly-guided representative' of God did was right. Even the lifestyle of the pleasure-loving al-Walid II, who while a claimant to the throne had led a life of wine, women and song, was excused as divinely willed. In a poem he remarks that a Muslim, as long as he does not fall away from the faith, enters paradise immediately—regardless of his transgressions. This view was widespread in these circles.

Naturally, opposite tendencies developed 'from below', in the milieu of the urban culture of new classes of merchants and educated people and in the face of this exaggerated religious ideology of rule. There was a firm insistence that human beings are responsible for evil; it cannot simply be attributed to God. Every individual is created by God for good but is free to do evil. Each is addressed as an individual and so has his own *qadar*, his own self-determination and responsibility. We can immediately recognize the political explosiveness of such a seemingly theological controversy: if human beings are responsible for their evil deeds, they can be called to account for them before God—be they subject or caliph.

This spiritual and religious current, which cannot always be precisely delineated, soon became highly controversial. It began in Iraq among ascetics who had an almost pietistic consciousness of sin, and was called Qadariyah. To begin with, this movement was not militant, but in Syria, where such thought had possibly circulated since Christian times, it became virtually a political party. Even if these bold advocates of human self-determination—including leading theologians in the service of the state—did not at first adopt direct political alternatives to the caliphate, the 'representatives of God' inevitably found such teaching disturbing. I shall look at this more closely, initially concentrating on two leading figures, one in Basra (Iraq) and the other in Damascus (Syria).

Human self-determination—politically dangerous: the Qadarites

Qadarite thinking appeared early in Iraq. Basra was a cosmopolitan city, with many Persians, Indians and East Africans. It is situated about ten miles from Shatt al-'Arab, from where according to tradition the apostle Thomas is said to have taken ship for India. In general, its people were loyal to the ruling caliphs and did not approve of Yazid III's coup. However, intellectually Basra was a very lively city, in which some people loved *kalam* (theological disputation) and poetry but there were also irrational tendencies: ecstatics and 'heretics' of the most different kinds. Basra has been called the cradle of Islamic asceticism and mysticism. There were also traces of free thinking:[65] alongside bold poems, writings against Islam circulated, in which contempt for the religion was expressed in a way unparalleled in the Arab sphere either before or after. There was also a parody of the Qur'an, which had the effrontery to show how its style could be imitated very well and the effect of the Qur'anic surahs could be achieved with rhyming prose.

All in all, though, the spiritual climate of this city had an ascetical orientation. In Basra, the sense of being chosen was countered, more strongly than in Kufa, by a sense of personal sinfulness and the lowliness of the world. No one proclaimed more impressively than al-Hasan al-Basri (died 728),[66] son of an Iranian, for a short time qadi under 'Umar II, that election was not without cost. Pious but no mystic, concerned with becoming one with God, he was a highly influential preacher of the consciousness of sin. The religious idea of the fear of God (*taqwa*)—a central concept of the Qur'an and the basic Muslim virtue, in which Muslims show their election in faith by observing the commandments—now seemed to be surpassed by the ideal of turning away from the world (*zuhd*), though this was aimed at performing work pleasing to God within the world.

Caliph 'Abd al-Malik seems to have asked Hasan al-Basri what he thought of the *qadar*. Hasan was undoubtedly a Qadarite, in an 'asymmetrical' way: for him the date of a person's death, his personal circumstances, visitations and good works, were predestined by God. However, sins did not come from God but from human beings (or from Satan). In his reply to the caliph (if, as is quite possible, it is authentic[67]), al-Hasan did not hesitate, explaining that this teaching was by no means an innovation; rather, the ancestors in the original Muslim community had attributed personal responsibility and a degree of self-determination to human beings, based on Qur'anic sayings such as, 'I have not created the invisible beings and men to any end other than that they may worship Me.'[68] By contrast, a strict predestinarianism which attributed total predestination to God was an innovation.

Evidently al-Hasan could not convince the caliph. For theologians to allow each individual *qadar*, which according to the official view belonged only to God and his representative, seemed to him to be a subversive teaching that endangered the state, with unforeseeable effects. Understandably, 'Abd al-Malik sought to dam this current—but only achieved the opposite result.

What was the situation in Syria? Under 'Abd al-Malik's successor al-Walid the Qadarites sharpened their teaching with an anti-Umayyad thrust. Ghaylan al-Dimashqi (who died in 732)[69] was one of their spiritual leaders. Although his father was a Coptic convert and thus he was a *mawlah* ('associate'), under 'Umar II he seems to have held an important position in the administration of the mint in Damascus. He even accompanied the caliph Hisham on his pilgrimage to Mecca. Ghaylan was not a speculative thinker but more of a social critic and writer of letters. His concern was that the rulers should not regard their power as a 'gift of God' with which they could do what they liked. Rather, they were to be aware of their responsibility for people before God.

Some historical–critical questions arise from this. Did Ghaylan focus the doctrine of individual responsibility for salvation on the bold thesis that not only a Qurayshi, but anyone who applied the Qur'an and Sunnah rightly, could be caliph? Josef van Ess thinks that this is not a Syrian but a later Iraqi thesis. Did Ghaylan claim that if a caliph did not do this he was to be driven from the throne? Did he even assert that if all Muslims really obeyed God and his law, there would be no need at all for a 'representative of God' on earth? We cannot know all the answers, but one thing is certain: later many people referred to Ghaylan.

Whatever the historicity of such political applications may be, for the caliphs these Qadarites had transgressed the limits that had been laid down. Wasn't power really given by God himself as a due portion (*rizq*)? Did it have to be earned by right action? The caliph took action against the Qadarites and Ghaylan, who was at that time in Armenia, which had been overrun by the Turkic Khasars, was arrested. After his return he was finally executed, along with a like-minded colleague, probably as a conspirator. Some Qadarites were banished (to the Dahlak islands in the Red Sea, opposite present-day Eritrea) but there was no general persecution.

Whereas Ghaylan was banished from the collective memory, a second leader of the Syrian Qadarites, Abu 'Abd-Allah Makhul[70] (he too was not an authentic Arab but originally a Persian prisoner of war, though perhaps of aristocratic origin), came into the foreground. In the pious tradition he becomes virtually the father figure of this 'pietistic' movement. He was a foreign sage, jurist and promoter of *jihad*, who likewise spoke critically about the rulers and escaped execution only thanks to the intercessions of a confidant of Caliph Hisham.

Still no theological orthodoxy

This brief sketch of two leading figures, al-Hasan al-Basri and Ghaylan, and of the conflict between caliphs and 'heretics', gives only a very feeble impression of all that developed in Islamic theology, especially in the last decades of the Umayyad epoch (P II), in Damascus, Basra, Kufa, Iran, Egypt, the Hijaz and southern Arabia. Josef van Ess has collected all the relevant texts, explained them philologically and published them in translation, with commentaries. If we investigate this history of Islamic theology, we can see how many theologians there were alongside the great leaders who made this literally a school, but also how their names were later classified in unhistorical schemes by later Islamic heresiographers, and often given false or wrong labels. It takes considerable effort today to replace them with real portraits, to discover hidden lives behind the names and, in the light of the concrete persons (Greek *prosopon*) if they can still be ascertained from the literature, recognize some structures of this theology (this constitutes van Ess's 'prosopographic method').

The dispute between the predestinarians and the advocates of human free will lasted for many more generations. It developed undisturbed, particularly in Basra. No 'orthodoxy' had yet formed at this time; theology was still in search of its identity. Only in the coming period would Islamic thought become unified—with all the concomitant advantages and disadvantages. There were further special developments, quite different from one another and depending on the culture of the provinces. They are extremely difficult to reconstruct but from a survey two things can be inferred:

– During the time of the conquests (P I) only beginnings of a theology, implicit theology, were to be observed, but now (P II) quite explicit and very different theologies developed, though none yet claimed to be generally binding ('orthodoxy') as opposed to the others.
– At the beginning (P I) there was a simple distinction between the elect (*ahl al-jannah*—Muslims—often only one's own party) on the one hand and the damned (*ahl an-nar*—unbelievers, including Jews and Christians) on the other, now (P II) the consciousness of sin in the ascetic milieu especially of Basra brought out sharply the possibility of damnation even for Muslims.

It would go beyond my limits to describe all the movements that played a role at this time. I have space only for the most important. I have already discussed the Qadarites and the Shiites at length. Now I shall turn to the far more radical and rigorous Kharijites.

Recourse to the Qur'an: the Kharijites

As I have already described,[71] these 'secessionists' had opposed 'Ali's submission to a court of arbitration.[72] Their hatred of 'Ali was powerful: he had defeated them and literally decimated them. This hatred had led one of them to murder 'Ali and it drove them to reject any form of rule which based itself on legitimation by descent. Thus, the Kharijites fought not only against 'Ali and the 'Alids but also against their counterparts Mu'awiyyah and the Umayyads. Indeed, they rejected the whole development of Islam after the first two caliphs, Abu Bakr and 'Umar, and called for a return to Medinan origins and the Qur'an

(P I). With reckless personal commitment and in unconditional obedience to their leader, true Muslims were to fight resolutely against the 'friends of Satan'. With a martyr's death as an immediate entry to paradise before their eyes, they were to understand themselves as the ones who had 'sold' their lives to 'God's cause' (therefore they called themselves *ash-Shurat*, with reference to particular passages in the Qur'an).[73]

The Kharijites, whose social roots were in Arab nomadic groups, as new Muslims with inferior rights and members of the less reputable professions, opposed the growing social divisions among the Muslims. They called for equal rights and practised the original Islamic democracy. They chose their own leaders (imams) regardless of their origins and formed their own communities, from Iran to North Africa. Above all they insisted rigorously on the fulfilment of Muslim duties. Only those who fulfilled these duties were true believers. Belief was what mattered. However, their way of believing meant that, from the start, they had little coherence and soon became hopelessly splintered. Although they posed a constant threat to the power of the state through guerrilla wars until the 'Abbasid period, they had political success only in certain regions. Only among the Berbers in North Africa (the Rustamids of Tahert in the central Maghreb, who established themselves as a dynasty between 761 and 908) could they form a Kharijite kingdom, and in Oman a small principality.

However, the Kharijites made a decisive contribution to the formation of an Islamic theology. They constantly referred to the Qur'an as the irrevocable standard for all Muslims. However, this starting point allowed a broad spectrum of different models of interpretation:

– On the one hand there were the extreme Azariqah (adherents of Nafi' ibn al-Azraq)[74] who, with fanatical stubbornness, looked for salvation in emigration from the Muslim community, in a new Hijrah. Anyone who did not join them, or concealed his attitude, was to be expelled and treated as an unbeliever. They did not object even to the killing of opponents, along with their wives and children. Killing Jews, Christians and Zoroastrians was not allowed. Very strong to begin with, but weakened by constant changes of ruler and inner splits, these fanatical Kharijites were defeated by 'Abd al-Malik, thus ending the most dangerous threat to the unity of the empire.

– On the other hand there were the Ibadites (*ibadiya*),[75] who wanted to preserve unity with the Islamic community and further reform from within. They still exist today, above all in Oman, Libya and the area of the Maghreb bordering the Sahara in southern Algeria. They claim to originate from 'Abdallah ibn Ibad of Basra; however, in recent research he has been moved back further and further into the unknown. A letter of his to Caliph 'Abd al-Malik, long regarded as authentic, is now attributed to Ibn Ibad's successor Jabir ibn Zayd. (And it was not sent to the caliph but to 'Abd al-Malik ibn al-Muhallab, who represented the governor in Basra at that time.)[76]

In reality, Abu 'Ubaydah seems to have been more important than these two. Head of the 'community of Muslims' towards the end of Umayyad rule, he was the rigorous leader of the Ibadite community leading a hidden life in Basra and above all of the Ibadite mission. The Ibadites had an influence throughout the Islamic sphere, from North Africa to India, as their leaders were mostly great merchants who handled long-distance trade to India and China. However, as the status of merchants in Basra was always precarious, they argued for the ideal of equality and for those who received short shrift: women had relatively great influence among them. They thought it all-important to observe the commandments of the Qur'an, to show solidarity (*wilayah*, friendship) with those who lived in the spirit of Islam and conversely to dissociate themselves (*bara'a*) from those (the government governors, tax collectors) who did not. However, unlike the Azariqah, the Ibadites abhorred the meaningless battles, indiscriminate slaughter and political murder among the Quraysh. They are known for not pursuing a Muslim who had fled. Still, that did not prevent them from agitating against the Umayyads and, ultimately, joining in a rebellion when the time was ripe (at least in their outposts in Yemen, the Maghreb and in Oman).

Theologically, the Ibadites under Abu 'Ubaydah and his successors sharply dissociated themselves from Qadarism, which they originally tolerated. The vast majority of them were regarded as predestinarinans, though they did not advocate complete determinism: how else would they have rebelled against unjust rulers? The strict Abu 'Ubaydah also imposed a ban on those who had incorrect ideas about the anthropomorphic-sounding statements about God in the Qur'an and understood the relevant words literally instead of metaphorically. As if God's 'hand' did not mean his knowledge or his protection and his bared 'calf' in the last judgement his resolution!

In the context of the Ibadiyah, there is an interesting statement by Khalil ibn Ahmad, a well-known lexicographer, founder of Arabic metrical poetry and author of a work on the image of God (*fi t-tawhid*: 'On the confession of unity'). A single fragment of his has been handed down as the following description of God's transcendence: 'You who ask to understand the Eternal! When you ask "Where is He?", you have already localized him; when you ask "How is He?" you have already qualified him. He is +A, +A (but also) –A, –A , or +A, –A and –A, +A.' This is the last sentence, following the translation of Louis Massignon.[77] Van Ess's translation is equally possible: 'He is the entity of an entity and the non-entity of a non-entity, the entity of a non-entity and the non-entity of an entity.'[78] This uncompromising expression of divine transcendence, by an author writing in Basra, seems to me not so much 'hyperdialectic', which is what Massignon calls it, as a parallel to the four-stage dialectic of the great Indian Buddhist Nagarjuna (second century CE), who denies all four possibilities in respect of the absolute: that it is so in reality; that it is other; that it is both so and other; that it is neither so nor other.[79] But what is everything for? So that human beings may be free for the highest, religious–mystical truth, which transcends mythical thought and metaphysical speculation and can dawn on human beings only in the act of immersion.

The theological controversies among the Ibadites, who now increasingly withdrew into themselves, focused on quite practical questions, from the validity of Friday prayer under an unjust ruler through the validity of the prohibition of wine to the permissiveness of anal intercourse (customary in Mecca but taboo in Medina, possibly due to Jewish influences). The tendency towards Puritanism among the Ibadiyah (for example in the regulations about purity and food and even in respect of shaking hands with strangers) and to scrupulousness in the fulfilling of the law (with public penance) is undoubtedly connected with the central point of Ibadite teaching, the relationship between faith and sin, belief and unbelief. This controversy was played out in the following era. In the meanwhile, there was a very considerable group in these controversies which did not want to take any position on what is 'hidden' from human beings.

Postponement of judgement: the Murjites

After the first civil war, and in view of the unprecedented bloody clashes among Muslims, which were felt to be a tribulation (*fitnah*—temptation, examination), voices were raised, especially in Kufa, claiming that it was impossible to decide who was right and who was wrong and therefore the verdict should be 'postponed' (*arja'a*): there should be a 'postponement' (*irja'*) of judgement. The representatives of this view were therefore called Murjites (*murji'a*). Their original rallying-cry—'restraint'—was presumably presented for the first time in the 'Letter of Restraint' (*kitab al-irja'*) writtem between 692 and 695.[80] However, the first reliable evidence not only for the activity but also for the thought of the Murjites is two poems from the late Umayyad period.[81]

The original call was for the postponing of judgement in political questions relating to the first Islamic schism. The question was not so much the status of the salvation of Muslims as the status of the first four caliphs. The verdict on 'Ali and 'Uthman was to be postponed and not made a matter of belief or unbelief. This was a double front, on the one hand against the Shiites who had attached themselves to 'Ali, and on the other against the Umayyads who regarded Abu Bakr, 'Umar and 'Uthman as rightly-guided caliphs. The Murjites wanted to preserve the unity of the Muslim community, to avoid excommunication and to leave the verdict to God himself on the Last Day.

It is quite evident that postponing judgement on political matters arises from theological motivations that were developed subsequently. The political principle of 'restraint' became a theological doctrine: *irja'* was to be practised when something was 'hidden' or 'doubtful' among unseen or long-dead people, and about whose salvation in the world to come no verse of the Qur'an provides any information.[82] Such a judgement about the belief of Muslim brothers in the faith was not to be appropriated by human beings. However, in practice, disparate Murjite groups in different camps, places and times behaved very differently: the original cry of 'restraint' could not always be maintained.

All these disputed questions finally came together in one great question: how was Islam to continue? After the second civil war, which cost the blood of so many Muslims (its end was celebrated in 691 as the 'year of harmonious community', *'am al-jama'ah*), it became clear to an increasing number of Muslims that Islam could not go on like this. Instead of referring to the Qur'an in all things, like the Shiites and Kharijites (yet achieving no unanimity), or acting as neutrally as possible, like the Murjites, there was another possibility: to reflect on the merits of the ancestors, following the path that the ancestors had already shown. If there were more reflection on this common 'Sunnah' ('custom'), wouldn't it be easier to avoid future splits and wars and the infinite sorrow at the Islamic world? The 'Sunnis' began to assemble. To the present day this 'Sunni' Islam embraces the great majority of Muslims, who regard all other groups as 'heretical' sects.

8. The crisis of the empire

Under the caliphs who followed 'Abd al-Malik and al-Walid it became increasingly clear that the Arab movement was no longer the power base of the government. Rather, this base consisted of elite Syrian troops, the increasingly powerful government apparatus and the propagation of an ideology of obedience towards the caliphs who represented the state. Would it be sufficient to hold together an enormously extended state, the greater part of whose population was no longer made up just of Arabs?

What is to be done with the new Muslims? The reform caliphate of 'Umar II

Strong as this Arab–Islamic empire appeared from the outside, it had been weakened internally by increasing tensions and polarizations. Alongside the 'pious opposition' that had always existed in the Arab tribal lands, which accused the Umayyads of Damascus of betraying Islamic principles with their *Realpolitik*; alongside the Iraqis who constantly rebelled against the hated Syrian rule and alongside the Shiites agitating from the underground, new classes and groups appeared everywhere, demanding their rights. Because of the progressive Islamization, the social movement which put Arab rule in question (an essential component of P II) became ever stronger. It wanted

- non-Arab soldiers to be entered on the lists for state pensions (*diwan*);
- non-Arab farmers who converted to Islam to be free from the discriminatory poll tax;
- the mawali who were active in the army and the administration to be given completely equal rights and the same privileges as the Arabs.

If one 'idealist' caliph could be trusted to find a realistic solution in this difficult situation it was 'Umar II ibn 'Abd al-'Aziz (717–20).[83] He had much to recommend him. First, he was born in Medina and had a traditional upbringing there. Second, on his mother's side he was descended from the family of 'Umar I and on his father's side from the long-lived viceroy of Egypt. Third, having married 'Abd al-Malik's daughter he was in every respect a pious, learned, almost ascetic man who was respected even by the traditional Muslims and the Shiites. Finally, and above all, although he was only thirty-five, he was politically clear-sighted enough to understand that the rule of one ethnic group over all the others, which his great-grandfather and namesake, the second rightly-guided caliph, had proclaimed, was out of date. If the empire were to survive, opposition between Arabs and non-Arabs, which led to so much conflict, had to be overcome. Under 'Umar II for the first time Islamic scribal learning, hitherto quite hostile to the Umayyad caliphate, had considerable positive influence.

'Umar II was not interested in wider external expansion of the empire. Soon after his election he broke off the very expensive siege of Constantinople which Caliph Sulayman, his immediate predecessor, had begun. He would also have loved to surrender Arab outposts such as Transoxania, but didn't succeed in doing so. Rather, from the beginning he concentrated on the pressing problems of domestic politics. He turned his attention inwards: unpopular governors were deposed and new officials appointed to the most important posts. He was concerned not for the increase of his power but for the preservation of law. For him, it was most important to return to the original principles of Islam and restore the internal unity of the Ummah. To a greater extent than with any of his Umayyad predecessors, his Muslim piety governed his personal life and his public action. Thus he hoped to halt the collapse of the Umayyad empire and to restore the widest possible basis of trust among the Muslim population. He was very concerned for the extension of Islamic faith; he had the Bedouins given religious instruction and even sent ten scholars to the Berbers.

'Umar II was not a tactician who wanted to soothe converts with concessions while preserving Arab rule. Rather, in a realistic policy of understanding, he worked for reconciliation with the Iraqis and Shiites and for fundamental equal rights for non-Arab Muslims. He introduced a comprehensive administrative reform: all non-Arab Muslims in the army, the administration, trade and the crafts, who played a leading part in the extension of Islam, were to be accepted into the empire as partners with equal rights. Something that had previously been unthinkable now happened: he nominated clients as judges and even governors.

With this was combined a tax reform that was to be fairer, but in no way left the financial interests of the empire out of account. Converts were to pay full land tax, but so too were Arab landowners. On the basis of the equality of all Muslims, there followed an equalization of taxes, but at a higher level, which burdened relatively few Arab landowners. Non-Muslims (Christians, Jews, Zoroastrians) still had to pay poll tax but all Muslims had to give alms (which amounted to much less). In part this compensated the state for tax income which did not materialize.

Instead of the existing antagonism between Arabs and non-Arabs there was to be a universal Muslim unity, instead of a purely Arab empire the empire of all Muslims. This was a grandiose programme, more difficult to put into practice than 'Umar II expected, and it took time to realize. He died at the age of thirty-nine. It was rumoured that he had been poisoned, but this is improbable. Be this as it may, 'Umar II was the 'saint of the Umayyads'.[84] He was held in grateful remembrance by all Muslim tendencies (even the new dynasty which succeeded him!) as a model of Islamic righteousness and piety. Would his successors be able to implement his programme?

A coup and an inaugural sermon

For about fifty years, following their successful suppression of the rebellions, the Umayyad rulers had been able to hold things together. However, around 640 unrest broke out, which was to lead to the fall of the dynasty in the next decade. The caliphs following 'Umar II were not of his stature. The next but one more important caliph, Hisham (caliph from 724 to 743),[85] actively attempted to put 'Umar's principles into practice in the war against the Byzantines and the Turkic peoples of Central Asia in Khorasan, Mesopotamia and Egypt but with little success and even fewer consequences. The last decade of the Umayyad dynasty was characterized by countless intrigues, revolutions, depositions, appointments, murders, executions and the public display of severed heads.

Nothing is more significant for this late period of the Umayyads than the internal Umayyad power struggle over the caliphate: Yazid III's rebellion against al-Walid II. Julius Wellhausen already described it vividly,[86] and Joseph van Ess has made a precise analysis of its religious dimensions.[87] Presumably the historical sources, which come from the circles of the pious, exaggerate the oppositions, but it is historically certain that:

– Al-Walid II[88] (743–4), the legitimate caliph and successor to Hisham, was regarded by his enemies as a heretic (*zindiq*), homosexual, teller of dirty jokes and a libertine. He was finally attacked by the people, who used even the weapon of the hadith. Living mostly in his desert castles, he was indeed a vigorous hunter, drinker and lady-killer, but he also read books and was wrote poetry. According to Wellhausen he even preached 'occasionally in verse': 'He could do anything, but for him everything was just a whim and his whims changed in the twinkling of an eye. He would steep himself in learned theological conversation and then go off and mock the saints. He could not refuse anyone a request, yet he was not merely angry, but also as cruel as a child. It was a curse that he had power.'[89]

– His challenger, the Caliph Yazid III (caliph in 744), was regarded as an ascetic. He disliked music and entertainments and is said to have ridden into Damascus on an ass, as Jesus the Messiah once rode into Jerusalem. In contrast to al-Walid, who was said to be close to the official predestinarianism, he was a Qadarite, the son of a non-Arab mother. He was able to put into political practice at the decisive moment the Qadarite conviction about the self-determination of human beings. Supported above all by young people who were not yet established, he had himself set up as anti-caliph, entered the main mosque of Damascus one Friday, commandeered the large stores of weapons kept there, and had various officials and the governor arrested. The caliph's troops were in the provinces and Yazid, having received the homage of the people of Damascus the following day, needed only a small army to go out against al-Walid. Al-Walid remained remarkably passive and fought only at the end, though bravely, with a small group of troops, before he was abandoned by them and retreated into his fortress. There, while reading the Qur'an, he died from repeated sword blows, as Caliph 'Uthman had died in Medina. His head was cut off and brought to Yazid, who carried it around everywhere and only had it handed over to the murdered man's brother a month later. However, the brother did not dare to bury it, out of cowardice.

How did the revolutionary justify his rebellion against the legitimate ruler of Damascus? Yazid's inaugural sermon, his declaration of government,[90] is extremely noteworthy. Like revolutionaries before and since, he justified his *coup d'état* by saying that he had carried it out 'out of anger about God and his religion and as an advocate of his holy scripture and the Sunnah of his Prophet'.[91] In view of the public criticism of the waste of money and the nepotism of previous Umayyad rulers, he promised to construct no new buildings or canals and to accumulate no treasure. The money raised in the provinces was to be used there, non-Muslim landowners would be spared excessive taxation and those eligible for military service would not be kept too long in the field.

What are astonishing (and of abiding topicality) are Yazid's concluding remarks about obedience to God: 'Obedience is due only to God. Thus there should be obedience to a [man] only in obedience to God, as long as he himself obeys [God]. If he opposes God and calls for lawlessness [that is, for sin], he deserves that people should be opposed to him and that he should be killed.'[92] This statement was aimed at al-Walid but it had consequences for the whole of state policy. Putting it plainly, Wazid's argument meant that 'reasons of state' were theologically relativized. Religion and morality stand above politics, above any ruler. Typical of this is the saying 'No obedience to anyone who opposes God' which would often be quoted. It was finally attributed to the first caliph, Abu Bakr.

Nevertheless, the downfall of the Umayyad dynasty could not be stopped even in this way, especially as Yazid III ruled for less than a year and his *coup d'état* failed to command a consensus. In 744, he died what was apparently a natural death.

Towards the third civil war

The inevitable happened: that same year the new caliph, Marwan II (caliph from 744 to 750), proclaimed himself the avenger of al-Walid. He felt that the Qadarite criticism of the Umayyads was a provocation. On his entry into Damascus he had the corpse of Yazid III exhumed and publicly nailed to a cross, head downwards.

Now internal unrest shook the empire: there were also attacks from external enemies. These had been going on for some time. The Berbers, now Muslim, had been true allies against West Goths and Franks. However, because after the death of 'Umar II they were treated by the Arab officials as slaves who had to pay tribute, under the leadership of Kharijites they sparked off a fearful rebellion from Morocco to Kairouan and, in the name of Islam, inflicted their worst-ever defeat on the Arabs, even though these were reinforced by Syrian government troops. Many thousands died. The Arabs took revenge for this the next year but by this time they were on the defensive not only in North Africa but also in Transoxania, which was over-run by the Turks. The same happened in Armenia, where the semi-nomadic people of the Khasars, from the north of the Caucasus, whose nobility had turned to Judaism out of an antipathy both to Byzantium and to Islam, defeated the Arabs. Finally it even happened in Anatolia, where the Byzantines routed a larger Syrian army.

From inside as from outside, it became increasingly evident that the Umayyad state, so long on the offensive, had reached military exhaustion. The well-tried, glorious Syrian army had been increasingly misused for the political control of the Arabs and at the same time had gradually shifted to the frontiers of the vast empire. So the Umayyad regime lacked the military force to defend itself effectively against its enemies. As Yazid's coup showed, a few thousand soldiers could decide who held power.

Between 744 and 750 opposing forces fought over the caliphate. Marwan II, who was recognized as caliph only as far as his army reached, was to be the last caliph of Damascus. The strict religious circles of the Sunnis maintained the institution of the caliphate and, in principle, its religious significance but now even more sharply than before they criticized the worldly policy and lifestyle of the caliphs of Damascus, their claim to quasi-imperial authority and their constant interventions in religious affairs for political motives. Some religious thinkers, who had kept a positive attitude to the dynasty under ʻUmar II, now became completely hostile. These were years of terror, and many people, above all the south Arabian party (the 'Yemenites'), waited in apocalyptic excitement for a turning point.

The Shiite circles had never given up hope that they would take over the caliphate and now, as they awaited a Mahdi who would restore the caliphate in the line of the Prophet, they found more support than before among many dissatisfied Arabs and new Muslims. They had already gone over to public agitation in Kufa between 736 and 740, which had led to arrests and executions. In the meantime a much more dangerous movement had developed, which was to deal the death blow to the Umayyads: the ʻAbbasids.

The end of the Arab empire

The Umayyads were not the only important clan of the Quraysh, the Prophet's tribe. A look at Muhammad's genealogy (see the table on p. 195) shows that he had another uncle, ʻal-Abbas, whose descendants had been seen less on the political stage. Now, in the great crisis over the dynasty of the Umayyads, the ʻAbbasids raised a claim to the caliphate. Their justification was that a nephew of ʻAli, Abu Hashim, had transferred the leadership of the Prophet's family, now understood in a broad sense as the Hashim, to them. Under the name and programme of the Prophet's family, the Hashim, and to the exclusion of all the other Qurayshi (especially the Umayyah), there was a campaign for a new legitimizing principle: the 'Hashimiyah', with a long-term strategy. Through genealogy, an opposition movement was called to life and a massive policy was carried out.

In Kufa, the 'Alid branch of the Hashim clan tested the anti-Umayyad rebellion (in favour of the 'Alids). Meanwhile, for two decades the 'Abbasid branch had been preparing in remote Khorasan in north-east Persia to overthrow the Umayyads. They were skilled at political and ideological agitation: the Hashimiyah were first built up on a broad basis as an underground movement. The great agitator and outstanding organizer of this movement (in practice a secret army and a secret government), sent by the 'Abbasid family to Khorasan, was a certain Abu Muslim.[93] He was a man of uncertain origin, but highly gifted and highly respected. He united Arabs and Iranians in an anti-Umayyad coalition with a common agenda. His words kindled sparks and found assent in all social strata. Vengeance for 'Ali! Fight against the Umayyads! A new order of peace and justice for those who have not had their due!

How could the early Arab conquerors of Khorasan not take these battle-cries positively? They were cultivating the land and living in villages but were being exploited by harsh taxes and treated as a subject people, like the Berbers. Having been promised a fair tax reform under 'Umar II, how could they not fight now, since this promise had proved to be empty? Many were also convinced that the end of the world, the final battle and the appearance of the Mahdi, as proclaimed by popular apocalyptic writings, were imminent.

Abu Muslim hoisted the black banner of the arrival of the Mahdi, the banner of revolution, in Marv, in the remote east of the empire, in 747. This was the sign to get things moving: black was also the colour of some Hashimites. Three thousand enthusiastic and amazingly disciplined men succeeded in defeating their rivals in Khorasan. They also found support in west Iran and among the Shiites in Mesopotamia. For the Shiites had set all their hopes on finally making a descendant of 'Ali caliph at this time.

This was to prove a mistake. As soon as it happened, the 'Abbasids unscrupulously overtrumped their Shiite allies. To the enormous disappointment of the Shiites, the new caliph, proclaimed in Kufa in 750, was not an 'Alid but someone who wanted to help the 'Alids secure their rights: Abu l-'Abbas as-Saffah,[94] allegedly the only eligible Hashimite. From then on 'Alids and 'Abbasids each went their own way: there were now two groups of Islamic nobility. Unmoved, the 'Abbasids appealed, as motivation for their one-sided bloody act of revenge, to 'Ali's descendant Zayd, who had fallen in 740 in a rebellion against the Umayyads and allegedly wanted to take his revenge. They succeeded in winning a definitive victory in northern Mesopotamia near Mossul over Caliph Marwan II, who was still reigning, and soon afterwards occupied Damascus. Caliph Marwan, left in the lurch by his own side, had to flee through the Jordan valley and Palestine to Egypt, accompanied by only a few loyal followers. He was killed in 750 in Upper Egypt by henchmen of the new caliph. As was customary, his head was sent to his successor, Abu l-'Abbas.

That was not enough. The first 'Abbasid caliph could not rest until the Umayyad élite had been utterly liquidated. Last to capitulate was the great garrison town of Wasit: most of the Syrian officers found there were executed—in contravention of the conditions of capitulation. The 'Abbasids now celebrated their blood orgies everywhere: the surname of the first caliph, as-Saffah ('the generous one'), was now understood as the 'bloodthirsty'. The horrific climax was a feast disguised as a 'reconciliation banquet' which more than eighty completely unsuspecting Umayyads attended. All were murdered; only one survived the bloodbath. Julius Wellhausen remarks that Abu l-'Abbas's executioners 'were utterly merciless, they inflicted the divine wrath and legitimate revenge ... Of course their motive was political; they wanted to make the fallen dynasty utterly harmless.' Alluding to the history of Israel he adds: 'In all this one is reminded of the extermination of the house of Omri carried out by the prophets.'[95] Wellhausen could also have recalled the moral degeneration in France of the Merovingians who had become Christians or Charlemagne's mass annihilations and deportations of the Saxons—not to mention the 'blood wedding' staged by Catherine of Medici on St Bartholomew's Eve in Paris in 1572 and the slaughter of several thousand Huguenots throughout the land.

Only 'Abd ar-Rahman, a nephew of Hisham, the 'falcon of the Quraysh', was able to avoid the massacre. He took flight, with many adventures, and reached North Africa where, as he had a Berber wife (sent to his father by a governor as a gift), he won the sympathies of the Berbers. In 755 he was able to move to Spain and brought almost the whole peninsula under his rule. He initially gave himself the modest title of emir (*amir*) and did not dispute the authority of the caliphate. He founded the most important dynasty of Muslim Spain, which lasted until the eleventh century: the Umayyad caliphs of Cordoba. By the eighth century, for the first time in the extreme West, there was an Islamic empire independent of the caliphate.

Things went differently with Abu Muslim, who had become so popular. In gratitude for his services the 'Abbasids nominated him governor of Khorasan. On this occasion we hear for the first time of 'people experienced in discussion' (*mutakallimun*) who were to convince the inhabitants of Marv that Abu Muslim was on the right way: whether there were already real controversial theologians is an open question.[96] Abu Muslim soon evidently became too powerful for the new rulers. The next caliph, al-Mansur, had him liquidated in an insidious way. He was summoned to court and as he entered the caliph's tent unarmed he was struck down by two assassins. This murder of a friend and legendary popular hero was to inspire some rebellions in future: Abu Muslim became the symbol of religious and social opposition to the 'Abbasids.

The 'Abbasids decisively pursued their agenda. Not only did a change of dynasty take place here but a change of overall constellation, which I shall analyse in the next chapter. The paradigm of the Arab empire (P II) came to a political end with the Umayyads but lived on in another form.

The paradigm of the Arab empire as a vision of hope: Pan-Arabism

With the aid of mathematics and experiment, scientific paradigms (like the Ptolemaic paradigm) can be definitively superseded by a new paradigm (the Copernican paradigm). However, in the sphere of the religions (and also art) earlier paradigms do not necessarily disappear. The paradigm of the Arab empire showed a considerable capacity to maintain itself and survive. Despite the shameful downfall of the caliphs of Damascus, down the centuries the memory was cultivated among the people of this glorious period of a purely Arab dynasty and a purely Arab great empire—and not only in Syria. It was to remain the conviction of many Muslims that the Arabs are the best of all peoples: it is not by chance that God addressed his final and universal revelation to them.

When the confrontation of Islam with European modernity reached a climax and thus also a crisis of identity in the nineteenth century—I shall discuss this development in the paradigm of modernity—people in Damascus, Beirut and Cairo again began to reflect on Arabic. The 'renewal' movement was at first concerned with the Arabic language of the early period and the study and modernization of the classic high Arabic of the Middle Ages. Its adherents saw this as a way to cultivate a nation with an Arab civilization.

At the beginning of the twentieth century a political Arabism took shape alongside cultural Arabism. Arabic-speaking people were politically to form a single 'Arab nation' on the basis of their great common history. The Pan-Arab movement came into being chiefly in reaction against European colonialism and imperialism but also against Pan-Ottomanism and Pan-Turkism. In cultivating Arab culture, the Arabic language and Arabic religion, it had in view, consciously or unconsciously, the image of the Umayyad empire and, on this basis, strove for the supra-national union of all Arab states.

Finally, however, a pragmatic economic Arabism established itself. The foundation of OPEC in 1960 and OAPEC (Organization of Arab Petroleum Exporting Countries) in 1968 and the formation of the Arab Common Market in 1964/5 had considerable significance for the formulation of a unitary petroleum policy. They therefore have to be seen as part of this historical continuity, even if no political collaboration followed the economic collaboration.

I shall return to all this in connection with the modern age. But what was to happen after the ʿAbbasid revolution, undertaken in the name of Islam? Would the reformation of Islam that was urgently necessary now come about?

C III

The Classical Paradigm of Islam as a World Religion

Historians may have often seen earlier paradigm changes more as a change of regime than as a change of overall constellation, of the kind that I have attempted to describe. The paradigm change from the Arab empire of the Umayyads to the Islamic empire of the ʿAbbasids is different. Traditional historiography also understands it as more than a mere change of ruling family. Tilman Nagel is correct in writing: 'The events of the years 129/747 to 132/750 mark a change which embraced all spheres of the Islamic commonwealth and the young Muslim culture, so that scholars such as M.A. Shaban have not hesitated to speak of a revolution.'[1]

1. A new era begins

In their revolutionary euphoria the ʿAbbasids at first called their government 'the turning point' (*dawlah*): after the corrupt past there was to be a revaluation of all values and a 'new era'. There was indeed a powerful upheaval, a paradigm change *par excellence*. After the fall of the 'usurpers', which seemed to justify the streams of blood, the universal empire was to be renewed, in religious terms, from the bottom upwards. After the 'turning point' the ʿAbbasids, who had come to power in unpleasant circumstances, did everything they could:

– to discredit the Umayyads (with the exception of the exemplary ʿUmar II) as unbelievers. They claimed that theirs had not been an authentic caliphate but only a 'kingly rule' of 'tyrants' resting on arrogance, force and oppression. Moreover it had given the non-Arab Muslims a status secondary to Arab Muslims;

– to legitimize their own rule. They said that this rule followed from the four 'rightly-guided' caliphs, whose direct successors they were. In this way their 'revolution' established itself as an institution and *dawlah* came to mean simply 'dynasty' or 'empire'. Their ideology of rule was aimed at a commonwealth grounded in, fortified and pacified by the Islamic faith. Its undisputed centre was the caliphate, which the 'Abbasids subsequently claimed. Finally, they belonged to the 'house' (*bayt*, which can also mean 'family') of the Prophet: al-'Abbas was the Prophet's uncle, whereas 'Ali was only his cousin and owed his legitimacy to his wife Fatimah.

Baghdad, the new cultural metropolis of Islam

The foundation of a new capital is often the symbol of a new beginning. The Assyrians had demonstrated that when they founded Nineveh and the Romans when they founded Constantinople. What about the 'Abbasids? To begin, with they only transferred the seat of government to Kufa. They did not destroy Damascus, the seat of the enemy, but they did abandon it as a capital. Only then did the Syrians notice that with the fall of the Umayyads, to whom they had also become superfluous, they had lost their own power. It was of no avail that they showed sympathy for the old dynasty, fomented unrest in Syria and Egypt and for centuries still visited Mu'awiyyah's tomb as a sanctuary.

The hegemony of Syria, which had lasted for almost a century, was replaced by the predominance of Iraq, which had already held such a position for a short period under 'Ali. The new dynasty came from Kufa, the citadel of the 'Alids, but they drew their power from Khorasan ('land of the sunrise'). So, the Iranian Central Asian Khorasans took the place of the Mediterranean Syrians. Extraordinarily powerful in military terms and moulded in a spirit of unconditional obedience, they formed the highly-disciplined guard of the caliph and the core of his standing army; they were also given other positions of power. They were soldiers who owed no allegiance to tribe or clan, and were blindly obedient to their often divinized leaders. However, precisely because of this they later became a danger to the caliph.

The new order became apparent under the second 'Abbasid caliph, al-Mansur (caliph from 754 to 775),[2] who, because of the sudden death of his brother Abu-l-'Abbas as-Saffah, was the real founder of the 'Abbasid caliphate. He did all he could to consolidate the regime (with the help of the Sunnis) after its revolutionary beginnings (with the help of the 'Alids), on the one hand guiding the eschatological expectations of its own extremist followers (Rawandites) along ordered ways[3] and on the other suppressing the old (Umayyad) and new ('Alid) enemies of the new dynasty.

Al-Mansur had Abu Muslim, the bold champion of the 'Abbasids and leading exponent of the Iranian enthusiasts, murdered, turned against his former allies, the 'Alids (in so far as they could not be won over by pensions) and finally crushed the opposition in Medina. Only then did this great, gaunt ruler who lived a simple life, found a new capital. At first he may have thought simply of a garrison town for his Khorasans, a safer residence than unruly Kufa, the citadel of the 'Alids, but the new city became the great imperial centre.

Al-Mansur started building in 762. A good deal of the material came from neighbouring Ctesiphon, the capital of the last indigenous Iranian dynasty. He called his new capital 'city of peace' (*Madinat as-Salam*), but it was usually called by the name of the little village of Baghdad (a word of uncertain origin, perhaps the Persian for 'gift of God') which had long been in existence.[4] The place was chosen strategically, on a site which was extremely favourable in military, climatic and economic terms. It lay on a fertile plain at the crossroads of the trade routes between Khorasan, Iran, Iraq, Syria and Egypt, protected by the river and canal system of the Tigris and the Euphrates and with links to the rest of Mesopotamia and the Persian Gulf. Soon, trade relations extended as far as India and East Africa, indeed to East Asia and the Atlantic. Commodities and cultural items from all over the world could be brought to the seat of the caliph and Islam succeeded in infiltrating, quietly and without violence, both Africa and South and South-East Asia.

Baghdad was not an Arab city but a city in the Persian style, in keeping with the Khorasan Iranian rule. Its ground plan was circular, probably following east Iranian patterns, with a diameter of perhaps a mile and a half. It was conceived of in accordance with clear geometrical principles, with the splendid buildings of the mosque and the caliph's palace in the centre. From here four streets, with four city gates, radiated and divided the city into four equal quarters at the four points of the compass, symbolizing the claim to universal rule. However, this government centre, safeguarded by two rings of walls—to get there visitors had to go through beautifully decorated and well-guarded gates—would not have existed without the great army, which had its own quarters (*al-Harbiyah*) to the north-west, and the vast workforce (thousands of building workers, textile workers, paper and leather workers from Iraq, Iran, Syria and Egypt) who with their countless markets, craft businesses and factories were likewise lodged in their own suburb (*al-Karkh*) south of the city. Everything was admirably planned.

Only the court, the harem, the guard and the top administrative authorities, together with an enormous number of slaves and servants, resided in the circular city. But even when it was being prepared, this well-organized and controlled military, economic and cultural centre was too small. Time and again al-Mansur and his successors built new palaces and administrative complexes (with countless gardens and baths with benches) on both sides of the Tigris. Thus this military and administrative city soon became an international and world city, ten times as big as Sasanid Ctesiphon, bigger even than Constantinople. Baghdad was the biggest and most splendid city in the world at that time (outside China), more than four miles long and three and a half miles wide, with a population of between 300,000 and 500,000, which in the tenth century rose to perhaps 1.5 million. For centuries it was the cultural metropolis of the Muslim world. And this was at the very beginning of the ninth century, when in Europe the empire of Charlemagne, with its still very primitive cities, was divided into three part-empires, all of which suffered an economic and cultural decline, threatened by attacks from the Normans in the west, the Hungarians in the east and the Muslim Saracens (to whom Sicily had belonged since 827!) in the south.

Baghdad made its powerful presence felt. From the middle of Mesopotamia, the rich, international capital of Islam, which incorporated both Arab and non-Arab elements, brilliantly embodied the new overall constellation (P III):

- Instead of the Umayyads, whose political tendency was Arabic and Syrian (P II), the 'Abbasids now ruled. Their political tendency was anti-Syrian, Iraqi, indeed cosmopolitan.
- The historical and theological legitimacy of the new revolutionary regime was based on the link that it claimed with the original Islamic paradigm of the caliphs of Medina (P I), who now, with the inclusion of 'Ali, were regarded as 'the four rightly-guided' (*ar-rashidun*), in contrast to their successors.
- Non-Arab tribes now represented the main contingent of the army: first the Khorasans and later the Turks. They were the most powerful supporters of the 'Abbasid regime.
- This was a renewal of the empire, not on an Arab but on an Islamic basis. In religious terms, the 'Abbasid caliphs saw themselves as leaders of the Ummah of all Muslims and champions of Islam, as a universal religion that embraced and united all peoples.
- The essence of Islam—the one God and Muhammad his Prophet—was sustained and re-emphasized.

No longer an empire dominated by Arabs? It cannot be overlooked that 'the turning point' had dramatically changed the position of Arabs throughout the kingdom.

Islam as a world religion instead of the Arab nation

Three factors need to be distinguished which took on a new status as the basis of the revolutionary social policy of the 'Abbasids in the new constellation:

- the Arab people: the 'nation' of the Arabs;
- Arab culture, with the Arabic language as its most important form of expression;
- the Arab religion: Islam.

This had tangible consequences:

– The rule of the Arab people was over. The old Arab structure of a 'nation in arms', cherished by the second rightly-guided caliph 'Umar, had collapsed. Only the Umayyads and the Syrians had upheld it. Now it was no longer enough to be an Arab to be a member of the ruling élite. The Arabs, whose exclusive status originally rested on martial law, were ousted from their positions of military power and became active in the civil sector. The numerous non-Arabs, who had previously been excluded from the élite, finally had access to the top military and administrative positions.

What the Umayyad 'Umar II had seen as the vision of a renewed empire, but could not bring about, now became reality: the Arabs lost their privileges, the Arab tribes were no longer the cadres of the divine state and their aristocracy no longer extended over the whole empire as a network of powerful elites interconnected by genealogy (it had already been weakened under the Umayyads). The more new Muslims had been accepted into the genealogical order by affiliation, the more it was undermined. Now all Muslims, whether Arabs or not, could fully acknowledge the Muslim empire. This was a return to the ideal of all believers, as the Prophet foresaw it in the Qur'an!

Particularly in Khorasan (Merv), from where the 'Abbasids had conquered the whole empire, Arabs had integrated themselves to such a degree that they no longer named themselves by their tribes but by their places of abode. The numerous new Muslims of alien origin (*mawali*) had made a decisive contribution to the 'Abbasid victory. Now they had equal rights, and in a time of population growth and economic boom had equal rights and duties in the army and the administration, in trade and in the crafts—indeed they often dominated. Even if the ruling family remained Arab (at least in its male representatives) and the majority of the homelands of the Arabs also remained Arab, in the future non-Arabs would make up the majority of the Islamic population. After a century of 'Abbasid rule, the designation mawali fell into disuse, because it had become meaningless, although tensions between the two population groups remained.

– Arab culture became a common possession. It did not collapse with the collapse of the Arab 'nation'; rather, it became an international culture in which all Muslims shared. Arabic did not disappear, as it remained the language of the

Qur'an and thus of Islam. It increasingly came to be used, also by very many non-Arabs, as a *lingua franca.* Arabic became established in writing and scholarly usage even among the Iranians. Only poetry—now cultivated even more in Persia—remained Persian.

As far as non-Muslims were concerned, Arabization was more effective in Syria and Egypt than Islamization—it was the other way round in Persia. In time Arabic absorbed the languages of the Christian people of the Middle East. It became established as the vernacular in the territories of the former Byzantine empire which had a predominantly Aramaic population. It even found its way into the Christian liturgy. To the present day, in that region, part of the Christian liturgy is celebrated in Arabic. No less importantly, wherever Islam established itself, the Arabic alphabet suppressed older alphabets. That was true not only of the Persian alphabet but also of the Turkic alphabet, though Arabic script was not very suitable for it.

– Islam became a world religion. It did not suffer in the dissolution of the Arab 'nation'; on the contrary, it was strengthened. The Islamic religion remained the foundation of Arab culture but lost its ethnic fetters. On the basis of equal rights, Islam became the religion of the Egyptians, the Berbers, the Greeks, the Persians, the inhabitants of Central Asia and the Turks. So:

- whereas in Arabia, the homeland of Arabs and Islam (P I), conditions were increasingly chaotic, so that soon not even pilgrimages to Mecca could be undertaken in safety, Islam freed itself from its provincial imprisonment and developed its universal power;
- traditional Arab tribal loyalty was replaced by universal Islamic order and brotherhood;
- even if Arabia now played only a very peripheral role economically and politically, its religion continued to be important for Muslims. Islam became a world religion in a real sense.

Islamization now made more rapid progress. For example, in Persia Islam almost completely replaced Zoroastrianism and in the Maghreb, where Christianity was established only in the form of a colonial church, a majority of the Berbers went over to Islam. Christianity offered resistance only in closed Christian areas of Syria, Mesopotamia and Egypt. Egypt's original inhabitants, the Copts, though Arabized, remained true to their Christian faith.

The cosmopolitan splendour of the caliphate

The caliphs disturbed little of this. Not only every possible nationality but also Jews and Christians—not to mention secret 'pagans'—came to their court.

Despite separatist tendencies in the outer provinces and occasional unrest this heterogeneous population was integrated into a society shaped by Arab culture and Islamic religion, whose centre was Baghdad: a rich, splendid and cosmopolitan court.

In Baghdad, the caliphate was more imposing than ever. Arab tribal princes no longer had to be consulted, tribal structures no longer had to be heeded. The caliph still officiated in leading Friday prayer, and from time to time held a court with due pomp. The centralization which had made great progress under the Umayyads now reached its climax: the 'Abbasid caliphs were sovereign rulers, who soon far surpassed the Umayyads in their absolutism and luxury.

On festive occasions the caliph—with his family a successor to the Prophet and the supreme embodiment of Islam—wore the *burdah*, the Prophet's mantle. Though he had stopped appearing to the people, he showed great generosity. Indeed, since all the differences between Arabs and non-Arabs and thus also important class differences had disappeared, the caliph 'by the grace of God' stood over against the all other Muslims as 'prince of the believers' (*amir al-mu'minin*) and 'God's representative' (*khalifat Allah*): in accordance with the Persian, ancient Near Eastern model. He was high above the people and also high above the aristocracy, endowed with a fullness of power which was to be possessed centuries later only by the Roman popes after Gregory VII (*vicarii Dei*, representatives of God) and the French kings after Louis XIV: '*L'état, l'église, l'ummah –c'est moi!*' Such 'sole rulers' took no notice of objections that they were not 'representatives of God' but only 'representatives of the Prophet', only 'representatives of Peter or Christ'. They all thought that they could dispense with a senate, an 'advisory' organ (*shurah*).

The caliphs were autocrats, as state interests and their own interests dictated. Who could have opposed them? Arab or non-Arab, all were subjects, nothing but subjects. If the new regime made efforts to take their complaints seriously, it did so in order to encourage their political passivity. The state was largely reduced to the court. The plebeian Khorasans had taken the place of the aristocracy, blood relations of the Damascene caliphs in the broadest sense; they were visible in the centre of the residence and drilled to obedience. Chosen by the 'Abbasids as their 'Praetorian guard', they could execute a command of the ruler at any time. Alongside the caliphs' officers there were also a large number of members of their own clan, the Hashimites (*hashimiyah*). Endowed with the self-confidence of those who feel that they are the sole representatives of the Prophet's clan, they enjoyed the luxurious life of the court—often including the wine that was forbidden to the pious—and had numerous servants of both sexes. Harem intrigues and other machinations were the order of the day.

Three significant court officials who had not existed either in Medina or in Damascus attended the absolute ruler:

- the court astrologer, who was consulted over all important undertakings (for example, laying the foundation-stone of Baghdad) and was taken on campaigns;
- the postmaster who, as head of the excellently organized news service, supervised all post and even (by means of selected informers) the provincial governors;
- the executioner who, wearing a leather hood on the Iranian pattern, stood directly beside the throne and could be employed for immediate execution or torture.

The 'Abbasids had announced 'the turning point', a better, more just order, and al-Mansur himself implemented the reform with energy and harshness. Through revolutionary changes in the army and administration he was able to put the new regime on a sure footing. The organization of the army underwent a micro-paradigm change.[5] Arab privileges were done away with and new armies were built up whose allegiance was not to any tribal or class interests but solely to the caliphate. The Umayyads had noticed that the concept of an Arab 'nation in arms', made up of the different tribes, which had been advocated by the second rightly-guided caliph 'Umar (P I), had become anachronistic and needed to be replaced by a professional army responsible only to the caliphate and paid by it. However, as long as the world conquests had continued under the Umayyads (P II), the regime had been dependent on loyal Arab tribal troops.

Under the 'Abbasids this era ended. The Arab troops were now used above all for the protection of the frontiers: in Anatolia, Yemen, Armenia and Egypt. Elsewhere mawali or even local non-Muslims could equally well be recruited. That happened in the central army of the caliphate, which consisted of Khorasan Arabs, their descendants and clients. This army now took on capital importance, both for attacks against the Byzantine empire, which still withstood all assaults, and also for the suppression of internal unrest (P III). Therefore, a considerable reserve of the army remained in the residence instead of going on expeditions and in Baghdad—in contrast to Medina and Damascus—the heads of the army formed part of the court. This meant that the Arabs in Iraq, Syria, Egypt and Khorasan could now be exempt from military service and engage in civil activity.

How the caliphs ruled

Even more important than the reform of the army was administrative reform. The caliphs of Damascus had attempted to build up a bureaucracy committed to them alone but it was modest by comparison with that of the caliphs of Baghdad. Under them it above all comprised favourites and henchmen (usually freemen) of the ruler. Anyone could be elevated to the loftiest heights and could fall again just as easily—there was no lack of intrigues. All titles, uniforms or marks of honour depended on the caliph's favour. Arabs still held important positions—in the dynasty itself and in the court—but a large number of officials were now non-Muslim: Persian scribes from Khorasan, Nestorian Christians from Iraq and, in the financial realm, quite a number of Jews. All in all, they often drew the hatred of the population down upon their heads instead of on the caliph. The attitude expected of an official or soldier in this state was clear:

- no allegiance to a tribe or in a clan but obedience to the ruler;
- privileges of origi- were no longer crucial for a position in the administration or army; beside professional qualifications, all that mattered was unconditional loyalty to the dynasty.

The 'Abbasids referred back to old experiences, old traditions and sometimes also to the old personnel of the Umayyads. At the same time they substantially increased the official court hierarchy (almost according to the 'law' of the British historian C. Northcote Parkinson, which states that administrators make work for one another so that they can increase their staff and heighten their own prestige). To begin with, everything was requested personally from the caliph. Then, quite rationally, three departments or offices (*diwan*[6]) were instituted: the chancellery (*diwan ar-rasa'il*), the tax authority (*diwan al-kharaj*) and, most importantly, the army office (*diwan al-jaysh*). As well as completely new office systems (for example, correspondence, seal, administrative court), they all developed an increasing number of sub-divisions, which of course in turn needed controlling bodies. There were numerous 'secretaries' (*kuttab*, singular *katib*), professionals or officials, who, aware of their status and well-trained, made up a bureaucracy which outlasted all caliphs and their governors. However, there was no 'cabinet', no small group of officials with independent spheres of responsibility.[7]

The fact that the caliphs were absolute rulers did not mean that they could easily impose their will down to the lowest levels of the empire.[8] The empire was too big and complex for that. Only the provinces closer to the centre were under the direct control of the caliph; the more remote ones were so to speak affiliates and the very remote ones were ruled by local dynasties on behalf of the caliph. Theoretically, the caliphate could impose its will by force if necessary, through the army, police and inspectors, but that was possible only to a limited degree. The provinces of the vast empire were composed of very different small communities. Especially in the numerous villages, where the ownership of property was often unclear and calculations of income proved difficult, the central and provincial authorities were often dependent on the collaboration of the local notables, family patriarchs and landowners, who were now mostly associated with the provincial governments and the central government through family, client, financial and administrative relationships. They were the ones who made the systems of administration, communication and taxation, which took such different forms everywhere, function at all.

The ʻAbbasid regime showed great tolerance to the old religions (Zoroastrianism and also Christianity), which were already very disorganized. The main interest of the caliphate was to bring together, on a religious basis, the local and central élites, of whatever ethnic or religious origin, into the most coherent system possible: 'This system of alliances was based on a concept of the empire as a product of God's will. By God's will the exalted person of the Caliph reigned in expectation of passive obedience from all his subjects.'[9]

The caliph could no longer supervise his vast administrative apparatus, so that a head of state administration was needed for co-ordination, supervision and control. While al-Mansur is said still to have looked after everything personally, his son and successor—in an eschatological mood named al-Mahdi (caliph from 755 to 785), 'the guided one'[10]—appointed a vizier (*wazir*—'one who bears a burden') to supervise all central authorities; at first his mandate depended completely on the authority of the caliph, but he soon began to play an ever greater role.

Al-Mahdi attempted to do justice to his eschatological, messianic name. He had prisons emptied, established courts of appeal, restored mosques, signposts and wells on the pilgrim routes and made gifts to Mecca and Medina. It is also worth mentioning once more that he carried on a religious conversation with the Nestorian patriarch Timotheos I, which was recorded on the Christian side.[11]

Under al-Mahdi, theologians (*mutakallimun*) were for the first time invited to discuss with the 'heretics' (*zanadiqa*); indeed, under him 'heretics' were crucified. His successor al-Hadi (caliph from 785 to 786) held office as a 'heretics' judge'. The administrative apparatus made it easy for a person to be suspected of being a 'heretic' (*zindiq*); there was a real purge. The Manichaeans (already persecuted under the Zoroastrian–Sasanian state religion of Persia) were particular victims of persecution; their dualistic confession of a good and an evil primal principle was especially offensive to the Muslim belief in unity. However, often people who were only politically unpopular were accused of being 'heretics', for example, Ibn al-Muqaffaʻ, the first important prose writer and translator from the Persian, who was executed under al-Mansur.

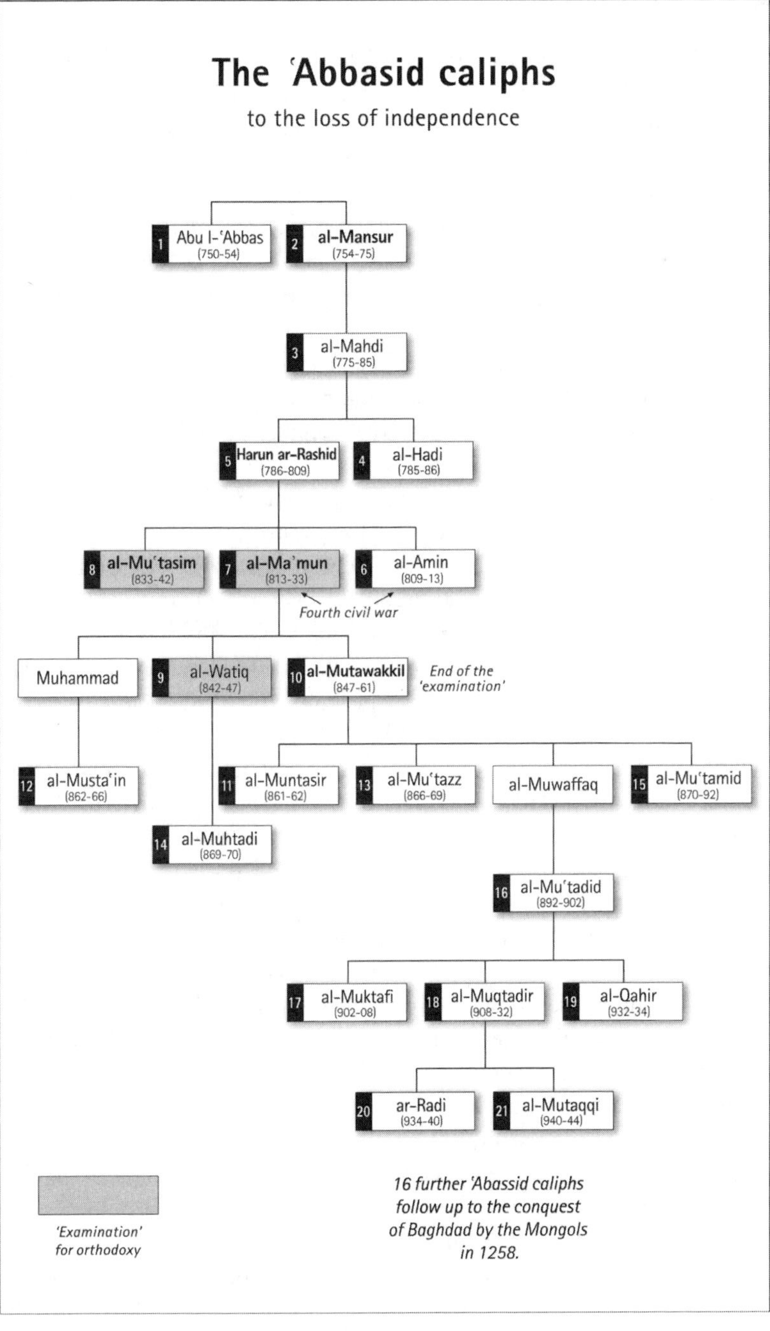
The 'Abbasid caliphs
to the loss of independence
1 Abu l-'Abbas (750-54)
2 al-Mansur (754-75)
3 al-Mahdi (775-85)
5 Harun ar-Rashid (786-809)
4 al-Hadi (785-86)
8 al-Mu'tasim (833-42)
7 al-Ma'mun (813-33)
6 al-Amin (809-13)
Fourth civil war
Muhammad
9 al-Watiq (842-47)
10 al-Mutawakkil (847-61)
End of the 'examination'
12 al-Musta'in (862-66)
11 al-Muntasir (861-62)
13 al-Mu'tazz (866-69)
al-Muwaffaq
15 al-Mu'tamid (870-92)
14 al-Muhtadi (869-70)
16 al-Mu'tadid (892-902)
17 al-Muktafi (902-08)
18 al-Muqtadir (908-32)
19 al-Qahir (932-34)
20 ar-Radi (934-40)
21 al-Mutaqqi (940-44)
'Examination' for orthodoxy
16 further 'Abassid caliphs follow up to the conquest of Baghdad by the Mongols in 1258.

A tale from The 1001 Nights?

Later Muslim generations are reminded of this period of the early 'Abbasid caliphs by the stories of *The 1001 Nights*, which sounds much more poetic in the Arabic original: *Alf layla wa-layla.* This collection of more than three hundred stories in different genres, with origins in the folk epics of different countries from India to Egypt, is without doubt the most famous collection of stories in world literature. In the final version, all the stories are told by a wise woman, Sheherazade,[12] who is associated with the name of Caliph Harun ar-Rashid. What do we have here? Pure fairy tales or pure reality? Probably more fiction than reality.

The stories, set in a courtly urban milieu of unimaginable wealth and luxury, certainly have a real background, the world of Harun ar-Rashid ibn al-Mahdi (caliph from 786 to 809),[13] the fifth 'Abbasid caliph. He was the son of al-Mahdi (third caliph) and grandson of al-Mansur (second caliph). His brother al-Hadi (fourth caliph) had him thrown into prison to ensure that his own son succeeded to office. Al-Hadi had therefore been murdered six months after his accession (with the connivance of his own mother, who preferred Harun). In the fairy tales, Harun appears as an exemplary prince, but in reality he had neither a very attractive character nor any remarkable stature as ruler. Even according to the fairy tales, he used to go through Baghdad by night incognito, often accompanied by a poet of a frivolous disposition, Abu Nuwas—and the executioner.

Events in the year 803 shows how problematical his character was. Harun, who for a long time had relied on a politically experienced hierarchy of officials from the Barmakids as viziers and generals, suddenly changed his mind and had his foster brother and long-standing personal friend, the Barmakid Ja'far, executed, together with several members of his family, and dismissed the rest. Presumably, he simply wanted to free himself from a tutelage which had become burdensome (in what was unfortunately the customary way). Rumours about homosexual relations with Ja'far or the impregnation of his own sister by a Barmakid friend cannot be verified. What is unmistakable is that under Harun the degeneration of the caliphate had already begun: as a 'down payment', he guaranteed the Aghlabids in Tunisia *de facto* independence under his purely formal supremacy, but refused this recognition to the rebellious Idrisids in Morocco.[14] So there is no reason to glorify Harun as the ideal of an oriental ruler.

Nor was he particularly tolerant. As a prince, he had carried out an expedition to the Bosphorus and made a particularly advantageous peace treaty with the empress Irene (after which he was called 'ar-Rashid', 'the one who follows the right path'). Now he sent a state letter to the ruling Byzantine emperor, warning the Byzantine ruler against false advisers (bishops) and offering arguments against the Trinity and the divine sonship of Jesus. This letter represents 'the earliest apologia for Muhammad as Prophet':[15] it contains prophecies from the Old Testament[16] and the New[17] and for the first time a reference to miracles (however, the 'argument from the shooting star' was later given up in connection with Muhammad because it was pre-Islamic). It also seems that under Harun ar-Rashid, the supreme qadi Abu Yusuf drafted special regulations for the 'protected', that is, the non-Muslims: they were ordered to wear different clothes from Muslims. Even worse, after a vigorous military confrontation with emperor Nikephoros I, Harun had many churches pulled down, not only in the frontier regions with Byzantium but also in Basra and elsewhere. Indeed, he mercilessly had Qurayshi who had converted to Christianity executed, even though they were remotely related to him.

Despite all this, it remains beyond dispute that under Harun Baghdad reached an unprecedented economic and cultural peak, with far-reaching international relations. Harun even exchanged embassages with his contemporary Charlemagne and sent a white elephant to him in Aachen. Muslim merchants reached the Chinese port of Canton in the year of Charlemagne's coronation as Roman emperor (800). There were also mention contacts with Russia and the Khasar empire. The economic basis of this prosperity were the textile, metal and paper industries, which brought prosperity to a wide range of people and made possible an unprecedented development in pomp and power, both for the caliph and for the ruling class. Harun's mother, a former Yemeni slave, ate only from gold and silver plates decorated with precious stones. Harun's tremendous palace was full of eunuchs, concubines, singing girls and male and female servants of every description. Harun was great not as a statesman but as a sybarite: as a lavish promoter of the arts and artists and a connoisseur in music and poetry (at that time the sciences, apart from philology, were not very developed in the Islamic world). Much that presented itself as Arab culture was, in reality, taken from elsewhere—in astronomy and medicine above all from the Greeks.[18]

Time and again there were revolts, but Harun was able to put them down relatively easily. There were great discussions about what policy the empire should adopt. Here two parties emerged. On the one hand were the officials, many Persians and people from the eastern provinces, initially supported by the Barmakids. On the other hand were the religious scholars, many of them Arabs, supported by the new vizier. How would things develop? The lack of a strict hereditary succession (from father to oldest son, and so on) once again proved pernicious. Harun thought that he could overcome the conflict by dividing his inheritance: bequeathing almost all the Arab lands to al-Amin, his son by a free Arab woman and his legitimate spouse; the Iranian provinces to al-Ma'mun, the son of a Persian slave girl; and the Byzantine border regions to his third son al-Mu'tasim.

However, this division of the inheritance furthered the collapse of the empire. When Harun ar-Rashid travelled to Khorasan in 808 to put down a revolt which had already lasted for two years and died (in Tus, near present-day Meshed) after an illness of only a few months, al-Amin[19] succeeded him in Baghdad as the sixth caliph. Al-Amin's efforts were at first directed towards excluding his brother al-Ma'mun from power. In 810, there was open confrontation in the dispute over the succession, which ended three years later with the violent death of the sixth caliph.

Al-Ma'mun[20] was the victor; he led the 'Abbasid dynasty for the next twenty years (813–33) as seventh caliph. As the sponsor of the Academy of Baghdad he was certainly of more cultural significance than his father; I shall discuss him at length above all in connection with the controversies over rationalistic theology. From then on, like him, almost all caliphs were sons of slave-concubines. This was because the caliph's family, which claimed the sole right to exercise the caliphate, wanted to avoid the complications of marrying into the families of subjects. This meant that there could no longer be any talk of the pure Arab blood of the caliphs.

2. Classical Islam: a world culture

We may legitimately describe the early 'Abbasid period, a glorious epoch in human culture, as the epoch in which Islam reached its classical form. This was not just because of the unprecedented economic boom and the development of the organs of government, administration and legislation which now became 'classic', but above all because of three developments which still shape Islam. We must deal with them in detail. In the framework of this paradigm (P III) there was

- an elaboration of specifically Islamic culture founded on classical Arabic, the Persian lifestyle and Hellenistic science;
- a development of Islamic law (*fiqh*) in which the four legal schools which still exist today came into existence;
- the formation of Islamic theology (*kalam*) in which a kind of 'scholasticism' came into being which still has an influence on the theological and systematic thinking of Muslims.

The heyday of Islam, its law, its theology and its culture, was and remains what from a European perspective is the early Middle Ages. In the tenth century, the time of the 'Abbasids in Baghdad and the Fatimids in Egypt, medieval Rome was going through its *saeculum obscurum* (dark century), dominated by cliques of the nobility and incompetent, indeed criminal, popes. During these centuries Islamic science was far ahead of its European counterpart. Even today, countless Arabic loan words—from alcohol, algebra and arsenal through magazine, masque and mocca to zenith—bear witness to this.[21]

Something that began to emerge at an early stage in Islamic architecture now realized itself generally in Islamic culture under the 'Abbasids: Arabic mixed with Hellenistic and Persian and entered the higher unity of a world culture in which Islam was embedded. The mix of population in the great centres, the international trade relations and the pilgrimages, contributed to this. Ira M. Lapidus has analysed the individual Arabic, Persian and Hellenistic elements of this 'cosmopolitan Islam' precisely,[22] so I can make clear the differences from the preceding constellations.

Arabic as a language of communication and a high language

I have already remarked that, although the political importance of the Arabs had declined under the new 'Abbasid regime, this in no way meant a general retreat of the Arabic language, which still served as the *lingua franca* of the vast empire. Even the opponents of the Arabic hegemony wrote in Arabic. Arabic remained the foundation of the common culture of the empire's very different peoples. Both at court and in the urban and scholarly milieus there was an intensive preoccupation with Arabic, even pre-Islamic, literature, so as to proclaim the praise of the Arab conquerors and the caliphate; the language of old Arabic poetry and the Qur'an were not fundamentally different. It goes without saying that in the urban milieu the study of Arabic was largely bound up with the study of the Qur'an.

As time went on, the Arabs had the disturbing experience that under local influence the Arabic dialects in the various provinces, which were very different from one another, were departing from the pure Arabic of the Qur'an—in vocabulary, grammar, syntax and style. What was to be done? With admirable energy, above all the religious scholars in the schools of grammar in Kufa and Basra, and then in Baghdad, turned to the pure Arabic of Mecca and the desert tribes. The roots of words were described systematically, the vocabulary was explained and rules of grammar and syntax were developed. In this way, in the light of the needs of the 'Abbasid period, what is now called classical Arabic or high Arabic was reconstructed: it remains the model and pattern for the language of educated people today. Its origins in pre-Islamic poetry and linguistic wisdom were investigated and a major grammar and several dictionaries were produced.

At the same time, classical Arabic historiography developed. It focussed on the life (*sirah*) of the Prophet and the Qur'anic revelations, then on the conquests and the lives of the first Muslim leaders. Its high point was at-Tabari's monumental 'Annals of the Prophets and Kings' (839–923), a collection of all the events in world history in chronological order, the biographies of the Prophet by Ibn Ishaq (died 767) and Ibn Hisham (died 834), and al-Baladhuri's (died 892) 'Book of Conquests'. All of these have been mentioned previously. The 'Abbasids were extremely interested in them as reinforcement of the religious legitimacy of their rule.

Completely secular interests in worldly life, at court and in the city, also found their literary reflection in poetry, which from time immemorial had had its home in Arabia (see A II, 2). All the worldly knowledge of the time was collected in encyclopedias. So in literature, too, a new paradigm becomes evident:

– In Arabic Bedouin poetry there had been much talk of camels, the heroic deeds of tribal warriors and the remote beloved in the desert; this literature was now collected in anthologies.
– The newer poetry spoke more of palaces, gardens and hunts, passions and intrigues and wine, women (and also beautiful boys) and song'. Its chief exponent was Abu Nuwas (died *c.* 815), who has already been mentioned. Ibn ar-Rumi ('the Roman', i.e. 'Byzantine'), son of a Byzantine captive and a Persian woman, who lived in the second half of the ninth century, was more of a mystic: I shall return to his passionate existential poetry later. This cultural heyday might lack epic and dramatic poetry, but by comparison with the contemporaneous Carolingian and Byzantine literature, Arabic literature is considerably more highly developed.

This literary development had important religious consequences. Parallels to the development and then the isolation of Latin in Western Christianity are abundantly clear:

– The whole of Arab culture contributed to reflecting on the Qur'an and illuminating it.
– Conversely, anyone who really wanted to get to know the Qur'an had to be at home in high Arabic and its literary traditions.
– Despite all these efforts over high Arabic, which remained the literary language, the vernacular largely grew away from the language of the Qur'an. In words and pronunciation, in forms and word order, Arabic was markedly simplified. From as early as the end of the eighth century it was this popular Arabic and no longer high Arabic that was spoken by the people. The Arabic of the Qur'an had largely become an antiquated, sacred, language, understood only

with difficulty even by Arabs—not to mention non-Arab Muslims (though it did not cause as much difficulty as did the Latin of the Western church to its members). To the present day, the five Arabic dialect groups—those of the Arabian peninsula, Mesopotamia, Syria and Palestine, Egypt and the Sudan and North Africa—differ considerably in vocabulary, syntax, morphology and phonetics not only from one another but also from high Arabic. However, high Arabic is the common form of language for Muslim literature and the media.

Persian education and way of life

By comparison with the Arabs and their original desert culture, Persian represented an age-old high culture. For the court and the educated élites it offered a serious literary and cultural alternative to Arabism and Islam: *adab*—'protocol', 'lifestyle', 'fine education'—for all those who attached importance to cultivated forms of conversation and polished style. Here Ibn Qutaybah (828–89) is a reliable guide. The Persian influence had already intensified among the late Umayyads: under them, the first translations were made from Persian political documents. In 'Abbasid Baghdad, the Persian lifestyle was preferred even more and Persian scientific and technical knowledge was taken over, above all from medicine, mathematics, astronomy, agronomy and weapons technique.

There was even a literary movement (*su'ubiyah*) which, without questioning Islam, emphasized the equality of all Islamic peoples (*su'ub*)[23] and above all the equality of Persian culture with Arabic; it sought to gain influence at court. This movement was therefore passionately attacked by al-Jahiz (776–868), the creator of Arabic prose and the most prolific writer in Arabic literature. He was the author of books about, among other things, eloquence and animals. In his 'Book of the Miserly' he wittily mocks the meanness of the non-Arabs.

It is not surprising that, in these circumstances, rivalries developed between Arab and Persian courtiers and scholars:

- From the start Arab thought had a more egalitarian orientation and maintained that the ruler had no legislative competence in religious matters, for which the community of Muslims remained responsible.
- However, from the start Persian thought had a more hierarchical stamp: the ruler was someone chosen by God who therefore had unlimited, absolute authority; every person had his unchangeable place in society on the basis of his status; sympathies for Zoroastrianism, Manichaeism or Gnosticism had by no means died out.

But the Arab scholars knew how to defend themselves: after precise critical examination they attempted to integrate Persian ideas into their thinking. Thus Ibn Qutaybah, in his remarks on government, law, scholarship, asceticism, friendship, love and women, combined Persian ideas, Indian stories and Aristotelian philosophy with quotations from the Qur'an, the hadith and Arabic literature; he simply ignored anti-Islamic elements in the other traditions. This gave rise to an Arabic–Persian cultural synthesis which left Islam intact, indeed even strengthened by the acceptance of a legacy that embraced not only Persian but also Hellenistic elements.

Hellenistic philosophy and science

I have already remarked how much the Arab conquerors learned from those whom they conquered, often Hellenistic scholars, above all about government, administration and the tax system. In time, they also took over philosophical ideas, less those of classical Greece than of the neo-Platonism that was then dominant. Some occult sciences, such as alchemy or neo-Pythagorean mathematics (number mysticism), which hoped to discover a hidden, higher spiritual world through esoteric revelations instead of by way of the Qur'an and obedience to the Islamic law, also became popular.

Hellenistic thought was first presented to the Arab élite in theological discussions. There had already been discussions between Arabs and Christians at the liberal caliphs' court in Damascus. They had worked with a sophisticated Greek–Christian vocabulary, using modes of argumentation and literary methods which immediately attracted the interest of the Arabs. Intellectuals from different provinces came together at the round table (*nudama'*: 'drinking companions', 'friends') of the caliphs of Baghdad: religious disputations were also carried on there.

People became increasingly open to the rich world of Hellenistic cultural material. The Greek academies of Athens and Alexandria were important for this transfer of education. Because of pressure from the Orthodox Church, they had first moved into the Christian, but not Byzantine, areas of the Middle East: the school of Athens to the Nestorians of Edessa and Nisibis, then to Persia and finally to Baghdad; the school of Alexandria to Antioch in Syria, later to Merv in Khorasan and then to Harran in Mesopotamia and finally, at the end of the ninth century, also to Baghdad.

Intense scholarly research developed in the cultural metropolis of Baghdad. Intensive translation work was done in the 'house of science' (*bayt al-hikmah*) there. Numerous Greek and Syriac works were translated into Arabic, usually by Syrian Christians or converts, to serve as models: these include theological treatises of Aristotle and medical works by Galen and Hippocrates. The quest for knowledge was widespread. In Baghdad, where among the many markets (which all, as was the Hellenistic custom, had an overseer) there was also a market of book traders, at times there were more than a hundred bookshops. Soon the original contributions of Muslims to mathematics, astronomy, medicine, chemistry, mineralogy, zoology and meteorology surpassed what they had been able to take over from the Greek, Persian and Indian legacy. Europe largely owes it to Islam that it could rediscover its own ancient heritage and understand it again.

Thus Islam, as religion and theology, came into close contact with Hellenistic philosophy, logic, natural philosophy and metaphysics, indeed with a strictly rational thought that was new to Arabs and posed completely new problems. The traditional Islamic views of the nature of God and his predicates, of revelation, prophecy and ethics seemed to be put in question: wasn't philosophy taking the place of religion? Which had the primacy, in theory and practice? Perhaps not the Qur'an, God's revelation, but human reason, which attempted to find the divine truth independently.

If one accepted Greek philosophy a dilemma seemed to arise, not dissimilar to that encountered by classical scholasticism two centuries later—not least through translations from the Arabic (one thinks of the dispute between Abelard and Bernard of Clairvaux):

– Either one believed in the revelation, in the Qur'an and the prophets and the priority of faith over reason, in order to find religious truth, in which case the doctrines of the Qur'an needed no philosophical justification and one need not take seriously the opposed philosophical doctrines of Plato and Aristotle. The sole function of reason was to contribute later philosophical explanation and depth to the revealed doctrine.

– Or one accepted the priority of reason and philosophical reflection: in that case one thought of God, the highest being, in philosophical and rational terms as one thought of the world and human beings. Islam certainly appeared to be the true religion, but as for the wider population it represented a still very anthropomorphic approximation to the divine truth, it had to be transcended by philosophical sages.

This dispute inevitably led to a crisis in Islamic thought. You may be eager to discover what the outcome was to be, in this and later periods. More important though, indeed decisive for the 'Abbasid era, was not so much the confrontation with philosophy as the definitive construction of Islamic law, which would be more important than philosophy and theology for the future.

The new role of the religious scholars

The Muslim population needed spiritual orientation and moral leadership. Officially the Muslim community was led by the caliphs and the governors, who possessed political power. However, the gulf between the absolutist government and society was becoming wider and wider. So, in practice, the faithful increasingly took their guidance from the religious scholars, who embodied religious and moral authority and were now becoming increasingly numerous.

A development that had been prepared for in the last decade of the Umayyads (P II) became fully established under the 'Abbasids (P III): the official recognition of the self-organization of religious scholars, who increasingly specialized as exegetes, theologians and above all legal scholars. This development was epoch-making.

- The religious scholars, whose activities were still quite 'private' under the Umayyads, were now publicly recognized and encouraged by the state as a professional class: they were the pioneer philosophers of the new Islamic concept of state and society which the 'Abbasids had undertaken to realize.
- The 'Abbasids recognized the religious law, as was taught by the pious specialists, as the only legitimate norm in Islam.
- The gulf between the pragmatic legislation of the qadis and the Islamic theory of law taught by the religious scholars was largely overcome, since more and more of the Ulama were attracted to the office of judge (*qadi*).

The political and religious system of the 'Abbasids could never have functioned without an extended law and a developed jurisprudence. In the Umayyad period that was coming to an end people suffered particularly under the legal uncertainty and arbitrariness of the governors and their helpers and the legal decisions of the qadis, which were often subjective. But it has already become clear that Islamic law is not a rigid, unchangeable system, embracing norms of absolute, eternal validity. It has undergone a history, even if this has so far been little investigated by Islamic scholars. What the Islamic Ummah regarded as law developed only in a long complex process, lasting three centuries (from the seventh to the ninth), through the interaction of different groups and personalities.

As we have discovered, there are only a few written sources for the history of the development of Islamic law before 750 (P II), which are mostly anti-Ummayad in tendency. Only from the 'Abbasid period (P III) does the period of Islamic law attested to by literature begin and the development of law becomes to some degree historically certain. Only then can it be followed step by step, person by person: in Iraq, for example, from Hammad (died 748) through Ibn Abi Laylah (died 765) and Abu Hanifah (died 767) to the supreme qadi Abu Yusuf (died 798) and the more theoretically orientated ash-Shaybani (died 805). Only then did legal schools form. It was not until around the middle of ninth century, under the 'Abbasid regime—two centuries before the legal pronouncements and collections of laws made by the absolutist popes of the

Gregorian 'reform'—that this development was closed to any degree. What was the course of this highly momentous process?[24]

Classical Islamic law: the Shariah

Although they declared themselves to be 'successors to the Prophet' and 'representatives of God', unlike the Umayyads, the powerful caliphs of Baghdad wanted to observe the traditional legal framework as given in the Qur'an and Sunnah. They claimed to be servants, not masters of the law, but although existing law also applied to them, they increasingly offended against it. There were few possibilities for them to intervene directly in the development of the law. They could not lay down law, though they could influence its exposition and application.

For this the caliphate was dependent on collaboration with the specialists of 'scholarship' (*'ilm*). The understanding, interpretation and adaptation of this divine 'law' (*fiqh*) lay within the competence of an independent guild which had become very powerful: it consisted of legal scholars (*'ulama'*, singular *'alim*) who were concerned with the knowledge of the law and its principles and of legal scholars (*fuqaha'*, singular *faqih*) who were concerned with individual legal precepts and the casuistry associated with them. Under the 'Abbasids, in the process of their discussions of the law a comprehensive and thoroughly structured law developed (for cultic, private and criminal law) which still remains in force unaltered for traditionally-thinking Muslims: the holy 'law', the Shariah (*shar'iah*), the totality of the canonical precepts of the law (including cultic and social obligations).

What was important, however, was that the Shariah itself was not codified, nor has it ever been—unlike Roman church law. In 757, in view of the great differences in the law and uncertainties about it, Ibn al-Muqaffa', a secretary of state who came from the Persian–Sasanian tradition, proposed in a memorandum to the caliph al-Mansur that the collecting and surveying of the modes of procedure, judgements, norms and analogies was very urgently needed for administrative and legal purposes. But the 'successor of the Prophet' did not have the authority and competence for the kind of codification that later the 'successors to St Peter' were to claim as a matter of course.

It is not surprising that, given the natural discrepancy between what the religious scholars emphasized as the ideal Islamic legal order and the real legal practice of those in power, there were constant disputes about whether particular decisions of the 'Abbasid caliphs were in accordance with Islam or un-Islamic. At a very early stage 'innovation' (*bid'a*, plural *bida'*) became a watchword with which it was easy to ward off any progress or reform in law or theology. If people could not agree, the legal question usually became a pure question of power, of who in fact came out on top.

What had happened? The Umayyads had increasingly opposed the experts on the Qur'an and the Sunnah, whose theories were often burdensome, but the 'Abbasids, who had made the legal scholars their allies from the start, brought important Sunnah scholars to Baghdad and asked for their opinions on all the difficult practical questions. At the same time, the state supported the leading juristic school of Kufa. However, ultimately there was an intellectual impoverishment in Kufa and Basra because so many scholars moved to Baghdad (a brain-drain), in the hope that they would at least be given an audience by the caliph or even be appointed by him (much like the artists in Renaissance Rome).

However much the 'Abbasids tied themselves to the religious scholars, they also made political use of them. By 'embracing' the religious scholars in this way the caliphs did not just indicate that they wanted to decide all political questions in a legally correct form but also made some of the religious scholars their pliant servants (though some did refuse). Thus the caliphs domesticated a considerable proportion of the scriptural scholars and as court theologians and court jurists also made them justify the arbitrary measures which soon accumulated. To make the pious opposition part of the government at the same time was to disarm them.

The public was to know that everything was now in order in the state, as the rulers observed the holy law like everyone else. Now at last 'peace and order' could prevail, since politics and religion were again closely connected. Surely that had to be welcome, after all the battles and slaughter, blood and tears? However, the 'Abbasid theocracy (not wholly unlike the later papal theocracy) soon proved to be a disguised form of absolute despotism which, through administrative measures, appropriated every possible legislative competence and was supported and flattered by droves of scholars and literary men who basked in the splendour of the 'Abbasid capital.

Reconciliation between the legal doctrine of the scholars and the legal practice of the law courts was at first helped by the way in which it was now normal for religious scholars to be appointed not only as legal experts but also as judges (*qudat*). Their task was to pronounce law to the Muslim population in civil and criminal matters, in accordance with the holy law of God. In contrast to earlier times, the qadis could no longer simply reflect and pronounce their own personal opinions (*ra'y*); rather, they were to feel indebted to the Shariah. However, customary law (whether of early Arabic and pre-Islamic, early Islamic, Byzantine or Sasanid origin) often remained in force, whereas special judges were active in real matters of state.

Caliph Harun ar-Rashid put all qadis under a Grand Qadi, Abu Yusuf, who in theory combined the functions of scholar and judge and, at the request of the caliph, even wrote the 'Book of Land Taxes', a treatise on tax law and criminal law. From the tenth century this 'qadi of the qadis', who was not an appeal authority but a supervisor (especially in important aptitude tests, but also afterwards), might even nominate the qadis in the provinces. However, the difference between legal theory and practice remained an abiding, even a growing, problem for Islam.

3. The formation of the 'traditions of the Prophet', the Sunnah

A further development no less epoch-making than the recognition of the legal scholars was the acknowledgement of particular sayings and actions of the Prophet as the Sunnah of the Prophet. The exponents of this movement argued that not what the theologians and legal experts said but what the Prophet had said and done was to be normative for all believers. The Prophet stood above all human parties and disputes. Consequently, everything which in any form could serve as an authoritative example for the shaping of one's own life by the standards of the Prophet was collected, not out of primarily historical or theological interest but as an utterly practical matter. However, doubts arose at a very early stage doubts: did everything really come from the Prophet? There was great discussion about this in classical Islam—there is even greater discussion in recent historical research.

What the Prophet said and did: the hadith

By the beginning of the eighth century people had begun to collect the hadith (*hadith*: 'report', 'tradition', plural *ahadith*),[25] usually short traditions of remarks or actions of the Prophet. The hadith is both the individual tradition and the sum of the tradition which makes up the Sunnah of the Prophet.

What is the content of the hadith? They are authoritative statements about ritual, moral and religious concerns. There is almost nothing important for the life of a Muslim for which there is not a saying of the Prophet, from questions of faith (the character traits of the Prophet and his descendants, the significance of the Qur'an and its exegesis or religious duties) and moral life (dealings in the family, the treatment of slaves and business relationships) to those relating to the just ordering of the state (character traits of the ruler and criminal justice). Everyday questions, for example about food and clothing, are also discussed. In the hadith Muslims could now find specific examples and rules for everything on which the Qur'an had made no statements. They could take their guidance from them, since in them they heard unequivocally the voice of the Prophet.

In what form were these stories of sayings or actions of the Prophet presented? In the hadith 'verbal discourse is the real vehicle of the content'. 'The standardized scenes serve merely to give the speakers, especially the companions of the Prophet and the Prophet himself, a plausible setting.'[26] Towards the middle of the eighth century, this scheme had found such widespread recognition that people thought that lists without these characteristics were insufficient. In the 'Abbasid period they were revised in accordance with it. Even where demonstrable written records existed, an oral tradition was claimed. Why? Readers were to get the impression that they were taken up directly into the words and activity of the Prophet.

However, the principle of oral tradition made it necessary to indicate the situation behind every word of this oral tradition and to identify specific informants. But now many centuries had passed since the time of the Prophet, so people resorted to making distinctions: between Muhammad's companions as the primary source and the 'later ones' (*tabi'un*), who had had no direct connection with the Prophet. From the beginning it was presupposed that there were good and bad traditions, authentic and inauthentic hadith. But what criteria were used for selection?

The science of the hadith

Now a whole hadith science developed for 'discerning the spirits', which attained perfection and high social prestige alongside the Qur'anic and legal sciences. In view of the enormous mass of sayings and traditions in circulation, the task of the hadith scholars was first to investigate the truth-content of the authentic text (the *matn*, 'back') of the hadith and undertake a detailed classification and secondly to test the chain of informants (*isnad*, 'support'). In this way the Shiites excluded all hadith which could not be attributed to 'Ali and his followers. The consequences were obvious. The study of the chains of tradition led to an extensive biographical literature on the 'science of the men' (*'ilm ar-rijal*), whose first representative, Ibn Sa'd (died 845), wrote the first important work.

In the ninth century the great collections of hadith came into being, ordered either by those who handed them down or—with greater success—by the themes discussed. The first great work, which has proved the most respected, is by al-Bukhari (died 870).[27] It bears the programmatic title 'as-Sahih' = 'The Healthy One'. Al-Bukhari (named after his home town of Bukhara) began to learn hadith by heart at the age of eleven. He made it his life's work to travel from his homeland in central Asia to Mecca, Medina and Egypt, to examine texts and chains of tradition carefully and take into his collection only the 'sound' (*sahih*), and not the 'weak' and false hadith. He eventually published ninety-seven books of hadith accompanied by Qur'anic verses and his own notes. They are divided in an extremely practical way according to the themes of the juristic handbooks: faith, purification, prayer, almsgiving, fasting, pilgrimage, trade, inheritance, testaments, oaths and vows, crimes, murder and legal proceedings. The hadith in this collection number 7397; after removing those repeated under different rubrics they number 2762.

Five further canonical hadith collections, recognized by the Sunnis as authoritative, followed in the ninth century: those of Muslim (died 875), Abu Dawud (died 889), Ibn Maja (died 886), at-Tirmidhi (died 892) and an-Nasa'i (died 915). Collections were also made by the founders of the different law schools, which were just as highly valued. What is the explanation of this tremendous blossoming of traditions? The hadith became the second source of Islamic jurisprudence (*fiqh*) after the Qur'an. To begin with, this was a challenge for that jurisprudence. Initially the hadith people were still in opposition to the legal scholars, but in the end they proved the victors. How did this come about?

The victory of the traditionists

At a very early stage, opposition movements had formed to the old law schools, which in the 'consensus (*ijma'*) of the scholars' represented the majority view. They likewise had to appeal to great names for their very manifold concerns. The Prophet's cousin 'Ali, who as caliph had long had his headquarters in Kufa, an intellectually more open place and the leading juristic city, was the obvious name to whom to refer the very different views.

Medina lagged behind somewhat in legal matters, since around 770 a quite different and very much more rigorous opposition movement arose which was to complete the paradigm change in law: the movement of the 'traditionists' or preservers of the tradition. Soon they formed their own groups in all the great centres of the empire. These 'people of the tradition' (*ahl al-hadith*) rejected the logical methods of the 'people of opinion' (*ahl ar-ra'y*), who in theological and legal questions concerned themselves with rational clarification and systematization, the formation of free opinion (*ra'y*), analogous derivation (*qiyas*) or argument (*ijtihad* or *ijtihad ar-ra'y*). Such rational decisions had been characteristic of Islamic legal science from the beginning, since they were practised both by the qadis and by the pious specialists (for example, the analogy between the minimal value of stolen property and the minimal level of a dowry). In these circles, it was said that as long as a particular practice did not contradict an explicit instruction of the Qur'an, it should be tolerated.

The very much stricter traditionists, who required the precepts of the Qur'an to be followed precisely, were different. Their basic intention was less juristic than ethical and religious. Whereas the 'Sunnah of the school', the living tradition of law schools which argued rationally, referred to the companions of the Prophet for their authority, the traditionists referred quite simply and directly to the higher 'Sunnah of the Prophet'. They did so, not generally and vaguely to confirm their own teaching, as the old law schools did, but specifically, citing particular sayings and actions of the Prophet, the hadith. The real conflict was over the legitimacy of the law. The unconditional concern of the traditionists to follow the Prophet led to the attribution to him of as many sayings and stories as possible, though not with any intent to deceive. These people acted in good faith, guided by the conviction that these words and stories expressed the authentic Islamic norm. They were convinced that the Prophet would have acted like this when confronted with the same problem.

There are exceptions, but the overall tendency of the hadith was towards greater strictness and narrowness in disputed questions. The traditionists were not primarily interested in technical questions of law but in the strict subordination of the whole of the law to the religious and moral authority of the Prophet. Thus, for example, they launched as a 'tradition of the Prophet' a prohibition against forcing prices up, in order to fight against the raising and lowering of prices.

What about the old law schools? After resistance and polemic, their only alternative was to accept the importance of these traditions, which were becoming increasingly popular. However, they did all they could to minimize their significance by interpretation and to confirm their own attitudes and teaching by their own hadith. Thus, many old legal principles were now attributed to the Prophet. The result was that, although the old schools attempted to accept the prophetic traditions only as far as they corresponded with their own traditions, the traditionists won through. This led to contradictions between traditional Islamic law and the hadith tradition, so that a new synthesis was needed. However, it would be many centuries before one could be presented. In the meantime tradition became yet more important in Islam, making the question of the authenticity of the hadith all the more urgent.

Are the hadith authentic?

Some extremely difficult historical and methodological questions lie behind this simple question. Many hadith manuscripts have been edited and published in our time, both in the Arabic world and in India and Pakistan, but most Muslim hadith scholars content themselves with the study of the earlier treatises and commentaries. By contrast modern scholars, led by Ignaz Goldziher,[28] have submitted the hadith to radical historical criticism. Joseph Schacht, whose understanding of Islamic history was criticized in the 1930s but who has been virtually canonized by historians in recent decades, argued that the traditionists had either put a large number of the hadith, previously completely unknown, into circulation for use in party disputes and for other purposes or had partly changed them and in time also attributed a further chain of tradition (*isnad*) to each of them: 'They were put into circulation, no doubt from the loftiest of motives, by the traditionists themselves from the first half of the second century onwards.'[29] So should we assume a gap of almost a century in Muslim tradition?

More conservative scholars, such as N. Abbott,[30] F. Sezgin[31] and M.M. Azami,[32] say that that is improbable. To assume that a tradition is invented if its authenticity has not been proved by present-day historical criteria to be beyond doubt seems to them to be an exaggerated critical demand. Scholars such as F. Rahman,[33] H. Motzki[34] or the British Islamic expert Noel J. Coulson take a middle line. Coulson, for all his basic agreement with Schacht over the mass of fictional material, wants to assume an 'authentic core' which may have preserved 'the substance of the actions and words of Muhammad, particularly in non-controversial matters'.[35] Therefore, we should accept as a 'reasonable principle of historical enquiry' that 'an alleged ruling of the Prophet should be tentatively accepted as such unless some reason can be adduced as to why it should be regarded as fictitious'.[36]

The fronts between the conservatives and the sceptics seem to have hardened with time and on both sides to rest on prior assumptions, as Herbert Berg has discovered in an acute analysis of the state of scholarship: 'The sceptics will continue to dismiss the evidence of the *isnad* [chain of tradition] and to assume that it obscures the true origin of the *matn* [text]. That origin is normally much later than the *isnad* purports, for the *isnad*'s function is precisely to project the *matn* into the past. The sanguine scholars will continue to accept the evidence of the *isnad*, which is thought to convey, for the most part, authentic and useful information. Any conclusion drawn therefore will be a product of these underlying assumptions.'[37]

The great majority of Muslims have little knowledge of this state of research. Just as many Christians still often understand the Bible literally, untouched by any exegetical insights, so too many Muslim spiritual and political leaders—perhaps more out of ignorance—are unaware of the results of hadith research. However, Christian and Muslim theologians must ask themselves:

– Didn't historical research into the Old and New Testaments also undergo a phase in which everything was either defended in a more or less fundamentalist way as historical or was hypercritically put in question (for example, Jesus never lived, the earliest Gospel is allegedly the invention of an 'Ur-Mark', and so on)? Such extreme positions tend to be relativized in the course of history.

– Why then should we exclude the historical possibility that, in an 'oral culture', authentic words and actions of the Prophet were handed down only orally for one or two centuries? Why should there have been no continuity between the first paradigm and the third? That must be assumed, at least where a tradition does not stand in contradiction to the historical situation of the Prophet in Medina (no anachronisms!).

– Doesn't a middle way then commend itself: to decide without 'dogmatic' prejudgements for or against form criticism from case to case (with the help of variants) which of the hundreds of hadith and their variants are authentic and which inauthentic? This will be the work of more than a generation of scholars.

A second source of revelation?

Alongside the first and original source of revelation, the Qur'an, a second has now clearly taken its place. One can hardly find a clearer demonstration of the paradigmatic change in a religion. For Muslim believers, the hadith are closely connected with the Qur'an and it can also be established that, in some cases, hadith have later been adapted to the Qur'an. The hadith are not there to correct or even replace the Qur'an but to clarify it, supplement it and make it tangible. Thus, an originally independent hadith can be transformed so that it functions as a commentary on a particular surah.[38] In this paradigm (P III) there has been a decisive development: the Qur'an and the hadith have become sources of equal rank for the orientation of Muslims.

Parallels to the development in Judaism and Christianity should not be overlooked: Torah and Talmud, scripture and tradition, Qur'an and Sunnah. As in Judaism and Christianity, an 'oral' tradition now appeared alongside the original holy scripture, the Qur'an, which could not be ignored. It had equal rights; indeed it was often set above it. That is worth thinking about: to give what was subordinate equal status is to demote what was above it. Just as the halakhah in Judaism and the dogmas and canons of the Christian church are often fixed before being given a biblical basis, so now in the Muslim tradition particular doctrines and laws were fixed in advance, and scholars could limit their exegesis to giving a later 'foundation' to the traditional doctrine, showing that it was in conformity with the Qur'an. Thus in all the three prophetic religions much is carried along in the tradition which claims to be 'grounded' in the original scripture, but can hardly be understood today and much that was once intended for a completely different situation is subsequently adapted (often by devious interpretation).

However, I must immediately emphasize an important distinction. Neither Judaism nor Islam has anything like a universal magisterium, council or pope, as there is in Christianity in its Hellenistic Byzantine (Christian P II) or its Roman Catholic form (Christian P III), which could simply declare other views heretical or excommunicate those who held them. We shall see that the caliph who claimed such a magisterium came to grief. The wide range of specific

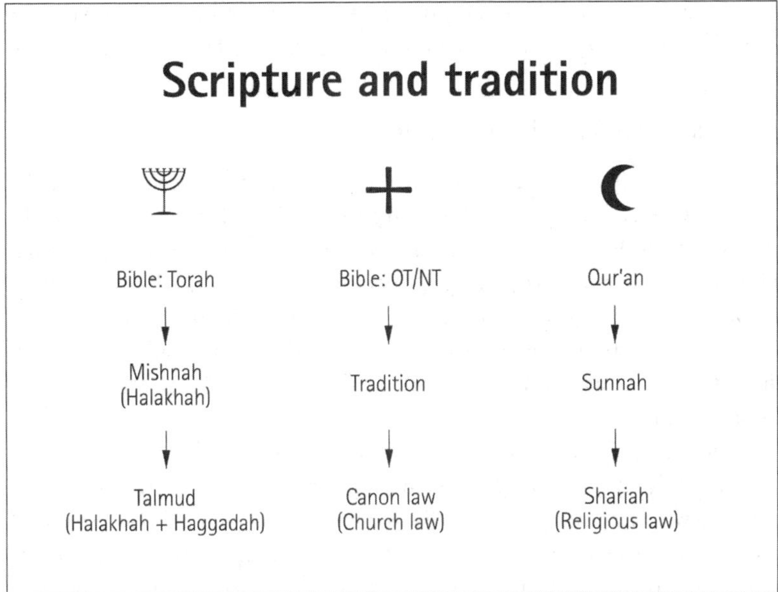

problems and answers in the hadith in any case allows very different statements and instructions. The hadith, like the Talmud, are not a handbook (*enchiridion*), a catechism of legally prescribed texts (such as the Roman Catholic 'Denziger'). They are the principal official collection of often contradictory statements and commandments: some are observed, but others are neglected, some are reinterpreted and some are simply no longer understood. Did this openness of the tradition and the absence of a universal teaching authority also lead to Islam existing more in parties than did Christianity and its mainstream church, as is sometimes claimed? Hardly, for both the West-East and the Catholic-Protestant splits in the church were chiefly caused by Roman absolutism and centralism in questions of faith and leadership.

4. The four great law schools

Islamic legal science, which had begun in such a simple and elementary way with analogies, became increasingly perfect. More and more traditions of the Prophet came to light and had to be incorporated into the legal system and more and more ethical and religious considerations were mixed with systematic arguments. In consequence, several great law schools (*madhhab*, plural *madhahib*) formed in the provinces with their different cultures– adapted to the very different conditions of the different parts of the empire. However, only four of them can still claim to be significant: the Malikite, Hanafite, Shafi'ite and Hanbalite.

The Malikite and Hanafite law schools

To the 'right' of the spectrum is the great legal scholar from Medina, Malik ibn Anas (710–95). He summed up the legal custom of the Hijaz and especially the practice of the Prophet's city, Medina. The Malikite law school (*malikiyah*) derives from him (and from his pupil Ibn al-Qasim). It once held sway from Arabia through Egypt to Spain, and remains influential in the Maghreb, on the coast of Eastern Arabia, in Upper Egypt, Mauritania and Nigeria. It is characterized by its strict observance of the Sunnah and an unmistakable conservatism.

Malik wrote the first handbook of Islamic law, 'The Levelled Way' (*al-muwatta'*); although it was preserved only in copies by pupils, it was often to be provided with commentaries. It is divided into 'books' which follow the different sections of existing law (marriage, treaties, punishments and so on). In each of these a whole mass of often very different topics and legal regulations are discussed, without general principles or definitions of concepts being given at the beginning. Malik begins the discussion of each topic by quoting the relevant tradition: numerous hadith on ritual and legal questions are included. He keeps to the hadith and the legal practice dominant in Medina but quite often rejects the former in favour of the latter, which shows that his conservatism has its limits. He reflects not only on the tradition but also on the utility of the law (*maslahah*) for the Ummah. Malik's supreme criterion remains the customary law sanctioned by the local consensus (*ijma'*) of Medina, so his handbook was completely accepted by the establishment there. In 762 he justified a revolt in the holy cities as legal; however, it was quickly put down by the caliph.

On the other side of the spectrum, the representative figure is Abu Hanifah (699–767), a rich silk manufacturer and mawla from Kufa, whom Abu Yusuf, the first Grand Qadi, regarded as his teacher. For a time Abu Hanifah was imprisoned because he refused to become a judge, but that did not damage his reputation as a legal scholar. Although no authentic juristic writings by him have been handed down, the Hanafite legal school (*hanafiyah*), which replaced the old school of Kufa, derives its origin from him, though presumably Abu Yusuf and above all ash-Shaybani made a much greater contribution to it. Under the 'Abbasids it formed the official law school, then lost its importance with their downfall, though it later became the official school of the Ottoman empire. To the present day it remains strong in Egypt, Syria, Iraq, Turkey and the Balkans, but also has prominent representatives in India, Pakistan and

Central Asia. The largest group of Muslims, around a third, must have belonged to this school, which was the most generous and tolerant in its interpretation of the Islamic law. To the present day, the Hanafites are regarded as representatives of free decision and the use of juristic dialectic. Opponents therefore accuse them of 'legal tricks', by which they attempted to get round or adapt burdensome precepts of the law.

Abu Hanifah's school takes the Qur'an and the Sunnah seriously but leaves considerable scope for a judge's freedom of decision (*ra'y*). If it is impossible to make progress with an analogy, use is made of one's own 'holding-to-be-good' (*istihsan*: 'opinion'). The school was generally interested in penetrating Muslim faith rationally and did not want to exclude the assessment of an experienced jurist. Sometimes opinions were expressed which were closer to the Persian views than those of the Arab Sunnah scholars, who were primarily concerned with appropriating the model of the Prophet in faith in accordance with the tradition of the Sunnah. Probably also for that reason Abu Hanifah expressed some heterodox views, which were later rejected. His tomb is in Baghdad.

The classical juristic synthesis: ash-Shafi'i

The great juristic synthesis was created a few generations later by Muhammad ibn Idris ash-Shafi'i (767–820). Born in Palestine, he was a widely travelled scholar who did not found a new law school but rather wanted to unify Islamic law, with its great local differences, against all conflicting tendencies.[39] After being entangled in rebellious activities in Yemen and being imprisoned in Syria for a short time, under Harun ar-Rashid, he studied at most of the great centres of jurisprudence: in Mecca, in Medina with Malik, then in Baghdad with ash-Shaybani. Eventually he settled in Fustat (Cairo) in Egypt. There, in the last five years of his life, he wrote the academically and stylistically brilliant work 'Risalah', which was to make him the father of Muslim jurisprudence. So great was his reputation that his tomb soon became a place of pilgrimage.

With ash-Shafi'i, the paradigm change from the old legal schools (P II) to a new jurisprudence that integrated the prophetic hadith reached its consummation (P III). He was a master of the juristic method, introducing few new concepts and ideas into the law but reinterpreting them and linking them together in a strictly systematic way to exclude, as far as possible, any arbitrary findings in the future. Thus, he made a fundamental contribution to the juristic methodology for the use of these traditions. He summed up much that was already taking shape in his well-formed doctrine of the four principles (*usul*: sources, roots) of legal science (*fiqh*): the Qur'an, the Sunnah, analogy (*qiyas*) and consensus (*ijma'*). He elevated the Sunnah to the level of the

Qur'an, decisively rejecting any argument with the help of analogy or the consensus of scholars.

Methodologically ash-Shafi'i was superior to the old law schools in that he was able to reconcile and combine the 'party of reason' and the 'party of tradition', which previously had been opposed or at best loosely interconnected.

– Like the representatives of the old law schools, ash-Shafi'i was a master of rational argument; in his works this occupied more space than in those of most of his predecessors. Since the process of the Islamization of the law was essentially complete before his time, he did not need constantly to bring specifically religious or moral perspectives into play. He could distinguish between the moral and legal aspects in principle better than his predecessors and unlike the traditionists he did not need to declare as 'invalid' all that was forbidden.

– On the other hand, however, like the traditionists and in a different way from the old schools, ash-Shafi'i took the prophetic traditions as a basis for his juristic reflections. He emphatically put forward the view that these could not be deprived of their force by any higher authority. For him, too, the Sunnah was no longer the living local tradition of the school but exclusively the word and actions of the Prophet himself, even if sometimes they were attested only by a single person in a generation.

What about the countless contradictions between the different prophetic traditions? According to ash-Shafi'i, in some cases a particular tradition can be preferred because the chain of tradition is more strongly attested while in others a particular tradition is to be understood as an exception to the general rule. But at the centre of his juristic expositions is the concept of the refutation (*naskh* –: abrogation) of an earlier legal norm by a later one; in some inconvenient cases this can make possible a way out of the difficulties. Ash-Shafi'i put forward the momentous view that the Qur'an can be abrogated only by the Qur'an and the Sunnah only by the Sunnah. He had two reasons:

- the Sunnah cannot refute any regulation of the Qur'an because its sole function is to interpret the Qur'an;
- the Qur'an cannot refute any regulation of the Sunnah because this would put in question the interpretative role of the inspired Sunnah.

This second point meant an enormous rise in the valuation of oral tradition. What were the consequences?

The traditionalist principle becomes established

This point makes ash-Shafi'i's specific approach clear: it goes far beyond the previous positions and at the same time represents a highly problematic contribution to Islamic jurisprudence. For ash-Shafi'i, too, the Qur'an remains the first source of revelation but since 'Obey God and his Prophet' is called for in the Qur'an in a variety of places, he concludes that the words and actions of the Prophet that have been handed down are to be regarded as divinely inspired.

There is no mistaking a paradigm change in the significance of the Prophet:

- for the old legal scholars the Prophet as an interpreter of the Qur'an was only the *primus inter pares*, who could be contradicted with good reasons (and especially with the help of the Qur'an);
- but now that the Prophet had become *the* lawgiver and at the same time the divinely inspired interpreter of the Qur'an, it was forbidden to contradict his hadith.

The result was a significant unification of the law: instead of the many local traditions of the law schools, there was now only the one inspired universal 'tradition of the Prophet'. This rose to be the second source of the revelation of the divine law which, though not on the same footing as the Qur'an, is in practice even more important, in so far as the Qur'an is to be interpreted in the light of this Sunnah. Whatever has remained undefined in the Qur'an can now be decided by one of the thousands of hadiths, on the basis of divine authority.

Ash-Shafi'i could thus present his approach systematically and rationally and as deeply bound up with tradition: analogies and learned consensuses were utterly subordinated to the Sunnah.

– In contrast to Abu Hanifah, he limited independent opinion (*ra'y*) obtained by analogies and rejected 'opinions' (*istihsan*), so that subjective views and decisions were hardly possible. His proposition was crystal clear: analogy results in a lack of discipline unless it starts from and is covered by the three other primary sources of law; therefore a legal argument may never arrive at a result which is in contradiction to the Qur'an, the Sunnah or the consensus. Only in this way can the differences between different views be reduced to a minimum.

– At the same time, he rejected reference to the use of the law (*maslahah*) in the Malikite sense. He replaced the authority of the local 'consensus of scholars' with the universal 'consensus of Muslims' (scholars and laity). This consensus had preserved the traditions of the Prophet entire and could not contain any error. It had to be 'infallible' but as a legal argument it came into play only for very elementary questions (for example the performance of daily prayer). At the same time, unlike Malik, ash-Shafi'i extended the binding consensus to all Islamic law, so that individual deviations were no longer possible. The teaching of the community and the authority of the prophetic traditions thus coincided.

The result of ash-Shafi'i's great wager was a comprehensive, coherent and self-contained system, which was much more logical and stringent than those of his predecessors. However, as the authority of the prophetic tradition had now been irrevocably established with an appeal to divine inspiration, any further natural development of the doctrine, of the kind that had still been taken for granted by the old legal scholars and their living tradition, was blocked. The tradition was raised to the status of a universal principle and in the long run this necessarily resulted in immobility and rigidity. Even an appeal to the spirit of the Qur'an, which formerly was quite customary, was no longer of any avail against a particular prophetic tradition,.

Ash-Shafi'i's hermeneutic had made provisions here in every respect: the Qur'an was to be interpreted in the light of the prophetic tradition and not vice versa. No more room was left for personal judgement than in the Roman Catholic system, where the Bible is to be interpreted in the light of the tradition by the 'authentic magisterium' and no appeal can be made to scripture that bypasses tradition and magisterium. You can no more argue against the divinely inspired Prophet and his words that have been handed down than you can against the Pope, assisted by the Holy Spirit and his defined statements. In both cases, you can no longer examine the truth of the statement itself but only the modalities of the tradition which are bound up with it. That is why Islamic legal science concentrates completely on questions of the chain of tradition.

Ash-Shafi'i's tradition was not established immediately and some points were subsequently modified. However, his central approach, the divine authority of the Sunnah of the Prophet, now generally appeared irrefutable. He put it like this: 'On points on which there is an explicit decision of Allah or a Sunnah of the Prophet or a consensus of Muslims, no deviant meaning is allowed; on other points the scholars must exercise their own judgement by seeking a reference in one of these three sources.'[40]

The other law schools had no alternative than to adapt to ash-Shafi'i's basic positions on the authority of the tradition. Even the Hanafites had to bring themselves to base their solutions on the hadith. However, neither in Medina, where people were still more orientated towards local practice, nor in Kufa, where they preferred free rational argument, was there a readiness to accept the binding character of every individual tradition, if this contradicted their own established teaching. In this way these two schools succeeded to a limited degree in keeping their own character.

Subsequently the Shafi'ite legal school spread from Egypt and Baghdad. It reached its zenith in Egypt between the 'Abbasid and Ottoman periods and produced such famous theologians as al-Ash'ari and al-Ghazali, whom I will discuss later. To the present day it has many adherents in Upper Egypt, Syria, southern

Arabia, East Africa and South East Asia. Unfortunately there is no overlooking the fact that in establishing Islamic legal science ash-Shafi'i also did a great deal towards ossifying it.

Is the door of 'legal findings' closed? Ibn Hanbal

What the great systematician ash-Shafi'i tried to avoid nevertheless came about: the foundation of a new law school based specifically on his teachings, but with an even more rigorous approach. Ahmad ibn Hanbal (870–55), who had studied with ash-Shafi'i, came from a pro-'Alid family in Merv; he lived mostly in Baghdad and collected more than 80,000 hadith. He thought that ash-Shafi'i had still too much room for personal reflection and decision; one should depart as little as possible from the literal sense of the Qur'an or the hadith. Ibn Hanbal is typified by the tradition that he had never eaten a water-melon because there was no precedent for that in the tradition of the Prophet. Paradoxically, his rigorous approach also had 'liberal' consequences, for one might not order what was not clearly commanded and one might not forbid what was not explicitly prohibited. Ibn Hanbal, who was inclined to regard both the Umayyad and 'Abbasid dynasties as legitimate, rejected the official teaching of rational theology (*mu'tazilah*), which at that time was being promoted by the 'Abbasids; between 833 and 835 he was thrown into prison, as we shall hear in more detail later, and only in the last five years of his life could he gather pupils round him again.

The fourth law school, the Hanbalite law school, goes back to him; it is well known for its interpretation of the Qur'an and Sunnah in a way that is faithful to the letter and its strict observance of the Shariah. But its rigorism in cultic and dogmatic questions is combined with liberality in questions that are not decided in the sources of revelation, such as those relating to contracts over debts and trade law so that, for this school, the principle of freedom of contract did not cause any difficulty, as it did for the others.

This school was especially widespread in Iraq, where it played a great role in controversies with the Shiites, but it was then repressed by the Ottomans and the Hanafite law school. Its rigorism influenced the Wahhabi reform movement in the eighteenth century through the conservative reformer Ibn Taymiyyah and, although numerically the weakest law school, it is still of great importance because it continues to have support today in Saudi Arabia and the United Emirates.

How were things to continue with Islamic legal science? Was it to continue at all? Within the framework of the 'Abbasid paradigm (P III) there was an amazing blossoming of Islamic legal science—centuries before the blossoming of canon law in the Latin Middle Ages. However, in contrast to earlier times, the religious scholars (*ulama*) in Islam were no longer free. It was in the interest of the ʿAbbasids that the development of religious law should come to an end in the eighth century. After the ninth century, the interpretation of Qur'an and Sunnah was allowed only within the four law schools. This was the heyday of the great hadith collections of al-Bukhari and his successors, which have already been mentioned.

The increasingly marked reference to tradition and consensus more and more limited formation of independent judgements (*ijtihad*), until their creative power was quenched altogether. However, there is no documentation anywhere that after the tenth century, at least in Sunni Islam, the 'door of independent judgement' (*bab al-ijtihad*) was regarded as closed, as has often been claimed (a century beforehand, a unitary papal church law had been formulated). More quickly than anyone could have guessed, the hopeful spring of Muslim legal science was followed by the autumn of traditionalism.

Does innovation become fossilized tradition?

For Islam, as for Judaism and Christianity, the question of the importance of tradition is vital and arises not only for outsiders but primarily for Muslims themselves. Within the Islamic community, many serious believers (though often they do not dare to speak openly) find the role of revelation that has accrued to the hadith problematical, because it has forced the Qur'an almost completely into the background. Muslims too, have objections, not primarily because from a present-day historical perspective it is difficult to distinguish authentic hadith from inauthentic hadith and doubts arise about the authenticity of the majority of them. Many hadith seem to reflect less the time of the Prophet than the discussions in the early Muslim community. Indubitably there are also quotations from Greek philosophers and even from the Bible in the hadith. Present-day Muslims seek to return to the origins, to the purest essence of Islam, so as to have more freedom from fossilized traditions. The Qur'an appears to them (as does the Bible to many Jews and Christians) deeper, more simple and more open than much that is later, even on such difficult questions as the position of women and non-Muslims, and in particular on questions of criminal law.

Here, too, it is paradoxical that Islam entered Arab life with a tremendous thrust towards innovation, successfully questioning the age-old Arab Sunnah, the local and regional tradition, and thus transforming much in Arab customary law. That was difficult enough but the Arabs felt that, by tradition and precedents, they were bound together much more closely than, for example, the Greeks. In principle, wasn't what had always been customary right and good? Could the ancients have been wrong? However, against all the resistance put up by the old Arab Sunnah, the Prophet with his message of one God and his righteousness was able to prevail (P I).

Yet when Islam had conquered, didn't the Islam of innovation become the Islam of tradition? The first caliph, Abu Bakr (P I), seems to have appealed to the Sunnah of the Prophet (albeit understood in a quite general way). And soon

Questions: Traditionalism

Many Christians recognize that the church tradition was absolutized at the cost of the biblical message. Thus, in the Hellenistic–Byzantine paradigm (P II) the tradition of the fathers and the councils and in the medieval Roman Catholic paradigm (P III) the authority of Rome in teaching morality and discipline became the highest norm of Christianity. Hasn't Christianity in this way obscured part of its essence? Doesn't Christian traditionalism exist decidedly at the expense of being Christ-like? Mustn't particular traditions be reformed, corrected or abolished in respect of the essence of Christianity, as the Reformation (P IV) required?

Many Jews recognize that in Judaism the Torah (P I) was overgrown by a second 'oral Torah' (P III): complicated 'traditions of the fathers' (P IV) which, in practice, became the normative basis for religious teaching and religious law. But didn't this make the tradition more important than the 'instruction' (Torah) of God himself? Doesn't a Jewish traditionalism exist all too much at the expense of the spirit of Judaism? Mustn't particular traditions be capable of being overcome to re-open the essentials?

Many Muslims recognize that where Islam has constructed and idealized its past all too strongly, the Sunnah has become a substitute institution for the guidance of the Prophet and the hadith have become a direct revelation of God. For Islamic legal science, which determines everything, the hadith have become more important than the Qur'an. The teachings of the ancestors have been largely taken over and often preserved only in mechanical formulae. However, can what is not itself the revelation of God but the result of a historical development be prescribed for all time and for people of all ages? Hasn't Islam as a living religion damaged itself by its absolutizing and fossilization of tradition and its exaggerated respect for earlier heads of schools? Hasn't the essence of the great prophetic message often been obscured in a traditionalist way? Mustn't there be freedom from particular traditions when referring to the essence of Islam?

there was a great controversy over whether the third caliph, 'Uthman, had deviated from the Sunnah of Abu Bakr and 'Umar and thus from the Qur'an and the Sunnah of the Prophet—a charge which the religious conservatives in Medina then levelled against the Umayyads (P II) and which was repeated as a foundation for the 'Abbasid revolution (P III). Following this, there was an absolutization and thus a fossilization of tradition. Law based on independent legal findings (*ijtihad*) was now replaced by the obligation of 'imitation' (*taqlid*). A legal school was inconceivable without this but it degraded the individual jurist so that he became a pure 'imitator' (*muqallid*), who simply followed the teaching laid down by his praised and idealized predecessors.

At least in theology, many Muslim scholars were clear that the repetition of Qur'anic verses and quotations from the Prophet was not everything; the important thing was the rational exegesis of Qur'an and Sunnah. However – after the first theological dispute over God's predestination and human predestination – this intention led to a second great theological dispute, over revelation and reason (P III).

5. The second theological dispute: revelation and reason

The conversion of the Arabs to faith in the one God now lay generations back in the past. Only on the periphery of the vast empire, in India, in Central Asia among the Turkic peoples and in Africa among the tribal religions, did Muslims have to do with large numbers of 'unbelievers' in the strict sense, with polytheists. The Muslim view was that, theologically, this 'pure' superstition no longer needed to be taken seriously.

Things were different with those of other faiths, the Jews and Christians. After all, these were also 'people of the book', to whom God had given a revelation of their own. Muslims were bound up with Jews and Christians through faith in the one God of Abraham but nevertheless were distinct from them, especially from Christians, who could easily be accused of 'polytheism' because of the Trinity. Any 'association' (*shirk*) which threatened belief in the one and only God had to be fought, whether it came from outside, from Christian doctrine, or from within, from all that could divert a Muslim from God. Theology, theological reason, had a special task here.

The new importance of reason

Just as the time of the 'Abbasids was the great age of the development of Islamic law, so too it was the time of the development of Islamic theology. In theology, too, within the framework of this paradigm (P III), classical positions were adopted which, for the most part, are still valid. However—as each paradigm change is prepared for in the preceding paradigm—they already announced themselves in the late Umayyad period, though only in the early 'Abbasid period did the outlines of the new paradigm for theology become clear:

- The centre of gravity of theology had shifted eastwards. Theologically, Syria, Egypt and even the Hijaz now lay on the periphery; theological decisions were made above all in Baghdad and in Iran.
- What was decisive now was no longer the opposition of the 'sects' or the cities but an opposition of method: traditional science (the *muhaddithun*, the hadith scholars) or rational theology (= the *kalam* of the *mutakallimun*).
- The substantive problem shifted from the group of topics surrounding 'God's predestination and human self-determination' to the problems of 'divine revelation and human reason' and consequently to the nature of the Qur'an—is it created or uncreated?
- In P II belief in the unity of God was largely accepted without question and needed no special reflection but now God's unity and oneness (*tawhid*) became a widely-discussed theological topic, sometimes even said to be the first truth of Islamic faith: the first of five 'foundations' (*usul*) of faith (*iman*) which paralleled the five 'pillars' ('members', *arkan*) or practical commandments.
- Previously the idea of God had been widely regarded as innate in human beings: the human being (even the unbeliever!) could know God by himself. But now, as later in Christian scholasticism, two levels of the knowledge of God began to be differentiated: what human beings could know of themselves (at least the existence of God) and what they know through God's revelation. Thoroughly formulated proofs of God (both from teleology and from the contingency of the world) and a well-thought-out doctrine of God's characteristics (attributes), of which there were only the beginnings in the Qur'an, were now developed rationally.
- There was a unification of Islamic thought and the zenith of Islamic theology.

To begin with this theology seemed strongly polarized, exposed to rising tensions between the advocates of the hadith and those of the *kalam*, both of whom struggled for the favour of the caliphs.

– On one side was the tradition theology of the 'people of tradition' (*ahl al-hadith*), and allied with them the law school of Ahmad ibn Hanbal (780–855), which I have already discussed. The often very aggressive Hanbalites called for a literal interpretation of Qur'an and Sunnah (hadith) and had no logical methods in the treatment of juristic and theological questions; for them human reason was by no means normative for theological knowledge. The social environment of this theology was that of the petty-bourgeois and the lower classes, who had been unsettled in the melting-pot of the metropolis. This theology made Islam seem smaller than it is.

– On the other side was the rational theology of the so-called Mu'tazilah, which had emerged at the end of the Umayyad period and reached its high point under the 'Abbasids. (I shall be looking at it more closely later.) It did not seek to replace or domesticate revelation by reason: to this degree it was not 'rationalistic', as it is often labelled, but 'rational'. While holding on to the revelation, with the help of reason it sought to understand, explain and ground the Qur'an and the Sunnah and defend them against their opponents (Jews and Christians), from whom it learned and adopted much. This rational theology was part of the discourse of the intellectuals in a lofty city culture and made Islam appear to be a practical religion, open to the world.

I shall now turn my attention to it, since it produced questions, concepts and arguments which dominated the next decades and have persisted to the present day, despite the later downfall of the school. Unfortunately, we have hardly any original works from this early period: we know it only from refutations and later reports or revisions. However, here too the work of Josef van Ess has brought decisive insights.[41]

The beginnings of rational theology: Wasil and 'Amr

After the civil war between the two sons of Harun ar-Rashid and the victory of al-Ma'mun over al-Amin, the Mu'tazilah was affirmed as the state theology. It has a complex background and originally was not a theology that would support the state. On the contrary, most recent research into the origin of the name Mu'tazilah[42] shows that it is primarily to be understood politically and goes back to the time of the first civil war between Mu'awiyyah and 'Ali:

– *Al-mu'tazil* (singular, not yet written with an initial capital) is someone who remains neutral in a dispute and 'distances himself', 'keeps aloof' (*i'tazala*) from all fellow-believers who, in an un-Islamic way, raise the sword against one another.

– *Al-Mu'tazilah* (singular) is the movement of those who keep aloof: 'The Mu'tazilah kept aloof from any political party', not just from the Umayyads but also from the 'Abbasids and their 'Alid opposition (thus J. van Ess[43] against H.S. Nyberg[44]).

Two pupils of the famous Hasan al-Basri, both the same age, are regarded as the founders of the Mu'tazilah in the theological sense; as yet there was no confrontation between them and the traditionists.

– One is the mawla Wasil ibn 'Ata' (699–748/9), who perhaps came from Medina.[45] He was a well-to-do carpet merchant (who perhaps, for that reason, was denounced as petty-bourgeois), highly educated (but with a speech defect), a moving orator (a *khatib* who could skilfully avoid the 'r' that he could not say). Influenced by Hasan's Qadarite-inspired asceticism, he organized a missionary movement. He advocated a moderate this-worldly asceticism, appealing not to the feelings but to rational insight. He became famous as the result of a highly impressive extempore speech before 'Abdallah, the son of 'Umar II, governor of Iraq, which surpassed all the other speeches; however, he died immediately before the 'Abbasid revolution.

– His fellow student, another mawla, 'Amr ibn 'Ubayd (699–762),[46] was taciturn rather than an orator, debater or scribe. He was even more ascetic than Wasil, by whom he is said to have been 'converted' in a disputation—though this cannot be verified historically. He thought little of money and luxury but attached much importance to constant prayer and the pilgrimage to Mecca. His last pilgrimage, from which he was not to return alive, was a dozen years after Wasil's death. 'Amr's influence during his lifetime lay in an alliance of young people which, in the face of the manifest political and social injustice, represented something like a network of communities, a civic self-help organization.

Legend brings Wasil and 'Amr very close together, so that they appear paired, like Goethe and Schiller or Marx and Engels. But they differ, although as Qadarite representatives of the freedom of the will they could have a close political collaboration in Basra. The Mu'tazilite theological fellowship that is often assumed hardly existed between them. Their pupils were also different: Wasil's were primarily jurists and 'Amr's above all traditionists. 'Amr was active as a teacher in Basra, whereas Wasil sent his pupils to work with the caravans; as missionaries, they created a basis of trust by giving advice on the law bringing religious questions into the discussion. Wasil sent his messengers, whom we know by name,[47] not only across the Arabian peninsula, to Medina and Bahrain and into Yemen, but also into the Maghreb, to Khorasan and Armenia. What was the theology of these two men?

To unite the community, split over the question, Wasil resolutely claimed that there was a special interim state for grievous sinners; this view later came to be regarded as typically Mu'tazilite. For example, he argued that a murderer was not a believer who enters paradise, far less an unbeliever who is destined for hell; he could convert. Moreover, good works were balanced against evil works—an interesting parallel to certain Catholic doctrines of penance. However, according to the more tolerant Muslim theologians, young children, whom (if they had not been baptized) Catholic church teachers such as Augustine damned to hell, were not called to reckoning but entered paradise.

The theology of ʻAmr was by no means revolutionary. He felt so close to his highly-respected teacher Hasan al-Basri that he edited the latter's commentary on the Qur'an. As a jurist, he also relied strongly on his teacher in the interpretation of the Qur'an. Otherwise he worked independently, as is attested by his writing on the division of the Qur'an into 360 parts, his only writing which has survived (two other works of his are known only by their titles). At some points, ʻAmr seems to surpass his teacher. Generally, he attached no importance to an exegesis supported by the analysis of words but also interpreted some verses of the Qur'an in a decisively Qadarite way, in the sense of human freedom of the will. However, he did not as yet advocate the rational positions of the later Muʻtazilah, except that he readily rejected hadith which were dogmatically predestinarian or contradicted the juristic practice customary in Basra. In his view God did not just determine evil, nor did he determine good.

Confrontation with the caliphate?

Neither Wasil nor ʻAmr preached armed resistance against the Umayyads or the ʻAbbasids (as did Bashir ar-Rahhal, who was, like them, a Muʻtazilite). Rather, even under the ʻAbbasids they kept their distance from the authorities and called for social and political justice. Possibly the circle around ʻAmr had already dissociated themselves from the Quraysh under the impact of the execution of Ghaylan (in 732), which has already been mentioned, but kept quiet after the victory of the ʻAbbasids.

ʻAmr's encounter with Caliph al-Mansur in 759 is surrounded by legends (and sometimes is considerably inflated). People have puzzled a great deal about the occasion for this encounter: did al-Mansur see ʻAmr as a trusted friend, even a spiritual father (thus H.S. Nyberg[48])? Did he receive him at least out of respect and for his counsel in moral and religious questions (thus W.M. Watt[49])? Or were there political reasons: the suspicion of conspiracy and machinations against the state among his followers, who numbered thousands? That is the latest view, after the comprehensive new investigation of the sources by Josef van Ess.[50] With its network of communities, which were not just religious groups but also political forces, the Muʻtazilah were a power factor in the ʻAlid agitations. However, when, in 759, Muhammad the son of ʻAbdallah ibn al-Hasan ibn ʻAli from Medina appeared in Basr, the caliph reacted rapidly with a demonstration of power. This impressed the Muʻtazilah so much that they forced ʻAmr to seek out the caliph, despite his resistance, and make a confession of loyalty. When the revolt then nevertheless broke out in 762, ʻAmr, who had previously been humiliated by the caliph, had been dead for a year. His followers later split into militant activists under the leadership of Bashir ar-Rahhal, among whom no theologians were to be found, and moderates, but the latter have likewise left hardly any historical traces.

Subsequently, there was increasingly an alliance with the caliphate: at the time of Caliph al-Mahdi, the Mu'tazilites still had no access to the court but in the time of Harun ar-Rashid they were very welcome in the disputation groups of the vizier's family, the Barmakids, where scholars of all kinds met. In the latter days of Harun they had to leave the palace, as the traditionists were in the supremacy; they returned to dominance under his son al-Ma'mun.

The paradigm of a rational theology

Under the 'Abbasids, the Mu'tazilah succeeded in working out a new paradigm of theology in which rationality, from 'physics' to the understanding of God and eschatology, played a completely new role. No one in Islam had adopted Greek philosophy and the other sciences as resolutely as the Mu'tazilah. Only in this way were they able to build up a coherent scientific system, expand the questions of Islamic theology, sharpen the formation of concepts and intensify their argument. The pioneer thinkers were two scholars who had been drawn to court under the Barmakids: the very productive Dirar ibn 'Amr, in whom ancient thought (Aristotelian) and Islamic thought (Qur'anic exegesis) met for the first time, and Mu'ammar, who was chiefly in the natural sciences (in mirrors and balances).[51]

When looking at the shaping of the paradigm we need particularly to examine the developed positions of the great systematicians, through which the classical Mu'tazilah reached its high point. Interestingly, an uncle and a nephew form the two poles: Abu l-Hudhayl and his nephew and former assistant an-Nazzam, who disputed with him. I shall concentrate more on Abu l-Hudhayl, who had a stronger influence than the outsider an-Nazzam, a highly original figure who became famous as a poet and artist in language (and notorious as a lover of boys) and made his name with 'philosophy' (the explanation of nature).

As a Christian, I am astounded how, centuries before any Latin scholasticism, at a time when Europe was threatened with a loss of continuity with its own antiquity (which was prevented only by the monks), in the Arab sphere under Greek influence, there should have been a highly sophisticated discussion between these two systematicians.[52] It was about:

- 'physics': about atomism, bodies and accidents (permanent and impermanent), movement, air and light, fire and burning, sense perceptions, theories of colours and acoustics, equality and difference and the position of the earth in space.

- anthropology: about bodies and the life-giving principle ('life', 'spirit'), the unity of person and action, perception and knowledge and about resurrection, eternal life, Satan and demons.
- hermeutical–criteriological questions: about the exegesis of the Qur'an and the reliability of the tradition about the Prophet, about juristic method and the problems of analogy and consensus.

It would be interesting to discuss, for example, Abu l-Hudhayl's idiosyncratic 'metaphysics of created being', constructed with the help of atomism (atoms, as invisible elements of the entity, are put together as bodies by God himself and possibly also dissolved again) and theology in the strict sense, as the doctrine of God. The Mu'tazilites have often been vilified as sheer rationalists but Abu l-Hudhayl and an-Nazzam no more wanted to give up the Qur'an as the basis of their theology than Albert the Great and Thomas Aquinas wanted to give up the Bible. They all attached more importance to reason than their predecessors; they were all deliberately rational but not rationalists.

Historically, Abu l-Hudhayl and an-Nazzam stand between two tendencies. The traditionalist anthropomorphists were content with a literal understanding of the Qur'an (and the hadith), excluded any transferred meaning of the Qur'an and had no difficulty with its numerous anthropomorphisms, descriptions of God in human terms. The extreme transcendentalists or Jahmites (*Jahmiyah*) emphasized in an exaggerated way the otherness of God for human knowledge. The Jahmites and the Mu'tazilites are often identified with each other, but they are different.

A God without properties? Jahm

The extreme transcendentalists go back to the rhetorically gifted and politically committed mawla Jahm ibn Safwan[53] (who was executed in 746). Jahm was from Khorasan but lived chiefly in Tirmid (Bactria, in present-day northern Afghanistan), where his doctrine was held in high esteem for several generations more. At that time, Tirmid was a centre of central Asian Buddhism, in the environs of which there were numerous Buddhist monuments.

According to all that we know, Jahm held conversations with 'Sumanites',[54] alleged to be sensualists, who did not believe in any spiritual reality and certainly not in any personal God. They were Indians (Sanskrit *sramana*, Middle Indian *samana*), probably ascetics of the Buddhist faith, possibly even Buddhist monks. It was not easy to defend the concept of a personal God against them. But perhaps this contact with Buddhists (if one does not want to see Neoplatonic sources behind all this) explains why Jahm, while holding on to the personality of God, radically sharpened many of his positions:[55] on the understanding of God (the rejection of all divine attributes) and on the understanding of faith (the knowledge of God, in this Islamic missionary region, if need be without an explicit confession). His radical determinism is quite isolated in Islam.

For Jahm, understanding God was a central problem: he believed in one omnipresent God who alone governs all that happens, creates every good deed in human beings, engenders faith and brings about everything in nature, even the rising and setting of the sun. His is a universal determinism, to which God wholly delivers human beings, who have no illusions about it.

The human beings delivered over in this way cannot really know God. For Jahm, it is fundamental that for all the essential immanence of God, God's radical transcendence is preserved for knowledge. Although God is at work in everything, he is the wholly other; he is not 'something' (*shay'*) and not a 'thing'; he is utterly incomparable with anything, as the Qur'an says.[56] Rather, God is the creator 'of each thing',[57] whose being infinitely transcends the being of any thing. Therefore, no property of a 'thing', no property at all that we can observe in our world—extension or colour, direction or limits—may be attributed to God,. The divine predicates in the Qur'an are metaphors: not really God's speech (self-predications), but human talk about God. God in himself is unknowable and has neither names nor properties.

No wonder that the Jahmites were called 'emptiers', who practised an 'emptying' of the divine being. Perhaps this would not have displeased them too much, as 'emptiness' (Sanskrit *sunyata*) is a term for the highest reality in Mahayana Buddhism. However, the other Buddhists vilified the Jahmites, claiming that they had robbed God of all attributes. The Sunni ad-Darimi (who died in 869) remarked: 'They (the Jahmites) spoke great words of God and scorned him in the most shameful way, attributed ignorance to him and gradually robbed him of the attributes with which he is described. Finally they also took away his prior knowledge [of events], speaking, hearing, seeing, indeed everything.'[58]

As I have already mentioned (see C II, 7), the Ibadite leader Abu 'Ubaydah had imposed a ban on those who wanted to understand statements about God which sounded metaphorical literally instead of metaphorically; they argued that God's 'hand' meant his power or his reward or that his 'eye' meant his knowledge or his protection. Jahm and the Jahmites went even further, if the accounts are authentic: for them God was the boundless one in space and time; present everywhere and at no place more present than at another. The unity of God is to be understood as the omnipresence of his being but this escapes any conceptual definition by human beings. Yet God has given himself to be known in revelation which, like the things of this world, is creaturely and temporally limited.

This teaching was inevitably opposed, not only by the traditionists, who limited themselves to the sacred text, but also by theologians who argued rationally. How could such a God intervene in the destiny of peoples and individuals? How could he speak directly to his Prophet? How could he have communicated himself in a book? For some, this questioned not only the action of God and the Qur'an as his revelation but possibly also such practical rites as mandatory prayer in the direction of Mecca or the pilgrimage to the Ka'bah, to the place where a special presence of God is experienced.

How was it possible to give a theological answer to the challenge of the Jahmites, which accorded with the Qur'an yet did not fall back below the level of reflection achieved here? It took a great systematician who was able to deal with and transcend extremes.

God has properties: Abu l-Hudhayl's rational system

The great systematician of the Mu'tazilah, Abu l-Hudhayl al-'Allaf, was a theologian, probably of Iranian origin. He was born in 752 and worked for a long time in Basra as a pupil of and successor to Dirar ibn 'Amr, leader of its circle of theological teachers. At the time of Caliph al-Mahdi he was apparently brought to Baghdad for interrogation, despite the protests of his followers, but now, more than sixty years old, he went to Baghdad of his own accord to gain influence at al-Ma'mun's court. With a comprehensive philosophical and theological education and the ability to shape systems, characterized by wit, irony and argumentative certainty, he could engage in polemical discussions with Jews, Christians and Zoroastrians and especially with his Muslim contemporaries. He introduced himself to the caliph, who believed in astrology, with a skilful speech against it. Subsequent generations regarded him as *the* representative of *kalam*, rational theology, but he would occupy his due place in modern scholarship only at a late date.[59]

It is not important in an analysis of the theological paradigm to consider Abu l-Hudhayl's 'physics' and anthropology or his very idiosyncratic eschatology which, more than some other topics, brought him into dispute with simpler minds. He thought that in the consummation, paradise and hell would not cease to exist because, as Jahm had claimed, God had stopped his creative action. Finally everything would enter an eternal, abiding rest. So the blessed would one day no longer eat, drink, visit one another and sleep together. Such remarks about the next world did not make him popular with the wider population.

Unlike his teacher Dirar, Abu l-Hudhayl did not fight against the traditionists but, in view of the contradictory and often falsified testimonies, laid down strict criteria for the hadith: twenty persons, including at least one exemplary Muslim, must unanimously attest a report. (For an-Nazzam the chief criterion was that the content must be enlightening.) The main point of interest is Abu l-Hudhayl's image of God: here the differences between the Mu'tazilites, as represented by him, and the Jahmites are particularly clear:

- According to the Jahmites, human beings cannot know God at all; according to the Mu'tazilites human beings cannot know God by the senses but they can know God by the mind.
- According to the Jahmites, there are no proofs of God; according to the Mu'tazilites there are: Abu l-Hudhayl was the first theologian in Islam to formulate a proof of God (constructed in four stages, from the movement and contingency of the world).

The whole discussion comes to a head over the doctrine of God's properties, developed systematically and in a positive way for the first time by Abu l-Hudhayl. He wanted to do away with extremes. Anthropomorphisms had to be interpreted by philosophical reflection (as they were by Jahm) but at the same time justice had to done to the Qur'an so that people were not led astray (as by Jahm) into a barren 'negative theology'.

Abu l-Hudhayl, building on Qur'anic exegesis, shows no inhibitions in attributing omnipotence to God (which, if need be, the Jahmites could also do to explain God's activity everywhere). Furthermore, accepting all the predicates which occur in the Qur'an, but only these, he firmly attributes greatness, majesty, grandeur and glory to God, as an expression of God's eternal perfections. These characteristics must not be distinguished from God but must be stated 'with him' or 'in him', indeed substantially 'by him'. Why? Because they are identical with his essence. Also identical with God are attributes which have no object, such as 'life', or which have no opposite, such as the 'countenance' or the 'self' (*nafs*). In respect of God's knowledge that means—and this is a test case for the doctrine of attributes—that to say 'God is knowing' means not only that God is not unknowing or that God 'has' knowledge, but rather that God 'is' knowledge. Knowledge is identical with God's being; God is knowledge.

So is, for example, God's power, which is likewise identical with God's essence, also identical with his knowledge? In that case, mustn't God then consistently do everything that he knows? Abu l-Hudhayl's solution, which calls for differentiation, is open to discussion—above all from the perspectives of formal logic. Moreover it was discussed not only within the Mu'tazilah but also by a contemporary Christian theologian from Basra, 'Ammar al-Basri. Was it possible for Muslims to discuss the argument of Christians? He had made precisely the opposite deduction from the doctrine of attributes, namely that wisdom and life were not only attributes of God but divine persons, Son and Holy Spirit who, in a substantial way, are independent and eternal. It was against him in particular that Abu l-Hudhayl wrote a treatise.[60] Whereas for the Jahmites God's personality (*nafs*) is a useless hypothesis, the Mu'tazilites, like all Muslims, radically reject the 'association' of two persons with the one personal God. As for God's wisdom or knowledge, it should be reflected that God does not become knowing through an act of knowledge but, as an-Nazzam puts it, is knowing 'through himself' or 'from himself'. Each different attribute would describe only another aspect of God.

What are the consequences for the image of human beings?

The controversies over the image of God were also recorded in discussions about the image of human beings. I need report these only briefly, since I have already discussed the old oppositions of Qadarites and predestinarians and the new oppositions:

– Those who, like the Jahmites, advocate an abrupt separation between God and the world and universal determinism cannot, in practice, attribute any kind of power and activity to human beings of themselves: no will and no possibility of free choice. In that case, how is the responsibility of human beings for their salvation to be combined with the metaphorical character of the action generally?

– Those who, like the Mu'tazilites, see a connection between God and the world, together with the preservation of God's transcendence, recognize an inner connection between God's action in creation and human action: human beings bear responsibility; they 'produce' their consequences (for example wounding and causing pain through the throwing of a stone) and are to be blamed at least for the foreseeable consequences of their actions. Can't a connection between cause and effect be observed everywhere in nature? The Mut'azilites laboured over their precise explanation as they did over their analysis of the impulses of the will and the motivations for human action.

In all this intellectual labour, we should not overlook the fact that such rational theology is in danger of getting entangled in detail and producing arbitrary constructions. Nevertheless, something that Abu l-Hudhayl had already worked out remained a comfort for the Mu'tazilites: God is in every respect gracious and merciful and in every case does good (that which is 'useful'). More precisely, an-Nazzam, who concerned himself with the question of theodicy, argued that God, the perfect, can do only what is perfect and so he always brings about what is most 'wholesome' for the individual (not the 'best' in the sense of the best of all possible worlds). However, human beings should respond to God's action by recognizing the divine law. But could such optimism be maintained in the face of the real world of Islam?

Abu l-Hudhayl died in Baghdad (presumably in 842) at the age of about ninety, almost blind; his nephew probably died only three years later: his dates are uncertain. The otherness of God (Abu l-Hudhayl called God the 'opposite of the world') remains characteristic of the Muslim image of God to the present day—but need not mean that God is alien, cold or unattainable. Isn't a degree of consensus possible here between Muslims and Christians? Christian scholasticism would likewise discuss this question, but not for two centuries: the debate started in Europe for the first time in the age of the Carolingians. In Baghdad, meanwhile, people had long mastered the politics of these delicate theological questions and had adopted certain positions. The new paradigm of Islam reached its climax in the ninth century, but also began on its decline.

6. The state and theology

The issue is one of theology and politics at the same time. The central concern of the Mu'tazilah was consistent monotheism. The later Mu'tazilites wanted to be 'fighters for God's unity and justice' but—for reasons which I shall give later—what would eventually produce the most vigorous of all controversies was the Mu'tazilite thesis of the created nature of the Qur'an, elevated to the status of a state dogma. However, this happened only after a fourth Muslim civil war.

The fourth civil war and its consequences for theology

Who would have thought that the Mu'tazilah, so long distanced from the authorities, would come to power and that an opposition theology would become a state theology?[61] This became possible through a fraternal dispute—with a theological background which I have already mentioned—in the house of 'Abbas, between the two sons of Harun ar-Rashid, the same age but very different.

- Al-Amin, son by a legitimate wife of Arab blood, whom Harun appointed his successor after a long delay, supported Arab culture and the religious tradition; no sooner had he become caliph (809) than he attempted to force his brother into second place behind his own son.
- Al Ma'mun, al-Amin's half brother, born of an Iranian concubine, was only six months younger than him and much more intelligent. He became autonomous ruler over the eastern half of the empire with his residence in Merv (Khorasan); he was open to new trends of thought and influences from outside and had the Eastern provinces, the great men of Iran and the Khorasan troops behind him when in 810 a confrontation with his half-brother became unavoidable.

Thus came about the wearisome fourth Muslim civil war, waged mercilessly for three years. After winning a battle at what was later Teheran and a long siege of Baghdad with bloody street battles, in 813 al-Ma'mun's generals decided it in their favour.

Al-Ma'mun, who had at first remained in the safety of Merv, now proclaimed a new 'turning point' (*dawlah*)—an allusion to the first 'Abbasid 'turning point'. This was to usher in a new age. Everywhere he had the black banners (of the 'Abbasids) replaced with green ones (of paradise, also of the 'Alids). He wanted to mend the split in the Islamic community between Sunnis and Shiites. To the amazement of all and to the dismay of his family he promised the succession to an 'Alid ('Ali ar-Rida). However, instead of a reconciliation between the two rival families in Baghdad there came the election of an 'Abbasid anti-caliph, his uncle Ibrahim al-Mahdi. Al-Ma'mun set off for Baghdad without delay. During the long journey his vizier was murdered by officers of the bodyguard and his 'Alid candidate for the throne died an unexplained death (by poisoning?). This was not inconvenient for al-Ma'mun, and in 818 it made possible a peaceful reconciliation with his family. The 'Abbasid black once again became his banner.

After his entry into Baghdad, the caliph appealed trustingly to the reason of all involved to restore peace. Al-Ma'mun, a thoughtful and successful ruler, originally more a Shiite than a Mu'tazilite, was already fond of religious and scientific debates when he lived in Merv. He even wrote dissertations himself. In Baghdad, he arranged debates every Thursday evening (with food) which were devoted largely to questions of theology and jurisprudence. Twenty selected scholars, whom he called 'brothers', took part in them; half of them were theologians but there were also grammarians, such as the two sons of the Mu'tazilite guardian of his youth.

Thus the Mu'tazilites, originally concerned with a theology which was very near to the people, gained access to the court after the civil war. Their theology, grounded in revelation and reason, seemed to the caliph an appropriate support for his work of reconciliation and renewal. Unlike his father Harun, who towards the end of his life had banished the Mu'tazilites from his palace, al-Ma'mun, universally accepted and also interested in medicine and the natural sciences, felt no religious scruples: it was confirmed to him in a dream that there was no conflict between Aristotle (and Greek culture generally) and revelation. There could be a synthesis. That was an intellectual work which the caliph's round table could not achieve, not even those *mutakallimun* who were in the court circle and did not belong to any school. A synthesis was quietly produced by the great Mu'tazilite systematicians who have already been mentioned.

An Islamic magisterium: al-Ma'mun and the Mu'tazilites

However, there was stubborn resistance from large parts of the Baghdad population. What was this crowd from Khorasan doing in their city? What was the purpose of this incomprehensible theology of the mind, which needed neither the Prophet nor the first rightly-guided caliphs? The 'people of the Sunnah' reacted and agitated against the caliph, who as 'imam of right guidance' wanted to proclaim and implement an allegedly infallible teaching. Al-Ma'mun lost patience and in his later years the renewal that had once begun so hopefully took a sharp 'turn' for the worse. More than any previous caliph, al-Ma'mun presented himself as teacher of the faithful, attempting to regulate the religious life of the people by sovereign decree. The introductory formula to all his decrees ran: 'In the name of God, the merciful one who has mercy'! In Western categories one could speak here of 'caesaropapism': politics and religion in the hand of an absolute ruler, a state of affairs that for the Mu'tazilite theologians mentioned earlier (here they resembled the Byzantines) was that of the ideal caliph.

How was it that the caliph

- in 826 in a decree threatening the loss of civic rights prohibited any praise of the Umayyad Mu'awiyyah?
- in 827 had 'Ali proclaimed the most admirable man after Muhammad and also proclaimed the created nature of the Qur'an (*haqq al-Qur'an*)?
- in 831, on his anti-Byzantine campaign of faith in Syria, ordered the troops who had remained behind in Baghdad to add a threefold *Allahu akbar* at the end of each Friday prayer?
- in 833 ordered the examination of all competent scholars of religion and jurists (especially those holding office) for their orthodoxy with respect to the created nature of the Qur'an?

Scholars today seem to have reached a consensus about the religious and political motives behind these measures and the introduction of innovations which again led the empire into a dangerous crisis. Previously, it had been thought that everything should be attributed to the caliphs' pro-'Ali, Shiite-friendly policy[62] but that doesn't fit with the controversial dogma of the created nature of the Qur'an, which could hardly have been pleasing to the Shiites. It is now emphasized that the caliph, who was remote from the people and maintained links only with the Iraqi intelligentsia, wanted, by his measures, to protect the 'stupid people' from popular but dangerous scholars.[63] This view is illuminating only when seen against a theological background:[64] the scholars criticized by the caliph and the 'people of the Sunnah' in fact based themselves on the very anthropomorphic picture of God in the tradition, whereas the caliph and the Mu'tazilites tried to put forward a 'progressive' image of God which emphasized God's transcendence.

This was evidently the key point in the discussion: for the Mu'tazilites the truth about the created nature of the Qur'an was bound up with the transcendence, unity and oneness of God, because in their view nothing was equal to God. Since what is not equal to God must be created, the Qur'an is also created.

This was explained theologically in different ways. For example, Abu l-Hudhayl designated the Qur'an (already God's word of creation) as an accident which needed a substratum: the Qur'an, as God's word, exists in a book, in human memory or in recitation, indeed already beforehand somewhere in heaven on the 'well-preserved tablet'—but always only as an accident. It is therefore created. For an-Nazzam, God's discourse is created in the moment of revelation and much of it is expressed in language that is hard to understand. The Qur'an is rhetorically beautiful but not unsurpassable. An-Nazzam was preparing for the later doctrine of unsurpassability by being the first theologian to accept the Qur'an—not because of its style but because of its content—as proof of Muhammad's status as Prophet.[65] Is it so astounding that these and similar arguments for the created nature of the Qur'an finally dawned on the caliph as the true faith, which must be defended by every possible means?

Is inquisition ('examination') in keeping with the mind of the Prophet?

Tilman Nagel has worked out more clearly than others that, by his decrees, al-Ma'mun was reacting to the religious naivety of the people and the scholars, which could have destructive political consequences. Therefore, in the introduction to his religious decrees, the caliph made it clear that it was his duty before God to protect the true faith (*din Allah*) and preserve the legacy of the Prophet, especially against 'those who with false dialectic appeal to their doctrine and designate themselves Sunnis'; these 'openly proclaim that they represent the truth, religion and the community (*jama'ah*) and that everyone else advocates only what is wrong, unbelief and division. In this way they exalt themselves over people and deceive the ignorant ...' The caliph goes on, 'The master of the believers thinks rather that they are the worst in the community, the heads of heresy, who no longer have any part in the confession of unity.'[66]

At issue, then, is the confession of unity (*tawhid*) which must be maintained in unconditional purity: 'Whoever does not recognize that the Qur'an is created has no *tawhid*', as he 'provides something that God has created and made with that characteristic which is due to God alone (namely being eternal)'.[67] Al-Ma'mun was firmly resolved to use the powers of state for this true faith in order, for both religious and political reasons, to educate and examine those believers who thought anthropomorphically in the right spirit and in accordance with particular principles of a speculative dogmatics.

So, this teacher of the faithful, in Baghdad (as in Christian Byzantium beforehand and in Christian Rome subsequently) brought into being a regular state religious inquisition—for the first time in Islam. This action, carried out on the orders of the chief of police in Baghdad, was called *mihnah*—'examination'.[68] Not all officials were 'investigated', but the supreme judges, the qadis, who were to be responsible for the further examination, certainly were. Anyone who did not confess the unity of God and the created nature of the Qur'an was not allowed before the court as a 'witness' (*shahid*): the witness was not just as, in modern law, a witness to facts; he guaranteed the correctness of the proceedings and was therefore the closest adviser of the qadi. The ideological examination of the apparatus of justice did not just take place in Baghdad; in his authoritarian 'infallible' demand for obedience the caliph sent similar documents to other provinces, possibly to all of them. The leading figures of the Sunnis were likewise examined: he invited the seven leading hadith scholars of Baghdad to his residence in Raqqa (in western Upper Mesopotamia) for examination and there they had no alternative but to grit their teeth and follow the caliph's view. Otherwise, in some circumstances they were threatened with torture, even death.

From a present perspective, critical questions arise. Not only does this inquisition darken the image of a caliph such as al-Ma'mun, who otherwise was so extraordinarily open to the world. It also raises a far more basic question. Was the examination in accord with the Qur'an and the Sunnah of the Prophet? Did the Prophet ever require or practise inquisition among his believers? Was it in keeping with the mind of the Prophet for inquisitions to be carried on with reference to him?

The Mu'tazilites gain and lose power

After ruling for twenty years, Caliph al-Ma'mun died unexpectedly in Tarsus in 833, in the middle of his campaign. His testament spoke of the 'created Qur'an'. Did that also mean an end to the 'examinations'? No, because the eighth 'Abbasid caliph, al-Mu'tasim (caliph from 833 to 842), a third, younger son of Harun, continued his religious policy. However, al-Mu'tasim's prime concern was to create a bodyguard of Turkic slaves dedicated solely to him—a momentous decision, as we shall see. Likewise, for reasons of security, he founded a new capital in Samarra, barely seventy years after the building of Baghdad. He encouraged the general recognition of the Mu'tazilah, but without his brother's theological sense of mission; the inquisitorial interrogations were not made by him personally but by the scholars present.

This caliph had Ibn Hanbal (the founder of the Hanbalite law school) examined a second time, although he had been arrested and interrogated under al-Ma'mun. Ibn Hanbal had begun to study the hadith only when he was more than fifty years old, though from the beginning he had advocated a traditional image of God in the sense of the hadith. He had not claimed that the Qur'an was 'eternal', any more than the other hadith scholars had, for this statement does not occur in the tradition that preceded him; the earlier view was that the Qur'an was 'neither creator nor created' but was 'discourse or word of God' (*kalam Allah*).[69] Al-Ma'mun had been the first to sharpen the controversy: if it was 'not created', then logically it was 'uncreated', 'eternal'. In his examination Ibn Hanbal, driven into a corner, seems to have protected himself: he said that he was not a theologian and did not want to interpret God's word.

We do not know the precise outcome of his examination, since here the reports contradict one another. Some say that the punishment was cruel but that Ibn Hanbal remained faithful to the end. Others say that the flogging consisted only in thirty light strokes but Ibn Hanbal finally recanted. It can hardly be assumed that he was freed without concessions. Be this as it may, Ibn Hanbal lived from then on in utter seclusion and was left in peace by the authorities. He was able to found a school and only then seems to have taken the step towards a positive statement—from 'not created' to 'uncreated' or 'eternal'. He died in Baghdad in 855. For the Sunnis he remains the great witness, the only one to have offered resistance to the unjust worldly state. He was a key witness for the traditionists, who in the meanwhile had become a popular movement.

The inquisition took very different courses in the provinces—depending on local authorities. The often sparse sources for Syria, Mesopotamia, Egypt, the Hijaz, the Maghreb and Iran frequently report more individual cases: for example that in Mecca the qadi had all members of the indigenous old nobility examined and caused a loyal member of the 'Abbasid 'black banner' party to proclaim, round the holy precinct, that the Qur'an was created. In Kufa, 118 of the 120 court witnesses were dismissed, but in Egypt the great jurist families were spared the 'examination'. Nowhere were believers generally persecuted but depending on the situation, judges and theologians were imprisoned, flogged or interned. Apart from some stubborn cases, the theologians, usually not the bravest of people, fell into line. They kept silent, fled, sought compromise formulae, conformed without protest and waited for better times.

The repression lasted for about twelve years and huge resources were wasted. Under Mu'tasim's successor al-Watiq (caliph from 842 to 847), the ninth 'Abbasid caliph, the disputed Qur'an dogma was even disseminated in elementary schools. However, now came the first unrest: rebellions and finally an attempted coup. This coup was supported by the hadith people but started prematurely, with the result that those involved were brought to Samarra and their leader was beheaded.

The repressive religious policy initially continued under the tenth caliph, al-Mutawakkil (caliph from 847–61).A year after his accession the powerful Grand Qadi Ibn Abi Duwad, who since al-Ma'mun's time had been regarded as the driving force in the 'examination' or persecution,[70] was paralysed by a stroke and almost completely lost his speech. He was succeeded by his son but, only a year later, the caliph proposed a change of direction: traditionists might not present prohibited doctrines publicly in the mosques. This quickly led to a change of course: in the longer term no policy might be practised which went against the people, supported by the traditionists. The inquisition was stopped and the new Grand Qadi deposed. He was sent to Baghdad with his semi-paralysed father, where he died in 854, a month before his father, who had been publicly cursed by a popular preacher. The followers of the Sunnah had won. After two decades of 'examination' under al-Ma'mun and another fifteen under his two successors (from 833 to 847) there was a restoration. The tenth caliph was wholly on the side of the traditionists and thus opposed the Mu'tazilites and also the Shiites, as is attested by the destruction of Husayn's tombstone in Karbala. Later, however, he was murdered by his own son.

Although the 'examination' was clearly the personal initiative of al-Ma'mun, in later tradition the caliph himself is exonerated, at the expense of his Grand Qadi, who presumably was not a Mu'tazilite. However, in more recent research the chief responsibility for the persecution is often attributed to the Mu'tazilah. They had long had their advocates but their downfall was inevitable, for they increasingly rested on the laurels of the past in a kind of late scholasticism: their arguments became increasingly sterile, their system increasingly dry, and the gulf between the original intellectual elite, concerned to be close to the people, and the ordinary people themselves, grew wider. In the tenth century a strong opponent arose from their own ranks.

Rational theology is subsumed into traditional theology: al-Ash'ari

The long underestimated Abu l-Hasan al-Ash'ari[71] did for theology what ash-Shafi'i did for Islamic law. He was born in Basra in 873/4 and died in Baghdad in 935/6—ten years before the downfall of the 'Abbasid empire. We know little of this descendant of Abu Musa al-Ash'ari, the companion of the Prophet: he was the favourite pupil of al-Jubba'i, the supreme head of the Mu'tazilah in Basra, perhaps also a rival of his highly-gifted son Abu Hashim. For whatever reasons, internal or external, at the age of forty al-Ash'ari moved over from the Mu'tazilah to the traditionists. In a later phase of his life he settled in Baghdad.

This was a puzzling shift. Can it be explained by the legend that al-Ash'ari had three dreams or visions of the Prophet Muhammad in the month of Ramadan, in which the Prophet commanded him to adhere to the true doctrine but in the third vision admonished him not to give up rational theology? The story of his conversion, told in very different variants, precisely describes al-Ash'ari's position between the Mu'tazilah and the traditionists: he represented the theology of those who preserved the tradition but defended it with the method of the 'moderns' of the time. In his theology, rational argument was utterly at the service of orthodox teaching and the *kalam* utterly at the service of the Sunnah.

So al-Ash'ari succeeded in doing what others—including the mystically orientated Muhasibi—had not been able to do: he combined the naive faith of the adherents to tradition with rational argument, thus eventually convincing the great majority of orthodox traditionalists. To overcome the resistance of the Hanbalites to the rational mode of proof, al-Ash'ari referred to numerous hadith in which the Prophet himself argues rationally, indeed to the Qur'an itself where, for example, there is an argument for the uniqueness of God, to the effect that two Almightys could have prevented the creation of the world.[72] Al-Ash'ari conceded to the traditionists that there was no intrinsic need of a rational theology (in the twenty-first century it remains forbidden in conservative Arab states such as Saudi Arabia) but because of the decline in belief since the original community, it was indispensable as an emergency solution.

In resolutely making revelation, Qur'an and hadith the basis of his theology, al-Ash'ari thought that he was standing the Mu'tazilah on its head, even if it was his pupils who first gathered his insights into a closed system. He was less concerned for a 'reconciliation' of rational and traditional theology, as is often claimed, than for subsuming the former in the latter. A Christian theologian might be reminded of the change from modern liberal theology to the dialectical method after the First World War: all al-Ash'ari's theology after his conversion is deeply concerned with taking seriously and in a new way the overwhelming reality of God, on which human being and activity are totally dependent. How did the content of this undertaking work out: for the understanding of God, the understanding of the Qur'an and the understanding of nature and human beings?[73]

For the understanding of God the new synthesis initially meant a victory of the concrete Qur'anic picture of God over the abstract philosophical picture of God.

– The Mu'tazilah assumed that God has no attributes which are different from his essence. Expressions such as God's 'hand' or God's 'countenance' are to be understood as God's 'grace' or 'essence'. Since God's essence manifests itself in creation, one can infer his attributes from his action in and with his creation (albeit in a restrained way) and thus move from the manifest to the ultimately hidden. Even in the consummation, human beings cannot 'see' God in the strict sense; this would bring God down to the level of a material and limited being.

– Al-Ash'ari wanted to form a stronger bond with the wording of the revelation to bring the picture of God alive. He claimed that the one essence of God expresses itself in various eternal attributes like knowing, seeing and speaking. However, these basic concepts also embrace other synonyms: thus 'knowing' also embraces 'knowledge', 'insight', 'understanding', 'feeling' and 'saying' also embraces 'speaking' and 'talking'. However, a complete assimilation of the creator to his creatures and the naive anthropomorphism of many of those who believe in the tradition are to be guarded against: expressions such as God's 'hand' or 'countenance' or 'sitting on the throne' have no bodily and human reference but are real attributes, even if we do not know their precise nature. Restraint is also appropriate over those attributes which we infer through an argument from the manifest to the hidden, on the basis of the analogy between creator and creature: for example, anyone who in a particular region gets to know only black people, or on a lake gets to know only fresh water, should not conclude that black people or fresh water are the only possibilities. We perceive only tiny selections of God's activity and essence. Alongside God's knowing, seeing and speaking there are quite different names for God, important for the religious disposition: for example 'the one who abides', 'the helper', 'the noble'. Ninety-nine names have been collected (see B II, 1).[74] These attributes make the otherwise pale, purely rational picture of God, which is always exposed to the danger of 'emptying', alive, vivid and edifying in its fullness of being, so that one can also really pray to God. Only in paradise will human beings finally be able to see God: the vision of God will be a reality, even though we cannot explain the mode of the seeing.

For the understanding of the Qur'an the new integration of the theologies meant the victory of belief in the eternity of the Qur'an over its historicity:

– For the Mu'tazilah, it was clear that the Qur'an can only be a created reality, God's created word. The Qur'an itself is the real miracle (by virtue not of its style but of its content) and confirms the Prophet's task. A sceptical attitude is appropriate for the miracles which are recorded in the hadith, but not those in the Qur'an.

– For al-Ash'ari, on the other hand, the Qur'an is not a word different in essence from God, any more than are the other names of God, God's knowledge and power or God's unity. Rather, the Qur'an is God's discourse, and as such an eternal, uncreated attribute of God. Anyone who speculates in natural philosophy, denies the eternity of the Qur'an and doubts the miracles of the Prophet attested in the tradition attacks the essence of Islam.

For the understanding of nature and human beings this 'sublation' of the theology of reason into the theology of tradition means a victory of metaphysics over physics.

– The Mu'tazilites attached the utmost importance to the human capacity to choose, to free decision and thus to moral responsibility. The link between cause and effect had to be taken seriously, both in human beings and in nature outside human beings. Analyses of the causality in nature could help human beings to understand God's activity better and thus also God's reward and punishment of responsible human beings at their end. However, mortal sinners were not to be regarded either as unbelievers or as believers: they could still convert before the end. But if the various eschatological images of the individual's end, such as the washing bowl, the bridge, the scales and the Prophet's intercession were to be accepted at all, they were to be interpreted rationally.

– Al-Ash'ari attached great importance to God's power, indeed omnipotence: everything, whether good or evil, is willed by God. In the sphere of creation outside the human race al-Ash'ari rejected the doctrine of the 'natures' of created things and the causal link between them. Rather, each 'thing' is immediate to God, and each action is directly caused by God. All events are acts of God; they rest on his will, choice, guidance and measure. God creates the human capacity to realize each individual act. Al-Ash'ari attempted to prove, from the Qur'an, that God can will sinfulness and folly without himself being sinful and foolish. He paid little attention to human responsibility: the doctrine of the 'acquisition' by human beings of actions really performed by God was possibly first developed in his school; at all events the view became established that this 'acquisition', too, in all its aspects, must be caused by God. As for mortal sinners, they remain believers but are destined to be punished by fire. The eschatological images are to be taken seriously, especially the Prophet's intercession, although it is nowhere mentioned in the Qur'an.

The school of al-Ash'ari, the Ash'ariyah, finally triumphed in the great battle between the traditionists and the rational thinkers. In this way a rational–traditional form of Sunni theology was achieved. What ash-Shafi'i had brought about a century earlier in Islamic law, al-Ash'ari now brought about in theology: a fixation on the traditionist principle. Al-Ghazali later developed this theology and made it the leading dogmatic school in Sunni Islam, the teachings of which have lasted to the present day.

7. The disintegration of the empire

During the brilliant rule of Harun ar-Rashid no one would have thought that in only a few decades the power and reputation of the ʿAbbasid caliphate would collapse almost completely. This collapse of the universal Near Eastern empire, in the ninth and tenth centuries, was not caused by blows from outside or the incursion of new nomadic peoples (as happened to the contemporary Frankish empire) but by the internal disintegration of its fundamental institutions.

The crisis of the institutions

The crisis in the making involved all three power factors of the ʿAbbasid empire: the caliph himself, the military and the bureaucracy. The crisis of the caliphate and the inner contradictions of society grew into a crisis of Islam, at the end of which came its regionalization, the splitting of the one great Islamic empire into different regional part-empires. This resulted in a new paradigm of Islam.[75]

Power factor 1: the caliph. The highly complex bureaucracy got increasingly out of hand and could no longer be supervised, directed and controlled by the caliph. The office of vizier brought some relief in the administration but over time this central office, originally conceived as that of a simple assistant, became that of a kind of prime minister; after all, the vizier usually had an advantage in gaining information and was closer to subordinates. For the sake of simplicity his orders were carried out without question and officials and petitioners had less and less to do with the caliph in person. This meant that the loyalty of the élites to the caliph necessarily decreased—and that had been the unifying force of this empire. This could hardly be good for an empire which had become tremendously varied and operated at many levels; which consisted of Arab and Khorasan soldiers, Iraqi, Iranian and Egyptian landowners, Jewish merchants, Nestorian scribes and central Asian generals. The theocratic claim of the ʿAbbasids became sheer ideology.

Some caliphs were quite grateful when they were relieved of many of the oppressive cares of the everyday business of government. Under Harun ar-Rashid, the vizier assumed so many tasks that in the eyes of some people the caliph had time to be a man of leisure. There was certainly more time for pleasant occupations and increasingly refined diversions. However, the caliph thus became a mysterious figure, to some degree hidden behind a curtain, although this did not prevent him from deposing a vizier who displeased him. That happened often and gradually the length of the vizier's period in office declined and the number of successive viziers increased. That did not diminish the court intrigues, and shameless self-enrichment increasingly took the place of unselfish service. Thus the stability of the leadership of the state was shaken.

Power factor 2: the military. The 'Abbasids were not spared the old experience that armies are expensive. As the border regions in central Asia and the Indus valley were unsafe, military interventions were constantly necessary, especially as the ideologically-driven wars against Christian Byzantium continued under Harun's successors. All this constantly increased military expenditure but what proved fateful was the decision, taken in view of the decline of the Arab military organization, to enlist more and more troops from slaves and prisoners of war in the border regions (such as Turks and Slavs). Unlike mercenaries, such slaves could rise as freemen to the ranks of officer, general and governor: the Berbers in the army had the same status as the free Arabs. During the war of the brothers, al-Mu'tasim, later successor to the caliph al-Ma'mun (833–42), surrounded himself with a bodyguard of Turks. Later, so many Turkic military slaves were taken into the army that whole Turkic regiments could be formed of them. They had their own quarters, mosques and markets and their on commanders who trained them, looked after them and paid them; these felt more indebted to their commander (often from the Turkic nobility) than to the caliph. This was a fatal innovation in the military history of the Near East, which in the long run made the caliphs dependent on their own slave regiments and their generals.

An alarm should have been heard when the former 'praetorians', the Khorasans, planned a conspiracy; it failed and there was a break with the caliph. In addition, the unpopular Turkic regiments alienated the caliph from his people, were rivals and were often entangled in disputes. To isolate them from the often rebellious population and to ensure his own security, in 847 Caliph al-Mu'tasim founded a second residence city, Samarra, 125 kilometres north of Baghdad. The alienation of the caliphate from the people could hardly have been demonstrated more clearly. Until 870, Samarra was the military and administrative centre of the caliphate; there, as well as the army there was a separate Turkic quarter. However, Baghdad survived the temporary emigration of the court and its officials. Yet the number of mercenaries constantly increased and more and more Turkic officers were appointed to important positions of command; in the second half of the ninth century there were Turkic governors of Syria and Egypt. Independent dynasties of governors were now beginning to form (the Tulunids in Egypt and the Ikhshidids in Egypt and Syria) who extended their influence to Palestine.

There were two Turkic generals in the body that elected Caliph al-

Mutawakkil (847–61). When this caliph attempted to avoid Turkic influence by recruiting Arab and Persian mercenaries and planning to shift the capital to Damascus, a conspiracy of Turkic generals murdered him at a banquet. His son and successor al-Muntasir (caliph from 861 to 862), who was implicated in the crime and died soon afterwards, was presumably also murdered. What a tragic change! The early 'Abbasids had depended on the military support of their own subjects, but the later 'Abbasids depended on foreign troops, which they needed to keep their own population under control. Indeed the 'Abbasid caliphate increasingly became the plaything of the Turkic war slaves.

Power factor 3: finances and bureaucracy. The high military expenditure completely ruined the state finances. A soldier received three times the wages of a craftsman, and a cavalryman very much more. There were also the costs of weapons, clothing and everyday living. The more slaves enlisted, the greater the expenses of the state became. Taxes had to be levied to pay for the army and this accelerated the collapse of the state finances, especially since the proven separation between financial and military administration had been abandoned. As the provinces became more and more independent, thus reducing the income of headquarters, the caliph's finances were increasingly hard pressed. When wages could be paid only with difficulty and often late, the consequences were protests and revolts among the war slaves. The caliph had no alternative but to give the military land from the state domains instead of cash. Senior officers thus quickly became landowners at the expense of the state. Indeed some private landowners put their own land under the 'protection' of a military leader in exchange for payment, so as to be armed against both high taxes and attacks.

The increase in the power of the military went hand in hand with the corruption of the bureaucracy. This bureaucracy worked less and less for the caliph and the empire and more for the personal and partisan interest of warring cliques and parties. What was true of the vizier was true of his following: the motto was no longer 'serve the state' but 'enrich yourself'. If the vizier had come to power by bribing the caliph and senior court officials, he felt justified in recouping his large 'investment' (and very much more) though his office. There was not only individual bribery at every level but what, in many ways, was institutionalized corruption. It began as soon as a young scribe was taken for his education into the house of a protector, to whom he would then feel indebted for the rest of his life.

The end of the world empire

To the destructive changes in the caliphate, its officials and its army, to the fiscal exploitation and political destabilization, there was added an economic recession which had been unthinkable in a formerly prosperous empire. For more than a century the caliphs of Baghdad, absorbed in other interests, had neglected investment in the irrigation system and land reclamation; they had allowed vast areas in the Tigris to become desolate and depopulated as a result of the constant wars, endangering some international trade routes. In the ninth and tenth centuries the economy seemed to be largely in ruins, especially in Iraq. This once-prosperous country became one of the poorest regions in the Middle East and remained so until the twentieth century. Egypt suffered a similar economic decline but not Iran.

The economic crisis intensified the political crisis and the great 'Abbasid empire soon collapsed. (Three centuries later, in 1258, the dynasty finally perished when, in the Mongol storm which destroyed everything in its wake, Baghdad was captured and with it the last caliph.) After 945 there was effectively no longer a world empire. In that year the Iranian Buwayhids, a dynasty from the south coast of the Caspian Sea which had converted only late to Shiite Islam after conquering central and west Iran, conquered Iraq (which had been contested by Turks and Arabs) and finally captured Baghdad. To support their foreign policy against the Samanids, who were powerful in east Iran, and the Fatimids, who were establishing themselves strongly in Egypt, they allowed the caliphate to remain in name. However, by 'saving' the caliph they made him their political tool. The 'grand emirs' ('house emirs') were now the real masters, and they treated the caliphs as their puppets (as the Pippinids in France, a little earlier, had treated the Merovingian kings). However, the Buwayhids were able to play a decisive role for only a few decades; their policy, orientated on an Iranian agricultural society, could not solve the problems of the rapidly growing cities or overcome the social tensions, accompanied by revolts of African slaves. The Seljuks followed them.

The paradigm of a world religion, which was established with the 'Abbasid revolution (P III), came to a political end because of the crisis of the caliphate, the military, the bureaucracy and the economy. Baghdad still remained the seat of the caliphs but the caliphs were no longer masters of the empire. The centrifugal forces in the provinces proved stronger and led finally to a multiplicity of regional rulers. However, the paradigm retained much of its light and splendour for many Muslims over the centuries to come.

The classical paradigm of a world religion as an image of hope: Pan-Islamism

The classical paradigm of Islam as a world religion showed a remarkable capacity for persistence and survival. Despite the hostile political circumstances, because of the free competition of intellectual forces in the tenth century something like a spiritual 'renaissance' became possible, in comparison with the 'classical period' of the first 'Abbasid glory. For centuries, the caliph remained the symbol of Muslim unity, although he no longer had any political power, and the culture of the '1001 nights' was idolized. For centuries, Islamic writers still mourned the unprecedented splendour of Babylon, then seen as the spiritual centre of the world (like pre-Christian Rome beforehand and papal Rome very much later). There was a good deal of literary stylization, but three factors were of abiding significance: the Islamic theology which was developed then, the Islamic law which was fully formed and the cosmopolitan Islamic culture for which the foundations were laid. This paradigm—for all its dark aspects—held together a multicultural society in many respects more tolerant also to those of other beliefs than contemporaneous Latin or Byzantine Christianity.

What I said right at the beginning of the analysis of this paradigm I can endorse here at its end: in this period, despite wars, disputes over the faith and crimes, of a kind that can be found in all religions, the essence of Islam—the one God and Muhammad his Prophet—was not only preserved but in some respects more sharply accentuated. As never before, people had laboured to describe this essence in accordance with reason and to defend it against the two other prophetic religions. In this period, Islam became a highly reflective religion, even for those who were more inclined to the tradition. Despite the incorporation of ever greater cultural spheres, the individual Muslim perhaps became more conscious than before of the essence of his faith.

It is not surprising that, particularly in modern times, when Islam split and increasingly went on the economic, military and cultural defensive against 'Christian' Europe, many Muslims recalled the glorious times of the classical paradigm of Islam as a world religion, when all Muslim peoples were united under the one caliph in one great empire, based on Islamic core values. Could it be possible to restore the unity of the Islamic Ummah? Since the nineteenth century, many religious scholars in colleges and mosques have asked this question on the basis of their Islamic 'knowledge' and so, too, have many intellectuals holding public positions, on the basis of the European scholarship that they have taken over. And so too have some neo-Sufi orders, on the basis of their experience of the one 'true Islam'.

Therefore at the highpoint of European modernity (P V), in the nineteenth century, the so-called 'Pan-Islamic' movement developed. It was fundamentally different from the Pan-Arabism (P III) which I have already discussed thoroughly (see D II, option 1). The goal of Pan-Islamism was the alliance not just of the Arab but of all Islamic peoples, if possible under one caliph, and a renewal of an Islamic state or even a unitary Islamic world. On this basis it was hoped to be able effectively to counter the economic and political superiority and colonial expansion of the European powers from North Africa to Indonesia.

We shall have to concern ourselves further with the ideas and notions of the leaders of this movement, such as Jamal ad-din al-Afghani, and then also with 'Abdallah as-Suhrawardi, who brought about the Pan-Islamic Conference in Mecca. The sultan, deposed by the Young Turks in 1908, had previously attempted once more to gain the assent of all Muslims to his claim to leadership as caliph with the help of a Pan-Islamic vision but his effort was in vain. The question would arise whether the (Arab) nationalism which had then broken through in Turkey and many Muslim countries, a typical product of European modernity, could bring a solution to the basic problems of Islam.

We shall see. At all events Pan-Islamism in the twentieth century would be achieved only in the framework of independent nation states; this was the aim of both the Muslim Brotherhood in Egypt and the followers of Muhammad Iqbal in India, a goal that seemed to have been realized with the foundation of Muslim Pakistan in 1947. However, the intended bloc of all-Islamic states has yet to be achieved—despite the Islamic World Congress (MAI) formed in Karachi in 1949, the Islamic General Congress (MIAQ) founded in Jerusalem in 1953 and the Islamic World League (RAI) founded in Saudi Arabia in 1962. Nevertheless, particularly in the face of this splitting and the rival organizations, the fascination with a Pan-Islamic union of the Muslim nation states has never been completely quenched and could become a political tool at any time.

After the decline of the caliphate, Islam no longer had an efficient monarchical leadership, as at the time of the Prophet and the rightly-guided caliphs (P I). The Umayyads (P II) and the 'Abbasids (P III) contributed decisively to its crisis after the ninth century. The new model of leadership that had thus become necessary is the reason why we must now turn to the new paradigm (P IV).

C IV

The Paradigm of the Ulama and Sufis

In all previous paradigms it has been possible to describe the history of Islam in a historical perspective, whether focussed on Mecca/Medina and Arabia, Damascus and Syria or Baghdad and Mesopotamia. This is now no longer possible. What follows is a complex period of history that cannot be evaluated from a single, central, viewpoint. It is comparable to the late Middle Ages in Europe, when the imperial–papal universal empire broke apart and nation states took its place. And just as in fifteenth-century Christianity there were three popes at the same time, so too as early in tenth-century Islam there were three rival caliphs: in Baghdad, Cairo and Cordoba. Thus—in contrast to the view of many Muslims—the Islamic Ummah was split long before the crusades, not as a result of external alien forces but from within. There are clear indications of an epoch-making paradigm change. I cannot go into all the many developments and complicated, fluctuating inter-connections but it may be helpful at first to give a brief survey of the different rules (see the box on the following page) before I describe some important developments more precisely and then undertake a systematic analysis of the new paradigm.

1. After one empire, many states

Marked regionalization replaced the one empire under central leadership. The centrifugal forces which had already become increasingly strong under the 'Abbasids and had led to the virtual autonomy of parts of the empire (for example, Spain, Morocco, Algeria, Egypt, Khorasan and Transoxania) also became established in the central regions. Smaller states came into being—at first

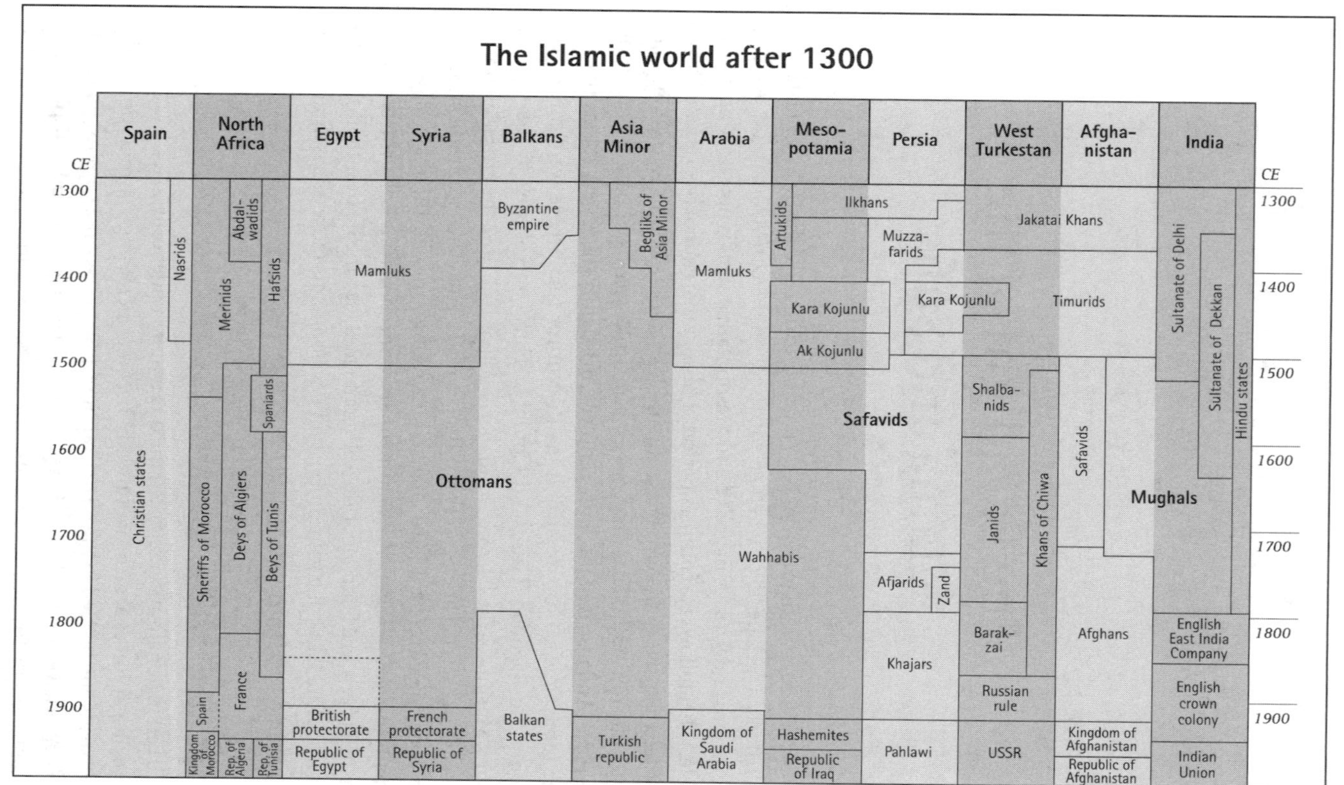
The Islamic world after 1300
Spain
North Africa
Egypt
Syria
Balkans
Asia Minor
Arabia
Meso-potamia
Persia
West Turkestan
Afgha-nistan
India
CE
1300
1400
1500
1600
1700
1800
1900
Christian states
Nasrids
Merinids
Abdal-wadids
Hafsids
Spaniards
Sheriffs of Morocco
Deys of Algiers
Beys of Tunis
France
Spain
Kingdom of Morocco
Rep. of Algeria
Rep. of Tunisia
Mamluks
British protectorate
Republic of Egypt
French protectorate
Republic of Syria
Ottomans
Byzantine empire
Balkan states
Begliks of Asia Minor
Turkish republic
Mamluks
Wahhabis
Kingdom of Saudi Arabia
Artukids
Ilkhans
Kara Kojunlu
Ak Kojunlu
Hashemites
Republic of Iraq
Muzza-farids
Safavids
Afjarids
Zand
Khajars
Pahlawi
Jakatai Khans
Kara Kojunlu
Timurids
Shalba-nids
Janids
Khans of Chiwa
Barak-zai
Russian rule
USSR
Safavids
Afghans
Kingdom of Afghanistan
Republic of Afghanistan
Sultanate of Delhi
Sultanate of Dekkan
Hindu states
Mughals
English East India Company
English crown colony
Indian Union

without central government or bureaucratic élites. These small states were ruled by different, often anti-centralist, landowners and military leaders, who based their power solely on paid troops. This happened in both east and west, as a short panoramic survey will make clear. Only with time did great empires arise once more but none of them ever again represented a wide spread of Islam. I shall look first at the east and then at the west.

Regionalization in east and west

In the east the 'Abbasids were followed by:

- the 'major-domos' dynasty' of the Shiite Buwayhids, which we came across in Iraq and in western Iran, which for around 110 years exercised dominance and protective rule over the 'Abbasid caliphs (from 945 to 1055);
- the Samanids in eastern Iraq and in Transoxania (beyond the Oxus or Amudarja); until 999 Bukhara was their splendid focal point and cultural centre;
- the Ghaznavids (they were descended from the Turks) in Khorasan (in north-east Iran); their centre was at Ghazna in Afghanistan, they practised a pro-Sunni policy and undertook campaigns as far as India (until 1040).

However, after the internal disintegration of the eleventh century, the frontiers between the cultural areas and the nomadic regions collapsed and the nomadic Turkic people began to infiltrate the region, resulting in social upheavals and new political orders. Empires of nomadic peoples formed one after another:

- in the tenth century, the Karachanids conquered Transoxania;
- in the eleventh century, the Sunni Seljuks (first under Arslan ibn Saljuq, then under Togril Beg, victor over the Ghaznavids) conquered Iran and Anatolia;
- in the thirteenth century, the Mongols (mostly shamanists and Buddhists) conquered the whole region. This Mongol storm left behind almost only negative traces: in 1258 Baghdad was captured and destroyed, the last 'Abbasid was murdered and the caliphate came to a physical end.

The end of the caliphate also removed the political symbol. All attempts to restore it (for example the substitute caliphate from 1261 to 1517) failed. The irony is that, through the vast Mongol empire, in which many people later converted to Islam, Islam made a massive invasion of China. In the second half of the fourteenth century, Timur (1336–1405), a Turkic Muslim Mongol from Samarkand (Transoxania), who claimed to be a distant relative of the legendary conqueror Genghis Khan (1167–1227), for a second time brought together the great Mongol–Turkic tribal alliances against the Islamic world, in the process dealing a cruel death blow to the churches in the Middle East and Iran. At the same time, though, he made possible an Islamic culture in the small states which then came into being.

In the west, the following great upheavals can be observed:

- in the eighth century, Spain left the great Arab empire following the 'Abbasid revolution: there was an independent emirate and then caliphate of Cordoba, which ended in 1031;
- in the ninth century, in Tunisia and Tripolitania, the Arab Aghlabids (whose capital was Kairouan) detached themselves from the central authority and conquered Sicily; in the Nile valley the Tulunids (commemorated by the Ibn Tulun mosque in present-day Cairo) also broke away;
- in the tenth century, the Shiite Fatimids moved from Tunisia to Egypt and Syria (with which they had a special bond); they founded the city of Cairo and a Shiite anti-caliphate but could not establish themselves as a dynasty capable of succeeding the 'Abbasids and in 1171, under Saladin, they were replaced by the Sunni Ayyubids;
- in the tenth century, Byzantium succeeded in winning back the north of Syria. Between the eleventh and the thirteenth centuries, European crusaders, in the course of seven crusades, succeeded in occupying Palestine and establishing a 'kingdom of Jerusalem'—in the face of the Turkic Seljuks, who had reached as far as Asia Minor.

The third confrontation between Islam and Christianity: the crusades

Following the Prophet, Islam was undoubtedly a warlike religion. What about Christianity? Contrary to the non-violent Jesus of Nazareth, Christianity had developed no less into a warlike religion. The champion of the absolutist papacy, Gregory VII (Hildebrand, 1073–85), was the first to be preoccupied with a plan for a great campaign eastwards—to compel the obedience of Byzantium and to conquer Jerusalem—twenty years before the First Crusade actually took place. Under his personal leadership, as pope and general, the primacy of Rome was to be established in Byzantium and the West–East schism was to be ended. In his own way, Gregory was a champion of 'holy war': he not only sent the 'banner of Peter' (that is, the blessing of Peter) to the war parties he favoured and thus hallowed wars but was the first pope to grant those who took part in a war—for example, to reconquer Spain—'remission' of the punishments for their sins, on the basis of the Petrine 'full authority', allegedly bestowed on him by Christ.

Gregory VII has, not unjustly, been called the most warlike pope ever to sit on the throne of Peter. He recruited troops, promoted warlike undertakings and often rode out to battle in person with pomp and splendour. He seemed to have forgotten the principle that the church should not shed blood. He was fond of quoting a saying of Jeremiah, 'Accursed is he who withholds his sword from blood!'[1] So it is no coincidence that, just ten years after Gregory's death, the First Crusade (1096–99)[2] was launched—into and for the 'holy land', to liberate the holy places from the 'unbelievers'! After the murder of the prominent Grand Vizier Nizam al-Mulk in 1092, the Seljuk empire was in crisis and threatened to collapse, so that the crusader army did not encounter a united Islamic great power.

A crusade is rather different from a pilgrimage, an adventure or an emigration, although the element of pilgrimage played an essential role and the desire for adventure (based on fabulous ideas about the East) and escapism (from debts and other wretched conditions at home) a substantial one. A crusade is essentially a holy war, which claims the authority of God under the sign of the victorious cross (here we are reminded of Constantine). Bernard of Clairvaux (1090–1153, like Hildebrand a monk) was the first Christian theoretician of the holy war and gave theological justification for the killing of unbelievers.[3] However, without the initiative and blessing of the papacy, which helped with privileges for crusaders (for example indulgences, exemption from taxes and tolls and the remission of private debts), it would never have come about. The anti-Islamic crusades were, from the beginning, papal enterprises, even if the papacy often dissociated itself from the specific way in which they were carried on.

So crusades are not historical disasters or chance by-products of church history; they are a typical phenomenon of the Roman Catholic paradigm (P III).[4] In the West, people were generally convinced that they were a deeply Christian undertaking:

- The crusades were regarded as the business of the whole of (Western) Christianity, even though the First Crusade was under French, the Second Crusade under French and German, and the Third Crusade under German leadership.
- The crusades were thought to be approved by Christ himself, since the Pope as Christ's spokesman had issued a personal summons to them.
- The crusades, which involved a journey of thousands of miles, usually through foreign countries, with no basis for provisions and indescribable tribulations, would have been impossible without religious enthusiasm, passion and often mass psychosis. The enterprise was presented as a kind of pilgrimage; some crusaders even took part because of an explicit desire to go on pilgrimage. The name 'Jerusalem', the holy city of the beginning and end of the history of

Christianity, had a magic ring. Despite the unspeakable suffering, anxiety and loss and everything else, the amazing 'success' of the First Crusade seemed to confirm to the crusaders that it was God's will.[5] This was the only crusade that at least achieved its military aim and founded crusader states: the kingdom of Jerusalem and the feudal fiefdoms of Antioch, Edessa and Tripolis, which immediately became the objects of quarrels between the European powers.

Innocent III, who praised the crusade as a 'means of salvation', initiated the Fourth Crusade (1202–4). This crusade led to the disastrous conquest and three-day plundering of Orthodox Christian Constantinople, the establishment of a Latin emperor and Latin church organization, and the enslavement of the Byzantine church. This was not originally Innocent's intention, but afterwards he praised the development as a work of divine providence; the papal goal since the fifth century, namely also to establish the primacy of Rome in Constantinople, seemed to have been achieved. Sadly, the opposite was the case: this crusade sealed the West–East schism.

We must understand the crusaders, too, 'in the light of the times', without using that as an excuse. Behind the crusades lies Augustine's theology of the legitimate use of force, by the legitimate authority, for a just cause. The 'cause of Christ' had to be defended or established and this Christ, seen with very human features, was understood as a 'political Christ' and the Roman primacy as a primacy of domination. Therefore, at that time, people might criticize the crusaders, whose sins were regarded as the cause of the failures, but not the crusades, at any rate not as long as they believed in their success.[6] The crusades contributed indirectly to a broadening of the spiritual horizon of the West, an economic boom in trade in the Mediterranean and the Italian cities, the formation of a nobility built up on shared ideals (chivalry) and a rise in urban living standards. In connection with this public, political and military reinterpretation of the Christian message it is worth noting that, at that time, despite increasing doubt about the utility of the crusades, the high taxes connected with them and the claim of Christian doctrine to be the only right doctrine, hardly anyone audibly put the obvious critical questions in the light of the gospel.

In the glorious history of Islam, the crusades—however much they remain rooted in Muslim memory as aggression—remain merely episodes which took place on the frontier of the empire and did not shake the power of Islam. The world empire of the 'Abbasids was not destroyed primarily from outside; rather, it dissolved itself from within.

Questions: The crusader mentality

Some clear questions must be put to Islam about the politicization and militarization of religion but first, in view of the crusader mentality against Islam which is currently being revived (for example in the phrase 'the war against terrorism' and in the light of the 2003 Iraq war), Christians should ask themselves:

- Isn't it a perversion of the cross of Jesus of Nazareth if, instead of inspiring people truly to bear it every day, it is used to legitimize the bloody wars of crusaders who wear the cross on their garments?
- Is the Pope truly the spokesman of Christ if he describes a crusader expedition as an act of Christian 'love' and 'repentance' and a 'meritorious work', particularly for lay people and especially knights, since monks and priests are not allowed to shed blood?
- Shouldn't the bloody persecution of Jewish communities in France, in the Rhineland, Bavaria and Bohemia, which was associated with the first wave of crusaders, and the persecution of Orthodox Christian communities by the Latin crusaders have been a warning sign that all this was far more a matter of hatred, revenge and greed than of repentance and love?
- Don't the strategy of massacring and driving out the Muslims from important places that were conquered (in the expectation of Western settlers) and the fearful bloodbath of Jews and Muslims after the entry into Jerusalem stand in blatant contradiction to the Jesus who rode without violence on an ass into Jerusalem?
- Aren't the newly-founded crusader states and the military orders which engaged in armed service (the Knights of St John and the Templars) disowned by the preacher from Nazareth, according to whom the non-violent shall possess 'the land'?
- May one therefore regard the fallen warriors, contrary to the old tradition, as martyrs who go directly into paradise?

The post-imperial period: anti-caliphs

A loss of external power followed the internal dissolution of the caliphate, from both the periphery and the centre of the kingdom.[7] The Umayyad emir of Cordoba had long had himself addressed as caliph, thus casting doubts on the supremacy of the caliph of Baghdad over his Spanish kingdom. In 909, the Fatimids founded a third caliphate in Tunisia,[8] which by 969 already ruled over almost all of North Africa and Egypt from its new capital of Cairo. This made the Fatimids the immediate neighbours and most dangerous rivals of the 'Abbasids, to whom the Islamic West was definitively lost—apart from Syria, which was fought over. The Fatimids, who belonged to the political revolutionary Sevener or Ismaili Shiah, were not just political enemies, whose propagandists and agitators undermined the 'Abbasid empire and made it unsafe, but also religious and ideological opponents. They claimed direct descent from the Prophet Muhammad through his daughter Fatimah (more important than his uncle 'Abbas!) and by taking the title of caliph claimed descent from the Prophet for the whole Ummah—though the Fatimids could not establish themselves in the face of the two rival caliphs, of Baghdad in the Arab east and of Cordoba in the Arab west.

Egypt was indebted to the fourth Fatimid caliph al-Mu'izz for its new palace city of Cairo (*al-Qahirah* = 'the powerful, victorious'), built a few miles north of the old Arabic garrison town of Fustat. He also founded the palace mosque of al-Azhar ('the brightly shining') which soon had thirty-five professorial chairs of law; eventually it became, and remains, the most renowned centre of teaching in the Islamic world. The Fatimid empire was at first very successful in its administration, economy and culture; although it was Shiite, it was extremely tolerant, and not only towards the Sunni majority. As the Tübingen Islamicist, H. Halm, rightly remarks: 'Under no other Islamic regime did the Egyptian Christians and Jews enjoy such far-reaching freedoms and privileges as under the first Fatimid caliph.'[9]

Things were very different under the notorious sixth Fatimid caliph, al-Hakim (caliph from 996 to 1021). Although not a bloodthirsty savage, as he is portrayed in Christian and pro-'Abbasid propaganda, he was a deeply mistrustful and brutal 'fundamentalist', who regarded himself as the incarnation of the divine intellect. He re-introduced discriminatory measures against Christians and Jews and in 1009 had the Church of the Holy Sepulchre, built in Jerusalem by Constantine, torn down.

Towards the end of the eleventh century the first crusader armies captured the coasts of Syria and Palestine and in 1099 took Jerusalem. After more than 200 years of a Shiite anti-caliphate, in 1171 the Fatimid caliph, who had been reduced to the status of ruler of a limited territory, was overthrown. This was done by a thirty-one-year-old Kurdish officer, the vizier since 1168, Salah ad-din, Saladin, who brought Egypt back under the formal authority of the Sunni caliph of Baghdad. For the next eight decades the Ayyubid dynasty,[10] founded by Saladin, son of the Kurd Ayyub, ruled in Cairo. Unlike the Fatimids, Saladin relied on the loyalty of his numerous relatives, ruling with the help of a family federation. By a shrewd policy and superior military strategy, in 1187 he succeeded in destroying the kingdom of Jerusalem. Despite many later wars, the dynastic ruler association of the Ayyubids stayed in power until they were replaced by a dynasty of their own mercenaries, the Mamluks, in 1252. Thus the 'Turks' followed the 'Kurds' as rulers.

Despite, and partly because of, the crusades in the twelfth and thirteenth centuries, the Christian West had made powerful economic and scientific gains, through intensified trade between Europe and the Islamic countries of the eastern Mediterranean. The Italian sea republics of Genoa, Pisa and Venice with their fleets became immensely rich, as is shown, for example, by the twelfth-century cathedral, baptistery and campanile of Pisa.

It is time to return to the Buwayhids (945–1055), whom I have already mentioned; they ruled over the East from the late period of the 'Abbasids.[11] Of Iranian origin, they belonged to the politically quietist Twelver Shiah. Although they could have, they did not want to found an anti-caliphate but wanted (like the Ghaznavids after them) to preserve the 'Abbasid caliphate. Why? Not because they did not have the power to remove it: a suspect caliph was blinded by a Buwayhid and replaced. It was because of their sober calculation that, in the political situation in the second half of the tenth century, the formal preservation of the caliphate was advantageous, with respect both to the hostile Fatimids and their pseudo-caliphate and to the Byzantines, who were pressing southwards in a threatening way; they had already advanced from Cilicia to Antioch and conquered Cyprus.

The Buwayhids could not demonstrate better to the whole world the legitimacy of their own rule in a deeply divided and very insecure Ummah than by an alliance with the venerable caliphate of Baghdad; they therefore had themselves named, with the caliph, at Friday prayer. The new 'barbarians' bathed in the splendour of this great name, as the Germanic 'barbarians' bathed in the splendour of the Roman popes who crowned them. They were happy to have certain functions of the caliph's rule formally transferred to them: the leading of prayer, military administration and the courts. The Turkic Ghaznavids and Seljuks, who followed them, would do the same.

The Turks as heirs of the Islamic empire: sultans instead of caliphs

The Islamic world was, and remained, split. Like the Arabs, the Iranians could not maintain their dominant position: others, especially the Turks, were heirs to the empire. It was this period of weakness that made the Christian reconquest, the crusades, possible. The future of Islam lay in Turkic hands, and the foundations of this predominance had been laid at the time of the decline of the 'Abbasids, for their earliest troops had been recruited from the Turks, a people from the Central Asian steppes who had been converted from Persia to Sunni Islam of a Hanafite tendency. The Ghaznavids, the masters of a great eastern state with its centre in present-day Afghanistan and later also in northern India, were also Turks, as were the Seljuks, who in the first half of the eleventh century conquered the whole of Persia and in

1055 Baghdad, thus making the puppet caliphs of the Buwayhids the puppets of the Seljuks.

The Seljuks mostly resided in Persian Isfahan. Their upper class was Persian (and rarely learned Arabic) and the south-west Turkic (Oghuz) population barely literate. They came forward as protectors and promoters of the caliphate and Sunni Islam, a policy which culminated in the marriage of the Seljuk leader Togril Beg to the daughter of a caliph. What was the real authority of the caliph? For the eleventh-century Seljuks it was purely nominal and symbolic, even in the east, extending over only part of the former empire.

Just as, eight hundred years later, in the face of the loss of their political power, the popes increasingly emphasized their spiritual power, so the disempowered caliph sought to be a 'symbol of the rule of the Islamic law to which all Muslims were subject'.[12] And just as, from the eleventh to the twenty-first century, Catholic theologians attempted to derive the authority of all offices in the Catholic Church from the Pope so, among the weak Buwayhids, the Shafi'i Grand Qadi al-Mawardi (died 1058) sought to demonstrate, on behalf of Caliph al-Qa'im, that the caliph was the focal point of all legitimate power, indeed the 'pillar on which the foundations of the community of faith rest and by whom the well-being of the community is ordered. Consequently all general affairs are grounded in the imamate, and all special offices derive from him.'[13]

Against this background, in 1056 Togril Beg was the first Islamic ruler on whom the title sultan was officially bestowed by the caliph: the title had originally denoted the power of the ruler, then from the tenth century the ruler himself. Now it meant the ruler empowered by the caliph. So, only the Seljuk rulers were sultans in this official sense. There was usually tension between the caliph and the sultan, though there could be no doubt of the caliph's political dependence on the sultan. Although they resided in Baghdad only for a short time, the Seljuk sultans, backed by their army, had a firm grip on the city; they drove the Fatimids out of Syria and inflicted an annihilating defeat on the Byzantines in 1071 (marking the beginning of Turkish Anatolia), thus gradually coming to rule the centre and east of the empire. The Seljuks even succeeded in what the Arabs had never done: after the destruction of the great Armenian empire in 1071, the greater Seljuk empire could spread to Asia Minor, where the Turks live to the present day. Later, other regional rulers gave themselves the title of sultan. The legitimization of these usurpers by a caliph eventually became as superfluous as the caliph as a symbolic figure of Muslim unity.

In the thirteenth century, the Turkic Mamluks came to power in Egypt and Syria. They were originally military slaves (*mamalik*: 'slaves'). In 1260, in Palestine, they had prevented the further advance of the Mongols, who two years previously had destroyed Baghdad in their victory at 'Ain Jalut. They also finally shattered the crusader possessions in Palestine and Syria. Thus they established a stable rule in the Middle East for around two hundred years; this made possible a late blossoming of traditional Sunni Islam. Sunni orthodoxy, embodied in the Mamluk pseudo-caliphate in Cairo, gave them legitimacy; the military aristocracy made up of Turkic military slaves, who were constantly recruited anew, guaranteed them political power; entry and transit tolls and the income from domains financed the state budget, and loans the army. However, in its later decadence, the Mamluk empire was overcome by the expanding power of the Ottomans.

The Ottomans, who originally settled in north-west Asia Minor (and later in Bursa), were grounded in the Seljuk tradition and led by Osman I (from 1281 to 1326). They replaced the Seljuks in Anatolia (or East Rome: hence they were called 'Rome Seljuks'). In 1354 they crossed Bosphorus, established their residence in Adrianople (Edirne), and subjugated Serbs and Bulgarians in the Balkans. On 29 May 1453 they achieved what for six centuries had been a vain Arab dream: they conquered Constantinople which, as Stamboul or Istanbul, became the capital of Turkey and the centre of the new great Islamic western empire; Mesopotamia, Syria, Palestine, Egypt and Arabia soon also belonged to it.

The Mongol invasion and its devastating consequences

At the time of the gradual dissolution of the Seljuk sultanate, the last 'Abbasids attempted to establish at least an 'Abbasid regional kingdom. In the course of the clashes with the Seljuks one caliph was executed, his successor driven out of office and a third murdered. However, a vigorous caliph-vizier succeeded in establishing a small 'Abbasid regional kingdom, about the size of present-day Iraq. With the help of the militant ascetic 'Futuwa alliances', originally chivalrous alliances of men from the cities who came from the lowest classes, this long-ruling caliph, an-Nasir li-din Allah (caliph from 1180 to 1225), was able first to form a household power and then to integrate many local dynasties from Afghanistan to Asia Minor into his empire. But this empire had no more than regional significance.

Even before an-Nasir's death, the Mongols had reached the frontier; within a few years they subjugated Iran and in 1258 stood at the gates of Baghdad. When Caliph al-Musta'sim (caliph from 1242 to 1258) did not capitulate, the Mongol ruler Hülagü stormed the city and rode into the palace on his horse, right up to the throne of the last caliph of Baghdad. The caliph was wrapped in a carpet and killed; a large part of the population of Baghdad also perished. Wherever the Mongol storm went, it left behind countless dead, destroyed cities and neglected irrigation systems, the foundation for agriculture. A centuries-old economic, social, cultural and religious development, promoted by many generations, ended everywhere.

Undoubtedly this was a catastrophe. For the first time broad central areas of Islam were under non-Islamic rule. At the same time, the Mongol invasion drove many Turkic people further, to western Asia as far as Anatolia. Only over time did the Mongols of Iran, under the Ilkhanid dynasty, adopt the religion of their Muslim subjects, eventually taking Sunni Islam also to central Asia, so that even the 'golden horde' which spread all over Russia converted to Islam. The Christian mission in Central Asia largely collapsed. Eventually, however, both the European and the rival Islamic powers succeeded in developing trade and cultural contacts as far as the Far East—guaranteed for around two centuries by the *pax Mongolica.*

The 'Abbasid paradigm of the caliphate, which had ended politically in 945, perished irrevocably with the invasion of the Mongol tribes from Central Asia in 1258. The area from the Far East to the Balkans completely changed between the thirteenth and fifteenth centuries. From the middle of the tenth century, no caliph as 'leader of the faithful' any longer had influence in the sphere of Islamic rule. Everywhere, those who now called the tune were Turkic nomadic warriors, slave war lords and their sultans. For my analysis of the paradigm change this means:

- Nomadic élites, military slaves and local war lords, who were not interested in collaborating with a central government, came to power in place of the former bureaucratic and land-owning classes which had controlled the empire.
- Genealogy, which traditionally had been highly prized, since most Islamic rulers had attempted to derive their descent from the Prophet Muhammad, lost significance. The new sultans were usually not Arabs but did attempt to legitimize themselves on the basis of the Islamic tradition.
- The Turks as an ethnic group, instead of the Arabs and then the Persians, now shaped Islamic society and religion. The centre of Islamic culture shifted westwards from ruined Iraq: from Baghdad to Damascus and Cairo and later to Istanbul.
- Instead of an 'Islamic empire' as a political institution, all that remained was the 'Islamic cultural circle' ('the Islamic world'), for whose vast territories no one political or religious authority was responsible but which continued to be characterized by similar religious forms or sacral organizations. Only at the beginning of the sixteenth-century world did three great Islamic empires form: the empires of the Mughals, the Safavids and the Ottomans.
- The former sacral regime, under a 'representative of God' who determined both religion and politics, was now increasingly replaced by a separation between the state and religious élites and institutions, the Ulama or Sufis.

Regardless of who was politically in power and controlled the state, believers were no longer guided by caliphs and sultans in religious, ethical and legal matters. They were guided by the religious scholars, the Ulama and—increasingly—by the mystics, the Sufis and religious orders. I shall now turn my attention to these; both have great religious (and sometimes also political) significance even in our day, at least in certain Islamic countries and milieus.

2. The Ulama: legal schools become popular movements

After the downfall of the Jewish state, the destruction of the second temple (70) and the city of Jerusalem, Judaism could not have survived the political end of the post-exilic theocracy paradigm (Jewish P III) without the rabbis. These Jewish religious scholars, who with their synagogues and the codification of the tradition of exegesis (Talmud) laid the foundations for the new medieval paradigm of the rabbis and the synagogue (Jewish P IV), secured the survival of Judaism down the centuries. A similar thing happened in Islam. It could not have survived the end of the classical Islamic paradigm of the caliphate (P III) after its disempowerment (945) and downfall (1258) without the Ulama (*'ulama'*, singular *'alim*).These scholars of the Qur'an and the hadith, of law and theology were always separate from the caliphate and had gained public recognition; they long had an autonomous authority in religious matters. Under alien regimes, in a completely new political constellation, they were able not only to preserve this authority but also to strengthen it substantially.[14]

Functions: training cadres, forming communities, networking

The new rulers, often uncultivated and barely educated, were dependent on the old élites, particularly in training their cadres. The Ulama, most of whom were both theologians and legal scholars, gradually became responsible for higher education. They formed law schools, with well-organized bodies of teachers and pupils. They took pains to train judges, notaries, legal experts and justiciaries. Alongside the law schools were special schools of theologians which, though they had no judicial and administrative functions, acquired a coherent social identity, much like the Mu'tazilah and the Ash'arite schools.

These cadre schools were not remote scholarly academies but institutions completely rooted in the people, with their own following. They had never been supported and maintained by the state but always by patrons and adherents, especially from the class of business people and craftsman. They earned their living from those communities in which they worked and whose qadis, imams and pulpit preachers (*khatib*) they trained. These schools served not only to train cadres but also to provide community education. Social ties within the schools were often stronger than political relations with the state authority.

The legal and theological schools were by no means fixed locally and encapsulated territorially. Although they were based completely on the personal relationship of the student to his teacher, who was also his religious upbringer and from whom at the end of his studies he received a certificate listing the books he had worked through, some of the professors made long journeys, especially if they were in search of hadith or if they had made themselves too unpopular with the political authorities. Students too liked to travel from one great teacher of law and theology to another in order to gain instruction over a broad palette of different studies. Thus, all the legal and theological schools had numerous international relationships. These affected the occupation of the posts of judges and other officials, to which appointments were made in accordance with law schools, giving rise to an informal but highly effective international network of communication among Muslim scholars.

The Ulama had performed these three functions—training cadres, forming a community and networking—in the previous paradigm (P III) but in the new paradigm, lacking a central political focus, they took on another function, of higher quality and greater political importance.

The new form of organization: the madrasah

Anyone who travels through Persia or Morocco will come upon madrasahs (*madrasah*, school); they are often architectural gems, especially in Isfahan and in Fez.[15] They were places of higher Islamic education which now essentially contributed to the formation of Islam, though later, with the general stagnation in Islam, they lost their reputation and importance; by the sixteenth century their great days were behind them. The madrasah is a symbol of this paradigm.

Originally, the education of the Ulama took place quite informally, mostly within the mosque, where often one or more special rooms and later also a library were set up for the purpose of study. In this period these became largely independent institutions with their own complexes of buildings, which served both as places of teaching and residences for the students and teachers. There were forerunners to the madrasah in Khorasan, in the framework of the Shafiʿite legal school; here legal instruction at first took place in private houses, which were then transformed into houses for students and scholars who were travelling through. The Ghaznavids officially founded the first madrasah at the beginning of the eleventh century. The Seljuks made madrasahs into state institutions and founded Hanafite or Shafiʿite madrasahs in all the larger cities—for Sunni Islam this soon became the usual course of legal and theological training.

Thus these educational institutions spread from Iraq to the West; by the end of the twelfth century there were thirty in Baghdad, six in Mosul and twenty in Damascus. In the thirteenth and fourteenth centuries they also existed in the Maghreb, indeed even in Granada.

The madrasah also represented a new development in architecture.[16] Its four-iwan scheme (from the time of the Seljuks in the form of a cross) is of Persian origin: four buildings (with two or more storeys) and a large vaulted hall (*iwan*) opening on to a courtyard were grouped around a square or rectangular inner courtyard which was often decorated with fountains. Opposite the main entrance was the main iwan and, not dissimilar to the apse of a Christian basilica, the prayer niche (*mihrab*) in the direction of Mecca; this was usually clad in ceramics, tiles, marble, plaster or woodwork and decorated with inscriptions from the Qur'an or with floral and geometrical ornamentation. Here the person leading the prayer (the imam) stood in worship. In the buildings there were cells, a kitchen and a bath, usually also a library and sometimes even a hospital and the mausoleum of the founder.

The madrasah thus combined the functions of a mosque, a law school and a theological seminary. It lodged teacher and pupils; in it they received teaching, food and lodging and often free medical care. The madrasah was financed by a religious foundation (*waqf*) through which the founders avoided it being divided up on their deaths; they appointed their heirs as administrators, who could largely determine the orientation of the teaching. For the Ulama who worked there this meant a secure regular income and an elevation of status. Although they were not sacral persons, they developed into a class of their own (with higher prestige than secular professions) with distinctive clothing and certain privileges—not unlike the Christian clergy in some respects, except that they did not have to observe Roman celibacy.

There was no real curriculum, with academic grades. Efforts were made to see that students learned as much as possible of the Qur'an by heart and the various professors taught the 'Islamic sciences': law (of one or more law schools), theology, history and auxiliary disciplines such as grammar, lexicology and rhetoric. In general the 'non-Islamic sciences', such as philosophy, medicine, mathematics, natural sciences and secret knowledge, were not taught. The student could subsequently teach what he could demonstrate by his certificate that he had learned.

Popular movements and party factions

Originally only the scholars, judges and their students, along with officials, rich patrons and their followers from the city made up the core of the law school, but gradually the law schools spread to the wider population: they not only offered charitable, educational and legal services but increasingly played a role in political and social leadership.[17]

The controversy over who should succeed Ibn Hanbal in imposing the 'examination' proved how easily the Ulama could mobilize the masses. Without disputing the authority of the caliph in matters of state, they claimed authority in religious questions, which could be judged rightly only from the Qur'an and the hadith. The Hanbalites were the first to establish such a religious authority and social leadership independent of the state; in Sunni Islam this was the first Muslim community to be separated from the caliphate. Here a new model of the relationship of religious scholars to the political rulers was tried out; it was to attain much greater importance during the impotence and then the disappearance of the caliphate. Other law schools developed into religious communities that followed their own authority and rules of behaviour regardless of the caliph and could, in principle, function even without the caliphate. The Ulama made this possible.

The Ulama strengthened their social position: confronted with military powers unfamiliar with the local traditions, through their religious and intellectual prestige the religious scholars, originally remote from politics, became the social and political élite. With merchants, landowners and administrative officials, because of the instability of the political regime in some cities and territories they exercised the *de facto* power. They owed their authority not to a nomination, nor to a group that they had represented, but to their teacher, their education and their recognition by the people. There was no central authority or church-like organization superior to the Ulama with the power of consecration. This underlines how much, in the period after the caliphate, there was a new Islamic paradigm.

Thus the law schools learned more and more about how to secure mass support or to get direct influence over public demonstrations. The madrasahs functioned as centres of religious propaganda and political agitation, not only of the Sunnis against the Shiites, who were always active, but also of the Sunni law schools among one another. The law schools had always been rivals and had disputed over the posts of judges, the control of doctrine and political decisions but now the squabbling between schools and parties took on quite different features.

The Hanbalites set in motion their own inquisition from below. They attempted to establish their religious views among others by force. For the first time in Islam, guardians of the faith appeared, who sought with every means at their disposal to suppress immoral activities such as prostitution and drinking wine; they did not hesitate to use violence against their opponents from the Mu'tazilah and the Ash'arite school. The notorious case of Ibn 'Aqil[18] shook

Baghdad in the years 1068 to 1072 because the Hanbalites first drove this scholar into exile and then forced him, publicly and in writing, to give up his Mu‘tazilite ties and recant his own views in favour of a strictly Hanbalite creed.

Is there an alternative to an Islam of the law?

In contrast to the early paradigms, at this time the view became established among most Muslims and their religious teachers that the truth lay with the majority. As we saw, the significance of the community for the question of truth was always emphasized in Islam. However, whereas earlier that community had been the Muslim community as such (Ummah), as opposed to all non-Muslim communities, now it was that of the ‘established majority’ (*al-jama‘ah*) within the Ummah, that is, the community of those who held fast to the Sunnah. They claimed orthodoxy solely for themselves, as opposed to other (minority) Muslim communities. This is similar to the practice of the mainstream church in the Roman Catholic paradigm (P III) over against the Eastern churches and special developments in the West. Muslim scholars found enough hadith in which the Prophet said that the true Muslim always had to follow the majority and the minorities were on the way to hell. Indeed, it was thought that God's special support was so much with the majority that they could not be in error. This developed into the view of the majority loyal to the Sunnah, who thus attributed to themselves infallibility in questions of faith, morality and law.

The Sunnis did not go so far as to attribute infallibility to an individual religious leader. Despite the condemnation of schism and the vilification of dissent, in practice people were very tolerant of the differences. Fortunately, there was a famous hadith about this: that differences of opinion were a blessing for the community. So there were far fewer formal excommunications and great schisms over the faith in Islam than there were in either Hellenistic (P II) or Roman Catholic Christianity (P III). In principle, the Sunnis were concerned with adaptation, integration and synthesis. The Kharijites and the Mu‘tazilites had shown where moral rigorism or doctrinaire uniformity led. As long as a group continued to believe in the one God and the definitive Prophethood of Muhammad—and the Shiites, the great opponents of the Sunnis, who believed in the infallibility of their imams, did that—some of their peculiarities and ‘heresies’ were allowed to slip through. While they were regarded as erring, they were regarded as erring Muslims.

However, in the paradigm without a caliph, the controversies between the schools, and between Sunnis and Shiites, came to a climax. Shiites celebrated their own feasts, to strengthen and propagate their faith, in particular venerating their martyrs, who had been persecuted by the majority, whereas the different

Sunni schools, although remaining in the framework of the one Ummah, developed increasingly into exclusive and mutually hostile communities. Sometimes one district of a city rose up against another; sometimes walls were built between different districts, to separate Sunnis from Shiites. In the middle of the twelfth century, the city of Nishapur (in north east Iran) was completely shaken by violent clashes between the Hanafite and Shafi'ite law schools. Identification with one's own religious sect became more important than identification with the Ummah: 'In this guise, the schools resembled the neighbourhood, lineage, or other parochial bodies into which Middle Eastern towns had always been divided. Religion now superseded tribal or quarter identifications.'[19]

The Shariah formed the uniting centre of Sunni Islam. But, some Muslims asked (and still ask), don't all the legal scholars and all the legal learning express only quite particular aspects of Islam and neglect others? Indeed, and it would become increasingly clear that the existing religious needs of individuals and later the broad population of Shariah Islam could not really be satisfied. A strong structure of legal procedure helped people to find the right answers for all the questions of everyday life in the Qur'an and Sunnah. Institutions for the cultivation of the law, culminating in the office of the judge, the qadi, likewise helped law to break through, as did the muftis (the rulers' expert advisors). But people,

Questions: The Islam of the law

- Islam, as an imposing political system, has shaped vast areas of the earth. But didn't heightened political power bring with it a secularization of religion and an externalization of piety, which largely concealed the original religious impulses of the Prophet Muhammad and the original community, and which therefore resolutely called for a new detachment from the world, for asceticism and internalization?
- Islamic law, now fully developed, comprehensively ordered Muslim society in all spheres. But doesn't the dry legal casuistry for all circumstances of life cover up direct religious knowledge and leave the human need for religious experience unsatisfied? Does repetition of individual regulations of the Shariah and brooding over possible transgressions really lead to peace in the soul? Is submission to the law itself 'submission to God', *'islam'*?
- The central concern of all Islamic law schools was justice, and rightly so. But are justice and legal learning really the highest things in human life? Isn't that rather love, human love as an image of love of God and as a response to God's mercy and right guidance? Isn't getting nearer to God more important than the fulfilment of the Shariah?

and especially religious people, required more than just 'law'. Many of the critical questions raised then about the Islam of the law have remained topical to the present day: questions from the past have become questions for the future.

It is not surprising that the popular movements of the law schools did not remain the only social groups that structured the new paradigm without a caliph. Indeed, particularly in the eleventh century, when Sunni Shariah Islam seemed complete and what the great lawyers of the eighth and ninth centuries had proclaimed and lived out became common knowledge, for many people, other goals and ideals came into the foreground: striving for the immediate experience of God instead of study of the over-complicated law and its countless applications in everyday life. A quite different kind of community from the law schools became ever more important. This community came from the 'mystics'. Only in this paradigm did these mystics form real brotherhoods which, in many spheres, went beyond the law schools and attained general social significance. That is why, although they were founded very much earlier, they are introduced for the first time here.

3. The Sufis: mystics form themselves into brotherhoods

Both Judaism and Christianity had a somewhat divided attitude to mysticism. As prophetic religions, both were fundamentally concerned, not with becoming one with God but with an abiding encounter between God and human beings, the encounter of creator and creature, the just and holy judge and human beings who had time and again incurred guilt. Any identification of human beings with God or the divine was therefore met with great restraint. In principle, it was the same in Islam, the third great religious force with a monotheistic prophetic character.

However, just as for a while an important mystical movement could form in Judaism under the influence of the Kabbala, though it tragically failed,[20] and just as in Christianity time and again individual mystics and small mystical communities appeared, which were suspected and persecuted by the Inquisition,[21] so too there was a mystical movement in Islam. It became extremely powerful and in the new paradigm without a caliph (P IV) developed dominant structures alongside the law schools (different from those in Judaism and Christianity). The movement of the Sufis, despite many overlaps, represents a different type of Muslim from the Ulama. From the tenth to the fourteenth century it became a real popular movement, with a considerably greater social dynamic than the law schools, which were fundamentally orientated towards preserving the *status quo*. With their own forms of piety, their own institutions and their own theology, the Sufis became the most popular and widespread form of Islam, its 'mystical' form. But is what arose here really 'mysticism'?

Is mysticism an original element of Islam? Asceticism at the beginning

Sufi (*sufi*, plural *sufiyun, sufiyah*—Sufism) is all too often translated 'mystic'. But what is a mystic? In everyday terminology the words 'mystic', 'mystical' or 'mysticism' are often used very vaguely and equated with the enigmatic, strange, mysterious or even simply irrational. But 'mystical' comes from the Greek *myein*, meaning to close the mouth or the eyes: the 'mysteries' are therefore 'secrets', 'secret teachings', 'secret cults', about which it is best to keep silent in the presence of those who have not been initiated. So, 'mystic' does not denote any form of spirituality. Understood precisely, it denotes that form of religion which closes the mouth (and eyes) in the face of the mysteries hidden from profane ears, as it seeks to attain salvation within and a direct, intuitive, experience of unity with God, whether this is designated 'gnosis' or 'knowledge', *sophia* or 'wisdom' or 'light' and 'love'.[22]

It can easily be inferred from the previous chapter why in Islam, as in Judaism and Christianity, mysticism exercised a fascination at a very early stage: in a religion of the law some features must have seemed attractive to Muslims:

- a tendency towards internalization and deepening;
- inner freedom from the compulsions of legality and in some cases also from the political power;
- finally, the overcoming of authoritarianism and formalism by thinking of and experiencing unity.

However, in Islam the experience of unity was not primary, so that the question must be asked: what is Islamic mysticism?[23] Is it identical with the Sufi movement? The sources relating to the early Sufi texts are confusing; specialists do not agree on either the dating or the authenticity of the early eighth-century witnesses. But one thing is certain: the Arabic word for mysticism, *tasawwuf*, literally means 'clothing oneself in wool'. So *sufi*, from which, since the nineteenth century, the word 'sufism' has been derived, goes back to the word *suf* ('wool'; that there is an allusion to the Greek word *sophos*, wise man, is unproven). This reminds us that the first Sufis were not identified with a particular 'philosophy' or spirituality. They stood out by wearing a coarse woollen cloth: that very woollen cloth which, much earlier, was the penitential garment for Christian (especially Nestorian) ascetics. But were the Sufis really mystics? From the beginning, some followers of the Prophet strove for a closer inner relationship with God. But whether there were really mystics in Islam as early as the seventh century has not so far been demonstrated. Sufis do not date from the beginning of Islam, but only from the eighth century.

Where does Sufism have its origins? Islamic and Western scholars have long looked outside Islam. We can note many influences in the later history of Sufism:

- neo-Platonic: ideas of the One, of reason and of the soul through the so-called 'theology of Aristotle' (which in fact comes from Plotinus's *Enneads*,[24] translated into Arabic in 840);
- Christian: through Syrian monks and hermits;[25]
- Indian: through Buddhist ascetics in respect of techniques of meditation and breathing (however, this is particularly disputed for the beginnings of Sufism);[26]
- Turkestan: shamanic influences,[27] only local, relating to particular customs and morals, with no significance for the spiritual content of Sufism.[28]

Present-day scholars—chiefly influenced by the great pioneering works of the French orientalist Louis Massignon[29]—have largely departed from dependence theories: not just because Muslims attach importance to originality, but because the methodological problems of authenticity and dating are almost insuperable. Today, critical research begins from an independent development: the origins of Sufism are to be found in Islamic asceticism.[30] With good reason the Sufis, who wore coarse woollen cloth, the material of poor people, were also called the 'poor'—*fuqara'* (plural of the Arabic *faqir*, in Persian *darwesh*, later *darwish*, from which the English loan words fakir and dervish derive).

An important insight follows from this. The original Sufis were not mystics in the real sense, proclaiming a doctrine and experience of unity, but rather ascetics, including many who despised and provoked existing society and were even active fighters for the glory of the faith (*jihad*) in the Muslim frontier settlements.[31] These Muslims who fled from God's threat and anger into God's protection and arms were not primarily concerned with 'unity' with God but with meeting God's demands.

Al-Hasan al-Basri (died 728), whom later the mystics as well as the theologians claimed as their ancestor, was not a mystic who strove to become one with God. He was an ascetic, who simply wanted to live a right life, pleasing to God, in the midst of the world. The pious men in Basra and its neighbourhood who reacted to the increasing worldliness, luxury and collapse of morality under the Umayyads (P II) were ascetics: in mourning and fear they meditated on the words of the Qur'an about the coming day of judgement. They were called 'the ones who constantly weep' (*al-bakka'un*), which could also be understood, probably ironically, as 'the whiners'. Unlike the average Muslim, these pious men proclaimed and practised renunciation and purity, submission to God and assimilation to his Prophet and, in the face of the widespread indifference and superficiality of religious life, attached great importance to scrupulous observance of the commandments of the Qur'an and the tradition. They sought to be taken up into God by self-abasement and transcending the self.

However, mysticism, in whichever of its countless variants, is more than asceticism and obedience to the law. Mysticism in the real sense is a deliberate striving for direct inner experience of God's reality. There are a number of Islamic mystics in this sense (in contrast to the many 'clad in wool') only from the late ninth century onwards, that is, under the 'Abbasids (P III). Even then this was by no means a mass movement which would define a paradigm, but a group of élite individuals and their pupils, friends and followers, especially in Baghdad. From this comes a second important insight, which has been too little stressed by lovers of Islamic mysticism, Western and Eastern: mysticism is not part of original Islam (P I), however much it can refer to individual verses of the Qur'an and even though, in the period of the conquests, there were pious individuals who thought and spoke about their own relationship and that of other human beings to God. This confirms the view of the essence of Islam given earlier (and likewise applies to Judaism and Christianity): originally Islam was not a mystical but a prophetic religion.[32] But does that mean that mysticism is un-Islamic?

Is mysticism un-Islamic? Personal experience of God

Later Sufis put an extraordinarily strong emphasis on asceticism. However, different answers were given to the question whether a Sufi might be rich. A clear distinction between ascetics and mystics is neither possible nor necessary but the classical Islamic mysticism that formed in the ninth century does not have one characteristic of the early ascetics: constant mourning about the wretched state of the world and separation from the human race. In general it affirmed a turning away from the world; not, however, necessarily in the sense of a radical flight from the world but predominantly in the sense of a partial inner 'letting go' and spiritual freedom in the midst of human society. Sufism accepts asceticism (*zuhd*) but also transcends it as one of the 'stations' on the 'way'. Turning inwards and striving for immediate unity with God is characteristic of the Sufis in the classical sense. They wanted to be 'friends of God': *awliya'* (singular *wali*) *Allah*. Such an experience of unity cannot be said to be impossible, even within the framework of the prophetic religions.

According to the masters of mysticism, this experience should not be wild and arbitrary but should take place in an ordered and methodical progress in stages, beginning with the purification of the will through different physical and psychological means, contemplation in which one forgets oneself and finally, if possible, enchanted or immersed ecstasy in which a person unites himself with the immeasurable Absolute, with the deity. Some of the exercises in mystical immersion (which continue to the present day) have played a special role from the classical period of Sufism, so as to achieve closer contact with God and possibly exceptional psychological and spiritual conditions:

– The thought of God (*dhikr Allah*): the incessantly repeated, litany-like invocation of God and his ninety-nine names and the repetition of particular formulae (especially the confession of faith), originally a simple prayer[33] (whispered or said aloud, alone or in community), become the means of attaining ecstatic states. This 'admonitory recollection of God' was commended to soldiers serving on the frontier to raise their morale and give the *jihad* meaning.[34]

– Listening to poetry and music (*sama'*): from the middle of the ninth century the Sufis not only cultivated brotherliness but above all aroused and intensified a feeling of love for God. They gave a symbolic interpretation to love songs written by poets in a purely earthly sense.[35]

– Dance: at a very early stage intensified movement and ritualized dance were associated with this as an outward expression of inner arousal. Onlookers were allowed to join in and the ecstatics sometimes tore their garments or threw them off (often as a gift for musicians and singers). People not only lost their turbans but could even get into a trance. In the thirteenth century, among the Mawlawis (the order of the great poet Jalal ad-din Rumi), dance became an art form and took on a symbolic character.[36]

The example of the Prophet as attested in the hadith led the way for the Sufis: his righteousness and friendliness, his compassion and mercy. He had attained what the Sufis sought: familiarity with God. Anyone who attempted to imitate the Prophet's career would be capable of attaining a similar familiarity with God.

Although, in some manifestations and persons, such mysticism had a revolutionary and offensive element, it was by no means automatically in opposition to the Shariah but sought (like asceticism) to transcend it. The aim was to move from the Islamic law (*shari'ah*) on the mystic path (*tariqah*) to the truth (*haqiqah*), to the most real reality, to God. This could be achieved with the help of the three exercises in immersion mentioned above. The aim was not separation from the Islamic community, since a mystic could also belong to one of the law schools. Rather, it was internalization: instead of legal scholarship, work under the guidance of the master, direct knowledge and personal experience of God stood at the centre. This was practical guidance of the soul instead of rational teaching.

In general the Sufis rejected philosophy with its Hellenistic thought material and abstract language, which thought that it could find wisdom without prophets and revelation. But they practised theology in a new sense, as the Basle orientalist Fritz Meier, one of the best Western experts on Sufism, puts it: as a 'science of pious introspection and an inner contemplation of the Islamic holy scriptures aiming at that'; this was also called a 'science of within' or a 'doctrine of the works of the heart'.[37] The classical Sufi is a scholar and a guide of the soul in one. In principle, Ulama who observed the Qur'an, hadith and Shariah could also labour for deeper religious knowledge, spiritual insight and ethical discipline through special practices and thus be both Ulama and Sufis.

Whatever external influences there may have been—Neoplatonic, Christian, Indian or central Asian—the decisive fact is that mysticism could never have been established in Islam had it not been in deep accord with the spirit of the Qur'an. Moreover the Sufis, who regarded themselves as special 'friends of God' and thus the real heirs of the Prophet, felt encouraged and legitimated by the Qur'an. The attentive reader can find in the Qur'an not only the constant expression of God's transcendence but also individual indications of God's immanence. God is nearer to a man 'than his neck-vein'.[38] Certainly, 'no human vision can encompass Him',[39] but they should know that 'wherever you turn, there is God's countenance'.[40] And God has set signs of his omnipotence and goodness not only in nature but also 'within your own selves'.[41]

For Muslim mystics, the covenant or primal treaty made before the beginning of time by God with humankind, the basis of which one can see in surah 7.172, became particularly important. In this surah God calls forth future humankind from the loins of Adam, who is not yet created, and asks them, 'Am I not your Sustainer?' They reply, 'Yea, indeed, we do bear witness thereto.' The Qur'an also speaks of a privileged class of 'friends of God',[42] the Sufis refer this to themselves. The Qur'an also speaks, in various places, of the lower or fleshly soul (*nafs*) and the spirit (*ruh*) which, according to the Sufis, often stand in contradiction in the human heart (*qalb*).

Against this background there is a reorientation of the reading of the Qur'an, marked more by strictness and sharpness than by gentleness and warmth. It is to be read not only with the eyes of the head but also with the eyes of the heart which, under God's illumination, can see and understand the inner nature and significance of things.[43] Whereas the earlier ascetics constantly referred to the surahs about the threat of judgement, which for them was the occasion for criticism, anxiety and mourning, the mystics chiefly referred to the core quotations I have cited, in particular the one verse which speaks of God's love orientated on mutuality: 'He loves them and they love Him.'[44]

Sometimes scholars therefore talk of a mysticism of love. The great German orientalist Annemarie Schimmel, who investigated the 'mystical dimensions of Islam' by means of the poems and their glowing images from the realm of earthly love and drunkenness,[45] constantly makes it clear that this love, love of the absolute, distinguishes authentic mysticism from an ascetic attitude. The joy of union, not the sorrowfulness of renunciation, stamps the mystic. 'What is Sufism?', the greatest mystical poet, Rumi, asked (very much later). His reply was: 'To find joy in the heart when grief comes.'[46]

Islamic mysticism no more draws directly on the Qur'an than Christian mysticism draws directly on the Bible. Quite strange ideas can be hidden under Qur'anic words. Specialists differ widely not only over the different influences but also over the dating and authenticity of the early eighth-century Sufi texts; it is not for a Christian theologian to be an arbiter here.

The difficulty becomes clear if we examine the testimony of Rab'iah al-'Adawiyyah (died 801), a pious woman from Basra, who is explicitly included in the list of 'non-Sufis' created by the famed Arabic writer Jahiz. She never designated herself a Sufi. According to some interpreters,[47] she was the first to live out the ideal of selfless love of God: a love independent of all fear of hell and reward of paradise, a love for love's sake, of the kind that we find expressed by Christian hermits. But according to other interpretations,[48] this emphasis on love in Islam rests on verses attributed to her (as to four other figures) only by a source which is 200 years later (and scholars have discovered a second Rab'iah in tenth-century Syria). What is important for our context is that in early mysticism a woman was given such an important role: indeed in both Iraq and Syria we can point to a series of women mystics.[49]

The goal of mysticism—abiding life in God: Muhasibi and Junayd

Classical mysticism was not about a unitive thought in the sense, for example, of early Indian all-unity mysticism but about piety with prophetic roots. With good reason classical mysticism has also been called 'moral mysticism' (*at-tasawwuf al-khuluqi*). A whole series of early Islamic mystics put unconditional trust (*tawakkul*) in God at the centre of their lives, so that—used exclusively in connection with God—it became a central concept of Sufism.[50] This emphasis on absolute trust in God (trusting faith) confirms that classical Islamic mysticism is completely within the framework of the prophetic religions, which have also been designated 'religions of faith' (as opposed to the early mystical unity religions of Indian origin). Whether one regards this trust in God as an attribute of believers generally or as a consequence of perfect faith, or distinguishes different degrees of faith, for the Islamic mystics unconditional trust, trusting surrender to God, follows from the recognition of the oneness of God (*tawhid*), which allows no association (*shirk*) of a created being nor any hidden polytheism (*shirk khafi*), since the wisdom, power and mercy of the one God are absolutely all-embracing and bring about everything (there is even talk of all-embracing forgiveness among Persian mystics of trust in God such as Yahyah ibn Muʿadh ar-Razi).

However, an exaggerated trust in God with an appeal to God's predetermination and universal activity can lead to complete human passivity. Thus it is reported in an anecdote that a Sufi who went through the desert without food, trusting only in God, was eaten by a lion and another, who did nothing to save himself, drowned in the Tigris. If such extreme contempt for everything worldly as polluted, of all physical work as dirty and of all possessions and all money as reprehensible had become generally established, the Islamic economy and social life would have been completely paralysed. That is one good reason why leading Sufis constantly insisted on trust in God as an inner attitude rather an external practice. The theory of inner intuitive knowledge of God or gnosis, which seems to have been put forward for the first time by an elusive historical figure, the Nubian Dhu 'n-Nun (died 859 or 860), the head of the Egyptian Sufi school, is important in this connection.

It is especially to the Iraqi school of mysticism, founded by al-Muhasibi (died 857), that the Sufis owe many themes of a knowledge of the soul and a differentiated terminology—developed not for the sake of anthropological reflection but for the sake of religious purification. Muhasibi is still more in line with the ascetics than with the mystics; he does not designate himself a 'Sufi', although in practice he is a kind of 'church father' of mystical piety. Only later did 'Sufi' become a designation for the Islamic mystics. Muhasibi speaks of an earthly vision of God 'more like a cautious and sober theologian than like a mystic caught up in his inner experience'.[51] He does not reject asceticism; however, he does not see it as an end in itself but as a means of purifying the soul in order to prepare for communion with God.[52]

The undisputed leader of classical Sufism, the Iranian Abu l-Qasim al-Junayd (died 910), was a pioneer of real mysticism in this Iraqi school, which attaches much importance to psychological insight, precise observation of the self and strict self-control. He was born in Iraq and studied at the Shafiʿite legal school; later, all chains of tradition, legitimization and initiation of the Sufis go back to him.[53] Junayd was a perceptive thinker of great sobriety and pious seriousness, utterly filled with the notion of divine majesty. He knew that the Sufi has to undergo a long course of purification and spiritual battle. He emphasized a return to the origin, to the covenant which God made with humankind before time. All are to return to God in constant worship, obedience and reflection on his name. A man may thus attain, through the various states and stages, to a mystical love in which he no longer reflects on God's attributes but is transformed into them.

The mystic realizes, in reflection and meditation, that as an earthly temporal individual he has no true existence, that he gains his true existence only in turning away from himself and to God. Junayd thought little of momentary mystical states of intoxication (*sukr*) which utterly quench human properties. He treasured sobriety (*sahw*), the second sobriety in which the human being becomes aware of himself again after ecstasy, in which all his attributes are restored to him, albeit spiritually transformed. The ultimate goal of the mystic is not 'un-becoming' (*fana'*), submersion, but 'abiding' (*baqa'*), abiding life in God.[54]

The classical Islamic mysticism of the ninth and tenth centuries therefore does not break up the framework of the prophetic religions. It does not matter whether it is called a mysticism of love (in contrast to asceticism), personal mysticism (in contrast to all-unity mysticism) or moral mysticism (in contrast to a Gnostic mysticism of knowledge); the decisive point is that none of the great mystics was concerned with a pantheistic experience of identity, an alleged unity of human beings with the whole, with nature, the cosmos, 'life'. They were concerned that, after a long journey with many 'stations' and 'states' (a common distinction is that the former are achieved through work and the latter given by God), at least in moments of ecstasy a unity of the whole human being should be experienced with the mysterious primal ground of reality: with that inexpressible, all-embracing, comprehensive, all-determining, very first and very last reality, before which human speech begins to stammer, concepts fail and notions melt away, indeed before whose mystery silence seems more appropriate. The aim was not to alienate human beings from the world but to have them lead a life from God in the world.

This is a third important insight. The classical Islamic mystics of the ninth and tenth centuries did not want either to make the things of nature God (the divinization of the universal) or even to make themselves God (self-divinization). But everyone, by whatever method, wanted to experience God's overwhelming reality directly: not as an ontic unity of God and human being which is a given but as a personal encounter which leads through God's grace, mercy and love to the presence of God, to fellowship with God and finally to unity in God.

What about that mysticism which seems not to observe the boundaries between God and human beings but definitively does away with them and therefore was (and is) vigorously contested by Islamic orthodoxy? Didn't even such a significant mystic as Junayd express hesitations about the doctrines of the man who stood at the centre of the controversy here and remains a disputed figure in Islam to the present day, namely al-Hallaj? Don't he and his followers represent an un-Islamic mysticism which no longer knew any boundaries between them and God?

Does mysticism have limits? The conflict over al-Hallaj

Some orthodox Muslims had already been deeply disturbed by the remarks of another leading mystic of the Persian school who is mentioned in poetry almost as often as Hallaj: Abu Yazid (Persian/Turkish Bayazid) al-Bistami (who died in 874),[55] who probably came from a small place called Bistam in north-east Iran. He had played a leading role in laying down the doctrine of the annihilation of the self, of 'un-becoming', which was so important for later Sufism, probably less under the influence of Indian Vedanta doctrines[56] than on the basis of his own authentic experiences of faith. Bayazid was the first to describe his mystical experiences using the image of the 'heavenly journey' (*mi'raj*) of the Prophet, the appropriation of a privilege of the Prophet which is said to have earned him expulsion from his homeland.[57] He not only stimulated later mystical poets through his own arbitrary symbolism but also ventured statements such as 'Praise be to Me, how great is My Majesty'[58]—one of those statements which, as H. Ritter puts it, 'point to his arrogant religious self-confidence'. However, according to Ritter, it does not seem impossible that 'despite all the proud language, at some point he came up against the limit which is set to all the religious experience of created, finite human beings': 'In this sense Junayd was right in asserting that Bayazid did not attain to God. But Bayazid could retort with one of his sayings, "You poor thing, does anyone ever get to him?" '[59]

A generation later, al-Husayn ibn Mansur al-Hallaj thought that 'the poor Abu Yazid' reached only the threshold of the divine.[60] Al-Hallaj had grown up in Wasit (south-east of Baghdad) and Tustar (south-west Iran); for a while he was also a pupil of Junayd but then made the great pilgrimage to Mecca, remaining there a whole year, engaged in the harshest ascetical exercises. After his return he is said to have knocked on Junayd's door in Baghdad. When Junayd asked, 'Who is there?', he replied: 'I am (*ana*) the true one (*al-haqq*)'—a saying used from an early date and frequently of God.

No Sufi saying is more notorious than this *ana l-haqq*, which, although attested in the writings of al-Hallaj, had not been verified in its precise context and was hardly meant as a 'dogmatic' statement. It was not just this statement which led Junayd to turn away from his former pupil. Junayd thought that al-Hallaj was disseminating false religious claims; he was notorious for his critical remarks about traditional Islam and current Sufism. Soon things got very unpleasant for al-Hallaj in Baghdad and he travelled around for many years: a second time to Mecca, allegedly accompanied by four hundred disciples, then by ship to India (on a mission or, as some of his opponents thought, to learn magic), then from Sind to Khorasan and Turkestan, where he finally settled in Turfan, increasingly suspect politically because of his contacts with the Shiite Karmates (in Sind and Multan).

After another great pilgrimage and a two-year stay in Mecca, al-Hallaj, by then known everywhere as a great ascetic and miracle-working ardent preacher of mystical love, again settled in Baghdad, where he had many friends at the caliph's court. However, he was so suspect for both his religion and his politics that his friends could not prevent his arrest on a journey in Susa in 912. He was put in the pillory for three days, imprisoned for years and finally executed on the orders of the vizier. This happened in 922, precisely three hundred years after the Hijrah. He is said to have danced while in fetters and, on his way to execution, to have recited a four-line verse about mystical intoxication. His last words that have been handed down are: 'It is enough for the lover that he should make the one single—i.e., that his existence should be cleared away from the path of love.'[61]

He was hanged on the gallows with hands and feet cut off and finally beheaded. He was not allowed a grave: his body was burned and the ashes scattered in the Tigris. Only fragments of his work have survived: the *Kitab at-tawasin* (an untranslatable made-up title of a little book probably written during his imprisonment), in rhyming prose, discusses questions of the divine unity and prophetology and has hymns in honour of the Prophet; there are also various prayers, poems, letters and statements.

Was this man, who seems to have longed for death out of love of God, perhaps like the moth he describes, which approaches the flame and burns in it so as to unite itself with the 'reality of reality'? This radical mystic still remains a controversial figure: Persian poets venerate him and enthusiastic Sufis take him as their model, but some Orthodox Ulama regard him as an arch-heretic who, among other things, is said to have asserted that one could make the pilgrimage to Mecca even if one remained at home and fed orphan children. Even some moderate mystics criticized him, not because he taught love through suffering but because he saw the deepest being of the deity expressed in passionate overflowing love (expressed with the sensuous word *'ishq* rather than the restrained *hubb*) and thus had unveiled the mystery of the loving unity. The statement 'I am God' makes not only many Muslim mystics but also many Western scholars (including August Tholuck, the Protestant revival theologian who, at the age of twenty-one, wrote the first comprehensive book about Sufism),[62] see al-Hallaj as a pantheist.

The great French orientalist Louis Massignon was the first to deal comprehensively with al-Hallaj in a scholarly way. As a scholar he researched all his life in the libraries of Europe and the Middle East. In 1922, exactly one thousand years after al-Hallaj's execution, he produced, in two imposing volumes, the life and work of the *Martyr mystique de l'Islam* ('The Mystical Martyr of Islam'). In 1976, after Massignon's death, the work was reissued in four volumes. Thanks to this scholar, who also did great service in promoting a new attitude to Islam in the Roman Catholic Church after Vatican II, al-Hallaj's original intentions are now understood better and he is protected against unjustified criticism. Despite all his problematical statements, al-Hallaj apparently never denied God's absolute transcendence, even if he wanted to see God in all things and especially in the human heart: 'When thirsty I do not drink a single drop of water without finding your image in the glass.'[63]

Later Sufic or theosophical thinkers, who tend towards a unitary notion of God and the world (monism), took up some of al-Hallaj's notions. Usually they developed their system in the framework of a gradated outflowing (emanation) of all things to God and a rise of the human being from matter and darkness back to God. Yahya as-Suhrawardi (who was executed in 1191) understood God as absolute light and the most famous monistic thinker, Ibn 'Arabi (who died in 1240), understood God as absolute being). In the current view Ibn 'Arabi was able to integrate philosophy and theology into Sufism, but according to other interpreters, as a Sufi he wanted to have nothing at all to do with philosophy.[64] He was venerated by his adherents as a saint but accused by the orthodox of pantheism.

This is a fourth important insight: how far the human spirit can and may unite itself with the divine spirit in moments of ecstasy (and al-Hallaj seems to have identified himself with 'the True', with God, only in this sense) was, and still is, disputed. There is hardly any theoretical argument against the mystic's experiential testimony of entering into an ultimate unity (in the original basic material of light and being). However, is there perhaps even a theoretical argument for such an experiential testimony, that is, that a coincidence of God and human being is, or is almost, conceivable? On the other hand, the suspicion of projection, which Muslim critics expressed long before modern critics of religion, can hardly be removed.

4. Sufism as a mass movement

In the time of the 'Abbasids (P III), who felt no sympathy for the mystics, as they were critical of authority and despised worldly honour, classical Sufism remained a marginal social phenomenon. Non-Sufi literature barely mentions them and in their religious life they could easily dispense with the official forms of worship. Only in the post-classical paradigm without a caliph (P IV), from the tenth and the fourteenth centuries (but before the Mongol storm), did the Sufi movement develop—in parallel to the law schools—into a power of paradigmatic significance which determined culture. Sufism underwent a deep change which differed from region to region. I shall now analyse its historical development systematically—on the premise of a great deal of continuity.

The regulation of the Sufi communities

The transformation of Sufism within the framework of the new post-classical paradigm can be summed up under the following headings:[65]

- The élite religion of individuals or individual small groups suspect to the government became a Sufi mass movement, open to all (though only to a lesser degree to women). It was usually in good standing with the government, as long as it did not become a powerful political opponent.
- Contrary to the individual arbitrariness and immoral excesses of eccentric Sufis, a degree of regulation developed over time, but this recognized as utterly legitimate the visionary element which was only tolerated by the classical mystics and even promoted it.
- On the basis of the regionalization of Islam, purely Arabic mystical literature became a multi-lingual mysticism (especially Persian).
- In the course of the expansion of Sufism beyond a regional level, which was based on individuals and largely dependent on itself, a loose organization developed which resembled religious orders, often supported by patrons and the government in power, though its basis remained the local Sufi master, his disciples and a lay following.
- The sheikh (*shaykh*), who had been a teacher of Sufi wisdom and practices, from whom the students took instruction, became a spiritual leader and master of groups of neophytes, who were trained to be obedient adepts.
- Whereas classical Sufism was not counted among the generally recognized religious disciplines, in the post-classical period Sufism became a regular classical discipline in which all theologians recognized themselves.
- The philosophical and metaphysical interest lacking in classical mysticism now became evident almost everywhere. There was an integration of Sufi thought and practice with other forms of Islamic faith and worship.

A kind of school had already developed in classical Sufism (P III). The word *tariqah* ('path'), the Sufi way of life, was now also used for the Sufi school (later brotherhood or order). At first, there were only cells of Sufis, extending beyond the small circle of the pupils of the master or sheikh, but all related to him as their spiritual leader and maintaining a common spiritual discipline. After the tenth century, many Sufis who previously gathered in the dwelling (or shop) of their master, or in mosques, had their own meeting houses. They were supported by voluntary, often regular, contributions and thus developed into pastoral and charitable centres.[66] Sufi centres were founded everywhere, on the model of the *ribat* (originally the name for a fortress of Islamic front-line fighters), a kind of hospice or lodge (Persian *khanaqah*). After the twelfth and thirteenth centuries—the time of the foundation of the great religious orders in Christian Europe—several such cells, existing independently of one another and referring only to the name and authority of their sheikh, founder or patron, now formed more or less loosely-connected networks which, given the nature of their spiritual affinity, could rightly be called brotherhoods or 'orders'. They were held together more by the shared spiritual culture of the different Sufi masters than by a highly developed organizational structure.[67]

In the wake of the controversies over al-Hallaj, and with the Shiah, which had been substantially strengthened in the tenth century (the Buwayhids in Baghdad were moderate Shiites, the Fatimids in Egypt radical Shiites), from the tenth and eleventh centuries onwards there was a growing need for demarcation. In the face of some over-excited eccentrics and often libertine, itinerant Sufis with no fixed affiliation (*qalandar*), who thought that the Sufis had divine rather than human attributes and were allowed anything, institutional and doctrinal limits were instituted within Sufism to consolidate the thousands of Sufi communities spiritually and regulate them at least minimally. This happened through:

- Sufi books of doctrine, which made an appropriate selection (with counter-examples) from the statements of classical mystics and gave instructions for correct behaviour (*adab* = etiquette);
- Chains of Sufi authorities (*salasil*, singular *silsilah*) who, as with the hadith, legitimized their own teachings and practices by going back to predecessors (especially Junayd), to early caliphs (especially 'Ali), or to the Prophet himself. These chains provided the spiritual genealogy of an authoritative 'Sufi succession', of 'representatives' (*khulafa*, singular *khalifah*);[68]
- Sufi boarding schools which provided better instruction, stricter upbringing of the pupils and strict subordination to the master or sheikh, so that free instruction with changing teachers was replaced by basic schooling from one teacher.

By the end of the eleventh century, with the revival of the Sunnis, mysticism had also established itself—not only in public opinion but also in professional theology, where as early as the tenth century it had favoured al-Ash'ari's new foundation of a rational 'orthodoxy' between the Mu'tazilah and the traditionists. Towards the end of the eleventh century, Muhammad al-Ghazali created the basis for the complete integration of Sufism into theology; he succeeded in connecting Shariah Islam and Sufi Islam organically, something that I shall evaluate in a later chapter.

Parallels to Christian religious orders

In the twelfth and thirteenth centuries, when the patched garment or habit (*khirqah*) became first a sign of acceptance into a quite specific Sufi community and then a sign of membership, the Sufi networks increasingly took on the features of religious orders—despite essential differences they were not unlike the Christian religious orders which were developing at the same time in Europe.[69] As in Christian orders, so among the Sufis we find:

- the ideals of love of God, discipleship, brotherliness and service to fellow human beings;
- subordination to superiors (sheikhs) who, as the *khalifah* of the founder of the order, indeed as representatives of God, might require unconditional obedience;
- a distinctive rule, differing from other rules by virtue of the sheikh and the order, which regulated everything in the smallest detail, from the initiation ceremonial, novitiate and hair-cutting through reflecting on God and 'liturgical' musical arrangements to earning one's living and dying;
- a distinctive dress, differing in colour, form and individual parts depending on the order. However, a Sufi could belong to as many orders as he liked and own several forms of dress (many garments, much honour—for both sides!);
- a special type of prayer with numerous prescribed formulae, wordy litanies and many devotions;
- disputes between rival orders, especially when individual orders worked zealously for their sheikh, their doctrine, method and membership and even made absolute claims (the sheikh as the 'seal of the saint', even an eschatological Mahdi, resulting in countless apocalyptic and revolutionary movements);
- an organization extending beyond a region under an over-sheikh ('sheikh of sheikhs'), usually nominated by the government as a control, though he often did not make much headway against the communities of the individual orders, which were usually more powerful.

Social work, mission, war

The parallels to the Christian orders go still further: the Sufi 'monastery' (in the eastern areas of Islam called *khanaqah*, Turkish *tekke*, Arabic *zawiyah*), which was often in competition with the madrasah of the law schools, was a centre not only of public preaching, religious instruction and common worship but also of social and charitable activity at the service of those in need, the poor, the sick and travellers. Through it, the Sufis won an extraordinarily broad and committed following among the population and also gained influence in the law schools.

The Sufi communities, which were very capable of adaptation, were also active in mission. The force of their convictions, their authentic and simple way of life and their proximity to the people convinced and attracted many. They did not teach an abstract law but demonstrated the Islamic way of life in practice. They were particularly active in the frontier regions of Islamic expansion, and for their preaching did not use the Arabic of the Qur'an and the scholars but the vernacular, thus performing a great service in developing languages such as Turkish, Urdu, Sindhi and Punjabi as literary languages. Albania, India, Indonesia and black Africa were largely Islamized by Sufi preachers; they were as active among Mongols as among Tatars; the Persian Safavid movement and dynasty emerged from a Sufi order; in India or in West Africa the tariqah structure, with its strong lay participation, virtually formed the foundation for the political and social organization of Islamic society; later orders became active throughout the Muslim world.

The Sufis, who regarded the fight against their own weaknesses and bad tendencies as the supreme *jihad*, also took part in the *jihad* wars; they were entangled in countless military and revolutionary enterprises. For example, the order of the Bektashis was responsible for the spiritual care of the janissaries, Turkic élite units composed of young Christian men selected at an early age. Some Sufis 'collaborated' even with unjust regimes without many inhibitions, but others, from sub-Saharan Africa to Central Asia and India, were active revolutionaries against tyrannical regimes (though also in the fanatical messianic revolts of so many self-appointed mahdis).

Whatever remarkable forms Sufism may sometimes have assumed and however much it was criticized even by Muslims, the Sufis were unsurpassed in loyalty to their Prophet. From the fifteenth century, a type of veneration of the Prophet developed in Sufism which one may rightly call Muhammad mysticism.[70] This meant a tremendous striving to experience the appearance of the Prophet in dreams and efforts to have occult, visionary and auditory experiences while awake. Litanies in which (as in Catholic litanies to the 'name of Jesus' or 'heart of Jesus') the thought of God was transferred to the invocation of the Prophet became particularly popular: 'O God, bless the Prophet' and other blessings for Muhammad were repeated incessantly, in assemblies which, in some circumstances, could last all night and were therefore called 'vigils' (*mahya*).[71]

From the eighteenth century, real Muhammad mystics appeared, who concentrated wholly on expecting a mystic togetherness with the Prophet and perhaps communicating it: they and their followers regarded the miracles which they could perform as miracles of the Prophet. Above all in Arabic-speaking lands from Arabia through the Sudan to West Africa, orders were founded whose main aim was to attain such a presence of the Prophet. The positive achievements of Muhammad mysticism should certainly not be overlooked.

No progress for women

From the beginning—regardless of all doctrinal differences—there was an unmistakable structural difference between Islamic and Christian orders. In theory, there is neither monastery nor monasticism in Islam; like the Prophet, Islam attaches no importance to the ideal of celibacy. With few exceptions[72] the Sufis, too, were not celibate monks but married men and fathers with large families who engaged in a great variety of professions;[73] therefore Sufism was particularly attractive to the often-despised craftsman. When applied to Sufi centres, Christian designations such as 'monastery' or 'convent' can easily give a wrong impression. The first Sufi cells were family undertakings. Only from the twelfth and thirteenth centuries onwards was the frontier to brotherhood and order crossed, and the link to the founding cell and headquarters very often remained.

I cannot conceal the fact that, even in Sufism, women did not attain equal rights. Although the eighth-century mystic Rabi'ah was by no means the only female representative of mysticism, and at that time many women chose the mystical path, it is striking that there were no women's orders. In the time of the Sufi mass movement, however, there were centres which were reserved for women and could be led by a woman as sheikh (*shaykha*). Although Islam has no compulsory celibacy, which devalues women, it is clear that both in society and in religious orders women are second-class: female Sufis had to lead their own religious lives or join one of the existing male orders—albeit with a clearly inferior status. Even as mystical pupils and disciples they had to maintain a certain distance from men: this was achieved by veils and curtains which divided the sexes. The 'gazing' of men 'on beardless youths', also condemned by some Sufi masters, is often justified as looking at the divine beauty in human form; in the literature there is a distinction between 'Platonic' love, which was allowed, and sexual love, which was not.

The family status of the Sufis meant that the Islamic orders often show a genealogical structure—which was impossible in the Christian orders. This had both an economic and financial and a religious and spiritual effect. Some Sufi masters owned their 'convents', had already become rich and administered great estates and (tax-free) foundations; sometimes they owned whole villages and tracts of land. Descent through the family also had a religious effect: personal spiritual authority and knowledge went from the Sufi master, indeed from the Prophet himself, through the descendants, who in this way shared in the holiness and blessing (*barakah*) of their saint.

However, in those centuries the ruling class in Islamic countries was no longer Arab but Turkic: peoples who had advanced from central Asia to north-west India, Iraq, Iran, Syria and present-day Turkey. They had been converted to Sunni Islam from Iran when still in their central Asian homeland. They attempted to establish rigorous Sunni norms and made use of the Sufi institutions to do so, both for internal social control and for warding off enemies. Thus Sufism came under the influence of a nomadic tribal religion which contained many ecstatic and shamanistic elements.

In the thirteenth century, many Sufis rose to be the most respected leaders of the people, in place of the school jurists. They made skilful use of the Mongol attacks to take the top places on the social ladder under the new rulers, as the 'friends of God';[74] in this period Ulama belonged to the brotherhoods and, with the Sufis in the leading social role, the Ulama–Sufi paradigm of Islam was solidly established.

Shadow sides of Sufism

Every system has its disadvantages and even in Sufism abuses could not be avoided. The development of Sufism from an elitist religion to a mass religion understandably led to a levelling which seems markedly to have diluted the high ideals of the classical period. From the twelfth and thirteenth centuries the shadow sides of Sufism seem to have increased, a development to which again there are countless parallels in the Christian Middle Ages:

– Now, visionary, auditory and occult experiences (often produced by 'mechanical' means) were treasured ever more highly, whereas in classical mysticism they had been forced to the periphery or excluded, though in principle they had been justified by al-Ghazali (as the 'lesser tradition' of mysticism, which confirms the 'greater tradition' of religion).[75]

– Many sheikhs and their successors were deified, if not divinized, in poetry, religious propaganda and popular belief ('the sheikh losing his being' and 'the sheikh losing his being in the Prophet'). Sheikhs often lived the life of feudal rulers rather than the life of the 'poor' (the office was often hereditary and became a 'family possession').

– The tomb of the sheikh or founder, often in his own convent and richly adorned, became a place of pilgrimage (it was frequently on the site of a pre-Islamic sanctuary) where masses of pilgrims awaited a spiritual and material blessing (*barakah*), often in a magical way.

– Everywhere there developed a veneration of the saints, which hallowed the Sufi as a 'friend of God' who was able to do much by his intercession that was unattainable by the suppliants themselves; the cult at the tomb of the saint became the main vehicle of Sufi Islam.

– There was also abundant belief in miracles: countless miracle stories attached themselves both to the living sheikh and to the tomb and there were often public demonstrations of thaumaturgical capacities (skills with poisonous snakes and knives and similar miraculous actions).

Ira M. Lapidus is thus right in saying: 'From the thirteenth to the end of the eighteenth century, the veneration of shrines and holy places became the most widespread form of Islamic religious life. The Sufis and shrines provided ritual and spiritual counsel, medical cures, and mediation between different groups and strata of the population. Sufis helped to integrate corporate bodies such as guilds and to form political organizations among diverse lineage groups.'[76] They were responsible not only for settling disputes, selecting the clan chief, celebrating feasts and organizing long-distance trade but also for circumcision, marriage and burial. They taught children and healed the sick, distributed amulets, practised white magic and functioned as mediators between the human world of human beings and the world of spirits and the divine. This was a dilution of the religious substance of Islam and a change of focus that inevitably provoked criticism.

Criticism of Sufism is as old as Sufism itself. From the beginning, a distinction was made between true and false Sufis. It is relatively easy to pretend to mystical experiences and knowledge. However, it would not have occurred to anyone in the Middle Ages, Muslim or Christian, to label all mystical experiences abnormal, simulated, projected, pathological phenomena so as to be able to dismiss even authentic mystical experience as pseudo-mysticism. Can authentic mystical experiences really be denied like that? In contrast to the often sterile legalistic learning of the jurists and a rational ossified 'scholastic' theology Sufism, quite rightly, expressed certain neglected aspects of Islam.

However, even its admirers[77] cannot deny that, despite all these legitimate concerns, Sufism often fell into an aggressive anti-intellectualism and irrationalism. Not only did mystics and poets mock the founders of great law schools, such as Abu Hanifah and Shafi'i, and vigorously attack the philosophers in particular, even Ibn Sina (Avicenna), who was himself also a mystic, in their predilection for immediate knowledge. Anyone who, like them, thought that all wisdom is comprised in the first letter of the alphabet, A (*alif*), the symbol for Allah, could easily mock the asses who burdened themselves with books—although they themselves often wrote books which were no more understandable than the theological treatises criticized in their poetry.

It is not surprising that this anti-intellectualism produced remarkable 'Sufis', such as the 'enraptured ones' who ran naked through the streets like madmen; the 'holy ones', who as illiterates allowed themselves all kinds of shamelessness; and the 'fakirs', who performed miracles as itinerant dervishes (it was not by chance that for the first Europeans who travelled to the East, 'fakir' became synonymous with cheats and tricksters). No wonder, too, that some seemed to see the essence of Sufism in the mystical dance concerts in which intoxicated 'howling dervishes' twirled round and round. No wonder, finally, that some modern Muslim mystics no longer want to be called 'Sufi', because of all the deviations.

Criticism of the Sufi veneration of saints, cult of tombs, musical events, divinization of sheikhs and self-divinization was already expressed in medieval Islam, beginning with the early Hanbalite law school in the tenth century. This school was known for its loyalty to the sayings of the Prophet and sought to prevent a departure from the original witnesses to the faith by the use of reason. Criticism of the excesses of Sufism also came from reform efforts in Egypt and Morocco and from the fourteenth-century Syrian Hanbalite dogmatic theologian Ibn Taymiyyah, until the eighteenth- and nineteenth-century Wahhabi movement in Arabia abolished Sufism and the Saudi-Arabian monarchy offered its own ideological basis. Everywhere conservatives called for a return to the original Islam, but often in vain. Since mystical leaders and 'saints' quite often played a pernicious role in politics, it is not surprising that, in 1925, Kemal Atatürk banned the politically and religiously reactionary order of dervishes from his modern Turkey. Muhammad Iqbal, the spiritual father of Pakistan, who was orientated towards mysticism, regarded 'pirism' (from the Persian *pir* = sheikh) as one of the most dangerous developments of Islam and Annemarie Schimmel, the expert on Islam, could not avoid coming to the conclusion that: 'The mystical fraternities that grew out of a need for spiritualizing Islam became, in the course of time, the very cause contributing to the stagnation of the Islamic religion.'[78] Many critical intellectuals and politicians of the twentieth century would therefore see the mystical orders and their practices as smacking of popular religion and an outdated tradition which needed to be shaken off.

A religion of the heart instead of a religion of reason?

Critics of Sufism should not overlook the fact that Sufism still speaks to many Muslims. By attaching themselves to a sheikh, they experience something like 'pastoral' care. However, the objections of believing Muslims must not be concealed. For Sufic Islam, as for the Islam of the law, critical questions arise which had been raised very much earlier, some of which are still topical today: questions from the past as questions for the future:

Questions: Sufism

- In many respects Sufism met the religious needs of the broad population; instead of just proclaiming 'doctrine', it allowed the expression of religious feelings in meditation, song, music, dance and festivals, and in an often enthusiastic veneration of the Prophet Muhammad. But many Muslims ask: isn't there a danger that the veneration of the one God will be overshadowed by a heightened veneration of the Prophet (like a heightened worship of Christ in Christianity)?
- Sufism increasingly attached importance to the veneration of saints, belief in miracles, the cult of tombs and the divinization of sheikhs, and could also point to a large number of charitable and social achievements. But many Muslims also ask: can't the considerable shifts in emphasis which medieval piety brought about in Islam (as in Christianity) lead people away from the original centre of the religion, despite all the veneration of the Prophet?
- Sufism addressed not just the reason but also the heart, the 'eye of the heart', intuitive holistic knowledge, the emotions, the imagination, the disposition, experience and spontaneous, instinctive faith, though some Muslims criticize this as anti-intellectualism. They think that a prophetic religion which is meant to be preserved, taught, considered and understood should always depend on scholarly knowledge and methodical rational thought if it is not to lose itself in irrationalism, obscurantism, superstition and a desire for miracles.

One Islamic theologian attempted to bring reason and the heart into harmony, and did not simply try to combine Shariah Islam and Sufi Islam organically, but sought to formulate theologically the normative form of Sunni Islam. To bring theological depth to my analysis of the medieval paradigm (P IV) I shall now describe him at some length.

5. Normative theology

The 'Abbasid paradigm of Islam as a world religion which was now beginning to dissolve gave Islam an even greater inner pluralism. There was a broad spectrum, from the piety of the Qur'an and hadith that was faithful to the letter, through all possible forms of philosophical and theological rationalism, to complete scepticism. The Islamic world was in a political and spiritual turmoil. Muhammad al-Ghazali (died 1111), one of the many theologians who were thrown into the whirlpool of the eleventh century, spoke of 'a confusion of the directions of the schools (*firaq*, singular: *firqah*) which have split into paths and ways'. He said that the 'diversity of men in religions and creeds' (*milal*, singular *millah*) and 'the multiplicity of sects and the divergency of methods' were 'a deep sea in which most men founder' and from which 'only a few' were saved.[79] Did he exaggerate? The 'sea of uncertainty' is undoubtedly a literary theme which had already been conjured up in very similar words by the great ninth-century mystic Muhasibi.[80] However, there is no question that existential experiences also underlie such themes.

I do not need to describe all these directions of faith and schools for my paradigm analysis: historians of theology have attempted to do this as far as the present state of scholarship allows.[81] I shall simply bring out what finally established itself in the Ulama-Sufi paradigm and has remained normative to the present day.

The long way of theology

Law is, and remains, the central discipline in higher Islamic education. However, legal science would have been incapable by itself of achieving an organic synthesis with the increasingly powerful movement that Sufism now represented. To achieve such a synthesis it needed theology, which had come a long way in a relatively short time.

In the first decades of the conquest (P I) there was no Islamic theology—to compare, for example, with the great theological schemes of the apostle Paul. At best there were the beginnings of local theologies. Only under the Umayyads (P II) had greater theological disputes come about over a core problem posed by the Qur'an itself: how God's omnipotence and inner-worldly causality, God's omnipotent predestination and human free self-determination, could be combined. Thus at this time explicit theologies were first worked out; however, these were very different from one another and raised no claims to be universally binding ('orthodoxy').

Only with the shift of the theological centre of gravity to the East, under the 'Abbasids, did a new paradigm of theology (P III) form, for which the decisive factor was no longer the opposition of cities or 'sects' but an opposition of methods: traditional science (the *muhaddithun*, the hadith scholars) and rational theology (the *kalam* of the *mutukallimun*). This was speculative dogmatics and apologetics (and thus only partially identical with the Christian concept of 'theology', which also embraces exegesis, history, ethics, pastoral care and law). The substantive problem in Islamic theology shifted increasingly from 'God's predetermination versus human self-determination' to 'God's revelation versus human reason'. As later happened in Christian scholasticism, a distinction was made between two levels of knowledge of God: what human beings can know of themselves and what they know through God's revelation. This led to a formulation of proofs of God and a well-thought-out doctrine of God's properties.

It was al-Ash'ari (who died in Baghdad in 945, ten years before the 'Abbasid empire lost power), a convert from the Mu'tazilah to the traditionists, who formulated the synthesis of theology which largely applied in this third paradigm—just as Shafi'i had done for Islamic law a century earlier. His was a rational form of Sunni theology which, nevertheless, was powerfully opposed by the traditionist majorities in many law schools.[82] Al-Ash'ari represented the theology of those who preserved the tradition but he defended it with the 'modern' speculative method of that time: rational argument, the *kalam*, was completely at the service of orthodox teaching, the Sunnah.

Al-Ash'ari's synthesis convinced many people in traditionalist orthodoxy but could not prevent the Ash'arite school in the tenth and eleventh centuries, which had settled between the rational Mu'tazilah and the literalistic Hanbalites, from moving to a more philosophical form of theology. Whereas the influence of philosophy as a whole declined, philosophical methods and arguments became increasingly at home in theology and led to ever greater purely philosophical reflection. What al-Ash'ari himself employed apologetically (in controversy with Jewish, Christian, Manichaean and heretical Islamic positions) came to be taken for granted as an element of theological method.

In the eleventh century, there was a restoration of traditionalism (with a Hanbalite or Shafi'ite stamp), centred in Baghdad. Usually supported by the caliph, people wanted the Shariah to apply without compromise in public life and—with the help of guardians of virtue—were not afraid of supervising public morality.[83] Opposition to the Mu'tazilite and Ash'arite theologians, and above all the Shiites and the Jewish and Christian merchants associated with them, often involved bloody controversies (*fitan*, singular *fitnah*) in which youths with long hair, breastplates and weapons played very active roles. However, at first theologians took little note of this.

The theologian 'Abd al-Malik al-Juwayni (died 1085), working in Nishapur (in north-east Iran), which was then an important spiritual centre, strove to achieve a systematic form for the literary presentation of his theology and to strengthen the rational argumentation of Aristotelian syllogisms, so as to derive his conclusions from universal principles and logical presuppositions without abandoning the old juristic logic and atomistic natural philosophy.[84] However, at the end of his life, al-Juwayni leaned towards traditionalism and, as people mockingly remarked, returned to 'old women's beliefs'.[85] Ash'arite theology in this rational form was unsuitable for integrating the Sufi movement and its emphasis on experience, which was becoming increasingly strong. Who would be up to this great task?

A synthesis of Shariah Islam and Sufi Islam: al-Ghazali

Muhammad al-Ghazali (1058–1111), a pupil of the Ash'arite al-Juwayni, was the theologian who, because of his personal history and indefatigable work as a legal scholar, was capable of combining the Islam of the law (dominated by the Ulama) and the mystical Islam (supported by the Sufi communities). He was given the honorific name 'the argument of Islam' (*hujjat al-Islam*). Western scholarship has perhaps isolated him far too much from his predecessors and contemporary theologians and overestimated him as a metaphysician and a mystic,[86] but one falls from uncritical admiration to the other extreme if today one attempts to dismiss this undoubtedly unusual personality as a man of the establishment and an inconsistent popularizer and then even denies him subjective honesty.[87] Possibly 'in composing his writings he is going by the intellectual capacity of the people whom he is addressing'[88]and moreover writing from very different existential situations.

Undoubtedly there were numerous respectable Sufis before al-Ghazali—and numerous less respectable ones after him. He experienced much opposition, above all from self-interested Hanafites; in later periods his theological works were not quoted as much as his legal works. However, that is no reason for ignoring al-Ghazali's extraordinarily comprehensive juristic and theological *oeuvre* (of the four hundred works attributed to him seventy are still in existence, and the authenticity of the most important of them is certain). He succeeded in integrating a complete concept of Sufi practice into his theology. He was as much at home in the madrasah, the college of jurisprudence, as in the khanaqah, the centre of Sufic activities. To the end of his life he remained a theologian and jurist and his example was a major factor in leading many Ulama later to join the Sufi movement.

Al-Ghazali never had the supreme authority in matters of Sunni orthodoxy that has sometimes been attributed to him but he was indisputably one of the most acknowledged and influential scholars in the history of Islamic thought. Through his first exemplary synthesis of traditional theology and Sufism he created, for the Ulama–Sufi paradigm of the post-classical period (P IV), a theology that finally became widely normative for the Sunni majority. His role in Islam is comparable to that played a good century later in Catholic theology by Thomas Aquinas, whose singularity, likewise, must not be isolated and whose authority must not be exaggerated. Like Thomas, al-Ghazali became the *doctor communis*, the 'universal doctor' (though he was recognized only long after his death), who, as Mahmoud Zakzouk, professor of philosophy at the al-Azhar university in Cairo and Egypt's minister of religion in the first years of the twenty-first century, remarks, 'still exercises a marked influence on the spiritual development in the Islamic world'.[89] Because al-Ghazali is a paradigmatic theologian, representative of the Ulama–Sufi paradigm like no one before him or since, I shall devote a relatively long section to him, culminating in a comparison with a paradigmatic theologian from the Christian Middle Ages, Thomas Aquinas.

How did al-Ghazali arrive at his synthesis? This is interesting for us not only because so many books have been and will be written about him and because he himself wrote so many books but also because he wrote a very personal account of his career and standpoint in a famous book: *Deliverance from Error* (*al-Munqidh min ad-dalal*). This work, for all its biographical information, does not give us an autobiography in a precise chronological order. It is a systematized and stylized invitation to all those with a mind to seek the truth[90] and thus also the author's skilful '*Apologia pro vita sua*—Justification of his own life.' This becomes particularly clear in the last of the four chapters.[91] It has often been compared with Augustine's *Confessions*, though a better comparison would be with Descartes' *Discourse on Method* ('in order to guide the mind well and to seek the truth in the sciences').[92]

Where does fundamental certainty come from? A forerunner of Descartes?

In 1055, the Turkic Seljuk dynasty, who saw themselves as champions of Sunni Islam, overthrew the rule of the Shiite Buwayhids over Iraq.[93] Muhammad al-Ghazali was born in Tus (Khorasan) in 1058 and thus under Seljuk military rule. After the early death of his father, who was presumably a yarn seller (*ghazzal*, spinner[94]), and together with his brother Ahmad, who was later to become a famous legal scholar and mystic, he was accepted into a madrasah there and received teaching, free board and lodging. However, very early the brilliant and gifted young man realized the questionability of the naive belief in authority (*taqlid*, blind 'imitation') which simply took over and 'imitated' the dogmas and external forms of religion. It struck him that the children of Christians, Jews and Muslims simply took over the religion of their parents. Independent thought (*ijtihad*) was not called for, far less independent research. This left the growing young theologian dissatisfied.

At the age of twenty, al-Ghazali arrived in Nishapur. This was one of the training centres for theologians founded by the most important Seljuk Grand Vizier, Nizam al-Mulk (and therefore called Nizamiyah madrasah) to establish his policy aimed at the unity of the empire and the renewal of Sunni Islam—

with the help of high schools that he founded in various cities of the empire and the support of rational Ash'arite theology. He had to work against the most vigorous opposition from the traditionist Hanbalites, who thought the mediating Ash'arites as dangerous as the rational Mu'tazilites. In the Nizamiyah high school al-Ghazali studied jurisprudence and Ash'arite theology. Once he had broken what he calls the 'fetters of servile conformism' in his early youth, his whole effort was 'to seek knowledge of the true meaning of things', 'that certain knowledge in which the thing known is made so manifest that no doubt clings to it'.[95]

A modern Western reader, reading this way of raising the problem, may well be reminded of René Descartes, the first modern European philosopher, who wanted to expose himself to doubt, not in order to attain the sphere of despair but to achieve a certainty free of doubt.[96] Therefore it has sometimes been conjectured that Descartes knew al-Ghazali's book *al-Munqidh*.[97] Some of his works, above all his critiques of philosophy, had been translated into Hebrew and Latin long before Descartes's time. Descartes was a friend of the famous orientalist Jakobus Golius (died 1667) of Leiden, who brought back numerous Arabic manuscripts from his travels to Morocco, the Near East and Persia. His pupil Levinius Warner, later Dutch ambassador to Istanbul, left a copy of *Munqidh* to another Leiden university library. In Descartes's time, another copy of this book was owned by Giulio Mazarin, who possibly got it from the famous Paulan father Marin Mersenne, a friend of Descartes. Indeed, in the German edition of his book 'Al-Ghazali's philosophy in comparison with Descartes', Mahmoud Zakzouk[98] cites a report by the Tunisian historian Osman al-Kaak (Algiers 1976) that he has seen a fourteenth-century Latin translation of the *Munqidh* in which the passage stating that doubt is the first step to certainty has been underlined by Descartes himself.

So far no one has found this copy. In any case, correspondence in substance is more important than the question of historical dependence—which will perhaps never be finally decided—and there is universal doubt about this, at least in respect of the approach of the two thinkers. Al-Ghazali confesses that in his quest for a truth and certainty that are beyond doubt he fell into complete scepticism and agnosticism. Thus, six centuries before Descartes, a Muslim thinker states (though he could have learned this from ancient sceptics) that one can doubt almost everything, particularly material things: 'This protracted effort to induce doubt finally brought me to the point where my soul would not allow me to admit safety from error even in the case of my sense-data.'[99]

If 'reliance on sense-data has become untenable', then is 'trust in what is given by reason'[100] unjustified? Indeed, for 'there may be, beyond the perception of reason, another judge. And if the latter revealed itself, it would give the lie to the judgements of reason, just as the reason-judge revealed itself and gave the lie to the judgements of sense.'[101] Descartes later wrote of the possibility of a deceiving 'evil spirit' (*genius malignus*),[102] which makes everything appear as 'the deceptive play of dreams'. Moreover, al-Ghazali already sees a confirmation of his doubt in a dream: 'Don't you see that when you are asleep you believe certain things and imagine certain circumstances and believe they are fixed and lasting and entertain no doubts about that being their status? Then you wake up and know that all your imaginings and beliefs were groundless and the unsubstantial thing that you believed in your waking state through the senses or through reason is true in relation to the state in which you find yourself?'[103] In short, reason likewise cannot be relied on; 'the intellectual truths which are first principles',[104] in other words the principles of reason, cannot be demonstrated. This basic problem cannot be resolved with rational arguments once the value of the reason which argues is put in question: 'the knowledge of first principles requires a proof; and as this has not been given, it is impossible to give a proof'.[105]

The consequence for al-Ghazali was an intellectual crisis: for two months he was struck down by the 'malady' of scepticism and found himself 'a sceptic in fact'. How was he healed from this 'malady' and how did he find a state of health and balance? How did 'the self-evident data of reason' become acceptable once again, so that they could be 'relied on with safety and certainty'? Al-Ghazali's answer is clear: 'That was not achieved by constructing a proof or putting together an argument. On the contrary, it was the effect of a light which God Most High cast into my breast. And that light is the key to most knowledge.'[106]

But how is this 'light' that overcomes philosophical doubt and creates certainty and security to be understood? If it is not the return to the unilluminated belief in authority (*taqlid*), nor a rational proof and certainly not an irrational decision, then isn't it at least—as some interpreters have said—naive[107] or thought-out[108] evidence of these rational principles? If they had compellingly imposed their evidence, whether a priori or a posteriori, al-Ghazali would hardly have had to toil over a solution for months. Or, rather than a deduction, is this an 'intuition' of first principles?[109] But—the question still arises—why did a man of al-Ghazali's stature have to struggle so long to gain such knowledge immediate to himself? And why did he attribute it not to himself but to a light given by God? Mahmoud Zakzouk, whose differentiated comparison with Descartes produces some very remarkable parallels, explains this 'intuition' by saying that 'in an act ... reason at the same time recognizes God (who sends it the light) and sees itself grounded in him'.[110] He sees the similarity between al-Ghazali and Descartes in the fact that 'at the centre of the two solutions is the knowledge of God attained through intuition'.[111]

This, in particular, seems to me to be questionable. For however much both regard the idea of God as innate and attach high importance to intuitive knowledge, Descartes does not introduce the knowledge of God to solve the problem of fundamental certainty.[112] I also ask myself whether, for al-Ghazali, it is really true that 'self-knowledge and knowledge of God are achieved in a single act'.[113] Here the fundamental difference between him and Descartes is clear: knowledge of God is introduced by Descartes into the argument only much later. Descartes grounds the primary certainty in the human subject, with his famous '*Cogito*' ('I think') that can be experienced in all doubt and which seems to him to justify an '*ergo sum*' ('therefore I am') as a spontaneous insight. Since Kant, he has been accused of arguing wrongly from thought to the substantial truth of an 'I'.

For his part, al-Ghazali spoke from the beginning of a 'trust' in reason—initially defective, but ultimately necessary. Yet he was convinced that human beings cannot arrive at such a trust without God and the gift of God's inner light.[114]

Which way of life: theology, philosophy, esotericism?

Still unmarried and independent, in 1091, at the age of thirty-four, al-Ghazali was called to the Nizamiyah high school in Baghdad, to probably the most important chair in the Sunni Islamic world of the time. The call came from the Grand Vizier Nizam al-Mulk (also from Tus), a powerful figure, more than seventy years old. It was at this court that al-Ghazali had probably lived for six years after the death of his teacher and got to know its confusing multiplicity of opinions. Clad in gold and silk and mounted on a costly horse, he made an imposing entry, soon afterwards to supervise three hundred students and perform public functions. What he presents to us in a perfect systematic and didactic form in his *Deliverance from Error* is doubtless not so much the four stages of his biographical development, to be distinguished with chronological precision, as the four fundamental spiritual positions to which he reduced the countless trends of faith and schools. It is almost impossible to establish clearly what theological view he had advocated before he studied theology and took the way to Sufism. Before al-Ghazali, the Persian mathematician 'Umar Khayyam, who was unknown to him, had distinguished four quite similar classes in a philosophical treatise.[115] What were the four great positions, movements, groupings of the time, between which the thoughtful Muslim had to decide? The jurist and theologian, who was also a skilled educator, teacher and orator, showed his contemporaries a way through the spiritual confusion.

The first group was formed of the Islamic scholastics (the *mutakallimun* with an Ash'arite tendency), the people of insight and speculative thought. However, the goal of their speculative dogmatics (*kalam*)—the preservation of the substance of faith revealed in the Qur'an and Sunnah and its defence against heretical innovations—did not seem adequate to al-Ghazali. These dogmaticians based too much of their work on the premises of their opponents; they accepted as a matter of course, in blind imitation (*taqlid*), the consensus (*ijma'*) of the community or the unthinking acceptance of Qur'an and Sunnah. They contented themselves with pointing out contradictions and false conclusions in their opponents' positions and did not meet the demands of Aristotelian logic. And once they moved from mere apologetic to the quest for the inner truth of things, they lost themselves in endless discussions over substance and accidents, nature and properties, without penetrating through the darkness of errors to the truth. Such speculative dogmatism could not provide rational justification for their own assumptions and presuppositions, so al-Ghazali turned, in his systematic exposition, to philosophy.

The second group was made up of the philosophers, the men of logic and proofs. Al-Ghazali was by no means a fundamental enemy of all philosophy. On the contrary, he accepted it completely. For several years he studied the sciences of the Greek philosophers (mathematics, logic, physics and metaphysics, politics and ethics) and was particularly attracted by Aristotelian logic, since it was far superior to traditional juristic logic because of its use of the syllogism (a logical conclusion drawn from two premises). In his treatise on 'The Goals of the Philosophers' (*al-maqasid al-falasifah*) he presents the ideas of Avicenna and his pupils with amazing objectivity, showing that he has a profound knowledge of philosophy.

Just as some people thought that al-Ghazali had gone over to philosophy, he published his differentiated 'Refutation of the Philosophers' (*tahafut al-falasifah*). He remained true to argument based on syllogistic logic and still took neo-Platonic philosophy seriously but his criticism now focused on those philosophical doctrines that clearly contradicted the religious teachings of Islam. He acutely analysed twenty problematical philosophical maxims and refuted the doctrines of the eternity of the world, time and movement, and also of the impossibility of a proof of God from creation and of God having no properties and being incapable of knowing individual things (instead of universals). Finally, he analysed the doctrines of the impossibility of the bodily resurrection and the material existence of hell and paradise. Al-Ghazali held seventeen of these maxims to be heretical and three even to be 'unbelief'; anyone who advocated them put himself outside Muslim society.

Al-Ghazali's sharp and brave controversy with philosophy had a double effect: those philosophical disciplines (in particular Aristotelian logic, about which he wrote two treatises) and all the neo-Platonic doctrines which were neutral to the Islamic revelation could now be broadly accepted into theology, so that from then on it had a philosophical stamp.[116] However, al-Ghazali's criticism led to a decisive weakening of the concerns of pure philosophy.

The third group was the movement of the revolutionary Shiites (Batinites, Ismailites), mostly supporters and propagandists of the hostile Shiite Fatimids and their anti-caliphate in Cairo, which was now growing stronger. They claimed to be bearers of true instruction and privileged recipients of knowledge through an infallible imam: the true, esoteric knowledge of the inner meaning (*batin*) of all external symbols could be attained only through this infallible imam, the guardian of truth. At the command of the Baghdad caliphate, al-Ghazali described Shiite doctrines accurately—all too accurately for some Sunnis—and at the same time refuted them, to the best of his ability. Arguing against the extreme Shiites who held that there was need of instruction and a teacher, and that only one infallible teacher was fit for that purpose, al-Ghazali pointed first to the Prophet Muhammad as the inspired teacher and then remarked that the Prophet and religious leaders had always 'referred men to the exercise of personal judgement ... despite their knowledge that men might err': 'The Apostle of God—God's blessing and peace be upon him!—even said: "I judge by externals, but God undertakes to judge the hearts of men! This means: 'I judge according to the most probable opinion resulting from the witnesses' statements, but they may err about the matter.' Thus according to this tradition, al-Ghazali concludes, 'the prophets had no way to be safe from error in such cases involving personal judgement', even in 'dogmatic questions'.[117] Moreover he described the way in which one does away with disputes over principles of faith in his work 'The Right Measure'.

After the negative assessment in respect of scholastic theology, philosophy and Shiite belief in infallibility, there remains the fourth group: the Sufis, the elect of the divine presence, vision and illumination, who over and above the dry science of the law and élitist theological speculation press for an internalization of faith and a more intimate relationship to God.

The crisis and the turn towards mysticism

Al-Ghazali was clear that with this group, unlike the philosophers, a purely academic discussion was not enough: theory alone, all the books of Muhasibi, Junayd and Abu Yazid, were not enough for understanding the mystical way. What was needed to follow the mystics' discourses and states of experience was praxis, personal experience, 'tasting' and existential change. Although al-Ghazali never wavered in his belief in God, prophecy and the last judgement,[118] for six months he was torn as to whether or not he should begin a completely new life. In his previous activity,hadn't he been more concerned with praise and glory than with the love of God? The beloved professor, now thirty-eight years old, got into such a serious psychosomatic crisis that he had to break off his lectures because of speech problems ('my tongue would not utter a single word'[119]). The political situation in Baghdad, burdened with terror of which al-Ghazali does not speak in his apologia, had dramatically worsened. His patron, Nizam al-Mulk, was murdered in 1092 by the 'Assassins', a secret Shiite alliance based on the fortress of Alamut (in the Alburz mountains) which committed murders (hence the word 'assassin', murderer) and the sultan died two weeks later. There were disputes over the throne, a collapse of central government, increasing provincialization and causing a deep crisis for the Seleucid state. In short, there was no longer a political authority with which al-Ghazali could identify.[120]

Then, in July 1095, only ten years after his accession to office and having married, the great legal scholar made the momentous decision to give up his professorship and abandon his family, friends, chair, fame and wealth to lead the life of a Sufi instead of pursuing his career as a school theologian. It caused a sensation in Baghdad. On the pretext of making a pilgrimage to Mecca (because otherwise he would certainly have been restrained) the admired scholar fled to Damascus, wearing a coarse woollen garment. There (mostly in the solitude and poverty of a cell of the great mosque) for two years he followed the Sufi way of life—'the best of all ways of life': beyond all intellectual knowledge and externals. Faithfulness to the law was completely concentrated on 'utter absorption of the heart in the remembrance of God' (*dhikr*), on the 'total purification of the heart', and as a last goal 'being completely lost (*fana'*) in God'.[121] However, al-Ghazali did not retreat into an esoteric mysticism or a Sufism free of the law; he engaged in hard scholarly work for the believers. This was no longer a barren dogmatics far from reality and a dialectical skill at disputation which despised the laity and had never yet led to the conversion of an unbeliever but a theology for those who strove for comprehension and depth of experience.

Time and again, though, his Sufi immersion was disturbed by family news and contemporary events and problems. After a lengthy stay in Jerusalem (shut up in the Dome of the Rock), a pilgrimage to Mecca and Medina and eight years of itinerant preaching and working, at the request of his children al-Ghazali returned to a great theological work. He did not, however, return to Baghdad and the luxurious life there but to his home town of Tus in Khorasan, where as well as the madrasah he founded a Sufi khanaqah. Something that he kept quiet about in his memoirs but can be established beyond doubt from his correspondence is that in 1095 in Hebron, at the tomb of Abraham, he had made a threefold vow: not to accept money from the government, not to appear before a ruler and not to take part in public disputations, the show-fights of scholars.[122] He kept this oath until his death, but perhaps transgressed against its spirit. Pangs of conscience could be the unspoken background to the amazingly long closing chapter of the *Munqidh*, in which he describes why a decade later he has again returned to his teaching activity (albeit without great show and disputation).[123]

What made him return to this institution which, though private, played an eminent political role? Al-Ghazali's answer was, first, the manifest paralysis of the faith of the people, then the command of the sultan's vizier, a son of Nizam al-Mulk (in which he later he recognized the will of God), and finally something that he states quite openly, the Muslim conviction that at the beginning of each century a renewer (*mujaddid*) of religion will appear. After the caliph 'Umar in the first Islamic century, this renewer was the legal scholar ash-Shafi'i in the second, the theologian al-Ash'ari in the third, the qadi al-Baqillani in the fourth and now in the fifth century, confirmed in his self-confidence by many friends, himself, al-Ghazali. He encountered the almost apocalyptic anxiety of many Muslims about the Islamic year 500 (beginning on 2 September 1106 CE). A few weeks before the beginning of the sixth century he left his Sufi seclusion in Tus and went back to the Nizamiyah high school in Nishapur, only to return to Tus after barely three years, presumably for health reasons. Having indefatigably studied and published, when he felt that his end was approaching, he is reported to have completed washing himself, been handed his shroud, kissed it and put it on his eyes with the words: 'I hear and obey, for my entrance to the king.' So, on 18 December 1111, died the man whom some later were to regard as the greatest figure after the Prophet.

What would have been lost to Islam if this Sufi had not remained a jurist and a theologian to the end? Only in the second half of his rich life did he write his main work, 'The Revival of the Sciences of Religion' (*ihya' 'ulum ad-din*),[124] which for him embraced all the spheres of human life, from table manners to the secrets of the heart. It is a classical *Summa Theologiae* (the classic term used to denote a whole compendium of theology), quite comparable with the Christian *Summa* of Thomas Aquinas.

6. Theological *Summa*

To think that the apparently dead science of a religion needed 'revival' is a very pessimistic starting point for a *Summa* of religion. But that was al-Ghazali's view. In the very first of the approximately forty books of his *Summa*, entitled *'ilm* ('knowledge', 'science', from the same root as *'ulama*—singular *'alim*), al-Ghazali speaks bitterly about scholars with fossilized religion and impenetrable theology. Instead of preparing people honestly for the coming world, before

God and in trust in him, these jurists and theologians are discussing, in academic isolation, legal questions remote from life and engaging in fruitless speculation—for their own intellectual self-confirmation instead of to help the people. In the face of the collapsing political order al-Ghazali is concerned with the renewal of society from below.

However, it would be a misunderstanding to think that al-Ghazali is against jurisprudence in itself and against theology as such. Even as a Sufi he remained a jurist and a theologian but understood both in a higher sense, a new way. He thought it important that he should continue to be regarded as an acknowledged member of the Shafi'ite law school and the Ash'arite theological school. To do that, having so regularly made critical statements about their views, he did not need to identify with all of them. He distinguished three levels of assent (what someone puts forward in a scholastic disputation, what he presents as public teaching and instruction and what he believes quite privately) but this should not suggest that for al-Ghazali himself they are in contradiction, whatever modern authors may reconstruct and interpret from perhaps too great a historical distance.[125]

Two masters of theology: al-Ghazali and Thomas Aquinas

Criticism of a particular mode of jurisprudence and theology, which he does not want to give up despite all the misuse of it, forms the constant background to al-Ghazali's one great *Summa Theologiae*, which is to give people tangible help towards finding their way to God. It is about God, before whom every human act is performed directly. Presumably this Muslim theologian, at the beginning of the twelfth century, could have described his task just as a Christian theologian formulated it 150 years later: 'I am aware that I owe it to God as the very first task of my life to let him speak in all my words and senses.'[126] That is the opening of Thomas Aquinas's *Summa contra gentiles* (1259–64), against the 'pagans', by whom primarily he means those Arab philosophers whose heretical or unbelieving views al-Ghazali had contested long before him. Both could have described it as 'responsible speech before God', even if one calls it 'theology' and the other 'science of religion'.[127]

Thomas Aquinas did not know al-Ghazali's theology. In the Christian Middle Ages only the works of Islamic philosophy (including al-Ghazali's account of Arabic philosophers, but ironically without his refutation) were at all widespread. No single significant work of Islamic theology (as distinct from philosophy) appears on the lists of translated works from Toledo, Burgos or Italy.[128] Thomas learned individual arguments against Islamic theology from the Jewish philosopher of religion Moses Maimonides (for him, 'Rabbi Moses') for his *Summa contra gentiles*. However, even the theological–philosophical

Summa theologiae for Christian faith, with which he supplemented the philosophical–theological *Summa contra gentiles* from 1265 till he broke it off in 1273, lacks any deeper insight into the overall context of the *kalam*, Islamic scholasticism.[129]

It makes no sense to seek to establish some univocal agreements between the two great theological *Summas*. However, as Louis Gardet and Georges Anawati (a pupil of Massignon) say, if certain 'correspondences (*coincidences*) are taken as guidelines and are thought through each in its own context, they could be extremely illuminating'. These two advocates of a '*théologie comparée*' most usefully compare the function and methods of theology in the different Islamic and Christian eras,[130] but without going into the decisive differences in content.[131]

The possibility cannot be excluded that Thomas learned from the Arabs for his *Summa Theologiae*, at least indirectly. The American Islamic expert George Makdisi of the University of Pennsylvania, a Catholic of Lebanese origin, has become particularly interested in this problem. In his knowledgeable book he attempts to demonstrate the relations between the scholarly institutions of Islam and the West:[132] he argues that the juristic structure of the early University of Paris goes back to the Islamic foundation (*waqf*). The beginnings of scholastic method, the dialectical *sic-et-non* ('thus and not thus') method, appeared before Abelard with the famous Photius, in 855 Byzantine ambassador to Caliph al-Mutawakkil in Baghdad and later Patriarch of Constantinople. He also argues that the method of Thomas' *Summa Theologiae* has its origin in Islam. In fact the formal parallels between the *Summa* (*al-wadih fi usul al-fiqh*) of the Hanbalite theologian and strict moralist Ibn 'Aqil (in Baghdad 1040–1119), a contemporary of al-Ghazali, who was forced to recant because of his youthful leaning towards the Mu'tazilah, and Thomas are perplexing: they make Ibn 'Aqil and Thomas seem kindred spirits. There were many lines of communication between Baghdad and the West through Syria, Italy, Sicily and Spain. The hypothesis seems illuminating. However, Makdisi, who died in 2003, did not succeed in establishing direct literary traces which really prove a dependence beyond conjecture.

Parallels in life

Al-Ghazali and Thomas lived not only in two different centuries but in two different worlds. A comparison between the Muslim and the Christian 'systematicians of religion' may seem problematical to specialists on both sides, even if no attempt is being made to claim dependence. However, al-Ghazali, too, was a theologian in a European sense, despite serious objections to the scholastic theology that he long practised, and there are some illuminating parallels between al-Ghazali and Thomas which call for a structural comparison. This will be helpful for an analysis of the medieval paradigm and enable us to get a closer view of the decisive difference between Muslim and Christian theology.

There are already parallels in the biographical backgrounds of the two men:

– Both were deeply religious and at an early stage underwent an intensive spiritual training.

– Both were marked by an insatiable intellectual curiosity, a critical spirit and a power of synthesis and at the peak of their careers worked at the most important academic positions in the spiritual centres of their worlds, one at the high school in Baghdad and the other at the University of Paris (1252–9), the supreme teaching authority in Christendom.

– Both were critical of the power of theological offices and dignities: Thomas rejected the bishopric of Naples and the dignity of cardinal successfully; al-Ghazali was driven into crisis by an inner conflict and fled from office.

– Both were attracted by the simple monastic life and lived a different form of life in a different world. One, the scion of an aristocratic family with large estates, entered the mendicant order of the Dominicans against the resistance of his family. The other, an already well-established court theologian, decided to take the Sufi way of humility and poverty and at the end of his life founded a convent of his own.

– Neither man was (Thomas) or was primarily (al-Ghazali) a mystic; they were 'systematic theologians', governed not by the mystical fire but by the intellect.

– Both, great intellectual workers, experienced a physical and psychological breakdown, one as a crisis of life which inhibited his speech until he turned to Sufism, the other in the final period of his life which brought inhibitions in writing that he did not overcome before his death.

– After initial strong resistance from the traditionalist side (Augustinianism or Hanbalism) both had their works disseminated very widely. Down to the twenty-first century their work has remained the basis for study in their respective religions.

Parallels in work

There are also important parallels in the standpoints of their theology:

– What al-Ghazali uses as the title to his four-volume work is very much in keeping with the approach of Thomas Aquinas: a 'revival' of the science of religion. After numerous theological–juristic or theological–philosophical works, both offer the quintessence of their decades of reflecting on God, the world and human beings, seeking to make it as comprehensive as possible.

– Both had their predecessors, from whom they learned. For Thomas these were especially Augustine, Peter Lombard and Albert the Great; for al-Ghazali they were al-Muhasibi and Abu Talib al-Makki. Al-Ghazali simply takes over from the former an important scheme of construction and from the latter whole chapters of his 'Nourishment of the Heart' (originality is a modern Western criterion!).

– Their philosophical and theological positions are comparable. Both have to do on the one hand with a traditionalist or rationalistic theology and on the other with an 'unbelieving' philosophy of Aristotelian provenance. The Arab Aristotelian Ibn Rushd (Averroes, died 1198), who, as I shall describe later, wrote a 'Refutation of the Refutation' in response to al-Ghazali's 'Refutation of the Philosophers', inspired the Averroistic philosophy of Siger of Brabant (died before 1284), in Paris the great philosophical challenge for Thomas Aquinas.

So it is no coincidence that there are parallels in the layout and content of their main theological works:

– Just as, for al-Ghazali, previous authorities (Qur'an, Sunnah) were not sufficient, so Aquinas was not satisfied with the authority of the Bible, the church fathers, councils and popes; for both, reason had an essential function alongside scripture and tradition, that of clarification.

– For both theologians, Aristotle has an unusual authority: although in many questions of faith he is a dangerous opponent, under other aspects 'the philosopher' appears as a strong ally. However, it is not the study of Aristotle—here too both theologians could agree—but discipleship of Christ or a deeper orientation on the Qur'an which form the spiritual basis of their existence as theologians.

– Like the 'Revival of the Science of Religion', so too the *Summa Theologiae* begins with God and ends with God: human beings and all their actions are constantly seen before God, so that in both works no separation of dogmatics and ethics can be recognized. Both emphasize this strongly.

– Both works discuss human vices (often the same ones) at length: al-Ghazali devotes the whole of the third part of his *Ihya'* to 'the healing of the sicknesses of the soul' (from excessive greed for food and sexual desire through anger, hatred and falsity to avarice, greed and pride); he diagnoses these sicknesses from their roots and attempts to provide therapy through formation of the soul and character training. But both also write at length, though in different dispositions, about the human virtues: al-Ghazali in Part IV about the positive properties and states of the soul, beginning with repentance and conversion through patience and gratitude, fear and hope to the pure love of God; Thomas in Part II/2 first about the theological virtues of faith, hope and love, then about the four cardinal virtues of wisdom, righteousness, bravery and moderation and finally about prophecy, though this has a quite different value for him from the value that it has for al-Ghazali.

It is neither possible nor necessary to go into these and other parallels in detail. It is more important to set the very considerable differences against the background of these parallels and investigate which are decisive for the relationship between Islamic and Christian theology and which are not.

Differences of style, method and interest

Of course there are differences of style, though both authors write in an extraordinarily clear and logical way. Al-Ghazali, a 'prophetic intellectual',[133] intended his main work generally for educated Muslims and wrote a very personal, warm and rhetorically beautiful Arabic. Thomas, a scholastic through and through, composed his *Summa* as an introduction to theology for theological students (whose ability, as so often, he overestimated) and theological colleagues and wrote a quite impersonal, coolly objective, even monotonous medieval scholar's Latin. However, it would be foolish to conclude a difference in religion from this. A Christian theologian, too (for example Augustine), can write in a more personal, warm-hearted style, whereas Muslim theologians can write in coolly and analytically (for example, the Mu'tazilites).

More important than the differences in style are differences in method. Both great thinkers make use of Aristotelian logic and syllogisms. However, in his main work al-Ghazali constantly refuses to operate with categories from Greek philosophy (such as substance, accidents, atoms and the void), though he had previously used them, to discuss the problems which arise from them and to mix natural philosophy with statements of faith.[134] By contrast Thomas Aquinas appropriated not only Aristotelian logic but also Aristotelian physics and metaphysics and attempted to rethink the whole of the Christian revelation with the help of Aristotelian categories, principles and lines of thought; everywhere there are analyses with acute definitions of concepts and formal distinctions, with numerous divisions and subdivisions, objections and responses. But in method, too, there is no decisive difference between Islamic and Christian theology. There was a tremendous expenditure of highly-developed, and often over-complicated, scholastic technique (long before Latin scholasticism, which at that time was still lagging behind) among the Mu'tazilites and Ash'arites (who are therefore criticized by al-Ghazali). On the other hand, in the Christian Middle Ages there was also a more existential Christian theology sceptical of or even hostile towards scholasticism (one might think of Bernard of Clairvaux's Commentary on the Song of Songs and his battle against Abelard).

Beyond the differences of style and method in the two great compendia there is a difference of interest, which is not purely academic. Al-Ghazali, the theologian jurist, is above all interested in advancing the reconciliation of the Muslim faith with Sufism, though not necessarily at the expense of the Shariah as this had developed since the classical period (P III). On the contrary, everything is to lead to a more precise and understanding observance of it. An overall concept of Sufi practice, in accord with Sunniism and with Sunni insights, was to arise which illuminated every detail of the Shariah for the individual Muslim. In his great theological–juristic–Sufi synthesis, al-Ghazali wants to help the average Muslim to a truly Muslim way and view of life: instead of an opposition between the Shariah and Sufi piety he sees the Shariah as the foundation of authentic mystical life and the mystical ascent as a supplement to and perfecting of the Shariah.

Thomas Aquinas, the theologian–philosopher, is above all interested in providing the basis for a reconciliation of the Christian faith with philosophy. However, this is by no means at the expense of dogma as it was worked out by Hellenistic theology (Christian P II) and Augustine (Christian P III). Rather, the rational responsibility and comprehensibility of church dogma are to be brought out clearly and convincingly. Thomas is less focused on the individual believer than al-Ghazali and more on theology, the university and the church as an institution. On the basis of his theological, philosophical and ecclesiastical synthesis, which interprets biblical Christian talk of God and human beings in a contemporary way with concepts of Greek Aristotelian philosophy, Thomas wanted, first, to help theologians and churchmen towards a practice of faith which was responsible to reason (*rationabile obsequium*) and thus to do the church a service. Instead of a 'double truth' of philosophy and theology, philosophy is the 'handmaid' (*ancilla*) of theology.

This difference of interest, too, is not exclusive. Both scholars have a pedagogical scholarly aim and combine a theological pastoral intention with strict methodology, logical order and didactic skill. Both want to survey the whole of 'sacred teaching' and, despite all the rational arguments, constantly presuppose Qur'anic or biblical faith. Just as the Muslim theologian–jurist uninhibitedly uses particular philosophical elements and arguments but avoids a purely allegorical interpretation of the faith (in the manner of the Ash'arites against the 'anthropomorphic' theology of the popular Hanbalites), so the Christian theologian philosopher takes juristic insights as far as possible and very carefully formulates the legal consequences of his theology for the church and individuals. Their different scholarly interests by no means require them to belong to different religions. So, what are the decisive differences?

Different overall structures

When we survey the whole of the two giant works the difference of overall structure stands out. Al-Ghazali keeps to a principle of form with a Sufic orientation which progresses by stages. The life of the Muslim is described, beginning with the confession of faith and ending with entry into paradise, without any cosmic drama of redemption: freed from false ties and avoiding all dangers, human beings are to progress from 'stage' to 'stage' towards the goal of eternal bliss.

Possibly this ascent is already indicated in the strictly schematic division of the work: four parts, each of ten chapters, that is, forty 'stages' in all, by which according to the mystical view human beings can rise to God. Part I lists human obligations towards God: the confession of faith and the other four pillars of Islam, thoughts of God and recitation of the Qur'an. Part II lists the obligations of human beings towards their fellows: behaviour when eating, acquisitions, friendship, marriage and travelling. Parts III and IV contain the doctrine of vices and virtues, culminating in the confession of God's unity and unconditional trust in God. All this is crowned, in the last books, with a more mystical colouring about the way of true love with a closing chapter on death and the beyond.

Although Thomas is Aristotelian in his method of working, he applies a cyclical principle of form derived from neo-Platonism: a scheme of going out and returning. Part I deals with God as origin and the going forth of creatures from God, their creation and their original sin. Part II describes the movement of the rational creation towards God as its goal. This scheme of departure and return is to be imagined primarily in spatial terms: Thomas does not orientate himself on historical epochs as do Augustine and Joachim of Fiore, inspired by the Bible, though this is not of course to be found in al-Ghazali either. Rather, he thinks primarily in stages of being and cause. This is particularly evident in his interpretation of the Christ who descends from heaven and returns to heaven. Here we come to the decisive difference between the two theological *Summas*, which makes it clear where, despite all the parallels and convergences, the theologian–lawyer and the theologian–philosopher differ fundamentally in their religious allegiance.

The abiding fundamental difference

This is not just a question of detail but the central question, which leads directly to the central message, to the essence of Islam and the essence of Christianity (see B II). It is not a random point of doctrine but the 'core' from which the totality receives its driving force and its emanating light. That is already evident, in purely external terms, in the system of the two *Summas*, if we look at the 'core' which determines each of them, in other words if we look, not at their identical coming forth from God and their return to God, which doubtless express what Islam and Christianity (and Judaism) have in common, but at their centre, which expresses what is peculiar to each religion.

– Al-Ghazali put the core of his theology precisely in the middle of his work, in chapter 20 of the forty chapters, at the end of the first two parts. The Prophet Muhammad (no surprise here!), his character, his moral qualities, his personality as revealed in the Qur'an as a gift of God is recommended for the imitation of believers: Muhammad, the 'seal of the prophets', who stands with the one God in the Islamic confession of faith.

– Thomas, however, has his whole theology after the two major parts about the coming forth and return of all things culminate in Part III, which is devoted to the one who guarantees this return, the Christ as the way to God (and this is a significant structural innovation): 'On Christ who as man is the way (*via*) for us to strive for God.'[135]

Is Muhammad the example in the one case and Christ in the other? One might think that this difference was important but not decisive. Isn't Muhammad as the prophet (born after Christ) the model for the Muslim way of life of Muslims and Jesus as the Messiah, the Christ (so also designated in the Qur'an, though not in the biblical Christian understanding of these terms), the model for the Christian way of life? Such a view is superficial because the prophetology of al-Ghazali and the christology of Thomas are essentially different.

– Al-Ghazali emphasizes the mediator of the Qur'an as a figure of light beyond compare and illustrates all his virtues with numerous words and actions, so that the Prophet could appear as the 'way' to God. However, he does not leave the slightest doubt that this Prophet is only a man.

– By contrast, Thomas Aquinas attaches much importance to the fact that precisely as a human being Jesus is the way to God, and also discusses his teachings, life and suffering more than later dogmatic theologians. However, at the same time he takes every conceivable trouble to prove, and then to spell out, that this Christ is not only man but Son of God (understood ontologically) and therefore God–man.

It is precisely at this point that al-Ghazali would contradict Thomas Aquinas most energetically. Today, no one would expect that Thomas's fifty-nine long christological *quaestiones* with all their *articuli* would cause al-Ghazali to yield intellectually and to believe in the one divine person in two natures. The sixteen highly differentiated *quaestiones* on the distinction between the persons in the one divine nature (following the twenty-seven *quaestiones* about the one nature of God) would seem to al-Ghazali to be not only superfluous but a blasphemous questioning of the unity of God. All that Thomas has set forth about the *mysterium trinitatis* and the *mysterium incarnationis* with the help of Hellenistic Latin conceptualities and forms of argument (Christian P II and P III) is incomprehensible to Muslim thought.

At this decisive point we recognize how far the two prophetic religions have moved apart. From the starting positions in the framework of the Jewish–Christian paradigm (Christian P I) and the original Islamic paradigm (Islamic P I), inter-religious dialogue would have been uncomplicated despite all the differences: Jesus understood in the overall Semitic context as the Messiah, friend, messenger of God, the word of God. However, in the Middle Ages, in the face of these tremendously complicated christological and trinitarian constructions built with the help of Greek and Latin concepts (Christian P II), an understanding with a medieval Muslim theologian (Islamic P III) became almost impossible. And despite all speculative approaches from the Christian side, that remains the case today. But need it be in the future?

Fossilization or renewal of theology?

From the beginning—and probably more than Judaism and Christianity—Islam was bound by certain regulations of faith and law which had to be handed down unchanged. These were, first, the holy statements of the Qur'an, all of which had been dictated to the Prophet Muhammad, and, secondly, the statements of the Sunnah, the tradition, which comprise the literal statements of the Prophet and the actions that accompanied the words. Through the centuries, Muslims have taken infinite pains, from childhood on, to learn by heart as many of these statements as possible, so as to be able to apply them at any time to a quite specific situation.

These statements about faith and law remained unchanged even when times changed. The transformation of the religion which came into being in an Arab tribal culture (P I) into the new historical constellation under the Umayyads (P II) and then again in the new paradigm under the 'Abbasids (P III) went very well. As times changed, religious scholars and theologian–jurists might not change the legacy that had been set down, but they could interpret it, adapt it and above all increase it. This they did with countless sayings of the Prophet, old and new (*hadith*), which resulted in a formal hadith scholarship. These scholars saw their task as distinguishing the 'sound' from the 'unsound' tradition, and this sound tradition was preserved for posterity in six large canonical collections.

That meant that from the middle of the ninth century the corpus of 'sound' tradition was essentially fixed: new additions were almost impossible. So, when a new paradigm change (P IV) made itself felt but new sayings and actions of the Prophet were no longer conceivable, and the 'door of independent judgement' (*ijtihad*—in fact only analogies) seemed to many to be closed, both theology and the law risked becoming fossilized. Al-Ghazali, who could hardly have found the didactic method of memorizing standard texts without independent thought satisfactory, formally called for a 'revival'.

Was al-Ghazali's revival successful? In the short term, barely at all, since the resistance from the law schools was too great, but in the medium term it was very successful. Al-Ghazali's synthesis made the non-Sufis more tolerant of the Sufis, while preventing the rise of a Sufism beyond the Shariah and thus established itself, in the new constellation, for the Sunni majority as the normative theology for the centuries to come.

Even as a Sufi, al-Ghazali did not want escape from society. He was not concerned with a 'great refusal' but with a 'great renewal', which he hoped to bring about, even after his departure from Baghdad, through his sermons, his study and his publications. Precisely when the Seljuk state threatened to collapse after the murder of the Grand Vizier Nizam al-Mulk, Islamic society was shown the right way. And for the thinker, al-Ghazali, who knew the great pre-Islamic tradition of this principle—beginning with Aristotle's definition of virtue as the mean between two extremes—the right way was deliberately a middle way: the *via media* as the guideline for thought and action.[136]

The *via media* was the religious and political concept ('order of rule') of al-Ghazali's patron Nizam al-Mulk, an ethically motivated yet realistic statesman who, although a Shafi'ite and promoter of Ash'arite theologians, stood apart from the general religious orientation of the ruler and tolerated the respected representatives of all the doctrinal opinions around him. Nizam's own rule for rulers hands down a saying of the Prophet that human beings are to choose the middle way in all things: 'The best thing is your midst.'[137]

The *via media* was and remained the theological and political concept of al-Ghazali, a thinker who was as perceptive as he was concerned for integration. Although he was likewise indebted to the Shafi'ite law school, he did not preach Ash'arite theology and fought against the widespread partisanship, rigid dogmatism, blind actionism and wild fanaticism. He offers a series of variants on the principle of the middle way and formulates them in his *Ihya'*: 'Know that the mean is most highly desirable in all things and virtues.'[138] So, what would help Islamic society on its way? Questions from that time are questions for tomorrow.

Questions: Theology

- Is Islamic society helped by a renewed restoration of traditionalism, of the kind that took place as early as the eleventh century and was advocated both by the Ulama, which at that time was rigidly moralistic, and the lower classes (*'awamm*), whom the Ulama could no longer control? Didn't ideal notions of a Sunni orthodoxy and orthopraxy lead to the confrontation of religious parties which often resulted in long-drawn-out urban disputes (*fitan*) which were like civil wars, the mass hysteria of the mob, murder squads (*fida'iyun*) and numerous planned acts of terror?
- Doesn't Islamic society need, rather, a programme of tolerance, as put forward by the statesman Nizam al-Mulk and, in his footsteps, the theologian al-Ghazali, contrary to the partisanship of the different tendencies of faith and law schools? According to this programme, doesn't an unpartisan sovereign state rightly affirm religious plurality and allow the different religious parties to experience tolerance and justice, so as to achieve a balance of opposites by a balanced religious policy rather than excluding the opponent?

In the long term, however, one could doubt whether the thorough fixation of the Shariah on a Sufi theological basis would stand the test of a new epoch-making change. There was a danger that what H. Laoust has called a 'legalistic Sufism' would prove to be the great obstacle for Islam in a new paradigm change, because it left too little room for the new historical and thus theological developments.

The same question could have been put to Thomas' new synthesis. In the short term, it was blocked by the church's magisterium; in the middle term it had tremendous success. But again, in the long term one must doubt whether the fixing of Catholic dogma on an Aristotelian–Thomistic basis would prove itself in the transition to a new epoch-making constellation. Such an 'official church Thomism' was to be the great block for Christianity because it, too, left no room for a historical dynamic. The crisis of a paradigm that had become tradition could be stopped, thus postponing the rise of the new age which was making itself felt; however, in the end it could not be avoided.

7. The rise and fall of Arabic philosophy

The crisis of the Thomistic synthesis and of medieval Christianity generally, long held up by hopes of reform, proposals for reform and reform councils, finally broke in the confrontation with the Lutheran Reformation. But the crisis of al-Ghazali's synthesis and medieval Islam generally already became evident in the conflict with Arabic philosophy, which traditional Islam won at the time, so that the crisis would break out only at a late date, in the confrontation with European modernity. Decisive questions emerged at an early stage.

Can there be an independent Islamic philosophy?

The premises are already well known to us: Islamic philosophy (*falsafah*)[139] is a typical phenomenon of the classic paradigm of Islam as a world religion (P III). Only under the 'Abbasid caliphs did an Islamic world culture develop which was able to integrate Hellenistic science and philosophy with Persian education and lifestyle. Theology formed the background for the Islamic philosophers (*falasifa*, singular *faylasuf*) and presented them with many questions about God and the world, such as that of the one and the many and the compatibility of revelation and reason. Many theologians had given increasing room to human reason and its arguments. Theological disputations were carried on in which 'sound reason' played a major role alongside the Qur'an and Sunnah.

However, the real origin of Islamic philosophy lies in the translation of the works of Greek philosophers in the period from 750 to 850, above all in Baghdad. Individual translations of Greek texts had been made under the Umayyads (P II), but planned and comprehensive translation work was done only under the 'Abbasids, especially under those caliphs close to the theological school of the Mu'tazilah with its rational arguments (see C III). A beginning had been made with the translation of Greek works of science, medicine and mathematics, and this was followed by the translation of the works of philosophy. From a very early stage cosmopolitan Baghdad had a valuable philosophical library of a kind that had been vainly sought in Rome, the city of the popes, which had come down in the world, or at the court of Charlemagne, the emperor of the Franks. This library contained philologically accurate translations (into Arabic, of course, not Latin) of the works of Plato and the main works of Aristotle. Paradoxically, Syrian Christian scholars, who produced the translations from the Greek, served as models. This was one of the main reasons why, in the early European Middle Ages, Islam was so far ahead of Latin Christianity in philosophy and science.

The Arabs came to know the classical Greek philosophy of Plato and Aristotle (fourth century BCE) as interpreted by the now dominant neo-Platonic philosophy of Plotinus (third century CE). This offered an explanation of the world which understood the order of the world as built up dynamically in stages: like all material things, the spiritual forces which formed and moved the world 'emanated' in stages from the unchangeable divine One, as the rays of light emanate from the sun. There was a constant 'emanation', an 'outflowing' of all things from a deity thought of as impersonal—not a unique creation from nothing by a God thought of as personal. In the eternal creative cycle there was a return from evil matter to the utterly spiritual deity: the descending divine self-revelation through such self-emptying and individualization in the realm of matter was said to correspond to the ascent of individual spiritual souls from the world of the senses to mystical unity with the Godhead.

On the basis of their ever-increasing knowledge of Greek philosophy, the Arab thinkers finally showed themselves capable of working out an independent Islamic philosophy—but against growing opposition. Some Muslim theologians asked very critically from the beginning whether a philosophy (*falsafah*) was at all legitimate in Islam alongside the rational theology (*kalam*) being developed from the non-religious practical and theoretical sciences, setting itself no limits other than reason itself, a worldview on a purely rational basis. The Arab philosophers, like the Christian scholastics later, were believers. They did not see the truth of reason as being in any way a contradiction of the truth of the revelation; rather, if both were understood rightly, reason was in accord with revelation. Philosophy and theology were allies—and differed both from pure traditional science and from Sufism by virtue of rational argument. They were related but independent disciplines; of course the philosophers usually attributed the primacy to philosophy.

So, could there be an Islamic philosophy? Only theology was 'Islamic' in the strict sense: practised by Muslims within the Muslim community of faith. Islamic philosophy was Islamic only in a broader sense: practised by Muslims but also by Christians and Jews, some of whom contributed to it, first in Baghdad and later in Spain. From the ninth to the twelfth century there was certainly an 'Arabic' philosophy, but this too existed only in a broad sense: a philosophy in Arabic in the lands ruled by Arabs. However, this was not the philosophy of the Arabs, which was supported by all. For from the beginning there were doubts: could, should, might Islamic philosophers establish themselves in Islam alongside the Ulama and the Sufis? Would Islamic philosophy, in time, perhaps be able to develop as strong a paradigmatic force for the whole Islamic Ulama or would it remain merely a marginal phenomenon in the framework of the medieval paradigm (like mysticism in Christianity)?

To anticipate the answer, in Islam philosophy remained a marginal phenomenon and so for my paradigm analysis it will be enough to make a brief survey of the development by considering prominent philosophical personalities who are significant for the beginning, high point and end of Arabic philosophy. This philosophy began with the classical paradigm of Islam as a world religion (P III) and gradually disappeared again with the post-classical Ulama–Sufi paradigm (P IV), though a revival of Islamic philosophy was attempted a couple of centuries later in Iran. I shall concentrate on the Arabic

Islamic philosophy that proved to be so influential on the history of European intellectual development alone.

Beginnings of Arabic philosophy: al-Kindi, ar-Razi, al-Farabi

Abu Yusuf al-Kindi, 'the philosopher of the Arabs' (born about 800, died about 870),[140] who came from Kufa, is generally regarded as the first Islamic philosopher. At the time of the triumph of the Mu'tazilah, unlike the theologians he opened himself unreservedly and enthusiastically to Greek wisdom. From astronomy to psychology, physics and metaphysics he evaluated all the sciences accessible to him in an original and eclectic way. However limited his knowledge of Plato and Aristotle may have been, in their spirit he reflected intensively on the relationship between the constantly-changing physical world and the unchanging eternal world of forms. He saw no difference between the purely human knowledge of things through reason and knowledge on the basis of special religious experience. On the contrary, philosophy helped him to understand and confirm the revelation of the Qur'an.

The view of the excellent Persian physician and philosopher Abu Bakr ar-Razi (in Latin Rhazes), who lived from 865 to 925,[141] was quite different. On the basis of five eternal and primal principles—the creator God, world soul, space, time and matter—he developed a rational theory of the emergence of the world from God. Theologians who discussed with ar-Razi claimed that he relied only on reason and rejected any authority in the sphere of knowledge; he believed in progress in the sciences and not in a prophetic message or a divine law. Here, by way of exception, a philosophy developed in opposition to revelation.

The first systematic philosopher in Islam, the first significant logician and political thinker, was Abu Nasr al-Farabi (in Latin, Alpharabius).[142] Born in Farab, Turkestan, in 870, the son of an officer of the caliph's Turkic bodyguard, he grew up in Baghdad and was introduced to Greek philosophy there. He later worked as a philosopher, mathematician and music theorist in Aleppo and died in Damascus in 950, at the age of eighty. He rejected both al-Kindi's view that prophets and philosophers had an independent way to the highest truth and ar-Razi's view that philosophy was the only way to the supreme truth. He had a Christian teacher in Baghdad and sought not only to make a synthesis of Platonic and Aristotelian philosophy but also to integrate the Islamic religion into philosophy. He developed an Islamic idealistic spiritualism which was strongly coloured by the Neoplatonic doctrine of emanation. Like almost all Arabic thinkers his starting point was that the so-called 'theology of Aristotle' was authentic (in fact it is part of Plotinus' *Enneads*). In this way he thought that he could remove the contradiction between Aristotle (the eternity of the world) and

Islam (creation from nothing) by his doctrine of the 'relatively necessary'. Al-Farabi wanted to reconcile philosophy and revelation.

Muslims soon regarded him as the greatest philosophical authority after Aristotle. Whereas al-Kindi and ar-Razi were primarily philosophers of nature, al-Farabi developed a system of sciences (though this is preserved in only a few works). Inspired by Plato's treatise on the model state (the *Republic*), this system culminates in political science. All the elements of Muslim society are subjected to philosophical investigation, thus introducing a rational basis to politics in Islam. As God himself is the embodiment of reason, human beings created by God are endowed with reason and can determine themselves. However, both as individuals and as a commonwealth they must go by moral principles (virtues). The state is to be led by a philosopher guided by reason—wholly in accordance with Plato's ideal of the philosopher king.

The high point of historic Arabic philosophy: Ibn Sina

Islamic philosophy reached its systematic high point with al-Farabi's Persian pupil Abu 'Ali Ibn Sina (Latin Avicenna), who lived from 980 to 1037. Beyond doubt he had the most influence in the Arab world.[143] Whereas al-Kindi and al-Farabi practised their philosophy so to speak under the protection of the 'Abbasid caliphs, Ibn Sina had personal experience of the regionalization of Islam and the paradigm change that was in the making. The caliphate in Baghdad had lost control of the new 'family states', which were all too often entangled in warlike controversies, as were the Samanids, rulers over east Iran and Transoxania, and the Ghaznavids, rulers over Khorasan and Afghanistan. Ibn Sina was born near Bukhara, the brilliant centre of the Samanids, the son of a court official. According to his autobiography, he knew the Qur'an at the age of ten and by sixteen was a physician; he gained entry to the court in Bukhara with its rich library, held state offices and, as a leading doctor and philosopher, led a life free of religious duties and rites. Some religious and military opponents grudged him this. Political entanglements eventually forced him to lead an itinerant life at different courts and he even spent some months in prison. Only the last fourteen years of his life, with a prince in Isfahan, were relatively peaceful. However, in 1030 the ruler of Ghazna conquered Isfahan, Ibn Sina's house was plundered and his library taken to Ghazna. He died, in flight, in 1037 in Hamadan.

What a fate for this universal scholar and the most important physician of the Arab Middle Ages. In the West he was known for centuries chiefly for his medicine: an 'Arabic Galen' whose 'canon of medicine' became the basic medical textbook for medieval Europe! However, in the Islamic world his philosophy was most influential. He was the first Islamic philosopher to create a coherent system of the sciences. His main work, 'The Healing (of the Soul from Error)' (*ash-shifa'*), discusses logic, physics, mathematics and metaphysics and for the whole subsequent period became the normative and influential synthesis of Aristotelian Neoplatonic metaphysics. The theologian al-Ghazali had it most in view when he criticized philosophy; for him, Avicenna's Neoplatonic ideas about an emanation of the world from God and eternal matter outside God seemed to contradict revelation.

Ibn Sina remained the most effective communicator of Greek thought; in his doctrine of being he impressively worked out the distinction between essence and existence in every entity (which had already been seen by al-Farabi): only in God, the necessary being, do essence and existence coincide; only from God can the whole chain of things that exist be explained. God is the simple and eternally existing Being from whom, as unchangeable primal ground, all changeable and contingent entities proceed in a series of dynamic stages: first the light world, imagined as being outside time, then the temporal and material world. The fact that Ibn Sina (unlike Aristotle) attributes its own forces to matter hardly justifies later Marxist attempts at interpretations which in the twentieth century seek to commandeer this mystically-orientated thinker for an 'Aristotelian left' with a materialistic disposition.[144]

In connection with the return of the world to God, Avicenna provides a rational argument even for the immortality of the simple spirit-soul that, unlike the composite body, cannot fall apart. On this philosophical basis he finally also explains, with the aid of a rational exegesis of Qur'an and hadith, the possibility of prophetic knowledge, revelation and miracle and the laws and institutions through which God attains his goal. In this way faith in God becomes the mystical ascent of the soul to the first being, which is essentially knowledge, truth, goodness and love all in one—just how Sufism experiences God. Here, then, is a harmony of philosophy and religion in a philosophical mysticism which Ibn Sina also expresses in allegorical poems—though at the price of understanding the revealed texts at decisive points as allegories of truths that can be seen in a purely philosophical way even without revelation. But does that mean that we have to renounce the riches of this great synthesis?

Not until the twelfth century did the writings of al-Farabi, Ibn Sina and al-Ghazali find their way into the West: to Spain, where people had long been closed to influences from hostile 'Abbasid Baghdad, allowing the study only of medicine, pharmacology, mathematics, astronomy and logic. Strikingly, even after Ibn Sina's death in 1037 there was hardly a philosopher in the heartlands of Islam who knew history. Did Arabic Islamic philosophy, unloved, indeed hated and fought against by both the Ulama and the Sufis, die out?

The end of Arabic Islamic philosophy: Ibn Rushd

The Western philosophical tradition in Morocco and Spain was the final phase of Islamic Arabic philosophy. In 1061 the Berber dynasty of the Almoravids had replaced the two dozen 'party-kings' (*muluk at-tawa'if*, Spanish *reyes de taifas*) who, from 1031, had succeeded the Umayyads. Eighty years later (in 1147), the Almoravids were overthrown by the Almohads, another Berber dynasty from the High Atlas. Their second ruler, al-Mansur ('the victorious'), had at first been able to repel the Spanish Reconquista, and when in 1195 he ceased to favour the most important philosopher of Spain, Abu l-Walid Muhammad Ibn Rushd, Latinized as Averroes,[145] and dropped him, his action was doubtless seen as a sign for critical spirits. Ibn Rushd was banished from the court of the city of Cordoba as a heretic and his philosophical writings were prohibited and burned. How could this have come about? Ibn Rushd, born in Cordoba in 1126, was a grand judge, grandson and son of grand judges; he too was a universal scholar, with an excellent education in the religious sciences, jurisprudence and medicine.

At the wish of the first Almohad ruler, Ibn Rushd had composed the first commentaries on the *Corpus aristotelicum* at the age of twenty-seven in the Moroccan residence city of Marrakesh. As grand judge in Seville and Cordoba he wrote further commentaries and medical treatises, becoming the leading commentator on Aristotle. He wanted to interpret the great Greeks authentically, not Neoplatonically, as his predecessors had done, and he helped towards a breakthrough of the 'pure' Aristotle among the Arabs. Instead of offering paraphrases of the concentrated texts of Aristotle, like Ibn Sina, he offered extremely precise commentaries, as clear as judicial arguments, sentence by sentence, word by word. No one had hitherto succeeded in explaining the difficult Aristotelian teaching of the principles of all things—matter and form, reality (act) and possibility (potency)—in such an illuminating way as he did. However, consciously or unconsciously, he also borrowed from Neoplatonism: he assumed not only a single first cause of the universe but also a single universal active intellect in which all human beings participate.

At first, Ibn Rushd was highly regarded as a grand judge in Cordoba. However, his philosophical writings, in particular his answer to al-Ghazali's 'Refutation of the Philosophers' (*tahafut al-falasifah*), with the smug title 'Refutation of the Refutation' (*tahafut at-tahafut*, later Latinized as *destructio destructionis*), aroused the enmity of the religious legal scholars. His concern with logic and philosophy were said to undermine the authority of the revelation and those who expounded it, cause unrest and unsettle believers and lead to confusion and hypocrisy in religious questions. However, he simply wanted to underline the role of reason in the face of the believing scepticism of the theologian al-Ghazali who, for example, rejected the application of the principle of causality to metaphysical questions, not least by saying that any polemic against reason presupposed the use of reason.

Ibn Rushd separated revelation and philosophy in order to remove the contradictions between them. He has thus, wrongly, had foisted on him the thesis of a 'double truth', as though in his view the truth of revelation and the truth of reason were contradictory. Rather, for him, the truth of faith and the truth of reason are in principle the same—even if they sometimes arrive in contradictory statements. One must distinguish hierarchically between three categories of thinkers, as is indicated in the Qur'an: philosophers, theologians and simple believers. To avoid dispute, all must keep to their limits, respect one another and not attempt to rise into the higher category. Philosophy proves, in the concepts of fundamental scientific thinking, what religion expresses for the people in images. Ibn Rushd argues against al-Ghazali that the eternity of the world (philosophy) and its createdness (theology) are no more mutually exclusive than God as first cause (philosophy) and God as creator (theology); the world, though eternal, is created and spatially limited because of its divine grounding. He used a similar argument in the question of the bodily resurrection.[146] However, some of his opponents got the impression that this distinction served as a 'Spanish wall', behind which was hidden a rationalist who put reason above religion and philosophy above theology.

It cannot be doubted that Ibn Rushd sought to maintain the primacy of autonomous reason. In accordance with Aristotelian principles, he wanted to offer a scientifically consistent and well-structured understanding of the world. However, there is equally no doubt that: 'He believed firmly in God, in God's Prophet Muhammad, and in the miraculous character of the Qur'an, and not a single text of Ibn Rushd's can be interpreted in the opposite sense. That is the essential point; all the other points—the eternity of the world, the divine knowledge which does not grasp details, divine providence which is limited to universal principles—are discussible questions which do not damage the ground of faith, and al-Ghazali is wrong to regard them in this way, as if they necessarily entailed the qualification of unbelief.'[147]

Years of polemic and struggle followed. In the end, the caliph yielded to the fanatical orthodox, since he depended on their support in the fight against the advancing Catholic *reconquistadores* (who by 1085 had won back Toledo and by 1115 Saragossa). Eventually, in 1195, Ibn Rushd was banished, first to the Jewish city of Lucena, just over sixty miles from Cordoba, which had no libraries, and two years later to the second residence city of the caliph, Marrakesh, where he was finally rehabilitated. He died shortly afterwards, in December 1198, at the age of seventy-two and his mortal remains were taken to Cordoba. He left no pupils.

Al-Andalus: an Arabized Christianity

For almost eight centuries, since the decisive battle of Jérez de la Frontera in 711, the greater part of Spain had been under the rule of the 'Moors' (*los moros*), as the Spaniards called the Muslims of Arab–Berber descent. They had been called in after dissension among the Christian West Goths. The church that was now called 'Mozarabic' (Arabic *musta'rib* = 'Arabized') was allowed to keep three of its metropolises, above all the seat of the primate in Toledo, with twenty-nine dioceses, which were largely self-administered. However, very soon the majority of the Christian population converted to Islam and only small Christian minorities, such as the Mozarabians, held firm to Christian faith and life. Among these linguistically and culturally Arabized Christian groups of the population with Muslim elements there developed a distinctive Mozarabic architecture, and also a distinctive Mozarabic liturgy with a chant. Nowhere was the Christian West in such close contact with the Arab cultural world as in Spain.

An independent Christian theology, which has been investigated more precisely only in recent times, also developed under the Mozarabians.[148] This was in contrast to, for example, North Africa, where in the view of the Muslim scholar Mohamed Talbi, after various Christian waves of emigration the failure of spiritual resources was the main reason why Christianity, which had flourished earlier, went out like a lamp that had run out of oil.[149] Unlike the Jews, who fell into line with Arab culture in various ways, the Christians of North Africa did not develop any specifically Arab Christian culture and so finally died out. However, in Spain, Christian theology maintained itself to a modest degree, though its representatives were obviously unknown to the great scholars among the Muslims (such as Averroes) and Jews (such as Moses Maimonides). In the twelfth century Gundisalivi (Latin Dominicus Gundissalinus), archdeacon of Segovia and the translator of al-Farabi's *Introduction to Science*, attempted a synthesis between Arabic Aristotelian science and Christian early scholastic thought. In the thirteenth century, Mozarabic theology had an influence on the important Catalan scholar, apologist and missionary Ramon Llull, who has already been mentioned and his intellectual rival, the Dominican Ramon Martí, both of whom, in our day, have been designated Neo-Mozarabians.[150]

In al-Andalus, in the highest church circles, alongside the orthodox theology there was a heterodox theology: Primate Elipandus of Toledo and Bishop Felix of Urgel—as Pope Hadrian I wrote in a sharp rebuke to Spain—had not been ashamed 'to confess the Son of God as an adopted son and so to speak purely human'.[151] Here was a 'christology from below' which, like the earliest Gospel (Mark), began with the narrative of the baptism of Jesus on whom the spirit of God came ('You are my beloved son, in you I am well pleased'[152]). This was a doctrine that had already been advocated in Jewish Christianity (see A II, 2) and in the Antiochene school (Paul of Samosata). In all probability it was formulated anew in Spain, in response to Muslim criticism,[153] for in this way the divine sonship of Jesus could be made comprehensible to Muslims. 'He has been accepted in place of the Son.' This view, adoptionism, denounced as heretical, had been fought against by Charlemagne's theologian Alcuin and condemned at several synods in France and Germany (Frankfurt, Regensburg, and so on), but the christological problem, called to life again by Islam, had not been solved. I shall pay particular attention to it in the interest of today's dialogue (see D IV, 2 below).

One curiosity is an Arabic 'Gospel according to St Barnabas'. This is not, as had been conjectured, the work of a Christian forger from the eleventh century who wanted to use the 'westward travels' of the apostle Barnabas through Cyprus to Europe for his own missionary purposes. Rather, it is a Muslim defence in the situation of persecution after the fall of the last Muslim city, Granada, in 1492, which attempted to argue for the orthodoxy of the Islamic view of the prophet and messiah Jesus.[154]

Al-Andalus: a fertile symbiosis of Muslims and Jews

Individual Jews also converted to Islam voluntarily, influenced either by the Islamic milieu or by fear of persecution. The Jews fared considerably better under Islam than under either the rule of Christianity or the Roman and West Gothic empires. This was not simply because of the hostility of the Christians; there were also positive reasons and background facts which explain why, on many points, Muslims and Jews were closer together than Christians and Jews:[155]

– For all its restrictions, the Islamic world empire had a universally binding basis of law for the Jewish minority, which gave them assured rights (including rights to personal possessions). Because of the migration of the peoples and the downfall of the Roman legal order associated with it, this was lacking in the Christian West and in the Byzantine empire it was gradually replaced by a legislation directly hostile to the Jews.

– Jews regularly served the Islamic world empire through trade in the East and the Mediterranean after the departure of the Christian Syrians; they could use Arabic, which is related to Hebrew, as an international language of commerce and trade. In the Christian sphere they had to surrender long-distance trade with the Islamic world to the Italian cities at a very early stage and in the late Middle Ages these cities took over the leadership in the Islamic sphere.

– Jews were closer to Muslims than Christians in religious terms because of their clear monotheism, with no mysterious dogmas, and because of similar commandments about cleanness and food. Both Jews and Muslims were separated even more markedly from the Christians through the Hellenistic–Latin doctrines of the Trinity and the incarnation than through the original Palestinian dispute over the law and circumcision.

– In the Islamic sphere, from an early stage Jews were confronted with Islamic philosophy and only to a degree with the theological claims of Islam, whereas they were confronted with Christian theology from the twelfth century onwards and had to grapple directly with the Christian claim to revelation (the court of the emperor Frederick II in Sicily in the thirteenth century was an exception).

Jews could still engage in agriculture to a greater extent in Spain than in other European countries. However, Jews were also heavily engaged in the flourishing slave trade, from the Middle East to Eastern Europe.

In Cordoba and other centres the Jews (at least the upper class) adopted the Arabic language, Arab clothing and Arab customs. They played a full part in economic, political and cultural life and stood out from the Jews of other lands by their prominence and self-confidence. Thus in Spain in particular, by far the most fruitful symbiosis between Jews and Muslims developed, which expressed itself in an incomparable blossoming of Jewish sciences and arts: Jewish philosophy and theology, linguistics and profane poetry (including the first Jewish love poem since the biblical Song of Songs, written by Jehuda ben Halevi), natural sciences and medicine and a wide range of translations (Arabic–Hebrew–Latin). By the tenth century, Moorish Spain had largely replaced Babylonia, where in the ninth and tenth centuries there had likewise been a fruitful exchange between Muslim and Jews, as the spiritual centre of Judaism. The relatively harmonious co-existence of Muslims and Jews, despite the Muslim rule and all kinds of restrictions, gives the lie to the widespread cliché of a 'hereditary Jewish–Arab hostility' based on religion.

The great symbolic figure of Spanish Judaism remains the most famous Jewish scholar of the Middle Ages, Moshe ben Maimon (1135–1204, in Arabic *Musa ibn Maymun*),[156] in the West called Moses Maimonides. He came from Cordoba but worked chiefly in Morocco and Egypt. A physician, jurist, philosopher and theologian, in his main work *Guide for the Perplexed* he tried to reconcile religious faith and reason (like the Muslim philosophers earlier or Albert the Great and Thomas Aquinas later in Christianity). He is still the great model for Jewish scholars. Avicebron, regarded by the Christian scholastics as an Arab philosopher, was also a Spanish Jew: Solomon ben Jehuda ibn Gevirol (1020–70). Without the intellectual exchange with Islam Judaism would hardly have produced so many significant scholars, doctors, officials, administrators and stewards and with the decline of Islam in the twelfth century the creative power of Judaism also declined.[157]

One dominant religion, two recognized minorities

In the tenth and eleventh centuries the caliphate had its capital in Cordoba. The 'jewel of the earth' in both an economic and a cultural respect—tens of thousands of shops, thousands of mosques, baths, running water, paved streets with lighting and the caliph's library of 400,000 volumes (just one of seventy libraries)—has been described by many scholars, most recently in a wider historical context by María Rosa Menocal of Yale University.[158] The tolerance and cultural exchange in Cordoba and throughout al-Andalus were unprecedented. Some Spanish historians have a positive view of the co-existence of the three religions (M. Asín Palacios[159] and A. Castro[160]); others (S. Fanjul[161]) are more sceptical. In Cordoba, the Christians did not play the same role as the Jews, who were intellectually and economically more efficient, though as members of the diplomatic corps at European courts Catholic bishops may have given reports about the miraculous city on the Guadalquivir.

There is no question that Cordoba—like Toledo, which was later also recaptured by the Christians—showed that members of the three Abrahamic religions could live together well, retaining the forms of life which their religions prescribed however much they differed in their theological focus. Thus, instead of the excommunication often practised elsewhere in Europe, there was living communication. Even under medieval conditions, a 'dialogue of civilizations' rather than a 'clash of civilizations' was possible.

Under medieval conditions: I am speaking of the medieval paradigm (P III–IV), and it would be illusory to expect freedom of religion in the modern sense. One of the best experts on the situation in Andalusia, the Spanish historian Mikel de Epalza, has described the co-existence of the three religions from the beginning of the eighth century to the beginning of the sixteenth century, the date of the forced conversion of Muslim and Jews, as 'one dominant religion and two recognized minorities'. First, Islam is the predominant religion: 'In broad outline this scheme describes the Muslim period. Only the religion of the Muslims, Arab–Muslim culture, could develop completely. Little was left of the Christian culture of pre-Islamic origin: it manifested itself only in the spheres of religion and language, by the use of Latin and alongside that—and this is not at all certain—through some material and local customs which were wholly incorporated by the dominant culture. Apart from religion and culture we must speak of an Arab culture of Christians, as is very well indicated by the terms "Mozarabic" or "Arabized". The same can be said of the Jews throughout al-Andalus. The sacred language (Hebrew) and religion formed their own cultural peculiarity.'[162]

The same scheme can then be found the other way round after the *reconquista*, the Christian reconquest of 1085, in Christian Toledo. Now Christianity was the dominant religion: 'The norms of social life were Christian in every respect. Muslim and Jewish culture were tolerated as sub-cultures or micro-cultures, which are characteristic of restricted religious communities, and are exposed to new abuse of every kind.'[163]

There was peaceful co-existence in Andalusia, not just under Christian rule but also under the preceding Islamic rule; however, there were no equal rights in the modern sense: there were numerous restrictions, for both Jews and Christians.[164] As I explained earlier, on the basis of the 'laws of 'Umar', which derive from the seventh and eighth centuries, theoretically, for the members of the two other 'religions of the book', the rules were: no Muslims as slaves, no riding on horses, no houses higher than one's Muslim neighbours' houses, no new places of worship and no prominent practice of one's own religion. Special clothes had to be worn, and there was a special land tax and poll tax.

For centuries, Islam was culturally far ahead of the West. Then, in 1031, the caliphate of Cordoba collapsed because of a revolt of the Arab nobility, and the rebellions of its militia in North Africa. Various local 'party' (*taifa*) kingdoms replaced the central power for the next decades. Then, summoned to the country by the ruler of Seville, the Berber political and religious reform movement of the strictly traditionalist Almoravids conquered the Muslim part of the Iberian peninsula. They were replaced, in the twelfth century, by a second Berber reform movement, the Almohads, who were more open. However, after the decisive battle of Las Navas de Tolosa in 1212 the Almohads gradually lost rule over almost all the Spanish territories in the Christian kingdoms of Aragon, Castile-Leon, Catalonia and Portugal. 1269 saw the collapse of the Almohad empire, the last great empire of Western Islam, embracing North Africa and Spain. From this, in the course of time, under three Berber dynasties the countries of Morocco, Algeria and Tunisia emerged, maintaining a very fragile equilibrium between refractory tribal alliances and the cities. In the meantime, a great fourteenth-century Arab historian could have warned the Muslims against over-estimating themselves and being too confident of victory.

History as a cycle of rise and decline: Ibn Khaldun

The universal history (*kitab al-'ibar*), in fact only of the Arabs and Berbers, by al-Hasan ibn Khaldun, born in Tunis in 1332, is based on the bitter experience of times of upheaval.[165] In an extended introduction (*al-Muqaddimah*), this prominent religious scholar, judge and writer presented the brilliant outline of a philosophy of history and society which contains lengthy reflections on the flourishing and decline of empires, dynasties and states.

In these turbulent and dangerous times Ibn Khaldun, evidently a restless and not always convenient scion of an old Arab family, served a series of rulers in Islamic Spain and in the Maghreb as general, politician and even 'prime minister'. However, he failed everywhere, and to explain the social and political mistakes, in 1375, in a castle in present-day Algeria, far from all politics, he examined the various forces which ruled the Muslim societies known to him. First, he discussed criteria for distinguishing historical truth and error and then reconstructed the main currents of social development over several centuries. His work was far in advance of Western historiography.

Ibn Khaldun developed some universal laws about the rise, flourishing and decline of tribes, dynasties and states. He was practising a new science, the science of culture (*'ilm al-'umran*)—something like a sociology of society in general, of politics, urban life, the economy and knowledge. The central concept in the development is 'social cohesion' (*'asabiyah*). As long as this cohesion is strengthened by various factors (not least religious factors), the relevant society rises. Conversely, after a certain high point the society is unavoidably weakened by the neglect of this social cohesion. This leads to the decline of a dynasty or an empire, which gives place to a new one with stronger cohesion. This is a history without real progress, except from the primitive to a cultivated society.

Later, Ibn Khaldun worked in Cairo and in 1400 in Damascus even negotiated with the cruel Tatar conqueror Timur, who wanted to take him into his service. He died in Cairo in 1406, without having found a worthy successor among the Muslim historiographers. Ibn Khaldun's view of history had no real influence on Islamic thought in the following centuries. For a long time people failed to recognize the crisis because in political and military terms Islam continued to advance. Then barely fifty years after Ibn Khaldun's death, Constantinople was captured by the Turks (in 1453), a great triumph for Islam and a shock for the whole of Christianity. After the Balkans could Islam in time also capture Vienna, the capital of the Habsburg empire? Yet there were signs of a coming shift in favour of Christianity. In the fifteenth century, Western Christianity was on the eve of an epoch-making paradigm change that had been in the making from the twelfth century and in which the crisis of Islam was also becoming evident.

8. The crisis of medieval Islam

Ibn Rushd's work marks the end of the Arabic Islamic philosophy that, from the ninth to the twelfth centuries, long before Christian scholasticism, had produced such important achievements. People continued to do philosophy after Averroes—especially following Avicenna. Doubtless historians can produce a series of names and works for the period.[166] However, only Avicenna and Averroes made any impact on history. The successors of these great philosophies had hardly any influence worth mentioning on the overall development of Islam. Even the revival of Islamic philosophy in Iran in the seventeenth century, intensively researched by Henri Corbin[167]—after a period of stagnation and the spread of Sufism—introduced by Mir Damad and reaching its highpoint with Mollah Sadra Shirazi, important though it is, was essentially restricted to the Shiah. In practice, these philosophers remained unknown not only in the Christian West but also in the Western Islamic world.[168]

The beginning of Western Christian philosophy

Faced with Shariah Islam and Sufi Islam, Arabic Islamic philosophy hardly had a chance. It did not achieve any accepted normative validity and could not develop any permanent dominant structures and institutions, for example in universities. Arabic Islamic philosophy had a great history but was not historically influential in Islam. At an earlier stage religious scholars such as the Sufis regarded it as alien, so it had a limited effect on the development of Islam. Arabic–Islamic philosophy had ended by the twelfth century; as would become evident only very much later, that was an ominous development for the intellectual future of Islam.

Only a few decades after Ibn Rushd's death, translators and translation schools (there was a great translation school in Toledo, then Catholic once more) were making his commentaries on the main works of Aristotle available to Latin Christianity. Michael Scotus, who worked at this school in Toledo, spent his last years (from about 1227 to 1236) as court scholar, physician and translator at the court of Frederick II in Sicily. His translation of Aristotle's works on natural philosophy (including the *Metaphysics*), each with the great commentary by Averroes, also probably date from this period. Philosophically, the thirteenth century would belong to Christian scholasticism. Averroes may not have been influential in Islam, but he was in Christianity; if he represents an end-point for Arabic Islamic philosophy, for medieval Christian philosophy he represents a beginning. One sign of this is that his writings have largely been preserved in Latin (and Hebrew) translations. The French orientalist Ernst Renan (1823–92), in the pioneering work of his youth, *Averroès et l'averroïsme*,[169] the first work to point out the tremendous influence of Averroes on Jewish philosophy (above all Maimonides) and scholasticism, believed that he could detect traces of an 'Averroism' as early as the first half of the thirteenth century. More recent research[170] indicates that Averroes was unknown in the Latin West before 1230 and was first translated around this time in the environs of the Sicilian imperial court.[171] After that date there were translations of Averroes at the University of Paris, the centre of Christian learning. From the middle of the century one may presuppose that all scholastics had his commentaries at their disposal.

Western philosophy, as engaged in by theologians (though it could also be practised independently of their theology) and urged on above all by the many translations of Aristotle and Arabic commentaries, was responsible for the birth of the intellectual. The French historian Jacques LeGoff has devoted a brilliant book to this.[172] He sees the appearance of this new social and professional type, in the blossoming cities of the twelfth and thirteenth centuries, as a decisive moment in the history of the West. The new role of university professor arose, a person who engages in the new intellectual work as a combination of research and teaching in an urban and no longer in a monastic setting.[173] The *magistri* of the university were particularly experienced in grappling with the philosophy of the 'Arabs'.

Thus, Christianity inherited the Arabic philosophy of Islam. No Arab philosopher stimulated scholastic discussion—about the eternity of the world, the theory of the active intellect and the relationship between reason and faith—as much as Averroes. His towering importance is evident in the fact that, from about 1250, he is cited as 'the commentator' on Aristotle without his name being mentioned. Scholastics everywhere used the precise and extensive explanations in his commentaries to help them understand the compact and difficult texts of Aristotle: down to the twentieth century, scholarly editions of the works of Aristotle followed the divisions he made.

Whereas Albert the Great (Albertus Magnus) paraphrased Avicenna, Thomas Aquinas was his first disciple and most important opponent. He used Avicenna's commentaries on Aristotle lavishly while, like al-Ghazali a century earlier, clearly dissociating himself from some of his unorthodox doctrines, such as the Aristotelian idea of eternal matter and the Neoplatonic notion, taken over by al-Farabi and Avicenna, of a single, universal active intellect (the divine *nous*) which activates the passive human intellect until, at death, it is detached from the individual soul, so that the soul cannot be regarded as immortal. In 1270 Thomas Aquinas wrote a treatise on the 'Unity of the Intellect against the Parisian Averroists' against this view (which mentions Aristotle only in passing); he argued that the intellect is a capacity of the soul peculiar to each individual. After that, Averroes had two faces in scholastic theology: great commentator and dangerous heretic.

The leader of the 'Averroists', who in Paris since 1260 had been advocating a radical Aristotelianism with no heed to orthodoxy, was Siger of Brabant of the arts faculty (the seven free arts, *artes liberales*). He fought for the correct interpretation of Aristotle and the rights of the philosophers ('artists') against the powerful position of the theologians in the running of the university. However, during his lifetime, thirteen Averroist theses were condemned by Stephan Tempier, Bishop of Paris, on 10 December 1270, and two hundred and nineteen, including theses of Thomas himself, on 7 March 1277. This was a severe blow to Thomas's reputation, though only for the short and middle terms. For whereas in Islam, as we saw, the great systematician al-Ghazali was interested chiefly in the reconciliation of the Muslim faith with Sufism and pure philosophy was decisively weakened by his criticism, in Christianity Thomas Aquinas worked above all to reconcile the Christian faith with philosophy (of the pagan Greeks), and by his rational method prepared the way for pure philosophy. As a result, in the long term he became established in the church.

Alain de Libera[174] has worked out how, alongside the 'organic' intellectuals established in the university, the 'critical intellectual' always also developed: someone who did not want to bind himself to university, church or state. At the same time de Libera champions the theologians: 'If by "philosophy" one understands the practice of argument, in the end of the day the medieval theologians philosophized as much as, indeed more than, the "professional" philosophers. Today it is an evident truth that analytical philosophy arose in the Middle Ages, among the theologians.' For both theologians and philosophers 'the medieval university is the place of reason'. He argues that 'mastery of disputation' is the 'element that unites all the philosophical attitudes of the Middle Ages': 'the law of discussion applies to everyone'.[175] Delight in intellectual discussions seized broad portions of the population.

At that time Islam was still far ahead of Christian Europe in scholarly research, as has been demonstrated by the Turkish scholar Fuat Sezgin (of Istanbul and Frankfurt), pupil of the famous Arabist Hellmut Ritter. His 'History of Arabic Writing', which by 2000 comprised twelve volumes, covers the humanities, medicine and the natural sciences from geography to chemistry.[176] Nothing would be more wrong than to regard Islam as a religion hostile to scholarship but the importance of the various disciplines in Christianity constantly increased.

In the fourteenth century, some scholastics identified fully with Averroes and took over his interpretation of Aristotle as a closed system, even if this meant an irreconcilable opposition between their philosophical demands and the true but unprovable beliefs of the church. Such assertions of orthodoxy which, for opportunistic reasons, describe the revealed Christian statements of faith as truth, can hardly be taken seriously. Especially in Padua—for three centuries the stronghold of Averroism—a self-confident, pure, rational philosophy developed which, together with a revived Neoplatonism, became an important element in the Renaissance. Special mention should be made of the influential and controversial Aristotelian Pietro Pomponazzi (1462–1525), in whom the theoretical approach of Averroism breaks through completely in the self-assertion of the demonstrable knowledge of philosophy over against revelation and religious faith and thus the possibility of autonomous moral behaviour and inner human dignity. Such an assertion of the autonomy of profane scholarship in a believing world was possible, though difficult, in Christianity.

A continuation of the Middle Ages instead of a renaissance

A side-effect of the conquest of Constantinople by the Turks in 1453, which is little noted by Muslims, is the flight of numerous Greek scholars from Byzantium to Italy. In that century, from about 1420 to 1500—the Italian Quattrocento of the Florentine early Renaissance—Italy took the lead in European art and culture. For the Muslims, used to victory, this should have been a warning that world history is decided not only on the battlefields but also in the studies and workshops of thinkers, inventors, engineers and artists, and in the lower and higher schools.

The Renaissance began with the revival of the study of Latin and Greek and a historical–critical cultivation of, and disputation with, the writings of the ancient Romans and then also of the Greeks. In Florence this process had already been encouraged by the Union Council with the Greeks (in 1439), striven for through fear of Islam but unsuccessful, and by the flight of Greek scholars after the fall of Constantinople. With the philosophy of Plato and Aristotle,they reinforced and made concrete the new image of an independent world and autonomous human beings. The final contribution was made by the Platonic Academy, founded by Marsilio Ficino in 1459.

A boom in ancient education would also have been possible in Islam, but could a similar blossoming of the graphic arts? Donatello's David, Fra Angelico's frescoes, Botticelli's paintings are works of art of the very first rank but such religious or secular art would not have been possible in Islam with its hostility to images. But in connection with the Graeco-Roman traditions of education and the departure from medieval scholasticism, could there have been a completely new link between philosophy and humanism? Could there perhaps have been in Islam personalities such as the humanist Nicholas of Cusa, Erasmus of Rotterdam or the statesman Thomas More? No, this too would have been hardly conceivable in Arabic Islam, which with Averroes had bidden farewell to its Greek-inspired philosophy, whereas Persian philosophy could still be inspired by the Greeks through Avicenna.

No one at that time could have guessed what historical consequences would follow from the fact that Islam, previously so progressive, missed out on the cultural link with European humanism in the late Middle Ages. In the thirteenth and fourteenth centuries, and even more in the European Renaissance, individuals recognized their own value as earthly and historical personalities, now reflected in the mirror of antiquity. Already at that point a free, responsible view of the human being appeared. What began with the 'birth of the intellectual' in the high Middle Ages was extended in humanism by the discovery of the natural man and the free citizen. A new spirit of technical invention and striving for material prosperity were evident everywhere—the basis for the development of trade and crafts, which would replace agriculture as the main source of wealth and the occasion for new forms of investment and banking. In the 'house of Islam', however, from Anatolia to India people were above all interested in new European weapons rather than in the new European picture of human beings and the world.

Thus Islam remained largely closed to the new shift towards the individual, towards freedom, towards nature, indeed towards the worldliness of the world. Nor were there the makings of any separation between worldly and religious concerns. A difference between the 'Islamic world' and the 'West' had been becoming evident since the Investiture Dispute between the pope and the emperor in the eleventh and twelfth centuries (though there were signs of it in early Christianity). In Islam there was no late-medieval period of transition and upheaval to a still indeterminate new time, as there was in Europe, embracing aesthetic, social, economic and political changes: there was no Renaissance as a prelude to a new age, marked off from the Middle Ages and its narrow world of belief on the one hand and the rising 'enlightened' modernity and its new picture of human beings and the world on the other.

Antiquity had provided a criterion for detaching human beings from many medieval forms of life and created a new self-awareness for the pious individual (the mystic!). By contrast, the spiritual development of Islam remained largely tied to the traditional thought and way of life of its own Middle Ages and did not enable the individual to gain a new self-awareness and a new freedom.

There has been much discussion as to whether personal autonomy is a European invention or whether it can also be found in other cultural circles. If by autonomy we understand autarky (inner self-contentment and independence), then this appears in ancient Egypt. A self can be recognized in the Indian concept of the soul, Atman, and in the Greek conception of the agonal (sporting, musical, combative) self. However, autonomy in the sense of an integration of different concepts of freedom was, in the full sense, a European achievement.[177]

So in the following centuries Islam remained spiritually in the medieval paradigm of the Ulama and Sufis (P IV). Its élites and representatives noticed too late that in Europe an epoch-making paradigm change was making itself felt which in the long run forced the cultural sphere shaped by Islam increasingly on the defensive. In the twelfth and thirteenth centuries, when the 'light' of reason began to play a completely new role in theology, germs of the Enlightenment were planted which could develop in Christianity but were stifled in Islam. No longer did independent thinkers such as al-Farabi, Ibn Sina, Ibn Rushd and Ibn Khaldun set the spiritual tone in the Islamic world. A strongly rational worldview could not establish itself. The traditionalists fixated on the Qur'an and Sunnah dominated the field. And because under Muslim rulers, despite all the good beginnings, there could be no independent thinkers in philosophy, the understanding of the state and the natural sciences, there was no Renaissance, no Reformation, no Enlightenment.

The victory of traditionalism: al-Mawardi, Ibn Taymiyyah

Instead of the philosophers, the religious scholars called the tune, especially the representatives of legal science (*fiqh*), grounded in the Qur'an and Sunnah. Later generations appealed to Abu 'l-Hasan al-Mawardi,[178] born in 974 in Basra and living in Baghdad until 1058. A Shafi'ite court jurist and later grand judge, he had to experience how three years before his death the Turkish Seljuks, under Togril Beg, captured Baghdad and ended the predominance of the Persian Buwayhids. This marked the end of classical Islam; the authority of the caliphate was decisively weakened, to the benefit of the regional rulers. Understandably, al-Mawardi was concerned for the unity of the Ummah, writing one of the earliest and most significant constitutional dissertations on 'The Rules of Ruling'. However, he did not seem very interested in an ideal state ordered on the basis of reason (*al-'aql*), of the kind that philosophers were calling for. Rather, he was concerned with the real state, which was to be brought into harmony with the Qur'an and hadith with the help of the religious law. In his view, there was only one Ummah and therefore only one caliph; a second caliph, of the kind that the Fatimids were attempting to establish in Cairo, was impossible.

Ahmad Ibn Taymiyyah appeared two centuries later.[179] From the nineteenth century onwards he became the great historical ideologist of a community life orientated completely on the Ulama (the religious scholars), which alone could sustain the Islamic order in an era of decline. Born in Harran in Mesopotamia in 1263 (five years after Baghdad had been captured by the Mongols and the caliphate had been dealt a death blow), he fled before the Mongols to Damascus. There he became famous not only through his call to resistance but also through his campaign for the execution of a Christian who insulted the Prophet Muhammad. A Hanbalite jurist even stricter than Mawardi, in his sermons, speeches, opinions and writings he vigorously attacked his enemies, including theologians and Sufis and of course Aristotelian philosophers. At the same time he attacked the Shiites and the cult of saints and tombs then spreading even across Sunni Islam. Ibn Taymiyyah was against all 'innovation'. For him, 'innovation' was apostasy from the 'right mean': heresy and unbelief which was to be fought with every possible means.

For Ibn Taymiyyah, the only things that mattered were the Qur'an as the word of God and the tradition of the Prophet as authoritatively collected in the Shariah. As a jurist he interpreted them in a binding way, case by case—like the Roman church lawyers, who with their formal reference to scripture and tradition in the Catholic church took over its governance in the thirteenth century with their canon law. The most important popes of the Middle Ages were church lawyers and the Reformer Martin Luther was condemned by a Roman commission consisting almost exclusively of church lawyers. However, unlike church lawyers who were fixated on the pope, Ibn Taymiyyah was the first Islamic legal teacher to be content with the fact that there was no longer a central authority in Islam. Instead of the one caliph there were several political rulers ('emirs': *wulat al-umur*, singular *wali al-'amr*) but they were always to be advised by the Ulama. Only in this way could they expect the unconditional obedience of their subjects and serve the Islamic community (Ummah) in the various states. There was no Islamic right to resist; rather, the Shariah called for draconian punishments. Ibn Taymiyyah also spoke out against worldly music and any form of dance.

Ibn Taymiyyah lived in Syria, under the rule of the Turkish Mamluks, who wanted to make Cairo the new centre of Islam. Although he first served the Mamluk sultan al-Malik al-Mansur, his rigorous orthodoxy brought him into conflict with the political authorities and he was imprisoned in Cairo from 1306 to 1307, Alexandria from 1309 to 1320 and Damascus, where he wrote several of his works. He died in prison in Damascus in 1328 at the age of sixty-five. After his death his work became even more popular, especially his treatise on public law, the 'politics of law' (*as-siyasah ash-shari'ah*)—not a rationally-based politics (*siyasa*), as with al-Farabi, but one subordinate to religion (*shari'ah*)—which became a catechism of Islamic fundamentalists, although he himself was perhaps not a real fundamentalist.

In the fourteenth century, Islam missed an opportunity in world politics: the rational Islam of the philosophers and thinkers who wanted to interpret the

Qur'an and Sunnah on a rational basis failed to become established alongside the Islam of the law practised by the Ulama, which concentrated on loyalty to the Shariah, and the mystical Islam of the Sufis, whose faith in Allah culminated in the love of God. For that to have happened, this rational Islam would likewise have had to be institutionalized—not only in an academy of the sciences as had formerly happened in Baghdad, but in the influential madrasahs, the higher Islamic places of education, where the Ulama cultivated the training of cadres, the formation of communities and an international network. However, the madrasahs rejected rational philosophy and, in part, theology.[180] Nor were the Sufi brotherhoods, increasingly involved in social work, Islamic mission and often war, interested in philosophy.

Unitive thinkers, able to combine the religion of reason and the religion of the heart in the love of God, remained the exception. Only the mystical theosophy of Ibn 'Arabi (1165–1240) exercised any great influence alongside the 'oriental' theosophy (philosophy of light) of as-Surhawadi (who, on the orders of Sultan Saladin, was executed in 1191 as a 'deviant' from Islam). Ibn 'Arabi taught the unity of being (*wahdat al-wujud*). Like many Sufis, he was convinced that human knowledge, gained by the senses and the mind, is lower than religious knowledge, which rests on divine inspiration. Human beings can finally attain to God, who is ineffably pure light and absolute being, by following a spiritual mystical path. However, this did not mean that believers should give up the duties of a Muslim, prayers, fasting and so on, on the way to unity with God.

We shall see more clearly (see D II, 1, option III) that neither Averroes and rational philosophy nor Ibn 'Arabi and mysticism were to have a historical influence on Sunni Islam. That influence came from Ibn Taymiyyah and traditionalism. The fundamentalists of all coming centuries would appeal to him, including Ibn 'Abd al-Wahhab in the eighteenth century, whose puritanical 'Wahhabism' would become the ideology of the house of Sa'ud. In the nineteenth and twentieth centuries this house contested Ottoman rule over Arabia and finally established the kingdom of Saudi Arabia—guardian of the holy places of Mecca and Medina.

Freedom, reason, human dignity?

Questions arise from looking back on the whole long development of the Ulama–Sufi paradigm (P IV) and philosophy, which was dropped all too soon, and even more looking to the rising paradigm of modernity (P V) and the new emphasis on freedom, reason and human dignity.

At the end of a chapter which has been extraordinarily long, because of the diversity of peoples, the confused nature of developments and the complexity

Questions: Philosophy

- Couldn't a new, relevant, philosophy again become a corrective (not a regulating factor) for the Islam of the law in the law schools and their legal system against a legalistic type of scholarship
  - when this identifies submission (Islam) to God completely with submission to the Shariah;
  - when it thinks that it can settle all individual cases in life with juristic casuistry;
  - when it uses revelation to justify the repetition of manifestly irrational stipulations of the Shariah?

Or are Islam and autonomous human freedom mutually exclusive?

- Couldn't philosophy act as a corrective for Sufism against an anti-intellectual 'mysticism'
  - when it shifts the accent from the centre of religion to the veneration of saints, belief in miracles, the cult of tombs and the personal cult of the sheikh;
  - when it sinks into irrationalism, obscurantism and superstition by despising scientific knowledge and methodical rational thinking?

Or are Islam and autonomous human reason mutually exclusive?

- Couldn't philosophy serve as a corrective for theology: even in the face of a theological–juristic–Sufi synthesis in the manner of al-Ghazali
  - when, in its combination of Shariah and Sufi piety, it trusts too self-confidently in God and in the inner light that God gives;
  - when it won't allow an understanding of the world structured in accordance with philosophical principles;
  - when it doesn't reflect that there are human beings who trust in reason and reality without an explicit belief in God: a rationally responsible 'fundamental trust' which has the inner rationality without which science is inconceivable and also a universal ethic binding on both believers and non-believers on the basis of the humanity of all human beings?

Or are Islam and primal human dignity mutually exclusive?

of themes, I have to state that in the high Middle Ages the tremendous spiritual life characteristic of Islam in the early Middle Ages—in Baghdad, in Iraq and Iran—had emigrated to Christian Europe: to Paris, France and the Italian states. Whereas Baghdad and many of the cultural centres and art treasures of the 'Abbasid empire had been destroyed by the Mongol hosts, in Europe, despite some conflicts between church and state, philosophy, theology, the sciences and the arts developed creatively. In Europe, the new status of the intellectual, the 'organic' and the 'critical', played an important role, as did the foundation of universities all over Europe.

It is significant for the situation in the late Middle Ages that the ecumenical Council of Constance (1414–18), the only council to take place north of the Alps and the only one which effectively remedied a schism in the church (of three popes at the same time), was a gathering essentially governed by scholars, *magistri* and *doctores*. The most important 'pre-Reformers' were the Oxford scholar John Wyclif and the Prague professor Jan Hus (the burning of this Bohemian patriot and reformer, contrary to the promise of free passage, is a blemish on the otherwise successful reform council of Constance). Again it was *doctores*, not church leaders or state rulers, who sparked off the paradigm change in Christianity which had long been in the making: Dr Martin Luther, a professor in Wittenberg, and Jean Calvin, a jurist, theologian and organizer trained in Paris and active in Geneva, were the two leading figures of the Reformation which laid the foundations for European modernity. In the next centuries, and until the present day, this modernity would be the great challenge for Islam.

CV

The Paradigm of Islamic Modernization

1492 would prove more important in the long run for Islam than 1453, which saw the downfall of Christian Constantinople. In Spain it marked the completion of the Christian *reconquista* with the capture of Muslim Granada and the merciless expulsion of all Muslims and Jews who would not convert. It also saw the 'discovery' of America, followed two years later by the conquest of Mexico and the foundation of a Christian colonial empire fabulously rich in precious metals. In the sixteenth century the Islamic empires, which had previously had a strong position on the European continent, in Spain and the Balkans, and dominated sea trade in the Mediterranean and the Indian Ocean as far as Java, were still expanding and flourishing culturally. However, without their noticing it at first, within a few decades they were overtaken in science, technology, commerce and culture by the European powers. How could Islamic culture, which for many centuries was superior to Christian Western culture, fall so far behind? When did the stagnation of the Islamic world begin?

I shall investigate this question without making a 'European claim to a monopoly on modernity' and ignoring the process of the 'intercultural communication' between the European and the Islamic worlds. Islamic history must not be understood as a radical counter-scheme to the modern paradigm; however, the essential stimulation from Europe must not be underestimated.[1]

1. Confrontation with European modernity

Is Islam to blame for the stagnation?

It is not very helpful to play the blame game, looking for new scapegoats (Crusaders, Mongols, Spaniards, French, English or Americans), to excuse the fact that what was for a long time the strongest, richest and intellectually most progressive civilization in the world withered into one that was, on the whole, politically weak, economically poor and with a stagnant culture and intellectual world. Since the 1960s the Arab world has been overtaken by all the developing regions except for sub-Saharan Africa. Now, at the beginning of the twenty-first century, even the Arabs have noted that the Arab world is lagging behind in the international competition over development. The 2002 UN *Arab Human Development Report*,[2] produced by recognized Arab scholars and politicians, notes that, despite great progress in education and health, the group of twenty-two Arab states comes bottom of the list (even behind some African states) in withholding civil rights and economic freedoms. There are defects in the realms of education (the illiteracy rate is fifty per cent), research and the productive use of knowledge and weak participation of women in areas of public responsibility and production. Despite all the wealth from petroleum, the income of all the Arab states put together ($530 billion US in 1999) is no larger than that of a single European country such as Spain. Whereas in 1960 the per capita income in Arab countries was on a similar level to that of other developing regions, since then a tremendous gap has opened up, above all with the countries of East and South-East Asia. Compare the following incomes:

- Egypt $1490, Syria $940, Morocco $1180, Iran $1680, Pakistan $440;
- South Korea $8910, Malaysia $3380, Singapore $24,640, Hong Kong $25,290.

There is a similar contrast in child mortality per 1000 births:

- Egypt 42, Syria 24, Morocco 47, Iraq 93, Iran 33, Pakistan 83;
- South Korea 8, Malaysia 8, Singapore 3, Hong Kong 3.[3]

In the face of such facts, conspiracy theories in search of external causes may be comfortable and emotionally satisfying for those concerned, but at best they help authoritarian Muslim governments which seek to conceal domestic repression and economic, political and social failure in this way. Happily, since 11 September 2001, more and more thinking Muslims argue, in view of the disappointing developmental results, that the question should be reversed. These include the British Islamic scholar Bernard Lewis, Professor at Princeton University, who has collected a set of such questions under the title 'What went wrong?'[4] No more self-pity: 'Who has done this to us?', but self-criticism: 'What did we do wrong?', in order to ask the constructive question: 'How can we put it right?'

Lewis is Jewish and his book was given an angry review by an Arab expert on Islam, no less knowledgeable and by no means reactionary, the Palestinian Christian Professor Edward W. Said, author of *Orientalism*, which I quoted earlier (A I, 1).[5] He argues that Lewis has not taken note of the diversity of Islam and has argued almost exclusively from the Turkish Ottoman tradition. He says that a blatant example of Lewis's erroneous criticism is his assertion that, while Islamic society was fond of adopting Western weapons, it completely rejected Western music. Said cites many Arab examples to contradict this. Elsewhere, however, he replaces constructive counter-arguments with tirades against Lewis, who in 1990 provided Samuel Huntington with the title and theme of his notorious 'Clash of Civilizations' and now through generalizations, trivialities and unfounded assertions is reviving the old, religiously-motivated cliché of a violent, anti-rational, anti-modern and monolithic Islam.

Despite justified objections, some of Lewis's arguments nevertheless seem to me to be worthwhile and I shall take them into account when I describe the Islamic response to the four great European thrusts towards modernization. However, on the basis of my account so far (C IV, 7–8) I must make two corrections. The lagging behind of Islam

– must not be explained superficially only by military, economic and political factors; the spiritual and intellectual dimension must also be noted, as it is expressed in philosophy, theology, law and mysticism. The struggle for military victory, economic prosperity and political freedom is accompanied by the struggle for knowledge and understanding; new ideas and innovations can become established only in a culture of intellectual curiosity;

– does not begin in European modernity but as early as the twelfth century, with the end of philosophy and with it profane scientific autonomy, which it remained possible to assert in Christianity, despite all the difficulties. At that time new freedom of thought and action in Islam, any creative shaping of life, was made impossible; a brake was put on the dynamics of Islamic culture, science and technology, and the 'birth of the intellectual' was prevented and postponed for many centuries.

It was not just external forces, such as crusades, Mongol invasions and colonialism that resulted in the downfall of Islam in the late Middle Ages, as Muslims have long thought. Rather, it essentially dried out from within: the victory over philosophy and theology of an orthodoxy hostile to reason and freedom completely blocked the development of modern science and technology in the realm of Islam on the eve of the European Renaissance. Where universities and educational institutions are wholly dominated by a fixed science of law and tradition, the joy of intellectual discussion cannot arise. Where thinkers cannot breathe spiritually, they will not develop new ideas, scientific innovations, technical inventions and social initiatives. Where self-criticism is not allowed and people remain fixated on the status quo, they resist enlightenment. The Syrian Muslim political scientist Bassam Tibi of the University of Göttingen had the courage to look to his own roots for the main reasons for the humiliating lack of productivity in Islamic culture and formulated them in a pointed way: 'In fact Ibn Khaldun ... was the last great thinker in Islam. Up to the encounter with modernity, whether in a military or a colonial framework, the Ottomans were almost exclusively concerned with their military conquests. For five centuries there was no thinker worth mentioning in Islam.'[6]

After 11 September 2001 the Tunisian Muslim writer and literary scholar Abdelwahab Meddeb of the University of Paris X-Nanterre also published a much-noted diagnosis of the 'sickness of Islam'.[7] Just as intolerance was the sickness of Catholicism, he said, so '*intégrisme*' was the sickness of Islam. It is amusing to note that the word 'integralism'—preserving the faith '*integer*, intact'—became most popular in the Catholic Church at the beginning of the twentieth century: as the battle-cry of the Roman Curia and its French supporters against the bogey of 'modernism', which they themselves had invented. Here the issue was the integral interpretation of Roman Catholic doctrine; in Islam, according to Meddeb, it was the integral interpretation of Qur'an and Sunnah. Beside the external reasons for 'the sickness of Islam' Meddeb seeks the inner grounds internal to Islam, integralism bound up with anti-Western feeling. He researches into the long history of Islam and comes up with a genealogy for this attitude: in the eighteenth century Ibn Taymiyyah, Ibn 'Abd al-Wahhab and in the twentieth century Rashid Rida, Hasan al-Banna', Abu l-A'la Mawdudi and Sayyid Qutb (who also appear in this book, albeit in the context of the great epoch-making constellations, the different paradigms).

Is Islam itself to blame for the striking lack of spiritual productivity in the Islamic world? Even Bernard Lewis does not think this. It is indisputable that at least in the early Middle Ages the great centres of civilization and progress were neither in the old cultures of the East nor in the young cultures of the West but in the world of Islam, which lay in between. Here old sciences were discovered and new sciences created, new industries came into being and both production and trade attained previously unprecedented levels as did art and poetry. It was under Islam, where governments and societies had attained a high degree of tolerance, that persecuted Jews and even Christian deviants sought refuge: 'The medieval Islamic world offered only limited freedom in comparison with modern ideals and even with modern practice in the more advanced democracies, but it offered vastly more freedom than any of its predecessors, its contemporaries and most of its successors.'[8]

So who is to blame? Bernard Lewis does not answer this question precisely. By way of anticipation, my reply would be: Islam is not in itself to blame, nor is a particular paradigm, as long as it is appropriate to the times; what is to blame is the perpetuation of a paradigm beyond the period which is appropriate for it. The Ulama–Sufi paradigm was as appropriate for medieval Islam as the Roman Catholic paradigm was for medieval Christianity. But to have persisted in this paradigm beyond the Middle Ages, in completely changed circumstances, led to a time lag and thus to a spiritual lack of productivity. This is true of the church, the theology of the Counter-Reformation and anti-modernism (apart from baroque art)[9] and of the Islam of modernity, which in a not dissimilar way rejected reformation and enlightenment. Religious paradigms have a high capacity to persist and survive, especially with the institutionalization of religion.[10] In both Christianity and Islam this can result in a lack of spiritual productivity, as will emerge in the following sections.

Islamic expansion in India, South Africa and South-East Asia

The gradual internal collapse of the Islamic world was hardly visible to begin with, since in the early modern period Islam first expanded further. However, this now happened less through military conquests than through merchants, settlers and Sufis. Islam expanded:

- from the tenth to the twelfth century from Arabia towards India and East Africa;
- from the thirteenth to the fifteenth century from Arabia and India to the Malay peninsula and the Indonesian archipelago;
- increasingly from the coasts of the continents and islands into the interior.

It was not Muslim armies of occupation but networks of trade, family ties, Sufi communities and teacher–pupil relationships that played the primary role here. Only in West Africa and in the Sudan did Islam spread through wars in which African Muslims seized political power and tried to extend it as far as possible. But even in Africa processes of conversion were usually slow and led to highly different forms of Islam.

The more Islam spread, the less monolithic it became. It mixed with the practices and convictions of the popular cultures in which it found itself taking root. In this way it succeeded in penetrating groups of peoples, integrating them into states and often giving them a new social identity. To differing degrees, it was the Middle Eastern forms of the Ulama–Sufi paradigm that were taken over. Thus whereas strong cultural and artistic energies were released everywhere, there was no fundamental paradigm change in the religious sphere.

The new Islamic world was shaped more than ever in two ways: by shared faith and religious practices and by highly varied local cultures. Islam proved to be a universal religion which was at the same time regionally rooted and strongly diversified: the Arab regimes remained orientated on traditional Islam, as did the Turkic regime, but the Indian Mughal empire developed syncretistically. The Malaysian–Indonesian region remained deeply grounded in non-Islamic cultures, with only a somewhat thin Islamic veneer.[11]

Different social structures

The density of social structuring developed in different and momentous ways in Islam and Christianity. In Islam there were essentially three levels: tribal relationship, religious community and empire. However, after the downfall of Rome and the dissolution of both the Carolingian and the Holy Roman empires the all-powerful state retreated and a richly differentiated society developed, with a multiplicity of interlocking feudal obligations, loyalties and networks. It had many different power centres and specific forms of popular sovereignty (based on Roman and Germanic legal concepts).

A new type of society manifested itself in Christian Europe. After the historic conflict between pope and emperor in the eleventh and twelfth centuries, a separation of church and state took shape, which made possible a highly varied development in both the religious and the worldly spheres: a separation of faith and knowledge, religion and politics. It resulted in a great pluralism in both church and secular communities and offered individuals many possibilities for activity. Religious identity and worldly role could be distinguished, and this first functional differentiation led to others. Gradually independent secular literature, philosophy, jurisprudence, medicine and finally science developed and a non-clerical intelligentsia of writers, poets, jurists, doctors, professors, judges, administrative officials and scientists formed. Whereas in Islam total acceptance of the Shariah and insertion into the Ummah was still called for and the obligations of the individual were defined in that light, in Europe the legitimacy of different ethnic, religious or philosophical values and systems was increasingly recognized, as was, ever more clearly, the dignity which inalienably dwells in each individual and the inviolable rights based on it.

This complex development, driven by Christianity and humanism and leading to serious interest in the distinctive worth of the individual, reached its first climax in the Renaissance. It encouraged the spirit of technological invention and with it economic development and military striking power. Only slowly did Muslims note the many ways in which the world was changing: whereas the heavy Arab ships were still confined to the coasts, inventive Spanish and Portuguese shipbuilders constructed stronger and faster ships with the aid of new techniques (the classic ship with three masts and a large store of provisions), capable of remaining at sea for months. This enabled them to sail boldly over the open ocean in search of new sea routes. The Portuguese Vasco da Gama discovered India (with the help of a Muslim pilot), and in 1492 America, a continent still unknown in Europe, was discovered by Christopher Columbus, the supreme master of seafaring and cartography. And all this happened without the Arabs being able to prevent it!

Sailing the oceans and discovering America did not of themselves bring about an epoch-making paradigm change for Christianity at that time; the first discoverers were, in many respects, still utterly medieval men with crusading ideas. Only in the seventeenth century would the new philosophy (Descartes), the new natural sciences (Galileo) and the new understanding of state and society (Hobbes and Locke) bring about the great change to modernity (P V) and only in the eighteenth century would Islam resolutely be forced on to the defensive. Before that, in Europe there was a religious revolution. But there was no Islamic reformation.

Why was there no Islamic reformation?

Only twenty-five years after the discovery of America there was a successful epoch-making religious upheaval in Europe which had long been in the making(C IV, 8): the revolution against the centralist absolutist medieval Roman church system (Christian P III) which refused to reform the church—Martin Luther's Reformation (Christian P IV). This revolution took up the impulses of humanism and the Renaissance and, with corrections and errors, thought them through in religious terms in respect of the position of the responsible individual before God. At the same time, under Calvin's influence and against the background of the fear of divine predestination and the personal salvation of the soul, a very effective work ethic also developed: material prosperity as a sign of God's gracious election. Max Weber's famous thesis of the 'spirit of capitalism'[12] is grounded in this.

Was there also a reformation in the world of Islam? This question, which has been posed time and again by Muslims, especially since the nineteenth century, is hard to answer. It was posed again after 11 September 2001, for example by the Pakistani Muslim Tariq Ali, who lives in England: 'Why was there no reformation in Islam, in contrast to other world religions such as Christianity or Judaism? Why did we have no renewal in this era?' Ali, a writer, journalist and film-maker, replies: 'This reformation would have taken place had Islamic culture in al-Andalus remained intact. For the first great ethnic cleansing in Europe took place in Spain, when Jews and Muslims either converted to Islam or had to leave the country. Europe reshaped its identity and wanted no alien presence.'[13]

However, this answer is hardly convincing. The European Reformation began shortly after the conquest of Granada, at the beginning of the sixteenth century, and many centuries have passed since then without there being any great 'reformation' in Islam. So is Islam a completely static religion? By no means. Long before the challenge from Western imperialism, there were several renewal movements which were not provoked from outside but were a response to the inner weaknesses and abuses of Islamic society itself.[14] I have shown how:

- under the Umayyads (P II) the 'secessionists' (Kharijites) called for a return to the origins at Medina and the Qur'an;
- the 'Abbasid 'turning point' (P III) was propagated as a renewal of original Islam against the Umayyad secularization;
- in the time of al-Ghazali (P IV) people were convinced that a renewer of Islam would appear at the beginning of every Muslim century;
- belief in a Mahdi ('the rightly-guided one'), in a 'hidden imam', the true successor to Muhammad and Ali, who had been taken up and would one day return, was central to Shiite Islam. He would restore the 'true Islam';
- also in Sunni popular belief the hope of a messianic Mahdi was widespread at an early stage.

The hope of an eschatological renewer is rather different from an effective reform here and now and a limited reform movement in certain regions is different from a reformation that moves the whole community of faith. As Islam had no church-like structures and, since the downfall of the caliphate, no universal leadership, it would have been difficult to focus the reform movements as they were focused in Christianity in reaction to the papal universal primacy. So there could be no universal reformation but only regional reform movements. These were often more successful in smaller countries. Thus in Africa some politically militant *jihad* movements from reformist Sufi orders even led to Islamic states. Early African reformers include 'Uthman dan Fodio (1754–1817) in northern Nigeria, Ahmad ibn Idris (died 1837) in Morocco and his pupil Muhammad ibn 'Ali as-Sanusi (1787–1853) in Libya. In the Sudan, Muhammad Ahmad (1844–85) proclaimed himself Mahdi, defeated the Egyptian forces of occupation and even the British under the governor general C.G. Gordon. Ahmad established a theocratic state that lasted until 1898, when it was defeated by an Anglo-Egyptian army under Sir Herbert Kitchener. Shah

Wali Allah of Delhi (1702–62) and his disciple Sayyid Ahmad Barelwi (1786–1831) were active in India; Barelwi succeeded in establishing an Islamic state on the territory of present-day Pakistan against the repressive Sikh regime, before falling in battle. However, the situations in the three great Islamic empires which formed at the beginning of modernity in India, Iran and Turkey were different.

2. Three great Islamic empires: Mughals, Safavids, Ottomans

At the beginning of the sixteenth century, apart from some peripheral Islamic territories such as Morocco, Central Asia and Indonesia, three great Islamic empires replaced the smaller Islamic states. They were marked out by a high spiritual and material culture, parts of which found their way to Europe (such as 'Turkish music' and also food, spices, materials and so on). They were:

- the Indian Mughal empire,
- the Persian Safavid empire,
- the Turkish Ottoman empire.[15]

Because of the spiritual and religious situation described above, all three empires had long been rooted in the Islamic Middle Ages (P IV). In the sixteenth century, absolute monarchies triumphed everywhere—in complete contradiction to the originally egalitarian orientation of Islam—with well-organized officialdoms and strong armies. However, soon all three empires were exposed to European modernity, which, thanks to its technical superiority, revolutionized world trade and world politics. The exploitation of the colonies brought vast imports of gold, silver and spices to Europe and led to a redistribution of the world's wealth, combined with a new international division of labour: raw materials (now more important than luxury goods) came from the colonies and high-quality industrial products were exported from the European countries. In the eighteenth century this development, which a century before had robbed the Islamic states of much income from tax and trade and so considerably weakened their governments, sparked off the economic, political and cultural downfall of the Islamic empires. However, Islam showed itself to be largely immune to Christianity as a religion. I shall now look at certain aspects of these three great empires in more detail.

The Indian Mughal empire: Akbar's unitary religion

There had been Islamic invasions of India as early as the eighth century—usually from Afghanistan—and from the beginning of the thirteenth century the sultanate of Delhi (1206–1526) was ruled by an Afghan Turkic military dynasty.

But from the beginning Islam in India was marked by a great variety of communities and groups—Sufi brotherhoods, individual sheikhs or teachers—each with a different doctrine and different schools.[16]

In India, too, Islam showed the essential features of the Ulama–Sufi paradigm but there was no unitary Muslim establishment and no uniform Muslim community. Here the Muslims had a new experience: they were, and remained, a minority ruling over a population which on the whole, unlike the Near East, North Africa, Central Asia and Indonesia, did not convert to Islam.

In time, the Sufis became even more important than the Ulama promoted by the state; the Indians could recognize their 'holy men' or gurus in them. The mystical philosophy of, for example, Ibn 'Arabi (1165–1240), who taught the unity of all being, corresponded very closely to the Indian mentality. The Sufis were more concerned than the Ulama, which was committed to Arabic, about the integration of the Indian languages, music and poetry into Islamic life. Hindi became their vernacular but they also inspired the rise of Urdu, a literary version of Hindi, which became the Muslim language in India and, in the twentieth century, the official language of Pakistan. The Sufis kept a more critical distance from the state than the Ulama, who often served as judges, officials and teachers.

A spiritualized form of monotheism had spread in India in the fourteenth and fifteenth centuries. Guru ('teacher') Nanak (1469–1539), founder of the religion of the Sikhs (Hindi 'disciples'), came from these circles. His great vision was the union of Hindus and Muslims on the basis of an aniconic monotheism—God beyond all forms—combined with a doctrine of reincarnation but he succeeded only in certain regions. Under his nine successors, the 'gurus', Sikhism spread in the Punjab. The Golden Temple ('Hari Mandir') in Amritsar is its main sanctuary and the 'Adi Granth' ('first book'), consisting mostly of poems and hymns of the gurus, is its holy scripture.

The Indian Mughal empire (Arabic *maghul*, Persian *mughol*, 'Mongol') was founded by Zahir ad-Din Muhammad Babur (1438–1530) at the beginning of the sixteenth century—at the time of the Reformation in Europe—in the turmoil surrounding the sultanate of Delhi. This Jagatai Turk claimed descent on his father's side from Timur and on his mother's side from Genghis Khan. He was an insatiable conqueror but also a highly sensitive literary figure whose memoirs, 'The Book of Babur' (Turkish *Babur-name*), have become part of world literature. It is 'regarded as one of the richest and most beautiful prose works', indeed as 'the most lively example of Turkish literature'.[17] With superior cavalry, fighting and weapons technique Babur conquered Kabul in 1504, Kandahar in 1506 and, after a decisive battle in 1526, the whole of north India. After the fall of Agra, Babur had himself proclaimed 'Emperor of Hindustan' in the mosque in Delhi but died only four years later.[18]

After some turbulence, the most important Mughal emperor of India was his grandson, Akbar the Great (1542–1605).[19] With great sacrifice, Akbar advanced the territorial expansion south and east and by the age of thirty-four ruled over a vast empire which embraced the whole of north India well down into the middle of the sub-continent. Akbar was not only a great general; although he could not read or write, he was highly successful in the thorough organization of administration, finances, the tax system and, under his direct command, the army. He also promoted the arts and sciences.

When Akbar, who had been brought up by a mystic, married a Hindu princess on a pilgrimage in Jaipur at the age of nineteen, she was allowed to continue to practise her faith and Akbar even accompanied her to her temple. At a very early stage he sought a balance between the small ruling minority of the Muslims and the great Hindu majority by practising unusual tolerance in his religious policy: there was a ban on enslaving Hindu prisoners of war, poll tax was abolished and Hindus were admitted to offices. What was created for the many different peoples of India was not an exclusively Muslim culture but a cosmopolitan Islamic Indian culture which cultivated an Islamic–Hindu style in painting, music, literature and architecture.

'Peace for all' was the later designation of Akbar's religious policy: the religions of the empire were encouraged to take one another seriously, as partners of equal standing, and a 'universal reconciliation' between them was to be striven for. In his new palace city in Fatehpur Sikri, west of Agra, he expressed this policy with a variety of religious symbols and from 1575, in the 'House of Worship' which was erected, scholars of the different religions had an opportunity to explain their own religion and discuss it with others.

This tolerant policy was criticized, especially by the circles of the Ulama loyal to the Shariah, but they often proved disunited and inferior in the discussions about both theological and practical questions. Akbar wanted to be a Muslim who was in principle faithful to the Qur'an; strengthened by a deep spiritual experience, he believed in the one God who could also reveal himself in other religions. Extremely well-educated Jesuit missionaries also took part in the scholarly discussions of Muslims with Hindus, Jains and Parsees; at court they even built their own chapel and were allowed to preach and carry on their mission there. However, even after efforts lasting several years, they were unable to convert the emperor.

Increasingly under pressure from the traditional religious scholars, on the occasion of a legal dispute over a disputed death sentence in 1579, Akbar made the scholars issue an official certificate giving him, as head of the community of believers (*al-Imam al-'Adil*), the right to decide in disputes. Having long been associated with a Sufi order, at the age of forty he had the confidence to found his own mystical order ('Divine Oneness') in the service of the one 'divine religion ' (*din ilahi*), which consisted of elements of the religions he knew. The emperor's last years were overshadowed by the rebellion of his son Salim (later called Jahangir). Akbar died on 25 October 1605, after a severe illness lasting four weeks: he had reigned for almost fifty years. Historians call him 'the Great', and rightly so, for his influence is still felt today—in the age of religious dialogue.

To his last days, Akbar was not interested in a Shariah that regulated the whole of life. His military and political élite comprised Afghans, Iranians and Turks and also Hindus; loyalty, not religion, was the criterion. His unitary religion did not become established but in the religious bond with their ruler the members of the orders ('Murids', 'aspirants', 'disciples') remained an important factor in the preservation of the Mughal dynasties. In Indian popular piety the boundaries between Muslims and Hindus remained fluid; it seemed to many that God might be beyond the difference between temple and mosque and behind all forms. Under Akbar and his successors Jahangir and Shah Jahan, in Agra and Delhi there arose perhaps the greatest buildings in Islamic art, witness to a bewitching Persian–Indian court culture. Akbar's grandson Shah Jahan (1628–58), builder of the Taj Mahal, the monumental tomb for his beloved wife and a wonder of world architecture to the present day, leant more towards the Shariah than Sufism. However, a craze for building and tremendous expenditure on court and army, intensified by neglect of agriculture, quickly led to serious economic difficulties.

'Re-islamization' and decline

The classical system of the Mughal empire lasted until the rule of the darkly puritanical Aurangzeb (1658–1707). Under him, the Mughal empire attained its greatest extent but it also had an economic crisis: it was over-extended and therefore endangered. Aurangzeb saw deliverance in strict orientation on a discipline regulated by the Shariah: instead of equal rights for Hindus there was a clear Islamic dominance. However, in the now powerful Hindu empire of the Marathas he soon had an opponent of equal stature. Aurangzeb hated 'heretics' and unbelievers; he avoided Hindu festivals as far as possible, again excluded Hindus from public office and fought both Shiites and Sikhs, whose leaders he had executed. He banned alcohol, games, prostitution and even music at court. Above all he ordered the destruction of all Hindu temples throughout the land, including that in Rama's birthplace, Ayodhya. To the present day he has not been forgiven this, as was shown by the destruction by fanatical Hindus in 1992 of the mosque erected there and the continued acts of violence by radical Hindus against Muslims.

Despite all its 'modern' approaches, the Mughal empire remained trapped in the medieval Ulama–Sufi paradigm—with serious consequences. Hindus and above all the militant Sikhs revolted; they wanted their own state in the Punjab (and indeed attained it for half a century, with its capital in Lahore). On his deathbed, the eighty-nine-year-old ruler (he too was in power for fifty years) had to concede his failure. The proud Mughal empire was now in a lamentable state and would soon collapse into numerous feudal regimes.

The European colonial powers were already bringing India under their rule. First came the Portuguese in the sixteenth century, followed by the Dutch in the seventeenth; then the French and above all the English were involved. The East India Company, active in India since 1600 as a trading organization, advanced British colonialization powerfully in the eighteenth century. But in 1857 there was a great mutiny of the Muslim and Hindu members of the Company which was put down by the British with draconian measures: the Mughal emperor was deposed and the Muslims were punished, having been made the main culprits for the rebellion. This was probably unjust.

These events were decisive for the development of the Muslim reformer Sayyid Ahmad Khan (1817–98) who, in many books and articles, attempted to convince the British that the Muslims were not the chief culprits in the revolt and wanted to educate his fellow-believers in a tolerant, enlightened understanding of Islam. He succeeded in opening Muhammad College in Aligarh in 1878; it was organized on the Oxbridge model and teaching was given in English. Before any other Muslim, he saw the need for a radical revaluation of Islamic thought, open to modern science and philosophy. So in India, at an earlier date than in Egypt and in the Ottoman empire, Islamic modernism became a real option for many people. But how did the situation develop in the adjacent second great Islamic empire, in Iran?

The Persian Safavid empire: the first Shiite state

Under the impact of the devastating Mongol invasions, Sufis had often formed groups and organizations for the political protection and the spiritual care of the people. For Iran the most significant was the Safavid movement, founded by the Sunni Safi ad-Din (died 1334), master of an order, from a Kurdish family in north-west Iran. The Safavids were able to establish themselves as a new dynasty which would reunite Iran and reign from 1501 to 1722.[20]

Isma'il I proclaimed himself Shah of Persia in Tabriz in 1501, conquered the whole of Iran with the help of a Turkman army, united the nation which was internally torn apart, and brought it together as a nation-state under a strong central authority. Isma'il declared himself the hidden imam of the Shiites and the reincarnation of 'Ali. He did not shrink from any act of violence to establish the Twelver Shiah as the state religion. The Sunnis—initially the majority in Iran—were persecuted; they—especially their Ulama—fled or were deported, even liquidated. Only now did the Shiites exist in clear geographical separation; they were also persecuted by the Sunnis as their opponents: this was a similar kind of hostility to that which existed in Europe between Catholics and Protestants in that same sixteenth century. For the first time in an Islamic heartland a stable, powerful Shiite state came into being, capable of defending itself; it has survived to the present day through all the vicissitudes of time.

Under 'Abbas I the Great (1588–1629), who renewed the army, administration and trade organizations, the now solidly established Safavid dynasty reached the pinnacle of its power. The symbol of its legitimacy was the new capital, Isfahan, a masterpiece of Middle Eastern city planning: all the businesses, the seat of government and the royal mosque were on a rectangular open space (*maydan*) extending for a third of a mile. Next to it was the giant bazaar and on the other side planted avenues led to the summer palace of the shah and the residences of the courtiers and ambassadors. To the present day Isfahan, with its more than a hundred mosques, remains Iran's architectural jewel.

At the same time 'Abbas brought a whole series of Arab Shiite Ulama into the country. These 'mullahs' established a clear doctrinal structure and instructed the people. 'Abbas formally incorporated them into his centrally organized military state: a state-controlled religious bureaucracy that performed tasks in the administrative, educational and judicial sectors. This was a religious establishment dominated by the land-owning aristocracy. On the basis of a literal exegesis of the Qur'an, these mullahs represented an Islam orientated wholly on the law instead of on philosophy and mysticism.

Shiite piety and politics

Instead of Sufi exercises in piety (*dhikr Allah*), ceremonies and rituals in honour of 'Ali's son Husayn were promoted and instead of the pilgrimage to Mecca, a pilgrimage to Karbala was commanded. There every year the Shiites celebrated Ashura Day (Arabic '*ashura*', presumably a loan word from the Aramaic, 'tenner'), the tenth day of the lunar month Muharram. From 963 this had been the official day of mourning for the murder of Husayn. The day is marked with fasting and passion plays with scenes depicting the life and suffering of the Prophet's nephew end with a great procession in which individual groups even engage in bloody flagellation. However, Husayn was no longer venerated as a champion against injustice (this would have been too dangerous for the Safavid system), but as a guarantor for entry into paradise.

Some mullahs continued loyal to the older reforming tradition; the Shiite mullahs never declared, as did some Sunnis, that 'the door of the *ijtihad* is closed'; rather, they argued that religion must adapt itself to current needs. That was demonstrated again in the Second Iraq War of 2003/4, when Karbala proved to be a centre of resistance.

The 'great' 'Abbas was both cruel and purposeful. He had most of his sons killed, as possible rivals, so only grandsons and great-grandsons succeeded him. Under them, the state rapidly fell apart, despite the cultural boom. In 1722 the first Shiite state collapsed and Isfahan was captured by the Afghans. Wars with neighbours and turmoil in the provinces were the result; Afghanistan, which remained Sunni, became independent.

Only towards the end of the eighteenth century did the dynasty of the Qajars (originally Turks in the service of the Safavids) reunite the land. But like the Indian empire, in the nineteenth century the Persian empire was in religious crisis: its élites saw themselves increasingly exposed to the political and spiritual influence of the West. A positive consequence was that the mullahs distanced themselves again from the political system and no longer wanted to see the shah as the hidden imam. However, the strong Shiite establishment, often in opposition to the political system, was maintained. From 1786, the capital was Teheran. In the nineteenth century an attempt at modernization was made from here, inspired by France and then by Great Britain. However, Persia came increasingly under Russian influence. In 1907 Russia concluded a partition treaty with England in St Petersburg—a Russian sphere of influence in the north and a British sphere of influence in the south-east. Only the Ottoman empire preserved its independence. What were the developments in this third great empire, the neighbour and ancestral enemy of the Persian Shiites?

The Turkish Ottoman empire: the new Muslim world power

At an early stage the Sunni empire of the Ottomans had spread in Anatolia, which became a completely Muslim country—on the basis of both Turkic immigration and the suppression and conversion of Christians.[21] For long a Christian territory after the mission of the apostle Paul, in 650 Asia Minor still had more than thirty metropolises and around 440 dioceses. After the advance of Islam, hardly a trace was left of them. By 1354 the Ottomans had advanced across the straits of the Bosphorus to the Balkans and conquered northern Greece, Bulgaria and Serbia. The decisive battle on the Field of the Blackbirds in Kosovo in 1389 is still a trauma for Serbia. However, there was no systematic persecution of the Christians, but a comparatively tolerant regime, so that these countries largely remained Christian.

After the conquest of Constantinople in 1453 by Sultan Mehmet II, the 'conqueror', the thrust of the Ottomans seemed limitless. Mehmet saw himself as successor to the Byzantine emperor and adopted some Byzantine practices. The sixteenth century saw new and highly aggressive expansion. The sultan was glorified as a warrior ruler, caliph and imperial conqueror. Under the established dynasty of sultans there was a military and administrative state with a rationalized and centralized organization headed by the Grand Vizier and the other ministers (viziers). The Ottoman empire became the chief Islamic power, with Sunni Islam as the state religion and a strong regular army. Its core was modernized artillery and élite infantry from the janissaries (Turkish 'new troops'), select Christian boys, brought up in isolation as Muslims, without Turkic relatives and committed to the sultan alone.

Sultan Selim I (1512–20) was the real founder of the Ottoman empire: he controlled the whole of the eastern Mediterranean and conquered Azerbaijan, northern Mesopotamia, Syria and Egypt. The Mamluks, who had military power over Egypt and Syria, had long been a political, religious and cultural bulwark against the Mongols, but proved to be hopelessly inferior to the Ottomans, as they had no artillery. In subsequent decades Ottoman supremacy was extended to Arabia, the holy cities of Mecca and Medina, Yemen and the states of East Africa as far as Morocco: this powerful East-West empire extended from Iran to the Western Mediterranean and from the Ukraine to Yemen. After the imprisonment of the last Mamluk anti-caliphs in Cairo in 1517, the title caliph, that they had earlier claimed, was hardly a matter of dispute any longer. Finally, the caliph embodied not only patrimonial (Ottoman) and Islamic authority (guardian of the Shariah and protector of the holy places[22]) but also imperial authority, grounded in a cosmopolitan culture with Arab, Persian, Byzantine and European elements. The Turks, whose governors and troops were present everywhere, had now replaced the Arabs as the privileged class; like the Balkan peoples, the Arabs would play no further independent political role until the twentieth century.

Sultan Selim's only son, Suleiman the Magnificent (1520–66), strengthened the state, reorganized the army, built remarkable mosques (after the model of Hagia Sophia) and extended the empire to Baghdad, Basra and Bahrain. In alliance with Christian France, he marched against the Christian emperor Charles V and after occupying the kingdom of Hungary (after the battle of Mohács, 1526) he even laid siege to the capital of the Habsburg empire, Vienna. However, this was in vain. Suleiman died in 1566 on a campaign in Hungary. In 1571 the Ottoman fleet lost the sea battle of Lepanto, against a Christian alliance. The Ottoman empire had passed the zenith of its power, though it was to maintain itself at an impressive level for another one hundred and fifty years.

If the sixteenth century was the century of expansion, the seventeenth century was the century of preservation. A second siege of Vienna in 1683 also ended in failure with defeat at the Kahlenberg. The advance of the Turks had been definitively stopped; the Ottoman empire had over-extended its power—the mistake of all empires. It was less and less able to maintain the great disciplined armies and could no longer finance them. The eighteenth century was the century of defeats. The Russian Tsar replaced the Roman-German emperor as champion against the Ottomans. He moved from the north to conquer the territories occupied by the Turks and, as we shall see, he was successful.

The difference in South-East Asian Islam

By the sixteenth century the Ottoman empire had succeeded in bringing both the Sufi orders, who were very powerful in the land, and the Ulama completely under state control: the Sheikh al-Islam supervised the Ulama aristocracy (made up of prominent families) and the lower Ulama—which resembled a hierarchy of higher and lower clergy. What had been a greater openness (for example, towards philosophy) was also increasingly suppressed. The quality of the religious élite declined: a state career became more important than piety and education. In the seventeenth and eighteenth centuries the Ulama formed a powerful conservative community of interest, whose members—teachers, preachers, heads of foundations, judges and provincial officials—were always on the side of the political establishment and legitimized it. However, their backwardness and their remoteness from the people took their toll, for the Ulama–Sufi paradigm in which they were trapped was directly challenged by the Christian West: new military techniques, economic organization and cultural renewal were increasingly seen as a direct commercial, territorial and religious threat to the Ottoman empire.

Islam developed in South-East Asia in a completely different way from Turkish state Islam, but also in a different way from the Mughal empire, where political splintering, rather than an imperial unity, was the rule. South-East Asia had never been conquered and united by Muslim tribes. The pre-Islamic world of Malaya, Sumatra and Java, with undiminished strong Hindu or Buddhist influence, remained the political and cultural foundation of Indo-Malayan Islam. This was introduced by merchants, Sufis or teachers of the law and so developed in a decentralized way: around individual village Ulamas, Sufis or other popular teachers. It had no state organization, and sometimes even resisted the state authority. Brotherhoods and Ulama schools could develop only to a limited degree. Village Muslims, the majority, were little marked by Islamic rituals, concepts, institutions and customs. Islam was more a matter of personal identification than social organization.[23]

At the beginning of modernity, a look at the Islamic world between Istanbul and Jakarta shows that there is no such thing as 'Islam', but a broad spectrum of different Islamic countries and systems. They were challenged, right across the spectrum, in an unprecedented way by science, culture, politics, military development, technology and industry.

3. How Europe challenged the world of Islam

The traditional conviction of Muslims everywhere was that through the Qur'an, revealed word for word by God, God had promised them the leading place in the world. The victorious progress of Islam to this point, far from being completed, had triumphantly confirmed this promise. With such a sense of superiority, grounded in religion, even at the *Porte Sublime* (*Bab-i 'Ali*)—the name of the splendid gate to the residence of the Grand Vizier, head of government in Istanbul and used generally for the government of the Ottoman empire—people realized too late that with the rise of European modernity the economic and political world situation had begun to change fundamentally. Under the influence of the traditionalist orthodox Ulama, both the spiritual and the social life of the Ottoman empire had fossilized.

The decisive geopolitical change—the 'discovery' of America and the circumnavigation of Africa (the sea route to India)—had an increasing effect. The Mediterranean, the great trading power Egypt and oriental trade through Islamic lands became secondary. With the shift of the economic centre the focal point of world history moved from the Mediterranean to the Atlantic. The modern European world system was taking shape; it was to prevail for about three centuries and would finally dominate the three great Islamic empires. This was a colonial five-power rule, first of Portugal and Spain, and increasingly of France, England and The Netherlands. New metropolises developed on the European Atlantic coast that would soon become more important than those in the Mediterranean. After Seville and Lisbon, Antwerp, Amsterdam and London came to dominate; the two latter also had the leading stock exchanges.

Even more important than the intellectual and cultural change was that autonomous reason, which had been dismissed in Arab Islam along with philosophy long before the Italian Renaissance in favour of the Ulama–Sufi paradigm, became the driving force of developments in Europe in the middle of the seventeenth century. European modernity was in keeping with the Renaissance and its basically optimistic mood. However, while the Renaissance was still orientated backwards on Graeco-Roman antiquity, European modernity was orientated forwards: belief in human reason and a common human nature became belief in a better future and in progress. A sense of superiority, grounded in a belief in reason and progress, was the force behind four epoch-making thrusts towards modernization, which also affected the Islamic world.[24]

The thrust towards modernization I: the scientific and philosophical revolution

The seventeenth-century revolution of European modernity was primarily a revolution of the spirit and of science, which became the first great power of modernity.[25] The new, truly revolutionary, world system, which had been presented by Copernicus in a purely theoretical and hypothetical way, seemed to threaten the biblical picture of the world only at the moment when the Italian Galileo Galilei irrefutably confirmed it with experiments. Galileo became the founder of modern empirical science, which opens up the laws of nature in an investigation of nature that is, in principle, boundless. Two generations later, Isaac Newton constructed a convincing new system in an utterly rational way and became the father of classical theoretical physics.

At the same time as Galileo was working in astronomy, the mathematician and scientist René Descartes founded modern philosophy. The precision and certainty of mathematics were the new ideals of knowledge. Given radical doubt, the foundation of all certainty was the fact of one's own existence, which could be experienced in the act of thinking: '*Cogito, ergo sum*—I think, therefore I am.' This was an epoch-making turning point: the point of original certainty had shifted from God to human beings. The English empiricists Thomas Hobbes, John Locke and David Hume put human experience (empiricism), on which all knowledge rests, in the foreground. Immanuel Kant then combined continental rationalism and English empiricism consistently in a great philosophical synthesis to construct the whole of reality from the human subject. In questions of the knowledge of God, Kant no longer appealed to 'theoretical' but to 'practical' reason, which manifests itself in human moral action. However, the existence of God is the condition for the possibility of this action. Human reason was the prime modern value and, increasingly, became the supreme arbiter on all questions of truth, in opposition to the religious authorities.

How did Christianity react to this 'Copernican shift' in science and theology? Luther and Melanchthon rejected the work of Copernicus because it contradicted the Bible, but Protestantism as a whole remained open to new developments. However, the Catholic Church became less and less characterized by intellectual effort, empirical assimilation and cultural competence and more and more by a rejection of all that was new. Out of fear of defeat and a loss of power the Inquisition was brought into play. Giordano Bruno, Lucilio Vanini, Tommaso Campanella, Galileo Galilei and others fell victim to it. In 1633 Galileo, blind and broken, was condemned to lifelong house arrest by the Roman Inquisition, having forsworn the teaching of Copernicus that the earth goes round the sun, allegedly contrary to the Bible. He died, alone and embittered, in Florence in 1642. Fear of inquisitors, denouncers and nunciatures spread among leading figures; Descartes postponed indefinitely the publication of his treatise 'On the World or Treatise on Light'. There was an almost silent emigration of natural scientists from the church: there were scarcely any new scientists in Catholic countries in the following centuries. How did people react in Islam?

A paradigm change in Islam?

The old Islamic societies, confronted with European modernity, were not static, decadent and incapable of resistance: they too were constantly subjected to changes from within. However, it cannot be denied that these societies were forced to make fundamental changes by the new European technology, international trade, new kinds of communication and education and new forms of administration and jurisprudence (often, too, by their own governments!). Albert Hourani of the University of Oxford, author of a history of the Arab peoples, is right in his view of this period as a 'complex interaction' which, for the Muslims, also includes preservation and change.[26] This was no simplistic opposition between the modern rational West and the unmodern religious East:[27] that is why, in these sections, I have always first put critical questions to the Christians. However, we cannot overlook the fact that the decisive impulses for modernity came from the West: hence there are clear questions to Islam. As far as possible I shall try to combine a synchronous and a diachronous consideration of history.

In the Ottoman empire and the empire of the Persian Safavids the great cities, centres of traditional manufacture, were dominated by three groups: the merchants, the master craftsman and the Ulama. These groups legitimized the rulers, who increasingly ruled the surrounding areas from the city and ensured that the Shariah as the Islamic legal system remained in force and was applied.

The Ulama did not necessarily have to oppose the new heliocentric picture of the world: the Qur'an, which like the Bible as a matter of course presupposes the geocentric picture of the world, differs from the Bible in not offering an exact description of the creation of the world and human beings in six days. Therefore there is no equivalent to the Galileo case in Islam. However, the Ulama did not encourage the adoption of the insights of the new Western philosophy and science, orientated on mathematics; they had long since bidden farewell to independent philosophy and autonomous thinking. Islam, increasingly focused on itself, therefore at first simply ignored the philosophical and scientific development of the West. A paradigm change to modernity, like that in the West, did not occur anywhere in the Islamic sphere in the seventeenth and eighteenth centuries, even in Iran, where philosophy underwent a revival.

Western superiority first struck the Muslims in the diplomatic and military spheres. At the peace of Karlowitz (Serbia) in 1699, the sultan, presenting himself to the West as caliph and 'protector of all Muslims', for the first time could not dictate the peace terms but had to engage in the play of modern 'diplomacy', which had been developing in the West since the sixteenth century and was based on permanent missions, with special rights, to foreign governments. The sultan lost Hungary, Slavonia and Croatia, and in 1774 also the Crimea. This was a truly a century of defeats.

Forced on to the defensive, the Ottoman empire imported Western weapons, telescopes, field glasses and clocks and, finally, above all Western experts. The consent of the Ummah was needed to bring 'unbelieving' teachers into the country to educate 'believing' Muslim pupils. At the same time, Turkish ambassadors, delegations and individual travellers attempted to get behind the secrets of Western society and their successes.

For a long time, there had been no independent scholarship in Islamic societies. Proud of what they had achieved, scholars limited themselves to the repetition and veneration of traditional—above all religious—knowledge. Even in areas such as mathematics or medicine, where they had been leaders for centuries, they stagnated, so that here too a remarkable change in the flow of knowledge can be observed.[28] The Arabs had been amazingly open to ancient medicine. This had been made possible by the followers of the patriarch Nestorius, who had been banished from the Byzantine empire in the middle of the fifth century because of christological disputes. These 'Nestorians' established important medical training centres in Syria and Persia, where Galen and other classic Greek texts were translated into Syriac. These were then translated by Arabs in centres in Damascus, Cairo, Antioch, Basra and Baghdad (above all in the time of the caliph al-Ma'mun, P III). Thus as early as the tenth century, Arab medicine experienced its first heyday through systematization, extension and expansion of the ancient writings. Arab, Persian, Islamic medicine remained superior to the monastic medicine which dominated in the West until the thirteenth century and then to that of the secular medical schools which developed from the twelfth to the sixteenth centuries. Avicenna's compact and unitary *Canon medicinae* was the basic medical work for the Western Middle Ages, and was thought unsurpassable.

In the Ulama–Sufi paradigm (P IV), after the Mongol storm Islamic medicine made no further decisive progress. In the West, though, doubt about traditional medicine, nurtured by the plague and syphilis, led to fundamental corrections to Galen's medicine, to reflection on the theoretical foundations and eventually to the founding of modern medicine. That came about in 1543 with the first medical textbook of anatomy (by Andreas Vesalius), containing plates based on systematic dissections of human bodies; in 1628 William Harvey demonstrated the circulation of the blood and thus laid the foundation for physiology as an experimental and quantifying science.

In the Ottoman empire, where—in view of the abundantly rich Arabic, Persian and Turkish literature—for a long time there was little interest in learning Western languages, people were dependent on the relatively rare translations of Western works. In medicine these were largely limited to works on syphilis, which was spreading at the beginning of the sixteenth century. Not until 1655 was the sultan given a relevant volume of writings and all of these came from the previous century.[29]

The thrust towards modernization II: the cultural and theological revolution

In eighteenth-century Europe, the scientific and philosophical revolutions led to the cultural revolution of the Enlightenment, which finally also resulted in a political revolution.[30] The old word 'modern' became modern itself: it was the designation for the new feeling of the time. In a universal sea-change of cultures there was a marked cooling-down over religion: in the seventeenth century order, authority and discipline, church, hierarchy and dogma had still been highly prized—the preacher, theologian of history and court bishop Bossuet was the leading spiritual figure in France. However, in the eighteenth century these traditional values and institutions were largely rejected, indeed mocked, by the intellectual élite, particularly in Catholic France. The leading figure of the French Enlightenment was Voltaire, philosopher and critic of the church, and its standard work the thirty-five-volume *Encyclopédie* of the sciences and arts edited by Diderot and d'Alembert. A large-scale process of secularization and emancipation began, which later spilled over to Germany, albeit in a weakened form. Culture and religion, society and the church momentously moved apart.

Belief in the omnipotence of reason and the possibility of controlling nature became the foundation for a belief in progress that extended to all spheres of life. Progress was given almost divine attributes, such as eternity, omniscience, omnipotence and all-goodness. 'Progress' (now also used in the singular) became the second leading value of modernity: people expected it to produce happiness in this world, not just in the next.

How did the church react to the Enlightenment? Medieval and Reformation belief in the devil, demons and magic, witch trials and the burning of witches, did not fit into the progressive age of reason. Wars of religion were increasingly regarded as both inhuman and un-Christian. Religious toleration, utterly alien to the Reformers, became almost a keyword of modernity. The political realization of human rights was being demanded loudly and freedom of conscience and religious practice were top of the list. The playwright Gotthold Ephraim Lessing who wrote *Nathan the Wise* was an important figure in Germany (1779, see above A I, 1: 'Enlightenment').

Christian theology and scholasticism were not spared the cultural revolution in the name of Enlightenment. Here a key role was played by biblical criticism, which even subjected Holy Scripture to a historical–critical analysis. However, within the Catholic Church, the spirit of biblical research was stifled before it could begin to blossom. The critical history of the Old Testament by the French Oratorian Richard Simon, far in advance of any Protestant exegesis of the time, was confiscated on its appearance in 1678, on the initiative of Bossuet. The consequence of the repression was the emigration from Rome of critical exegesis and thus of the *avant garde* of theology. It was thanks to the tremendous work of generations initially only of Protestant exegetes that the Bible became by far the most thoroughly investigated book in world literature. This made possible a text-critical theology, capable of translating the original Christian message for a new time.

Enlightenment in Islam?

'Enlightenment', which according to Kant is the departure of human beings from a self-imposed tutelage, might perhaps have been demanded in the ninth century by Mu'tazilites but hardly by an eighteenth-century Muslim. The Enlightenment, prepared for in Europe by the Renaissance, could not establish itself in the Ottoman empire because the great European literature, from Descartes to Voltaire and Kant, was barely known in Turkey: initially there were only a few translations into Turkish.[31]

In addition, the printing of books was first allowed only to minorities; therefore to begin with, remarkably enough, there were printed books only for Jews, Greeks and Armenians. There was a religious taboo: no books were to be printed in the 'holy language of the Qur'an', Arabic, or in Turkish; that is what the Ulama and, in part, the calligraphers wanted. Only in the nineteenth century was the printing press generally allowed. This meant a tremendous time-lag in the communication of information. At first, there were hardly any Turkish newspapers either; those that eventually appeared were for a long time only government papers. So there was no need for the profession of journalism, which was becoming increasingly important in the West, a vital element in the new critical intelligentsia.

In these circumstances, public criticism of the existing political and religious system, and getting rid of prejudices generally, was difficult, as was a critical historiography which was not just conformist protocol. This applied especially to critical research into the sources of faith, the Qur'an and the hadith. Critical Christians now regarded both the writings of the Hebrew Bible and those of the New Testament as the products of human authors who wrote them under the inspiration of the Spirit of God but the surahs of the Qur'an were regarded as having been personally dictated by God and thus as the literal word of God: nothing in them could be altered and they could be interpreted only within very narrow limits.

However, in the context of the second theological dispute—over reason and revelation in the ninth century (P II)—I established that at that time the dominant view of Islamic theologians and the caliphs was that the Qur'an was created. This could have been the basis for a text-critical Islamic theology which was in keeping both scripture and its time. But belief in the un-createdness and infallibility of the Qur'an finally triumphed over belief in its historicity. The signs for a historical–critical investigation of the Qur'an were considerably less favourable than those for such an investigation of the Bible and in later periods not a single Muslim scholar took up Qur'anic criticism. The question arises as to whether whether it can be prevented in Islam in the long run, and whether, if it is not practised by Muslims, it will be practised by Western scholars. Only at the end of the nineteenth century and in the twentieth century did commentaries on the Qur'an stress the value of reason and the acquisition of rational knowledge and, in some cases, present Islam as a religion of reason (see D VI, 2–3). However, the controversy concentrated initially on politics.

The thrust towards modernization III: the political and democratic revolution

The political revolution—after the American Revolution—was the French Revolution, at the end of the eighteenth century.[32] The medieval church theocracy, embodied in the pope, was a thing of the past, as was the notion of the king as sovereign 'by the grace of God', the Protestant authority of a prince or city council and the early modern enlightened absolutism of Frederick II of Prussia or Joseph II of Austria. In France, the hour of democracy had arrived. The people (Greek *demos*), embodied in the National Assembly, were sovereign. The nation became the third leading modern value; its ideology was '*liberté*' (political), '*égalité*' (social) and '*fraternité*' (spiritual). On 26 August 1789, following the American model (1776), the French National Assembly passed the Declaration of the Rights of Men and Citizens—the Magna Carta of democracy, one of the great documents of human history.

What about the Catholic Church? Unlike the democratically inclined local Catholic clergy (such as the great Abbé Grégoire, in the Revolution a champion of human rights and the equality of all human beings), the Vatican, the bulwark of anti-democratic reaction, rejected the revolutionary slogan 'Freedom—Equality—Brotherhood'. Massive resistance followed, also from the clergy, after the nationalization of church property, the restriction of clerical office, the dissolution of all monasteries and spiritual orders and finally the 'Civil Constitution on the Clergy'. Pope Pius VI declared the 1791 Civil Constitution invalid and, with reference to the divine revelation, rejected 'the abhorrent philosophy of human rights', especially the freedom of religion, conscience and the press and the equality of all human beings. The Roman Catholic Church presented itself as the great enemy of revolutionary transformation and thus became the main victim of the national revolution.

In France, this resulted in a split between clericals and anti-clericals, indeed the formation of two hostile cultures: the new militant republican lay culture of the dominant liberal bourgeoisie and the deeply-rooted Catholic conservative, clerical and royalist (later papalist) counter- or sub-culture of the church. The march of the Catholic Church into a cultural ghetto had begun. However, the Reformed Church of France, which had been mercilessly persecuted for a century, welcomed the revolution as liberation and adopted its humanistic values.

Islam and the French Revolution

In the late eighteenth century, the control system of the *Porte Sublime*, the central Ottoman government in Islam, had been loosened considerably. Though the sultan's authority remained undisputed because of the power of the army, fleet and provincial governors, the military commands in Syria, Baghdad and especially Cairo enjoyed growing independence. On the periphery of the empire, in Central Arabia, Muhammad ibn Sa'ud (died 1765) and his son 'Abd al-'Aziz I (1803) founded a state in close collaboration with the reform movement of the Wahhabis. In 1926 their successor established a kingdom in Arabia, made themselves independent and captured the cities of Mecca and Medina.

The French Revolution in 1789 seemed to Muslims to be the first European movement that was not Christian but even anti-Christian. How should Islam react to the demand for democracy, human rights and civil rights, toleration and the separation of state and church propagated by the revolution? As we have seen, to some extent the toleration of other religions by Islam was greater than that exercised by Christianity. However, even the much-quoted Qur'an verse 'No compulsion in religion' (2.256) still presupposes the pre-eminence of Islam and the rule of Muslims, and people were even less willing to consider a dissolution of the close connection between religion and political power.

Paris was a long way away, and people in the Islamic countries hoped that they could keep this European movement far from their own territory. However, in 1798, the thunder of the cannons of Napoleon Bonaparte, who had set out to conquer Egypt, shook the Muslim world and showed what the novel 'machines' used by the French were capable of. Terror spread widely: a small European army could evidently penetrate Muslim heartlands with impunity. Traditional military means could not oppose it.

It became irrevocably clear to the Muslims that a new time had dawned: Islam could no longer avoid European modernity. Muslims, too, increasingly took up the new ideas and models of the French Revolution: a new freedom and equality attracted their peoples. Soon patriotism and nationalism proved to be driving forces that could shatter and finally dissolve the multi-people empire of the Ottomans as they could that of the Habsburgs. In this complex process, the economy became increasingly important.

The thrust towards modernization IV: the technological and industrial revolution

A hundred years before the bloody French Revolution, Britain had carried through its 'glorious revolution' and introduced a parliament into the political system. So in the nineteenth century, undisturbed by political revolutions and restorations, it could provide economic impulses and technological achievements such as steam engines, railways and factories. In this way it initiated the technical and industrial upheavals that were to change the European world no less deeply than the political revolution: industry became the fourth modern leading value.[33]

In several European countries, anti-revolutionary restoration and romanticism already proved to be a trough in the revolutionary wave of 1848, though reaction once again proved victorious. Democracy continued its victorious course, as did the technological revolution. Lightning conductors, spinning machines, mechanical looms, coal-fired steam engines; the building of roads, bridges, canals and the first railway lines; the development of locomotives, steam ships, telegraphy—all this was the foundation for new methods of production and the organization of work.

An epoch-making change in the economic and social conditions of life began to spread, what came to be called the Industrial Revolution. This embraced revolutions in technology, production processes, the generation of energy, transport, the rural economy, the markets and in social structures and ways of thinking, combined with a population explosion, an agricultural revolution and headlong urbanization. As a consequence of industrialization, a proletariat of factory workers, without possessions and often living in great misery, formed below the 'third estate'. In the *Communist Manifesto* of 1848, Karl Marx and Friedrich Engels summoned the proletariat to class warfare and the abolition of the capitalist order that owned property and business and ordered society. In the first third of the nineteenth century industrialization spread from Britain to The Netherlands, Belgium, France and Switzerland; in the middle of the century to Germany; and eventually to the rest of Europe, Russia and Japan. Industrial technique, previously implemented purely empirically, was now practised on a scientific basis and became technology.

How did the church react to the Industrial Revolution? The break with tradition brought about by democratization and industrialization came as a shock for the churches, whether Catholic, Protestant or Anglican, but also as a challenge to win back the working class that they had lost through a series of new forms of church action. The result, especially in Germany, was many social activities within the church; however, in the Catholic Church these were counteracted by controversies between a reactionary papacy and liberalism, and tensions between the papal primacy and the episcopacy and over the claim to the infallibility of the Pope in matters of faith and morals proclaimed at the First Vatican Council in 1869/70.

It became clear that modern democracy, which abolished the absolutist system, and the Roman system formed in the eleventh century, which put a religious brake on absolutism and bureaucratized it, were totally incompatible. Soon a large number of representative spirits, from Copernicus to Kant, stood on the Index of books prohibited to Catholics. This shows how, with the Roman-Catholic medieval paradigm (P III), Rome had gone on the defensive. And Islam too?

Reforms in Islam?

After the Napoleonic wars, which ended in 1815, the Islamic countries were increasingly confronted with a new kind of trade: European ships brought more and more mass-produced goods, above all textiles and steel, into the ports of the eastern Mediterranean, along with precious spices and coffee from the eastern colonies. Since the 1830s, transport had been speeded up by steamships, later supported by telegraphs. The Middle Eastern countries, by contrast, could provide only raw materials for the European factories: corn, dried fruits and cotton from Anatolia, silk from the Lebanon, cotton from Egypt and olive oil from Tunisia. These one-sided trade relations necessarily led to a growing economic dependence of the Islamic countries on the European powers, which would be followed by political dependence—unless reforms were implemented in Islam.

The situation of Islam became increasingly complex in the nineteenth century, although all Islamic countries faced the same challenge. Even if we leave aside Islam in central and South East Asia, in West and East Africa, and concentrate on the Islamic heartlands, it is striking what different state and religious structures and social institutions were dominant in Turkey, in Egypt or in the Arab 'fertile crescent'. Whereas Turkey represented an established Ottoman state and Egypt, Tunisia and Algeria were something like Ottoman sub-states, in the 'fertile crescent', while there were the important government centres of Damascus, Aleppo, Mosul and Baghdad with small provinces separated from one another, there was no state regime with any degree of independence which had its own history and united ruling élite. This would remain the case until the Second World War—an important factor in understanding the conflict that would arise between the Palestinians, who were not organized into a state, and the Israelis.

The Ottoman empire was particularly important. It was the chief Islamic power, even if in North Africa and Egypt it could maintain its supremacy only formally. The Ottoman empire reflected, in exemplary fashion, the problems of reform in Islam generally. The issue everywhere was how Islam could find a way from the medieval Ulama–Sufi paradigm (P IV) into an appropriate modernity, an Islamic modernization paradigm (P V). Since the middle of the seventeenth century Christianity, and since the eighteenth century Judaism, had begun to realize a paradigm of modernization—with great difficulties but ultimately successfully. By the nature of things, such a paradigm change would not take place in Islam without controversies. Reforms were almost always disputed. Even in the discussion of the entry of Turkey into the EU at the beginning of the twenty-first century, people are asking how far the Turkish nation has really appropriated the 'achievements of modernity', above all at a political level. This is a question of fundamental importance, not only for Islamic Turkey but also for Europe with a Christian stamp. So, let me pose some questions specifically from the Islamic perspective.

Questions for European modernity

This necessarily broad description of the four main European challenges to the world of Islam should not give the impression that the achievements of European modernity were not problematical and that critical questions from Islam are unjustified. However, at the high point of European modernization, only some of its shadow sides had become evident. Today faith in the leading modern values of reason, progress, nation and industry have been shattered by two world wars; Communism, Nazism and Fascism; the Holocaust, the Gulag Archipelago and the atom bomb—and so too has faith in the modern ideologies of nationalism, liberalism and socialism.

But critics could have put questions to modernity as early as the nineteenth century and some are certainly put by Muslims, both from the more conservative and the more liberal side. From a present-day perspective we could formulate them like this:

Questions: Modernization

- Muslims cannot ignore the tremendous progress made by scientific research, but many are asking where the moral progress is which would have been able to prevent the misuse of science.
- Muslims admire and make use of the highly-efficient forms of technology which have been developed, but many are wondering why the spiritual energy which could have brought the risks of technology under control has not been developed to the same extent.
- Muslims are themselves part of an expanding worldwide economy, but many are asking what the resources of ecology are to oppose the worldwide destruction of nature by industrialization.
- Muslims see themselves confronted with developments towards the realization of democracy and human rights in their countries, but many of them are asking whether a morality is also developing which could work against the massive interests of the great variety of individuals and groups with power and which could provide the necessary impulses for the realization of human rights.

In the nineteenth century, these questions could not be put in this polished form, but they were in play in the battle over reforms which was affirmed by many, in particular in the Ottoman empire, but resolutely rejected by others.

4. Between reform and reaction

The impetus to reforms (Turkish *tanzimat*) in the Ottoman empire always came from above, from the rulers, the sultans, and initially reached only an élite.[34] Sultan Selim III (1789–1807) introduced systematic reforms and Mahmud II (1808–39) continued them in the army and administration, while Mahmud's son 'Abd al-Majid I (1839–61) undertook a fundamental reform of the laws. Not only the military but also the administration, law, the economy and education were to be modernized. The Islamic state was successively modernized, i.e. centralized, rationalized and in fact also secularized. Of course, the sultans did not want to carry out these reforms against Islam, but for Islam. The Ottoman empire remained the last bulwark against the advance of Western colonialism and imperialism, which had to be defended with every possible means.

Ulama for reforms: Islamic reformism

How were reforms to be realized without the collaboration of the powerful body of religious scholars, the Ulama (often called mullahs in the Ottoman empire, as among the Iranian Shiites), who dominated the religious institutions, justice and education and occupied important points in public administration, politics and diplomacy? In this transitional period of the first half of the nineteenth century, it is of both historical and contemporary interest to investigate the question of what attitude the clergy of the last Islamic great power adopted towards the modernization and Westernization of state and society and how they assimilated the Western impulses in a way specific to their culture. Here we can see an Islamic reformism which ultimately became an Islamic modernism.

It may seem surprising that, as more recent research indicates,[35] the Ulama were by no means automatically opposed to reforms. On the contrary, they essentially supported Islamic reformism. Precisely because the heads of the Ulama were utterly bound up with the Ottoman political system and formed a part of the ruling class, they had a strong interest in defending their empire against the West. The Shaykh al-Islam and the senior Ulama—who came from a few prosperous families—were the only aristocracy in the empire. They maintained a variety of relationships with the court and the sultan and were given a great variety of political, diplomatic and social tasks. Four influential positions were traditionally occupied by high-ranking Ulama: the sultan's chief physician, the chief astrologer and the two personal imams.

The senior Ulama supported the reforms and sanctioned them by *fatwahs* (legal opinions);[36] they prompted these and sometimes even conceived them themselves; they were also represented in the newly-established advisory bodies. The introduction of printing presses, the Western bayonet, modern uniform and the red fez instead of turbans in the army, the first (official) Turkish newspaper, the first census and the fight against plague through a quarantine station in Istanbul would all have been impossible, given the manifold religious prejudices in the people, without the collaboration of the Ulama and important sheikhs of certain dervish orders. A religious scholar who, as the chief doctor, was also a confidant of Sultan Mahmud wrote a treatise at his request on fighting cholera. He did so with the help of an Austrian handbook, and thousands of copies of the resultant work were officially disseminated throughout the empire; he went on to found a new army medical school where, in the face of all resistance, he dissected human bodies, documenting this in his handbook of anatomy with the depiction of parts of the human body (which was traditionally forbidden).

The corporation of the Ulama could not show open resistance to the sultan; it had already lost considerable credibility and influence even before the reform period because of disunity, nepotism and corruption. The sultan was able to oppose the Ulama by being an absolute and autocratic ruler who mercilessly imprisoned, deposed or even executed those who opposed him. These opponents might be individual Sufi protesters or the janissaries who had ventured several revolutions against the sultan, sometimes as the tools of the Ulama. In 1826, the janissaries and the allied Bektashi Sufi order (which was likewise proletarian and illiterate)—were abruptly dissolved by the sultan and their property was confiscated. The abolition of the janissaries by Mahmud II was a decisive step towards the modernization of the empire and one supported by the Ulama. Out of gratitude, the sultan put the palace of the supreme commander of the janissaries at the disposal of the Shaykh al-Islam.

However, here the dilemma in which the leading Ulama found themselves became increasingly evident:

- On the one hand they had justified many reforms contrary to the Shariah as unavoidable, especially those forced on them by the European great powers in peace treaties and other agreements (for example, the rights of diplomats and their wives and the possession of land by Christians or Islamic apostates within the Ottoman empire).
- On the other hand the Ulama undermined their own authority as guardians and watchmen of the Shariah. Even constant new *fatwahs* for reforms could not end the people's tacit opposition to modernization.

Opposition to the reforms: Islamic traditionalism

Sultan Mahmud II established the red fez, which he himself also wore, not only in the army but also among officials. He robbed the Ulama of so much power that they were forced to accept the self-portraits distributed by the sultan—which was clearly against the precepts of the Shariah. However, the Ulama would not be stripped of the white turbans which marked them out from other believers, despite the urgings of the sultan; Kemal Atatürk abolished them a century later.

These measures largely silenced the opposition to the reforms but could not end it. It was kept alive by the class opposition between the higher and lower clergy: between the immensely rich aristocratic senior Ulama, exempt from taxes, who in their own interests also supported the reforms, and the lower Ulama in the city and country, who were closer to the often-fanatical masses of the Islamic people and had little time for the violations of the Shariah by the reformers. The allies of this reactionary Ulama were the merchants, craftsmen and lower classes of the people: they defended themselves against both Western influences and their own intelligentsia.

The thousands of students of the Islamic schools (*softas*) were particularly hostile to reform: whether they lived in madrasahs or outside, they were often desperately poor and undernourished and sometimes had to wait decades for a post as imam, whereas the privileged got posts even without adequate qualifications. No wonder that there were also demonstrations and revolts by these religious students, who wanted to have nothing to do with European reforms because they had been trained only in the traditional Islamic sciences and therefore saw both their Islamic faith and their economic future endangered.

The reforms were not imposed by officials in accordance with a revolutionary programme on the basis of a new order of values but pragmatically, on the basis of Islamic teaching and history. The official reason was that at a time of threats to the empire and Islam from the West the command for *jihad* in both Qur'an and Shariah required effort and sacrifice from all ('we are all in the same boat'). Islamic history shows that, from the beginning, the Muslims had taken over military techniques from their opponents. Moreover, where the Shariah did not pronounce against it, the sultan was always to be obeyed, as the legitimate authority. So the *de facto* ignoring or violating of the Shariah was tolerated, as long as there was no attempt to question it in principle or to reform it.

The reforming sultans used Islam for their own political ends and did everything they could to take the wind out of the sails of the critics of their reforms. There was:

- public endorsement of Islamic ideals at every opportunity and the derivation of the empire not only from Osman I but from the Prophet Muhammad and the community of Medina;
- an insistence on times of prayer and Islamic instruction even in the modernized army, with the help of special army imams;
- the building or restoration of countless mosques, holy tombs and dervish monasteries;
- regular participation in religious occasions;
- a raising of the salaries of the lower Ulama and numerous other signs of favour towards the Ulama.

Under these conditions, which were externally favourable for religion, the Ulama did not immediately recognize the possible consequences of this creeping secularization and totally failed to see the deterioration in their economic situation brought about by the state control of all religious institutions and foundations. Under Sultan 'Abd al-Majid I after 1839 there were comprehensive new methods of administration and legal codices with civil rights and civil responsibilities, along with an improvement in schooling. However, despite these changes, the strictly Islamic character of the kingdom was preserved externally: it was still a nominally Islamic empire, built on the Shariah with the Ulama as the leading class. So convinced were the Ulama of the absolute superiority and inexhaustible power of their religion, and so little did they know and understand the four revolutionary thrusts towards modernization which were having an increasingly strong effect on the West, that it did not even occur to them that one day Islam, like Christianity, could lose its public importance and that they too, the Ulama, like the Christian clergy, would experience a decisive loss of power through modernization.

An Islamic system that integrated the representatives of religion into society as an essential element could not avoid the conflicts between state and church, politics and religion, that were going on in the West but it did not take into account either a split between the higher and lower Ulama or a split in the spirit of the leading Ulama, who were exhausting themselves in political and administrative tasks and were scarcely concerned about the ongoing spiritual development of Islam. Would such a medieval system, built on the Shariah and Ulama (P IV), which had been internally weakened, be able to resist the clash with a largely secularized Western culture (P V)?

The new élites: Islamic modernism

For the French, Napoleon Bonaparte's expedition to Egypt was a military and financial catastrophe: its fleet was destroyed by the English under Admiral Nelson at Abukir (north of Alexandria); the army, cut off from home and decimated by plague, had no success in Syria either. However, in Paris Napoleon presented and propagated this expedition as a scientific and cultural success. For the Arab world, it was the starting point of independence from the Ottoman empire.[37]

After the brief occupation of Egypt by Napoleon's troops, an Albanian upstart and general by the name of Muhammad 'Ali (1805–48), who had been nominated governor general (Pasha) by the Turks, seized power with the help of a new military élite from the Balkans and Anatolia. With the aid of European capital and advisers, he introduced modernization of the army, the administration and the law. Unlike the Ottoman sultans, who had been restrained in this respect, the new Egyptian governor general nationalized the tremendous resources of the Ottoman sultans and boldly shaped Egyptian society on the model of European law and European financial practices. He encouraged irrigation and the cultivation of cotton and made possible a tremendous expansion of the capitalist economies of Europe and especially Great Britain. He built roads and reformed the health system. But at the same time he blocked the development of the Egyptian economy by a trade monopoly and high export tolls. Muhammad 'Ali did not achieve the independence from Turkey that he strove for, despite a successful military advance on Syria, but his governorship was made hereditary and after 1867 the governor general was given the title 'Viceroy' (Persian *khedive*, 'Lord').

Like the Egyptian reformers, the Ottoman and other Muslim reformers achieved more and more: a strong state and a productive and socially integrated society were fundamentally important for modernization. So corresponding social, legal and educational programmes had to be introduced which undermined the traditional role of the religious élite but precisely by so doing could lead to modern systems of justice and education. It was no longer the Ulama who worked vigorously for the adoption of European military techniques and the modernization of the economy and education but the new political élites educated in the West—the military, bureaucrats, landowners—and the rapidly growing political, technical and literary intelligentsia. To this degree Islam caught up with the 'birth of the intellectuals'. The medieval forms of Islam had to be given up but not Islam itself. Rather, in the view of the reformers this needed renewal of the often-neglected principles of nationality, patriotism and ethical activism.

In the first half of the nineteenth century, the reformers were still confident about the superiority of Islam and Eastern culture but in the second half of the century more and more reforms boldly conceded the lamentable state of Islam and called for a return to the original pure Islam with which important elements of modern European culture could be combined. Such ideas were not only put forward in Egypt but also by the 'young Ottomans' of the 1860s and 1870s. In India, Sayyid Ahmad Khan (1817–98), whom I have already mentioned, was far ahead in founding the college of Aligarh which, as Aligarh Muslim University, increasingly became the spiritual centre of Indian Islam.

From the 1870s, Islamic modernism was disseminated above all by Jamal ad-Din al-Afghani (1839–97).[38] He stood between the traditionalists, who wanted to go back to the Qur'an and the beginning in Medina, and the secularists, who wanted to give up Islam in favour of European education. Almost an Islamic Martin Luther, he emphasized the need for an Islamic reformation. He rightly said that European progress had been possible only because the Reformation had preceded it.

Born and brought up in Iran, al-Afghani was active throughout the Islamic world from India through Istanbul to Egypt as an inspiring political activist and journalist. He taught philosophy, theology and jurisprudence and in all these fields canvassed for a dynamic, creative and progressive Islamic religion and civilization. He argued that if Islam were not understood in a medieval way but as it originally was, there would be no difficulties in combining it with Western reason, science and technology. After all, this had previously been done with

Hellenistic and Persian science. Al-Afghani argued for a contemporary Islamic identity and unity of the Ummah. At the same time he promoted Muslim nationalism and pan-Islamism and ultimately always had in view freedom from the colonial yoke.

Al-Afghani's inspired Egyptian pupil Muhammad 'Abduh (1849–1905)[39] was also very interested in the continuity between Islamic heritage and modern change. He got to know al-Afghani in Cairo in 1873 and became professor at the al-Azhar university there but because of his entanglement in the revolt against the British after the occupation of Egypt he was banished by the British army and then, with al-Afghani, organized resistance in Paris. After his return in 1881 he worked hard for reform and in 1899 rose to become Mufti of Egypt, which gave him the power to interpret the Shariah authoritatively in a modern way. In his interpretation, the reform of justice became possible and European clothing and usury were allowed. He carried through a reform of Islamic law, Islamic theology and education. The distinction that he made was that duties towards God such as prayer, fasting and pilgrimage are unchanging but duties towards others are not. 'Abduh was particularly critical of polygamy and its extremely negative effects on family life. In addition to his commentary on the Qur'an and his dissertation on mystical experience, he wrote 'The Theology of Unity' (*Risalat at-tawhid*). His fellow-fighter, Qasim Amin (1863–1908), state advocate and judge, wrote a bold controversial book on the emancipation of women, 'The Liberation of Woman' (1899), followed by 'The New Woman' (1901). She was later praised as the hero and founder of the feminist revival. After 'Abduh's death the Lebanese journalist and religious scholar Rashid Rida (1865–1935) became the intellectual leader of the reformist movement in Egypt. In his battle against nationalism and secularism he even argued for a renewal of the caliphate in his book 'The Caliphate or the Greatest Imamate' (1923).

Whereas the Ottoman and Indian reformers concentrated on their local and national situation, al-Afghani, in grand style, propagated an international union of all Muslim people who felt committed to modernization, so that they were politically united in resisting Western oppression. For in the meantime the Muslims had been forced to note that the colonialism of the European great powers had entered a new phase, described even in the West as European imperialism.

European imperialism: a paradigm of confrontation and aggression

In the 1856 Peace of Paris (after Turkey had defeated Russia in the Crimean War with the support of Great Britain, France and Sardinia) the independence of Turkey was confirmed and the sultan recognized as one of the European heads of state. That same year, the Ottoman empire introduced equal status for all nationalities in the service of the state; there was resistance only to putting the religions on an equal footing. Many Turks saw the collapse of the Ottoman empire on the horizon.

Egypt became increasingly dependent on England for the financing of all its projects. The opening in 1869 of the Suez Canal, the new trade artery to India, East Asia and Australia, by 'Ali's nephew Isma'il, tremendously increased the strategic importance of Egypt for Great Britain and with it Egyptian debt. Because of a ruinous taxation and financial economy, coupled with a ring of British politicians who were concerned for their own advantage, the economy and finance of the country kept deteriorating. I do not intend to go into the various analyses and theories of how, in a complex process, first Egypt went bankrupt followed by the state administration of debts incurred by foreigners (1882) and occupation by British troops (1882), probably to prevent an independent Egyptian military government. There is no doubt that the whole Arab world, indeed the whole Islamic world, saw the subjection of this Arab heartland by a single European power as an unparalleled shame.

But towards the end of the nineteenth century it could not be overlooked that, even in the Islamic countries, all the European great powers had moved on from colonialism (which strove for a few economic and military points of support above all on the coasts) to imperialism. In a feverish competition for protectorates and colonies, there was fighting for the economic, military and political control of whole countries and their integration into empires. The European great powers divided Africa up between them at the Berlin Congo conference of 1884–5. In the first half of the nineteenth century France had occupied Algeria and later Tunisia and in 1912 it established a protectorate over Morocco. The statesmen responsible did not take seriously that this modern policy of national interest, power and prestige of the European powers would inflame them against one another in the paradigm of confrontation, aggression and revenge that ultimately led to the catastrophe of a world war.

Around 1900 the world, in particular the Islamic world, was divided by the European great powers into areas of rule and spheres of influence:

– Russia, which had begun its expansion into Central Asia and Siberia in the sixteenth century with the conquest and colonization of the Tatar khanates of Kasan and Astrakhan and in the eighteenth century had incorporated the Crimea and the coastland on the Black Sea, in the nineteenth century seized rule over the Kazakh population of the northern steppes and annexed Transoxania and the trans-Caspian regions.

– China made East Turkestan a Chinese province, so that the majority of the Muslim peoples of Central Asia were controlled by Russia and China.

– The Netherlands gained control of South-East Asian trade in the seventeenth century and in the middle of the eighteenth century established territorial rule over the central island of Java; during the nineteenth century it extended this over the whole of the Indonesian archipelago. Belgium conquered the Congo and Ruanda-Urundi in 1881.

– During the nineteenth century, after occupying Algeria and Tunisia, France won rule over West and Equatorial Africa and the Levant (Syria and Lebanon). In 1885 Italy occupied Eritrea, in 1889 Somalia and in 1911 Libya. Germany founded 'protectorates' in South-West Africa, Cameroon, Togo and East Africa and in the Pacific bought the Caroline, Marshall and Palau Islands from Spain. As compensation for the loss of its colonial empire in South America and the Caribbean, Spain sought a substitute in Morocco. Since the fifteenth and sixteenth centuries Portugal had possessed and retained Guinea, Angola and Mozambique.

– Great Britain, which had established a trading empire in the seventeenth century with the help of its East India Company, seized political power over Bengal in the late eighteenth century and in the nineteenth century extended this over all India, thus ending Islamic rule. In 1858 India was put directly under control of the British crown. Great Britain also controlled Palestine, Transjordan and Iraq and, to secure its empire, controlled the Indian Ocean from bases in Malaya, the Persian Gulf, the Red Sea and East Africa. In 1907 there was a British–Russian agreement that Iran should be divided into two spheres of influence and later Great Britain made possible the discovery and exploitation of Iranian oil. In the Iran of the Qajars there were no reform laws, as there were in the Ottoman empire.[40]

European imperialism reached its high point at the time of the First World War: the colonial powers of France, England, Italy, Germany and The Netherlands had North Africa, the Middle East, India and Indonesia under their control—the whole vast Muslim territory from Morocco to the Indonesian peninsula! Some people, who want to frighten Europeans about an Islamic invasion, talk of this tremendous 'green girdle'. They should reflect that, barely a century ago, the same 'green girdle' was completely controlled and exploited politically, economically and culturally by the European powers.

Secular nationalism: the downfall of the Ottoman empire

In the nineteenth century, only the Ottoman empire had been able to preserve its independence—albeit increasingly limited to the Turkish heartlands. Not only had it lost Egypt and North Africa but early in the nineteenth century the Ottomans had to grant Serbia autonomy and in 1833—after a four-year freedom struggle—had to grant Greece its independence. In both Tunis and Cairo, what was in practice an independent regime had been ruling for a long time. The struggle of the Christian Armenians for independence, with Russian support, was met by the Kurds and Turks with deportations and massacres which took place from 1895 to 1897, in 1909 and, finally, under the revolutionary 'Young Turks' during the First World War in 1915/16, when around 400,000 Armenians were driven from the Armenian settlement area and more than 200,000 perished on the journey. Armenian historians speak of more than a million dead. It is still disputed whether the Young Turkish government controlled the pogroms itself.[41] The sovereignty of the sultan was increasingly limited to the central provinces and lasted only because the European powers virtually neutralized one another in the fight for this sphere of influence.

Millions of Muslims in the poor districts of cities and above all in the country still lived and thought in a traditional way. Their values and standards largely continued to be determined by the spiritual authorities of the former paradigm (P IV)—the Shariah, the Ulama and the Sufis—but slowly, in the capitals of Istanbul and Cairo and in other trade centres of the Ottoman empire, the number of officers, officials, teachers and doctors with a European training grew, and they had made the paradigm change to modernity (P V) in dress, dwelling and lifestyle. They formed an 'enlightened' modern class. Instead of Islamic modernism, their ideology was increasingly a secular nationalism on the European model.

Modern means of communication helped here: printing works and publishers, books, newspaper and journals contributed to the education of a critical class of independent-minded intellectual. Among them, modern nationalistic ideas from the West found more and more adherents: solidarity and unity no longer related to the throne and to rulers but to a nation state, based on the constitution and controlled by the people and its representatives, a democracy.

In 1876 the sultan had agreed to a constitution but this was soon suspended. In 1908 it was reinstated by a revolution of Young Turks,[42] mostly army officers, and the influence of the sultan on the government was heavily restricted. Islam remained the state religion but other religions were tolerated. In reaction to the pan-Islamic policy of Sultan 'Abd al-Hamid II (1876–1909), the Young Turks brought about a change from Islamic modernism to secular constitutional patriotism. For a modern government, administration, army and society, not Islam but nurture and education on the European model was of decisive significance. A modern middle class emerged from the modern schools—which were now open to girls—and especially schools teaching French and English (usually with the support of Christian institutions). These now produced the new élite. By comparison the traditional Islamic schools declined; they served only to train the Ulama, who now had far fewer professional possibilities, since modern legal works had replaced the Shariah—except in personal and family law. From Tunis through Cairo and Damascus to Aligarh, the spiritual centre of Indian Islam, a nationalistic ideology became established which, after the fading of the Islamic Ummah, promised a spiritual home with its national and secular symbols.

Most Young Turks still believed in a revived and strengthened Ottoman empire on the model of the Danube monarchy with its many peoples. They worked on political mobilization, economic planning, new social services and the promotion of women's work, laying the social and psychological foundations for a new civil society. However, they thought that the Ottoman empire could survive only with the help of a European protector. Therefore, on the eve of the First World War, they made a disastrous alliance with Germany and entered the war on Germany's side. However, the operations of war interrupted the import of the European goods and capital on which the Ottoman economy depended. The result was complete paralysis.

The Turks were now among the losers: the end of the First World War brought the end not only of the Russian, German and Habsburg empires but also of the Ottoman empire. There was a cease-fire on 30 October 1918 and in spring 1919 Istanbul was occupied by the Allies. The British and French advanced to the south-east, the Italians to the south and the Greeks occupied Izmir/Smyrna. In August 1919, the peace treaty of Sèvres was signed. Only a small territory in Anatolia was left to the sultan. Egypt became a British protectorate. Iraq, Palestine and Transjordan were also administered by the British under a 'mandate' from the newly-founded League of Nations, with a commitment to make possible a Jewish homeland (not a state—thus the declaration by the British Prime Minister Balfour in 1917) in Palestine. Lebanon and Syria were administered by the French, also under a mandate. Only on the Arabian peninsula had the Saudis been able to found their own state in 1832, on the basis of a strict Islamic Wahhabism: Saudi Arabia. Arabia was again making an entrance on the world stage.

Arab renaissance?

Scarcely had Egypt overcome the terror over the Napoleonic invasion and its own impotence than Muhammad 'Ali, the new ruler, sent a commission to Paris, in 1826, to study the scientific and technical, political, cultural and intellectual progress of the French. The leader of this commission, Rifa'ah at-Tahtawi, is still regarded as the pioneer of the 'rebirth' (*nahdah*), the Arabic Renaissance—four centuries after the Italian Renaissance. The great question was: would it be possible to bring about an Arab renaissance in the Islamic world?

It must never be forgotten that Islam was originally the religion of the Arabs (P I). So when the Islamic empire extended through conquest, new Muslims had to attach themselves to an Arab tribe as 'clients' (P II). But as these 'clients' became ever more numerous and influential, other nationalities had to be recognized as having equal rights. Islam then formed the great spiritual bond which held all these different nationalities together (P III). When the caliphate succumbed to the Mongol storm and Muslims came to be ruled by a number of sultans in place of the one sole caliph as the representative of the Prophet, the Shariah, protected by the Ulama, largely guaranteed the unity of Islamic society (P IV). This was and remained the case when in the sixteenth century the Turkish Ottomans took over rule from the Arabs for four centuries.

After the fall of the Ottoman empire, shouldn't there have been reflection on 'true Islam' and thus on the Arab origin of Islam, the great Arab history, the Arab kingdom and the Arabic language?[43] An increasing number of Arab intellectuals spoke out, questioning the right of the Turks to rule over the Arabs, especially since non-Islamic societies had experienced equal legal rights in the Ottoman empire. They recognized in the new ideology, Arabism, the answer to the basic questions of the time. This Arab awakening was provoked by the encounter with the West. This was first highlighted in a book by at-Tahtawi, written in 1834 after a five-year stay in France. This 'Travel Diary of my Stay in Paris' was of great interest to both Arabs and Turks (it included a translation of the French Constitution of 1814). In it, at-Tahtawi spoke in a very European way of Egypt as his country and of the Egyptians as a people who should love their homeland. Just as he sought to promote Egyptian patriotism, so the Turkish reformers tried to promote Ottoman patriotism. Both sides were convinced of the downfall of Islamic culture and the need for reforms on the European model.

In the nineteenth century, to the great displeasure of the Muslim Arabs, there were Arabs of a Christian cast, who propagated a secular Arabism. First, European modernization in the Lebanon—where the influence of Maronite clergy trained in Rome led to a civil war with the Druse—resulted in a novel, secular, Arab consciousness. A modern literary élite emerged from the new schools run by Europeans. The Protestant Syrian College, founded in 1886, eventually became the famous American University of Beirut, and the French-orientated Université de St-Joseph appeared beside it in 1875. At the end of the nineteenth century there was increasing anti-Turkish resentment, indeed a newly-aroused sense of superiority among the Arabs, who thought that they might once again seize the leadership of Islam. Here for the first time a call rang out for the formation of a secular Arab state, in which Christians and Muslims could live together peacefully under a constitutional regime: instead of religion and a particular dynasty the Arab nation was to be the foundation of the state. Whereas Ottoman reformers strove for a single Ottoman nation made up of the different ethnic elements of the Ottoman empire, these Arabists wanted to unite all Arabs as a single people in a single nation: to replace Pan-Islamism there was a—now secular—Pan-Arabism. This gave rise to a new Pan-Arab consciousness, which first above all turned against the rule of the sultan and then, after the collapse of the Ottoman empire, gained wide assent.

If we look back at the process of modernization in Islam (P V), we can see that at the end of the nineteenth and beginning of the twentieth century the inner situation of Islam had dramatically sharpened—through the contemporaneity of divergent and rival paradigms which was now recognizable. All had their problems: Islamic reformism, Islamic traditionalism, Islamic modernism, secular nationalism and supranational Arabism.

Even more urgent and serious than the questions from outside, from the modern West, were the questions from within, from Islam itself. Would Islam remain merely conservative and preservative or would it develop into a progressive and liberating social force? How far could there be a renewal of Islam that sought to be orientated on the future, aware of problems and ready for change? How far would readiness for change go in the twentieth and twenty-first century world? Despite sometimes spectacular technological modernizations, was the state still to be dominated by religious institutions governed by medieval theology, medieval laws and a medieval social constitution?

After the analysis of the five macro-paradigms of the long history of Islam, we have arrived at the immediate present, though of course this continues to be governed by the paradigms of the past.

D. CHALLENGES OF THE PRESENT

How do things stand with Islam in the twenty-first century? At the beginning of the twentieth century, Judaism seemed in some ways better prepared to cope with the modernization process. Because they had been dispersed widely, the Jews of Western and Central Europe, among whom the Enlightenment established itself at the turn of the eighteenth and nineteenth centuries, had been more radically exposed to modernity than the Muslims. Spiritually, too, they had come out of the ghetto.[1] In Germany there was a great controversy over the reform of Judaism: not, as in Christianity, a religious reformation as a foundation for rational enlightenment but rational enlightenment as the basis for a religious reformation. From the form of worship to modern universal education and the training of rabbis, the reform embraced everything, including the modernization of Jewish clothing and diet—not forgetting the imposing 'science of Judaism' (Judaistics).[2] As a result, in Judaism there was a paradigm change in the nineteenth century, from the medieval rabbinic paradigm (P IV) to the paradigm of modernity (P V), the paradigm of enlightened reform Judaism.

And in Islam? Would the paradigm change from the Muslim Middle Ages (P IV) to modernity (P V), so powerfully initiated in India, Egypt and Turkey, be able to consolidate itself? Forces and counter-forces determined the picture and the present was still largely dominated by the paradigms of the past.

In the following chapters I cannot present a complete contemporary history of Islamic countries or societies; for that I refer readers to the most recent histories of Islam.[3] Rather, to help towards a better understanding of the present Islamic world, I intended to sketch out some typical developments. I see the most recent history of the most important Islamic countries of the Near and Middle East as offering case studies which not only demonstrate the dynamic of the Islamic world, often overlooked, but also indicate some political, social and spiritual options for the future. In this difficult survey I have been helped not only by the standard works on recent history which I have quoted and the ever-helpful *History of Islamic Societies* by Ira M. Lapidus, but also above all by *The Modern Middle East*, edited by Albert Hourani, Philip S. Khoury and Mary C. Wilson, with contributions by outstanding specialists.[4]

D I

Competition between Paradigms

The present-day problems of the Islamic world are largely to do with the new ordering of the world after 1918. Unfortunately, what arose was not the world order sketched out on 8 January 1918 by the American President Woodrow Wilson in his 'Fourteen Points': 'a just peace' without any peoples being vanquished and the 'self-determination of peoples' without annexations and demands for reparation.[5] The 'Versailles' of the real politicians Clemenceau and Lloyd George prevented the realization of the new paradigm: instead of a just peace there was a 'dictated peace' without the participation of those who had been defeated. Little can be seen of the self-determination of the peoples called for by President Wilson either in the sphere of the former Danube monarchy or in the former Ottoman empire. There were very different developments and contradictory constellations: different groups of Muslims, who lived briefly in the same land with quite different theologies, forms of life and pictures of the world, dependent on quite different paradigms.

1. The secularist way

The victorious powers divided the Ottoman empire into two language spheres: the Turkish-speaking north and the Arabic-speaking south. In order to win the Arabs over in the fight against the Turks, during the war they had been promised a single, large, Arab kingdom but this promise was immediately broken by a secret agreement made in 1916 between England and France, the Sykes–Picot Agreement, which I shall discuss later. Completely in their own interests, the English and French divided the Arab sphere into different states, zones of influence and autonomous areas: for the most part, these were artificial constructions of imperialism. Thus, they removed from the map the

Ottoman empire, which had formed the political framework for the peoples of the Middle East for four hundred years.

Turkish secularism: Mustafa Kemal Atatürk

Thanks above all to a charismatic statesman, Mustafa Kemal Atatürk,[6] the Turkish-speaking north did not experience the same kind of division as the Arabic-speaking south. Mustafa Kemal was the first leader to establish a radically modernized and secularized paradigm in an Islamic country. He was born in 1881 in the cosmopolitan city of Saloniki, the son of a junior Ottoman official. He graduated from the Istanbul military academy but was banished to Damascus for being co-founder of the secret organization 'Fatherland and Freedom'. He did not study the Qur'an and Sunnah but Montesquieu, Rousseau, Voltaire and especially the positivist Auguste Comte. He did not see himself as the 'Martin Luther of Islam'; he did not want a reformation of religion but a thorough transformation of Turkish society. He was more of a Jacobin, a radical modernizer, who had studied the French Revolution in every detail. He did not strive for a renewed Ottoman empire, of the kind that the reforming 'Young Turks' (who likewise came from Saloniki and to whom he belonged) dreamed. He wanted a modern, bourgeois, secular Turkish republic, on the model of laicist France and its separation of church and state (1905).

Although such a state had already been introduced by the *de facto* secularization of the reforming sultans, this was a bold, indeed rash, project, given the predominantly traditional leaning of the Anatolian rural population. However, Mustafa Kemal was predestined for it. He had a brilliant military career; as a young general he had gained the admiration of the nation by a successful defence of the Dardanelles against the British. After the cease-fire with the Ottoman government in October 1918, Istanbul and other parts of Turkey were occupied by the British, French, Italians and Greeks. In August 1919 the peace treaty of Sèvres, part of the dictated peace of Versailles, left the sultan only an insignificant piece of territory in Anatolia with no sovereignty over it: the hour of decision had struck. Should the army be demobilized in accordance with the command of the sultan, who was controlled by the Allies? No, the general resolutely recruited partisans and regular army forces in Anatolia. He founded the 'Union for the Defence of National Rights', not against the sultan, but against the 'unbelievers' who had invaded.

In 1920, Kemal convened a great Turkish National Assembly in Ankara, a provincial city but centrally located and connected to Istanbul by rail. The assembly had legislative and executive authority and consisted chiefly of urban intellectuals and professionals along with the military. Kemal was president and supreme commander. All were united in freeing the Turkish nation under his leadership. In March 1921, a new Turkish constitution was passed and a peace treaty made with the Soviet Union. There was a victory over the Armenians, who were seeking their own state, in which cruel massacres of the civil population were again perpetrated. 1922 saw several victories over Greek troops who had occupied large parts of Anatolia and an advance towards Istanbul. By his triumphal victory, Kemal forced the allies to sign the peace treaty of Lausanne, which was favourable towards him: on 24 April 1923 the Turkish national state was recognized, with firmly fixed frontiers, encompassing Anatolia and the area around Istanbul but excluding the Armenian and Kurdish provinces. The foreign troops left Istanbul.

In this way the Turkish Republic was founded but not realized. However, with stupendous energy and breath-taking speed, Mustafa Kemal worked towards this realization. His work recalls the French Revolution—and it shocked the Islamic world. In 1922, in the new capital Ankara, a 'national assembly' dared to abolish the sultanate and in 1924 the caliphate, the religious and political institution which had lasted for a millennium. In the name of the sovereignty of the people the assembly proclaimed the Turkish Republic. At the same time the office of the supreme clergyman, the Shaykh al-Islam, was dissolved and the Shariah courts, responsible for family and hereditary law, were abolished. The last Ottoman sultan, Mehmet VI, secretly left his palace on the Bosphorus in a British army ambulance and from a British warship said farewell to his country for ever. Soon the Qur'an schools (the madrasahs) were also closed, Sufi orders and monasteries abolished and compulsory state schools and co-education for all children and young people were introduced. The property of religious foundations was put under state control. In this way all the organized institutions of Islam were abolished and the foundations of the social power of the Ulama were removed.

The way in which Mustafa Kemal planned reforms with his general staff in the presidential palace of Ankara and did not have them discussed at length by parliament but simply passed, is reminiscent of Napoleon. The constitution of 20 April 1924 contains the six principles of Kemalism that made Turkey a thoroughly modern state: the principles of action were nationalism (the nation state), secularism (laicism) and modernism (the emancipation of women and the abolition of the prohibition of alcohol) and the principles of organization were republicanism (the form of government), populism (the sovereignty of the people) and statism (a controlling role of the state in the economy, state capitalism and modern legislation on work and social welfare). How were these principles turned into political reality?

Radical rejection of the Shariah

Mustafa Kemal dictatorially introduced a new legal system, fundamental to the functioning of a new state. This was no 'Code Napoléon', nor even a 'Code Kemal'; Kemal thought the French, Austrian and Italian civil laws out of date. His model was rather the Swiss civil law book, the content and language of which he thought to be the best in the world. This law book—essentially the work of one individual, the legal scholar Eugen Huber of the universities of Basle and Berne—is simpler and more comprehensible even than the German Civil Law Book. So the Swiss Law Book was translated word for word into Turkish, ordained by the president and passed by parliament with few changes. This was indisputably the core of the Turkish revolution.

At the same time Mustafa Kemal did all he could to help the Turks develop a sense of nationhood. He was not just the inventor of the Turkish nation but also the founder of Turkish identity. That explains why, in 1934, the National Assembly gave him the honorific name 'Father of the Turks', 'Atatürk'. Despite changes of government his portraits and memorials still adorn the schoolrooms, offices, public institutions and public squares of present-day Turkey. Whereas formerly the 'Ottoman' élite had despised the 'Turks' as ignorant peasants and shepherds, now the saying went: '*Ne mutlu Türküm*—How great to say, "I am a Turk!" ' Unlike earlier reforms, this revolution reached not only the urban middle classes but also, and particularly, Anatolian villagers.

Without delay, Swiss family and divorce law was extended to women, most of whom still wore the veil; monogamy was introduced, the professional world was opened up to women and (far more progressively than even Switzerland at that time) they were granted the vote. The 'lifting of the veil' followed as a matter of course. All over Turkey the international reckoning of time (the Gregorian calendar) was applied, along with new weights and measures. New music and architecture (in the Bauhaus style) were promoted; new universities and schools were founded and theatres and concert halls built. There was a consistent Westernization and secularization of state and society, a true cultural revolution.

Kemal Atatürk never let slip the reins of power; alongside his Republican People's Party other organizations were, at best, tolerated. He could deal brutally with opponents. The revolt of the Kurds in 1925 was put down bloodily, as had been the Armenian revolt; its leader Sheikh Sait (*Sa'id*), who wanted to march under the Prophet's green banner to Anatolia against the 'unbelievers' of south-east Anatolia, was executed together with his closest followers and the assimilation of the Kurds into the Turkish population was enforced by compulsory resettlement in western Turkey (1927). To the present day, the conflict between the Turkish state and the Kurds, which periodically flares up, has found no solution. Only with Greece did Atatürk seek an agreement in a treaty of friendship (in 1930).

In the course of the reforms, Islamic forms of dress were abolished and the fez—mocked as an Ottoman 'carnival piece'—replaced by the European hat; this measure was enforced by the military even in the mosques. But perhaps nowhere is the radical paradigm change to modernity so clear as in the law of 1928, replacing Arabic script with Latin script. Atatürk said that eighty per cent of Turks were illiterate because they could not understand Arabic characters, so now all Turks had to learn the simple Latin alphabet. Atatürk travelled through the province with his modern wife, a lawyer, who did not wear the veil, explaining Latin script with blackboard and chalk. Arabic and Persian were removed from school curricula. A few weeks after the law was enacted all officials were tested on their knowledge of the script and only a month later all newspapers and books had to appear in it. This was an unparalleled break in culture; soon only specialists could read books published before 1929.

What was the position of the Qur'an, written in Arabic, the holy scripture of Muslims? Atatürk, a positivist and atheist, was not interested. He thought nothing of religion, which he first used strategically in the fight against the 'unbelievers'. For him Muhammad was an Arab Bedouin and Islam a religion fit for Arabs, not Turks. The passage declaring Islam the state religion was removed from the constitution in 1928. Religion was a private matter and being a Muslim was significant only as a distinguishing mark for being Turkish. In the new Turkey, non-Muslim communities led a more marginal existence than before. What did the true Kemalists believe in? In Atatürk, science, the nation and its future and themselves.

Towards the end of his life Atatürk was exhausted, his health ruined by nocturnal 'sessions' and the consumption of alcohol and cigarettes. He died alone, at the early age of fifty-seven, on 10 November 1938, in the Ottoman Dolmabahçe Palace in Istanbul. He needed no religious comfort. He died in the conviction that the new Western worldview and laicist culture offered a substitute of equal value for the obsolete Islamic religion and religious culture. Soon the difficulties inherent in this radically modernized and secularized paradigm (P V) would emerge. Yet could there have been an alternative?

2. The Islamist way

In contrast to the Turkish-speaking north of the former Ottoman empire, in the Arabic-speaking south, especially in Arabia, the homeland of Islam, people attempted to counter the unavoidable scientific and technological modernization with the restoration of the tradition Ulama–Sufi paradigm (P IV). The development of the Ottoman empire shows us that the resistance of the Ulama to Westernization was by no means limited to a sterile defence. Since the eighteenth century, before the European invasion, there had been premodern restoration movements in Egypt and Arabia which were in fact forerunners of Islamism:[7] informal Ulama and Sufi groups which strove for a purified form of Islamic faith and practice. There was what approached a miniature Islamic reformation, founded on a combination of the study of the Qur'an, the hadith and the Shariah with Sufi asceticism. The Prophet Muhammad, the original community of Medina and the first caliphs (P I) were the model for individual and community Muslim life. The reformers attacked not only alien influences and the official toleration of other religions but above all abuses in their own house, which they blamed on the economic, political and military decline of Islam. There was a resolute call for the abolition of Muslim veneration of saints, the cult of tombs and many superstitious ideas and magical practices: there was no longer to be blind adoption of old traditions but the reform of medieval Islam.

Stricter monotheism was again called for: the unity and oneness of God for both the individual Muslim and the Islamic community. A religion of moral responsibility, personal discipline and an obligation towards the universal Muslim community was striven for. This meant the segregation of the sexes in all realms of life, strict observance of times of prayer and precise observance of dress codes. Women wore the veil; theatres put on only plays by men for men; wine, coffee and tobacco were prohibited. A moral police supervised the observance of the religious order. From Arabia and Egypt, itinerant scholars, students and Sufis, merchants and craftsmen took these strict ideas to India and Indonesia, North and West Africa. From the eighteenth to the twentieth century there were countless Muslim reform and restoration movements.[8]

Feudal Arabic Islamism: the Wahhabism of Saudi Arabia

In the long run the most successful of the reformers was Muhammad Ibn 'Abd al-Wahhab (1703–92), the son of an educated jurist and theologian, who studied in Mecca and Medina and joined the strict Hanbalite law school, taking Ibn Taymiyyah as his model. In the face of the moral laxity and spiritual malaise of the time, he wanted to restore Islam to its original, pure form. He wanted to eradicate all innovations after the Qur'an, especially the views and practices of Sufism, the veneration of saints and the cult of tombs, which were especially widespread in the popular religion of Arabia but were often superstitious. Ibn 'Abd al-Wahhab demanded that Sufism should not only be purged but suppressed. Even the monumental tombs of Muhammad and his first followers in

Medina were destroyed, along with the tomb of Husayn in Karbala, the most important Shiite pilgrimage place in present-day Iraq. The Shiites have not forgiven this even today. Ibn 'Abd al-Wahhab's ideas led to a rigoristic Puritanism, which rejected any assimilation to the present. He successfully joined forces with a local tribal head, the emir of ad-Dar'iya, Muhammad Ibn Sa'ud, who in 1744 took over the political and military leadership of the movement. The restoration movement of the Wahhabis (*Wahhabiyah*) was born and Wahhabism became the official ideology of the Sa'ud family of central Arabia.[9] On the basis of this new ideology, which transcended tribes, the Sa'uds succeeded in bringing together various Arab tribal groups into a political and religious movement. Religious zeal was combined with military power and was able, against all resistance, to conquer the greater part of the peninsula.

One characteristic of the Arabian peninsula—the westernmost of the three great South Asian peninsulas, at the heart of the great desert girdle and only thinly populated—was that for centuries it had no political central authority. However, in the eighteenth and nineteenth centuries Muhammad Ibn Sa'ud (died 1765) and his son 'Abd al-'Aziz I, in alliance with Wahhabism as the official religious tendency, created the first sovereign state in central Arabia, the capital of which since 1821 has been the oasis city of Riyadh (*ar-Riyad*, 'the garden'). After the death in 1792 of the religious leader Ibn 'Abd al-Wahhab, the Sa'ud princes combined the roles of supreme worldly and spiritual leader. Expelled by other tribes and exiled in 1884, 'Abd al-'Aziz III Ibn Sa'ud recaptured Riyadh in 1920 and subsequently steadily extended his rule: in 1924 he occupied Mecca, in 1926 he was proclaimed king and in 1932 the territory over which he ruled was constituted Saudi Arabia. The Saudi kings, now adorned with the title 'guardian of the holy places', professed an ordering of state and society moulded by Islam, but which they later tried to combine with a modernization of the economic infrastructure.

In the First World War, which revived the idea of an Arab empire, 'Abd al-'Aziz III maintained a neutrality which was friendly to Britain, whereas the grand sheriff (*sharif*) and then prince (*amir*) of Mecca, Hussein, a Hashemite (from Hashim, the great-great-grandfather of Muhammad), firmly took the British side. To win over the Arabs, as I have already said, the British government promised them a single 'Arab nation'; the bold British scholar, officer and guerrilla leader T.E. Lawrence ('of Arabia') put himself at its service. Under him, a small band of Arab warriors liberated the town of 'Aqaba at the north-east end of the Red Sea after a bravura two-month march through the desert. The Turks defended it in vain. At the same time Hussein's son Faisal, later king of Iraq, invaded Transjordan with Arab troops, supporting the Palestine offensive led by the British general E.H.H. Allenby, which led to the collapse of the Turkish front. With his Arabs, Lawrence took part in the victory parade over the Turks in Jerusalem and also captured Damascus.

However, in 1916 the British government (represented by Sir Mark Sykes) with the French government (represented by Georges Picot) had concluded the Sykes–Picot Agreement, an agreement which was disastrous for the Arabs. This divided the territory in the 'fertile crescent': Syria and the Lebanon were to come under the French sphere of influence; Palestine, Iraq and Kuwait and the Saudi coast west of the Persian Gulf were to become a British mandate and the territory west of the Jordan was to remain separate from the Arab territory in the east. When this Anglo-French (and Russian) secret agreement was published at the end of 1917 by Russian revolutionaries, Lawrence, who had been promoted to colonel by the age of thirty, resigned after thirty-four years service, returned to England and renounced his royal honours in protest.

The exploitation of its rich petroleum resources—the greatest in the world—quickly made Saudi Arabia one of the richest countries on earth. In 1933, the Arabian American Oil Company (ARAMCO) was founded by four US petroleum companies. It later ceded its rights to Saudi Arabia, but without losing influence. Only after the death of 'Abd al-'Aziz, in 1953, was the Saudi Arabian tribal society organized as a state with ministries, provinces and regions. However, the important posts in ministries, provincial administration and the army were occupied by royal sons, nephews, and grandsons, linked with other tribes through marriage and other kinds of ties. As sovereign, both by law and *de facto*, through this extended family the king maintains undisputed power in this state with a ninety-eight per cent Sunni Muslim population—today with 21 million inhabitants.

There was a conflict over foreign policy between conservative Islamic Saudi Arabia under King Faisal, son of 'Abd al-'Aziz III Ibn Sa'ud, and the Egyptian president Gamal Abd el-Nasser, who was working for a Greater Arabia.[10] Saudi Arabia became involved in the 1962 Yemeni civil war, as the protector of the royalist forces in Yemen. Only after the defeat of Nasser and the Arab states in the Six-Day War against Israel in June 1967 did Saudi Arabia shift: it made an agreement with Egypt in Yemen and joined in the fight of the Arab states against Israel. In alliance with other oil-producing states working together in OAPEC (the Organization of Arab Petroleum Exporting Countries), after the Yom Kippur War of 1973 Saudi Arabia instituted an oil embargo against the states of Europe and North America regarded as friendly to Israel.

However, a threat to the Sa'ud dynasty emerged from quite another angle: the Islamic revolution in Iran in 1979 manifested a radical Islamism of a Shiite stamp which was also political and social, and made waves as far as Arabia. In November and December 1979—the beginning of the year 1400 after the

Hijrah, in the heated mood of the start of a new century—militant Shiite pilgrims occupied the great mosque in Mecca. Only after bloody battles and with foreign support was the army able to end the occupation. The shadow of Khomeini had fallen on Arabia.

Political–social radical Islamism: Khomeini's Islamic revolution

In Iran, Islam had undergone quite a different development from that in Arabia.[11] Influenced by the ideas of Kemal Atatürk in neighbouring Turkey, as early as 1921 General Reza Khan Pahlawi took power in Teheran at the head of a Cossack brigade. In 1925 Parliament elected him Shah and he was crowned. Supported by the army and the bureaucracy, he energetically reorganized the army, the financial and judicial systems, introduced European criminal and civil legislation, advanced industrialization and the use of technology (especially railways) and, by introducing European dress, abolished the compulsory veil. In foreign policy, in 1932–33 he granted the Anglo-Persian Oil company more favourable contracts. Since 1934 the old name 'Iran' ('Land of the Aryans') has been the official name of the state.

Because the Shah encouraged German influence and in the Second World War proved to be the friend of the Axis powers, following the occupation of his country by British and Soviet troops in 1941 he was forced to resign in favour of his son Muhammad Reza. The nationalization of the Anglo-Iranian Oil Company by Muhammad Mussadiq, who was elected prime minister, was stopped when Mussadiq was toppled by a military *coup* staged by the CIA. However, the nationalization was not reversed and after the 1960s, persistent strikes above all in the petroleum industry led Shah Muhammad Reza to implement a 'white revolution' of land reforms, with the help of agricultural associations: in some cases workers shared in business profits, health care was developed and women were granted political rights. However, unrest was brutally put down by force of arms: it is reckoned that more than four thousand died. As the influence of foreign businesses grew, so did Iranian debt and large sectors of the population were impoverished.

The intensified military and political reliance on the West increased discontent in many circles, above all the bazaar traders and the Shiite clergy. More and more people resented the tremendous corruption in the upper classes and the suppression of any opposition by the police and the secret services. (According to Amnesty International, the number of political prisoners increased in 1977 from 25,000 to 100,000.) In 1963, Ayatollah Ruhollah Khomeini had been banished from Iran because of his opposition to the un-Islamic direction taken by the Shah's regime. He had gone into exile in Iraq, to the Shiite holy city of Najaf. In 1971, the neglect of the religious values of Islam culminated in the bombastic celebration of the (fictitious!) 2500th anniversary of the Iranian monarchy in old Persepolis, under the aegis of the Persian great kings. The Islamic calendar was replaced by a calendar based on the years of individual rulers, devised by the Shah, son of an upstart, and in a coronation ceremony this evident megalomaniac presented himself to state guests from all over the world as the successor to Cyrus the Great (559–530 BCE). In more than fifty years of alliances with Muslim potentates and dictators, the USA had become used to ignoring the street protests of the masses against the continuing repressions, from Morocco to Indonesia, thus missing all the warning signs of a political change of weather in Iran.

The resistance against the Shah now reached boiling point, directed (and also disseminated on audio cassettes) by Ayatollah Ruhollah Khomeini, who in 1978 had moved from his exile in Iraq to Neauphle-le-Château, near Paris. His revolutionary movement ultimately caused the fall of the Shah and his regime: in 1979 Muhammad Reza and his family left Iran for ever. On 1 February Ayatollah Khomeini returned to Teheran in triumph, amidst mass demonstrations. As charismatic as Atatürk, he pursued the opposite political plan: belonging in speech, dress and behaviour to an earlier paradigm, he aimed at a fundamental Islamization of Iranian society, instead of the secularization that had already progressed a long way under the Shah. In all areas—administration, law, education, business—Iranian society, in contrast to its old rival Turkey, was to be transformed in the spirit of a fundamentalist Islam. In Turkey anything Western was regarded as a model; in Iran it was condemned as un-Islamic. In Turkey a new intelligentsia became established; many intellectuals left Iran because they felt threatened.

Soon, in Khomeini's Iran, an almost medieval violence prevailed over human rights. The violent attempts by the Marxist 'people's *mujahaddin*' to seize power were mercilessly suppressed by the followers of Khomeini and the moderate prime minister Medhi Bazargan, who had been appointed by Khomeini, having often been imprisoned for his opposition to the Shah, was deposed together with his provisional government; all power was handed over to the revolutionary council formed on 12 February 1979. Revolutionary courts supported by Islamic popular militia carried out a bloody 'cleansing' of the whole country, directed especially against the deposed representatives of the Shah's regime—in the administration, the army and the secret services. On 30 March 1979, after a positive referendum, Khomeini proclaimed Iran an Islamic republic; he was supported by the Shiite clergy and opponents were persecuted mercilessly. As Amnesty International reports, there were thousands of executions. Regardless of international protests, followers of the enlightened universalist Baha'i religion, who venerate their founder, the Persian Baha'u'llah

(1817–92) as a prophet after Muhammad and the 'glory of God', were systematically persecuted: many were tortured and many executed.

In foreign policy Khomeini turned against the 'great Satan', the United States, hated because of its policy and its base in the Middle East, the state of Israel. He also distanced himself from the 'godless' Soviet Union and proclaimed a 'third way'. The nadir of relations with the USA was a hostage affair: contrary to all international law, the staff of the American embassy in Teheran were taken prisoner by revolutionary forces. These called for the Shah to be handed over, his possessions to be given back to the people and Iranian bank accounts frozen by the US government to be freed. All the efforts of the International Court of Justice and the United Nations were fruitless and in 1980 a failed military rescue operation organized by the CIA contributed to the electoral success of Ronald Reagan against Jimmy Carter, then president. Whether the liberation of the hostages was delayed until after the election by Reagan's people can no more be explained than can the whole background to Reagan's Iran–Contra scandal (involving the sale of American weapons to Iran as payment to the Nicaraguan counter-revolutionaries). Only the death of the Shah on 20 January 1981 and the fulfilment of reduced Iranian demands enabled the release of the hostages, thanks to Algerian mediation.

In the 1980s Iran came under strong external pressure: Saddam Hussein, the ruler of neighbouring Iraq, thought that he could exploit Iran's weakness to open up new sources of oil and dominate the Middle East. In a war against Iran, which he began in September 1980, the United States took his side, though he used poison gas in his aggression. With the help of other Western nations, the United States armed him powerfully with conventional and chemical weapons. The Islamic Republic of Iran had to concentrate all its military economic and political efforts on a war which lasted eight years and led to a fearful slaughter, with more than a million dead. When, in March 1985, during the first inter-religious conversations in the Khomeini era, the people of Isfahan experienced the explosion of one of Saddam's bombs, they had little sympathy for the American arms suppliers, who only two decades later self-righteously waged war, with unknown numbers of victims, for the 'disarming' of Iraq.

In 1988, on the initiative of the UN, a cease-fire was arranged between Iran and Iraq. The Iranian regime, with its doctrinaire attitude, largely remained isolated in foreign politics, as it was feared even by the moderate Arab regimes. Khomeini's 1989 call for the murder (Arabic *fatwah*: the legal statement of a religious scholar which is not legally binding) of the author Salman Rushdie contributed to enraging the world public and to the breaking off of diplomatic relations with Great Britain. Later that year, on 3 June, Khomeini died; in accordance with the new constitution the Islamic 'Guardian Council' nominated the religious scholar Ali Khamenei as *rahbar*, the spiritual and political leader of Iran's seventy-one million inhabitants, ninety-nine per cent of whom are of the Shiite Muslim faith. I shall discuss whether Iranian Islamism can represent a successful option for the Muslim world in the next chapter, after I have reflected on other options.

3. The socialist way

After the Second World War, three countries in the Middle East were ruled by a military élite in the shadow of the East–West conflict and were committed to a socialist economic order; however, they went different ways to achieve it. These were Egypt, Syria and Iraq—to be treated as a special case.[12]

Arab socialism: Egypt

Egypt, the most populous Arab country (of its sixty-nine million inhabitants, ninety-four per cent are Sunni Muslims) was a British protectorate after the collapse of the Ottoman empire, and from 1922 a kingdom, under the supervision of Great Britain, which controlled its foreign and domestic policy. Egypt did not declared war on Germany until 1945. After the Second World War, Great Britain withdrew its troops from Egypt to the Suez Canal Zone. In July 1952, in a situation of economic and political crisis, the secret organization of 'Free Officers' overthrew King Farouk. The Revolutionary Council was headed by General A.M. Nagib, who served as prime minister; he also became state president after the proclamation of the republic.

Two years later, Nagib had to resign both offices in favour of the radical Colonel Gamal Abd el-Nasser. Nasser introduced land reform, encouraged Egyptian private capital and banned all political parties, including the Islamic Muslim Brotherhood. He was elected president in 1956. In that year, in reaction to the withdrawal of promised Western financial contributions, he proclaimed the nationalization of the Suez Canal, to the protests of France and Great Britain, who had only just left the Canal Zone. In autumn 1956 this action led to the Suez War. The blockade of the canal and the closure of the Gulf of 'Aqaba to Israeli ships provoked the advance of Israeli troops into the Sinai peninsula, while British and French forces undertook well-coordinated air and land operations in the Suez Canal area. However, the combined pressure of the USA (which at that time was still against preventive wars contrary to international law) and the USSR made Britain and France retreat, while Egypt agreed to compensate the Suez Canal shareholders.

President Nasser supported the efforts at decolonialization in Africa, especially in Algeria, promoted the Pan-Arab movement and in 1958 allied Egypt with Syria as the United Arab Republic (UAR); however, Syria withdrew three years later. In 1964 Egypt, supported by the USSR, was given a new constitution. Nasser and his Unity Party, the Arab Socialist Union, attempted, under a programme of Arab socialism, to improve the economic and social structures of his country. With Nehru's India and Tito's Yugoslavia, Nasser's Egypt became a leader of the non-aligned countries and thus received development help from both East and West. What did 'socialism' mean for Nasser? Not primarily nationalization but land reform, industrialization, new labour laws with the right of employee participation and the building of the Aswan Dam. Egypt, with a political identity rooted in history and long accustomed to a central government, could afford a relatively flexible regime. Its socialism was less rigid doctrine than a pragmatic policy which left some economic sectors in private hands.

As in all socialist states, internal opposition was resolutely fought against. However, this opposition was long-standing. In 1928, the elementary school teacher Hasan al-Banna' (1906–49), a pupil of Rashid Rida, had founded the Muslim Brotherhood, which spread across the Middle East. Its aim was an Islamic order based on Qur'an and Sunnah, a 'social Islamism' with its own factories, shops, schools, groups and newspapers. In this way, a Muslim ethos for the modern world was to develop which would prove itself in charitable and social institutions.

At the same time, the Muslim Brothers wanted to take action against the British occupation of the Canal Zone and against Zionism in Palestine. A radical 'political Islam' formed within the Brotherhood around Sayyid Qutb (1916–66), an originally pro-Western journalist who turned anti-Western in the USA. After fighting colonizers and Zionists, this group now also fought against its own socialist regime (which had no religious foundation) when, under Nasser, the Socialists claimed sole power. The group's terrorism and assassinations (including, in 1948, the murder of the Egyptian prime minister) led to a wave of arrests and executions, in the wake of which al-Banna' was executed at the beginning of 1949. In 1954, further confrontations with the regime led to the banning of the Muslim Brotherhood. Sayyid Qutb, its leading ideologist, who denounced the Egyptian regime as un-Islamic, spent nine years in a concentration camp and was finally executed in August 1966. Repeated arrests followed later, but despite being banned, the Muslim Brotherhood, which had been forced underground, kept emerging in public and published newspapers and books.

When it sent troops into Yemen (1962–7), Egypt came into conflict with Saudi Arabia, which was resisting Nasser's efforts towards hegemony. The conflict with Israel also intensified. Increasingly supported by the military help of

Communist states, Nasser blocked the Gulf of 'Aqaba to Israeli ships. In 1967, as I have said, this sparked off the Six-Day War, in which Israel occupied the Sinai Peninsula as far as the Suez Canal. After this defeat Nasser, deeply humiliated, attempted a war of attrition but he died in 1970, and with him the socialist experiment.

His successor, Anwar as-Sadat, at first continued Nasser's policies. In October 1973, Egypt and Syria launched a surprise attack on Israel on the Jewish Day of Atonement (Yom Kippur), which largely drove the Israelis from Sinai but eventually ended with a ceasefire. Not until 1978, under pressure from President Jimmy Carter, was the Camp David Agreement secured—one of his historic achievements. The year after that, a peace treaty was signed between Israel and Egypt, which led to the withdrawal of Israel from Sinai but not to a solution of the Palestine question. Neither the USA nor Israel has subsequently made a constructive contribution to this. In 1981, Sadat, who had undertaken a bold journey of reconciliation to Jerusalem, was assassinated by militant Muslim Brothers during a military parade. After Sadat and his successor Hosni Mubarak (since 1981), little remained of Nasser's programme of an Arab socialism.

The mainstream of the Muslim Brotherhood was prepared to collaborate with the regimes of Sadat and of his successor Hosni Mubarak against socialism and authoritarianism. In this way, they could create more of a place for Islam in private and public life. In the 1990s, there were also attacks by numerous extremists, chiefly on tourists in Upper Egypt. But prominent Islamists were now sitting in parliament and had influence in professional organizations and publishing houses, while many mosques had extended their functions and offered cheap medical and social services. Moreover, the Muslim Brothers lacked inspiring leadership so that, in time, a group of 'new Islamists' formed outside them: where possible, these stood for democracy and pluralism. In the First Gulf War, they were against the Iraqi invasion of Kuwait but rejected military solutions in favour of diplomatic ones. It is clear that Islam is again playing an important role in Egyptian civil society and in politics.

Pan-Arabism: Syria

Even in the Syria of the Ottoman empire the idea of a 'Pan-Arabism' had developed: the union of all Arab countries in a common state (see C V, 4). Following the French and British partition of the Arab world after the First World War, the great Umayyad Arab empire (P II), with its capital in Damascus, was a brilliant memory for the Syrians. One language, one culture, one caliphate and one empire: shouldn't a modern form of that be a vision for the future? In Syria a party was founded which called itself 'Baath' (Arabic *ba'th*, Arabic rebirth). Its founder and chief ideologist was a Christian, Michel Aflaq, whose ideas had been shaped by French socialism and German nationalism. The aim of the Baath party was to bring about the cultural renewal of the Arab world and the union of all Arab countries in a single great state, stretching from Morocco to Iraq.

In 1944 Syria was granted independence by France, the mandate power which, after 1918, had separated Lebanon from Syria in its own interests. Under the leadership of a national party, the vehicle of the independence movement, *coup* followed *coup*. Under a series of presidents, policy was determined above all by the development of external relations with the Arab states. At the end of the 1940s, Syria found itself confronted with the Iraqi plan to unify the lands of the 'fertile crescent' in an Arab union under Hashemite rule. However, Syria was fascinated by the rise of the Egyptian president, Nasser, and in 1945 the Arab League was founded in Cairo, as a forum for discussion and negotiation. In 1958 Syria joined Egypt in the United Arab Republic but, as I have said, this lasted for only three years. Syrian independence was restored after a *coup* by the Syrian military.

In 1963 a final *coup* brought the Baath Party to power as the leading political party. The full name of this Pan-Arabic party with a socialist orientation that transcended the region was 'Socialist Party of Arab Rebirth'. As well as its Syrian wing it also had an Iraqi wing, which likewise came to power through a *coup*. It, too, shared the historic, linguistic and cultural confession of the joint Arab nation, but this was not enough to move it towards joint action. Rather, at an early stage, the pan-Arab programme of the Baath was effectively countered by efforts to form sovereign nation states within the newly created frontiers. Couldn't Syrian or Iraqi nationalism create a state more easily than Syrian–Iraqi–Egyptian Pan-Arabism?

Moreover the Syrian regimes were dominated by the splinter group of the Shiite Alawis ('those who belong to 'Ali'), which attempted to create a socialist system with a marked ideological stamp. The doctrinaire, socialist, Baath government eventually appointed its own head of state, which placed a heavy burden on relations with Iraq and the Iraqi Baath leadership. For Syria, too, the Middle East conflict became fateful, since it maintained a line that was markedly hostile to Israel and, in the Six-Day War, lost the Golan Heights; it is still not prepared to sign a peace treaty with Israel unless it regains them.

In Syria also the Muslim Brothers formed an opposition to the regime's socialist and secularist agenda. They organized a number of rebellions, though these were limited to the cities, since the poor rural population and the Syrian minorities (Druses, Alawis, Christians and Ismailis) had no sympathy with Islamists. Syria regained some of the Golan Heights under General Hafis al-Assad, who came to power in 1970 through a *coup* and established a one-man dictatorship. Instead of a Middle East dominated by Israel, Assad sought a peace which was founded, not on the dominance of the Arabs or the Israelis, but on a balance of power between a Middle East centred on Damascus (Levant) and an Israel within its 1948–49 frontiers. President Assad was a wily and shrewd tactician, who represented stability in the country—with the help of the military, the secret service and the Baath party. His thirty years of iron rule (which saw the massacre of at least 10,000 Muslim Brothers in the old city of Hama in 1982) led to growing isolation and stagnation. The personality cult that now held sway over the sixteen million inhabitants drove out all socialism. Assad exploited a favourable moment in the Israel–Lebanon conflict to occupy Beirut and, in practice, to control Lebanon. In the Iraq–Iran war, Syria was on Iran's side.

The Syrian Muslim Brothers had split into three parties, one of which was prepared to collaborate with the regime. While the regime maintained a strict separation of religion and politics, it did not attempt to undermine the place of religion in Syrian culture and society. The University of Damascus has a faculty of Islamic law and its Arabic division offers courses on early Islamic literature. Although in 1967 the Baath party nationalized all Muslim and Christian private schools, Muslim and Christian, religious instruction continues to be given in them. Islam is very much present in newspapers, books and other media. Assad even had many mosques and Qur'an schools (with a strong Wahhabi influence) built and in this way promoted the revitalization of a more conservative, though still unpolitical, Islam.

After his death on 19 June 2000, Hafis al-Assad was succeeded—for the first time in an Arab republic—by his son, Bashar al-Assad, an opthalmologist. Bashar wanted to introduce internal reforms, counter widespread corruption and defend Syria's position against Israel and the USA. Syria is the first 'hereditary republic' in the Arab world, a status which is making heads of state in Egypt and elsewhere think of such a solution to the succession. After Iraq's defeat in the Second Gulf War (2003), Syria came under pressure from the USA but this declined when, in 2004, the USA had to devote all its energy to the chaotic situation in Iraq which it had itself produced.

Aggressive nationalism: Iraq

Iraq is a relatively young state, with twenty-three million inhabitants (ninety-seven per cent of them Muslims, mostly Shiite). Its territory is the area of perhaps the earliest high culture on earth. Humankind is indebted to Mesopotamia for writing, the wheel, the division into weeks, the solar year, the earliest legal system and the first laws. Mesopotamia has a rich past: in antiquity it held the temple cities of the Sumerians, the empires of the Babylonians,

Assyrians and Chaldaeans and in the Middle Ages the empires of the Sasanians, Umayyads and 'Abbasids. Wasn't such a country also destined to play a leading role today? However, Iraq is also a country without a connected history. The total destruction of 'Abbasid Baghdad, by the Mongols in 1258, which caused the devastation of the ingenious irrigation system and led to the slaughter of thousands of people, is as firmly rooted in Iraqi consciousness as the Thirty Years War is rooted in the German consciousness. Not until the seventeenth century, after centuries of Mongol rule and wearisome clashes with the Shiite–Iranian Safavids (whose capital was Isfahan), did the Sunni Ottoman empire succeed in incorporating Iraq and dividing it into three provinces (Mosul, Baghdad and Basra)—the impoverished interior of the Ottoman empire. However, the Ottoman concessions to the Germans in 1899 for the building of the Baghdad railway alarmed the British and during the First World War they occupied Iraq.

The present Iraqi state was constructed artificially by the British under a mandate of the League of Nations after the First World War with no attention to ethnic frontiers.[13] The Kurdish people, who live in northern Iraq, Turkey, Syria and Iran, were denied their own state. Instead, a kingdom was created with three very different populations: in the north, around Mosul, the Kurds; in the south, around Basra, the Shiites, who were in the majority; and in the middle Baghdad and its Sunni minority.[14] The British intended this country to be held together by the Hashemite King Faisal, who came from Mecca. In 1932 the kingdom was formally granted independence by the British. However, in 1933 the king was murdered—with the result that there was no strong figure to integrate the Arabs. In the Second World War, anti-British, pro-German activities were the occasion for renewed British occupation. After the war there was constant unrest, which in 1958 led to a *coup d'état* by the Arab nationalist military: King Faisal II was murdered, along with several members of his family. A republic was proclaimed, whose head of state was an army officer, Abd al-Kaim Kassem. He exercised his power in an increasingly dictatorial way and emphasized Iraqi independence, thus coming into conflict with Pan-Arab forces at home and with the Egypt president Nasser abroad. Under him, Islam played hardly any role.

Changes of power in Iraq were usually bloody. In 1963, Kassem was deposed by the socialist Baath party with its Pan-Arab orientation and murdered. However, it soon became evident that the original Pan-Arabism, chiefly popular with the urban middle classes, was gradually being replaced by a nationalism centred on Iraq, which stabilized the position of the political class of the young state and its military leadership.[15] For a time Iraq, Syria and Egypt collaborated but plans for a union failed. There were further *coups d'état*. In 1968, the Arab

Sunni general Ahmad Hassan al-Bakr came to power amid mass arrests and public executions. He introduced land and labour law reforms, and in 1972 nationalized the oil industry. The billions earned by oil financed not only the growth of the army during the 1970s but also an extensive modernization programme and other measures including a free national health system and the massive development of education, which included women's education.

Al-Bakr's brutal chief of secret police was Saddam Hussein. He was the opposite of a believing Muslim, a powerful man capable of any trickery and any barbarism. He made the security apparatus his power base. In 1979 he toppled his mentor al-Bakr and became president of the Revolutionary Council, state president and general secretary of the Baath party. He continued developments in education and upbringing, requiring equal rights for women (leading to the opening up of the labour market) and promoting archaeological research (including the 'restoration' of Babylon). He pressed for an organic combination of the ancient Mesopotamian and Muslim legacies. His model was not Stalin and his terror, as is sometimes claimed in the West, but Harun ar-Rashid or Saladin in their glory. He wanted to create a model state, with a well-functioning bureaucracy and health system, and provide a basic wage for every Iraqi.

However, even the Baath regime, which from the beginning had a secular stamp, did not succeed in really integrating the Kurdish peoples in the north and the Shiite population in the south. Saddam Hussein, a Sunni, had Shiite sanctuaries restored and regularly visited the holy places of Najaf and Karbala but this exploitation of religion was too simplistic not to be seen through when Saddam had inconvenient Shiite religious leaders and Kurdish opposition members cruelly murdered. This was repression, not integration. The sense of an Iraqi state could hardly develop among the heterogeneous groups in this way.

The arbitrary frontier drawn in the 1920s between Iraq and Kuwait (which also belonged to the Ottoman empire and was a British protectorate until independence in 1960) helped the Armenian oil magnate Calouste Gulbenkian and the Anglo-Dutch and American oil companies. After the separation of Kuwait, Iraq's only access to the Gulf was the Shatt al-Arab, the confluence of the Euphrates and the Tigris south of Basra. This strategically and economically important access to the sea was guaranteed to it by the British in 1937 but challenged in 1969 by the Shah of Iran. The Shah was supported by the USA, which at the same time encouraged the Kurds to rebel against Baghdad. In 1975, in the treaty of Algiers, Saddam Hussein finally agreed to draw the frontier with Iran in the deep-water channel of the Shatt. Thereupon, the USA for the first time dropped the Kurds and handed them over to Saddam's henchmen (which explains why Saddam abrogated the treaty of Algiers in 1980).

After Khomeini's Iran had challenged the USA in 1979, by driving out the Shah and taking hostages in the American embassy, the Americans again sought contact with Khomeini's opponent Saddam Hussein, to whom they gave massive weapons support. With such encouragement, in 1980 Saddam began the invasion of a weakened Iran. However, relying on bad information (not least in reports from the American Secret Service, he underestimated the power of resistance of Khomeini's troops. In 1983, in violation of international law, he used poison gas. Ironically, the American special ambassador who negotiated personally with Saddam Hussein (after the war increasingly the sole ruler) was Donald Rumsfeld (and he is not on record as opposing the use of poison gas); in 2002/3, when US Secretary of State for Defense, was one of the main advocates of war against Saddam and in 2004 was chiefly responsible for the American abuses in Iraq (including the maltreatment and torture of Iraqi prisoners of war by US soldiers). By March 1984, UN experts had absolute proof that Saddam had begun to use gas on the battlefields. Nevertheless, the US continued to extend its help towards him; after all, Iraq had the world's second greatest oil resources. In 1984 diplomatic relations, the supply of satellite images of Iranian troop movements and further secret service operations were resumed. Between 1985 and 1990, the USA gave Iran breeding materials for biological weapons, such as anthrax and plague bacilli. Other Western nations joined in. There was a transitory cooling off of relations between the countries after the Americans' double play under President Reagan in the Iran–Contra scandal which I have already mentioned (like much else, it was passed over in utter silence in Reagan's theatrical funeral ceremony in June 2004). Not even Saddam's war against the Kurds and the attack by Iraqi troops with chemical weapons on the Kurdish village of Halabsha in 1988, which left five thousand people dead, could precipitate the breaking off of American support.

Since the Iraq–Iran war, the Shatt al-Arab had been blocked by wrecks and mines and Iraq, the second greatest nation on the Gulf, was in practice cut off from the sea. This was another reason for Saddam Hussein to plan the violent reincorporation of Kuwait into Iraq. In a conversation on 27 July 1990, the American ambassador April Glaspie, an orientalist, assured Saddam Hussein that the USA would regard this as an internal Arab concern. On 2 August 1990 Iraqi troops marched into the Emirate of Kuwait.

In Washington and London, it was suddenly noticed that the conquest of Kuwait endangered Saudi Arabia, which had the world's greatest oil resources. Influenced by the British prime minister Margaret Thatcher, George Bush, Sr (the first American president to have been head of the CIA), resolved to forge a great coalition for war against Iraq. In military terms, Bush won this first American Gulf War in January–February 1991 (it was named Desert Storm). In political terms he lost it: by not setting a clear aim and by a premature end to the military action. For the first time in this war Saddam Hussein used Islam on a grand scale as an ideological weapon. The misuse of religion to legitimize dictators has happened repeatedly in Arab countries. However, before the advent of Khomeini, the secularized regimes—whether the Shah or socialist rulers—had treated Islam as politically insignificant and as folklore. Saddam was now able finally to set himself up as a Muslim against Khomeini. He could easily play himself off against the Americans, the Saudis and the Israelis as the guardian of the holy places (Mecca, Medina and Jerusalem), and use Islam for his own political ends.

So the Iraqi despot remained in power. Moreover, in his regime's fight for national integration, a certain Iraqi national feeling had developed after the eight long years of war against Iran. The Shiites felt loyal to the state, which through the oil boom had brought them a certain degree of prosperity. The disarmament of Iraq, now totally in debt, proceeded. Military installations were destroyed until, in the estimate of the US Defense Secretary Richard Cohen, a member of the Clinton administration, the markedly-weakened Iraq no longer posed a danger to its neighbours. It was the civil population who suffered under the American and British bombardments in the no-fly zones.

Was there still Arab socialism in Iraq? Less so than ever, after the collapse of the Soviet system. Many of Saddam's contemporaries, like himself and al-Bakr, came from the city of Tikrit and its surrounding areas. After the Iraq–Iran war, Saddam built up his power base there and—contrary to the principles of the Baath party—relied on the traditional Iraqi clans, above all those around his home city. Pan-Arabism and socialism cloaked a growing economy run by favouritism and nepotism at the expense of the state structures.

How rotten the Iraqi regime and its army were had become evident in the first Gulf War; the second showed how small a threat it posed to its neighbours, let alone to the USA and Great Britain. This second war was begun on 20 March 2003 by the American president George W. Bush and the British prime minister Tony Blair—following months of media campaigning and the massing of powerful forces on land, at sea and in the air. After the capture of Baghdad on 1 May, the war was declared to be, in principle, at an end (thus for the second time the Americans and British completely misunderstood the situation). The first Gulf War under President Bush, Sr, after Saddam's attack on Kuwait, was clearly a defensive war and thus covered by international law and the UN charter and given the approval of the UN Security Council. However, the second Gulf War was clearly a war of aggression, a preventive war based on suspicion and thus clearly forbidden by international law and the UN charter. President George W. Bush even declared it to be a 'crusade'. The war was not approved by the UN

Security Council and world public opinion; indeed, it stirred up the Islamic world even more against the USA.

However, this Iraq war was very much in line with the aggressive imperialistic foreign policy of the only remaining superpower (after the implosion of the Soviet Union) under the regime of George W. Bush. Moreover, the main architect of this new American policy of hegemony since the beginning of the 1990s, Deputy Defense Secretary Paul Wolfowitz, who persuaded President George W. Bush of the need for the Iraq war, and its main propagandist, Richard Perle, were both prominent members of the lobby which advised Israel to break off the Oslo Accords with the Palestinians and, in agreement with the Israeli Prime Minister Ariel Sharon, demanded the Iraq war at an early stage. In such a US strategy the state of Israel has a leading role in the Middle East but, since its foundation in 1948, for all its Arab neighbour states has been the hated bridgehead of the West, recklessly supported (though often in a disguised fashion) especially by the USA and parts of the West at the expense of the Palestinians.

The fragmentation of Iraq was intensified, not overcome, by the US invasion of 2003. The outcome remains uncertain.

– The fate of Iraq continues to be decided in Baghdad, where the Sunnis (who represent some thirty-two to thirty-seven per cent of the population) still want to play the main role. The opposition in the south has so far not managed to obtain any co-operation worth mentioning.

– The Shiites in the south, who form between fifty-five and sixty per cent of the population, are the majority. They are governed by a conglomerate of religious rulers and their networks. After the fall of the Sunni-dominated Baath regime, the Shiite majority legitimately called for more political influence. With their traditional pilgrimage centres of Najaf and Karbala, they see themselves as the centre of a Shiite world extending far beyond the frontiers of Iraq, which spiritually embraces the Shiites in Iran, in Lebanon and even in Pakistan.

– The Kurds in the north, with between fifteen and twenty per cent of the population—geographically divided between the northern and southern halves of their territory by two different dialects—want a political voice in Baghdad but they are primarily committed to autonomy, which was previously successful both economically and politically; the traditional secessionist call for a Kurdistan for all Kurds in Turkey, in Iraq and in Syria is in retreat.

At the time of writing it is difficult to foresee what effect the purely formal return of sovereignty from the US army to the provisional Iraqi government which it has appointed, and the planned elections for the country, will have. For the moment, a withdrawal of the Americans, who are chiefly concerned to control oil production, is improbable; nor is it desirable, given the chaotic internal political situation.

However, what kind of Islam will establish itself is a question not just for Iraq but for the Islamic countries generally.

So in the next section I shall reflect on the different options for Islam at the present time and ask which of them would be most desirable in the interests of the Islamic world and world peace.

D II

What Kind of Islam do Muslims Want?

What will be decisive for the future is not what kind of Islam 'the world' or even 'the West' wants, but what kind of Islam Muslims in all their different contexts themselves want and aim at. There is a variety of options. The paradigms are very different and compete with one another. In the future, too, Islam will not present itself as a monolith but offer a different picture in different regions and countries. As I have often pointed out,[1] in the natural sciences the old paradigms are eliminated as soon as they have been refuted by mathematics and experiment. They are no longer viable, and no student of, for example, astronomy would study the old Ptolemaic model of the world that has been replaced by Copernicus. However, in the history of religions nothing can be proved or refuted by mathematics and experiment—any more than it can be in art. As in Judaism and in Christianity, in Islam there were internal oppositions which were no less important than the external oppositions to the other two religions. This gave rise to a contemporaneity of diverging and converging paradigms with very different theologies or ideologies, images of the world and forms of life.

1. The contemporaneity of competing paradigms

After my brief description of the typical ways taken by Islam (see D I), it is time for me to attempt a provisional interim assessment for the present. Some fundamental paradigm dependences already emerge from the scheme of this book:

- The original Islamic community paradigm (P I) remains something like the ideal of Muslims of all periods: an irrevocably lost gold age, but also time and again a court of appeal. However, the later paradigms have also remained alive as something to remember and long for and with them their own elements and structures, embodied in leading figures and lived out in communities, large and small.

- The paradigm of the Arab empire (P II) is still present in Pan-Arabism, the idea of a single Arab nation, and also in the different Arab nationalisms.
- The classic paradigm of Islam as a world religion (P III) influences ideas of the unity of all Muslims beyond all nations, in the dream of a Pan-Islamism.
- The medieval Ulama–Sufi paradigm (P IV) perpetuates itself in the different forms of Islamic traditionalism and, as a programme, in radical Islamism.
- The modernization paradigm (P V) has an effect on all forms of Islamic reformism and an extreme effect on Islamic secularism.

The question is, which paradigm will establish itself in the long term in the epoch-making transition from modernity (P V) to a postmodern period? If mathematics and experiment cannot help us here, in the religious sphere the question of acceptance also arises, that is: to what extent a paradigm can be appropriated by people today, can be experienced as helpful; whether only small groups are attracted by it or whether great masses can be enthused by it and whether particular élites or broad areas of the population accept it or reject it. Where the typical ways of Islam in the twentieth century have led has become clear, as have the options on offer in the twenty-first century. I can sketch them out only briefly here.[2]

Option I: Pan-Islamism?

A first option, which at one time was a reality, was whether it was possible to reunite all Islamic peoples, Arab and non-Arab, in a great Islamic empire or a great Islamic federation. The classical period of Islam (P III) was when, under the 'Abbasids, all Islamic peoples from Morocco to India and Central Asia were held together by a common Islamic faith and the one caliph of Baghdad: this was the great time of Islamic law, Islamic philosophy and theology, the Islamic world culture.

It is understandable that, as I described, in the 1870s such Pan-Islamic ideas were developed on the Arabian peninsula—to ward off European colonialism—above all by al-Afghani and his disciple 'Abduh.[3] It is understandable that some organizations and parties strove later for a union of the different Islamic peoples, the Arabs, Turks, Persians and many others, under the leadership of the sultan in Istanbul. It is even more understandable that the Ottoman reform sultan, 'Abd al-Hamid II (1876–1909), should have gratefully taken up this Pan-Islamic idea to support his endangered claim to rule.

However, at the same time this sultan suppressed the Arab national movement for precisely such political considerations. And when the Young Turks came to power in 1908–9 they opposed all Pan-Islamic efforts under the banner of Pan-Ottomanism[4]—until the Ottoman empire collapsed in 1918 and the caliphate was abolished by Atatürk in 1924, so that Pan-Islamism lost its leading figure. Five Pan-Islamic conferences of religious scholars followed: in Mecca (1924), Cairo (1926), Mecca (1926), Jerusalem (1931) and Geneva (1935)—all without tangible results. After the Second World War, Pan-Islamism received fresh impetus with the foundation in 1949 of the Islamic World Congress in Karachi, in 1962 of the World Muslim League in Mecca and in 1970 of the Organization of the Islamic Conference in Jeddah as an umbrella organization for Islamic governments. However, none of these organizations was able to integrate the national liberation movements in the individual Islamic countries. In 1947, after the partition of India, Pakistan became the first independent Islamic state; others followed. The Islamic movements and conferences could at best spread the idea of solidarity among Muslims and warn of the need for a common solution to economic and social problems. But to the present day, the creation of an Islamic federation remains a daydream. Other movements proved more attractive.

Option II: Pan-Arabism?

In view of the failure of Pan-Islamism, wouldn't it have been more realistic to bring together just the Arab countries instead of all the Islamic countries—into a great Arab empire or a great Arab federation? Despite today's secularization, couldn't the Arab Umayyad empire (P II) have been a model here, since it held its peoples together efficiently: not only through the Islamic faith but also through the Arabic language, Arab culture, the many common features in their historic and cultural traditions and their political and economic interests? As I described, in the middle of the nineteenth century, in the course of the *nahda*, the cultural, scientific and political 'uprising' which followed Napoleon's expedition to Egypt, Syrian, Lebanese and Egyptian intellectuals founded the Pan-Arab movement, which was also joined by Arabic-speaking non-Muslims (Maronites, Copts, Druses etc., see C V, 4). Pan-Arabism established itself as a political current in the conflict with the Pan-Ottomanism of the Young Turks, against the centuries of alien Ottoman rule and European colonialism.[5]

However, instead of leading to the promised great Arab empire, the 1916 secret Anglo-French Sykes–Picot agreement led to the splitting up of Arab territory into individual kingdoms, mandates and protectorates. The following year the British foreign minister, Arthur Balfour, promised the Jews a 'national homeland' in Palestine, which made the situation even more complicated and almost insoluble. Only in the 1950s and 1960s did Pan-Arabism have new opportunities, on the one hand through the activity of the Egyptian President Nasser and the movement of Arab nationalists, and on the other through the Baath party in Syria and Iraq. However, all the state alliances in Arab countries failed:

- 1958–61: The United Arab Republic: Egypt and Syria;
- 1958: The Arab Federation: Iraq and Jordan;
- 1971: The Federation of Arab Republics: Egypt, Libya and Syria;
- 1984: The Arab–African Union: Morocco and Libya.

The political interests of the various regions and states and their governments were too great. Even an Arab Common Market, founded in 1965, established itself only to a very limited degree, because of differing economic and political interests. Only the Arab League, founded in Cairo in 1945, was able to express the political, economic and cultural interest of all Arabs—though with varying degrees of success. The creation of an Arab federation or even of just a common Arab foreign policy remains a utopian ideal—apart from fundamental opposition to the state of Israel founded in 1948. The Second Gulf War of 2003–4 showed this once more.

Option III: Islamism?

Given the political difficulties of Pan-Islamism and Pan-Arabism, many Muslims ask themselves whether it would be better to give up all visions of Islamic or Arab unity and concentrate on a religious and social renewal of Islam in every country. Especially after all the disappointments with Western modernization, wouldn't it be better to reflect on the tradition, the Qur'an and the Shariah, as the basis of the social order? And who could introduce these better than the religious scholars, the Ulama (in the Arab sphere) and the mullahs (in Iran), who, after the downfall of the caliphate, are holding together Muslim communities everywhere and (often with the Sufis) seek to create a rich community life (P IV)? I shall examine two versions of Islamic traditionalism or, more radically, Islamism:[6] the Saudi Arabian and the Iranian.

Traditionalist Islamic Saudi Arabia has long been admired and envied for its oil wealth—'Allah's gift to the Arabs'. It has succeeded in modernizing the country technologically and not only sparing its population taxes (the population is small in comparison with the vastness of the territory: today twenty-one million, of whom probably thirty per cent are foreigners) but also giving it largely free health care and schooling. The five thousand princes of the Saʿud ruling house, all provided with the wherewithal for a high standard of living, who hold key positions in politics, business and the army, would seem to guarantee stability. The conservative Wahhabi Ulama hierarchy ensures the observance of strict moral norms. (As I was able to see for myself when in Saudi Arabia, one can park a car unlocked in front of a supermarket without being afraid that something might be stolen.) So, is Saudi Arabia a model of a traditional Islam, a state religion, which it helps to disseminate worldwide by donating money for propaganda and the building of mosques?

However, the economic situation has deteriorated considerably because of the fluctuation in the price of oil, excessive spending on armaments, the wasteful luxury of the royal family and the recent increase in violence. There are no political parties, no trade unions and no free press. Around fifteen per cent of the population is unemployed. The living standard of the average person (Saudi Arabian citizens, like citizens of Western welfare systems, have learned to avoid the dirty work) has generally become lower. Dissatisfaction with the archaic legal system and the lack of freedom of the media and of public opinion is spreading widely. The government has appointed a consultative council, but so far has not implemented a single serious plan for reform: despite timid small steps towards reform, there is no clear concept of reform. Time and again, critics who ask for more are imprisoned. A National Human Rights Commission nominated by the government has so far contented itself with inconsequential statements on cases of the violation of human rights. So far, the 'national dialogue' announced by Crown Prince Abdullah in July 2003 has led only to discussions that have got nowhere. Democracy is rejected by individual conservative Ulama as un-Islamic. Even in Saudi Arabia itself, people do not understand why women are often discriminated against: for example, they are even forbidden to drive cars (this is rather different from the situation in the south-east of the Arabian peninsula, in the sultanate of Oman). The lack of tolerance towards other religions—for example the prohibition of any public Christian worship and even of the sign of the cross (including the Red Cross)—means that the Saudi regime has a bad image. In its present condition, Saudi Arabia is unfortunately not a model for Arab states.

After the terrorist attacks on the World Trade Center and the Pentagon on 11 September 2001—of the nineteen alleged perpetrators, fifteen were Saudis—and especially after the bomb attacks in Riyadh and also against the oil industry in 2003–4, people in Saudi Arabia have begun to reflect. The average Saudi wants to assume more responsibility for his or her life, but fears the chaos that Islamic activists and terrorists could unleash. The USA, previously highly regarded, has no moral authority because of its support of Israel and the Iraq war. Although, under the influence of the religious leaders, any criticism of Wahhabis is met with harsh punishment, more and more voices are being heard which trace the roots of the evil to the Wahhabi ideology itself. For many generations, in many mosques and schools, everything foreign has been discriminated against as 'unbelieving'; hatred and enmity have been preached against liberals, supporters of women's rights, secularists, Christians and Jews, and also against Shiites and Sufis. It has even been said that in some circumstances violence may be used against them.

Therefore bold Saudis are beginning to say that 'Islam is not Wahhabism, and other forms of liberation can be preached'. These are the words of Mansur an-Nogaidan, a columnist on the newspaper *Ar-Riyad*, who was a religious extremist but learned this lesson when in prison by reading liberal Muslim philosophers. 'And this is what Saudi Arabia, as a nation, also needs: a rebirth. We need to accept the pain of it and learn how to accept change. We need patience and the ability to withstand the consequences of our crimes over the past two decades.'[7] In Saudi Arabia, too, where both democratic reformers and radical Islamists have been persecuted, democracy must grow from within: it cannot be imported from America or even bombed in.

At the present time it is impossible to see what effect the terrorist attacks on skilled foreign workers in the Saudi oil industry will have in the extremely unsafe situation following the Iraq war. It will be impossible to win the battle against terrorism without guaranteeing fundamental structural reforms, human rights and a minimum of political participation. The first independent survey of opinion in Saudi Arabia (based on 15,000 answers) supports efforts at reform. Only 4.7% would back Osama bin Laden for president but 48.7% endorse his concerns: 'When we hear bin Laden storming against the West and attacking the corruption and incompetence of Arab governments and the suffering of the Palestinians, it is as if we were in a dream ... When we see the pictures of innocent people who have been killed for this ideology, it is as if we were having a nightmare'.[8] The results of the questionnaire on concrete reform concerns are amazing: 85% are in favour of political reform, more than 90% want more rights for women and 63% think that women should be allowed to drive cars. However, less than 59% support the religious establishment, not because they are against the Ulama in principle but because they think that it no longer has any contact with them and the problems of their families. For 79.6%, unemployment is the most urgent concern. If the royal family could tackle this concern constructively, they would undoubtedly have the vast majority of the people behind them; in that case a transition from an absolute to a constitutional monarchy could not be ruled out.

Whereas the feudal Islamism of Saudi Arabia never had any particular attraction for those living elsewhere, things were quite different with the radical Islamism of the Iranian Khomeini regime. At first, this aroused hopes and generated enthusiasm in the Arab world. Its attempts to combine a strict Islamic faith with the original Islamic ideal of social justice won sympathy beyond the Islamic world—the clash with the USA aside. It cannot be denied that the mullahs' regime did much for schools and education; the level of illiteracy dropped markedly. More than 60% of students beginning at the universities are women; women have been integrated into professional life with amazing speed and they have gained markedly in self-confidence and economic independence: every third marriage ends in divorce, often at the wife's request.

However, despite all its success, even in Iran itself (which has the third largest oil reserves and the second largest natural gas reserves in the world) the Islamic political system has been largely rejected. The 1997 elections which, although they did not bring the moderate mullah Muhammad Khatami to power, did bring him the presidency, showed that the great majority of Iranians (above all women and young people) want more freedom of opinion, more democracy and less economic mismanagement, corruption and arbitrary law. Two-thirds of the Iranian population is below the age of thirty. Young people have a different view of the world, do not like to be tied by official regulations and long for a life which promises personal satisfaction and prosperity, the kind that they can see on satellite television and via the internet. In private, there is a high degree of freedom of opinion and lifestyle.[9]

At the beginning, the violence of the regime could still be regarded as a response to the violence of the popular *mujahiddin* but the execution of numerous peaceful Baha'is caused repulsion everywhere and severely damaged the reputation of both Iran and Islam. For the great majority in Iran and throughout the Islamic world, the award of the Nobel Peace Prize in 2003 to an Iranian woman, Shirin Ebadi, was an acknowledgement and encouragement in the fight to establish and apply human rights.[10]

Just as the self-righteous and rigid Roman Catholic hierarchy has shaken the credibility of Christianity in the eyes of many people, so too the intolerant and dogmatically rigid Muslim hierarchy has shattered the credibility of Islam. In Iran, many of the younger generation think that Islam is out of date. It is worth reflecting that today the Turks in their secular state, without moral guardians, practise Islam more than the Iranians in their clerical republic. For all these reasons Iranian Islamism can hardly be the model which today is longed for by a majority of Muslims, in any country. The French sociologist of religion, Gilles Keppel,[11] is right in his sophisticated analysis of the rise and fall of Islamism in the last twenty-five years of the twentieth century when he says that militant Islamism has already passed its peak, because its promise of a free, social, democratic development of the Muslim masses has not been fulfilled. Some Muslims are asking: can this be better achieved in another way?

Option IV: Socialism?

Shouldn't a socialist economic order in Arab countries, with their tremendous differences between rich and poor, be able to bring about more social justice? After the Second World War, in Europe, too (outside the Federal Republic of Ludwig Erhard!), the nationalization of key industries seemed to be the patent recipe for solving social problems. At the time of decolonialization hopes on all sides were pinned on socialism. However different the regimes, Sukarno in Indonesia and Muhammad Mussadiq in Iran, but also Kwame Nkrumah in Ghana, Sekou Touré in Guinea, Modibo Keita in Mali, Julius Nyerere in Tanzania and Patrice Lumumba in the Congo (although he was murdered very early on), all applied similar methods in a socialist planned economy.[12]

None of these socialist experiments produced any convincing economic successes—even in Egypt. In the 1960s, numerous inhabitants of Upper Egypt or the Nile Delta were made to move because of Nasser's socialist castles in the air. That period saw the formation of the 'informal regions': areas without an urban infrastructure (lacking schools, hospitals, running water, drainage and sewage systems) in which two-thirds of the population live. (For example, the capital, Cairo has grown to almost twenty million inhabitants.) During the same period it proved less and less possible to provide jobs for the enormous number of students in the inflated state service. Bourguiba in Tunisia and Senghor in Senegal with their free market economies had far more success than Nasser. Even the great Soviet Union increasingly failed as the model of a successful state socialist economy and society. Therefore, the Egyptian President, Anwar as-Sadat, dissociated himself from the USSR, abrogated the 1976 Egyptian–Soviet treaty of friendship (after winning the Yom Kippur War against Israel in 1973) and, in a surprise visit to Jerusalem, introduced a peace initiative towards Israel in 1977. He concluded a peace agreement with the Israeli Prime Minister Menahem Begin in 1978, receiving back the whole of the Sinai peninsula which had been occupied by Israel since the Six-Day War of 1967, even if he initially forfeited the sympathy of the Arab nations. In his domestic policy, in 1976 Sadat introduced the transition to a multi-party state (albeit strictly controlled) and political and economic liberalization was introduced in stages: the Arab Socialist Union was dissolved and the National Democratic Party founded.

After Sadat's murder by an Islamicist fanatic on 6 October 1981, under his successor Hosni Mubarak relations were restored with the USA, Egypt's Arab neighbours and the Palestine Liberation Organization (PLO). In 1990, the headquarters of the Arab League moved to Cairo. Arab socialists in Egypt faced the end. The country, whose population is increasing by a million every eight months, faces immense economic and social problems. Since the 1990s, the influence of Islamic groups has again increased and has been expressed in hostile actions against Christian Copts, liberal writers and foreign tourists; the state has been able to respond only with oppression and mass arrests. But isn't secularism the best remedy against rigid and violent Islamicism?

Option V: Secularism?

Isn't the only consistent solution to realize the modern paradigm (P V) radically and to adopt the allegedly superior Western worldview and secular culture in place of outdated Islamic religion and culture? Shouldn't Islam become the private religion of any independent individual who wants to profess it, with no influence on society and politics? Kemal Atatürk has served as the model for very different reforms or revolutionaries: Shah Reza Pahlawi (Iran), President Habib Bourguiba (Tunisia), President Gamal Abd el-Nasser (Egypt) and the revolutionary leader Muammar al-Gaddafi (Libya).[13]

But everywhere religion keeps returning! After Atatürk's death, secularism was increasingly criticized even in Turkey. No one questioned the separation of state and religion in principle but the ideological and political spectrum became increasingly broad. Thus in 1960 the military—the generals as guardians of the Kemalistic revolution—thought it their duty to intervene against the government of the New Democratic Party and the National Salvation Party of Necmettin Erbakan with its neo-Islamic orientation. Subsequently the fear grew that the secular basis of the republic would be undermined by 'a new order with an Islamic orientation'.

Why was there a return of religion, a constant growth of the religious party in parliament, the rise of new religious groups and the resurrection of the Sufi schools and brotherhoods? Why was the observance of Ramadan in the country and in the Anatolian cities reflected on? Turks today think that Atatürk's reforms were aimed at the collective and freed the individual from the compulsions of the Islamic Ummah, but an individual isn't given a new identity simply by a secular republic: identity comprises more than rational ideas and national symbols. Atatürk and his followers could not and would not understand the role that Islam played and still plays for the personal identity of Turks, which has always also had an emotional existential component.

The Turkish historian Serif Mardin argues: 'It is a truism, but still one worth emphasizing, that Islam has become stronger in Turkey because social mobilization has not decreased but on the contrary increased the insecurity of the men who have been projected out of their original setting. This insecurity is sometimes "cognitive" and appears as a search for a convincing political leadership or a bountiful economic system. Here Islam assumes an ideological guise and competes with Marxism. In many cases, the insecurity is deeper-seated, more truly ontological, and Islam appears in its aspect of a cosmology and an eschatology.'[14]

For, as the Turkish specialist Udo Steinbach remarks, 'at the end of the 1940s it became evident that they (the Kemalists) had applied too rational, too European, a standard to Turkey'.[15] Therefore, religious instruction was allowed again and later even made statutory. A new theological faculty was opened in Ankara in 1949. Courses on the Qur'an, organized by the state, attracted large numbers, new mosques were built and old ones restored. Moderate Islamists could hold state posts. Newspapers, magazines, publishing houses, schools and businesses with an Islamic orientation and self-help groups were founded.

Alongside state Islam, which was shaped by the Department for Religion (*diyanet*), a popular Islam developed again, with brotherhoods and a cult of saints, mysticism and superstition. Finally, political Islam became established. I cannot trace all the stages of domestic politics since 1945[16] but ultimately this development led to the elections of November 2002 and the overwhelming victory of the moderate Islamists, the religious–modernistic Party for Justice and Development (AKP), founded shortly beforehand by Recep Tayyip Erdogan. Happily, the state president, government and parliament were not led into active participation in the Iraq war despite a maximum of political and economic pressure from the US government. Nor did Erdogan allow himself to be deterred from a visit of friendship to Greece in 2004 by the incomprehensibly negative vote of the Greek Cypriots on the reunion plan for Cyprus proposed by the United Nations. His option for Turkey is Europe.

2. Islam in a constant state of change

The reactions of Muslims to the invasion of their world by modernity shaped by Europe were very different: Turkish secularism, Arab and Iranian Islamism, Pan-Islamism, Pan-Arabism and Arab socialism. Many questions arise from my sketches of these different paradigms in the Islamic world of the twentieth century.

Questions to traditionalists, secularists and reformers

It has become clear that the Islamic world is not a unitary block, an 'Islam' that one can set against the West—which is just as little a unity. As a result of the US wars against Muslim countries, that view, held by the Pentagon adviser S.P. Huntington, who speaks of a 'clash of civilizations', superficial and politically dangerous as it is, will become a self-fulfilling prophecy and make Muslims all over the world aware of the unity of the Ummah. However, the plurality of rival paradigms still embraces very different trends, groups and parties, which often bitterly contradict one another or are even engaged in massive feuds.

The twentieth century in particular found the Islamic world in constant change. Individual Islamic countries were often led by governments with completely different orientations (pro-Western and anti-Western, capitalist and socialist, more or less authoritarian or democratic). The frontiers between the different movements are fluid and the alliances between the different parties and groups keep changing.

Questions: The future

- To the traditionalists: is it possible to live in a 'semi-modernity'? Can one accept the technological and economic possibilities of the modern world and at the same time detach oneself in spiritual, cultural and religious terms from modern social development, appealing to the divine revelation to avoid democracy, discriminate against women and forbid religious minorities to worship in public and build new buildings? Can Islam still remain the sole universally recognized complete book of laws and rules for the shaping of public and social life if society modernizes itself everywhere and extends religious tolerance? Isn't a separation between state and religion, within certain limits, unavoidable in an Islamic context?
- To the secularists: can one or should one, in a fascination with technological progress, give up membership of the Islamic religion regardless of one's own history and tradition, in order to live a 'god-less' life and, by industrialization and imitation of Western social structures, attempt to catch up with the West? Have people really had good experiences under deliberately atheistic regimes (for example, the Soviet Union, Nazi Germany, Mao's China, the Khmer Rouge)? Should one simply forget the Islamic religion and treat and rule a nation that has grown great in Islam as if Islam were a negligible factor? Mustn't a secular regime reckon with Islamic criticism as well as Islamic hopes? Can't renewed reflection on the original Islamic way of life even lead to the fall of a government which denies Islam?
- To the reformers: can one or should one reform Islamic nurture and education and limit the observance of the Islamic law to the purely ethical? Wouldn't this touch on basic questions of Qur'an interpretation, without sacrificing what is specifically Islamic and endangering the core of Islamic faith and the Islamic community? In the future, too, won't religion create emotional group identity, solidarity and demarcation and also authority and legitimacy?

The future of Islam in the twenty-first century is therefore by no means predetermined along a single line but is open to different models. In Islam, too, there is a pluralism of thought and action. No one can predict the future; different prognoses are possible, but some fundamental questions can be raised.

Western science, technology and media cannot in the long run be adopted successfully without adopting their intellectual and cultural background: the freedom to think and doubt and the right to criticize and put in question authorities and statements of faith. Those seriously concerned with reform therefore cannot avoid investigating the authority of the Qur'an (as the word of God, is it also a human word?), the hadith (divine revelation or time-conditioned prophetic instruction?) and the Shariah (unchangeable divine law or has it become historical)? In the view of many Muslims, 'here in particular lies the key to serious and far-reaching reforms'.[17]

A chasm in knowledge that is growing dramatically

What is the use of knowledge about the Qur'an if there is a lack of knowledge about the world, if secular education is defective? The second report of the UN Development Programme (UNDP) on human development in North Africa and in the Middle East[18] was published in October 2003; it was produced on behalf of the United Nations and the Arab League by around fifty Arab scholars. Like the first report, published in 2000, on freedom, the acquisition of knowledge and the role of women in the Arab world, the results of this second report on the state of education and the exchange of knowledge at the beginning of the twenty-first century are dramatically negative. Despite the considerable 'human capital', there is a gulf in knowledge between the Arab countries and the Western and the Far Eastern world: bad elementary schools, no independent science, over-full classes, out-of-date teaching methods and a lack of communication of knowledge. The average ownership of computers per 1000 in the Arab world is only eighteen; the world average is 78.3. And this with a dramatically increasing population: in Saudi Arabia, for example, from 3.2 million in 1950 to 22 million in 2004, three-quarters of whom are below the age of twenty-five.

According to the Arab scientists who produced the report, the Arab world is heading for a crisis of an unsuspected degree. The factors to be feared are a sustained economic decline, a drastic reduction in per capita income and a drop in productivity. This is in a region of the world consisting of twenty-two countries with 300 million inhabitants, of whom two-thirds are below thirty years of age, a population which, it is calculated, may grow to 410–459 million by 2020. What kind of future do people have in these circumstances? Should they emigrate? But only graduates can do that: in 1995/6 25% of

Islam on the way to postmodernity?

Traditionalist Islamism

Islam in **religious isolation**, religious substance with no relation to the modern world.

A medieval substitute world: legalism, fixated on the Qur'an and Sunnah as **law**.

Islam prescribed as the **state religion**: the Shariah provides the comprehensive regulations.

Radical secularism

Islam **emptied of religion**, a relation to the modern world with no religious substance.

A modern substitute religion: Pan-Arabism, nationalism or socialism, fixated on history as **progress**.

Islam tolerated as a **private religion**: priority of science, technology and democracy.

Postmodern Islam?

Religious emancipation of Islam, religious substance with a relation to the modern world.

The original Islamic religion:
No God but God,
Muhammad his Prophet.

Its constant point of reference:
the **revelation of the Qur'an** and the **Hijrah** (622=1).

Islamic identity through renewed **belief in the one God** and God's **righteousness**; an uncurtailed Islamic sense of history, but in the postmodern paradigm.

Consequence: **postmodern emancipation** and communication with today's world of nations and religions.

graduates emigrated; between 1998 and 2000 15,000 doctors left the Arab world. The report stresses that this is not a chance result but a structural problem connected with bad government, planning and politics: excessively high military expenditure, systematic nepotism in the economy and shameless self-enrichment.

In 2003 the former prime minister of Malaysia, Mahathir bin Mohamad, who was extremely successful despite all his authoritarianism, sharply criticized Muslims in his much-noted farewell speech at the Islamic summit in the newly founded capital, Putrajaya. Mahathir reminded his Muslim audience, which included numerous heads of state and government, of the golden age of Muslim science in the early Middle Ages, when Europe was still going through its dark ages. He criticized those Islamic scholars who since then had moved away from the practical knowledge of science and to the present day contented themselves with religious struggles. 'Whether we like it or not, we have to change, not by changing our religion but by applying its teachings in the context of a world that is radically different from that of the first Islamic century.' Here Jews are models: 'They survived 2000 years of pogroms not by hitting back, but by thinking.'

Mahathir has been criticized in the world press for some critical statements about the 'financial and media power of Judaism' and the state of Israel. In context they read differently. As he asks critically in respect of Palestine, was there really no other possible reaction for Muslims 'than to ask our young people to blow themselves up and kill people and invite the massacre of more of our own people'?[19] In Palestine, he argues, all this has achieved nothing, but has made the situation even worse. So Mahathir calls on Muslims to give up radical fundamentalism and suicide bombings and apply themselves fundamentally and practically to modernization and co-existence with non-Muslims. He argues that the Islamic world must adopt these values in order to overcome poverty, dissatisfaction and the growing gulf with the West, which only help the radicals on both sides.[20] But what is to be done?

How is the gap in education to be closed?

According to the UN report, educated society must be reinforced in all Arab countries. This rests on five pillars: a guarantee of basic freedoms, a dissemination of qualitatively good education, a social rooting of society, a shift to science-backed production and the development of an enlightened Arab model of knowledge. The report realistically acknowledges that in Arab culture, knowledge is communicated by religion, culture, history and a desire for success. If defective social, economic and above all political structures get in the way, they need to be removed or reformed.

What measures would help against the chronic technological, scientific and economic backwardness? The Arab states should be supported by the world powers and the international organizations in the following reforms:[21]

- The armaments expenditure of Arab countries (on average 6% of their Gross Domestic Product) needs to be restricted (in most Western states the figure is under 2% and in the USA only 4.5% of their GDP).
- Instead of this, investment is needed in education and research (in Arab countries the average level is only 0.5% of GDP) in order to overcome the two-class educational system—private schools and universities for the well-to do and state schools and universities for the middle and lower class—and thus make social mobility possible.
- It is not enough to reproduce the knowledge of other regions of the world in the Arab countries; rather, their own creativity and power to shape things must be strengthened. The level of new knowledge can be measured by research products, patents, inventions, technical innovations and developments.
- Education must change from teacher-centred education to pupil-centred, so that pupils learn to act independently; instead of merely learning things by heart they must work independently and as far as possible co-operatively.
- The urgent gap in education that needs to be filled is not only quantitative (more schools, text books, teachers, universities and research institutes) but also qualitative: there is need for a better culture of learning through a political and social climate friendly to education.

These five points are shared by many in the Arab world. So why haven't they been implemented long ago? The main problem of the Arab states is the rejection of fundamental reforms by rulers and their advisers, all of whom fear for their power. Just as the Vatican establishment likes to withhold knowledge (for example, the results of critical exegesis and the history of dogma) from the Roman Catholic laity and uses every possible means to produce a log-jam in reforms, so the Ulama establishment prefers to keep its people in ignorance. In authoritarian structures, of whatever kind, regimes work for the power interests of relatively small cliques that are not at all interested in enlightening the majority of the population. Transparency would make control possible and control would lead to the sharing of power. What is feared above all is accountability, so free expression of opinion is suppressed and dissenters are marginalized. Knowledge, research, development and creativity could only be disruptive. Those who currently hold power would much prefer the *status quo* to remain for the long term but that must be prevented. The UN report recommends the exertion of economic and political pressure from outside on the Arab autocrats, so that they are less concerned with prestige and retaining power and more concerned with the future of their countries and their young people. Ultimately, however, only the Muslims will be able to help themselves.

However, the democratization of the Arab states is bound up with a solution to the Palestine question. For there can be no peace between Israelis and Arabs, Jews and Muslims, without a peaceful solution of the Israel–Palestine conflict. I shall therefore now have to turn to this conflict, its genesis, the five wars bound up with it and a possible peaceful solution.

D III

The Middle East Conflict and a New Paradigm

The hostility between Muslims and Jews is not a historical inevitability. In many respects, Muslims and Jews are closer to each other than either are to Christians. Over the centuries, they have often lived together well, not only in Spain but also in Istanbul and the Balkans. Deep antagonism between Muslims and Jews has existed only since the twentieth century and does not primarily have to do with religion but with the political Middle East conflict between Israelis and Palestinians, Israelis and Arabs. The relationship between Jews and Muslims cannot essentially be improved without a solution to this conflict.

1. Causes of conflict

In the nineteenth century, long before Arab nationalistic efforts turned into a Pan-Arab movement, a Jewish national movement, political Zionism, came into being. In the twentieth century, despite resistance on many sides, this succeeded not only in establishing a 'Jewish homeland' (in the Balfour Declaration of 1917) in the historic land of the people of Israel (a land which in the meantime and from the seventh and eighth centuries had above all been an Arab homeland) but in building up a real Jewish state. The roots of the Palestine conflict lie in this dispute between two peoples over the same land and the resultant clash of two nationalisms; with the foundation of the state of Israel this expanded into an Arab–Israeli conflict and with the one-sided support of Israel by the USA even into an Arab–Western conflict. Often neither Jews nor Arabs are aware of the changing history of Palestine.

The state of Israel on Palestinian land

More than fifty years after the Holocaust and the foundation of the state, the state of Israel remains the centre of passionate dispute, a political dispute between Israelis and Arabs and a religious dispute between Jews, Christians and Muslims. The state of Israel is therefore still both a political and a theological challenge of the first order. This has to be recognized if peace is to come in this part of our world which has no peace. There will be no permanent, real peace until all sides not only seek an external diplomatic solution but also find a deeper political, ethical and religious understanding from within. Jews, Christians and Muslims have to agree on this. The Middle East must not remain a symbol for political fanaticism, national passions and religious blockades.

Far from all the party-political involvement, the remarks that follow must be understood as those of a Christian theologian, intended to contribute towards understanding and peace. Here I am presupposing what I have said at length on the prehistory of the state of Israel in my book *Judaism*:[1] about the Jewish people without a land and Zionism which was born out of need; about Theodor Herzl's view of a Jewish state (1896); about the Balfour Declaration in favour of a 'national home' for the Jewish people (1917); about the five Jewish immigrations ('Aliyah') to Palestine since the 1880s and the native Palestinian population; and about the Jewish terrorism in the 1930s and 1940s and the reaction of the British and Arabs.

From the beginning, a deep shadow fell on the state of Israel—completely contrary to the intentions of Herzl and many other Zionists. Both sides would have been spared an infinite amount of suffering had people listened more to Theodor Herzl, to Nahum Goldmann, the president of the Jewish World Congress, and to other great figures of Judaism such as the philosopher of religion Martin Buber, all of whom were opposed to terror and war and had worked for collaboration between Jews and Arabs. The dream of a homeland entertained by many Zionists was only half-fulfilled in Palestine. A land had been found, even *the* land of the Jews, but even here peace and quiet did not return for the Jewish people. On the contrary, the difficulties in Palestine went further and became even more intense when Zionism, which had become an autonomous community in the inter-war period, attained a wide range of self-administration and even a parliament, Israel's Knesset. The Second World War and Holocaust did not form the basis for all this but did accelerate it.

In the face of more conciliatory elements, in 1942, David Ben-Gurion, the rival of the liberal Chaim Weizmann, established his position at a Zionist conference in New York with the help of militant American Zionists: his 'Biltmore Programme', put forward at the Biltmore Hotel, aimed at a state embracing the

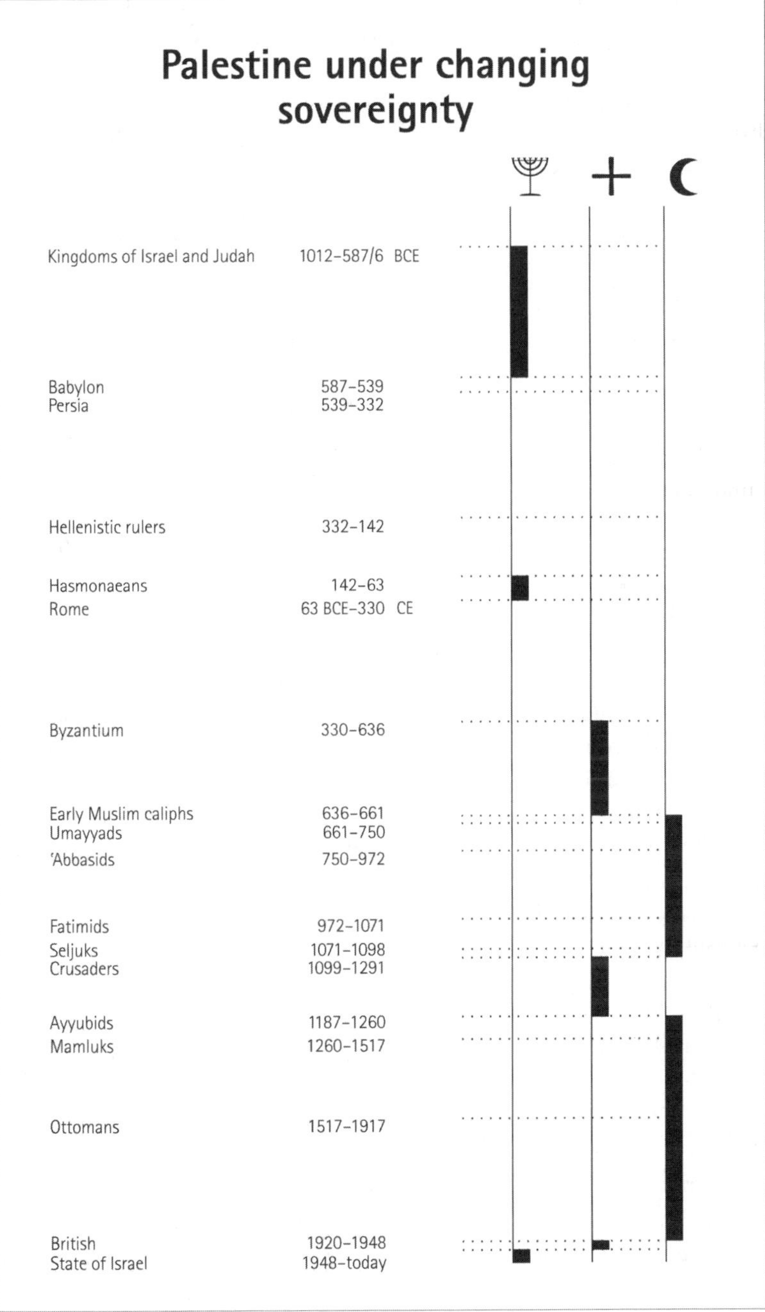
Palestine under changing sovereignty
Kingdoms of Israel and Judah 1012–587/6 BCE
Babylon 587–539
Persia 539–332
Hellenistic rulers 332–142
Hasmonaeans 142–63
Rome 63 BCE–330 CE
Byzantium 330–636
Early Muslim caliphs 636–661
Umayyads 661–750
'Abbasids 750–972
Fatimids 972–1071
Seljuks 1071–1098
Crusaders 1099–1291
Ayyubids 1187–1260
Mamluks 1260–1517
Ottomans 1517–1917
British 1920–1948
State of Israel 1948–today

whole of Palestine. Neither the participation of the Arabs nor any frontiers were mentioned. Ben-Gurion's aim was not a Jewish state in Palestine but Palestine as a Jewish state.

However, under the new constellation of powers that arose towards the end of the Second World War and the newly-formed United Nations, things turned out differently. The British mandate was to end on 14 May 1948. Time was pressing. Nahum Goldmann had argued for a partition and the creation of a viable Jewish state in an appropriate part of Palestine and Chaim Weizmann also drafted a plan for partition, which was to change markedly.

On 29 November 1947, a solid UN majority (with the USA and USSR!) voted to divide Palestine into a Jewish and an Arab state—with clearly defined borders, an economic union of the two states and the internationalization of Jerusalem under UN administration. The Jews, who at this point possessed ten per cent of the land of Palestine, were to receive fifty-five per cent, around 15,000 square kilometres; the Arab population, which at 1.3 million was almost twice as large, only 11,000. The main powers of the Arab League (the Palestinians, since the sixteenth century under Ottoman rule and since the First World War under British rule, still had no political representation and organization) rejected this unfair division. This was a fatal mistake, as even Palestinians recognize in retrospect today: in this way the Arabs forfeited the foundation of their own Palestinian state, which they still vainly long for.

There is no doubt that with their rejection the Arabs played into the hands of Ben-Gurion, now head of the Labour Party, the Jewish Agency and the Zionist executive in Palestine: he still secretly strove for a Jewish state comprising the whole of Palestine. Politically shrewder than the Arabs, Ben-Gurion assented to the partition plan despite objections—and moved forward decisively towards the foundation of the state. On 15 May 1948 the state of Israel was proclaimed by the National Council of Jews. That David Ben-Gurion, the first prime minister and defence minister (1948–53 and 1955–63), omitted to mention the frontiers laid down by the United Nations in the declaration of independence caused a stir but was not taken seriously.

In addition to the foundation of the state, steps were taken towards political reconciliation with Germany—a reparation agreement over the Holocaust was made with the Federal Chancellor Konrad Adenauer in 1952. This is undoubtedly Ben-Gurion's greatest achievement as a statesman and deserves unqualified acknowledgement. Ben-Gurion also made other decisive contributions towards the technological–economic and scientific–cultural development of the state of Israel and the incorporation of the vast number of immigrants from all over the world but he could not make peace for his state. His legacy in both foreign and domestic policy was therefore highly ambivalent: because the whole policy of this 'armed prophet' was aimed at the greatest possible territorial expansion of Israel and thus *ipso facto* against a state of Palestine, not only did he fail to seek reconciliation with the Arabs but he laid the foundations for the disastrous development of the next decades: the arms race in the Middle East; a series of wars, Israel's high budget deficit and an economic and—in the view of some Israelis—also a moral decline. From 1948, all Arab efforts were aimed at reversing the foundation of the state of Israel and deciding the situation in Palestine in their favour by force of arms. The consequence was that from the day of its foundation the young state in fact found itself in a state of war with its Arab neighbours.

The Arab dilemma: Israel either un-Jewish or undemocratic

Five bloody wars were fought between Israelis and Arabs in the next fifty years, a new war in each decade: the War of Independence (15 May 1948 to 24 February 1949); Israel's Sinai campaign (29 October to 8 November 1956); Israel's Six-Day War (5–11 June 1967); the Arab Yom Kippur War (6–25 October 1973); and Israel's invasion of Lebanon (6 July 1982). The two-fold result was, first, that the small state of Israel fighting for independence became the military power of Greater Israel occupying broad Arab territories and, second, the five million settled Palestinian people became a people of the oppressed, fugitives and freedom fighters, the breeding ground for that terrorism which is contemptuous of humanity.

To establish rights to this land and to settle people of different nations, languages, cultures and economic classes from all over the world on it, the Zionists, the majority of whom were secularists, had to refer back to religion: to the religious tradition which is binding on all Jews, the memory of the state sovereignty which they lost more than 2000 years previously and the frontiers of the great empire of David and Solomon when, for a few decades, the old Israel had possessed the sovereignty which it now demanded.

From the beginning it was evident that different paradigms were at work and simultaneously in dispute in the Jewish state founded in 1948: elements of the Enlightenment–modern paradigm (P V: a parliamentary democracy), but also the Davidic imperial paradigm (P II: the kingdom of Judah and the northern kingdom united with Jerusalem as the capital and the borders as wide as possible). Small religious parties and the Chief Rabbinate ensured that an independent judiciary was introduced (the post-exilic theocracy paradigm P III) and that the medieval rabbinic paradigm (P IV) was applied rather than modern reform Judaism.[2]

Both Christians and Muslims must try to understand that, for Jews and especially for Israelis, 'people' and 'land' in principle belong together: this is the essence of Judaism.[3] However, since the Jewish resettlement of this country and even more since the foundation of a Jewish state it has become abundantly clear that here two peoples stand over against each other—the Jewish people and the Arab–Palestinian people—both of whom can appeal to a consciousness, deeply rooted over three thousand or thirteen hundred years, that this land legitimately belongs to them and to them alone. The Jews refer above all to the empire of David and Solomon after 1000 BCE (Jewish P II), the Palestinians refer to the conquest of the land by the Arabs in 636 CE (Islamic P I). So it is legitimate to put the question that the British historian James Parkes chose as the title of his history of the peoples of Palestine: 'Whose Land?'[4]

By its policy of occupation after the 1967 war, the state of Israel put itself in an increasingly difficult situation and—apart from the one-sided support of the USA—manoeuvred itself into widespread international isolation. This critical situation was accentuated by the settlements on the occupied territories; these were slow at first but the policy was pursued energetically after the right-wing Likud block under Prime Minister Menahem Begin gained a parliamentary majority in 1977 (the former terrorist leader had been made politically respectable by the government of national unity that had proved necessary). The areas involved were east Jerusalem, 'Judaea and Samaria' (the biblical terms are employed now instead of west Jordan, although for centuries Samaria was an opponent of Judaea) and the Gaza strip. While the official Israeli government policy used simply to deny the Palestinians as a political entity on Israeli territory, whether in Israel or abroad one cannot close one's eyes to the fact that by 2010 the Arab 'minority' within the present *de facto* state frontiers will be half the total population. According to the *New York Times* of 17 September 2003, this now numbers 1.3 million in Israel and 3.2 million on the West Bank and in Gaza, making 4.5 million Palestinians in all—compared with 5.4 million Jews. However, by the temporary closing of frontiers (the 'green line') the Israeli military authorities have made it clear to the world that the occupied territories of 'Judaea and Samaria' are not part of the state of Israel. The building of the wall in 2003–4 (euphemistically called the 'security fence'), begun under Ariel Sharon and for the most part on Palestinian territory, like the invasion of Lebanon in 1982, recalls the worst methods of the Cold War.

There are clear Jewish majorities simply because the birth-rate of the Arab part of the population is more than twice as high only in the big cities and in the 'defensive villages'. If, as all the forecasts predict, within the foreseeable future the number of Arabs overtakes the number of Jews—a demographic time bomb—what will Israel's future look like? At the beginning of the twenty-first century, in its practical policy the Jewish state faced the alternative of collapse—as the former Knesset speaker Avraham Burg clearly pointed out in a moving

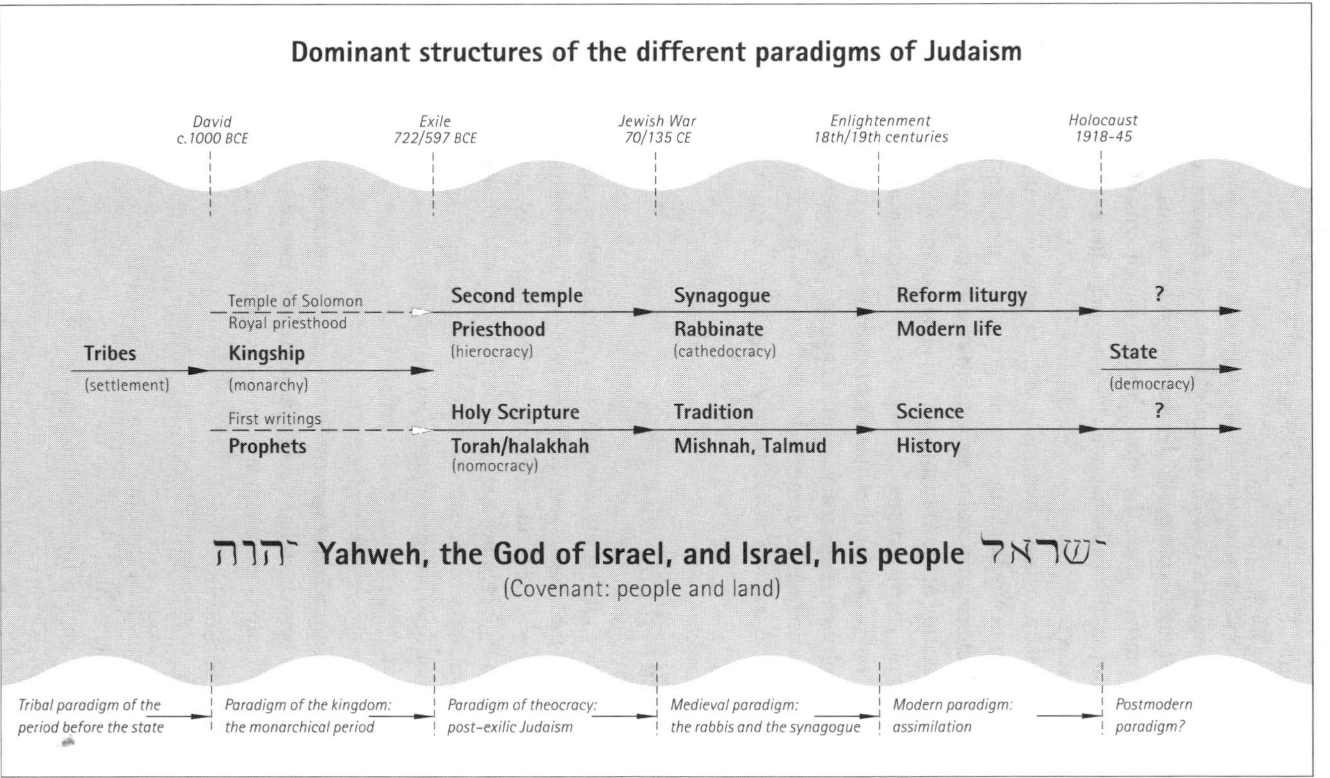
Dominant structures of the different paradigms of Judaism
David
c.1000 BCE
Exile
722/597 BCE
Jewish War
70/135 CE
Enlightenment
18th/19th centuries
Holocaust
1918–45
Temple of Solomon
Royal priesthood
Second temple
Priesthood
(hierocracy)
Synagogue
Rabbinate
(cathedocracy)
Reform liturgy
Modern life
?
Tribes
(settlement)
Kingship
(monarchy)
State
(democracy)
First writings
Prophets
Holy Scripture
Torah/halakhah
(nomocracy)
Tradition
Mishnah, Talmud
Science
History
?
יהוה Yahweh, the God of Israel, and Israel, his people ישראל
(Covenant: people and land)
Tribal paradigm of the period before the state
Paradigm of the kingdom: the monarchical period
Paradigm of theocracy: post-exilic Judaism
Medieval paradigm: the rabbis and the synagogue
Modern paradigm: assimilation
Postmodern paradigm?

article in 2003 under the title 'A Failed Israeli Society is Collapsing'.[5] (In 2000 Burg had presided over the first speech given to the Knesset by a German Federal President, Johannes Rau.)

– Either Israel acts in a consistently democratic fashion, in which case it runs the risk of becoming un-Jewish, for constitutionally the large Arab 'minority' must be given the same rights as the citizens of Jewish descent, which would result in a bi-national, Jewish–Arab state: a Zionism which was abolishing itself.

– Or the state of Israel remains Jewish, in which case it runs the risk of becoming un-democratic. It is quite possible that if its policy remains unchanged, the country will be exposed to ever greater internal tensions: further radicalization of the Arab minority will be accompanied by the radicalization of small Jewish groups, the settlers and also the army—the former murdering out of despair, the latter out of revenge. The occupied territories are still ruled only by an emergency law under a state of emergency. Is what used to be Israel's much-vaunted democracy only for Jews, whereas Palestinian Arabs experience it as military dictatorship and aggressive colonialism and largely attack it?

2. No end to the tragedy?

When will the endless dispute over the Holy Land ever be settled? When will the war be ended, the tragedy—which deeply depresses all the friends of the state of Israel, among whom I include myself—be over? In the present world situation, inflamed by 11 September 2001 and the Iraq War of 2003, the Jewish state is, unhappily, in danger of remaining even more fixated on the past, instead of facing the present and being open to the future.

Persisting in the old paradigm

From the beginning, there was a potential conflict in Israeli society, allowed by Ben-Gurion, between religious and non-religious Jews, a conflict which has never been resolved and which now provides dangerous fuel for blockades and confrontations within Israel:

– Some people persist in the medieval paradigm of the orthodox (Jewish P IV), which includes theocratic elements and can become very aggressive (in no Western state other than the Vatican state are there as many restrictions grounded in religion as there are in Israel).

– Others persist in an outdated modern paradigm of the secularists (Jewish P V) often also governed by nationalism, racism and militarism. Internal political peace between the two Israeli camps is all the more important for political peace with the Arabs.

The state of Israel therefore paradoxically resembles some Islamic countries, which likewise seem to be suppressing the challenges of a postmodernity which—as in the European Union and similar processes in Latin America or South East Asia—has more of an international than a national orientation, despite old and new political, ethnic and religious oppositions. This postmodernity no longer promotes aggressive antagonism but good neighbourliness and peace between the nations and no longer strives for fanaticism but for peaceful co-existence, indeed the pro-existence of the different religions: it works for understanding, reconciliation and integration instead of the confrontation, revenge and war which used to be customary.

What is to be done in Israel? For the survival of both Israelis and the Arabs, realism and pragmatism are called for, rather than national mythologies and illusions. But are there still realistic chances for the new paradigm in the Middle East? As Avraham Burg wrote in the article I mentioned above: 'The Jewish people did not survive for two millennia in order to pioneer new weaponry, computer security programmes or antimissile missiles. We were supposed to be a light unto the nations. In this we have failed. It turns out that the 2000-year struggle for Jewish survival comes down to a state of settlements, run by an amoral clique of corrupt lawbreakers who are deaf both to their citizens and to their enemies. A state lacking justice cannot survive.'[6]

That Israeli policy is increasingly being rejected also by European Jews had been shown in a marked way by the best-known Swiss Jew, Sigi Feigel, honorary president of the Israelite Worship Community in Zurich. In an open letter he addressed Ariel Sharon bluntly: 'No one has caused greater insecurity and no one has endangered the peace as much as you have; no one has put Israel to shame and brought it into disrepute as often as you have, Prime Minister.' Feigel concluded by saying that Israel had never been brought 'so near to the edge of the abyss of self-destruction'. His demands were: 'The wall must go. The excessive acts of retribution by the army must cease. The settlements need to be removed. And Jerusalem must be shared with the Palestinians.' He was 'aware that a peace for Israel involves risks and sacrifice. But all in all they are certainly less than those of the present situation.'[7]

What could be

A solution to the apparently insoluble Israeli–Palestine conflict is possible only on the basis of a conclusive and fair overall plan that requires concessions from both sides and promises gains to both. From a view which I developed in the

1990s,[8] and which has again been confirmed from various sides recently, in the context of 2004, I shall attempt to indicate some realistic chances for a new paradigm: not with apparently sure predictions, but in the mode of 'it could be that'. I do this in full awareness of the very real uncertainties of the future, which can bring about fundamental changes more quickly but not always for the worse. There is also an anti-Murphy's law: 'What can go wrong need not always go wrong ...'

It could be that an increasing number of Israelis realize that they were led astray by demagogy when their politicians promised them peace through the policy of the 'strong hand' without reflecting that the capacity of the oppressed for suffering is greater and more persistent than that of the oppressors.

It could also be that the majority of Jews in the USA and Europe, long challenged by the scandalous oppression of a people, will no longer keep silent but will help those who want peace to prevail in Israel, so that in the present chaotic stalemate a different policy from that of the Sharon government can be implemented as soon as possible, or another government be elected that really wants the peace and prosperity of Israelis and Palestinians.

It could be that an Israeli government could withdraw its troops from all the occupied territories, as it did from Lebanon in 2000 after two decades of occupation (Israel's 'Vietnam'), under the following conditions: the recognition of the state of Israel by all Arab states with normal political and economic relations; the establishment of an autonomous and viable (not fragmented) Palestinian state and if possible an economic union between Israel, Palestine and Jordan (on the model of the Benelux states) which would be a blessing for the whole region and especially for Israel.

It could be that then the Palestinians, who react with the same logic of violence as the Israelis, would stop their bloody terrorist activities and suicide attacks; that they would guarantee the state of Israel and its security; that they would therefore realistically limit their 'right of return' to a symbolic return in some particularly harsh cases—in favour of new Palestinian settlements, the take-over of Israeli settlements and substantial financial and economic reparations on the part of Israel, of the kind that the state of Israel and many Jews received from Germany after the Second World War.

It could be that, finally, the Islamic world, under the pressure of the terrorist attacks and after 11 September 2001, with a view to a better future, found itself ready for a comprehensive self-examination and condemnation of Islamic terrorism and further suicide attacks and collaboration with a peaceful Israel.

It could be that the Jerusalem question, too, could find a solution, similar to the solution of the 'Roman question' which dragged on, likewise for many decades, in the nineteenth and twentieth centuries while the Vatican and the

Italian state disputed sovereignty over the holy city of Rome, until a relatively simple solution was found in the 1929 Lateran treaties: a single city with one administration but two sovereignties, Italy on the left bank of the Tiber and the City and State of the Vatican on the right. For Jerusalem this would mean that in the one Old City (it alone is of religious and political significance) there would be two sovereignties and two flags but a single joint city administration—if possible with a mayor of the stature of the Jewish Teddy Kollek, who was mayor for many years.

I again feel that I am supported by Avraham Burg: 'That's what the prime minister should say to the people. He should present the choices forthrightly: Jewish racism or democracy. Settlements or hope for both peoples. False visions of barbed wire, road-blocks and suicide bombers, or a recognized international border between two states and a shared capital in Jerusalem.'[9]

Even clearer and more welcome to me is the confirmation of this by an unofficial peace plan which was worked out with the support of the Swiss Confederation in months of efforts by important representatives of both sides under the leadership of the former Israeli minister of justice, Yossi Beilin, and the former Palestinian information officer, Yassir Abd Rabbo. It was published in Geneva on 1 December 2003. This was not just a vague 'road map', leaving the decisive questions open, but a realistic peace plan which responded constructively to the questions addressed above in terms of a consistent two-state solution within the frontiers of the Six-Day War of 1967, a partition of Jerusalem and a solution to the refugee problem. Sharon and Arafat were against it. However, the Middle East must not remain an eternal breeding ground of Arab terrorism and the main occasion for it.

Opportunities for the new paradigm

The important thing is to convince people on both sides that according to some surveys more people are ready for compromise than their stubborn leaders. Tactical manoeuvres lead nowhere. That must be made clear by fundamental considerations of the situation in world politics. The vision of peace for Israel and Palestine will seem considerably more convincing if it is seen in the context of the epoch-making paradigm change from the modern nationalistic and imperialistic paradigm (P V) to the postmodern co-operative world order (P VI).

Particularly at a time of international political failure by an American president, I am glad to recall that the initiative for a new paradigm in international relations came from the USA: first in 1918, with the US president Woodrow Wilson's 'Fourteen Points' and the League of Nations and second in 1945 with the Bretton Woods agreement on a new ordering of the world economy, the foundation of the International Monetary Fund and the World Bank and the Universal Declaration of Human Rights in 1948, followed by American economic help for the rebuilding of Europe and its incorporation into a system of free trade.

Whereas in 1945 the Islamic world, like the Asian and African world generally, continued largely to be governed by national power politics (imported from Europe!), in the Western European countries from which nationalism, imperialism and racism originated and which had caused the majority of wars (especially the two world wars) an international political paradigm change could be established: in the direction of a novel overall political model of regional co-operation and integration, which could peacefully overcome centuries of opposition. This was the European Union. Here the USA also played a leading role: the result was fifty years of peaceful democracy, not only for the EU but for the whole sphere of the OECD (Organization for Economic Cooperation and Development, founded in 1948 and re-founded in 1960, i.e. the Western industrialized states, including Japan). This was a successful paradigm change not only in theory but also in practice, a model for South East Asia (ASEAN), Latin America (MERCOSUR) and South Asia (India and Pakistan).[10]

The new political overall constellation confirms in principle that instead of the modern policy of national interest, power and prestige there is a policy of regional understanding, convergence and reconciliation. This calls for mutual co-operation, compromise and integration instead of the former confrontation, aggression and revenge. It has been implemented in exemplary fashion by France and Germany and reconciliation is also proceeding between Germany and Poland and Germany and the Czech Republic.

Could such a development also be commended for the Islamic world, for regions of conflict such as Afghanistan, Kashmir and Cyprus and above all for the Middle East? It is hard to see why such a paradigm change couldn't also be set in motion between Israel and the Arab nations—with massive support from the USA and the EU. However, this presupposes a change of mentality in the population, especially among those who make the decisions, which goes far beyond the politics of the day. New organization is not enough; a new mind-set is needed. As long as Israelis regard Arabs as second-class citizens and Arabs regard Israelis as monsters, no fundamental transformation of their relationship can be expected. What needs to be achieved is to understand national, ethnic and religious differences not as threats but as potential enrichments. Thinking in the old paradigm always presupposed an enemy, even an arch-enemy. Thinking in the new paradigm (as the EU has shown) no longer needs an enemy but needs partners, rivals and often opponents. Economic competition should replace military confrontation.

Questions: Living together

In this political situation all three Abrahamic religions and their global, regional and local representatives are challenged to develop a new peaceful attitude and actions in keeping with it.

'Recompense no one evil with evil' (Romans 12.17). Isn't this saying from the New Testament also addressed to those American and European Christian 'crusaders' of the Iraq war who seek only the evil in the other, think that a religious motivation hallows every military means and through shameful acts and shameful photographs must discover the evil in their own ranks and hearts?

'An eye for an eye, a tooth for a tooth' (Exodus 21.24). Isn't this saying in the Hebrew Bible on the limitation of violence also addressed to those Jewish fanatics among the settlers and military who prefer to take two eyes from their opponents instead of one and who by using their tanks, helicopters and rockets forget that, as Mahatma Gandhi put it, 'an eye for an eye makes the whole world blind'?

'But if they incline to peace, incline thou to it as well' (Surah 8.61). Isn't this saying from the Qur'an also addressed to those Palestinian 'warriors of God' who, with no understanding of the history of the Jewish people, comprising many centuries of suffering, still wish to expunge the state of Israel from the map? Isn't it also addressed to those who respond to the state terror of Israel with desperate and cruel suicide attempts, which also hit innocent civilians, women and children? As soon as the Israelis withdraw, Palestinian terrorism must also stop, so that the reasonable demands of the Palestinians can be met and the guarantees of security for Israel be realized.

The Middle East has proved that democracy and national prosperity cannot be promoted by war but only by peace, not by confrontation or uninvolved juxtaposition, but by co-operation. Because different interests continue to be virulent, both sides must make efforts to calm the situation down by an interweaving of interests. This would make possible a policy between Arabs and Israelis which was no longer a zero-sum game in which some constantly win at the expense of others but a positive-sum game in which everyone profits from constructive (not lazy) compromises. Sometimes, of course, there is need for a stimulus from outside to encourage completely split parties to join in the game.

The three Abrahamic religions, which are at least indirectly entangled in these clashes, should become aware of their ethical responsibility and use their spiritual resources to achieve peace and make it permanent.

However, ethical questions are not the only questions in dispute between Jews, Christians and Muslims. Ethics is essential for every religion, but religion does not just consist of ethics, nor can it be reduced to ethics: ritual and community, which I have already discussed at length, are also essential dimensions. Finally, there are questions of the fourth dimension, doctrine and the interpretation of the holy scriptures, which traditionally divide Muslims and Christians. Politicians, businessmen and scientists in particular should note these.

D IV

New Approaches to Theological Conversation

In societies sensitive to religion, conflicts with a social or political basis quickly become religious controversies and conversely religious controversies have an effect on the social and political 'basis': both Karl Marx and Max Weber are correct on this point—with qualifications. For this reason alone it is also politically of the utmost importance to work on religious differences and reach the widest possible agreement between Christians and Muslims, Christianity and Islam. There can be no political peace without observing the religious dimension of political controversies—that is evident both in the Israel–Palestine conflict and in Iraq.

1. Yesterday's methods

The classical Muslim objections to christology and the doctrine of the Trinity are already known from the Qur'an and have been constantly repeated by Muslim authors. I shall go into them briefly in what follows but it makes little sense to accumulate a multiplicity of Muslim testimonies. Nor can it be the task of a book on Islam to report at length on the discussion about christology and the Trinity in Christian theology. Readers will find the theological background in my earlier books *On Being a Christian* and *Christianity*, which include a broad description and documentation of the development of dogmatic christology in the first centuries. In the two sections that follow I want to further the theological discussion between Christians and Muslims and to offer ways towards constructive solutions on the disputed points. First, though, I shall discuss briefly the traditional controversies and the defensive strategies on both sides.

The traditional controversy

The theological discussion is made difficult by the literal reference to the Qur'an, widespread in Muslim circles, which takes too little note of changing contexts in interpretation. The positive contribution of Islam—compared with dogmatic Christianity and its belief in the Trinity and the incarnation—is its lesser complexity and its doctrine, which is more rational and in some respects illuminating. There is no question that this greater simplicity had a decisive influence on so many Christians who converted to Islam, leading to the almost complete disappearance of Christianity, from the countries in which it originated (the Middle East and North Africa). It also often represents a reason for conversion to Islam.

Muslim theologians from the famous al-Azhar university in Cairo know that the traditional belief in Trinity and incarnation often comes up against criticism, misunderstanding and indeed rejection in Europe and North America, since it easily deviates into the tritheism of popular theology. This is one of the reasons why quite a few Muslims in the Middle East—under the impact of increasing Muslim missionary literature which contains reports of successful conversions and photographs of new mosques—seriously think that the West is on the way towards Islamization and Islam on the way to becoming the greatest world religion.

This view is not as absurd as it might seem. In contrast to Christian dogmatics, which seems over-complicated and not very rational, Islamic theology and propaganda praises the complete accord of the Qur'an with reason, indeed with the newest science. Certainly people in the West may laugh at the way in which Muslim ancestry is sought for every science—from mathematics and astronomy to physics, chemistry and medicine—and the origins, for example, of depth psychology are found quite directly in al-Ghazali in the twelfth century.[1] However, not very long ago Catholic theologians, too, wanted to see everything (apart from a modern view of history or Einstein's theory of relativity) prefigured in Thomas Aquinas in the thirteenth century. While there are some surahs in the Qu'ran which refer to the creation, there is no extended creation narrative in the style of the Bible, except possibly at the beginning. So the Qur'an poses far fewer problems for compatibility with modern science than does the Bible.[2]

Arabic-speaking Christians had great difficulty in countering Islamic arguments against their belief in Christ, especially if they knew no Western theological literature (often this was the fault of the church leaders) and read about Jesus only from a Qur'anic perspective. Instead of unenlightened Christian edifying and devotional literature, what is needed is biblically-based theology.

However, one question arises: won't the situation have its revenge if Muslim theologians make the mistake of suspecting more recent research by Western orientalists of anti-Islamic motives and think that they needn't take its results seriously, thus leaving their own communities uninformed?

The defensive strategies on both sides

W. Montgomery Watt, one of the best English-language experts on the life of Muhammad and the early history of Islam, made an important contribution to dialogue some time ago in his book *Islam and Christianity Today*.[3] With great openness, he began by pointing out to both sides the defensive strategies which Christian and Muslim theologians have developed over the centuries so as not to have to take note of the other side.

First came the Greek-speaking Christian theologians of the East. They classified Islam as a 'Christian heresy' and provided a detailed catalogue of the allegedly false assertions of the Qur'an and the moral weakness of the Prophet.[4] The western Christian theologians, who gained a more precise knowledge of Islam only after the crusades, were similar. Not least out of a cultural inferiority complex they disseminated a formal caricature of Islam, although they now had access to the Qur'an and Muslim books. I referred in the opening chapter of this book (A I, 1) to Norman Daniel's *Islam and the West: The Making of an Image*,[5] and in an early book by W.M. Watt, *The Influence of Islam on Medieval Europe*[6] there is evidence for the following charges: Islam is a religion of violence which has been spread by the sword, a religion with no moral and particularly no sexual inhibitions, a religion of numerous false assertions and twistings of the truth. With all his moral weaknesses, Muhammad could only be the founder of a false religion, a tool or an agent of the devil. Watt, a Scottish Anglican minister, remarks succinctly: 'No objective historian today can accept any of these points.'[7]

It would take a long time to explain why such a caricature—handed down by some Christians even now and, as we saw, again recently favoured by political developments—burdens any substantive conversation between Muslims and Christians from the start, indeed makes it impossible. In October 2003, General William G. Boykin, the man in the Pentagon in charge of the hunt for Osama bin Laden, Saddam Hussein and others, declared that he was fighting 'against Satan', but that he knew 'that God is greater': this God was the 'real God' and the God of his opponents was 'an idol'. However, he said that he was 'no zealot or extremist, but only a soldier with a deep faith'.[8] American commentators pointed out that there were many evangelicals among those around President George W. Bush who thought in similarly exclusive terms and that such belief was also widespread in the Vatican. One example of this is the document

Dominus Iesus produced by the Vatican Congregation for the Doctrine of the Faith in 2000, in which it is sweepingly said of members of other religions that 'objectively speaking they are in a gravely deficient situation'.[9]

Does there seem to be more openness and readiness for understanding on the Islamic side? Unfortunately not. Many Muslim theologians have attempted, on the basis of an obscure verse of the Qur'an, to develop all-too-clear a doctrine of what they call 'falsification' (*tahrif*) of the Jewish and Christian scriptures. Muslim authors interpret this very differently: it might be falsification by deliberately changing the text or merely by different interpretations of the text.

This 'dogma' of the 'falsification' of the Jewish and Christian scriptures—which is nowhere convincingly proved[10]—has often been sufficient to immunize Muslims against any argument from the original Jewish and Christian scriptures: the Qur'an knows better. Moreover, it has compelled Christians to enter the controversy on the basis of the Qur'an: read the Qur'an instead of the Bible. The dogma of the self-sufficiency of Islam is combined with the dogma of falsification: every truth is contained in the Qur'an. This dogma has contributed towards making Muslims reject any possible borrowing of the Qur'an from non-Islamic sources from the start. It has also kept them from learning from the West—with the negative consequences that I have described for the scientific, technological, economic and finally also military spheres and for society generally.

Christian or Muslim, traditionalistic immunization against the insights of the other side, indeed against modern 'infection' generally, has so far produced no longer-term successes. It therefore seems that both sides have every reason to take the arguments of their opponents very seriously and to work on them self-critically. The truth can be perceived only by listening to one another and approaching one another. The result will not be the weakening of the religions but mutual correction, supplementation and enrichment, combined with a demolition of prejudices and a strengthening of credibility.

In my experience, Christian–Muslim dialogue needs to do two things: first, to include the most influential conservative Muslims, in particular theologians, in the conversation. Secondly, the conversation will be a serious one only if the difficult questions are not excluded. However, some church people who call for critical dialogue have little idea about other religions. Yet only on a solid, scholarly, theological basis will progress be made in mutual understanding.

I would therefore like to quote a text that in an epoch-making way has laid the foundation for a new theological dialogue. For the Roman Catholic Church, it makes the paradigm change from that of modernity: it does not breathe the spirit of rejection and condemnation but the spirit of ecumenical understanding. It comes from the Second Vatican Council's Declaration on the Non-Christian Religions: 'The Church has a high regard for the Muslims. They worship God, who is one, living and subsistent, merciful and almighty, the Creator of heaven and earth, who has also spoken to men. They strive to submit themselves without reserve to the hidden decrees of God, just as Abraham submitted himself to God's plan, to whose faith Muslims eagerly link their own. Although acknowledging him as God, they venerate Jesus as a prophet, his virgin Mother they also honour, and even at times devoutly invoke. Further they await the day of judgement and the reward of God following the resurrection of the dead. For this reason they highly esteem an upright life and worship God, especially by way of prayer, almsdeed and fasting. Over the centuries many quarrels and dissension have arisen between Christians and Muslims. The sacred Council now pleads with all to forget the past, and urges that a sincere effort be made to achieve mutual understanding; for the benefit of all men, let them together preserve and promote peace, liberty, social justice and moral values.'[11] This leads me immediately to the central point of the theological controversy: Jesus.

2. Dialogue about Jesus

Just as Muslims—as we shall see in more detail—can learn something from Christians about a modern understanding of the *word* of God, so Christians can learn something from Muslims and Jews about a simpler, more original understanding of the *son* of God. Christians who concern themselves with Islam in a way that is not only apologetic and defensive but also critical and self-critical, will be challenged to reflect again and more sharply on their own Christian roots. In looking at the picture of Jesus we shall move from the Qur'an to the New Testament.

Jesus in the Qur'an: God's messenger, not son

Jesus of Nazareth plays a highly significant role in the Qur'an: fifteen surahs mention him, and more than a hundred verses are devoted to him. Islam does not dispute that Jesus was a Jew, and that his first disciples were Jews.[12] Jesus, called 'Isa in the Qur'an (the derivation is uncertain but the name is possibly formed in parallel to 'Musa', Moses), the 'son of Mary', *'Isa ibn Maryam*, is given more honorary titles and names than anyone else in the Qur'an. Only once is he called '*nabi*' = 'prophet', for according to the Qur'an there are very many prophets. Above all he is called '*rasul*' = 'sent'.[13] This is a lofty title: only the few who have received a book of revelation—Moses (the Torah) and David (the Psalms), Jesus (the Gospel) and of course Muhammad—are 'sent'.

A Muslim–Christian dialogue can begin at the level of prophecy, but it should not begin with the titles, though initially they seem to promise still more:

– Eleven times in the Qur'an Jesus is called 'the Messiah' (*al-masih*);[14] however, this does not denote a divine dignity of mission in salvation history but the anointed one who is cleansed from sin or blessed.

– In the Qur'an Jesus is also called 'word of God' (*kalimah min Allah*),[15] probably in some connection with the notion of the Logos in the prologue of the Gospel of John. However, this does not mean a pre-existent divine being, even a divine person, but the creative word of God, to which Jesus also, and particularly, goes back.

– In the Qur'an Jesus is also called 'spirit of God' (*ruh min Allah*),[16] because Mary conceived him as a virgin through an action of the spirit; here the relationship of the spirit to the Angel Gabriel remains unclear. The announcement of the birth of Jesus and his virginal conception is narrated at length twice,[17] not as proof of the divinity of Jesus but as a sign of God's omnipotence—in an utterly theocentric way.

– In the Qur'an Jesus performs miracles ('proofs', 'signs') at a very early stage: he even addresses people from the cradle, makes clay birds fly and food come from heaven. However, he performs all the miracles, including healing the sick and raising the dead, with God's permission and power: as the 'servant of God' (*'abd Allah*),[18] which, fundamentally, every human being is.

Thus the Qur'an clearly has a christology with a prophetic, theocentric, stamp. Jesus points away from himself to God. All prophets have fundamentally the same dignity and preach the same message of the one and only God. Just as Moses brings the Jews the Torah, so Jesus brings people 'the gospel'; thus his followers are 'people of the book', like Jews and Muslims. The Qur'anic Jesus shows himself to be warm-hearted and gentle; he confirms the Torah and at the same time makes it easier. However, like any prophet he, too, is attacked and accused of 'manifest sorcery',[19] indeed is even threatened with death. We shall see later how his fate is portrayed in the Qur'an.

Despite its use of biblical honorific titles, Qur'anic christology has nothing to do with classical Christian christology in the sense of doctrines of pre-existence, incarnation and two natures, of the kind that theologians since the eighth-century John of Damascus, the dogmatic theologian of the Orthodox Church (see A I, 1), have repeatedly advanced against Islam. The New Testament title that is most important for dogma, 'son of God', does not appear in the Qur'an. The reason is understandable even for Christians: for the Prophet Muhammad the title 'son of God' had negative associations with the old Arabian polytheistic tribal religions, as did 'daughter of God'. They seem to express a sexual physical descent from God, like that in numerous Greek, Roman and Germanic mythologies. Muslims understood this as a devaluation of, indeed an insult to, the transcendence of God and, as is well known, this led to misunderstandings in Christian christology and popular piety. Therefore Jesus is never called 'son of God' in the Qur'an, just as one word, 'Father', is absent from the 'ninety-nine beautiful names of God'. It would similarly be misunderstood mythologically.

As mother of Jesus, Mary has a special place in the Qur'an (and therefore in Islamic popular piety). The nineteenth surah bears her name, the important third surah that of her father, who here is called Imran ('Imran): these two surahs even mention the begetting of Jesus by the Spirit and the virgin birth. In Islam, Mary is regarded as chief of all women in piety and is set on the same level as Khadijah, 'A'ishah and Fatimah. However, here too there are clear limits: there is no question of Muslims using the title 'Mother of God'. Probably also because of this Christian title, there is a misunderstanding of the Christian Trinity in the Qur'an. According to surah 5.116 Mary is the second person of the Trinity with God the Father first, and Jesus, the Son, third.

In the Qur'an—in complete contrast to later Jewish writings, for example the *Toledot Yeshu*—Jesus is neither ignored nor defamed but regarded with great reverence and sympathy. There is protest against only one thing: that people make him, God's messenger, God's messiah, God's word, God himself: 'Indeed, the truth deny they who say, "Behold, God is the Christ, son of Mary"—seeing that the Christ [himself] said, "O children of Israel! Worship God [alone] who is my Sustainer as well as your Sustainer." Behold, whoever ascribes divinity to any being beside God, unto him will God deny paradise, and his goal shall be the fire.'[20] However, it must surely be of interest also to Muslims how the Christian New Testament answers the question of divine sonship without denying belief in one God.

What does it mean for Jesus to be God's son?

It will surprise not only Muslims but also some Christians that if we want to understand why Jesus' disciples came to proclaim him as son of God our starting point should not be Jesus' birth but his death. The New Testament, including the letters of Paul, knows nothing anywhere of a virgin birth except in the two great Gospels of Matthew and Luke. The earliest Gospel, that of Mark, begins immediately with John the Baptist, Jesus' forerunner, and Jesus' public life, and thus has no birth narrative at all. So, unquestionably, belief in a virgin birth does not belong at the centre of the Christian message. Hence we can understand that even those in the early church who knew nothing or thought nothing of virgin birth could be convinced, like Mark, Paul or John, that Jesus was the 'Messiah' (Greek 'Christ') or could confess him 'Son of God', the centre of the Christian message.

As a pious Jew, Jesus himself preached a strict monotheism. He never called himself God, on the contrary: 'Why do you call me good? No one is good save God alone.'[21] According to the same Gospel, Jesus answers a scribe's question about what is the highest commandment with Israel's confession of faith, the '*shema Israel*': 'The greatest commandment is: "Hear, Israel, the Lord your God is one God." '[22] There is no indication in the New Testament that Jesus understood himself as the second person in God and was present at the creation of the world.[23] In the New Testament, God himself ('*ho theos*', 'the God', 'God') is always the one God and Father—not the Son.[24]

Only after Jesus' death, when on the basis of certain Easter experiences, visions and auditions people might believe that he had not remained in suffering and death but had been taken up into God's eternal life, had been 'elevated' by God to God, did the believing community begin to use the title 'son' or 'son of God' for Jesus. At first, people recalled the experience of God and union with God by which Jesus of Nazareth had lived, preached and acted: how he had taught people to see God as the Father of all human beings ('Our Father') and had called him Father ('Abba, dear Father'). So for Jews who followed Jesus there was a substantive reason and an inner logic that the one who had called God 'Father' should explicitly be called the 'son' by those who believed in him and followed him. The one who was in a unique way God's son was not, as formerly, the king of Israel, since there had long been no kings, but Jesus, the expected Messiah who had come.

At a very early stage people began to sing the songs of the Psalter, understood messianically, in honour of the one who had been raised from the dead, especially the accession psalms. Jews at that time could easily think of the elevation to God as analogous to the accession of the Israelite king. Just as the king was appointed 'son of God' at the moment of his accession to the throne—probably a borrowing from the royal ideology of the ancient Near East—so now the crucified Jesus was understood to be 'son of God' by virtue of his resurrection and exaltation. In particular Psalm 110, in which King David sang to his future 'son', who at the same time was his 'Lord', must have been sung and quoted time and again: 'The Lord said to my lord, "Sit at my right hand" ' (v. 1). For the Jewish followers of Jesus, this verse answered the burning question of the 'place' and function of the risen Jesus.[25] To the question 'Where is the Risen One now?' one could reply: with the Father, 'at the right hand of the Father', not in a community of essence but in a 'throne community' with the Father.

In Psalm 2.7, an accession ritual, the Messiah king is explicitly addressed as 'son': 'You are my son; today I have begotten you.' In this verse, 'begotten' is a synonym for enthronement, exaltation. Neither in the Hebrew Bible nor in the New Testament is there any trace of a physical–sexual begetting as in the case of the Egyptian God-king and the Hellenistic sons of god, nor of a metaphysical begetting along the lines of the later Hellenistic ontological christology.

Therefore, one of the oldest confessions of faith (probably even pre-Pauline) in the introduction to the Letter to the Romans can say that Jesus Christ was 'appointed son of God in power after the resurrection from the dead'.[26] So this accession Psalm 2 could be taken up in the Acts of the Apostles and applied to Jesus: 'He (God) said to me (according to Psalm 2.7 to the king, to the anointed, but according to Acts 13.33 to Jesus), "You are my son, today I have begotten you."' How could all this come about? Because here in the New Testament the thought is still thoroughly Jewish: 'begotten' as king, 'begotten' as the anointed one (= Messiah, Christ) means being 'appointed' as representative and 'son'. And by 'today' (in the psalm the day of enthronement) the Acts of the Apostles clearly does not mean Christmas but Easter; not the feast of a descent, incarnation, but the day of resurrection, the exaltation of Jesus to God. That is why Easter is the main feast in Christianity.

What did first Judaism and then the New Testament mean by 'son of God'? Regardless of how this was later defined by Hellenistic councils with Hellenistic terms, in the New Testament what is unquestionably meant is not descent but an appointment to a position of justice and power in the Hebrew Old Testament sense. This is not a physical divine sonship, of the kind that occurs in the Greek myths, which is often supposed and rightly rejected by Jews and Muslims, but an election and authentication of Jesus by God, completely in keeping with the Hebrew Bible, in which sometimes the people of Israel can collectively be called 'son of God'. In the light of the Jewish belief in one God no fundamental objection could be made to such an understanding of divine sonship; otherwise it would not have been put forward in the original Jewish–Christian community. If the original understanding of divine sonship were emphasized again today, then probably Islamic monotheism too would have no fundamental objection to it.

In the view of orthodox Muslims, the Prophet Muhammad received the teaching laid down in the Qur'an about Jesus, the Messiah, directly through divine revelation. But divine revelation by no means excludes prior human knowledge. The Qur'an often speaks of Muhammad's contacts with Jews and Christians. Revelation always takes place in a particular individual and social context.

What could Muhammad have known?

The Qur'an presupposes considerable knowledge of the religious situation of its time. One question that is not just motivated by historical curiosity is: from whom could Muhammad have gained his thoroughly positive picture of Jesus which nevertheless diverges sharply from that in Christianity? From the Jews? Certainly not: the majority of them rejected Jesus from the beginnings of the Jesus movement, or ignored him. From the Hellenistic Christians? Likewise not: they over-exalted Jesus as Muhammad thought of him and made him equal to God, using Greek categories. This was true above all of the 'Monophysites' in nearby Egypt and Syria, who under the influence of Cyril, Patriarch of Alexandria, did not want to attribute a human 'physis', nature, to Jesus but only a single divine 'physis'. Cyril forced through this view on his own initiative at the Council of Ephesus in 431 (before the arrival of his opponent, Nestorius, Patriarch of Antioch, and the opposing party).[27] It was also held, however, by the orthodox Byzantine Christians, though they corrected Ephesus with the Council of Chalcedon in 451, when they put forward the doctrine of two natures in Christ, one divine and one human. But these were united in one divine person![28] So according to this council, too, Jesus was not a human person—which for Muhammad would have been completely unacceptable.

That makes the question all the more fascinating: in Muhammad's positive picture of Jesus (with its negative demarcations), which Christians are being referred to if the Monophysite and the orthodox (Dyophysite) Christians cannot be meant? According to the Qur'an they must have held a belief in Jesus stamped by

- a strict Jewish monotheism,
- an eschatology totally orientated on the day of judgement,
- an affirmation of the law of Moses.

This, then, was a basic faith in the one God and his 'Prophet' or 'Messiah', which could accept narratives such as the virgin birth but had to reject later Hellenistic speculations on a second divine person or eternal hypostasis beside the one personal God—an 'association' (*shirk*) or 'partnership'. If we look for such believers, there is only one 'group' which fits: the Jewish Christians, that early form of Christianity whose members, mostly of Jewish origin, had combined their belief in Jesus as the Messiah with the observance of the ritual law of Moses. That immediately raises the further question: could Muhammad have known such Jewish Christians?

There are various mentions of Christians in the Qur'an and Muhammad must also have known several personally. However, he did not read the Bible, even supposing that he could read and write at all. Arabia, always outside the

Roman–Byzantine empire, was never a systematic field of mission. But Christianity was dominant in Ethiopia and Syria and according to credible Muslim tradition, as a merchant Muhammad would travelled to adjacent cultivated lands on his trading journey, especially into Syria, which at that time was one of the most highly Christianized areas of the world. As we know, there were also not only self-contained, strongly Arabized, Jewish communities in the general area of Mecca and Medina but also a great, ethnically diverse, Christian community south of Mecca in the oasis of Najran, on the territory of the old Sabaean empire (in present-day Saudi Arabia) on the border with Yemen. There were even isolated Christians in the few cities of Arabia and also in Mecca, just as Christian merchants will have kept coming to this, the most important trading centre on the Arabian peninsula, especially to its annual market.

It is not easy to verify what lies behind the reports, some of which occur in biographies of the Prophet only around 150 by the Islamic calendar. However, in connection with Muhammad's relationship with Christians, we can be certain that:

– Muhammad's first wife had a Christian cousin, Waraqah ibn Nawfal, who had a good knowledge of the Christian scriptures; he would hardly have been a Hellenistic Christian but rather a Jewish Christian, as he spoke Aramaic. At an early stage he drew Muhammad's attention to the correspondence between his experience of revelation and that of Moses. Moreover, one of Muhammad's later wives was a Christian.

– Muhammad encountered Christian monks during his caravan journeys and they spoke their sacred texts in Aramaic, the language of Jesus and the Jewish Christians.

– In the Qur'an great respect is shown to the Christians (they are called 'Nazoreans'): 'Thou wilt surely find that, of all people, the most hostile to those who believe [in this divine writ] are the Jews as well as those who are bent on ascribing divinity to aught beside God; and thou wilt surely find that, of all people, they who say, "Behold, we are Christians," come closest to feeling affection for those who believe [in this divine writ]: this is so because there are priests and monks among them, and because these are not given to arrogance.'[29] According to the most recent research, which I have reported at length (see A II, 2), these are clearly Jewish Christians.[30] I must now return to them in connection with Muhammad's picture of Jesus.

An affinity between the Qur'anic and the Jewish–Christian understandings of Christ

In the original Jewish Christian community, belief in the one God was so much taken for granted that the notion of rivalry through another being equal to God could not arise. The executed Jesus had been exalted by God to God and now (according to Psalm 110) occupied the place of honour 'at God's right hand'; he had been 'made Lord and Messiah by the resurrection from the dead' (see Acts 2.22–36) and was now the pioneer, bringer of salvation and coming judge of the world. In the Jewish paradigm—and also in Paul and John—this was not regarded as competition with belief in the one God but as its consequence. Jesus Christ was, for Jewish Christians, the embodiment of the rule and kingdom of God, which could now be experienced in the spirit.

Whatever may be said about Muhammad's historical knowledge, there are unmistakable parallels between the Qur'an and the understanding of Christ in Jewish–Christian communities. They were worked out, around a century ago, by Adolf von Harnack and Julius Wellhausen and later by the conservative Protestant exegete Adolf Schlatter and the Jewish scholar Hans-Joachim Schoeps. However, these parallels have so far found few echoes either in Islam or in Christian dogmatics or in Jewish–Christian–Muslim dialogue. Not only Muslim theologians but also Christian dogmatic theologians of all confessions often simply ignore inconvenient results of exegetical and historical research, whereas some of those involved in dialogue have a defective knowledge of dogmatics, exegesis and the history of dogma. However, the parallels and analogies compel them all to face the question why Muhammad—although he rejected orthodox (or Monophysite) christology—nevertheless always spoke with sympathy of Jesus as the great 'messenger' (*rasul*) of God, indeed as 'Messiah' (*masih*), who brought 'the gospel'. In his 'Theology and History of Jewish Christianity'[31] Hans-Joachim Schoeps endorses Harnack, Wellhausen and Schlatter: 'While it may not be possible to demonstrate the context precisely, the indirect dependence of Muhammad on sectarian Jewish Christianity is beyond any doubt. That gives rise to a paradox of truly historic dimensions, namely that while Jewish Christianity went under in the Christian church it conserved itself in Islam and in some of its driving impulses extends down to the present day.'[32]

What does 'sectarian Jewish Christianity' mean here? Were the Jewish Christians who combined their belief in Jesus as the Messiah with the observance of the ritual law of Moses sectarian, as it were, heretical? By no means: the very early church father Justin Martyr (*c.*150), who came from Palestine (Nablus) and was the first to report on this Jewish Christianity, was well able to make a distinction. On the one side were the majority of the completely orthodox Jewish Christians, who observed the Jewish ritual law and circumcision but did not seek to impose them on the Gentiles (here resembling Paul and the Apostolic Council) and on the other were those legalistic Jewish Christians who were really 'heretical' and who wanted to impose the law on

Gentiles also, as being necessary for salvation. According to Justin, Jewish Christians accepted Jesus as Messiah/Christ but claimed that he was 'a man of men' and had been 'chosen' to be the Messiah/Christ.[33] In principle, they observed law and circumcision and put forward a christology with a Jewish stamp which offered an illuminating combination of messianic belief and observance of the law, which was only later labelled 'heretical' (because it was allegedly 'natural' or 'adoptionist'). The handbook on heresies, the *Panarion*, written by Epiphanius of Salamis, had a bad influence, since he includes the 'Nazoraeans' as a matter of course among his eighty heresies.

We should not forget that, like Jesus himself, his first disciples, the greater part of the original community and all the Christian missionaries known to us, were Jews, or more precisely 'Jewish Christians'. (What else could they be?) They were by no means all heretics simply because they observed the law and circumcision and 'only' advocated an 'apocalyptic' son of man christology or an 'adoptionist' son of God christology. New Testament christology began modestly, with quite human questions such as 'Who is this?'[34] and 'Can anything good come out of Nazareth?'[35] Titles for Jesus 'from below' were 'son of David', 'new Moses', 'high priest' and then 'from above' 'son of man', 'word of God', 'son of God'. If we wanted to judge all Christians before the Council of Nicaea (325) in the light of the statements of this council, which put Christ on the same level as God ('of the same substance' as him), then not only the Jewish Christians but also almost all the Greek church fathers of the first three centuries would in fact be heretics, since as a matter of course they taught a subordination of the 'Son' to the 'Father' ('subordinationism'). Who would have been orthodox at all in the church of the first three centuries?

However the Jewish–Christian sources are to be assessed in detail, present-day research sees more the continuity of Jewish Christianity with the beginnings of early Christianity and less its heretical caricatures. Thus, the Jewish Christians are regarded as legitimate heirs of early Christianity, whereas the rest of the New Testament largely reflects the view of Gentile Christianity as it was defended—rightly—by Paul and his followers.[36]

Reflecting on the cross

Muslims will hardly find an answer in the Qur'an to the theodicy question, namely the question of the justification of God in the face of all the suffering in the world. A fearful event such as a plague in the Syrian village of Emmaus (which Josef van Ess investigated in a detailed investigation extending of more than 450 pages)[37] was seen as fate, destiny. People were convinced that God holds human destinies in his hands and that this God is a good God, from whom even such a visitation must be understood as a sign of mercy. So sickness was simply accepted and prophylactic measures were neglected: 'The religious obligations, daily common prayer, burials, evidently continued to be observed as a matter of conscience. But charitable orders never came into being in the Islamic world which saw the care of the sick as their task; just as little did the victims form themselves into brotherhoods, as did the lepers in the kingdom of Jerusalem at the time of the crusades.'[38]

In Christianity the question of theodicy is connected with the crucifixion of Jesus. This is perhaps the most difficult point in dialogue about Jesus: the fact of the crucifixion, which according to all the earliest Christian, Jewish and pagan sources is historically indisputable and needs no proof. The Qur'an mostly points out that people have repeatedly attempted to kill the messengers sent to them because of their message. And Jesus was accused of 'manifest sorcery'[39] because of his miraculous actions and therefore threatened with death. According to the Qur'an, the Jews boast: ' "Behold, we have slain the Christ Jesus, son of Mary, [who claimed to be] an apostle of God." ' But according to the Qur'an this did not correspond with historical reality: 'However, they did not slay him, and neither did they crucify him.'[40]

These verses about the cross have become the '*crux interpretum*', the burden and pain of exegetes.[41] As the Qur'anic verse about the crucifixion of Jesus is not really clear, other interpretations are possible, for example that strictly speaking only the view that Jesus was killed by the Jews is rejected here. However, it is striking how much the prophetic figure of Jesus in the Qur'an corresponds to the figure of the Prophet Muhammad, whose coming he foretold.[42] As the last prophet before Muhammad to be chosen by God at God's command, Jesus performed prayer, gave alms and behaved in a pious way towards his mother.[43] How could Jesus have failed totally at the end, unlike the Prophet Muhammad? Islam knows no idea of a 'redemption', since human beings are not imprisoned in an inherited sin; in principle they can fulfil the will of God by 'right guidance'.

The Qur'an's answer to this is: 'But (another) seemed to them similar (so that they confused him with Jesus and killed him).'[44] This verse is understood in docetic terms by some Muslim commentators: 'It only *seemed* to them (that they had crucified Jesus)', an interpretation which is still put forward by the Ahmadiyyah movement: Jesus was taken down from the cross in a helpless state and then cared for; went in search of the lost ten tribes of Israel in the East; and died in Kashmir at a great age; his tomb is pointed out in Shrinagar.[45] However, the majority of both classical and modern Qur'an exegetes interpret it in terms of a substitution or replacement: another was executed in his place—a view widespread in the circles around Muhammad; the Christian Gnostic Basilides had claimed that another (Simon of Cyrene) was executed in place of Jesus.[46]

The Qur'an seems to think in terms of a natural death of Jesus and his resurrection to life.[47] God 'called away' Jesus and 'elevated' him (to heaven) when the time was right.[48] The 'exaltation' is understood in different ways in the Islamic tradition: some interpreters assume that Jesus had died and was rescued by God from death to himself, others think that he did not die but was taken up into heaven alive from where he will return as Mahdi—though this notion does not occur in the Qur'an. The Qur'an speaks of Jesus appearing at the last judgement, not, however, as judge but as 'witness' (*shahid*) who bears witness to God for the Christians.[49]

The Muslim scholar Mahmoud Ayoub, author of the pioneering study *Redemptive Suffering in Islam* (1958),[50] has examined all the tormented Muslim interpretations of this disputed verse of the Qur'an in an article entitled 'Towards an Islamic Christology. The Death of Jesus, Reality or Delusion?'[51] He goes on to ask self-critically: 'Why ... does the Qur'an deny the crucifixion of Christ in the face of apparently overwhelming evidence? Muslim commentators were not capable of refuting the crucifixion convincingly ... Commentators have taken the verse as a historical statement. However, this statement, like all the other statements about Jesus in the Qur'an, does not belong to history, but to theology in the broadest sense.'[52] What is the theological meaning of this verse of the Qur'an, which Ayoub attempts to put in the framework of an 'authentic Islamic understanding of Christ', an 'Islamic christology'? His answer can be understood only in the context of the elevation of Christ to new life with God which the Qur'an affirms at the same point: 'Therefore the denial of the death of Jesus is a denial of the power of human beings to compel and destroy the divine word, which is eternally victorious.'[53]

The Christian theologian, Martin Bauschke, emphasizes the decisive point: 'Christians and Muslims are agreed that however Jesus may have died and whatever happened to him after his death—this death did not and does not have the last word about his life and activity on behalf of God. Rather, this death was the way through, the transition, the way back into the presence and nearness of the one who sent him.'[54]

Jesus fully integrated into the Islamic tradition

Numerous hadith bear witness to Jesus' coming again, and also to this or that saying or action of Jesus. Western scholars conjecture that some Jesus hadith may have been introduced by Christian or Jewish converts to Islam from the biblical wisdom tradition or the New Testament (often apocryphal sources). Jesus also plays a major role in the mystical tradition. The French Islamologist, Roger Arnaldez of the Sorbonne, has not only written a study of Jesus in the Qur'an[55] and Qur'anic commentaries but also one on Jesus in Islamic thought, especially in mysticism.[56] In it he discusses an adequate number of representative figures of the various streams to draw general conclusions which, for him as a Christian, seem conflicting, welcome and disappointing.

It is welcome that Jesus is very present in Islamic thought, whether as a guide or as a Sufi. He is a spiritual and moral example, a 'master of Sufism', together with Abraham, Moses, David and the Prophet Muhammad, to whom of course he is subordinate. Jesus takes on special significance in esoteric mysticism: for Ibn 'Arabi the returning Christ became the seal of holiness; for al-Hallaj he became the type of mystical union; for the Shiites, he became a pointer to the Mahdi, though the Mahdi will be one of their imams and not Jesus. The figure of Jesus is fully 'integrated' into the moral and spiritual culture of the Muslims, but this integration has its shadow side.

It is disappointing that this is a fully Islamicized Jesus, reduced to what is known from the Islamic tradition, the hadith or Sufism, with or without him. His behaviour, his words and the states of his soul make him seem the perfect Sufi but he loses his own profile in the process and so is difficult for Christians to recognize. In this Jesus, we do not find the slightest echo of the Sermon on the Mount, the Beatitudes and many other aspects of his life and conduct which are important for Christians. The Jesus of the Gospels had distinctive things to say about poverty, humility and other mystical values but in the works of the Sufis he is only to confirm these values: 'In the end of the day Jesus appears as a mystic who has his status in the midst of other mystics as great as, if not greater than, him, just as he is also only one prophet among others and in any case subordinate to Muhammad.'[57]

Any reader, whether Muslim or Christian, will appreciate the way in which the Islamologist Arnaldez formulates his personal standpoint as a Christian, openly and clearly, at the end. He is convinced that 'Islamic mysticism offers a favourable ground for the development of Muslim–Christian dialogue' but also that 'this dialogue cannot and should not begin with Jesus'.[58] If in amazement one asks why, it becomes clear on the last page of the book that, on this question, Arnaldez ultimately adopts a standpoint which is grounded in Christian dogma with a Hellenistic formulation: 'For Christians,' he says, 'it is Jesus as the Word become human, as Son of God, who grounds them and creates them.'[59] Thus he unwittingly makes it clear that this dogmatic basis of dialogue with Muslims over Jesus is blocked from the start. He thinks that Jesus' saying 'He who is not for me is against me, and he who does not gather with me scatters' may be applied to Muslims.[60]

What would be the alternative for entering into a conversation about Jesus with Muslims? My proposal is that if the dialogue—or, with the inclusion of Jews, the 'trialogue'—about Jesus is to be fruitful, it must begin with the Jesus of the Jewish Christians.

What are the opportunities for a 'trialogue' on Jesus? Does it ask too much?

Which historical references in the Qur'an point with what intensity to what specific Christian group must possibly be left open but there can be no disputing the decisive point that the analogies in content between the Qur'anic picture of Jesus and a christology with a Jewish–Christian stamp are indisputable. The parallels remain perplexing and open up surprising possibilities for conversation between Christians, Jews and Muslims.

It has to be said, once again, to Muslim conversation-partners that one is not putting the authenticity of the Qur'anic revelation in question if one sees links with the Christian scriptures. I have not cited parallels and analogies in order to prove the superiority of Christianity or doubt the authenticity of the Qur'anic revelation. I want nothing to do with any strategy of 'commandeering' or an over-cautious strategy of treading lightly which does not allow the conversation-partner to grapple with the historical facts. Rather, I wish, emphatically and constructively, to refer to the affinity between Christianity and Islam. This asks a great deal of all those involved in the dialogue but in my view also offers great opportunities.

Unless the signs of the time are deceiving, despite tremendous political difficulties, the ethnic and religious tensions and violent conflicts, we are at the beginning of new theological conversations which do not deny the well-known differences between the great monotheistic religions but put them in a different light.

After centuries of mutual contempt, the Jewish–Christian dialogue about Jesus made substantial progress once Jews and Christians together began to take seriously the abiding Jewish features of the message and figure of Jesus for their faith. Insight into the affinity between primitive Christianity and primitive Islam also needs to be utilized for Muslim–Christian dialogue—the earlier the better: Christians should no longer see the Qur'anic understanding of Jesus as Muslim heresy but as a christology with a primitive Christian colouring on Arabian soil. For all the prophetic religions, these insights would at first be extremely inconvenient but if there is to be real understanding, the questions that are now urgent must be answered:

Questions: Jesus

Faced with Muslims, may Christians still exclusively appeal to the high christology of the Hellenistic councils and make them the sole norm for belief in Jesus as the messenger of God for all the 'children of Abraham'? What significance do they attach to the Jewishness of Jesus of Nazareth? What status do they give him for their faith? How far are they prepared to take seriously the much more original christology of the Jewish disciples of Jesus and the early Christian communities, as reflected in the Qur'an?

Faced with Christians, may Jews still polemically put on one side the figure of Jesus, in whose name much suffering has been inflicted on them, or even ignore him for the Jewish life of faith? What significance can Jesus have today for the life of Jews, if he is taken seriously as the last great prophet of the Jewish people with abiding Jewish features, as he is by the Qur'an and some Jewish scholars?

Faced with Christians, may Muslims content themselves with criticism of Hellenistic christology (which endangers monotheism)? How ready are they also to regard the religious significance of Jesus from the perspective of the New Testament, so as to understand the authentic figure of Jesus more comprehensively and to avoid constricting it and looking at it in a one-sided way? Three times the Qur'an calls Jesus a 'sign' of God for people all over the world.[61] Precisely what does this mean?

There is no question that, in this new situation for discussion, all three Abrahamic religions are called on to set out from the traditional view of things towards a new future. The inconvenient insight into the affinity of Jewish–Christian and Qur'anic christology will prove extremely fruitful. All three prophetic religions are above all offered an opportunity:

- An opportunity for Jews: they can hold on to their faith in the one God of the fathers, Abraham, Isaac, Jacob, and on to the Torah. Yet they can look at the challenge of Jesus of Nazareth, the great son of Israel who, for the sake of God and human beings, relativized the absolute validity of descent, Sabbath and halakhah and by his message and fate proved himself to be a successor to Moses and indeed 'more than Moses'.
- An opportunity for Christians: they need not remove the slightest element of their belief in Jesus as the one Messiah or son of God or even of their discipleship of Jesus. Yet, they could explain their understanding of 'sonship' in

a way that is more comprehensible to Jews and Muslims. They can show how, in the light of the Hebrew Bible and the Jewish community, there could be no notion of any sexual-physical or even metaphysical ontic 'begetting' in this divine sonship; the notion is that of the 'appointment' and enthronement of Jesus by God himself as 'messiah (anointed king) in power'[62] on the basis of his resurrection.

- An opportunity for Muslims: they can absolutely and completely maintain their belief in the one and only God and the impossibility of an 'association' or 'partnership' of an earthly being with God. Could they also attempt to understand more comprehensively Jesus, the 'messenger', the 'word', the 'messiah' of God who, according to the Qur'an, was elevated to God, in the light of the New Testament, as God's 'pointer', as 'God's friend and servant', perhaps even, in the originally Jewish sense, as 'son of God'?

Supposing that the opportunities I have indicated were taken: would not a conversation between Jews and Muslims on the one hand and Christians on the other ultimately come to grief on the Christian doctrine of the Trinity (for many Christians the 'central truth'), on the assertion of a divine tri-unity?

D V

Speculative Questions

A question which is not just for Christian theologians but which constantly comes up especially in dialogue with conservative Muslims is: how are monotheism and the Christian doctrine of the Trinity related? Aren't they contradictory? Some Christian apologists think that the Christian doctrine of the Trinity 'heightens' the unity of God. But is belief in the Trinity really 'the golden mean between monotheism and polytheism', as they boldly claim?

1. Monotheism and Trinity

Together with Jews and Muslims, some Christians ask: can one 'heighten' unity, and do so by trinity? May mystery mean contradiction? Shouldn't the Jewish and Islamic criticism of the dogma of the Trinity which was first formed in the fourth century be understood as a challenge to reflect on an interpretation of the relationship between Father, Son and Spirit which, in principle, was also understandable to Jesus' Jewish disciples (less Graeco-Latin than 'Semitic')? Strikingly, the doctrine of the Trinity was not originally an object of rabbinic polemic and initially there was no departure from belief in one God—above all among Jewish Christians, with whom the rabbis had to deal. So what is the origin of the doctrine of the Trinity, against which Jews and Muslims finally engaged in vigorous polemic?

The Muslim belief in one God versus the Christian Trinity

The Greek word *trias* appears first in the apologist Theophilus of Antioch in the second century and the Latin *trinitas* first in the African Tertullian in the third century. The trinitarian formula was shaped in a highly complex, sometimes contradictory and at all events wearisome process of thought. Its classic form was spelt out by three Cappadocian church fathers (Cappadocia is in the centre of present-day Turkey), Basil, Gregory of Nazianzus and Gregory of Nyssa: God is threefold in the 'persons' ('hypostases', 'subsistences', 'prosopa') but one in 'nature' ('physis', 'ousia', 'substance'). In short: *Deus triunus*, triune God, God three in one.

At the beginning—in the New Testament—threefold formulas appear without emphasis on a unity: simple triadic (not 'trinitarian') confessional statements. The triadic baptismal formula in Matthew's community tradition ('Baptize in the name of the Father, and of the Son, and of the Holy Spirit'[1]) developed from the simple christological baptismal formula ('Baptize in the name of Jesus Christ'[2]). A trinitarian speculation which was intellectually highly demanding and which emphasized the unity of the three entities came increasingly to be built on this. The result was something like a higher trinitarian mathematics which, despite all the efforts to attain conceptual clarity, hardly led to permanent solutions. Practical preaching continued to be about the Father, the Son and the Spirit but largely passed over this doctrine of the Trinity—God in three persons but in one nature. The liturgy of the Trinity (propagated in the Gallican sphere from the eighth century in the face of persistent Roman resistance) and the feast of the Trinity (introduced as late as 1334 by the French Pope John XXII in Avignon) for the Sunday after Pentecost changed little. This was the first feast dedicated not to a saving event but to a dogma and while hardly disputed—except by the Unitarians, who emphasize the unity of God—it was largely ignored. In the twenty-first century, preachers who 'have to' preach about this dogma on the festival are usually unaffected by critical exegesis and the history of dogma and employ lofty trains of thought about the Three who are yet one God. No Muslim who heard such a sermon would be ever be convinced by such speculative reflections.

In seventh-century Islam the doctrine of the Trinity was brought into the centre of criticism. This criticism is formulated harshly in the Qur'an: 'O followers of the Gospel! Do not overstep the bounds [of truth] in your religious beliefs, and do not say of God anything but the truth. The Christ Jesus, son of Mary, was but God's Apostle—[the fulfilment of] His promise which He had conveyed unto Mary—and a soul created by Him. Believe, then, in God and His apostles, and do not say "[God is] a trinity." Desist [from this assertion]. God is but one God.'[3] However, in the Qur'an we sometimes find as the Christian Trinity not the Trinity of God the Father, Son and Spirit but the Trinity of God the Father, Mary mother of God and Jesus son of God. Could this also be found in popular Christian belief at that time and indeed today?[4]

The background to the polemic of the Qur'an, as the Qur'an also observes, is the vigorous Christian controversies and church–political battles which began with the formulation of christology in Hellenistic categories and notions and led to disunity and disruption in the church.[5] Therefore in 325, the emperor Constantine invited all the bishops of the Roman empire to a first ecumenical council, to take place in his residence at Nicaea, near Constantinople. However, the formula which the emperor personally imposed, that as Son of God Jesus Christ is 'of the same substance' (*homo-ousios*) [6] as God himself, only increased the difficulties which it claimed to solve. How was one to describe the relationship of Jesus to God in accordance with scripture and reason? Both historically and substantively, this christological problem was the occasion for the origin of the trinitarian problem and not, for example, the question how in God three can be one (described as an impenetrable mystery). Only when some 'spirit fighters' (*pneumatomachoi*) described the Holy Spirit as a mere 'creature' did the Second Ecumenical Council of Constantinople (in 381) feel compelled also to state that the Holy Spirit was of the same substance as God. This concluded the formation of the dogma of the Trinity, and the 'Niceno-Constantinopolitan' creed based on this is still in liturgical use today.

Is criticism of the Qur'an legitimate?

Thirty years ago, I called for critical reflection on the traditional doctrine of the Trinity on the basis of the evidence of exegesis and the history of dogma. I asked whether this Greek speculation, which was far removed from its biblical basis and attempted boldly to spy into the dizzying heights of God's mystery, wasn't comparable with the story in Greek mythology of the flight of Icarus, the son of Daedalus. As he came too near to the sun, his wings made of feather and wax fell off.[7]

In the meantime, Catholic church historians such as Norbert Brox have confirmed the degree to which Hellenistic speculation on the Trinity represented a threat to the belief in one God held by 'simple believers' and to the unity of the church. The ecumenical councils of the fourth to eighth centuries had not been able to restore it by the time of the Prophet Muhammad: 'Many people felt that also to use the word "God" for the Logos made the monarchy and uniqueness of God dangerously unclear ... Those theologians who began to distinguish the Logos as God clearly from the Father or even to speak of a threeness (trinity) in God (as did Hippolytus, Novatian and Tertullian) thus came up against bitter resistance from the many simple believers, who charged them with teaching two or three gods ... The beginnings of the church's theology of the Trinity were felt to be polytheism, and rejected as heresy in the name of the biblical God.'[8]

The Catholic fundamental theologian Hans Zirker remarks how the voice of these 'simple believers' were 'put to silence within the church': 'So even if it contains no detailed account of these historical circumstances, the Qur'an intercedes at a considerable distance for those who centuries beforehand were put in a minority by church policy and suppressed by state policy, although they were simply keeping their confession close to biblical language and wanted to preserve it from the dispute of speculative differentiation.' According to Zirker, this does not of course mean that Christian theology should measure the significance of its history of dogma solely by the Qur'an, or even rewrite it in the sense of the Qur'an. However, Christian theology could recognize in the Qur'an 'what was not resolved in the formulation and implementation of fundamental Christian articles of faith and indeed was prevented by violence'.[9]

The Catholic dogmatic theologian Herbert Vorgrimler has recently investigated the Qur'anic criticism of the Christian doctrine of the Trinity in an amazingly open way. He asks: 'Are Christians "polytheists"? They need not be seen as such. But unfortunately there are Christian ways of expressing the trinity of the one God, both in popular piety and in theology, which could be misunderstood in the direction of polytheism, a belief in many gods.'[10] He argues that God reveals himself in his relationship to us: 'Speaking about the life of God before creation in childlike human terms, human beings do not need to experience what God did before there was a cosmos and human beings.'[11]

Vorgrimler explicitly attacks the unbiblical trinitarian constructions of some theologians. His teacher Karl Rahner would certainly have asked, 'How do we know that?' For example, he says that the Catholic theologian Hans Urs von Balthasar speaks 'in such a way of a "drama" performed by the divine persons, as only three independent subjects, three Godheads, could perform it. And this view is not grounded in the revelation of God.'[12] He points out that the Protestant dogmatic theologian Jürgen Moltmann also constructs an unbiblical theology of the Godforsakenness of Jesus and 'in his remarks about the triune God firmly and explicitly denies the traditional belief in one God, Jewish–Christian monotheism'. 'But since, according to Moltmann, the time of monarchs in the church and in the world has finally come to an end, the notions of contemporary social democracy must be incorporated into ideas about God. For him God consists of three person-subjects who form this democracy. This view is incompatible with Jesus' confession of faith. Is his faith so out of date?'[13] According to the Catholic dogmatic theologian Gisbert Greshake, Christian prayer may 'certainly use the address "You three"': 'However, his technical language is not generally understandable: these are the esoterics of the initiated. So he says that "person in God" is "a relationship, pure being-from-one-another and for-one-another, whereas human beings emphasized being I or being in myself. But how can one be relationship without being I? The explanation of the triunity of God is like a conjuring trick: in God unity is multiplicity.'[14]

Critics say that it is a pity that Herbert Vorgrimler himself could not resolve to say 'old things in a new way' and 'for this programme cites only a rather verbose confession by his teacher (Rahner)'. Any reform of the church today first needs a reform of the faith. This calls for a 'paradigm change, a reshaping of the models of understanding the faith in liturgy, addressing God, prayer and language'.[15] One can only agree with this and, accentuating the problem, ask whether there is a distinction in God.

Is there a distinction in God?

Time and again, Christians with one-sided information think that they can justify their notion of the Trinity over against Islam with the cliché of the remote, unfeeling, abstract God in Islam who contrasts with the Christian God of boundless love and self-surrender: 'In the depths of his heart—has he a heart?—the God of Muhammad is completely indifferent as to who goes to paradise and who goes to hell.'[16] But as we heard, this God is 'closer to man than his neck-vein',[17] and if they ask after him, 'I am near; I respond to the call of him who calls, whenever he calls unto Me.'[18]

It is useless to tell Jews and Muslims that they have to accept a trinitarian distinction in God because of the greater nearness of God to human beings. The confession of the one and only God, who is also the covenant God of the people of Israel, is and remains the foundation and basic concern of Judaism. Therefore there may be three-member formulae (triads), but not triunity (trinity) within God. There may be liveliness, mobility, sympathy, compassion, indeed suffering of God, but no distinction and difference within God.

A Muslim theologian could echo a retort once made by the Jewish theologian Pinchas Lapide to the Protestant theologian Jürgen Moltmann: 'We know no conflict between the immanence and transcendence of God ... For the God who dwells in the heaven of heavens and was present in the sanctuary, when it still stood, but who also makes known his presence with the oppressed, is not for me a God who can be divided or, as Rosenzweig says, a God of self-distinction; he is the one ineffable. However, our tiny human brain cannot grasp this all-unity and therefore divides it into two or three.' Lapide retorts to Moltmann in respect of the Spirit. 'For me, the Spirit of God, too, is not hypostatized and has no special existence, but in good Hebrew terms is an emanation of God, in other words an emanation of the one God. The Spirit is as integral a part of God as, for example, the word of God, the love of God or the mercy of God. As a Jew I could not pursue this logic further and hypostatize the mercy and give it special existence. For me that would be almost blasphemous. For me this God with all his attributes is the one and only, and if my human brain does not go along with that, so much the worse for my brain.'[19]

As far as Christianity is concerned, what is distinctively Christian is Christ Jesus himself, in his decisive relationship with God, his Father, and thus also with the Spirit of God. However, the number three, which has exercised a fascination from the beginnings of human thought (because it was the most original unity in multiplicity), and has been uncommonly important for religion, myth, art and literature and everyday life, is clearly not specifically Christian, any more than the trios of gods who can be found from Rome and Greece to India and China. Nor is the 'triple beat of life' (a going-out and returning to oneself from identity with oneself) or the 'triple step of dialectic' (thesis–antithesis–synthesis). What is specific is christology, from which, in the Bible and the history of dogma all that is trinitarian seems to be derived.

Any Christian theologian who does not just speculate uncritically on the basis of the Hellenistic development of doctrine in the fourth and fifth centuries but who follows Protestant and Catholic theologians in thinking in the light of the New Testament will notice that, while there are many triadic formulae in the New Testament, there is not a word about the 'unity' of these three extremely different entities, that is, a unity on the same divine level. At one point in the First Letter of John there was a clause (known as the *Comma Johanneum*) which was in the context of a saying about the Spirit, the water and the blood, and went on to speak of the Father, the word and the spirit as being 'one'.[20] However, historical criticism has shown this statement to be a forgery which arose in North Africa or Spain in the third or fourth century and it did not help the Roman Inquisition at all by trying to defend the authenticity of the sentence at the beginning of the twentieth century;[21] it would have done better to adopt the results of historical criticism. However, out of a fear that it would have to correct much more, it has not been able to bring itself to do this, even now.

2. Reflection on the Bible

Is it at all possible to communicate to Muslims what Christian belief in the Father, Son and Spirit is all about? If Christians want Muslims to understand better, first they must understand themselves better. To do this they must start from the Bible again. In the Bible they will quickly find that in Jewish Christianity, indeed throughout the New Testament, whereas there is belief in God the Father, in Jesus the Son and in God's Holy Spirit, there is no doctrine of one God in three persons (modes of being), no doctrine of a 'tri-une God', a 'trinity'.[22] Nor is there any mention of a' trinity' in the traditional Apostles' Creed. So how can the relationship between Father, Son and Spirit be explained to Muslims in the light of the New Testament?

How do we speak of Father, Son and Spirit in biblical terms?

There is probably no better example in the New Testament by which to imagine the original relationship between Father, Son and Spirit than the speech which Stephen, the first martyr, makes in his own defence as handed down by Luke in his Acts of the Apostles.[23] During this speech, Stephen has a vision: 'Filled with the Holy Spirit, he looked up to heaven, saw the glory of God and Jesus standing on the right hand of God and cried: "I see heaven open and the son of man standing on the right hand of God." '[24] Here God, Jesus the son of man and the Holy Spirit are mentioned, but Stephen does not see a God with three faces, far less three men in the same form; he sees no triangular symbol of the kind that would be used later in Western Christian art. Rather:

– The Holy Spirit is at Stephen's side, is in him. The Spirit, the invisible power and might that goes forth from God, fills him completely and thus opens his eyes: 'in the Spirit' heaven reveals itself to him.
– God himself ('*ho theos*' = *the* God) remains hidden and is not in human form; only his 'glory' (Hebrew *kabod*, Greek *doxa*) is visible: God's splendour and power, the splendour of light which emanates fully from him.
– Finally Jesus, visible as the son of man, stands 'at the right hand of God', that is, sharing the throne with God and having the same power and glory. Raised from death and taken up into God's eternal life, he is now appointed as God's son, God's representative for us and the human representative of human beings before God.

So the belief in the one God, taken over from Israel and shared with Islam, need not be given up even in a 'Gentile Christian' doctrine of the Trinity: there is no God but God. To think of the relationship between God, God's Spirit and Jesus (as the bearer of God's Spirit, Messiah, Christ, Word, Son) and, in the light of the New Testament, to emphasize the true difference and undivided unity, is the task of theology: the legitimate basic intention of the traditional doctrine of the Trinity is to give a correct definition of the relationship between God, Son and Spirit. Any attempt at a critical new Christian interpretation will have to be accountable to this great tradition. Traditional dogmatic or liturgical formulations must not be rejected unthinkingly, but interpreted in a differentiated way for the present in the light of the New Testament.

Christ and the Trinity: from the Bible to dogma

In my book *Christianity*, I briefly described a development which, in all its details, occupies hundreds of pages of New Testament exegesis and the history of dogma.[25] To help readers to understand the development as it is depicted in the two tables on pages 513 and 514, I shall give a short account of the different positions in chronological order. This should make the development of christology and the doctrine of the Trinity comprehensible for Muslims as well:

– In one of the oldest documents of the New Testament (I Corinthians from the years 54–56, two decades after Jesus' death), the whole gospel of Jesus Christ is concentrated on the crucifixion and resurrection against the background of his imminent return: there are only allusions to Jesus' public activity, and there is not a word about his childhood, far less about a virgin birth.

– The oldest (and shortest) Gospel, that of Mark (written not long before the destruction of Jerusalem in the year 70), reports at length the baptism of Jesus, in which God reveals Jesus through the spirit as his son, and then Jesus' public activity. However, here too there is no story of Jesus' childhood and no mention of a virgin birth.

– Only the two great Gospels of Matthew and Luke (written after the destruction of Jerusalem) offer childhood narratives and the narrative of a virgin birth.

– The latest Gospel, that of John (*c.* 100), again does not mention any virgin birth, but does contain a prologue which speaks of the eternal pre-existence of the Logos (the wisdom) of God, which has assumed flesh in the human being Jesus of Nazareth.

– Starting from the prologue to the Gospel of John, the Greek church fathers (for example, Origen in the third century) developed the notion of three pre-existent eternal entities: Father, Son and Spirit.

– In the fourth century, the Alexandrian presbyter Arius gave the Logos an existence before all that is created but explicitly says that he is a creature.

– Against Arius, the First Ecumenical Council of Nicaea (325) stated that Jesus Christ, the Son of God, is 'of one substance' (*homoousios*) with God the Father.

– However, there were those who did not want to attribute such a pre-existence to the Holy Spirit (the spirit fighters).

– Against them, the Ecumenical Council of Constantinople (381) defined the deity of the Holy Spirit also.

– The conceptual solution for the extremely complicated problem of oneness and threeness in God that had now arisen was offered by the three Cappadocian church fathers (Basil, Gregory of Nazianzus and Gregory of Nyssa) in the fourth century; their terminology ('three *hypostases*—one *physis*') finally also became established in the West ('three persons—one nature').

– The African, Augustine, the most important church father of the Latin West, explained this threeness in unity using psychological categories: in the light of the one divine nature as mutual knowledge of the Father and the Son, from which the Holy Spirit proceeds 'as love'.

Christian theologians will have to ask of this series of interpretations whether it isn't possible to observe, particularly in the doctrine of the Trinity, the paradigm change (see the box below) from the original Jewish–Christian paradigm (P I) to the Hellenistic paradigm of the early church and the medieval Latin paradigm. Aren't the attempts at interpretation, laboriously developed with many contradictions (especially by the Cappadocian church fathers) in the Hellenistic paradigm (P II) and the dogmatic formulations of this relationship between God, Jesus Christ and God's Spirit which finally emerged from them, as time-conditioned as the later Latin theologies of the Trinity constructed by Augustine in the fifth century and Thomas Aquinas in the thirteenth (P III)? One thing is certain: they are not simply identical with the New Testament message of Christ.

To take up a central Jewish figure of thought, the unity of Father, Son and Spirit is to be understood as a revelation event, as a unity of revelation: not how God is in himself (ontologically) but how he encounters himself, reveals himself (in the economy of salvation). That means that the one God and Father reveals himself, in the Spirit, through Jesus as the Son. That all the classical prayers of the old Roman liturgy are not addressed to a Trinity, but solely to the one God and Father through the Son in the unity of the Holy Spirit, is in complete agreement with this.

I ask myself: couldn't the concern of Christians be better communicated to Jewish and Muslim conversation-partners in such an original New Testament perspective? It would be better than using the ever-new problematical (and for Jews and Muslims unacceptable) ontological, psychological, sociological, indeed gynaecological speculations—about the Hellenistic doctrine of the two natures (with its discussions of '*homoiousios*', of similar being, or '*homoousios*', of the same being) or about the no less problematical Latin doctrine of the Trinity (with its complexities of one divine nature, two processions, three persons or hypostases, four relations).

Instead of this, in dialogue with Muslims, in the light of the New Testament the following critically thought out basic statements should be the starting point:

- The *Father* is the one and only God of Abraham, beside whom there are no other Gods and who to us (as we must say in present-day metaphorical language) is both 'Father' and 'Mother'. Belief in one God must not be put in question indirectly either: there is no third way between monotheism and polytheism.
- The *Son* is none other than the historical person Jesus of Nazareth, who personally reveals the word and will of this one God: in him the one true God is really manifest, present and effective.

Shifts of accent in the proclamation of Christ

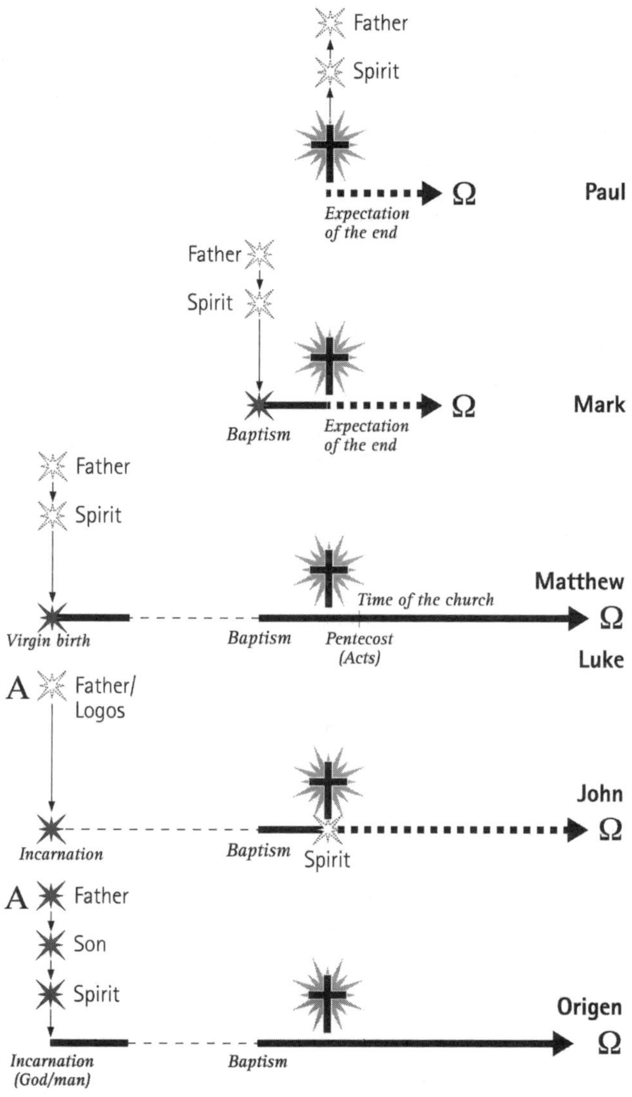

Father
Spirit
Ω
Paul
Expectation of the end

Father
Spirit
Ω
Mark
Baptism
Expectation of the end

Father
Spirit
Matthew
Time of the church
Ω
Virgin birth
Baptism
Pentecost (Acts)
Luke

A Father/ Logos
John
Ω
Incarnation
Baptism
Spirit

A Father
Son
Spirit
Origen
Ω
Incarnation (God/man)
Baptism

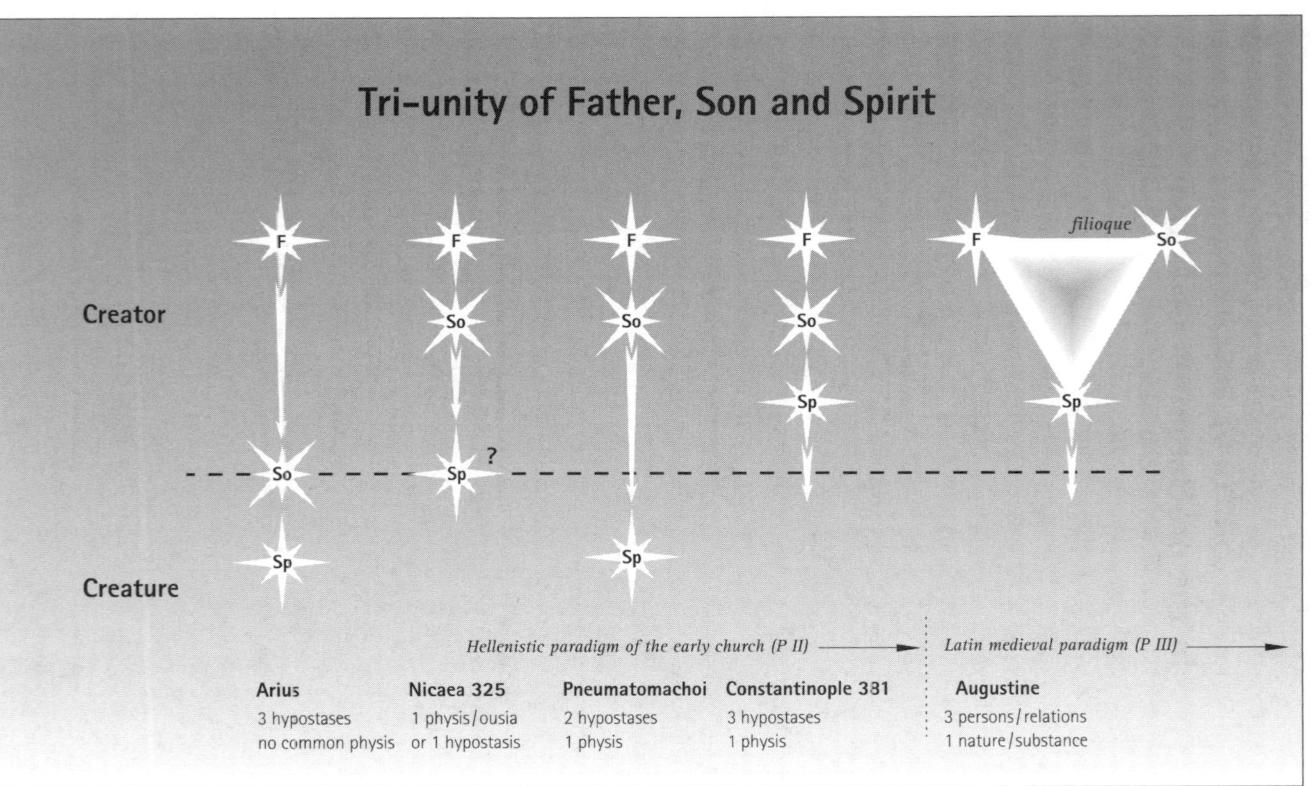
Tri-unity of Father, Son and Spirit
Creator
Creature
F
So
Sp
?
filioque
Hellenistic paradigm of the early church (P II)
Latin medieval paradigm (P III)
Arius
3 hypostases
no common physis
Nicaea 325
1 physis/ousia
or 1 hypostasis
Pneumatomachoi
2 hypostases
1 physis
Constantinople 381
3 hypostases
1 physis
Augustine
3 persons/relations
1 nature/substance

- The *Spirit* is the holy emanation, might and power of God and Jesus Christ who is exalted to him, which is effective in the believer and in the community of faith and which makes all human beings the sons and daughters of God. Thus the Spirit is not a third party between God and human beings but is none other than God himself, God's powerful spiritual presence and reality.

Or, as one can sometimes say in a quite elementary way in preaching or religious instruction: what we are concerned with is not a hidden, enigmatic divine triangle in heaven, but God the Father over me; Jesus as his Son, our brother, alongside and with me; the Holy Spirit as God's power and might in me. Mightn't the unity of Father, Son and Spirit seem less nonsensical to Jews and Muslims (as well as Christians who are alienated by the traditional formulae) if presented in this way?

In theological terms, according to the New Testament (in contrast to later Christian dogmatics) the issue is not an 'immanent' unity of three persons in God 'in himself' in his eternity, far less the identity of an eternal divine 'nature'. Rather, it is the salvation–historical ('economic') unity of God 'for us' in history: the way in which God himself has acted, spoken, made himself known and revealed himself through Jesus in the gift of his Holy Spirit to us, to our very unholy spirit and for our salvation. This is an identity of the revealer with the revealed; as Christ, interpreted by the Fourth Gospel, says: 'He who sees me, sees the Father.'[26]

The situation of interreligious dialogue

However, Christians might ask in return: isn't this simply to abandon the truth of the Christian councils—for the sake of dialogue with the Muslims? Do these councils still play any role in the epoch-making paradigm change of theology, church and society? Doesn't this totally relativize them and make them merely optional? I don't want to be misunderstood: as a European 'Gentile Christian' I can understand the Hellenistic–Latin development of christology (from the Jewish–Christian paradigm I through the Hellenistic paradigm II to the medieval Latin paradigm III); I can accept the truth of the christological councils from Nicaea to Chalcedon and I can interpret Augustine's and Thomas's doctrine of the Trinity and survey and affirm their great intentions and statements in the light of the New Testament. So I do not think that Christians today have naively to begin again un-historically at zero, to become, as it were, Jewish Christians. Any paradigm change brings losses as well as new insights.

However, we no longer live in the Middle Ages or in the period of the Reformation. Our situation is not that of a theological–dogmatic conversation but of a modern, postmodern inter-religious conversation. The repetitive conversation among theologians about the Trinity, with its ever new approaches, has become barren and boring but the conversation with Jews and Muslims is an intellectual challenge. In this context, every Christian theologian should be really oppressed by the question: how can I explain, to a Muslim or a Jew, why Christians believe in this Jesus as the Messiah, the Christ, God's revelation? As a European 'Gentile Christian', should I really expect them to accept the Hellenistic councils of the fourth and fifth centuries or even the Roman Catholic development of the views of Augustine and the Latin Middle Ages? Should I expect this in particular of Jews, who have to experience Jesus, the great son of their people, as a stranger when he shows himself to them in Greek or Latin garb? Or of Muslims, whose religion appeared on the stage of history when Hellenistic culture began to outlive itself?

As a Christian, I also ask myself: would I be ready, for the sake of belief in the one God of Abraham, to accept the Talmud and the halakhah, as well as the Hebrew Bible? Would I be ready, for the sake of common faith in the God who is also attested in the Qur'an, to acknowledge the Islamic Shariah as binding on me? Christians must not expect others to accept expansions of the tradition and possibly also excrescences that they rightly regard as being excessive.

For Eastern Hellenistic and Western Latin Christianity, the great councils and their doctrinal statements, some of which have found their way into the creeds, will always be important. For understanding within Christianity, between Orthodox, Catholics and Protestants, the creeds will remain criteria for discovering the truth, standards for faith, thought and prayer which in turn are to be measured by the supreme criterion of the New Testament. But what about inter-religious dialogue? Here the Greek and Latin tradition may not claim to be the sole criterion of truth.

Stages of time and systems of language

A conversation with Jews and Muslims, or with Hindus and Buddhists, Chinese and Japanese, is doomed to failure if the linguistic tradition of a regional culture, whether that of the Greek East or the Latin West, makes absolute claims. What is a problem for understanding between Christians of the West (in view of the collapse of the plausibility structures of traditional doctrine) is even more of an obstacle to inter-religious dialogue. There must therefore be a way of speaking and confessing Christian truth without making a particular Christian language absolute.

One urgent practical need follows from these theological discussions: Christians, Jews and Muslims must first of all read one another's holy scriptures. If one considers that even al-Ghazali had virtually no knowledge of the Gospels (which were available in Arabic) and even Thomas Aquinas had no knowledge of the Qur'an (which had long since been translated into Latin), it is not surprising that the same is still true of many theologians of both religions. However, if these theologians were to look at the others' holy scriptures and grapple with the different paradigm changes, they could note that, as in Christianity, so in Islam there are many stages and language systems. One can be a Christian or a Muslim without having to appropriate and integrate them all at the same time. Even in the New Testament there were quite distinct christologies and outspoken differences between Jewish Christians and Hellenists, between Mark and Luke, Paul and John. In Islam, too, from the very beginning there were different traditions in law, the understanding of faith and morality.

We need to reflect again on what language system, together with what Ludwig Wittgenstein called its different language games, will prove to be viable in dialogue with Jews and Muslims. Our reflections should not be tactical, but driven by the conviction that an original truth manifests itself in many forms of language. For the Christian faith this original truth has its basis in the historical Jesus of Nazareth; to understand him as the Christ of the one God with all its practical consequences, theologians must have the right to take up christological options which were pushed to the side and covered up but are nevertheless completely legitimate, indeed original. These are the options from which the disciples of Jesus and the oldest Jewish–Christian community also began. And theologians should do this in the hope that here, possibly, are categories that will make this Jesus more understandable as the revelation of God to Jews and Muslims.

But what about the original truth, which for Islam is grounded in the Qur'an? Shouldn't Muslims, and Muslim theologians, allow a certain degree of freedom in the interpretation of the Qur'an if they want to make the Qur'an comprehensible to themselves and others?

DVI

From Biblical Criticism to Qur'anic Criticism?

The Qur'an itself emphasizes in a variety of places that Jews and Christians are also 'people of the book', that they have scriptures. This common feature of the three monotheistic prophetic religions of revelation should not be underestimated. But are Judaism and Christianity really 'religions of the book' in the strict sense, as Islam is? Do their scriptures contain the *ipsissima verba* (the very own words) of God and are they inspired, indeed dictated, by him word for word? Is the Bible, like the Qur'an, in every respect—linguistic, stylistic, logical, historical, scientific—a miraculous, absolutely perfect, holy book, which has to be accepted literally? Some Christians have believed, and still believe, in such verbal inspiration of the Bible, so here I am not just concerned with the Muslim view of the Qur'an.

1. Literal revelation?

Is this a clear case of a law of development in the history of religion that seems to apply to both Christianity and to Islam? Later generations of adherents of a very human religion try to avoid a crisis that has gradually arisen over the legitimation of their faith and its claims by exaggerating their theology, usually referring the legitimacy back to divine origins. What does that achieve? They immunize themselves against competition, legitimize their own claim to truth, consolidate their powers of conviction and hold their group.

The Bible—is every word inspired?

Muslims must concede that, according to the Christian understanding, the Bible was not written by an author in heaven (which is what is believed about the Qur'an) but by many very different authors on earth, as the letters of Paul and the beginning of the Gospel of Luke and the Acts of the Apostles in the New Testament openly attest. It follows from this that the Bible is not without defects and mistakes, concealment and confusion, limitations and error; it is a very diverse collection of documents of the faith, which are not simply God's revelation and word but attest the revelation and word of God in human form: the one word of God in many human words.

Had this original view of the Bible been maintained, Christianity would have been spared many conflicts with the natural sciences (since Galileo and Darwin) and with history (since the Enlightenment). First in Judaism, then in Catholicism and then in Protestantism, attempts were made to suppress historical criticism of the Bible by force. The mistakes of Jews and Christians should make Muslims think:

– In his 1670 *Tractatus theologico–politicus*, Baruch de Spinoza, the rabbinic pupil and philosopher, called for freedom of historical–critical investigation of the Bible as a human, and therefore often contradictory, document of human faith.[1] He was the first to dispute that Moses was the author of the 'five books of Moses'. He thus became the father of modern biblical criticism. Having already been put under the ban and excluded from his synagogue in Amsterdam for his heterodox views, he was finally banished completely.

– In 1678 the Paris Oratorian Richard Simon, stimulated by Spinoza, was the first Christian author to write a 'Critical History of the Old Testament'.[2] He too disputed that the five books of Moses (the Pentateuch) could have been written by one and the same author and thus became the father of Catholic biblical criticism. His book was confiscated at the prompting of the famous court bishop and preacher Bossuet and Simon was excluded from his Oratory (community of priests).

– Precisely a century later, a Protestant 'lay theologian', the most eloquent polemicist in classical German literature, Gotthold Ephraim Lessing, published the 'Fragments of an Unknown' (Hermann Samuel Reimarus) on 'The Aims of Jesus and his Disciples'.[3] This work inaugurated the modern Protestant quest of the historical Jesus, to the indignation of Protestant orthodoxy. As the Duke of Brunswick's librarian, Lessing had enjoyed freedom from censorship, but a few months after the publication of the book it was revoked; this amounted to a ban on publication of works with theological problems, but it provoked him to compose his great Enlightenment play *Nathan the Wise* (1779). I investigated this right at the beginning of the present book (see A I, 1).

Despite these setbacks, biblical criticism became established, in Protestant theology in the first half of the nineteenth century in Protestant theology, in Reform Judaism in the second half of the century and in Catholic theology in the first half of the twentieth century (definitively only with the Second Vatican Council of 1962–5). The church that could have been first was last.

More than two hundred years of historical–critical research into the Bible have made it clear that it is not the infallibility and inerrancy of the authors that guarantees the truth; the truth of the content, the testimony, the message, must stand by itself. It needs no 'external' divine legitimacy, but legitimizes itself on the basis of testimony 'from within' itself—inspired and inspiring. But what about the Qur'an?

The Qur'an—the question of historical contingency

It should not be disputed that the Qur'an, too, is inspired and has been and is inspiring. As analysed by religious scholars, it is a seventh-century testimony, but for countless people it is a twentieth-century document: a foundation document which is by no means dead, but very much alive, a document which is not only literary but also deeply religious. It is a book with a challenging message which is to be not only studied and analysed but also recited and proclaimed, a book for living and acting, beginning with questions of faith and religious practice and extending to questions of law and morality. Theologians and specialists of all kinds may, and should, reflect on the Qur'an in a scholarly way but it is to be hoped that they will also understand how many Muslims simply hear, read and delight in the verses of the Qur'an.

In the chapter in this book about the Qur'an as the centre of Islam, as 'the way, the truth and the life' of Muslims, the foundation document of God's final revelation (see B I, 1), I developed the universal Muslim understanding of the Qur'an, which is that the subject, author, of the Qur'anic revelation is the one God and God alone. The Prophet is only the object, the one who is addressed and the spokesman of the revelation. I also argued, on the basis of the Bible and early church tradition, that today Christians too can recognize the Qur'an as the word not simply of a human being but, in principle, of God himself.

If Christians do recognize the religious transcendence of the Qur'an, they will also want to raise the question of the historical contingency and the historical conditioning of this holy scripture—even if this complex of problems initially seems as threatening to traditional Muslims as the parallel set of problems does to traditional Christians. Western religious scholarship hasn't taken the Qur'an seriously enough as a living religious document of the present but does that mean that all the insights of this scholarship into the historical genesis, literary structure and social content of the Qur'an must be dismissed as a Western 'imperialistic' undermining of Muslim faith and completely irrelevant to believing Muslims? That would damage both Islam and the credibility of the Qur'an.

2. Critical exegesis

In the chapter about the periods of the Qur'anic revelation and the wearisome process of the origin and canonization of the Qur'an (see B I, 2) I made it clear that, in the Islamic view, the Qur'an did not 'fall from heaven' as a book; rather, it sank 'into the heart' of the Prophet, was first proclaimed by him orally, only then written down and finally collected, ordered and edited. The holy book, in its present form, appeared only decades after the Prophet's death. To this degree the historical contingency of the Qur'an, too, is recognized by Muslims but for fourteen centuries the question has repeatedly arisen in a different form: how is the Qur'an to be understood?

The exegesis of the Qur'an—phases and problems

The Qur'an seems obscure and contradictory in some places and difficult to read, since to begin with it was transmitted without vowels. However, it never existed without interpretation, without exegesis. If we recall the history of Islam which I described at length in previous chapters (see C I–V), it is easy to understand how Qur'anic exegesis takes its place in the different paradigms.[4] Hardly had the Qur'an come into being as a canonical book (P I) than the process of Qur'anic exegesis began. Usually it followed the text word for word, somewhat unsystematically; it was not concerned philologically with the vocabulary and did not want to emphasize the peerless literary quality of the Qur'an. The earliest commentaries, though known only in fragments from later quotations, come from as early as the seventh century (P II).

Qur'anic exegesis was developed professionally down to the last detail by the legal scholars. From the beginning Islam was more interested in law than in theology so these scholars also had to act as exegetes for all legal questions. In the period of classical Islam (P III), they organized themselves into the four schools I have described, each with its own specific legal principles. Each school was interested in justifying its own view from the Qur'an, and in some circumstances also read it into the Qur'an. Here the traditions of the Prophet (hadith) became increasingly important; in the classical synthesis of ash-Shafi'i (died 820), whose principles eventually became established, the tradition (Sunnah) was established as a universal principle for Qur'anic exegesis. The Qur'an had to be interpreted in the light of the tradition, the divinely inspired and authorized words and actions of the Prophet, and not vice versa. In these circumstances, little room remained for personal judgement.

By the tenth century some Sunnis had come to regard the 'door of independent legal findings (*ijtihad*)' as closed, though there is no evidence for a general decision. The comprehensive and structured Islamic law, the Shariah, was formed at this time, though unlike Roman church law it was never codified. The autumn of traditionalism that all too soon followed the hopeful spring of the legal sciences also affected Qur'anic exegesis, which came to a climax with the compilation of the rich exegetical material in the thirty-volume commentary of the Iranian historian and exegete Abu Ja'far at-Tabari (died 923). The establishment of the law on traditionalist principles was further intensified by the analogous development in theology. What ash-Shafi'i accomplished in the law was achieved in theology a century later by al-Ash'ari (died 936): the victory of the principle of the tradition, by taking up rational theology into traditional theology and transcending it.

For decades the rational theology of the Mu'tazilites set the tone in Baghdad, under the 'Abbasids in the ninth century. They attempted to interpret the Qur'an and the anthropomorphic characteristics of God rationally and with philological precision. The Mu'tazilites argued against popular and all too human ideas of God for the transcendence, unity and oneness of God, so for them the Qur'an could not be like God but had rather to be 'created'—if not as an accident of God, then as his creature at the moment of revelation. However, although this view was supported by Caliph al-Ma'mun and two of his successors with almost inquisitorial measures, it did not become established. The contrary thesis, which previously had not been put forward explicitly, prevailed, namely that the Qur'an was 'uncreated, eternal'.

The historicity of the Qur'an was forced into the background, indeed suppressed, by the decision for its 'uncreatedness' and thus its unsurpassed and perfect 'eternity'. In the longer term this resulted in a traditionalist fossilization and ossification of law, theology and exegesis. From then on any criticism of the Qur'an had to be blasphemy. In these circumstances, how should the Qur'an be interpreted, comprehensibly and effectively, for a new time with new problems and methods?

In the paradigm of the Ulama and Sufis (P IV) which followed that of the caliphs, the now dominant Ulama could refer to a wealth of different interpretations in difficult cases of the Shariah (which had not been codified); it could appeal to divergent hadith or explain particular contradictions simply as a sign of the unfathomability of the word of God. On the other hand, attempts were made in Sufism, which had now become popular, to pass over the external meaning of the text that lay in the foreground by an allegorical interpretation in terms of a mysterious inner sense. Alongside the literal exegesis (*tafsir*, 'explanation') an interpretative, allegorical interpretation (*ta'wil*) became established. However, the exegesis of individual verses (*ayat*) still stood at the centre.

Al-Ghazali's (died 1111) theological and juristic synthesis sought to combine Shariah and Sufi piety but neither his exegesis nor that of traditionalists such as Ibn Taymiyyah (died 1328) could stand up to the challenges of rising European modernity and the Enlightenment. First, people simply ignored the modern theology, science and views of society and history that brought a critical investigation of the sources of faith. I have already noted that despite attempts at modernization, no paradigm change towards modernity took place throughout the sphere of Islam in the seventeenth and eighteenth centuries (see C V, 3). Discussion repeatedly centred on the old question of how the 'inimitability' (*al-i'jaz*) of the Qur'an was to be justified: was it inimitable in content or in style and what arguments could be used to determine this?[5]

Beginnings of a modern exegesis of the Qur'an

Only in the second half of the nineteenth century did Islamic reformism (P V) dawn with Al-Afghani, who called for an Islamic reformation. People began to connect the Qur'an with the demands of reason, new scientific knowledge and social and political developments (see C V, 4). From 1900, a consecutive commentary appeared in the journal *al-Manar* ('The Lighthouse') by Muhammad 'Abduh (1848–1905), Mufti of Egypt, which was completed after his death by his Syrian pupil, Rashid Rida. This work, which was fundamental to countless later interpretations of the Qur'an in the various Arab countries, was an interpretation of the Qur'an with a philological orientation and contained practical moral instruction for Muslim behaviour in modern everyday life. In 'Abduh's view, the Qur'an was to be read above all as an ethical guide.

'Abduh, an educational reformer, also wanted to give a scientific–religious interpretation which, contrary to the thesis of the French philosopher Ernest Renan (namely that Islam was absolutely incompatible with modern philosophy and science), proved the correspondence between religion and science in Islam; indeed, it even looked in the Qur'an for references to new scientific knowledge. The stories of the Qur'an, 'Abduh argued, are not modern historiography; he left some difficult passages unexplained. The door of *ijtihad*, which had closed for many Sunnis, had to be opened again. Proud of their great past, Muslims should find a new identity and orientation by creative new interpretation of the Qur'an in accord with modernity. According to Helmut Gätje at the end of his brief account of the Islamic exegesis of the Qur'an, this modern interpretation of the Qur'an, too, which found many advocates after Muhammad 'Abduh is the 'explication of a particular theology and worldview by the Qur'an and not historical–critical research into the Qur'an'.[6] These early Muslim reformers could not bring themselves to apply literary–critical or strictly historical–critical methods in the service of a comprehensive theology and a systematic programme of reform.

Diversity of approaches and forms

In the twentieth century, new tendencies in Qur'anic exegesis developed, some of which can be found in classical exegesis, some outside it. The Islamologist Jacques Waardenburg of the University of Lausanne has given an analysis that is both knowledgeable and perceptive.[7] First, there are new tendencies in the traditional exegesis of the Qur'an:

- The unique character of the Qur'an, as the final revelation of God and the miracle of the Arabic language, is further intensified by some scholars and preachers, also in the media.
- At a practical level, the return to the sources of Islam, Qur'an and Sunnah, is making a separation from burdensome elements of the tradition possible.
- Reformers are emphasizing the rationality of the Qur'an, which often uses rational arguments and emphasizes the need to acquire knowledge.
- Many interpretations of the Qur'an are insisting on an emphasis on social values such as human dignity, the fight for social justice and the moral aspects of life: human freedom and responsibility, rights and obligations and the need for moral orientation.

New, predominantly practical, forms are arising outside classical exegesis of the Qur'an:

- a strict reforming exegesis, which aims to purify Islam from later forms of popular piety by a restoration of original Islam (such as the Hanbalite tradition in Saudi Arabia);
- a political–activist exegesis, which wants to shape state and society on the basis of the Shariah in a 'truly Islamic' way, both from below (for example, the Muslim Brothers) and from above by the establishment of an Islamic state (for example, Ayatollah Khomeini);
- a modernizing exegesis, which wants to orientate individuals and society on the modern norms accepted world-wide and discover these universal values in the Qur'an also;
- a spiritual exegesis, which aims to develop a broad religious worldview, on the basis of mystical experience or a theological metaphysic;
- an even more markedly spiritualistic exegesis which, with the help of texts from the Qur'an, seeks to communicate a spiritual worldview which goes beyond Islamic teaching and practice and forms communities to match;

- a theoretical investigation which aims to develop new methods of interpreting the Qur'an and its message on the basis of rational arguments, often with the help of philosophical currents.

The first attempts at historical criticism also appeared as theoretical investigations around the middle of the twentieth century, above all in Egypt.[8] Amin al-Khuli (1895–1966), professor of Arab studies at the (later) University of Cairo, was the first to put forward the thesis of the existence of different literary genres in the Qur'an, which provoked an enormous scandal. His pupil Muhammad Ahmad Khalafallah (1916–98) argued that not all the texts of the Qur'an could be understood in a strictly historical sense; they were primarily addressed to the pagan Arabs of the seventh century. He was not allowed to say this in his 1947 dissertation but that did not prevent him finally from becoming professor at the Institute for Arab Studies in Cairo (from 1958 he worked in the Ministry of Culture).

At the end of the twentieth and the beginning of the twenty-first century a series of pioneer thinkers are working for a contemporary and viable Islam. Some of them are particularly concerned with a contemporary exegesis of the Qur'an: they include the Pakistani professors Fazlur Rahman and Riffat Hassan and the Iranian philosopher Abdolkarim Soroush; the South Africans Farid Esack and Abdul Karim Tayob; the Egyptians Hasan Hanafi and Nasr Hamed Abu Zayd; the Sudanese jurist Abdullahi Ahmed an-Na'im; the Tunisian Mohamed Talbi; the Kuwaiti Abul-Fadl. In France the Algerian Mohammed Arkoun and in Ankara several young Turkish scholars are engaged in hadith criticism.[9] These scholars all differ from other Muslim intellectuals by their profound knowledge of the Islamic heritage and from the traditional Ulama by their capacity to interpret this heritage using the present-day humanities—history, anthropology, sociology, linguistics and hermeneutics.

So will it be possible in future permanently to suppress a historical account of the Qur'an in Islamic countries, when today this is shared not only by Western scholars but also by some Muslim scholars and thousands of intelligent and critical Muslim students at foreign universities? Won't books by Western authors about Islam be read with more interest by Muslims if they show more empathy and sympathy for Islam? Aren't the doubts about the verbal inspiration of the Qur'an among Muslim intellectuals far more widespread than is conceded and tolerated by traditionalist scholars? Unless appearances are deceptive, in the long term, in Islam too, what the sociology of knowledge calls the 'plausibility structure' of belief in the verbal inspiration of the Qur'an will also collapse—and that is the presupposition for the belief of the broad masses.

Insights and hypotheses of Western exegesis of the Qur'an

According to the Islamic self-understanding, Muhammad received the Qur'an directly from God: it is God's word and one may not raise the question of any Jewish or Christian influence on it. This conviction needs to be taken seriously, because countless generations have drawn strength, courage and comfort from it, in their individual and social lives. It accords with historical reality, to which Muslim scholars attach the utmost importance, that Muhammad—although presumably he was not illiterate—had neither read the Bible nor had it read to him. At that time there was no Arabic translation of the Bible; otherwise Qur'anic references to the Bible would have been presented more clearly, more accurately and in a less fragmentary way.

In his major account of Islam,[10] evaluating Muhammad's character, W.M. Watt worked out that Muhammad was utterly convinced that he could distinguish between God's revelations and his own thoughts. However, this leaves many questions (perhaps the most fundamental ones) open. The nineteenth-century Jewish scholars Abraham Geiger[11] and Hartwig Hirschfeld[12] attempted to demonstrate the Prophet's dependence on Judaism.

Muhammad's role in the origin of the Qur'an certainly cannot be left aside, and the early influence of oral tradition from Judaism and Christianity can hardly be denied. In connection with Jewish Christianity (see D V, 2) I demonstrated that prior knowledge on the part of Muhammad does not put the authenticity of revelation in question:

- There were connections in Muhammad's time not only with the great Christian power of Byzantium but also with Jews and with both Jewish and Gentile Christians in neighbouring territories, on the Arabian peninsula, indeed even in Mecca and Medina.
- The Qur'an itself repeatedly refers to biblical figures: not only to Abraham (and two old Arabian prophets) but above all to the three other great 'messengers', Moses, David and Jesus, and also to Noah, Solomon, Joseph, Jonah, John the Baptist and the Virgin Mary. Why shouldn't Muhammad have known all this—or much of it—even before his revelation experience and thought it important?

Only in recent times have Western scholars put the highly developed instruments and techniques of biblical criticism at the service of a form–critical analysis of the Qur'an—though with contradictory results. According to the revolutionary *Quranic Studies* (1977) by the American Arabist John Wansbrough (he learned Old and New Testament exegesis as a student in Germany) the Qur'an was above all formed by the community—interpreting particular sayings of the Prophet, worked out from different traditions, on biblical patterns. Like the Christian model, the process of the formation of the canon took almost two hundred years.[13] According to an investigation by a British Arabist—John Burton, *The Collection of the Qur'an*[14] (it too appeared in 1977)—the present-day text of the Qur'an derives from the Prophet himself. Günter Lüling's 'Rediscovery of the Prophet Muhammad'[15] (1981), based on his earlier thesis 'On the Ur-Qur'an'[16] (1974), claims even to have discovered pre-Islamic Christian strophic songs in the Qur'an; he distinguishes between three different versions: a Christian-Arabic Ur-Qur'an, a Qur'an of the Prophet and the post-prophetic Qur'an (the one accepted today).

In 2000 a 'German semitic scholar' (really an oriental Christian clergyman from Iraq, teaching in Germany) writing under the name of Christoph Luxenberg—allegedly he feared suffering the fate of Salman Rushdie—wrote a study entitled 'The Syro-Aramaic Reading of the Qur'an. A Contribution towards Deciphering the Language of the Qur'an'.[17] It had long been known (see A II, 2) that Aramaic with a Syriac Christian stamp was the vernacular of the Near East in the time of Muhammad, that there are some Aramaic loan words in the Qur'an and that Christianity was indigenous to Arabia before Muhammad. Over and above this Luxenburg wanted to demonstrate that, in its oldest parts, the Qur'an contains a considerable Christian stratum of text: 'a basic core of which the Qur'an as a Christian liturgical book originally consisted'.[18] This was said to clarify many passages of the Qur'an which had previously not been understood or had been understood wrongly: for example, 'huri' does not mean 'white-eyed maidens' but 'white, crystal-clear grapes'. If true, this would rob polemic against the erotic Islamic notions of paradise of its foundations.

There is hypothesis upon hypothesis in a discussion that seems to move in extremes, as the investigation of the Bible sometimes does. As a Christian theologian who is not an Arabist, I am cautious about passing judgment but sometimes I am reminded of the early days of historical–biblical criticism, between 1840 and 1880, when radical critics such as Bruno Baur wrote big books to prove that the whole of the New Testament was a second-century forgery, that the picture of Jesus in the Gospels was the product of the creative idea of an 'Ur-evangelist' and that Christianity was a product of the Greek spirit, born not in Palestine but in Alexandria and Rome. This was a challenge to New Testament research but not an answer that finally gained scholarly assent.

As for the Qur'an, I go along with Angelika Neuwith's precise 'Studies on the Composition of the Meccan Surahs'.[19] Trained in the form criticism of the Old Testament, she demonstrates that at least the Meccan surahs were put together for liturgical recitation by the Prophet himself and that behind the present text a single will is engaged in the shaping. It is not enough to think of a mere redactor who has cobbled together variants with 'scissors and paste'.

New insights of Muslim exegesis of the Qur'an

Given time, will yet more Islamic scholars allow themselves to be convinced of the value of such solid and cautious historical–critical research? If there is biblical criticism (in favour of a contemporary biblical faith), why not a historical criticism of the Qur'an with a thoroughly constructive, not destructive intent (in favour of a contemporary Muslim faith)? Christians and Muslims need to continue to keep talking about this difficult but fundamental point of the understanding of revelation. To make progress we need not only Christian scholars of Islam but also Muslim scholars of Christianity—and, so far, these hardly exist. We shall not make any real advances in Christian–Islamic dialogue if we do not give an account of the understanding of truth that is necessary for the application of the tools of historical criticism. In the longer term, the possibility cannot be excluded that in the more self-confident Islam which is also disseminated in the West, and which in many respects seeks to assimilate Western science and culture, historical criticism of the holy book will also be allowed and put into practice.

It can only help Islamic faith if Islamic scholars begin to tackle the historical problems. This can still be dangerous for a Muslim today, just as a heterodox view was for a Catholic at the height of the Inquisition or for a liberal Protestant in Calvin's Geneva. In 1971, in Kabul, at that time still the peaceful capital of Afghanistan, I reached agreement with a Muslim professor in a long evening discussion among friends that the Qur'anic word of God is at the same time the human word of the Prophet. I asked my conversation-partner whether he could put forward such a view at the university. His reply was a clear no: 'If I did, I would have to emigrate.' And indeed he did, some years later. What positive possibilities are there for a Muslim to take the historicity of the Qur'an seriously?[20]

The problem does not disappear if one ignores it. The interpretation of the Qur'an remains fundamental. So in his 'Manifesto for an Enlightened Islam'[21] the anthropologist and Islamologist, Malek Chebel, asks in the very first of his twenty-seven theses on reform for 'a new interpretation of the texts' and in the second for an 'affirmation of the superiority of reason to every other form of thought or belief.'

3. A time-sensitive understanding of the Qur'an

By way of example, I want to sketch out the methods of three contemporary Muslim authors to make it clear how today Muslims, too, are attempting to 'understand' the Qur'an in a time-sensitive way (by which I mean the 'hermeneutics' or 'theory of understanding' which underlies any exegesis). The three approaches are:

- historical–critical hermeneutics: Fazlur Rahman,
- historical–anthropological hermeneutics: Mohammed Arkoun and
- pluralist–political hermeneutics: Farid Esack.

Historical–critical hermeneutics of the Qur'an

The Pakistani Fazlur Rahman, whom I have already mentioned, also felt compelled to emigrate. After his studies at the universities of Oxford and the Punjab, he was the first believing Muslim to understand in historical–critical terms the question of the origin of the Qur'an in the historical context of the Prophet and interpret the Qur'an for people in the present socio-historical context.

In his early book *Prophecy in Islam: Philosophy and Orthodoxy* (1958),[22] Rahman had made it clear that in classical Islam, views on this question were by no means as monolithic as is often supposed. In his later book *Islam* (1979), he returned to the classic controversy under the 'Abbasids in which, contrary to the prevailing rational view of the Mu'tazilites of the createdness and historicity of the Qur'an, a dogmatic orthodoxy was forming in favour of the uncreatedness and eternity of the Qur'an (see C III, 5–6). As Rahman unambiguously states: 'But orthodoxy (indeed, all medieval thought) lacked the necessary intellectual tools to combine in its formulation of the dogma the otherness and verbal character of the Revelation on the one hand, and its intimate connection with the work and the religious personality of the Prophet on the other, i.e. it lacked the intellectual capacity to say both that the Qur'an is entirely the word of God and, in an ordinary sense, also entirely the word of Muhammad.' [23] According to Rahman, against this hermeneutical background the important thing is not to practise a fragmentary *ad hoc* exegesis but to understand the Qur'an as a unity from within.

Finally, in his book *Major Themes of the Qur'an* (1980),[24] Rahman, who from his emigration until his death in 1988 was a professor at the University of Chicago, describes the state of things in the Qur'an as follows. According to the earliest accounts Muhammad, at around the age of forty and prepared by a lengthy process of development, had one or more authentic ecstatic experiences, chiefly the experience of his call, which (like the Old Testament prophets) he did not strive for. The experience of his call was followed by further experiences of revelation, which Muhammad experienced through the 'spirit' or 'spiritual messenger' (who is sometimes identified with Gabriel) in his 'heart', i.e. deep within him. Only later did orthodoxy objectify this inner spiritual experience, which may have been accompanied by somatic phenomena, in the form of an angel who appeared publicly (or a voice which was heard). Doubtless, Muhammad had shaped his insights in the course of his further activity in Mecca and Medina, but regular community prayers and collecting alms contributed as much to the solidarity typical of the Muslim community as did his proclamation. The revelation of the Qur'an lasted twenty-three years. Rahman concludes: 'There is no doubt that whereas on the one hand, the Revelation emanated from God, on the other, it was also intimately connected with his deeper personality.'[25]

Historical–anthropological hermeneutics of the Qur'an

Unlike Rahman, who did not set out to engage in hermeneutics professionally, Mohammed Arkoun, an Algerian of Berber descent, who completed his doctorate at the Sorbonne and for decades taught in Paris, thought through the problems of Qur'anic exegesis in a sophisticated way against the background of the hermeneutical discussion in France (Paul Ricoeur, Emmanuel Lévinas, Edgar Haulotte).[26] He worked out a highly complex hermeneutics of metaphors and symbols in the light of which the Qur'an is to be understood.[27] By avoiding all dogmatic definitions and theological constructions, Arkoun wanted to understand the revelation above all as a linguistic and cultural phenomenon.

Arkoun saw three scriptural traditions, the Hebrew Bible, the New Testament and the Qur'an, together. Like Paul Ricoeur before him, he differentiates three levels of the word of God for all prophetic religions:

- the first is the word of God itself that, transcendent and infinite, has been revealed to prophets only in fragments;
- the second is formed by the historical manifestations of the word of God through the prophets of Israel (in Hebrew), through Jesus of Nazareth (in Aramaic) and through Muhammad (in Arabic): messages that were originally oral statements, heard and handed down by the disciples (Qur'anic discourse);
- the third is formed by the textual objectification of the word of God in which the Qur'an, like the Hebrew Bible and the New Testament, becomes a written text (*mushaf*, Qur'anic text) finally present in a closed corpus (canon), on which countless further books (exegesis, theology, law, translations) are then based. However, the theological syntheses, exegeses and law books should not be confused with the Qur'anic text.

In the Qur'anic text, the sequences of surahs and verses are neither chronologically, rationally or formally ordered. However, this 'disorder' conceals a semiotic order which, as in the Bible, makes it possible to distinguish five different types of speech (discourse): prophetic, legislative, wisdom, narrative and hymnic.

At a time when literacy programmes for the mass of the population have made exegesis possible for anyone, Arkoun regrets that the philological criticism of scholars (chiefly German scholars) as applied to the Hebrew Bible and the New Testament 'is largely rejected by Muslim scholarly opinion'. This has happened for both political and psychological reasons: 'In a political respect the Qur'an provides legitimation for the new states; this is all the more indispensable when democratic mechanisms of legitimation are lacking. From a psychological perspective, after the failure of the school of the Mu'tazilites over the created Qur'an (*mushaf*), it has always been an integral element in the Muslim consciousness that all the pages brought together in the Qur'an as *mushaf* represent the word of God itself. Accordingly the written Qur'an has been identified with the Qur'anic discourse or the Qur'an as recitation, where this recitation is seen as the direct expression of the primal writing of the book.'[28]

Arkoun does not reject the sacral, spiritual and transcendent but argues that we must note that the vocabulary of the Qur'an is completely subject to historicity, even where it relates to stable, immaterial values. Faith never exists independently of human beings but is always shaped, expressed and actualized in and through human discourse. The believer can interact only on the third level with the word of God and thus also with the community of faith and salvation history. The community can be renewed in the light of the original message, so it has a fundamental function in the process of understanding.

Arkoun thinks that a demystifying or demythologizing of the holy books is unavoidable, especially as many societies have been undergoing this process for centuries without really coming to terms with it. However, Arkoun does not want, like the Christian exegete Rudolf Bultmann, 'to reduce myth to an object of rationalistic knowledge, to be understood exclusively in a historical and positivistic way' (but does Bultmann do this?). Rather, he wants to 'abandon the dualistic framework of knowledge in which reason is set over against imagination, history over against myth, the true over against the false, good over against the evil, reason over against faith, and instead of this go over to a pluralistic, changeable, open rationality that can embrace all the psychological processes which the Qur'an has assigned to the heart and which present-day anthropology is attempting to reintroduce under the name of the "imaginary"'.[29] He wants to be freed from the 'naivety' of the exegesis of someone such as at-Tabari, who introduced each of his commentaries with the words 'God said', 'by which he implicitly postulated that his exegesis coincided completely with the intended meaning and of course also the semantic content of each verse'.[30]

Pluralistic–political hermeneutics of the Qur'an

The young South African Muslim scholar Farid Esack, who has studied, among other places, in Britain and Germany, takes up Rahman's historical–critical and Arkoun's historical– anthropological exegesis of the Qur'an in a differentiated way and wants to lay the foundation for political–pluralist exegesis of the Qur'an.[31]

– In his hermeneutics he takes present-day pluralistic society more seriously than Rahman: for example, the necessity for interreligious solidarity, the structural causes of injustice and the dovetailing of knowledge and practice.
– More than Arkoun, as a child of apartheid, in the exegesis of the Qur'an he wants to take account of the specific context of the fight for justice against oppression by racism, capitalism and patriarchy; in other words, with welcome clarity, as he announces in his title, he seeks a Qur'anic hermeneutics of pluralism for liberation.

Taking up above all the hermeneutics of the Catholic theologian David Tracy of the University of Chicago, who has adopted many impulses from Hans-Georg Gadamer and Jürgen Habermas, Esack says that there is 'no innocent interpretation, no innocent interpreter and no innocent text, and no interpreter can simply escape his or her own history, language and tradition'.[32] 'A political' ('spiritual') interpretation is not 'neutral' but is often at the service of a conservative political and religious establishment.

Esack cites Gustavo Gutiérrez, the founder of Latin American liberation theology: 'The last systematic obstacle for any theology committed to human liberation' is 'a certain type of academism which posits ideological neutrality as the ultimate criterion'.[33] In seeking the meaning of a text, one cannot ignore the situation of the time and the faith community in favour of an intellectual 'objectivity'. To do this would finally put a small group of 'objective' intellectuals outside or above the great majority of believers, for whom the text is a living document. For Esack, the fundamental question, which is also a political one, remains: 'For whom and in whose interests does one pursue the hermeneutical task?'[34]

Beyond doubt Farid Esack's book provides many valuable impulses for the Islamic hermeneutics of the Qur'an. But more than those of Fazlur Rahman and Mohammed Arkoun his remarks provoke critical questions:

– Despite the 'radical plurality of our differential languages and the ambiguity of all our histories',[35] mustn't a pluralistic exegesis be demarcated more clearly from an arbitrary exegesis which simply reads certain (personal or political) interests out of the text that it uses?

– Mustn't a 'hermeneutics of liberation' be aware of its proneness to become an ideology? Isn't there also 'slavery' in the name of liberation? Shouldn't a stand be taken not only against a capitalism which despises human beings but also against a socialism which despises human beings? Don't victims of racism, when they come to power, sometimes themselves become racist oppressors (for example, in Africa or Israel)?[36]

Unquestionably Rahman, Arkoun and Esack, for all their differences, have made Muslim contributions to a new understanding of the Qur'an which are well thought out and extremely helpful. In my dialogue with Muslims I have seen how great the interest is in a contemporary hermeneutic of the Qur'an. In such dialogue one can also learn from biblical hermeneutics, for example about the 'hermeneutical circle': every interpreter of the Qur'an approaches the holy text with a 'pre-understanding' but this pre-understanding must be corrected by the text.

The efforts of the 'Ankara school', a group of younger high-school teachers who, since the 1990s, have been attempting to clarify a historical understanding of the book of revelation without abandoning faith in the divine origin of the Qur'an, are an encouraging sign for a new understanding of the Qur'an: 'The Ankara school came to the conclusion that the Qur'an is on the one hand a concretization of timelessly valid ethical principles bound to a historical context, which in a different historical situation cannot simply be continued literally by the faithful; it must be reworked by the standard of their own insights. On the other hand it emphasizes that any knowledge of the ethical principles of the Qur'an, including that of the present-day interpreter, remains bound up with its place and limited to its context. This makes possible a great deal of flexibility, say, in dealing with the Qur'anic legal prescriptions and the consolidated dogmatic views of the Sunni tradition. However, the school remains very aware that it cannot make any claims for the eternity and absoluteness of its own attempts as a solution.'[37] That brings me to a last question: what could a time-sensitive understanding of the Qur'an mean today?

What could a time-sensitive understanding of the Qur'an mean today?

On the basis of three Muslim hermeneutists who are so different and yet who correspond in so many ways, here are two delimitations and a possible definition:

- The Qur'an should not be understood, any more than the Bible should be, as a system of fixed formulae, rigid doctrines, unchangeable legal principles, as if it could be handed down unhistorically with no heed to time, place and persons. History cannot be dispensed with. Anything else would be an uncritical dogmatic understanding of the Qur'an—whether with a Muslim or a Christian stamp.

- Nor should the Qur'an be understood, any more than the Bible should be, as a river of interpretations which constantly change depending on time, place and persons; as though the meaning of the Qur'an were none other than the history of its meanings. Criticism cannot be dispensed with. Anything else would be an uncritical phenomenological understanding—whether with a Christian or a Muslim stamp.
- The Qur'an should be understood, like the Bible, as a living message, repeatedly perceived anew in its recitation as the great prophetic testimony to the one and only powerful and merciful God, the creator and perfecter, his judgement and his promise. It is a completely constant testimony which can and should be handed down in a form that is constantly renewed, varying with time, place and person, so that certain conflicts with nature and history, with modern ethics and awareness of law can be given an unambiguous and constructive solution. That would be a historical–critical–topical understanding with a Muslim or Christian stamp, which takes up the concerns of pluralistic anthropological and political hermeneutics and which does not contradict a believing positive basic attitude to the religion.

I remain aware that at first the distance between the modern attitude to the Bible and the traditional attitude to the Qur'an seems immense but, as I have attempted to make clear, it must not simply remain unchangeable and unbridgeable. As I have indicated, a convergence seems to me to be necessary—for the sake of the renewal of Islam, understanding between Islam and Christianity and world peace.

Or will understanding between Jews, Christians and Muslims be reserved for the end of time? As I hope has become clear, no unitary religion is being striven for; better mutual understanding is possible even now, as is collaboration not only on a political or humanitarian but also on a religious basis. Thus far only the beginnings of this are recognizable but, happily, more recent Protestant and Catholic documents on the relationship between Christians and Jews end with hopeful and constructive sections on the 'shared tasks' in the present world situation, in which Muslims should be involved despite difficulties that are all too well known. On the basis of what is held in common the following possibilities could be realized:

- a shared perception of responsibility for shaping the world in accordance with the maxims of the realization of the will of God;
- a shared prophetic protest against injustice in the economic and social spheres and against all political oppression, in favour of freedom, justice, true humanity and human rights;

- a shared expectation of the kingdom of God and final salvation, which will not be brought about by scientific and technological evolution or by political and social revolution but by God alone, when God, manifest to all, becomes all in all. All our efforts at dialogue, understanding and encounter are only a beginning but what has been achieved in recent decades gives us courage resolutely to follow in theology and practice the way that has already been taken.

With my Iranian Muslim colleague, Seyyed Hossein Nasr, formerly Professor of Islamic Studies at Washington University, Washington DC, I think 'that the destinies of Islam and Christianity are intertwined, that God has willed both religions to exist and to be ways of salvation for millions of human beings'.[38] The way into the future must not once again be the way of war. In the face of all hatred, all fanaticism and all intolerance, with Nasr I hope that in the end the voice of understanding and harmony will prevail, for (as he remarks) 'it is based upon the truth and surely Christ whose second coming is accepted by both Christians and Muslims shall not come but by truth, that truth which he asserted himself to be according to the Gospel statement, and which the Qur'an guarantees as being triumphant at the end, for there will finally arrive the moment when it can be asserted with finality that "Truth has come and falsehood has perished" (surah 17.81)'.[39]

Let an economist and Middle Eastern specialist have the last word on the transition from the challenges of the present to the possibilities of the future and from the problems of theology and religion to those of society, politics and economics: 'The struggle to achieve a viable interpretation of Islam between the enlighteners and the orthodox must be taken seriously. If that happens, experience shows that a conversation will also be possible about options for economic and social political schemes and their concrete forms that are conceivable, but which cannot be decided clearly.'[40]

E. POSSIBILITIES FOR THE FUTURE

Now that I have surveyed the paradigms of the past (C I–V) and considered the challenges of the present (D I–VI), the question arises: where does Islam stand today, at the threshold of a new world era? Or more precisely, how can its identity crisis, provoked by the encounter with modernity, be overcome? What religious options will Islam follow? What are the possibilities for Islam in the immediate future? This chapter will open up the way through modernity to postmodernity (not 'postmodernism'), the contours of which are still largely unclear. I do not want to don the garb of a seer or futurologist but to continue a sober analysis. If I ask about the possibilities of Islam in a postmodern period and speak sweepingly of 'Islam', the preceding chapters have made it sufficiently clear how much this religion manifests itself in aspects which are extremely different, both regionally and culturally, and how different developments run their course at the same time. I am concerned with an 'overall trend', with the tendencies which the overall picture, which characterize an overall constellation, the macroparadigm that is coming into view.

E I

Islamic Renewal

From Feuerbach and Marx to Nietzsche and Freud, those who have cited modern achievements to prophesy the end of religion have been discredited. From a global perspective religion is alive, however problematical its forms, which are often to be criticized. Religion—which in European modernity has been ignored, neglected and persecuted, often because of the faults that have already been described—is again also playing a role in public life. This is a symptom of the transition from modernity to a postmodernity, even if in some societies religion still has to carry on a critical discussion with modernity. Undoubtedly, Islam has performed a special service in bringing about a new global awareness of the religious dimension, for this religion has experienced a true revival.

1. The programme

At the beginning of the twenty-first Christian and the fifteenth Muslim century '*tajdid*', 'renewal', has become a rallying-cry in Islam, from Africa, through the Middle East to Pakistan, Malaysia and Indonesia. For some in the West this is a disturbing and, for many theoreticians and strategists of development, an extremely surprising phenomenon. Some of these strategists had been quite content with the religious, intellectual and political stagnation of the Islamic countries, which formerly had had such highly-developed cultures, and had left the ethical and religious dimensions of the development completely out of account. They have had to note that the political collapse of the modern colonialist Eurocentric paradigm (P V) and the transition to a postmodern post-colonialist polycentric paradigm (P VI) have been accompanied by a revival of Islam.

Factors in the revival

Some decisive factors in this amazing development are:

– The cultural stagnation of Islam, prepared for from the twelfth century and manifest since the fifteenth century, its loss of political power since the nineteenth century and an acute identity crisis, accompanied by a sense of powerlessness and alienation and the loss of self-confidence and dignity in the face of Western colonialism and imperialism, form the dark background to a possible paradigm change.

– The political liberation of many Islamic countries in the late 1950s and 1960s, made possible by the way in which the European colonial powers tore one another to pieces in the First and Second World Wars and heralded by the withdrawal of Great Britain from India in 1948 and the simultaneous founding of the Islamic republic of Pakistan, created the necessary free space for a new development of the religion of these Islamic states as well (today there are more than fifty of them, brought together in the Organization of the Islamic Conference, OIC). In Istanbul on 12 and 13 February 2004, the OIC and EU, in opposition to the geopolitical concept of the 'conflict of civilizations' which had long been reflected on and, after 11 September 2001, had been frantically propagated by the 'neo-conservative' American snipers, announced reinforced commitment to a 'dialogue of civilizations' (more about this at the end of the chapter).

– After all the unfulfilled promises of Arab nationalism, Pan-Arabism and Arab socialism, from 1973 onwards, military and economic successes—the Arab–Israeli war and the oil embargo, the victory of Ayatollah Khomeini over the Shah and the humiliation of the United States (the Teheran hostage affair)—initially helped Islam to a heightened self-awareness and sense of power.

– Disappointment over the West and the inability of the governments of Islamic countries with a Western orientation to cope with home-made economic and social problems led to fundamental doubts in the modern paradigm in both its socialist–Soviet–Chinese and its capitalist–European–American forms. In one case there was social justice at the expense of freedom, in the other freedom at the expense of social justice.

– In view of the concentration on the satisfaction of material needs in both East and West, voices from the Islamic world have called for greater attention to spiritual, moral and religious values. The technological blood transfusion from the West that was meant to help the Islamic countries towards a new convalescence had failed; nowhere was this clearer than in Iran, the prime example of Western development policy after the Second World War.

So the question arises: how is the Islamic revival to be assessed at the beginning of the twenty-first century? Is it a militant political reaction to Western colonialism and imperialism on the one hand and the collapse of Soviet Communism on the other or the worryingly ambivalent consequence of Western development policy through the transfer of technology or simply the reactionary and religious ebb of the revolutionary–secular wave that broke in vain? It is all these things. But these assessments remain on the political surface. They overlook the moral and religious roots of this renewal, which in many places has found its way into private, social and political life. However, it is not a completely new phenomenon.

Renewal as a return to the origins

Since the ninth century, when Islam consolidated itself and the 'Sunnah', the 'tradition' of the Prophet, there have been repeated calls for renewal (which have sometimes been revolutionary). Renewal always takes place through a return to the foundations of Islam, Qu'ran and Sunnah, though the meaning and methods vary according to time and place.

On the one hand there were the conservative reformers whom we met earlier: from the Wahhabi reform movement in eighteenth-century Saudi Arabia to the reform efforts of the Muslim Brotherhood in twentieth-century Egypt.[1] And on the other hand there were the great Islamic 'modernists' such as al-Afghani and 'Abduh who, despite all criticism of forms of thought and religion, moulded by the spirit of the Middle Ages, did not understand themselves as Westernized assimilators but as religious reformers who acknowledged Qur'an and Sunnah and called for a return to original Islam. There is an inner connection here between them and those who inspired the later Islamic renewal, even if the latter reject their 'modernistic' interest in reason, rationality and science: in India (Muhammad Iqbal and Mawlana Abu l-A'la Mawdudi), in Egypt (Sayyid Qutb) and in Iran ('Ali Shari'ati).[2]

Islam is and remains rooted in the spiritual world in which its people live, more strongly than many Western experts assume. Moreover, in its revival it reminds the nations of the West of their own religious roots, which are often hidden. As many Muslims see it, the West, one-sidedly imprisoned in the modern paradigm, has ignored the depth-dimensions of society and neglected the deepest force in human beings, religious faith.

The Islamic renewal is supported and furthered by the world-wide transition from a modern colonialist paradigm to what I have called a postmodern polycentric paradigm, which has the following characteristics: global interaction and interdependence, the rejection of an allegedly 'value-free' science and technology, a growing awareness of social morality, and a constructive revaluation of religion as a social force which is not only conservative and preservative (and unfortunately often also reactionary) but progressive and liberating (sometimes even revolutionary).

Is a new age also dawning for Islam, for a world religion which now hopes to make a great breakthrough in the southern hemisphere and become the greatest religion in the world in the new millennium—with far more than one billion Muslims at the beginning of the millennium? Is Islam the heir to Christianity which, as a consequence of its compromise with colonialism and imperialism and the social development towards individualism and secularism, has lost its credibility in southern lands? Whether these are dreams or not, the West is confronted with an Islamic renewal which has many aspects:

- the re-Islamization of the Muslim states,
- an intensification of the Muslim mission in Africa and Asia,
- and the activation of the Muslim minorities in Western states.

Islam—the 'third force' for the future?

This renewal shows different shadings and intensities in different countries: sometimes it is more sectarian, sometimes more universalistic (embracing Sunnis and Shiites); often it is nationalist and often internationalist (orientated on the whole Muslim Ummah); at times it is isolationist, at other times it is capable of co-operation. To regard this Islamic renewal as hostile to science, technology and industry is a naïve Western prejudice which is misled by the pronouncements of Muslim extremists. However, it is true that whereas in the modern West the Christian faith is fighting to assert itself against science, in some Islamic countries science must still fight for its place over against faith.

To put it simply: identity through modernity, modernity through identity is a definition of the standpoint of the Islamic renewers, in so far as their attitude is not simply conservative and reactionary but critical and conservative. At issue is the acceptance of the challenge of European modernity in a positive and creative way, without modernist assimilation to the present or traditionalist preservation of the past. Aren't such famous converts to Islam as the French philosopher Roger Garaudy or the former German ambassador in Algeria and Morocco, Murad Hofmann, right when they speak of Islam as the 'third force'?

In view of the religionless materialism which is widespread in industrial societies, the Islamic renewal is attempting to go its own way: to create a new basis for economics, culture and science through belief in the one God (*tawhid*) in submission (*islam*) to his will by observing his commandments. This faith is meant to penetrate all realms of both personal and social life and wasn't it precisely this faith which, from the beginning, was the tremendous force behind

Islam which made its unprecedentedly victorious course possible? Isn't it the basis for the equality of all human beings before the one God, uniting the Muslim community of faith and transcending all differences of race, caste and class? So why shouldn't it be possible to achieve an intellectual, moral, social, cultural, political and even economic renewal on this foundation: a new society? Are these great ambitions—or great illusions?

The Islamic renewal movement is by no means simply a criticism of Western culture. It also represents internal criticism of the Islamic *status quo* and 'Islamic' regimes, in the light of the Qur'an and the Sunnah. It is not just a matter of a new political and social start but also of the development of faith: 'the social order is definitely important but the starting point is reawakening and strengthening faith and rebuilding the moral personality and the character of the individual. There is an upsurge of spirituality and idealism, generating a new sense of direction and a commitment to reconstruct their world, whatever be the sacrifice.'[3] Are these great intentions—or great frustrations?

Such an Islam does not want to be just an other-worldly religion (as Christianity is alleged to be), nor does it want to be just a this-worldly religion (as Judaism is alleged to be). It seeks to be both: God is one and his revelation is one, so religion and politics cannot simply be separated. What Islamic renewal wants is a modernization of society without compromising Islamic principles and values, a preparation for the future which mediates between old and new with support from every possible part of the population. This means Islam as a third force, which rejects Westernization and secularization but not development and modernization. Are these great plans—or great theories?

The beginnings of a real change, which will be viable for the future, can be seen.

2. Approaches towards realization

Both in the West and in the Islamic world there are still governments which in practice draw no distinction between radically violent and politically moderate Islamists, which exclude religious forces from the national dialogue with every possible means, which see the political relevance of the mass phenomenon of Islamism at best as a security problem and ban religious parties and banish them underground. At present, this is true of Egypt, Algeria and Tunisia. Jordan and Morocco are attempting to integrate Islamist forces in a democratic way. However, an extension of violent Islamism threatens in the Central Asian states that followed the Soviet Union: Kazakhstan, Kirghistan, Tajikistan, Turkmenistan and Uzbekistan, which are terribly poor and ruled by ex-Communist autocrats. They are all unstable dictatorships and have an uncertain future; however, they are used by the USA as bases for its anti-terror campaign in Afghanistan and are therefore tolerated, as other countries are not. It should be remembered that radical Islam is primarily a reaction to poverty, an absence of freedom and a lack of democratic, secular alternatives.[4]

Turkey—a laboratory for Islamic democracy?

One development is unmistakable: many originally radical Islamists have learnt from their experiences the uselessness of violent confrontation with the autonomous power of the state, and increasingly support parliamentary democracy and human rights. They are also involved in social institutions for the impoverished Muslim population and the foundation of Islamic banks and educational institutions.

Developments in Turkey, the advance guard of a radical secularism, could serve as an example. In 1998[5] I stood looking at the tremendous suspension bridge over the Bosphorus in Istanbul, once thought impossible to build, a bridge between Europe and Asia, the West and the East, the old time and the new, and several questions occurred to me. What is the future of this city, this state full of oppositions? What will be the future for Islam, here and in other countries? Who will be the heirs of this almost fourteen-hundred- year-old religion and culture?

– Will it be the modernists and secularists who think that they can dispense with Islam and religion altogether?
– Or will it be the traditionalists and fundamentalists who think that they can give a new spiritual and moral foundation to these societies with a literal observance of the religious writings?

I would like to hope that neither will win the day completely but that those who want to preserve the substance of Islam while attempting to translate the message of the Qur'an for today will again become more important. This means neither a godless secularism nor a fundamentalism alien to the world but a religion that can communicate to people of today a horizon of meaning, ethical criteria and a spiritual home.

– It will be a religion that does not separate and divide but unites and reconciles. What our age needs above all is bridge-builders who, despite all the difficulties, clashes and confrontations, have a shared worldview, ethical values and attitudes; bridge-builders who profess these shared ethical values and criteria and put them into practice in their lives.

Was what I thought in Istanbul in 1998 only an illusion, a theory, sheer utopia? At that time, Turkey was in an extremely precarious situation: facing a financial crisis, loss of confidence, an economic collapse and a demand by the IMF to reduce state subsidies for agriculture. The political landscape was fragmented: both the right-wing conservative parties (the Motherland Party Anap and the Party of the Right Way, DVP) and the social democrats (the democratic left-wing party DSP and the republican popular party CHP) were agreed that the further rise of the Islamist party, which despite numerous bans imposed by the government and the army kept reappearing under new names (Prosperity Party/Virtue Party), had to be prevented at all costs. Dominated by the rich Erbakan family (and the Naqshbandiyyah, one of the largest Sufi orders), this party of the poor gained only 15.3% of the seats in the 1999 parliamentary elections.

However, the crisis became increasingly acute. The parties that hitherto had been in power were incapable of coping with it. In the meantime the Islamic party had recreated itself under new leadership. Recep Tayyip Erdogan, the successful former mayor of Istanbul, who comes from a simple background and is socially committed, is also a highly-gifted politician who, in contrast to Erbakan, could speak to the new and increasingly Islamicized middle class which had come into being. In November 2002 his Party for Justice and Development won a landslide victory: it even forced the Atatürk party out of parliament and had only the social democratic Republican Party as opposition.

So far, Erdogan has been a bridge-builder. His party does not want to engage in any policy of active Islamization (radical Islamic parties, which called for the introduction of the Shariah, received only about 2.5% of the vote): religion remains a private matter. However, the new party does affirm a personal Muslim faith and practice which may have an indirect effect on the public—for example, through Islamic garments for women, which are now allowed but not prescribed. This is a religious conservative people's party which, when founded, took the Christian Democrat party in Germany as its model: an Islamic democratic party. Anyone who heard Erdogan spontaneously answering questions at the World Economic Forum in Davos in 2003 will have heard his profession of democracy. The fact that the Turkish parliament and government kept out of the 2003 Iraq war, despite immense political and financial pressure from the USA, does them great credit. One can only hope that Erdogan can stabilize the political situation and human rights question in Turkey, bring the Kurdish question nearer to a solution and master the difficult economic situation.

The whole of the Arab world, both conservative Islamists and liberal intellectuals, is following developments in Turkey closely. The Syrian philosopher, Sadik al-Azm, expects them to produce a boom in enlightened Islam. In 2004, at the University of Tübingen, he was awarded the important Leopold Lucas prize, founded by Franz Lucas, Consul General in London, son of the German rabbi Leopold Lucas, who was killed in a concentration camp. In his acceptance speech, al-Azm said: 'After the collapse of the allegedly progressive systems in Communist countries it is now in fact possible to see a revival of the values of the Enlightenment. Ideas such as human rights, democracy, civil freedoms, civil government, the separation of powers, elections, control of the administration are now regarded as key values by large parts of Arab society and as the only way out of the desperate situation in which the Arab countries find themselves. Here the example of Turkey is very important: the fact that political Islam in Turkey could become part of the democratic system without a catastrophe. In Egypt just a month ago the organization of Muslim Brothers passed a basic programme that reads almost like the ideas of Diderot. They have abandoned the demand for the caliphate and the notion that the Qur'an replaces a constitution. The Turkish example has sparked off a great debate on all these values in the Arab world.'[6]

There are signs of hope that the legal situation of the religious minorities in Turkey will also improve. The Christian minority, which makes up 0.2% of the overall population, leads a miserable life and is legally insecure: officially it does not exist, since churches as institutions are not provided for under Turkish law; consequently it may not possess land or erect church buildings. Numerous buildings bequeathed to the long-established Orthodox churches by founders have been appropriated by the state. As *primus inter pares* the supreme head of 250 million Orthodox Christians all over the world, the Ecumenical Patriarch of Constantinople, Bartholomew I, who is very open to the current situation, hopes that at least the educational institution for Greek Orthodox theologians in Halki (Turkish *Heybeli Ada*), on an island in front of Istanbul, closed in 1971, will be reopened. It is to be hoped that reports about a 'mood of new beginnings in Turkey' prove true: 'In view of the clearly relaxed climate the Christian churches of the country at the end of 2003 felt encouraged to present joint demands to the government. These include the recognition of the patriarchs and churches as persons in law, the permission of foreign priests to have residence, and permission to set up seminaries for the training of priests.'[7] In present-day Turkey no one need have any fears about Christian proselytism.

Erdogan reacted peacefully and thoughtfully to the horrific terrorist attacks by Islamist extremists on a synagogue and the British consulate in Istanbul in the autumn of 2003. The message read out at the end of November 2003 in all Turkish mosques (also in Germany) at the conclusion of the month of Ramadan is also hopeful: 'Unfortunately today we live in the shadow of war, violence and terror, which are signs of helplessness and rage. If the wounds are to stop bleeding, the members of the three world religions of Islam, Christianity and Judaism must make great efforts. Religions cannot be a ground for war ...; war and terror cannot have a human message. What they create are fear and suspicion ... In the end every war and act of terror swallows up those associated with them. History is full of countless examples of this.'[8]

Pioneer Islamic thinkers

Democracy cannot be introduced with bombs, which is what the USA, Great Britain and their allies have attempted in Iraq. Democracy cannot be forced on Islamic countries from outside. Democracy must grow from within—even if at first, in free elections, 'more Islamic' parliaments and governments come to power. Long-unnoticed by the public of the West (and particularly of America), in recent years a moderate Islam has formed as a 'civil alternative' to the 'clerical' Islamists established in Iran after the Islamic revolution in 1979:[9] a 'political class' between conservative clerics and secularist intellectuals.

Many influential pioneer thinkers developing a contemporary Islam capable of surviving in the world community (some of them are personally known to me) have long been working in this direction despite resistance and obstacles:

- the Algerian Mohammad Arkoun (Arabist and philosopher at the Sorbonne),[10]
- the Egyptian Hasan Hanafi (professor of philosophy in the University of Cairo),[11]
- the Iranian Abdolkarim Soroush (Iran and USA),
- the Indonesian Abdurrahman Wahid (for a short time state president),
- the Malaysian Anwar Ibrahim (thinker and politician, former finance minister and deputy prime minister).[12]

That they all come up against difficulties of very different kinds in their respective countries in presenting their different concepts of how Islam is to be reconciled with the modernity of our days is no argument for not taking them seriously. To them should be added Ismail Raji al-Faruqi (Palestine and USA), a pioneer of Muslim–Christian relations; Khurshid Ahmad (India and Pakistan), an 'activist-economist'; Maryam Jameelah (Pakistan and USA), a voice of conservative Islam and Rashin Ghannoushi (Tunisia), an activist in exile.

Regrettably, these leading thinkers of a modern political Islam are hardly known in the West. Thanks to the distinguished American Islamic scholars John L. Esposito and John O. Voll (both of Georgetown University, Washington DC), we have eloquent portraits of these 'Makers of Contemporary Islam',[13] which present their very different ideas to the Western public. To them, from personal experience, I would also add Prince Hassan bin Talal of Jordan, who has been working for many years for Islam interpreted in a humane way, for

Christianity in the Arab world and for the dialogue of the three Abrahamic religions;[14] he founded the Royal Interfaith Academy in Amman, was president of the Club of Rome, and, since 1999, has been moderator of the World Conference of the Religions for Peace (WCRP). Similarly, Chandra Muzaffar in Malaysia, founder of the International Movement for a Just World (JUST), has worked untiringly and incorruptibly all over the world for a renewed Islam and inter-religious understanding.[15] Finally, there is the Pakistani professor Riffat Hassan, passionately committed to feminism and inter-religious dialogue,[16] on whose bold initiative in February 1984 I gave a lecture on religion and world peace to the Philosophical Society of Lahore and engaged in Islamic–Christian dialogue with important figures in Islamabad and Karachi.

In the West there is often criticism of the alleged cowardice of moderate Muslims. The American Stanley A. Weiss, founder of Business Executives for National Security, has spoken out against such criticism: 'Western critics should look closer. From Africa to Southeast Asia, a battle is raging for the soul of Islam. Progressive Muslim clerics, intellectuals, journalists and activists are bravely taking on the fundamentalists and risking their lives in the process. They are the best hope for saving the world's fastest-growing religion from the grip of religious totalitarianism.'[17] As examples of Muslims who are risking their lives in their work he mentions Ulil Abshar-Abdalla in Indonesia, founder of a liberal Islamic network; the Iranian academic Hashem Aghajari, who was condemned to death because he called for an 'Islamic Protestantism'; the Afghan doctor Sima Samar, who worked for the rights of women in Afghanistan; the journalist Jamal Khashoggi, who criticizes the 'fanaticism' of the ultra-conservative Shiites; the Pakistani physicist Pervez Hoodbhoy, who attacks the 'subversion of science' by a 'religious orthodoxy'; and the professor of philosophy Sari Nusseibeh, who teaches in the East Jerusalem university of Al-Quds and was arrested by the Israelis.

It would be wrong to see all these pioneer thinkers in isolation. The intellectual *avant garde* is finding a following. The information from Katajun Amirpur, reporting on her Iranian homeland, is important: 'Today in the allegedly fundamentalist theocracy, in the Islamic republic of Iran, there are hundreds of reform theologians—men and women. They are all attempting to argue that Islam need not be in conflict with human rights, democracy and religious pluralism.'[18]

Critical dialogue also with moderate Islamists

The thinking of the Tunisian scholar Mohamed Talbi, whom I have already mentioned, resonates particularly strongly in the West; he has made a name for himself as an unconventional thinker and with works on the history of the Maghreb. Talbi, winner of the Tübingen Lucas Prize in 1985, has not been afraid to describe Tunisia, formerly progressive and secularist and now under the dictatorship of President Ben Ali, as 'an immense gulag of the spirit' and to publish a 'plea for a modern Islam'.[19] However, though he has a modern education he does not like to describe himself as a 'modern Muslim': 'I really do not like this label. Most Muslims associated with it have been to some degree "de-Islamized". By contrast I feel myself in no way alienated from Islam. I am a believing Muslim. I practise my religion and accept the Qur'an as the word of God. If I have to be given a label at all, then I would prefer "Qur'anic Muslim". This is because I feel myself bound only by the Qur'an. A "Qur'anic Muslim" has made the Qur'an his own as the divine word out of free choice. For those who accept it into themselves, the Qur'an is no compulsion, but rather part of their consciousness, their conscience. That is precisely how I feel. I am completely free towards God, who is freedom. And God is with me in the sense of the word, in the sense of the Qur'an, which says that there is a part of the divine in every human being.'[20]

Whereas some representatives of a secularized Islam are often uninterested in a dialogue between cultures and religions and the representatives of a radical–violent Islamism often prove to be hostile, moderate Muslims are mostly sympathetic. They are convinced that the religious dimension should not be ignored in the life of the individual or society but rather brought to awareness in an enlightened way.

Amr Hamzawy was born in Cairo and teaches at the Free University of Berlin and the University of Cairo; he writes about Islamists, Arab élites and the capacity of the Arab world for reform. He rightly warns the West not to evade dialogue with future political leaders of the Arab world, who have become religious democrats. Since the 1970s, he says, there has been uninterrupted talk about steps towards modernization and liberalization but the ruling élites have no serious interest in reforms, for fear of losing power. They allow the discussion of reform and practise the art of cosmetic democracy. There are no middle classes in Arab countries, no strong self-confident groups which can exercise the necessary social pressure for reform. For their part, the radical Islamists preach a return to the original community and the special nature of the Islamic way, by which they all too often mean an authoritarian rule.

Only the moderate Islamists, Hamzawy says, such as the Party of Justice and Development in Morocco or parts of the Muslim Brotherhood in Egypt and Jordan or the not yet legalized Centre Party in Egypt, are serious partners for the West. They are very often the only effective opposition to the authoritarian Arab regimes, against which secular agents of civil society, human rights associations and women's associations are largely isolated, producing only discourse by experts: 'Only the moderate Islamist groups, both traditional and modern, have roots in society and are politically in a position to mobilize large parts of Arab societies. They will be the true agents of democratic transformation if they are not excluded and if their tendencies towards moderation are encouraged. It is time for the West to enter into serious dialogue with them. Granted, most governments in the Middle East criticize such a reorientation. In the West, too, the secular moral preachers and the real politicians will issue their warnings. They will declare this to be irrational behaviour or conjure up the destabilization of the region. Nevertheless, dialogue with the moderate Islamists is the only way of setting democracy in motion in the region.'[21]

That all this is not sheer utopia is shown by the final communiqué of the Organization of the Islamic Conference and the Foreign Ministers of the EU, mentioned above, on 13 February 2004 in the 'European-Asian metropolis' of Istanbul. In it the representatives of seventy-one states unanimously affirm that 'cultures in all their differences mutually supplement and further one another' and that 'harmony between the cultures' is desirable and attainable. In addition to this 'the best means of furthering coherence and solidarity and fighting against racist, religious and cultural prejudices lies in improving our knowledge of the other through communication and co-operation in implementing shared universal values'.[22] All those committed to a global ethic will be particularly pleased that there is emphasis on the implementation of shared universal values.

However, only a critical dialogue will prove fruitful and that means that inconvenient questions must be considered clearly by both sides. Here attitudes to the Shariah and human rights take first place but there is also a need to pay attention to the relationship between state and religion and the relationship of Islam to violence, war and democracy. In this dialogue, political theory and theology, Islamic studies and religious studies, must work together. My own contribution will be to put questions to Islam, Judaism and Christianity and to combine criticism and self-criticism in an appropriate way, using a trilateral method. Because the changing differences and parallels for the different periods of time have hardly ever been analysed in detail, I shall not hesitate, for the sake of transparency, to mark these diachronic–synchronic paradigm comparisons with the abbreviations that I have constantly used (P I, II, III, etc.): first for the phenomenon of legalization, second for the relationship of state and theology, third for attitudes to violence and war and finally for the problems of the economy and the everyday world.

E II

The Future of the Islamic Legal Order

The practical implementation of modernization, which in theory is easy to see as a necessity, poses considerable problems to Islam. Despite their fundamental identification with Islam, many people today, particularly younger Muslims (even in Iran), are questioning the role of the Shariah. May a religion today still be such a comprehensive system of rules that dictate life down to the last detail? Can Islam be a 'total way', revealed by God for the whole of intellectual, cultural, social, political and economic life? Are the commandments of God a 'system' which permeates all spheres and in which religion is utterly bound up with economics, politics and culture?

1. The challenge to traditional legal systems

I need to issue a warning about rushing to hasty conclusions on the Christian side. Islam is by no means the only religion that has had massive difficulties with modernization because of its medieval legal system. Hence my trilateral method: whether Islam, Judaism or Christianity, the more strongly a religion is legalized and has committed its believers to a narrow web of commandments and prohibitions then, paradoxically, the more intensively it opposes the codification of basic rights. Basic rights are the rights which all human beings have as human beings, independent of religious or political institutions, and which should protect their freedom from attacks not only by other human beings but also by institutions—state, religion or hierarchy (of whatever kind).

The spread of legalism—in all three prophetic religions

Islam, like Judaism or Christianity, must not be judged solely according to its fundamental holy scripture (Torah, New Testament, Qur'an); the legal elaboration (halakhah, church law, Shariah) of that scripture and its current practice must be included. Here the following development becomes evident.

All three prophetic religions, which began as spiritual and intellectual renewal movements, became rigid as their legal systems and societies developed. Today, their future depends to no small degree on their capacity to overcome this rigidity, which has been there since the Middle Ages. I shall use the paradigm analysis which I have now made for all three prophetic religions in the three volumes of 'The Religious Situation of our Time' to survey the problems of halakhah, church law and Shariah in context.

In Judaism, the Torah (P I) was supplemented by the second, 'oral Torah' (P III): complex commentaries and 'traditions of the fathers' in the Talmud (P IV), which became the basis for all rabbinical legal decisions in everyday life. Thus, in practice the tradition made by human beings became more important than the 'Torah', the instructions of God himself. Two centuries before the development of Islamic sacral law, in Judaism the 'halakhah' (that part of the Talmud that contains the binding regulations in religion and civil law) was essentially fixed. Today the Babylonian Talmud is the normative basis for the religious teaching and the religious law of Orthodox (and often also of Conservative) Judaism. Even in the 'Talmudic period', nothing might be changed and supplemented. As all the countless precepts of the Torah and Talmud (going far beyond the original five books of Moses) are regarded directly or indirectly as the revealed word of God, they must be scrupulously observed—to the smallest rules about the Sabbath, food, cleanness, prayer and worship.[1]

In Christianity with a catholic stamp, the tradition was also increasingly set over against the biblical message (P I). In the early church Byzantine paradigm (P II) the tradition of the fathers and the councils became the supreme authority but from the beginning the church remained incorporated into the empire by law. By contrast, after the eleventh century (the 'Gregorian reform') the Catholic Church of the West (P III) developed its own church law (the *ius canonicum*) and its own science of church law, which is as complex and as differentiated as state law but is focused on the Pope as absolute ruler, legislator and judge. The twelfth-century popes issued more legal decisions for the whole church than all their predecessors put together. In time, three official collections of decrees came into being which (although important parts of them were forged by Frankish clergy) form the *Corpus Iuris Canonici*. On 10 December

1520, in Wittenberg, Martin Luther (P IV) burned not only the papal bull of excommunication but also the books of papal canon law, thus restoring the primacy of the Bible over tradition, though this did not prevent the spread of legalism in the Lutheran state churches. The Roman Catholic Church, persisting in the medieval paradigm, retained a centralist church law orientated on the Pope and reinforced it by the *Codex Iuris Canonici of* 1917–18, which still applies: it was revised, but not reformed, in 1983. Even after the Second Vatican Council (1962–65) the Catholic Church thus remained imprisoned in the authoritarian Roman system, cemented, at the First Vatican Council of 1870, by the papal dogmas (on the Pope's primacy and infallibility).[2]

In Islam, the tradition (Sunnah) became an institution that replaced the Prophet's right guidance and the hadith became a direct revelation from God. The hadith became more important than the Qur'an itself for legal scholarship, which became ever more determinative (P III). Centuries before the high point of medieval church legalism, Islamic legal science was experiencing its heyday (P III).

During the first three centuries of Islam (the seventh to ninth centuries), because of the changed social and political conditions, Muslim legal scholars had derived the regulations of the Shariah (*shar'iah*, literally 'way to the watering hole') from the Qur'an and the Sunnah and developed them into a comprehensive system (see C II, 4 and III, 3–4). However, after the tenth century, as I described, many Muslims regarded 'the door of independent judgement (*ijtihad*)' as closed. After the eleventh century, when the philosophy and truly innovative thought of orthodoxy had been excluded, the teachings of the ancestors were usually simply taken over and often repeated, rather than interpreted. For many Muslims, everything that had been 'derived' from the normative sources of Qur'an and Sunnah, with the help of analogies and the consensus of the legal scholars, was the holy law of God. Thus, an Islamic law which was not the revelation of God but manifestly the result of a historical development and a human disclosure was prescribed for all ages and for Muslims of all times. However, unlike the Roman *ius canonicum*, the Shariah, the totality of canonical (and cultic and social) legal precepts, was never codified; only a civil law book (Turkish *Mecelle*, Arabic *Majalla*) was established in 1869 as the basis of Islamic law for the Ottoman empire.

Just as Islam has no 'church', so it has no central teaching office. What has not already been decided by Qur'an and Sunnah (from permission to take photographs, through birth control to organ transplants and eating caviar) is decided by the Ulama, the religious experts.[3] Anyone can raise questions (today also in newspapers and on the television) but only those with special qualifications (among the Shiites only the supreme Ayatollahs) may give answers.

However, in contrast to Roman Catholicism, in Islam there is no magisterium with a claim to infallibility. Neither the most senior mufti in a country nor the highest body of experts at the al-Azhar University in Cairo can automatically count on absolute assent; their opinions are not binding and depend on the reputation and authority of the expert and the number of those who assent. Even the notorious death sentence by Ayatollah Khomeini on the writer Salman Rushdie received divided support in Iran and in Islam generally.

In the modern paradigm (P V) these three traditional religious legal systems—whether Jewish, Christian or Muslim—are confronted with secular political and legal demands, which are meant to guarantee every human being, of whatever religion and country, fundamentally equal freedoms, 'human rights'. However, instead of this confrontation being understood as an opportunity to reflect on the tradition, the tradition is usually maintained in an uncritical and defensive way.

Catching up with the Reformation

Europeans and Americans should remain modest: as the peace scholar, Dieter Senghaas of the University of Bremen, impressively makes clear, neither the key word 'progress', dominant in the modern paradigm, nor a sense of moral superiority were responsible for bringing an awareness and formulation of human rights.[4] Rather, numerous painful experiences of injustice were their foundation: oppression by the modern absolutist state and dominant church, genocide of the Indians and the intercontinental slave trade, exploitation of workers in early capitalism and colonialism, and so on. In the eighteenth century all this prompted the wish, the demand and the will among European and American peoples to proclaim and realize human rights. In the twentieth century, the inhumanities of the two world wars which broke out in Europe, Stalinism and Nazism and above all the crime against humanity that is the Holocaust—'the barbarous acts which have outraged the conscience of mankind' (preamble)[5]–generated even more moral energy, to pass the 1948 Universal Declaration of Human Rights.

Similarly, in the twenty-first century, various forms of injustice, also in Islamic countries, have provoked demands for a decisive realization of human rights. More than ever after the two Gulf Wars waged by the Western superpower and its allies on Arab soil, malaise among Arab peoples has spread and deepened so that, also for purely political reasons, the desire for a fundamental change in the economic, political and social situation and a realization of human rights has become increasingly strong.

How far will this readiness for reform go in the world of the twenty-first Christian and the fifteenth Muslim century? Doesn't history suggest that

Islam—in comparison with the European development—is trapped in the medieval paradigm more than Judaism and Christianity? Despite some spectacular technological modernization, in many parts of the Islamic world the states still seem to be dominated by religious and political institutions and their representatives and by medieval theology, medieval law and medieval social constitutions. Many Islamic societies seem to be living in a 'semi-modernity'.

If I take the development of Europe and Christianity and its paradigm changes as a comparison, it seems that today the Islamic renewal with its slogan 'back to the origins' is attempting no more and no less than to catch up with the paradigm change of the Reformation. Al-Afghani, the father of reform-orientated Islam, appealed to Luther's Reformation (see C V, 4). Today, instead of '*tajdid*' ('renewal'), people use the synonymous word '*islah*' ('reform'). Parallels of both form and content between Islamic reform and the Protestant Reformation are manifest. Although the situation of Islam in individual countries looks very different, because of the different degrees to which modernization has advanced and the different kinds of political regime, in the Islamic reform, as once in the Protestant Reformation, there is recourse to the normative and permanently binding foundation documents of the origin, to open up a future for the faith community of the present in the face of the ballast of tradition.

However, in one point the Muslim reform seems to differ from the Protestant Reformation: the emphasis is not (as in Luther, referring back to Paul) explicitly on the justification of human beings by trusting faith but more on justification by works. Original Islam, too, was less a religion of the law than the religion of an ethic, grounded in unconditional submission to God (see C I, 2). Nor is the widespread Western prejudice correct that the conscience of the individual—which was so important for the Protestant Reformers—plays no role in Islam. In the Islamic view, the function of the conscience is identical with that of the 'heart' (Arabic *qalb*) which, according to the Qur'an, is the criterion for human actions.[6] However, in the fight against alleged 'Western' moral decay and criminality Islamic renewal concentrates wholly on the law, on right, on what the conscience has to observe. What theology is to Christians, the religious law is to Muslims—and the state has to help to apply it.

Reintroduction of the Shariah? Nigeria, the test case

For a long time, Islamist activists world-wide, from the Muslim Brotherhood to Hizbollah and the Pakistani Jamaat-i Islami, have been calling for a reintroduction of the Shariah, which had been largely restricted in the modernization of the state, legislation and administration in the nineteenth and twentieth centuries.[7] Today, this demand is echoed in the wider population, far beyond radical groups and parties. Most Islamic states therefore use some form of the Shariah to gain religious legitimacy for themselves and to ward off the pressure of the Islamist movement (hardly ever through a democratic process of consultation or decision but by government decree). Sometimes, though, they use it to be able to proceed more easily against internal critics and opponents.

However, the profession of the Shariah in no way means that the traditional norms of the Shariah are really applied. In any case, the Shariah is less normative for trade and criminal law shaped on a European model than it is for family law. Nevertheless, it should not be overlooked that, for example in the Muslim northern half (in twelve out of thirty-six federal states) of Nigeria, Africa's most populous state, the introduction of Islamic criminal law has also proved particularly popular. Why?

Visited by waves of violence, the citizens of the federal republic of more than 130 million inhabitants long for legal security and an ordered society. Experience tells them that they can no longer hope for this from the complicated and sometimes incomprehensible democratic legal system, with its endless legal proceedings which often favour the powerful; rather, it will come from the rules of the Shariah, which are simple and formulated in an understandable way. According to the careful analysis by the ethnologist Johannes Harnischfeger, the vast majority of northern Nigerians hope that the Shariah will make it possible 'to call the rulers to account or at least to set limits on their arbitrariness. They want to incorporate the arrogant élite into a moral community in which the poor and the rich are united by the same cultures—as in the mythical beginnings of Islam.'[8] 'Immediate justice' and public executions are prized for their deterrent effect even by Christian citizens, who have had an increasingly hard time because of the progressive Islamization of the north and the associated hegemonial politics and appropriation of land by the Muslim tribes of the Haussa-Fulani. They have therefore converted to Islam, in large numbers. However, the Shariah campaign is actually colonialization with a religious brake on the part of the Muslims, who are concerned with conquest rather than with a balance of ethnic interests. Intent on de-escalation, the Nigerian president Olusegun Obasanjo (a Christian) together with Christian and Muslim leaders, on 5 January 2004, at a benefit performance for a mosque, called for non-violence between the fifty per cent Muslims and the fifty per cent Christians of the country.

Even in Muslim countries where the introduction of the medieval Shariah criminal law has been rejected, it remains a symbol of cultural identity, justice and order for many Muslims, especially in view of allegedly failing Western models and economic and social decline. Even many critical Muslims in Islamic countries hardly ever call for an abolition of the Shariah, but for a better interpretation of it; for them, the Shariah, by virtue of its character, seems to offer more possibilities than other legal systems. This is because:

- even educated Muslims know that the Shariah is not simply a holy law of God but largely juristic law (*fiqh*), prescribed neither by God nor by the Prophet;
- the Shariah is pluralistic in origin (it comes from several law schools) and capable of adaptation (there is no central authoritative standard interpretation);
- it had never been codified down to the modern period;
- today the norms, procedures and institutions said to be 'Islamic' are extremely different in different countries and allow many possibilities of evasion.

Noting these possibilities of interpretation, some Western experts recommend that Western people and institutions should not engage in a counter-productive course of confrontation for the abolition of the Shariah: 'It is a more appropriate approach to use the existing framework of interpretation with a view to wider participation. In this way the forms of economic activity and life furthered by collaboration in development will not be perceived as having resulted in an (unavoidable) break with "Islam".'[9]

That does not exclude the question why reform should be only in retrospect and within. Why cannot reform be forward-looking innovation, directed outwards?

2. The challenge of modern legal systems

Whatever is said about the economic or political situation in countries such as northern Nigeria or Iran which have introduced the Islamic criminal law, in the long run—in the middle of the transition in the Western world from modernity to post-modernity—can a religious reformation (reflections by the reformers on origins) replace a secular Enlightenment (liberation from restraint on autonomous human reason often caused by religion)? The answer of many radical Islamists is: modernization, yes; secularization no. However, can there be real modernization without at least limited—and I cannot avoid the word which so annoys orthodox Muslims—'secularization'? Secularization should not be confused with secularism, the ideology which ends up in Westernization, understood as religiouslessness, godlessness. The present Muslim identity crisis cannot finally be overcome simply by a religious reformation; this makes Muslims continue to doubt which world they really belong to, the Islamic world or the modern world, both or neither. The test cases for the transition to modernity are science and business, but above all human rights confront all three prophetic religions with a serious problem, given the trend towards legalism which I have just described.

Human rights—a test case for Christianity and Judaism

Historically, it is just not true that the West wants to force human rights on the 'rest' of the world. The movement for human rights in Europe by no means had all classes and estates behind it. Primarily secular forces, not the Christian churches in Europe, championed rights peculiar to each human being by virtue of being human, with no distinction of gender, race, skin colour, language and religion, rights which can or cannot be granted by a dominant institution or religious or state rulers. In this understanding of human rights, the obligation to the same human dignity and freedom is bound up with the political principle of the rule of law.

The great programme of the French Revolution, 'Freedom (political), equality (social) and brotherhood (spiritual)', was mostly rejected by the churches, although at that time thinking Christians had already seen the earliest Christian concerns in them. The Declaration of the Rights of Man (*Déclaration des droits de l'homme et du citoyen*), proclaimed in Paris in 1789, the year of the Revolution on the American model (the 1776 Virginia Declaration of Rights), to which Catholic clergy friendly to the Revolution, such as Abbé Grégoire and various Reformed pastors, made a decisive contribution, was rejected by Pope Pius VI in 1791 with reference to divine revelation as 'an abominable philosophy of human rights';[10] he was against freedom of religion, conscience and the press, and in particular against the equality of all human beings. This was a fatal decision for the Catholic Church, though it was repeatedly confirmed by Rome in the nineteenth century.[11]

After this condemnation of human rights, Rome was finally to be led to affirm them by Pope John XXIII, with his encyclical *Pacem in terris* (1963), and the Second Vatican Council, with its Declaration on Religious Freedom, strongly fought against even there, and its Declaration on the Relation of the Church to the Non-Christian Religions (1965). However, even this did not end the broken relationship between the Catholic Church and human rights, as is shown by the fact that up to the end of the twentieth century many of the cruellest dictatorships existed in Catholic countries: Spain, Portugal and military dictatorships of Latin America, often supported and courted by church leaders.

The Declarations of Human Rights issued by the American and French Revolutions brought a decisive improvement in the living conditions of Jews. In the USA, Jewish immigrants were free citizens from the start. In

France, after a controversial debate, this status was made clear by a resolution of the National Assembly that also granted all Jews who took the oath as French citizens unlimited civil rights as individual citizens; the resolution was solemnly confirmed by Napoleon in 1806.[12] However, the Dreyfus Affair in Paris (1898–99) showed in France (and later even more in Nazi Germany) what shallow roots the consciousness of human rights had. The Holocaust, the most fearful of all crimes against humanity, with six million Jews murdered, made it evident to the whole world how fundamental human rights are for preserving the human dignity of each individual and for maintaining the humanity of humankind.

As Jews had to suffer more massive violations of human rights than any other people, it might have been expected that the state of Israel, founded under the monstrous impact of the Holocaust in 1948, the year of the UN Universal Declaration of Human Rights, and supported by the Western democracies, would have done all it could to grant these human rights to everyone within its borders and to realize them in an exemplary way. Regrettably, this expectation has not so far been fulfilled. For as long as Israel grants full human and civil rights in its own territory only to Jews, and every day violates them brutally for Palestinians, its claim to be the only democracy in the Middle East lacks credibility. Conservative Israelis point to the terrible suicide attacks by Palestine extremists and think that fifteen years after the fall of the Berlin Wall, over which there was worldwide rejoicing, they can justify the building of a new wall and state terrorism against the Palestinians. But the question of human rights is a pressing one for Muslims, regardless of the Israeli–Palestine conflict.

Human rights—a test case for Islam

The situation is by no means hopeless. The Catholic Church, for so long a bulwark of anti-democratic reaction (because it rightly feared for its medieval hierarchical power structures), has finally acknowledged human rights, at least in theory (though in the first instance outside the church!). So shouldn't such a fundamental change also be possible for Islam, even though it doesn't have the institution of an ecumenical council? In Islamic countries, European colonial powers and most churches notoriously did little to promote human rights, so we can see why today many Muslims are indignant when former colonial rulers now arrogantly require human rights to be implemented 'overnight'. The European states took almost two hundred years to implement human rights (for example, women's rights) to any degree. Therefore, a certain degree of understanding must also be allowed to the Islamic states in respect of the tempo and mode of their realization of human rights, without trivializing blatant violations.[13]

When the Universal Declaration of Human Rights was passed by the UN General Assembly in 1948 there was Muslim opposition: Saudi Arabia abstained, as did South Africa and six Communist states. The reason given was that the Declaration did not recognize that rights are a gift of God and scorned the Qur'an by its recognition of a right to change religion. Interestingly, the Muslim Foreign Minister of Pakistan defended the Declaration in the name of his government, arguing that the Qur'an allowed one to believe it or not to believe it.[14] Since 1948, South Africa has abolished apartheid and the vast majority of Communist states have shaken off regimes hostile to human rights. However, Saudi Arabia still faces reorientation and in many places the way to the recognition of individual human rights is still a long one.

The Universal Declaration of Human Rights posed a tremendous challenge to Islamic self-understanding: it called for equal rights for women and religious minorities and the abolition of rigorous physical punishments. Under the influence of conservative thinkers, such as the Pakistani Mawlana Abu l-A'la Mawdudi,[15] important Muslim organizations attempted to harmonize Islam and human rights, but in reverse, by integrating human rights into the existing system of the Shariah and leaving unmentioned those rights which simply could not be integrated into it. In 1990 the Cairo Declaration of Human Rights in Islam[16] was accepted by the Organization of the Islamic Conference. Though the Cairo Declaration is not legally binding, it has great political weight.

In view of the Cairo Declaration, critical Muslims[17] ask whether the tensions between the Shariah and the Universal Declaration of Human Rights can be glossed over, by making the Cairo Declaration an integral element of the Islamic tradition and keeping quiet about essential differences. For example, in Article 5 of the Cairo Declaration on the right to marriage, there is no mention of the non-discrimination on grounds of religion that is called for by the Universal Declaration. By contrast, Article 10 grants Islam a privileged status over against other religions: 'Islam is a religion of unspoiled nature. It is prohibited to exercise any form of compulsion on men or to exploit their poverty or ignorance in order to convert them to another religion or to atheism.'[18] This article attempts to exclude conversion from Islam and missionary activity of other religions among Muslims; this is in blatant contradiction to the Universal Declaration of Human Rights, which explicitly declares conversion to another religion, or to no religion, to be a human right. It is doubtful whether such an 'Islamization of the Declaration of Human Rights' does justice to its real content. But could human rights be given a specifically Muslim basis and if so, how?

An Islamic basis for human rights?

For me, unquestionably human rights can also be grounded in the Islamic tradition, above all in the Qur'an itself. Only faith in the one God, who is a God not only of Muslims but of all men and women, can be the Muslim basis for human rights. In the Bible, man and woman are created in the 'image of God',[18] which for the Qur'an assimilates human beings all too much to God; the Qur'an emphasizes the dignity of the human being in another way: God has put human beings on earth as 'representatives', 'governors', 'deputies' (*khulafa'*)—the angels (?).[19] At the same time the human being is a 'servant' (*'abd*) of God; the popularity of the first name 'Abd-allah shows that this designation is not seen as being humiliating, but rather as an honour.

There is a fundamental text for the equal dignity of all human beings in surah 5.32: '... We did ordain unto the children of Israel that if anyone slays a human being—unless it be [in punishment] for murder or for spreading corruption on earth—it shall be as though he had slain all mankind; whereas, if anyone saves a life, it shall be as though he had saved the lives of all mankind.' In Islam the human person has absolute value, because the individual reflects humankind as a whole: 'The value of the individual is neither numerical nor rational nor social; it is a gift of God himself, a gift for human beings as such—taking no account of cultural peculiarities, historical importance or striking self-confidence.'[20]

There are verses in the Qur'an, especially from the Meccan period of the Prophet, which emphasize freedom of belief and the equal dignity of all human beings before God regardless of faith or gender. The most famous verse, repeatedly cited by Muslims for freedom of religion, is 'There is no compulsion in religion.' The foundation for tolerance is also laid by the fundamental justification for a plurality of religions: 'Had thy Sustainer so willed, all those who live on earth would surely have attained to faith, all of them; dost thou, then, think that thou couldst compel people to believe?'[21] Another surah emphasizes the equal dignity of man and woman as God's creatures.[22] Yet another says that God cares for all the children of Adam.[23]

These positive statements are only one side of the message of the Qur'an; unfortunately many Muslims keep silent about the other. Equal rights of all human beings must surely follow from the equal dignity of all human beings. However, the Qur'an does not mention this: in law men seem to be clearly and massively privileged above women and Muslims above non-Muslims. Still, here, too, a trilateral approach to the problem will allow us to take a more differentiated view.

3. Religions and women—a relationship of tension

Critical questions need to be asked about the rights of women and minorities, not just in Islam. In most male-dominated world religions, the role assigned to women is problematical. For ages, women have been subjected to men, regarded as second-rate in the family, politics and the economy, and restricted in their social and religious rights and their involvement in worship. The status of women in the religions is one of the most controversial inter-cultural themes.

Equal rights for women in Christianity and Judaism?

The many Christians who have already have made up their minds (negatively) about the role of women in Islam should show some self-critical restraint.[24] Christianity did not bring forth women's liberation; in the society of late antiquity, women had achieved a high degree of emancipation for the time. However, from the third century on, there were more and more prohibitions against women exercising leadership in the church, in contrast to the friendly attitude of the man from Nazareth towards women and despite the leading functions of women in the communities of the apostle Paul (P I). This suggests a fight by the church authorities against the emancipation of women at a church or a social level (P II).

In the Middle Ages, the church contributed to raising the value of women in society by its theology and practice of marriage but women were also legally suppressed. (This has remained characteristic of the Roman Catholic paradigm, P III.) It was symptomatic of the time that the wife always had to put herself at a decent distance behind her husband. On an Old Testament basis, the law of inheritance was restricted to the male (patrilinear) succession (unless there were no male descendants). Even more importantly, church law (e.g. the fundamental *Decretum Gratiani* around 1140) established the status of women as subject to men with an argument from natural law. The ideal for women in the church was the nun. Women remained excluded from all church offices, and even preaching was repeatedly forbidden them because of the attractiveness of the Cathar and Waldensian movements, which were friendly to women.

The Reformation abolished compulsory celibacy for the clergy and revalued marriage. Wives, and especially pastors' wives, took on a completely novel field of activity in the community—on the model of Martin Luther's wife, Katherine von Bora. However, women continued to be excluded from all important church ministries and they were normally even forbidden to preach (P IV). Since the English 'man' and the French '*homme*' can mean both human being and male, the American and French Declarations of Human Rights were at first interpreted as purely male affairs, especially in connection with the vote and the right to own property, to assemble and to speak (P V).

Only at the beginning of the twentieth century did many (but not all) European countries also give women the vote. In the following decades many Protestant, Anglican and Old Catholic churches made great progress in promoting the equal rights of women, even in the structures of leadership (such as allowing ordination to the priesthood and even the episcopate). However, the Roman Catholic Church continues to resist, with every possible means, the equal rights for women that have been taken for granted in society, though ultimately its opposition will prove unsuccessful. The joint opposition to birth control by the Vatican and a few small Islamic states at the 1994 UN Population Conference in Cairo was not fortuitous but dictated by the system. The Roman hierarchy still does not grant women the right to decide on contraception or abortion and refuses them the ordination necessary for functions of leadership in the church. This attitude is making a major contribution to the striking loss of membership and credibility of the church in Western societies.

How do things stand in Judaism?[25] For countless Jewish women and Jewish men the status and role of the women, as regulated in the halakhah, are decisive test cases for the future understanding of the law. According to the Orthodox understanding a wife cannot request a dissolution of her marriage; only the husband can do that. In some circumstances this law has impossible consequences: a married woman remains tied to her husband even if he has disappeared or left her. In Hebrew, such a woman is called *'aguna*. Women's groups and lawyers estimate that there are about ten thousand of these *'agunot* in Israel. Complaints from women are numerous, not least about the way in which they are disadvantaged at hearings in exclusively male rabbinic courts, where some Orthodox rabbis sometimes make women in distress wait ten or twenty years before compelling the husband to consent to a divorce. Divorce laws two thousand years old still prevail, and act as chains on women.[26] Women are also strikingly under-represented in Israeli political life. Only a few members of the Knesset are women and hardly any woman holds a ministerial or deputy ministerial post, although women have to perform military service, 'with equal rights'. (The former Prime Minister, Golda Meir, is the famous exception to the rule.) Here is patriarchy instead of equal dignity and rights.

Despite the official blockages to women's emancipation, there has been progress in Judaism. Unlike a century ago, women in Orthodox Jewish families now receive a full education and training; the time when a Jewish woman had to dress as a man to be able to study, as in the film *Yentl*, is past. Nevertheless, much has still to be done before full equal rights are achieved. Although the very first chapter of the Bible[27] says that human beings have been created in God's image as man and woman, in his daily morning prayer the Orthodox male Jew thanks God that he has not been born a woman. This is a passage which cannot be reinterpreted by any apologetics, so it has been omitted or altered in Jewish prayer books of the Conservative, Reformed and Liberal movements.

As in Christianity, so too in Judaism an increasing restriction of the active involvement of women in public worship can be observed. Women were eventually no longer allowed to read aloud from the Torah nor did they count in the quorum (*minyan*) required for holding a public service. According to Orthodox understanding, at least ten men (!) are needed for this. To the present day, men and women are strictly separated in Orthodox synagogues. However, in Reform Judaism and also in Conservative and Liberal Judaism, the position of women has substantially improved. Women are also ordained to the rabbinate and a considerable number are already active in this profession. At the same time as the more recent international women's movement, a feminist theology has developed in all Jewish synagogues. For more than thirty years, Judith Plaskow has been one of its most prominent representatives and there are many others:[28] in Germany, Pnina Navè Levinson (Germany), Susannah Heschel (USA)[29] and Evelyn Goodman-Thaus (Israel) from Orthodox Judaism have made a name for themselves. Judaism is a religion in transition. Is Islam also?

Equal rights for women in Islam?

The Muslim scholar Fazlur Rahman, whom I have already quoted frequently, remarks, probably rightly: 'The Qur'an immensely improved the status of the woman in several directions, but the most basic is the fact that the woman was given a fully-fledged personality.'[30] I have already drawn attention to improvements in the legal situation of women in respect of property, the implementation of divorce and dowries in connection with the constitution of the earliest Islamic community (see above, C I, 3).

It is interesting for Christians that in the creation story according to the Qur'an[31] the woman is not depicted as having seduced the man. Certainly, the first human couple committed a primal sin which resulted in their expulsion from paradise but there is no original sin which was transmitted to every child by sexuality from the first moment of life—the reason why, in traditional Christian practice, children are to be baptized as soon as possible. However, this idea does not occur in the Bible either, whether in the book of Genesis or the New Testament (Romans); it is an invention of the great church teacher Augustine, who in his early years belonged to the Manichaean religion. Scarcely any idea in the Latin church (P III as opposed to P II) contributed so much to the vilification of sexuality and the demotion of the woman as this unbiblical idea of an original sin and the extreme fear of sin (which likewise goes back to

Augustine), coupled with a corresponding need for redemption which, in this form, is alien to Islam (and also to Judaism).

Sin is taken with the utmost seriousness in Islam, but the sinner can turn directly to the merciful God, who forgives the penitent sinner at any time and in any place, without a mediator or 'church'. There is a realistic view of human beings in the Qur'an. They are not 'good by nature', as Rousseau and some optimistic figures of the Enlightenment thought; they keep proving to be weak, fickle and unreliable. However, they are not 'corrupt by nature' either, as Augustine and the Reformers assumed: they remain God's creatures and representatives. Adam was 'disobedient'; he erred (from the right way) and therefore had to leave paradise.[32] Human beings are divided, beings with freedom of choice, prone to forgetfulness and irresoluteness and in need of right guidance. They have responsibilities: 'Whatever good happens to thee is from God; and whatever evil befalls thee is from thyself.'[33]

In Islam, as in traditional Christianity, the woman's role is generally limited to that of spouse, housewife, mother and the one who brings up children. Islam attaches extraordinary value to marriage and family, the wider family as a cell of society. For that reason it does not have the law of celibacy for dignitaries which contributes to the contempt for women among Catholic clergy. In Roman Catholic Christianity Mary, virgin and mother, excessively venerated and idealized, serves for unmarried clergy as a compensating figure with whom they can experience intimacy, loving-kindness, femininity and motherliness in a 'spiritual way'. In Shiite Islam Fatimah, the ascetic and hard-working daughter of the Prophet who is orientated on the family, serves as an example and role model against both Western consumerism and the widespread enslavement of the women by their fathers and then by their husbands. So she can become a symbol of freedom, equality and integrity.

However, this does not make the position of women in Islam satisfactory, and this disturbs many women today. According to official Sunni teaching,[34] women may not offer prayer in the mosque in the company of men. In political activity, the exercise of public office and jurisprudence, women are subject to restrictions, as they are under laws relating to marriage and children and in professional activity. Contacts between men and women are not allowed outside the domestic sphere, as the public sphere is reserved for men.

The restriction of the role of women to the domestic sphere has a negative effect on the whole of society. According to recent research, one of the main reasons for the lack of competitiveness in the Islamic states, from Morocco to Iran, is a lack of working women: 'Among the fifteen states in the world with the lowest quota of working women, thirteen are Arab or Islamic.' The more open a regime is to the non-Islamic world, the higher is the quota of working women: 'However, it would be wrong to put all the blame for the low quota of working women on the Islamic system of faith. Working women are also the exception in Arab countries with secular regimes such as Syria and Iraq.' Things look very different in more eastern Muslim countries: 'Bangladesh (42.3%), Indonesia (40.6%) and Malaysia (37.7%) are examples of how not all states with a majority Muslim population necessarily want to do without half their national talents and capabilities.'[35] In Turkey, in both percentage and actual terms, the number of female university professors is higher than it is in Germany.

Muslim women for women's rights

Under the influence of the European and American women's movements, in Islam too a beginning has been made on investigating which aspects of the role of women are originally Islamic and which are culture-dependent, resembling what happened in neighbouring ancient cultures. Some women today see the Qur'an as the main support for an improvement of their status.

Like other Muslim women,[36] the Pakistani professor Riffat Hassan of the University of Louisville, Kentucky,[37] has concentrated on the position of women in the Qur'an. She blames the hadith literature and patriarchal jurists (P II–III) for forcing Qur'anic statements about the equal rights of women into the background and bringing particular verses of the Qur'an into the foreground as evidence for male superiority. Surah 4.34 is particularly famous (or notorious): 'Men shall take full care of women with the bounties which God has bestowed more abundantly on the former than on the latter, and with what they may spend out of their possessions. And the righteous women are the truly devout ones, who guard the intimacy that God has [ordained to be] guaranteed. And as for those women whose ill-will you have reason to fear, admonish them [first]; then leave them alone in bed; then beat them.' According to Riffat Hassan, if this verse is looked at more closely, there is nothing about the husband (as *qawamuna*) being ruler over his wives; rather, it speaks of him as their protector; the root word *daraba* has other meanings than 'beat'. Unfortunately the three stages of the 'taming of a refractory woman'—conversation, avoiding the marital bed and beating—have normally been understood in the current sense, indeed have been used by some Muslims to justify acts of violence against their wives. Islamic penal law goes considerably beyond the Qur'an and commands that adulteresses should be beaten or stoned.

The Islamic expert Johann Christoph Bürgel, of the University of Berne, has pointed out with reference to Arabic and Persian sources that even before Islam Arab women had an inferior position and numerous limitations were imposed on them by the Qur'an.[38] Riffat Hassan does not deny this but contests what was laid down by the Shariah, 'derived' from the Qur'an and Sunnah: the unconditional duty of obedience of wives towards husbands, the right of the husband to marry up to four wives and also to buy an unlimited number of concubines on the slave market; and finally the right to cast off a wife at any time without giving a reason, indeed to kill her if she is unfaithful to him. Women are permanently disadvantaged in the law of inheritance (the woman's share is half that of the man) and in courts, where they may speak as witnesses only in civil trials, not in serious criminal cases. But there have to be two women with one man—if there are not two men.[39] In one hadith the wife is described as the husband's captive; even the great theologian al-Ghazali (P IV) gives ten reasons for this, though he concludes that the husband must therefore treat the wife mercifully. That makes all the more welcome the appointment of women in various Islamic states as social ministers, education ministers or culture ministers and the elections of Benazir Bhutto as prime minister of Pakistan (in 1989 and 1993) and of Tansu Çiller as prime minister of Turkey (1993). The award of the Nobel Peace Prize in 2003 to the Iranian jurist and human rights activist Shirin Ebadi, whose work for equal rights was internationally recognized as representative of many others, is particularly noteworthy.[40]

In most modern Muslim world states, the Shariah has been replaced by secular law with a Western orientation (with the removal of the *shari'ah* and *fiqh*, described as *qanun*). Even in countries such as Saudi Arabia, Western elements have been tacitly incorporated into the legal system and therefore many discriminatory principles no longer apply (P V). Thus the Qur'anic demand for equal and just treatment for all wives is often interpreted as an indirect invitation to monogamy and in more recent marriage contracts, marriage with a second wife is excluded. However, in principle, most of the traditional laws concerning family and inheritance, which in many respects are contrary to human rights, remain in force and still have a major influence on the behaviour of people in everyday life, political and private. In Egypt in 1999, a draft government law that would have allowed women to leave a violent husband was rejected by the conservative majority in parliament, despite being supported by the Supreme Mufti of the land. The discrepancy between the claims of the Shariah and the context of modernity becomes particularly clear when different cultures meet: if, for example, Western wives live in Islamic countries[41] or second- and third-generation Islamic girls and women live in Western countries. The worldwide indignation at the sentence of stoning passed on Amina Lawal of northern Nigeria (where the Shariah had been once again introduced)[42] shows that there is an urgent need for critical reflection on the Shariah. The sentence was eventually repealed by the Nigerian central government.

Indisputably, many Muslim societies still do not regard women as having equal rights, even within marriage, despite the affirmation of the fundamental equality of man and woman before God in the Qur'an. In general, men have a legal pre-eminence which has extremely insidious effects on society. However, in recent decades the number of women writers, and the literary quality of their work (whether poetic, journalistic or academic), has increased considerably. It has given powerful help to the women's emancipation movement, whether organized or not.[43] The Pakistani feminist Riffat Hassan agrees with the Moroccan sociologist Fatima Mernissi when she writes:

> An important characteristic of Muslim sexuality is its territoriality, which reflects a specific concept of society and power. The territoriality of Muslim sexuality defines status, tasks and the pattern of authority. Kept within narrow bounds spatially, the woman has been materially looked after by the man who possessed her as a reward for her absolute obedience and her sexual and reproductive services. The whole system was organized in such a way that the Islamic 'Ummah' in fact represented a society of citizens who among other things also possessed the female half of the population ... Muslim men had increasingly more rights and privileges than Muslim women, even including the right to kill their wives ... The husband compelled the wife to an existence which was constricted both physically and intellectually.[44]

In a constructive and profound way Mernissi has investigated both the hadith which are hostile to women and the verses in the Qur'an which are friendly to women and in all this has brought out how well disposed the Prophet was towards women.[45]

The circumcision of girls and young women (*khafd* or *khifad*) is a particularly dramatic example of a traditional attitude to feminine sexuality. Like the circumcision of boys, this is probably a pre-Islamic custom which was taken over by Islam and in many Islamic countries was part of the preparation of girls for marriage. The Qur'an does not mention the circumcision of either boys or girls; the latter was not regarded as obligatory, merely commended.[46]

Today, this practice, in which either the foreskin of the clitoris or the whole organ and sometimes parts of the inner labia are removed, is increasingly recognized as cruel genital mutilation, not only because every year a considerable number of girls die from the consequences of the intervention but also because it markedly impairs sexual feelings. Nevertheless, genital mutilation is still customary today in twenty-eight countries (mainly African) and affects four thousand girls a day—despite the fact that in some of these countries, such as Egypt, it is forbidden by law.

The insight that genital mutilation represents a severe violation of the human right to bodily integrity was not established until the second half of the twentieth century. In December 1993, the UN General Assembly spelt out the formulations of the concluding document of the UN Conference on Human Rights in Vienna with its own Declaration on the Abolition of Violence against Women. Among countless forms of human rights violations against women, in both the private and the public spheres, this mentions genital mutilation and other traditional practices which violate women. Great contributions towards developing awareness here have been made by personal testimonies of women who have themselves been victims of genital mutilation. One example is Waris Dirie of Somalia, whose autobiography *Desert Flower* became a bestseller in twenty-one countries and who is now active all over the world as a special ambassador of the United Nations Organization against the circumcision of women.[47] Women's rights organizations have now taken up this problem, for example in Germany 'Terre des Femmes', which is based in Tübingen.[48] The initiative Target, launched by Rüdiger Nehberg and his Pro-Islamic Alliance against Genital Mutilation, which includes Muslims, is also very effective.

Even Saudi Arabia has taken up the fight for the rights of women, as is shown by the third round of the national dialogue in Medina in June 2004, which the government proposed should be devoted for the first time to the question of women.[49] A vigorous challenge was made not only to the universal ban on driving for women, for which there is no direct Qur'anic justification, but above all to the Saudi laws which require a male guardian in the first degree of affinity (*mahram*) for almost every action in the public sphere (buying tickets, travelling, banking, business transactions, etc.). The Saudi rulers make it possible for tens of thousands of women to study and engage in diplomacy but so far the pressure that women have exerted in efforts to have a part in professional life has not led to an opening up of the male world. Instead, parallel worlds of schools, banks and even shopping centres purely for women have been created, which have only virtual connections with the male world (through the telephone, video, internet). A manifesto by around a hundred clergy shows the degree to which the Islamic justification of patriarchal customs of Bedouin society within Arabia is preventing a professional discussion. Following the example of 'A'ishah, the Prophet's wife, who rode her camel through the desert, one day around fifty women they drove their cars through Riyadh. They were given prison sentences.

Despite everything, the fight for women's rights is not hopeless as is shown, for example, by Morocco. Unexpectedly, its young king Muhammad VI proposed a new family law which was accepted on 23 January 2004 with few changes. The obligation for wives to be obedient to their husbands was abolished and the family was made the responsibility of both partners. The age at which women might marry was raised from fifteen to eighteen.[50]

Don't misunderstand me: in the long history of Christianity there are many parallels to many practices in Islam hostile to women. The actual social position of women often depends less on religion than on the social environment and cultural setting. What is customary in modern districts of Cairo or Istanbul can be taboo in country areas or in the suburban settlements which have come into being as a result of flights from the land. That makes it all the more important for shared life in the twentieth century that all Abrahamic religions should agree on some principles which at present are still recognized and implemented in the various religions in very different ways. These might be:

- Instead of the subordination of wives to husbands, which is not of the essence of marriage, there should be equal dignity and rights for women.
- Child marriage, the marriage of girls without their consent and the confinement of women to the house are archaic customs with no basis in revelation.
- Responsibly practised birth control and, if need be, abortion are not a matter for a state, religious or medical institution; they are solely the affair of the woman concerned.
- Given the fact that in many places the structures of leadership and power are still largely dominated by men, there is an urgent need to press for equal education (including university study) of women and equal involvement in public and political life, including access to leadership roles.

4. Reforms are indispensable

For a long time, neither Christianity nor Islam was very tolerant of minorities, 'those of other faiths', 'unbelievers', and drastic corporal punishment was inflicted.

Protection of minorities?

The balance sheet of the Catholic Church is also extremely ambiguous in respect of the protection of minorities: the church of the persecuted all too quickly became the church of the persecutor. In the church after Constantine, from the time of the emperor Theodosius (died 395) onwards, heresy was regarded as a crime against the state: the enemy of the church was also the enemy of the empire and was punished accordingly. The first executions of Christian heretics took place in Trier in 385. Since the Middle Ages, the dreaded name of the Inquisition has filled the darkest pages of church history: 1209 saw the first crusade against fellow-Christians, the Cathar Albigensians in southern France, and later came the persecution of women who 'stood out' in religious, physical and social terms; many thousands were burned as witches. The crusades against the Muslims played a central role in this 'criminal history of Christianity': during the first three crusades there were fearful massacres of Jews in France, in the Rhineland, in Bohemia and Palestine. Luther's heated discourses against 'enthusiasts', peasants and Jews, along with the inquisition, torture and the stake in Calvin's Reformed Geneva also hardly bear witness to a 'church of freedom and love'.

Compared to the church and worldly leaders of Christianity, in many respects Islam proved to be more tolerant. The *dhimmi* status of Christian and Jewish minorities made it possible for them to live a tolerable life (with guarantee of life and property) but rights were very limited, even in tolerant Moorish Spain (see C IV, 7). However, here too, in the final phase of the *reconquista*, the Inquisition murdered thousands of Jews by burning and in 1402 gave them the stark alternative of 'baptism or emigration': around one hundred thousand Jews emigrated. The Islamic empire proved tolerant and hospitable; later, Christian minorities and dissidents often preferred life under Muslim rule to persecution by their fellow-Christians in the Byzantine or Habsburg empires. All in all, Islam has a better record of religious toleration than Christianity.

However, in neither Christian nor Muslim countries was there freedom of religion in the modern sense. According to the 'Laws of 'Umar' (see C I, 5), in theory the rules for Jews and Christians were: no Muslims as slaves, no houses higher than those of Muslim neighbours, no riding on horses, no new houses of God, no prominent practice of their own religion and the prescription of special dress and special taxes (land tax and poll tax). Although non-Muslim religions had considerable autonomy in respect of self-administration, family law and religious law, pluralistic forms of society could not form spontaneously. At best there were enclaves of communities with a Jewish or Christian structure. Jews and Christians were forbidden to marry Muslim wives but a Muslim might marry several wives from other religions.

Against this background, we can formulate more clearly where Islamic teachings are in conflict with human rights as articulated in the 1948 UN Declaration:

– Prohibition of mixed marriages: Muslim men may marry one or more non-Muslim women but Muslim women may not marry non-Muslim men. This guarantees that the children are brought up as Muslims and thus Muslim society is not weakened. In a patriarchal system, it is presupposed that the husband controls the education of the children, so Muslim domination is guaranteed.

– Intolerance against 'unbelievers' (polytheists and atheists): 'Slay those who ascribe divinity to aught beside God wherever you may come upon them, and lie in wait for them at every conceivable place.'[51] 'Fight against those who do not believe in either God or the Last Day and do not consider forbidden that which God and His Apostle have forbidden, and do not follow the religion of truth.'[52] However, 'unbelievers' living in certain countries are in practice treated as 'non-Muslim believers'; otherwise it would have been impossible for Muslims and non-Muslims to live together, for example as in India.

– Drastic corporal punishment (*hudud* punishments: *hadd*, 'limit', as the punishment is laid down by God in the Qur'an and Sunnah). This includes eighty lashes for drinking alcohol or false accusations of adultery; cutting off the right, then the left hand, and finally the right and left foot in cases of (repeated) theft and stoning for adultery.

Fortunately these punishments are seldom imposed today and are totally absent from the law books of most Islamic states. However, Saudi Arabia has retained them on the basis of the Shariah and other states such as Nigeria, Iran, Pakistan and Sudan have reintroduced them. Unlike amputation, flogging is still widespread. I shall examine this again in the context of state and religion (see E III), in connection with the death penalty threatened in Saudi Arabia in cases of 'apostasy'.

Is the Shariah simply a code of life?

Christianity is no stranger to inhuman punishments, as we can see from the 'Christian' Middle Ages. Then, too, people were flogged, tortured, mutilated, impaled and beheaded with an appeal to God and his word. Freethinkers, heretics, 'apostates' and above all women who were alleged to be witches had to fear the fire. In principle Christians were certainly not better than Muslims. However, all that happened in the Middle Ages and in early modern times; in the Enlightenment, under secular but also Christian influences, the European states emancipated themselves from this justice practised by state and church. These social changes were also accompanied by a change in the sense of justice. Physical integrity was recognized to be an essential expression of human dignity, even in criminal law, to the degree that Article 5 of the Universal Declaration of Human Rights states: 'No one shall be subjected to torture or to cruel, inhuman or degrading treatment or punishment.'

So, despite all the arguments for the Shariah, Christians and Muslims must be allowed to ask: how long will the justification of inhuman practices with an appeal to the divine origin of the Qur'an go on? How long will conservative Muslims still be able to claim that such cruel punishments are the rights and punishments of the just God himself? May they suggest that human behaviour has hardly improved since the Middle Ages? Surely theft (punished with cutting off the hands) and adultery (punished with stoning) are now about the restoration of trust in a particular society and its most important institutions, property and family? Are mercy, humanity and liberality appropriate only in the implementation and adaptation of those unchangeable divine norms that apply beyond time? Are human rights to apply only because and in so far as the divine law of the Qur'an applies—and therefore not in the same way for men *and* women, Muslims *and* non-Muslims?

This is the problem: can medieval sacral law, in which independent legal opinion was largely sacrificed to the consensus of the Sunni law schools, still be applied literally, even to Christians and Jews living in the Muslim sphere or to foreigners who have immigrated? The issue here is not merely of distance in time but of application and implementation, use and misuse, understanding and misunderstanding—and so of more than reformation. Can an Islamic law, formed more than a thousand years ago on the basis of the Qur'an and Sunnah, which attempted to regulate the whole of life (at that time!) in minute detail but finds it impossible to regulate whole spheres of life (today!) such as science, technology and industry, serve as *the* code of life and form of life in the completely different social conditions of the twenty-first century?

Since the development of Qur'anic exegesis, the majority of Muslims have accepted that there are some surahs which mitigate or even abolish (*nasikh* and *mansukh* = 'obliterating' and 'obliterated'). It is also well known that many commandments and prohibitions were bound up with practical experiences which are quite different today. Muslims attach the utmost importance to the rationality of their religion and therefore the Shariah is seldom applied fully and completely. As in real Catholicism, so too in real Islam, there is a considerable gulf between the formal ideal of the law and its material reality. Muslims, too, ask whether this gulf can be bridged. Only a differentiated and corrective interpretation, not direct abolition, promises real progress—in the sense of also being able to live out Islam in completely changed conditions. How could such an interpretation be justified within Islam?

Towards a modern Shariah

Muslims affirm that Qur'anic verses from the Mecca period emphasize the freedom of faith and equal dignity of all human beings regardless of faith and gender but verses of the Medina period restrict the rights of women and non-Muslims. Discrimination against women and non-Muslims is intensified when legal scholars regard the verses from the Mecca period as being 'abrogated, abolished' by the later verses from Medina. By contrast, the Sudanese Muslim legal scholar Abdullahi Ahmed an-Na'im (who is able to put forward his view only in North America) conjectures that 'this process of abrogation should be reversed in order to develop a modern version of the Shariah which guarantees the equal rights of women and non-Muslims. Before that can happen, however, we must openly concede and identify the discrimination contained in the historical formulations of the Shariah ... Reference may not only be made to the way in which the Qur'an has been interpreted; it must also integrate the Sunnah and other sources of the Shariah, because that is the context in which the Qur'an is understood and used by Muslims.'[53]

This conceals a fundamental problem, expressed by an- Na'im's teacher, the engineer, scholar and mystic Mahmud Muhammad Taha.[54] Taha was highly respected in the Sudanese capital Khartoum but executed by the dictator Numeiri in 1985 at the age of seventy-six. Taha and his followers, the Republican Brothers, had argued for a modernization of Islamic teaching and the Shariah, claming that a distinction had to be made between the abiding valid message of the Mecca surahs and the time-conditioned application of them to the society of the time in the Medina surahs. Taha called for a scholarly exegesis of the Qur'an and Shariah for the present day, instead of a fundamentalist and literal exegesis of Islamic law (the Shariah of President Numeiri, reintroduced two years before his fall).

The question is not just for the Sudan: in the twenty-first century, can such reformers still be condemned as heretics and atheists and even executed publicly as 'apostates'? This is a particularly serious violation of human rights. Happily, the post-Numeiri Sudan government supported freedom of religion and withdrew strict Shariah punishments such as stoning or amputating hands. Yet, even in 2001, the newly-elected president Ahmed al-Bashir invited Sudanese men to marry several wives because of underpopulation, the many war widows and the fact that the Qur'an not only allowed but demanded polygamy (which is not in fact true). Be this as it may, peace negotiations began in Switzerland in 2002 between representatives of the Arab Muslim Sudanese government (in the north) and the Sudan People's Liberation Army (SPLA, Christian animist, in the south) to end the civil war which had broken out in 1983. In his Global Ethic Lecture, given in Tübingen on 12 December 2003, the UN secretary-general Kofi Annan expressed his well-founded hope that a peace treaty in the Sudan could be achieved in a relatively short time. Peace would also relax the controversial attitudes to the Shariah.

Ahmed an-Na'im is convinced that 'the historical version of the Shariah is incapable of preserving the most fundamental human rights today'. The mistake does not lie in the historical Shariah, which the early Muslims attempted to interpret in the light of their own historical context, 'in order to create a coherent and practicable system which achieved important improvements in human rights compared to its predecessors and contemporaries'. However, he argues, it is the right and duty of present-day Muslims to do what was done then, 'to create a modern Shariah for the present, radically changed context'.[55]

Islam today—like Roman Catholicism before the Second Vatican Council—needs to implement a double paradigm change: not just that of the Reformation but also that of modernity, the Enlightenment. It is important to make a great leap from the Middle Ages, over modernity, into postmodernity. In this situation, anyone on the Western side who simply calls for human rights by pointing the finger runs the risk of falling into ideological narrow-mindedness.

General ethical framework: rights and responsibilities

Many Muslim fears about the dissolution of community bonds as a result of human rights seem to us in the West unjustified, at least in theory. In practice, however, Western societies look different: shaped, often split and frequently undermined by unfettered individualism, selfish libertinism and random pluralism. Many Muslim objections (and those of other religious communities) could be countered if human responsibilities were emphasized as well as human rights and responsibility for society as well as the freedom of the individual. For centuries, the religions (including Islam) emphasized only human obligations (to God, to the ruler, to employers or parents). However, modern philosophy, the Enlightenment and the American and French Revolutions put the emphasis on rights due to human beings as human beings. It is now important to note that human dignity includes both rights and responsibilities.

Are human rights really an expression of Western cultural imperialism, as Muslims often suspect? It would doubtless be easier for Islamic governments to struggle towards the acknowledgement of human rights if these were not isolated, but put in a general ethical context. The 1948 Universal Declaration of Human Rights was drafted in such a context: the references to 'reason and conscience' and the 'spirit of brotherliness' expressed in its Article 1 clearly presuppose a basic ethical attitude and ethical action. That is even more the case with the concluding Article 29, which contains a clear affirmation that 'everyone has duties to the community' and talks of the 'just requirements of morality, public order and the general welfare in a democratic society'. If human rights are used in the spirit of a power struggle instead of being used in a spirit of brotherliness, concerned for the common good and universal ethical standards, then the unconditional and heedless implementation of them can lead to crude violations of human dignity and inhumanity (for example the 'Terror' and Robespierre's guillotine).

It was the advocate Maximilien Robespierre who, in the revolutionary parliament of 1789, put obstacles in the way of the supplementation of the Declaration of the Rights of Men with an enumeration of human duties ('*les devoirs de l'homme*') which was wanted by almost half the delegates (it was rejected by the Constitutive Assembly in the session of 4 August 1789 by 570 votes to 433). Muslims, Hindus, Buddhists and many other believers in Asia and Africa prize the fact that human obligations are many centuries or even millennia older than the human rights formulated in the European Declaration. A saying of Mahatma Gandhi, who is said to have wanted an extended mention of human responsibilities in the 1948 Declaration, has been handed down: 'The Ganges of rights rises in the Himalaya of responsibilities.'

Most recent discussion of the philosophy of law also comes to this conclusion. The American John Rawls has convincingly demonstrated[56] that a distinction must be made between the concept of political justice, which relates to the most important social institutions, and a comprehensive philosophical and legal doctrine which contains more than rights. In his view human rights do not represent a comprehensive view of the world, a way of life, a criterion for judging the different cultures or a moral ideal. Human rights do not set out to replace the Christian demand for love, the Buddhist ethic of compassion or Muslim solidarity. They make only limited demands, which concentrate on political and legal standards of political justice.[57]

In these circumstances, the question of the foundation for human rights becomes all the more important: a positivistic insistence on the UN Declaration will convince few. It is more important that human rights can be connected with various philosophical or religious doctrinal systems, ideas and values—Christian, humanist and particularly also Islamic. They do not do away with the pluralism of cultures, religions and philosophies but presuppose them. Human dignity is a central concept which has its roots in various European cultures[58] and includes a fundamental obligation to the reciprocal recognition of human beings. This inalienable dignity of each human being can be grounded in many ways: in Judaism and Christianity (human beings as the image of God), in Stoic philosophy (universal reason) and also in Islam (the human being as God's creature and deputy). In so far as human rights presuppose and promote human dignity they of course also influence the different religions and societies over and beyond law and politics and contribute to their humanization. They are also norms for the religions, if these seek to be human and not inhuman.

So human rights and human responsibilities belong together. They are the two sides of human dignity:

- Human rights without human responsibilities lead to self-opinionatedness, legal disputes and pseudo-righteous wars.
- Human responsibilities without human rights lead to authoritarianism, blind obedience and dictatorship. Respect for human rights may never be made dependent on the fulfilment of certain human responsibilities, for example towards the state.

Human rights are rights of the individual but not individualistic rights. Everywhere they presuppose the social dimension and should always be seen in the context of the human community. Therefore the Declaration of Human Rights speaks not only of individual freedom of thought, conscience and religion but also of the religious community and the public practice of religion.[59] There is also express mention of the family as the 'natural and fundamental unity of society', which 'has a claim to protection from society and the state'.[60] Social, economic and cultural rights have equal value to civic and political human rights.

The Norwegian Johan Galtung is a pioneer in research into peace and conflict. In the 1960s and 1970s he analysed the compulsions imposed on the individual from a system of domination as forms of 'structural violence'. In his creative reflections on the future of human rights, he remarked: 'What we are looking for is a thick cocoon made up of reciprocal rights and responsibilities—of individuals, for individuals and about individuals. Neither rights nor responsibilities are enough by themselves. The key word is *sympathy*, embedded in individuals and about individuals.' On the way to a 'more intensive, richer culture of ethics than the one that we have today in many places', he argues for a 'balanced normative input' for human rights in which, so far, the impulses of Jewish–Christian normative culture are strongly represented. It will certainly encourage Muslims when he asks: 'But what contribution can Islam make? How can an institution such as the *zakat*, a mandatory tax on the poor, be integrated into this plan? It makes it a duty for everyone to make a contribution to the satisfaction of others ... What is there against the United Nations taking an Islamic norm as a model for the benefit of all non-Muslims?'[61]

E III

The Future of Islamic State Order and Politics

Many Muslim states are ruled by autocrats who claim the unlimited power of the state for themselves in the name of God (or in the name of the people). Such autocratic regimes conflict with democracy, the 'rule of the people by the people for the people', to quote the classic definition formulated by the US president Abraham Lincoln in his speech on the battlefield of Gettysburg on 9 November 1863, at the end of the Civil War. Are the USA and the West doing enough to promote democracy in a peaceful way in Iraq, in Saudi Arabia, in the Arab world and indeed in the Islamic world generally?

1. State and religion—united or separated?

In the West, many people argue that this system of the sovereignty of the people, bound up with a separation of powers (legislative, executive and judicial), is incompatible with Islam. I think differently, but I do see the problem. So in this chapter I shall first illuminate the relationship of the three prophetic religions to 'power' in the positive sense (*potestas, pouvoir*), that is, to legitimate power, whether grounded in God or in society. Then I shall discuss the relationship of the three religions to power in the negative sense (*vis, violentia, violence*), that is, to repressive power, which is what legitimate power becomes where it is exercised apart from or contrary to the will of the citizens.[1]

A trilateral comparison

It is a widespread cliché in the West that Islam identifies the state and religion, whereas Christianity distinguishes between them. But it isn't as simple as that.

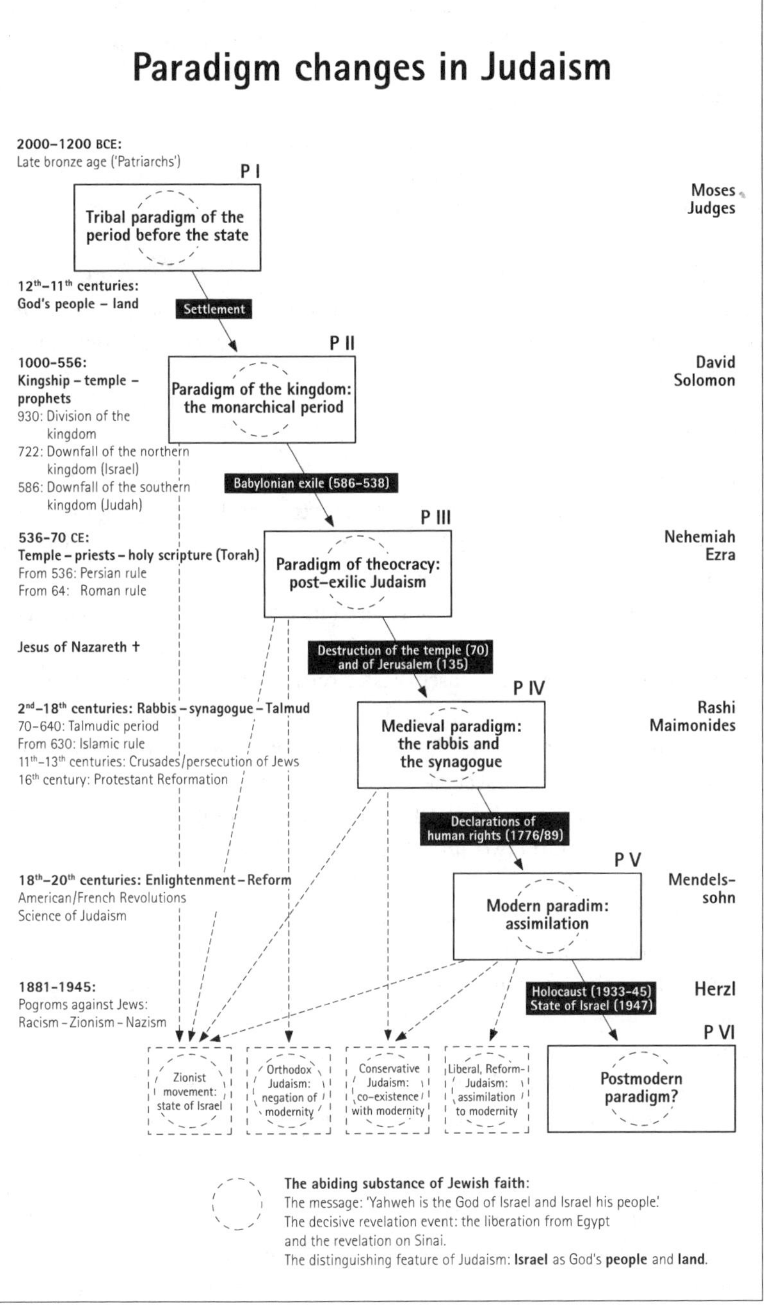
Paradigm changes in Judaism
2000–1200 BCE:
Late bronze age ('Patriarchs')
P I
Tribal paradigm of the period before the state
Moses
Judges
12th–11th centuries:
God's people – land
Settlement
P II
1000–556:
Kingship – temple – prophets
930: Division of the kingdom
722: Downfall of the northern kingdom (Israel)
586: Downfall of the southern kingdom (Judah)
Paradigm of the kingdom: the monarchical period
David
Solomon
Babylonian exile (586–538)
P III
536–70 CE:
Temple – priests – holy scripture (Torah)
From 536: Persian rule
From 64: Roman rule
Paradigm of theocracy: post-exilic Judaism
Nehemiah
Ezra
Jesus of Nazareth †
Destruction of the temple (70) and of Jerusalem (135)
P IV
2nd–18th centuries: Rabbis – synagogue – Talmud
70–640: Talmudic period
From 630: Islamic rule
11th–13th centuries: Crusades/persecution of Jews
16th century: Protestant Reformation
Medieval paradigm: the rabbis and the synagogue
Rashi
Maimonides
Declarations of human rights (1776/89)
P V
18th–20th centuries: Enlightenment – Reform
American/French Revolutions
Science of Judaism
Modern paradim: assimilation
Mendels-sohn
1881–1945:
Pogroms against Jews:
Racism – Zionism – Nazism
Holocaust (1933–45)
State of Israel (1947)
Herzl
P VI
Zionist movement: state of Israel
Orthodox Judaism: negation of modernity
Conservative Judaism: co-existence with modernity
Liberal, Reform-Judaism: assimilation to modernity
Postmodern paradigm?
The abiding substance of Jewish faith:
The message: 'Yahweh is the God of Israel and Israel his people.'
The decisive revelation event: the liberation from Egypt and the revelation on Sinai.
The distinguishing feature of Judaism: Israel as God's people and land.

The question of the unity or separation of religion and state is a problem for all three prophetic religions: a problem which poses itself in different ways at different periods of history and which has led to a diversity of models of this relationship with different nuances. A trilateral method can be instructive in analysing it. On the basis of the analysis of the different paradigms and paradigm changes in the three religions worked out in this trilogy, I can now offer a comparative account which allows a differentiated picture for discussion of the options for the future.

To simplify the diachronic–synchronic comparison of paradigms, I shall recapitulate the paradigm changes in Judaism, Christianity and Islam which form the temporal and spatial framework for developments in different spheres of life and society.

Religion and state in Judaism

Judaism[2] did not begin as a state society but as a tribal society (P I). Only under King David (*c.* 1000 BCE) did a first relatively extensive Israelite kingdom come into being, with internal political divisions; it had Jerusalem as its political and religious centre (P II). Around seventy years after David's accession there was a fatal split of the kingdom into the northern kingdom of Israel (with Samaria as its capital) and the southern kingdom of Judah (with Jerusalem as its capital). The period of the Israelite monarchy lasted only around four hundred years—up to the destruction of Jerusalem and the First Temple (of Solomon) and the deportation of the whole upper class to Babylon in the sixth century. If we pass over the interlude of the Maccabaean period, this was the end of the political and state independence of the Jewish people and of Jerusalem as the capital of a Jewish state—for around two and a half millennia, until the refounding of the state of Israel in 1948.

After the Babylonian exile, the state and political order changed fundamentally. In the following centuries political power lay first with the Persians, then with Alexander the Great and his Greek followers, then with the Romans and finally, up to the twentieth century, with the Muslims. The theocracy of the temple hierarchy that formed after the exile (P III) did not extend to the state but only to the community of Yahweh believers—by means of the priesthood (hierocracy) and the law of God now collected in writings (nomocracy). The separation of religion and state was enforced by the occupying power. After the defeat of the Jews in the national religious war against Rome, Jerusalem and the Second Temple were destroyed in 70 CE.

The end of the theocracy had come and the long Jewish Middle Ages began. Until the eighteenth century in Europe this was shaped by the paradigm of the rabbis and the synagogue (P IV). Judaism was no longer a national religion, since by far the greater part of the Jews lived 'among the nations', dispersed all over the world from the Hindu Kush to Gibraltar in the Diaspora ('dispersion'). In the Christian empire they formed a minority subject to more and more restrictions, so that in Palestine, in particular, the Muslim conquest in 638 was felt to be liberation from Byzantium. In the Western Latin empire the Byzantine restrictions were accentuated. During the period of the crusades and in the centuries that followed, there were more and more pogroms and massacres of Jews. There were numerous forcible measures even at the time of the Reformation and even more in the Counter-Reformation, with its anti-Jewish popes. However, Judaism survived: through the oral Torah, fixed in the Talmud, the Hebrew language and the continued teaching of Torah and Talmud from generation to generation through feasts and religious custom—all this supported by the authority of the rabbis. There was no need for a Jewish state.

Not until the Enlightenment and the French Revolution, as we saw, were individual Jews given human and civil rights and eventually integrated legally, politically and socially into the modern nation state (P V). This process often led to assimilation, but was brutally interrupted by National Socialism and totally broken off by the catastrophe of the Holocaust. Only the foundation of the state of Israel again helped the people of the Jews towards existence as a state. Yet the great hope of the visionary pioneer Theodor Herzl, that Israel would become a model democratic state, was deceptive from the beginning and was destroyed by the regime of occupation which has lasted since 1967 and finally by the state terrorism in Palestine.

From the beginning, the Orthodox religious parties have not allowed either civil marriage or civil divorce in the state of Israel—the situation is as it used to be in the authoritarian Catholic states (Italy, Spain, Portugal, Ireland and the countries of Latin America) because Catholicism was the state religion. In some other areas, too, since the founding of the state the regulations of the Jewish religious law (the halakhah) have become state law—as the Shariah is in some Islamic countries. Religious pluralism or a single state religion is Israel's alternative for the future. At the beginning of the twenty-first century Israel is being torn apart between the growing influence of the Orthodox religious on politics and the legal system and the demands of non-religious and liberal Jews for a clearer separation of state and religion, in accordance with the spirit of the time of Israel's foundation. How are things in Christianity?

Separation of religion and state with Jesus of Nazareth?

There is no doctrine of the state in the New Testament. The original Christian community and the apostle Paul lived in expectation of the imminent return of

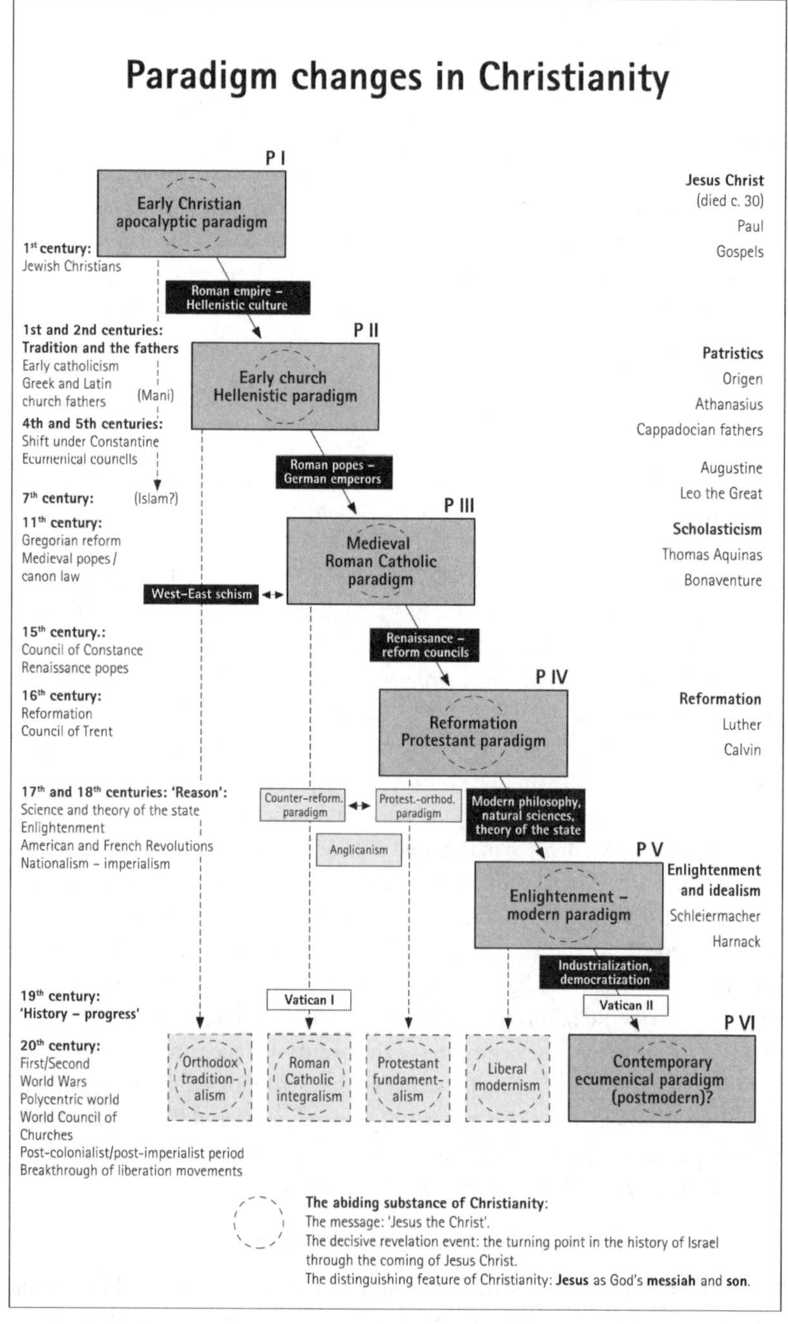

Paradigm changes in Christianity
P I
Early Christian apocalyptic paradigm
Jesus Christ
(died c. 30)
Paul
Gospels
1st century:
Jewish Christians
Roman empire – Hellenistic culture
1st and 2nd centuries:
Tradition and the fathers
Early catholicism
Greek and Latin church fathers
(Mani)
P II
Early church Hellenistic paradigm
Patristics
Origen
Athanasius
Cappadocian fathers
4th and 5th centuries:
Shift under Constantine
Ecumenical councils
Roman popes – German emperors
Augustine
Leo the Great
7th century:
(Islam?)
P III
11th century:
Gregorian reform
Medieval popes / canon law
Medieval Roman Catholic paradigm
Scholasticism
Thomas Aquinas
Bonaventure
West–East schism
15th century.:
Council of Constance
Renaissance popes
Renaissance – reform councils
P IV
16th century:
Reformation
Council of Trent
Reformation Protestant paradigm
Reformation
Luther
Calvin
17th and 18th centuries: 'Reason':
Science and theory of the state
Enlightenment
American and French Revolutions
Nationalism – imperialism
Counter-reform. paradigm
Protest.-orthod. paradigm
Modern philosophy, natural sciences, theory of the state
Anglicanism
P V
Enlightenment – modern paradigm
Enlightenment and idealism
Schleiermacher
Harnack
Industrialization, democratization
19th century:
'History – progress'
Vatican I
Vatican II
P VI
20th century:
First/Second World Wars
Polycentric world
World Council of Churches
Post-colonialist/post-imperialist period
Breakthrough of liberation movements
Orthodox tradition-alism
Roman Catholic integralism
Protestant fundament-alism
Liberal modernism
Contemporary ecumenical paradigm (postmodern)?
The abiding substance of Christianity:
The message: 'Jesus the Christ'.
The decisive revelation event: the turning point in the history of Israel through the coming of Jesus Christ.
The distinguishing feature of Christianity: Jesus as God's messiah and son.

the Lord (P I) and consequently were uninterested in establishing structures of worldly power. However, an evocative saying of Jesus (in the earliest Gospel, Mark 12.17) had given a certain guideline about the power of the state: 'Render to Caesar that which is Caesar's and to God that which is God's.' The historian Leopold von Ranke thought that this was probably Jesus' most important and most momentous saying. That may be putting it too sweepingly, but in comparison with the basic attitude of the Prophet Muhammad, statesman and general (although in a quite different historical and political context), its historical significance is obvious. How are we to understand the saying?[3]

With the help of a Roman silver coin (a dinar) bearing the emperor's image, Jesus gave a disarming answer to the political catch-question whether one should pay the emperor the tax he required. He asked one of his opponents, who evidently used the coin, to give him one and agreed with them: God is to be given what is his; worship and sacrifice are due to him alone. But at the same time the emperor is to be given what is his; Jesus did not reject the emperor's position of power and justice. However, Jesus of Nazareth belonged neither to the religious or the political establishment, which collaborated with the Romans (he was not a priest or rabbi), nor was he an unpolitical enthusiast, the adherent of an apocalyptic anarchism which expected God's intervention against the Roman forces of occupation; nor, finally, was he a political revolutionary, advocate of a theocratic zealotry which hoped to weaken the Roman powers with guerrilla war and conquer them with a military rebellion. Regardless of what historical event may lie behind it, Jesus' cleansing of the temple[4] was not a revolutionary occupation of the temple against the Romans; it was a provocative prophetic symbolic act against the secularization of the house of God by the current practice of piety.

Jesus' saying is not against Roman rule. The Gospels accept state power as a fact: it is not trivialized but relativized and robbed of its absoluteness. Its limits are God's claim and it rules only over the non-godly, secular, 'profane' sphere. For Jesus, state power, in so far as it may and must be criticized, is not demonic or essentially evil but a necessary authority to regulate political problems. The attitude of Jesus' disciples should therefore be neither an anarchistic denial nor an ideological divinization of the state, neither political inwardness nor the politicization of religion, but a life in accordance with God's will, lived for the welfare of neighbours and fellow human beings, in both the divine and the worldly sphere. For the apostle Paul, too, the power of the state—as ordained by God[5]–belongs to the form of this world; the abolition of all earthly power is foreseen only for the end time.[6] However, to give God and the emperor each what is his own is not simple, either for the individual or for a community; it is constantly fraught with conflict.

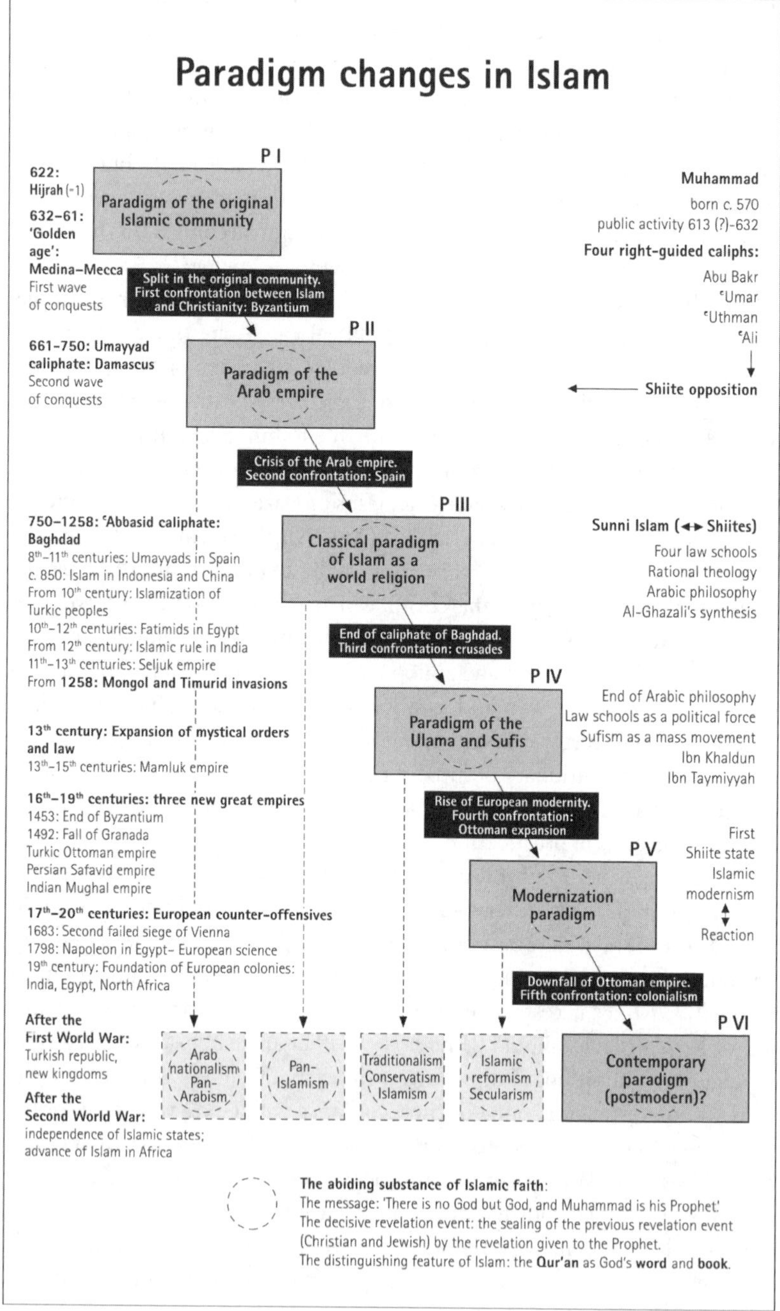
Paradigm changes in Islam
P I
Paradigm of the original Islamic community
622: Hijrah (-1)
632–61: 'Golden age': Medina–Mecca
First wave of conquests
Muhammad
born c. 570
public activity 613 (?)-632
Four right-guided caliphs:
Abu Bakr
ʿUmar
ʿUthman
ʿAli
Shiite opposition
Split in the original community. First confrontation between Islam and Christianity: Byzantium
P II
Paradigm of the Arab empire
661–750: Umayyad caliphate: Damascus
Second wave of conquests
Crisis of the Arab empire. Second confrontation: Spain
P III
Classical paradigm of Islam as a world religion
750–1258: ʿAbbasid caliphate: Baghdad
8th–11th centuries: Umayyads in Spain
c. 850: Islam in Indonesia and China
From 10th century: Islamization of Turkic peoples
10th–12th centuries: Fatimids in Egypt
From 12th century: Islamic rule in India
11th–13th centuries: Seljuk empire
From 1258: Mongol and Timurid invasions
Sunni Islam (◄► Shiites)
Four law schools
Rational theology
Arabic philosophy
Al-Ghazali's synthesis
End of caliphate of Baghdad. Third confrontation: crusades
P IV
Paradigm of the Ulama and Sufis
13th century: Expansion of mystical orders and law
13th–15th centuries: Mamluk empire
End of Arabic philosophy
Law schools as a political force
Sufism as a mass movement
Ibn Khaldun
Ibn Taymiyyah
16th–19th centuries: three new great empires
1453: End of Byzantium
1492: Fall of Granada
Turkic Ottoman empire
Persian Safavid empire
Indian Mughal empire
Rise of European modernity. Fourth confrontation: Ottoman expansion
P V
Modernization paradigm
First Shiite state
Islamic modernism
Reaction
17th–20th centuries: European counter-offensives
1683: Second failed siege of Vienna
1798: Napoleon in Egypt– European science
19th century: Foundation of European colonies: India, Egypt, North Africa
Downfall of Ottoman empire. Fifth confrontation: colonialism
P VI
Contemporary paradigm (postmodern)?
After the First World War: Turkish republic, new kingdoms
After the Second World War: independence of Islamic states; advance of Islam in Africa
Arab nationalism Pan-Arabism
Pan-Islamism
Traditionalism Conservatism Islamism
Islamic reformism Secularism
The abiding substance of Islamic faith:
The message: 'There is no God but God, and Muhammad is his Prophet.'
The decisive revelation event: the sealing of the previous revelation event (Christian and Jewish) by the revelation given to the Prophet.
The distinguishing feature of Islam: the Qur'an as God's word and book.

The different context of the Prophet Muhammad

The situation of the Prophet Muhammad in Arabia, six centuries later, was fundamentally different from that of Jesus of Nazareth in Palestine. Muhammad did not live in an excessively powerful empire with a strict military, political, legal and economic organization. As I have already described (see C I, 4–5), he grew up in the tribal and clan society of a desert people between two empires which, militarily exhausted after decades of a policy of rivalry and revenge, had left behind a political vacuum in the Near East. Arabia at the time of the Prophet Muhammad was a society that was most definitely not a state; it comprised disconnected, mobile and rival tribes and cities.

But the Prophet, too, was not originally the founder of a state and a lawgiver. Only when he was called from Mecca to Medina to overcome the tribal conflicts which had long been endemic there and to integrate the tribes into a commonwealth was he to some degree 'compelled', as a religious authority, to become politically active. This meant building up a commonwealth and functioning as a 'statesman'. On the basis of his prophetic message, he attained a political union with a religious basis. To expect a 'separation of religion and state' in this situation would be to be blind to history.[7]

In retrospect, whether Muhammad had any other option is hardly relevant. What is relevant is that Jesus of Nazareth was fundamentally against war and the use of violence and for non-violence and peace, whereas in order to attain his goals, above all to ensure a peaceful existence for the new society, the prophet from Mecca and Medina accepted the use of violence and war. Thus, the starting points for Islam and Christianity were very different and it would be an unfair simplification to contrast the two religions as a 'religion of battle' and a 'religion of peace'. The different paradigms of Christianity follow the line prescribed by the Christ in word and deed less than the different paradigms of Islam follow Muhammad's line. How could that have come about?

State and religion in Christianity and Islam

The difference between Islam and Christianity in the original phase (P I) is immediately striking. Whereas the Christian church came into being outside the state (first Jewish, then Roman), was in conflict with the state and sometimes even persecuted by it, the original Muslim community formed the core around which the Islamic 'state' was built—at first a confederation of the Arab tribes with Islam as a common religious basis. This Islamic commonwealth was, from the beginning, both a religious and a political community, a 'divine state' whose religious and state institutions were fundamentally identical. State and religion could hardly be separated. Here was the rule of God in the comprehensive sense, of a kind that we also find in Christianity—but only in exceptional cases, for example in the Geneva of the Reformer Calvin, in the Baptist kingdom of Münster and especially in the Roman church state, the foundations of which were laid in the eighth century and which persist today as the Vatican state.

There are exceptions. Even the Christian–Byzantine model of the 'symphony' of throne and altar (P II) differentiated church and state, for all their unity, whereas the first Arab empire, that of the Umayyads (P II), which took over the Byzantine administrative apparatus with many of its organizational structures, remained a theocracy in keeping with its origins—its head was the caliph as God's representative. He had not only political but also religious authority and ultimately even claimed a dynastic succession.

In later Christianity, in the Roman Catholic model under the influence of Augustine and the leadership of the bishops of Rome, despite all the dovetailing of church ('city of God') and state ('city of this world'), an explicit antagonism developed between them. By contrast, in the classical Islamic paradigm of the 'Abbasids (P III), the caliphs of Baghdad, seeking to secure the historical and theological legitimacy of their revolutionary regime, were interested (even more than the former caliphs of Damascus) in their link with the original Islamic caliphs of Medina. Only now were the latter—including the previously defamed 'Ali—regarded as the four 'rightly-guided' caliphs (see the table on page 195, The Prophet's family). The 'Abbasid caliphs (in emphatic opposition to the Umayyad 'kings') again deliberately understood themselves in religious terms as the leaders of the Ummah of all Muslims (both Arabic and non-Arabic) and as champions of a religion which embraced all peoples. They soon far surpassed the Umayyads in absolutism and luxury. As 'commander of the faithful (*amir al-mu'minin*)' and 'God's representative' (thus not just the Prophet's representative), despite considerable differences the caliphs can be compared with the Roman popes after Gregory VII. These popes likewise felt called to rule the world as representatives of 'God' and not just of Peter or Christ but from the start had powerful opponents in the emperors of the Holy Roman empire.

The basic foundations of the Roman Catholic paradigm were first shaken by the epoch-making paradigm change of the Reformation in the sixteenth century (P IV) and a further splitting of Christianity. However, the 'Abbasid paradigm of the caliphate came to a political end as early as the tenth century and disappeared irrevocably in the Mongol storm of the thirteenth. In the regionalization which followed, no 'commander of the faithful' any longer had universal authority in the sphere of Islamic rule: for the first time a separation of state and religious élites or institutions, as it had existed in Latin Christianity long before the Protestant Reformation and was deepened by that Reformation, replaced the former sacral regime of 'God's representative', who determined both religion and politics. In religion, ethics and law believing Muslims were no longer guided by the caliphs and sultans but by the Ulama and Sufis (P IV). In the paradigm without a caliph, Islam would no more have survived without Ulama and Sufis than Judaism after the fall of the Second Temple and its priests would have survived without the rabbis.

To this degree the three great Islamic empires that came into being at the beginning of European modernity, the Ottoman even more than the Persian and the Indian, were already prepared for the wider separation of state and religion prompted by European modernization (P V), as promoted radically under the last Ottoman sultans and implemented by Atatürk. In 1918, the thousand-year era of the Christian state came to an end in Germany and the Austro-Hungarian empire, as the 560-year-old era of the Muslim state did in Istanbul. Since then a pluralistic democracy has been increasingly established in Europe; however, as we have seen, there are several options for Muslim states, from the secularist Turkish model of the state to the conservative Saudi Arabian model of the monarchy. None satisfies the majority of Muslims. Fundamental questions arise here.

2. Secularity without secularism

Is any institutionalization of religion bad? The institutionalization of Christianity within the framework of a secular empire should not be interpreted simplistically in retrospect by a Protestant theory of decline as 'falling away from Christ and his gospel'. Nor, however, should it be interpreted along the lines of a Roman Catholic glorification as a 'victory of Christ and his church'. Rather, it should be regarded as an almost unavoidable, but ambivalent, process of socio-political development. Islamic institutionalization cannot be seen as negative only because the confession of Islam became a relationship of loyalty resembling a law and thus supportive of the state, and a criterion for the citizen's loyalty to an Islamic state. However, this process, too, is ambivalent and needs a critical survey.[8]

Farewell to aggressive universalistic Christian and Muslim claims

In these socio-political developments Christians often overlook and ignore the fact that both Christianity and Islam have made aggressive claims to universality and have preached and practised an ideology of war rather than peace. Not only in Islam but also in Christianity, above all in Roman Catholic Christianity up to the Second Vatican Council (1962–5), the starting points were that:

- one's own religion was in full possession of the truth and represented the best and most perfect society;

- one's own religion had a privileged place and if other faith communities were recognized at all, they were to be granted only limited freedoms and possibilities of development;
- one's own religion should therefore be the state religion and one could not be content with a religiously indifferent, neutral state;
- one's own order of life, sanctioned by God's authority, was universally valid and therefore binding on all communities and states;
- one had an obligation to extend one's own religious sphere of rule as far as possible and to use political means for this mission, to bring about a society with a unitary religion embracing as many people as possible: the final goal was the conversion of all men and women to one's own God and the establishment of one's own religion all over the world.

Defensive wars against attackers (Huns, the Germanic migration, Arabs, Turks) who threatened the West were once unavoidable for historical self-assertion. Conversely, Muslim peoples must be granted the right to self-defence in the cases of the crusades and of European and American colonialism and imperialism. However, for both Islam and Christianity, the final goal of the victory of the religion has proved unattainable and illusory. Moreover, this is theologically in conflict with statements of faith in both religions, to the effect that it is for God himself to bring in the goal of history. There are more realistic political alternatives and alternatives with a religious foundation.

Future perspectives for Islam and Christianity

What follows from my comparison of paradigms with respect to religion and state for the Islam and Christianity of the future?[9]

- There is no such thing as 'the' Islamic state and 'the' Christian state, serving as a criterion for all time. Like Christianity, Islam has very different views and forms of the relationship between religion and state.
- In its historical development, Christianity came to be more in conflict with its founder-figure, who called for non-violence and peaceableness, than did Islam, which can appeal to the Prophet for the use of violence and wars.
- From its origin Christianity has tended more towards a distinction between religion and state, and Islam more to their identification. This meant that Christianity was better prepared than Islam for the autonomy of numerous spheres of life called for in the modernization process.
- In both Christianity and Islam, over the course of history, original impulses and ideals were often overlaid by authoritarian political power-structures. Just as, for example, Luther's Reformation did not simply lead to the realization of a free Christian church, so too Ibn 'Abd al-Wahhab's reform did

not lead to a Muslim Ummah in keeping with the origins but to a new princely rule.

- Neither the Christian character of the state called for by the popes up to the middle of the twentieth century, nor the Islamic character, still propagated by the Ulama of the twenty-first, are compatible with the secularity of the modern state and the separation of state and religion. A modern democracy rests on legislation, independent justice, the political separation of powers, an efficient administration, a critical public and a lively civil society.

The conclusion for the future is that the secularity (worldliness) of the state, which guarantees freedom of religion, does not contradict the essence of Christianity or Islam. This essence does, however, conflict with a total secularization in the spirit of an ideological secularism (hostility to religion) which seeks to banish religion completely from public life. Here a special question arises for both religions: that of 'apostasy'.

Religious freedom—even to change religion?

According to the United Nations Universal Declaration of Human Rights, freedom of religion as a human right includes freedom of faith and conscience, freedom to belong to a religious confession or no religion, and freedom to engage in private and public worship. This essentially includes—and this is the critical point, which calls for investigation—freedom also to change religion: to give up the religion into which one has been born or which one chose. Within the group concerned this is often called apostasy from the faith, an extremely sensitive matter even among pseudo- and non-religious ideological groups and one which is usually condemned strongly. Neither Christianity nor Islam has shown tolerance here.

As we have already seen, when Christianity rose to become the state religion under the emperor Constantine in the fourth century, heresy and especially apostasy, a capital sin from earliest times, became a crime against the state punishable by both church and state (see E II). The first killing of Christians by other Christians for deviations from the faith seems to have been the execution of the Spanish heretic Priscillian and six companions in Trier in 385. Over the course of time the original objection by the church authorities to violent action gave way to what had become custom. The leading Latin church teacher Augustine in his latter years was influential here; he affirmed the use of violence against heretics but rejected the death penalty.

In contrast, eight centuries later the most famous theologian of the high Middle Ages, Thomas Aquinas, even commended the death penalty, arguing: 'To accept the faith is a matter of the will; but to maintain the faith once accepted is a matter of necessity.'[10] This attitude gave rise to an established institution: the Inquisition, whose victims numbered many thousands over the course of the centuries. The most prominent example was the pantheistic philosopher Giordano Bruno, who in 1600 was cruelly tortured and burnt alive in public in Rome.[11] Even after the Second Vatican Council, according to Canon 1364 of the *Codex Iuris Canonici*, an 'apostate' is automatically excommunicated.[12]

Against the background of the development in Christianity it is hardly surprising that Islam, too, does not show the slightest toleration of apostasy (*irtidad, riddah*), however tolerant it may be towards Jews and Christians as 'possessors of scripture'.[13] The Qur'an threatens apostasy with severe penalties only in the other world;[14] repentance and forgiveness are possible, but the Sunnah contains the unmistakable and often-cited statement of the Prophet, justifying punishment in this world: 'Whoever changes his religion, kill him!'[15] Thus, it became the dominant teaching that apostasy is to be punished with death. Here the boundary between apostasy (falling away from the faith) and heresy (a deviant view within the faith) is fluid, since often those who are regarded as apostates, who deny a truth of faith, may continue to regard themselves as Muslims.[16]

But what about the principle from surah 2, 256 that is quoted so often by Muslims, 'No compulsion in religion'? This applies only to the recognized 'religions of the book' and not to 'unbelievers', the polytheists and atheists (see E II). According to the traditional exegesis it may not be understood to mean that a Muslim may give up Islam and accept another religion or worldview. Even today, in Muslim states, the right to change religion applies only to conversion to Islam. Islamic fundamentalists who condemn apostasy do so not because they see it as a violation of God's law, as formerly; in view of the lack of understanding in non-Islamic countries they condemn it as a threat to the stability of the state and the well-being of society, which are based on the stability of the religion. This has priority over the right of Muslims to give up Islam.

However, Article 18 of the 1948 UN Universal Declaration of Human Rights says unambiguously: '... This right (to freedom of thought, conscience or religion) includes freedom to change his religion or belief.' This formulation was rejected at the time by Afghanistan, Iraq, Pakistan, Saudi Arabia and Syria. In the UN Declaration on Intolerance and Discrimination on Grounds of Religion of 25 November 1981, a group of Islamic states ensured that the phrase 'change of religion' was absent from Article 1, paragraph 1.

My question therefore relates particularly to the 1981 Islamic Declaration of Human Rights.[17] The Islamic expert Martin Forstner, of the University of Mainz, praises the fact that this declaration introduces human rights to the

Islamic peoples: 'This could also oblige governments which accept this declaration on human rights to observe human rights.' However, Forstner attacks any relativization of the right to religious freedom: 'On the other hand, this is at the least relativized, if not completely done away with, if one notes on closer consideration of the Arabic text that the human rights which are proclaimed here do not correspond completely to those of the United Nations, and that those which are important, for example the right to change one's religion, are not even mentioned.'[18]

My question is: wouldn't it result in chaos in the understanding of the law if one were to make the content of the Declaration of Human Rights dependent on different value-conceptions of the different cultures, in an attitude of cultural relativism? 'The task, therefore, is to work out a core of values which despite all the different conceptions of value and ways of thinking are contained in human rights and which include absolute freedom of religion and faith, to declare them binding, to incorporate them into each distinctive conception of value, and to establish it.'[19] That is precisely the aim of a global ethic: a basic stock of shared elementary ethical values, standards and attitudes.[20]

3. Religion, violence and 'holy wars'

Now that I have analysed the relationship of the three prophetic religions to legitimate political power I want to turn to political power in the negative sense. What is the attitude of the three prophetic religions to repressive violence and war? All are confronted with the charge that as 'monotheistic' religions they are more exposed to the temptation to use force than 'polytheistic' and 'non-theistic' religions (for example, Buddhism).

Does monotheism have a special propensity to violence?

Could it be that every religion contains aspects of violence? Are monotheistic religions particularly intolerant, lacking in peace and ready for violence because of their bond to a single God? Some Christian theologians think that they must attribute an anti-monotheistic feeling to certain secularist intellectuals. Don't such theologians underestimate the strong anti-religious feelings held by those representatives of the church who, in the name of God, address self-righteous and highly moral demands to the community without solving the problems they have at home? Anti-monotheistic feelings are sometimes also evident among Christian dogmatic theologians, who attempt to support their speculations on the Trinity with polemic against a belief in one God on the part of Jews, Christians and Muslims, claiming that this is responsible for intolerance and an absence of peace. Weren't crusades carried on in the name of

Christ, and heretics, Jews and witches burned in the name of the 'Most Holy Trinity'?

I approach the problems of religion and war[21] by noting soberly that there has been religion ever since there have been human beings, and that ever since human beings have existed there has been violence. There has never been a non-violent paradisical society in the world of human beings, who evolved from the animal world. The picture of the uncorrupted peaceful 'noble savage' has long been unmasked as a myth created by the optimistic Enlightenment, to which even such a well-known cultural anthropologist as Margaret Mead fell victim when investigating the inhabitants of Samoa, whom she alleged to be utterly peaceful.

Even Christian ethicists acknowledge that specific ethical norms, values and attitudes have formed through an extremely complicated sociological process. Wherever existential needs and urgent human requirements have become evident, regulations for human behaviour have emerged. This is the origin of human culture. Over generations, human beings have had to get used to these ethical norms and test whether they prove themselves; the norms include reverence for the life of others, not killing other human beings for a lower purpose, not murdering. However, since early times there have been wars, above all (it is been supposed) to gain power (mana) and respect, or to restore a divine order which has allegedly been disturbed.

'Holy' wars are understood to be wars of aggression, waged with a missionary claim at the command of a deity. Whether they are waged in the name of one God or several gods is of secondary importance. It would be wrong to attribute all the wars waged by 'Christians' in the last few centuries to religious motivations. When white colonizers in Latin America, North America and Australia killed countless Indians and Aborigines, when German colonial rulers in Namibia murdered tens of thousands of Hereros, when British soldiers shot down protesting Indians in large numbers, when the Israeli army in Lebanon and Palestine killed hundreds of civilians or when Turkish soldiers massacred hundreds of thousands of Armenians, this could not all be blamed on belief in one God. Next, I shall look more closely at what wars with a religious motivation can be found in the three prophetic religions.

Holy wars of Yahweh?

A new stage of cultural development was reached when ethical norms which, for instance, already appear in the old Babylonian Codex Hammurabi from the eighteenth and seventeenth centuries BCE were put under the authority of the one God and proclaimed as God's commandment. This happened in the Decalogue, the 'Ten Words'.[22] Old Testament scholars largely agree that polytheism was widespread in Israel even at the time of the monarchy (P II) and that to begin with there was only monolatry: of the many gods which existed in Israel, only Yahweh was worshipped as the one God; the existence of other gods in other peoples was not denied. Strict monotheism, the denial of the existence of other gods, existed only after the Babylonian exile, in the late strata of Deuteronomy and in II Isaiah (Deutero-Isaiah), that is, in the age of theocracy (P III), when all the scriptures were revised from beginning to end in the spirit of a strictly exclusive monotheism.[23]

In terms of religion and violence, this means that long before the relatively late rise of monotheism the world was full of violence. It cannot be proved that proneness to violence increased with the rise of monotheism. In this time of changing polytheistic alien rule, Israel was more the victim of violent acts than their perpetrator.

The Hebrew Bible stands out for the way in which it sees the violence of both nature and human beings as part of earthly reality; the power of evil can be held in check only provisionally. It bluntly reports acts of violence, whereas in other ancient cultures (as René Girard has shown)[24] violence is covered with a veil of silence, either mentioned only indirectly, seen through rose-tinted spectacles or exalted in myths. Violence is a constant theme of the biblical books, which confront human beings with their violent nature: beginning with the murder by Cain of his brother Abel out of sheer rivalry,[25] through the anti-war speeches of the prophets, to a vision of a peace among nations, established by Yahweh, in the prophets Micah and Isaiah.[26] There will be an end-time free of violence, in which swords are forged into ploughshares. This is a key text for the peace movements of our days and also for the peace movement in Israel.

Reports about early acts of violence were often edited hundreds of years later and are almost impossible to verify, though this has not prevented the political misuse of these texts (for example, in the Middle East conflict). The Yahweh war narrated in the context of the settlement of Israel and Judah[27]—probably a slow infiltration or upheaval within Palestine rather than a military conquest[28]—is a construction edited five hundred years later, presumably to act as counter-propaganda against the threat of Assyrian terror: there is no evidence that the Israelites annihilated the whole population of a city as a sacrifice to God (Hebrew *herem* = dedicate to destruction), but the inscription of a Moabite king in the ninth century attests that the Moabites did this. However, 'there is not a single text in the Old Testament from which we could infer reliable information about an Israelite *herem* action for any period of Israel'.[29] Such an act of annihilation cannot be excluded, even for Israel, but the perpetration of these acts is by no means a specific characteristic of Israel from which an argument could be constructed showing a great readiness for violence in monotheism.[30] The heroic saga of the prophet Elijah, surrounded with legends, relates how this ruthless champion of Yahweh religion destroyed all the prophets of Baal and the asherah;[31] however, the saga was likewise fixed in writing only centuries later and therefore it is impossible now to discover how far it corresponds to historical reality. This is not an argument against Israelite monotheism, since previously all the prophets of Israel but Elijah had been killed in the name of the god Baal and his pantheon.

The reports of wars and violent acts must be seen in the overall context of the Hebrew Bible. In describing the creation of human beings, the biblical creation stories do not offer a fairy-tale narrative of a first human being in the garden of paradise but simply describe the human situation. According to the Hebrew Bible, Adam is not the first Jew nor even the first Christian, nor of course is he the first Muslim (unless we simplify and equate Muslim with monotheist). Adam is simply *the* human being: the human being as God's image and likeness.[32] After the model story of Cain's fratricide of Abel, the climax of the creation narratives comes with the story of the flood in which, more than in any other flood narrative in the environment of Israel, the problem of violence is put at the centre: humankind is 'corrupt in God's eyes, full of violence' and therefore doomed to destruction.[33] Only the one righteous man, Noah, and his family are spared and makes a new beginning of humankind possible under the sign of the rainbow, which overarches the whole earth; this symbolizes the covenant of God with all of humankind, indeed the whole of creation.

From then on, God protects human life with sanctions against acts of violence, 'for God has made human beings in his own image'.[34] An ethic of humanity should correspond with God's covenant with humankind, a minimal basic ethic of reverence for life (the theologian and doctor Albert Schweitzer took this as the basis of ethics generally): not to murder, nor to eat the flesh of animals which are still alive. Rabbinic Judaism later derived seven 'Noachic commandments' from this ethic: beside the prohibition of murder and cruelty to animals, there is the prohibition of robbery, unchastity, idolatry and blasphemy and the command to practise the law (including setting up law courts).[35] This accords with an ethic of humanity which *a priori* applies not only to Jews but to all human beings (see B II, 2).[36]

So is an 'anti-monotheistic feeling' justified? No, for the belief of Jews, Christians and Muslims in one God contradicts any quasi- or pseudo-religion which makes a relative absolute. Even today, this means a radical repudiation of divinized powers of nature and of all earthly entities with quasi-divine functions, to which human beings sacrifice everything, which they are to hope for or fear more than anything else in the world—regardless of whether modern men and women worship profit, sex, power, sport, science, nation, church, party, leader or pope as 'God'. When 'supermen' such as Stalin and Hitler with their 'will to power' wanted to replace belief in the one God with belief in a socialist society or the Germanic race and ultimately with their own divinization, the cost was millions of lives. Martin Luther summed it up well: 'Only the trust and faith of the heart makes both God and idols. That to which your heart clings, that is really your God.'[37]

Belief in the one God gives Jews, Christians and Muslims great freedom from all spiritual bonds: through their bond with the one true absolute, human beings become free from all that is relative, which can no longer be idolatrous. So no mythologically retarded return to the gods is called for today in the transition to postmodernity. Artificial remythologization is countered by a new return to the one true God who, as the God of Jews, Christians and Muslims, tolerates no false gods beside him. Precisely this can give tolerance among human beings a basis: because God is one for all human beings, all, every human being—even the non-Jew, non-Christian, non-Muslim—is in his image and as such demands respect for his dignity. But what is the Christian standpoint on violence and war?

Violence in the sign of the cross

After the elevation of Christianity to become the state religion of the Roman empire it became necessary (both for Greek East Rome and the Byzantine empire and for Latin West Rome and the Holy Roman Empire of the German Nation which began with Charlemagne) for state and church power to protect, support and promote each other despite the rivalry which soon developed. In this dovetailing of the profane and secular spheres, the worldly rulers understood themselves to be protectors of the church and the church hierarchs often legitimated and inspired the secular authorities. An expansion of worldly rule always resulted in an expansion of the church and a mission of the church resulted in an expansion of worldly rule. State and church law supplemented each other; church measures governed civil life and civil authorities punished the violation of the moral and religious order. Thus the 'secular and spiritual' arms helped each other. However, this meant that Christianity was necessarily burdened with secular acts of violence; the church often played a part in violent developments and actions that were in conflict with the peaceful non-violent spirit of its founder. Just think of what was not only tolerated but also approved in the name of Christ!

The cross of Jesus of Nazareth, who was executed by the Romans, to which the cold and at the same time superstitious politician Constantine attributed the decisive victory over his rival Maxentius at the Milvian Bridge in 312, increasingly came to be used as a sign of conflict and battle which gave even the worst bloodshed and atrocities a Christian 'seal'. This was by no means an inevitable development, yet at a very early stage people in this Christian empire proceeded violently against enemies at home and abroad. In the approximately thirty years of war waged by Charlemagne, the first Christian emperor of the Franks, against the pagan Saxons thousands were executed or deported. In the church of the martyrs, people got used to seeing those of other faiths, deviants, and later Jews and witches, executed.

In the high Middle Ages a militant church waged 'holy wars'. The Orthodox churches of the East (P II) were entangled in most of the political and military conflicts of the secular power and often gave wars theological legitimation, even inspired them. Only in the Latin Christianity of the West (P III) did the (Augustinian) theory of the legitimate use of violence for attaining spiritual ends apply, which finally allowed the use of violence to extend to Christianity. Contrary to the tradition of the early church, there were wars of conversion, wars against pagans, wars against heretics, indeed—completely perverting the cross—crusades.

The supreme representatives of Christianity, Pope Urban II and the powerful preacher and mystic Bernard of Clairvaux, the founder of a religious order, issued a summons to war in the name of Jesus Christ, to snatch the 'holy land' from the 'unbelievers', the Muslims. The crusades were regarded as the affair of all (Western) Christianity. They were said to be approved by Christ himself; the Pope as the voice of Christ called for them. Innocent III, who initiated the Fourth Crusade (with the disastrous conquest and plundering of Constantinople and the establishment of a Roman primacy), was the first also to proclaim a great crusade in the West against fellow-Christians. This led to the cruel Albigensian war in the south of France, which lasted for two decades, with bestial cruelties on both sides and the extermination of whole sections of the population.

Even then, many people asked whether the Jesus of the Sermon of the Mount, who proclaimed non-violence, the renunciation of law and love of one's enemy, would have allowed such warlike enterprises. Wasn't the cross of Jesus being turned into its opposite when, instead of inspiring Christians to bear real crosses every day, it legitimized bloody wars by crusaders who bore the cross on their garments? In the Middle Ages, non-violence ('the peace of God') was institutionalized only locally and temporarily, with places of sanctuary being granted to the persecuted. In Protestantism (P IV) the Mennonites, the Brethren movement and especially the Quakers (the 'historic peace churches') offered a free-church alternative to the traditional legitimizing of violence in the state churches.

This should be food for thought for those Christians, including statesmen who emphatically claim to be Christian, who think that, in the twenty-first century, it is necessary to wage a crusading 'war against terrorism' in Muslim countries with concealed colonialist and imperialist aims ('God bless America'). In the Iraq War, such statesmen totally ignored the classic criteria of a 'just war', developed in the long Christian tradition (for the sake of a 'just peace'). The political theorist Alois Riklin, of St Gallen, has summed up these criteria and applied them to the 2003 Iraq War.[38] He found that the following were lacking:

- just cause: self-defence;
- honourable intentions: weapons of mass destruction in Iraq;
- proportionality: humanitarian catastrophes;
- legitimate authority: the UN Security Council;
- the last and only means: war instead of sanctions;
- international law: observing the Geneva conventions.

All six criteria should have been fulfilled to justify a war, given the state of threat at the time, but not one was. This war was clearly immoral, and would have been even if it had been sanctioned by the UN Security Council. Moreover, it is incomprehensible that a US President who is a 'born–again Christian' and publicly professes Christian values could wage a second war against a Muslim country after Afghanistan, under false pretences, and could and would also like to wage other similar wars. Fundamentalist Christians in America have an answer: for centuries the Muslims waged 'holy wars' against Christianity and today are fighting against the basic order of freedom and democracy.

'Holy wars' of Muslims?

The Arabic word *jihad* does not mean precisely the same as the two English words 'holy war';[39] it covers a broad semantic field. Initially it means simply 'effort', and in some passages of the Qur'an is understood as 'striving hard' on the way of God: 'And strive hard in God's cause with all the striving that is due to Him: it is He who has elected you.'[40] The combination of 'holy' and 'war' does not occur in the Qur'an: in the Islamic view, war can never be 'holy'.

However, in other passages *jihad* is understood as violent 'struggle', in the sense of a warlike conflict: 'You are to believe in God and His Apostle, and to strive hard in God's cause with your possessions and your lives.'[41] The verb *jahada*, 'strive for', with one's own possessions and one's own person, here means fight, 'wage war', with immediate entry into paradise promised as a reward: 'He will admit you into gardens through which running waters flow, and into goodly mansions in gardens of perpetual bliss: that [will be] the triumph supreme.'[42] There are several similar Qur'anic verses: 'O Prophet! Strive hard against the deniers of the truth and the hypocrites, and be adamant with them. And [if they do not repent,] their goal shall be hell—and how vile a journey's end!'[43]

One thing is clear: whereas Jesus' disciples were committed to non-violence by the message, conduct and fate of their Messiah, the followers of the Prophet Muhammad are committed, if necessary, to militant conflict and do not shrink from the use of violence. War as a policy is affirmed, waged and—in most cases—won. From the start Islam has indisputably had a militant character, even if the summons to battle at first related to the polytheistic Meccans and the Arab tribes hostile to the Muslims, and so to a quite particular historical situation in which the new Muslim community was threatened.

However, it should be emphasized that the Prophet attested not only a will to fight but also a will for peace—for example in the peace treaty with the Meccans or with Christian communities and the Jews who still remained—and that the *dhimmi* status of those whose protection was commanded always made possible a toleration which went far beyond what was customary in Christian kingdoms. In the holy months 'there shall be no fighting',[44] and in principle 'not at the holy place of worship' (of Mecca). In general 'no transgressions' are to be committed in battle.[45]

The explanation of present-day Muslim authors[46] that in the Meccan surahs *jihad* does not mean 'war' but 'effort' in bringing forward arguments and that an armed battle which would have been hopeless was not allowed, are understandable from the Prophet's biography: it was in the Medinan surahs that Muhammad received the first revelations which gave permission for armed combat against the idolatrous Meccans. Thus *jihad* in self-defence became an obligation. In further revelations *jihad* is formulated increasingly clearly as the 'armed struggle of faith against unbelievers'.

However, the apologetic argument often advanced by Muslims that armed *jihad* refers only to wars of defence cannot be maintained. It is contradicted by the testimonies of the Islamic chroniclers, who show that the *jihad* was of the utmost political and military significance. It is hard to imagine a more effective motivation for a war than the 'struggle' (often expressed with the clear term *qital*, armed 'struggle') which furthers God's cause against the unbelievers. This is a highly meritorious struggle, declared in the Qur'an to be an obligation. Above all in the first wars of expansion, this obligation was a motive for all the tribal warriors involved and the leaders on and around the Arabian peninsula who fought with them (P I). It was less markedly a motive when, under the Umayyad caliphs, imperial wars were strategically planned from Damascus, targeted on remote destinations and waged with the help of non-Arab troops and leaders (P II). Under the 'Abbasids, the Arabs increasingly left the waging of war to Turkic troops (P III), so that after the downfall of the caliphate Turks (with the Mughals in India) became the heirs of the Islamic empire and in turn used the motive of *jihad* as legitimation for their wars of conquest in the Balkans and in India.

4. War or peace?

The wars of Muhammad against the pagan Meccans and the first wars of conquest led to a discussion of the concept of 'war' in Islam. The classic doctrine of *jihad* later emerged from this, taking account of the Qur'an and Sunnah. In the Shariah, *jihad* with all its conditions and modes occupies long chapters.[47] How is this to be judged from a present perspective and with regard to the future?

Realm of Islam—realm of war

We have seen (see C I) that the cliché that Islam spread its faith with 'fire and sword' was not true. The early conquests were primarily concerned with the territorial expansion of the Islamic state, not with conversions to the Islamic faith. Only later, in the further development of Islamic war, did the schematic notion arise of a world divided into two camps: on the one hand the 'territory (abode) of Islam' (*dar al-Islam*) and on the other the 'territory (abode) of war' (*dar al-harb*).This bisection of the world into a territory in which a Muslim ruler ensured the observance of the norms of faith and law and a territory surrounding the Islamic territory which was the occasion for campaign of robbery and conquest hardly helped to promote peace: it suggested that the aim of every pious Muslim was to make the non-Islamic world Islamic, which inevitably resulted in an endless war of religion.

Since a permanent state of war could not be sustained, it was enough if the ruler carried out, or at least planned, an annual expedition for robbery or plunder or a slave raid. The people against whom the *jihad* was waged were invited to accept Islam. If they yielded, they might be given the status of those 'commanded to be protected'; otherwise, in some circumstances, after the conquest they could be enslaved and their possessions given to the victors as plunder. The Islamic world became a state of many peoples not only as a result of the conquests but also through the slaves plundered and bought from many countries.[48] The threats of war and the treatment of the conquered Christian people—quite apart from other reasons (see C I)—explain why so little remained of the Christian population in the territories of the Near East and North Africa where Christianity originated.

During the great Islamic conquests, the doctrine of *jihad* almost came to occupy the position of a sixth pillar of Islam. In contrast to Christianity, in Islam one could become a 'witness' (Greek *martys*), in Arabic also in the sense of blood witness (Arabic *shahid*, plural *shuhada'*), not only passively, through endurance for the faith, but also actively, through fighting. Anyone who sacrificed his life in such dedication would immediately go to paradise: 'Now when you meet [in war] those who are bent on denying the truth, smite their necks (with the sword) ... And as for those who are slain in God's cause, never will He let their deeds go to waste; He will guide them [in the hereafter as well] and will set their hearts at rest, and will admit them to the paradise which He has promised them.'[49]

In modern times, the *jihad* was increasingly given up under the pressure of European colonialism. The last Ottoman sultan, Mehmet V, called for a *jihad* against the powers of the Entente on 23 November 1914 and even today *jihad* is proclaimed on this occasion or that. However, many moderate advocates of a modern Islam have reflected on the original sense of *jihad*, namely moral effort. From the late eighth century, a distinction was made in the case of Sufi frontier battles between the 'small effort' as armed struggle against external foes and the non-violent 'great effort' of self-control and the realization of higher values. What form of *jihad* will the future bring?

Radicalization of the idea of jihad*?*

In the twentieth century, *jihad* was given new political interpretations. Modern fundamentalists could refer not only to the law books but also to conservative theologians, especially to the Hanbalite scholar Ibn Taymiyyah (see C IV, 7), who was thus elevated to become the spiritual father of the radical Islamists. Ibn Taymiyyah, in his *fatwahs*, had struggled with the situation under the Mongol rulers, who for him had to be treated as unbelievers, although they called themselves Muslims, because they did not observe the Shariah. Thus, it was easier for the ideologists of radical Islamism in the twentieth century to wage *jihad* not just externally, in the struggle for liberation from colonialism, but also internally, against the Westernized autocratic rulers whom they claimed no longer to be practising Islam. The term *jihad* can easily be used as a political instrument: depending on the need, it can be interpreted (like the military term 'campaign') as the struggle against underdevelopment, the struggle against tourism, the struggle for economic reform or even the murder of liberal politicians, writers and journalists.

Since the 1970s, it has been possible to observe a radicalization of the idea of *jihad* (*jihad* -Islam) among numerous small but highly-committed extremist groups. Under the influence of the Egyptian Umar Abd ar-Rahman and the Palestinian Abdallah Azzam, ideologist of the Hamas movement (first encouraged by Israel as a counter to Yasser Arafat), particular groups have resolved on *jihad* as an armed struggle, in view of the increasing occupation of Palestine and the rigidity of many Arab regimes. In 1981, a terrorist group using the name Hamas was responsible for the murder of the Egyptian president Anwar as-Sadat, following his peace initiative in Israel. It is a terrifying fact that more and more people are joining these radical groups out of despair at the catastrophic situation of the Palestinian people, the poverty and misery of the Arab masses, and the insensitivity and repressive mechanisms of the élites in so many countries. This is not least also because of their social institutions for the poorer strata of the population.

Since 11 September 2001, it has become increasingly clear what a disastrously ambiguous role has been played by Saudi Arabia, America's greatest ally in the Arab Middle East (there are business links between the Bush family and bin Laden), not only in the export of oil but also in the export of terrorism. The core of al-Qaida (Arabic *al-qa'ida* = 'foundation', 'basis') around Osama bin Laden is made up of Saudis rebelling against the royal family, which tolerates a permanent presence of American troops (thirty thousand soldiers on Saudi soil). Al-Qaida has financed rigidly Wahhabi groups in neighbouring Arab countries and beyond. We cannot overlook the fact that Wahhabism, both in Saudi Arabia itself and in the Islamic world generally, is promoting intolerance and xenophobia.

The Tunisian writer Abdelwahab Meddeb (see C V, 1) proposes cures for the inner causes of the Islamic 'sickness' of 'fundamentalism', especially as it manifests itself in Wahhabism, on three levels: tradition, law and school education. He says that it is important: 1. To recall the countless controversies and debates in the Islamic tradition, so as to create within Islam today a freedom of pluralistic discourse with a critical awareness. 2. In the effort to humanize law appropriately for our time, to seek out erroneous points in norms which seem to be inhuman in the tradition (the principle of *talfiq*). 3. To purge school curricula of extremism: 'Diffuse Wahhabism infects the consciousness through instruction given in schools and supported by television.'[50]

However, Americans, Israelis and Europeans should have noted, at least since the Iraq war, that it will not be possible to stop terrorism with military strategies of retaliation, especially since these clearly do not deter the equipping of suicide bombers or the comparatively harmless stone-throwers. It is important to grasp the evil of terrorism at its roots and invest in social reforms the astronomical sums of money that have so far been spent on arms, both in the West and in the Arab countries. It is necessary not only to attend to the violent excesses of Islamic extremists but also to reflect on Islam's potential for peace.

A hermeneutic of peacemaking

In contrast to antiquity and the Middle Ages, in the twenty-first century humankind can destroy itself with novel technical means. Therefore all religions, including the three prophetic religions which are often so aggressive, should be concerned to avoid wars and promote peace. A careful re-reading of one's own religious traditions is unavoidable. A contemporary understanding of the Qur'an is vitally important (see D VI): statements about war may not be taken uncritically either as dogmatic doctrines or as rigid legal principles. Rather, they must be understood historically and critically and translated from the situation of their time into the situation today. A two-fold change is urgently needed in the service of a hermeneutic of peacemaking:

First, the warlike words and events each tradition should be interpreted historically, on the basis of the situation at the time, without excuses. This applies to all three religions:

– The cruel 'wars of Yahweh' and the inexorable psalms of revenge in the Hebrew Bible are to be understood in terms of the situation of the settlement and of later defensive situations against far superior enemies.
– The Christian missionary wars and the 'crusades' are grounded in the situation of the ideology of the church in the early and high Middle Ages.
– The calls to war in the Qur'an reflect the particular situation of the Prophet in the Medina period and the special character of the Medinan surahs. In particular, the calls to battle against the polytheistic Meccans cannot be transferred to the present day as a justification for the use of violence.

Secondly, the words and actions in each tradition that make for peace should be taken seriously as stimuli for the present. That must be easiest for Christians, as the memories of their origin are not of militant prophetic heroes such as Moses or Elijah or of an aggressive king such as David, but of a preacher of non-violence and an original church which, at least at the beginning, spread through the Roman empire not through violence but through a message of justice, love and eternal life. Not only military service, but even the profession of butcher, was initially forbidden to Christians. Muslims who are committed to war and violence will possibly refer to sayings and actions of the Prophet from the Qur'an. Christians who use violence and wage wars cannot appeal to their Christ.

However, in view of the threats and dangers to world peace today, challenging practical questions arise which are not simple to answer. Alongside a hermeneutic of peacemaking there is also need for a pedagogy and pragmatic of peacemaking.

A pedagogy of peacemaking

Many Christians are unaware that the Qur'anic statements about war and violence comprise relatively few verses and that 'mercy' and 'peace' occur far more often than *jihad*. According to the Qur'an, God is not the lord of war (this is not a name of God), but 'the merciful, the one who has mercy'. This is revealed in the very first words of the opening surah (which Muslims cite at the beginning of every prayer or utterance). God's ninety-nine names include such peaceful attributes as the Sensitive, the Long-suffering, the Lovable, the Gracious, the One who is Full of Forgiveness.

Moreover the *islam* (submission) that human beings are to show God is formed from the same root as the word 'peace' (*salam*). Hence the Muslim greeting: 'Peace be with you' (*as -salam 'alaykum*). God can forgive and anyone who forgives is following God's example.[51] There is even a kind of Golden Rule in the Qur'an: the invitation to recompense evil with good and thus to make an enemy into a warm-hearted friend.[52] Above all, peace should be made between disputing parties of believers and peace is to be made even with enemies—I have already quoted the relevant verse in connection with the Palestinian question (see D III): 'If they incline to peace, incline thou to it as well.'[53]

Today, a pedagogy of peacemaking is called for, both individual and collective, for children and for their parents, for the Ulama and for politicians. Here it should be noted that:

– A heightened sense of self-worth among Muslims is welcome, as long as it does not turn into a sense of self-righteousness and xenophobia (as happened with many Jews and Christians) that can lead to attacks and terrorism.

– The fought-for self-control of the great *jihad* is to be welcomed, as long as it does not end in suicide for political ends; this is rejected by the Muslim tradition, as only God may decide on life and death.

– An intensive fight against terror is necessary, provided that it does not degenerate into hysteria over security and the suppression of the basic democratic rights of prisoners of war and citizens. A terrorist network cannot be overcome by military means but only by removing its breeding ground: the social need and the oppression of large strata of the population. The extremists have to be isolated from the social environment that supports them and non-violent reform movements have to be supported.[54]

Islam has a significant potential for peace and it is important to activate this in the light of the latest experiences—not least the events of 11 September 2001. However, assurances of peace are not enough by themselves. There is need not only for a new hermeneutics and pedagogy, but also for a pragmatic of peacemaking.

A pragmatic of peacemaking

If a policy is to be successful, it needs an 'art of action'. An ideological military policy, without ethical principles, which serves only the interests of economic and political élites and justifies any means—lies, deception, political murder, war and torture—for political ends must be rejected. So too must an ideological peace policy which is focused only on mere disposition and is not concerned with the real conditions of power, concrete practicability and possible negative consequences.

The art of a responsible peace policy is tested by combining the necessary political calculations with an ethical judgement. What ethical principles are to be observed in the question of war and peace, in respect of a new and better world order?[55]

- In the twenty-first century, too, wars are neither 'holy', 'just' nor 'clean'. Given the unforeseeable sacrifice of human life, the immense destruction of the infrastructure and cultural treasures and the ecological damage, modern 'wars of Yahweh' (Sharon), 'crusades' (Bush) and *jihad* (al-Qaida) are irresponsible.
- Wars are never unavoidable: better co-ordinated diplomacy, supported by efficient arms control, would have been able to prevent the wars in Yugoslavia and the two Gulf wars.
- A policy of national interest without ethics—for example for the sake of the oil reserves or hegemony in the Middle East—is partly to blame for war. An examination of consciences after the First Gulf War could have shown that it was not simply a matter of 'rogue states' and innocent democracies, good and evil, God and Satan. The demonizing of the opponent often serves only to provide a moral excuse for the party that makes war. For example, Saddam Hussein was equipped above all by the West with arms, money, technology and advisers as a bulwark against an Islamicized Iran and was uninhibitedly supported by the USA (represented by Donald Rumsfeld, later to become Secretary of Defense).
- Absolute pacifism, for which peace is the highest good and for which everything must be sacrificed, is politically impracticable and can even be irresponsible as a political principle.
- In the Muslim tradition, time and again importance is attached to the right to self-defence, expressly affirmed in Article 51 of the UN Charter: 'God sees to the defence of those who believe ... Those who fight (against the unbelievers) have been given permission (to fight) because injustice has been done to them (previously).'[56] At the 1993 Parliament of the World's Religions in Chicago it was important to the Muslim representatives in

> particular that the right to self-defence was emphasized in section III.1 of the Declaration Toward a Global Ethic on non-violence. If a new Holocaust threatens, peace at any price is irresponsible. Megalomaniac dictators and mass murderers (such as Stalin, Hitler and Saddam) must be opposed. Those who have committed crimes against humanity should appear before the International Court of Criminal Justice, which one hopes will also finally be supported, in the best American tradition, by the American administration which follows that of George W. Bush.

There are still many questions about state and religion, state and violence, war and peace but it is time for me to turn to the equally important questions of the Islamic economy and the everyday world of Islam.

E IV

The Future of the Islamic Economic Order

As well as in manifold political and military confrontations in the Middle Ages, from the Near East and North Africa to Spain and the Balkans, it is clear that the Christian world very often also acted as an opponent in the economic sphere.

1. Is Islam the solution?

With the loss of vast territories to the Muslims, the Christians suffered an enormous loss of economic markets and areas of production. For a long time Islam was stronger in military and economic terms. The Muslims, who for many centuries had been masters of the whole of the eastern and southern Mediterranean, controlled the trade with the East that was so important for Europe, whether this went by the silk roads from China or the incense route from southern Arabia to the coasts of the Mediterranean. However, sea trade also brought piracy.

The Mediterranean between piracy and good neighbourliness

As the Italian historian Franco Cardini has worked out,[1] the activities of Muslim pirates were 'important factors in the crisis, indeed sometimes decisive, producing social and economic as well as psychological and cultural distress: there was a drastic decline in navigation in general, a reduction in the number of Christian ports and coastal towns, widespread impoverishment, a contraction in the monetary economy and, finally, general fear and anxiety.' From the eighth century onwards Muslims launched raids from the coasts of Africa and Spain not only to the Greek islands but also to Sicily and Sardinia; this resulted in a decline of the settlements along the coast as a result of the flight of the population into the trackless but safe interior: 'Usually the raiders' objectives was a rapid foray, the kidnapping of young people for the slave trade and the occasional imposition of taxes or ransom. Occasionally they would establish a "nest" of corsairs, who would form a small commercial and military colony.' In 846 CE the Saracens advanced as far as Ostia, sailed up the Tiber and plundered the basilica of St Peter, causing Pope Leo VI to enclose St Peter's and that part of the city within a fortification—still called the 'Civitas Leonina'.

However, relations between the Christian and Islamic powers in the Mediterranean were characterized not only by attacks and warlike clashes but also by 'fairly good commercial relations': 'Somewhere around the beginning of the eleventh century, however, the initiative changed sides: during the earlier period the Saracens were consistently more active and dynamic, always the first to attack. Later, however, their position became a defensive one, whilst Christian strength and power showed a steady increase.'[2] As well as slaves, weapons and hides, all large quantities of iron ('Frankish swords') and wood (very rare in Muslim territories) were transported to the East.

The paradigm change to modernity (see C V, 3) brought about a fundamental change in economic relations. The world of Islam increasingly went into economic decline, although for a long time this remained unnoticed because of constant military expansion. Here I must return once more (see C V, 1) to the reasons for this decline, now from an economic perspective.

Why the economic backwardness?

The Ottoman empire lost its superiority first in the technical and military spheres but soon also in medicine, printing and the other technical achievements which became the foundation of European industry. The uncertainty that seized these peoples, accustomed to victory and trusting in the promises of the Qur'an, reached a first climax in 1798 with Napoleon's invasion of the Islamic heartland, Egypt. This was the signal for the ruling classes in Cairo and Istanbul to overcome their lethargy and catch up with the scientific and technological revolution in order once again to compete economically on equal terms with the Western states, which in the nineteenth century were rapidly developing into industrial states.

This was not as simple as it first appeared. It was not just a matter of adopting scientific knowledge, technical achievements and economic methods of production but involved the radical change of mentality without which modern science and a modern economy cannot function. Islam now felt the effect of the rejection in the ninth century of the theology of the Mu'tazilites, with their emphasis on reason, free will and the need to understand the Qur'an in a historical context and in the eleventh century of autonomous philosophy and thus the secular spirit of invention which had already created new instruments for itself in the Italian Renaissance (see C IV, 8). Islam also felt the effect of having had no religious reformation which would have led to a comparable revaluation of worldly occupations: of professional work as a vocation and service of God (Martin Luther) and of economic success as a sign of God's favour (Jean Calvin). According to Max Weber's famous investigation, it is no coincidence that the 'Protestant ethic' was the essential religious driving force behind the increasingly successful 'spirit of capitalism'.[3]

The Islamic economy had hardly comparable stimuli from religion. Changes of mentality were at best superficial. Immobility, intellectual laziness and economic incompetence were widespread. The Islamic economic system could not become the equal of the European. It was also vitally important that until well into the twentieth century, almost all Islamic countries were economically dependent on the European colonial powers. The discovery of oil gave some Arab states extraordinary economic power but they did not know how to use it for their internal development. At the beginning of the twenty-first century, because of the failure of their economic and social policies, the Arab countries are the losers from globalization rather than the winners—in contrast to many East Asian and South-East Asian threshold countries.[4]

Most Islamic countries are caught in a permanent crisis, incapable of structural reforms. The problems are well known: excessively high birth rates and illiteracy rates and terrifyingly low per capita incomes. There are too many military conflicts and unresolved conflicts over the distribution of land, water and energy resources. There have been reform coalitions which have not really been able to take action; there has been too much nepotism, and the potential of women has lain unused. What is particularly disastrous is the neglect of 'human capital': there is not the freedom of critical thought and the social scope necessary for research and development, creativity and innovation.

In this crisis is 'Islam the solution'? This is the slogan of the Islamists. However, some Muslims are asking secretly—it is still dangerous to ask aloud in most Islamic states—whether the unhistorical exegesis of the Qur'an isn't partly to blame for the backward economic position of Muslims. One might think of the unconditional prohibition against usury, which is hardly compatible with the modern international financial system.

The prohibition of usury—required and evaded

At the time of the Prophet Muhammad, 'usury' was a serious problem: debts not paid back immediately were doubled and this could finally result in slavery for the debtor. Hence the warning in the Qur'an against usury: 'Those who gorge themselves on usury (*ribah*, 'increase') behave but as he might behave whom Satan has confounded with his touch; for they say, "Buying and selling is but a kind of usury"—the while God has made buying and selling lawful and usury unlawful ... O you who have attained to faith! Remain conscious of God, and give up all outstanding gains from usury, if you are [truly] believers.'[5] In her investigation,[6] the Scottish theologian Susan Buckley has shows how various economic systems developed in the writings of these three monotheistic religions, in accord with the teachings on 'usury', and how these teachings still influence economic systems.[7]

It is clear from the Qur'anic verses on usury that the Prophet Muhammad, himself a merchant—in the city state of Medina on the incense route which, like Mecca, was dependent on trade—never dreamed of limiting trade and vilifying profit. Nor did he see poverty freely chosen as a religious ideal; rather, he affirmed an appropriate standard of living, without luxury and greed. Justice, together with belief in the one God, is part of the central message of the Qur'an (see B II, 2). Here the Prophet presupposed contemporary economic structures and gave no concrete instructions for business.

Zakat, one of the five pillars of Islam (see B III, 2), was an important innovation: this voluntary social tax was meant to reduce the poverty of the poor and limit the wealth of the rich. It is vitally necessary today in countries in which there is no system of social security. Therefore, for Islamists the prohibition of usury, almsgiving and the foundations (which I shall discuss later), are the three main elements of a contemporary Islamic economic model. However, Muslim financial experts emphasize that present-day state policy cannot be limited to *zakat*; this can only be the indispensable, minimal, part of the tax income of an Islamic state. All three elements must be understood in the light of their historical context.

The Prophet Muhammad was by no means alone in prohibiting usury. The Hebrew Bible forbids Jews to exact usury—in the first place from fellow-Jews, but also, unless there is an emergency, from aliens.[8] The New Testament recognizes the possibility that usury will be levied, but says nothing about its ethical side.[9] However, under the influence of the Old Testament, the Christian churches also rigorously prohibited usury, at least in the first four centuries (thus the Pan-Spanish Council of Elvira in 306). 'Usury' continued to be identified with 'extortion' (the Latin word *usura* is used for both), the exploitation of the debts of the poor. After the collapse of the Roman empire, the prohibition of usury was relaxed but between the eighth and fourteenth centuries it was again made stricter.

The prohibition against usury was never completely implemented in practice. The money business and the exaction of usury were largely left to the

Jews. From the Middle Ages onwards, there were widespread historical prejudices about the Jews as 'money men', 'money Jews' and 'Christian Jews'. As if the Christians had not driven the Jews out of the high offices of state, the judiciary and the army, and also out of agriculture and the crafts![10] The Christians themselves forced the Jews into the money business, as this was the only way in which the Jews could earn a living. Jewish landowners could not employ Christian workers, and the Christian order of guilds excluded the Jews from the crafts. At the same time Jews had to pay for almost everything in cash—the right to come and go, to buy and sell, to pray together, to marry, to bear a child. The effect of this was long-lived: Christians cannot evade the sorry truth that the centuries-old anti-Judaism in Christianity and the church was a presupposition for the racist antisemitism of the National Socialists.[11]

From an early stage Christians also devised methods by which big bankers, popes and rulers could get round the prohibition of usury:[12] out of 'gratitude' a debtor might give a 'gift', subscribe to a higher debt (sometimes even double) or pay an agreed 'forfeit' because he had 'exceeded the date', or simply engage in a pseudo-transaction. From the fourteenth century, usury was allowed if financial damage (Latin *damnum emergens*) threatened the creditor through the credit, if no other possible credit was viable (Latin *lucrum cessans*), if a credit was bound up with a high risk of defection (Latin *periculum sortis*) or if repayment was late (Latin *titulus morae*).[13] The Reformers were firm opponents of usury, Zwingli even more than Luther.[14] Only Calvin, in upward-striving Geneva, had to recognize that the banking which was developing in Italy had produced a capital as well as a commodity market, which needed to be guided with the help of usury.

The ban on usury comes from a time when there was an almost purely natural economy, when most people had to borrow everyday goods only in times of need. For Christians, the profit from such distress-driven credit amounted to a violation of the Christian love of neighbour, and was therefore repeatedly forbidden by the church for Christians from Christians. However, by the middle of the sixteenth century, with the rise of the modern monetary economy, money changed its character and became a directly profitable thing (Latin *res fructifera*). Loans became increasingly autonomous; it had been a long time since credit had been needed primarily for survival, so a moderate rate of interest could hardly be seen as unjustified gain. Thus the prohibition of usury lost its original sense and was tacitly abandoned by the churches, though only after much argument.

During the sixteenth and seventeenth centuries, the question of usury had been thoroughly discussed and finally resolved in Christian Europe.Another symptom of the late entry of the Islamic countries into modernity is that the question of usury became pressing in them only in the twentieth century, in connection with the demand for an Islamic banking system.

2. Islamic traditions rediscovered

Islamic countries became independent after the Second World War. The more Muslims were tied into the Western financial system, the more they called for financial institutions that followed the principles of the Shariah, for religious, political or purely commercial reasons.

Islamic banking systems

First in Egypt and Pakistan and then in Saudi Arabia, Islamic savings banks and banks were established, and these soon founded branches and daughter societies in many countries. Although they were at first small in number, they had considerable significance, since they had a capital of tens of billions of US dollars. While these banks had weaknesses (such as a lack of trained staff and of co-ordination with conventional banks, political complications and all too short-term trade), they succeeded in developing a broad range of financial instruments which harmonized the needs of modern life with the Shariah;[15] here the Islamic legal scholars came to very similar solutions to those of the Roman church lawyers:

- profit-sharing systems, in which the bank finances an investment project and the creditor makes his contribution in the form of management (*mudarabah*);
- business partnerships, in which the bank and entrepreneur finance a project jointly and profits and losses are agreed on in advance (*musarakah*);
- purchase contracts to the bank, with a subsequent additional margin of profit (*murabahah*);
- a kind of leasing contract, with higher payment of rates (*ijarah*);
- Islamic assurance (*takaful*).

The Islamic banks were so successful with these models (not recognized by all Muslims in the same way) that eventually the international world of finance was ready to co-operate with them. Individual Western big banks even offered special Islamic financial products to their Muslim customers or founded Islamic daughter banks. Cultural experts, often committees of legal scholars and bankers, advise the banks and give legal decisions (*ijtihad*) as to what is lawful (*halal*) and what is contrary to the law (*haram*).

On 29 May 1991, Sheikh al-Azhar Muhammad Tantawi, the highest spiritual authority in Sunni Islam, published a declaration which allowed the fixing of capital gain to a firm rate, so that the bank authorities, having obtained the rate from the scholars and experts ('Shariah board'), could establish interest on capital in advance. Since clergy increasingly understand modern banking and bankers increasingly understand the principles of Islam, collaboration with these Shariah boards has improved considerably. On 1–2 March 2003 the *New York Herald Tribune* had three pages on 'Islamic banking' with the headline: 'Islamic finance, now twenty-five years old, has become a global enterprise which is rapidly spreading into new markets and products.' According to this article, more than 200 financial institutions with a capital of more than $US 200 billion are active in 23 countries (the central bank is Bahrain); however, this is only a small part of the $800 billion which Muslims have at their private disposal in the Middle East alone. People who, for religious reasons, prefer not to buy gold, jewellery and furniture can thus put what they have saved into an interest-bearing bank account.

Here, however, it should not be overlooked that the majority of private and public financial operations in the Islamic sphere have followed Western patterns, since legislation in most Arabic countries allows the levying of interest. Transactions in the stock market are no longer forbidden, so long as they do not relate to forbidden things such as pork, alcohol, weapons, pornography or games of chance.

Islamic foundations

In addition to almsgiving and the absence of usury, countless religious, charitable and family foundations (*waqf*, plural *awqaf*) are a third important component of Islamic society. I have already described them in the early Islamic period (P I–II, see B III, 2) when they were legally regulated within the framework of the formation of the Shariah (P III). They were made possible by a testament or by registration with the qadi, and originally served to support a mosque and its staff or a group of needy people. Equally, they safeguarded the continuation of property within a family and thus provided protection against confiscation by the state. In the paradigm of the Ulama and Sufis (P IV), foundations for every possible purpose serving the common good multiplied, as they did in the Christian Middle Ages. Foundations were not burdened with taxes and duties; their contributions went primarily to the mosques, then to education and only in third place to the poor and needy.

In the colonial period, the nineteenth and twentieth centuries (P V), the introduction of Western educational and economic systems and the general Muslim decline also affected the property of the *waqf*, which was largely confiscated. The preference had always been to use this property in favour of the family, to avoid the obligation of social redistribution. Religious foundations were now often replaced by the public hand or by private welfare associations, which took over both traditional religious and modern social tasks.

After independence, some Muslim states (Syria, Egypt, Turkey and Tunisia) nationalized the property of the *waqf* (and the land was redistributed); in these countries the government took over responsibility for financing mosques and some religious schools (for example, the al-Azhar university in Cairo). Many Muslim governments appointed ministries of *awqaf* and religious affairs to administer the foundations. Some countries, such as Lebanon, Jordan, Turkey and recently Algeria, attempted to revive the *waqf* properties with new laws and to develop and even encourage new foundations. In view of an often ultra-liberal economic policy and the privatization and commercialization of social contributions even in Muslim countries, the work of the welfare organizations is of enormous significance; at the same time they represent an appeal to individual responsibility for society and are an expression of the community sense within Muslim society which is particularly evident today.[16]

3. Commerce and ethics

Having discussed three features peculiar to Islam—the prohibition of usury, almsgiving, and foundations—I shall ask a more fundamental question: what can contribute to a fairer economic life in the special conditions of Islam, which is the state religion in many Islamic countries?

Ethical principles for commerce in keeping with Islam

Islam rejects the separation of economy and ethics. Today, this is echoed in the West, now that Westerners have begun to see the problems of neo-liberal economics orientated exclusively on the laws of the free market. Even in a completely economized world, the principles of an Islamic ethic of business and society would need to be reflected on and applied:

- the reference to the one God as the ultimate Lord of all resources and the view of human beings in this world as God's deputies and temporary trustees;
- the same basic rights for all human beings: a right to life, freedom, dignified treatment and possessions if legitimately obtained (by work, inheritance or alms), though there are divinely willed differences in gifts and social position which are to be respected;
- solidarity, brotherliness and responsibility for the well-being of neighbours and the social group;
- personal modesty and social justice.

Is this a middle way between unbridled capitalist individualism and equally unacceptable totalitarian state socialism,[17] a way which could command a consensus among the religions? The economist and Middle East expert, Dieter Weiss, says this about the Islamic guidelines for economic action: 'We see the model of an economy based on social justice, economic independence, personal responsibility and achievement. Work done with care guarantees the satisfaction of material and spiritual needs. There is an emphasis on emotional and social balance and a prohibition against doing damage to the social environment by uncontrolled greed. Resources may not be misused unproductively and in an ethically questionable way. For their sole owner remains Allah, who leaves them to human beings as trustees for a limited lifespan. Such ideas manifestly hardly differ from Christian norms. They largely agree with remarks on the ethics of business by church fathers such as Augustine down to the contemporary demands of Catholic social teaching.'[18]

All this means that there are no objections to the ethical and religious basis of an Islamic economy as long as economic power is not made into a political weapon for ideological reasons (for example, an oil embargo) in a way which has all too often happened in the West, a way that makes impossible effective collaboration with the world economy which, in the meantime, has become increasingly interdependent.

However, here the Shariah again becomes the problem. Why? Because it connects these basic ethical principles capable of forming part of a consensus with a system of detailed regulations which are understood to have been revealed, but which in fact come from the world of the first four paradigms, the city cultures from Medina to Baghdad, and, in some circumstances, are obstacles to better regulations. This is true of the traditional prohibition of usury, which is largely evaded and in any case is only a means to an end. The Islamic economy does not stand or fall by it but, in the present situation, for many Islamists it is still the visible sign of an 'Islamic economy'. That also applies to the almsgiving of 2.5% of income which has been reintroduced in some places. At best this makes up a small percentage of the state income and needs to be rethought; a comparison used by experts is that its place in a modern tax system is like that of a hand pump in a complex hydraulic installation. Lending without interest, or at very low interest, would be of the utmost importance, particularly for the poor population of the southern hemisphere, as has been shown in Bangladesh with great success by the Grameen bank (founded by Muhammad Yunus), which also makes personal loans to women.

Muslim legal scholars say that what the Shariah does not directly allow or forbid is left to human judgement. It is difficult to imagine in what country a popular economy organized on Islamic principles could function: those intent on Islamic renewal still tend to evade the more fundamental questions. But instead of arguing over almsgiving and interest-free banking, there is a much more urgent fundamental question: what would a modern tax system, reshaped in the spirit of Islamic social justice, look like in the framework of a viable state financial, economic and social policy? As I have indicated, a wealth of starting points for the foundation of a modern economic and social system (or several competing systems) can be discovered in the foundation documents of Islam.[19]

However, there is a presupposition to all these considerations: that an open interpretation of such notions of order, orientated on the future, is theologically permissible. No consensus among Muslims seems to be in sight here: 'The central question is that of an open interpretation which on the one hand corresponds to the religious, social and emotional climate within the heterogeneous Arab/Islamic societies and on the other hand is compatible with the structures, mechanisms and forms of organization of the international economic system that have developed in the meantime, in which the Arab states participate and indeed the majority of them want to participate.'[20]

The need for an ethical framework

Islamic economists ask whether, in the long run, the market can exist without morals. The falling away of religious ties in the modern world brought the European economy a new freedom which, with the development of science and technology, gave it a tremendous and unprecedented dynamic. However, many moral ties fell away with the religious ties. The leading theoretician of the liberal economic system, Adam Smith, still took it for granted that the economy[21] is embedded in a moral 'framework' with the three elementary virtues of wisdom, justice and goodness,[22] but today's economic systems have not only emancipated themselves from church and theology but also detached themselves from the overall structure of the world in which we live, with all its norms and laws, including morality, and sometimes also from the state and its legal order. This has led to a rampant ultra-liberalism, with all its well-known consequences: financial bubbles, the falsification of balance sheets, exaggerated managerial salaries and scandalous compensation payments coupled with mass dismissals for the sake of shareholder value.

Stimuli from Protestant social ethics and Catholic social teaching—for example the principles of solidarity and subsidiarity—helped to shape the free market economy into a social market economy in post-war Europe. Similarly, it is conceivable that some of the ethical principles of Islam could help to improve the economic order in Islamic countries. One need think only of the inequalities in the petroleum states that mock all Muslim ideas of justice: the luxurious lifestyle of the rulers is scandalous to many Muslims, so it is not surprising that some of the al-Qaida activists who are also against it come from Saudi Arabia.

The globalization of the economy, technology and communication has also brought with it a globalization of problems from ecology, nuclear and gene technology to the internationalization of the drug problem, crime, the Mafia and terrorism. Numerous business scandals have prompted many people to reflect on the existing system. They have brought the insight that it is by no means guaranteed that the system of market economy will last. At the beginning of the twenty-first century the financial crisis in South-East Asia, the Wall Street scandals, the Californian energy crisis and the falsification of the balance sheet of an Italian company to the tune of billions have shown that the new globalized economy also brings new risks. There will usually be not just one reason for the failure of the system of the market economy but several. As the British economic theorist John H. Dunning has analysed,[23] it is always possible that there will be:

- a failure of the market,
- a failure of institutions,
- a failure of morality.

This prompts the conclusion that if one wants to protect a striving for profit which is in principle justified, but to prevent a boundless greed for profit, there is need for a 'moral framework' which is interdependent on both the markets and the political and social institutions and interactive with them but which must not be identified with a legalization of ethics in every detail.[24]

Islamic commercial principles as a bridge

Ethics is a structure of constants and variables:

– Those who want to see only moral constants everywhere—whether grounded in the Bible or in the Qur'an—will end up in a rigid moral dogmatism or fundamentalism alien to the world.

– Those who think that they can see only variables in ethics, grounded in different cultures or situations, will fall victim to destructive relativism or scepticism.

– But those who combine constants and variables are capable of doing justice to economic laws and ethical imperatives at the same time.

Neither an Islamic nor a Christian business ethic can allow itself to offer the alternative God or money. That would be a grotesque over-simplification. However, there is no question that:

– According to Christian, Muslim and Jewish views, it is not money that rules or should rule the world, but God.
– All believers, whether poor or rich, have to decide whether their hearts are fixed on God or on mammon, whether money is a necessary 'means of payment and living' or an idol for them.
– Everyone is called by the message of the Bible and the Qur'an to be understanding and ready to offer generous help.
– In short, economic values cannot and may not be at the top of the scale of values.

An Islamic market economy with a morality: the selfish *homo oeconomicus* has to become the *homo Islamicus* who is aware of his responsibility. Striving for profit is ethically justified provided that higher values are preserved, the maximization of profit as a leading political and economic principle is not. But may the maximum of (financial) profit be striven for if at the same time it incurs a maximum of (social or ecological) costs? As Umer Chapra, born in Pakistan and adviser to the Saudi Arabian Central Bank, writes: 'We are for a market economy, but with a moral filter.' His book on *Islam and the Economic Challenge*[25] is a standard work of Islamic economic theory. Along these lines, it is possible to formulate guidelines that are capable of attaining a general and inter-religious consensus:

- Only the actions of realistic economists, with ideals and an ethic of responsibility, can benefit the new world economic order. Such an ethic presupposes commitment to ideals of conscience and values in business but asks realistic questions about the foreseeable, and especially the negative, consequences of economic decisions. It also takes responsibility for them.
- Responsible commerce in the postmodern period consists in combining economic strategies and ethical judgement convincingly.
- This new paradigm of a business ethic is realized in the examination of economic activity—for all the legitimacy of profit—to see whether it violates higher goods or values and whether it is compatible with society, the environment and the future: sustainability is a guiding principle of present-day commerce. Because such an argumentative examination of ethical justifications is difficult at an individual level, political part-ordinances are called for.

It is understandable, in view of the progressive globalization and liberalization of the markets and the threat of the economization of all spheres of life, that Muslims want to preserve their own identity. As the economist Steffen Wippel remarks:

> Islamic business principles can contribute towards building a bridge from (supposed) tradition to modernity (in its many forms). By taking up

historical elements and adapting them to present-day demands, on the one hand they attempt to satisfy the motives of strata of the population whose attitude is religious and traditional. On the other hand they also contribute towards legitimizing the principle of capital reimbursement in the form of profit-sharing. In addition they can help to break up structures that have become inflexible as a result of the intervention of state bureaucracies—such as the unattractive upper limits to interest prescribed in Egypt up to the beginning of the 1990s. Thus the concept of an Islamic economy is best understood as an expression of the striving for a free but at the same time socially responsible market economy.[26]

EV

The Future of the Islamic Way of Life

Muslims, too, realize the spiritual reorientation that modernization requires. The Iranian philosopher Abdolkarim Soroush, a former ally of Ayatollah Khomeini who now teaches in America, has expressed the challenge in sharp antitheses. He could make them more differentiated, but his succinct 'contrast between modernity and (Islamic) tradition' makes one think:

> A modern person is critical and demanding (not placid and inert), in search of change (not merely of understanding), in favour of revolution (not just reform), active (not passive), at home with scepticism and anxiety (not certitude), interested in clarity and causality (not bewilderment and enchantment), prone to pride and joy (no sorrow of separation), mindful of life (not death), in pursuit of rights (not only duties), sponsor of creative (not imitative) art, oriented to the external (not just the internal) world, a lover (not a despiser) of life, an intervener in (not merely user of) the world, a user of reason in the service of criticism (not just for understanding). Modern humanity is, in a word, oblivious to its limits and proud of its creative possibilities.[1]

1. Do clothes make people?

In Europe, too, Islam has been an issue in domestic politics, where it often leads to vigorous debates. Believers, and Muslims especially, live out their religion not just in a special ritual sphere but also in their everyday life. Here clothing has always played a role of prime importance. One need think only of questions about wearing the veil or the headscarf. Difficult questions arise here, and not just for Islam.

Problems for Christian churches with the veil

The veil, or scarf which covers the head and often the face and body (usually of women), presumably comes from the East. Wearing the veil offers protection from curious looks, and removing it grants intimacy. Islamic rulers such as the 'Abbasid caliphs, and also the Chinese emperors, used a veil or curtain as a garment, and among the Tuareg of the Sahara today, only men are veiled. Among many peoples the woman had to cover her head completely or partially, especially in public.[2] In the ancient East, there is evidence of the wearing of a veil in Middle Assyrian laws for the second half of the second millennium BCE—from the beginning a sign of the prominent and/or married woman.

So it was not extraordinary that the veil was also widespread in Judaism and in Jewish–Christian communities. When the apostle Paul wanted to introduce this custom for women into the Gentile–Christian community of Corinth, he probably hadn't reflected sufficiently that in the Hellenistic world the veil was worn only on a wedding day or as a fashion accessory. The Corinthian women refused to wear veils. Paul found himself on the defensive and therefore argued, deeply wounded,[3] in his first letter to the community at Corinth (1 Cor.11.2–16), that the head of the man is Christ but the head of the woman is the man: the man may not veil his head because he is the image and splendour of God, but the woman is only the radiance of the man. According to Genesis 2, the woman is made after and from the man; Paul wants to argue from this that, just as men may not come to worship with long hair, so women may not come without a veil (or with their hair let down). For men, long hair is a dishonour, but for women it is an honour and given to them as a quasi-natural veil.

Paul himself immediately goes on to limit this argument: the woman is nothing without the man and the man is nothing without the woman; each is dependent on the other.[4] Women, too, occupy positions of leadership in his communities and he explicitly affirms the charisma of prophecy for women. Paul is attempting to find a way between patriarchalism and misogyny on the one hand and uniformity of the sexes on the other. He does not advocate any relationship of partnership, but he does not advocate one-sided subordination of the woman either; he emphasizes the dependence of the man and the support of the woman. Finally, in an unusual way he breaks the discussion off impatiently, as if he did not trust his own argument, with a reference to the custom now observed in the communities.

Where Paul (in the transition from P I to P II) still differentiated, the church fathers called for complete subordination of the women to men in a very crude way. At the beginning of the third century, in his writing *De virginibus velandis* ('On the veiling of virgins'), the very first Latin theologian, the North African lawyer Tertullian (P III), calls for the veiling of all virgins not only in the church but in public. This was a postulate later realized above all by the sisters in religious orders. The argument became established, even more in Latin theology than in Greek theology, that according to Genesis 1.27, while man and woman are the image of God, according to Genesis 2.21–3 the woman has only a derived image of God. Other shortcomings of women were associated with this.

Down the centuries, the inferiority of the woman was affirmed and emphasized with similarly devious arguments by theologians and bishops: the woman is subordinate to the man and subject to his rule. Even in the twenty-first century, the Catholic Church is still fighting against the emancipation of women. To the present day, when entering church many Italian Catholic women wear a veil, a head-covering or at least a handkerchief, put on quickly; the protocol for papal audiences at a high level provides for an artistically made veil, like that customary elsewhere at burials, while brides still often wear white veils at weddings.

The Reformers (P IV) did not want to change the head covering of women, though occasionally, as in the case of Calvin, the time-conditioned nature of this custom appears on the periphery. Since modern times (P V), in industrial countries, the liturgical use of the veil for women has become increasingly unusual, so that the issue no longer represents a problem for the church authorities. This is an example of how the time-conditioned character of biblical statements can be recognized and in fact they can no longer be applied.[5] Things are different—so far—in Islam.

The commandment for head coverings for Muslim women—not in the Qur'an

No other item of clothing today symbolizes a lifestyle shaped by Islam so much as the veil or the headscarf. Is this because this head covering is prescribed for women in the Qur'an? To be quite clear, we need to look closely at the relevant terminology.[6]

In three passages (33.53; 33.59; 24.31) the Qur'an calls for appropriate and demure covering for women. In the Qur'an, the Arabic word *hijab* (from *hajaba*, 'conceal'),[7] which is customary today, does not mean 'head and shoulder scarf', as it does in present-day Arabic. The word appears seven times in the Qur'an,[8] but it has the meaning 'screen, separation, partition, dividing wall'. Only in surah 33.53 is it at all connected with the Muslim woman: 'And [as for the Prophet's wives], whenever you ask them for anything that you need, ask them from behind a screen; this will but deepen the purity of your hearts and theirs.' The background to this verse is the protection of the private sphere for Muhammad's wives: in his house a curtain separated the reception area, constantly filled with many visitors, from the private rooms. So originally the rule applied to dealings with the wives of the Prophet in their home; *hijab* later underwent a change of meaning to include the female head covering and thus became the norm for all women.

Another key word, *jilbab*, also occurs in surah 33.59: 'O Prophet! Tell thy wives and thy daughters, as well as all [other] believing women, that they should draw over themselves some of their outer garments [when in public]; this will be more conducive to their being recognized [as decent women] and not annoyed. But God is indeed much-forgiving, a dispenser of grace!' The background to this verse is that women in the Prophet's family and other Muslim women were to pull part of their upper garment over their heads when they went out, so that they could be distinguished from slaves and treated with respect. At the time of the Prophet concealment was regarded as a sign of the élite: a free, honourable woman veiled herself on the street but a woman slave did not. However, the verse gives no indication of the nature and extent of the veiling; only in the tradition and in later commentaries on the Qur'an were precise descriptions of how women were to veil themselves developed.

Finally, the term *khimar* is also used in connection with the covering of women, as in surah 24.31. The verse stands in a wider context of rules of behaviour for the encounter between believing women and men: 'And tell the believing women to ... draw their head coverings (*khimar*) over their bosoms.' This kind of covering, which also includes the neck and shoulders, served to distinguish Muslim women from women of other tribes, who simply joined their headscarves at the neck and let the ends fall down behind. However, the word *khimar* can also denote a man's head covering.

So, the Qur'an does not impose any general religious obligations for women's clothing but simply gives guidelines for social decency; discontinuing the clothing of Bedouin women and slave girls, the ideal of urban clothing is commended as being the most decent. However, in subsequent periods, the passages of the Qur'an that I have mentioned were interpreted in a stricter and more limited way, based on certain hadith. Two people above all determined women's head coverings: 'Umar, later the second caliph, a very ascetic man who regulated the lives of Muhammad's widows, and the Prophet's wife 'A'ishah (see B II, 2, 3), a pious, self-confident and politically active wife who soon became the embodiment of the ideal Muslim woman.

Today, many Sunni and Shiite law schools see the Qur'an verses mentioned above as a binding religious instruction for women to wear the headscarf. However, many modern Muslim men and women interpret the surahs and hadiths as instructions conditioned by time and culture, which do not amount to a general obligation to wear the headscarf. After commenting on the verse of the Qur'an that I have quoted,[9] the Arabist Jacqueline Chabbi, who lectures on the history and thought of medieval Islam in the University of Paris, remarks that 'in the Qur'an, from a historical perspective how to dress oneself is not a religious but a social question. Moreover, no passage obliged the Muslims of that time to wear a religious garment.' Hence Chabbi's unambiguous conclusion: 'The allegedly Islamic veil cannot in any way be supported by a passage of the Quran.'[10]

Examined more closely, what fundamentalists describe as 'Islamic clothing' for women is not a return to a traditional Islamic custom of dress but an adaptation to an already Europeanized form of clothing orientated on fundamentalist views of 'divinely willed decency': an ankle-length garment with a high neck and long sleeves which loosely covers the form of the body and a headscarf which, tied fast, shows neither hair nor neck. In contrast, men mostly adapt European clothing but wear shirts with open necks and not ties (which are seen as Western neo-colonialist).

Today for many people such clothing, especially for women, is far more than just clothing or a fashion accessory without religious significance; it has become a symbol of a religious and political attitude. Those who wear it are demonstrating to the outside world their deliberate decision for Islam and against the secularist state. That brings us to the dispute which at present is agitating the public in various countries of Europe more than other religious controversies.

What is at issue in the dispute over the headscarf?

Around 3.1 million Muslims (including more than half a million German Muslims) live in the Federal Republic of Germany, as many as 7 million in France and around twenty million in the member states of the EU. This makes it clear that this question, which is visibly moving societies and in part dividing them, is of the utmost importance. I shall try to deal with it in a matter-of-fact way.

Almost from the beginning of human history, clothing has been more than just a replacement for animal skins. Clothing is an expression of gender, culture, age group, social status, political convictions, attitudes to life and religious allegiance: these are inner values which are communicated non-verbally to others by particular codes.

It is no coincidence that, for millennia, women's clothing has repeatedly been the subject of normative texts—after all, women more than men are regarded as symbolic representatives of social and religious orders. The present-day media reflect this: barely a report on Islam, far less about Islamic fundamentalism, is not illustrated with a woman who is either veiled or wearing a headscarf.

The dispute over the headscarf can be limited if we recognize that every controversial religious position usually has an opposite in which everyone can recognize themselves:

– Women wearing a Muslim headscarf cause no problem on the streets of Europe, where they have become commonplace. But would Christians in, for example, clerical dress or the dress of religious orders remain as untroubled in such traditional Muslim states as Saudi Arabia?

– Women wearing a Muslim headscarf pose no problem in the workplace, where they are valued for their qualities and people care little about their head-dress. But in traditional Muslim states, would the same toleration be accorded to sales girls with, for example, a cross as an expression of their profession of the Christian faith?

– Women wearing a Muslim headscarf pose no problem in society, if they choose to express their membership of the religious and cultural tradition of the land of their origin in this way. But would Muslim relatives be as tolerant towards a Christian wife in a mixed marriage involving a Muslim husband?

In Europe, the headscarf is normally:

– tolerated and acknowledged where it simply represents a religious symbol; in all European states individual freedom of faith and confession is protected by the constitution;

– discussed where it is intended as a political feminist symbol for the dignity of women; many non-Muslims affirm that feminine identity must be protected, whether with a headscarf or in some other way, in a sexist, man's world;

– suspected and doubted where it is a political symbol for the patriarchal oppression of the woman and the aggressive dissemination of Islam; a democratic constitutional state must defend itself against any threat to its basic order of freedom and democracy.

Having marked out the problem, I shall proceed to analysis.

2. Walking the tightrope between Islamism and secularism

Discussion chiefly focuses on the question whether the Muslim headscarf, which in the present situation appears simultaneously as both a religious and a political symbol, may be worn by girls or indeed by women teachers in state institutions, especially in state schools, which in democratic states are obliged to be neutral. The fact that neither governments nor parties nor European courts have a clear opinion shows how difficult the question is to decide. To clarify it, I shall first describe the two extreme positions, as it were the two fundamentalisms, which seem to stand over against each other and to be apparently irreconcilable. At one extreme is a religious fundamentalism which accepts and presents the Islamic religion (and correspondingly the Christian or Jewish religion) as the sole true religion and wants to impress the standards of that religion on the whole of society, and at the other is a secularist fundamentalism which with equal conviction wants to keep any expression of religion out of state institutions and especially out of schools.

An Islamist fundamentalism

When women in the poorer districts of the city of Teheran or in the villages of Iran wore headscarves, this was no more the expression of an ideology than when country women wore them in Germany or Switzerland. It was simply a practical piece of clothing in a society in which the hairdressing was expensive. So for a long time, for Muslim women in Europe wearing a headscarf was not a point of dispute.

Only in 1979 did Ayatollah Ruhollah Khomeini and the Islamic revolution prescribe the headscarf, which covers head and neck, for all women in Iran as an Islamic obligation; this ruling gave women a certain subordinate role and the headscarf became a politically loaded symbol. With a reference to the Qur'an, it became a sign of victory for the new Islam that was triumphing over 'godless modernity'.

Since the headscarf has been made a political instrument by Islamists, every Muslim woman in Europe or America who wears a headscarf must reckon that the majority of contemporaries will see her as a sympathizer with, if not a supporter of, Islamism, however she personally may regard her headscarf. Therefore, in Europe and America, the vast majority of believing Muslim women have freely chosen not to wear the headscarf, despite all the Islamist propaganda. That makes it all the more evident that individual Muslim protagonists of the headscarf enjoy support from Islamic organizations whose Islamizing intentions go far beyond the headscarf. They fail to note that the supreme authority in Sunni Islam, the Sheikh al-Azhar Muhammad Tantawi, has stated (with reference to France): 'If a Muslim woman lives in a land whose laws do not allow the veil, she is to observe the laws.'[11]

It is not surprising that critical Muslim women and Western feminists are against such Islamization. The most prominent German feminist, Alice Schwarzer, shows her customary perception in attacking the Muslim teacher Fereshta Ludin, a German woman born in Afghanistan and given a religious education in Saudi Arabia: 'For twenty-five years the veil for women has been the flag of the Islamic crusader. It is the symbol of separation. So it is time finally to put an end to the patronizing pseudo-toleration—and to show serious respect, respect above all for the millions of Muslim men and women who are even more threatened by the terror from their own camp than we are.'[12] Other women, including Christian theologians, warn against legal action against the headscarf and a cultural battle of the kind which has threatened in France since 2002, in which Islamic and secularist fundamentalists have goaded one another on. They are afraid that bans on headscarves will encourage the withdrawal of many Muslims into separation and further strengthen the fundamentalist Islamists, instead of furthering integration.

A secularist fundamentalism

In France, the integration debate is symbolized by the question whether Muslim girls may wear the headscarf in state schools; this is regarded by the President, the government and Parliament as a litmus test for the lay character of the French Republic. The historical background explains this: the Catholic Church and thus religion, for centuries allied with the monarchy and the nobility, was the main support of the *Ancien régime* and was therefore fought against and persecuted in the Revolution. The 1801 concordat between the papacy and Napoleon restored much power to the church in the state and in schools. The reactionary documents of Popes Gregory XVI and Pius IX (the 1864 *Syllabus errorum*, 'List of errors', and the 1870 definition of papal infallibility) gave the anti-clericals a wealth of ammunition for the battle which was waged under the Third Republic (1870–1914) under the new term *laïcité*. There was laicization of elementary schools that had hitherto been confessional (1882) and a legal separation of state and church (1905). This French laicism was not monolithic but anticlericalism was widespread and, for some, associated with positivism and atheism.

The experiences of the two world wars, of Fascism, Nazism and Communism, the 1965 Declaration on Religious Freedom by the Second Vatican Council and the social reorientation of French theology and pastoral practice associated with it have fundamentally changed the situation in France and relaxed relations between the French state and the Catholic Church. Moreover, President Jacques Chirac's programmatic speech on 17 December 2003 was very well-disposed towards the religions. However, in almost every sentence he conjured up *laïcité* with an almost religious ardour (it was 'the heart of our Republican identity', the 'pillar of our constitution', the 'cornerstone of the Republic'). In Chirac's view, laicity guarantees the cohesion of a society threatened by 'centrifugal forces, by the high esteem for separative particularisms'. The danger is that 'people want to put particular rules above the common law'.[13]

Laïcité, an anticlerical secularism, has remained the French state ideology, though in a more flexible and less aggressive form: in 'a Republic which is one and indivisible' there is not only 'freedom of religion' but also 'freedom from religion', not only are there no clergy in state schools and in official public life, there is no religion at all and there are no religious symbols. School secularism in particular is still regarded as the foundation of religious peace and the integration of all inhabitants into the French Republic and its ideals, which are grounded above all in the freedom of the individual. The almost two thousand years of the history of Christian Gaul/France play not the slightest role in this concept.

Today, however, the French Republic is no longer confronted with an overpowerful, ultramontane political Catholicism (the religion which embraces the majority of the French) but with an often marginalized Muslim minority[14] to whom the freedom of the individual brings little, for whom the 'equality' of the citizens exists only in theory, and who, in this society, hardly experience 'brotherhood'. In France, people attach less importance to multiculturalism than in Germany because, in the law, everyone born in the country is French, regardless of where his or her parents come from. However, for many people, becoming 'French' in this way does not achieve its structural aim. Many children of Muslim immigrants might not accept their parents' values, but they cannot make anything of the secularist identity offered by the French state. Although they are citizens of France in education and job-seeking, they often experience discrimination from the majority and therefore often have little hope for the future. In this situation, they again seek meaning in life and identity in Islam, since they are all too often refused real integration into French society, as can be seen, for example, in the ghettoization of the suburbs.

French citizens, including the élites, who have often grown up without any religious knowledge, are ill-prepared for these controversies with Islam. Under the ideological 'neutrality' of the state, private Christianity, which is certainly allowed, has largely died out and people have often lost a basic knowledge about the religious background to their own culture. So in his speech President Chirac also called for 'a development of instruction about the *fait religieux* in the state schools'. The French Ministry of 'Éducation nationale' is working out how a minimum of information about religion and ethics could be communicated within the framework of the laicist system of schools—something that is taken for granted in other countries.[15]

Neither Islamism nor secularism as a model

France is slowly facing the fact that the secularist French ideology is an exception even in the Western world—quite apart from the Asian, African and of course Muslim world—that has virtually no chance of becoming established, even in the framework of the EU. The French Islamologist, Olivier Roy, points out that outside France people cannot understand a universal law against wearing the veil in schools because it 'seems to prefer authoritarian laicism to democracy and freedom': 'It is the conflict-ridden history of *laïcité à la française*, set against religion, which people do not understand, either in Islamic countries or among our best European neighbours. In this respect France is more like Mexico, the Soviet Union or in part Turkey than countries such as Great Britain, Germany or Italy.'[16] In the USA, Great Britain, Italy and Germany, for all the separation between state and religion, there is a distanced collaboration.

The issue in the dispute over the headscarf in France is timely opposition to a political and religious fanaticism that, it is feared, might create an extra-territorial Islamic enclave in this secular nation. The headscarf could be used by the fundamentalist Islamic groups standing behind this demand (with the help of their lawyers) as a battering ram to break up the secularity of the republic and establish an anachronistic, inhuman, fanatical parallel society.

What would be the consequences? How far should one go to meet the various Muslim lobbying groups? Can the exclusion of Muslim girls from sport and biology teaching and class outings, under pressure from their parents, be tolerated? Can 'pauses for prayer' be inserted into examination timetables and special menus for lunch be requested in school canteens? Can Muslims in hospitals refuse investigation and treatment by personnel of the opposite sex? Can a limited Muslim sector (*carré musulman*) make claims for public cemeteries or urban land for mosques and perhaps for separate swimming baths? Can more and more teaching in vernacular languages be financed and French neglected? Can special broadcasting slots for vernacular programmes be called for? What if the principle of equal rights is flouted by the veiling of women and girls, often enforced by fathers and brothers until they enter into a marriage arranged by parents?

Despite these serious problems, it is an exaggeration to appeal, out of fear of an 'Islamization of the West' and the 'dissolution' of France, to 'French Christianity', as the right-wing conservative Catholic Church does. Some French people even fan such anxieties by quoting the early warning of General de Gaulle that he did not want his home town of Colombey-les-Deux-Églises one day to be given the name Colombey-les-Deux-Mosquées.

In Germany,[17] similar demands to those made in France are being made by some Muslim groups. Although some have been met, experiences so far are not just positive. The best example is the 2002 Schächt judgement of the Federal Constitutional Court which, in some conditions, allows the ritual slaughter of sheep, cattle or goats by cutting the neck, vein and windpipe without first stunning the animal—despite the objections of animal protectionists. What is needed is expert proof, which must be obtained in the Karlsruhe abattoir. According to serious research,[18] thousands of sheep and goats were slaughtered illegally for the Islamic sacrificial feast of Eid al-Adha in 2004. This is proved by the fact that although, during the two previous years, permits had been arranged in Karlsruhe for the slaughter of six hundred animals, not a single one was taken up.

Pessimists are afraid that future European courts will have to show an understanding of 'honour killings', 'forced marriages', the depriving of women and girls of their freedom, justice taken into people's own hands because of 'shame' that has been suffered, and genital mutilation: in all this, the cultural context must at least serve to mitigate the punishment. In 2004 an Institute for Civil Justice was set up in Canada to judge according to Islamic, not Canadian, law. At present people there are discussing whether the democratic constitutional state can allow a parallel (and rather cheaper) system of justice for a million Muslims in Canada to be introduced on the sly. This is rejected by many Muslim women, who prefer Canadian law.

3. Dialogue rather than clash

In both France and Germany, many expert observers of this highly complex situation are convinced that co-existence with Muslims in an originally Christian, secular country cannot be shaped simply by laws and prohibitions. Neither Islamist 'militancy' nor secularist 'neutrality' can lead to a solution satisfactory to all sides. Is there no better way? After the analysis, here is a synthesis, which cries out for dialogue.

Not prohibition but understanding

First, if a 'clash of cultures' over the position of Islam is to be avoided in European countries, dialogue is the only way to constructive solutions. Such dialogue presupposes that:

– the original majority population, with a Christian or laicist orientation, not only offers the other religious groups 'law and order' as the sole instrument of regulation but shows tolerance, if not respect, which ideally rests on serious knowledge. This can create a readiness for understanding, with the aim of peaceful co-existence with Muslims, and at the same time firmly reject and effectively ward off opponents of the constitutional order;

– the religious minorities, especially Muslims and their organizations, which have the constitutional right to practise their religion freely, unreservedly affirm the free democratic basic order, especially the equal rights of men and women guaranteed by the constitution, and the right of women and girls to self-determination.

Secondly, this dialogue will remain barren if it is limited to reciprocal gestures of friendship and courtesies and does not also lead to criticism of the other religion. However, if it is to be convincing, it must always include self-criticism. The peace researcher, Dieter Senghaas of Bremen, who has done great work in intercultural dialogue, warns Europeans and Westerners generally that they should always remember their real legal situation. They should think of all the effort it has taken finally to establish the recognition that all human beings are indeed born free and equal in dignity and rights: the right to tolerance, freedom of religion, equality of the sexes and yet more.[19]

The demand for self criticism applies to all three Abrahamic religions. Here are some topical and significant examples.

– Little conviction is carried by Christian church people who, while making great demands on society and other religions, conceal the past intolerance of the Christian churches and their dogmatic claim to offer salvation exclusively in the name of '*Dominus Iesus*' (the Vatican declaration that I have already mentioned) and who keep silent about and veil their own lack of readiness for change.

– Little conviction is carried by representatives of Judaism who on every occasion complain bitterly about increasing antisemitism in Europe but sweepingly denounce any criticism of the inhuman policy of oppression carried out by the Israeli government under Ariel Sharon as 'antisemitic' and do not utter a word of pity or even justice for the Palestinian people, who have been shamefully treated for decades.

– Little conviction is carried by the Muslim women headscarf activists living in Europe who demand human rights for themselves but quietly overlook the inhuman treatment of women in traditionally Muslim countries, who are robbed of their basic rights: in Saudi Arabia a woman cannot even drive a car or lead a life of her own.

Thirdly, if the dialogue is to lead to concrete solutions, there can be no avoiding negotiations which are inconvenient for both sides, most of which will be about rights. Any one-sided insistence on rights blocks the process of understanding and is counter-productive. It is an old legal maxim that the supreme justice is the supreme injustice. That means that if rights are over-exaggerated they tip over into injustice and inhumanity. Inter-personal relations in which one party constantly insists on its rights become 'self-righteous' and do not last. In a society in which excessive emphasis is put on rights, cohesion is endangered by constant litigation. Rights and responsibilities belong together (see E II).

Especially rights with a religious basis need to be considered responsibly. Again this applies to all the Abrahamic religions, as I shall demonstrate by some topical examples:

– A homosexual Anglican priest who rightly opposes discrimination against homosexuals in the church and in principle has the right to hold the office of bishop should reflect self-critically (if he and his partner want to enter the House of Bishops) whether he is not only legally but also morally right simply to pass over biblically-based objections to the practice of homosexuality, thus consolidating the discord in his diocese and risking a split in the world-wide Anglican Communion—a case from the USA in 2003.
– An Israeli settler who thinks that he has a sacred right to the land west of the Jordan and that he may fight for this right with armed force should reflect self-critically whether the frontiers of Israel, which has existed as a sovereign state for only a few decades of the past three millennia, are really defined clearly 'by God' in the Hebrew Bible, whether the implementation by force of this claimed right will not cost yet more Palestinian and Israeli lives and whether the oppression of a whole people with tanks and bulldozers, planes and rockets, really corresponds to the will of a just and merciful God.
– A Muslim woman teacher, appointed to a Muslim private school in Germany, who thinks that as one who wears the headscarf she must stubbornly fight through all the courts in the land for an appointment to a state school with full rights, should reflect self-critically whether she is not only legally but also morally in the right in understanding her right both to the headscarf and to a state position as the will of God, ignoring the millions of believing Muslim women who feel no obligation to wear the headscarf. Hasn't this vast majority of Muslim women possibly understood better what the people of ancient Rome, which was open to many ethnic and religious groups, expressed in the words 'When in Rome, do as the Romans do'?

Support for this position comes from the Egyptian Muslim cultural scholar Fuad Kandil of the University of Karlsruhe:

> One can only hope that the Muslim community here will succeed in producing *a responsible intellectual and theological élite which is open to the world* and has a correspondingly broad horizon; which understands [realizes] that fundamental rethinking and a degree of religious flexibility are necessary for life here and in other modern Western societies. This intellectual theological

> élite should be in a position to offer believers in the mosques and also members of the Muslim minority generally guidelines to life which would give them support in overcoming their imprisonment in archaic, if not often dogmatically rigid notions of religion and show new ways for religion in a secular world.[20]

What practical position can be commended in the dispute over the headscarf?

Pragmatic, not ideological solutions

It is improbable that the aggressive secularist state ideology *à la française*, which for ideological reasons wants to prohibit the Islamic headscarf to all children in state schools, will become established in Europe. A child is not a figure of authority for another child and it is hard to see why pupils may express their own identity with sporting idols or pop stars on their T-shirts but not religious symbols. Neither a pupil's headscarf, nor cross, nor kippah, must endanger religious peace. In France, too, it would be appropriate for the organs of state to work towards a constructive understanding of Islam, so as to counter the fear of obscurantism or clericalism and to avoid ghettoization and political and religious fanaticism.

It is equally improbable that an aggressively Islamic ideology will establish itself in Europe. In Germany, a vigorous dispute has flared up over whether believing Muslim women teachers may wear the Islamic headscarf in state schools and possibly claim further privileges. In the eyes of many people in the West—regardless of the intention of those who wear the Islamic headscarf—the widely-publicized experiences in Saudi Arabia, Iran and other Islamic countries have made it the symbol of the oppression of women and the rejection of equal rights for the sexes. In view of many Muslim demands, we are entitled to ask in return why, in traditionally Islamic cultures, women play a lesser public role, masculinity is expressed less in creativity than in warlike heroism and the cult of weapons, boys and girls are usually brought up separately and the use of force and corporal punishment is largely endorsed.

The dilemma is that the wearing of a headscarf does not automatically indicate that the person wearing it does not support the constitution; a woman without a headscarf can be just as hostile to the constitution. However, a teacher is regarded as a figure of authority who sets an example, who can have a direct or indirect influence on children and can provide Muslim parents with an argument for their girls to wear the headscarf—and all its implications.

At present, wearing the Islamic headscarf doubtless conveys a questionable political message that conflicts with the equal rights for women laid down in most European constitutions. Nevertheless, it is legitimate to ask whether a general ban on the headscarf for teachers in state schools is the (only) right answer to this problem in present circumstances. Perhaps a pragmatic solution would be preferable to what, in principle, would be a negative solution imposed from secularist or Christian motives. However, such a solution seems difficult, since the legal situation is completely unclear in many countries. A brief comparison between the German and French situations might be illuminating—and not just for these countries.

A short excursus on the German legal situation

In France the legal situation is quite clear: the French Parliament can pass a law in conflicts like that over the headscarf and has done so in this case at the prompting of the President and on the proposal of the government. Legislature, executive and judiciary agree on the matter. Only time will tell whether the law can then be imposed and the policy be ultimately successful or whether it will lead to a dead end.

In Germany, the legal situation is highly complicated: unlike the French Parliament, the German Bundestag cannot just resolve on a law to regulate such conflicts. This is because since 1919 Germany, too, has not been a Christian state but—apart from the National Socialist period and the German Democratic Republic—a pluralistic, constitutional democracy based on the fundamental values of freedom and equality. The general principle of equality (Article 3.1 of the Basic Law) also applies to the religions, interpreted as a prohibition of arbitrariness and discrimination (Article 3.3), which does not allow a preferential position to be given to the Christian religion. However, freedom of faith, conscience and confession is formulated in Article 4, without any legal proviso. This came about after the Second World War because of the catastrophic experiences with National Socialism and a society which at that time was still to some extent homogeneous. As a basic right, freedom of religion is not subject to simple legal restriction. However, the Federal Administrative Court in Leipzig has decided (in June 2004) that the prohibition by the government of Baden-Württemberg of the wearing of a headscarf by a Muslim woman teacher was lawful. A first decision by the EU court concurred.

This raises the question whether, instead of a general ban on headscarves, a provisional examination of their suitability would not be sufficient and appropriate in individual cases: that is, to determine whether the Muslim teacher concerned affirmed the basic Christian character of the school and would be ready to dispense with the headscarf if it disrupted the school peace or if a bias in her teaching activities became evident. Why shouldn't a teacher who gave positive answers to these questions be appointed?[21]

Until now, how far a state allows religious symbols in school and public life seems largely to have been a question of judgement but here the history and culture of the country concerned should also be taken into account—this is easily overlooked by jurists, who think unhistorically and formally. Just as the thousand-year history of an Arab country cannot be understood without the Qur'an, so the thousand-year history of a European country—its literature, art, music and politics—cannot be understood without the Bible. Germany is a secular state, but it has a Christian history that extends to the present: Christianity is a 'formative factor in culture and education'. The cross hangs in schools or courts with a Christian stamp not as a sign of oppression and a lack of equality but, as in the case of the Red Cross, as an admonition to humanity, justice, mercy and love of neighbour. It is a pious custom, going back centuries: even the Nazi Gauleiter Adolf Wagner had to 'creep to the cross' in 1941 when he attempted to replace the crucifixes with 'contemporary decorations'.

However, a consideration of Christian history and culture suggests that Catholic politicians, in particular, should maintain an independence from church (or more precisely Catholic) pressures which seek to undermine the separation of state and church in such questions as contraception, abortion and assisted euthanasia and—as happened through a declaration by the Roman Congregation for the Doctrine of Faith as recently as 2002—attempt to tie Catholic politicians to rigorous Roman moral positions. Most recently, there have also been attempts by bishops to impose a moral monopoly in a secular state. For example, in 2004, the Spanish Conference of Bishops denied the government the right to legislate where it sees the protection of human life endangered.[22] Instead of helping nations to arrive at a reasonable consensus between libertinism and rigorism in disputed moral questions, the Roman Curia is attempting to hold the national episcopates to positions on issues from contraception to assisted euthanasia which are rigoristic and therefore polarize society.

In questions relating to schools, dialogues between parents, teachers and school governors are in most cases defusing the dispute. Likewise, Christians must not expect that in Islamic countries Islamic symbols or inscriptions (for example that on the Dome of the Rock in Jerusalem) will be removed in the name of secularity. However, in our age of religious pluralism the population must become accustomed to a change in the 'religious landscape' expressed in the frequent presence of symbols and buildings of other religions. Christians and Muslims often speak out together against the banishment of religion from the public sphere, for a society cannot dispense with all religious symbols as messages which give meaning without suffering damage in the long term.

I cannot go into more detail on the very important question of Islamic religious education, which is very important for the integration of Muslims into

European societies, since the presuppositions and conditions for this vary in Europe from country to country, and even by state or canton within lands with a federal structure such as Germany and Switzerland. Among other things, this is connected with the different models of the relationship between the state and religious communities and the possibility of religious instruction in public schools generally. Moreover, this question is particularly fluid and the number of models and pilot projects is almost too big to take in. In principle, state and society are still concerned that Muslim children in European countries should neither be brought up without any religious education nor with a radical Islamist attitude (in some circumstances guided by imported imams with no knowledge of the language and culture of the land). This insight is spreading. The Tübingen Professor of Ecumenical Theology, Urs Baumann, has given a comprehensive description of the problem in Germany, with glances at Great Britain, The Netherlands and Austria.[23]

4. Controversies centred on the mosque

As is evident from fears in France, there are many potential matters of dispute between the Muslim minority and the majority, usually Christian, population. It would make little sense to go into them all: the social conditions and the legal situation in the different regions, countries and cities are so different. In Germany the number of Muslims has grown from virtually none in the 1950s to more than four per cent of the population; at 3.2 million, after the two great churches they are the third largest faith community (though by comparison with the fifty-three million Christians are still a clear minority). Questions are about permissions for building mosques and minarets and the permissibility of call to prayer on loudspeakers are therefore being raised with increasing frequency. The law in these relatively novel situations is in flux.

Mosques

The legal situation about the building of mosques, the number of which has increased markedly everywhere, needs to be clarified within the European Union. Buildings for church, cultural and social purposes are generally allowed in residential areas. So in a state which is neutral about religions and worldviews this permission must be extended to corresponding Muslim institutions and, in principle, the building of mosques must be allowed in these areas.

It is very welcome that today, even in the 'holy city' of Rome, not only has there long been a synagogue but for some years there has also been a large mosque, of the kind that have existed for decades in Paris, London and many other European cities. As a guest at the opening of the new al-Manaar mosque in London, in 2001, in the presence of Prince Charles, heir to the British throne, I saw for myself how well Muslim representatives and the city authorities had collaborated in its building. In 1997 in a speech on the occasion of the award of the Karl Kübel prize to the largest mosque in Germany, in Mannheim, a splendid building with dome and minaret, I was able to support the local forces which were arguing, against all tendencies towards ghettoization, for integration and co-operation between the Muslim minority and the majority Christian secular society.

Comparison betweens mosques and churches as places of worship hold only up to a point, because today a Christian church building does not normally exert the same political or social influences on Christians as a mosque does on Muslims. The model of all mosques—the house of the Prophet Muhammad in Medina—was a multi-purpose building: a place for worship, for political gatherings, for negotiations and judgement, for personal prayer and for religious instruction and study (see B III). Young Muslim architects in Germany, Iran and elsewhere are by preference again designing mosques today as multi-purpose buildings, more in a sober modern than in a traditional style.[24]

In the Islamic world, mosques were and are often also centres for the formation of political opinion, indeed agitation. Dissatisfaction with rulers could often be expressed only in mosques, which is why some present-day governments, with their chronic lack of credibility, maintain strict control of the mosques. The globalization of communication which has also embraced the Muslim world gives imams, preachers and teachers in mosques better information about Islam in other regions of the earth, especially in crisis areas such as Bosnia, Palestine and India. It also gives them the possibility of contributing to a trans-national identity and solidarity among Muslims which sometimes even overcomes the split between Sunnis and Shiites. Muslims often gathered in the main mosque of a city to discuss great international problems such as Salman Rushdie's *The Satanic Verses*, the Gulf War, the massacre of Muslims in Bosnia, and the Afghanistan and Iraq wars.

However, there are also tensions and splits within Islam over the mosques. Wahhabi organizations from Saudi Arabia have been increasingly active in Bosnia since the end of the Yugoslav war: they are building a number of new mosques with associated institutions completely dominated by Wahhabi personnel and thus attempting to put their stamp on Bosnian Islam. All this is very much to the displeasure of the majority of Bosnian Muslims, who do not recognize in them their familiar, strongly 'Europeanized', Islam.

As Akbar S. Ahmed, who holds the Chair of Islamic Studies at American University, Washington, reports in his publications, similar developments can be seen in many non-Muslim countries, especially Great Britain where, in great political controversies, those responsible for the mosques as political leaders and spokesmen were more important to the media than the often 'Westernized' leaders of official Muslim associations or those with less traditional roots.[25] In Germany, which is generally peaceful, repeatedly individual mosques are politicized. So the building of mosques is not just about legal questions. This applies even more to the building of highly visible minarets.

Minarets

There are political, aesthetic and socio-psychological aspects to the building of minarets. In Europe, the building of a minaret for the mosque often provokes vigorous resistance from the local people, especially in rural areas. It is understandable that Muslims, with their growing self-confidence, are seeking to utilize to the full their spheres of freedom within the democratic state and thus are using the possibilities provided by a constitutional state. Nevertheless, the question arises how far such disputed questions should be resolved primarily in the law courts.

There is no obligation on Muslims to build a minaret for every mosque, just as a tower or spire is by no means an essential part of a Christian church: minarets are not even mentioned in the Qur'an. At first, the mosque did not have a tower. The minaret became a constituent part of the mosque only after the Umayyad period (mostly in regions which had formerly been Christian). All over the world there are countless mosques without minarets.

It makes a difference whether a high minaret is built in the middle of a big modern big city amidst other tall buildings, with the agreement of those who live there, or in a small traditional town against the will of the populace. Experience shows that, in the course of social development, people get used to much that was originally felt to be 'alien' but they don't get used to some things, small or great. Much needs time.

The legal questions must remain open. In any event, it is questionable whether legal judgements serve religious and social peace in such sensitive issues. Wounds are left on both sides that do not heal quickly. Both sides would do better to work towards a fair compromise, for the sake of a good future life together.

The question of the one who calls Muslims to prayer, the muezzin, is even more tricky than the question of the minaret.

The call to prayer

Happily, so far, the Islamic faith community in Germany has in practice unanimously dispensed with the prayer call (Turkish *ezan*) of the muezzin, amplified through a loudspeaker, which is alien to many of the native population and is disruptive. If given at all, the call is given only within the mosque: no fears of a threat are to be generated, no resentment aroused and social peace is not to be disturbed. However, this consensus has crumbled since in Germany some mosques have begun to appeal to the legislation on the ringing of church bells and are demanding to be allowed to issue the call to prayer in the open air, if not (yet) five times a day, at least for Friday midday prayer. Nevertheless, most communities reject the call to prayer by loudspeaker.

If legal decisions are not only to be formally unassailable but also in keeping with the situation and generally convincing, in religious questions more account needs to be taken of the religious, historical, cultural, religious and social-political dimension of the issue in dispute. Despite certain parallels, Muslims can recognize the important differences between the call of the muezzin and the Christian ringing of bells.

– There was a call to prayer in original Islam by a man, not calling from a minaret but probably, according to old and not only Arab custom, going through the streets with the brief invitation 'Come to prayer' (see B III); this is a parallel to church bell-ringing.
– Later, the Muslim call to prayer usually consisted of a brief sevenfold formula, which contained the confession of faith not only in the one God but also in the Prophet Muhammad—an essential difference from Christian bell-ringing, which contains no verbal message and can be heard in purely musical terms as chimes.
– The call of the muezzin clearly has a religious function, whereas ringing bells can also have purely secular significance (such as warning of a storm or as part of festivities).
– Over the centuries, the call of the muezzin has been made without a loudspeaker system; this has only been introduced very recently and is felt by many to be a disturbance. Today many mosques think that it is a matter of prestige for the call not to be given live by a muezzin but by a tape recording.

For all these reasons, it is clear that the call to prayer is more than a noise problem and that the difference from Christian bell-ringing is important. This does not mean that the ringing of bells should not also be limited. If bell-ringing is not a liturgical sound which indicates a religious observance, but merely marks the course of time, it is right that it should be in keeping with noise regulations. For a long time now, wise pastors have limited bell-ringing, especially in the early hours of the morning, at the request of the members of their own congregations.

At the end of this chapter on some current controversies, it may be appropriate to offer some basic reflections for both Muslims and Christians.

Legal standpoint or dialogue?

In all these disputed issues, both in principle and in practice the question arises whether a legal course is always to be recommended or whether in particular cases it would be better to attempt to resolve the conflict in a different way. In many controversies between the Muslim minority and the Christian–secular majority both sides often think that they are in the right. Both sides can usually advance reasons for their claims and rights—legal, historical, economic, cultural and political—and will always find sufficient advocates to fight through all the legal bodies for their 'well-founded' claims and rights. This doesn't just happen with the Muslim headscarf.

If there is inflexible insistence on a legal standpoint—by whichever side—an atmosphere of suspicion and collective doubt easily arises. There is a vicious circle of mistrust, which makes any readiness for understanding questionable from the start, since it is seen as a weakness or a tactic of the other side. So a deadlock comes about, because neither party sees why it and not the other should renounce a position of right or of power.

Christians (and why not also Muslims?) should also recognize that a voluntary renunciation of legal action for the sake of peace, not generally and always but in individual cases, can be honourable. Indeed, in accordance with Jesus' Sermon on the Mount, such renunciation can lead to great freedom and a new quality of relationship; it can amount to going two miles with someone who has asked for one.[26] This is no small challenge for all those who erroneously think that power and violence, getting one's own way and exploiting the other, wherever that is possible to avoid risk to oneself, is the most advantageous and wisest course.

In dialogue, in an atmosphere of understanding and co-operation, it is possible to arrive not only at a good agreements on individual cases but over time and beyond individual cases, at changes in whole social structures, attitudes and prejudices. Forms of pre-juristic agreement like settlements and mediations have happily increased in recent years. And the Truth and Reconciliation Commission, set up in South Africa specifically by people with a religious motivation, has contributed more to the reconciliation of groups of peoples at enmity with one another than all the courts of the land could have done.

Here the law should not be declared superfluous but it should be applied in a more flexible, more humane way, so that it serves people, Muslims and non-Muslims alike, rather than people serving it. In this way reconciliation and satisfaction become possible in difficult cases, even within the existing legal order.

Muslims, Christians and Jews—together in prayer?

Religions can easily have too high an opinion of themselves but basically they know—and here Jews, Christians and Muslims agree—that it is not the religions but God himself who is the origin and ultimate goal of humankind. In a time when the world is increasingly growing together, when the world economy is becoming global and the other religions are not remote alien entities but close everyday realities, for many people the question is becoming pressing whether the believers of different religions—despite their very different teachings and rites—do not have something in common over and above shared ethical values and norms. May they not also turn together in shared prayer to the one God?

If we are clear that Jews, Christians and Muslims serve one and the same God (see B II, 1), the question of whether one may pray together is, in principle, easy to answer: people of different religions, and especially adherents of the three Abrahamic religions, may, indeed should, pray together more frequently. There are still considerable differences in thinking about God—even within the Christian communities—but God's reality transcends human understanding and imagining. So a different understanding of God need not prevent shared prayer to the one God.

It is harder to see how one can pray together. In my book *Judaism*,[27] I remarked that there are few difficulties in Christians and Jews wanting to pray together psalms or other prayers from the Hebrew Bible or the Jewish tradition. Christians who have taken part in a Jewish service know that one can join in most prayers, even if one understands the term 'torah'—like some Jews—more in the sense of a 'spiritual law'. Conversely, it may not cause many Jews insuperable difficulties, for example, to join in praying the Our Father, since in its essential ingredients this prayer goes back to the Hebrew Bible.

Similarly, it need not cause theological difficulties for Christians and Jews to say some of the fine prayers from the Qur'an with Muslims. After all, the Qur'an maintains that the same God has spoken to Abraham, the prophets, Jesus and Muhammad. Those Christians who have experienced the impressive shared prayer of Muslims will know that it can be meaningful to prostrate oneself before the one God of Abraham, even if the Christian does not confess the Prophet Muhammad in the same way. Conversely, in time, particularly in Diaspora Islam, which is becoming increasingly important for the coming Abrahamic ecumene, there may be greater readiness in some circumstances to join in Jewish or Christian prayers to the one all-merciful God. All this means that within the three prophetic religions it must time and again be possible also to speak to one and the same God through a common prayer.

However, despite all that is held in common, the limits to such shared prayer must also be seen: one cannot expect members of another religion to join in a prayer which expresses the specific character of a religion, what is utterly peculiar and special to its faith. At best, they would join in without seriousness or in a ritualistic way, out of sympathy for their friends of another religion or perhaps not really thinking seriously about what they were doing.

One cannot expect Jews to end their prayer to the God of Israel with the addition 'through Christ our Lord', any more than one can expect Muslims to utter the trinitarian formula 'Glory be to the Father, and to the Son, and to the Holy Spirit'. Conversely, one cannot expect any Christian to join with Jews in the confession of faith that the land of Israel is territory promised by God or to add the confession of the Prophet Muhammad to that of the one God. Here prayer would not unite but divide, would not reconcile but endanger the identity of the other. Much inter-religious sensitivity is therefore needed in the formulation of shared prayer texts and the shaping of shared celebrations.

An ecumenical prayer

A certain consensus is developing here among Christians: 'Interreligious prayer is an expression of the coming together of all the "scattered children of God". It is a sharing in the common journey towards the fulfilment of the Kingdom of God ... Prayer together is an invitation to friendship, to share the reality of a loving God who is our Creator, Redeemer and Sustainer. It is an invitation to enter into the mystery of God which is beyond human intellectual grasp and understanding.'[28]

God alone knows what will be possible in the distant future. After all, the religions have only just begun to get to know each other more closely, to exchange some spiritual experiences and to make some first tentative attempts towards praying together. Think how long it took for Christians of different confessions to understand that they could at least pray together!

What is to be done in the meantime? Theologians and scholars of religion may work out the real religious convergences, despite all the real divergences. At the same time they may help to collect good and usable prayer texts from the different religions and translate them for possible prayers together.[29] However, new prayers should also be written. So I would like to end this chapter about controversial questions of Islamic life with an expression of community, with a prayer that I have composed. I think it could be prayed together by Jews, Christians and Muslims:

> Hidden, eternal, immeasurable God, rich in mercy,
> there is no other God than you.
> You are great and worthy of all praise.
> Your power and grace sustain the universe.
> God of truth without falsity, righteous and true,
> you chose Abraham your submissive servant
> to be the father of many peoples
> and spoke through the prophets.
> Hallowed and praised be your name in all the world,
> and let your will be done wherever people live.
> Living and gracious God, hear our prayer:
> our guilt has become great.
> Forgive us children of Abraham our wars,
> our enmities, our misdeeds against one another.
> Redeem us from all distress and give us peace.
> Guide of our destiny,
> bless the leaders and rulers of the states,
> that they do not lust after power and glory
> but act responsibly for the well-being of their subjects
> and peace among all.
> Guide our religious communities and their leaders,
> so that they not only proclaim the message of peace
> but live it out themselves.
> And to all of us, and those who are not of us,
> give your grace, mercy and all good things,
> and lead us, God of the living,
> on the right way to your eternal glory.

Epilogue: Islam, an Image of Hope

The way along which I have led readers through ever more new paradigms and problem areas to this point has been long: we started from the hostile image and the ideal image of Islam with the aim of surveying the real image. Now, at the end, we can turn our attention to the image of hope.

1. From a hostile image to an image of hope

By means of the original document of Islam, the Qur'an as God's word, I analysed the central message of the One God and of Muhammad his Prophet and the five central structural elements or 'pillars'—the confession of faith, prayer, almsgiving, fasting and pilgrimage. We have been able to see that the 'essence' of Islam shows itself in constantly changing forms, as I have followed a laborious way through fourteen hundred years of history to describe more precisely and investigate the five epoch-making constellations which Islam has undergone: from the paradigm of the original Islamic community (P I) and the paradigm of the Arab empire (P II) through the classic paradigm of Islam as a world religion (P III) and the following paradigm of the Ulama and Sufis (P IV) to the Islamic paradigm of modernization (P V).

Two things have become clear. While these paradigms have lasted down to the present in some structures and tendencies, the political options associated with them—Pan-Arabism, Pan-Islamism, Islamism, socialism and secularism—have not proved helpful in solving the fundamental problems in recent decades. If, despite all the pessimistic economic forecasts for the Muslim world, there is to be revival and an Islamic renewal, the problem areas which are decisive for the future need to be energetically ploughed and recultivated: the Shariah and human rights, state and religion, violence and 'holy' wars, the Islamic economy and morality, Islam and the everyday world. Will it prove possible in the foreseeable future to find a middle way here between an ideological Islamism and an equally ideological secularism which strives for pragmatic, not ideological, solutions, rather than being preoccupied with prohibitions against understanding?

The fateful question for Islam

To conclude, I shall now sketch out an image of hope for Islam which is diametrically opposed to the hostile image I described at the beginning of this book. It must not be confused with an ideal image, because it presupposes the analyses of history and the present and at the same time sketches out realistic prognoses for the future. It is a 'best-case scenario', as opposed to Samuel Huntington's well-known 'worst-case scenario'; as an encouraging vision, it allows realistic hopes for the future.

The decisive question remains: in some Islamic key countries, sooner or later will there be the necessary space to combine the substance of Islam with the challenges of the twenty-first century? This is decisive not only for an interpretation and discussion of Islam orientated on the future but also for an honest application and consistent implementation of the results of this discussion, which are of the utmost importance for science and society generally. What political tendencies will finally establish themselves—in legal science and jurisprudence, Ummah and state, science and society? As I asked earlier, who will be the heirs of a fourteen hundred-year-old religion and culture with views relevant for today: the orthodox traditionalists, the ideological secularists or the religious and political innovators? With a clear view of the paradigm change which has taken place in the meantime and in the face of insistence on the tradition (*taqlid*), these last are opening the door of independent interpretation (*ijtihad*) that has been closed for centuries and undertaking a translation of the original message of Islam for the present day so as to make possible a democratic society and creative culture with innovative science and a viable economy. If they succeed, Islam could make its contribution to world society, a contribution in which, despite all the cultural differences, human rights and human responsibilities would be seen as a common basis.

Particularly in view of the resistance and the pressures in many places,[1] I regard the question of space as the fateful question for Islam; the question is both political and theological.

In politics, many Muslims, from Morocco to Iran, from Afghanistan to Indonesia, hope more or less openly that:

– Islam and modern democracy will come together and that Islam, which theoretically is obligated to Muslim brotherliness (as in the Sunni caliphate and the Shiite imamate), does not continue to remain authoritarian in political practice. There should be no kind of theocratic clerical state in which self-nominated representatives of God on earth take it upon themselves to come forward as rulers, legislators and judges, allegedly responsible to God alone and not to the people and no 'holy scripture' which replaces or fully determines the national constitution (to the point of imposing a universal ban on pork and alcohol and allowing polygamy);

– a democratic system will be established with a separation of powers: a government independent of the clergy and independent parties, freedom of faith and conscience, the right to resist and a legal opposition. For women there is a need for the right to personal responsibility and involvement in all spheres of public life, in all stages of education and all political decisions, in other words the same human rights as for men. This would be a state in which non-Muslims do not just occupy the position of a tolerated minority (exemplary though this may have been in the Middle Ages), but have full civil rights.

In religion, many educated Muslims, an open Ulama and interested 'laity' similarly hope that their efforts for an interpretation of the Qur'an and hadith in accordance with today's insights and demands will finally become a majority view. They hope that:

– Muslims of the twenty-first century need not maintain the uncreatedness and therefore the perfection, infallibility and immutability of the seventy-eight thousand words of the Qur'an (and, indirectly, the words of the Sunnah of the Prophet and the Shariah);

– Muslims may take seriously the historical character of the divine revelation (God's word in the word of the Prophet, God's word attested by the human word). So in practice there should be no fixed literal interpretation and no pattern of argumentation tied to tradition, but an interpretation in accordance with the spirit and meaning of the whole prophetic book. There should be no legalistically overgrown religious heritage but a religious heritage purged in accordance with the criteria of original Islam and reinterpreted for our time. Islam as a foundation should not be understood fundamentalistically but in keeping with our time.

Contemporary Islam

Many Muslims recognize that Arab-Islamic culture, insistently fixated on its heyday long past, suppressed all tendencies towards reform and enlightenment which could have led to a paradigm change and thus remained in permanent crisis. It is not a chance happening of history that in contrast to European countries, Islamic countries did not manage to develop from trade capitalism to an industrial society. The well-known consequence was a complete isolation from scientific and technological progress and thus a scientific, technical, military and cultural subordination to the West, which some individual Muslim groups still compensate for by fighting against the 'unbelieving West'. A dependence on European colonial powers, which lasted into the twentieth century, made this fatal situation worse.

Many though the reasons may be for the underdevelopment of Islamic countries, given the accelerated processes of innovation in the present-day world economy and future falls in oil revenues, the danger of becoming blockaded behind an Islamic defensive culture and the growth of a dangerous potential for frustration in Islamic countries seems to be particularly great. The UN investigations by Arab specialists which I have quoted have shown that although some of the Islamic countries began on modernization very early, their development has lagged behind many countries of East and South-East Asia to a terrifying degree. These—along with the policy of the state of Israel on Palestine—are probably the main roots of the terrorist acts by Arab extremists, chiefly against the United States, which feels that it is the leading Western power.

There is also an increasing realization in the Islamic countries that their difficulties do not lie in a lack of capital but in the 'human factor', in people, their basic attitudes and values, the level of their education and their sense of responsibility. These structures and processes are in turn determined by the cultural and religious 'infrastructure': 'From their own perspective the majority of Islamic societies, in contrast to the cultures of East Asia, have not managed satisfactorily to assimilate Western—secularized Christian—concepts of a scientific worldview and way of shaping the world and to integrate this into their own pattern of values.'[2] The most recent high technology does not reduce the problems but exacerbates them, in so far as they no longer require mechanical capacities, as did earlier techniques, but call for a lack of prejudice and a capacity for adaptation, flexibility, creativity and a potential for innovation. None of these can be bought with petro-dollars, nor can they be given with developmental help; they can be acquired only at the price of granting intellectual freedom. A life in a 'semi-modernity', in which technological innovations are taken over but not social and political achievements, is a balancing act that cannot long be maintained.

The paradigm comparison demonstrated that in the West the Reformation (P IV) and Enlightenment (P V) created the individual—for the first time in world history human dignity, human rights and freedom were guaranteed institutionally against the attacks of religion and the state. This has consequences for the Islamic sphere, whether or not they are wanted. Because of the lack of intellectual freedom, an élite of Muslim scholars and scientists, who did not want either to be hampered and targeted by the existing regime or to be seduced by money, have emigrated to Western Europe and America—not to mention all the Muslim refugees from Palestine, Afghanistan and Iran. Similarly, millions of Muslims have felt compelled by 'circumstances', some of which they have brought upon themselves, to emigrate to non-Muslim countries—Turks to Germany, Algerians to France, Pakistanis to Great Britain. To this extent, too, the paradigm change for Islam is evident: the characteristic of modern times is not, as in European modernity, a Western colonialism imposed by military force but a more or less voluntary Muslim emigration to the West.

The consequences of this emigration for Islam as a whole are now evident: European and American Islam, the growing élites among these millions of Muslims living in the Diaspora, all of them living in lands without a month of fasting and a ban on alcohol, but with intellectual freedom and in principle equal rights for women, will already be sending out a message over the networks of the world's media (like the Jews of the Diaspora formerly and today) about the understanding of Islam that will become established in the future. This will probably not be an orthodox and excessively literal interpretation orientated on the past but a constructive–reformation interpretation orientated on the future. As the Muslim scholar Malek Chebel, whom I have quoted above, writes: 'One must recall the hope of millions of Muslims who reject a radical Islam (many are even fighting against it at risk of their lives) and who attach importance to rediscovering a positive Islam, that of Averroes, of critical thought or of the nineteenth-century "Renaissance" (*nahdah*), in a word an Islam of the Enlightenment, an enlightened Islam.'[3]

2. An enlightened sense of religion

It is to be hoped that more and more Muslims will become convinced that modernization cannot be carried through without enlightenment, without a certain decree of secularization (not to be confused with secularism). Here a notable process has been set in motion, especially among Muslim intellectuals in France.[4] The secular development is in no way a pure privatization of faith, a complete separation of the political and the religious. Rather, here a new form of enlightened religion is manifesting itself. But what, many unsettled Muslims are asking, would be the result of such serious modernization and limited secularization in Islam, which in any case would have to include modern science, technology and democracy?

The modern differentiation of religion

The basic attitude of Islam to spiritual and scientific progress was originally positive, as many verses of the Qur'an and hadith attest: the first five centuries of Islam, when it was culturally ahead of the 'West', speak for themselves. Couldn't Muslims today learn from the Western process of modernization (in a positive and a negative way) and thus avoid certain Western mistakes?

Here first of all we must note the fatal failure of the Christian churches (the Catholic Church above all but in part also the Protestant churches) which, blinded by belief in their tradition and anxious for their spiritual power and rule, declared war on modern science, technology and democracy. Conversely, it was a basic mistake for modernity (evident today) to think that it could suppress, ignore or privatize religion. Thus the Christian church and modernity are together responsible for the way in which the autonomy of the secular spheres in Europe has often turned into a lawlessness that is criticized by Muslims, a loss of orientation and godlessness, and that a rational secularization has turned into a not very rational atheistic agnostic secularism with many negative consequences.

Islam is not bound to repeat the mistakes of Christian Europe. However, if it is to succeed, its spiritual leaders must examine the problems of secularization more consistently. Modern sociologists of religion—following Max Weber, Talcott Parsons and Niklas Luhmann—have made a very precise analysis of the social structure of the transition from premodern to modern society. They have noted that premodern society was primarily differentiated according to social strata (nobility, clergy, citizens, peasants), whereas modern society is primarily differentiated by social function. In contrast to the earlier unitary social system in modern European industrial society, plural, relatively independent secular part- or sub-systems slowly developed, according to different social functions: politics, law, economics, science, education, art, health systems and social welfare. These spheres were emancipated from church, theology and religion and had their own institutions, modes of behaviour, scales of value and overall orientations.

So religion is no longer, as it was in the Middle Ages and the Reformation, an institution set over the social system to guarantee its unity, but merely a factor, a sphere, one part-system among several. But is it so simple? Isn't such a way of looking at things too superficial? For Islam that is an important question.

Islam—only a part-system?

In Islam, such a differentiation must come up against considerable resistance. But can Islam really be closed to this process in the longer term? The transition began long ago. In premodern societies, both Islamic and Christian, with their relatively unitary self-understanding, moulded by the upper classes (of the religious and political élite), the whole person with all his or her functions was integrated into a unitary religious and moral system firmly defended against the forces of change. Family and family law above all assigned each person his or her place in a specific social class. Religion legitimized and guaranteed the existing social system.

Although this medieval system was long fortified by religion and institutionally safeguarded in Christian Europe, it did not last, either in Europe or in North America—except in some Roman Catholic countries and cultural enclaves that remained backward until the time of the Second Vatican Council. So will it also maintain itself in the Islamic world?

We should realistically concede that if, in a modern society, traditional class structures necessarily retreat behind the new functional structures and if neither membership of a family nor membership of a religion governs the new sub-systems which have formed, then in Islamic societies in the process of modernization religion can no longer occupy the central role of institutional guarantor of the unity of the social system as it traditionally did. In Islamic countries, too, politics, law and the economy, science, education and art will slowly develop into autonomous, secular spheres that can no longer be controlled by religion but have been emancipated in a worldly way. This process has already, imperceptibly, begun. In particular, modern educational systems, if they are to be efficient, must become largely independent and free of all religious supervision. Indeed, they have already attained this status in many Islamic countries—with the help of the political (state) and scholarly (university) sub-systems.

This complex process of secularization is not a product of an evil will, as some clergy (both Christian and Islamic) keep insinuating. It is a process that was unavoidable and necessary if the modernization in all spheres which was striven for from the seventeenth century onwards by the West—and is still being striven for by Islam—was to be completed. For Islamic countries, such a development is not a harmful Western import that can be diluted or removed by religious education but is unavoidable for any modern society. It was not the Christian missions that decisively shook Islam, as Muslims keep claiming, but the modernization which embraced the whole world and cannot be reversed, even in Islamic countries.

However, one thing must not be overlooked. The price that the West had to pay for the differentiation of society and the epoch-making change in values and norms in the society of late modernity associated with it was a high one: the other spheres of life were left with no religious and indeed largely also with no moral basis and ultimate horizon of meaning. In the long term, the self-interest of individuals and social groups, which can easily degenerate into naked egotism, is not a sufficient foundation for life. Living standards are no substitute for meaning in life. From this follows a deep crisis of orientation and an often almost desperate search for meaning, criteria and a shared basis for values. Like absolutized faith, so too absolutized reason can set free destructive energies, with devastating effects in the form of unreligious or pseudo-religious ideologies. If many Muslims are showing themselves dissatisfied not only with Marxist–materialist but also with Western–technological modernization and are returning to the traditions of their religion, it is because of such anxieties—which are certainly not unjustified. Here is a new task for Muslims and Christians together.

Ethics as the foundation of democracy—in Islam too

'The free secular state lives by presuppositions which it can no longer itself guarantee without putting its freedom in question.' This is an oft-quoted remark by the constitutional lawyer Ernst-Wolfgang Böckenförde.[5] The ideologically neutral state may not decree a meaning in life nor prescribe any supreme values by law; it has to presuppose them if its own mechanisms are to function at all and its laws are to be observed. The democratic state needs a fundamental ethical consensus, supported by all social groups, to which all religions, philosophies and worldviews contribute—in Islamic countries primarily Islam, in countries with a Christian character Christianity. It needs a fundamental consensus, that is, not a 'strict' or total' consensus but what John Rawls calls an 'overlapping consensus'[6] on binding values, irrevocable criteria and basic personal attitudes.

In such a situation, a religion will certainly fall victim to ethically unproductive ideological secularism which, from a global perspective, represents an exceptional phenomenon in Western and Central Europe and among American élites. However, if it is wise, religion will not strive once again for a clerical domination of secular spheres (an approach that can be seen behind the papal Roman plea for 'the truth' which the absolute ruler thinks that he can state 'infallibly'). Rather, religion will bring about, inspire, motivate and possibly also correct 'secularity', 'affirmation of the world', from the perspective of faith.

- If, for example, a majority (of whatever size) says that it will legitimize torture or violently suppress a minority (of whatever kind), then religion must defend the inalienable dignity of every human being and protest.
- If super-rich potentates shamelessly exploit their people or in a modern business system individual managers dismiss thousands of staff in the name of

globalization and vote themselves massive remuneration, then religion may, indeed should, call for social justice.

– If a power or superpower thinks that it may unilaterally achieve its aims of hegemony, violate international law, ignore the United Nations and wage a preventive war, then the religious leaders must argue together for peace and against war.

In principle, politics, the economy, the law, science, the education of individuals and society need a moral framework. I call this an ethic of humanity or a global ethic. And all religions, especially Islam, Judaism and Christianity, can make an important contribution to this. Although it is often misused, the Qur'an, like the Hebrew Bible or the New Testament, can give such a 'global ethic' a solid basis and spell it out in a convincing way. To this degree, religion is more than just a 'factor' or 'sub-system' alongside others. It is interdependent with, and interacts with, all the other sub-systems (which are allegedly completely 'self-referential'); indeed it functions for the different sub-systems as the depth dimension that can always be appealed to in the ethical discourse of a society. However, a humanistic ethic, with no religious foundation, can also play this social role.

Islam as a help in life

Today Muslims, even those living in Islamic countries, are increasingly confronted with a plurality of possibilities for living and lifestyles and are forced to make choices: education, profession, marriage partner, number of children and how to spend their leisure time. In such countries religion, too, is also affected by individualization and pluralization. The question arises: what can Islam offer individuals to help them live in a modern democracy? Briefly and schematically, two things:

– In view of growing individualization, a Muslim conviction that is sensitive to the times can help people towards a right personal experience, self-discovery, self-determination and self-fulfilment. Self-fulfilment does not necessarily lead to an over-estimation of the self and self-centredness but is combined with responsibility for the self and the world and responsibility for fellow human beings and society.

– In view of the growing pluralization, a Muslim conviction which is sensitive towards the times can keep people from cobbling together, from the free market of religious possibilities, a private religion made up of religious, para-religious and even pseudo-religious elements which is all too convenient and all too orientated on their own needs ('patchwork religion'). What is binding on all believers must not be replaced with randomness, but with the expansion, enrichment, deepening of Islamic religious practice through the insights, symbols, ethical demands and religious practices of other religions and alternative movements.

Such a contemporary Islam will not over-hastily condemn modernity but affirm its human face: there must be no Muslim sub-culture in the ghetto. At the same time, a contemporary Islam will avoid the inhuman constrictions and destructive effects of modernity: there will be no modernistic concessions and no selling out of the substance of Islam. A rational relationship to the modern world and trust in a 'personal' God could support each other. Such an Islam, sensitive to the times, is challenged to become a new, differentiated, pluralistic holistic synthesis which, with good reason, one would call postmodern.

To give an example: it is remarkable how in Egypt a young Islamic preacher, Amr Khalid, has appeared. In contrast to the Ulama he is modern in his dress (suit and tie), language (Egyptian dialect instead of classical Arabic) and forms of expression (friendly admonitions instead of threats of punishment). He has found a great following in the media. He combines Islam, understood in a traditional way, with a modern way of life by emphasizing subjectivity, self-development and personal responsibility. He does not reject daily prayers, abstinence from alcohol and a conservative sexual morality. Many people in Egypt are asking: does Amr Khalid, as a modern Muslim—not an Islamist but not a member of the old-fashioned Ulama either—perhaps represent the model of the future?[7]

The problems that Islam faces in the twenty-first century are not very different from those of Christianity, though there is something of a time lag. Four problem areas can be marked out for both Islam and Christianity, relating to different dimensions of reality—individual everyday life and global problems—and needing intense reflection and wise practical implementation:

- the cosmic dimension: human beings and nature (the concern of the ecological movement);
- the anthropological dimension: men and women (the concern of the women's movement);
- the socio-political dimension: rich and poor (the concern of the social organizations);
- the religious dimension; human beings and God (the concern of the Christian and interreligious ecumene).

Islam and world problems: the population explosion as a test case

Islam can certainly make a contribution on individual problems and provide help for living. But what is its position on the great problems of the world, for example, human rights, scarcity of resources, environmental pollution, extinction of forests, climate change, traffic problems, waste, mass unemployment, government, debt crises, the gulf between North and South, Third World problems, over-armament, gene manipulation and the nuclear threat? It would be asking far too much for a religion to make a substantial contribution to all these problem areas but it should have something to say on one or the other of them. Islam can do this, as I can illustrate using a test case.

Population policy is a test case not only for Islam but for all religions. Excessively high population growth, above all in the poor countries, poses one of the greatest threats to the survival of humankind with a life worth living: according to the 'median' projection of the UNO the world's population will rise from 6.3 billion in 2004 to seven billion by 2015 at the latest, to around nine billion by 2050 and then possibly to as high as eleven billion before a reversal can be expected.[8] The effects of population growth are already catastrophic in many places: millions of people have no schools, no jobs, and not even enough food and water. However, counter trends are developing in some countries, including those of the southern hemisphere. Lower growth rates decisively depend on more couples using contraception; there are further causes for this decline, negatively the rise of mortality rates through Aids and the lowering of life expectancy in some countries, and positively the fight against poverty and better educational opportunities.

By comparison with other religions, the position of Christianity is not very strong over questions of population policy, because the Pope and episcopate of the Roman Catholic Church have for years stubbornly rejected any form of contraception (not just the pill) as immoral, against the overwhelming majority of their own faithful and pastors, thus indirectly making a massive contribution to the population explosion. At the 1994 UN World Population Conference in Cairo a controversy erupted over the relationship between the population explosion and contraception: an unholy alliance between Catholic Vatican fundamentalists and Islamists from the smaller Islamic states did all it could to impose a narrow-minded sexual morality and so irresponsibly to give free rein to uncontrolled population development.

A welcome counter-movement developed: large and populous Islamic countries did not go along with this policy of obstruction but supported the UN programme. Most recent investigations show that the equation 'Islam equals abundant children' can no longer be used sweepingly, any more than can the equation 'Catholic equals abundant children'. The study *Population Policy in the Islamic Countries* by Ahad Rahmanzadeh[9] demonstrates that everything depends on the policy that Islamic leaders pursue over this set of problems.

Developments in Islamist Iran are illuminating here: in the twentieth century the Iranian population increased sevenfold, from nine million to over sixty-three million. In the mid-1980s, population growth reached a dramatic climax at an annual 3.4%. After the 1979 revolution the clerical authorities, like the papacy, had initially banned family planning, for religious but also for strategic reasons. Later, however, this policy was corrected, so that population growth in Iran has continuously slowed and by 2003 had sunk to 1.2% per annum. Without the intervention of the religious leaders in the programme, family planning in Iran, in contrast to other Islamic countries, could never have been implemented so successfully and so consistently nationwide. The direct dovetailing of state and religion was thus more an advantage than a disadvantage in this decision, which was more pragmatic than dogmatic. It also helped that health education and information, for example about different methods of contraception, were at the centre of the programme rather than a legal ordinance. Laicist Turkey was not as successful as Islamist Iran, because its family planning was based less on information and advice. In Iran in 1999, around fifty-seven per cent of married couples used a modern method of contraception; in Turkey it was only thirty-eight per cent.

So Islam has resources which can contribute not only to coping with central questions of life but also to solving the great problems of the world. Does this apply to the central problem of war and peace: clash or dialogue among civilizations?

3. The Muslim contribution to dialogue among civilizations

In 1998, three years to the day before 11 September 2001, the UN General Assembly announced in a resolution its 'firm determination to facilitate and promote dialogue among civilizations' and, in the face of all the Cassandra-like cries of a 'clash of civilizations', proclaimed 'the year 2001 as the United Nations Year of Dialogue among Civilizations'.[10]

Bridges into the future

Unexpectedly, the prompting for this resolution came from the Muslim side, from the Islamic republic of Iran and its president Seyed Mohammad Khatami (increasingly attacked and hindered in his own country by the conservatives, although elected by an overwhelming majority). In his speech to the UN General Assembly on 21 September 1998 he stated: 'In the name of the Islamic Republic of Iran I would like to propose that the United Nations, as a first step, designates the year 2001 as the "Year of Dialogue among Civilizations", in the earnest hope that through such a dialogue the realization of universal justice and liberty may be initiated. Among the worthiest achievements of this century is the acceptance of the necessity and significance of dialogue and the rejection of force, the promotion of understanding in the cultural, economic and political fields, and the strengthening of the foundations of liberty, justice and human rights. The establishment and enhancement of civility, whether at the national or international level, is contingent upon dialogue among societies and civilizations representing different views, inclinations and approaches. If humanity at the threshold of the new century and new millennium, devotes all its efforts to institutionalizing dialogue, replacing hostility and confrontation with discourse and understanding, it will leave an invaluable legacy for the benefit of future generations.'[11]

The events of 11 September 2001, the war in Afghanistan and the escalating situation in the Middle East tragically confirmed the urgent need for such an initiative. On 8 and 9 November 2001, the UN General Assembly again met to discuss the dialogue between civilizations—the activities of the year, the report by the group of experts and the wider agenda. Under the leadership of the former deputy UN secretary-general Giandomenico Picco, some members of this group, the Group of Distinguished Persons convened by the UN secretary-general Kofi Annan, which on the Islamic side included Dr A. Kamal Aboulmagd (of Egypt), Prince El Hassan bin Talal (of Jordan) and Dr Javaad Zarif (of Iran),[12] gave the UN secretary-general a printed copy of the American original of their report *Crossing the Divide. Dialogue among Civilizations.*[13] As I have written in the context of the Israel–Palestine conflict (see D II), this manifesto aimed at a new paradigm of international relations on the basis of a global ethic. Unfortunately, in the USA (in contrast to Germany) neither the motto of the international year nor this publication caught the attention of the media, the public or politicians, although it would have been highly topical and politically explosive in the country.

After two days of discussion in the General Assembly, the delegations of the various states, including very many Islamic states, spoke out against the clash of civilizations and for the dialogue among civilizations. Finally, on 9 November, the General Assembly passed a resolution (initiated above all from the Muslim side) with a 'global agenda for dialogue among civilizations'.[14] It recalled the previous resolutions and stressed the great importance of a dialogue between civilizations. Nine articles describe at length the aims, principles and participants in this dialogue: Article 1 describes the dialogue between the civilizations as a process which is grounded in the 'collective desire to learn, to open up prejudices and to investigate and develop common meaning and core values' and Article 2 specifically calls for 'the development of better understanding on the basis of shared ethical standards and universal human values'.[15]

Shared ethical standards and universal human values

In this resolution, the UN General Assembly expressed what the Group of Distinguished Persons had set out at length in its report: the view that there will only be real co-existence, authentic community, on this globe when 'people live together, share an ethos and a practicable civil ethic and are unified in their commitment to a common good'.[16] What does this mean? It does not mean Western cultural imperialism, as Muslims sometimes fear: the aim is not a single world religion or a uniform world culture but a juxtaposition of 'diversity in lifestyles and differences in belief', though that is possible without conflict only 'so long as the diversity and differences do not infringe upon the fundamental freedoms and rights of others'.[17]

It was natural to the authors of the report, very much in line with the 1993 Chicago Parliament of the World's Religions, to emphasize, as the first great shared ethical value of humankind, the Golden Rule rooted in all religious and humanist traditions. It calls for 'the awareness, recognition, acceptance and celebration of the other in our own self-understanding'; it can help us 'to learn to be humane'.[18] Humanity, mutuality and trust are the basic attitudes which have to be practised for a life in the spirit of the golden rule: 'Without humanity and trust there is no common ground for exploring values as a joint spiritual venture of like-minded dialogical partners.'[19]

Finally, from the perspective of reconciliation as an answer to the vicious circle of hatred and violence—an approach dramatically confirmed by the events of 11 September and their consequences—those four irrevocable directives are recalled which alongside the Golden Rule and the principle of humanity make up the nucleus of a global ethic: the demands for non-violence, justice, truthfulness and the partnership of men and women.[20]

How can these values and standards be confirmed and empowered from the Muslim tradition?

The Islamic foundation for a global ethic

Asghar Ali Engineer, a leading Indian Muslim scholar, has compared the Parliament of the World's Religions' 1993 Declaration toward a Global Ethic with the message of the Qur'an. His succinct conclusion is 'that the Declaration toward a Global Ethic completely corresponds to the spirit of Islam'.[21]

Taking account of the insights of his work, I shall describe briefly how the four elementary ethical obligations that occur in all the great religious and philosophical traditions are also grounded in the holy book of Muslims, the Qur'an. I shall keep to the core statements of the 1993 Declaration toward a Global Ethic, confirmed by 'A Call to our Leading Institutions' made at the 1999 Parliament of the World's Religions in Cape Town, South Africa, and finally the report *Crossing the Divide. Dialogue among Civilizations* of 2001.

- A culture of non-violence and respect for life:
  'Have respect for life'—'You shall not kill', torture, torment, violate!
  Respect for life, for all life, is deeply rooted in Islamic ethics. The Qur'an says that the killing of an innocent person is equivalent to killing the whole of humankind[22] and the Prophet's concern for the animals and for nature emerges from the hadith.
- A culture of solidarity and a just economic order:
  'Deal honestly and fairly'—'You shall not steal', exploit, bribe, corrupt.
  For the ethic of the Qur'an, justice is so central that only a just person can be a right believer. 'O you who have attained to faith! Be ever steadfast in your devotion to God, bearing witness to the truth in all equity; and never let hatred of anything lead you into the sin of deviating from justice. Be just: this is closest to being God-conscious.'[23] An unjust social order cannot be an Islamic order. The Qur'an requires that the surpluses beyond actual need shall be distributed to the needy and poor. Mandatory almsgiving, the *zakat*, is one of the five pillars of Islam.
- A culture of tolerance and a life of truthfulness:
  'Speak and act truthfully'—'You shall not lie', deceive, falsify, manipulate.
  The ethic of the Qur'an is essentially grounded in faithfulness to the truth. Truth (*haqq*) is one of the names of God and as central a value in Islam as justice. A just social order cannot be realized without truthfulness as a fundamental postulate.
- A culture of equal rights and partnership between men and women:
  'Respect and love one another': 'Do not abuse sexuality', do not deceive, humiliate, dishonour.
  In principle, the Qur'an gives women and men the same status: 'The rights of the wives [with regard to their husbands] are equal to the [husbands'] rights with regard to them, although men have precedence over them [in this respect].'[24]

The principle of humanity, the most elementary principle of the global ethic, the human dignity of each individual, appears in the basic statements of the Qur'an: God has chosen human beings before all other creatures,[25] and appointed them his governors on earth.[26] The golden rule of mutuality has been handed down in the Sunnah: 'None of you is a believer as long as he does not wish for his brother what he wishes for himself.'[27]

All this is so obviously the common heritage of the three Abrahamic religions that many bitter controversies of the past could be overcome in its spirit.

It is made historically specific in the famous Islamic code of responsibilities in surah 17.22–38, which closely corresponds with the biblical Decalogue (see B II, 2: Box on 'The common basic ethic').

The basis for an understanding between Islam and the West

With the debate and resolution by the UN General Assembly the dialogue among civilizations and thus the idea of a global ethic have entered the fundamental considerations of the United Nations, stimulated above all by the initiatives of its secretary-general (and winner of the Nobel Peace Prize) Kofi Annan. The secretary-general confirmed this personally in a major, and much noted, Global Ethic Lecture, 'Are There Still Universal Values?', which he gave at the University of Tübingen on 12 December 2003 at the invitation of the Global Ethic Foundation.[28]

Kofi Annan is convinced that 'universal values are more acutely needed, in this age of globalization, than ever before. Every society needs to be bound together by common values, so that its members know what to expect of each other, and have some shared principles by which to manage their differences without resorting to violence. That is true of local communities and of national communities.'

This applies especially to the relationship between the West and Islam. For all the condemnation of the attacks of 11 September 2001 on the United States 'we must not allow them to provoke a "clash of civilizations", in which millions of flesh-and-blood human beings fall victim to a battle between two abstractions—"Islam" and "the West"—as if Islamic and Western values were incompatible'. 'They are not, as millions of devout Muslims living here in Germany, and elsewhere in the West, would be the first to tell you. Yet many of those Muslims now find themselves the objects of suspicion, harassment and discrimination, while in parts of the Islamic world anyone associated with the West or Western values is exposed to hostility and even violence.'

Kofi Annan emphasizes 'that the validity of universal values does not depend on their being universally obeyed or applied. Ethical codes are always the expression of an ideal and an aspiration, a standard by which moral failings can be judged rather than a prescription for ensuring that they never occur.'

For Christianity and for Islam, 'no religion or ethical system should ever be condemned because of the moral lapses of some of its adherents. If I, as a Christian, for instance, would not wish my faith to be judged by the actions of the Crusaders or the Inquisition, I should be very careful not to judge anyone else's faith by the actions that a few terrorists may commit in its name.'

'So if it is wrong to condemn a particular faith or set of values because of the actions or statements of some of its adherents, it must also be wrong to abandon the idea that certain values are universal just because some human beings do not appear to accept them. Indeed, I would argue that it is precisely the existence of such aberrations that obliges us to assert and uphold common values. We need to be able to say that certain actions and beliefs are not just contrary to our own particular morality, but should be rejected by all humanity.'

Kofi Annan is well aware that values and norms can never be applied in an abstract way but always only concretely, taking into account the situation of the individual and the culture. This allows a certain range of different interpretations and realizations: 'Of course having such common values does not solve all problems, or eliminate the scope for different societies to solve them in different ways.'

The secretary-general spells this out by means of the four directives of the Parliament of the World's Religions' Declaration toward a Global Ethic:

- We may all be sincerely committed to non-violence and respect for life, and yet disagree about whether it is legitimate to take the lives of those who have themselves taken life, or to use violence to defend the innocent when violence is being used against them.
- We may all be genuinely committed to solidarity with our fellow human beings and a just economic order, and yet not agree which policies will be most effective in bringing about that order.
- We may all be deeply attached to tolerance and truthfulness, and yet not agree how tolerant we should be of states or systems that seem to us *in*tolerant and *un*truthful.
- And we may all be genuinely committed to equal rights and partnership between men and women, without agreeing on how far the social roles of men and women should be differentiated, or whether it is the responsibility of society to enforce the sanctity of the marriage bond.[29]

This was the verdict of the secretary-general of the United Nations, who in 2003 led the world organization in the best possible way in what was perhaps its most difficult period so far.

Conclusion

With these developments (and I cannot conceal a sigh of relief) I have come to the end of my trilogy 'The Religious Situation of Our Time'. I am well aware that in these three volumes, *Judaism* (1991, ET 1992), *Christianity* (1994, ET 1995) and *Islam* (2004, ET 2007), I have made some uncomfortable remarks about each of the three Abrahamic religions which have been my main scholarly preoccupation over the last twenty-five years. At the same time I have opened up perspectives on the future that sometimes may have seemed all too utopian. But the whole work is borne up by a threefold unshakable hope:

- that each of the three prophetic religions has an effective potential for the future on the basis of its spiritual and ethical wealth;
- that all three can come to share more thorough understanding and collaboration;
- that all three world religions together will make an indispensable contribution to a more peaceful and more just world.

I would like to end the trilogy with the programmatic statements with which I began it twenty-five years ago. However, having completed the investigation of the foundations of the religions that I called for there, I can revise them and make them more precise, in a way which Jews, Christians and Muslims may affirm even more:

No peace among the nations
without peace among the religions.

No peace among the religions
without dialogue between the religions.

No dialogue between the religions
without global ethical standards.

No survival of our globe without
a global ethic, a world ethic,
supported by both
the religious and the non-religious.

Notes

Short bibliography of works frequently cited

Lexica

Encyclopedia of Islam, new edition, ed. H.A.R. Gibb et al. (6 vols), Leiden 1960–90, cited as *EncIsl*
Oxford Encyclopedia of the Modern Islamic World (4 vols), New York 1995, cited as *EncModIsl*
Encyclopedia of the Qur'an (4 vols), Leiden 2001ff., cited as *EncQur*
Handwörterbuch des Islam, ed. A.J. Wensinck and J.H. Kramers, Leiden 1976, cited as *HdI*

Encyclopaedia Judaica, ed. C. Roth and G. Wigoder (17 vols), Jerusalem nd
Die Religion in Geschichte und Gegenwart. Handwörterbuch für Theologie und Religionswissenschaft, ed. K. Galling (6 vols), Tübingen [3]1957–62
Theological Dictionary of the New Testament, ed. G. Kittel, ET G.W. Bromiley (10 vols), Grand Rapids 1964ff.
Theologische Realenzyklopädie, ed. G. Krause and G. Müller (30 vols), Berlin 1966ff., cited as *TRE*
Lexikon für Theologie und Kirche, ed. J. Höger and K. Rahner (10 vols), Freiburg 1957ff.

Dictionnaire des Religions, ed. P. Poupard, Paris [2]1985
Encyclopaedia of Religion, ed. M. Eliade (16 vols), New York 1987, cited as *EncRel*
Lexikon religiöser Grundbegriffe: Judentum, Christentum, Islam, ed. A.T. Khoury, Graz 1987

Works by Hans Küng (the date of the original German publication is in brackets)

Christianity and the World Religions (1984, Part A on Islam with J. van Ess), New York 1986 and London 1987
Christianity and Chinese Religions (1988, with Julia Ching), New York 1989 and London 1993

Tracing the Way. Spiritual Dimensions of the World Religions (*Spurensuche*, 2000), London and New York 2002
Judaism (1991), London and New York 1992
Christianity (1994), London and New York 1995

On Being a Christian (1974), London and New York 1977
Does God Exist? An Answer for Today (1978), London and New York 1980
Eternal Life? (1982), London and New York 1984
The Church (1967), London and New York 1967
Women in Christianity (2001), London and New York 2001

Global Responsibility (1990), London and New York 1991
A Global Ethic. The Declaration of the Parliament of the World's Religions (ed. with Karl-Josef Kuschel) (1993), London and New York 1993
A Global Ethic for Global Politics and Economics (1997), London and New York 1997
Crossing the Divide. Dialogue among Civilizations, South Orange, NJ 2001

The Aim of this Book

1. Cf. H. Küng and D. Senghaas (eds), *Friedenspolitik. Ethische Grundlagen internationaler Beziehungen*, Munich 2003. In my introduction, at an early stage I gave a precise analysis of 'How the Iraq War came about', which was confirmed by subsequent events. I am deeply grateful for their collaboration not only to my co-editor Dieter Senghaas, but also to Ernst-Otto Czempiel, Otfried Höffe, Helmut Fahrenbach, Volker Rittberger, Manfred Mols, Norbert Brieskorn, Alois Riklin, Andreas Hasenclever, Rainer Tetzlaff and Klaus M. Leisinger.

A. Origin

1. Because, as I remarked in the introduction, the view expressed in this book is the end-product of a long course of thinking which has matured over decades, the structural elements which support the view need to be made quite clear at this point. This will show the reader that my view is comprehensive and well-founded. Consequently, from time to time I refer in the notes to earlier writings. This is not ritualized self-quotation, but a documentation of the way I have described.

A I. A Controversial Religion

2. Cf. S. Huntington, 'The Clash of Civilizations?', in *Foreign Affairs* 72.3, 1993, 22–49.
3. H. Nicklas, 'Feindbilder', in *Pipers Wörterbuch zur Politik*, Vol. V (ed. A. Boeckh), Munich 1984, 148–50: 148; cf. for what follows also G. Sommer et al. (eds), *Feindbilder im Dienste der Aufrüstung. Beiträge aus Psychologie und anderen Humanwissenschaften*, Marburg ²1988; G. Stein and V. Windfuhr (eds), *Ein Tag im September: 11. 9. 2001. 1. Hintergründe—Folgen—Perspektiven*, Heidelberg 2002.

4. Cf. G. Rotter, *Allahs Plagiator. Die publizistischen Raubzüge des 'Nahost-experten' Gerhard Konzelmann*, Heidelberg 1992.
5. Cf. V. Klemm and K. Hörner (eds), *Das Schwert des 'Experten'. Peter Scholl-Latours verzerrtes Araber- und Islambild*, Heidelberg 1993.
6. Cf. the texts translated into English in J.W. Sweetman, *Islam and Christian Theology*, Part I, Vol. I, London 1945; Part II, Vol. 1, London 1955. Cf. also J. Assfalg, 'Agapios, melchitischer Bischof von Hierapolis', in *Lexikon für Theologie und Kirche.*
7. Cf. Patriarch Timothy, *Apology for Christianity* (ed. A. Mingana), Woodbrooke Studies, Vol. II, Part I, Cambridge, MA 1928, 1–162.
8. Cf. the dispute, handed down in two forms, which for a long time was attributed to John of Damascus: *Disputatio Christiani et Saraceni*, in *Johannes Damaskenos und Theodor Abu Qurra, Schriften zum Islam*, Greek and German texts with a commentary by R. Glei and A.T. Khoury, Würzburg 1995, 167–83.
9. Cf. John of Damascus, 'Über die Haresien (742/43)', in *Schriften zum Islam*, 73–83.
10. Cf. A.T. Khoury, *Polémique byzantine contre l'Islam*, Leiden 1972.
11. Cf. R.W. Southern, *Western Views of Islam in the Middle Ages*, Cambridge, MA 1962, 1–33.
12. Ibid., 37.
13. E. de Beer, 'St Francis and Islam', *Concilium* 149, 1981, 11–20: 16.
14. Probably after his *Summa contra gentiles*, at the request of a cantor from Antioch Thomas Aquinas wrote 'On the Reasons for Faith' (*De rationibus fidei*), in which he attempted to demonstrate that the Trinity, the divine sonship of Jesus and the crucifixion were rational.
15. Ramon Llull, *Disputatio Raymundi christiani et Hamar saraceni (De fide catholica contra saracenos)*, in *Selected Works of Ramon Llull*, edited and translated by A. Bonner, Princeton 1985.
16. Cf. R.W. Southern, *Western Views of Islam* (n. 11), 67–109. There is a very informative new survey of the image of Muhammad in antiquity, the Middle Ages and modern times by the British theologian C. Bennett, *In Search of Muhammad*, London 1998; for the new development see ch. 4, 'Non-Muslim Lives of Muhammad from the Renaissance to Today' (especially Henry Stubbe, le Comte de Boulainvilliers, Voltaire, Humphrey Prideaux, George Sale, Washington Irving, Charles Forster, etc.).
17. The very titles of Luther's writings are significant: *On War against the Turks* (1529); *A Campaign Sermon against the Turks* (1529); *A Book on the Life and Customs of the Turks* (1530); *Appeal to Prayer against the Turks* (1541); *Brother Richard's Refutation of the Qur'an* (1542).
18. Cf. A. Ross, *Pansebeia or: A View of all Religions in the World*, London [4]1672, esp. 162–79. What underlies the title *Pansebeia* is made clear by the German translation: *Unterschiedliche Gottesdienste in der ganzen Welt. Das ist: Beschreibung aller bewusten Religionen, Secten und Ketzereyen, so in Asia, Africa, America und Europa von Anfang der Welt bis auf diese gegenwärtige Zeit theils befindlich theils annoch*

gebräuchlich, Heidelberg 1668 ('Various religions throughout the world. That is, a description of all known religions, sects and heresies, which can be found in Asia, Africa, America and Europe from the beginning of the world to this present time, some of which are still practised'). The author, who had already published other works (e.g. *A Caveat for reading the Alcoran*), discusses Islam comprehensively in section 6.

19. Cf. N. Daniel, *Islam and the West: The Making of an Image*, Edinburgh 1960, reprinted Oxford 1997.
20. Cf. A. Reland, *De Religione Mohammedica Libri Duo*, Utrecht 1705, expanded edition 1717. The first part is a compendium of Muslim theology written in Arabic and Latin; the second discusses teachings falsely attributed to Islam, both of course with a view to Christian apologetics.
21. Cf. G. Sale, 'Preliminary Discourse', in *The Koran* (1734), reprinted London nd, 1–145.
22. Cf. G.E. Lessing, *Nathan the Wise* (1779), Everyman Library, London 1930.
23. Cf. W. Jens and H. Küng, *Dichtung und Religion. Pascal, Gryphius, Lessing, Hölderlin, Novalis, Kierkegaard, Dostojewski, Kafka*, Munich 1985, 82–101.
24. K.-J. Kuschel, *'Jud, Christ und Muselmann vereinigt'? Lessings 'Nathan der Weise'*, Düsseldorf 2004, 13.
25. Ibid., 18f.. For the further context see id., *Vom Streit zum Wettstreit der Religionen. Lessing und die Herausforderung des Islam*, Düsseldorf 1998.
26. Cf. J.W. v. Goethe, *Poems of the West and East: West-Eastern Divan—West-Östlicher Divan*, translated by John Whaley, Berne 1998; also 'Noten und Abhandlungen. Zu besserem Verstandnis des West-östlichen Divans', in *Sämtliche Werke* (ed. F. Beutler), Vol. 3, Zurich 1977, 413–566.
27. Cf. T. Carlyle, 'The Hero as Prophet. Mahomet: Islam' (1840), in id., *On Heroes, Hero-Worship, and the Heroic in History*, Berkeley 1993, 37–66.
28. Cf. W.M. Watt and A.T. Welch, *Der Islam, Vol. 1: Mohammed und die Frühzeit—Islamisches Recht—religiöses Leben*, Stuttgart 1980, 28–38.
29. Cf. J. Waardenburg, *Islam dans le miroir de l'occident. Comment quelques orientalistes occidentaux se sont penchés sur l'Islam et se sont formés une image de cette religion* (I. Goldziher, C. Snouck Hurgronje, C.H. Becker, D.B. Macdonald, L. Massignon), The Hague 1962.
30. Cf. E.W. Said, *Orientalism*, London 1978. Cf. K.U. Syndram, 'Der erfundene Orient in der europäischen Literatur vom 18. Jahrhundert bis zum Beginn des 20. Jahrhunderts', in *Europa und der Orient 800–1900*, ed. G. Sievernich and H. Budde, Gütersloh 1989, 324–41.
31. For the author's biographical background cf. E.W. Said, *Out of Place. A Memoir*, New York 1999.
32. Cf. M. Rodinson, *La fascination de l'Islam*, Paris 1980.
33. Cf. B. Johansen, 'Politics and Scholarship. The Development of Islamic Studies in the Federal Republic of Germany', in *Middle East Studies. International Perspectives on the State of the Art*, ed. T.Y. Ismael, New York 1990, 71–130.

34. S. Widmer, 'Ein Kritiker und Gentleman. Zum Tod von E. Said', *Neue Zürcher Zeitung*, 27/28 September 2003.
35. Stein and Windfuhr (eds), *Ein Tag im September: 11. 9. 2001* (n. 3), 179–87: 187.
36. Cf. the survey of the various positions in E. Rudolph, *Westliche Islamwissenschaft im Spiegel muslimischer Kritik. Grundzüge und aktuelle Merkmale einer innerislamischen Diskussion*, Bonn 1991, 60–6.
37. Cf. Klemm and Hörner, *Das Schwert des 'Experten'* (n. 5). The first Islamic scholar in Germany who dared to contradict popular television experts to their faces was the Tübingen professor Heinz Halm, 'Die Panikmacher. Wie im Westen der Islam zum neuen Feindbild aufgebaut wird', *Süddeutsche Zeitung*, 16/17 February 1991. The same composite volume also contains an article by the long-time and knowledgeable Middle East correspondent of the *Neue Zürcher Zeitung*, A. Hottinger, on the problem 'Der Journalist als Historiker' (180–99): 'Specialists wrote for specialists. That produced a technical language which thought it important not to be too comprehensible. The specialist books were published by specialist publishers. When printing became increasingly expensive the specialist world published with the help of state and private support. This was given on the commendations of other specialists, so it was best not to depart from specialist language and a specialist mentality. It was not appropriate for professors to concern themselves with "vulgarisation". Most of them do not seem to have noticed that in adopting this course they have handed over the "oriental field" as a happy hunting ground to the demagogues of information ... By contrast, in England and in France the specialists see it as a worthwhile task to write books which can be read with interest by educated contemporaries. This is very rare in the specialist German-speaking world, especially in the case of such "exotic" disciplines as oriental studies' (191f.). The same volume contains illuminating remarks by K. Hörner on the hostile image and by A.K. Reulecke on B. Mahmoody's novel *Not without my Daughter.*
38. M.A. Rassoul, *Was ist Islam?*, Cologne ^{2}1984, 7f.
39. *Kleiner Islamischer Katechismus*, ed. Mehmet Soymen, *Mufti in Isparta*, Veröffentlichungen der Behörde für religiöse Angelegenheiten 79, Ankara 1975. The Pakistani I.S. Hussain, *The Qur'an and Modernism. Beyond Science and Philosophy*, Lahore 2000, 1f., offers what is almost a hymn to Islam. The introduction has the significant title 'The Qur'an: An Immaculate Conception'.
40. Cf. I. Goldziher, *Tagebuch*, ed. A. Scheiber, Leiden 1978, 55–74.
41. Ibid., 57, 59, 71.
42. R. Garaudy, *Promesses de l'Islam*, Paris 1981; German *Verheissung Islam*, Munich 1989, 19; cf. id., *L'Islam habite notre avenir*, Paris 1981 (with impressive illustrations). Garaudy argued at an early stage for a dialogue of civilizations: *Pour un dialogue des civilisations*, Paris 1977.
43. M.W. Hofmann, *Der Islam als Alternative*, Munich 1992, 7f. Cf. id., *Die Religion im 3. Jahrtausend. Eine Religion im Aufbruch*, Munich 2000; id., *Der Islam*, Munich 2001.
44. Cf. W.C. Smith, *On Understanding Islam*, The Hague 1981.

45. The German word *Gestalt* (from the verbs *stellen, gestalten*), which has also been taken over into English and other languages, is generally used to translate the Latin *forma*, form which can be seen in space. In the broader sense *Gestalt* is a structure (a melody, a nation) which is not composed of individual elements perceived as such but presents itself as a total experience.
46. German has the words *Wesen* and *Unwesen*, used here in the original, which conveniently express opposites. It would be possible to translate them by 'nature' and the neologism 'unnature', as in the English translation of H. Küng's *The Church* (1967), where they were first used. However, 'nature' here is too general and weak; *Wesen* means 'essence'. So I have opted for 'essence' and 'perversion'. [Tr]
47. Cf. the Second Vatican Council, 'Declaration of the Church on the Non-Christian Religions *Nostra aetate*', Rome 1965.
48. Cf. World Council of Churches, *Guidelines on Dialogue with People of Living Faiths and Ideologies*, Geneva 1979, fourth revised edition 1990; developed further in *Guidelines for Dialogue and Relations with People of Other Religions. Taking stock of 30 years of dialogue and revisiting the 1979 Guidelines*, Geneva 2002. There is a comprehensive account and analysis of the Christian-Muslim dialogue in Jutta Sperber, *Christians and Muslims. The Dialogue Activities of the World Council of Churches and their Theological Foundation*, Berlin 2000.

A II. Problems of the Beginning

1. Cf. H. Küng, *Does God Exist?*, C III, 2: The disputed origins of religion.
2. Cf. I.J. Gelb, *A Study of Writing. The Foundations of Grammatology*, Chicago 1952; M. Cohen, *La grande invention de l'écriture et son évolution* (3 vols), Paris 1958; D. Diringer, *Writing*, New York 1962; J. Friedrich, *Geschichte der Schrift. Unter besonderer Berücksichtigung ihrer geistigen Entwicklung*, Heidelberg 1966; C.H. Gordon, *Forgotten Scripts*, New York [2]1982; H. Haarmann, *Universalgeschichte der Schrift*, Frankfurt am Main 1990.
3. For the history of pre-Islamic Arabia cf. I. Shahid, 'Pre-Islamic Arabia', in *Cambridge History of Islam*, I, ed. P.M. Holt, A.K.S. Lambton and B. Lewis, Cambridge 1970, 3–29; id., *Byzantium and the Arabs in the Fifth Century*, Washington, DC 1989, esp. Part II, 'The Arabic Sources'; I.M. Lapidus, *A History of Islamic Societies*, Cambridge 1988, 3–20. For the pre-Islamic religions of Arabia see M. Höfner's article in H. Gese, M. Höfner and K. Rudolph, *Die Religionen Altsyriens, Altarabiens und der Mandäer*, Die Religionen der Menschheit, 10, 2, Stuttgart 1970, 233–402. For further literature on the history of Islam cf. C 1,1 below.
4. Cf. T. Weiss Rosmarin, *Aribi und Arabien in den babylonisch-assyrischen Quellen*, Würzburg dissertation 1931, New York 1932.
5. Cf. H. Küng, *Judaism*, Part I, A II, 5: The establishment of monotheism.
6. Isa. 45.21.
7. Cf. Gen. 10.26–2.
8. Cf. Gen. 25.1–4.

9. Cf. 1 Kings 10.1–13 (cf. 9.26–8: so far it has not proved possible to identify the location of Ophir precisely); 2 Chron. 9.1–12.
10. Cf. H.Z. Hirschberg, 'Arabia', in *Encyclopaedia Judaica.*
11. Cf. I. Shahid, *The Martyrs of Najran. New Documents*, Brussels 1971. The Arabist and Byzantinist Shahid attempts to elucidate the historical background to the persecution of Christians especially through an analysis of newly-discovered letters and the Arabic, Ethiopian and Greek versions of the *Martyrium Arethae*, which is based on the 'Book of the Himyarites'. A more recent investigation of the background, course and circumstances of the persecution finally arrives at a figure of between 700 and 1000 martyrs: R. Tardy, *Najran. Chrétiens d'Arabie avant l'Islam*, Beirut 1999, Part 2, ch. III, 'Najrân dans les tourments'.
12. Cf. R. Paret, *Der Koran* (2 vols), Stuttgart [2]1980, on surah 85. 4–7. Shahid, *The Martyrs* (n. 11), 193, differs: 'The majority of Qur'anic exegetes take it to be a reference to the martyrs of Najran.'
13. Cf. Tardy, *Najrân* (n. 11), 'Conclusion: La rencontre de Medine'.
14. Cf. also G.D. Newby, *A History of the Jews of Arabia. From Ancient Times to their Eclipse under Islam*, Columbia, SC 1988.
15. I. Goldziher, *Muhammedanische Studien* (3 vols), Halle 1889–90, I, 12.
16. Cf. K. Cragg, *The Arab Christian. A History in the Middle East*, Louisville, KY 1991.
17. Cf. ibid., ch. 2, but also already W.M. Watt, *Muhammad at Medina*, Oxford 1953, 23–9.
18. Cf. Prince El Hassan bin Talal, *Christianity in the Arab World*, London 1998.
19. Cf. Acts 2.11.
20. Cf. Gal. 1.17. Cf. M. Hengel and A.M. Schwemer, *Paul between Damascus and Antioch: The Unknown Years*, London and Minneapolis 1997, above all ch. 3; id., *Paulus und Jakobus*, Kleine Schriften III, Tübingen 2002, ch. 3, 'Paulus in Arabien'. Hengel identifies Paul's 'Arabia' with the great Arab kingdom of the Nabataeans, which extended from southern Syria over the Dead Sea to the southern Negev.
21. Cf. J.M. Fiey, 'Nasara', *EncIsl*[2].
22. Cragg, *The Arab Christian* (n. 16), 44. That is impressively confirmed by Shahid, *Byzantium and the Arabs* (n. 3), esp. Part IV: Synthesis and Exposition.
23. Cf. N. Abbott, *The Rise of the North Arabic Script and its Kur'anic Development, with a Full Description of the Kur'an Manuscripts in the Oriental Institute*, Chicago 1939, 1–5.
24. Cf. C. Rabin, "Arabiyya (II. The literary language. Classical Arabic)', *EncIsl*[2]. The role of Christian poets of Hira and other instances of Arabian Christianity is discussed by Abbott, *The Rise of the North Arabic Script* (n. 23), 5–14: 'There are … evidences which point to pre-Islamic Christian writings' (13).
25. Cf. R.A. Nicholson, *A Literary History of the Arabs* (1907), Cambridge [2]1930, XXIf., 137f. The question is passed over completely by A.G. Chejne, *The Arabic Language. Its Role in History*, Minneapolis 1969.
26. Cf. A. Jeffery, *The Foreign Vocabulary of the Qur'an*, Baroda 1938, 240, 242f.

27. Cf. surah 96.4 and surah 68 entitled 'The Reed'.
28. Cf. surah 1.6, etc.
29. Cf. L. Gardet, 'Allah', *EncIsl²*.
30. Shahid, 'Pre-Islamic Arabia' (n. 3), 20.
31. Cragg, *The Arab Christian* (n. 16), 16.
32. Ibid., 18.
33. Cf. H. Küng, *Christianity and the World Religions*, A IV 2, 'Jesus as the Servant of God'.
34. In what follows I am summing up in respect of Arabia and Islam some results that I have already worked out in connection with Christianity (C 1, 7: The fate of Jewish Christianity; C 1, 8: Jewish Christianity and the Qur'an). H.-J. Schoeps, *Theologie und Geschichte des Judenchristentums*, Tübingen 1949, is still a basic work on the history of Jewish Christianity. For the individual Jewish–Christian groupings which appear in the patristic (non-Gnostic) sources (Cerinthians, Ebionites, Nazoraeans, Symmachians, Elkesaites), there is a fairly complete presentation of the material in A.F.J. Klijn and G.J. Reinink, *Patristic Evidence for Jewish–Christian Sects*, Leiden 1973. Klijn also produced the first comprehensive study of the Jewish–Christian Gospel tradition (with texts and commentaries): *Jewish–Christian Gospel Tradition*, Leiden 1992. Cf. also R.A. Pritz, *Nazarene Jewish Christianity. From the End of the New Testament Period Until its Disappearance in the Fourth Century*, Jerusalem 1988. The historical development is reconstructed on the basis of the most recent research by G. Strecker, 'Judenchristentum', *TRE*; cf. id., 'On the Problem of Jewish Christianity', appendix 1 to W. Bauer, *Orthodoxy and Heresy in Earliest Christianity*, Philadelphia 1971 and London 1972, 241–84. S. Légasse, 'La polémique antipaulinienne dans le judéo-christianisme hétérodoxe', *Bulletin de Littérature Ecclésiastique* 90, 1989, 5–22, 85–100, investigates the individual Jewish–Christian documents from the perspective of anti-Paulinism. For an archaeological perspective cf. B. Bagatti, *Alle origini della chiesa, Vol. I: Le comunità giudeo-cristiane*, Rome 1986 (Vol. II deals with the Gentile–Christian communities). For the earlier literature see E. Manns, *Bibliographie du judéo-christianisme*, Jerusalem 1979. The material on both 'conservative' and 'liberal' Christianity is skilfully presented by T. Carran, *Forgetting the Root. The Emergence of Christianity from Judaism*, New York 1986.
35. Cf. Eusebius, *Church History* III, 5, 3a.
36. With reference to the Jewish–Christian Pseudo-Clementines (*Recognitiones* 37,39) and Luke 21, and following the historians E. Meyer and M. Simon, who argue for its historicity, cf. J. Wehnert, 'Die Auswanderung der Jerusalemer Christen nach Pella—historisches Faktum oder theologische Konstruktion?', *Zeitschrift für Kirchengeschichte* 102, 1991, 231–55. Likewise C. Koester, 'The Origin and Significance of the Flight to Pella Tradition', *The Catholic Biblical Quarterly* 51, 1939, 90–106.
37. Cf. Wehnert, 'Die Auswanderung' (n. 36), 252.
38. Cf. Eusebius, *Church History* IV 5, 1–4. For the complex question of Jesus' kin cf. R. Bauckham, *Jude and the Relatives of Jesus in the Early Church*, Edinburgh 1990.

For the Letter of Jude which is brought in here cf. R. Heiligenthal, *Zwischen Henoch und Paulus. Studien zum theologiegeschichtlichen Ort des Judasbriefes*, Tübingen 1962.

39. I was given valuable pointers by Professor James Robinson, Director of the Institute for Christianity and Antiquity in Claremont, CA, during a semester in which he visited our Institute for Ecumenical Research.
40. It is generally recognized that the sayings source (known to scholars as Q, translated by good fortune from Aramaic into Greek and integrated into the Gospels of Matthew and Luke) which contains sayings of Jesus from the very earliest period is of Jewish–Christian origin. The Gospel of Matthew (possibly written around 80 in Antioch) also has its home in a Jewish–Christian milieu, as does the letter of James and—precisely because in it the controversy with the Jews is even sharper than it is in Matthew—also the Gospel of John (around 100). In addition to the New Testament writings there are three non-canonical Jewish–Christian Gospels (which can be reconstructed from fragments in the church fathers): the Gospel of the Hebrews, the Gospel of the Nazarenes and the Gospel of the Ebionites, which must be related to the Gospel of Matthew but like the earliest canonical Gospel (Mark) has no infancy narrative and understands the divine sonship of Jesus in terms of the descent of the Holy Spirit in baptism. If we may accept the hypothesis of the American New Testament scholar Louis Martyn, even in the second century Jewish Christians were still engaged in a mission to the Gentiles which called for observance of the law; they must already lie behind the opponents of Paul in Galatia (and Philippi). Evidently they wanted to see Christ in the light of God's law—whereas Paul saw the law in the light of Christ—and because they observed the law (circumcision, festivals, regulations about purity), understood themselves to be the true children of Abraham. The Jewish–Christian work the *Ascension of Isaiah* (*c.* 100–130) is also interesting; in it a group of prophets attributes revelations to the prophet Isaiah against an apostolic background and in this way they express their loyalty to Jesus as the Messiah.
41. Pseudo-Clementine Recognitions 1, 33–71. On this, after H. Waitz, O. Cullmann, E. Schwartz and H.-J. Schoeps, see above all G. Strecker, *Das Judentum in den Pseudoklementinen*, Berlin 1957, [2]1981.
42. This interpretation was developed by R.E. van Voorst, *The Ascents of James: History and Theology of a Jewish–Christian Community*, Atlanta 1989, esp.163–80.
43. Cf. Jerome, *On Famous Men* 3; cf. id., *In Jes 40,9–11*. Also Strecker, 'Judenchristentum' (n. 34), 312, 321.
44. Cf. Ignatius, *To the Magnesians* 8–10.
45. Cf. Irenaeus, *Against the Heresies* I, 26, 2; III, 15, 1; V, 1, 3.
46. This is emphasized by C. Colpe, *Das Siegel der Propheten. Historische Beziehungen zwischen Judaism, Judenchristentum, Heidentum und frühem Islam*, Berlin 1990, 166f.
47. Strecker, 'Judenchristentum' (n. 34), 323.
48. Docetism (from the Greek *dokein* = 'seem') is the doctrine that attributes to Christ only a phantom body and denies that he personally died on the cross.

49. I find at least indirect confirmation in F. Heyer, *Die Kirche Äthiopiens*, Berlin 1971, 222f.; E. Isaac, *A New Text–critical Introduction to Mashafa Berhan*, Leiden 1973 (from this important Ethiopian book the author conjectures two parties: Judaizing Christianity and Coptic Monophysite Christianity).
50. Cf. S. Weil, 'Symmetry Between Christians and Jews in India. The Cananite Christians and the Cochin Jews of Kerala', in T.A. Timberg, *Jews in India*, New Delhi 1986, 182–94; J. Kollaparambil, *The Babylonian Origin of the Southists Among the S. Thomas Christians*, Rome 1992.
51. Cf. Eusebius, *Church History* V, 10.
52. The Cologne Mani Codex (inventory no. 4780) was published in 1975/81 with a commentary by A. Henrichs and L. Koenen. There is now a standard edition by L. Koenen and C. Roemer, *Der Kölner Mani-Kodex. Abbildungen und diplomatischer Text*, Bonn 1985.
53. A. Böhlig, foreword to L. Cirillo (ed.), *Codex Manichaicus Coloniensis. Atti del Simposio Internazionale 1984*, Cosenza 1986 (the contributions by J. Maier, K. Rudolph, G. Strecker, L. Cirillo and A.F.J. Klijn are particularly important here). For Manichaeism cf. especially K. Rudolph, *Gnosis. The Nature and History of Gnosticism*, New York 1977; G. Widengren (ed.), *Der Manichäismus*, Darmstadt 1977; H.-C. Puech, *Sur le manichéisme et autres essais*, Paris 1979; E. Rose, *Die manichäische Christologie*, Wiesbaden 1979. I am grateful to my Tübingen colleague Professor Alexander Böhlig, a specialist in gnosticism who died in 1996, for numerous suggestions.
54. Cf. H. Küng and J. van Ess, *Christianity and the World Religions*, A IV 2: Jesus as the Servant of God.
55. A. Schlatter, *Geschichte der ersten Christenheit*, Gütersloh 1926, 367f.
56. Cf. A.von Harnack, *Lehrbuch der Dogmengeschichte*, II, Tubingen [4]1909, reprinted Darmstadt 1964, 529–38.
57. Cf. Schoeps, *Theologie* (n. 34, taking up the work of C. Clemen, T. Andrae and H.H. Schaeder), 342: 'This produces the paradox of truly historic significance that while Jewish Christianity was swallowed up in the Christian church, it preserved itself in Islam, and some of its most powerful impulses extend down to the present day.'
58. C. Buck, report to the American Academy of Religion, *Abstracts AAR/SBL* 1983.
59. Strecker, 'Judenchristentum' (n. 34), 323.
60. On this see C. Buck, 'Exegetical Identification of the Sabi'un', *Muslim World* 73, 1982, 95–106; G. Quispel, 'The Birth of the Child. Some Gnostic and Jewish Aspects', in *Jewish and Gnostic Man*, Eranos Lectures 3, Dallas 1986, 3–26. For the Elkesaites as propagandists for Jewish Christianity cf.—after A.von Harnack and the early monograph by W. Brandt (1912)—more recently G.P. Luttikhuizen, *The Revelation of Elchasai. Investigations into the Evidence for a Mesopotamian Jewish Christian Apocalypse of the Second Century and its Reception by Judeo-Christian Propagandists*, Tübingen 1985: the apocalyptic book of revelation, originally written in Aramaic by a Mesopotamian Jew of the second century, was used a century

later by Syrian Jewish Christians for religious propaganda in Christian churches of Rome and Palestine.

61. Cf. also U. Rubin, 'Hanifiyya and Ka'ba: An inquiry into the Arabian pre-Islamic Background *of din Ibrahim*', *Jerusalem Studies in Arabic and Islam* 13, 1990, 85–112.
62. Cf. J. Wellhausen, *Reste arabischen Heidentums*, Berlin ^{2}1927, 231–3.
63. Cf. Colpe, *Das Siegel der Propheten* (n. 46), 237f.
64. Surah 33.40.
65. Cf. Tertullian, *Adversus Judaeos* VIII, 12. The correct reading, following Colpe, is *Signaculum omnium prophetarum*, not *prophetiarum* (prophecies), as conjectured by E. Kroymann (in Corpus Scriptorum Ecclesiasticorum Latinorum 70 and in Corpus Christianorum Series Latina II/2, 1361, contradicting 1383, *prophetarum*).
66. Cf. Colpe, *Das Siegel der Propheten* (n. 46), 28–34.
67. Ibid., 238.
68. Ibid., 169f.
69. Cf. S. Pines, 'The Jewish Christians of the Early Centuries of Christianity According to a New Source', in *Proceedings of the Israel Academy of Sciences and Humanities* 2, 1968, 237–309.
70. Cf. also Colpe, *Das Siegel der Propheten* (n. 46), 171f.
71. Prince El Hassan bin Talal, *Christianity in the Arab World* (n. 18), 10–11. I received impressive confirmation of my view immediately before the typesetting of this book from an article by the French Iranian specialist François de Blois, 'Elchasai—Manes—Muhammad. Manichäismus und Islam in religionshistorischem Vergleich', *Der Islam* 81, 2004, 31–48. The author points out 'that the *nasara* of the Qur'an were in fact Nazarenes, i.e. so-called Jewish Christians, and that this name only later became the general Arabic designation for Christians'. He concludes: 'The recognition that the *nasara* of the Qur'an are in fact Nazarenes now brings primitive Islam in direct contact with Jewish Christianity. For the first time that produces a plausible historical model for the theological proximity of Jewish Christianity to Islam which has long been noted' (47). He concludes: 'Thus some essential elements of a current of early Christianity which for a long time had been submerged within Christianity now continue in one of the great world religions of the present day' (48). For future research it would be worthwhile for de Blois to recognize that Jewish Christianity should be evaluated not just as a current of early Christianity but as the very first paradigm of Christianity (Christian P I), as I have demonstrated in extensive chapters in both *Judaism* and *Christianity*.
72. For Abraham (or Ibrahim) cf. the articles in: *Dictionnaire des Religions* (H. Cazelles, E. Cothenet, K. Hruby, G. Harpigny); *Die Religion in Geschichte und Gegenwart* (E. Blum, H.W. Attridge, G.A. Anderson, J. Dan, T. Nagel); *Encyclopedia Judaica* (I.M. Ta-Shma, D. Kadosh, S.D. Goitein, J. Dan, H. Rosenau); *Encyclopaedia of Islam* (R. Paret); *Encyclopaedia of the Qur'an* (R. Firestone); *Islam–Lexikon* (L. Hagemann); *Jüdisches Lexikon* (A. Spanier, A. Kristianpoller, A. Sandler); *Lexikon für Theologie und Kirche* (V. Hamp, J. Schmid); *Lexikon religiöser Grundbegriffe* (P. Navè Levinson, G. Evers, S. Balić); *The Encyclopedia of Religion* (J. van Seters); *Theologische*

Realenzyklopädie (R. Martin-Achard, K. Berger, R.P. Schmitz, J. Hjärpe); *Theologisches Wörterbuch zum Neuen Testament* (J. Jeremias). Cf. also H. Donner, *Geschichte des Volkes Israel und seiner Nachbarn in Grundzügen*, I, Göttingen 1984, 72–84. The study by K.-J. Kuschel, *Abraham. A Symbol of Hope for Jews, Christians and Muslims*, London and New York 1995, is particularly helpful. Further important works are: Y. Moubarac, *Abraham dans le Coran. L'histoire d'Abraham dans le Coran et la naissance de l'Islam*, Paris 1958; R. Martin-Achard, *Actualité d'Abraham*, Neuchâtel 1969; W. Gross, *Glaubensgehorsam als Wagnis der Freiheit. Wir sind Abraham*, Mainz 1980; F.E. Peters, *Children of Abraham. Judaism—Christianity—Islam*, Princeton 1982; W. Zuidema (ed.), *Isaak wird wieder geopfert. Die 'Bindung Isaaks' als Symbol des Leidens Israels. Versuche einer Deutung*, Neukirchen 1987; J.G. Butler, *Abraham. The Father of the Jews*, Clinton, Iowa 1993; A. Ségal, *Abraham. Enquête sur un Patriarche*, Paris 1995; T. Römer (ed.), *Abraham. Nouvelle jeunesse d'un ancêtre*, Geneva 1997, in this on Islam: J.-C. Basset, 'Ibrahim à la Mecque, prophète de l'Islam', 79–92. R.G. Kratz and T. Nagel (eds), *Abraham, unser Vater. Die gemeinsamen Wurzeln von Judentum, Christentum und Islam*, Göttingen 2003.

73. For the book of Genesis, in addition to earlier works by H. Gunkel, J. Skinner and O. Procksch, see the important commentaries by G. von Rad (1953, ET [2]1972), R. de Vaux (1956), A. van Selms ([3]1979), W.G. Plaut (1974), E.A. Speiser (1981) and C. Westermann (1981, ET 1984–6, 3 vols).

74. That many biblical narratives have the character of sagas was first worked out by H. Gunkel and H. Gressmann, and then later comprehensively by A. Alt, M. Noth and many other German Old Testament scholars—often with negative conclusions on their historicity. Against this some American scholars especially from the circle around W.F. Albright called for more detailed attention to the results of archaeology. Summary works are: W.F. Albright, *The Archaeology of Palestine*, Harmondsworth 1949, Gloucester, MA 1971; G.E. Wright, *Biblical Archaeology*, Philadelphia 1957; J.B. Pritchard, *Archaeology and the Old Testament*, Princeton 1958; K.M. Kenyon, *Archaeology in the Holy Land*, London [4]1979 (this gives a good survey of Kenyon's excavations in Jericho and puts them in context); V. Fritz, *Einführung in die biblische Archäologie*, Darmstadt 1985. The Frenchman A. Parrot wrote an illuminating series of books in the 1950s, including *Discovering Buried Worlds*, London 1955; *Babylon and the Old Testament*, London 1958; and *Samaria*, London 1958.

75. On this see G.W. Coats, *Genesis, with an Introduction to Narrative Literature*, Grand Rapids 1983; id. (ed.), *Saga, Legend, Tale, Novella, Fable: Narrative Forms in Old Testament Literature*, Sheffield 1985.

76. See H. Haag, *Das Land der Bibel. Gestalt—Geschichte—Erforschung*, Stuttgart 1989, 50–63.

77. Cf. Gen. 11.

78. For his origin from Ur: Gen. 11.28, 31; 15.7; from Haran: Gen. 11.31; 24.4,10; 27.43.

79. Cf. Gen. 12.6–9.

80. Gen. 23.4.

81. Cf. Gen. 23.19f.
82. Gen. 14.13.
83. For the 'Hebrews/Apiru' cf. M. Weippert, *The Settlement of the Israelite Tribes in Palestine*, London 1971, 63–102, which confirms the views of G.E. Mendenhall. O. Loretz, *Habiru—Hebräer. Eine sozio-linguistische Studie über die Herkunft des Gentiliziums* 'ibri *vom Appellativum* habiru, Berlin 1984, differs.
84. For the genealogy cf. Westermann, *Genesis* (n. 73), I, 6–18.
85. Cf. Gen. 25.1, 6.
86. Cf. Gen. 21.2f.
87. Cf. Gen. 16.15.
88. Cf. Gen. 25.12–18. The tribes of Ishmael, Nebayot and Kedar, Adbeel, Massa and Tema, listed here, are Arab tribes which are also mentioned in Assyrian inscriptions.Whether the 'sons of Ishmael' are the real ancestors of the Arabs is disputed. Cf. I. Eph'al, '"Ishmael" and "Arab(s)": A Transformation of Ethnological Terms', *Journal of Near Eastern Studies* 35, 1976, 225–35; id., *The Ancient Arabs. Nomads on the Borders of the Fertile Crescent 9th-5th Centuries* BC, Leiden 1982, esp. 233–40. There is a critical discussion of Eph'al and a detailed argument for the opposite thesis in Shahid, *Byzantium and the Arabs* (n. 3), 332–49. Cf. also Donner, *Geschichte des Volkes Israel* (n. 72), I, 58; also E.A. Knauf, *Ismael. Untersuchungen zur Geschichte Palästinas und Nordarabiens im 1. Jahrtausend vor Christus*, Wiesbaden 1985: '"Ishmael" was a proto-Bedouin confederation which embraced the whole of northern Arabia from the Nefud to the periphery of the fertile crescent' (113).
89. Cf. Gen. 25.1–6.
90. Cf. Gal. 4.22–6.
91. Cf. Kuschel, *Abraham* (n. 72), A III, 1: Cast out—yet blessed.
92. Gen. 16.11.
93. Cf. Gen. 17.23–6.
94. Gen. 16.7–11; 21.17–19; 22.11–13.
95. Gen.16.10.
96. Gen. 17.20; cf. also Gen. 21.13, 18.
97. Cf. Gen. 21.10–14.
98. Gen. 25.9.
99. Cf. R. de Vaux, *The Early History of Israel*, Vol.1, London and New York 1971, 274–82, 454–62.
100. Cf. Westermann, *Genesis* (n. 73), I, 314, excursus on circumcision.
101. Cf. Lev. 12.3.
102. Gen.15.6.
103. Cf. Gen. 22.1–12.
104. Cf. H. Küng, *Global Responsibility*, C III, 3: The Three Great Currents of Religious Systems Today; id., *Tracing the Way*.
105. R. Paret, *Mohammed und der Koran. Geschichte und Verkündigung des arabischen Propheten*, Stuttgart 1957, [7]1991, 20.
106. Cf. the summary in Kuschel, *Abraham* (n. 72), A III: Abraham and Islam.

107. Cf. surahs 2.125; 3.97; 22.26–31.
108. As well as Paret's article in *EncIsl²* cf. C. Snouck Hurgronje, *Het Mekkaansche Feest*, Leiden 1880; also J. Eisenberg and A. J. Wensinck, 'Ibrahim', *HdI.*
109. See the criticism of Hurgronje by the Christian pupil of Massignon, Y. Moubarac, *Abraham dans le Coran* (n. 72), though it misses the point. In the Arabic edition of *EncIsl* ² Wensinck's article has been provided with an extensive critical commentary from a Muslim perspective.
110. Dismissed by Snouck Hurgronje as interpolations.
111. Thus E. Beck, 'Die Gestalt des Abraham am Wendepunkt der Entwicklung Muhammeds. Analyse von Sure 2, 118 (124)–135 (141)', *Le Muséon. Revue d'études orientales* LXV, 1952, 73–94: 93f.
112. Cf. surah 2.127: 'Raising the foundations'.
113. Cf. surah 2.125: 'Purify my Temple'.
114. Cf. W.M. Watt and A.T. Welch, *Der Islam. Vol. I, Mohammed und die Frühzeit—Islamisches Recht—Religiöses Leben*, Stuttgart 1980, 122–4 (quoted in what follows under W.M. Watt, except in the case of Part E, which is by Welch). It was above all the works by A. Geiger, *Was hat Mohammed aus dem Judenthume aufgenommen*, Leipzig ²1902, and Snouck Hurgronje, *Het Mekkaansche Feest* (n. 108), which resulted in a big discussion about the development of Muhammad's attitude to Abraham and Ishmael. Cf. Paret, 'Ibrahim' (n. 72); id., *Mohammed und der Koran* (n. 105), 119–122; R. Firestone, 'Abraham', *EncQur.*
115. Surah 4.125.
116. Surah 3.67.
117. Cf. surahs 6.74–81; 21.55–67.
118. Cf. surahs 2.124; 37.102–6.
119. Cf. Kuschel, *Abraham* (n. 72), A III, 2: Key witness against the idols: Abraham.
120. Cf. Gen.18–19.
121. Surah 2.124.
122. P. Antes concludes his precise account of 'Abraham im Judentum, Christentum und Islam', in id. et al., *Christen und Juden. Ein notwendiger Dialog*, Hanover 1988, 11–15: 15, with this legitimate question.
123. Jesus Christ as a descendant of Abraham is spoken of particularly clearly right at the beginning of the New Testament in Matt. 1.1–17 and also in Luke 3.23–34.
124. Acts 3.13.
125. Cf. Rom. 4.
126. Cf. Gal. 5.6.
127. Cf. John 8.39.
128. Cf. James 1.22–5.
129. Cf. H. Strack and P. Billerbeck, *Kommentar zum Neuen Testament aus Talmud und Midrasch*, III, Munich 1926, 186–201; four passages are brought together here.
130. Cf. J.J. Petuchowski and C. Thoma (eds), *Lexikon der jüdisch-christlichen Begegnung*, Freiburg 1989, 'Abraham'.

131. D. Flusser, 'Christianity', in A.A. Cohen and P. Mendes-Flohr (eds), *Contemporary Jewish Religious Thought. Original Essays on Critical Concepts, Movements, and Beliefs*, Jerusalem 1972, new edition New York 1988.
132. K. Rudolph, 'Juden—Christen—Muslime. Zum Verhältnis der drei monotheistischen Religionen in religionswissenschaftlicher Sicht', *Judaica* 44, 1988, 214–32: 223.
133. H. Denzinger, *Enchiridion*, no. 1351(the collection of documents by H. Denzinger, *Enchiridion Symbolorum*, which has appeared in a series of new editions, is quoted in this book from the 31st edition, Freiburg im Breisgau 1960).
134. Ibid., nos. 1295, 1379.
135. Second Vatican Council, Constitution, *Lumen gentium*, Rome 1965, Art. 16. For the discussion over this constitution at the council cf. H. Küng, *My Struggle for Freedom. Memoirs*, London 2004, ch. IX.
136. *Lumen gentium*, Art. 16.

B. Centre

B I. God's Word has Become a Book

1. Cf. H. Küng, *Judaism*, Part I, B I, The Central Structural Elements.
2. Cf. id., *Christianity*, B II, The Central Structural Elements.
3. The following overall accounts of Islam are important for this book as a whole: L. Gardet, *Connaître l'Islam*, Paris 1958; F. Rahman, *Islam*, Chicago 1966, [2]1979; K. Cragg and R.M. Speight, *The House of Islam*, Belmont, CA 1975, [3]1988; id., *Islam from Within. Anthology of Religion*, Belmont, CA 1980; S. Balić, *Ruf vom Minarett. Welt-Islam heute—Renaissance oder Ruckfall? Eine Selbstdarstellung*, Vienna 1979; H.M. Azzam, *Der Islam. Plädoyer eines Moslem*, Stuttgart 1981; M. Hamidullah, *Der Islam. Geschichte, Religion, Kultur*, Aachen [2]1983; C. Bouamrane and L. Gardet, *Panorama de la pensée islamique*, Paris 1984; E.M. Denny, *An Introduction to Islam*, New York 1985; S.H. Nasr (ed.), *Islamic Spirituality. Foundations*, New York 1987; id. (ed.), *Islamic Spirituality. Manifestations*, New York 1991; J.L. Esposito, *Islam—the Straight Path*, Oxford 1988; G. Galbiati, *La diversità dell'Islam*, Florence 1992; H. Halm, *Der Islam. Geschichte und Gegenwart*, Munich 2000. The most comprehensive introduction to Islam, to which I keep referring, is that by W.M. Watt and A.T. Welch, *Der Islam* (3 vols), Stuttgart 1980–90. The great encyclopaedias on Islam are indispensable tools: *Encyclopedia of Islam, The Oxford Encyclopedia of the Modern Islamic World, Encyclopedia of the Qur'an, Handwörterbuch des Islam* (cf. the bibliography given at the head of these notes); but shorter, usually one-volume, reference works are also helpful: C. Glassé, *Dictionnaire Encyclopédique de l'Islam*, Paris 1991; A.T. Khoury, L. Hagemann and P. Heine (eds), *Islam–Lexikon*, Freiburg im Breisgau 1991; K. Kreiser and R. Wielandt (eds), *Lexikon der islamischen Welt*, Stuttgart 1992; G. Barthel and K. Stock (eds), *Lexikon Arabische Welt*, Wiesbaden 1994; G.D. Newby, *A Concise Encyclopedia of Islam*, Oxford 2002.

4. John 1.14.
5. The most important Western translations of the Qur'an are as follows: 1. The fundamental English translation is that of R. Bell, *The Qur'an. Translated, with a Critical Re-arrangement of the Surahs* (2 vols), Edinburgh 1937–9; see also the much-praised introduction, *Introduction to the Qur'an, Completely Revised and Enlarged*, by W.M. Watt, Edinburgh 1970, and Bell's commentary: *A Commentary on the Qur'an* (2 vols), ed. C.E. Bosworth and W.E.J. Richardson, Manchester 1991. However, the translation of the Qur'an used in most quotations here is that of M. Asad, *The Message of the Qur'an*, Gibraltar 1980. 2. The classical German translation of the Qur'an (with commentary and concordance) is that of R. Paret, *Der Koran*, Stuttgart 1966; pocket-book edition in two volumes, Stuttgart [2]1980. The theologically thoughtful translation by A.T. Khoury, *Der Koran*, Gütersloh 1987, is also helpful; see also the multi-volume commentary *Der Koran. Arabisch–Deutsch. Übersetzung und wissenschaftlicher Kommentar* (12 volumes to date), Gütersloh 1990. 3. The most important French translation has been produced (in a historical reconstruction of the order of the surahs with a commentary) by R. Blachère, *Le Coran. Traduction selon un essai de reclassement des sourates*, 3 vols, Paris 1947–51 (Vol. III, *Introduction au Coran*, has also appeared separately, Paris [2]1977). There is a new French translation, modestly sub-titled 'Essai de traduction', by the Arabist J. Berque, *Le Coran*, Paris 1990; the numerous notes and the exegetical study in the appendix (711–93), which discuss the structure, language, meaning and truth of the Qur'an, are valuable; cf. id., *Relire le Coran*, Paris 1993. Further important literature on the Qur'an is: J. Horovitz, *Koranische Untersuchungen*, Berlin 1926; R. Paret, *Grenzen der Koranforschung*, Stuttgart 1900; id. (ed.), *Der Koran*, Darmstadt 1973 (articles and reviews on research into the Qur'an between 1921 and 1971); H. Birkeland, *The Lord Guideth. Studies on Primitive Islam*, Oslo 1956; F. Sezgin, *Geschichte des arabischen Schrifttums*, Vol. I, Leiden 1967, ch.1, 'Qur'anwissenschaften'; H. Gätje, *Koran und Koranexegese*, Zurich 1971; E. Kohlberg, 'Some Notes on the Imamite Attitude to the Qur'an', in S.M. Stern, A. Hourani and V. Brown (eds), *Islamic Philosophy and the Classical Tradition*, Oxford 1972, 209–24; G. Lüling, *Über den Ur-Qur'an. Ansätze zur Rekonstruktion vorislamischer christlicher Strophenlieder im Qur'an*, Erlangen 1974; L. Hagemann, *Der Kur'an in Verständnis und Kritik bei Nikolaus von Kues. Ein Beitrag zur Erhellung islamisch–christlicher Geschichte*, Frankfurt 1976; J. Burton, *The Collection of the Qur'an*, London 1977; J. Wansbrough, *Quranic Studies. Sources and Methods of Scriptural Interpretation*, Oxford 1977; id., *The Sectarian Milieu. Content and Composition of Islamic Salvation History*, Oxford 1978; Watt, *Der Islam* (n. 3), I, C: Der Koran; M. Arkoun, *Lectures du Coran*, Paris 1982; T. Nagel, *Der Koran. Einführung—Texte—Erläuterungen*, Munich 1983; A.T. Welch, 'Al-Kur'an', in *EncIsl*[2]; M.M. Ayoub, *The Qur'an and its Interpreters* (2 vols), Albany, NY 1984, 1992; S. Abu al-A'la Mawdudi, *Towards Understanding the Qur'an*, Leicester 1988ff. (7 vols so far); P. Schwarzenau, *Korankunde für Christen*, Hamburg 1990; M.M. Ayoub, V.J. Cornell and M. Mir, 'Qur'an', in

EncModIsl; Ibn Warraq (ed.), *The Origins of the Koran. Classic Essays on Islam's Holy Book*, Amherst, NY 1998; H. Bobzin, *Der Koran. Eine Einführung*, Munich 1999; N. Kermani, *Gott ist schön. Das ästhetische Erleben des Koran*, Munich 1999; B. Maier, *Koran–Lexikon*, Stuttgart 2001; M. and U. Tworuschka, *Der Koran und seine umstrittenen Aussagen*, Düsseldorf 2002. A thorough historical and theological introduction into the spirit of the Qur'an from a Christian perspective can be found in K. Cragg, *The Event of the Qur'an. Islam in its Scripture*, London 1971; id., *The Mind of the Qur'an. Chapters in Reflection*, London 1973; A. Rippin (ed.), *The Qur'an. Formative Interpretation*, Aldershot 1999; id., (ed.), *The Qur'an. Style and Contents*, Aldershot 2001. There is a helpful account of research above all into the language and literary form of the Qur'an by the Arabist scholar A. Neuwirth, 'Koran', in H. Gätje (ed.), *Grundriss der arabischen Philologie*, Vol. II, Wiesbaden 1987, 96–135. The most complete bibliography of articles is in J.D. Pearson, *Index Islamicus. A bibliography of articles on Islamic subjects in periodicals and other collective publications*, London 1958ff. The volume edited by W.H. Behn, Millersville, PA 1989, is particularly valuable for the earlier literature between 1665 and 1905.

6. Surah 1.1–7; translation following R. Paret, *Der Koran* (n. 5), but the translation of the first verse (= Basmala, which precedes all surahs with the exception of surah 9) follows Khoury, *Der Koran. Arabisch–Deutsch*, Vol. I (n. 5).
7. Asad, *The Message of the Qur'an* (n. 5), 1.
8. E. Gellner, *Muslim Society*, Cambridge 1981.
9. B. Tibi, *Der Islam und das Problem der kulturellen Bewaltigung sozialen Wandels*, Frankfurt 1985, 13.
10. A. Schall, 'Islam I', *TRE* XVI, 316. It is the great achievement of Ignaz Goldziher and C. Snouck Hurgronje that they began to understand Islam 'as a self-contained cultural whole in its own terms'; in so doing, as C.H. Becker points out in his portraits of well-known Islamic scholars, they 'founded Islamic studies as a separate discipline' (*Islamstudien*, Leipzig 1932, Vol. II, 500f.).
11. Schall, 'Islam I' (n. 10), 315.
12. Cf. S. Rushdie, *The Satanic Verses*, London and New York 1989.
13. T. Fahd, 'L'Islam et les sectes islamiques', in H.-C. Puech (ed.), *Histoire des Religions*, III, Paris 1976, 3–179: 5, 8.
14. J. W. Fück, *Arabiya. Untersuchungen zur arabischen Sprach- und Stilgeschichte*, Berlin 1950, 1.
15. A good explanation of this rhyming language (partly for liturgical use) which can be easily understood by readers who do not know Arabic is provided by H. Bobzin, *Der Koran* (n. 5), pp. 87–98; he also gives concrete examples. A standard work on the aesthetics of the Qur'an has been written by the Iranian Navid Kermani, *Gott ist schön. Das ästhetische Erleben des Koran*, Munich 1999.
16. *Der Koran in der Übersetzung von Friedrich Rückert*, ed. H. Bobzin, Würzburg 1995, 468.
17. Surah 12.1–3.
18. Surah 2.97.

19. Surah 56.77–80.
20. Surah 85.21f.
21. Surah 2.185.
22. Cf. surahs 52.34; 17.88; 11.13f.; 10.38; 2.23.
23. An edition with commentary comprising 22 fascicles (around 3000 pages) appeared in association with the mosques in Munich: *Die Bedeutung des Korans*, Munich 1991–6, [2]1998. However, the monumental twelve-volume edition already cited, by the Christian religious scholar A.T. Khoury, *Der Koran. Arabisch–Deutsch* (n. 5), is also bilingual in Arabic and German.
24. Surah 4.82.
25. Surah 2.97.
26. As well as the Qur'an literature indicated (above all Nagel and Watt), see also the precise summary by A. Neuwirth, 'Koran', in K. Kreiser and R. Wielandt (eds.), *Lexikon der Islamischen Welt*, Stuttgart 1992, 159–62, for its account of research, mentioned above.
27. For the critical objections see Watt, *Der Islam* (n. 3), I, 176–8.
28. One example is surah 80, which is made up of five passages that do not hang together very well.
29. Cf. Kohlberg, 'Some Notes' (n. 5), 219.
30. Watt, *Der Islam* (n. 3), I, 182; likewise T. Nagel, *Der Koran. Einführung—Texte—Erläuterungen*, Munich 1983, 33.
31. Thus for example there is no 'Dictionary of the Qur'an' comparable to the ten-volume *Dictionary of the New Testament*, founded by G. Kittel.
32. Cf. G. Weil, *Historisch–kritische Einleitung in den Koran*, Bielefeld 1844, [2]1878.
33. Cf. T. Nöldeke, *Geschichte des Qorans* (1860), second edition completely revised by F. Schwally and developed by G. Bergstrasser and O. Pretzl (3 vols), Leipzig 1909–38 (henceforth cited as Nöldeke-Schwally).
34. Cf. Blachère, *Le Coran* (n. 5).
35. Cf. Watt, *Der Islam* (n. 3), I, 188–214.
36. Cf. the brief survey by A.T. Khoury, 'Koran', *Islam–Lexikon* (n. 3) 462–7, which is parallel to Nöldeke and Blachère.
37. Nöldeke–Schwally, *Geschichte des Qorans* (n. 33), I, 74.
38. Ibid., 118.
39. Ibid., 143.
40. Cf. ibid., 164–234 (Vol. II is devoted to the assembling of the Qur'an, Vol. III to the history of the Qur'an text and the readings).
41. M.M. Ayoub, 'Qur'an', *EncModIsl* III, 385.
42. Cf. W.C. Smith, *On Understanding Islam*, The Hague 1981, ch. 6: Is the Qur'an the Word of God?
43. Illustration in Bobzin, *Der Koran* (n. 5), 16.
44. Quoted from ibid., 17.
45. Even the great Protestant theologian Karl Barth, who in an earlier phase contrasts the other religions with the Christian revelation as purely human work, saw

himself compelled in the last complete volume of his monumental *Church Dogmatics* to concede that alongside the one 'light' of Jesus Christ (which he had emphasized so much all his life), other lights were to be accepted. Cf. *Church Dogmatics* IV/3. Edinburgh 1963, § 69, 2, The Light of Life.

46. Clement XI, Dogmatic Constitution *Unigenitus* (1713), in Denzinger, *Enchiridion* no. 1379.

B II. The Central Message

1. Cf. H. Kung, *Judaism*, Part I, B I: The Central Structural Elements.
2. Cf. id., *Christianity*, B I: Basic Form and Original Motif.
3. Cf. D. B. Macdonald, 'Tawhid', *HdI.*
4. Cf. L. Gardet, 'Islam', *EncIsl*[2]: I. Definitions and Theories of Meaning.
5. Surah 22.34: cf. 2.112.
6. Surah 3.18f.
7. *Der Koran in der Übersetzung von Friedrich Rückert*, ed. H. Bobzin, Würzburg 1995, 23.
8. Cf. L. Gardet, 'Iman', *EncIsl*[2].
9. Cf. H. Küng, *Christianity*, C I, 6 (Jewish Christianity), C II, 5 (Hellenistic christology), C III, 2 (Augustine's doctrine of the Trinity).
10. Surah 23.91.
11. Cf. surahs 37.35; 47.19.
12. Surah 37.4.
13. Surah 2.116.
14. Surah 5. 72f.; cf. 9.30.
15. Cf. surah 22.73.
16. Surah 13.16.
17. Gen.1.3.
18. Surah 40.68.
19. Surah 32.4.
20. Cf. surahs 7.54; 10.3; 11.7; 25.59; 50.38; 57.4.
21. Cf. surah 41.9–12.
22. Surah 50.38.
23. There is a connection between the six-days' work and the creation of human beings only in surah 32.7.
24. Surah 96.1f.
25. Cf. surah 23.12–14.
26. Surah 51.56.
27. Surah 19.93.
28. Cf. surah 2.30: 'And (then) when your Lord said to the angels, "I will appoint a successor on earth!" They said, "Will you impose on them someone (from the race of men) who is bent on your disaster and sheds blood, where we (angels) celebrate you and praise your holiness?" (He said, "I know [much] that you do not").'
29. Surah 8.7.
30. Cf. surah 57.22f.

31. Surah 9.51; cf. 57.22f.
32. Surah 16.93.
33. Cf. Ex. 4.21 (8.15 differs): 'But when the Pharaoh saw ... his heart was hardened'; Isa. 6.9f.
34. Cf. Isa. 45.7.
35. Surah 2.26; cf. 16.104.
36. This is conjectured by some, following surah 17.110; after this the name *ar-rahman* in the Qur'an retreats again.
37. Cf. H. Küng, *Eternal Life?*, ch. IX: End of the World and Kingdom of God.
38. Cf. surahs 56.1–7; 69.13–16; 77. 8–13; 78.18–20; 81.1–14; 82.1–5; 84.1–6.
39. Cf. surah 7.46.
40. Cf. surah 75.22f.
41. Cf. surahs 44.54; 55.46–78; 78.31–4.
42. Cf. Mark 14.25.
43. Cf. Matt. 25.1–13.
44. Cf. Luke 14.15–24.
45. Surah 74.27–9.
46. Surah 73.13.
47. Surahs 44.43–6; cf. 37.62–8; 56.51–6.
48. Cf. surahs 3.54; 7.99; 8.30.
49. Surah 7.180.
50. Gen 1.26f.
51. Surah 2.40, 83f.
52. Cf. A. d'Alverny, 'La prière selon le Coran', *Proche-Orient Chrétien* 10, 1960, 212–26, 303–17; 11, 1961, 3–16. Cf. also H. Zirker, *Islam. Theologische und gesellschaftliche Herausforderungen*, Düsseldorf 1993, 161–85.
53. Cf. A.J. Wensinck, 'Rabb', in *HdI.*
54. Cf. F. Buhl, 'Allahumma', *EncIsl*[2] (= *EncIsl*[1]).
55. Surah 2.201.
56. Surah 27.19.
57. Surah 3.26.
58. Abu Hurayrah, in A.T. Khoury, *Der Koran. Arabisch—Deutsch. Übersetzung und wissenschaftlicher Kommentar*, I, Gütersloh 1990, 150–1. For the interpretation cf. H. Molla-Djafari, *Gott hat die schönsten Namen. Islamische Gottesnamen, ihre Bedeutung, Verwendung und Probleme ihrer Übersetzung*, Frankfurt am Main 2001.
59. Surah 50.16.
60. M. Heidegger, *Identität und Differenz*, Pfullingen 1957, 51.
61. Cf. Mark 6.15; Luke 7.16; John 9.17.
62. This is Jesus' verdict on John the Baptist in Luke 7.26; the verdict on Jesus himself is that he is 'more than Solomon' and 'more than Jonah' (Luke 11.31f.).
63. Cf. H. Küng, *Christianity and the World Religions* (with H. v. Stietencron), 174–7: Mystic and Prophetic Religion; id., *Christianity and Chinese Religions* (with J. Ching), 110–14: A Third Basic Type of Religiosity.

64. Surah 41.6.
65. Surah 33.22.
66. Surah 24.47; cf. 5.55; 8.46.
67. Surah 72.23.
68. Surah 3.144; the other 3 passages are 33.40 ('seal of the prophets'); 42.3; 48.29.
69. Cf. Ibn Ishaq, *Das Leben des Propheten. Aus dem Arabischen übertragen und bearbeitet von G. Rotter*, Tübingen 1976. For Ibn Ishaq, the father of Islamic historiography, cf. R. Sellheim, 'Prophet, Chalif und Geschichte. Die Muhammed-Biographie des Ibn Ishaq', *Oriens* 18/19, 1965/66, 33–91.
70. For the historical quality of the qualitatively very varied source material on the life of the Prophet cf. W. M. Watt, *Der Islam*, I, Stuttgart 1980, 47–51.
71. For the biography of Muhammad: the commendable early historical–critical biographies come from A. Sprenger, *Das Leben und die Lehre des Mohammad, nach bisher grösstentheils unbenutzten Quellen bearbeitet*, I–III, Berlin 1861–5, and W. Muir, *The Life of Mahomet. With Introductory Chapters on the Original Sources for the Biography of Mahomet, and on the Pre-Islamite History of Arabia*, I–IV, London 1861 (reprint in one volume, Edinburgh 1923). The standard European biography was originally the work of the Dane F. Buhl, *Muhammeds Liv med en Indledning om Forholdene i Arabien för Muhammeds Optraeden*, Copenhagen 1903 (German *Das Leben Muhammeds*, Leipzig 1930). This book was basic to Buhl's article 'Muhammed' in *EncIsl*[1], which was completely revised by A.T. Welch for *EncIsl*[2]. Then there was T. Andrae, *Mohammed. Sein Leben und sein Glaube*, Göttingen 1932. The standard studies of Muhammad's life, based on a thorough analysis of the Arabic texts, have been written by W.M. Watt, *Muhammad at Mecca*, Oxford 1953; id., *Muhammad at Medina*, Oxford 1956. A summary of the two volumes in more of a chronological order appeared under the title *Muhammad: Prophet and Statesman*, London 1961. Watt has summarized his studies on the biography of Muhammad and brought them up to date in *Der Islam* (n. 70), I, C II. Other important works are: R. Paret, *Mohammed und der Koran. Geschichte und Verkündigung des arabischen Propheten*, Stuttgart 1957, [2]1991; R. Blachère, *Le problème de Mahomet. Essai de biographie critique du fondateur de l'Islam*, Paris 1952; E. Dermenghem, *Mahomet et la tradition islamique*, Paris 1955; E. Gabrieli, *Muhammad e le prime conquiste arabiche*, Milan 1967; M. Rodinson, *Mahomet*, Paris 1965; id., 'Bilan des études mohammadiennes', *Revue historique* 87, 1963, 169–220; S.H. Nasr, *Muhammad, the Man of Allah*, London 1982; M. Cook, *Muhammad*, Oxford 1983; M. Lings, *Muhammad: His Life Based on the Earliest Sources*, Cambridge 1983; R. Caratini, *Mahomet*, Paris 1993, [2]2002; J.M. Buaben, *Image of the Prophet Muhammad in the West. A Study of Muir, Margoliouth and Watt*, Leicester 1996; J. Chabbi, *Le Seigneur des Tribus. L'Islam de Mahomet*, Paris 1997; U. Rubin (ed.), *The Life of Muhammad*, Aldershot 1998; H. Motzki (ed.), *The Biography of Muhammad. The Issue of the Sources*, Leiden 2000; Ibn Warraq, *The Quest for the Historical Muhammad*, Amherst, NY 2000. In what follows I keep above all to the accounts by Watt, Paret and Rodinson.

72. The chronology follows R. Bell, *Introduction to the Qur'an*, new edition by W.M. Watt, Edinburgh 1970, 15.
73. Cf. A.T. Welch, 'Muhammad', *EncModIsl*: Life of the Prophet.
74. Cf. W.M. Watt, 'Kuraysh', *EncIsl²*.
75. F.M. Donner, *The Early Islamic Conquests*, Princeton 1981, ch. I, State and Society in Pre-Islamic Arabia, is fundamental to the understanding of pre-Islamic tribal society.
76. On all the questions relating to the prehistory and history of the call of Muhammad cf. Watt, *Muhammad at Mecca* (n. 71).
77. Id., *Der Islam* (n. 70), I, 53. This text finally found its way into the history by at-Tabari, *Annales*, I, 1147f.
78. Surah 53.2–12. The second vision is described immediately afterwards, in 53.13–18.
79. Surah 6.103.
80. According to al-Bukhari, quoted by Bobzin (ed.), *Der Koran* (n. 7), 34.
81. Surah 42.51.
82. Surah 2.97.
83. R. Paret, *Der Koran* (2 vols), Stuttgart ²1980, commentary on surah 53.1–18.
84. Most Muslim scholars share with Ibn Ishaq the conviction that the opening of surah 96 (as quoted above) is the first revealed passage; however, sometimes surah 74.1–7 is also regarded as the first revelation.
85. Ibn Ishaq, *Das Leben des Propheten* (n. 69), 45.
86. Surah 74.2.
87. Surah 87.9.
88. Surah 90.13–17; cf. 92.5–11; 93.9–11.
89. Surah 104.1–3.
90. Surah 22.52.
91. Surah 53.19f. Cf. also H. Busse, 'Die Versuchung Muhammads. Die "satanischen Verse" in der Koranexegese', in *Festgabe fur Hans-Rudolf Singer*, ed. M. Forstner, Frankfurt am Main 1991, 477–92.
92. Text following Paret, *Der Koran* (n. 83), commentary on surah 53.19–25; for the interpretation cf. id., *Mohammed und der Koran* (n. 71), ⁷1991, 103f.; Watt, *Der Islam* (n. 70), I, 88–93.
93. Surah 53.21–3.
94. Surah 109.1–6.
95. Surah 4.48; 4.116.
96. Over against a 'predominantly Muhammad-centred perspective', with reference to the book by F.M. Donner cited above, 'the Quraysh' view of things' is convincingly depicted by A. Noth, 'Früher Islam', in U. Haarmann, *Geschichte der arabischen Welt*, Munich 1987, ²1991, 18–28.
97. For the early history of Medina cf. Watt, *Muhammad at Medina* (n. 71), 151–74.
98. Cf. ibid. for the whole of Muhammad's period in Medina.

99. Ibn Ishaq, *Das Leben des Propheten* (n. 69), 109.
100. Ibid.
101. Ibid.,110.
102. Ibid.
103. R. Paret, 'Umma', in *HdI.*
104. The fundamental work on the Prophet's relation to the Jewish tribes was written at a very early stage by the leading Dutch Islamologist A.J. Wensinck, *Mohammed en de Joden te Medina*, Leiden 1908; new English edition *Muhammad and the Jews of Medina*, Freiburg im Breisgau 1975, Berlin [2]1982. A more recent account is given by J. Bouman, *Der Koran und die Juden. Die Geschichte einer Tragödie*, Darmstadt 1990.
105. Particularly clearly in surah 5.44–8.
106. Surah 5.44.
107. Surah 5.46f.
108. Surah 5.48.
109. Ibid.
110. Ibid.
111. Cf. above, A II, 3: Abraham—the common ancestor of the 'people of the book'.
112. Surah 3.160.
113. Surah 5.82.
114. Surah 9.29–31.
115. Cf. Paret, *Koran* (n. 83), commentary on surah 9.29f.
116. M. Hamidullah, *The Battlefields of the Prophet Muhammad, with Maps, Illustrations and Sketches: A Contribution to Muslim Military History*, Hyderabad 1973, is written on the basis of field research.
117. M.M. Ali, *Muhammad the Prophet*, Lahore 1924, [2]1933, 295f.; cf. id., *The Living Thoughts of the Prophet Muhammad*, London 1947.
118. I shall return to this criticism of Muhammad in my discussion of the individual paradigms and then document the attitude of Christianity to Islam in the different periods. Here we are concerned with the results of the historical research which is to be found in all the biographies of Muhammad, in my view best in W.M. Watt and R. Paret, on whose results I base my own assessments.
119. Cf. surah 4.3.
120. Cf. surah 80.2f.
121. Cf. surah 4.23.
122. Surah 33.37.
123. Ibid.
124. Cf. at-Tabari, Commentary XXII, 9; quoted in Paret, *Mohammed* (n. 71), 159.
125. Surah 33.50.
126. Quoted in Paret, *Mohammed* (n. 71), 151.
127. Surah 33.52.
128. Cf. H. Küng, *The Church*, E II, 2: The diaconal structure.
129. Cf. 1 Cor. 12.28.

B III. The Central Structural Elements

1. Cf. D.B. Macdonald, ‘Mala’ika’, in *EncIsl*^{2} (= *EncIsl*^{1}), revised and supplemented by W. Madelung.
2. Cf. A.J. Wensinck, ‘Iblis’, in *EncIsl*^{2} (= *EncIsl*^{1}), revised by L. Gardet.
3. Cf. D.B. Macdonald, ‘Djinn’, in *EncIsl*^{2} (= *EncIsl*^{1}), revised by H. Massé; E. Zbinden, *Die Djinn des Islam und der altorientalische Geisterglaube*, Berne 1953.
4. For prayer, in addition to the earlier publications by E. Mittwoch and E.E. Calverley see especially A.J. Wensinck, ‘Salat’, in *HdI.* A.T. Welch, ‘Das religiöse Leben der Muslime’, in W.M. Watt, *Der Islam*, I, Stuttgart 1980, 262–347, esp. 262–84, offers a convincing attempt at a reconstruction of the early development of *salat*; cf. also A.T. Khoury, *Gebete des Islams*, Mainz 1981, and the scrupulous invitation to prepare to pray and pray by M. Rassoul (ed.), *As-Salah. Das Gebet im Islam*, Cologne 1983. A. Zaki Hammad, *Lasting Prayers of the Quran and the Prophet Muhammad*, Quranic Literacy Institute, Bridgeview, IL 1996, is a fine edition of prayers from the Qur’an and Sunnah for every possible occasion.
5. Cf. surah 11.114.
6. Cf. surahs 2.238f.; 73.20.
7. Welch, ‘Das religiöse Leben der Muslime’ (n. 4), 271. In what follows Welch investigates the two groups of aetiological legends, both of which date the origin of the five *salat* back to Muhammad’s lifetime, assigning an important role to the angel Gabriel (and Moses).
8. Cf. surahs 4.43; 5.6.
9. Surah 1.5.
10. Surah 1.6.
11. Surah 1.7.
12. Cf. S.D. Goitein, ‘Djum’a’’, in *EncIsl*^{2}.
13. Cf. surah 62.9f.
14. Cf. F. Kluge and E. Seebold, *Etymologisches Wörterbuch der deutschen Sprache*, Berlin ^{22}1989, 489.
15. For the mosque see the two-volume standard work by K.A.C. Creswell, *Early Muslim Architecture*, Oxford ^{2}1969, which has been compiled with great scrupulousness; also U. Vogt-Göknil, *Die Moschee. Grundformen sakraler Baukunst*, Zurich 1978; A. Papadopoulo, *L’islam et l’art musulman*, Paris 1976 [German *Islamische Kunst*, Freiburg 1977, 218–97, 578–88], plates nos 112–73; J.E. Campo, A. Kuran, A.S. Ahmed, P.D. Gaffney and J. Waardenburg, ‘Mosque’, in *EncModIsl*; J.M. Bloom, ‘Mosque’, in *EncQur.*
16. Welch, ‘Das religiöse Leben der Muslime’ (n. 4), 279.
17. Surah 17.110.
18. Cf. Kluge and Seebold, *Etymologisches Wörterbuch der deutschen Sprache* (n. 14), 479f.
19. For the minaret cf. R. Hillenbrand, J. Burton-Page and G.S P. Freeman-Grenville, ‘Manara, Manar (minaret)’, in *EncIsl*^{2}; Papadopoulo, *Islamische Kunst* (n. 15), 226–91; J.M. Bloom, *Minaret. Symbol of Islam*, Oxford 1989.

20. A.T. Khoury (ed.), *Lexikon religiöser Grundbegriffe*, Graz 1987, is helpful for the comparison of analogous religious phenomena in Judaism, Christianity and Islam. For the Islamic terms cf. A.T. Khoury, L. Hagemann and P. Heine, *Islamlexikon*, Freiburg 1991; K. Kreiser and R.Wielandt (eds), *Lexikon der Islamischen Welt*, new edition Stuttgart 1992.
21. For almsgiving, in addition to the older treatment by N.P. Aghnides and J. Schacht, 'Zakat', in *HdI*, see more recently A. Zysow, 'Zakat', in *EncIsl*[2]; A. al-Sheikh, 'Zakat', in *EncModIsl*.
22. Cf. surah 9.5, 11.
23. Surah 2.83.
24. Cf. surah 9.60.
25. Cf. surah 73.20.
26. For the origin and history of the *waqf* cf. the Saudi-Arabian economist Monzer Kahf, 'Waqf', in *EncModIsl*.
27. Cf. Lev. 16.29ff.; 23.27ff.
28. Matt. 6.16–18.
29. For fasting, in addition to the older work by G. Jacob see especially C.C. Berg, 'Sawm', in *HdI*; M. Plessner, 'Ramadan', in *HdI*; A.J. Wensinck, '*'Ashura*', in *EncIsl*[2] (= *EncIsl*[1], supplemented by P. Marçais); K. Hiridjee, *Le Ramadan, ses rites, ses bienfaits*, Cachan 1950; K. Wagtendonk, *Fasting in the Koran*, Leiden 1968; K. Lech, *Geschichte des islamischen Kultus. Rechtshistorische und hadit-kritische Untersuchungen zur Entwicklung und Systematik der 'Ibadat, I. Das Ramadan-Fasten*, I, Wiesbaden 1979; L. Clark, 'Sawm', in *EncModIsl*.
30. Cf. surah 2.184–7.
31. Cf. surah 9.36f.
32. Cf. surah 2.187.
33. Cf. Ex. 23.17; 34.23; Deut. 16.16.
34. For the pilgrimage, in addition to the classic account by C. Snouck Hurgronje, *Het mekkaansche Feest*, Leiden 1880, and the older publications by R. Burton, A. Rhalli, S. Spiro Bey and M. Gaudefroy-Desmombynes, cf. especially A.J. Wensinck, 'Hadjdj', in *EncIsl*[2] (= *EncIsl*[1], partly revised by J. Jomier and supplemented by B. Lewis); C. Rathjens, *Die Pilgerfahrt nach Mekka. Von der Weihrauchstrasse zur Ölwirtschaft*, Hamburg 1948; F.E. Peters, *The Hajj. The Muslim Pilgrimage to Mecca and the Holy Places*, Princeton 1994 (especially the historical development of the Hajj); R. Bianchi, 'Hajj', in *EncModIsl*. M. Wolfe, *The Hadj. A Pilgrimage to Mecca*, London 1994, gives a personal account of his own pilgrimage.
35. Surah 3.97.
36. E. de Vitray-Meyerovitsch (text) and H.Y. Hirashima (photographs), *La Mecca e Medina. Le città del Profeta*, Milan 1981, provide an impressive photographic documentation for non-Muslims, who are not allowed to visit Mecca and Medina. Cf. also J. Roman, *Le pélérinage aux lieux saints de l'Islam*, Algiers 1954. A film documentation of the pilgrimage is given in the seventh film on Islam in the television series made by Sudwest Rundfunk, Germany/ DRS Switzerland and

presented by H. Küng, *Spurensuche*, Munich 1999. It is available on video, CD-ROM and DVD.

C. History

C I. The Original Paradigm of the Islamic Community

1. T.S. Kuhn, *The Structure of Scientific Revolutions*, Chicago 1962, 175.
2. Cf. H. Küng, *Theology for the Third Millennium. An Ecumenical View*, London 1991, B II–IV C I; also id., *Global Responsibility*, Part C.
3. The accounts by H. Busse, B. Radtke, W. Ende and R. Peters in W. Ende and G.T. Steinbach (eds), *Der Islam in der Gegenwart*, Munich 1984, 17–131, were very helpful to me as a first orientation. Cf. also G. Endress, *Der Islam. Eine Einführung in seine Geschichte*, Munich 1982, [2]1991.
4. Cf. P.M. Holt, A.K.S. Lambton and B. Lewis (eds), *The Cambridge History of Islam*, Vols I–II, Cambridge 1970, and K. Armstrong, *Islam. A Short History*, London 2000.
5. Cf. J.L. Esposito, *Oxford History of Islam*, Oxford 1999.
6. Cf. C. Cahen, *Der Islam I. Vom Ursprung bis zu den Anfängen des Osmanenreiches*, Frankfurt 1968, [2]1987.
7. Cf. M.G.S. Hodgson, *The Venture of Islam. Conscience and History in a World Civilization*, Vols I–III, Chicago 1974.
8. Cf. U. Haarmann (ed.), *Geschichte der arabischen Welt*, Munich 1987.
9. Cf. I.M. Lapidus, *A History of Islamic Societies*, Cambridge 1988.
10. Cf. T. Nagel, *Geschichte der islamischen Theologie. Von Mohammed bis zur Gegenwart*, Munich 1994.
11. Cf. J. van Ess, *Theologie und Gesellschaft im 2. und 3. Jahrhundert Hidschra. Eine Geschichte des religiösen Denkens im frühen Islam* (6 vols), Berlin 1991–7.
12. Cf. *The Encyclopaedia of Islam, New Edition, Prepared by a Number of Leading Orientalists*, Leiden 1986–2002 (11 vols, with supplements and indices = *EncIsl*[2]). But the first *Encyclopedia of Islam*, edited by M.T. Houtsma (5 vols, Leiden 1913–38, = *EncIsl*[1]), which appeared simultaneously in German, English and French, or the shorter version, edited by A.J. Wensinck and J.H. Kramers, *Handwörterbuch des Islam*, Leiden [2]1976 (= *HdI*), are still important (some articles in *EncIsl*[2] have been taken over from *EncIsl*[1]).
13. Cf. H. Küng, *Christianity*, C I: The Jewish–Apocalyptic Paradigm of Earliest Christianity.
14. Cf. B, Centre, in the present work.
15. The standard treatment in terms of social history is that of F.M. Donner, *The Early Islamic Conquests*, Princeton 1981. Donner's results are accepted by A. Noth, 'Früher Islam', in Haarmann (ed.), *Geschichte der arabischen Welt* (n. 8), 11–100, and Lapidus, *History* (n. 9), Ch. 1: Arabia.
16. J. Schacht, *An Introduction to Islamic Law*, Oxford 1964, 11; cf. id., *The Origins of Muhammadan Jurisprudence*, Oxford 1950, [2]1953.

17. Id., *Introduction* (n. 16), 11.
18. Cf. N.J. Coulson, *A History of Islamic Law*, Edinburgh 1964, 12, which is a good supplement to Schacht.
19. Cf. J. Schacht, 'Kisas', in *EncIsl*^{2} (= *EncIsl*^{1}).
20. Cf. B. Farès, *L'honneur chez les Arabes avant l'Islam. Étude de sociologie*, Paris 1932.
21. Cf. surah 5.45: 'We have prescribed for them (in the Torah): A life for a life, an eye for an eye, a nose for a nose, an ear for an ear, a tooth for a tooth and wounds (likewise. In all cases) retribution (is prescribed).'
22. Surah 2.179.
23. Cf. surah 17.33.
24. Cf. surahs 16.126; 17.33; 42.40.
25. Cf. surah 2.178. Cf. E. Tyan, 'Diya', in *EncIsl*^{1} (remarkably without a single instance from the Qur'an).
26. Cf. surah 22.60.
27. Cf. J. Schacht, 'Riba', in *HdI*; M. Rodinson, *Islam et capitalisme*, Paris 1966.
28. Surah 30.39.
29. Surah 3.130.
30. Surah 2.275.
31. Surah 4.161.
32. Cf. surahs 2.282f.; 17.34; 23.8.
33. Surah 17.35.
34. Cf. surah 62.9.
35. Cf. A.J. Wensinck, 'Khamr', in *EncIsl*^{2} (= *EncIsl*^{1}); P. Heine, *Weinstudien. Untersuchungen zu Anbau, Produktion und Konsum des Weins im arabisch-islamischen Mittelalter*, Wiesbaden 1982.
36. Cf. surah 16.67.
37. Surah 2.219.
38. Surah 4.43.
39. Surah 5.90.
40. Cf. B. Carra de Vaux, 'Maisir', in *HdI*.
41. Cf. surahs 5.3; 6.121, 145; 16.115.
42. Cf. surahs 2.30; 6.165; 35.39.
43. Surah 2.269.
44. Surahs 4.36; 31.18.
45. Surah 16.23.
46. Cf. surah 41.1.
47. Surah 3.144.
48. Cf. surah 3.103.
49. Cf. surah 9.71.
50. Cf. surah 16.126.
51. Cf. surah 24.22.
52. Surah 41.34f. The Paris dissertation by M.A. Draz, *La morale du Koran*, Paris 1951, supervised by Louis Massignon and Renz Le Senne, compares the doctrine of the

Qur'an on the one hand with the classical schools and on the other with modern Western moral theories (especially Kant).

53. Cf. W.M. Watt, *Der Islam*, I, Stuttgart 1980, 132–5.
54. Surah 16.72.
55. Cf. surahs 23.12–14; 75.36–9; 86.5–7.
56. Surah 30.21.
57. Surah 24.33.
58. Cf. surah 70.31.
59. Surah 4.3.
60. Ibid.
61. The translation by Watt, *Der Islam*, I (n. 53), 133, differs from that of Paret. However, Paret too thinks that the emphasis is on the fact that 'a man should in some cases marry more than just one woman, but not that it may be no more than four' (R. Paret, *Der Koran* [2 vols], Stuttgart [2] 1980, commentary on surah 4.3).
62. For the practice of temporary marriage (*mut'a* marriage), forbidden by the second caliph 'Umar, by the Shiites (Imamites), who did not recognize 'Umar as the legitimate caliph, but still allowed it on the basis of surah 4.24, as for everything else above, see Watt, *Der Islam* (n. 53), I, 135.
63. Cf. surahs 7.189; 42.11.
64. Surah 16.97.
65. Thus the working definition of 'state' in the comprehensive investigation by T. Nagel, *Staat und Glaubensgemeinschaft im Islam. Geschichte der politischen Ordnungsvorstellungen der Muslime* (2 vols), Zurich 1981, quotation I, 8f.
66. Cf. Donner, *Early Islamic Conquests* (n. 15), 251–67. Noth, 'Früher Islam' (n. 15), 30–40, 100, prefers to speak of 'confederation' or 'Muslim ecumene'.
67. Donner, *Early Islamic Conquests* (n. 15), 258.
68. Noth, 'Früher Islam' (n. 15), 37.
69. Lapidus, *History* (n. 9), 226.
70. Ibid.
71. The earliest example (dating from 691) and bibliographies (L. Massignon, F. Meier) are to be found in van Ess, *Theologie* (n. 11), I, 3.
72. Cf. surah 33.40.
73. For the early history of Islam, in addition to the overall accounts mentioned at the beginning of C I (especially I.M. Lapidus), see first of all the ninth-century Arabic history by A. al-Baladuri, *Kitab Futuh al-Buldan*; English translation by P.K. Hitti and E.C. Murgotten (2 vols), New York 1916–24, reprinted 1968. The classic modern history is that by J. Wellhausen, *Das arabische Reich und sein Sturz*, Berlin 1902, [2]1960. The most important more recent works are: C. Cahen, *Der Islam I. Vom Ursprung bis zu den Anfängen des Osmanenreiches*, Frankfurt am Main 1968; M. Lombard, *L'islam dans sa première grandeur (VIIIe–XIe siècle)*, Paris 1971; Nagel, *Staat und Glaubensgemeinschaft im Islam* (n. 65); Donner, *Early Islamic Conquests* (n. 15); id., 'Muhammad and the Califate', in J.L. Esposito, *Oxford History of Islam*, Oxford 1999, ch. I. There are illuminating articles in G.H.A. Juynboll, *Studies of the*

First Century of Islamic Society, Carbondale, IL 1982. A succinct and concentrated account in terms of social history is given by Noth, 'Früher Islam' (n. 15).

74. Of course there can be no question of 'writing about Islamic history—and this is particularly the case with early Islamic history—in terms of domination', as Noth critically observes ('Früher Islam' [n. 15], 30). Full account will be taken of Noth's remarks on social history in what follows.
75. I have given my own integrative hermeneutic of history in *Christianity*, ch. C 1, 1: The need for a basic orientation.
76. For the concept of the caliph see D. Sourdel and A.K.S. Lambton, 'Khalifa (I–II)', in *EncIsl²*; Nagel, *Staat und Glaubensgemeinschaft im Islam* (n. 65); J.M. Landau, *The Politics of Pan-Islam. Ideology and Organization*, Oxford 1990. In his earlier work Nagel speaks of 'three substitute institutions for the principle of direct jurisprudence': the Qur'an, the imamate and the Sunnah (*Rechtleitung und Kalifat. Versuch über eine Grundfrage der islamischen Geschichte*, Bonn 1975).
77. For Abu Bakr cf. C.H. Becker, *Islamstudien*, I, Leipzig 1924, 70–4; W.M. Watt, 'Abu Bakr', in *EncIsl²*.
78. For the charismatic and traditional form of rule and for making the charisma an everyday matter cf. M. Weber, *Economy and Society*, New York 1966, I, 241–54.
79. Cf. van Ess, *Theologie* (n. 11), I, 3.
80. Cf. id., *Prémices de la théologie musulmane*, Paris 2002, 101f.
81. Cf. E. Shoufani, *Al-Riddah and the Muslim Conquest of Arabia*, Toronto 1973.
82. Cf. van Ess, *Theologie* (n. 11), I, 4.
83. Donner, *Early Islamic Conquests* (n. 15), 269.
84. Ibid., 270.
85. For the military potential of the Muslims cf. Noth, 'Früher Islam' (n. 15), 86–90.
86. Cf. ibid., 87f.
87. Cf. id., *Quellenkritische Studien zu Themen, Formen und Tendenzen frühislamischer Geschichtsüberlieferung*, I, Bonn 1973, 72f.
88. Cf. B. Spuler, *Iran in frühislamischer Zeit. Politik, Kultur, Verwaltung und öffentliches Leben zwischen der arabischen und der seldschukischen Eroberung 633 bis 1055*, Wiesbaden 1952; M.G. Morony, *Iraq after the Muslim Conquest*, Princeton 1984.
89. A.J. Butler, *The Arab Conquest of Egypt and the Last Thirty Years of the Roman Dominion*, Oxford 1902, revised version by P.M. Frazer, Oxford 1978 (on Islam from ch. XI), is still usable.
90. Cf. surah 9.29.
91. E.g. surah 10.31.
92. Cf. van Ess, *Theologie* (n. 11), I, 48f.
93. Ibid., 49.
94. Cf. H. Küng, *Christianity*, C I, 5: Excommunication by the synagogue: John's community.
95. Nagel, *Geschichte der islamischen Theologie* (n. 10), 94.
96. Cf. van Ess, *Theologie* (n. 11), I, 46.

97. Cf. P. Crone and M. Hinds, *God's Caliph. Religious Authority in the First Centuries of Islam*, Cambridge 1986, 58–96.
98. Cf. van Ess, *Theologie* (n. 11), I, 38 (with reference to Goldziher).
99. Schacht, *Introduction* (n. 16), 19.
100. Cf. ibid., 20–2.
101. Cf. L. Veccia Vaglieri, ''Ali b. Abi Talib', in *EncIsl²*. As there are no contemporary sources, there is also much dispute over the dating of 'Ali's caliphate. The first monographs, from Kufa and therefore anti-Umayyad, were in fact written down only in the eighth century. A critical investigation has been made of them by E.L. Petersen, *'Ali and Mu'awiya in Early Arabic Tradition. Studies on the Genesis and Growth of Islamic Historical Writing until the End of the 9th Century*, Copenhagen 1964. For the course of events and their dating I follow the investigation by my Tübingen colleague Heinz Halm, *Die Schia*, Darmstadt 1988, 10–17.
102. Cf. G. Rotter, *Die Umayyaden und der Zweite Bürgerkrieg (680–692)*, Wiesbaden 1982, 14.
103. Cf. L. Gardet, 'Fitna', in *EncIsl²*.
104. Cf. A. Sachedina, 'Najaf', in *EncModIsl.*
105. For these and all other questions about 'Ali's caliphate which are disputed between Shiites and Sunnis cf. Halm, *Die Schia* (n. 101), 10–17.
106. Cf. H. Laoust, *Les schismes dans l'Islam. Introduction à une étude de la religion musulmane*, Paris 1964, new edition 1983. Chapters I and II discuss the schism between 'Ali und Mu'awiyyah and the development of the schisms under the Umayyads.
107. Cf. J. van Ess, *Prémices de la théologie musulmane*, Paris 2002, 103f.

C II. The Paradigm of the Arab Empire

1. D.P. Little, 'Mu'awiyah I', in *Encyclopaedia Britannica*, Vol. 8, Chicago [17]1987, 389. J. Wellhausen, *Das arabische Reich und sein Sturz*, Berlin 1902, remains a basic account of the history of the Umayyads. C.H. Becker, *Islamstudien*, II, Leipzig 1932, 474–80, gives a brilliant account of Wellhausen's scholarly achievement. There is a good survey of the period of the Umayyads (661–750) by C. Cahen, *Der Islam* I. *Vom Ursprung bis zu den Anfängen des Osmanenreiches*, Frankfurt am Main 1968, [2]1987, ch. 4.
2. For the fluctuating history of Damascus, which rose to become an imperial capital under the Umayyads and under the 'Abbasids sank to being a provincial town, cf. N. Elisséeff, 'Dimashk', in *EncIsl²*.
3. In addition to Wellhausen, the early work by H. Lammens, *Études sur le règne du calife omaiyade Mo'awia Ier*, Beirut 1906, is fundamental to an understanding of Mu'awiyyah. It is summed up in his article 'Mu'awiya', in *EncIsl¹* (1936). The most recent state of research can be found in M. Hinds, 'Mu'awiya I', in *EncIsl²* (1993). For the whole period of the Umayyads cf. the collection of articles by H. Lammens, *Études sur le siècle des Omayyades*, Beirut 1930.

4. Cf. J. van Ess, *Theologie und Gesellschaft im 2. und 3. Jahrhundert Hidschra. Eine Geschichte des religiösen Denkens im frühen Islam* (6 vols), Berlin 1991–7, I, 68f.
5. P. Crone, *Slaves on Horses. The Evolution of the Islamic Polity*, Cambridge 1980, 30. There is an analysis of the 'Sufyanid Pattern' and the significance of the *ashraf* for the power-structure on pp. 29–33. For the development of the caliphate from a nomadic kingship to the monarchy cf. also I.M. Lapidus, *A History of Islamic Societies*, Cambridge 1988, 54–67.
6. Quoted following S. Brock in Hinds, 'Mu'awiya'(n. 3).
7. Thus against Watt, Paret, Nagel and Rotter, P.Crone and M. Hinds, *God's Caliph. Religious Authority in the First Centuries of Islam*, Cambridge 1986, ch. 2: 'The title khalifat Allah'.
8. Cahen, *Der Islam* (n. 1), 65–8, refers to the concept of the hereditary monarchy in which the power passes from the father to the oldest son or another of the closest relations; this has remained alien to the mentality of the Near East.
9. Hinds, 'Mu'awiya' (n. 3), with reference to Lammens (n. 3).
10. J. Wellhausen, *Die religiös-politischen Oppositionsparteien im alten Islam*, Berlin 1901 (as well as the Shiah in Part II, in Part I Wellhausen discusses the Hawarij) is still the basic work on the beginnings of the Shiah. In addition to the relevant sections in the histories of Arabic (C. Brockelmann, F. Sezgin) and Persian literature (E.G. Browne, C.A. Storey), particularly important critical investigations include M. Momen, *An Introduction to Shi'i Islam. The History and Doctrines of Twelver Shi'ism*, New Haven 1985, and W.M. Watt, *The Formative Period of Islamic Thought*, Edinburgh 1973. A.S.M.H. Tabatabai, *Shi'ite Islam*, London 1975 (systematic), and S.H.M. Jafri, *Origins and Early Development of Shi'a Islam*, London 1979 (historical), write from an emphatic Shiite perspective. A. Falaturi, 'Die Zwölfer-Schia aus der Sicht eines Schiiten: Probleme ihrer Untersuchung', in E. Graf (ed.), *Festschrift Werner Caskel*, Leiden 1968, 62–95, reflects on the problems of communicating convictions of faith and an academic approach. H. Halm, *Die Schia*, Darmstadt 1988, gives the most recent survey, both brief and well-documented, not only of the Twelver Shiah but also of the Shiah as a whole. Y. Richard, *L'Islam chi'ite. Croyances et ideologies*, Paris 1991, is more systematic.
11. Cf. L. Veccia Vaglieri, '(al-) Hasan b. 'Ali b. Abi Talib', in *EncIsl*^{2}; Halm, *Schia* (n. 10), 17f.
12. Cf. H. Lammens, *Le Califat de Yazid I*^{er}, Beirut 1910–1913 (4 fascicles).
13. Cf. L. Veccia Vaglieri, '(al-) Husain b. 'Ali b. Abi Talib', in *EncIsl*^{2}; Halm, *Schia* (n. 10), 18–21.
14. Cf. E. Honigmann, 'Karbala', in *EncIsl*^{2}.
15. I. Goldziher, *Vorlesungen über den Islam*, Heidelberg ^{2}1925, 233.
16. Cf. the title of Wellhausen's study of the 'opposition parties' mentioned above.
17. Cf. G.R. Hawting, 'al-Mukhtar b. Abi 'Ubayd al-Thakafi', in *EncIs1*^{2}.
18. Cf. F. Buhl, 'Muhammad ibn al-Hanafiyya', in *EncIsl*^{2}.
19. For the origin and early development of the term Mahdi, its further development under the 'Abbasids, and the central role of the expectation of the Mahdi in the

radical Shia, cf. W. Madelung, 'al-Mahdi', in *EncIsl*[2]. For the various Mahdi movements cf. also Halm, *Die Schia* (n. 10), passim.

20. Cf. Madelung, 'al-Mahdi' (n. 19).
21. Using new Ismaili texts from private collections, the Twelver-Shiite Iranian F. Daftary has written *A Short History of the Ismailis. Traditions of a Muslim Community*, Edinburgh 1998. For a history of the different Aga Khans cf. Y. Kerlau, *Les Aga Khans*, Paris 1990.
22. See below D I, 2: Politically and socially radical Islamism: Khomeini's Islamic revolution.
23. For 'Abd al-Malik cf. H.A.R. Gibb, "Abd al-Malik b. Marwan', in *EncIsl*[2].
24. For al-Hajjaj's politics and person (simply because he was of plebeian origin, he was disliked by the Iraqi authorities as a representative of state authority) cf. what is still a valid and fair assessment by Wellhausen, *Das arabische Reich* (n. 1), 141–60. Also A. Dietrich, 'al-Hadjdjadj b. Yusuf', in *EncIsl*[2].
25. This is brought out clearly by van Ess, *Theologie* (n. 4), I, 9f.
26. Ibid., 9.
27. Cf. Wellhausen, *Das arabische Reich* (n. 1), 135f.
28. Cf. H. Gaube, *Arabosasanidische Numismatik*, Brunswick 1973, 10 (plate 1), 18–37.
29. Cf. M.L. Bates, *Islamic Coins*, New York 1982, quoted in van Ess, *Theologie* (n. 4), I, 10.
30. For the complex linguistic situation of post-classical 'Middle Arabic' cf. J.W. Fück, *Arabiya. Untersuchungen zur arabischen Sprach- und Stilgeschichte*, Berlin 1970; id., "Arabiyya, II, 3: Middle Arabic', in *EncIsl*[2].
31. For the development of Islamic art cf. O. Grabar, *The Formation of Islamic Art*, New Haven 1973, second revised and expanded edition 1987; A. Papadopoulo, *L'islam et l'art musulman*, Paris 1976.
32. Grabar, *The Formation of Islamic Art* (n. 31), 209.
33. For the development of Islamic architecture, in addition to the works on art mentioned above cf. especially K.A.C. Creswell, *A Short Account of Early Muslim Architecture*, London 1958, second edition revised and expanded by J.W. Allan, Aldershot 1989; G. Michell (ed.), *Architecture of the Islamic World. Its History and Social Meaning*, London 1978; U. Vogt-Göknil, *Die Moschee. Grundformen sakraler Baukunst*, Zurich 1978.
34. Cf. M. Rosen-Ayalon, *The Early Islamic Monuments of Al-Haram Al-Sharif. An Iconographic Study*, Jerusalem 1989. J. van Ess, 'Abd al-Malik and the Dome of the Rock. An Analysis of Some Texts', in J. Raby (ed.), *'Abd al-Malik's Jerusalem*, Oxford 1992, has made a new attempt to interpret the 'Dome of the Rock' (in English transcription 'Qubbat as-Sakhra') as 'tent' (Arabic *qubba*) over the throne of God on the rock (there is an extensive bibliography at the end of the volume).
35. Quotation in van Ess, *Theologie* (n. 4), I, 13.
36. Cf. J. Schacht, *The Origins of Muhammadan Jurisprudence*, Oxford 1950; id., *An Introduction to Islamic Law*, Oxford 1964.
37. Cf. N.J. Coulson, *A History of Islamic Law*, Edinburgh 1964.

38. F. Rahman, *Islamic Methodology in History*, Karachi 1965, 6–12.
39. A.A.A. Fyzee, *Outlines of Muhammadan Law*, New Delhi 1964, ^{2}1974, 24–31.
40. Cf. M.M. al-Azami, *On Schacht's Origins of Muhammadan Jurisprudence*, Riyadh 1985 (there is more on Azami's criticism in the chapters which follow).
41. Coulson, *History* (n. 37), 35.
42. For the origin and practice of the office of qadi cf. Schacht, *Introduction* (n. 36), 24–6; Coulson, *History* (n. 37), 28–30; P.G. Dannhauer, *Untersuchungen zur frühen Geschichte des Qadi-Amtes*, Bonn 1975. Also, summarizing his earlier works, E. Tyan, 'Kadi', in *EncIsl*^{2}.
43. Cf. id., 'Hakam', in *EncIsl*^{2}.
44. Cf. the portrait by van Ess, *Theologie* (n. 4), II, 123–33.
45. Cf. Schacht, *Introduction* (n. 36), ch. 5.
46. Ibid., 27.
47. Cf. ibid.
48. Ibid., 29.
49. Coulson, *History* (n. 37), 41.
50. Lapidus, *History* (n. 5), 61.
51. Cf. P. Crone and M. Hinds, *God's Caliph. Religious Authority in the First Centuries of Islam*, Cambridge 1986, 5.
52. Lapidus, *History* (n. 5), 61f.
53. Cf. ibid., 45–53.
54. Cf. van Ess, *Theologie* (n. 4), I, 40–2.
55. In respect of the paradigm analysis I can only summarize very briefly what histories of Islam or the Arab peoples narrate at greater length; Cahen, *Der Islam* I (n. 1), 32–6, gives a good survey.
56. Cf. H. Küng, *Christianity*, C III, 5: The great counter-force: Islam.
57. Cf. H. Pirenne, *Mohammed and Charlemagne* (1937), New York 1957. E. Gabrieli (ed.), *Maometto in Europa*, Milan 1982, is very illuminating here.
58. Cf. Lapidus, *History* (n. 5), ch. 5 (cosmopolitan Islam) and ch. 6 (urban Islam).
59. Cf. W.M. Watt, *Der Islam*, II, Stuttgart 1985.
60. Cf. T. Nagel, *Geschichte der islamischen Theologie. Von Mohammed bis zur Gegenwart*, Munich 1994.
61. Cf. W.M. Watt, *Free Will and Predestination in Early Islam*, London 1948, 20–31.
62. For Qadarism cf. id., *Der Islam*, II (n. 59), ch. 4: The determination of events by God; J. van Ess, 'Kadariyya', in *EncIsl*^{2}; id., *Theologie* (n. 4), I, 72–135; Nagel, *Geschichte* (n. 60), II, 3.
63. Cf. surahs 15.21; 20.40; 23.18, etc.
64. For what follows cf. van Ess, *Theologie* (n. 4), I, 23–5.
65. Cf. ibid., II, 4–41 (the 'Ketzera').
66. Cf. ibid., 41–121 (Hasan al-Basri and his spiritual successors).
67. For a long time the authenticity of this letter was accepted almost unanimously by scholars, but recently it has been disputed by J. Wansbrough and M. Cook. Van Ess leaves the question open (cf. *Theologie* [n. 4], II, 46f.).

68. Surah 51.56.
69. Cf. van Ess, *Theologie* (n. 4), I, 73–83.
70. Cf. ibid., 75–80.
71. Cf. above C 1, 7: the split between Sunnis, Kharijites and Shiites.
72. For the history of the Kharijites cf. Watt, *Der Islam* (n. 59), II, ch.1; Nagel, *Geschichte* (n. 60), ch. II, 4.
73. Cf. e.g. surah 4.74f.
74. Cf. R. Rubinacci, 'Azarika', in *EncIsl*[2].
75. For the community of Ibadites in Basra and the further developments cf. the pioneering study by T. Lewicki, who has summed up various studies in his article 'Ibadiyya' in *EncIsl*[2]. Also, directly from an Ibadite perspective, A.K. Ennami (an-Nami), *Studies in Ibadism* (al-Ibadiyah), Cambridge dissertation 1971 (there is also an Arabic version). Finally, taking account of the dissertations of Cuperly, Rebstock and Schwarz and the Arabic study by 'Iwad Hulaifat, Amman 1978, van Ess, *Theologie* (n. 4), II, 186–233.
76. For the case of 'Abdallah ibn Ibad cf. M. Cook, *Early Muslim Dogma. A Source-Critical Study*, Cambridge 1981, 51–67; van Ess, *Theologie* (n. 4), II, 187–9.
77. L. Massignon, 'Interférences philosophiques et percées métaphysiques dans la mystique hallagienne: Notions de "l'essentiel desir"', in *Opera Minora*, II, Beirut 1963, 226–53: 245.
78. van Ess, *Theologie* (n. 4), II, 223.
79. Cf. H. Küng, *Christianity and the World Religions*, C III, 2: Self-Immolation of Thinking by Thought Itself.
80. Thus the first editor of this text (1974/5), J. van Ess (against M. Cook, who argues for a later date), *Theologie* (n. 4), I, 174–9; German edition of the text in vol. V, 6–12 (Text II, 1). There is confirmation in W. Madelung, 'Murdji'a', in *EncIsl*[2], who himself published a draft 'On the history of the Murjites' as early as 1965. There is a broad treatment (application of the term, reconstruction of the development, membership of the community, problems of doctrine) in Watt, *Der Islam* (n. 59), II, ch. 5, and a brief summary of the theological problems in Nagel, *Geschichte* (n. 60), II, ch. 6.
81. Cf. the analysis of the two Murjite poems in van Ess, *Theologie* (n. 4), I, 166–71; German edition of the texts, Vol. V, 17–24 (Text II, 3–4).
82. Ibid., I, 171.
83. Cf. the still convincing interpretation by Wellhausen, *Das arabische Reich* (n. 1), 166–94, which defends 'Umar II against the charge of political incompetence.
84. Cf. ibid., 228.
85. Cf. E. Gabrieli, *Il califfato di Hisham. Studi di storia omayyade*, Alexandria 1935; id., 'Hisham', in *EncIsl*[2].
86. Cf. Wellhausen, *Das arabische Reich* (n. 1), 226–8.
87. Cf. van Ess, *Theologie* (n. 4), I, 83–6.
88. For Walid II, in addition to Wellhausen and van Ess see the dissertation by D. Derenk, *Leben und Dichtung des Omaiyadenkalifen al-Walid ibn Yazid. Ein quellenkritischer Beitrag*, Frankfurt 1974.

89. Wellhausen, *Das arabische Reich* (n. 1), 223.
90. Cf. the precise analysis of the inaugural sermon in van Ess, *Theologie* (n. 4), I, 86–8.
91. Ibid., 86.
92. Ibid., 87.
93. Cf. S. Moscati, 'Abu Muslim', in *EncIsl*^{2}, which summarizes his earlier works.
94. Cf. id., 'Abu l-'Abbas as-Saffah', in *EncIsl*^{2}.
95. Wellhausen, *Das arabische Reich* (n. 1), 344.
96. van Ess, *Theologie* (n. 4), I, 51.

C III. The Classical Paradigm of Islam as a World Religion

1. T. Nagel, 'Das Kalifat der Abbasiden', in U. Haarmann, *Geschichte der arabischen Welt*, Munich ^{2}1991, 101–65: 101. Cf. M.A. Shaban, *The 'Abbasid Revolution*, Cambridge 1970, who wanted above all to correct Wellhausen, who remains fundamental: he argues that the background to this revolution is not only the endless tribal battles among the Arabs and the rebellion of the Persians against the Arabs; its aim is the assimilation of Muslims to the empire, Arabs and non-Arabs, in the one Muslim society with the same rights for each member of this society (XV). Also important for the 'Abbasid seizure of power is F. Omar, *The 'Abbasid Caliphate 132/750—170/786*, Baghdad 1969; M. Sharon, *Black Banners from the East. The Establishment of the 'Abbasid State—Incubation of a Revolt*, Leiden 1983. There is a good survey of the whole 'Abbasid period in C. Cahen, *Der Islam I. Vom Ursprung bis zu den Anfängen des Osmanenreiches*, Frankfurt 1968, ^{2}1987, chs 6–7.
2. Cf. H. Kennedy, 'al-Mansur', in *EncIsl*^{2}. For the successes and failures of Mansur's policy of internal consolidation (capital, bureaucracy, jurisprudence) cf. Nagel, 'Kalifat' (n. 1), 110–18.
3. For al-Mansur's clash with the chiliastic Rawandiyah, and their appeal to the spirit of Jesus (or Adam) who is to return at the end as Mahdi, cf. J. van Ess, *Theologie und Gesellschaft im 2. und 3. Jh. Hidschra. Eine Geschichte des religiösen Denkens im frühen Islam* (6 vols), Berlin 1991–7, III, 10–17.
4. Cf. A. A. Duri, 'Baghdad', *EncIsl*^{2}.
5. Cf. Nagel, 'Kalifat' (n. 1), 118–20.
6. For the many varied meanings of the word *diwan*—in the caliphate, in Egypt, in the Muslim West, in Iran and in India—cf. the composite article *diwan* in *EncIsl*^{2}. Because Western travellers encountered the 'diwan' on the frontier, the word was adopted for the customs post (Italian *dogana*, French *douane*); the piece of furniture on which writers sit also came to be known in the West as a divan, and it was used of a 'list', 'display', 'collection' of poems.
7. There is more about Islamic state administration in C. Cahen, *Der Islam I* (n. 1), 102–19; Cahen has also written a number of articles on tax in *EncIsl*^{2}.
8. Cf. the survey in I.M. Lapidus, *A History of Islamic Societies*, Cambridge 1988, 73–80.
9. Ibid., 80.
10. Cf. H. Kennedy, 'al-Mahdi (3. Abbasiden-Kalif)', in *EncIsl*^{2}.

11. Cf. the analysis of the report of the discussion, which has possibly been revised, in van Ess, *Theologie* (n. 3), III, 22–8.
12. Cf. W. Walther, 'Alf Laila wa-Laila', in *Kindlers Literaturlexikon*, Vol. 18, Munich 1992, 97–101.
13. Cf. F. Omar, 'Harun al-Rashid', *EncIsl*^{2}; W.M. Watt, 'Harun ar-Rashid', in *The New Encyclopaedia Britannica*, Vol. V, Chicago ^{15}1987, 731.
14. For the crisis in the empire which already begins with Harun cf. Nagel, 'Kalifat' (n. 1), 120–7.
15. van Ess, *Theologie* (n. 3), III, 26.
16. Esp. Isa. 21.6–9: saying 'from the desert'.
17. Esp. John 14.26: on the 'support which the Father will send in my name'.
18. Cf. D. Gutas, *Greek Thought, Arabic Culture. The Graeco-Arabic Translation Movement in Baghdad and Early 'Abbasid Society (2nd–4th/8th–10th centuries)*, London 1998.
19. Cf. F. Gabrieli, 'al-Amin', in *EncIsl*^{2}.
20. Cf. M. Rekaya, 'al-Ma'mun', in *EncIsl*^{2}, for al-Ma'mun and the sometimes very confused history of the conflict with al-Amin. Moreover al-Qasim was involved in this as the third designated successor to the caliphate. However, he wisely held back, to appear later under the name al-Mu'tasim (not al-Mu'tamin) as the eighth 'Abbasid caliph.
21. Cf. N. Osman, *Kleines Lexikon deutscher Wörter arabischer Herkunft*, Munich 1982.
22. Cf. Lapidus, *History* (n. 8), 89–97.
23. Cf. surah 49.13.
24. In this chapter, too, my reflections are based on J. Schacht, *The Origins of Muhammadan Jurisprudence*, Oxford 1950, ^{2}1953; id., *An Introduction to Islamic Law*, Oxford 1964, chs 7–9; cf. N. J. Coulson, *A History of Islamic Law*, Edinburgh 1964, chs 3–5.
25. For the hadith cf. T. Nagel, *Geschichte der islamischen Theologie. Von Mohammed bis zur Gegenwart*, Munich 1994, ch. III, l.
26. Nagel, *Geschichte* (n. 25), 82.
27. There is a new bilingual edition (Arabic–English) of the work of al-Bukhari: *The Translation of the Meanings of Sahih Al-Bukhari*, ed. M. Muhsin Khan (9 vols), sixth revised edition, Lahore 1986. There is also the well-known French translation, *Les traditions islamiques*, ed. O. Houdas and W. Marçais (4 vols), Paris 1903–14. There is also a selection of hadith by G.H. Bousquet (ed.), *El Bokhârî. L'authentique tradition musulmane*, Paris 1964. Cf. J. Robson, 'al-Bukhari', in *EncIsl*^{2}. Hadith from various collections have been brought together by Abu-r-Rida' (ed.), *Von der Sunna des Propheten*, Cologne ^{2}1994.
28. Cf. I. Goldziher, *Muhammedanische Studien*, Vols I–II, Halle/Saale 1889/90, new edition in one volume Hildesheim 1971: for the development of the hadith see Vol. II, 1–274 (and the excuses on hadith and the NT and women in the hadith).
29. Schacht, *Introduction* (n. 24), 34. N. Calder, *Studies in Early Muslim Jurisprudence*, Oxford 1993, gives a more recent example of a critical estimate of the dating of the hadith.

30. Cf. N. Abbott, *Studies in Arabic Literary Papyri, Vol. II: Qur'anic Commentary and Tradition*, Chicago 1967.
31. Cf. F. Sezgin, *Geschichte des arabischen Schrifttums, Vol. I: Qur'anwissenschaften, Hadith etc. bis ca.430 H.*, Leiden 1967 (as early as 1956 the author wrote a fundamental study on al-Bukhari in Turkish).
32. Cf. M.M. Azami, *Studies in Hadith Methodology and Literature*, Indianapolis 1977; id., *Studies in Early Hadith Literature: With a Critical Edition of some Early Texts*, Indianapolis 1978. On Schacht see id., *On Schacht's Origins of Muhammadan Jurisprudence*, Riyadh 1985, esp. 115–53. The distinguished Muslim expert on the hadith concedes that copyists made mistakes even in the hadith and were sometimes deceived in their memory; deliberate falsifications also occurred (cf. 111). However, according to Azami the following methodological assumptions must be investigated critically (and Western experts have hardly grappled sufficiently with his criticism): 'a. That if a certain hadith was not mentioned by a certain scholar, it is proof of that scholar's ignorance of that hadith. b. That all the works of the early scholars have been printed and nothing is missing, so that we possess all that they compiled. c. That one scholar's ignorance of a particular hadith is sufficient proof that the hadith did not exist. d. That knowledge known to one scholar at a particular time must have been known to all his contemporaries in that branch of knowledge. e. That when a scholar writes on a subject, he uses *all* the evidence available to him at that time' (118f.).
33. Cf. F. Rahman, *Islam*, Chicago [2]1979, ch. 3.
34. Cf. H. Motzki, 'The Prophet and the Cat. On Dating Malik's Muwatta' and Legal Traditions', *Jerusalem Studies in Arabic and Islam* 22, 1998, 18–83 (critical discussion of N. Calder); id., *Die Anfänge der islamischen Jurisprudenz: ihre Entwicklung in Mekka bis zur Mitte des 2./8. Jh.*, Stuttgart 1991.
35. Coulson, *History* (n. 24), 42.
36. Ibid., 65.
37. H. Berg, *The Development of Exegesis in Early Islam. The Authenticity of Muslim Literature from the Formative Period*, Richmond, Surrey 2000, 226.
38. Cf. the example in Nagel, *Geschichte* (n. 25), 79–82.
39. For ash-Shafi'i cf. Schacht, *Introduction* (n. 24), 58–60; Coulson, *History* (n. 24), ch. I, 4, 'Master-Architect ...'.
40. Ash-Shafi'i, quoted from Schacht, *Origins* (n. 24), 97.
41. Cf. van Ess, *Theologie* (n. 3), III, which is wholly devoted to the Mu'tazilah. Cf. also T. Nagel, *Rechtleitung und Kalifat. Versuch über eine Grundfrage der islamischen Geschichte*, Bonn 1975; D. Gimaret, 'Mu'tazila', in *EncIsl*[2].
42. Cf. van Ess, *Theologie* (n. 3), II, 335–42.
43. Cf. ibid., 339.
44. Cf. H.S. Nyberg, ''al-Mu'tazila', in *HdI*.
45. Cf. A.J. Wensinck, 'Wasil b. 'Ata', in *HdI*; van Ess, *Theologie* (n. 3), II, 234–80.
46. Cf. W.M. Watt, ' 'Amr b. 'Ubayd', in *EncIsl*[2]; van Ess, *Theologie* (n. 3), II, 280–310.
47. Cf. van Ess, *Theologie* (n. 3), II, 310–16.

48. Cf. H.S. Nyberg, "al-Mu'tazila', in *HdI.*
49. Cf. W.M. Watt, "Amr b. 'Ubayd', in *EncIsl*[2].
50. Cf. van Ess, *Theologie* (n. 3), II, 287–95.
51. Van Ess has also made a thorough investigation of Dirar and Mu'ammar, *Theologie* (n. 3), III, 31–92, and of Bishr ibn al-Mu'tamir, 107–30.
52. Cf. ibid., 224–70 (Abu l-Hudhayl), 309–92 (an-Nazzam). A more systematic treatment can be found in id., *Les prémices de la théologie musulmane,* Paris 2002, ch. 3, 'La théologie et la science. L'atomisme mu'tazilite'.
53. Cf. W. M. Watt, 'Djahm b. Safwan', in *EncIsl*[2].
54. For the Sumanites see van Ess, *Theologie* (n. 3), II, 20–2, 503f.
55. For the discussion between F. Zimmermann and R.M. Frank, which for the first time has brought out the Neoplatonic parallels, cf. van Ess, *Theologie* (n. 3), II, 499f.
56. Cf. surah 42.11.
57. Cf. surah 39.62.
58. Quoted by Nagel, *Geschichte* (n. 25), 103.
59. After a first introductory monograph by 'Ali Mustafa Gurabi (in Arabic, Cairo 1949) the basic work is by R.M. Frank, *The Metaphysics of Created Being according to Abu 1-Hudhayl al-'Allaf. A Philosophical Study of the Earliest Kalam,* Istanbul 1966. The most comprehensive investigation of the life of Abu l-Hudhayl together with an analysis of his whole work is in van Ess, *Theologie* (n. 3), III, 209–96.
60. Cf. van Ess, *Theologie* (n. 3), III, 275f.
61. Cf. Nagel, 'Kalifat' (n. 1), 123–7.
62. Thus already W.M. Patton in his pioneering work *Ahmed ibn Hanbal and the Mihna. A Biography of the Imam including an Account of the Mohammedan Inquisition Called the Mihna, 218—234 a.h.,* Leiden 1897; it has been confirmed and qualified by W.M. Watt and D. Sourdel.
63. Cf. I.M. Lapidus, 'The Separation of State and Religion in the Development of Early Islamic Society', *International Journal of Middle East Studies* 6, 1975, 363–85, esp. 378f. ('an authoritarian response'); Nagel, *Rechtleitung* (n. 41), 442; id., 'Kalifat' (n. 1), 127–30.
64. Thus van Ess, *Theologie* (n. 3), III, 446–52.
65. Cf. ibid., 283–6 (for Abu l-Hudhayl), 408–13 (for an-Nazzam).
66. Quoted from ibid., 453.
67. Quoted from ibid.
68. Cf. M. Hinds, 'Mihna', in *EncIsl*[2].
69. This has been worked out by W. Madelung, 'The Origins of the Controversy Concerning the Creation of the Koran', in *Festschrift Pareja,* Leiden 1974, Vol. I, 504–25, esp. 520f.; Ibn Hanbal is said to have remarked before the controversy: 'Whoever asserts that the Qur'an is created is a Jahmite, and whoever affirms that it is uncreated is a heretical innovator (*mubtadi'*).' Cf. also Nagel, *Rechtleitung* (n. 41), 330–2.
70. For Ibn Abu Duwad's biography cf. van Ess, *Theologie* (n. 3), III, 481–502.

71. Cf. W.M. Watt, "al-Ash'ari, Abu l'Hasan', in *EncIsl²*; id., *Der Islam*, Vol. II: *Politische Entwicklungen und theologische Konzepte*, Stuttgart 1985, 303–12; R.J. McCarthy, *The Theology of al-Ash'ari*, Beirut 1953 (with the Arabic–English text of *Kitab al Lima'* and the *Risalah*); D. Gimaret, *Théories de l'acte humain en théologie musulmane*, Paris 1982, ch. II, 2; id., *La doctrine d'al-Ash'ari*, Paris 1990.
72. Cf. surah 21.22.
73. This is emphasized by Nagel, *Geschichte* (n. 25), 143–53, who gives the evidence for the following remarks on image of God, Qur'an and human responsibility.
74. Cf. D. Gimaret, *Théologie des noms divins en Islam. Exégèse lexicographique et théologique*, Paris 1988.
75. For the downfall of the 'Abbasid caliphate cf. Lapidus, *History* (n. 8), ch. 8; Nagel, *Rechtleitung und Kalifat* (n. 41), chs 6–7. D. Pipes, *Slave Soldiers and Islam. The Genesis of a Military System*, New Haven 1981.

C IV. The Paradigm of the Ulama and Sufis

1. Jer. 48.10.
2. For the crusades cf. C. Erdmann, *Die Entstehung des Kreuzzugsgedankens*, Stuttgart 1935, reprinted 1955; S. Runciman, *A History of the Crusades* (3 vols), Cambridge 1951–4; J. Richard, *Le Royaume latin de Jérusalem*, Paris 1953; id., *Croisades et états latins d'Orient. Points de vue et documents*, Aldershot 1992; K.M. Setton et al. (eds), *A History of the Crusades* (6 vols), Philadelphia 1955–89; id., *The Papacy and the Levant (1204–1571)* (4 vols), Philadelphia 1976–84; A. Waas, *Geschichte der Kreuzzüge* (2 vols), Freiburg 1956; F. Gabrieli (ed.), *Storici arabi delle crociate*, 1957; H.E. Mayer, *Geschichte der Kreuzzüge*, Stuttgart 1965, [9]2000; id., *Kreuzzüge und lateinischer Osten*, London 1983; E. Sivan, *L'Islam et la croisade. Idéologie et propagande dans les réactions musulmanes aux croisades*, Paris 1968; J. Prawer, *Histoire du royaume latin de Jérusalem* (originally in Hebrew) (2 vols), Paris 1969f.; M. Purcell, *Papal Crusading Policy. The Chief Instruments of Papal Crusading Policy and Crusade to the Holy Land from the Final Loss of Jerusalem to the Fall of Acre 1244–1291*, Leiden 1975; T.P. Murphy (ed.), *The Holy War*, Columbus 1976; R.C. Schwinges, *Kreuzzugsideologie und Toleranz. Studien zu Wilhelm von Tyrus*, Stuttgart 1977; E.-D. Hehl, *Kirche und Krieg im 12. Jahrhundert. Studien zu kanonischem Recht und politischer Wirklichkeit*, Stuttgart 1980; L. Riley-Smith and J. Riley-Smith, *The Crusades. Idea and Reality, 1095–1274*, London 1981; R. Pernoud, *Les hommes de la Croisade*, Paris 1982; A. Maalouf, *Les croisades vues par les Arabes*, Paris 1983; P. Rousset, *La croisade. Histoire d'une idéologie*, Lausanne 1983; B.Z. Kedar, *Crusade and Mission. European Approaches towards the Muslim*, Princeton 1984; E. Siberry, *Criticism of Crusading 1095–1274*, Oxford 1985; J. Riley-Smith, *The First Crusade and the Idea of Crusading*, London 1986; id., *The Crusades. A Short History*, London 1987; R. Chazan, *European Jewry and the First Crusade*, Berkeley 1987; A. Dupront, *Du Sacré. Croisades et pélerinages, images et langages*, Paris 1987; R. Delort (ed.), *Les croisades*, Paris 1988; J.A. Brundage, *The Crusades, Holy War and Canon Law*, Hampshire 1991; P.J. Cole, *The Preaching of*

the Crusades to the Holy Land, 1095–1270, Cambridge 1991; S. Schein, *Fideles Crucis. The Papacy, the West, and the Recovery of the Holy Land, 1274–1314*, Oxford 1991; J. Flori, *La première croisade. L'Occident chrétien contre l'Islam*, Brussels 1992; B.N. Sargent-Baur (ed.), *Journeys Toward God. Pilgrimage and Crusade*, Kalamazoo 1992; '"Militia Christi" e Crociata nei secoli XI–XIII' was also the topic of a study week in Mendola (proceedings published Milan 1997); B. Tibi, *Kreuzzug und Djihad. Der Islam und die christliche Welt*, Munich 2001. The big exhibition in Mainz in 2004 was also very informative; catalogue and illustrations ed. H.-J. Kotzur, *Die Kreuzzüge. Ausstellung*, Mainz 2004.

3. Cf. Bernard of Clairvaux, *De laude novae militiae ad milites templi*, in *Opera omnia*, Paris 1862, Vol. I, cols 921–40.
4. In the part of his book dealing with 'ideologies' (107–217), the French historian J. Flori, *La première croisade* (n. 2), makes an important contribution to the history of the mentality of this time by working out precisely the various elements of the 'Western ideology' now taking shape in the clash with Islam (231–8). For the whole context see H. Küng, *Christianity*, C III: The Roman Catholic Paradigm of the Middle Ages.
5. This is convincingly depicted by J. Riley-Smith, *The First Crusade* (n. 2).
6. Cf. Siberry, *Criticism of Crusading* (n. 2).
7. For this whole development see T. Nagel, 'Das Kalifat der Abbasiden', in U. Haarmann (ed.), *Geschichte der arabischen Welt*, Munich ^{2}1991, chs 10–13.
8. Cf. H. Halm, 'Die Fatimiden', in Haarmann (ed.), *Geschichte der arabischen Welt* (n. 7), 166–99.
9. Ibid., 172.
10. Cf. id., 'Die Ayyubiden', in U. Haarmann (ed.), *Geschichte der arabischen Welt* (n. 7), 200–16.
11. Cf. Nagel, 'Das Kalifat' (n. 7), 141–6.
12. Cf. ibid., 154.
13. Quoted ibid., 154f.
14. There is a good survey of the development from 945 to 1200 in I.M. Lapidus, *A History of Islamic Societies*, Cambridge 1988, 137–237.
15. Cf. J. Pedersen, 'Madrasa (I. The Institution in the Arabic, Persian and Turkish Lands)', in *EncIsl*^{2} (= *EncIsl*^{1}, revised by G. Makdisi).
16. Cf. R. Hillenbrand, 'Madrasa (III. Architecture)', in *EncIsl*^{2}.
17. Cf. Lapidus, *History* (n. 14), 166f.
18. Cf. G. Makdisi, 'Ibn 'Akil', in *EncIsl*^{2}.
19. Lapidus, *History* (n. 14), 167.
20. Cf. H. Küng, *Judaism*, Part I, C V, 1: The Kabbala—not a new paradigm.
21. Cf. id., *Christianity*, C III, 10: Mysticism under suspicion.
22. For the concept of mysticism cf. R. Otto, *West–östliche Mystik. Vergleich und Unterscheidung zur Wesensdeutung*, Gotha 1926, pocket book edition of the third revised edition, Gütersloh 1979; R.C. Zaehner, *Mysticism, Sacred and Profane*, Oxford 1957; id., *Concordant Discord. The Interdependence of Faiths*, New York

1970; G.C. Anawati and L. Gardet, *Mystique Musulmane. Aspects et tendances—expériences et techniques*, Paris 1961, [2]1968; A. Bharati, *The Light at the Center. Context and Pretext of Modern Mysticism*, Santa Barbara, CA 1976; R. Woods (ed.), *Understanding Mysticism*, Garden City, NY 1980; S.T. Katz (ed.), *Mysticism and Religious Traditions*, New York 1983; E. Bock, *Meine Augen haben Dich geschaut. Mystik in den Religionen der Welt*, Zurich 1991.

23. For Islamic mysticism in general cf. T.Andrae, *Islamische Mystiker*, Stuttgart 1960 (Swedish original Stockholm 1947); M. Molé, *Les Mystiques Musulmans*, Paris 1965; A. Schimmel, *Mystical Dimensions of Islam*, Chapel Hill, NC 1975; F. Meier, 'The Mystic Path', in *The World of Islam*, ed. B. Lewis, London 1975, 117–28; id., *Bausteine. Ausgewählte Aufsätze zur Islamwissenschaft*, ed. E. Glassen and G. Schubert (3 vols), Stuttgart 1992 (on Sufism, Vol. I, part B); J. Baldick, *Mystical Islam. An Introduction to Sufism*, London 1989. There are numerous up-to-date popular introductions to Sufism, including I. Shah, *The Sufis*, Garden City, NY 1964; M. Lings, *What is Sufism?*, London 1975; L. Bakhtiar, *Sufi. Expressions of the Mystic Quest*, London 1976; 'Abd al-Qadir as-Sufi, *The Way of Muhammad*, Berkeley, CA 1975; R. Gramlich, *Der eine Gott. Grundzüge der Mystik des islamischen Monotheismus*, Wiesbaden 1998; K.P. Bahadur, *Sufi Mysticism*, New Delhi 1999. For the various regional developments, which it was impossible to survey here, see the extensive composite volume edited by F. de Jong and B. Radtke, *Islamic Mysticism Contested. Thirteen Centuries of Controversies and Polemics*, Leiden 1999; A. Knysh, *Islamic Mysticism. A Short History*, Leiden 2000. The professor of the theological faculty of the Marmara University in Istanbul gives a good brief introduction on the basis of the Qur'an: Y.N. Öztürk, *The Eye of the Heart*, Istanbul 1988. I am grateful to Professor Fritz Meier of Basle, who died on 10 June 1998, for reading through the whole chapter on Sufism.

24. Cf. R.A. Nicholson, *The Mystics of Islam*, London 1914, [2]1963, 12; E. Zimmermann, 'The Origins of the so-called "Theology of Aristotle"', in *Pseudo-Aristotle in the Middle Ages*, ed. J. Kraye et al., London 1986, 110–240.

25. Cf. T. Andrae, *Islamische Mystiker* (n. 23), especially the chapter on Islam and Christianity. The monk and mystic Isaac of Nineveh (died *c.*700), first brought into the discussion by J. van Ess, *Die Gedankenwelt des Harit al-Muhasibi anhand von Übersetzungen aus seinen Schriften dargestellt und erläutert*, Bonn 1961, is given a major role by Baldick, *Mystical Islam* (n. 23), 17, as a witness to the 'Christian character of Islamic mysticism', but Baldick cannot demonstrate any links with Islamic mystics; Isaac resigned as bishop of the Nestorian church (*c.* 670) after only five months, presumably because of his approach towards orthodox christology, at all events not to the Qur'anic Jesuology.

26. Cf. M. Horten, *Indische Strömungen in der islamischen Mystik* (2 vols), Heidelberg 1927/28; R.C. Zaehner, *Hindu and Muslim Mysticism*, London 1960.

27. Cf. R. Hartmann, 'Zur Frage nach der Herkunft und den Anfängen des Sufitums', *Der Islam* 6, 1915, 31–70.

28. Cf. S.M. Demidow, *Sufismus in Turkmenien. Evolution und Relikte*, Hamburg 1988 (original Russian 1978).
29. Cf. L. Massignon, *Essai sur les origines du lexique technique de la mystique musulmane*, Paris 1922, considerably enlarged second edition 1954. Far beyond what is indicated in the title, this work offers a fundamental investigation of the possible dependence and real originality of Islamic mysticism from its beginnings to its classical formation in the third century after the Hijrah. Further works by Massignon on the topic are collected in the three volumes edited by Y. Moubarac, *Opera minora*, Vol. II, Beirut 1963, 1–484. A comprehensive bibliography of the publications of Massignon (with indexes of names and topics) was also published by Moubarac in *Mélanges Louis Massignon*, Vol. I, Damascus 1956, 3–56.
30. Thus already C. Cahen, *Der Islam I. Vom Ursprung bis zu den Anfängen des Osmanenreiches*, Frankfurt 1968, [2]1987, 220f.
31. Cf. J. van Ess, *Theologie und Gesellschaft im 2. und 3. Jh. Hidschra. Eine Geschichte des religiösen Denkens im frühen Islam* (6 vols), Berlin 1991–7, I, 141f.
32. For the distinction between the mystical and the prophetic type see the classical work by E. Heiler, *Prayer: A Study in the History and Philosophy of Religion*, Oxford 1932.
33. Cf. surah 13.28: 'Hearts find their rest in the remembrance of God.'
34. Cf. L. Gardet, 'Dhikr', in *EncIsl*[2]; van Ess, *Theologie* (n. 31), I, 141.
35. Cf. J. During, 'Sama' ' (1. In music and mysticism)', in *EncIsl*[2].
36. Cf. F. Meier, 'Der Derwischtanz. Versuche eines Uberblicks', in id., *Bausteine* (n. 23), 1, 23–52.
37. Id., 'The Mystic Path' (n. 23), 117. Id., *Abu Sa'id-i Abu l-Khayr (357–440/967 –1049). Wirklichkeit und Legende*, Leiden 1976, contributes a brilliant illustration to this compact and informative overall survey of Sufism, convincingly bringing out the 'pious introspection' of the Sufis. In the introduction to this volume, on the basis of Muslim sources Meier explains the 'diversity of Sufism' from personal differences, local differences, individual characteristics and deviations over the same point (for example with relation to eating, travelling, loneliness, suffering, etc.).
38. Surah 50.16.
39. Surah 6.103.
40. Surah 21.15.
41. Surah 51.21.
42. Surah 10.62f.
43. Cf. surah 24.35: 'Light upon light. God guides unto his light him that wills, and God propounds parables unto men, since God has full knowledge about all things.' Verses 35–40, which are so important for the Sufis, are called light verses.
44. Surah 5.54.
45. Cf. A. Schimmel, *Mystical Dimensions* (n. 23). Stimulating articles on the literary and aesthetic dimensions of Sufism can be found in the *Festschrift* dedicated to A. Schimmel: A. Giese and J.C. Burgel (eds), *Gott ist schön und Er liebt die Schönheit. God is beautiful and He loves beauty*, Berne 1994.

46. Quoted in Schimmel, *Mystical Dimensions* (n. 23), 17.
47. Cf. M. Smith, *Rabi'a the Mystic and her Fellow-Saints in Islam*, Cambridge 1928.
48. Cf. Baldick, *Mystical Islam* (n. 23), 29f. (without instances).
49. Examples in van Ess, *Theologie* (n. 31), II, 101f. (relating to Rabi'ah); I, 144f. (relating to parallel developments in Syria); 397f. (relating to female ascetics in Kufa).
50. Cf. the extensive study by B. Reinert, *Die Lehre vom* rawakkul *in der klassischen Sufik*, Berlin 1968.
51. van Ess, *Gedankenwelt* (n. 25), 215; examples 215–18.
52. In the same way in Christian mysticism the *via purgativa*, the cleansing of the heart, has been seen as a presupposition for the *via illuminativa*, the giving of illumination in order to attain to the *unio mystica*, the soul's vision or union in love with God.
53. Cf. Abu l-Qasim al-Junayd, *Dawa' al-arwah*, edited and translated into English by A.J. Arberry, 'The Book of the Cure of Souls', *Journal of the Royal Asiatic Society*, 1937, 219–31. Cf. A.H. Abdel-Kader, *The Life, Personality and Writings of al-Junayd. A Study of a Third/Ninth Century Mystic with an Edition and Translation of his Writings*, London 1962.
54. One then 'loses being' and 'remains' in God, but continues in the world on the basis of the great experience. Junayd says that 'Sufism is not (achieved) by much prayer and fasting, but it is the certainty of the heart and the generosity of the soul' (quoted in Schimmel, *Mystical Dimensions* [n. 23], 14; cf. 57–9). But he wants to speak of the ultimate mystery of love and union at best in allusions and hints—not only because of the tangible hostility of orthodox circles and the mistrust of the government (Junayd's private correspondence was opened by the 'postal service') but out of an ultimate reverence for the great mystery.
55. Cf. H. Ritter, 'Die Aussprüche des Bayezid Bistami. Eine vorläufige Skizze', in *Westöstliche Abhandlungen, Festschrift für R. Tschudi*, ed. F. Meier, Wiesbaden 1954, 231–43; id., 'Abu Yazid (Bayazid)', in *EnclIsl²*.
56. The Indian influence is emphasized by Zaehner, *Hindu and Muslim Mysticism* (n. 26), in the chapter on 'Vedanta in Muslim Dress' (86–109).
57. Cf. Schimmel, *Mystical Dimensions* (n .23), 47–51; cf. surah 17.1.
58. Abu Yazid (Bayazid) al-Bistami, quoted in Schimmel, *Mystical Dimensions* (n. 23), 49.
59. Ritter, 'Die Aussprüche' (n. 55), 239.
60. Quoted in Schimmel, *Mystical Dimensions* (n. 23), 50.
61. Al-Husayn ibn Mansur al-Hallaj, quoted in Schimmel, *Mystical Dimensions* (n. 23), 69.
62. Cf. F.A.D. Tholuck, *Sufismus sive theosophia Persarum pantheistica*, Berlin 1821.
63. Al-Husayn ibn Mansur al-Hallaj, quoted in Schimmel, *Mystical Dimensions* (n. 23), 71.
64. Cf. W.C. Chittick, *The Sufi Path of Knowledge. Ibn al-'Arabi's Metaphysics of Imagination*, Albany, NY 1989.
65. A precise description of the historical development of post-classical Sufism is given by Meier, 'The Mystic Path' (n. 23), 119–22. For an analysis of the paradigm

change see the summary of the various differences between the classical mysticism of the ninth century and the post-classical mysticism of the fourteenth century in id., 'Hurasan und das Ende der klassischen Sufik', in id., *Bausteine* (n. 23), 1, 131–56.

66. The dervish organization of Abu Ishaq al-Kazaruni (died 1035) is a well-investigated example of a network of intensive works of charity (on the basis of gifts of money) which survived its founder by centuries. Cf. F. Meier (ed.), *Die Vita des Scheich Abu Ishaq al-Kazaruni in der persischen Bearbeitung von Mahmud b. 'Urman*, Leipzig 1948.
67. The organizational aspect of Sufism, the brotherhoods or orders, was investigated in the nineteenth century by the colonial official L. Rinn (1884) and the missionary A. le Chatelier (1887) for the 'Littérature de surveillance'. Only in more recent times have they been thought worthy of a comprehensive investigation: J. Spencer Trimingham, *The Sufi Orders in Islam*, Oxford 1971, new edition 1998 (with several genealogical charts of the various orders). Important psychological aspects are discussed by F. Meier, *Zwei Abhandlungen über die Naqsbandiyya*, Stuttgart 1994; Part I discusses 'Binding the heart to the Master', Part II 'Act of power and force of the Holy'. There is a comprehensive survey of the Sufi orders in the big composite volume by international specialists edited by A. Popovic and G. Veinstein, *Les Voies d'Allah. Les ordres mystiques dans le monde musulman des origines à aujourd'hui*, Paris 1996. J.W. Frembgen, *Reise zu Gott. Sufis und Derwische im Islam*, Munich 2000, gives vivid insights into the practice of Sufism.
68. Cf. R. Gramlich, *Die schiitischen Derwischorde Persiens* (2 vols), Wiesbaden 1965/76. In Vol. I Gramlich engages in an exemplary discussion of the affiliation of three orders of Shia; Vol.II is illuminating for faith and love.
69. For the first Sufi brotherhoods which still exist today—above all the Qadiriyyah (founded on the tomb of 'Abd al-Qadir al-Jilani, who died in Baghdad in 1166) and the Suhrawardiyyah (founded by 'Umar Abu Hafs as-Suhrawardi, died 1234)—cf. also Schimmel, *Mystical Dimensions* (n. 23), 244–58. There continued to be individual Sufis, in the form of serious scholars or 'holy fools'.
70. For Muhammad-mysticism cf. already T. Andrae, *Die Person Muhammeds in Lehre und Glauben seiner Gemeinde*, Stockholm 1918.
71. Cf. F. Meier, 'Kehrreim und *mahya*', in *Festschrift Ewald Wagner*, ed. W. Heinrichs and G. Schoeler, Vol.II, Stuttgart 1994, 462–89.
72. The Afghan Hujwiri (died *c.*1071), himself unmarried, commended celibacy and continence in marriage; later there was the celibate branch of Bektashis, strongly influenced by Byzantine Christianity.
73. This is clearly emphasized by Baldick, *Mystical Islam* (n. 23), 169–71.
74. Cf. ibid., 74, 171.
75. Despite a fundamental difference over ecstasy there are parallels between Islam and Christianity: 'If we compare the circumstances in which these raptures took place and the phenomena which accompanied them with those which have been

collected for Christian ecstasy by Antoine Imbert-Gourbeyre in his *La stigmatisation, l'extase divine et les miracles de Lourdes*, and more recently by Herbert Thurston in his *The Physical Phenomena of Mysticism*, it has to be conceded that there were the same psychological and physiological processes on both sides ... However, there is the fundamental difference between Christian and Islamic ecstasy that from a very early stage the Sufis did not leave the stimuli wholly to chance, but often introduced them deliberately,' Meier, 'Derwischtanz' (n. 36), 35–7. Id., *Die Fawa'ih al-gamal wa-fawatih al-galal des Nagm ad-Din al-Kubra. Eine Darstellung mystischer Erfahrungen im Islam aus der Zeit um 1200 n. Chr.*, Wiesbaden 1957, is very illuminating on the knowledge of the mystical consciousness.

76. Lapidus, *History* (n. 14), 256.
77. For the critique of Sufism which follows see the remarks by Schimmel, *Mystical Dimensions* (n. 23), 12–22 (who is suspected of having an uncritical attitude to Sufism).
78. Ibid., 238.
79. Muhammad al-Ghazali, *Deliverance from Error* (*al-Munqidh min ad-dalal*), translated by R.J. McCarthy, Louisville, KY nd. Cf. W.M. Watt, *Muslim Intellectual: A Study of Al-Ghazali*, Edinburgh 1963, which contains an excellent commentary on the 'Munqidh'. H. Laoust, *Pluralismes dans l'Islam*, Paris 1983, discusses and illustrates the pluralism of the 'sectes et familles spirituelles'; pp. 257–67 contain an excellent article on the pedagogy of al-Ghazali in his last work, 'Mustasfa', completed after the 'Munqidh', two years before his death.
80. For the literary clichés in al-Ghazali see J. van Ess, 'Quelques remarques sur le Munqid min ad-dalal', in *Table ronde UNESCO*, 57–68.
81. Cf. the major accounts by L. Gardet and G.C. Anawati, *Introduction à la théologie musulmane. Essai de théologie comparée*, Paris 1948, [3]1981; M. Marmura (and W.M. Watt), *Der Islam II: Politische Entwicklungen und theologische Konzepte*, Stuttgart 1985, Part V, Die islamische Theologie, 950–1850; T. Nagel, *Geschichte der islamischen Theologie. Von Mohammed bis zur Gegenwart*, Munich 1994, esp. chs VI–VIII.
82. Cf. G. Makdisi, 'Ash'ari and the Ash'arites in Islamic Religious History', *Studia Islamica* 17, 1962, 37–80; 18, 1963, 19–39.
83. Cf. id., *Ibn Aqil et la Resurgence de l'Islam traditionaliste au XIe siècle (Ve siècle de l'Hégire)*, Damascus 1963.
84. Gardet and Anawati, *Introduction* (n. 81), 72–6, describe al-Ghazali, in connection with the great Islamic philosopher of history Ibn Khaldun, as a first representative of the *via moderna* in theology by contrast with the *via antiqua*, which is represented for example by the Ash'arite Baqillani. His teaching was characterized by atomism, by a close connection between philosophical principles and dogmas, and by the assertion that the falsity of a proof already indicated the falsity of the matter to be proved. Accordingly al-Juwayni should be seen as a theologian of transition between the *via antiqua* and the *via moderna*.
85. The evidence for this is given in V.M. Poggi, *Un classico della spiritualità Musulmana: saggio monografico sul Munqid di al-Gazali*, Rome 1967, 26 f.

86. This is true above all of the older, and quite worthwhile, literature—D.B. Macdonald (*EncIsl* 1914), H. Frick (1919), J. Obermann (1921)—which interpreted al-Ghazali with the categories of bourgeois liberalism. In his dissertation, A.T. van Leeuwen, *Ghazali als apologeet van de Islam. Bijdrage tot de interpretatie van zijn persoon en zijn werk*, Leiden 1947, gives a survey of the Roman Catholic, cultural–historical and modernist interpretations and enters into discussion with Frick and Obermann.
87. Thus Baldick, *Mystical Islam* (n. 23), 10, 65f.
88. E. Glassen, *Der mittlere Weg. Studien zur Religionspolitik und Religiosität der späteren Abbasidenzeit*, Wiesbaden 1981, 80.
89. Cf. M. Zakzouk, *Al-Ghazalis Philosophie im Vergleich mit Descartes*, Frankfurt am Main 1992, 21.
90. Poggi, *Un classico* (n. 85), 16–36, explains that certain contradictions with other sources can be explained in terms of this literary genre.
91. This aspect is particularly emphasized by H. Laoust, *La politique de Gazali*, Paris 1970, 138, 141–4.
92. Cf. H. Frick, *Ghazalis Selbstbiographie. Ein Vergleich mit Augustins Konfessionen*, Leipzig 1919.
93. Cf. Zakzouk, *Al-Ghazalis Philosophie* (n. 89). Glassen, *Der mittlere Weg* (n. 88), gives a convincing reconstruction of the political and religious background to the time of al-Ghazali.
94. Another derivation of the name is from a woman or a village named Ghazala.
95. Al-Ghazali, *Deliverance from Error* (n. 79), 56. For the problems of truth and certainty in al-Ghazali see F. Jabre, *La notion de certitude selon Ghazali dans ses origines psychologiques et historiques*, Paris 1958, second enlarged edition, Beirut 1986; M. Arkoun, 'Revelation, verité et histoire d'après l'oeuvre de Gazali', *Studia Islamica* 31, 1970, 53–6.
96. Cf. R. Descartes, *Discourse on the Method of Properly Conducting One's Reason and of Seeking the Truth in the Sciences* (1637); id., *Meditations on the First Philosophy in which the Existence of God and the Real Distinction between the Soul and Being of Man are Demonstrated* (1641), Harmondsworth 1968.
97. For further information see the introduction by A.A. Elschazli to his German edition of 'al-Munqidh', *Der Erretter aus dem Irrtum*, Hamburg 1988, XXXI–XXXVI.
98. Cf. Zakzouk, *Al-Ghazalis Philosophie* (n. 89), 10.
99. Al-Ghazali, *Deliverance from Error* (n. 79), 56.
100. Cf. ibid.
101. Ibid.
102. Cf. Descartes, *Meditations* (n. 96) I, 11ff.
103. Al-Ghazali, *Deliverance from Error* (n. 79), 57.
104. Ibid. Here I follow, rather, the English translation by W.M. Watt, *The Faith and Practice of al-Ghazali*, London 1963, 'Intellectual truths which are first principles.'
105. Al-Ghazali, *Deliverance from Error* (n. 79), 57. Translation again corresponding to Watt, *The Faith* (n. 104), 25.

106. Ibid.
107. Thus van Leeuwen, *Ghazali* (n. 86), 45: 'the compass of evidential certainty had not shown him (Ghazali) the way sufficiently convincingly'.
108. Thus Poggi, *Un classico* (n. 85), 169: 'it has to be recognized that such principles are self-evident and as such can also be accepted in reflection'.
109. Thus Zakzouk, *Al-Ghazalis Philosophie* (n. 89), 68: 'an insight which, in contrast to discursive knowledge, is based on a direct spiritual vision. So this is an intuition.'
110. Ibid., 70.
111. Ibid., 85.
112. Zakzouk himself has to concede this when he observes that 'Descartes has distinguished various levels, whereas in al-Ghazali's solution, knowledge of self and knowledge of God are achieved in a single act' (ibid., 88, though he does not take this recognition sufficiently seriously). This is the decisive point.
113. Ibid.
114. Here I can only indicate that the truth perhaps lies in the middle—between *cogito* and *credo* (cf. the critical discussions of Descartes and Pascal in H. Küng, *Does God Exist?*, Part A: 'Reason or Faith?'). On the one hand today even Descartes would have to recognize that his '*Cogito ergo sum*' is by no means evident and that reason cannot function without a particular 'trust in reason' (cf. my remarks on fundamental trust in ibid, Part E: 'Yes to Reality—Alternative to Nihilism'). On the other hand, today even al-Ghazali could hardly fail to see that there are many people who have such trust in God, such a fundamental trust, but without an explicit belief in God. However, science is not possible at all without a rationally responsible fundamental trust which has an inner rationality (once again see the chapter 'Fundamental trust as basis for science' in *Does God Exist?*, 460–1); moreover there is no generally compelling ethic (ibid., 'Fundamental trust as basis of ethics', 461–5) without such trust.
115. Cf. van Ess, 'Quelques remarques' (n. 80), 65f.
116. R.M. Frank, *Creation and the Cosmic System: Al-Ghazali and Avicenna*, Heidelberg 1992, thinks that he can prove against the present consensus that al-Ghazali made important philosophical theories of Avicenna the basis of his theology: the world is a closed deterministic system of second causes the activities of which are regulated by the first created beings ('angels' or 'intellect'). God cannot intervene in the activities of second causes. Whether Frank's exegesis of al-Ghazali, which is contradicted by other al-Ghazali texts, is convincing must be left to the specialists.
117. Cf. al-Ghazali, *Deliverance from Error* (n. 79), 73f.
118. Cf. ibid., 79.
119. Ibid.
120. For the contemporary context cf. again Glassen, *Der mittlere Weg* (n. 88), esp. 131–75. J. van Ess, 'Neuere Literatur zu Gazzali', *Oriens* 20, 1967, 299–308, observes: 'In genre the *Munqidh* is paraenesis: not only a description of how

things have been but just as much an indication of how things should be, depicted in his own exemplary case. It is conceivable that the motives for the decision have also been "internalized", or that the "internal" components of a complex decision, in which some other, political, pressure, had also played a role, as the only thing worth reporting, indeed imitating, played a part' (300f.).

121. Al-Ghazali, *Deliverance from Error* (n. 79), 81.
122. Cf. D. Krawulsky, *Briefe und Reden des Abu Hamid Muhammad al-Gazzali*, Freiburg 1971, 66; Glassen, *Der mittlere Weg* (n. 88), 169f.; van Ess, 'Quelques remarques' (n. 80), 60–4.
123. Al-Ghazali, *Deliverance from Error* (n. 79), 87–98.
124. Cf. id., *Die Neubelebung der Wissenschaften von der Religion* (*ihya' 'ulum ad-din*). Only a few books of this giant work have been translated into English (*The Book of Knowledge*, Lahore 1962) and German (*Lehre von den Stufen zur Gottesliebe*, Wiesbaden 1984). There is a survey of the individual books by N. Koribaa, *Restauration des sciences religieuses (ihya ulum ad-dine) d'al-Ghazali*, Algiers 1984. Al-Ghazali himself wrote a summary in Persian under the title 'The Elixir of Happiness' (*kimiya-i sa'adat*); German edition *Das Elixier der Glückseligkeit* by H. Ritter (Munich 1959, new edition 1993).
125. In a further more comprehensive account, R.M. Frank, *Al-Ghazali and the Ash'arite School*, Durham 1994, has attempted to demonstrate that in his public teaching and instruction al-Ghazali put forward the Ash'arite views, but quite personally agreed with basic views of Avicenna—and this is expressed in his last publications: 'It is the dialectical interplay of these several levels, in many works and in many ways, that has caused difficulties for students of al-Ghazali's works and given some the impression of gross inconsistency' (101).
126. Thomas Aquinas, *Summa contra gentiles*, 1, 2.
127. For the biography of Thomas Aquinas cf. H. Küng, *Great Christian Thinkers*, London 1994, ch. 4; in the framework of the paradigm analysis cf. id., *Christianity*, C III, 9.
128. For the Latin translations from the Arabic cf. M. Steinschneider, *Die europäischen Übersetzungen aus dem Arabischen bis Mitte des 17. Jahrhunderts*, Vienna 1904/5, reprinted Graz 1956; J.M. Casciaro, *El diálogo teológico de Santo Tomás con Musulmanes y Judíos. El tema de la profecía y la revelación*, Madrid 1969, 40–2.
129. For the complex Thomas Aquinas, *falsafah* and *kalam* (in discussion above all with the Spanish orientalist M. Asín Palacios) see Gardet and Anawati, *Introduction* (n. 81), 282–90.
130. Cf. ibid., 289.
131. Nor is there any thematic discussion of the differences relating to christology and the doctrine of the Trinity in L. Gardet's second volume on *Les grands problèmes de la théologie musulmane*, entitled *Dieu et la destiné de l'homme*, Paris 1967.
132. Cf. G. Makdisi, *The Rise of Colleges. Institutions of Learning in Islam and the West*, Edinburgh 1981, 245–60; id., *Ibn 'Aqyil. Religion and Culture in Classical Islam*, Edinburgh 1997, XVf., 57f.

133. Watt, *Muslim Intellectual* (n. 79), 180.
134. Cf. what is said in n. 84 about *via antiqua* and *via moderna.*
135. Cf. Thomas Aquinas, *Summa theologiae*, pars I, quaestio 2 (prologue).
136. I was given important insights into assessing this set of problems by Glassen, *Der mittlere Weg* (n. 88).
137. Quotation ibid., 78.
138. Quotation ibid., 79.
139. The article by the Harvard Arabist M.S. Mahdi, 'Islamic philosophy', in *Encyclopaedia Britannica*, Vol. 22, Chicago [15]1987, 24–31, towers above the introductions to Arabic/Islamic philosophy in the big lexica of philosophy, theology and the study of religion; it is developed at length in his two-volume *History of Islamic Philosophy*, New York 1986. After the early studies by F. Dieterici (1858–79, reprinted 1969); I. Goldziher (1896/1910); M. Horten (1924) and P.J. de Menasce (1948), the following more recent works should be noted: C. Brockelmann, *Geschichte der arabischen Litteratur* (2 vols), Leiden [2]1943–9, 3 supplementary volumes 1937–42; M.M. Sharif (ed.), *A History of Muslim Philosophy* (2 vols), Wiesbaden 1963–6; H. Corbin, *Histoire de la philosophie islamique*, new edition Paris 1986, ET London and New York 1993; M. Fakhry, *A History of Islamic Philosophy*, New York [2]1983; M. Marmura, 'Die islamische Philosophie des Mittelalters', in W.M. Watt and M. Marmura, *Der Islam*, II, Stuttgart 1985, 320–92; O. Leaman, *An Introduction to Classical Islamic Philosophy*, New York 1985, [2]2002 (mainly about al-Ghazali's attack on philosophy); C.E. Butterworth (ed.), *The Political Aspects of Islamic Philosophy. Essays in Honor of Muhsin S. Mahdi*, Cambridge, MA 1992; S. Pines (ed. S. Stroumsa), *Studies in the History of Arabic Philosophy. The Collected Works of Shlomo Pines*, Vol. III, Jerusalem 1996 (especially about Avicenna and Averroes); S.H. Nasr and O. Leaman (eds), *History of Islamic Philosophy* (2 vols), London and New York 1996; W.G. Lerch, *Denker des Propheten. Die Philosophie des Islam*, Düsseldorf 2000; D. Gutas, *Greek Philosophers in the Arabic Tradition*, Aldershot 2000. H. Daiber, *Bibliography of Islamic Philosophy* (Vol. I: Alphabetical list of publications; Vol. II: Index of names, terms and topics), Leiden 1999, provides a survey of publications in the sphere of Islamic philosophy from the fifteenth century to the present.
140. Alongside the histories of philosophy mentioned above cf. J. Jolivet and R. Rashed, 'al-Kindi', in *EnclIsl*[2], E. Tornero Poveda, *Al-Kindi. La transformación de un pensamiento religioso en un pensamiento racional*, Madrid 1992, offers a recent synthetic account (incorporating earlier works) of al-Kindi's thought.
141. Cf. L.E. Goodman, 'al-Kazi', in *EncIsl*[2]; E. al-Sharqawi, 'Razi', in *EncRel.*
142. After the first studies of al-Farabi in a European language by M. Steinschneider (1889) and L. Madkour (1934), the following are important: R. Walzer, 'al-Farabi', in *EncIsl*[2]; T.-A. Druart, 'al-Farabi', in *EncRel*; D. Gutas, 'Farabi' (1. Biography, 4. F. and Greek Philosophy), in *Encyclopaedia Iranica*, Vol. IX, New York 1999; M.S. Wahdi, *Alfarabi and the Foundation of Islamic Political*

Philosophy, Chicago 2001; M. Fakhry, *Al-Farabi, Founder of Islamic Neoplatonism. His Life, Works and Influence*, Oxford 2002.

143. Cf. A.-M. Goichon, 'Ibn Sina', in *EncIsl²*; W.E. Gohlman, 'Ibn Sina', in *EncRel*; G.G. Hana, 'Ibn Sina (Avicenna)', in *Die Grossen der Weltgeschichte*, Munich 1973, Vol. III, 222–33; H. Corbin, *Avicenne et le récit visionnaire. Étude sur le cycle des récits avicenniens*, Paris 1954, new edition 1999; D. Gutas, *Avicenna and the Aristotelian Tradition. Introduction to Reading Avicenna's Philosophical Works*, Leiden 1988; id., 'Avicenna (2. Biography, 5. Mysticism)', in *Encyclopaedia Iranica*, Vol.III/1, London 1989; L.E. Goodman, *Avicenna*, London 1992; G. Strohmaier, *Avicenna*, Munich 1999.

144. Thus with others E. Bloch, *Avicenna und die aristotelische Linke*, Berlin 1952.

145. Cf. R. Arnaldez, 'Ibn Rushd' in *EncIsl²*; G.F. Hourani, 'Ibn Rushd', in *EncRel*; G.G. Hana, 'Ibn Rusd (Averroes)', in *Die Grossen der Weltgeschichte*, Munich 1973, Vol. III, 440–9; I.A. Bello, *The Medieval Islamic Controversy between Philosophy and Orthodoxy. Ijma' and Ta'wil in the Conflict between Al-Ghazali and Ibn Rushd*, Leiden 1989; D. Urvoy, *Ibn Rushd (Averroes)*, London 1991 (here there are bibliographical pointers to the history of Averroes studies, to the historical sources and texts, and to the Western interpreters); A. von Kügelgen, *Averroes und die arabische Moderne. Ansätze zu einer Neubegründung des Rationalismus im Islam*, Leiden 1994; R. Arnaldez, *Averroès—un rationaliste en Islam*, Paris ²1998; A. Badawi, *Averroès (Ibn Rushd)*, Paris 1998; G. Endress and J.A. Aertsen (eds), *Averroes and the Aristotelian Tradition. Sources, Constitution and Reception of the Philosophy of Ibn Rushd (1126–1198). Proceedings of the Fourth Symposium Averroicum (Cologne 1996)*, Leiden 1999 (the most recent and extensive bibliography); M. Fakhry, *Averroes (Ibn Rushd). His Life, Works and Influence*, Oxford 2001 (ch.11 makes an illuminating comparison between Averroes and Thomas Aquinas); R.G. Khoury (ed.), *Averroes (1126–1198) oder der Triumph des Rationalismus. Internationales Symposium, anlässlich des 800. Todestages des islamischen Philosophen. Heidelberg, 7.–11.10.1998*, Heidelberg 2002.

146. Bello, *The Medieval Islamic Controversy* (n. 145), 142–51, takes the side of al-Ghazali.

147. Badawi, *Averroès (Ibn Rushd)* (n. 145), 144.

148. Cf. T.E. Burman, *Religious Polemic and the Intellectual History of the Mozarabs, c. 1050–1200*, Leiden 1994; id. (ed.), *Religion, Text, and Society in Medieval Spain and Northern Europe: Essays in Honor of J.N. Hillgarth*, Toronto 2002.

149. Cf. M. Talbi, 'Le Christianisme maghrébin de la conquête musulmane à sa disparition: une tentative d'explication', in M. Gervers and R.J. Bikhazi (eds), *Conversion and Continuity: Indigenous Christian Communities in Islamic Lands, 8th to 18th Centuries*, Toronto 1990, 313–51.

150. Cf. Burman, *Religious Polemic* (n. 148), 200f.

151. H. Denzinger, *Enchiridion*, nos 309f.

152. Mark 1.11.

153. Cf. J.E. Rivera Recio, *El adopcionismo en España: siglo VIII; historia y doctrina*, Toledo 1980, 21.
154. Cf. M. de Epalza, 'Le milieu hispano-moresque de l'Évangile islamisant de Barnabé (XVIe–XVIIe siècles)', *Islamochristiana* 8, 1982, 159–83. It has been confirmed by a dissertation by L.F. Bernabé Pons, *El evangelio de San Bernabé. Un evangelio islámico espanol*, University of Alicante 1996, written under the direction of Epalza. There is a report on German-language scholarship in R. Kirste, P. Schwarzenau and U. Tworuschka (eds), *Wertewandel und religiöse Umbrüche*, Balve 1996, 133–88, on the truth and authenticity of the Gospel of Barnabas.
155. For the political environment and internal organization of Judaism from the Arab conquest to the expulsion from Spain (638–1492), see J. Maier, *Das Judentum. Von der biblischen Zeit bis zur Moderne*, Munich [2]1973, 383–434; A. Cohen, *Jewish Life under Islam. Jerusalem in the Sixteenth Century*, Cambridge, MA 1984.
156. Maimonides—abbreviated to Rambam—is described as a halakhist, philosopher and physician by A. Sandler, J. Guttmann, M.W. Rapaport and L. Lewin in the article 'Maimonides' in the *Jüdisches Lexikon*, and by L.I. Rabinowitz, J.I. Dienstag, A. Hyman and S. Muntner in the article 'Maimonides' in *Encyclopaedia Judaica*. Cf. also S.W. Baron, 'Moses Maimonides', in S. Noveck (ed.), *Grosse Gestalten des Judentums*, Vol. I, Zurich 1972, 103–30.
157. Cf. A. Castro, *España en su historia. Cristianos, moros y judíos*, Barcelona 1983, 448–54.
158. Cf. M.R. Menocal, *The Ornament of the World. How Muslims, Jews, and Christians Created a Culture of Tolerance in Medieval Spain*, Boston 2002.
159. Cf. M. Asín Palacios, *El Islam cristianizado. Estudio del 'Sufismo' a través de las obras de Abenárabi de Murcia*, Madrid 1931, above all the introduction.
160. Cf. Castro, *España en su historia* (n. 157), esp. 198–205.
161. Cf. S. Fanjul, *Al-Andalus contra España. La forja del mito*, Madrid [2]2002.
162. M. de Epalza, 'Pluralisme et tolérance, un modèle tolédan?', in L. Cardaillac (ed.), *Tolède, XIIe–XIIIe. Musulmans, chrétiens et juifs: le savoir et la tolérance*, Paris 1991, 241–51; German: 'Überlegungen zum religiosen Pluralismus (Muslime, Christen und Juden) und die Toleranz auf der iberischen Halbinsel im Mittelalter', in Kirste et al. (eds), *Wertewandel und religiöse Umbrüche* (n. 154), 365–78: 374. Cf. id., *Jésus entre judíos, cristianos y musulmanes españoles (siglo VI–XVII)*, Granada 1999; German: *Jesus zwischen Juden, Christen und Muslimen. Interreligiöses Zusammenleben auf der iberischen Halbinsel (6.–17. Jh.)*, Frankfurt 2002, esp. 221–35.
163. Epalza, 'Überlegungen' (n. 162), 375.
164. Cf. S.D. Goitein, *Jews and Arabs. Their Contacts through the Ages*, New York 1955; N.A. Stillman, *The Jews of Arab Lands. A History and Source Book*, Philadelphia 1979; Bat Ye'or, *Le Dhimmi. Profil de 1'opprimé en Orient et en Afrique du Nord depuis la conquête arabe*, Paris 1980; new English edition, *The Dhimmi. Jews and Christians under Islam*, Rutherford 1985; on p.187 see e.g. the burdens imposed on the *dhimmis* in Seville around 1100; B. Lewis, *The Jews of Islam*, Princeton 1984.

165. Cf. C. Issawi, 'Ibn Khaldun', in *Encyclopaedia Britannica*, Vol. 6, Chicago [15]1987, 222f.; M. Talbi, 'Ibn Khaldun', in *EncIsl²*; E. Rosenthal, 'Ibn Khaldun', in *EncRel.*
166. This is attempted by Dimitri Gutas (Yale) in his worthwhile research into Arabic and Iranian philosophy, which puts Avicenna at the centre and depicts Averroes only as one of Avicenna's many opponents.
167. Cf. Corbin, *Histoire* (n. 139), Part II. Cf. also A. Johardelvari, *Iranische Philosophie von Zarathustra bis Sabzewari*, Frankfurt am Main 1994.
168. Cf. R. Arnaldez, *Fakhr al-Din al-Razi: commentateur du Coran et philosophe*, Paris 2002. He criticizes Corbin's excessive leanings towards the Gnostic systems and says: 'Despite the protests of Henry Corbin against the historians of Islamic philosophy, who do not go beyond Averroes: apart from the philosopher of Cordoba (Averroes), the general public knew only Avicenna and al-Ghazali' (254).
169. Cf. E. Renan, *Averroès et l'averroïsme. Essai historique*, Paris 1852, reprint of the third edition, Paris 1860, ed. F. Sezgin, Frankfurt am Main 1985; pp. 236–46 on Thomas Aquinas.
170. Cf. E. van Steenberghen, *La philosophie au XIIIe siècle*, Louvain 1966; W. Kluxen, 'Averroismus im lateinischen Mittelalter', in *TRE*; C.E. Butterworth and B.A. Kessel (eds), *The Introduction of Arabic Philosophy into Europe*, Leiden 1994; J. Jolivet, *Philosophie médiévale arabe et latine*, Paris 1995; A. Pérez Estévez, *La Materia, de Avicena a la Escuela Franciscana. Avicena, Averroes, Tomás de Aquino, Buenaventura, Pecham, Marston, Olivo, Mediavilla y Duns Escuto*, Maracaibo 1998; M. Zanner, *Konstruktionsmerkmale der Averroes-Rezeption. Ein religionswissenschaftlicher Beitrag zur Rezeptionsgeschichte des islamischen Philosophen Ibn Ruschd*, Frankfurt am Main 2002 (contains an extensive bibliography particularly of more recent works).
171. Cf. Endress and Aertsen (eds), *Averroes and the Aristotelian Tradition* (n. 145), 17–23.
172. Cf. J. LeGoff, *The Intellectuals in the Middle Ages*, Oxford 1993, ch.1.
173. Ibid., 176.
174. Cf. A. de Libera, *Penser au Moyen Age*, Paris 1991; German *Denken im Mittelalter*, Munich 2003.
175. Ibid., 114, 118f.
176. Cf. F. Sezgin, *Geschichte des arabischen Schrifttums* (12 vols), Leiden 1967–2000.
177. This is the result of the work of an international group of scholars from Germany, Switzerland, the USA, England and Israel, which is documented in the conference report by K.-P. Kopping et al. (eds), *Die Autonomie der Person—eine europaische Erfindung?*, Munich 2002.
178. Cf. C. Brockelmann, 'al-Mawardi', in *EncIsl²*; D.P. Little, 'al-Mawardi', in *EncRel.*
179. Cf. H. Laoust, 'Ibn Taymiyya', in *EncIsl²*; G. Makdisi, 'Ibn Taymiyah', in *EncRel.* F. Rahman, *Revival and Reform in Islam. A Study of Islamic Fundamentalism*, Oxford 2000, ch. 4, 'Later Medieval Reform', gives a fair assessment of Ibn Taymiyyah in a present-day context.

180. Cf. Makdisi, *The Rise of Colleges* (n. 132), 75f.; id., *The Rise of Humanism in Classical Islam and the Christian West: with Special Reference to Scholasticism*, Edinburgh 1990.

C V. The Paradigm of Islamic Modernization

1. There are important insights into this in R. Schulze, *Geschichte der Islamischen Welt im 20. Jahrhundert*, Munich 1994, introduction. I warmly welcome *Einladung in die Geschichte*, Darmstadt 2001, by the Syrian German Islamologist Bassam Tibi, and simply on the basis of my own approach endorse the 'historical–sociological Islamology' which he (alone) practises. However, I cannot accept his numerous verdicts on German oriental and Islamic studies (which he claims to be totally dominated by Islamology); I have learned a great deal from these disciplines and they have also produced many works of historical sociology. In his book Tibi does not take account of the basic work by Reinhard Schulze mentioned above, nor of the publications of Dieter Weiss (along with some other studies, cf. E IV, 2).
2. Cf. United Nations Development Programme, *Arab Fund for Economic and Social Development, Arab Human Development Report 2002, Creating Opportunities for Future Generations*, New York 2002; also at http://www.undp.org.
3. According to statistical information from the World Bank, *World Bank Atlas 2002*, Washington, DC 2002, 28–9, 46–7; quoted in D. Weiss, *Vor einer Neuordnung des islamischen Orients? Alte Krankungen und neue Kooperationsperspektiven in einer globalisierten Welt* (manuscript 2004).
4. Cf. B. Lewis, *What Went Wrong? The Clash between Islam and Modernity in the Middle East*, London 2002.
5. Cf. E.W. Said, 'Impossible Histories. Why the many Islams cannot be simplified', *Harper's Magazine*, July 2002.
6. B. Tibi, *Der wahre Imam. Der Islam von Mohammed bis zur Gegenwart*, Munich 1998, 216.
7. Cf. A. Meddeb, *La Maladie de l'Islam*, Paris 2002.
8. Lewis, *What Went Wrong?* (n. 4), 156.
9. Cf. H. Küng, *Christianity*, C III, 12: Counter-Reformation? Back to the mediaeval paradigm; 13: From anti-Protestantism to anti-Modernism.
10. Cf. id., *Theology for the Third Millennium. An Ecumenical View*, London and New York 1991, C 1, 3: 'The survival of "outdated" paradigms in art and religion'.
11. For individual developments see the analytic and synthetic account in I.M. Lapidus, *A History of Islamic Societies*, Cambridge 1988, 'Part II: The Worldwide Diffusion of Islamic Societies from the Tenth to the Nineteenth Century', 239–547.
12. Cf. M. Weber, *The Protestant Ethic and the Spirit of Capitalism* (1904–6), New York 1958.
13. T. Ali, 'Krieg der Kulturen—Clash of Civilizations?', in H. Hoffmann and W. F. Schoeller (eds), *Wendepunkt 11. September 2001*, Cologne 2001.
14. Cf. J.O. Voll, 'Renewal and Reform in Islamic History: *Tajdid* and *Islah*', in *Voices of Resurgent Islam*, ed. J.L. Esposito, New York 1983, ch. 2, 32–47.

15. G.S. Hodgson, *The Venture of Islam. Conscience and History in a World Civilization*, Vol. III, Book 5, 'Second Flowering: The Empires of Gunpowder Times', Chicago 1974, offers an excellent survey.
16. Cf. J. Burton-Page and K.A. Nizami, 'Hind (IV. History, V Islam)', in *EncIsl²*; P. Hardy, *The Muslims of British India*, London 1972; Lapidus, *History* (n. 11), ch. 18, 'The Indian Subcontinent: the Delhi Sultanates and the Mughal Empire', 437–66; M.D. Ahmed, 'Indien', in W. Ende and U. Steinbach (eds), *Der Islam in der Gegenwart*, fourth expanded edition, Munich 1996, 313–30; D. Khálid and M.D. Ahmed, 'Pakistan', in W. Ende and U. Steinbach, *Der Islam in der Gegenwart*, Munich [4]1996, 330–58.
17. C. Schönig, 'Zahir ad-Din Muhammad Babur', in *Kindlers Neues Literaturlexikon*, ed. W. Jens, Vol. 2, Munich 1989, quotation p. 18.
18. There is a brief new assessment by F. Stammler, 'Babur der Tiger: Eroberer, Mensch und Dichter', in *Neue Zürcher Zeitung*, 12/13 April 2003.
19. Cf. A. Hottinger, *Akbar der Grosse (1542–1605), Herrscher über Indien durch Versöhnung der Religionen*, Zurich 1998.
20. Cf. A.K.S. Lambton and R.M. Savory, 'Iran (V. History)', in *EncIsl²*; R.M. Savory, *Iran under the Safavids*, Cambridge 1980; Lapidus, *History* (n. 11), ch. 13, 'Iran: the Mongol, Timurid, and Safavid Empires', 276–302; U. Steinbach, 'Iran', in Ende and Steinbach, *Der Islam in der Gegenwart* (n. 16), 246–63.
21. Cf. C.E. Bosworth and J.H. Kramers, ' 'Othmanli (I. Political and Dynastic History)', in *EncIsl²*; H. Inalcik, *The Ottoman Empire. The Classical Age 1300–1600* (from the Turkish), new edition London 1977; J. Matuz, *Das Osmanische Reich: Grundlinien seiner Geschichte*, Darmstadt [3]1994; Lapidus, *History* (n. 11), ch. 14, 'The Turkish Migrations and the Ottoman Empire', 303–43; U. Spuler-Stegemann, 'Türkei', in Ende and Steinbach, *Der Islam in der Gegenwart* (n. 16), 232–46.
22. F.E. Peters, *Mecca. A Literary History of the Muslim Holy Land*, Princeton 1994, gives an overall survey of the history of the holy places; chs V–VII provide valuable information about the Turkish period.
23. For Islam in South-East Asia cf. O. Schumann, 'Südostasien', in Ende and Steinbach, *Der Islam in der Gegenwart* (n. 16), 367–408; Lapidus, *History* (n. 11), ch. 19, 'The Formation of Islamic Societies in Southeast Asia', 467–88; for Islam in Africa ch. 20, 'Islam in Sudanic, Savannah, and Forest West Africa', 489–523; ch. 21, 'Islam in East Africa and the Rise of European Colonial Empires', 524–47.
24. There is an extensive account in H. Küng, *Christianity*, C V: The Paradigm of Modernity, Orientated on Reason and Progress.
25. Cf. ibid., C V, 3: The revolutions in science and philosophy.
26. Cf. A. Hourani, 'Introduction' to the composite volume *The Modern Middle East: A Reader*, ed. id., S. Khoury and M.C. Wilson, London 1993. This volume contains a whole series of articles on developments in reform since 1789.
27. This is the concern of the historian Schulze, *Geschichte* (n. 1), 12.
28. Cf. W.U. Eckar, *Geschichte der Medizin*, fourth revised and enlarged edition, Berlin 2001.

29. At least this detailed report by B. Lewis with reference to A. Adnan (pp.19, 116) is not disputed by E. Said.
30. Cf. H. Küng, *Christianity*, C V, 4: The revolutions in culture and theology.
31. Cf. Lewis, *What Went Wrong* (n. 4), ch. 2, The Quest for Wealth and Power.
32. Cf. Küng, *Christianity*, C V, 6: The revolutions in state and society.
33. Cf. ibid., C V, 7: The revolutions in technology and industry.
34. Cf. R.H. Davison, 'Tanzimat', in *EncIsl*^{2}. The author distinguishes three phases, from 1839 to the decree for a constitution in 1876.
35. The article by U. Heyd, 'The Ottoman 'Ulema and Westernization in the Time of Selim III and Mahmud II', in Hourani et al., *The Modern Middle East* (n. 26), 29–59, is particularly illuminating.
36. Cf. H. Gerber, *State, Society, and Law in Islam. Ottoman Law in Comparative Perspective*, Albany, NY 1994.
37. Cf. R. Owen, 'Egypt and Europe: from French Expedition to British Occupation', in Hourani et al., *The Modern Middle East* (n. 26), 111–24.
38. Cf. A. Hourani, *Arabic Thought in the Liberal Age, 1798–1939*, Cambridge 1983; N.R. Keddie, *Sayyid Jamal ad-Din 'al-Afghani': A Political Biography*, Berkeley, CA 1972.
39. Cf. A.E. Hillal-Dessouki, 'Abduh, Muhammad', in *EncRel*; C.C. Adams, *Islam and Modernism in Egypt*, London 1933 reprinted New York 2002.
40. Cf. A.K.S. Lambton, 'Social Change in Persia in the Nineteenth Century', in Hourani et al., *The Modern Middle East* (n. 26), 145–68.
41. Cf. Schulze, *Geschichte* (n. 1), 71, 360.
42. Cf. F.Ahmad, 'War and Society under the Young Turks, 1908–18', in Hourani et al., *The Modern Middle East* (n. 26), 125–43.
43. Cf. C.E. Dawn, 'From Ottomanism to Arabism: The Origin of an Ideology', in Hourani et al., *The Modern Middle East* (n. 26), 375–93.

D. Challenges of the Present

D I. Competition between Paradigms

1. Cf. H. Küng, *Judaism*, Part I, C V, The Modern Paradigm: Assimilation.
2. The abiding great testimony to the 'Science of Judaism' is the *Jüdische Lexikon. Ein enzyklopädisches Handbuch des jüdischen Wissens*, founded by G. Herlitz and B. Kirschner, Vols, I–IV/2, Berlin 1927, Frankfurt ^{2}1987 (involving more than 250 Jewish scholars and writers).
3. Cf. P.M. Holt et al. (eds), *The Cambridge History of Islam, Vol. I A: The Central Islamic Lands. From Pre-Islamic Times to the First World War*, Cambridge 1970: Part III, 'The Central Islamic Lands in the Ottoman Period'; G.E. von Grunebaum (ed.), *Der Islam, Vol. II: Die islamischen Reiche nach dem Fall von Konstantinopel*, Frankfurt am Main 1971; M.G.S. Hodgson, *The Venture of Islam*, Vol. III, Book 6, The Islamic Heritage in the Modern World, Chicago 1974; U. Haarmann (ed.), *Geschichte der arabischer Welt*, Munich ^{4}2001; R. Schulze, *Geschichte der Islamischen Welt im 20. Jahrhundert*, Munich 1994.

4. Cf. A. Hourani, P.S. Khoury and M.C. Wilson (eds), *The Modern Middle East. A Reader*, London 1993. G. Barthel and K. Stock (eds), *Lexikon Arabische Welt*, Wiesbaden 1994, also give brief and precise information on the most recent history of Arab countries. The most recent statistical information can be found in B. Harenberg (ed.), *Das Jahrbuch 1. Aktuell 2003*, Dortmund 2002.
5. Cf. H. Küng, *A Global Ethics for Global Politics and Economics* A II, 1, An attempt at a new politics: Wilson.
6. For Atatürk cf. S. Mardin, 'Religion and Secularism in Turkey', in Hourani et al., *The Modern Middle East* (n. 4), 347–74. For Islam in Turkey in the twentieth century see U. Spuler-Stegemann, 'Türkei', in W. Ende and U. Steinbach (eds), *Der Islam in der Gegenwart*, Munich [4]1996, 232–46.
7. Cf. J.L. Esposito, *Islam and Politics*, Syracuse, NY [3]1991, ch. 2: Revival and Reform.
8. Cf. the graphic survey in I.M. Lapidus, *A History of Islamic Societies*, Cambridge 1988, Table 16, 566.
9. Cf. G. Salamé, 'Political Power and the Saudi State', in Hourani et al., *The Modern Middle East* (n. 4), 579–600.
10. Cf. E. Picard, 'Arab Military in Politics: from Revolutionary Plot to Authoritarian State', in Hourani et al., *The Modern Middle East* (n. 4), 551–78.
11. Cf. N.R. Keddie, 'Iranian Revolutions in Comparative Perspective', Hourani et al., *The Modern Middle East* (n. 4), 601–23. For Islam in Iran in the nineteenth and twentieth centuries cf. U. Steinbach, 'Iran', in Ende and Steinbach (eds), *Der Islam in der Gegenwart* (n. 6), 246–63.
12. Cf. Lapidus, *History* (n. 8), ch. 15: The Arab Middle East. The articles on the Arab East by B. Kellner-Heinkele (Ottoman empire 1517–1800), A. Scholch (in the nineteenth century 1800–1914) and H. Mejcher (in the twentieth century 1914–1985) in Haarmann (ed.), *Geschichte der arabischen Welt* (n. 3), 33–501, are important for what follows. For Egypt cf. A. Flores, 'Ägypten', in Ende and Steinbach (eds), *Der Islam in der Gegenwart* (n. 6), 474–86.
13. C. Tripp, *A History of Iraq*, enlarged new edition, Cambridge 2002, is a new introduction to Iraqi history; cf. also H. Fürtig, *Kleine Geschichte des Irak*, Munich 2003. There are precise analyses on most recent developments in the composite volume edited by K. Hafez and B. Schabler (eds), *Der Irak. Land zwischen Krieg und Frieden*, Heidelberg 2003.
14. Cf. 'The complex mosaic of Iraqi society', *International Herald Tribune*, 13 March 2003, 3.
15. For this development cf. A. Rohde, 'Von Kaisers Kleiden. Wechselfälle des Nationalismus in Irak', in Hafez and Schabler, *Der Irak* (n. 13), 172–85.

D II. What Kind of Islam do Muslims Want?

1. For the question of the transference of the paradigm theory from the natural sciences to the history of religion cf. H. Küng, *Theology for the Third Millennium*, ch. 3, Paradigm Shift in Theology and Natural Science, C I: The paradigm shift in the world religions.

2. For the options developed in what follows cf. the standard works and studies of countries listed in D I. For the political background see especially J.L. Esposito, *Islam and Politics*, Syracuse [3]1991; id. (ed.), *Political Islam. Revolution, Radicalism or Reform?*, Boulder, CO 1997.
3. Cf. J.M. Landau, 'Pan-Islam', in *EncModIsl.*
4. Cf. E. Ahmad, 'Pan-Turanism', in *EncModIsl.* Pan-Turanism is a wider term than Pan-Turkism and includes peoples such as the Hungarians, Finns and Estonians.
5. Cf. B. Korany, 'Arab Nationalism', in *EncModIsl.*
6. Cf. G. Kepel, *Jihad. Expansion et déclin de l'islamisme*, Paris 2000.
7. M. an-Nogaidan, 'Telling the truth, facing the whip', in *International Herald Tribune*, 29/30 November 2003. The journalist had to appear at a police station on 20 November to receive 75 lashes on his back.
8. N. Obaid, 'Yes to bin Laden rhetoric; no to Al Qaeda violence. An unprecedented poll of Saudi opinion', *International Herald Tribune*, 28 June 2004. Nawaf Obaid is Managing Director of the Saudi National Security Assessment Project.
9. Cf. N. Kermani, *Iran—die Revolution der Kinder*, Munich 2003.
10. For Ebadi's attitude to Islam cf. her interview in *Le Monde des Religions*, July/August 2004, 66–9. My public discussion with the Nobel prizewinner Shirin Ebadi, planned to be held at the Parliament of the World Religions in Barcelona, took place in Tübingen in 2005.
11. Cf. Kepel, *Jihad* (n. 6).
12. Cf. P. Sluglett, 'Arab Socialism', in *EncModIsl.*
13. Cf. C.D. Smith, 'Secularism', in *EncModIsl.*
14. S. Mardin, 'Religion and Secularism in Turkey', in A. Hourani, P.S. Khoury and M.C. Wilson (ed.), *The Modern Middle East. A Reader*, London 1993, 372f.
15. U. Steinbach, 'Islam in der Türkei', in *Türkei. Informationen zur Politischen Bildung*, No. 277, 4/2002, 25.
16. Cf. ibid.; also id., *Die Türkei im 20. Jahrhundert. Schwieriger Partner Europas*, Bergisch Gladbach 1996.
17. B. Nirumand, 'Zwischen Mekka und Moderne. Alte und neue Zielsetzungen der islamischen Reformbewegung', *Neue Zürcher Zeitung*, 24 November 2003.
18. Cf. United Nations Development Programme, *Arab Human Development Report 2003.*
19. Cf. D.S. Mahathir bin Mohamad, *International Herald Tribune*, 22 October 2003.
20. Cf. ibid. More recent aspects are also provided by F.A. Noor, 'In Search of Islamic Economics: The Malaysian Model', in F.-J. Richter and P.M.C. Mar, *Asia's New Crisis. Renewal through Total Ethical Management*, Singapore 2004, 96–117. The former US ambassador in Pakistan, T.W. Simons, Jr, in his *Islam in a Globalizing World*, Stanford, CA 2003, expresses the hope of many Americans for an authentic Islamic modernity.
21. For the background cf. the report of the ARD correspondent in Cairo, Reinhard Baumgarten, dated 21 June 2004.

D III. The Middle East Conflict and a New Paradigm

1. Cf. H. Küng, *Judaism*, Part 2, A III, and Part 3, C I–IV (with full bibliographical details).
2. The analysis of these paradigms can be found in ibid., Part 1, C I–V History.
3. Cf. ibid., Part 1, B I: The Central Structural Elements.
4. Cf. J. Parkes, *Whose Land? A History of Palestine*, Harmondsworth ^{2}1970. Among the numerous more recent publications, J.W. Wright, Jr (ed.), *Structural Flaws in the Middle East Peace Process. Historical Contexts*, Basingstoke 2002, is particularly informative. For the more recent history of Palestine cf. G. Kramer, *Geschichte Palästinas: von der Osmanischen Eroberung bis zur Gründung des Staates Israel*, Munich 2003.
5. Cf. A. Burg, 'A failed Israeli society is collapsing', *International Herald Tribune*, 6/7 September 2003.
6. Ibid.
7. *Neue Zürcher Zeitung*, Sunday 4 January 2004.
8. Readers of this book, whether Muslims, Jews or Christians, believers or secular men and women, who are interested in a more detailed political and theological basis and explication of the 'opportunities' hinted at here should consult the relevant sections in my *Judaism*. There they will find answers to questions such as: Religious pluralism or a state religion in the Jewish state? Endure—withdraw—repress? Land for peace? Biblical arguments for state frontiers? Jerusalem: two flags over the 'city of peace'? The Dome of the Rock—a sign of unity for the Abrahamic ecumene?
9. Burg, 'A failed Israeli society' (n. 5).
10. Here I shall limit myself to defining in principle the new paradigm of international relations which I have laid out in books such as *Global Responsibility* (1991) and *A Global Ethic for Global Politics and Global Economics* (1997). Many of the ideas put forward here found their way in 2001 into the report for the United Nations, *Crossing the Divide. Dialogue Among Civilizations*, South Orange, NJ 2001. With the former Federal President R. von Weizsäcker I belonged to a twenty-member 'Group of Distinguished Persons' from all over the world, appointed by the UN General Secretary Kofi Annan to work out a manifesto for a new paradigm of international relations. The occasion was the International Year of Dialogue among Civilizations, proposed by a Muslim, the reforming State President of Iran, Mohammad Khatami. We presented our report on the dialogue of religions and a new paradigm of international relations to the Secretary General and the UN General Assembly on 9 November 2001. This view has been endorsed by a group of German-language political theorists, peace researchers and ethicists, who after a symposium in Tübingen in autumn 2002 published their contributions under the title *Friedenspolitik. Ethische Grundlagen internationaler Beziehungen*, ed. H. Küng and D. Senghaas, Munich 2003.

D IV. New Approaches to Theological Conversation

1. To be read in S. Hunke, *Allahs Sonne über dem Abendland*, Frankfurt 1963.

2. In 2003 Muslim students at the University of Toronto referred me with great enthusiasm to a work by a French surgeon who converted to Islam, M. Bucaille, *La Bible, le Coran et la science: les Écritures Saintes examinées à la lumière des connaissances modernes*, Paris [15]1993. The Arabic translation has become a bestseller and the book has also appeared in English: *The Bible, The Qur'an and Science: The Holy Scriptures Examined in the Light of Modern Knowledge*, Indianapolis 1979.
3. Cf. W.M. Watt, *Islam and Christianity Today. A Contribution to Dialogue*, London 1983 (with a preface by the Saudi Arabian oil minister Sheikh Ahmed Yamani). Cf. also C. Bennett, *In Search of Muhammad*, London 1998, Part II: Non-Muslim Lives of Muhammad: from the 7th to the 16th Centuries and Non-Muslim Lives: from the Renaissance to Today.
4. Cf. A.T. Khoury, *Polemique byzantine contre l'Islam, VIIIe–XIIIe siècles*, Leiden 1972.
5. Cf. N. Daniel, *Islam and the West: The Making of an Image*, Edinburgh 1960.
6. Cf. W.M. Watt, *The Influence of Islam on Medieval Europe*, Edinburgh 1972, 72–7.
7. Ibid., 4.
8. *International Herald Tribune*, 23 October 2003.
9. *Congregation for the Doctrine of Faith, Declaration Dominus Iesus on the Unicity and Salvific Universality of Jesus Christ and the Church*, 6 August 2000, no. 22.
10. This is also true of the comparison between the Qur'an and the Old and New Testaments by the well-known Muslim hadith scholar Muhammad Mustafa al-A'zami, *The History of the Qur'anic Text. From Revelation to Compilation. A Comparative Study with the Old and New Testaments*, Leicester 2003. For all its scholarship this work is ultimately written from a dogmatic standpoint: 'On Islamic issues—whether the Qur'an, tafsir, hadith, fiqh, history ... etc.—only the writings of a practising Muslim are worthy of our attention' (341). This means that the two parts of the book are written in black and white: 1. The history of the Qur'anic text is depicted without the objections of critical scholarship (Western or Muslim) being taken seriously; 2. In the second part, by contrast the biblical writings are subjected to critical investigation in order to destroy the credibility of the Old and New Testaments. The author understands the biblical sayings source Q as a kind of 'proto-Gospel'. Therefore he manages a piece of sleight of hand by writing about Jesus without even mentioning his crucifixion and what led up to it. However, New Testament research has brought out clearly that the Gospel of Mark is the oldest Gospel (it has been described as a passion narrative with an extended introduction) and that Matthew and Luke base themselves on Mark and the sayings source Q for their Gospels. Al-A'zami sees the development of the New Testament texts in negative terms as a falsification of this alleged original source and sets against that the complete immutability of the Quran'ic text as a criterion for its credibility and greater worth. I have demonstrated how the different New Testament traditions can be used constructively for an authentic understanding of the message and fate of Jesus on the basis of historical criticism in *On Being A Christian*, B II, C I–V. J.-D. Thyen, *Bibel und Koran. Eine Synopse gemeinsamer*

Überlieferungen, Cologne [2]1993, is helpful for a comparison of texts common to the Bible and the Qur'an.

11. Second Vatican Council, *Declaration on the Relationship of the Church to the Non-Christian Religions Nostra Aetate*, Rome 1965, no. 3.
12. On the christology of the Qur'an, for the older literature see D.B. Macdonald, ''Isa', in *HdI* (1941, [2]1976, taken over unaltered from *EncIsl*). For more recent literature cf. G.C. Anawati, ''Isa', in *EncIsl*[2] (1978: references in particular to the books by L. Bakker, M. Hayek, I. al-Husayni, H. Michaud and G. Parrinder). The most recent work is M. Bauschke, *Jesus im Koran*, Cologne 2001—an expanded version of ch. A of his comprehensive work *Jesus—Stein des Anstosses. Die Christologie des Koran und die deutschsprachige Theologie*, Cologne 2000. Jesus in the Qur'an and the broader historical context are discussed by N. Robinson, *Christ in Islam and Christianity. The Representation of Jesus in the Qur'an and the Classical Muslim Commentaries*, London 1991 (unfortunately Jewish Christianity is mentioned only on the periphery).
13. Surah 61.6 (one of the two 'I' sayings of Jesus already quoted, cf. surah 10.30).
14. There is dispute as to which verses should be included in the Qur'anic christology and which should not. In chronological order Bauschke (with a reference to Nöldeke/Schwally) counts six surahs which were revealed in Mecca (19.16–37; 19.88–93; 43.57–65; 23.50; 21.91; 42.13; 6.85) and nine surahs which Muhammad received in Medina (2.87; 2.116f.; 2.136; 2.253; 3.36; 3.39; 3.42–64; 3.14; 61.6,14; 57.27; 4.156–9, 163.171f; 33.7f.; 66.12; 9.30f.; 5.17,46f., 72–79, 110–119).
15. Surahs 3.39, 45; 4.171.
16. Surah 4.171.
17. Cf. surahs 19.16–22 and 3.42–7.
18. Cf. surahs 10.30; 21.26; 51.56.
19. Surah 5.110.
20. Surah 5.72; cf. also surah 5.17.
21. Mark 10.18.
22. Mark 12.29; cf. Deut. 6.4.
23. For the question of pre-existence see the comprehensive work by K.-J. Kuschel, *Born before All Time. The Dispute over Christ's Origin*, London and New York 1992.
24. The Catholic dogmatic theologian Karl Rahner devoted his biblical–theological article (almost the only one that he wrote), '*Theos* in the New Testament', in *Theological Investigations* I, Baltimore and London 1961, 79–148, to this topic.
25. Cf. M. Hengel, 'Die Inthronisation Christi zur Rechten Gottes und Ps 110, 1', in M. Philonenko (ed.), *Le trône de Dieu*, Tübingen 1993.
26. Rom.1.4.
27. Cf. H. Denzinger, *Enchiridion Symbolorum*, no. 111a.
28. Cf. ibid., no. 148.
29. Surah 5.82.
30. That 'Nazoreans' are the Jewish Christians has recently been confirmed by F. de Blois, 'Elchasai—Manes—Muhammad. Manichäismus und Islam in

religionshistorischem Vergleich', *Der Islam* 81, 2004; he cites not only the agreement between the Islamic and the Jewish–Christian understanding of prophet but also the prohibition of wine in Islam and in Jewish Christianity—which was rejected by both Judaism and Gentile Christianity (44f.). J.D. McAuliffe, *Qur'anic Christians. An Analysis of Classical and Modern Exegesis*, Cambridge 1991, discusses the picture of Christians in the Qur'an reflected in the rich commentary literature (*tafsir*).

31. Cf. H.-J. Schoeps, *Theologie und Geschichte des Judenchristentums*, Tübingen 1949.
32. Ibid., 342.
33. Cf. Justin, *Dialogue with the Jew Trypho*, 48.3f.; 49.1.
34. Mark 4.41; Luke 7.49; 8.25.
35. John 1.46.
36. Cf. G. Strecker, 'Judenchristentum', in *TRE*.
37. J. van Ess, *Der Fehltritt des Gelehrten. Die 'Pest von Emmaus' und ihre theologischen Nachspiele*, Heidelberg 2001.
38. Ibid., 394.
39. Surah 5.110.
40. Surah 4.157.
41. For the translation and history of the exegesis of the Qur'anic verse about the crucifixion cf. Bauschke, *Jesus—Stein des Anstosses* (n. 12), 163–78.
42. Thus the probable interpretation of surah 61.6.
43. Cf. surah 19.31–33.
44. Surah 4.157.
45. Starting from nineteenth-century 'travel accounts' and reports of an alleged tomb of Jesus in Srinagar (tombs of Jesus are also pointed out elsewhere), in the 1980s in his *Starb Jesus in Kaschmir? Das Geheimnis seines Lebens und Wirkens in Indien*, Düsseldorf 1983, S. Obermeier came forward with the thesis that Jesus died in Kashmir.
46. Thus at least according to Irenaus of Lyons, *Against the Heresies*, 1,24,4. The hypotheses of both a pseudo-death and a substitution contradict all the evidence in and outside the Bible and other results of historical research.
47. Cf. surah 19.33.
48. Surah 3.55.
49. Cf. Bauschke, *Jesus—Stein des Anstosses* (n. 12), 178–85. For the distinction between the 'christology of the Qur'an' and the 'christology of the Islamic tradition', cf. the table in ibid., 185.
50. Cf. M. Ayoub, *Redemptive Suffering in Islam. A Study of the Devotional Aspects of 'Ashura' in Twelver Shi'ism*, The Hague 1978.
51. Id., *Towards an Islamic Christology, II: The Death of Jesus, Reality or Delusion. A Study of the Death of Jesus in Tafsir Literature*, reprint of *The Muslim World*, 70, No. 2, April 1980, 91–121.
52. Ibid., 116.
53. Ibid.
54. Bauschke, *Jesus im Koran* (n. 12), 110.

55. Cf. R. Arnaldez, *Jésus, fils de Marie, prophète de l'Islam*, Paris 1980.
56. Cf. id., *Jésus dans la pensée musulmane*, Paris 1988.
57. Ibid., 242.
58. Ibid., 246.
59. Ibid., 248.
60. Matt. 12.30.
61. Cf. surahs 19.21; 21.91; 23.50.
62. Cf. Rom. 1.3–4; Acts 2.36; Phil. 2.9–10; 1 Tim. 3.16; 1 Peter 3.21; John 3.14.

D V. Speculative Questions

1. Matt. 28.19; cf. Paul's closing blessing in 2 Cor. 13.13.
2. Acts 2.38; cf. 8.16; 10.48; 1 Cor 1.13–15; Gal. 3.27; Rom. 6.3.
3. Surah 4.171; cf. 5.72f.
4. Cf. surah 5.116.
5. Cf. surah 23.52f.
6. Cf. Denzinger, *Enchiridion Symbolorum*, no. 325.
7. I first worked out the view of the doctrine of the Trinity which I present briefly here on the basis of philosophical problems in my book *The Incarnation of God. An Introduction to Hegel's Theological Thought as Prolegomena to a Future Christology* (1970), Edinburgh 1987, especially Part VIII, 2–3 and excursuses I–V; then on the basis of research into the New Testament and the history of dogma in *On Being a Christian* (1974), 436–44; finally I give a historical–critical account of the development of the doctrine of the Trinity in the first centuries in *Christianity* (1994), C I, 6; C II, 5–6.
8. N. Brox, *A History of the Early Church*, London 1994, 152.
9. H. Zirker, 'Der Koran in christlicher Perspektive', in A. Renz and S. Leimgruber (eds), *Lernprozess Christen Muslime. Gesellschaftliche Kontexte—Theologische Grundlagen—Begegnungsfelder*, Münster 2002, 183–97: 193.
10. H. Vorgrimler, *Gott. Vater, Sohn und Heiliger Geist*, Münster 2003, 114.
11. Ibid., 47.
12. Ibid., 118.
13. Ibid., 120f.
14. Ibid., 121.
15. Thus the criticism of P. Rosien, in *Publik Forum* 13, 2003, in his call for a paradigm change referring to J. Röser of *Christ in der Gegenwart.*
16. This was written in 1982 and repeated unchanged in a second revised edition twenty years later by the Tübingen Protestant church historian S. Raeder, *Der Islam und das Christentum. Eine historische und theologische Einführung*, Neukirchen-Vluyn 2003. There is a rightly critical review by the Protestant theologian and Qur'anic expert M. Bauschke in *Zeitschrift für Mission* 29, 2003, 375–9.
17. Surah 50.16.
18. Surah 2.186.
19. P. Lapide and J. Moltmann, *Jüdischer Monotheismus, christliche Trinitätslehre*, Munich 1979, 50f. I remember with gratitude the ecumenically-minded Jewish

theologian Pinchas Lapide, who died all too prematurely; at an early stage I gave public dialogue lectures with him at Tübingen University: H. Küng and P. Lapide, *Jesus im Widerstreit. Ein jüdisch-christlicher Dialog*, Munich 1976.

20. Cf. 1 John 5.7: 'There are three who bear witness: the spirit, the water (= baptism) and the blood (= eucharist); and these three are one' (i.e. the two sacraments are witnesses to the one power of the one spirit). Some textual witnesses make an insertion here which has been shown to be a forgery (known as the 'Comma Johanneum'): 'There are three who bear witness *in heaven—the Father, the Word and the Holy Spirit, and these three are one. And there are three who bear witness on earth*: the spirit, the water....' For the interpretation cf. R. Bultmann, *The Johannine Epistles*, Hermeneia, Philadelphia 1973, ad loc.
21. Denziger, *Enchiridion*, no. 2198.
22. I would refer once again to the basic work by K.-J. Kuschel, *Born before All Time. The Dispute over Christ's Origin*, London and New York 1992.
23. Cf. Acts 7.1–53.
24. Acts 7.55f.
25. Cf. H. Küng, *Christianity*, C I, 6: What Jewish Christians believe; C II, 5: Paradigm shift in christology; C III, 2: Augustine: the father of the new paradigm of theology.
26. John 14.9.

D VI. From Biblical Criticism to Qur'anic Criticism?

1. Cf. B. de Spinoza, *Tractatus theologico-politicus*, Hamburg (in fact Amsterdam) 1670; English, *A Theologico–political Treatise*, New York 1951.
2. Cf. R. Simon, *Histoire critique du Vieux Testament*, Paris 1678; with a new preface, Rotterdam 1685.
3. G.E. Lessing, 'Von Duldung der Deisten. Fragment eines Ungenannten' (1778), in *Werke in drei Bänden*, ed. H.G. Gopfert, Vol. III, Munich 1982, 309–48.
4. The basic masterly investigation is that of I. Goldziher, *Die Richtungen der islamischen Koranauslegung*, Leiden 1920; cf. J.M.S. Baljon, *Modern Muslim Koran Interpretation (1880–1960)*, Leiden 1961; H. Gätje, *Koran und Koranexegese*, Zurich 1971 (with an anthology of classical texts); J.J.G. Jansen, *The Interpretation of the Koran in Modern Egypt*, Leiden 1974; H. Lazarus-Yafeh, *Intertwined Worlds. Medieval Islam and Bible Criticism*, Princeton 1992; A. Rippin, 'tafsir', in *EncRel* (1987); id., 'tafsir', in *EncIsl*² (1998); id. (ed.), *Approaches to the History of the Interpretation of the Qur'an*, Oxford 1988.
5. Cf. N.H. Abu Zayd, 'Le dilemme de l'approche littéraire du Coran (1ère partie)', to be found on the internet under *www.etudes-musulmanes.com*; cf. id., *Islam und Politik. Kritik des religiösen Diskurses* (from the Arabic), Frankfurt am Main 1996.
6. Gätje, *Koran und Koranexegese* (n. 4), 66.
7. Cf. J. Waardenburg, 'Gibt es im Islam hermeneutische Prinzipien?', in H.-M. Barth and C. Elsas (ed.), *Hermeneutik in Islam und Christentum, Beiträge zum interreligiösen Dialog*, Hamburg 1997, 51–74.
8. Cf. Abu Zayd, 'Le dilemme de l'approche littéraire du Coran' (n. 5).

9. Cf. the dossier 'Les rénovateurs de l'Islam' in *Le Monde des Religions*, no. 1, 2003: 'Les axes de la récherche'.
10. Cf. W.M. Watt and A.T. Welch, *Der Islam, Vol. I: Mohammed und die Frühzeit—Islamisches Recht—Religiöses Leben*, Stuttgart 1980, 141–9, esp. 142, 148.
11. Cf. A. Geiger, *Was hat Mohammed aus dem Judenthume aufgenommen?*, Leipzig ^{2}1902.
12. Cf. H Hirschfeld, *Beiträge zur Erklärung des Korân*, Leipzig 1886.
13. Cf. J. Wansbrough, *Quranic Studies. Sources and Methods of Scriptural Interpretation*, Oxford 1977; id., *The Sectarian Milieu. Content and Composition of Islamic Salvation History*, Oxford 1978.
14. Cf. J. Burton, *The Collection of the Qur'an*, Cambridge 1977.
15. Cf. G. Lüling, *Die Wiederentdeckung des Propheten Muhammad. Eine Kritik am 'christlichen' Abendland*, Erlangen 1981.
16. Cf. id., *Über den Ur-Qur'an. Ansätze zur Rekonstruktion vorislamischer christlicher Strophenlieder im Qur'an*, Erlangen 1974.
17. Cf. C. Luxenberg, 'Die syro-aramäische Lesart des Koran', in *Beitrag zur Entschlüsselung der Koransprache*, Berlin 2000.
18. Ibid., 275. As one example of the numerous pertinent criticisms of Luxenberg's bold thesis (and also Lüling's hypothesis of a pre-Islamic Ur-Qur'an) see the article by the Bonn Islamic expert Stefan Wild, 'Die Sinnlichkeit des Koran ist alles andere als dunkel. Der Prophet Mohammed und sein Ur-Koran', *Süddeutsche Zeitung*, 24 February 2004. His final conclusion is: 'However, the systematic approach of a Syro-Aramaic reading of the Qur'an as the product of a mixed Aramaic–Arabic language and as a universal key to treating textual problems in the Qur'an raises greater difficulties than it resolves.'
19. Cf. A. Neuwirth, *Studien zur Komposition der mekkanischen Suren*, Berlin 1981.
20. J. Loop, *Auslegungskulturen. Grundlagen einer komparatistischen Beschreibung islamischer und christlicher Hermeneutiktraditionen*, Berne 2003, makes a critical comparison of Islamic and Christian hermeneutical concepts.
21. Cf. M. Chebel, *Manifeste pour un islam des Lumières. 27 propositions pour réformer l'Islam*, Paris 2004.
22. Cf. F. Rahman, *Prophecy in Islam. Philosophy and Orthodoxy*, London 1958.
23. Id., *Islam*, Chicago ^{2}1979, S. 31.
24. Cf. id., *Major Themes of the Qur'an*, Chicago 1980.
25. Ibid., 100.
26. Cf. P. Ricoeur et al., *La Révélation*, Brussels 1977.
27. Cf. M. Arkoun, *Lectures du Coran*, Paris 1982, second revised edition Tunis 1991; id., *Pour une critique de la raison islamique*, Paris 1984. Arkoun gives a very good introduction to his understanding of the Qur'an in *Ouvertures sur I'Islam*, Paris 1989, in the expanded third edition *L'Islam. Approche critique*, Paris 1992; German *Der Islam: Annäherung an eine Religion*, Heidelberg 1999; id., *The Unthought in Contemporary Islamic Thought*, London 2002.
28. Id., *Der Islam* (n. 27), 75.
29. Ibid., 77.

30. Ibid., 84.
31. Cf. F. Esack, *Qur'an, Liberation and Pluralism. An Islamic Perspective of Interreligious Solidarity Against Oppression*, Oxford 1997; there are critical discussions with Rahman and Arkoun on pp. 63–73. Cf. id., *The Qur'an. A Short Introduction*, Oxford 2002.
32. D. Tracy, *Plurality and Ambiguity: Hermeneutics, Religion, Hope*, San Francisco 1987, 79.
33. Esack, *Qur'an, Liberation and Pluralism* (n. 31), 72.
34. Ibid. 73.
35. Ibid., 76.
36. For the unambiguous commitment to liberation which has to guard against uncritical identifications see H. Küng, *On Being a Christian* (1974), D III 1: Being Christian as Being Radically Human.
37. This group includes e.g. Mehmet Paçac, Adil Çiftçi, Ömer Özsoy and Ilhami Güleray, who begin from the hermeneutical approach of Fazlur Rahman and insights of Gadamer's hermeneutics. Cf. the account by R. Wielandt, 'Zugänge zeitgenössischer Muslime zum Korantext', in *Zur Debatte. Themen der Katholischen Akademie in Bayern* 33, 2003, no. 5, 10–12: 12.
38. S.H. Nasr, 'The Islamic View of Christianity', *Concilium* 183, 1986, 10f.
39. Ibid., 11.
40. D.Weiss, *Vor einer Neuorientierung des islamischen Orients? Alte Kränkungen und neue Kooperationsperspektiven in einer globalisierten Welt* (manuscript 2004).

E. Possibilities for the Future

E I. Islamic Renewal

1. Cf. J.O. Voll, 'Renewal and Reform in Islamic History. Tajdid and Islah', in J.L. Esposito (ed.), *Voices of Resurgent Islam*, New York 1983, 32–47. There is a comprehensive bibliography in Y.Y. Haddad and J.L. Esposito, *The Islamic Revival since 1988. A Critical Survey and Bibliography*, Westport, CT 1997.
2. Cf. Part II, 'Pioneers of the Islamic Resurgence', in Esposito (ed.), *Voices of Resurgent Islam* (n. 1), 63–214; K. Cragg, *The Pen and the Faith. Eight Modern Muslim Writers and the Qur'an*, London 1985, has a more theological orientation. But cf. also J. Reissner, 'Die militant-islamischen Gruppen', in W.Ende and U. Steinbach, *Der Islam in der Gegenwart*, Munich [4]1996, 630–45.
3. A. Khurshid, 'The Nature of the Islamic Resurgence', in Esposito (ed.), *Voices of Resurgent Islam* (n. 1), 227.
4. There is a precise analysis in M. Lüders, *Tee im Garten Timurs. Die Krisengebiete nach dem Irak-Krieg*, Zurich 2003.
5. Cf. my 1998 statement at the end of the film on Islam in the television series *Spurensuche*, which can be read in H. Küng, *Tracing the Way*, London and New York 2002, 264–5.

6. S. al-Azm, 'Westliche Irrtümer und islamischer Selbsttäuschungen', *Schwäbisches Tagblatt*, 15 May 2004. There is a good insight into present-day Turkey in the 'sympathy magazine' edited by H.-J. Wald, *Türkei verstehen*, Ammerland and Starnberger See 2004.
7. R. Lang, 'Paradies mit Wachtürmen. Die Aufbruchstimmung in der Türkei verändert auch die Situation der dortigen Christen', *Zeitzeichen* 5, February 2004, 8–10.
8. 'Predigt wider den Terror', *Süddeutscher Zeitung*, 26 November 2003.
9. Cf. Haddad and Esposito, *The Islamic Revival since 1988* (n. 1); R. Benzine, *Les nouveaux penseurs de l'Islam*, Paris 2004; O. Safi (ed.), *Progressive Muslims: on Justice, Gender and Pluralism*, Oxford 2003.
10. Cf. F. Malti-Douglas, 'Arkoun M.', in *EncModIsl.*
11. Cf. I.J. Boullata, 'Hanati H.', in *EncModIsl.*
12. Cf. E. Jamil, 'Ibrahim A.', in *EncModIsl.*
13. Cf. J.L. Esposito and J.O. Voll, *Makers of Contemporary Islam*, Oxford 2001.
14. Cf. El Hassan bin Talal, *Christianity in the Arab World*, London 1998. For his services to dialogue between the religions Prince Hassan of Jordan was awarded an honorary doctorate in theology by the Catholic theological faculty in Tübingen on 14 May 2002. The *laudatio* was given by K.-J. Kuschel, published as 'Perspektiven des christlich–muslimischen Dialogs heute', *Theologische Quartalschrift* 181, 2001, 266–74. Prince Hassan's latest publication is a kind of catechism with forty-one questions: *To Be a Muslim. Islam, Peace, and Democracy*, Brighton 2004. The postscript, 'Toward a Universal Ethic of Human Understanding' (building on the 1993 Chicago Declaration toward a Global Ethic), is important.
15. Cf. the journal *Just Commentary*, edited in Malaysia by Chandra Muzaffar, the founder of the International Movement for a Just World (*www.just-international.org*).
16. Cf. e.g. R. Hassan, 'Rights of Women Within Islamic Communities', in J. Witte and D. van der Vyver (eds.), *Religious Human Rights in Global Perspective, Vol. 1: Religious Perspectives*, The Hague 1996, 361–86.
17. S.A. Weiss, 'The battle for the soul of Islam', *International Herald Tribune*, 28 February 2003.
18. K. Amirpur, 'Zu streng genommen', *Süddeutscher Zeitung*, 30 March 2004.
19. Cf. M. Talbi, ' "Mein Glaube ist die Freiheit". Plaidoyer pour un Islam moderne', *Neue Zürcher Zeitung*, 15 September 2003. Cf. id., *Plaidoyer pour un Islam moderne*, Tunis 1998. For the suppression of all freedom of opinion and prevention of access to the internet in Tunisia cf. *International Herald Tribune*, 26/27 June 2004: 'Tunisia is economically liberal but politically we live in the Soviet Union of the 1950s.' Significantly the dictator Ben Ali is supported by the Bush administration in the 'war against terror'; cynically a UN conference on information technology took place in Tunis in November 2005.
20. Id., '"Meine Glaube ist die Freiheit"' (n. 19).
21. A. Hamzawy, 'Der Westen muss jetzt mit den Islamisten sprechen', *Neue Zürcher Zeitung*, Sunday 4 January 2004; id., 'Das Reformtheater. Arabische Regime

behindern die Demokratisierung. Der Westen beschönigt das' (on the declaration of the G8 summit on the American Sea Island), *Die Zeit*, 17 June 2004.

22. Communiqué of the EU–OIC conference, Istanbul, 13 February 2004.

E II. The Future of the Islamic Legal Order

1. Cf. H. Küng, *Judaism*, Part I, C IV: The Mediaeval Paradigm: The Rabbis and the Synagogue.
2. I have worked out very briefly in *A Short History of the Catholic Church*, London 2001, the constitutional development of the Roman Catholic paradigm in the Middle Ages, Counter-Reformation and anti-modernity which I described at length in *Christianity* (C III).
3. For the institution of the expert opinion cf. 'Fatwa', in *EncModIsl*: M.K. Masud, 'Concepts of Fatwa'; B. Messick, 'Process and function'; A.S. Dallal, 'Modern Usage'.
4. Cf. D. Senghaas, *Zivilisierung wider Willen*, Frankfurt am Main 1998, on Islam esp. 71–90.
5. Universal Declaration of Human Rights of 10 December 1948, preamble.
6. Cf. J.D. McAuliffe, 'Heart', in *EncQur*, Vol. II, 409: 'The qur'anic depiction of the heart, rather than the brain, as the locus of understanding became a central theme in the elaboration of post-qur'anic anthropology, particularly that of medieval Sufism. The notion that religious knowledge and sensitivity, i.e. conscience, are lodged in the heart grew more formalized and systematized, generating an extensive literature on spiritual formation.'
7. The classical works on the development of Islamic law by I. Goldziher, J. Schacht and N.J. Coulson are basic for understanding the Shariah today. In addition to the numerous works on the legal situation in individual Islamic countries or on individual subjects and questions cf. J. Schacht, 'Shari'a', in *EncIsl*; M.B. Hooker, 'Shari'a', in *EncIsl²*; N. Anderson, *Law Reform in the Muslim World*, London 1976; A. El Baradie, *Gottes–Recht und Menschen–Recht. Grundlagenprobleme der islamischen Strafrechtslehre*, Baden-Baden 1983; R.J.A. De Seife, *The Shari'a. An Introduction to the Law of Islam*, San Francisco 1994; K. Dilger, 'Tendenzen der Rechtsentwicklung', in W. Ende and U. Steinbach, *Der Islam in der Gegenwart*, Munich [4]1996, 186–212; in the same volume, on pp. 213–555 there are contributions by specialists on the position of Islam and Islamic law in selected states. The articles in *EncModIsl*, N. Calder, 'Legal Thought and Jurisprudence'; F.H. Ziadeh, 'Sunni Schools of Law'; A. Sachedina, 'Shi'i Schools of Law'; A.E. Mayer, 'Modern Legal Reform', give a good survey.
8. J. Harnischfeger, 'Die Scharia—Gegenmodell zur Demokratie. Warum in Nigeria das islamische Strafrecht populär ist', *Neue Zürcher Zeitung*, 29/30 June 2002.
9. Thus the report of the academic adviser to the Ministry of Economic Collaboration and Development, 'Islam and Legal Systems: The Significance of an "Implementation of Shari'a" for Development Co-operation with Islamic Societies', in *BMZ aktuell*, No. 092, August 1998.

10. Pope Pius VI, brief *Quod aliquantum* of 10 March 1791.
11. Cf. H. Küng, *Christianity*, C, V 6.
12. Cf. id., *Judaism*, Part I, C V, 7.
13. For a survey of the development of human rights in Islam cf. A.E. Mayer, 'Human Rights', in *EncModIsl.*
14. Cf. R. Traer, *Faith in Human Rights*, Washington, DC 1991, 111.
15. A.A. Mawdudi, *Human Rights in Islam*, London 1976, 13.
16. The Cairo Declaration on Human Rights in Islam (1990) and other Islamic documentations on human rights can be found on the Internet on the home page of the 'University Committee on Human Rights Studies' of Harvard University: www.humanrights. harvard.edu /documents/regionaldocs/ cairo_dec.htm.
17. Cf. S. Balić, 'Die innerislamische Diskussion zu Säkularismus, Demokratie und Menschenrechten', in Ende and Steinbach, *Der Islam in der Gegenwart* (n. 7), 590–603, esp. 600f. The Muslim Balić mentions H.A. Amin, F. Rahman, M. Arkoun, H. Sa'b, H. Hanafi, M. Amara and I. Subuksu.
18. Gen. 1.27. Cf. D. C. Peterson, 'Creation', in *EncQur.*
19. Cf. surah 2.30.
20. M.A. Sinaceur, 'Islamic Tradition and Human Rights', in *Philosophical Foundations of Human Rights*, Paris, UNESCO 1986, 211, quoted here from Traer, *Faith in Human Rights* (n. 14), 114.
21. Surah 10.99.
22. Cf. surah 4.1.
23. Cf. surah 17.70.
24. For the role of women in the various Christian paradigms see the extended discussion in H. Küng, *Women in Christianity*, London and New York 2001.
25. For the position of women in Judaism and in Jewish feminist theology cf. id., *Judaism*, Part III, B II, 2: A test case—the position of women.
26. Cf. G. Frankel, 'Israel's 2,000-Year-Old Divorce Laws Turn Ties That Bind Into Chains', *International Herald Tribune*, 14 March 1989.
27. Cf. Gen. 1.27.
28. Among other things Judith Plaskow is the co-founder and long-time editor of the interreligious *Journal of Feminist Studies in Religion*, which regularly also publishes contributions from Jewish women, such as the discussion on Jewish theology by T. Drorah Setel, Marcia Falk, Anne M. Solomon and others, 'Feminist Reflections on Separation and Unity in Jewish Theology, Roundtable', *JFSR* 2, 1986, 1, 113–30; cf. also Martha Ackelsberg, 'Spirituality, Community, and Politics. B'not Esh and the Feminist Reconstruction of Judaism', *JFSR* 2, 1986, 2, 109–20. For Jewish feminism see the recent contribution by Marla Brettschneider, Judith Plaskow, Marcia Falk and others, 'Meeting at the Well: Multiculturalism and Jewish Feminism, Special Section', in *JFSR* 19, 2003 1, 85–128.
29. Cf. S. Heschel (ed.), *On Being a Jewish Feminist*, New York 1983. In the middle of the 1980s Susannah Heschel, daughter of the famous theologian Abraham J. Heschel, who managed to flee from the Nazis in Germany in time along with his

family, came to Germany to give a series of lectures and provoked a vigorous debate on the presence of Christian antisemitism also in Christian feminist theology. Cf. L. Siegele-Wenschkewitz (ed.), *Verdrängte Vergangenheit, die uns bedrängt. Feministische Theologie in der Verantwortung für die Geschichte*, Munich 1988 (with contributions by S. Heschel, S. Goodman-Thau and others).

30. F. Rahman, *Islam*, London[2] 1979, 38. The extraordinary complexity of the question of women in Islam already emerges from the fact that the *EncModIsl* devotes two articles to the topic of women and Islam: 1. Soraya Altorki, 'Role and Status of Women' (in the Qur'an and Sunnah and in the different countries); 2. Valerie J. Hoffmann-Ladd, 'Women's Religious Observances'. In addition there is a further article by Nadia Hijab, 'Women and Social Reform', followed by articles by various authors on the social reforms in the different Islamic regions. The Tübingen Arabist Wiebke Walther, *Die Frau im Islam*, Stuttgart 1980, has produced a richly illustrated basic work on the cultural–historical role of women in the Islamic world, taking into account the topics of religion and law; marriage and family; politics, art and literature. The last chapter, 'Tear off the veil!' (a quotation from the Iraqi political poet Jamil Sidqi az-Zahawi from the beginning of the twentieth century) is particularly significant (178–84). Walther has written an excellent survey article 'Die Frau im Islam heute' in Ende and Steinbach, *Der Islam in der Gegenwart* (n. 7), 604–29.
31. Cf. surahs 20.115–127; 2.34–39.
32. Surah 20.121.
33. Surah 4.79.
34. Cf. M. Forstner, 'Die Stellung der Frau nach neoislamischer sunnitischer Lehre', in *Kanon. Kirche und Staat im Christlichen Osten*, XVI, 2000, 282–36.
35. S. Richter, 'Verpuffte Frauenpower', in *Financial Times Deutschland*, 19 November 2001.
36. Cf. Margot Badran and Miriam Cook, *Opening the Gates. A Century of Arab Feminist Writing*, London 1990.
37. For Riffat Hassan's key interest, feminist theology in Islam and Jewish–Christian–Muslim trialogue, see e.g. her articles 'Jihad fi Sabil Allah. A Muslim Woman's Faith Journey from Struggle to Struggle', in L. Grob, R. Hassan and H. Cordon (eds), *Women's and Men's Liberation. Testimonies of Spirit*, New York 1991; R. Hassan, 'The Issue of Women–Man Equality in the Islamic Tradition', ibid; ead., 'Muslim Women and Post-Patriarchal Islam', in P.M. Cooey, W.R. Eakin and J.B. McDaniel (eds), *After Patriarchy. Feminist Transformations of the World Religions*, Maryknoll, NY 1991. Cf. also C. Schöning-Kalender, A. Neusel and M.M. Jansen (eds), *Feminismus, Islam, Nation. Frauenbewegungen im Maghreb, in Zentralasien und in der Türkei*, Frankfurt am Main 1997. I owe to my learned and brave colleague Riffat Hassan a lecture and fact-finding tour in Pakistan in 1984 with lectures in Lahore and Rawalpindi and dialogues in Islamabad and Karachi.
38. Cf. J.C. Bürgel, 'Der Islam und die Menschenrechte', in R. Kley and S. Möckli (eds), *Geisteswissenschaftliche Dimensionen der Politik. Festschrift für Alois Riklin zum 65. Geburtstag*, Berne 2000, 39.

39. Cf. surah 2. 282.
40. Cf. Katajun Amirpur, *Gott ist mit den Furchtlosen. Schirin Ebadi—die Friedensnobel-preisträgerin und der Kampf um die Zukunft Irans*, Freiburg im Breisgau 2003. See also Shirin Ebadi, *History and Documentation of Human Rights in Iran*, New York 2000.
41. Cf. the (tendentious) report by the American Betty Mahmoody, *Not without my Daughter*, New York 1988. One might compare with this the much more serious autobiographical account by the Muslim student Maryam Ansary, who fled from Khomeini's Iran via Kurdistan to Germany, *Flieh, bevor der Morgen graut. Die Geschichte einer iranischen Frau*, Munich 2003. See also the book by a Muslim woman who likewise fled her homeland—Uganda—for political reasons and now lives in Canada: Irshad Manji, *The Trouble with Islam*, New York 2003.
42. The 26 March 2003 press release of the International Society for Human Rights (IGFM, Frankfurt).
43. Cf. Margot Badran, 'Feminism', in *EncModIsl.*
44. R. Hassan, 'Feministische Interpretationen des Islam', in Schöning-Kalender, Neusel and Jansen (eds), *Feminismus* (n. 37), 217–33: 228; cf. F. Mernissi, *Beyond the Veil*, Cambridge 1975, 103.
45. Cf. F. Mernissi, *Le harem politique—le prophète et les femmes*, Paris 1987.
46. In *EncIsl*[2] we read in the (redactional) article 'Khafd': 'Under Islam, the circumcision of girls has never been regarded as obligatory, but has been considered as recommended ...; in fact, it is practised very irregularly in the Muslim world, where whole populations are unaware of it or confine themselves to a symbolic pricking of the clitoris' (Vol. IV, 913).
47. Cf. W. Dirie, *Desert Flower*, London 1999 (which also contains the statistics quoted in the text). Cf. also the continuation of her (auto)biographical report (with J.D'Haem), *Desert Daughter*, London 2002. It was a delight to me to exchange common concerns with Waris Dirie at the annual congress of the International Union of Publishers in Berlin on 24 June 2004.
48. Among the countless material cf. Terre des Femmes (ed.), *Schnitt in die Seele. Weibliche Genitalverstümmelung. Eine fundamentale Menschenrechtsverletzung*, Frankfurt am Main 2003.
49. Cf the report in the *Neue Zürcher Zeitung* of 16 June 2004.
50. Cf. C. Braendle and E. Spycher, 'Im Namen des Königs', *Neue Zürcher Zeitung*, 24/25 January 2004.
51. Surah 9.5.
52. Surah 9.29.
53. A.A. an-Na'im, 'Qur'an, Shari'a and Human Rights: Foundations, Deficiencies and Prospects', *Concilium* 1990/2, 61–9 (my italics). I am grateful to Abdullahi Ahmed an-Na'im for accepting my request to write on the question of human rights in Islam for the Christian journal *Concilium* as long ago as the end of the 1980s. Cf. his book published at the same time: A.A. an-Na'im, *Toward an Islamic Reformation*, Syracuse, NY 1989, esp. chs. 4 and 7.

54. Cf. M.M. Taha, *The Second Message of Islam* (Arabic 1967), Syracuse, NY 1987.
55. an-Na'im, 'Qur'an, Shari'a and Human Rights' (n. 53), 67.
56. Cf. J. Rawls, *Political Liberalism*, New York 1993, 13.
57. H. Bielefeldt, 'Muslim Voices in the Human Rights Debate', in *Human Rights Quarterly* 17, 1995, 587–617, gives a precise analysis of the questions connected with this. T. Mitri (ed.), *Religion and Human Rights. A Christian–Muslim Discussion*, Geneva 1996, documents a Christian–Muslim dialogue on human rights organized by the World Council of Churches.
58. Cf. J. Hersch (ed.), *Le droît d'être un homme. Recueil de textes*, Paris 1968.
59. Universal Declaration on Human Rights, art. 18.
60. Ibid., art. 16.
61. J. Galtung, *Die Zukunft der Menschenrechte. Vision: Verständigung zwischen den Kulturen*, Frankfurt am Main 2000, 97f.

E III. The Future of the Islamic State Order and Politics

1. Cf. H.-H. Schrey, 'Gewalt/Gewaltlosigkeit I (Ethisch)', in *TRE*.
2. Cf. the relevant chapter in H. Küng, *Judaism*, Part I, C 1-V: History.
3. For the exegesis of Mark 12.17 see above all W. Schmithals, *Das Evangelium nach Markus*, Gütersloh [2]1986. For the same passage see also J. Gnilka, *Das Evangelium nach Markus*, Vol. 2, Zurich 1979.
4. Cf. Mark 11.15–19.
5. Cf. Rom. 13. 1.
6. Cf. 1 Cor. 15. 24.
7. M. Arkoun, *Der Islam. Annäherungen an eine Religion*, Heidelberg 1999, ch. 3, 'Kirche und Staat', rightly attaches importance to this. However, Arkoun overlooks the fact that Jesus of Nazareth had a political option (and perhaps the Prophet Muhammad also had an unpolitical one?).
8. Cf. S. Balic, 'Die innerislamische Diskussion zu Säkularismus, Demokratie und Menschenrechten', in W.Ende and U. Steinbach, *Der Islam in der Gegenwart*, Munich [4]1996, 590–603. The Bosnian scholar Smail Balić, who died recently, worked for a democratic Islam in Europe not only in his own country but also in the German-speaking world.
9. This was not an option for Judaism until the foundation of the state in 1948; I have described the dilemma of the future for the state of Israel in D III 1.
10. Thomas Aquinas, *Summa theologiae*, pars II–II, quaestio 10, articulus 8, ad 3: *Accipere fidem est voluntatis, sed tenere iam acceptam est necessitatis.*
11. The Protestant theologian J. Moltmann paints a moving portrait of Bruno in his 'What would be a God who only intervened from outside?', in *History and the Triune God. Contributions to Trinitarian Theology*, London and Minneapolis 1991, 56–64.
12. Cf. H. Küng, *The Church*, C III, 4: The Church and the heretics.
13. The Mainz Islamologist M. Forstner, 'Das Menschenrecht der Religionsfreiheit und des Religionswechsels als Problem der islamischen Staaten', in *Kanon. Kirche*

und Staat im Christlichen Osten, Vol. X, 1991, 105–86, offers an empirically very well attested and analytically acute discussion which I follow here.

14. Cf. e.g. surahs 2.217; 47.25.
15. Handed down by al-Bukhari and others. Cf. A.J. Wensinck, *Concordance et indices de la tradition Musulmane*, Leiden 1936, Vol. II, 167.
16. A first (and of course controversial) book with testimonies by Muslims who have become alienated and have moved away from Islam appeared in 2003 under a pseudonym: Ibn Warraq, *Leaving Islam: Apostates Speak Out*, Amherst, NY 2003. These personal testimonies have been collected through the Internet: *www.Secularislam.org*.
17. Universal Islamic Declaration of Human Rights, published in 1981 by the Islamic Council for Europe in Paris: English version at *http://www.alhewar.com/Islamdecl.html*
18. Forstner, 'Das Menschenrecht der Religionsfreiheit' (n. 13), 150. The basic declaration of 20 February 2002 by the Central Council of Muslims in Germany (ZND, with an Arab orientation, the President is Dr Nadeem Elyas) on the relationship of the Muslim to state and society is happily clear: article 11 on freedom of religion states: 'Therefore they also accept the right to change religion, to have another religion or even none at all.' Reprinted in *WCRP-Informationen* No. 62, 2002. I do not know of a similar declaration by the 'Islamic Council' (which is dominated by Turks and co-operates with the right-wing radical Milli Görus).
19. Ibid., 148, here there is a reference to H. Küng, *Global Responsibility*.
20. Cf. H. Küng (ed.), *Dokumentation zum Weltethos*, Munich 2002.
21. P.Gerlitz, 'Krieg I (Religionsgeschichtlich)', in *TRE*, surveys the almost incalculable number of special investigations from the perspective of religious studies.
22. Cf. Ex. 20.1–17; Deut. 5.6–21.
23. Cf. 'The movement from polytheism through henotheism (monolatry) to monotheism' in H. Küng, *Judaism*, Part I, A II, 5: The establishment of monotheism.
24. Cf. R. Girard, *Violence and the Sacred* (1972), Baltimore 1979; id., *The Scapegoat* (1982), Baltimore 1989.
25. Cf. Gen. 4.
26. Cf. Isa. 2.4; Micah 4.1–3.
27. Cf. Deut. 1–3 and the book of Joshua.
28. H. Küng, *Judaism*, Part I, C I, 1: The settlement—three attempts at reconstruction.
29. N. Lohfink, 'heraem', in *Theologisches Wörterbuch zum Alten Testament*, Vol. III, Stuttgart 1982, cols. 192–213: 206.
30. Cf. J.A. Soggin, 'Krieg II (Altes Testament)', in *TRE*.
31. Cf. 1 Kings 18–19.
32. Gen. 1.26–28.
33. Gen. 6.11–13.
34. Gen. 9.6.
35. Cf. A. Lichtenstein, *The Seven Laws of Noah*, New York [3]1997.

36. For the importance of the Noachic commandments for a global ethic cf. also K.-J. Kuschel, *Abraham. A Symbol of Hope for Jews, Christians and* Muslims, London and New York 1995.
37. M. Luther, *Larger Catechism*, The First Commandment (beginning).
38. Cf. A. Riklin, 'Gerechter Krieg? Die sechs Kriterien einer neualten Theorie', in H. Küng and D. Senghaas (eds), *Friedenspolitik. Ethischer Grundlagen internationaler Beziehungen*, Munich 2003, 279–87. My explanation and assessment in the introduction to this book, pp.17–68, right at the beginning of the Iraq war, have recently also been confirmed by American publications, above all by President Bush Jr's former anti-terrorist chief Richard A. Clarke, *Against All Enemies. Inside America's War against Terror*, Old Tappan, NJ 2004.
39. For the holy war/*jihad* see A. Noth, *Heiliger Krieg und heiliger Kampf im Islam und Christentum*, Bonn 1966; R. Peters, *Islam and Colonialism. The Doctrine of Jihad in Modern History*, The Hague 1980; W.M. Watt and A.T. Welch, *Der Islam I: Mohammed und die Frühzeit—Islamisches Recht—Religiöses Leben*, Stuttgart 1980, esp. 150ff.; J.C. Bürgel, *Allmacht und Mächtigkeit. Religion und Welt im Islam*, Munich 1991, esp. 80f.; W. Ende and U. Steinbach (eds), *Der Islam in der Gegenwart. Entwicklung und Ausbreitung—Staat, Politik und Recht—Kultur und Religion*, Munich [4]1996, esp. 279–82.
40. Surah 22.78.
41. Surah 61.11.
42. Surah 61.12.
43. Surah 9.73.
44. Cf. surah 9.5.
45. Cf. surah 2.190–3.
46. Thus for example A. el Kalim Ragab (who teaches in Bamberg and Cairo), 'Die Lehre vom "jihad" im Islam. Eine kritische Diskussion der Quellen und aktueller Entwicklungen', in A. Renz and S. Leimgruber (eds), *Lernprozess Christen Muslime*, Münster 2002, 57–88.
47. Cf. R. Peters, *Jihad in Medieval and Modern Islam*, Leiden 1977; id., 'Jihad', in *EncModIsl.*
48. For this whole development cf. J. C. Bürgel, 'Der Islam und die Menschenrechte', in R. Kley and S. Möckli (eds), *Geisteswissenschaftliche Dimensionen der Politik. Festschrift für Alois Riklin zum 65. Geburtstag*, Berne 2000, 31–60. Here he refers to a work by Hans Müller, *Die Kunst des Sklavenkaufs nach arabischen, persischen und türkischen Ratgebern vom 10. bis zum 18. Jahrhundert*, Freiburg im Breisgau 1980. In his book *Allmacht und Mächtigkeit* (n. 39), Bürgel illuminates various phenomena and processes of Islamic cultural history by putting them in the field of tension between the power-claim of religion and the powers of the secular counter-forces which have to be subjected.
49. Surah 47.4–6.
50. A. Meddeb, *La Maladie de l'Islam*, Paris 2002; German *Die Krankheit des Islam*, Heidelberg 2002, quotation p. 247.

51. Cf. surah 64.14.
52. Cf. surah 41.33–35.
53. Surah 8.61.
54. Cf. V. Rittberger and A. Hasenclever, 'Religionen in Konflikten', in H. Küng and K.-J. Kuschel (eds), *Wissenschaft und Weltethos*, Munich 2001, 161–200; A. Hasenclever, 'Geteilte Werte—Gemeinsamer Frieden? Überlegungen zur zivilisierenden Kraft von Religionen und Glaubensgemeinschaften', in Küng and Senghaas (eds), *Friedenspolitik* (n. 3 8), 288–318; G. Gebhardt, *Zum Frieden bewegen. Die friedenserzieherische Tätigkeit religiöser Friedensbewegungen*, Hamburg 1994.
55. For this see at length H. Küng, *A Global Ethic for Global Politics and Economics*, A V: World Peace—A Challenge for the World Religions.
56. Cf. surah 22.38f.

E IV. The Future of the Islamic Economic Order

1. F. Cardini, *Europe and Islam*, Oxford 2001, 18–26: 18f.
2. Ibid., 23. Cf. R. Davis, *Christian Slaves, Muslim Masters. White Slavery in the Mediterranean, the Barbary Coast, and Italy, 1500–1800*, Basingstoke 2004.
3. Cf. M. Weber, *The Protestant Ethic and the Spirit of Capitalism* (1904–6), New York 1958).
4. Cf. D. Weiss, 'Entwicklung als Wettbewerb der Kulturen', in *Aus Politik und Zeitgeschichte*, B 29, 1995, 6f.; id., 'Entwicklungszusammenarbeit mit islamischen Ländern', in *Aus Politik und Zeitgeschichte*, B 12, 1996, 12f.; id., 'Europa und die arabischen Länder. Krisenpotenziale im südlichen Mittelmeerraum', in *Aus Politik und Zeitgeschichte*, B 19–20, 2002; id., *EU-Arab Development Cooperation, Scenarios and Options*, Berlin 1996. I am grateful to Dieter Weiss, Professor of the National Economy of the Near East at the Free University of Berlin, and also editor of the series Volkswirtschaft des Vorderen Orients since the middle of the 1980s, for important insights.
5. Surah 2. 275, 278.
6. S. Buckley, *Teachings on Usury in Judaism, Christianity and Islam*, Lewiston 2000.
7. Summed up in S. Buckley, 'Islamic Banking. Does it Offer a Paradigm for the Future?', in *Faith in Business*, I, 2, June 1997.
8. Cf. Ex. 22.24; Deut. 23.20f.; Lev. 25.36f.
9. Cf. Matt. 25.27.
10. Cf. H. Küng, *The Church*, C I, 4: The Church and the Jews.
11. Cf. id., *Judaism*, Part I, C IV, 5–8: The Jewish Middle Ages and the beginnings of Christian anti-Judaism; Part II, A I, 6: The fatal antisemitism of a Catholic: Adolf Hitler.
12. Cf. N. Monzel, *Die Katholische Kirche in der Sozialgeschichte. Von den Anfängen bis zur Gegenwart*, Munich 1980, 102f.
13. Cf. ibid., 98–102.
14. Cf. ibid., 101f.

15. Cf. I. al-Fallouji and D. Urech, 'Investitionen im Islam. Parallelen und Unterschiede zu anderen Wirtschaftssystemen', *Neue Zürcher Zeitung*, 13/14 June 1998 (which contains precise technical information about the various forms of replacing interest).
16. For the origin and history of the *waqf* cf. the article by the Saudi Arabian economist Monzer Kahf (from Jeddah), 'Waqf', in *EncModIsl.* There is a brief analysis of present-day problems in S. Wippel, 'Islam und Wirtschaft: Dynamik oder Desaster?', in K.H. Schreiner (ed.), *Islam in Asien*, Bad Honnef 2001, 30–51. As one example of the numerous studies on *waqf* in different countries see S. Khalid Rashid (ed.), *Awqaf Experiences in South Asia*, New Delhi 2002.
17. The literature on Islamic economic theory has become too extensive to survey. The classic work is the composite volume of reports given at the first international conference on Islamic economics in Mecca in February 1976, which for the first time brought together Islamic economists and theologians; it was published with extensive bibliographies by K. Ahmad (ed.), *Studies in Islamic Economics*, Jeddah 1980. It contains illuminating articles by M. Abu Saud on 'Money, Interest and Qirad' (59–84) and by E. R. Faridi on 'Zakat and Fiscal Policy' (119–130); cf. also T. Kuran and R. Wilson, 'Economics (Economic Theory—Economic Institutions)', in *EncModIsl.*
18. D.Weiss, 'Islamisch Ökonomie und christliche Wirtschaftsethik. Perspektiven eines interkulturellen Dialogs', *Die neue Ordnung* 57, 2003, 424–43: 426f.
19. Cf. id., 'Aspekte der Re-islamisierung der Wirtschaft im arabisch-islamischen Orient', a lecture given at the Sixth Tübingen Conversation on Development Questions, 'The World of Islam between Tradition and Progress', Institute for Scholarly Collaboration with Developing Countries, Tübingen, 17–18 May 1985.
20. Ibid., 15.
21. Cf. A. Smith, *Inquiry into the Nature and Causes of the Wealth of Nations*, London 1776, new edition Oxford 1976.
22. Cf. id., *The Theory of Moral Sentiments*, London 1759, new edition Oxford 1976.
23. Cf. J.H. Dunning, 'Whither Global Capitalism?', *Global Focus*, Vol. 12, No. 1, 2000; id. (ed.), *Making Globalization Good. The Moral Challenges of Global Capitalism*, Oxford 2003.
24. The UN Global Compact initiated by the UN Secretary General Kofi Annan and by 2003 adopted by 700 businesses all over the world offers a stimulus for such an ethical framework, as does the Declaration toward a Global Ethic by the Parliament of the World's Religions, Chicago 1993.
25. Cf. U. Chapra, *Islam and the Economic Challenge*, Leicester 1992.
26. S. Wippel, 'Islam und Ökonomie: Ethisches Wirtschaften ist ein globaler Trend', *Das Parlament*, 1 August 2003. The same author has displayed his special knowledge in his empirical–analytical study *Islamische Wirtschafts- und Wohlfahrtseinrichtungen in Ägypten zwischen Markt und Moral*, Münster 1996. M.A. Choudhury, *The Principles of Islamic Political Economy. A Methodological Enquiry*, New York 1992, contrasts the alleged value-free method of positivist

economists with an Islamic paradigm and an ethical theory with an empirical foundation and relevance. R.Wilson, *Economics, Ethics and Religions. Jewish, Christian and Muslim Economic Thought*, New York 1997, ch. 4, 115–63, argues for a combination of economics and ethics—with reference to Ellen Frankel Paul, Amartya Sen, Kurt Rothschild, Gay Meeks and Alan Lewis, and Karl-Eric Warneryd. Further recent works are: M.A. Khan, *Glossary of Islamic Economics*, London 1990; M.F. Khan, *Essays in Islamic Economics*, Leicester 1995; J.A. Khan, *Islamic Economics and Finance. A Bibliography*, London 1995; U. Ucum, *Wirtschaftsethik im Christentum und Islam. Eine volkswirtschaftliche Analyse und ein finanzwirtschaftliches Wettbewerbskonzept*, Frankfurt am Main 1998; J. Neusner (ed.), *Religious Belief and Economic Behavior. Ancient Israel, Classical Christianity, Islam, and Judaism, and Contemporary Ireland and Africa*, Atlanta 1999; for Islam see the article in id. by Tamara Sonn and the response by J.L. Esposito, 185–204; M. Kalisch, 'Islamische Wirtschaftsethik in einer islamischen und in einer nichtislamischen Umwelt', in H.G. Nutzinger (ed.), *Christliche, jüdische und islamische Wirtschaftsethik. Über religiöse Grundlagen wirtschaftlichen Verhaltens in der sakulären Gesellschaft*, Marburg 2003, 105–29. H. Leipold, 'Wirtschaftsethik und wirtschaftliche Entwicklung im Islam', in H.G. Nutlinger (ed.), *Christliche, jüdische und islamische Wirtschaftsethik*, 131–49.

E V. The Future of the Islamic Way of Life

1. A. Soroush, *Reason, Freedom, and Democracy in Islam*, ed. M. and A. Sadri, Oxford 2000, 54–69: 56.
2. Cf. A. Jeremias, *Der Schleier von Sumer bis heute*, Leipzig 1931; A. and J. Assmann (eds), *Schleier und Schwelle. Archäologie der literarischen Kommunikation V* (3 vols), Munich 1997–9; C. Knieps, *Geschichte der Verschleierung der Frau im Islam*, Würzburg 1993.
3. The most thorough exegesis of 1 Cor. 11.2–16, including the history of the tradition, has been given by Wolfgang Schrage, *Der erste Brief an die Korinther*, Solothurn 1995, Vol. II, 487–541 (he comes from Bonn, formerly from Tübingen).
4. Cf. ibid., 518.
5. Except by those Christian groups which interpret the Bible literally, such as the Hutterite Brethren or the Amish (a branch of the Mennonites), who also apply regulations about clothing directly from the Bible.
6. For what follows cf. H.D. Galter, *Kopftuch und Schleier. Kulturgeschichte eines orientalischen Phänomens*, Urania-Skripten 2, Graz 2001; J. Chabbi, 'Ce voile que l'on dit "islamique" ', in *Le Monde des religions*, No. 3, January/ February 2004, 32–3.
7. Cf. J. Chelhod, 'Hidjab', in *EncIsl*[2].
8. Cf. surahs 7.46; 17.45; 19.17; 33.53; 38.32; 41.5; 42.51.
9. Cf. surahs 24.30f., 60; 33.53; 49.2–4.
10. Cf. Chabbi, 'Ce voile que l'on dit "islamique" ' (n. 6), 32–3.
11. Matinternet of 31 December 2003.
12. A. Schwarzer, 'Die Machtprobe', in *Der Spiegel*, no. 26, 2003.

13. Cf. J. Chirac, Président de la République, *Discours relatif au respect du principe de laïcité dans la République*, Paris, 17 December 2003. Chirac wants a 'code de laïcité' and wants to establish an 'Observatoire de la laïcité'.
14. Cf. A. Escudier (ed.), *Der Islam in Europa*, Göttingen 2004.
15. Cf. also R. Debray, *L'enseignement du fait religieux dans l'École laïque. Rapport au ministre de l'Education nationale*, Paris 2002.
16. O. Roy, 'Le contexte est totalement incompris à l'étranger', interview in *Le Monde*, 4 February 2004. Roy is the author of *Globalized Islam*, London 2004.
17. Cf. U. Spuler-Stegemann, *Muslime in Deutschland*, Freiburg 2002; F. Sen, *Islam in Deutschland*, Munich 2004; Escudier, *Der Islam in Europa* (n. 14).
18. Press release by the Protestant press agency EPD at the end of January 2004, referring to research by the Norddeutschen Rundfunks NDR.
19. Cf. D.Senghaas, 'Interkulturelle Dialoge angesichts kultureller Globalisierung: Plädoyer für eine Reorientierung', in T. Fues and J. Hippler (eds), *Globale Politik. Entwicklung und Frieden in der Weltgesellschaft*, Bonn 2003, 318–34.
20. E. Kandil, 'Muslime in der säkularen Gesellschaft', in A. Renz and S. Leimgruber (eds), *Lernprozess Christen Muslime*, Münster 2002, 29–43: 43.
21. 'The way of careful and legally sustainable decisions in individual cases' is also recommended by a specialist on questions of human rights, H. Bielefeldt, *Zur aktuellen Kopftuchdebatte in Deutschland. Anmerkungen aus der Perspektive der Menschenrechte*, Deutsches Institut fur Menschenrechte, Berlin 2004.
22. Cf. 'Spaniens Kirche gegen die Regierung', *Neue Zürcher Zeitung*, 1 June 2004.
23. Cf. U. Baumann (ed.), *Islamischer Religionsunterricht. Grundlagen, Begründungen, Berichte, Projekte, Dokumentationen*, Frankfurt am Main 2001.
24. Cf. M. al-Asad, 'Architecture: Contemporary Forums', in *EncModIsl.*
25. Cf. A.S. Ahmed, *Postmodernism and Islam. Predicament and Promise*, London 1992; id, 'The Mosques in Politics', in *EncModIsl.*
26. Matt. 5.41.
27. Cf. H. Küng, *Judaism*, Part III, C IV, 6: Praying together?
28. Thus the concluding document of a meeting between the World Council of Churches and the Pontifical Council for Interreligious Dialogue held in 1997 in Bose, in *Pro Dialogo & Current Dialogue*, Bulletin 98, 1998/2, 237ff.: 240. Cf. *Christen und Muslime: 'Wie können wir Muslimen begegnen?'* and *'Christen und Muslime: Gemeinsam beten?'*, two working papers by the joint committee 'Islam in Europe' of the Conference of European Churches (KEK) and the Council of European Bishops' Conferences (CCEE), in *epd Dokumentation* no. 51, 15 December 2003.
29. Cf. the model joint publication by a Christian, a Jewish and a Muslim scholar, M. Bauschke, W. Homolka and R. Müller (eds), *Gemeinsam vor Gott. Gebete aus Judentum, Christentum und Islam*, Gütersloh 2004.

Epilogue: Islam, an Image of Hope

1. For the resistance of non-democratic structures in the Near East see the subtle analysis by P. Pawelka, 'Der orientalische Staat: zur Resistenz patrimonialer und

autoritärer Systeme in einer globalisierten Welt', in V. Rittberger (ed.), *Demokratie—Entwicklung—Frieden*, Baden-Baden 2003, 145–64.

2. D. Weiss, 'Zur wissenschaftliche Kooperation mit den Ländern des Vorderen Orients', in *Europa-Archiv Folge* 22, 1982, 681.
3. Malek Chebel, *Manifeste pour un islam des Lumières. 27 propositions pour reformer l'Islam*, Paris 2004, 20.
4. One expression of this is a new series published by Albin Michel, Paris, with the evocative title 'L'Islam des Lumières', which provides a forum for innovative Muslim thinkers. Cf. in this series R. Benzine, *Les nouveaux penseurs de l'Islam*, 2004. Cf. also the extensive special issue of the famous journal *Le Nouvel Observateur, Les nouveaux penseurs de l'Islam*, April/May 2004 (with more than 30 contributions).
5. E.-W. Böckenförde, 'Fundamente der Freiheit', in E. Teufel (ed.), *Was hält die moderne Gesellschaft zusammen?*, Frankfurt am Main 1996, 89–99: 89.
6. Cf. J. Rawls, *A Theory of Justice*, Cambridge, MA 1971, 387f.
7. Cf. the account reported by B. Stauffer of the political theorist P. Haenni, who is active in Egypt, in *Neue Zürcher Zeitung*, 9 February 2004, on 'Egypt's New Preachers and their Seductive Message'.
8. Cf. Stiftung Entwicklung und Frieden, *Globale Trends 2004/2005*, ed. I. Hauchler, D. Messner and F. Nuscheler, Frankfurt am Main 2003, 68.
9. A. Rahmanzadeh, *Population Policy in the Islamic Countries*, which appeared in the series produced by the Federal Ministry for Economic Collaboration and development, BMZ Special, August 2002.
10. UN Resolution A/RES/53/22.
11. Seyed Mohammad Khatami in his speech to the UN General Assembly on 21 September 1998: UN-Dokument A/53/PV.8 (the emphases in this and the following UN documents are mine).
12. The group also includes: Professor Lourdes Arizpe (Mexico), Dr Hanan Ashrawi (Palestine), Professor Ruth Cardoso (Brazil), Jacques Delors (France), Dr Leslie Gelb (USA), Nadine Gordimer (South Africa), Professor Sergei Kapitza (Russia), Dr Hayao Kawai (Japan), Ambassador Tommy Koh (Singapore), Professor Dr Hans Küng (Switzerland), Dr Graça Machel (Mozambique), Professor Amartya Sen (India), Dr Song Jian (China), Dick Spring (Ireland), Professor Tu Wei-Wing (China), Former Federal President Richard von Weizsäcker (Germany).
13. G. Picco, R. von Weizsäcker, H. Küng (et al.), *Crossing the Divide. Dialogue among Civilizations*, South Orange, NJ 2001.
14. Cf. UN Resolution A/RES/O6/6 of 9 November 2001.
15. Ibid., Art 1, Art. 2. For the whole process see. S. Schlensog, 'Weltethos bei den Vereinten Nationen', in H. Küng (ed.), *Dokumentation zum Weltethos*, Munich 2002, 251–266.
16. *Crossing the Divide* (n. 13), 68.
17. Ibid.
18. Ibid, 74.

19. Ibid., 78.
20. Ibid., 206.
21. A. Asghar Engineer, 'Die "Erklarung zum Weltethos", eine islamische Antwort', in K.H. Schreiner (ed.), *Islam in Asien*, Bad Honnef 2001, 114–22. Dr Ali Asghar Engineer is director of the Centre for Studies of Society and Secularism (CSSS) in Bombay. He researches into Islam and its cultural and political aspects.
22. Cf. surah 5.32.
23. Surah 5.8.
24. Surah 2.228.
25. Cf. surah 17.70.
26. Cf. surah 2.30.
27. *40 Hadith of an-Nawawi*, no. 13.
28. Kofi Annan, UN Secretary General, in the Third Global Ethic Lecture given in Tübingen on 12 December 2003; to be found at *www.weltethos.org*.
29. Ibid.

Index

A word of thanks

There is no more pleasant task for me as an author than to say thank-you. There are four people without whose support over the last decade I would not have been able to complete this extremely difficult work.

Without the fundamental researches of Professor Joseph van Ess, a star of the first magnitude in the heaven of Islamic studies and his readiness to give public lectures with me at the University of Tübingen in the 1980s, I could never have gained so comprehensive a knowledge of Islam and especially of its theology. Our conversations and shared involvement in scholarly gatherings have been countless, and the dangerous journey that the two of us made to a colloquium in Teheran in March 1985 during the Iran–Iraq war was unforgettable. I am particularly grateful to him for reading through my manuscript despite the many claims on his time and for improving it with many corrections and suggestions.

Without constant involvement with my colleague and friend Professor Karl-Josef Kuschel, who in the meantime has himself produced important works in the sphere of the theology of culture and inter-religious dialogue, I would not have had an expert theological companion who read through the whole book critically chapter by chapter and at the end read the whole of the revised manuscript all over again: I am indebted to him for many improvements in content and style.

Without the intensive collaboration of Stephan Schlensog, business manager of the Global Ethic Foundation, the production of the manuscript would not have been so smooth and successful: the design, the typesetting and the graphics for my schemes from *Judaism* and *Christianity* had already been in his hands. He accompanied me on the laborious filming trips for the television series *Spurensuche* (in English a book version appeared as *Tracing the Way*) on a journey that also went through Islamic countries, and was then responsible for the illustrated volume and the CD. As a result of this he has been able to make valuable suggestions on both method and content at every stage. He also produced the index of the book with its many hundreds of entries. His achievement is all the more remarkable since at the same time, so to speak 'on the side', he has also finished his dissertation on 'Hinduism: Faith—History—Ethic', which hopefully will be published in 2005. It will be a worthy continuation to my three volumes on 'The Religious Situation of our Time'.

Without the daily care of Marianne Saur, who for twenty-five years now, supported by Sybille Abt and Gerti Erichsen, has been in charge of my home, my life with its many commitments could not have been lived in so peaceful and joyful an atmosphere, which has made scholarly work easy. Over all these years she has also read all my manuscripts to make sure that they are easily understood.

The extensive task of obtaining literature from the university library, the constant correction of the manuscript and the checking of hundreds of notes has been carried out by Bettina Schmidt—sometimes assisted by Thomas Riplinger. In the last phase of work on this book the academic project co-ordinator of our Global Ethic Foundation, Dr Günther Gebhard, took over the bibliographical work; he too constantly corrected the manuscript and in other respects was a daily support. Jutta Flattes made the final corrections to the manuscript.

Finally, the last version of the manuscript was examined by specialists: by my Tübingen colleague in Islamics, Professor Heinz Halm, and by Mechthild Kellermann, who as the university library specialist in oriental studies was eminently qualified to correct and harmonize the Arabic words and their transcription, along with the place names in the maps. I have also expressed my thanks to other colleagues in the relevant sections.

I am again grateful to the Robert Bosch Jubilee Foundation which made available to me a generous grant for a research assistant and expensive computer system for the first phase of this research between 1989 and 1997, and thus created the material and personal basis for the whole project 'No World Peace without Religious Peace'.

But what would have become of this manuscript without the perfection of the work of our chief secretaries, first for many years Eleonore Henn and then Inge Baumann. It has never been too much for them to maintain their concern for this book in the midst of the countless letters, telephone calls and other claims from all over the world. However, the main responsibility for the manuscript lay in the hands of Anette Stuber-Rousselle, who cheerfully and indefatigable worked over the constantly new versions of individual chapters with thousands of improvements and in all this did not neglect the education of her four sons.

I thank all of these with all my heart. And finally I also thank Piper Verlag, to whom I may hand over this book so to speak as an anniversary gift to mark its centenary and my thirty years with Piper. Ulrich Wank has been the ideal editor and Hanns Polanetz—in collaboration with Stephen Schlensog—the ideal production manager. Both have had the complete trust of the board: first that of Viktor Niemann, now head of Bonnier, and later by the present director of Piper, Wolfgang Ferchl. I am grateful to them too for the outstanding collaboration.

Hans Küng
Tübingen, 2007

List of tables and maps

List of questions for discussion